PUBLISHER'S NOTE

MICRO-OFFSET BOOKS are published in editions of from 100 to 250 copies. The titles issued in this series consist largely of reprints of out of print and scarce books required by those doing research work, and for which only an extremely limited sale is possible. Copies of the original edition have become practically unobtainable at any price; the occasional one that might prove available generally is priced far beyond the means of most libraries or scholars.

It thus becomes necessary to employ some method of reproducing these books in very small editions and at a moderate price.

Our method of reprinting such volumes hence makes available again titles that might otherwise prove unobtainable, perhaps for all time.

THE ENGLISH UTILITARIANS

THE ENGLISH UTILITARIANS

By LESLIE STEPHEN

IN THREE VOLUMES

VOL. I

JEREMY BENTHAM

NEW YORK
PETER SMITH
1950

PREFACE

THIS book is a sequel to my *History of English Thought in the Eighteenth Century.* The title which I then ventured to use was more comprehensive than the work itself deserved. I felt my inability to write a continuation which should at all correspond to a similar title for the nineteenth century. I thought, however, that by writing an account of the compact and energetic school of English Utilitarians I could throw some light both upon them and their contemporaries. I had the advantage for this purpose of having been myself a disciple of the school during its last period. Many accidents have delayed my completion of the task ; and delayed also its publication after it was written. Two books have been published since that time, which partly cover the same ground ; and I must be content with referring my readers to them for further information. They are *The English Radicals*, by Mr. C. B. Roylance Kent ; and *English Political Philosophy from Hobbes to Maine*, by Professor Graham.

CONTENTS

CONTENTS

CHAPTER IV

PHILOSOPHY

CHAPTER V

BENTHAM'S LIFE

CHAPTER VI

BENTHAM'S DOCTRINE

INTRODUCTORY

THE English Utilitarians of whom I am about to give some account were a group of men who for three generations had a conspicuous influence upon English thought and political action. Jeremy Bentham, James Mill, and John Stuart Mill were successively their leaders; and I shall speak of each in turn. It may be well to premise a brief indication of the method which I have adopted. I have devoted a much greater proportion of my work to biography and to consideration of political and social conditions than would be appropriate to the history of a philosophy. The reasons for such a course are very obvious in this case, inasmuch as the Utilitarian doctrines were worked out with a constant reference to practical applications. I think, indeed, that such a reference is often equally present, though not equally conspicuous, in other philosophical schools. But in any case I wish to show how I conceive the relation of my scheme to the scheme more generally adopted by historians of abstract speculation.

I am primarily concerned with the history of a school or sect, not with the history of the arguments by which it justifies itself in the court of pure reason. I must therefore consider the creed as it was actually embodied in the dominant beliefs of the adherents of the school, not as it was expounded in lecture-rooms or treatises on first principles. I deal not with philosophers meditating upon Being and not-Being, but with men actively engaged in framing political platforms and carrying on popular agitations. The great majority even of intelligent partisans are either indifferent to the philosophic creed of their leaders or take it for granted. Its postulates are more or less implied in the doctrines which guide them in practice, but are not explicitly stated or deliberately reasoned out. Not the less the doctrines of a sect, political or religious, may be dependent upon theories which for the greater number remain latent or are recognised only in their concrete application. Contemporary members of any society, however widely they differ as to results, are employed upon the same problems and, to some extent, use the same methods and make the same assumptions in attempting solutions. There is a certain unity even in the general thought of any given period. Contradictory views imply some common ground. But within this wider unity we find a variety of sects, each of which may be considered as more or less representing a particular method of treating the general problem : and therefore principles which, whether clearly recognised or not, are virtually implied in their party creed and give a certain unity to their teaching.

One obvious principle of unity, or tacit bond of sympathy which holds a sect together depends upon the intellectual idiosyncrasy of the individuals. Coleridge was aiming at an important truth when he said that every man was born an Aristotelian or a Platonist.[1] Nominalists and realists, intuitionists and empiricists, idealists and materialists, represent different forms of

[1] *Table-Talk*, 3 July 1830.

a fundamental antithesis which appears to run through all philosophy. Each thinker is apt to take the postulates congenial to his own mind as the plain dictates of reason. Controversies between such opposites appear to be hopeless. They have been aptly compared by Dr. Venn to the erection of a snow-bank to dam a river. The snow melts and swells the torrent which it was intended to arrest. Each side reads admitted truths into its own dialect, and infers that its own dialect affords the only valid expression. To regard such antitheses as final and insoluble would be to admit complete scepticism. What is true for one man would not therefore be true— or at least its truth would not be demonstrable—to another. We must trust that reconciliation is achievable by showing that the difference is really less vital and corresponds to a difference of methods or of the spheres within which each mode of thought may be valid. To obtain the point of view from which such a conciliation is possible should be, I hold, one main end of modern philosophising.

The effect of this profound intellectual difference is complicated by other obvious influences. There is, in the first place, the difference of intellectual horizon. Each man has a world of his own and sees a different set of facts. Whether that which is visible from his parish steeple or from St. Peter's at Rome, it is still strictly limited : and the outside universe, known vaguely and indirectly, does not affect him like the facts actually present to his perception. The most candid thinkers will come to different conclusions when they are really provided with different sets of fact. In political and social problems every man's opinions are

moulded by his social station. The artisan's view of the capitalist, and the capitalist's view of the artisan, are both imperfect, because each has a first-hand knowledge of his own class alone : and, however anxious to be fair, each will take a very different view of the working of political institutions. An apparent concord often covers the widest divergence under the veil of a common formula, because each man has his private mode of interpreting general phrases in terms of concrete fact.

This, of course, implies the further difference arising from the passions which, however illogically, go so far to determine opinions. Here we have the most general source of difficulty in considering the actual history of a creed. We cannot limit ourselves to the purely logical factor. All thought has to start from postulates. Men have to act before they think : before, at any rate, reasoning becomes distinct from imagining or guessing. To explain in early periods is to fancy and to take a fancy for a perception. The world of the primitive man is constructed not only from vague conjectures and hasty analogies but from his hopes and fears, and bears the impress of his emotional nature. When progress takes place some of his beliefs are confirmed, some disappear, and others are transformed : and the whole history of thought is a history of this gradual process of verification. We begin, it is said, by assuming : we proceed by verifying, and we only end by demonstrating. The process is comparatively simple in that part of knowledge which ultimately corresponds to the physical sciences. There must be a certain harmony between beliefs and realities in regard to knowledge of ordinary matters of fact, if only because such harmony is essential

to the life of the race. Even an ape must distinguish poisonous from wholesome food. Beliefs as to physical facts require to be made articulate and distinct ; but we have only to recognise as logical principles the laws of nature which we have unconsciously obeyed and illustrated—to formulate dynamics long after we have applied the science in throwing stones or using bows and arrows. But what corresponds to this in the case of the moral and religious beliefs? What is the process of verification? Men practically are satisfied with their creed so long as they are satisfied with the corresponding social order. The test of truth so suggested is obviously inadequate : for all great religions, however contradictory to each other, have been able to satisfy it for long periods. Particular doctrines might be tested by experiment. The efficacy of witchcraft might be investigated like the efficacy of vaccination. But faith can always make as many miracles as it wants : and errors which originate in the fancy cannot be at once extirpated by the reason. Their form may be changed but not their substance. To remove them requires not disproof of this or that fact, but an intellectual discipline which is rare even among the educated classes. A religious creed survives, as poetry or art survives,—not so long as it contains apparently true statements of fact but—so long as it is congenial to the whole social state. A philosophy indeed is a poetry stated in terms of logic. Considering the natural conservatism of mankind, the difficulty is to account for progress, not for the persistence of error. When the existing order ceases to be satisfactory ; when conquest or commerce has welded nations together and brought conflicting creeds into cohesion ; when industrial development has modified the old class relations; or when the governing classes have ceased to discharge their functions, new principles are demanded and new prophets arise. The philosopher may then become the mouthpiece of the new order, and innocently take himself to be its originator. His doctrines were fruitless so long as the soil was not prepared for the seed. A premature discovery if not stamped out by fire and sword is stifled by indifference. If Francis Bacon succeeded where Roger Bacon failed, the difference was due to the social conditions, not to the men. The cause of the great religious as well as of the great political revolutions must be sought mainly in the social history. New creeds spread when they satisfy the instincts or the passions roused to activity by other causes. The system has to be so far true as to be credible at the time; but its vitality depends upon its congeniality as a whole to the aspirations of the mass of mankind.

The purely intellectual movement no doubt represents the decisive factor. The love of truth in the abstract is probably the weakest of human passions; but truth when attained ultimately gives the fulcrum for a reconstruction of the world. When a solid core of ascertained and verifiable truth has once been formed and applied to practical results it becomes the fixed pivot upon which all beliefs must ultimately turn. The influence, however, is often obscure and still indirect. The more cultivated recognise the necessity of bringing their whole doctrine into conformity with the definitely organised and established system; and, at the present day, even the uneducated begin to have an inkling of possible results. Yet the desire for logical consistency is not one which presses

forcibly upon the less cultivated intellects. They do not feel the necessity of unifying knowledge or bringing their various opinions into consistency and into harmony with facts. There are easy methods of avoiding any troublesome conflict of belief. The philosopher is ready to show them the way. He, like other people, has to start from postulates, and to see how they will work. When he meets with a difficulty it is perfectly legitimate that he should try how far the old formula can be applied to cover the new applications. He may be led to a process of 'rationalising' or 'spiritualising' which is dangerous to intellectual honesty. The vagueness of the general conceptions with which he is concerned facilitates the adaptation; and his words slide into new meanings by imperceptible gradations. His error is in taking a legitimate tentative process for a conclusive test; and inferring that opinions are confirmed because a non-natural interpretation can be forced upon them. This, however, is only the vicious application of the normal process through which new ideas are diffused or slowly infiltrate the old systems till the necessity of a thoroughgoing reconstruction forces itself upon our attention. Nor can it be denied that an opposite fallacy is equally possible, especially in times of revolutionary passion. The apparent irreconcilability of some new doctrine with the old may lead to the summary rejection of the implicit truth, together with the error involved in its imperfect recognition. Hence arises the necessity for taking into account not only a man's intellectual idiosyncrasies and the special intellectual horizon, but all the prepossessions due to his personal character, his social environment, and his consequent sympathies and antipathies. The philosopher has

his passions like other men. He does not really live in the thin air of abstract speculation. On the contrary, he starts generally, and surely is right in starting, with keen interest in the great religious, ethical, and social problems of the time. He wishes—honestly and eagerly —to try them by the severest tests, and to hold fast only what is clearly valid. The desire to apply his principles in fact justifies his pursuit, and redeems him from the charge that he is delighting in barren intellectual subtleties. But to an outsider his procedure may appear in a different light. His real problem comes to be: how the conclusions which are agreeable to his emotions can be connected with the postulates which are congenial to his intellect? He may be absolutely honest and quite unconscious that his conclusions were prearranged by his sympathies. No philosophic creed of any importance has ever been constructed, we may well believe, without such sincerity and without such plausibility as results from its correspondence to at least some aspects of the truth. But the result is sufficiently shown by the perplexed controversies which arise. Men agree in their conclusions, though starting from opposite premises; or from the same premises reach the most diverging conclusions. The same code of practical morality, it is often said, is accepted by thinkers who deny each other's first principles; dogmatism often appears to its opponents to be thorough-going scepticism in disguise, and men establish victoriously results which turn out in the end to be really a stronghold for their antagonists.

Hence there is a distinction between such a history of a sect as I contemplate and a history of scientific inquiry or of pure philosophy. A history of mathematical or

physical science would differ from a direct exposition of the science, but only in so far as it would state truths in the order of discovery, not in the order most convenient for displaying them as a system. It would show what were the processes by which they were originally found out, and how they have been afterwards annexed or absorbed in some wider generalisation. These facts might be stated without any reference to the history of the discoverers or of the society to which they belonged. They would indeed suggest very interesting topics to the general historian or 'sociologist.' He might be led to inquire under what conditions men came to inquire scientifically at all; why they ceased for centuries to care for science; why they took up special departments of investigation; and what was the effect of scientific discoveries upon social relations in general. But the two inquiries would be distinct for obvious reasons. If men study mathematics they can only come to one conclusion. They will find out the same propositions of geometry if they only think clearly enough and long enough, as certainly as Columbus would discover America if he only sailed far enough. America was there, and so in a sense are the propositions. We may therefore in this case entirely separate the two questions: what leads men to think? and what conclusions will they reach? The reasons which guided the first discoverers are just as valid now, though they can be more systematically stated. But in the 'moral sciences' this distinction is not equally possible. The intellectual and the social evolution are closely and intricately connected, and each reacts upon the other. In the last resort no doubt a definitive system of belief once elaborated would repose upon universally

valid truths and determine, instead of being determined
by, the corresponding social order. But in the concrete
evolution which, we may hope, is approximating towards
this result, the creeds current among mankind have been
determined by the social conditions as well as helped to
determine them. To give an account of that process it
is necessary to specify the various circumstances which
may lead to the survival of error, and to the partial
views of truth taken by men of different idiosyncrasies
working upon different data and moved by different
passions and prepossessions. A history written upon
these terms would show primarily what, as a fact, were
the dominant beliefs during a given period, and state
which survived, which disappeared, and which were
transformed or engrafted upon other systems of thought.
This would of course raise the question of the truth or
falsehood of the doctrines as well as of their vitality: for
the truth is at least one essential condition of permanent
vitality. The difference would be that the problem
would be approached from a different side. We should
ask first what beliefs have flourished, and afterwards ask
why they flourished, and how far their vitality was due
to their partial or complete truth. To write such a history would perhaps require an impartiality which few
people possess and which I do not venture to claim. I
have my own opinions for which other people may
account by prejudice, assumption, or downright incapacity.
I am quite aware that I shall be implicitly criticising
myself in criticising others. All that I can profess is
that by taking the questions in this order, I shall hope
to fix attention upon one set of considerations which are
apt, as I fancy, to be unduly neglected. The result of

reading some histories is to raise the question : how people
on the other side came to be such unmitigated fools? Why
were they imposed upon by such obvious fallacies? That
may be answered by considering more fully the conditions under which the opinions were actually adopted, and
one result may be to show that those opinions had a considerable element of truth, and were held by men who
were the very opposite of fools. At any rate I shall do
what I can to write an account of this phase of thought,
so as to bring out what were its real tenets ; to what
intellectual type they were naturally congenial ; what
were the limitations of view which affected the Utilitarians'
conception of the problems to be solved ; and what were
the passions and prepossessions due to the contemporary
state of society and to their own class position, which to
some degree unconsciously dictated their conclusions.
So far as I can do this satisfactorily, I hope that I may
throw some light upon the intrinsic value of the creed,
and the place which it should occupy in a definitive
system.

CHAPTER I

POLITICAL CONDITIONS

I. THE BRITISH CONSTITUTION

THE English Utilitarians represent one outcome of the
speculations current in England during the later part of
the eighteenth century. For the reasons just assigned I
shall begin by briefly recalling some of the social conditions
which set the problems for the coming generation and
determined the mode of answering them. I must put the
main facts in evidence, though they are even painfully
familiar. The most obvious starting-point is given by
the political situation. The supremacy of parliament
had been definitively established by the revolution
of 1688, and had been followed by the elaboration
of the system of party government. The centre of
gravity of the political world lay in the House of
Commons. No minister could hold power unless he
could command a majority in this house. Jealousy of
the royal power, however, was still a ruling passion.
The party line between Whig and Tory turned ostensibly upon this issue. The essential Whig doctrine is
indicated by Dunning's famous resolution (6 April
1780) that ' the power of the crown had increased, was
increasing, and ought to be diminished.' The resolution

was in one sense an anachronism. As in many other
cases, politicians seem to be elaborately slaying the slain
and guarding against the attacks of extinct monsters.
There was scarcely more probability under George III.
than there is under Victoria that the king would try
to raise taxes without consent of parliament. George III.,
however, desired to be more than a contrivance for
fixing the great seal to official documents. He had
good reason for thinking that the weakness of the execu-
tive was an evil. The king could gain power not by
attacking the authority of parliament but by gaining
influence within its walls. He might form a party of
' king's friends ' able to hold the balance between the
connections formed by the great families and so break up
the system of party government. Burke's great speech
(11 Feb. 1780) upon introducing his plan ' for the
better security of the independence of parliament and
the economical reformation of the civil and other establishments ' explains the secret and reveals the state of
things which for the next half century was to supply one
main theme for the eloquence of reformers. The king
had at his disposal a vast amount of patronage. There
were relics of ancient institutions : the principality of
Wales, the duchies of Lancaster and Cornwall, and the
earldom of Chester ; each with its revenue and establishment of superfluous officials. The royal household was
a complex ' body corporate ' founded in the old days of
' purveyance.' There was the mysterious ' Board of
Green Cloth ' formed by the great officers and supposed
to have judicial as well as administrative functions.
Cumbrous mediæval machinery thus remained which had
been formed in the time when the distinction between

a public trust and private property was not definitely drawn or which had been allowed to remain for the sake of patronage, when its functions had been transferred to officials of more modern type. Reform was foiled, as Burke put it, because the turnspit in the king's kitchen was a member of parliament. Such sinecures and the pensions on the civil list or the Irish establishment provided the funds by which the king could build up a personal influence, which was yet occult, irresponsible, and corrupt. The measure passed by Burke in 1782[1] made a beginning in the removal of such abuses.

Meanwhile the Whigs were conveniently blind to another side of the question. If the king could buy, it was because there were plenty of people both able and willing to sell. Bubb Dodington, a typical example of the old system, had five or six seats at his disposal : subject only to the necessity of throwing a few pounds to the 'venal wretches' who went through the form of voting, and by dealing in what he calls this 'merchantable ware' he managed by lifelong efforts to wriggle into a peerage. The Dodingtons, that is, sold because they bought. The 'venal wretches' were the lucky franchise-holders in rotten boroughs. The 'Friends of the People'[2] in 1793 made the often-repeated statement that 154 individuals returned 307 members, that is, a majority of the house. In Cornwall, again, 21 boroughs with 453 electors controlled by about 15 individuals returned 42 members,[3] or, with the two county members, only one member less than Scotland ; and the Scottish members were elected by close corporations in boroughs

[1] 22 George III. c. 82.   [2] Parl. Hist. xxx. 787.
[3] State Trials, xxiv. 382.

and by the great families in counties. No wonder if the House of Commons seemed at times to be little more than an exchange for the traffic between the proprietors of votes and the proprietors of offices and pensions.

The demand for the reforms advocated by Burke and Dunning was due to the catastrophe of the American War. The scandal caused by the famous coalition of 1783 showed that a diminution of the royal influence might only make room for selfish bargains among the proprietors of parliamentary influence. The demand for reform was taken up by Pitt. His plan was significant. He proposed to disfranchise a few rotten boroughs ; but to soften this measure he afterwards suggested that a million should be set aside to buy such boroughs as should voluntarily apply for disfranchisement. The seats obtained were to be mainly added to county representation ; but the franchise was to be extended so as to add about 99,000 voters in boroughs, and additional seats were to be given to London and Westminster and to Manchester, Leeds, Birmingham, and Sheffield. The Yorkshire reformers, who led the movement, were satisfied with this modest scheme. The borough proprietors were obviously too strong to be directly attacked, though they might be induced to sell some of their power.

Here was a mass of anomalies, sufficient to supply topics of denunciation for two generations of reformers, and, in time, to excite fears of violent revolution. Without undertaking the easy task of denouncing exploded systems, we may ask what state of mind they implied. Our ancestors were perfectly convinced that their political system was of almost unrivalled excellence : they held that they were freemen entitled to look down upon

foreigners as the slaves of despots. Nor can we say that their satisfaction was without solid grounds. The boasting about English freedom implied some misunderstanding. But it was at least the boast of a vigorous race. Not only were there individuals capable of patriotism and public spirit, but the body politic was capable of continuous energy. During the eighteenth century the British empire spread round the world. Under Chatham it had been finally decided that the English race should be the dominant element in the new world ; if the political connection had been severed by the bungling of his successors, the unbroken spirit of the nation had still been shown in the struggle against France, Spain, and the revolted colonies ; and whatever may be thought of the motives which produced the great revolutionary wars, no one can deny the qualities of indomitable self-reliance and high courage to the men who led the country through the twenty years of struggle against France, and for a time against France with the continent at its feet. If moralists or political theorists find much to condemn in the ends to which British policy was directed, they must admit that the qualities displayed were not such as can belong to a simply corrupt and mean-spirited government.

One obvious remark is that, on the whole, the system was a very good one—as systems go. It allowed free play to the effective political forces. Down to the revolutionary period, the nation as a whole was contented with its institutions. The political machinery provided a sufficient channel for the really efficient force of public opinion. There was as yet no large class which at once had political aspirations and was unable to gain a hearing.

England was still in the main an agricultural country : and the agricultural labourer was fairly prosperous till the end of the century, while his ignorance and isolation made him indifferent to politics. There might be a bad squire or parson, as there might be a bad season ; but squire and parson were as much parts of the natural order of things as the weather. The farmer or yeoman was not much less stolid ; and his politics meant at most a choice between allegiance to one or other of the county families. If in the towns which were rapidly developing there was growing up a discontented population, its discontent was not yet directed into political channels. An extended franchise meant a larger expenditure on beer, not the readier acceptance of popular aspirations. To possess a vote was to have a claim to an occasional bonus rather than a right to influence legislation. Practically, therefore, parliament might be taken to represent what might be called 'public opinion,' for anything that deserved to be called public opinion was limited to the opinions of the gentry and the more intelligent part of the middle classes. There was no want of complaints of corruption, proposals to exclude placemen from parliament and the like ; and in the days of Wilkes, Chatham, and Junius, when the first symptoms of democratic activity began to affect the political movement, the discontent made itself audible and alarming. But a main characteristic of the English reformers was the constant appeal to precedent, even in their most excited moods. They do not mention the rights of man ; they invoke the 'revolution principles' of 1688 ; they insist upon the 'Bill of Rights' or Magna Charta. When keenly roused they recall the fate of Charles I.; and their favourite toast is the cause for which Hampden died on the field and Sidney on the scaffold. They believe in the jury as the 'palladium of our liberties'; and are convinced that the British Constitution represents an unsurpassable though unfortunately an ideal order of things, which must have existed at some indefinite period. Chatham in one of his most famous speeches, appeals, for example, to the 'iron barons' who resisted King John, and contrasts them with the silken courtiers which now compete for place and pensions. The political reformers of the time, like religious reformers in most times, conceive of themselves only as demanding the restoration of the system to its original purity, not as demanding its abrogation. In other words, they propose to remedy abuses but do not as yet even contemplate a really revolutionary change. Wilkes was not a 'Wilkite,' nor was any of his party, if Wilkite meant anything like Jacobin.

II. THE RULING CLASS

Thus, however anomalous the constitution of parliament, there was no thought of any far-reaching revolution The great mass of the population was too ignorant, too scattered and too poor to have any real political opinions. So long as certain prejudices were not aroused, it was content to leave the management of the state to the dominant class, which alone was intelligent enough to take an interest in public affairs and strong enough to make its interest felt. This class consisted in the first place of the great landed interest. When Lord North opposed Pitt's reform in 1785 he said[1] that the Consti-

[1] *Parl. Hist.* xxv. 472.

tution was 'the work of infinite wisdom . . . the most beautiful fabric that had ever existed since the beginning of time.' He added that 'the bulk and weight' of the house ought to be in 'the hands of the country-gentlemen, the best and most respectable objects of the confidence of the people.' The speech, though intended to please an audience of country-gentlemen, represented a genuine belief.[1] The country-gentlemen formed the class to which not only the constitutional laws but the prevailing sentiment of the country gave the lead in politics as in the whole social system. Even reformers proposed to improve the House of Commons chiefly by increasing the number of county-members, and a county-member was almost necessarily a country-gentleman of an exalted kind. Although the country-gentleman was very far from having all things his own way, his ideals and prejudices were in a great degree the mould to which the other politically important class conformed. There was indeed a growing jealousy between the landholders and the 'monied-men.' Bolingbroke had expressed this distrust at an earlier part of the century. But the true representative of the period was his successful rival, Walpole, a thorough country-gentleman who had learned to understand the mysteries of finance and acquired the confidence of the city. The great merchants of London and the rising manufacturers in the country were rapidly growing in wealth and influence. The monied-men represented the most active, energetic, and growing part of the body politic. Their interests determined the direction of the national policy. The great wars of the

[1] The country-gentlemen, said Wilberforce in 1800, are the 'very nerves and ligatures of the body politic.'—*Correspondence*, i. 219.

century were undertaken in the interests of British trade. The extension of the empire in India was carried on through a great commercial company. The growth of commerce supported the sea-power which was the main factor in the development of the empire. The new industrial organisation which was arising was in later years to represent a class distinctly opposed to the old aristocratic order. At present it was in a comparatively subordinate position. The squire was interested in the land and the church ; the merchant thought more of commerce and was apt to be a dissenter. But the merchant, in spite of some little jealousies, admitted the claims of the country-gentleman to be his social superior and political leader. His highest ambition was to be himself admitted to the class or to secure the admission of his family. As he became rich he bought a solid mansion at Clapham or Wimbledon, and, if he made a fortune, might become lord of manors in the country. He could not as yet aspire to become himself a peer, but he might be the ancestor of peers. The son of Josiah Child, the great merchant of the seventeenth century, became Earl Tylney, and built at Wanstead one of the noblest mansions in England. His contemporary Sir Francis Child, Lord Mayor, and a founder of the Bank of England, built Osterley House, and was ancestor of the earls of Jersey and Westmoreland. The daughter of Sir John Barnard, the typical merchant of Walpole's time, married the second Lord Palmerston. Beckford, the famous Lord Mayor of Chatham's day, was father of the author of *Vathek*, who married an earl's daughter and became the father of a duchess. The Barings, descendants of a German pastor, settled in England early in the century

and became country-gentlemen, baronets, and peers. Cobbett, who saw them rise, reviled the stockjobbers who were buying out the old families. But the process had begun long before his days, and meant that the heads of the new industrial system were being absorbed into the class of territorial magnates. That class represented the framework upon which both political and social power was moulded.

This implies an essential characteristic of the time. A familiar topic of the admirers of the British Constitution was the absence of the sharp lines of demarcation between classes and of the exclusive aristocratic privileges which, in France, provoked the revolution. In England the ruling class was not a 'survival': it had not retained privileges without discharging corresponding functions. The essence of 'self-government,' says its most learned commentator,[1] is the organic connection 'between State and society.' On the Continent, that is, powers were intrusted to a centralised administrative and judicial hierarchy, which in England were left to the class independently strong by its social position. The landholder was powerful as a product of the whole system of industrial and agricultural development ; and he was bound in return to perform arduous and complicated duties. How far he performed them well is another question. At least, he did whatever was done in the way of governing, and therefore did not sink into a mere excrescence or superfluity. I must try to point out certain results which had a material effect upon English opinion in general and, in particular, upon the Utilitarians.

[1] Gneist's *Self-Government* (3rd edition, 1871), p. 879.

III. LEGISLATION AND ADMINISTRATION

The country-gentlemen formed the bulk of the law-making body, and the laws gave the first point of assault of the Utilitarian movement. One explanation is suggested by a phrase attributed to Sir Josiah Child.[1] The laws, he said, were a heap of nonsense, compiled by a few ignorant country-gentlemen, who hardly knew how to make good laws for the government of their own families, much less for the regulation of companies and foreign commerce. He meant that the parliamentary legislation of the century was the work of amateurs, not of specialists ; of an assembly of men more interested in immediate questions of policy or personal intrigue than in general principles, and not of such a centralised body as would set a value upon symmetry and scientific precision. The country-gentleman had strong prejudices and enough common sense to recognise his own ignorance. The product of a traditional order, he clung to traditions, and regarded the old maxims as sacred because no obvious reason could be assigned for them. He was suspicious of abstract theories, and it did not even occur to him that any such process as codification or radical alteration of the laws was conceivable. For the law itself he had the profound veneration which is expressed by Blackstone. It represented the 'wisdom of our ancestors' ; the system of first principles, on which the whole order of things reposed, and which must be regarded as an embodiment of right reason. The common law was a tradition, not made by express legislation, but somehow existing apart from any definite embodiment, and revealed

[1] See *Dictionary of National Biography.*

to certain learned hierophants. Any changes, required by the growth of new social conditions, had to be made under pretence of applying the old rules supposed to be already in existence. Thus grew up the system of ' judge-made law,' which was to become a special object of the denunciations of Bentham. Child had noticed the incompetence of the country-gentlemen to understand the regulation of commercial affairs. The gap was being filled up, without express legislation, by judicial interpretations of Mansfield and his fellows. This, indeed, marks a characteristic of the whole system. ' Our constitution,' says Professor Dicey,[1] ' is a judge-made constitution, and it bears on its face all the features, good and bad, of judge-made law.' The law of landed property, meanwhile, was of vital and immediate interest to the country-gentleman. But, feeling his own incompetence, he had called in the aid of the expert. The law had been developed in mediæval times, and bore in all its details the marks of the long series of struggles between king and nobles and parliaments. One result had been the elaborate series of legal fictions worked out in the conflict between private interests and public policy, by which lawyers had been able to adapt the rules fitted for an ancient state of society to another in which the very fundamental conceptions were altered. A mysterious system had thus grown up, which deterred any but the most resolute students. Of Fearne's essay upon 'Contingent remainders '(published in 1772) it was said that no work ' in any branch of science could afford a more beautiful instance of analysis.' Fearne had shown the acuteness of ' a Newton or a Pascal.' Other critics dispute this proposition ; but in any

[1] *The Law of the Constitution,* p. 209.

case the law was so perplexing that it could only be fully understood by one who united antiquarian knowledge to the subtlety of a great logician. The ' vast and intricate machine,' as Blackstone calls it, ' of a voluminous family settlement' required for its explanation the dialectical skill of an accomplished schoolman. The poor country-gentleman could not understand the terms on which he held his own estate without calling in an expert equal to such a task. The man who has acquired skill so essential to his employer's interests is not likely to undervalue it or to be over anxious to simplify the labyrinth in which he shone as a competent guide.

The lawyers who played so important a part by their familiarity with the mysteries of commercial law and landed property, naturally enjoyed the respect of their clients, and were rewarded by adoption into the class. The English barrister aspired to success by himself taking part in politics and legislation. The only path to the highest positions really open to a man of ability, not connected by blood with the great families, was the path which led to the woolsack or to the judge's bench. A great merchant might be the father or father-in-law of peers ; a successful soldier or sailor might himself become a peer, but generally he began life as a member of the ruling classes, and his promotion was affected by parliamentary influence. But a successful lawyer might fight his way from a humble position to the House of Lords. Thurlow, son of a country-gentleman ; Dunning, son of a country attorney ; Ellenborough, son of a bishop and descendant of a long line of North-country ' statesmen ' ; Kenyon, son of a farmer ; Eldon, son of a Newcastle coal merchant, represent the average career of a successful

barrister. Some of them rose to be men of political importance, and Thurlow and Eldon had the advantage of keeping George III 's conscience—an unruly faculty which had an unfortunately strong influence upon affairs. The leaders of the legal profession, therefore, and those who hoped to be leaders, shared the prejudices, took a part in the struggles, and were rewarded by the honours of the dominant class.

The criminal law became a main topic of reformers. There, as elsewhere, we have a striking example of traditional modes of thought surviving with singular persistence. The rough classification of crimes into felony and misdemeanour, and the strange technical rules about ' benefit of clergy ' dating back to the struggles of Henry II. and Becket, remained like ultimate categories of thought. When the growth of social conditions led to new temptations or the appearance of a new criminal class, and particular varieties of crime became conspicuous, the only remedy was to declare that some offence should be ' felony without benefit of clergy,' and therefore punishable by death. By unsystematic and spasmodic legislation the criminal law became so savage as to shock every man of common humanity. It was tempered by the growth of technical rules, which gave many chances of escape to the criminal ; and by practical revolt against its excesses, which led to the remission of the great majority of capital sentences.[1] The legislators were clumsy, not intentionally cruel ; and the laws, though

[1] See Sir J. F. Stephen's *History of the Criminal Law* (1883), i. 470. He quotes Blackstone's famous statement that there were 160 felonies without benefit of clergy, and shows that this gives a very uncertain measure of the severity of the law. A single act making larceny in general punishable by death would be more severe than fifty separate acts, making fifty different

sanguinary in reality, were more sanguinary in theory than in practice. Nothing, on the other hand, is more conspicuous than the spirit of fair play to the criminal, which struck foreign observers.[1] It was deeply rooted in the whole system. The English judge was not an official agent of an inquisitorial system, but an impartial arbitrator between the prisoner and the prosecutor. In political cases especially a marked change was brought about by the revolution of 1688. If our ancestors talked some nonsense about trial by jury, the system certainly insured that the persons accused of libel or sedition should have a fair trial, and very often something more. Judges of the Jeffreys type had become inconceivable, though impartiality might disappear in cases where the prejudices of juries were actively aroused. Englishmen might fairly boast of their immunity from the arbitrary methods of continental rulers ; and their unhesitating confidence in the fairness of the system became so ingrained as to be taken as a matter of course, and scarcely received due credit from later critics of the system.

The country-gentleman, again, was not only the legislator but a most important figure in the judicial and administrative system. As justice of the peace, he was the representative of law and order to his country neighbours. The preface of 1785 to the fifteenth edition of Burn's *Justice of the Peace*, published originally in 1755,

varieties of larceny punishable by death. He adds, however, that the scheme of punishment was 'severe to the highest degree, and destitute of every sort of principle or system.' The number of executions in the early part of this century varied apparently from a fifth to a ninth of the capital sentences passed. See Table in Porter's *Progress of the Nation* (1851), p. 635.

[1] See the references to Cottu's report of 1822 in Stephen's *History*, i. 429, 439, 451. Cottu's book was translated by Blanco White.

mentions that in the interval between these dates, some three hundred statutes had been passed affecting the duties of justices, while half as many had been repealed or modified. The justice was of course, as a rule, a superficial lawyer, and had to be prompted by his clerk, the two representing on a small scale the general relation between the lawyers and the ruling class. Burn tells the justice for his comfort that the judges will take a lenient view of any errors into which his ignorance may have led him. The discharge of such duties by an independent gentleman was thought to be so desirable and so creditable to him that his want of efficiency must be regarded with consideration. Nor, though the justices have been a favourite butt for satirists, does it appear that the system worked badly. When it became necessary to appoint paid magistrates in London, and the pay, according to the prevalent system, was provided by fees, the new officials became known as 'trading justices,' and their salaries, as Fielding tells us, were some of the 'dirtiest money upon earth.' The justices might perhaps be hard upon a poacher (as, indeed, the game laws became one of the great scandals of the system), or liable to be misled by a shrewd attorney ; but they were on the whole regarded as the natural and creditable representatives of legal authority in the country.

The justices, again, discharged functions which would elsewhere belong to an administrative hierarchy. Gneist observes that the power of the justices of the peace represents the centre of gravity of the whole administrative system.[1] Their duties had become so multifarious and

[1] Gneist's *Self-Government* (1871), p. 194. It is characteristic that J. S. Mill, in his *Representative Government*, remarks that the 'Quarter Sessions' are

perplexed that Burn could only arrange them under alphabetical heads. Gneist works out a systematic account, filling many pages of elaborate detail, and showing how large a part they played in the whole social structure. An intense jealousy of central power was one correlative characteristic. Blackstone remarks in his more liberal humour that the number of new offices held at pleasure had greatly extended the influence of the crown. This refers to the custom-house officers, excise officers, stamp distributors and postmasters. But if the tax-gatherer represented the state, he represented also part of the patronage at the disposal of politicians. A voter was often in search of the place of a 'tidewaiter' ; and, as we know, the greatest poet of the day could only be rewarded by making him an exciseman. Any extension of a system which multiplied public offices was regarded with suspicion. Walpole, the strongest minister of the century, had been forced to an ignominious retreat when he proposed to extend the excise. The cry arose that he meant to enslave the country and extend the influence of the crown over all the corporations in England. The country-gentleman had little reason to fear that government would diminish his importance by tampering with his functions. The justices of the peace were called upon to take a great and increasing share in the administration of the poor-law. They were concerned in all manner of financial details ; they regulated such police as existed ; they looked after the old laws by which the trades were still restricted ; and, in theory at least,

formed in the 'most anomalous' way; that they represent the old feudal principle, and are at variance with the fundamental principles of representative government (*Rep. Gov.* (1867), p. 113). The mainspring of the old system had become a simple anomaly to the new radicalism.

could fix the rate of wages. Parliament did not override, but only gave the necessary sanction to their activity. If we looked through the journals of the House of Commons during the American War, for example, we should get the impression that the whole business of the legislature was to arrange administrative details. If a waste was to be enclosed, a canal or a high-road to be constructed, there was no public department to be consulted. The gentry of the neighbourhood joined to obtain a private act of parliament which gave the necessary powers to the persons interested. No general enclosure act could be passed, though often suggested. It would imply a central commission, which would only, as was suggested, give rise to jobbery and take power out of the natural hands. Parliament was omnipotent ; it could regulate the affairs of the empire or of a parish ; alter the most essential laws or act as a court of justice ; settle the crown or arrange for a divorce or for the alteration of a private estate. But it objected to delegate authority even to a subordinate body, which might tend to become independent. Thus, if it was the central power and source of all legal authority, it might also be regarded as a kind of federal league, representing the wills of a number of partially independent persons. The gentry could meet there and obtain the sanction of their allies for any measure required in their own little sphere of influence. But they had an instinctive aversion to the formation of any organised body representing the state. The neighbourhood which wanted a road got powers to make it, and would concur in giving powers to others. But if the state were to be intrusted to make roads, ministers would have more places to give, and roads might be made which they did not want. The English roads had long been infamous, but neither was money wasted, as in France, on roads where there was no traffic.[1] Thus we have the combination of an absolute centralisation of legislative power with an utter absence of administrative centralisation. The units meeting in parliament formed a supreme assembly; but they did not sink their own individuality. They only met to distribute the various functions among themselves.

The English parish with its squire, its parson, its lawyer and its labouring population was a miniature of the British Constitution in general. The squire's eldest son could succeed to his position; a second son might become a general or an admiral; a third would take the family living; a fourth, perhaps, seek his fortune at the bar. This implies a conception of other political conditions which curiously illustrate some contemporary conceptions.

IV. THE ARMY AND NAVY

We are often amused by the persistency of the cry against a 'standing army' in England. It did not fairly die out until the revolutionary wars. Blackstone regards it as a singularly fortunate circumstance 'that any branch of the legislature might annually put an end to the legal existence of the army by refusing to concur in the continuance' of the mutiny act. A standing army was obviously necessary; but by making believe very hard,

[1] See Arthur Young, *passim.* There was, however, an improvement even in the first half of the century. See Cunningham's *Growth of English Industry, etc. (Modern Times)*, p. 378.

we could shut our eyes to the facts, and pretend that it was a merely temporary arrangement.[1] The doctrine had once had a very intelligible meaning. If James II. had possessed a disciplined army of the continental pattern, with Marlborough at its head, Marlborough would hardly have been converted by the prince of Orange. But loyal as the gentry had been at the restoration, they had taken very good care that the Stuarts should not have in their hand such a weapon as had been possessed by Cromwell. When the Puritan army was disbanded, they had proceeded to regulate the militia. The officers were appointed by the lords-lieutenants of counties, and had to possess a property qualification; the men raised by ballot in their own districts; and their numbers and length of training regulated by Act of Parliament. The old 'train-bands' were suppressed, except in the city of London, and thus the recognised military force of the country was a body essentially dependent upon the country gentry. The militia was regarded with favour as the 'old constitutional force' which could not be used to threaten our liberties. It was remodelled during the Seven Years' War and embodied during that and all our later wars. It was, however, ineffective by its very nature. An aristocracy which chose to carry on wars must have a professional army in fact, however careful it might be to pretend that it was a provision for a passing necessity. The pretence had serious consequences. Since the army was not to have interests separate from the people, there was no reason for building barracks. The men might be billeted on publicans, or placed

[1] See *Military Forces of the Crown*, by Charles M. Clode (1869), for a full account of the facts.

under canvas, while they were wanted. When the great war came upon us, large sums had to be spent to make up for the previous neglect. Fox, on 22nd February 1793, protested during a lively debate upon this subject that sound constitutional principles condemned barracks, because to mix the army with the people was the 'best security against the danger of a standing army.'[1]

In fact a large part of the army was a mere temporary force. In 1762, towards the end of the Seven Years' War, we had about 100,000 men in pay; and after the peace, the force was reduced to under 20,000. Similar changes took place in every war. The ruling class took advantage of the position. An army might be hired from Germany for the occasion. New regiments were generally raised by some great man who gave commissions to his own relations and dependants. When the Pretender was in Scotland, for example, fifteen regiments were raised by patriotic nobles, who gave the commissions, and stipulated that although they were to be employed only in suppressing the rising, the officers should have permanent rank.[2] So, as was shown in Mrs. Clarke's case, a patent for raising a regiment might be a source of profit to the undertaker, who again might get it by bribing the mistress of a royal duke. The officers had, according to the generally prevalent system, a modified property in their commissions; and the system of sale was not abolished till our own days. We may therefore say that the ruling class, on the one hand, objected to a

[1] *Parl. Hist.* xxx. 490. Clode states (i. 222) that £9,000,000 was spent upon barracks by 1804, and, it seems, without proper authority.
[2] Debate in *Parl. Hist.* xiii. 1382, etc., and see Walpole's *Correspondence*, i. 400, for some characteristic comments.

standing army, and, on the other, since such an army was a necessity, farmed it from the country and were admitted to have a certain degree of private property in the concern. The prejudice against any permanent establishment made it necessary to fill the ranks on occasion by all manner of questionable expedients. Bounties were offered to attract the vagrants who hung loose upon society. Smugglers, poachers, and the like were allowed to choose between military service and transportation. The general effect was to provide an army of blackguards commanded by gentlemen. The army no doubt had its merits as well as its defects. The continental armies which it met were collected by equally demoralising methods until the French revolution led to a systematic conscription. The bad side is suggested by Napier's famous phrase, the 'cold shade of our aristocracy'; while Napier gives facts enough to prove both the brutality too often shown by the private soldier and the dogged courage which is taken to be characteristic even of the English blackguard. By others,—by such men as the duke of Wellington and Lord Palmerston, for example, types of the true aristocrat—the system was defended[1] as bringing men of good family into the army and so providing it, as the duke thought, with the best set of officers in Europe. No doubt they and the royal dukes who commanded them were apt to be grossly ignorant of their business; but it may be admitted by a historian that they often showed the qualities of which Wellington was himself a type. The English officer was a gentleman before he was a soldier, and considered the military virtues to be a part of his natural endowment. But it

[1] Clode, ii. 86.

was undoubtedly a part of his traditional code of honour to do his duty manfully and to do it rather as a manifestation of his own spirit than from any desire for rewards or decorations. The same quality is represented more strikingly by the navy. The English admiral represents the most attractive and stirring type of heroism in our history. Nelson and the 'band of brothers' who served with him, the simple and high-minded sailors who summed up the whole duty of man in doing their best to crush the enemies of their country, are among the finest examples of single-souled devotion to the calls of patriotism. The navy, indeed, had its ugly side no less than the army. There was corruption at Greenwich[1] and in the dockyards, and parliamentary intrigue was a road to professional success. Voltaire notes the queer contrast between the English boast of personal liberty and the practice of filling up the crews by pressgangs. The discipline was often barbarous, and the wrongs of the common sailor found sufficient expression in the mutiny at the Nore. A grievance, however, which pressed upon a single class was maintained from the necessity of the case and the inertness of the administrative system. The navy did not excite the same jealousy as the army; and the officers were more professionally skilful than their brethren. The national qualities come out, often in their highest form, in the race of great seamen upon whom the security of the island power essentially depended.

[1] See the famous case in 1778 in which Erskine made his first appearance, in *State Trials*, xxi. Lord St. Vincent's struggle against the corruption of his time is described by Prof. Laughton in the *Dictionary of National Biography*, (*s.v.* Sir John Jervis). In 1801 half a million a year was stolen, besides all the waste due to corruption and general muddling.

V. THE CHURCH

I turn, however, to the profession which was more directly connected with the intellectual development of the country. The nature of the church establishment gives the most obvious illustration of the connection between the intellectual position on the one hand and the social and political order on the other, though I do not presume to decide how far either should be regarded as effect and the other as cause.

What is the church of England? Some people apparently believe that it is a body possessing and transmitting certain supernatural powers. This view was in abeyance for the time for excellent reasons, and, true or false, is no answer to the constitutional question. It does not enable us to define what was the actual body with which lawyers and politicians have to deal. The best answer to such questions in ordinary case would be given by describing the organisation of the body concerned. We could then say what is the authority which speaks in its name; and what is the legislature which makes its laws, alters its arrangements, and defines the terms of membership. The supreme legislature of the church of England might appear to be parliament. It is the Act of Uniformity which defines the profession of belief exacted from the clergy; and no alteration could be made in regard to the rights and duties of the clergy except by parliamentary authority. The church might therefore be regarded as simply the religious department of the state. Since 1688, however, the theory and the practice of toleration had introduced difficulties. Nonconformity was not by itself punishable though it exposed a man

to certain disqualifications. The state, therefore, recognised that many of its members might legally belong to other churches, although it had, as Warburton argued, formed an 'alliance' with the dominant church. The spirit of toleration was spreading throughout the century. The old penal laws, due to the struggles of the seventeenth century, were becoming obsolete in practice and were gradually being repealed. The Gordon riots of 1780 showed that a fanatical spirit might still be aroused in a mob which wanted an excuse for plunder; but the laws were not explicitly defended by reasonable persons and were being gradually removed by legislation towards the end of the century. Although, therefore, parliament was kept free from papists, it could hardly regard church and state as identical, or consider itself as entitled to act as the representative body of the church. No other body, indeed, could change the laws of the church; but parliament recognised its own incompetence to deal with them. Towards the end of the century, various attempts were made to relax the terms of subscription. It was proposed, for example, to substitute a profession of belief in the Bible for a subscription to the Thirty-Nine Articles. But the House of Commons sensibly refused to expose itself by venturing upon any theological innovations. A body more ludicrously incompetent could hardly have been invented.

Hence we must say that the church had either no supreme body which could speak in its name and modify its creed, its ritual, its discipline, or the details of its organisation; or else, that the only body which had in theory a right to interfere was doomed, by sufficient considerations, to absolute inaction. The church, from

a secular point of view, was not so much a department of the state as an aggregate of offices, the functions of which were prescribed by unalterable tradition. It consisted of a number of bishops, deans and chapters, rectors, vicars, curates, and so forth, many of whom had certain proprietary rights in their position, and who were bound by law to discharge certain functions. But the church, considered as a whole, could hardly be called an organism at all, or, if an organism, it was an organism with its central organ in a permanent state of paralysis. The church, again, in this state was essentially dependent upon the ruling classes. A glance at the position of the clergy shows their professional position. At their head were the bishops, some of them enjoying princely revenues, while others were so poor as to require that their incomes should be eked out by deaneries or livings held *in commendam*. The great sees, such as Canterbury, Durham, Ely, and Winchester, were valued at between £20,000 and £30,000 a year; while the smaller, Llandaff, Bangor, Bristol, and Gloucester, were worth less than £2000. The bishops had patronage which enabled them to provide for relatives or for deserving clergymen. The average incomes of the parochial clergy, meanwhile, were small. In 1809 they were calculated to be worth £255, while nearly four thousand livings were worth under £150; and there were four or five thousand curates with very small pay. The profession, therefore, offered a great many blanks with a few enormous prizes. How were those prizes generally obtained? When the reformers published the *Black Book* in 1820, they gave a list of the bishops holding sees in the last year of George III.; and, as most of these gentlemen were on their promotion at the end of the previous century. I give the list in a note.[1]

There were twenty-seven bishoprics including Sodor

[1] The list, checked from other sources of information, is as follows:—Manners Sutton, archbishop of Canterbury, was grandson of the third duke of Rutland; Edward Vernon, archbishop of York, was son of the first Lord Vernon and cousin of the third Lord Harcourt, whose estates he inherited; Shute Barrington, bishop of Durham, was son of the first and brother of the second Viscount Barrington; Brownlow North, bishop of Winchester, was uncle to the earl of Guildford; James Cornwallis, bishop of Lichfield, was uncle to the second marquis, whose peerage he inherited; George Pelham, bishop of Exeter, was brother of the earl of Chichester; Henry Bathurst, bishop of Norwich, was nephew of the first earl; George Henry Law, bishop of Chester, was brother of the first Lord Ellenborough; Edward Legge, bishop of Oxford, was son of the second earl of Dartmouth; Henry Ryder, bishop of Gloucester, was brother to the earl of Harrowby; George Murray, bishop of Sodor and Man, was nephew-in-law to the duke of Athol and brother-in-law to the earl of Kinnoul. Of the fourteen tutors, etc., mentioned above, William Howley, bishop of London, had been tutor to the prince of Orange at Oxford; George Pretyman Tomline, bishop of Lincoln, had been Pitt's tutor at Cambridge; Richard Beadon, bishop of Bath and Wells, had been tutor to the duke of Gloucester at Cambridge; Folliott Cornewall, bishop of Worcester, had been made chaplain to the House of Commons by the influence of his cousin, the Speaker; John Buckner, bishop of Chichester, had been tutor to the duke of Richmond; Henry William Majendie, bishop of Bangor, was the son of Queen Charlotte's English master, and had been tutor to William IV.; George Isaac Huntingford, bishop of Hereford, had been tutor to Addington, prime minister; Thomas Burgess, bishop of St. David's, was a personal friend of Addington; John Fisher, bishop of Salisbury, had been tutor to the duke of Kent; John Luxmoore, bishop of St. Asaph, had been tutor to the duke of Buccleugh; Samuel Goodenough, bishop of Carlisle, had been tutor to the sons of the third duke of Portland and was connected with Addington; William Lort Mansel, bishop of Bristol, had been tutor to Perceval at Cambridge, and owed to Perceval the mastership of Trinity; Walter King, bishop of Rochester, had been secretary to the duke of Portland; and Bowyer Edward Sparke, bishop of Ely, had been tutor to the duke of Rutland. The two remaining bishops were Herbert Marsh, bishop of Peterborough, who had established a claim by defending Pitt's financial measures in an important pamphlet; and William Van Mildert, bishop of Llandaff, who had been chaplain to the Grocers' Company and became known as a preacher in London.

and Man. Of these eleven were held by members of noble families; fourteen were held by men who had been tutors in, or in other ways personally connected with the royal family or the families of ministers and great men; and of the remaining two, one rested his claim upon political writing in defence of Pitt, while the other seems to have had the support of a great city company. The system of translation enabled the government to keep a hand upon the bishops. Their elevation to the more valuable places or leave to hold subsidiary preferments depended upon their votes in the House of Lords. So far, then, as secular motives operated, the tendency of the system was clear. If Providence had assigned to you a duke for a father or an uncle, preferment would fall to you as of right. A man of rank who takes orders should be rewarded for his condescension. If that qualification be not secured, you should aim at being tutor in a great family, accompany a lad on the grand tour, or write some pamphlet on a great man's behalf. Paley gained credit for independence at Cambridge, and spoke with contempt of the practice of 'rooting,' the cant phrase for patronage hunting. The text which he facetiously suggested for a sermon when Pitt visited Cambridge, 'There is a young man here who has six loaves and two fishes, but what are they among so many?' hit off the spirit in which a minister was regarded at the universities. The memoirs of Bishop Watson illustrate the same sentiment. He lived in his pleasant country house at Windermere, never visiting his diocese, and according to De Quincey, talking Socinianism at his table. He felt himself to be a deeply injured man, because ministers had never found an opportunity for

translating him to a richer diocese, although he had written against Paine and Gibbon. If they would not reward their friends, he argued, why should he take up their cause by defending Christianity?

The bishops were eminently respectable. They did not lead immoral lives, and if they gave a large share of preferment to their families, that at least was a domestic virtue. Some of them, Bishop Barrington of Durham, for example, took a lead in philanthropic movements; and, if considered simply as prosperous country-gentlemen, little fault could be found with them. While, however, every commonplace motive pointed so directly towards a career of subserviency to the ruling class among the laity, it could not be expected that they should take a lofty view of their profession. The Anglican clergy were not like the Irish priesthood, in close sympathy with the peasantry, or like the Scottish ministers, the organs of strong convictions spreading through the great mass of the middle and lower classes. A man of energy, who took his faith seriously, was, like the Evangelical clergy, out of the road to preferment, or, like Wesley, might find no room within the church at all. His colleagues called him an 'enthusiast,' and disliked him as a busybody if not a fanatic. They were by birth and adoption themselves members of the ruling class; many of them were the younger sons of squires, and held their livings in virtue of their birth. Advowsons are the last offices to retain a proprietary character. The church of that day owed such a representative as Horne Tooke to the system which enabled his father to provide for him by buying a living. From the highest to the lowest ranks of clergy, the church was as Matthew Arnold could

still call it, an 'appendage of the barbarians.' The clergy, that is, as a whole, were an integral but a subsidiary part of the aristocracy or the great landed interest. Their admirers urged that the system planted a cultivated gentleman in every parish in the country. Their opponents replied, like John Sterling, that he was a 'black dragoon with horse meat and man's meat'—part of the garrison distributed through the country to support the cause of property and order. In any case the instinctive prepossessions, the tastes and favourite pursuits of the profession were essentially those of the class with which it was so intimately connected. Arthur Young,[1] speaking of the French clergy, observes that at least they are not poachers and foxhunters, who divide their time between hunting, drinking, and preaching. You do not in France find such advertisements as he had heard of in England, 'Wanted a curacy in a good sporting country, where the duty is light and the neighbourhood convivial.' The proper exercise for a country clergyman, he rather quaintly observes, is agriculture. The ideal parson, that is, should be a squire in canonical dress. The clergy of the eighteenth century probably varied between the extremes represented by Trulliber and the Vicar of Wakefield. Many of them were excellent people, with a mild taste for literature, contributing to the *Gentleman's Magazine*, investigating the antiquities of their county, occasionally confuting a deist, exerting a sound judgment in cultivating their glebes or improving the breed of cattle, and respected both by squire and farmers. The 'Squarson,' in Sydney Smith's facetious phrase, was the

[1] *Travels in France* (1892), p. 327.

ideal clergyman. The purely sacerdotal qualities, good or bad, were at a minimum. Crabbe, himself a type of the class, has left admirable portraits of his fellows. Profound veneration for his noble patrons and hearty dislike for intrusive dissenters were combined in his own case with a pure domestic life, a keen insight into the uglier realities of country life and a good sound working morality. Miss Austen, who said that she could have been Crabbe's wife, has given more delicate pictures of the clergyman as he appeared at the tea-tables of the time. He varies according to her from the squire's excellent younger brother, who is simply a squire in a white neck-cloth, to the silly but still respectable sycophant, who firmly believes his lady patroness to be a kind of local deity. Many of the real memoirs of the day give pleasant examples of the quiet and amiable lives of the less ambitious clergy. There is the charming Gilbert White (1720-1793) placidly studying the ways of tortoises, and unconsciously composing a book which breathes an undying charm from its atmosphere of peaceful repose; William Gilpin (1724-1804) founding and endowing parish schools, teaching the catechism, and describing his vacation tours in narratives which helped to spread a love of natural scenery; and Thomas Gisborne (1758-1846), squire and clergyman, a famous preacher among the evangelicals and a poet after the fashion of Cowper, who loved his native Needwood Forest as White loved Selborne and Gilpin loved the woods of Boldre; and Cowper himself (1731-1800) who, though not a clergyman, lived in a clerical atmosphere, and whose gentle and playful enjoyment of quiet country life relieves the painfully deep pathos of his disordered

imagination; and the excellent W. L. Bowles (1762-1850), whose sonnets first woke Coleridge's imagination, who spent eighty-eight years in an amiable and blameless life, and was country-gentleman, magistrate, antiquary, clergyman, and poet.[1] Such names are enough to recall a type which has not quite vanished, and which has gathered a new charm in more stirring and fretful times. These most excellent people, however, were not likely to be prominent in movements destined to break up the placid environment of their lives nor, in truth, to be sources of any great intellectual stir.

VI. THE UNIVERSITIES

The effect of these conditions is perhaps best marked in the state of the universities. Universities have at different periods been great centres of intellectual life. The English universities of the eighteenth century are generally noted only as embodiments of sloth and prejudice. The judgments of Wesley and Gibbon and Adam Smith and Bentham coincide in regard to Oxford; and Johnson's love of his university is an equivocal testimony to its intellectual merits. We generally think of it as of a sleepy hollow, in which portly fellows of colleges, like the convivial Warton, imbibed port wine and sneered at Methodists, though few indeed rivalled Warton's services to literature. The universities in fact had become, as they long continued to be, high schools chiefly for the use of the clergy, and if they still aimed at some wider intellectual training, were sinking to be

[1] See *A Country Clergyman of the Eighteenth Century* (Thomas Twining), 1882, for a pleasant picture of the class.

institutions where the pupils of the public schools might, if they pleased, put a little extra polish upon their classical and mathematical knowledge. The colleges preserved their mediæval constitution; and no serious changes of their statutes were made until the middle of the present century. The clergy had an almost exclusive part in the management, and dissenters were excluded even from entering Oxford as students.[1] But the clergyman did not as a rule devote himself to a life of study. He could not marry as a fellow, but he made no vows of celibacy. The college, therefore, was merely a stepping-stone on the way to the usual course of preferment. A fellow looked forwards to settling in a college living, or if he had the luck to act as tutor to a nobleman, he might soar to a deanery or a bishopric. The fellows who stayed in their colleges were probably those who had least ambition, or who had a taste for an easy bachelor's life. The universities, therefore, did not form bodies of learned men interested in intellectual pursuits; but at most, helped such men in their start upon a more prosperous career. The studies flagged in sympathy. Gray's letters sufficiently reveal the dulness which was felt by a man of cultivation confined within the narrow society of college dons of the day. The scholastic philosophy which had once found enthusiastic cultivators in the great universities had more or less held its own through the seventeenth century, though repudiated by all the rising thinkers. Since the days of Locke and Berkeley, it had fallen utterly out of credit. The bright common

[1] At Cambridge subscription was abolished for undergraduates in 1775; and bachelors of arts had only to declare themselves ' *bona-fide* members of the church of England.'

sense of the polished society of the day looked upon the old doctrine with a contempt, which, if not justified by familiarity, was an implicit judgment of the tree by its fruits. Nobody could suppose the divines of the day to be the depositaries of an esoteric wisdom which the vulgar were not worthy to criticise. They were themselves chiefly anxious to prove that their sacred mysteries were really not at all mysterious, but merely one way of expressing plain common sense. At Oxford, indeed, the lads were still crammed with Aldrich, and learned the technical terms of a philosophy which had ceased to have any real life in it. At Cambridge, ardent young radicals spoke with contempt of this ' horrid jargon —fit only to be chattered by monkies in a wilderness.'[1] Even at Cambridge, they still had disputations on the old form, but they argued theses from Locke's essay, and thought that their mathematical studies were a check upon metaphysical ' jargon.' It is indeed characteristic of the respect for tradition that at Cambridge even mathematics long suffered from a mistaken patriotism which resented any improvement upon the methods of Newton. There were some signs of reviving activity. The fellowships were being distributed with less regard to private interest. The mathematical tripos founded at Cambridge in the middle of the century became the prototype of all competitive examinations; and half a century later Oxford followed the precedent by the Examination Statute of 1800. A certain number of professorships of such modern studies as anatomy, history, botany, and geology were founded during the eighteenth century, and show a certain sense of a need of broader views. The lectures

[1] Gilbert Wakefield's *Memoirs*, ii. 149.

upon which Blackstone founded his commentaries were the product of the foundation of the Vinerian professorship in 1751; and the most recent of the Cambridge colleges, Downing College, shows by its constitution that a professoriate was now considered to be desirable. Cambridge in the last years of the century might have had a body of very eminent professors. Watson, second wrangler of 1759, had delivered lectures upon chemistry, of which it was said by Davy that hardly any conceivable change in the science could make them obsolete.[1] Paley, senior wrangler in 1763, was an almost unrivalled master of lucid exposition, and one of his works is still a text-book at Cambridge. Isaac Milner, senior wrangler in 1774, afterwards held the professorships of mathematics and natural philosophy, and was famous as a sort of ecclesiastical Dr. Johnson. Gilbert Wakefield, second wrangler in 1776, published an edition of Lucretius, and was a man of great ability and energy. Herbert Marsh, second wrangler in 1779, was divinity professor from 1807, and was the first English writer to introduce some knowledge of the early stages of German criticism. Porson, the greatest Greek scholar of his time, became professor in 1790; Malthus, ninth wrangler in 1788, who was to make a permanent mark upon political economy, became fellow of Jesus College in 1793. Waring, senior wrangler in 1757, Vince, senior wrangler in 1775, and Wollaston, senior wrangler in 1783, were also professors and mathematicians of reputation. Towards the end of the century ten professors were lecturing.[2] A large number were not lecturing,

[1] De Quincey, *Works* (1863), ii. 106.
[2] Wordsworth's *University Life, etc.* (1874), 83-87.

though Milner was good enough to be 'accessible to students.' Paley and Watson had been led off into the path of ecclesiastical preferment. Marsh too became a bishop in 1816. There was no place for such talents as those of Malthus, who ultimately became professor at Haileybury. Wakefield had the misfortune of not being able to cover his heterodoxy with the conventional formula. Porson suffered from the same cause, and from less respectable weaknesses; but it seems that the university had no demand for services of the great scholar, and he did nothing for his £40 a year. Milner was occupied in managing the university in the interests of Pitt and Protestantism, and in waging war against Jacobins and intruders. There was no lack of ability; but there was no inducement to any intellectual activity for its own sake; and there were abundant temptations for any man of energy to diverge to the career which offered more intelligible rewards.

The universities in fact supplied the demand which was actually operative. They provided the average clergyman with a degree; they expected the son of the country-gentleman or successful lawyer to acquire the traditional culture of his class, and to spend three or four years pleasantly, or even, if he chose, industriously. But there was no such thing as a learned society, interested in the cultivation of knowledge for its own sake, and applauding the devotion of life to its extension or discussion. The men of the time who contributed to the progress of science owed little or nothing to the universities, and were rather volunteers from without, impelled by their own idiosyncrasies. Among the scientific leaders, for example, Joseph Black (1728-1799) was a

Scottish professor; Priestley (1733-1804) a dissenting minister; Cavendish (1731-1810) an aristocratic recluse, who, though he studied at Cambridge, never graduated; Watt (1736-1819) a practical mechanician; and Dalton (1766-1844) a Quaker schoolmaster. John Hunter (1728-1793) was one of the energetic Scots who forced their way to fame without help from English universities. The cultivation of the natural sciences was only beginning to take root; and the soil, which it found congenial, was not that of the great learned institutions, which held to their old traditional studies.

I may, then, sum up the result in a few words. The church had once claimed to be an entirely independent body, possessing a supernatural authority, with an organisation sanctioned by supernatural powers, and entitled to lay down the doctrines which gave the final theory of life. Theology was the queen of the sciences and theologians the interpreters of the first principles of all knowledge and conduct. The church of England, on the other hand, at our period had entirely ceased to be independent: it was bound hand and foot by acts of parliament: there was no ecclesiastical organ capable of speaking in its name, altering its laws or defining its tenets: it was an aggregate of offices the appointment to which was in the hands either of the political ministers or of the lay members of the ruling class. It was in reality simply a part of the ruling class told off to perform divine services: to maintain order and respectability and the traditional morality. It had no distinctive philosophy or theology, for the articles of belief represented simply a compromise; an attempt to retain as much of the old as was practicable and yet to admit as

much of the new as was made desirable by political considerations. It was the boast of its more liberal members that they were not tied down to any definite dogmatic system; but could have a free hand so long as they did not wantonly come into conflict with some of the legal formulæ laid down in a previous generation. The actual teaching showed the effects of the system. It had been easy to introduce a considerable leaven of the rationalism which suited the lay mind; to explain away the mysterious doctrines upon which an independent church had insisted as manifestations of its spiritual privileges, but which were regarded with indifference or contempt by the educated laity now become independent. The priest had been disarmed and had to suit his teaching to the taste of his patrons and congregations. The divines of the eighteenth century had, as they boasted, confuted the deists; but it was mainly by showing that they could be deists in all but the name. The dissenters, less hampered by legal formulæ, had drifted towards Unitarianism. The position of such divines as Paley, Watson, and Hey was not so much that the Unitarians were wrong, as that the mysterious doctrines were mere sets of words, over which it was superfluous to quarrel. The doctrine was essentially traditional; for it was impossible to represent the doctrines of the church of England as deductions from any abstract philosophy. But the traditions were not regarded as having any mysterious authority. Abstract philosophy might lead to deism or infidelity. Paley and his like rejected such philosophy in the spirit of Locke or even Hume. But it was always possible to treat a tradition like any other statement of fact. It could be proved by appropriate evidence. The truth of Christianity was therefore merely a question of facts like the truth of any other passages of history. It was easy enough to make out a case for the Christian miracles, and then the mysteries, after it had been sufficiently explained that they really meant next to nothing, could be rested upon the authority of the miracles. In other words, the accepted doctrines, like the whole constitution of the church, could be so modified as to suit the prejudices and modes of thought of the laity. The church, it may be said, was thoroughly secularised. The priest was no longer a wielder of threats and an interpreter of oracles, but an entirely respectable gentleman, who fully sympathised with the prejudices of his patron and practically admitted that he had very little to reveal, beyond explaining that his dogmas were perfectly harmless and eminently convenient. He preached, however, a sound common-sense morality, and was not divided from his neighbours by setting up the claims characteristic of a sacerdotal caste. Whether he has become on the whole better or worse by subsequent changes is a question not to be asked here ; but perhaps not quite so easily answered as is sometimes supposed.

The condition of the English church and universities may be contrasted with that of their Scottish rivals. The Scottish church and universities had no great prizes to offer and no elaborate hierarchy. But the church was a national institution in a sense different from the English. The General Assembly was a powerful body, not overshadowed by a great political rival. To rise to be a minister was the great ambition of poor sons of farmers and tradesmen. They had to study at the universities in the intervals, perhaps, of agricultural labour ; and if

the learning was slight and the scholarship below the English standard, the young aspirant had at least to learn to preach and to acquire such philosophy as would enable him to argue upon grace and freewill with some hard-headed Davie Deans. It was doubtless owing in part to these conditions that the Scottish universities produced many distinguished teachers throughout the century. Professors had to teach something which might at least pass for philosophy, though they were more or less restrained by the necessity of respecting orthodox prejudices. At the end of the century, the only schools of philosophy in the island were to be found in Scotland, where Reid (1710-1796) and Adam Smith (1723-1790) had found intelligent disciples, and where Dugald Stewart, of whom I shall speak presently, had become the recognised philosophical authority.

VII. THEORY

What theory corresponds to this practical order ? It implies, in the first place, a constant reference to tradition. The system has grown up without any reference to abstract principles or symmetrical plan. The legal order supposes a traditional common law, as the ecclesiastical order a traditional creed, and the organisation is explicable only by historical causes. The system represents a series of compromises, not the elaboration of a theory. If the squire undertook by way of supererogation to justify his position he appealed to tradition and experience. He invoked the 'wisdom of our ancestors,' the system of 'checks and balances' which made our Constitution an unrivalled mixture of monarchy, aristocracy, and democracy

deserving the 'dread and envy of the world.' The prescription for compounding that mixture could obviously be learned by nothing but experiment. Traditional means empirical. By instinct, rather than conscious reasoning, Englishmen had felt their way to establishing the 'palladia of our liberties': trial by jury, the 'Habeas Corpus' Act, and the substitution of a militia for a standing army. The institutions were cherished because they had been developed by long struggles and were often cherished when their real justification had disappeared. The Constitution had not been 'made' but had 'grown'; or, in other words, the one rule had been the rule of thumb. That is an excellent rule in its way, and very superior to an abstract rule which neglects or overrides experience. The 'logic of facts,' moreover, may be trusted to produce a certain harmony : and general principles, though not consciously invoked, tacitly govern the development of institutions worked out under uniform conditions. The simple reluctance to pay money without getting money's worth might generate the important principle that representation should go with taxation, without embodying any theory of a 'social contract' such as was offered by an afterthought to give a philosophical sanction. Englishmen, it is said, had bought their liberties step by step, because at each step they were in a position to bargain with their rulers. What they had bought they were determined to keep and considered to be their inalienable property. One result is conspicuous. In England the ruling classes did not so much consider their privileges to be something granted by the state, as the power of the state to be something derived from their concessions. Though

the lord-lieutenant and the justices of the peace were nominated by the crown, their authority came in fact as an almost spontaneous consequence of their birthright or their acquired position in the country. They shone by their own light and were really the ultimate sources of authority. Seats in parliament, preferments in the church, commissions in the army belonged to them like their estates; and they seemed to be qualified by nature, rather than by appointment, to act in judicial and administrative capacities. The system of 'self-government' embodies this view. The functions of government were assigned to men already powerful by their social position. The absence of the centralised hierarchy of officials gave to Englishmen the sense of personal liberty which compelled the admiration of Voltaire and his countrymen in the eighteenth century. In England were no *lettres de cachet*, and no Bastille. A man could say what he thought and act without fear of arbitrary rule. There was no such system as that which, in France, puts the agents of the central power above the ordinary law of the land. This implies what has been called the 'rule of the law' in England. 'With us every official from the prime minister down to a constable or a collector of taxes' (as Professor Dicey explains the principle) 'is under the same responsibility for every act done without legal justification as any other citizen'[1] The early centralisation of the English monarchy had made the law supreme, and instead of generating a new structure had combined and regulated the existing social forces. The sovereign power was thus farmed to the aristocracy

[1] Professor Dicey's *Lectures on the Law of the Constitution* (1885), p. 178. Professor Dicey gives an admirable exposition of the 'rule of law.'

instead of forming an organ of its own. Instead of resigning power they were forced to exercise it on condition of thorough responsibility to the central judiciary. Their privileges were not destroyed but were combined with the discharge of corresponding duties. Whatever their shortcomings, they were preserved from the decay which is the inevitable consequence of a divorce of duties from privileges.

Another aspect of the case is equally clear. If the privilege is associated with a duty, the duty may also be regarded as a privilege. The doctrine seems to mark a natural stage in the evolution of the conception of duty to the state. The power which is left to a member of the ruling class is also part of his dignity. Thus we have an amalgamation between the conceptions of private property and public trust. 'In so far as the ideal of feudalism is perfectly realised,' it has been said,[1] 'all that we can call public law is merged in private law; jurisdiction is property; office is property; the kingship itself is property.' This feudal ideal was still preserved with many of the institutions descended from feudalism. The king's right to his throne was regarded as of the same kind as the right to a private estate. His rights as king were also his rights as the owner of the land.[2] Subordinate landowners had similar rights, and as the royal power diminished

[1] Pollock and Maitland's *History of English Law*, i. 208.
[2] A characteristic consequence is that Hale and Blackstone make no distinction between public and private law. Austin (*Jurisprudence* (1869), 773-76) applauds them for this peculiarity, which he regards as a proof of originality, though it would rather seem to be an acceptance of the traditional view. Austin, however, retorts the charge of *Verwirrung* upon German critics.

greater powers fell to the aggregate of constitutional kinglets who governed the country. Each of them was from one point of view an official, but each also regarded his office as part of his property. The country belonged to him and his class rather than he to the country. We occasionally find the quaint theory which deduced political rights from property in land. The freeholders were the owners of the soil and might give notice to quit to the rest of the population.[1] They had therefore a natural right to carry on government in their own interests. The ruling classes, however, were not marked off from others by any deep line of demarcation; they could sell their own share in the government to anybody who was rich enough to buy it, and there was a constant influx of new blood. Moreover, they did in fact improve their estate with very great energy, and discharged roughly, but in many ways efficiently, the duties which were also part of their property. The nobleman or even the squire was more than an individual; as head of a family he was a life tenant of estates which he desired to transmit to his descendants. He was a 'corporation sole' and had some of the spirit of a corporation. A college or a hospital is founded to discharge a particular function; its members continue perhaps to recognise their duty; but they resent any interference from outside as sacrilege or confiscation. It is for them alone to judge how they can best carry out, and whether they are actually carrying out, the aims of the corporate life. In the same way the great noble took his part in legislation,

[1] This is the theory of Defoe in his *Original Power of the People of England* (Works by Hazlitt, vol iii. See especially p. 57).

church preferment, the command of the army, and so forth, and fully admitted that he was bound in honour to play his part effectively; but he was equally convinced that he was subject to nothing outside of his sense of honour. His duties were also his rights. The naïf expression of this doctrine by a great borough proprietor, 'May I not do what I like with my own?' was to become proverbial.[1]

This, finally, suggests that a doctrine of 'individualism' is implied throughout. The individual rights are the antecedent and the rights of the state a consequent or corollary. Every man has certain sacred rights accruing to him in virtue of 'prescription' or tradition, through his inherited position in the social organism. The 'rule of law' secures that he shall exercise them without infringing the privileges of his neighbour. He may moreover be compelled by the law to discharge them on due occasion. But, as there is no supreme body which can sufficiently superintend, stimulate, promote, or dismiss, the active impulse must come chiefly from his own sense of the fitness of things. The efficiency therefore depends upon his being in such a position that his duty may coincide with his personal interest. The political machinery can only work efficiently on the assumption of a spontaneous activity of the ruling classes, prompted by public spirit or a sense of personal dignity. Meanwhile, 'individualism' in a different sense was represented by the forces which made for progress rather than order, and to them I must now turn.

[1] The fourth duke of Newcastle in the House of Lords, 3 Dec. 1830.

CHAPTER II

THE INDUSTRIAL SPIRIT

I. THE MANUFACTURERS

THE history of England during the eighteenth century shows a curious contrast between the political stagnancy and the great industrial activity. The great constitutional questions seemed to be settled; and the statesmen, occupied mainly in sharing power and place, took a very shortsighted view (not for the first time in history) of the great problems that were beginning to present themselves. The British empire in the East was not won by a towering ambition so much as forced upon a reluctant commercial company by the necessities of its position. The English race became dominant in America; but the political connection was broken off mainly because English statesmen could only regard it from the shopkeeping point of view. When a new world began to arise at the Antipodes, our rulers saw an opportunity not for planting new offshoots of European civilisation, but for ridding themselves of the social rubbish no longer accepted in America. With purblind energy, and eyes doggedly fixed upon the ground at their feet, the race had somehow pressed forwards to illustrate the old doctrine that a man never goes so far as when he does

not know whither he is going. While thinking of earn-
ing an honest penny by extending the trade, our 'monied-
men' were laying the foundation of vast structures to be
developed by their descendants.

Politicians, again, had little to do with the great
'industrial revolution' which marked the last half of the
century. The main facts are now a familiar topic of
economic historians ; nor need I speak of them in detail.
Though agriculture was still the main industry, and the
landowners almost monopolised political power, an ever
growing proportion of the people was being collected in
towns ; the artisans were congregating in large factories ;
and the great cloud of coal-smoke, which has never
dwindled, was already beginning to darken our skies.
The change corresponds to the difference between a fully
developed organism possessed of a central brain, with an
elaborate nervous system, and some lower form in which
the vital processes are still carried on by a number of
separate ganglia. The concentration of the population
in the great industrial centres implied the improvement of the means of commerce ; new organisation of
industry provided with a corresponding apparatus of
machinery ; and the systematic exploitation of the
stored-up forces of nature. Each set of changes was
at once cause and effect, and each was carried on separately, although in relation to the other. Brindley,
Arkwright, and Watt may be taken as typical representatives of the three operations. Canals, spinning-
jennies, and steam-engines were changing the whole
social order.

The development of means of communication had been
slow till the last half of the century. The roads had

been little changed since they had been first laid down
as part of the great network which bound the Roman
empire together. Turnpike acts, sanctioning the construction of new roads, became numerous. Palmer's
application of the stage-coaches to the carriage of the
mails marked an epoch in 1784 ; and De Quincey's
prose poem, 'The Mail-coach,' shows how the unprecedented speed of Palmer's coaches, then spreading the
news of the first battles in the Peninsula, had caused
them to tyrannise over the opium-eater's dreams. They
were discharging at once a political and an industrial
function. Meanwhile the Bridgewater canal, constructed
between 1759 and 1761, was the first link in a great
network which, by the time of the French revolution,
connected the seaports and the great centres of industry.
The great inventions of machinery were simultaneously
enabling manufacturers to take advantage of the new
means of communication. The cotton manufacture
sprang up soon after 1780 with enormous rapidity.
Aided by the application of steam (first applied to a
cotton mill in 1785) it passed the woollen trade, the
traditional favourite of legislators, and became the most
important branch of British trade. The iron trade had
made a corresponding start. While the steam-engine, on
which Watt had made the first great improvement in
1765, was transforming the manufacturing system, and
preparing the advent of the steamship and railroad,
Great Britain had become the leading manufacturing
and commercial country in the world. The agricultural
interest was losing its pre-eminence ; and huge towns with
vast aggregations of artisan population were beginning
to spring up with unprecedented rapidity. The change

was an illustration upon a gigantic scale of the doctrines
expounded in the *Wealth of Nations*. Division of labour
was being applied to things more important than pin-
making, involving a redistribution of functions not as
between men covered by the same roof, but between
whole classes of society ; between the makers of new
means of communication and the manufacturers of
every kind of material. The whole industrial community might be regarded as one great organism.
Yet the organisation was formed by a multitude of
independent agencies without any concerted plan. It
was thus a vast illustration of the doctrine that each
man by pursuing his own interests promoted the interests of the whole, and that government interference
was simply a hindrance. The progress of improvement, says Adam Smith, depends upon 'the uniform,
constant, and uninterrupted effort of every man to
better his condition,' which often succeeds in spite of
the errors of government, as nature often overcomes
the blunders of doctors. It is, as he infers, 'the
highest impertinence and presumption for kings and
ministers to pretend to watch over the economy of
private people' by sumptuary laws and taxes upon
imports.[1] To the English manufacturer or engineer
government appeared as a necessary evil. It allowed
the engineer to make roads and canals, after a troublesome and expensive process of application. It granted
patents to the manufacturer, but the patents were a
source of perpetual worry and litigation. The Chancellor of the Exchequer might look with complacency
upon the development of a new branch of trade ; but it

[1] *Wealth of Nations*, bk. ii. ch. iii.

was because he was lying in wait to come down upon it
with a new tax or system of duties.

The men who were the chief instruments of the process were 'self-made' ; they were the typical examples of
Mr. Smiles's virtue of self-help ; they owed nothing to
government or to the universities which passed for the
organs of national culture. The leading engineers began
as ordinary mechanics. John Metcalf (1717-1810),
otherwise 'blind Jack of Knaresborough,' was a son of
poor parents. He had lost his sight by smallpox at
the age of six, and, in spite of his misfortune, became
a daring rider, wrestler, soldier, and carrier, and made
many roads in the north of England, executing surveys
and constructing the works himself. James Brindley
(1716-1772), son of a midland collier, barely able to
read or write, working out plans by processes which he
could not explain, and lying in bed till they took shape
in his brain, a rough mechanic, labouring for trifling
weekly wages, created the canals which mainly enabled
Manchester and Liverpool to make an unprecedented
leap in prosperity. The two great engineers, Thomas
Telford (1757-1834), famous for the Caledonian canal
and the Menai bridge ; and John Rennie (1761-1821),
drainer of Lincolnshire fens, and builder of Waterloo
bridge and the Plymouth breakwater, rose from the ranks.
Telford inherited and displayed in a different direction
the energies of Eskdale borderers, whose achievements
in the days of cattle-stealing were to be made famous
by Scott : Rennie was the son of an East Lothian
farmer. Both of them learned their trade by actual
employment as mechanics. The inventors of machinery
belonged mainly to the lower middle classes. Kay was

a small manufacturer ; Hargreaves a hand-loom weaver ; Crompton the son of a small farmer ; and Arkwright a country barber. Watt, son of a Greenock carpenter, came from the sturdy Scottish stock, ultimately of covenanting ancestry, from which so many eminent men have sprung.

The new social class, in which such men were the leaders, held corresponding principles. They owed whatever success they won to their own right hands. They were sturdy workers, with eyes fixed upon success in life, and success generally of course measured by a money criterion. Many of them showed intellectual tastes, and took an honourable view of their social functions. Watt showed his ability in scientific inquiries outside of the purely industrial application ; Josiah Wedgwood, in whose early days the Staffordshire potters had led a kind of gipsy life, settling down here and there to carry on their trade, had not only founded a great industry, but was a man of artistic taste, a patron of art, and a lover of science. Telford, the Eskdale shepherd, was a man of literary taste, and was especially friendly with the typical man of letters, Southey. Others, of course, were of a lower type. Arkwright combined the talents of an inventor with those of a man of business. He was a man, says Baines (the historian of the cotton trade), who was sure to come out of an enterprise with profit, whatever the result to his partners. He made a great fortune, and founded a county family. Others rose in the same direction. The Peels, for example, represented a line of yeomen. One Peel founded a cotton business ; his son became a baronet and an influential member of parliament ; and his grandson went to Oxford, and became the

great leader of the Conservative party, although like Walpole, he owed his power to a kind of knowledge in which his adopted class were generally deficient.

The class which owed its growing importance to the achievements of such men was naturally imbued with their spirit. Its growth meant the development of a class which under the old order had been strictly subordinate to the ruling class, and naturally regarded it with a mingled feeling of respect and jealousy. The British merchant felt his superiority in business to the average country-gentleman ; he got no direct share of the pensions and sinecures which so profoundly affected the working of the political machinery, and yet his highest ambition was to rise to be himself a member of the class, and to found a family which might flourish in the upper atmosphere. The industrial classes were inclined to favour political progress within limits. They were dissenters because the church was essentially part of the aristocracy ; and they were readiest to denounce the abuses from which they did not profit. The agitators who supported Wilkes, solid aldermen and rich merchants, represented the view which was popular in London and other great cities. They were the backbone of the Whig party when it began to demand a serious reform. Their radicalism, however, was not thoroughly democratic. Many of them aspired to become members of the ruling class, and a shopkeeper does not quarrel too thoroughly with his customers. The politics of individuals were of course determined by accidents. Some of them might retain the sympathy of the class from which they sprang, and others might adopt an even extreme version of the opinions of the class to which they

desired to rise. But, in any case, the divergence of interest between the capitalists and the labourers was already making itself felt. The self-made man, it is said, is generally the hardest master. He approves of the stringent system of competition, of which he is himself a product. It clearly enables the best man to win, for is he not himself the best man ? The class which was the great seat of movement had naturally to meet all the prejudices which are roused by change. The farmers near London, as Adam Smith tells us,[1] petitioned against an extension of turnpike roads, which would enable more distant farmers to compete in their market. But the farmers were not the only prejudiced persons. All the great inventors of machinery, Kay and Arkwright and Watt, had constantly to struggle against the old workmen who were displaced by their inventions. Although, therefore, the class might be Whiggish, it did not share the strongest revolutionary passions. The genuine revolutionists were rather the men who destroyed the manufacturer's machines, and were learning to regard him as a natural enemy. The manufacturer had his own reasons for supporting government. Our foreign policy during the century was in the long run chiefly determined by the interests of our trade, however much the trade might at times be hampered by ill-conceived regulations. It is remarkable that Adam Smith[2] argues that, although the capitalist is acuter that the country-gentleman, his acuteness is chiefly displayed by knowing his own interests better. Those interests, he thinks, do not coincide so much as the interests of the country-gentleman with the general interests of the country. Consequently the

[1] *Wealth of Nations*, bk. i. ch. xi. § 1. [2] *Ibid.* bk. i. ch. xi. conclusion.

country-gentleman, though less intelligent, is more likely to favour a national and liberal policy. The merchant, in fact, was not a free-trader because he had read Adam Smith or consciously adopted Smith's principles, but because or in so far as particular restrictions interfered with him. Arthur Young complains bitterly of the manufacturers who supported the prohibition to export English wool, and so protected their own class at the expense of agriculturists. Wedgwood, though a good liberal and a supporter of Pitt's French treaty in 1786, joined in protesting against the proposal for free-trade with Ireland. The Irish, he thought, might rival his potteries. Thus, though as a matter of fact the growing class of manufacturers and merchants were inclined in the main to liberal principles, it was less from adhesion to any general doctrine than from the fact that the existing restrictions and prejudices generally conflicted with their plain interests.

Another characteristic is remarkable. Though the growth of manufactures and commerce meant the growth of great towns, it did not mean the growth of municipal institutions. On the contrary, as I shall presently have to notice, the municipalities were sinking to their lowest ebb. Manufactures, in the first instance, spread along the streams into country districts : and to the great manufacturer, working for his own hand, his neighbours were competitors as much as allies. The great towns, however, which were growing up, showed the general tendencies of the class. They were centres not only of manufacturing but of intellectual progress. The population of Birmingham, containing the famous Soho works of Boulton and Watt, had increased between 1740 and

1780 from 24,000 to 74,000 inhabitants.   Watt's partner Boulton started the 'Lunar Society' at Birmingham.[1]   Its most prominent member was Erasmus Darwin, famous then for poetry which is chiefly remembered by the parody in the *Anti-Jacobin* ; and now more famous as the advocate of a theory of evolution eclipsed by the teaching of his more famous grandson, and, in any case, a man of remarkable intellectual power.   Among those who joined in the proceedings was Edgeworth, who in 1768 was speculating upon moving carriages by steam, and Thomas Day, whose *Sandford and Merton* helped to spread in England the educational theories of Rousseau.   Priestley, who settled at Birmingham in 1780, became a member, and was helped in his investigations by Watt's counsels and Wedgwood's pecuniary help.   Among occasional visitors were Smeaton, Sir Joseph Banks, Solander, and Herschel of scientific celebrity; while the literary magnate, Dr. Parr, who lived between Warwick and Birmingham, occasionally joined the circle.   Wedgwood, though too far off to be a member, was intimate with Darwin and associated in various enterprises with Boulton.   Wedgwood's congenial partner, Thomas Bentley (1731-1780), had been in business at Manchester and at Liverpool. He had taken part in founding the Warrington 'Academy,' the dissenting seminary (afterwards moved to Manchester) of which Priestley was tutor (1761-1767), and had lectured upon art at the academy founded at Liverpool in 1773.   Another member of the academy was William Roscoe (1753-1831), whose literary taste was shown by his lives of Lorenzo de Medici and Leo x.,

[1] Smiles's *Watt and Boulton*, p. 292.

and who distinguished himself by opposing the slave-trade, then the infamy of his native town.   Allied with him in this movement were William Rathbone and James Currie (1756-1805) the biographer of Burns, a friend of . Darwin and an intelligent physician.   At Manchester Thomas Perceval (1740-1804) founded the 'Literary and Philosophical Society' in 1780.   He was a pupil of the Warrington Academy, which he afterwards joined on removing to Manchester, and he formed the scheme afterwards realised by Owens College.   He was an early advocate of sanitary measures and factory legislation, and a man of scientific reputation.   Other members of the society were: John Ferriar (1761-1815), best known by his *Illustrations of Sterne*, but also a man of literary and scientific reputation ; the great chemist, John Dalton (1766-1844), who contributed many papers to its transactions ; and, for a short time, the Socialist Robert Owen, then a rising manufacturer.   At Norwich, then important as a manufacturing centre, was a similar circle. William Taylor, an eminent Unitarian divine, who died at the Warrington Academy in 1761, had lived at Norwich.   One of his daughters married David Martineau and became the mother of Harriet Martineau, who has described the Norwich of her early years.   John Taylor, grandson of William, was father of Mrs. Austin, wife of the jurist.   He was a man of literary tastes, and his wife was known as the Madame Roland of Norwich. Mrs. Opie (1765-1853) was daughter of James Alderson, a physician of Norwich, and passed most of her life there.   William Taylor (1761-1836), another Norwich manufacturer, was among the earliest English students of German literature.   Norwich had afterwards the

unique distinction of being the home of a provincial school of artists.   John Crome (1788-1821), son of a poor weaver, and John Sell Cotman (1782-1842) were its leaders ; they formed a kind of provincial academy, and exhibited pictures which have been more appreciated since their death.   At Bristol, towards the end of the century, were similar indications of intellectual activity. Coleridge and Southey found there a society ready to listen to their early lectures, and both admired Thomas Beddoes (1760-1808), a physician, a chemist, a student of German, an imitator of Darwin in poetry, and an assailant of Pitt in pamphlets.   He had married one of Edgeworth's daughters.   With the help and advice of Wedgwood and Watt, he founded the 'Pneumatic Institute' at Clifton in 1798, and obtained the help of Humphry Davy, who there made some of his first discoveries.   Davy was soon transported to the Royal Institution, founded at the suggestion of Count Rumford in 1799, which represented the growth of a popular interest in the scientific discoveries.

The general tone of these little societies represents, of course, the tendency of the upper stratum of the industrial classes.   In their own eyes they naturally represented the progressive element of society.   They were Whigs—for 'radicalism' was not yet invented— but Whigs of the left wing; accepting the aristocratic precedency, but looking askance at the aristocratic prejudices.   They were rationalists, too, in principle, but again within limits : openly avowing the doctrines which in the Established church had still to be sheltered by ostensible conformity to the traditional dogmas. Many of them professed the Unitarianism to which the old

dissenting bodies inclined.   'Unitarianism,' said shrewd old Erasmus Darwin, 'is a feather-bed for a dying Christian.'   But at present such men as Priestley and Price were only so far on the road to a thorough rationalism as to denounce the corruptions of Christianity, as they denounced abuses in politics, without anticipating a revolutionary change in church and state.   Priestley, for example, combined 'materialism' and 'determinism' with Christianity and a belief in miracles, and controverted Horsley upon one side and Paine on the other.

II. THE AGRICULTURISTS

The general spirit represented by such movements was by no means confined to the commercial or manufacturing classes ; and its most characteristic embodiment is to be found in the writings of a leading agriculturist.

Arthur Young,[1] born in 1741, was the son of a clergyman, who had also a small ancestral property at Bradfield, near Bury St. Edmunds.   Accidents led to his becoming a farmer at an early age.   He showed more zeal than discretion, and after trying three thousand experiments on his farm, he was glad to pay £100 to another tenant to take his farm off his hands.   This experience as a practical agriculturist, far from discouraging him, qualified him in his own opinion to speak with authority,

[1] Young's *Travels in France* was republished in 1892, with a preface and short life by Miss Betham Edwards.   She has since (1898) published his autobiography.   See also the autobiographical sketch in the *Annals of Agriculture*, xv. 152-97.   Young's *Farmer's Letters* first appeared in 1767 ; his *Tours* in the Southern, Northern, and Eastern Counties in 1768, 1770, and 1771 ; his *Tour in Ireland* in 1780 ; and his *Travels in France* in 1792.   A useful bibliography, containing a list of his many publications, is appended to the edition of the *Tour in Ireland* edited by Mr. A. W. Hutton in 1892.

and he became a devoted missionary of the gospel of agricultural improvement. The enthusiasm with which he admired more successful labourers in the cause, and the indignation with which he regards the sluggish and retrograde, are charming. His kindliness, his keen interest in the prosperity of all men, rich or poor, his ardent belief in progress, combined with his quickness of observation, give a charm to the writings which embody his experience. Tours in England and a temporary land-agency in Ireland supplied him with materials for books which made him known both in England and on the Continent. In 1779 he returned to Bradfield, where he soon afterwards came into possession of his paternal estate, which became his permanent home. In 1784 he tried to extend his propaganda by bringing out the *Annals of Agriculture*—a monthly publication, of which forty-five half-yearly volumes appeared. He had many able contributors and himself wrote many interesting articles, but the pecuniary results were mainly negative. In 1791 his circulation was only 350 copies.[1] Meanwhile his acquaintance with the duc de Liancourt led to tours in France from 1788 to 1790. His *Travels in France*, first published in 1792, has become a classic. In 1793 Young was made secretary to the Board of Agriculture, of which I shall speak presently. He became known in London society as well as in agricultural circles. He was a handsome and attractive man, a charming companion, and widely recognised as an agricultural authority. The empress of Russia sent him a snuff-box; 'Farmer George' presented a merino ram; he was elected member of learned societies; he visited

[1] *Annals*, xv. 166.

Burke at Beaconsfield, Pitt at Holmwood, and was a friend of Wilberforce and of Jeremy Bentham.

Young had many domestic troubles. His marriage was not congenial; the loss of a tenderly loved daughter in 1797 permanently saddened him; he became blind, and in his later years sought comfort in religious meditation and in preaching to his poorer neighbours. He died 20th April 1820. He left behind him a gigantic history of agriculture, filling ten folio volumes of manuscript, which, though reduced to six by an enthusiastic disciple after his death, have never found their way to publication.

The *Travels in France*, Young's best book, owes one merit to the advice of a judicious friend, who remarked that the previous tours had suffered from the absence of the personal details which interest the common reader. The insertion of these makes Young's account of his French tours one of the most charming as well as most instructive books of the kind. It gives the vivid impression made upon a keen and kindly observer in all their freshness. He sensibly retained the expressions of opinion made at the time. 'I may remark at present,' he says,[1] 'that although I was totally mistaken in my prediction, yet, on a revision, I think I was right in it.' It was right, he means, upon the data then known to him, and he leaves the unfulfilled prediction as it was. The book is frequently cited in justification of the revolution, and it may be fairly urged that his authority is of the more weight, because he does not start from any sympathy with revolutionary principles. Young was in Paris when the oath was taken at the tennis-court; and

[1] *Travels in France* (1892), p. 184 n.

makes his reflections upon the beauty of the British Constitution, and the folly of visionary reforms, in a spirit which might have satisfied Burke. He was therefore not altogether inconsistent when, after the outrages, he condemned the revolution, however much the facts which he describes may tend to explain the inevitableness of the catastrophe. At any rate, his views are worth notice by the indications which they give of the mental attitude of a typical English observer.

Young in his vivacious way struck out some of the phrases which became proverbial with later economists. 'Give a man the secure possession of a bleak rock and he will turn it into a garden. Give him a nine years' lease of a garden, and he will convert it into a desert.'[1] 'The magic of PROPERTY turns sand to gold.'[2] He is delighted with the comfort of the small proprietors near Pau, which reminds him of English districts still inhabited by small yeomen.[3] Passing to a less fortunate region, he explains that the prince de Soubise has a vast property there. The property of a grand 'seigneur' is sure to be a desert.[4] The signs which indicate such properties are 'wastes, *landes*, deserts, fern, ling.' The neighbourhood of the great residences is well peopled— 'with deer, wild boars, and wolves.' 'Oh,' he exclaims, 'if I was the legislator of France for a day, I would make such great lords skip again!' 'Why,' he asked, 'were the people miserable in lower Savoy?' '*Because*,' was the reply, '*there are seigneurs everywhere*.'[5] Misery in Brittany was due 'to the execrable maxims of despotism

or the equally detestable prejudices of a feudal nobility.'[1] There was nothing, he said, in the province but 'privileges and poverty,'[2] privileges of the nobles and poverty of the peasants.

Young was profoundly convinced, moreover, that, as he says more than once[3] 'everything in this world depends on government.' He is astonished at the stupidity and ignorance of the provincial population, and ascribes it to the lethargy produced by despotism.[4] He contrasts it with 'the energetic and rapid circulation of wealth, animation, and intelligence of England,' where 'blacksmiths and carpenters' would discuss every political event. And yet he heartily admires some of the results of a centralised monarchy. He compares the miserable roads in Catalonia on the Spanish side of the frontier with the magnificent causeways and bridges on the French side. The difference is due to the 'one all-powerful cause that instigates mankind . . . government.'[5] He admires the noble public works, the canal of Languedoc, the harbours at Cherbourg and Havre, and the *école vétérinaire* where agriculture is taught upon scientific principles. He is struck by the curious contrast between France and England. In France the splendid roads are used by few travellers, and the inns are filthy pothouses; in England there are detestable roads, but a comparatively enormous traffic. When he wished to make the great nobles 'skip' he does not generally mean confiscation. He sees indeed one place where in 1790 the poor had seized a piece of waste land, declaring that the poor were the nation, and that the

[1] *Travels in France*, p. 54.   [2] *Ibid.* p. 109.   [3] *Ibid.* p. 61.
[4] *Ibid.* p. 70.   [5] *Ibid.* p. 279.

[1] *Travels in France*, p. 125.   [2] *Ibid.* p. 131.   [3] *Ibid.* pp. 198, 298.
[4] *Ibid.* pp. 55, 193, 199, 237.   [5] *Ibid.* p. 43.

waste belonged to the nation. He declares[1] that he considers their action 'wise, rational, and philosophical,' and wishes that there were a law to make such conduct legal in England. But his more general desire is that the landowners should be compelled to do their duty. He complains that the nobles live in 'wretched holes' in the country in order to save the means of expenditure upon theatres, entertainments, and gambling in the towns.[2] 'Banishment alone will force the French nobility to do what the English do for pleasure—to reside upon and adorn their estates.'[3] He explains to a French friend that English agriculture has flourished 'in spite of the teeth of our ministers'; we have had many Colberts, but not one Sully[4]; and we should have done much better, he thinks, had agriculture received the same attention as commerce. This is the reverse of Adam Smith's remark upon the superior liberality of the English country-gentleman, who did not, like the manufacturers, invoke protection and interference. In truth, Young desired both advantages, the vigour of a centralised government and the energy of an independent aristocracy. His absence of any general theory enables him to do justice in detail at the cost of consistency in general theory. In France, as he saw, the nobility had become in the main an encumbrance, a mere dead weight upon the energies of the agriculturist. But he did not infer that large properties in land were bad in themselves; for in England he saw that the landowners were the really energetic and improving class. He naturally looked at the problem from the point of view of an

[1] *Travels in France*, pp. 291-92.   [2] *Ibid.* p. 132.
[3] *Ibid.* p. 66.   [4] *Ibid.* p. 131.

intelligent land-agent. He is full of benevolent wishes for the labourer, and sympathises with the attempt to stimulate their industry and improve their dwellings, and denounces oppression whether in France or Ireland with the heartiest goodwill. But it is characteristic of the position that such a man—an enthusiastic advocate of industrial progress—was a hearty admirer of the English landowner. He sets out upon his first tour, announcing that he does not write for farmers, of whom not one in five thousand reads anything, but for the country-gentlemen, who are the great improvers. Tull, who introduced turnips; Weston, who introduced clover; Lord Townshend and Allen, who introduced 'marling' in Norfolk, were all country-gentlemen, and it is from them that he expects improvement. He travels everywhere, delighting in their new houses and parks, their picture galleries, and their gardens laid out by Kent or 'Capability Brown'; he admires scenery, climbs Skiddaw, and is rapturous over views of the Alps and Pyrenees; but he is thrown into a rage by the sight of wastes, wherever improvement is possible. What delights him is an estate with a fine country-house of Palladian architecture ('Gothic' is with him still a term of abuse),[1] with grounds well laid out and a good home-farm, where experiments are being tried, and surrounded by an estate in which the farm-buildings show the effects of the landlord's good example and judicious treatment of his tenantry. There was no want of such examples. He admires the marquis of Rockingham, at once the most honourable of statesmen and most judicious of improvers. He sings the praises of the duke of Portland, the earl of Darling-

[1] e.g. *Southern Tour*, p. 103; *Northern Tour*, p. 180 (York Cathedral).

ton, and the duke of Northumberland. An incautious announcement of the death of the duke of Grafton, remembered chiefly as one of the victims of Junius, but known to Young for his careful experiments in sheep-breeding, produced a burst of tears, which, as he believed, cost him his eyesight. His friend, the fifth duke of Bedford (died 1802), was one of the greatest improvers for the South, and was succeeded by another friend, the famous Coke of Holkham, afterwards earl of Leicester, who is said to have spent half a million upon the improvement of his property. Young appeals to the class in which such men were leaders, and urges them, not against their wishes, we may suppose, and, no doubt, with much good sense, to take to their task in the true spirit of business. Nothing, he declares, is more out of place than the boast of some great landowners that they never raise their rents.[1] High rents produce industry. The man who doubles his rents benefits the country more than he benefits himself. Even in Ireland,[2] a rise of rents is one great cause of improvement, though the rent should not be excessive, and the system of middlemen is altogether detestable. One odd suggestion is characteristic.[3] He hears that wages are higher in London than elsewhere. Now, he says, in a trading country low wages are essential. He wonders, therefore, that the legislature does not limit the growth of London.

This, we may guess, is one of the petulant utterances of early years which he would have disavowed or qualified upon maturer reflection. But Young is essentially

[1] *Northern Tour*, iv. 344, 377.   [2] *Irish Tour*, ii. 114.
[3] *Southern Tour*, p. 326.

an apostle of the 'glorious spirit of improvement,'[1] which has converted Norfolk sheep-walks into arable fields, and was spreading throughout the country and even into Ireland. His hero is the energetic landowner, who makes two blades of grass grow where one grew before; who introduces new breeds of cattle and new courses of husbandry. He is so far in sympathy with the *Wealth of Nations*, although he says of that book that, while he knows of 'no abler work,' he knows of none 'fuller of poisonous errors.'[2] Young, that is, sympathised with the doctrine of the physiocrats that agriculture was the one source of real wealth, and took Smith to be too much on the side of commerce. Young, however, was as enthusiastic a free-trader as Smith. He naturally denounces the selfishness of the manufacturers who, in 1788, objected to the free export of English wool,[3] but he also assails monopoly in general. The whole system, he says (on occasion of Pitt's French treaty), is rotten to the core. The 'vital spring and animating soul of commerce is LIBERTY.'[4] Though he talks of the balance of trade, he argues in the spirit of Smith or Cobden that we are benefited by the wealth of our customers. If we have to import more silk, we shall export more cloth. Young, indeed, was everything but a believer in any dogmatic or consistent system of Political Economy, or, as he still calls it, Political Arithmetic. His opinions were not of the kind which can be bound to any rigid formulæ. After investigating the restrictions of rent and wages in different districts, he quietly accepts the conclusion that the difference is due to accident.[5] He

[1] *Southern Tour*, p. 22.   [2] *Annals*, i. 380.   [3] *Ibid.* vol. x.
[4] *Ibid.* iv. 17.   [5] *Southern Tour*, p. 262; *Northern Tour*, ii. 412.

has as yet no fear of Malthus before his eyes. He is roused to indignation by the pessimist theory then common, that population was decaying.[1] Everywhere he sees signs of progress; buildings, plantations, woods, and canals. Employment, he says, creates population, stimulates industry, and attracts labour from backward districts. The increase of numbers is an unqualified benefit. He has no dread of excess. In Ireland, he observes, no one is fool enough to deny that population is increasing, though people deny it in England, 'even in the most productive period of her industry and wealth.'[2] One cause of this blessing is the absence of the poor-law. The English poor-law is detestable to him for a reason which contrasts significantly with the later opinion. The laws were made 'in the very spirit of depopulation'; they are 'monuments of barbarity and mischief'; for they give to every parish an interest in keeping down the population. This tendency was in the eyes of the later economist a redeeming feature in the old system; though it had been then so modified as to stimulate what they took to be the curse, as Young held it to be the blessing, of a rapid increase of population.

With such views Young was a keen advocate of the process of enclosure which was going on with increasing rapidity. He found a colleague, who may be briefly noticed as a remarkable representative of the same movement. Sir John Sinclair (1754-1835)[3] was heir to an estate of sixty thousand acres in Caithness which produced only £2300 a year, subject to many encum-

[1] *Northern Tour*, iv. 410, etc. [2] *Irish Tour*, ii. 118-19.
[3] *Memoirs of Sir John Sinclair*, by his son. 2 vols., 1837.

brances. The region was still in a primitive state. There were no roads: agriculture was of the crudest kind; part of the rent was still paid in feudal services; the natives were too ignorant or lazy to fish, and there were no harbours. Trees were scarce enough to justify Johnson, and a list of all the trees in the country included currant-bushes.[1] Sinclair was a pupil of the poet Logan: studied under Blair at Edinburgh and Millar at Glasgow; became known to Adam Smith, and, after a short time at Oxford, was called to the English bar. Sinclair was a man of enormous energy, though not of vivacious intellect. He belonged to the prosaic breed, which created the 'dismal science,' and seems to have been regarded as a stupendous bore. Bores, however, represent a social force not to be despised, and Sinclair was no exception.

His father died when he was sixteen. When twenty years old he collected his tenants, and in one night made a road across a hill which had been pronounced impracticable. He was an enthusiastic admirer of Gaelic traditions; defended the authenticity of Ossian; supported Highland games, and brought Italian travellers to listen to the music of the bagpipes. When he presented himself to his tenants in the Highland costume, on the withdrawal of its prohibition, they expected him to lead them in a foray upon the lowlands in the name of Charles Edward. He afterwards raised a regiment of 'fencibles' which served in Ireland in 1798, and, when disbanded, sent a large contingent to the Egyptian expedition. But he rendered more peaceful services to his country. He formed new farms; he enclosed several thousand acres; as head

[1] *Memoirs*, i. 338.

of the 'British Wool Society,' he introduced the Cheviots or 'long sheep' to the North—an improvement which is said to have doubled the rents of many estates; he introduced agricultural shows; he persuaded government in 1801 to devote the proceeds of the confiscated estates of Jacobites to the improvement of Scottish communications; he helped to introduce fisheries and even manufactures; and was a main agent in the change which made Caithness one of the most rapidly improving parts of the country. His son assures us that he took every means to obviate the incidental evils which have been the pretexts of denunciators of similar improvements. Sinclair gained a certain reputation by a *History of the Revenue* (1785-90), and, like Malthus, travelled on the Continent to improve his knowledge. His first book finished, he began the great statistical work by which he is best remembered. He is said to have introduced into English the name of 'statistics,' for the researches of which all economical writers were beginning to feel the necessity. He certainly did much to introduce the reality. Sinclair circulated a number of queries (upon 'natural history,' 'population,' 'productions,' and 'miscellaneous' informations) to every parish minister in Scotland. He surmounted various jealousies naturally excited, and the ultimate result was the *Statistical Account of Scotland*, which appeared in twenty-one volumes between 1791 and 1799.[1] It gives an account of every parish in Scotland, and was of great value as supplying a basis for all social investigations. Sinclair bore the expense, and gave the profits to the 'Sons of the Clergy.'

[1] *A New Statistical Account*, replacing this, appeared in twenty-four volumes from 1834 to 1844.

In 1793 Sinclair, who had been in parliament since 1780, made himself useful to Pitt in connection with the issue of exchequer bills to meet the commercial crisis. He begged in return for the foundation of a Board of Agriculture. He became the president and Arthur Young the secretary;[1] and the board represented their common aspirations. It was a rather anomalous body, something between a government office and such an institution as the Royal Society; and was supported by an annual grant of £3000. The first aim of the board was to produce a statistical account of England on the plan of the Scottish account. The English clergy, however, were suspicious; they thought, it seems, that the collection of statistics meant an attack upon tithes; and Young's frequent denunciation of tithes as discouraging agricultural improvement suggests some excuse for the belief. The plan had to be dropped; a less thorough-going description of the counties was substituted; and a good many 'Views' of the agriculture of different counties were published in 1794 and succeeding years. The board did its best to be active with narrow means. It circulated information, distributed medals, and brought agricultural improvers together. It encouraged the publication of Erasmus Darwin's *Phytologia* (1799), and procured a series of lectures from Humphry Davy, afterwards published as *Elements of Agricultural Chemistry* (1813). Sinclair also claims to have encouraged Macadam (1756-1836), the roadmaker, and Meikle, the inventor of the thrashing-

[1] He was president for the first five years, and again from 1806 till 1813. For an account of this, see Sir Ernest Clarke's *History of the Board of Agriculture*, 1898.

machine. One great aim of the board was to promote enclosures. Young observes in the introductory paper to the *Annals* that within forty years nine hundred bills had been passed affecting about a million acres. This included wastes, but the greater part was already cultivated under the 'constraint and imperfection of the open field system,' a relic of the 'barbarity of our ancestors.' Enclosures involved procuring acts of parliament—a consequent expenditure, as Young estimates, of some £2000 in each case ;[1] and as they were generally obtained by the great landowners, there was a frequent neglect of the rights of the poor and of the smaller holders. The remedy proposed was a general enclosure act ; and such an act passed the House of Commons in 1798, but was thrown out by the Lords. An act was not obtained till after the Reform Bill. Sinclair, however, obtained some modification of the procedure ; which, it is said, facilitated the passage of private bills. They became more numerous in later years, though other causes obviously co-operated. Meanwhile, it is characteristic that Sinclair and Young regarded wastes as a backwoodsman regarded a forest. The incidental injury to poor commoners was not unnoticed, and became one of the topics of Cobbett's eloquence. But to the ardent agriculturist the existence of a bit of waste land was a simple proof of barbarism. Sinclair's favourite toast, we are told, was ' May commons become uncommon '—his one attempt at a joke. He prayed that Epping Forest and Finchley Common might pass under the yoke as well as our foreign enemies. Young is driven out of all patience by the sight of 'fern, ling, and other trumpery'

[1] *Northern Tour*, i. 222-32.

usurping the place of possible arable fields.[1] He groans in spirit upon Salisbury Plain, which might be made to produce all the corn we import.[2] Enfield Chase, he declares, is a ' real nuisance to the public.'[3] We may be glad that the zeal for enclosure was not successful in all its aims ; but this view of philanthropic and energetic improvers is characteristic.

It is said[4] that Young and Sinclair ruined the Board of Agriculture by making it a kind of political debating club. It died in 1822. Sinclair obtained an appointment in Scotland, and continued to labour unremittingly. He carried on a correspondence with all manner of people, including Washington, Eldon, Catholic bishops in Ireland, financiers and agriculturists on the Continent, and the most active economists in England. He suggested a subject for a poem to Scott.[5] He wrote pamphlets about cash-payments, Catholic Emancipation, and the Reform Bill, always disagreeing with all parties. He projected four codes which were to summarise all human knowledge upon health, agriculture, political economy, and religion. *The Code of Health* (4 vols., 1807) went through six editions ; *The Code of Agriculture* appeared in 1829 ; but the world has not been enriched by the others. He died at Edinburgh on the 21st September 1835.

I have dwelt so far upon Young because he is the

[1] *Northern Tour*, ii. 186.
[2] *Southern Tour*, p. 20.   [3] *Northern Tour*, iii. 365.
[4] Arthur Young had a low opinion of Sinclair, whom he took to be a pushing and consequential busybody, more anxious to make a noise than to be useful. See Young's *Autobiography* (1898), pp. 243, 315, 437. Sir Ernest Clarke points out the injury done by Sinclair's hasty and blundering extravagance ; but also shows that the board did great service in stimulating agricultural improvement.   [5] Scott's *Letters*, i. 202.

best representative of that 'glorious spirit of improvement' which was transforming the whole social structure. Young's view of the French revolution indicates one marked characteristic of that spirit. He denounces the French seigneur because he is lethargic. He admires the English nobleman because he is energetic. The French noble may even deserve confiscation ; but he has not the slightest intention of applying the same remedy in England, where squires and noblemen are the very source of all improvement. He holds that government is everything, and admires the great works of the French despotism : and yet he is a thorough admirer of the liberties enjoyed under the British Constitution, the essential nature of which makes similar works impossible. I need not ask whether Young's logic could be justified ; though it would obviously require for justification a thoroughly 'empirical' view, or, in other words, the admission that different circumstances may require totally different institutions. The view, however, which was congenial to the prevalent spirit of improvement must be noted.

It might be stated as a paradox that, whereas in France the most palpable evils arose from the excessive power of the central government, and in England the most palpable evils arose from the feebleness of the central government, the French reformers demanded more government and the English reformers demanded less government. 'Everything for the people, nothing by the people,' was, as Mr. Morley remarks,[1] the maxim of the French

[1] Essay on 'Turgot.' See, in Daire's Collection of the *Économistes*, the arguments of Quesnay (p. 81), Dupont de Nemours (p. 360), and Mercier de la Rivière in favour of a legal (as distinguished from an 'arbitrary') despotism.

economists. The solution seems to be easy. In France, reformers such as Turgot and the economists were in favour of an enlightened despotism, because the state meant a centralised power which might be turned against the aristocracy. Once 'enlightened' it would suppress the exclusive privileges of a class which, doing nothing in return, had become a mere burthen or dead weight encumbering all social development. But in England the privileged class was identical with the governing class. The political liberty of which Englishmen were rightfully proud, the 'rule of law' which made every official responsible to the ordinary course of justice, and the actual discharge of their duties by the governing order, saved it from being the objects of a jealous class hatred. While in France government was staggering under an ever-accumulating resentment against the aristocracy, the contemporary position in England was, on the whole, one of political apathy. The country, though it had lost its colonies, was making unprecedented progress in wealth ; commerce, manufactures, and agriculture were being developed by the energy of individuals ; and Pitt was beginning to apply Adam Smith's principles to finance. The cry for parliamentary reform died out : neither Whigs nor Tories really cared for it ; and the 'glorious spirit of improvement' showed itself in an energy which had little political application. The nobility was not an incubus suppressing individual energy and confronted by the state, but was itself the state ; and its individual members were often leaders in industrial improvement. Discontent, therefore, took in the main a different form. Some government was, of course, necessary, and the existing system was too much in harmony, even in its defects, with the social order to provoke any distinct revolutionary sentiment. Englishmen were not only satisfied with their main institutions, but regarded them with exaggerated complacency. But, though there was no organic disorder, there were plenty of abuses to be remedied. The ruling class, it seemed, did its duties in the main, but took unconscionable perquisites in return. If it 'farmed' them, it was right that it should have a beneficial interest in the concern; but that interest might be excessive. In many directions abuses were growing up which required remedy, though not a subversion of the system under which they had been generated. It was not desired—unless by a very few theorists—to make any sweeping redistribution of power; but it was eminently desirable to find some means of better regulating many evil practices. The attack upon such practices might ultimately suggest—as, in fact, it did suggest—the necessity of far more thorough-going reforms. For the present, however, the characteristic mark of English reformers was this limitation of their schemes, and a mark which is especially evident in Bentham and his followers. I will speak, therefore, of the many questions which were arising, partly for these reasons and partly because the Utilitarian theory was in great part moulded by the particular problems which they had to argue.

CHAPTER III

SOCIAL PROBLEMS

I. PAUPERISM

PERHAPS the gravest of all the problems which were to occupy the coming generation was the problem of pauperism. The view taken by the Utilitarians was highly characteristic and important. I will try to indicate the general position of intelligent observers at the end of the century by referring to the remarkable book of Sir Frederick Morton Eden. Its purport is explained by the title: 'The State of the Poor; or, an History of the Labouring Classes of England from the Norman Conquest to the present period; in which are particularly considered their domestic economy, with respect to diet, dress, fuel, and habitation; and the various plans which have from time to time been proposed and adopted for the relief of the poor' (3 vols. 4to, 1797). Eden[1] (1766-1809) was a man of good family and nephew of the first Lord Auckland, who negotiated Pitt's commercial treaty. He graduated as B.A. from Christ Church, Oxford, in 1787; married in 1792, and at his death (14th Nov. 1809) was chairman of the Globe Insurance Company. He wrote

[1] See *Dictionary of National Biography*.

various pamphlets upon economical topics; contributed letters signed 'Philanglus' to Cobbett's *Porcupine*, the anti-jacobin paper of the day; and is described by Bentham[1] as a 'declared disciple' and a 'highly valued friend.' He may be reckoned, therefore, as a Utilitarian, though politically he was a Conservative. He seems to have been a man of literary tastes as well as a man of business, and his book is a clear and able statement of the points at issue.

Eden's attention had been drawn to the subject by the distress which followed the outbreak of the revolutionary war. He employed an agent who travelled through the country for a year with a set of queries drawn up after the model of those prepared by Sinclair for his *Statistical Account of Scotland*. He thus anticipated the remarkable investigation made in our own time by Mr. Charles Booth. Eden made personal inquiries and studied the literature of the subject. He had a precursor in Richard Burn (1709-1785), whose *History of the Poor-laws* appeared in 1764, and a competitor in John Ruggles, whose *History of the Poor* first appeared in Arthur Young's *Annals*, and was published as a book in 1793 (second edition, 1797). Eden's work eclipsed Ruggles's. It has a permanent value as a collection of facts; and was a sign of the growing sense of the importance of accurate statistical research. The historian of the social condition of the people should be grateful to one who broke ground at a time when the difficulty of obtaining a sound base for social inquiries began to make itself generally felt. The value of the book for historical purposes lies beyond my sphere. His first volume, I may say, gives a history of

[1] *Works*, i. 255.

legislation from the earliest period; and contains also a valuable account of the voluminous literature which had grown up during the two preceding centuries. The other two summarise the reports which he had received. I will only say enough to indicate certain critical points. Eden's book unfortunately was to mark, not a solution of the difficulty but, the emergence of a series of problems which were to increase in complexity and ominous significance through the next generation.

The general history of the poor-law is sufficiently familiar.[1] The mediæval statutes take us to a period at which the labourer was still regarded as a serf; and a man who had left his village was treated like a fugitive slave. A long series of statutes regulated the treatment of the 'vagabond.' The vagabond, however, had become differentiated from the pauper. The decay of the ancient order of society and its corresponding institutions had led to a new set of problems; and the famous statute of Elizabeth (1601) had laid down the main lines of the system which is still in operation.

When the labourer was regarded as in a servile condition, he might be supported from the motives which lead an owner to support his slaves, or by the charitable energies organised by ecclesiastical institutions. He had now ceased to be a serf, and the institutions which helped the poor man or maintained the beggar were wrecked. The Elizabethan statute gave him, therefore, a legal claim to be supported, and, on the other hand, directed that he should be made to work for his living. The assumption is still that every man is a member of a

[1] See Sir G. Nicholls's *History of the Poor-law*, 1854. A new edition, with life by H. G. Willink, appeared in 1898.

little social circle. He belongs to his parish, and it is his fellow-parishioners who are bound to support him. So long as this corresponded to facts, the system could work satisfactorily. With the spread of commerce, and the growth of a less settled population, difficulties necessarily arose. The pauper and the vagabond represent a kind of social extravasation; the 'masterless man' who has strayed from his legitimate place or has become a superfluity in his own circle. The vagabond could be flogged, sent to prison, or if necessary hanged, but it was more difficult to settle what to do with a man who was not a criminal, but simply a product in excess of demand. All manner of solutions had been suggested by philanthropists and partly adopted by the legislature. One point which especially concerns us is the awkwardness or absence of an appropriate administrative machinery.

The parish, the unit on which the pauper had claims, meant the persons upon whom the poor-rate was assessed. These were mainly farmers and small tradesmen who formed the rather vague body called the vestry. 'Overseers' were appointed by the ratepayers themselves; they were not paid, and the disagreeable office was taken in turn for short periods. The most obvious motive with the average ratepayer was of course to keep down the rates and to get the burthen of the poor as much as possible out of his own parish. Each parish had at least an interest in economy. But the economical interest also produced flagrant evils.

In the first place, there was the war between parishes. The law of settlement—which was to decide to what parish a pauper belonged—originated in an act of 1662.

Eden observes that the short clause in this short act had brought more profit to the lawyers than 'any other point in the English jurisprudence.'[1] It is said that the expense of such a litigation before the act of 1834 averaged from £300,000 to £350,000 a year.[2] Each parish naturally endeavoured to shift the burthen upon its neighbours; and was protected by laws which enabled it to resist the immigration of labourers or actually to expel them when likely to become chargeable. This law is denounced by Adam Smith[3] as a 'violation of natural liberty and justice.' It was often harder, he declared, for a poor man to cross the artificial boundaries of his parish than to cross a mountain ridge or an arm of the sea. There was, he declared, hardly a poor man in England over forty who had not been at some time 'cruelly oppressed' by the working of this law. Eden thinks that Smith had exaggerated the evil: but a law which operated by preventing a free circulation of labour, and made it hard for a poor man to seek the best price for his only saleable commodity, was, so far, opposed to the fundamental principles common to Smith and Eden. The law, too, might be used oppressively by the niggardly and narrow-minded. The overseer, as Burn complained,[4] was often a petty tyrant: his aim was to depopulate his parish; to prevent the poor from obtaining a settlement; to make the workhouse a terror by placing it under the management of a bully; and by all

[1] *History*, i. 175.
[2] M'Culloch's note to *Wealth of Nations*, p. 65. M'Culloch in his appendix makes some sensible remarks upon the absence of any properly constituted parochial 'tribunal.'
[3] *Wealth of Nations*, bk. i. ch. x.
[4] See passage quoted in Eden's *History*, i. 347.

kinds of chicanery to keep down the rates at whatever cost to the comfort and morality of the poor. This explains the view taken by Arthur Young, and generally accepted at the period, that the poor-law meant depopulation. Workhouses had been started in the seventeenth century[1] with the amiable intention of providing the industrious poor with work. Children might be trained to industry and the pauper might be made self-supporting. Workhouses were expected that is, to provide not only work but wages. Defoe, in his *Giving Alms no Charity*, pointed out the obvious objections to the workhouse considered as an institution capable of competing with the ordinary industries. Workhouses, in fact, soon ceased to be profitable. Their value, however, in supplying a test for destitution was recognised; and by an act of 1722, parishes were allowed to set up workhouses, separately or in combination, and to strike off the lists of the poor those who refused to enter them. This was the germ of the later 'workhouse test.'[2] When grievances arose, the invariable plan, as Nicholls observes,[3] was to increase the power of the justices. Their discretion was regarded 'as a certain cure for every shortcoming of the law and every evil arising out of it.' The great report of 1834 traces this tendency[4] to a clause in an act passed in the reign of William III., which was intended to allow the justices to check the extravagance of parish officers. They were empowered to strike off persons improperly relieved. This incidental regulation, widened by subsequent interpretations,

[1] Thomas Firmin (1632-1677), a philanthropist, whose Socinianism did not exclude him from the friendship of such liberal bishops as Tillotson and Fowler, started a workhouse in 1676.
[2] Nicholls (1898), ii. 14.   [3] *Ibid.* (1898), ii. 123.   [4] *Report*, p. 67.

allowed the magistrates to order relief, and thereby introduced an incredible amount of demoralisation.

The course was natural enough, and indeed apparently inevitable. The justices of the peace represented the only authority which could be called in to regulate abuses arising from the incapacity and narrow local interests of the multitudinous vestries. The schemes of improvement generally involved some plan for a larger area. If a hundred or a county were taken for the unit, the devices which depopulated a parish would no longer be applicable.[1] The only scheme actually carried was embodied in 'Gilbert's act' (1782), obtained by Thomas Gilbert (1720-1798), an agent of the duke of Bridgewater, and an active advocate of poor-law reform in the House of Commons. This scheme was intended as a temporary expedient during the distress caused by the American War; and a larger and more permanent scheme which it was to introduce failed to become law. It enabled parishes to combine if they chose to provide common workhouses, and to appoint 'guardians.' The justices, as usual, received more powers in order to suppress the harsh dealing of the old parochial authorities. The guardians, it was assumed, could always find 'work,' and they were to relieve the able-bodied without applying the workhouse test. The act, readily adopted, thus became a landmark in the growth of laxity.[2]

[1] William Hay, for example, carried resolutions in the House of Commons in 1735, but failed to carry a bill which had this object. See Eden's *History*, i. 396. Cooper in 1763 proposed to make the hundred the unit.—Nicholls's *History*, i. 58. Fielding proposes a similar change in London. Dean Tucker speaks of the evil of the limited area in his *Manifold Causes of the Increase of the Poor* (1760).   [2] Nicholls, ii. 88.

At the end of the century a rapid development of pauperism had taken place. The expense, as Eden had to complain, had doubled in twenty years. This took place simultaneously with the great development of manufactures. It is not perhaps surprising, though it may be melancholy, that increase of wealth shall be accompanied by increase of pauperism. Where there are many rich men, there will be a better field for thieves and beggars. A life of dependence becomes easier though it need not necessarily be adopted. Whatever may have been the relation of the two phenomena, the social revolution made the old social arrangements more inadequate. Great aggregations of workmen were formed in towns, which were still only villages in a legal sense. Fluctuations of trade, due to war or speculation, brought distress to the improvident ; and the old assumption that every man had a proper place in a small circle, where his neighbours knew all about him, was further than ever from being verified. One painful result was already beginning to show itself. Neglected children in great towns had already excited compassion. Thomas Coram (1668?-1751) had been shocked by the sight of dying children exposed in the streets of London, and succeeded in establishing the Foundling Hospital (founded in 1742). In 1762, Jonas Hanway (1712-1786) obtained a law for boarding out children born within the bills of mortality. The demand for children's labour, produced by the factories, seemed naturally enough to offer a better chance for extending such charities. Unfortunately among the people who took advantage of it were parish officials, eager to get children off their hands, and manufacturers concerned only to

make money out of childish labour. Hence arose the shameful system for which remedies (as I shall have to notice) had to be sought in a later generation.

Meanwhile the outbreak of the revolutionary war had made the question urgent. When Manchester trade suffered, as Eden tells us in his reports, many workmen enlisted in the army, and left their children to be supported by the parish. Bad seasons followed in 1794 and 1795, and there was great distress in the agricultural districts. The governing classes became alarmed. In December 1795 Whitbread introduced a bill providing that the justices of the peace should fix a minimum rate of wages. Upon a motion for the second reading, Pitt made the famous speech (12th December) including the often-quoted statement that when a man had a family, relief should be 'a matter of right and honour, instead of a ground of opprobrium and contempt.'[1] Pitt had in the same speech shown his reading of Adam Smith by dwelling upon the general objections to state interference with wages, and had argued that more was to be gained by removing the restrictions upon the free movement of labour. He undertook to produce a comprehensive measure ; and an elaborate bill of 130 clauses was prepared in 1796.[2] The rates were to be used to supplement inadequate wages ; 'schools of industry' were to be formed for the support of superabundant children ; loans might be made to the poor for the purchase of a cow ;[3] and the possession of property was not to disqualify for

[1] *Parl. Hist.* xxxii. 710.
[2] A full abstract is given in Eden's *History*, iii. ccclxiii. etc.
[3] Bentham observes (*Works*, viii. 448) that the cow will require the three acres to keep it.

the receiving relief. In short, the bill seems to have been a model of misapplied benevolence. The details were keenly criticised by Bentham, and the bill never came to the birth. Other topics were pressing enough at this time to account for the failure of a measure so vast in its scope. Meanwhile something had to be done. On 6th May 1795 the Berkshire magistrates had passed certain resolutions called from their place of meeting, the 'Speenhamland Act of Parliament.' They provided that the rate of wages of a labourer should be increased in proportion to the price of corn and to the number of his family—a rule which, as Eden observes, tended to discourage economy of food in times of scarcity. They also sanctioned the disastrous principle of paying part of the wages out of rates. An act passed in 1796 repealed the old restrictions upon out-door relief ; and thus, during the hard times that were to follow, the poor-laws were adapted to produce the state of things in which, as Cobbett says (in 1821) 'every labourer who has children is now regularly and constantly a pauper.'[1] The result represents a curious compromise. The landowners, whether from benevolence or fear of revolution, desired to meet the terrible distress of the times. Unfortunately their spasmodic interference was guided by no fixed principles, and acted upon a class of institutions not organised upon any definite system. The general effect seems to have been that the ratepayers, no longer allowed to 'depopulate,' sought to turn the compulsory stream of charity partly into their own pockets. If they were forced to support paupers, they could contrive to save the payment of wages. They could use the labour of the

[1] Cobbett's *Political Works*, vi. 64.

rate-supported pauper instead of employing independent workmen. The evils thus produced led before long to most important discussions.[1] The ordinary view of the poor-law was inverted. The prominent evil was the reckless increase of a degraded population instead of the restriction of population. Eden's own view is sufficiently indicative of the light in which the facts showed themselves to intelligent economists. As a disciple of Adam Smith, he accepts the rather vague doctrine of his master about the 'balance' between labour and capital. If labour exceeds capital, he says, the labourer must starve 'in spite of all political regulations.'[2] He therefore looks with disfavour upon the whole poor-law system. It is too deeply rooted to be abolished, but he thinks that the amount to be raised should not be permitted to exceed the sum levied on an average of previous years. The only certain result of Pitt's measure would be a vast expenditure upon a doubtful experiment : and one main purpose of his publication was to point out the objections to the plan. He desires what seemed at that time to be almost hopeless, a national system of education ; but his main doctrine is the wisdom of reliance upon individual effort. The truth of the maxim '*pas trop gouverner*,' he says,[3] has never been better illustrated than by the contrast between friendly societies and the poor-laws. Friendly societies had been known, though they were still on a humble scale, from the beginning of the century, and had tended to diminish pauperism in spite of the poor-laws. Eden

[1] I need only note here that the first edition of Malthus's *Essay* appeared in 1798, the year after Eden's publication.
[2] Eden's *History*, i. 583.
[3] *Ibid.* i. 587.

gives many accounts of them. They seem to have suggested a scheme proposed by the worthy Francis Maseres[1] (1731-1824) in 1772 for the establishment of life annuities. A bill to give effect to this scheme passed the House of Commons in 1773 with the support of Burke and Savile, but was thrown out in the House of Lords. In 1786 John Acland (died 1796), a Devonshire clergyman and justice of the peace, proposed a scheme for uniting the whole nation into a kind of friendly society for the support of the poor when out of work and in old age. It was criticised by John Howlett (1731-1804), a clergyman who wrote much upon the poor-laws. He attributes the growth of pauperism to the rise of prices, and calculates that out of an increased expenditure of £700,000, £219,000 had been raised by the rich, and the remainder 'squeezed out of the flesh, blood, and bones of the poor.' An act for establishing Acland's crude scheme failed next year in parliament.[2] The merit of the societies, according to Eden, was their tendency to stimulate self-help; and how to preserve that merit, while making them compulsory, was a difficult problem. I have said enough to mark a critical and characteristic change of opinion. One source of evil pointed out by contemporaries had been the absence of any central power which could regulate and systematise the action of the petty local bodies. The very possibility

[1] Maseres, an excellent Whig, a good mathematician, and a respected lawyer, is perhaps best known at present from his portrait in Charles Lamb's Old Benchers.

[2] It may be noticed as an anticipation of modern schemes that in 1792 Paine proposed a system of 'old age pensions,' for which the necessary funds were to be easily obtained when universal peace had abolished all military charges. See State Trials, xxv. 175.

of such organisation, however, seems to have been simply inconceivable. When the local bodies became lavish instead of over-frugal, the one remedy suggested was to abolish the system altogether.

II. THE POLICE

The system of 'self-government' showed its weak side in this direction. It meant that an important function was intrusted to small bodies, quite incompetent of acting upon general principles, and perfectly capable of petty jobbing, when unrestrained by any effective supervision. In another direction the same tendency was even more strikingly illustrated. Municipal institutions were almost at their lowest point of decay. Manchester and Birmingham were two of the largest and most rapidly growing towns. By the end of the century Manchester had a population of 90,000 and Birmingham of 70,000. Both were ruled, as far as they were ruled, by the remnants of old manorial institutions. Aikin[1] observes that 'Manchester (in 1795) remains an open town; destitute (probably to its advantage) of a corporation, and unrepresented in parliament.' It was governed by a 'boroughreeve' and two constables elected annually at the court-leet. William Hutton, the quaint historian of Birmingham, tells us in 1783 that the town was still legally a village, with a high and low bailiff, a 'high and low taster,' two 'affeerers,' and two 'leather-sealers.' In 1752 it had been provided with a 'court of requests' for the recovery of small debts, and in 1769 with a body of commissioners to provide for lighting the town. This

[1] Aikin's Country Round Manchester.

was the system by which, with some modifications, Birmingham was governed till after the Reform Bill.[1] Hutton boasts[2] that no town was better governed or had fewer officers. 'A town without a charter,' he says, 'is a town without a shackle.' Perhaps he changed his opinions when his warehouses were burnt in 1791, and the town was at the mercy of the mob till a regiment of 'light horse' could be called in. Aikin and Hutton, however, reflect the general opinion at a time when the town corporations had become close and corrupt bodies, and were chiefly 'shackles' upon the energy of active members of the community. I must leave the explanation of this decay to historians. I will only observe that what would need explanation would seem to be rather the absence than the presence of corruption. The English borough was not stimulated by any pressure from a central government; nor was it a semi-independent body in which every citizen had the strongest motives for combining to support its independence against neighbouring towns or invading nobles. The lower classes were ignorant, and probably would be rather hostile than favourable to any such modest interference with dirt and disorder as would commend themselves to the officials. Naturally, power was left to the little cliques of prosperous tradesmen, who formed close corporations, and spent the revenues upon feasts or squandered them by corrupt practices. Here, as in the poor-law, the insufficiency of the administrative body suggests to contemporaries, not its reform, but its superfluity.

The most striking account of some of the natural

[1] Bunce's History of the Corporation of Birmingham (1878).

[2] History of Birmingham (2nd edition), p. 327.

results is in Colquhoun's[1] Treatise on the Police of the Metropolis. Patrick Colquhoun (1745-1820), an energetic Scot, was born at Dumbarton in 1745, had been in business at Glasgow, where he was provost in 1782 and 1783, and in 1789 settled in London. In 1792 he obtained through Dundas an appointment to one of the new police magistracies created by an act of that year. He took an active part in many schemes of social reform; and his book gives an account of the investigations by which his schemes were suggested and justified. It must be said, however, parenthetically, that his statistics scarcely challenge implicit confidence. Like Sinclair and Eden, he saw the importance of obtaining facts and figures, but his statements are suspiciously precise and elaborate.[2] The broad facts are clear enough.

London was, he says, three miles broad and twenty-five in circumference. The population in 1801 was 641,000. It was the largest town, and apparently the most chaotic collection of dwellings in the civilised world. There were, as Colquhoun asserts[3] in an often-quoted passage, 20,000 people in it, who got up every morning without knowing how they would get through the day. There were 5000 public-houses, and 50,000 women supported, wholly or partly, by prostitution. The revenues raised by crime amounted, as he calculates, to an annual sum of £2,000,000. There were whole classes of professional thieves, more or less organised in

[1] The first edition, 1795, the sixth, from which I quote, in 1800. In Bentham's Works, x. 330, it is said that in 1798, 7500 copies of this book had been sold.

[2] In 1814 Colquhoun published an elaborate account of the Resources of the British Empire, showing similar qualities.

[3] Police, p. 310.

gangs, which acted in support of each other. There were gangs on the river, who boarded ships at night, or lay in wait round the warehouses. The government dockyards were systematically plundered, and the same article often sold four times over to the officials. The absence of patrols gave ample chance to the highwaymen then peculiar to England. Their careers, commemorated in the *Newgate Calendar*, had a certain flavour of Robin Hood romance, and their ranks were recruited from dissipated apprentices and tradesmen in difficulty. The fields round London were so constantly plundered that the rent was materially lowered. Half the hackney coachmen, he says,[1] were in league with thieves. The number of receiving houses for stolen goods had increased in twenty years from 300 to 3000.[2] Coining was a flourishing trade, and according to Colquhoun employed several thousand persons.[3] Gambling had taken a fresh start about 1777 and 1778[4]; and the keepers of tables had always money enough at command to make convictions almost impossible. French refugees at the revolution had introduced *rouge et noir*; and Colquhoun estimates the sums yearly lost in gambling-houses at over £7,000,000. The gamblers might perhaps appeal not only to the practices of their betters in the days of Fox, but to the public lotteries. Colquhoun had various correspondents, who do not venture to propose the abolition of a system which sanctioned the practice, but who hope to diminish the facility for supplementary betting on the results of the official drawing.

The war had tended to increase the number of loose

[1] *Police*, p. 105.   [2] *Ibid.* p. 13.   [3] *Ibid.* p. 211.   [4] *Ibid.* p. 136.

and desperate marauders who swarmed in the vast labyrinth of London streets. When we consider the nature of the police by which these evils were to be checked, and the criminal law which they administered, the wonder is less that there were sometimes desperate riots (as in 1780) than that London should have been ever able to resist a mob. Colquhoun, though a patriotic Briton, has to admit that the French despots had at last created an efficient police.[1] The emperor, Joseph II., he says, inquired for an Austrian criminal supposed to have escaped to Paris. You will find him, replied the head of the French police, at No. 93 of such a street in Vienna on the second-floor room looking upon such a church; and there he was. In England a criminal could hide himself in a herd of his like, occasionally disturbed by the inroad of a 'Bow Street runner,' the emissary of the 'trading justices,' formerly represented by the two Fieldings. An act of 1792 created seven new offices, to one of which Colquhoun had been appointed. They had one hundred and eighty-nine paid officers under them.[2] There were also about one thousand constables. These were small tradesmen or artisans upon whom the duty was imposed without remuneration for a year by their parish, that is, by one of seventy independent bodies. A 'Tyburn ticket,' given in reward for obtaining the conviction of a criminal exempted a man from the discharge of such offices, and could be bought for from £15 to £25. There were also two thousand watchmen receiving from 8½d. up to 2s. a night. These were the true successors of Dogberry; often infirm or aged persons appointed to keep them out of the workhouse.

[1] *Police*, p. 523.   [2] *Ibid.* p. 397.

The management of this distracted force thus depended upon a miscellaneous set of bodies; the paid magistrates, the officials of the city, the justices of the peace for Middlesex, and the seventy independent parishes.

The law was as defective as the administration. Colquhoun represents the philanthropic impulse of the day, and notices[1] that in 1787 Joseph II. had abolished capital punishment. His chief authority for more merciful methods is Beccaria; and it is worth remarking, for reasons which will appear hereafter, that he does not in this connection refer to Bentham, although he speaks enthusiastically[2] of Bentham's model prison, the Panopticon. Colquhoun shows how strangely the severity of the law was combined with its extreme capriciousness. He quotes Bacon[3] for the statement that the law was a 'heterogeneous mass concocted too often on the spur of the moment,' and gives sufficient proofs of its truth. He desires, for example, a law to punish receivers of stolen goods, and says that there were excellent laws in existence. Unfortunately one law applied exclusively to the case of pewter-pots, and another exclusively to the precious metals; neither could be used as against receivers of horses or bank notes.[4] So a man indicted under an act against stealing from ships on navigable rivers escaped, because the barge from which he stole happened to be aground. Gangs could afford to corrupt witnesses or to pay knavish lawyers skilled in applying these vagaries of legislation. Juries also disliked convicting when the penalty for coining sixpence was the same as the penalty for killing a mother. It followed, as he shows by statistics, that half the persons committed for

[1] *Police*, p. 60.   [2] *Ibid.* p. 481.   [3] *Ibid.* p. 7.   [4] *Ibid.* p. 298.

trial escaped by petty chicanery or corruption, or the reluctance of juries to convict for capital offences. Only about one-fifth of the capital sentences were executed; and many were pardoned on condition of enlisting to improve the morals of the army. The criminals, who were neither hanged nor allowed to escape, were sent to prisons, which were schools of vice. After the independence of the American colonies, the system of transportation to Australia had begun (in 1787); but the expense was enormous, and prisoners were huddled together in the hulks at Woolwich and Portsmouth, which had been used as a temporary expedient. Thence they were constantly discharged, to return to their old practices. A man, says Colquhoun,[1] would deserve a statue who should carry out a plan for helping discharged prisoners. To meet these evils, Colquhoun proposes various remedies, such as a metropolitan police, a public prosecutor, or even a codification or revision of the Criminal Code, which he sees is likely to be delayed. He also suggested, in a pamphlet of 1799, a kind of charity organisation society to prevent the waste of funds. Many other pamphlets of similar tendencies show his active zeal in promoting various reforms. Colquhoun was in close correspondence with Bentham from the year 1798,[2] and Bentham helped him by drawing the Thames Police Act, passed in 1800, to give effect to some of the suggestions in the *Treatise*.[3]

Another set of abuses has a special connection with Bentham's activity. Bentham had been led in 1778 to attend to the prison question by reading Howard's book on *Prisons*; and he refers to the ' venerable friend

[1] *Police*, p. 99.   [2] Bentham's *Works*, x. 329 *seq.*   [3] *Ibid.* v. 335.

who had lived an apostle and died a martyr.'[1] The career of John Howard (1726-1790) is familiar. The son of a London tradesman, he had inherited an estate in Bedfordshire. There he erected model cottages and village schools; and, on becoming sheriff of the county in 1773, was led to attend to abuses in the prisons. Two acts of parliament were passed in 1774 to remedy some of the evils exposed, and he pursued the inquiry at home and abroad. His results are given in his *State of the Prisons in England and Wales* (1779, fourth edition, 1792), and his *Account of the Principal Lazarettos in Europe* (1789). The prisoners, he says, had little food, sometimes a penny loaf a day, and sometimes nothing; no water, no fresh air, no sewers, and no bedding. The stench was appalling, and gaol fever killed more than died on the gallows. Debtors and felons, men, women and children, were huddled together; often with lunatics, who were shown by the gaolers for money. 'Garnish' was extorted; the gaolers kept drinking-taps; gambling flourished: and prisoners were often cruelly ironed, and kept for long periods before trial. At Hull the assizes had only been held once in seven years, and afterwards once in three. It is a comfort to find that the whole number of prisoners in England and Wales amounted, in 1780, to about 4400, 2078 of whom were debtors, 798 felons, and 917 petty offenders. An act passed in 1779 provided for the erection of two penitentiaries. Howard was to be a supervisor. The failure to carry out this act led, as we shall see, to one of Bentham's most characteristic undertakings. One peculiarity must be noted.

[1] Bentham's *Works*, iv. 3, 121.

Howard found prisons on the continent where the treatment was bad and torture still occasionally practised; but he nowhere found things so bad as in England. In Holland the prisons were so neat and clean as to make it difficult to believe that they were prisons: and they were used as models for the legislation of 1779. One cause of this unenviable distinction of English prisons had been indicated by an earlier investigation. General Oglethorpe (1696-1785) had been started in his philanthropic career by obtaining a committee of the House of Commons in 1729 to inquire into the state of the gaols. The foundation of the colony of Georgia as an outlet for the population was one result of the inquiry. It led, in the first place, however, to a trial of persons accused of atrocious cruelties at the Fleet prison.[1] The trial was abortive. It appeared in the course of the proceedings that the Fleet prison was a 'freehold.' A patent for rebuilding it had been granted to Sir Jeremy Whichcot under Charles II., and had been sold to one Higgins, who resold it to other persons for £5000. The proprietors made their investment pay by cruel ill-treatment of the prisoners, oppressing the poor and letting off parts of the prison to dealers in drink. This was the general plan in the prisons examined by Howard, and helps to account for the gross abuses. It is one more application of the general system. As the patron was owner of a living, and the officer of his commission, the keeper of a prison was owner of his establishment. The paralysis of administration which prevailed throughout the country made it natural to farm out paupers to the master of a workhouse, and prisoners to the proprietor of a gaol.

[1] Cobbett's *State Trials*, xvii. 297-626.

The state of prisoners may be inferred not only from Howard's authentic record but from the fictions of Fielding, Smollett and Goldsmith; and the last echoes of the same complaints may be found in *Pickwick* and *Little Dorrit*. The Marshalsea described in the last was also a proprietary concern. We shall hereafter see how Bentham proposed to treat the evils revealed by Oglethorpe and Howard.

III. EDUCATION

Another topic treated by Colquhoun marks the initial stage of controversies which were soon to grow warm. Colquhoun boasts of the number of charities for which London was already conspicuous. A growing facility for forming associations of all kinds, political, religious, scientific, and charitable, is an obvious characteristic of modern progress. Where in earlier times a college or a hospital had to be endowed by a founder and invested by charter with corporate personality, it is now necessary only to call a meeting, form a committee, and appeal for subscriptions. Societies of various kinds had sprung up during the century. Artists, men of science, agriculturists, and men of literary tastes, had founded innumerable academies and 'philosophical institutes.' The great London hospitals, dependent upon voluntary subscriptions, had been founded during the first half of the century. Colquhoun counts the annual revenue of various charitable institutions at £445,000, besides which the endowments produced £150,000, and the poor-rates

£255,000.[1] Among these a considerable number were intended to promote education. Here, as in some other cases, it seems that people at the end of the century were often taking up an impulse given a century before. So the Society for promoting Christian Knowledge, founded in 1699, and the Society for the Propagation of the Gospel, founded in 1701, were supplemented by the Church Missionary Society and the Religious Tract Society, both founded in 1799. The societies for the reformation of manners, prevalent at the end of the seventeenth century, were taken as a model by Wilberforce and his friends at the end of the eighteenth.[2] In the same way, the first attempts at providing a general education for the poor had been made by Archbishop Tenison, who founded a parochial school about 1680 in order 'to check the growth of popery.' Charity schools became common during the early part of the eighteenth century and received various endowments. They were attacked as tending to teach the poor too much—a very needless alarm—and also by free thinkers, such as Mandeville, as intended outworks of the established church. This last objection was a foretaste of the bitter religious controversies which were to accompany the growth of an educational system. Colquhoun says that there were 62 endowed schools in London, from

[1] *Police*, p. 340.
[2] Wilberforce started on this plan a 'society for enforcing the king's proclamation' in 1786, which was supplemented by the society for 'the Suppression of Vice' in 1802. I don't suppose that vice was much suppressed. Sydney Smith ridiculed its performances in the *Edinburgh* for 1809. The article is in his works. A more interesting society was that for 'bettering the condition of the poor,' started by Sir Thomas Bernard and Wilberforce in 1796.

Christ's Hospital downwards, educating about 5000 children; 237 parish schools with about 9000 children, and 3730 'private schools.' The teaching was, of course, very imperfect, and in a report of a committee of the House of Commons in 1818, it is calculated that about half the children in a large district were entirely uneducated. There was, of course, nothing in England deserving the name of a system in educational more than in any other matters. The grammar schools throughout the country provided more or less for the classes which could not aspire to the public schools and universities. About a third of the boys at Christ's Hospital were, as Coleridge tells us, sons of clergymen.[1] The children of the poor were either not educated, or picked up their letters at some charity school or such a country dame's school as is described by Shenstone. A curious proof, however, of rising interest in the question is given by the Sunday Schools movement at the end of the century. Robert Raikes (1735-1811), a printer in Gloucester and proprietor of a newspaper, joined with a clergyman to set up a school in 1780 at a total cost of 1s. 6d. a week. Within three or four years the plan was taken up everywhere, and the worthy Raikes, whose newspaper had spread the news, found himself revered as a great pioneer of philanthropy. Wesley took up the scheme warmly; bishops condescended to approve; the king and queen were interested, and within three or four years the number of learners was reckoned at two or three hundred thousand. A Sunday School Association was formed in 1785 with well known men of business at its head. Queen Charlotte's friend, Mrs. Trimmer

[1] *Biographia Literaria* (1847), ii. 327.

(1741-1810), took up the work near London, and Hannah More (1745-1833) in Somersetshire. Hannah More gives a strange account of the utter absence of any civilising agencies in the district around Cheddar where she and her sisters laboured. She was accused of 'methodism' and a leaning to Jacobinism, although her views were of the most moderate kind. She wished the poor to be able to read their Bibles and to be qualified for domestic duties, but not to write or to be enabled to read Tom Paine or be encouraged to rise above their position. The literary light of the Whigs, Dr. Parr (1747-1825), showed his liberality by arguing that the poor ought to be taught, but admitted that the enterprise had its limits. The 'Deity Himself had fixed a great gulph between them and the poor.' A scanty instruction given on Sundays alone was not calculated to facilitate the passage of that gulf. By the end of the century, however, signs of a more systematic movement were showing themselves. Bell and Lancaster, of whom I shall have to speak, were rival claimants for the honour of initiating a new departure in education. The controversy which afterwards raged between the supporters of the two systems marked a complete revolution of opinion. Meanwhile, although the need of schools was beginning to be felt, the appliances for education in England were a striking instance of the general inefficiency in every department which needed combined action. In Scotland the system of parish schools was one obvious cause of the success of so many of the Scotsmen which excited the jealousy of southern competitors. Even in Ireland there appears to have been a more efficient set of schools. And yet, one remark must be suggested. There is

probably no period in English history at which a greater number of poor men have risen to distinction. The greatest beyond comparison of self-taught poets was Burns (1759-1796). The political writer who was at the time producing the most marked effect was Thomas Paine (1737-1809), son of a small tradesman. His successor in influence was William Cobbett (1762-1835), son of an agricultural labourer, and one of the pithiest of all English writers. William Gifford (1756-1826), son of a small tradesman in Devonshire, was already known as a satirist and was to lead Conservatives as editor of the *The Quarterly Review*. John Dalton (1766-1842), son of a poor weaver, was one of the most distinguished men of science. Porson (1759-1808), the greatest Greek scholar of his time, was son of a Norfolk parish clerk, though sagacious patrons had sent him to Eton in his fifteenth year. The Oxford professor of Arabic, Joseph White (1746-1814), was son of a poor weaver in the country and a man of reputation for learning, although now remembered only for a rather disreputable literary squabble. Robert Owen and Joseph Lancaster, both sprung from the ranks, were leaders in social movements. I have already spoken of such men as Watt, Telford, and Rennie; and smaller names might be added in literature, science, and art. The individualist virtue of 'self-help' was not confined to successful money-making or to the wealthier classes. One cause of the literary excellence of Burns, Paine, and Cobbett may be that, when literature was less centralised, a writer was less tempted to desert his natural dialect. I mention the fact, however, merely to suggest that, whatever were then the difficulties of getting such

schooling as is now common, an energetic lad even in the most neglected regions might force his way to the front.

IV. THE SLAVE-TRADE

I have thus noticed the most conspicuous of the contemporary problems which, as we shall see, provided the main tasks of Bentham and his followers. One other topic must be mentioned as in more ways than one characteristic of the spirit of the time. The parliamentary attack upon the slave-trade began just before the outbreak of the revolution. It is generally described as an almost sudden awakening of the national conscience. That it appealed to that faculty is undeniable, and, moreover, it is at least a remarkable instance of legislative action upon purely moral grounds. It is true that in this case the conscience was the less impeded because it was roused chiefly by the sins of men's neighbours. The slave-trading class was a comparative excrescence. Their trade could be attacked without such widespread interference with the social order as was implied, for example, in remedying the grievances of paupers or of children in factories. The conflict with morality, again, was so plain as to need no demonstration. It seems to be a questionable logic which assumes the merit of a reformer to be in proportion to the flagrancy of the evil assailed. The more obvious the case, surely the less the virtue needed in the assailant. However this may be, no one can deny the moral excellence of such men as Wilberforce and Clarkson, nor the real change in the moral standard implied by the success of their agitation. But another question remains, which is indicated by a later controversy. The followers of Wilberforce and of Clarkson were jealous of each other. Each party tried to claim the chief merit for its hero. Each was, I think, unjust to the other. The underlying motive was the desire to obtain credit for the 'Evangelicals' or their rivals as the originators of a great movement. Without touching the personal details it is necessary to say something of the general sentiments implied. In his history of the agitation,[1] Clarkson gives a quaint chart, showing how the impulse spread from various centres till it converged upon a single area, and his facts are significant.

That a great change had taken place is undeniable. Protestant England had bargained with Catholic Spain in the middle of the century for the right of supplying slaves to America, while at the peace of 1814 English statesmen were endeavouring to secure a combination of all civilised powers against the trade. Smollett, in 1748, makes the fortune of his hero, Roderick Random, by placing him as mate of a slave-ship under the ideal sailor, Bowling. About the same time John Newton (1725-1807), afterwards the venerated teacher of Cowper and the Evangelicals, was in command of a slaver, and enjoying 'sweeter and more frequent hours of divine communion' than he had elsewhere known. He had no scruples, though he had the grace to pray 'to be fixed in a more humane calling.' In later years he gave the benefit of his experience to the abolitionists.[2] A new sentiment, however, was already showing itself.

[1] *History of the Rise, Progress, and Accomplishment of the Abolition of the Slave-trade by the British Parliament* (1808). Second enlarged edition 1839. The chart was one cause of the offence taken by Wilberforce's sons.
[2] Cf. Sir J. Stephen's *Ecclesiastical Biography* (The Evangelical Succession).

Clarkson collects various instances. Southern's Oroonoco, founded on a story by Mrs. Behn, and Steele's story of Inkle and Yarico in an early *Spectator*, Pope's poor Indian in the *Essay on Man*, and allusions by Thomson, Shenstone, and Savage, show that poets and novelists could occasionally turn the theme to account. Hutcheson, the moralist, incidentally condemns slavery; and divines such as Bishops Hayter and Warburton took the same view in sermons before the Society for the Propagation of Christian Knowledge. Johnson, 'last of the Tories' though he was, had a righteous hatred for the system.[1] He toasted the next insurrection of negroes in the West Indies, and asked why we always heard the 'loudest yelps for liberty among the drivers of negroes'? Thomas Day (1748-1789), as an ardent follower of Rousseau, wrote the *Dying Negro* in 1773, and, in the same spirit, denounced the inconsistencies of slave-holding champions of American liberty.

Such isolated utterances showed a spreading sentiment. The honour of the first victory in the practical application must be given to Granville Sharp[2] (1735-1813), one of the most charming and, in the best sense, 'Quixotic' of men. In 1772 his exertions had led to the famous decision by Lord Mansfield in the case of the negro Somerset.[3] Sharp in 1787 became chairman of the committee formed to attack the slave-

[1] See passages collected in Birkbeck Hill's *Boswell*, ii. 478-80, and cf. iii. 200-204. Boswell was attracted by Clarkson, but finally made up his mind that the abolition of the slave-trade would 'shut the gates of mercy on mankind.'
[2] See the account of G. Sharp in Sir J. Stephen's *Ecclesiastical Biography* (Clapham Sect).
[3] Cobbett's *State Trials*, xx. 1-82.

trade by collecting the evidence of which Wilberforce made use in parliament. The committee was chiefly composed of Quakers; as indeed, Quakers are pretty sure to be found in every philanthropic movement of the period. I must leave the explanation to the historian of religious movements; but the fact is characteristic. The Quakers had taken the lead in America. The Quaker was both practical and a mystic. His principles put him outside of the ordinary political interests, and of the military world. He directed his activities to helping the poor, the prisoner, and the oppressed. Among the Quakers of the eighteenth century were John Woolman (1720-1772), a writer beloved by the congenial Charles Lamb and Antoine Benezet (1713-1784), born in France, and son of a French refugee who settled in Philadelphia. When Clarkson wrote the prize essay upon the slave-trade (1785), which started his career, it was from Benezet's writings that he obtained his information. By their influence the Pennsylvanian Quakers were gradually led to pronounce against slavery[1]; and the first anti-slavery society was founded in Philadelphia in 1775, the year in which the skirmish at Lexington began the war of independence. That suggests another influence. The Rationalists of the eighteenth century were never tired of praising the Quakers. The Quakers were, by their essential principles, in favour of absolute toleration, and their attitude towards dogma was not dissimilar. 'Rationalisation' and 'Spiritualisation' are in some directions similar. The general spread of philanthropic sentiment, which

[1] The Society determined in 1760 'to disown' any Friend concerned in the slave-trade.

found its formula in the *Rights of Man*, fell in with the Quaker hatred of war and slavery. Voltaire heartily admires Barclay, the Quaker apologist. It is, therefore, not surprising to find the names of the deists, Franklin and Paine, associated with Quakers in this movement. Franklin was an early president of the new association, and Paine wrote an article to support the early agitation.[1] Paine himself was a Quaker by birth, who had dropped his early creed while retaining a respect for its adherents. When the agitation began it was in fact generally approved by all except the slave-traders. Sound Whig divines, Watson and Paley and Parr; Unitarians such as Priestley and Gilbert Wakefield and William Smith; and the great methodist, John Wesley, were united on this point. Fox and Burke and Pitt rivalled each other in condemning the system. The actual delay was caused partly by the strength of the commercial interests in parliament, and partly by the growth of the anti-Jacobin sentiment.

The attempt to monopolise the credit of the movement by any particular sect is absurd. Wilberforce and his friends might fairly claim the glory of having been worthy representatives of a new spirit of philanthropy; but most certainly they did not create or originate it. The general growth of that spirit throughout the century must be explained, so far as 'explanation' is possible, by wider causes. It was, as I must venture to assume, a product of complex social changes which were bringing classes and nations into closer contact, binding them

[1] Mr. Conway, in his *Life of Paine*, attributes, I think, a little more to his hero than is consistent with due regard to his predecessors; but, in any case, he took an early part in the movement.

together by new ties, and breaking up the old institutions which had been formed under obsolete conditions. The true moving forces were the same whether these representatives announced the new gospel of the 'rights of man'; or appealed to the traditional rights of Englishmen; or rallied supporters of the old order so far as it still provided the most efficient machinery for the purpose. The revival of religion under Wesley and the Evangelicals meant the direction of the stream into one channel. The paralytic condition of the Church of England disqualified it for appropriating the new energy. The men who directed the movements were mainly stimulated by moral indignation at the gross abuses, and the indolence of the established priesthood naturally gave them an anti-sacerdotal turn. They simply accepted the old Protestant tradition. They took no interest in the intellectual questions involved. Rationalism, according to them, meant simply an attack upon the traditional sanctions of morality ; and it scarcely occurred to them to ask for any philosophical foundation of their creed. Wilberforce's book, *A Practical View*, attained an immense popularity, and is characteristic of the position. Wilberforce turns over the infidel to be confuted by Paley, whom he takes to be a conclusive reasoner. For himself he is content to show what needed little proof, that the so-called Christians of the day could act as if they had never heard of the New Testament. The Evangelical movement had in short no distinct relation to speculative movements. It took the old tradition for granted, and it need not here be further considered.

One other remark is suggested by the agitation against the slave-trade. It set a precedent for agitation of a

kind afterwards familiar. The committee appealed to the country, and got up petitions. Sound Tories complained of them in the early slave-trade debates, as attempts to dictate to parliament by democratic methods. Political agitators had formed associations, and found a convenient instrument in the 'county meetings,' which seems to have possessed a kind of indefinite legal character.[1] Such associations of course depend for the great part of their influence upon the press. The circulation of literature was one great object. Paine's *Rights of Man* was distributed by the revolutionary party, and Hannah More wrote popular tracts to persuade the poor that they had no grievances. It is said that two millions of her little tracts, 'Village Politics by Will Chip,' the 'Shepherd of Salisbury Plain,' and so forth were circulated. The demand, indeed, showed rather the eagerness of the rich to get them read than the eagerness of the poor to read them. They failed to destroy Paine's influence, but they were successful enough to lead to the foundation of the Religious Tract Society. The attempt to influence the poor by cheap literature shows that these opinions were beginning to demand consideration. Cobbett and many others were soon to use the new weapon. Meanwhile the newspapers circulated among the higher ranks were passing through a new phase, which must be noted. The great newspapers were gaining power. The *Morning Chronicle* was started by Woodfall in 1769, the *Morning Post* and *Morning Herald* by Dudley Bate in 1772 and 1780, and the *Times* by Walter in 1788. The modern editor was to appear during the war. Stoddart and Barnes of the *Times*, Perry and Black of the *Morning*

[1] See upon this subject Mr. Jephson's interesting book on *The Platform*.

Chronicle, were to become important politically. The revolutionary period marks the transition from the old-fashioned newspaper, carried on by a publisher and an author, to the modern newspaper, which represents a kind of separate organism, elaborately 'differentiated' and worked by a whole army of co-operating editors, correspondents, reporters, and contributors. Finally, one remark may be made. The literary class in England was not generally opposed to the governing classes. The tone of Johnson's whole circle was conservative. In fact, since Harley's time, government had felt the need of support in the press, and politicians on both sides had their regular organs. The opposition might at any time become the government; and their supporters in the press, poor men who were only too dependent, had no motive for going beyond the doctrines of their principals. They might be bought by opponents, or they might be faithful to a patron. They did not form a band of outcasts, whose hand would be against every one. The libel law was severe enough, but there had been no licensing system since the early days of William and Mary. A man could publish what he chose at his own peril. When the current of popular feeling was anti-revolutionary, government might obtain a conviction, but even in the worst times there was a chance that juries might be restive. Editors had at times to go to prison, but even then the paper was not suppressed. Cobbett, for example, continued to publish his *Registrar* during an imprisonment of two years (1810-12). Editors had very serious anxieties, but they could express with freedom any opinion which had the support of a party. English liberty was so far a reality that a very free discussion of

the political problems of the day was permitted and practised. The English author, therefore, as such, had not the bitterness of a French man of letters, unless, indeed, he had the misfortune to be an uncompromising revolutionist.

V. THE FRENCH REVOLUTION

The English society which I have endeavoured to characterise was now to be thrown into the vortex of the revolutionary wars. The surpassing dramatic interest of the French Revolution has tended to obscure our perception of the continuity of even English history. It has been easy to ascribe to the contagion of French example political movements which were already beginning in England and which were modified rather than materially altered by our share in the great European convulsion. The impression made upon Englishmen by the French Revolution is, however, in the highest degree characteristic. The most vehement sympathies and antipathies were aroused, and showed at least what principles were congenial to the various English parties. To praise or blame the revolution, as if it could be called simply good or bad, is for the historian as absurd as to praise or blame an earthquake. It was simply inevitable under the conditions. We may, of course, take it as an essential stage in a social evolution, which if described as progress is therefore to be blessed, or if as degeneration may provoke lamentation. We may, if we please, ask whether superior statesmanship might have attained the good results without the violent catastrophes, or whether a wise and good man who could appreciate the real position would have approved or condemned the actual policy. But to answer such problems with any confidence would imply a claim to a quasi-omniscience. Partisans at the time, however, answered them without hesitation, and saw in the Revolution the dawn of a new era of reason and justice, or the outburst of the fires of hell. Their view is at any rate indicative of their own position. The extreme opinions need no exposition. They are represented by the controversy between Burke and Paine. The general doctrine of the 'Rights of Men'—that all men are by nature free and equal—covered at least the doctrine that the inequality and despotism of the existing order was hateful, and people with a taste for abstract principles accepted this short cut to political wisdom. The 'minor' premise being obviously true, they took the major for granted. To Burke, who idealised the traditional element in the British Constitution, and so attached an excessive importance to historical continuity, the new doctrine seemed to imply the breaking up of the very foundations of order and the pulverisation of society. Burke and Paine both assumed too easily that the dogmas which they defended expressed the real and ultimate beliefs, and that the belief was the cause, not the consequence, of the political condition. Without touching upon the logic of either position, I may notice how the problem presented itself to the average English politician whose position implied acceptance of traditional compromises and who yet prided himself on possessing the liberties which were now being claimed by Frenchmen. The Whig could heartily sympathise with the French Revolution so long as it appeared to be an attempt to assimilate British principles.

When Fox hailed the fall of the Bastille as the greatest and best event that had ever happened, he was expressing a generous enthusiasm shared by all the ardent and enlightened youth of the time. The French, it seemed, were abolishing an arbitrary despotism and adopting the principles of Magna Charta and the 'Habeas Corpus' Act. Difficulties, however, already suggested themselves to the true Whig. Would the French, as Young asked just after the same event, 'copy the constitution of England, freed from its faults, or attempt, from theory, to frame something absolutely speculative'?[1] On that issue depended the future of the country. It was soon decided in the sense opposed to Young's wishes. The reign of terror alienated the average Whig. But though the argument from atrocities is the popular one, the opposition was really more fundamental. Burke put the case, savagely and coarsely enough, in his 'Letter to a noble Lord.' How would the duke of Bedford like to be treated as the revolutionists were treating the nobility in France? The duke might be a sincere lover of political liberty, but he certainly would not be prepared to approve the confiscation of his estates The aristocratic Whigs, dependent for their whole property and for every privilege which they prized upon ancient tradition and prescription, could not really be in favour of sweeping away the whole complex social structure, levelling Windsor Castle as Burke put it in his famous metaphor, and making a 'Bedford level' of the whole country. The Whigs had to disavow any approval of the Jacobins; Mackintosh, who had given his answer to Burke's diatribes, met Burke himself on friendly terms (9th July

[1] *France*, p. 206 (20th July 1789).

1797), and in 1800 took an opportunity of public recantation. He only expressed the natural awakening of the genuine Whig to the aspects of the case which he had hitherto ignored. The effect upon the middle-class Whigs is, however, more to my purpose. It may be illustrated by the history of John Horne Tooke[1] (1736-1812), who at this time represented what may be called the home-bred British radicalism. He was the son of a London tradesman, who had distinguished himself by establishing, and afterwards declining to enforce, certain legal rights against Frederick Prince of Wales. The prince recognised the tradesman's generosity by making his antagonist purveyor to his household. A debt of some thousand pounds was thus run up before the prince's death which was never discharged. Possibly the son's hostility to the royal family was edged by this circumstance. John Horne, forced to take orders in order to hold a living, soon showed himself to have been intended by nature for the law. He took up the cause of Wilkes in the early part of the reign; defended him energetically in later years; and in 1769 helped to start the 'Society for supporting the Bill of Rights.' He then attacked Wilkes, who, as he maintained, misapplied for his own private use the funds subscribed for public purposes to this society; and set up a rival 'Constitutional Society.' In 1775, as spokesman of this body, he denounced the 'king's troops' for 'inhumanly murdering' their fellow-subjects at Lexington for the sole crime of 'preferring death to slavery.' He was imprisoned for the libel, and thus became a martyr to the cause. When

[1] See the *Life of Horne Tooke*, by Alexander Stephens (2 vols. 8vo, 1813). John Horne added the name Tooke in 1782.

the country associations were formed in 1780 to protest against the abuses revealed by the war, Horne became a member of the 'Society for Constitutional Information,' of which Major Cartwright—afterwards the revered, but rather tiresome, patriarch of the Radicals—was called the 'father.' Horne Tooke (as he was now named), by these and other exhibitions of boundless pugnacity, became a leader among the middle-class Whigs, who found their main support among London citizens, such as Beckford, Troutbeck and Oliver; supported them in his later days; and after the American war, preferred Pitt, as an advocate of parliamentary reform, to Fox, the favourite of the aristocratic Whigs. He denounced the Fox coalition ministry, and in later years opposed Fox at Westminster. The 'Society for Constitutional Information' was still extant in the revolutionary period, and Tooke, a bluff, jovial companion, who had by this time got rid of his clerical character, often took the chair at the taverns where they met to talk sound politics over their port. The revolution infused new spirit into politics. In March 1791[1] Tooke's society passed a vote of thanks to Paine for the first part of his *Rights of Man*. Next year Thomas Hardy, a radical shoemaker, started a 'Corresponding Society.' Others sprang up throughout the country, especially in the manufacturing towns.[2] These societies took Paine for their oracle, and circulated his writings as their manifesto. They communicated

[1] *Parl. Hist.* xxxi. 751.
[2] The history of these societies may be found in the trials reported in the twenty-third, twenty-fourth, and twenty-fifth volumes of Cobbett's *State Trials*, and in the reports of the secret committees in the thirty-first and thirty-fourth volumes of the *Parl. History*. There are materials in Place's papers in the British Museum which have been used in E. Smith's *English Jacobins*.

occasionally with Horne Tooke's society, which more or less sympathised with them. The Whigs of the upper sphere started the 'Friends of the People' in April 1792, in order to direct the discontent into safer channels. Grey, Sheridan and Erskine were members ; Fox sympathised but declined to join ; Mackintosh was secretary ; and Sir Philip Francis drew up the opening address, citing the authority of Pitt and Blackstone, and declaring that the society wished ' not to change but to restore.' [1] It remonstrated cautiously with the other societies, and only excited their distrust. Grey, as its representative, made a motion for parliamentary reform which was rejected (May 1793) by two hundred and eighty-two to forty-one. Later motions in May 1797 and April 1800 showed that, for the present, parliamentary reform was out of the question. Meanwhile the English Jacobins got up a 'convention' which met at Edinburgh at the end of 1793. The very name was alarming : the leaders were tried and transported ; the cruelty of the sentences and the severity of the judges, especially Braxfield, shocked such men as Parr and Jeffrey, and unsuccessful appeals for mercy were made in parliament. The Habeas Corpus Act was suspended in 1794: Horne Tooke and Hardy were both arrested and tried for high treason in November. An English jury fortunately showed itself less subservient than the Scottish ; the judge was scrupulously fair : and both Hardy and Horne Tooke were acquitted. The societies, however, though they were encouraged for a time, were attacked by severe measures passed by Pitt in 1795. The 'Friends of the People' ceased to exist. The

[1] *Parl. Hist.* xxix. 1300-1341.

seizure of the committee of the Corresponding Societies in 1798 put an end to their activity. A report presented to parliament in 1799[1] declares that the societies had gone to dangerous lengths : they had communicated with the French revolutionists and with the 'United Irishmen' (founded 1791); and societies of 'United Englishmen' and 'United Scotsmen' had had some concern in the mutinies of the fleet in 1797 and in the Irish rebellion of 1798. Place says, probably with truth, that the danger was much exaggerated : but in any case, an act for the suppression of the Corresponding Societies was passed in 1799, and put an end to the movement.

This summary is significant of the state of opinion. The genuine old-fashioned Whig dreaded revolution, and guarded himself carefully against any appearance of complicity. Jacobinism, on the other hand, was always an exotic. Such men as the leading Nonconformists Priestley and Price were familiar with the speculative movement on the continent, and sympathised with the enlightenment. Young men of genius, like Wordsworth and Coleridge, imbibed the same doctrines more or less thoroughly, and took Godwin for their English representative. The same creed was accepted by the artisans in the growing towns, from whom the Corresponding Societies drew their recruits. But the revolutionary sentiment was not so widely spread as its adherents hoped or its enemies feared. The Birmingham mob of 1791 acted, with a certain unconscious humour, on the side of church and king. They had perhaps an instinctive perception that it was an advantage to plunder on

[1] *Parl. Hist.* xxxiv. 574-655.

the side of the constable. In fact, however, the general feeling in all classes was anti-Jacobin. Place, an excellent witness, himself a member of the Corresponding Societies, declares that the repressive measures were generally popular even among the workmen.[1] They were certainly not penetrated with revolutionary fervour. Had it been otherwise, the repressive measures, severe as they were, would have stimulated rather than suppressed the societies, and, instead of silencing the revolutionists, have provoked a rising.

At the early period the Jacobin and the home-bred Radical might combine against government. A manifesto of the Corresponding Societies begins by declaring that ' all men are by nature free and equal and independent of each other,' and argues also that these are the ' original principles of English government.' [2] Magna Charta is an early expression of the Declaration of Rights, and thus pure reason confirms British tradition. The adoption of a common platform, however, covered a profound difference of sentiment. Horne Tooke represents the old type of reformer. He was fully resolved not to be carried away by the enthusiasm of his allies. ' My companions in a stage,' he said to Cartwright, ' may be going to Windsor : I will go with them to Hounslow. But there I will get out : no further will I go, by God !' [3] When Sheridan supported a vote of sympathy for the French revolutionists, Tooke insisted upon adding a rider declaring the content of Englishmen with their own constitution.[4] He offended some of his allies by asserting that the ' main timbers ' of

[1] Mr. Wallas's *Life of Place*, p. 25 *n.*
[2] Ibid. xxv. 330.
[3] *State Trials*, xxiv. 575.
[4] *Ibid.* xxv. 390

the constitution were sound though the dry-rot had got into the superstructure. He maintained, according to Godwin,[1] that the best of all governments had been that of England under George I. Though Cartwright said at the trial that Horne Tooke was taken to ' have no religion whatever,' he was, according to Stephens, ' a great stickler for the church of England ' : and stood up for the House of Lords as well as the church on grounds of utility.[2] He always ridiculed Paine and the doctrine of abstract rights,[3] and told Cartwright that though all men had an equal right to a share of property, they had not a right to an equal share. Horne Tooke's Radicalism (I use the word by anticipation) was that of the sturdy tradesman. He opposed the government because he hated war, taxation and sinecures. He argued against universal suffrage with equal pertinacity. A comfortable old gentleman, with a good cellar of Madeira, and proud of his wall-fruit in a well-tilled garden, had no desire to see George III. at the guillotine, and still less to see a mob supreme in Lombard Street or banknotes superseded by assignats. He might be jealous of the great nobles, but he dreaded mob-rule. He could denounce abuses, but he could not desire anarchy. He is said to have retorted upon some one who had boasted that English courts of justice were open to all classes : ' So is the London tavern—to all who can pay.' [4] That is in the spirit of Bentham ; and yet Bentham complains that Horne Tooke's disciple, Burdett, believed in the common law, and revered the authority of Coke.[5] In

[1] Paul's *Godwin*, i. 147.
[2] Stephens, ii. 48, 477.
[3] *Ibid.* ii. 34-41, 323, 478-481.
[4] *Ibid.* ii. 483.
[5] Bentham's *Works*, x. 404.

brief, the creed of Horne Tooke meant 'liberty' founded upon tradition. I shall presently notice the consistency of this with what may be called his philosophy. Meanwhile it was only natural that radicals of this variety should retire from active politics, having sufficiently burnt their fingers by flirtation with the more thorough-going party. How they came to life again will appear hereafter. Horne Tooke himself took warning from his narrow escape. He stayed quietly in his house at Wimbledon.[1] There he divided his time between his books and his garden, and received his friends to Sunday dinners. Bentham, Mackintosh, Coleridge, and Godwin were among his visitors. Coleridge calls him a 'keen iron man,' and reports that he made a butt of Godwin as he had done of Paine.[2] Porson and Boswell encountered him in drinking matches and were both left under the table.[3] The house was thus a small centre of intellectual life, though the symposia were not altogether such as became philosophers. Horne Tooke was a keen and shrewd disputant, well able to impress weaker natures. His neighbour, Sir Francis Burdett, became his political disciple, and in later years was accepted as the radical leader. Tooke died at Wimbledon 18th March 1812.

VI. INDIVIDUALISM

The general tendencies which I have so far tried to indicate will have to be frequently noticed in the course

[1] He was member for Old Sarum 1801-2; but his career ended by a declaratory act disqualifying for a seat men who had received holy orders.
[2] Bentham's *Works*, x. 404; *Life of Mackintosh*, i. 52; Paul's *Godwin*, i. 71; Coleridge's *Table-Talk*, 8th May 1830 and 16th August 1833.
[3] Stephens, ii. 316, 334, 438.

of the following pages. One point may be emphasised before proceeding : a main characteristic of the whole social and political order is what is now called its 'individualism.' That phrase is generally supposed to convey some censure. It may connote, however, some of the most essential virtues that a race can possess. Energy, self-reliance, and independence, a strong conviction that a man's fate should depend upon his own character and conduct, are qualities without which no nation can be great. They are the conditions of its vital power. They were manifested in a high degree by the Englishmen of the eighteenth century. How far they were due to the inherited qualities of the race, to the political or social history, or to external circumstances, I need not ask. They were the qualities which had especially impressed foreign observers. The fierce, proud, intractable Briton was elbowing his way to a high place in the world, and showing a vigour not always amiable, but destined to bring him successfully through tremendous struggles. In the earlier part of the century, Voltaire and French philosophers admired English freedom of thought and free speech, even when it led to eccentricity and brutality of manners, and to barbarism in matters of taste. Englishmen, conscious and proud of their 'liberty,' were the models of all who desired liberty for themselves. Liberty, as they understood it, involved, among other things, an assault upon the old restrictive system, which at every turn hampered the rising industrial energy. This is the sense in which 'Individualism,' or the gospel according to Adam Smith—*laissez faire*, and so forth— has been specially denounced in recent times. Without asking at present how far such attacks are justifiable, I

must be content to assume that the old restrictive system was in its actual form mischievous, guided by entirely false theories, and the great barrier to the development of industry. The same spirit appeared in purely political questions. 'Liberty,' as is often remarked, may be interpreted in two ways, not necessarily consistent with each other. It means sometimes simply the diminution of the sphere of law and the power of legislators, or, again, the transference to subjects of the power of legislating, and, therefore, not less control, but control by self-made laws alone. The Englishman, who was in presence of no centralised administrative power, who regarded the Government rather as receiving power from individuals than as delegating the power of a central body, took liberty mainly in the sense of restricting law. Government in general was a nuisance, though a necessity ; and properly employed only in mediating between conflicting interests, and restraining the violence of individuals forced into contact by outward circumstances. When he demanded that a greater share of influence should be given to the people, he always took for granted that their power would be used to diminish the activity of the sovereign power ; that there would be less government and therefore less jobbery, less interference with free speech and free action, and smaller perquisites to be bestowed in return for the necessary services. The people would use their authority to tie the hands of the rulers, and limit them strictly to their proper and narrow functions.

The absence, again, of the idea of a state in any other sense implies another tendency. The 'idea' was not required. Englishmen were concerned rather with

details than with first principles. Satisfied, in a general way, with their constitution, they did not want to be bothered with theories. Abstract and absolute doctrines of right, when imported from France, fell flat upon the average Englishman. He was eager enough to discuss the utility of this or that part of the machinery, but without inquiring into first principles of mechanism. The argument from 'utility' deals with concrete facts, and presupposes an acceptance of some common criterion of the useful. The constant discussion of political matters in parliament and the press implied a tacit acceptance on all hands of constitutional methods. Practical men, asking whether this or that policy shall be adopted in view of actual events, no more want to go back to right reason and 'laws of nature' than a surveyor to investigate the nature of geometrical demonstration. Very important questions were raised as to the rights of the press, for example, or the system of representation. But everybody agreed that the representative system and freedom of speech were good things ; and argued the immediate questions of fact. The order, only established by experience and tradition, was accepted, subject to criticism of detail, and men turned impatiently from abstract argument, and left the inquiry into 'social contracts' to philosophers, that is, to silly people in libraries. Politics were properly a matter of business, to be discussed in a business-like spirit. In this sense, 'individualism' is congenial to 'empiricism,' because it starts from facts and particular interests, and resents the intrusion of first principles.

The characteristic individualism, again, suggests one other remark. Individual energy and sense of responsibility are good—as even extreme socialists may admit—if they do not exclude a sense of duties to others. It may be a question how far the stimulation of individual enterprise and the vigorous spirit of industrial competition really led to a disregard of the interests of the weaker. But it would be a complete misunderstanding of the time if we inferred that it meant a decline of humane feeling. Undoubtedly great evils had grown up, and some continued to grow which were tolerated by the indifference, or even stimulated by the selfish aims, of the dominant classes. But, in the first place, many of the most active prophets of the individualist spirit were acting, and acting sincerely, in the name of humanity. They were attacking a system which they held, and to a great extent, I believe, held rightly, to be especially injurious to the weakest classes. Possibly they expected too much from the simple removal of restrictions ; but certainly they denounced the restrictions as unjust to all, not simply as hindrances to the wealth of the rich. Adam Smith's position is intelligible : it was, he thought, a proof of a providential order that each man, by helping himself, unintentionally helped his neighbours. The moral sense based upon sympathy was therefore not opposed to, but justified, the economic principles that each man should first attend to his own interest. The unintentional co-operation would thus become conscious and compatible with the established order. And, in the next place, so far from there being a want of humane feeling, the most marked characteristic of the eighteenth century was precisely the growth of humanity. In the next generation, the eighteenth century came to be denounced as cold, heartless, faithless, and so forth.

The established mode of writing history is partly responsible for this perversion. Men speak as though some great man, who first called attention to an evil, was a supernatural being who had suddenly dropped into the world from another sphere. His condemnation of evil is therefore taken to be a proof that the time must be evil. Any century is bad if we assume all the good men to be exceptions. But the great man is really also the product of his time. He is the mouthpiece of its prevailing sentiments, and only the first to see clearly what many are beginning to perceive obscurely. The emergence of the prophet is a proof of the growing demand of his hearers for sound teaching. Because he is in advance of men generally, he sees existing abuses more clearly, and we take his evidence against his contemporaries as conclusive. But the fact that they listened shows how widely the same sensibility to evil was already diffused. In fact, as I think, the humane spirit of the eighteenth century, due to the vast variety of causes which we call social progress or evolution—not to the teaching of any individual—was permeating the whole civilised world, and showed itself in the philosophic movement as well as in the teaching of the religious leaders, who took the philosophers to be their enemies. I have briefly noticed the various philanthropic movements which were characteristic of the period. Some of them may indicate the growth of new evils; others, that evils which had once been regarded with indifference were now attracting attention and exciting indignation. But even the growth of new evils does not show general indifference so much as the incapacity of the existing system to deal with new conditions. It may, I think,

be safely said that a growing philanthropy was characteristic of the whole period, and in particular animated the Utilitarian movement, as I shall have to show in detail. Modern writers have often spoken of the Wesleyan propaganda and the contemporary 'evangelical revival' as the most important movements of the time. They are apt to speak, in conformity with the view just described, as though Wesley or some of his contemporaries had originated or created the better spirit. Without asking what was good or bad in some aspects of these movements, I fully believe that Wesley was essentially a moral reformer, and that he deserves corresponding respect. But instead of holding that his contemporaries were bad people, awakened by a stimulus from without, I hold that the movement, so far as really indicating moral improvement, must be set down to the credit of the century itself. It was one manifestation of a general progress, of which Bentham was another outcome. Though Bentham might have thought Wesley a fanatic or perhaps a hypocrite, and Wesley would certainly have considered that Bentham's heart was much in need of a change, they were really allies as much as antagonists, and both mark a great and beneficial change.

CHAPTER IV

PHILOSOPHY

I. JOHN HORNE TOOKE

I HAVE so far dwelt upon the social and political environment of the early Utilitarian movement ; and have tried also to point out some of the speculative tendencies fostered by the position. If it be asked what philosophical doctrines were explicitly taught, the answer must be a very short one. English philosophy barely existed. Parr was supposed to know something about metaphysics—apparently because he could write good Latin. But the inference was hasty. Of one book, however, which had a real influence, I must say something, for though it contained little definite philosophy, it showed what kind of philosophy was congenial to the common-sense of the time.

The sturdy radical, Horne Tooke, had been led to the study of philology by a characteristic incident. The legal question had arisen whether the words, ' She, knowing that Crooke had been indicted for forgery,' did so and so, contained an averment that Crooke had been indicted. Tooke argued in a letter to Dunning[1] that

---

[1] Published originally in 1778 ; reprinted in edition of ΕΠΕΑ ΠΤΕΡΟΕΝΤΑ or Diversions of Purley, by Richard Taylor (1829), to which I refer. The first part of the Diversions of Purley appeared in 1786 ; and the second part (with a new edition of the first) in 1798.

they did; because they were equivalent to the phrase, 'Crooke had been indicted for forgery: she, *knowing that*,' did so and so. This raises the question : What is the meaning of 'that'? Tooke took up the study, thinking, as he says, that it would throw light upon some philosophical questions. He learned some Anglo-Saxon and Gothic to test his theory and, of course, confirmed it.[1] The book shows ingenuity, shrewdness, and industry, and Tooke deserves credit for seeing the necessity of applying a really historical method to his problem, though his results were necessarily crude in the prescientific stage of philology.

The book is mainly a long string of etymologies, which readers of different tastes have found intolerably dull or an amusing collection of curiosities. Tooke held, and surely with reason, that an investigation of language, the great instrument of thought, may help to throw light upon the process of thinking. He professes to be a disciple of Locke in philosophy as in politics. Locke, he said,[2] made a lucky mistake in calling his book an essay upon human understanding ; for he thus attracted many who would have been repelled had he called it what it really was, 'a treatise upon words and language.' According to Tooke, in fact,[3] what we call 'operations of mind' are only 'operations of language.' The mind contemplates nothing but 'impressions,' that is, 'sensations or feelings,' which Locke called 'ideas.' Locke

[1] *Diversions of Purley* (1829), i. 12, 131.
[2] *Ibid.* ii. 362. Locke's work, says Prof. Max Müller in his *Science of Thought*, p. 295, 'is, as Lange in his *History of Materialism* rightly perceived, a critique of language which, together with Kant's *Critique of the Pure Reason*, forms the starting-point of modern philosophy.' *See* Lange's *Materialism*, (1873), i. 271.   [3] *Ibid.* i. 49.

mistook composition of terms for composition of ideas. To compound ideas is impossible. We can only use one term as a sign of many ideas. Locke, again, supposed that affirming and denying were operations of the mind, whereas they are only artifices of language.[1]

The mind, then, can only contemplate, separately or together, aggregates of 'ideas,' ultimate atoms, incapable of being parted or dissolved. There are, therefore, only two classes of words, nouns and verbs ; all others, prepositions, conjunctions, and so forth, being abbreviations, a kind of mental shorthand to save the trouble of enumerating the separate items. Tooke, in short, is a thoroughgoing nominalist. The realities, according to him, are sticks, stones, and material objects, or the 'ideas' which 'represent' them. They can be stuck together or taken apart, but all the words which express relations, categories, and the like, are in themselves meaningless. The special objects of his scorn are 'Hermes' Harris, and Monboddo, who had tried to defend Aristotle against Locke. Monboddo had asserted that 'every kind of relation' is a pure 'idea of the intellect' not to be apprehended by sense.[2] If so, according to Tooke, it would be a nonentity.

This doctrine gives a short cut to the abolition of metaphysics. The word 'metaphysics,' says Tooke,[3] is nonsense. All metaphysical controversies are 'founded on the grossest ignorance of words and the nature of speech.' The greatest part of his second volume is concerned with etymologies intended to prove that an 'abstract idea' is a mere word. Abstract words, he

[1] *Diversions of Purley*, i. 36, 42.   [2] *Ibid.* i. 373.   [3] *Ibid.* i. 374.

says,[1] are generally 'participles without a substantive and therefore in construction used as substantives.' From a misunderstanding of this has arisen 'metaphysical jargon' and 'false morality.' In illustration he gives a singular list of words, including 'fate, chance, heaven, hell, providence, prudence, innocence, substance, fiend, angel, apostle, spirit, true, false, desert, merit, faith, etc., all of which are mere participles poetically embodied and substantiated by those who use them.' A couple of specific applications, often quoted by later writers, will sufficiently indicate his drift.

Such words, he remarks,[2] as 'right' and 'just' mean simply that which is ordered or commanded. The chapter is headed 'rights of man,' and Tooke's interlocutor naturally observes that this is a singular result for a democrat. Man, it would seem, has no rights except the rights created by the law. Tooke admits the inference to be correct, but replies that the democrat in disobeying human law may be obeying the law of God, and is obeying the law of God when he obeys the law of nature. The interlocutor does not inquire what Tooke could mean by the 'law of nature.' We can guess what Tooke would have said to Paine in the Wimbledon garden. In fact, however, Tooke is here, as elsewhere, following Hobbes, though, it seems, unconsciously. Another famous etymology is that of 'truth' from 'troweth.'[3] Truth is what each man thinks. There is no such thing, therefore, as 'eternal, immutable, everlasting truth, unless mankind, *such as they are at present*,

[1] *Diversions of Purley*, ii. 18. Cf. Mill's statement in *Analysis*, i. 304, that 'abstract terms are concrete terms with the connotation dropped.'
[2] *Ibid.* ii. 9, etc.   [3] *Ibid.* ii. 399.

be eternal, immutable, everlasting.' Two persons may contradict each other and yet each may be speaking what is true for him. Truth may be a vice as well as a virtue; for on many occasions it is wrong to speak the truth.

These phrases may possibly be interpreted in a sense less paradoxical than the obvious one. Tooke's philosophy, if so it is to be called, was never fully expounded. He burned his papers before his death, and we do not know what he would have said about 'verbs,' which must have led, one would suppose, to some further treatment of relations, nor upon the subject, which as Stephens tells us, was most fully treated in his continuation, the value of human testimony.

If Tooke was not a philosopher he was a man of remarkably shrewd cynical common-sense, who thought philosophy idle foppery. His book made a great success. Stephens tells us[1] that it brought him £4000 or £5000. Hazlitt in 1810 published a grammar professing to incorporate for the first time Horne Tooke's 'discoveries.' The book was admired by Mackintosh,[2] who, of course, did not accept the principles, and had a warm disciple in Charles Richardson (1775-1865), who wrote in its defence against Dugald Stewart and accepted its authority in his elaborate dictionary of the English language.[3] But its chief interest for us is that it was a great authority with James Mill. Mill accepts the etymologies, and there is much in common between the two writers, though Mill had learned his main

[1] Stephens, ii. 497.   [2] *Life of Mackintosh*, ii. 235-37.
[3] Begun for the *Encyclopædia Metropolitana* in 1818 ; and published in 1835-37. Dugald Stewart's chief criticism is in his Essays (*Works*, v. 149-188). John Fearn published his *Anti-Tooke* in 1820.

doctrines elsewhere, especially from Hobbes. What the agreement really shows is how the intellectual idiosyncrasy which is congenial to 'nominalism' in philosophy was also congenial to Tooke's matter of fact radicalism and to the Utilitarian position of Bentham and his followers.

II. DUGALD STEWART

If English philosophy was a blank, there was still a leader of high reputation in Scotland. Dugald Stewart (1753-1828) had a considerable influence upon the Utilitarians. He represented, on the one hand, the doctrines which they thought themselves specially bound to attack, and it may perhaps be held that in some ways he betrayed to them the key of the position. Stewart[1] was son of a professor of mathematics at Edinburgh. He studied at Glasgow (1771-72) where he became Reid's favourite pupil and devoted friend. In 1772 he became the assistant, and in 1775 the colleague, of his father, and he appears to have had a considerable knowledge of mathematics. In 1785 he succeeded Adam Ferguson as professor of moral philosophy and lectured continuously until 1810. He then gave up his active duties to Thomas Brown, devoting himself to the

[1] Nine volumes of Dugald Stewart's works, edited by Sir W. Hamilton, appeared from 1854 to 1856; a tenth, including a life of Stewart by J. Veitch, appeared in 1858, and an eleventh, with an index to the whole, in 1860. The chief books are the *Elements of the Philosophy of the Human Mind* (in vols. ii., iii. and iv., originally in 1792, 1814, 1827); *Philosophical Essays* (in vol. v., originally 1810); *Philosophy of the Active and Moral Powers of Man* (vols. vi. and vii., originally in 1828); *Dissertation on the Progress of Philosophy* (in vol. i.; originally in *Encyclopædia Britannica*, in 1815 and 1821). The lectures on Political Economy first appeared in the *Works*, vols. viii. and ix.

completion and publication of the substance of his lectures. Upon Brown's death in 1820, he resigned a post to which he was no longer equal. A paralytic stroke in 1822 weakened him, though he was still able to write. He died in 1828.

If Stewart now makes no great mark in histories of philosophy, his personal influence was conspicuous. Cockburn describes him as of delicate appearance, with a massive head, bushy eyebrows, gray intelligent eyes, flexible mouth and expressive countenance. His voice was sweet and his ear exquisite. Cockburn never heard a better reader, and his manners, though rather formal, were graceful and dignified. James Mill, after hearing Pitt and Fox, declared that Stewart was their superior in eloquence. At Edinburgh, then at the height of its intellectual activity, he held his own among the ablest men and attracted the loyalty of the younger. Students came not only from Scotland but from England, the United States, France and Germany.[1] Scott won the professor's approval by an essay on the 'Customs of the Northern Nations.' Jeffrey, Horner, Cockburn and Mackintosh were among his disciples. His lectures upon Political Economy were attended by Sydney Smith, Jeffrey and Brougham, and one of his last hearers was Lord Palmerston. Parr looked up to him as a great philosopher, and contributed to his works an essay upon the etymology of the word 'sublime,' too vast to be printed whole. Stewart was an upholder of Whig principles, when the Scottish government was in the hands of the staunchest Tories. The irreverent young Edinburgh Reviewers treated him with respect, and to some

[1] *Works*, vi. ('Preface')

extent applied his theory to politics. Stewart was the philosophical heir of Reid; and, one may say, was a Whig both in philosophy and in politics. He was a rationalist, but within the limits fixed by respectability; and he dreaded the revolution in politics, and believed in the surpassing merits of the British Constitution as interpreted by the respectable Whigs.

Stewart represents the 'common-sense' doctrine. That name, as he observes, lends itself to an equivocation. Common-sense is generally used as nearly synonymous with 'mother wit,' the average opinion of fairly intelligent men; and he would prefer to speak of the 'fundamental laws of belief.'[1] There can, however, be no doubt that the doctrine derived much of its strength from the apparent confirmation of the 'average opinion' by the 'fundamental laws.' On one side, said Reid, are all the vulgar; on the other side all the philosophers. 'In this division, to my great humiliation, I find myself classed with the vulgar.'[2] Reid, in fact, had opposed the theories of Hume and Berkeley because they led to a paradoxical scepticism. If it be, as Reid held, a legitimate inference from Berkeley that a man may as well run his head against a post, there can be no doubt that it is shocking to common sense in every acceptation of the word. The reasons, however, which Reid and Stewart alleged for not performing that feat took a special form, which I am compelled to notice briefly because they set up the mark for the whole intellectual artillery of the Utilitarians. Reid, in fact, invented what J. S. Mill called 'intuitions.' To confute intuitionists and get rid of intuitions was one main purpose of all Mill's specula-

[1] *Works* (Life of Reid), x. 304-8.   [2] Reid's *Works* (Hamilton), p. 302.

tions. What, then, is an 'intuition'? To explain that fully it would be necessary to write once more that history of the philosophical movement from Descartes to Hume, which has been summarised and elucidated by so many writers that it should be as plain as the road from St. Paul's to Temple Bar. I am forced to glance at the position taken by Reid and Stewart because it has a most important bearing upon the whole Utilitarian scheme. Reid's main service to philosophy was, in his own opinion,[1] that he refuted the 'ideal system' of Descartes and his followers. That system, he says, carried in its womb the monster, scepticism, which came to the birth in 1739,[2] the date of Hume's early *Treatise*. To confute Hume, therefore, which was Reid's primary object, it was necessary to go back to Descartes, and to show where he deviated from the right track. In other words, we must trace the genealogy of 'ideas.' Descartes, as Reid admitted, had rendered immense services to philosophy. He had exploded the scholastic system, which had become a mere mass of logomachies and an incubus upon scientific progress. He had again been the first to 'draw a distinct line between the material and the intellectual world'[3]; and Reid apparently assumes that he had drawn it correctly. One characteristic of the Cartesian school is obvious. Descartes, a great mathematician at the period when mathematical investigations were showing their enormous power, invented a mathematical universe. Mathematics presented the true type of scientific reasoning and determined his canons of inquiry. The 'essence' of matter, he said, was space. The objective world, as we

[1] Reid's *Works* (Hamilton), p. 88.   [2] *Ibid.* 206.   [3] *Ibid.* 267.

have learned to call it, is simply space solidified or incarnate geometry. Its properties therefore could be given as a system of deductions from first principles, and it forms a coherent and self-subsistent whole. Meanwhile the essence of the soul is thought. Thought and matter are absolutely opposed. They are contraries, having nothing in common. Reality, however, seems to belong to the world of space. The brain, too, belongs to that world, and motions in the brain must be determined as a part of the material mechanism. In some way or other 'ideas' correspond to these motions; though to define the way tried all the ingenuity of Descartes' successors. In any case an idea is 'subjective': it is a thought, not a thing. It is a shifting, ephemeral entity not to be fixed or grasped. Yet, somehow or other, it exists, and it 'represents' realities; though the divine power has to be called in to guarantee the accuracy of the representation. The objective world, again, does not reveal itself to us as simply made up of 'primary qualities'; we know of it only as somehow endowed with 'secondary' or sense-given qualities: as visible, tangible, audible, and so forth. These qualities are plainly 'subjective'; they vary from man to man, and from moment to moment: they cannot be measured or fixed; and must be regarded as a product in some inexplicable way of the action of matter upon mind; unreal or, at any rate, not independent entities.

In Locke's philosophy, the 'ideas,' legitimate or illegitimate descendants of the Cartesian theories, play a most prominent part. Locke's admirable common-sense made him the leader who embodied a growing tendency. The empirical sciences were growing; and Locke, a

student of medicine, could note the fallacies which arise from neglecting observation and experiment, and attempting to penetrate to the absolute essences and entities. Newton's great success was due to neglecting impossible problems about the nature of force in itself—'action at a distance' and so forth—and attention to the sphere of visible phenomena. The excessive pretensions of the framers of metaphysical systems had led to hopeless puzzles and merely verbal theories. Locke, therefore, insisted upon the necessity of ascertaining the necessary limits of human knowledge. All our knowledge of material facts is obviously dependent in some way upon our sensations—however fleeting or unreal they may be. Therefore, the material sciences must depend upon sense-given data or upon observation and experiment. Hume gives the ultimate purpose, already implied in Locke's essay, when he describes his first treatise (on the title page) as an 'attempt to introduce the experimental mode of reasoning into moral subjects.' Now, as Reid thinks, the effect of this was to construct our whole knowledge out of the representative ideas. The empirical factor is so emphasised that we lose all grasp of the real world. Locke, indeed, though he insists upon the derivation of our whole knowledge from 'ideas,' leaves reality to the 'primary qualities' without clearly expounding their relation to the secondary. But Berkeley, alarmed by the tendency of the Cartesian doctrines to materialism and mechanical necessity, reduces the 'primary' to the level of the 'secondary,' and proceeds to abolish the whole world of matter. We are thus left with nothing but 'ideas,' and the ideas are naturally 'subjective' and therefore in some sense unreal.

Finally Hume gets rid of the soul as well as the outside world; and then, by his theory of 'causation,' shows that the ideas themselves are independent atoms, cohering but not rationally connected, and capable of being arbitrarily joined or separated in any way whatever. Thus the ideas have ousted the facts. We cannot get beyond ideas, and yet ideas are still purely subjective. The 'real' is separated from the phenomenal, and truth divorced from fact. The sense-given world is the whole world, and yet is a world of mere accidental conjunctions and separation. That is Hume's scepticism, and yet according to Reid is the legitimate development of Descartes' 'ideal system.' Reid, I take it, was right in seeing that there was a great dilemma. What was required to escape from it? According to Kant, nothing less than a revision of Descartes' mode of demarcation between object and subject. The 'primary qualities' do not correspond in this way to an objective world radically opposed to the subjective. Space is not a form of things, but a form imposed upon the data of experience by the mind itself. This, as Kant says, supposes a revolution in philosophy comparable to the revolution made by Copernicus in astronomy. We have completely to invert our whole system of conceiving the world. Whatever the value of Kant's doctrine, of which I need here say nothing, it was undoubtedly more prolific than Reid's. Reid's was far less thoroughgoing. He does not draw a new line between object and subject, but simply endeavours to show that the dilemma was due to certain assumptions about the nature of 'ideas.'

The real had been altogether separated from the

phenomenal, or truth divorced from fact. You can only have demonstrations by getting into a region beyond the sensible world; while within that world—that is, the region of ordinary knowledge and conduct—you are doomed to hopeless uncertainty. An escape, therefore, must be sought by some thorough revision of the assumed relation, but not by falling back upon the exploded philosophy of the schools. Reid and his successors were quite as much alive as Locke to the danger of falling into mere scholastic logomachy. They, too, will in some sense base all knowledge upon experience. Reid constantly appeals to the authority of Bacon, whom he regards as the true founder of inductive science. The great success of Bacon's method in the physical sciences, encouraged the hope, already expressed by Newton, that a similar result might be achieved in 'moral philosophy.'[1] Hume had done something to clear the way, but Reid was, as Stewart thinks, the first to perceive clearly and justly the 'analogy between these two different branches of human knowledge.' The mind and matter are two co-ordinate things, whose properties are to be investigated by similar methods. Philosophy thus means essentially psychology. The two inquiries are two 'branches' of inductive science, and the problem is to discover by a perfectly impartial examination what are the 'fundamental laws of mind' revealed by an accurate analysis of the various processes of thought. The main result of Reid's investigations is given most pointedly in his early *Inquiry*, and was fully accepted by Stewart. Briefly it comes to this. No one can doubt that we believe, as a fact, in an external world. We believe

[1] Stewart's remarks on his life of Reid: Reid's *Works*, p. 12, etc.

that there are sun and moon, stones, sticks, and human bodies. This belief is accepted by the sceptic as well as by the dogmatist, although the sceptic reduces it to a mere blind custom or ' association of ideas.' Now Reid argues that the belief, whatever its nature, is not and cannot be derived from the sensations. We do not construct the visible and tangible world, for example, simply out of impressions made upon the senses of sight and touch. To prove this, he examines what are the actual data provided by these senses, and shows, or tries to show, that we cannot from them alone construct the world of space and geometry. Hence, if we consider experience impartially and without preconception, we find that it tells us something which is not given by the senses. The senses are not the material of our perceptions, but simply give the occasions upon which our belief is called into activity. The sensation is no more like the reality in which we believe than the pain of a wound is like the edge of the knife. Perception tells us directly and immediately, without the intervention of ideas, that there is, as we all believe, a real external world.

Reid was a vigorous reasoner, and credit has been given to him by some disciples of Kant's doctrine of time and space. Schopenhauer[1] says that Reid's 'excellent work' gives a complete 'negative proof of the Kantian truths'; that is to say, that Reid proves satisfactorily that we cannot construct the world out of the sense-given data alone. But, whereas Kant regards the senses as sup-

[1] *The World as Will and Idea* (Haldane & Kemp), ii. 186. Reid's '*Inquiry*,' he adds, is ten times better worth reading than all the philosophy together which has been written since Kant.

plying the materials moulded by the perceiving mind, Reid regards them as mere stimuli exciting certain inevitable beliefs. As a result of Reid's method, then, we have 'intuitions.' Reid's essential contention is that a fair examination of experience will reveal certain fundamental beliefs, which cannot be explained as mere manifestations of the sensations, and which, by the very fact that they are inexplicable, must be accepted as an 'inspiration.'[1] Reid professes to discover these beliefs by accurately describing facts. He finds them there as a chemist finds an element. The 'intuition' is made by substituting for 'ideas' a mysterious and inexplicable connection between the mind and matter.[2] The chasm exists still, but it is somehow bridged by a quasi-miracle. Admitting, therefore, that Reid shows a gap to exist in the theory, his result remains 'negative.' The philosopher will say that it is not enough to assert a principle dogmatically without showing its place in a reasoned system of thought. The psychologist, on the other hand, who takes Reid's own ground, may regard the statement only as a useful challenge to further inquiry. The analysis hitherto given may be insufficient, but where Reid has failed, other inquirers may be more successful. As soon, in fact, as we apply the psychological method, and regard the 'philosophy of mind' as an 'inductive science,' it is perilous, if not absolutely inconsistent, to discover 'intuitions' which will take us beyond experience. The line of defence against em-

[1] 'We are inspired with the sensation, as we are inspired with the corresponding perception, by means unknown.'—Reid's *Works*, 188. 'This,' says Stewart, 'is a plain statement of fact.—Stewart's *Works*, ii. 111-12.
[2] See Rosmini's *Origin of Ideas* (English translation), i. p. 91, where, though sympathising with Reid's aim, he admits a 'great blunder.'

piricism can only be provisional and temporary. In his main results, indeed, Reid had the advantage of being on the side of 'common sense.' Everybody was already convinced that there were sticks and stones, and everybody is prepared to hear that their belief is approved by philosophy. But a difficulty arises when a similar method is applied to a doctrine sincerely disputed. To the statement, 'this is a necessary belief,' it is a sufficient answer to reply, 'I don't believe it.' In that case, an intuition merely amounts to a dogmatic assumption that I am infallible, and must be supported by showing its connection with beliefs really universal and admittedly necessary.

Dugald Stewart followed Reid upon this main question, and with less force and originality represents the same point of view. He accepts Reid's view of the two co-ordinate departments of knowledge; the science of which mind, and the science of which body, is the object. Philosophy is not a 'theory of knowledge' or of the universe; but, as it was then called, 'a philosophy of the human mind.' 'Philosophy' is founded upon inductive psychology; and it only becomes philosophy in a wider sense in so far as we discover that as a fact we have certain fundamental beliefs, which are thus given by experience, though they take us in a sense beyond experience. Jeffrey, reviewing Stewart's life of Reid, in the *Edinburgh Review* of 1804, makes a significant inference from this. Bacon's method, he said, had succeeded in the physical sciences, because there we could apply experiment. But experiment is impossible in the science of mind; and therefore philosophy will never be anything but a plaything or a useful variety of gymnastic. Stewart replied

at some length in his *Essays*,[1] fully accepting the general conception, but arguing that the experimental method was applicable to the science of mind. Jeffrey observes that it was now admitted that the 'profoundest reasonings' had brought us back to the view of the vulgar, and this, too, is admitted by Stewart so far as the cardinal doctrine of 'the common sense' philosophy, the theory of perception, is admitted.

From this, again, it follows that the 'notions we annex to the words Matter and Mind are merely relative.'[2] We know that mind exists as we know that matter exists; or, if anything, we know the existence of mind more certainly because more directly. The mind is suggested by 'the subjects of our consciousness'; the body by the objects 'of our perception.' But, on the other hand, we are totally 'ignorant of the essence of either.'[3] We can discover the laws either of mental or moral phenomena; but a law, as he explains, means in strictness nothing but a 'general fact.'[4] It is idle, therefore, to explain the nature of the union between the two unknowable substances; we can only discover that they are united and observe the laws according to which one set of phenomena corresponds to the other. From a misunderstanding of this arise all the fallacies of scholastic ontology, 'the most idle and absurd speculation that ever employed the human faculties.'[5] The destruction of that pseudo-science was the great glory of Bacon and Locke; and Reid has now discovered the method by which we may advance to the establishment of a truly inductive 'philosophy of mind.'

[1] Stewart's *Works*, v. 24-53. Hamilton says in a note (p. 41) that Jeffrey candidly confessed Stewart's reply to be satisfactory.
[2] *Ibid.* ii. 46.   [3] *Ibid.* ii. 45-67.   [4] *Ibid.* iii. 159.   [5] *Ibid.* v. 21.

It is not surprising that Stewart approximates in various directions to the doctrines of the empirical school. He leans towards them whenever he does not see the results to which he is tending. Thus, for example, he is a thorough-going nominalist;[1] and on this point he deserts the teaching of Reid. He defends against Reid the attack made by Berkeley and Hume upon 'abstract ideas.' Rosmini,[2] in an elaborate criticism, complains that Stewart did not perceive the inevitable tendency of nominalism to materialism.[3] Stewart, in fact, accepts a good deal of Horne Tooke's doctrine,[4] though calling Tooke an 'ingenious grammarian, not a very profound philosopher,' but holds, as we shall see, that the materialistic tendency can be avoided. As becomes a nominalist, he attacks the syllogism upon grounds more fully brought out by J. S. Mill. Upon another essential point, he agrees with the pure empiricists. He accepts Hume's view of causation in all questions of physical science. In natural philosophy, he declares causation means only conjunction. The senses can never give us the 'efficient' cause of any phenomenon. In other words, we can never see a 'necessary connection' between any two events. He collects passages from earlier writers to show how Hume had been anticipated; and holds that Bacon's inadequate view of this truth was a main defect in his theories.[5] Hence we have a characteristic conclusion. He says, when

---

[1] Stewart's *Works*, ii. 165-93; iii. 81-97. Schopenhauer (*The World as Will and Idea*, ii. 240) admires Reid's teaching upon this point, and recommends us not 'to waste an hour over the scribblings of this shallow writer' (Stewart).
[2] Rosmini's *Origin of Ideas* (English translation), i. 96-176.
[3] *Ibid.* i. 147 *n.*   [4] Stewart's *Works*, iv. 29, 35, 38, and v. 149-88.
[5] *Ibid.* ii. 97, etc., and iii. 235, 389, 417.

discussing the proofs of the existence of God,[1] that we have an 'irresistible conviction of the *necessity* of a cause' for every change. Hume, however, has shown that this can never be a logical necessity. It must then, argues Stewart, be either a 'prejudice' or an 'intuitive judgment.' Since it is shown by 'universal consent' not to be a prejudice, it must be an intuitive judgment. Thus Hume's facts are accepted; but his inference denied. The actual causal nexus is inscrutable. The conviction that there must be a connection between events attributed by Hume to 'custom' is attributed by Stewart to intuitive belief. Stewart infers that Hume's doctrine is really favourable to theology. It implies that God gives us the conviction, and perhaps, as Malebranche held, that God is 'the constantly operating efficient Cause in the material world.'[2] Stewart's successor, Thomas Brown, took up this argument on occasion of the once famous 'Leslie controversy'; and Brown's teaching was endorsed by James Mill and by John Stuart Mill.

According to J. S. Mill, James Mill and Stewart represented opposite poles of philosophic thought. I shall have to consider this dictum hereafter. On the points already noticed Stewart must be regarded as an ally rather than an opponent of the Locke and Hume tradition. Like them he appeals unhesitatingly to experience, and cannot find words strong enough to express his contempt for 'ontological' and scholastic methods. His 'intuitions' are so far very harmless things, which fall in with common sense, and enable him to hold without further trouble the beliefs which, as a matter of fact, are held by everybody. They are an excuse for not seeking any

---

[1] *Works*, vii. 13-34.   [2] *Ibid.* vii. 26, etc.

ultimate explanation in reason. He is, indeed, opposed to the school which claimed to be the legitimate successor to Locke, but which evaded Hume's scepticism by diverging towards materialism. The great representative of this doctrine in England had been Hartley, and in Stewart's day Hartley's lead had been followed by Priestley, who attacked Reid from a materialist point of view, by Priestley's successor, Thomas Belsham, and by Erasmus Darwin. We find Stewart, in language which reminds us of later controversy, denouncing the 'Darwinian School'[1] for theories about instinct incompatible with the doctrine of final causes. It might appear that a philosopher who has re-established the objective existence of space in opposition to Berkeley, was in danger of that materialism which had been Berkeley's bugbear. But Stewart escapes the danger by his assertion that our knowledge of matter is 'relative' or confined to phenomena. Materialism is for him a variety of ontology, involving the assumption that we know the essence of matter. To speak with Hartley of 'vibrations,' animal spirits, and so forth, is to be led astray by a false analogy. We can discover the laws of correspondence of mind and body, but not the ultimate nature of either.[2] Thus he regards the 'physiological metaphysics of the present day' as an 'idle waste of labour and ingenuity on questions to which the human mind is altogether incompetent.'[3] The principles found by inductive observation are as independent of these speculations as Newton's theory of gravitation of an ultimate mechanical cause of gravitation.

Hartley's followers, however, could drop the 'vibra-

---

[1] *Works*, iv. 265.   [2] *Ibid.* ii. 52.   [3] *Ibid.* v. 10.

tion' theory; and their doctrine then became one of 'association of ideas.' To this famous theory, which became the sheet-anchor of the empirical school, Stewart is not altogether opposed. We find him speaking of 'indissoluble association' in language which reminds us of the Mills.[1] Hume had spoken of association as comparable to gravitation—the sole principle by which our 'ideas' and 'impressions' are combined into a whole; a theory, of course, corresponding to his doctrine of 'belief' as a mere custom of associating. Stewart uses the principle rather as Locke had done, as explaining fallacies due to 'casual associations.' It supposes, as he says, the previous existence of certain principles, and cannot be an ultimate explanation. The only question can be at what point we have reached an 'original principle,' and are therefore bound to stop our analysis.[2] Over this question he glides rather too lightly, as is his custom; but from his point of view the belief, for example, in an external world, cannot be explained by association, inasmuch as it reveals itself as an ultimate datum.

In regard to the physical sciences, then, Stewart's position approximates very closely to the purely 'empirical' view. When we come to a different application of his principles, we find him taking a curiously balanced position between different schools. 'Common sense' naturally wishes to adapt itself to generally accepted beliefs; and with so flexible a doctrine as that of 'intuitions' it is not difficult to discover methods of proving the ordinary dogmas. Stewart's theology is characteristic of this tendency. He describes the so-called *a*

---

[1] *Works*, ii. 155.   [2] *Ibid.* ii. 337.

priori proof, as formulated by Clarke. But without denying its force, he does not like to lay stress upon it. He dreads 'ontology' too much. He therefore considers that the argument at once most satisfactory to the philosopher and most convincing to ordinary men is the argument from design. The belief in God is not 'intuitive,' but follows immediately from two first principles: the principle that whatever exists has a cause, and the principle that a 'combination of means implies a designer.'[1] The belief in a cause arises on our perception of change as our belief in the external world arises upon our sensations. The belief in design must be a 'first principle' because it includes a belief in 'necessity' which cannot arise from mere observation of 'contingent truths.'[2] Hence Stewart accepts the theory of final causes as stated by Paley. Though Paley's ethics offended him, he has nothing but praise for the work upon *Natural Theology*.[3] Thus, although 'common sense' does not enable us to lay down the central doctrine of theology as a primary truth, it does enable us to interpret experience in theological terms. In other words, his theology is of the purely empirical kind, which was, as we shall see, the general characteristic of the time.

In Stewart's discussion of ethical problems the same doctrine of 'final causes' assumes a special importance. Stewart, as elsewhere, tries to hold an intermediate position; to maintain the independence of morality without committing himself to the 'ontological' or purely logical view; and to show that virtue conduces to happiness without allowing that its dictates are to be deduced from

[1] *Works*, vi. 46; vii. 11.   [2] *Ibid.* vii. 46.   [3] *Ibid.* i. 357.

its tendency to produce happiness. His doctrine is to a great extent derived from the teaching of Hutcheson and Bishop Butler. He really approximates most closely to Hutcheson, who takes a similar view of Utilitarianism, but he professes the warmest admiration of Butler. He explicitly accepts Butler's doctrine of the 'supremacy of the conscience'—a doctrine which as he says, the bishop, 'has placed in the strongest and happiest light.'[1] He endeavours, again, to approximate to the 'intellectual school,' of which Richard Price (1723-1791) was the chief English representative at the time. Like Kant, Price deduces the moral law from principles of pure reason. The truth of the moral law, 'Thou shalt do to others as you wish that they should do to you,' is as evident as the truth of the law in geometry, 'things which are equal to the same thing are equal to each other.' Stewart so far approves that he wishes to give to the moral law what is now called all possible 'objectivity,' while the 'moral sense' of Hutcheson apparently introduced a 'subjective' element. He holds, however, that our moral perceptions 'involve a feeling of the heart,' as well as a 'judgment of the understanding,'[2] and ascribes the same view to Butler. But then, by using the word 'reason' so as to include the whole nature of a rational being, we may ascribe to it the 'origin of those simple ideas which are not excited in the mind by the operation of the senses, but which arise in consequence of the operation of the intellectual powers among the various objects.'[3] Hutcheson, he says, made his 'moral sense' unsatisfactory by taking his illustrations from the 'secondary' instead of the

[1] *Works*, vi. 320.   [2] *Ibid.* vi. 279.   [3] *Ibid.* vi. 297.

'primary qualities,'[1] and thus with the help of intuitive first principles, Stewart succeeds in believing that it would be as hard for a man to believe that he ought to sacrifice another man's happiness to his own as to believe that three angles of a triangle are equal to one right angle.[2] It is true that a feeling and a judgment are both involved; but the 'intellectual judgment' is the groundwork of the feeling, not the feeling of the judgment.[3] In spite, however, of this attempt to assimilate his principles to those of the intellectual school, the substance of Stewart's ethics is essentially psychological. It rests, in fact, upon his view that philosophy depends upon inductive psychology, and, therefore, essentially upon experience subject to the cropping up of convenient 'intuitions.'

This appears from the nature of his argument against the Utilitarians. In his time, this doctrine was associated with the names of Hartley, Tucker, Godwin, and especially Paley. He scarcely refers to Bentham.[4] Paley is the recognised anvil for the opposite school. Now he agrees, as I have said, with Paley's view of natural theology and entirely accepts therefore the theory of 'final causes.' The same theory becomes prominent in his ethical teaching. We may perhaps say that Stewart's view is in substance an inverted Utilitarianism. It may be best illustrated by an argument familiar in another application. Paley and his opponents might agree that the various instincts of an animal are so constituted that in point of fact they contribute to his

[1] *Works*, vi. 295. Cf. v. 83.   [2] *Ibid.* vi. 298-99.   [3] *Ibid.* v. 84.
[4] In *Works*, vi. 205-6, he quotes Dumont's *Bentham*; but his general silence is the more significant, as in the lectures on Political Economy he makes frequent and approving reference to Bentham's tract upon usury.

preservation and his happiness. But from one point of view this appears to be simply to say that the conditions of existence necessitate a certain harmony, and that the harmony is therefore to be a consequence of his self-preservation. From the opposite point of view, which Stewart accepts, it appears that the self-preservation is the consequence of a pre-established harmony, which has been divinely appointed in order that he may live. Stewart, in short, is a 'teleologist' of the Paley variety. Psychology proves the existence of design in the moral world, as anatomy or physiology proves it in the physical.

Stewart therefore fully agrees that virtue generally produces happiness. If it be true (a doctrine, he thinks, beyond our competence to decide) that 'the sole principle of action in the Deity' is benevolence, it may be that he has commanded us to be virtuous because he sees virtue to be useful. In this case utility may be the final cause of morality; and the fact that virtue has this tendency gives the plausibility to utilitarian systems.[1] But the key to the difficulty is the distinction between 'final' and 'efficient' causes; for the efficient cause of morality is not the desire for happiness, but a primitive and simple instinct, namely, the moral faculty.

Thus he rejects Paley's notorious doctrine that virtue differs from prudence only in regarding the consequences in another world instead of consequences in this.[2] Reward and punishment 'presuppose the notions of right and wrong' and cannot be the source of those notions. The favourite doctrine of association,

[1] *Works*, vii. 236-38.   [2] *Ibid.* vi. 221.

by which the Utilitarians explained unselfishness, is only admissible as accounting for modifications, such as are due to education and example, but 'presupposes the existence of certain principles which are common to all mankind.' The evidence of such principles is established by a long and discursive psychological discussion. It is enough to say that he admits two rational principles, 'self-love' and the 'moral faculty,' the coincidence of which is learned only by experience. The moral faculty reveals simple 'ideas' of right and wrong, which are incapable of any further analysis. But besides these, there is a hierarchy of other instincts or desires, which he calls 'implanted' because 'for aught we know' they may be of 'arbitrary appointment.'[1] Resentment, for example, is an implanted instinct, of which the 'final cause' is to defend us against 'sudden violence.'[2] Stewart's analysis is easygoing and suggests more problems than it solves. The general position, however, is clear enough, and not, I think, without much real force as against the Paley form of utilitarianism.

The acceptance of the doctrine of 'final causes' was the inevitable course for a philosopher who wishes to retain the old creeds and yet to appeal unequivocally to experience. It suits the amiable optimism for which Stewart is noticeable. To prove the existence of a perfect deity from the evidence afforded by the world, you must of course take a favourable view of the observable order. Stewart shows the same tendency in his Political Economy, where he is Adam Smith's disciple, and fully shares Smith's beliefs that the harmony between

[1] *Works*, vi. 213.　　[2] *Ibid.* vi. 199.

the interests of the individual and the interests of the society is an evidence of design in the Creator of mankind. In this respect Stewart differs notably from Butler, to whose reasonings he otherwise owed a good deal. With Butler the conscience implies a dread of divine wrath and justifies the conception of a world alienated from its maker. Stewart's 'moral faculty' simply recognises or reveals the moral law; but carries no suggestion of supernatural penalties. The doctrines by which Butler attracted some readers and revolted others throw no shadow over his writings. He is a placid enlightened professor, whose real good feeling and frequent shrewdness should not be overlooked in consequence of the rather desultory and often superficial mode of reasoning. This, however, suggests a final remark upon Stewart's position.

In the preface[1] to his *Active and Moral Powers* (1828) Stewart apologises for the large space given to the treatment of Natural Religion. The lectures, he says, which form the substance of the book, were given at a time when 'enlightened zeal for liberty' was associated with the 'reckless boldness of the uncompromising freethinker.' He wished, therefore, to show that a man could be a liberal without being an atheist. This gives the position characteristic of Stewart and his friends. The group of eminent men who made Edinburgh a philosophical centre was thoroughly in sympathy with the rationalist movement of the eighteenth century. The old dogmatic system of belief could be held very lightly even by the more educated clergy. Hume's position is significant. He could lay down the most

[1] *Works*, vi. 111.

unqualified scepticism in his writings; but he always regarded his theories as intended for the enlightened; he had no wish to disturb popular beliefs in theology, and was a strong Tory in politics. His friends were quite ready to take him upon that footing. The politeness with which 'Mr. Hume's' speculations are noticed by men like Stewart and Reid is in characteristic contrast to the reception generally accorded to more popular sceptics. They were intellectual curiosities not meant for immediate application. The real opinion of such men as Adam Smith and 'Stewart was probably a rather vague and optimistic theism. In the professor's chair they could talk to lads intended for the ministry without insulting such old Scottish prejudice (there was a good deal of it) as survived: and could cover rationalising opinions under language which perhaps might have a different meaning for their hearers. The position was necessarily one of tacit compromise. Stewart considers himself to be an inductive philosopher appealing frankly to experience and reason; and was in practice a man of thoroughly liberal and generous feelings. He was heartily in favour of progress as he understood it. Only he will not sacrifice common sense; that is to say, the beliefs which are in fact prevalent and congenial to existing institutions. Common sense, of course, condemns extremes: and if logic seems to be pushing a man towards scepticism in philosophy or revolution in practice, he can always protest by the convenient device of intuitions.

I have gone so far in order to illustrate the nature of the system which the Utilitarians took to be the antithesis of their own. It may be finally remarked that at present

both sides were equally ignorant of contemporary developments of German thought. When Stewart became aware that there was such a thing as Kant's philosophy, he tried to read it in a Latin version. Parr, I may observe, apparently did not know of this version, and gave up the task of reading German. Stewart's example was not encouraging. He had abandoned the 'undertaking in despair' partly from the scholastic barbarism of the style, partly 'my utter inability to comprehend the author's meaning.' He recognises similarity between Kant and Reid, but thinks Reid's simple statement of the fact that space cannot be derived from the senses more philosophical than Kant's 'superstructure of technical mystery.'[1]

I have dwelt upon the side in which Stewart's philosophy approximates to the empirical school, because the Utilitarians were apt to misconceive the position. They took Stewart to be the adequate representative of all who accepted one branch of an inevitable dilemma. The acceptance of 'intuitions,' that is, was the only alternative to thoroughgoing acceptance of 'experience.' They supposed, too, that persons vaguely described as 'Kant and the Germans' taught simply a modification of the 'intuitionist' view. I have noticed how emphatically Stewart claimed to rely upon experience and to base his philosophy upon inductive psychology, and was so far admitting the first principles and the general methods of his opponents. The Scottish philosophy, however, naturally presented itself as an antagonistic force to the Utilitarians. The 'intuitions' represented

[1] *Works*, v. 117 18. I have given some details as to Stewart's suffering under an English proselyte of Kant in my *Studies of a Biographer*.

the ultimate ground taken, especially in religious and ethical questions, by men who wished to be at once liberal philosophers and yet to avoid revolutionary extremes. 'Intuitions' had in any case a negative value, as protests against the sufficiency of the empirical analysis. It might be quite true, for example, that Hume's analysis of certain primary mental phenomena—of our belief in the external world or of the relation of cause and effect—was radically insufficient. He had not given an adequate explanation of the facts. The recognition of the insufficiency of his reasoning was highly important if only as a stimulus to inquiry. It was a warning to his and to Hartley's followers that they had not thoroughly unravelled the perplexity but only cut the knot. But when the insufficiency of the explanation was interpreted as a demonstration that all explanation was impossible, and the 'intuition' an ultimate 'self-evident' truth, it became a refusal to inquire just where inquiry was wanted; a positive command to stop analysis at an arbitrary point; and a round assertion that the adversary could not help believing precisely the doctrine which he altogether declined to believe. Naturally the empiricists refused to bow to an authority which was simply saying, 'Don't inquire further,' without any ground for the prohibition except the 'ipse dixitism' which declared that inquiry must be fruitless. Stewart, in fact, really illustrated the equivocation between the two meanings of 'common sense.' If by that name he understood, as he professed to understand, ultimate 'laws of thought,' his position was justifiable as soon as he could specify the laws and prove that they were ultimate. But so far as he virtually took for granted that the average beliefs of

intelligent people were such laws, and on that ground refused to examine the evidence of their validity, he was inconsistent, and his position only invited assault. As a fact, I believe that his 'intuitions' covered many most disputable propositions; and that the more clearly they were stated, the more they failed to justify his interpretations. He was not really answering the most vital and critical questions, but implicitly reserving them, and putting an arbitrary stop to investigations desirable on his own principles.

The Scottish philosophy was, however, accepted in England, and made a considerable impression in France, as affording a tenable barrier against scepticism. It was, as I have said, in philosophy what Whiggism was in politics. Like political Whiggism it included a large element of enlightened and liberal rationalism; but like Whiggism it covered an aversion to thoroughgoing logic. The English politician was suspicious of abstract principles, but could cover his acceptance of tradition and rule of thumb by general phrases about liberty and toleration. The Whig in philosophy equally accepted the traditional creed, sufficiently purified from cruder elements, and sheltered his doctrine by speaking of 'intuitions and laws of thought.' In both positions there was really, I take it, a great deal of sound practical wisdom; but they also implied a marked reluctance to push inquiry too far, and a tacit agreement to be content with what the Utilitarians denounced as 'vague generalities'—phrases, that is, which might be used either to conceal an underlying scepticism, or really to stop short in the path which led to scepticism. In philosophy as in politics, the Utilitarians boasted of

being thoroughgoing Radicals, and hated compromises, which to them appeared to be simply obstructive. I need not elaborate a point which will meet us again. If I were writing a history of thought in general I should have to notice other writers, though there were none of much distinction, who followed the teaching of Stewart or of his opponents of the Hartley and Darwin school. It would be necessary also to insist upon the growing interest in the physical sciences, which were beginning not only to make enormous advances, but to attract popular attention. For my purpose, however, it is I think sufficient to mention these writers, each of whom had a very special relation to the Utilitarians. I turn, therefore, to Bentham.

CHAPTER V

BENTHAM'S LIFE

I. EARLY LIFE

JEREMY BENTHAM,[1] the patriarch of the English Utilitarians, sprang from the class imbued most thoroughly with the typical English prejudices. His first recorded ancestor, Brian Bentham, was a pawnbroker, who lost money by the stop of the Exchequer in 1672, but was neither ruined, nor, it would seem, alienated by the king's dishonesty. He left some thousands to his son, Jeremiah, an attorney and a strong Jacobite. A second Jeremiah, born 2nd December 1712, carried on his father's business, and though his clients were not numerous, increased his fortune by judicious investments in houses and lands. Although brought up in Jacobite

[1] The main authority for Bentham's Life is Bowring's account in the two last volumes of the *Works*. Bain's *Life of James Mill* gives some useful facts as to the later period. There is comparatively little mention of Bentham in contemporary memoirs. Little is said of him in Romilly's *Life*. Parr's *Works*, i. and viii., contains some letters. See also R. Dale Owen's *Threading my Way*, pp. 175-78. A little book called *Utilitarianism Unmasked*, by the Rev. J. F. Colls, D.D. (1844), gives some reminiscences by Colls, who had been Bentham's amanuensis for fourteen years. Colls, who took orders, disliked Bentham's religious levity, and denounces his vanity, but admits his early kindness. Voluminous collections of the papers used by Bowring are at University College, and at the British Museum.

principles, he transferred his attachment to the Hanoverian dynasty when a relation of his wife married a valet of George II. The wife, Alicia Grove, was daughter of a tradesman who had made a small competence at Andover. Jeremiah Bentham had fallen in love with her at first sight, and wisely gave up for her sake a match with a fortune of £10,000. The couple were fondly attached to each other and to their children. The marriage took place towards the end of 1744, and the eldest son, Jeremy, was born in Red Lion Street, Houndsditch, 4th February 1747-48 (o.s.) The only other child who grew up was Samuel, afterwards Sir Samuel Bentham, born 11th January 1757. When eighty years old, Jeremy gave anecdotes of his infancy to his biographer, Bowring, who says that their accuracy was confirmed by contemporary documents, and proved his memory to be as wonderful as his precocity. Although the child was physically puny, his intellectual development was amazing. Before he was two he burst into tears at the sight of his mother's chagrin upon his refusal of some offered dainty. Before he was 'breeched,' an event which happened when he was three and a quarter, he ran home from a dull walk, ordered a footman to bring lights and place a folio *Rapin* upon the table, and was found plunged in historical studies when his parents returned to the house. In his fourth year he was imbibing the Latin grammar, and at the age of five years nine months and nineteen days, as his father notes, he wrote a scrap of Latin, carefully pasted among the parental memoranda. The child was not always immured in London. His parents spent their Sundays with the grandfather Bentham at Barking, and made

occasional excursions to the house of Mrs. Bentham's mother at Browning Hill, near Reading. Bentham remembered the last as a 'paradise,' and a love of flowers and gardens became one of his permanent passions.

Jeremy cherished the memory of his mother's tenderness. The father, though less sympathetic, was proud of his son's precocity, and apparently injudicious in stimulating the unformed intellect. The boy was almost a dwarf in size. When sixteen he grew ahead,[1] and was so feeble that he could scarcely drag himself upstairs. Attempts to teach him dancing failed from the extreme weakness of his knees.[2] He showed a taste for music, and could scrape a minuet on the fiddle at six years of age. He read all such books as came in his way. His parents objected to light literature, and he was crammed with such solid works as *Rapin*, Burnet's *Theory of the Earth*, and Cave's *Lives of the Apostles*. Various accidents, however, furnished him with better food for the imagination. He wept for hours over *Clarissa Harlowe*, studied *Gulliver's Travels* as an authentic document, and dipped into a variety of such books as then drifted into middle-class libraries. A French teacher introduced him to some remarkable books. He read *Télémaque*, which deeply impressed him, and, as he thought, implanted in his mind the seeds of later moralising. He attacked unsuccessfully some of Voltaire's historical works, and even read *Candide*, with what emotions we are not told. The servants meanwhile filled his fancy with ghosts and hobgoblins. To the end of his days he was still haunted by the imaginary horrors in the dark,[3] and he says[4] that they had been among the torments of his life. He had

[1] *Works*, x. 33.　　[2] *Ibid.* x. 31.　　[3] *Ibid.* ix. 84.　　[4] *Ibid.* x. 18.

few companions of his own age, and though he was 'not unhappy' and was never subjected to corporal punishment, he felt more awe than affection for his father. His mother, to whom he was strongly attached, died on 6th January 1759.

Bentham was thus a strangely precocious, and a morbidly sensitive child, when it was decided in 1755 to send him to Westminster. The headmaster, Dr. Markham, was a friend of his father's. Westminster, he says, represented 'hell' for him when Browning Hill stood for paradise. The instruction 'was wretched.' The fagging system was a 'horrid despotism.' The games were too much for his strength. His industry, however, enabled him to escape the birch, no small achievement in those days,[1] and he became distinguished in the studies such as they were. He learned the catechism by heart, and was good at Greek and Latin verses, which he manufactured for his companions as well as himself. He had also the rarer accomplishment, acquired from his early tutor, of writing more easily in French than English. Some of his writings were originally composed in French. He was, according to Bowring, elected to one of the King's scholarships when between nine and ten, but as 'ill-usage was apprehended' the appointment was declined.[2] He was at a boarding-house, and the life of the boys on the foundation was probably rougher. In June 1760 his father took him to Oxford, and entered him as a commoner at Queen's College. He came into residence in the following October, when only twelve

[1] Southey was expelled from Westminster in 1792 for attacking the birch in a schoolboy paper.
[2] *Works*, x. 38. Bowring's confused statement, I take it, means this. Bentham, in any case, was not on the foundation. See Welsh's *Alumni West.*

years old. Oxford was not more congenial than Westminster. He had to sign the Thirty-nine Articles in spite of scruples suppressed by authority. The impression made upon him by this childish compliance never left him to the end of his life.[1] His experience resembled that of Adam Smith and Gibbon. Laziness and vice were prevalent. A gentleman commoner of Queen's was president of a 'hellfire club,' and brutal horseplay was still practised upon the weaker lads. Bentham, still a schoolboy in age, continued his schoolboy course. He wrote Latin verses, and one of his experiments, an ode upon the death of George II., was sent to Johnson, who called it 'a very pretty performance for a young man.' He also had to go through the form of disputation in the schools. Queen's College had some reputation at this time for teaching logic.[2] Bentham was set to read Watt's *Logic* (1725), Sanderson's *Compendium artis Logicae* (1615), and Rowning's *Compendious System of Natural Philosophy* (1735-42). Some traces of these studies remained in his mind.

In 1763 Bentham took his B.A. degree, and returned to his home. It is significant that when robbed of all his money at Oxford he did not confide in his father. He was paying by a morbid reserve for the attempts made to force him into premature activity. He accepted the career imposed by his father's wishes, and in November 1763 began to eat his dinners in Lincoln's Inn. He returned, however, to Oxford in December to hear Blackstone's lectures. These lectures were then a novelty at an English university. The Vinerian professorship had been founded in 1758 in consequence of the success of a

[1] *Works*, x. 37.　　　[2] *Ibid.* viii. 113, 217.

course voluntarily given by Blackstone ; and his lectures contained the substance of the famous Commentaries, first published 1765-1769. They had a great effect upon Bentham. He says that he 'immediately detected Blackstone's fallacy respecting natural rights,' thought other doctrines illogical, and was so much occupied by these reflections as to be unable to take notes. Bentham's dissatisfaction with Blackstone had not yet made him an opponent of the constituted order. He was present at some of the proceedings against Wilkes, and was perfectly bewitched by Lord Mansfield's ' Grim-gibber,' that is, taken in by his pompous verbiage.[1]

In 1765 his father married Mrs. Abbot, the mother of Charles Abbot, afterwards Lord Colchester. Bentham's dislike of his step-mother increased the distance between him and his father. He took his M.A. degree in 1766 and in 1767 finally left Oxford for London to begin, as his father fondly hoped, a flight towards the woolsack. The lad's diffidence and extreme youth had indeed prevented him from forming the usual connections which his father anticipated as the result of a college life. His career as a barrister was short and grievously disappointing to the parental hopes. His father, like the Elder Fairford in Redgauntlet, had 'a cause or two at nurse' for the son. The son's first thought was to 'put them to death.' A brief was given to him in a suit, upon which £50 depended. He advised that the suit should be dropped and the money saved. Other experiences only increased his repugnance to his profession.[2] A singularly strong impression had been made upon him by the Memoirs of Teresa Constantia Phipps, in which

[1] Works, x. 45.   [2] Ibid. x. 51, 78, 83.

there is an account of vexatious legal proceedings as to the heroine's marriage. He appears to have first read this book in 1759. Then, he says, the 'Demon of Chicane appeared to me in all his hideousness. I vowed war against him. My vow has been accomplished !'[1] Bentham thus went to the bar as a 'bear to the stake.' He diverged in more than one direction. He studied chemistry under Fordyce (1736-1802), and hankered after physical science. He was long afterwards (1788) member of a club to which Sir Joseph Banks, John Hunter, R. L. Edgeworth, and other men of scientific reputation belonged.[2] But he had drifted into a course of speculation, which, though more germane to legal studies, was equally fatal to professional success. The father despaired, and he was considered to be a 'lost child.'

II. FIRST WRITINGS

Though lost to the bar, he had really found himself. He had taken the line prescribed by his idiosyncrasy. His father's injudicious forcing had increased his shyness at the bar, and he was like an owl in daylight. But no one, as we shall see, was less diffident in speculation. Self-confidence in a philosopher is often the private credit which he opens with his imagination to compensate for his incapacity in the rough struggles of active life. Bentham shrank from the world in which he was easily browbeaten to the study in which he could reign supreme. He had not the strong passions which prompt

[1] Works, x. 35, 77. References are given to this book in Works, vii. 219-20 ('Rationale of Evidence'). Several editions appeared from 1725 to 1761. See Works, vi. 465, for a recollection of similar experiences.
[2] Ibid. viii. 148 n.; x. 183.

commonplace ambition, and cared little for the prizes for which most men will sacrifice their lives. Nor, on the other hand, can he be credited with that ardent philanthropy or vehement indignation which prompts to an internecine struggle with actual wrongdoers. He had not the ardour which led Howard to devote a life to destroy abuses, or that which turned Swift's blood to gall in the struggle against triumphant corruption. He was thoroughly amiable, but of kindly rather than energetic affections. He, therefore, desired reform, but so far from regarding the ruling classes with rancour, took their part against the democrats. 'I was a great reformist,' he says, ' but never suspected that the " people in power " were against reform. I supposed they only wanted to know what was good in order to embrace it.'[1] The most real of pleasures for him lay in speculating upon the general principles by which the 'people in power' should be guided. To construct a general chart for legislation, to hunt down sophistries, to explode mere noisy rhetoric, to classify and arrange and re-classify until his whole intellectual wealth was neatly arranged in proper pigeon-holes, was a delight for its own sake. He wished well to mankind ; he detested abuses, but he hated neither the corrupted nor the corruptors ; and it might almost seem that he rather valued the benevolent end, because it gave employment to his faculties, than valued the employment because it led to the end. This is implied in his remark made at the end of his life. He was, he said, as selfish as a man could be ; but 'somehow or other' selfishness had in him taken the form of benevolence.[2] He was at any rate in the position of a

[1] Works, x. 66.   [2] Ibid. xi. 95.

man with the agreeable conviction that he has only to prove the wisdom of a given course in order to secure its adoption. Like many mechanical inventors, he took for granted that a process which was shown to be useful would therefore be at once adopted, and failed to anticipate the determined opposition of the great mass of ' vested interests ' already in possession.

At this period he made the discovery, or what he held to be the discovery, which governed his whole future career. He laid down the principle which was to give the clue to all his investigations ; and, as he thought, required only to be announced to secure universal acceptance. When Bentham revolted against the intellectual food provided at school and college, he naturally took up the philosophy which at that period represented the really living stream of thought. To be a man of enlightenment in those days was to belong to the school of Locke. Locke represented reason, free thought, and the abandonment of prejudice. Besides Locke, he mentions Hume, Montesquieu, Helvétius, Beccaria, and Barrington. Helvétius especially did much to suggest to him his leading principle, and upon country trips which he took with his father and step-mother, he used to lag behind studying Helvétius' De l'Esprit.[1] Locke, he says in an early note (1773-1774), should give the principles, Helvétius the matter, of a complete digest of the law. He mentions with especial interest the third volume of Hume's Treatise on Human Nature for its ethical views: ' he felt as if scales fell from his eyes' when he read it.[2] Daines Barrington's Observations on the Statutes (1766) interested him by miscellaneous sug-

[1] Works, x. 54.   [2] Ibid. i. 268 n.

gestions. The book, he says,[1] was a 'great treasure.' 'It is everything, *à propos* of everything; I wrote volumes upon this volume.' Beccaria's treatise upon crimes and punishments had appeared in 1764, and had excited the applause of Europe. The world was clearly ready for a fundamental reconstruction of legislative theories. Under the influence of such studies Bentham formulated his famous principle—a principle which to some seemed a barren truism, to others a mere epigram, and to some a dangerous falsehood. Bentham accepted it not only as true, but as expressing a truth of extraordinary fecundity, capable of guiding him through the whole labyrinth of political and legislative speculation. His 'fundamental axiom' is that 'the greatest happiness of the greatest number is the measure of right and wrong.'[2] Bentham himself[3] attributes the authorship of the phrase to Beccaria or Priestley. The general order of thought to which this theory belongs was of course

[1] *Works*, x. 121. [2] *Ibid.* x. 227.

[3] *Ibid.* x. 79, 142. See also *Deontology*, i. 298-302, where Bentham speaks of discovering the phrase in Priestley's *Essay on Government* in 1768. Priestley says (p. 17) that 'the good and happiness of the members, that is of the majority of the members, of any state is the great standard by which everything relating to that state must be finally determined.' So Le Mercier de la Rivière says, in 1767, that the ultimate end of society is *assurer le plus grand bonheur possible à la plus grande population possible* (Daire's *Economistes*, p. 470). Hutcheson's *Enquiry concerning Moral Good and Evil*, 1725, see iii. § 8, says 'that action is best which secures the greatest happiness of the greatest number.' Beccaria, in the preface to his essay, speaks of *la massima felicità divisa nel maggior numero*. J. S. Mill says that he found the word 'Utilitarian' in Galt's *Annals of the Parish*, and gave the name to the society founded by him in 1822-1823 (*Autobiography*, p. 79). The word had been used by Bentham himself in 1781, and he suggested it to Dumont in 1802 as the proper name of the party, instead of 'Benthamite' (*Works*, x. 92, 390). He afterwards thought it a bad name, because it gave a 'vague idea' (*Works*, x. 582), and substituted 'greatest happiness principle' for 'principle of utility' (*Works*, i.: 'Morals and Legislation').

not the property of any special writer or any particular period. Here I need only observe that this embodiment of the general doctrine of utility or morality had been struck out by Hutcheson in the attempt (as his title says) 'to introduce a mathematical calculation on subjects of morality.' This defines the exact reason which made it acceptable to Bentham. For the vague reference to utility which appears in Hume and other writers of his school, he substituted a formula, the terms of which suggest the possibility of an accurate quantitative comparison of different sums of happiness. In Bentham's mind the difference between this and the more general formula was like the difference between the statement that the planets gravitate towards the sun, and the more precise statement that the law of gravitation varies inversely as the square of the distance. Bentham hoped for no less an achievement than to become the Newton of the moral world.

Bentham, after leaving Oxford, took chambers in Lincoln's Inn. His father on his second marriage had settled some property upon him, which brought in some £90 a year. He had to live like a gentleman upon this, and to give four guineas a year to the laundress, four to his barber, and two to his shoeblack. In spite of Jeremy's deviation from the path of preferment, the two were on friendly terms, and when the hopes of the son's professional success grew faint, the father showed sympathy with his literary undertakings. Jeremy visited Paris in 1770, but made few acquaintants, though he was already regarded as a 'philosopher.' In 1778 he was in correspondence with d'Alembert, the abbé Morellet, and other philanthropic philosophers, but it

does not appear at what time this connection began.[1] He translated Voltaire's *Taureau Blanc*[2]—a story which used to 'convulse him with laughter.' A reference to it will show that Bentham by this time took the Voltairean view of the Old Testament. Bentham, however, was still on the side of the Tories. His first publication was a defence of Lord Mansfield in 1770 against attacks arising out of the prosecution of Woodfall for publishing Junius's letter to the king. This defence, contained in two letters, signed Irenæus, was published in the *Gazetteer*. Bentham's next performance was remarkable in the same sense. Among the few friends who drifted to his chambers was John Lind (1737-1781), who had been a clergyman, and after acting as tutor to a prince in Poland, had returned to London and become a writer for the press. He had business relations with the elder Bentham, and the younger Bentham was to some extent his collaborator in a pamphlet[3] which defended the conduct of ministers to the American colonies. Bentham observes that he was prejudiced against the Americans by the badness of their arguments, and thought from the first, as he continued to think, that the Declaration of Independence was a hodge-podge of confusion and absurdity, in which the thing to be proved is all along taken for granted.[4] Two other friendships were formed by Bentham about this time: one with James Trail, an

[1] A letter in the Additional MSS. 33, 537, shows that Bentham sent his 'Fragment' and his 'Hard Labour' pamphlet to d'Alembert in 1778, apparently introducing himself for the first time. Cf. *Works*, x. 87-88, 193-94.

[2] The translation of 1774. See Lowndes' *Manual* under Voltaire, *Works*, x. 83 n.

[3] *Review of the Acts of the Thirteenth Parliament, etc.* (1775).

[4] *Works*, x. 57, 63.

unsuccessful barrister, who owed a seat in Parliament and some minor offices to Lord Hertford, and is said by Romilly to have been a man of great talent; and one with George Wilson, afterwards a leader of the Norfolk circuit, who had become known to him through a common interest in Dr. Fordyce's lectures upon chemistry. Wilson became a bosom friend, and was one of Bentham's first disciples, though they were ultimately alienated.[1]

At this time, Bertham says, that his was 'truly a miserable life.'[2] Yet he was getting to work upon his grand project. He tells his father on 1st October 1776 that he is writing his *Critical Elements of Jurisprudence*, the book of which a part was afterwards published as the *Introduction to the Principles of Morals and Legislation*.[3] In the same year he published his first important work, the *Fragment on Government*. The year was in many ways memorable. The Declaration of Independence marked the opening of a new political era. Adam Smith's *Wealth of Nations* and Gibbon's *Decline and Fall* formed landmarks in speculation and in history; and Bentham's volume, though it made no such impression, announced a serious attempt to apply scientific methods to problems of legislation. The preface contained the first declaration of his famous formula which was applied to the confutation of Blackstone: Bentham was apparently roused to this effort by recollections of the Oxford lectures. The *Commentaries* contained a certain quantity of philosophical rhetoric; and as Blackstone was much greater in a literary than in a philosophical sense, the result was naturally unsatisfactory from a scientific point

[1] *Works*, x. 133-35. [2] *Ibid.* x. 84. [3] *Ibid.* x. 77

of view. He had vaguely appealed to the sound Whig doctrine of social compact, and while disavowing any strict historical basis had not inquired too curiously what was left of his supposed foundation. Bentham pounced upon the unfortunate bit of verbiage; insisted upon asking for a meaning when there was nothing but a rhetorical flourish, and tore the whole flimsy fabric to rags and tatters. A more bitter attack upon Blackstone, chiefly, as Bowring says, upon his defence of the Jewish law, was suppressed for fear of the law of libel.[1] The *Fragment* was published anonymously, but Bentham had confided the secret to his father by way of suggesting some slight set-off against his apparent unwillingness to emerge from obscurity. The book was at first attributed to Lord Mansfield, Lord Camden, and to Dunning. It was pirated in Dublin; and most of the five hundred copies printed appear to have been sold, though without profit to the author. The father's indiscretion let out the secret; and the sale, when the book was known to be written by a nobody, fell off at once, or so Bentham believed. The anonymous writer, however, was denounced and accused of being the author of much ribaldry, and among other accusations was said to be not only the translator but the writer of the *White Bull*.[2]

Bentham had fancied that all manner of 'torches from the highest regions' would come to light themselves at his 'farthing candle.' None of them came, and he was left for some years in obscurity, though still labouring at

---

[1] *Works*, x. 82.
[2] *Works*, x. 77-82. Blackstone took no notice of the work, except by some allusions in the preface to his next edition. Bentham criticised Blackstone respectfully in the pamphlet upon the Hard Labour Bill (1778). Blackstone sent a courteous but 'frigidly cautious' reply to the author.—*Works*, i. 255.

the great work which was one day to enlighten the world. At last, however, partial recognition came to him in a shape which greatly influenced his career. Lord Shelburne, afterwards marquis of Lansdowne, had been impressed by the *Fragment*, and in 1781 sought out Bentham at his chambers. Shelburne's career was to culminate in the following year with his brief tenure of the premiership (3rd July 1782 to 24th February 1783). Rightly or wrongly his contemporaries felt the distrust indicated by his nickname 'Malagrida,' which appears to have been partly suggested by a habit of overstrained compliment. He incurred the dislike not unfrequently excited by men who claim superiority of intellect without possessing the force of character which gives a corresponding weight in political affairs. Although his education had been bad, he had something of that cosmopolitan training which enabled many members of the aristocracy to look beyond the narrow middle-class prejudices and share in some degree the wider philosophical movements of the day. He had enjoyed the friendship of Franklin, and had been the patron of Priestley, who made some of his chemical discoveries at Bowood, and to whom he allowed an annuity. He belonged to that section of the Whigs which had most sympathy with the revolutionary movement. His chief political lieutenants were Dunning and Barré, who at the time sat for his borough Calne. He now rapidly formed an intimacy with Bentham, who went to stay at Bowood in the autumn of 1781. Bentham now and then in later years made some rather disparaging remarks upon Shelburne, whom he apparently considered to be rather an amateur than a serious philosopher, and who in the

House of Lords talked 'vague generalities'—the sacred phrase by which the Utilitarians denounced all preaching but their own—in a way to impose upon the thoughtless. He respected Shelburne, however, as one who trusted the people, and was distrusted by the Whig aristocracy. He felt, too, a real affection and gratitude for the patron to whom he owed so much. Shelburne had done him a great service.[1] 'He raised me from the bottomless pit of humiliation. He made me feel I was something.' The elder Bentham was impressed by his son's acquaintance with a man in so eminent a position, and hoped that it might lead by a different path to the success which had been missed at the bar. At Bowood Bentham stayed over a month upon his first visit, and was treated in the manner appropriate to a philosopher. The men showed him friendliness, dashed with occasional contempt, and the ladies petted him. He met Lord Camden and Dunning and young William Pitt, and some minor adherents of the great man. Pitt was 'very good-natured and a little raw.' I was monstrously 'frightened at him,' but, when I came to talk with him, he seemed 'frightened at me.'[2] Bentham, however, did not see what ideas they were likely to have in common. In fact there was the usual gulf between the speculative thinker and the practical man. 'All the statesmen,' so thought the philosopher, 'were wanting in the great elements of statesmanship': they were always talking about 'what *was*' and seldom or never about 'what ought to be.'[3] Occasionally, it would seem, they descended lower, and made a little fun of the shy and over-sensitive intruder.[4]

---

[1] *Works*, x. 115-17, 186
[2] *Ibid.* x. 100.
[3] *Ibid.* x. 122.
[4] *Ibid.* x. 118; i. 253.

The ladies, however, made it up to him. Shelburne made him read his 'dry metaphysics' to them,[1] and they received it with feminine docility. Lord Shelburne had lately (1779) married his second wife, Louisa, daughter of the first earl of Upper Ossory. Her sister, Lady Mary Fitz-Patrick, married in 1766 to Stephen Fox, afterwards Lord Holland, was the mother of the Lord Holland of later days and of Miss Caroline Fox, who survived till 1845, and was at this time a pleasant girl of thirteen or fourteen. Lady Shelburne had also two half-sisters, daughters of her mother's second marriage to Richard Vernon. Lady Shelburne took a fancy to Bentham, and gave him the 'prodigious privilege' of admission to her dressing-room. Though haughty in manner, she was mild in reality, and after a time she and her sister indulged in 'innocent gambols.' In her last illness, Bentham was one of the only two men whom she would see, and upon her death in 1789, he was the only male friend to whom her husband turned for consolation. Miss Fox seems to have been the only woman who inspired Bentham with a sentiment approaching to passion. He wrote occasional letters to the ladies in the tone of elephantine pleasantry natural to one who was all his life both a philosopher and a child.[2] He made an offer of marriage to Miss Fox in 1805, when he was nearer sixty than fifty, and when they had not met for sixteen years. The immediate occasion was presumably the death of Lord Lansdowne. She replied in a friendly letter, regretting the pain which her refusal would inflict. In 1827 Bentham, then in his eightieth year, wrote once more, speaking of the flower she had

---

[1] *Works*, x. 97; i. 252.
[2] *Ibid.* x. 219, 265.

given him 'in the green lane,' and asking for a kind answer. He was 'indescribably hurt and disappointed' by a cold and distant reply. The tears would come into the old man's eyes as he dealt upon the cherished memories of Bowood.[1] It is pleasant to know that Bentham was once in love; though his love seems to have been chiefly for a memory associated with what he called the happiest time of his life.

Shelburne had a project for a marriage between Bentham and the widow of Lord Ashburton (Dunning), who died in 1783.[2] He also made some overtures of patronage. 'He asked me,' says Bentham,[3] 'what he could do for me? I told him, nothing,' and this conduct —so different from that of others, 'endeared me to him.' Bentham declined one offer in 1788; but in 1790 he suddenly took it into his head that Lansdowne had promised him a seat in parliament; and immediately set forth his claims in a vast argumentative letter of sixty-one pages.[4] Lansdowne replied conclusively that he had not made the supposed promise, and had had every reason to suppose that Bentham preferred retirement to politics. Bentham accepted the statement frankly, though a short coolness apparently followed. The claim, in fact, only represented one of those passing moods to which Bentham was always giving way at odd moments.

Bentham's intimacy at Bowood led to more important results. In 1788 he met Romilly and Dumont at Lord Lansdowne's table.[5] He had already met Romilly in 1784 through Wilson, but after this the intimacy became close. Romilly had fallen in love with the

---

[1] Works, x. 118, 419, 558.　　[2] Ibid. i. 253.　　[3] Ibid. x. 116, 182.
[4] Ibid. x. 228-42.　　[5] Ibid. x. 186.

Fragment, and in later life he became Bentham's adviser in practical matters, and the chief if not the sole expounder of Bentham's theories in parliament.[1] The alliance with Dumont was of even greater importance. Dumont, born at Geneva in 1759, had become a Protestant minister; he was afterwards tutor to Shelburne's son, and in 1788 visited Paris with Romilly and made acquaintance with Mirabeau. Romilly showed Dumont some of Bentham's papers written in French. Dumont offered to rewrite and to superintend their publication. He afterwards received other papers from Bentham himself, with whom he became personally acquainted after his return from Paris.[2] Dumont became Bentham's most devoted disciple, and laboured unweariedly upon the translation and condensation of his master's treatise. One result is odd enough. Dumont, it is said, provided materials for some of Mirabeau's 'most splendid' speeches; and some of these materials came from Bentham.[3] One would like to see how Bentham's prose was transmuted into an oratory by Mirabeau. In any case, Dumont's services to Bentham were invaluable. It is painful to add that according to Bowring the two became so much alienated in the end, that in 1827 Bentham refused to see Dumont, and declared that his chief interpreter did 'not understand a word of his meaning.' Bowring attributes this separation to a remark made by Dumont about the shabbiness of Bentham's dinners as compared with those at Lansdowne House—a comparison which he calls 'offensive, uncalled-for, and groundless.'[4] Bentham apparently argued that a man

---

[1] Works, v. 370.　　[2] Souvenirs sur Mirabeau (preface).
[3] Works, x. 185.　　[4] Works, x. 185. Colls (p. 41) tells the same story.

---

who did not like his dinners could not appreciate his theories: a fallacy excusable only by the pettishness of old age. Bowring, however, had a natural dulness which distorted many anecdotes transmitted through him; and we may hope that in this case there was some exaggeration.

Bentham's emergence was, meanwhile, very slow. The great men whom he met at Lord Lansdowne's were not specially impressed by the shy philosopher. Wedderburn, so he heard, pronounced the fatal word 'dangerous' in regard to the Fragment.[1] How, thought Bentham, can utility be dangerous? Is this not self-contradictory? Later reflection explained the puzzle. What is useful to the governed need not be therefore useful to the governors. Mansfield, who was known to Lind, said that in some parts the author of the Fragment was awake and in others was asleep. In what parts? Bentham wondered. Awake, he afterwards considered, in the parts where Blackstone, the object of Mansfield's personal 'heart-burning,' was attacked; asleep where Mansfield's own despotism was threatened. Camden was contemptuous; Dunning only 'scowled' at him; and Barré, after taking in his book, gave it back with the mysterious information that he had 'got into a scrape.'[2] The great book, therefore, though printed in 1781,[3] 'stuck for eight years,'[4] and the writer continued his obscure existence in Lincoln's Inn.[5] An opinion

---

[1] Works ('Fragment, etc.'), i. 245, and Ibid. ii. 463 n.
[2] Ibid. i. 246, 250, 251.　　[3] Ibid. i. 252.　　[4] Ibid. x. 185.
[5] Bentham says (Works, i. 240) that he was a member of a club of which Johnson was the despot. The only club possible seems to be the Essex Street Club, of which Daines Barrington was a member. If so, it was in 1783, though Bentham seems to imply an earlier date.

which he gave in some question as to the evidence in Warren Hastings's trial made, he says, an impression in his favour. Before publication was achieved, however, a curious episode altered Bentham's whole outlook. His brother Samuel (1757-1831), whose education he had partly superintended,[1] had been apprenticed to a shipwright at Woolwich, and in 1780 had gone to Russia in search of employment. Three years later he was sent by Prince Potemkin to superintend a great industrial establishment at Kritchev on a tributary of the Dnieper. There he was to be 'Jack-of-all-trades—building ships, like Harlequin, of odds and ends—a rope-maker, a sail-maker, a distiller, brewer, malster, tanner, glass-man, glass-grinder, potter, hemp-spinner, smith, and copper-smith.'[2] He was, that is, to transplant a fragment of ready-made Western civilisation into Russia. Bentham resolved to pay a visit to his brother, to whom he was strongly attached. He left England in August 1785, and stayed some time at Constantinople, where he met Maria James (1770-1836), the wife successively of W. Reveley and of John Gisborne, and the friend of Shelley. Thence he travelled by land to Kritchev, and settled with his brother at the neighbouring estate of Zadobras. Bentham here passed a secluded life, interested in his brother's occupations and mechanical inventions, and at the same time keeping up his own intellectual labours. The most remarkable result was the Defence of Usury, written in the beginning of 1787. Bentham appends to it a respectful letter to Adam Smith, who had supported the laws against usury inconsistently with his own general principles. The

---

[1] Works, x. 77.　　[2] Ibid. x. 147.

disciple was simply carrying out those principles to the logical application from which the master had shrunk. The manuscript was sent to Wilson, who wished to suppress it.[1] The elder Bentham obtained it, and sent it to the press. The book met Bentham as he was returning. It was highly praised by Thomas Reid,[2] and by the *Monthly Review*; it was translated into various languages, and became one of the sacred books of the Economists. Wilson is described as 'cold and cautious,' and he suppressed another pamphlet upon prison discipline.[3] In a letter to Bentham, dated 26th February 1787, however, Wilson disavows any responsibility for the delay in the publication of the great book. 'The cause,' he says, 'lies in your constitution. With one-tenth part of your genius, and a common degree of steadiness, both Sam and you would long since have risen to great eminence. But your history, since I have known you, has been to be always running from a good scheme to a better. In the meantime life passes away and nothing is completed.' He entreated Bentham to return, and his entreaties were seconded by Trail, who pointed out various schemes of reform, especially of the poor-laws, in which Bentham might be useful. Wilson had mentioned already another inducement to publication. 'There is,' he says, on 24th September 1786, 'a **Mr. Paley**, a parson and archdeacon of Carlisle, who has written a book called *Principles of Moral and Political Philosophy*, in quarto, and it has gone through two editions with prodigious applause.' He fears that Bentham will be charged with stealing from Paley, and exhorts him to come home and 'establish a great literary

[1] *Works*, x. 176.   [2] Reid's *Works* (Hamilton), p. 73.   [3] *Works*, x. 171.

reputation in your own language, and in this country which you despise.'[1] Bentham at last started homewards. He travelled through Poland, Germany, and Holland, and reached London at the beginning of February 1788. He settled at a little farmhouse at Hendon, bought a 'superb harpsichord,' resumed his occupations, and saw a small circle of friends. Wilson urged him to publish his *Introduction* without waiting to complete the vast scheme to which it was to be a prologue. Copies of the printed book were already abroad, and there was a danger of plagiarism. Thus urged, Bentham at last yielded, and the *Introduction to the Principles of Morals and Legislation* appeared in 1789. The preface apologised for imperfections due to the plan of his work. The book, he explained, laid down the principles of all his future labours, and was to stand to him in the relation of a treatise upon pure mathematics to a treatise upon the applied sciences. He indicated ten separate departments of legislation, each of which would require a treatise in order to the complete execution of his scheme.

The book gives the essence of Bentham's theories, and is the one large treatise published by himself. The other works were only brought to birth by the help of disciples. Dumont, in the discourse prefixed to the *Traités*, explains the reason. Bentham, he says, would suspend a whole work and begin a new one because a single proposition struck him as doubtful. A problem of finance would send him to a study of Political Economy in general. A question of procedure would

[1] *Works*, x. 163-64. Cf. *Ibid*. x. 195, where Wilson is often 'tempted to think'—erroneously, of course—that Paley must have known something of Bentham's work. Paley's chief source was Abraham Tucker.

make him pause until he had investigated the whole subject of judicial organisation. While at work, he felt only the pleasure of composition. When his materials required form and finish, he felt only the fatigue. Disgust succeeded to charm; and he could scarcely be induced to interrupt his labours upon fresh matter in order to give to his interpreter the explanations necessary for the elucidation of his previous writings. He was without the literary vanity or the desire for completion which may prompt to premature publication, but may at least prevent the absolute waste of what has been already achieved. His method of writing was characteristic. He began by forming a complete logical scheme for the treatment of any subject, dividing and subdividing so as to secure an exhaustive classification of the whole matter of discussion. Then taking up any subdivision, he wrote his remarks upon sheets, which were put aside after being marked with references indicating their place in the final treatise. He never turned to these again. In time he would exhaust the whole subject, and it would then be the duty of his disciples simply to put together the bricks according to the indications placed upon each in order to construct the whole edifice.[1] As, however, the plan would frequently undergo a change, and as each fragment had been written without reference to the others, the task of ultimate combination and adaptation of the ultimate atoms was often very perplexing. Bentham, as we shall see, formed disciples ardent enough to put together these scattered documents as the disciples of Mahomet put together the Koran. Bentham's revelation was possibly less influential than

[1] See J. H. Burton in *Works*, i. 11.

Mahomet's; but the logical framework was far more coherent.

Bentham's mind was for the present distracted. He had naturally returned full of information about Russia. The English ministry were involved in various negotiations with Russia, Sweden, and Denmark, the purpose of which was to thwart the designs of Russia in the East. Bentham wrote three letters to the *Public Advertiser*, signed Anti-Machiavel,[1] protesting against the warlike policy. Bentham himself believed that the effect was decisive, and that the 'war was given up' in consequence of his arguments. Historians[2] scarcely sanction this belief, which is only worth notice because it led to another belief, oddly characteristic of Bentham. A letter signed 'Partizan' in the *Public Advertiser* replied to his first two letters. Who was 'Partizan'? Lord Lansdowne amused himself by informing Bentham that he was no less a personage than George III. Bentham, with even more than his usual simplicity, accepted this hoax as a serious statement. He derived no little comfort from the thought; for to the antipathy thus engendered in the 'best of kings' he attributed the subsequent failure of his Panopticon scheme.[3]

III. THE PANOPTICON.

The crash of the French revolution was now to change the whole course of European politics, and to bring

[1] Given in *Works*, x. 201-12.
[2] See Lecky's *Eighteenth Century*, x. 210-97, for an account of these transactions.
[3] Bowring tells this gravely, and declares that George III. also wrote letters to the *Gazette de Leyde*. George III. certainly contributed some letters to Arthur Young's *Annals of Agriculture*, and is one of the suggested authors of Junius.

philosophical jurists face to face with a long series of profoundly important problems. Bentham's attitude during the early stages of the revolution and the first war period is significant, and may help to elucidate some characteristics of the Utilitarian movement. Revolutions are the work of passion : the product of a social and political condition in which the masses are permeated with discontent, because the social organs have ceased to discharge their functions. They are not ascribable to the purely intellectual movement alone, though it is no doubt an essential factor. The revolution came in any case because the social order was out of joint, not simply because Voltaire or Rousseau or Diderot had preached destructive doctrines. The doctrines of the 'rights of man' are obvious enough to have presented themselves to many minds at many periods. The doctrines became destructive because the old traditions were shaken, and the traditions were shaken because the state of things to which they corresponded had become intolerable. The French revolution meant (among other things) that in the mind of the French peasant there had accumulated a vast deposit of bitter enmity against the noble who had become a mere parasite upon the labouring population, retaining, as Arthur Young said, privileges for himself, and leaving poverty to the lower classes. The peasant had not read Rousseau ; he had read nothing. But when his discontent began to affect the educated classes, men who had read Rousseau found in his works the dialect most fitted to express the growing indignation. Rousseau's genius had devised the appropriate formula ; for Rousseau's sensibility had made him prescient of the rising storm.

What might be a mere commonplace for speculative students suddenly became the warcry in a social upheaval. In England, as I have tried to show, there was no such popular sentiment behind the political theories : and reformers were content with measures which required no appeal to absolute rights and general principles. Bentham was no Rousseau ; and the last of men to raise a warcry. Passion and sentimentalism were to him a nuisance. His theories were neither suggested nor modified by the revolution. He looked on with curious calmness, as though the revolutionary disturbances were rather a transitory interruption to the progress of reform than indicative of a general convulsion. His own position was isolated. He had no strong reforming party behind him. The Whigs, his main friends, were powerless, discredited, and themselves really afraid to support any vigorous policy. They had in the main to content themselves with criticising the warlike policy which, for the time, represented the main current of national sentiment. Bentham shared many of their sympathies. He hated the abstract 'rights of man' theory as heartily as Burke. It was to him a 'hodge-podge' of fallacies. On the other hand, he was absolutely indifferent to the apotheosis of the British Constitution constructed by Burke's imagination. He cared nothing for history in general, or regarded it, from a Voltairean point of view, as a record of the follies and crimes of mankind. He wished to deal with political, and especially with legal, questions in a scientific spirit—but 'scientific' would mean not pure mathematics but pure empiricism. He was quite as far from Paine's abstract methods as from Burke's romantic methods.

Both of them, according to him, were sophists : though one might prefer logical and the other sentimental sophistries. Dumont, when he published (1802) his versions of Bentham, insisted upon this point. Nothing, he says, was more opposed to the trenchant dogmatism of the abstract theorists about 'rights of man' and 'equality' than Bentham's thoroughly scientific procedure (*Discours Préliminaire*). Bentham's intellectual position in this respect will require further consideration hereafter. All his prejudices and sympathies were those of the middle class from which he sprang. He was no democrat : he had no particular objection to the nobility, though he preferred Shelburne to the king's friends or to the Whig aristocracy. The reforms which he advocated were such as might be adopted by any enlightened legislator, not only by Shelburne but even by Blackstone. He had only, he thought, to convert a few members of parliament to gain the acceptance for a rational criminal code. It had hardly even occurred to him that there was anything wrong in the general political order, though he was beginning to find out that it was not so modifiable as he could have wished by the new ideas which he propounded.

Bentham's activity during the first revolutionary war corresponded to this position. The revolution, whatever else it might do, obviously gave a chance to amateur legislators. There was any amount of work to be done in the way of codifying and reforming legislative systems. The deviser of Utopias had such an opening as had never occurred in the world's history. Lord Lansdowne, on the 3rd January 1789, expresses his pleasure at hearing that Bentham intends to 'take up the

cause of the people in France.'[1] Bentham, as we have seen, was already known to some of the French leaders, and he was now taking time by the forelock. He sent to the Abbé Morellet a part of his treatise on Political Tactics, hoping to have it finished by the time of the meeting of the States General.[2] This treatise, civilly accepted by Morellet, and approved with some qualifications by Bentham's counsellors, Romilly, Wilson, and Trail, was an elaborate account of the organisation and procedure of a legislative assembly, founded chiefly on the practice of the House of Commons. It was published in 1816 by Dumont in company with *Anarchic Fallacies*, a vigorous exposure of the *Declaration of Rights*, which Bentham had judiciously kept on his shelf. Had the French known of it, he remarks afterwards, they would have been little disposed to welcome him.[3] An elaborate scheme for the organisation of the French judiciary was suggested by a report to the National Assembly, and published in March 1790. In 1791, Bentham offered to go to France himself in order to establish a prison on his new scheme (to be mentioned directly), and become 'gratuitously the gaoler thereof.'[4] The Assembly acknowledged his 'ardent love of humanity,' and ordered an extract from his scheme to be printed for their instruction. The tactics actually adopted by the French revolutionists for managing assemblies and their methods of executing justice form a queer commentary on the philosopher who, like Voltaire's Mamres in the *White Bull*, continued to 'meditate profoundly' in placid disregard of facts. He was in fact proposing that the lava boiling up in a volcanic

[1] *Works*, x. 195.   [2] *Ibid.* x. 198-99.   [3] *Ibid.* x. 317.   [4] *Ibid.* x. 270.

eruption should arrange itself entirely according to his architectural designs. But his proposal to become a gaoler during the revolution reaches the pathetic by its amiable innocence. On 26th August 1792, Bentham was one of the men upon whom the expiring Assembly, anxious to show its desire of universal fraternity, conferred the title of citizen. With Bentham were joined Priestley, Paine, Wilberforce, Clarkson, Washington, and others. The September massacres followed. On 18th October the honour was communicated to Bentham. He replied in a polite letter, pointing out that he was a royalist in London for the same reason which would make him a republican in France. He ended by a calm argument against the proscription of refugees.[1] The Convention, if it read the letter, and had any sense of humour, must have been amused. The war and the Reign of Terror followed. Bentham turned the occasion to account by writing a pamphlet (not then published) exhorting the French to 'emancipate their colonies.' Colonies were an aimless burthen, and to get rid of them would do more than conquest to relieve their finances. British fleets and the insurrection of St. Domingo were emancipating by very different methods.

Bentham was, of course, disgusted by the divergence of his clients from the lines chalked out by proper respect for law and order. On 31st October 1793 he writes to a friend, expressing his wish that Jacobinism could be extirpated ; no price could be too heavy to pay for such a result : but he doubts whether war or peace would be the best means to the end, and protests against the policy of appropriating useless and expensive colonies

[1] *Works*, x. 282.

instead of 'driving at the heart of the monster.'[1] Never was an adviser more at cross-purposes with the advised. It would be impossible to draw a more striking portrait of the abstract reasoner, whose calculations as to human motives omit all reference to passion, and who fancied that all prejudice can be dispelled by a few bits of logic.

Meanwhile a variety of suggestions more or less important and connected with passing events were seething in his fertile brain. He wrote one of his most stinging pamphlets, '*Truth versus Ashhurst*' in December 1792, directed against a judge who, in the panic suggested by the September massacres, had eulogised the English laws. Bentham's aversion to Jacobin measures by no means softened his antipathy to English superstitions ; and his attack was so sharp that Romilly advised and obtained its suppression for the time. Projects as to war-taxes suggested a couple of interesting pamphlets written in 1793, and published in 1795. In connection with this, schemes suggested themselves to him for improved systems of patents, for limited liability companies and other plans.[2] His great work still occupied him at intervals. In 1793 he offers to Dundas to employ himself in drafting Statutes, and remarks incidentally that he could legislate for Hindostan, should legislation be wanted there, as easily as for his own parish.[3] In 1794, Dumont is begging him to 'conquer his repugnance' to bestowing a few hints upon his interpreter.[4] In 1796, Bentham writes long letters suggesting that he should be sent to France with Wilberforce, in order to re-establish friendly

[1] *Works*, x. 296.   [2] *Ibid.* x. 304.   [3] *Ibid.* x. 292.   [4] *Ibid.* x. 300.

relations.[1] In 1798 he is corresponding at great length with Patrick Colquhoun upon plans for improving the Metropolitan police.[2] In 1801 he says[3] that for two years and a half 'he has thought of scarce anything else' than a plan for interest-bearing notes, which he carefully elaborated and discussed with Nicholas Vansittart and Dr. Beeke. In September 1800, however, he had found time to occupy himself with a proposed *frigidarium* or ice-house for the preservation of fish, fruits, and vegetables ; and invited Dr. Roget, a nephew of Romilly, to come to his house and carry out the necessary experiments.[4] In January 1802 he writes to Dumont[5] proposing to send him a trifling specimen of the Panopticon, a set of hollow fire-irons invented by his brother, which may attract the attention of Buonaparte and Talleyrand. He proceeds to expound the merits of Samuel's invention for making wheels by machinery. Dumont replies, that fire-irons are 'superfluities'— (fire-arms might have been more to Buonaparte's taste) —and that the Panopticon itself was coldly received.

This Panopticon was to be Bentham's masterpiece. It occupied his chief attention from his return to England until the peace of Amiens. His brother had returned from Russia in 1791. Their father died 28th March 1792, dividing his property equally between his sons. Jeremy's share consisted of the estate at Queen's Square Place, Westminster, and of landed property producing £500 or £600 a year. The father, spite of the distance between them, had treated his son with substantial kindness, and had learned to take a pride in

[1] *Works*, x. 315.   [2] *Ibid.* x. 329.   [3] *Ibid.* x. 366.
[4] *Ibid.* x. 346.   [5] *Ibid.* x. 381.

achievements very unlike those which he had at first desired.[1] Bentham's position, however, was improved by the father's death. The Westminster estate included the house in which he lived for the rest of his life. There was a garden in which he took great delight, though London smoke gradually destroyed the plants : and in the garden was the small house where Milton had once lived.[2] Here, with the co-operation of his brother and his increased income, he had all the means necessary for launching his grand scheme.

The Panopticon, as defined by its inventor to Brissot, was a 'mill for grinding rogues honest, and idle men industrious.'[3] It was suggested by a plan designed by his brother in Russia for a large house to be occupied by workmen, and to be so arranged that they could be under constant inspection. Bentham was working on the old lines of philanthropic reform. He had long been interested in the schemes of prison reform, to which Howard's labours had given the impetus. Blackstone, with the help of William Eden, afterwards Lord Auckland, had prepared the 'Hard Labour Bill,' which Bentham had carefully criticised in 1778. The measure was passed in 1779, and provided for the management of convicts, who were becoming troublesome, as transportation to America had ceased to be possible. Howard, whose relation to Bentham I have already noticed, was appointed as one of the commissioners to carry out the provisions of the Act. The commissioners disagreed ; Howard resigned ; and though at last an architect (William Blackburn) was appointed who possessed

[1] See his letter to Lansdowne, sending a portrait to Jeremy.—*Works*, x. 224.
[2] *Works*, xi. 81.   [3] *Ibid.* x. 226.

Howard's confidence, and who constructed various prisons in the country, the scheme was allowed to drop. Bentham now hoped to solve the problem with his Panopticon. He printed an account of it in 1791. He wrote to his old antagonist, George III., describing it, together with another invention of Samuel's for enabling armies to cross rivers, which might be more to his Majesty's taste.[1] In March 1792 he made a proposal to the government offering to undertake the charge of a thousand convicts upon the Panopticon system.[2] After delays suspicious in the eyes of Bentham, but hardly surprising at such a period, an act of parliament was obtained in 1794 to adopt his schemes. Bentham had already been making preparations. He says[3] (14th September 1794) that he has already spent £6000, and is spending at the rate of £2000 a year, while his income was under £600 a year. He obtained, however, £2000 from the government. He had made models and architectural plans, in which he was helped by Reveley, already known to him at Constantinople. This sum, it appears, was required in order to keep together the men whom he employed. The nature of their employment is remarkable.[4] Samuel, a man of singular mechanical skill, which was of great use to the navy during the war, had devised machinery for work in wood and metal. Bentham had joined his brother, and they were looking out for a steam-engine. It had now occurred to them to

[1] Works, x. 260. It is doubtful whether the letter was sent.
[2] The Panopticon story is confusedly told in Bowring's life. The *Panopticon Correspondence*, in the eleventh volume, gives fragments from a 'history of the war between Jeremy Bentham and George III.,' written by Bentham in 1830-31, and selections from a voluminous correspondence.
[3] Works, x. 301.   [4] Ibid. xi. 167.

employ convicts instead of steam, and thus to combine philanthropy with business. Difficulties of the usual kind arose as to the procurement of a suitable site. The site secured under the provisions of the 'Hard Labour Bill' was for some reason rejected; and Bentham was almost in despair. It was not until 1799 that he at last acquired for £12,000 an estate at Millbank, which seemed to be suitable. Meanwhile Bentham had found another application for his principle. The growth of pauperism was alarming statesmen. Whitbread proposed in February 1796 to fix a minimum rate of wages. The wisest thing that government could do, he said, was to 'offer a liberal premium for the encouragement of large families.' Pitt proceeded to prepare the abortive Poor-law Bill,[1] upon which Bentham (in February 1797) sent in some very shrewd criticisms. They were not published, but are said to have 'powerfully contributed to the abandonment of the measure.'[2] They show Bentham's power of incisive criticism, though they scarcely deal with the general principle. In the following autumn Bentham contributed to Arthur Young's *Annals of Agriculture* upon the same topic. It had struck him that an application of his Panopticon would give the required panacea. He worked out details with his usual zeal, and the scheme attracted notice among the philanthropists of the time. It was to be a 'succedaneum' to Pitt's proposal. Meanwhile the finance committee, appointed in 1797, heard evidence from Bentham's friend, Patrick Colquhoun, upon the Panopticon, and a report recom-

[1] The plan, according to Bentham (*Works*, xi. 102), was suggested by Ruggles, author of the work upon the poor-laws, first printed in Young's *Annals*.   [2] Works, viii. 440.

mending it was proposed by R. Pole Carew, a friend of Samuel Bentham. Although this report was suppressed, the scheme apparently received an impetus. The Millbank estate was bought in consequence of these proceedings, and a sum of only £1000 was wanted to buy out the tenant of one piece of land. Bentham was constantly in attendance at a public office, expecting a final warrant for the money. It never came, and, as Bentham believed, the delay was due to the malice of George III. Had any other king been on the throne, Panopticon in both 'the prisoner branch and the pauper branch' would have been set at work.[1] Such are the consequences of newspaper controversies with monarchs! After this, in any case, the poor Panopticon, as the old lawyers said, 'languishing did live,' and at last 'languishing did die.' Poor Bentham seems to have struggled vainly for a time. He appealed to Pitt's friend, Wilberforce; he appealed to his step-brother Abbot; he wrote to members of parliament, but all was in vain.

Romilly induced him in 1802 to suppress a statement of his grievances which could only have rendered ministers implacable.[2] But he found out what would hardly have been a discovery to most people, that officials can be dilatory and evasive; and certain discoveries about the treatment of convicts in New South Wales convinced him that they could even defy the laws and the Constitution when they were beyond inspection. He published (1803) a *Plea for the Constitution*, showing the enormities committed in the colony, 'in breach of Magna Charta, the Petition of Right, the Habeas Corpus Act, and the Bill of Rights.' Romilly in vain told him that the

[1] Works, xi. 102-3.   [2] Ibid. x. 400.

attorney-general could not recommend the author of such an effusion to be keeper of a Panopticon.[1] The actual end did not come till 1811. A committee then reported against the scheme. They noticed one essential and very characteristic weakness. The whole system turned upon the profit to be made from the criminals' labour by Bentham and his brother. The committee observed that, however unimpeachable might be the characters of the founders, the scheme might lead to abuses in the hands of their successors. The adoption of this principle of 'farming' had in fact led to gross abuses both in gaols and in workhouses; but it was, as I have said, in harmony with the whole 'individualist' theory. The committee recommended a different plan; and the result was the foundation of Millbank penitentiary, opened in 1816.[2] Bentham ultimately received £23,000 by way of compensation in 1813.[3] The objections of the committee would now be a commonplace, but Bentham saw in them another proof of the desire to increase government patronage. He was well out of the plan. There were probably few men in England less capable of managing a thousand convicts, in spite of his theories about 'springs of action.' If anything else had been required to ensure failure, it would have been association with a sanguine inventor of brilliant abilities.

Bentham's agitation had not been altogether fruitless. His plan had been partly adopted at Edinburgh by one of the Adams,[4] and his work formed an important stage in the development of the penal system.

[1] Works, xi. 144.
[2] For its later history see *Memorials of Millbank*, by Arthur Griffiths. 2 vols., 1875.   [3] Works, xi. 106.   [4] Ibid. x. 294.

Bentham, though he could not see that his failure was a blessing in disguise, had learned one lesson worth learning. He was ill-treated, according to impartial observers. 'Never,' says Wilberforce,[1] 'was any one worse used. I have seen the tears run down the cheeks of that strong-minded man through vexation at the pressing importunity of his creditors, and the indolence of official underlings when day after day he was begging at the Treasury for what was indeed a mere matter of right.' Wilberforce adds that Bentham was 'quite soured,' and attributes his later opinions to this cause. When the *Quarterly Review* long afterwards taunted him as a disappointed man, Bentham declared himself to be in 'a state of perpetual and unruffled gaiety,' and the 'mainspring' of the gaiety of his own circle.[2] No one, indeed, could be less 'soured' so far as his habitual temper was concerned. But Wilberforce's remark contained a serious truth. Bentham had made a discovery. He had vowed war in his youth against the 'demon of chicane.' He had now learned that the name of the demon was 'Legion.' To cast him out, it would be necessary to cast out the demon of officialism; and we shall see what this bit of knowledge presently implied.

IV. THE UTILITARIAN PROPAGANDA.

Bentham in 1802 had reached the respectable age of fifty-four. He had published his first work twenty-six years, and his most elaborate treatise thirteen years, previously. He had been brought into contact with many of the eminent politicians and philanthropists of the day. Lansdowne had been a friendly patron: his

[1] Wilberforce's *Life*, ii. 71.   [2] *Works*, x. 541.

advice had been treated with respect by Pitt, Dundas, and even by Blackstone; he was on friendly terms with Colquhoun, Sir F. Eden, Arthur Young, Wilberforce, and others interested in philanthropic movements, and his name at least was known to some French politicians. But his reputation was still obscure; and his connections did not develop into intimacies. He lived as a recluse and avoided society. His introduction to great people at Bowood had apparently rather increased than softened his shyness. The little circle of intimates, Romilly and Wilson and his own brother, must have satisfied his needs for social intercourse. It required an elaborate negotiation to bring about a meeting between him and Dr. Parr, the great Whig prophet, although they had been previously acquainted, and Parr was, as Romilly said by way of introduction, a profound admirer and universal panegyrist.[1] He refused to be introduced by Parr to Fox, because he had 'nothing particular to say' to the statesman, and considered that to be 'always a sufficient reason for declining acquaintance.'[2]

But, at last, Bentham's fame was to take a start. Bentham, I said, had long before found himself. Dumont had now found Bentham. After long and tedious labours and multiplied communications between the master and the disciple, Dumont in the spring of 1802 brought out his *Traités de Législation de M. Jérémie Bentham*. The book was partly a translation from Bentham's published and unpublished works,[3] and partly a statement of the pith of the new doctrine in Dumont's own language. It had the great merit of

[1] *Works*, x. 403.   [2] *Ibid.* x. 62.
[3] Bentham had himself written some of his papers in French.

putting Bentham's meaning vigorously and compactly, and free from many of the digressions, minute discussions of minor points and arguments requiring a special knowledge of English law, which had impeded the popularity of Bentham's previous works.

The Jacobin controversies were passing into the background: and Bentham began to attain a hearing as a reformer upon different lines. In 1803 Dumont visited St. Petersburg, and sent home glowing reports of Bentham's rising fame. As many copies of the *Traités* had been sold there as in London. Codes were wanted; laws were being digested; and Bentham's work would supply the principles and the classification. A magnificent translation was ordered, and Russian officials wrote glowing letters in which Bentham was placed in a line with Bacon, Newton, and Adam Smith—each the founder of a new science.[1] At home the new book was one of the objects of what Dumont calls the 'scandalous irreverence' of the *Edinburgh Review*.[2] This refers to a review of the *Traités* in the *Edinburgh Review* of April 1804. Although patronising in tone, and ridiculing some of Bentham's doctrines as commonplace and condemning others as criminal, it paid some high compliments to his ability. The irreverence meant at least that Bentham had become one of the persons worth talking about, and that he was henceforth to influence the rising generation. In January 1807 the *Edinburgh* itself (probably Jeffrey) suggested that Bentham should be employed in a proposed reform of the Scottish judicial system. His old friend, Lansdowne, died on 7th May 1805, and in one of his last letters expresses a hope that Bentham's principles

[1] *Works*, x. 407, 410, 413, 419.   [2] *Ibid.* x. 415.

are at last beginning to spread.[1] The hope was fulfilled.

During the eighteenth century Benthamism had gone through its period of incubation. It was now to become an active agency, to gather proselytes, and to have a marked influence not only upon legislative but upon political movements. The immediate effect upon Bentham of the decline of the Panopticon, and his consequent emancipation from immediately practical work, was apparently his return to his more legitimate employment of speculative labour. He sent to Dumont at St. Petersburg[2] part of the treatise upon Political Economy, which had been naturally suggested by his later work: and he applied himself to the Scottish judiciary question, to which many of his speculations had a close application. He published a work upon this subject in 1808. To the period between 1802 and 1812 belongs also the book, or rather the collection of papers, afterwards transformed into the book, upon Evidence, which is one of his most valuable performances.

A letter, dated 1st November 1810, gives a characteristic account of his position. He refers to hopes of the acceptance of some of his principles in South America. In Spain Spaniards are prepared to receive his laws 'as oracles.' 'Now at length, when I am just ready to drop into the grave' (he had still twenty years of energetic work before him), 'my fame has spread itself all over the civilised world.' Dumont's publication of 1802 is considered to have superseded all previous writings on legislation. In Germany and France codes have been prepared by authorised lawyers, who have 'sought

[1] Lord E. Fitzmaurice's *Life of Shelburne*.   [2] *Works*, x. 413.

to do themselves credit by references to that work.'[1] It has been translated into Russian. Even in England he is often mentioned in books and in parliament. 'Meantime I am here scribbling on in my hermitage, never seeing anybody but for some special reason, always bearing relation to the service of mankind.'[2] Making all due allowance for the deceptive views of the outer world which haunt every 'hermitage,' it remains true that Bentham's fame was emerging from obscurity.

The end of this period, moreover, was bringing him into closer contact with English political life. Bentham, as we have seen, rejected the whole Jacobin doctrine of abstract rights. So long as English politics meant either the acceptance of a theory which, for whatever reason, gathered round it no solid body of support, or, on the other hand, the acceptance of an obstructive and purely conservative principle, to which all reform was radically opposed, Bentham was necessarily in an isolated position. He had 'nothing particular to say' to Fox. He was neither a Tory nor a Jacobin, and cared little for the paralysed Whigs. He allied himself therefore, so far as he was allied with any one, with the philanthropic agitators who stood, like him, outside the lines of party. The improvement of prisons was not a party question. A marked change—not always, I think, sufficiently emphasised by historians—had followed the second war. The party-divisions began to take the form which was to become more marked as time went on. The old issues between Jacobin and Anti-Jacobin no longer existed. Napoleon had become the heir of the revolution. The

[1] This statement, I believe, refers to a complimentary reference to Bentham in the preface to the French Code.   [2] *Works*, x. 458.

great struggle was beginning in which England commanded the ocean, while the Continent was at the feet of the empire. For a time the question was whether England, too, should be invaded. After Trafalgar invasion became hopeless. The Napoleonic victories threatened to exclude English trade from the Continent: while England retorted by declaring that the Continent should trade with nobody else. Upon one side the war was now appealing to higher feelings. It was no longer a crusade against theories, but a struggle for national existence and for the existence of other nations threatened by a gigantic despotism. Men like Wordsworth and Coleridge, who could not be Anti-Jacobins, had been first shocked by the Jacobin treatment of Switzerland, and now threw themselves enthusiastically into the cause which meant the rescue of Spain and Germany from foreign oppression. The generous feeling which had resented the attempt to forbid Frenchmen to break their own bonds, now resented the attempts of Frenchmen to impose bonds upon others. The patriotism which prompted to a crusade had seemed unworthy, but the patriotism which was now allied with the patriotism of Spain and Germany involved no sacrifice of other sentiment. Many men had sympathised with the early revolution, not so much from any strong sentiment of evils at home as from a belief that the French movement was but a fuller development of the very principles which were partially embodied in the British Constitution. They had no longer to choose between sympathising with the enemies of England and sympathising with the suppressors of the old English liberties.

But, on the other hand, an opposite change took

place. The disappearance of the Jacobin movement allowed the Radicalism of home growth to display itself more fully. English Whigs of all shades had opposed the war with certain misgivings. They had been nervously anxious not to identify themselves with the sentiments of the Jacobins. They desired peace with the French, but had to protest that it was not for love of French principles. That difficulty was removed. There was no longer a vision—such as Gillray had embodied in his caricatures—of a guillotine in St. James's Street: or of a Committee of Public Safety formed by Fox, Paine, and Horne Tooke. Meanwhile Whig prophecies of the failure of the war were not disproved by its results. Though the English navy had been victorious, English interference on the Continent had been futile. Millions of money had been wasted: and millions were flowing freely. Even now we stand astonished at the reckless profusion of the financiers of the time. And what was there to show for it? The French empire, so far from being destroyed, had been consolidated. If we escaped for the time, could we permanently resist the whole power of Europe? When the Peninsular War began we had been fighting, except for the short truce of Amiens, for sixteen years; and there seemed no reason to believe that the expedition to Portugal in 1808 would succeed better than previous efforts. The Walcheren expedition of 1809 was a fresh proof of our capacity for blundering. Pauperism was still increasing rapidly, and forebodings of a war with America beginning to trouble men interested in commerce. The English Opposition had ample texts for discourses; and a demand for change began to spring up which was no

longer a reflection of foreign sympathies. An article in the *Edinburgh* of January 1808, which professed to demonstrate the hopelessness of the Peninsular War, roused the wrath of the Tories. The *Quarterly Review* was started by Canning and Scott, and the *Edinburgh*, in return, took a more decidedly Whig colour. The Radicals now showed themselves behind the Whigs. Cobbett, who had been the most vigorous of John Bull Anti-Jacobins, was driven by his hatred of the taxgatherer and the misery of the agricultural labourers into the opposite camp, and his *Register* became the most effective organ of Radicalism. Demands for reform began again to make themselves heard in parliament. Sir Francis Burdett, who had sat at the feet of Horne Tooke, and whose return with Cochrane for Westminster in 1807 was the first parliamentary triumph of the reformers, proposed a motion on 15th June 1809, which was, of course, rejected, but which was the first of a series, and marked the revival of a serious agitation not to cease till the triumph of 1832.

Meanwhile Bentham, meditating profoundly upon the Panopticon, had at last found out that he had begun at the wrong end. His reasoning had been thrown away upon the huge dead weight of official indifference, or worse than indifference. Why did they not accept the means for producing the greatest happiness of the greatest number? Because statesmen did not desire the end. And why not? To answer that question, and to show how a government could be constructed which should desire it, became a main occupation of Bentham's life. Henceforward, therefore, instead of merely treating of penal codes and other special reforms, his attention is directed to the previous question of political organisation ; while at times he diverges to illustrate incidentally the abuses of what he ironically calls the 'matchless constitution.' Bentham's principal occupation, in a word, was to provide political philosophy for radical reformers.[1]

Bentham remained as much a recluse as ever. He seldom left Queen's Square Place except for certain summer outings. In 1807 he took a house at Barrow Green, near Oxted, in Surrey, lying in a picturesque hollow at the foot of the chalk hills.[2] It was an old-fashioned house, standing in what had been a park, with a lake and a comfortable kitchen garden. Bentham pottered about in the grounds and under the old chestnut-trees, codifying, gardening, and talking to occasional disciples. He returned thither in following years ; but in 1814, probably in consequence of his compensation for the Panopticon, took a larger place, Ford Abbey, near Chard in Somersetshire. It was a superb residence,[3] with chapel, cloisters, and corridors, a hall eighty feet long by thirty high, and a great dining parlour. Parts of the building dated from the twelfth century or the time of the Commonwealth, or had undergone alterations attributed to Inigo Jones. No Squire Western could have cared less for antiquarian associations, but Bentham made a very fair monk. The place, for which he paid £315 a year, was congenial. He rode his favourite hobby of gardening, and took his regular 'ante-jentacular' and 'post-prandial' walks, and

---

[1] Bentham says that he reached these conclusions some time before 1809: *Works*, iii. 435. Cf. *Ibid.* v. 278.
[2] *Works*, x. 425.   [3] See description in Bain's *James Mill*, 129-36.

played battledore and shuttlecock in the intervals of codification. He liked it so well that he would have taken it for life, but for the loss of £8000 or £10,000 in a Devonshire marble-quarry.[1] In 1818 he gave it up, and thenceforward rarely quitted Queen's Square Place. His life was varied by few incidents, although his influence upon public affairs was for the first time becoming important. The busier journalists and platform orators did not trouble themselves much about philosophy. But they were in communication with men of a higher stamp, Romilly, James Mill, and others, who formed Bentham's innermost council. Thus the movements in the outside world set up an agitation in Bentham's study ; and the recluse was prompted to set himself to work upon elaborating his own theories in various directions, in order to supply the necessary substratum of philosophical doctrine. If he had not the power of gaining the public ear, his oracles were transmitted through the disciples who also converted some of his raw materials into coherent books.

The most important of Bentham's disciples for many years was James Mill, and I shall have to say what more is necessary in regard to the active agitation when I speak of Mill himself. For the present, it is enough to say that Mill first became Bentham's proselyte about 1808. Mill stayed with Bentham at Barrow Green and at Ford Abbey. Though some differences caused superficial disturbances of their harmony, no prophet could have had a more zealous, uncompromising, and vigorous disciple. Mill's force of character qualified him to become the leader of the school ; but his doctrine was

---

[1] *Works*, x. 479, 573.

always essentially the doctrine of Bentham, and for the present he was content to be the transmitter of his master's message to mankind. He was at this period a contributor to the *Edinburgh Review* ; and in October 1809 he inserted some praises of Bentham in a review of a book upon legislation by S. Scipion Bexon. The article was cruelly mangled by Jeffrey, according to his custom, and Jeffrey's most powerful vassal, Brougham, thought that the praises which remained were excessive.[1]

Obviously the orthodox Whigs were not prepared to swear allegiance to Bentham. He was drawing into closer connection with the Radicals. In 1809 Cobbett was denouncing the duke of York in consequence of the Mrs. Clarke scandal. Bentham wrote to him, but anonymously and cautiously, to obtain documents in regard to a previous libel case,[2] and proceeded to write a pamphlet on the *Elements of the Art of Packing (as applied to Special Juries)*, so sharp that his faithful adviser, Romilly, procured its suppression for the time.[3] Copies, however, were printed and privately given to a few who could be trusted. Bentham next wrote (1809) a 'Catechism of Parliamentary Reform,' which he communicated to Cobbett (16th November 1810), with a request for its publication in the *Register*.[4] Cobbett was at this time in prison for his attack upon flogging militia men ; and, though still more hostile to government, was bound to be more cautious in his line of assault. The plan was not published, whether because too daring or too dull ; but it was

---

[1] *Works*, x. 452-54 ; Bain's *James Mill*, 104.
[2] The case of the 'King *v.* Cobbett,' (1804), which led to the proceedings against Mr. Justice Johnson in 1805.—Cobbett's *State Trials*, xxix.
[3] *Works*, x. 448-49.   [4] *Ibid.* x. 458.

apparently printed. Bentham's opinion of Cobbett was anything but flattering. Cobbett, he thought in 1812, was a 'vile rascal,' and was afterwards pronounced to be 'filled with the *odium humani generis*—his malevolence and lying beyond everything.'[1] Cobbett's radicalism, in fact, was of the type most hostile to the Utilitarians. John Hunt, in the *Examiner*, was 'trumpeting' Bentham and Romilly in 1812, and was praised accordingly.[2] Bentham formed an alliance with another leading Radical. He had made acquaintance by 1811 with Sir F. Burdett, to whom he then appealed for help in an attack upon the delays of Chancery.[3] Burdett, indeed, appeared to him to be far inferior to Romilly and Brougham, but he thought that so powerful a 'hero of the mob' ought to be turned to account in the good cause.[4] Burdett seems to have courted the old philosopher ; and a few years later a closer alliance was brought about. The peace of 1815 was succeeded by a period of distress, the more acutely felt from the disappointment of natural hopes of prosperity ; and a period of agitation, met by harsh repression, followed. Applications were made to Bentham for permission to use his 'Catechism,' which was ultimately published (1818) in a cheap form by Wooler, well known as the editor of the democratic *Black Dwarf*.[5] Burdett applied for a plan of parliamentary reform. Henry Bickersteth (1783-1851), afterwards Lord Langdale and Master of the Rolls, at this time a rising barrister of high character, wrote an appeal to Bentham and Burdett to combine in setting forth a scheme which, with such authority, must command general acceptance.

---

[1] *Works*, x. 471, 570.   [2] *Ibid.* x. 471.   [3] *Ibid.* x. 461.
[4] *Ibid.* x. 471.   [5] *Ibid.* x. 490.

The result was a series of resolutions moved by Burdett in the House of Commons on 2nd June 1818,[1] demanding universal suffrage, annual parliaments, and vote by ballot. Bentham had thus accepted the conclusions reached in a different way by the believers in that 'hodge-podge' of absurdities, the declaration of the rights of man. Curiously enough, his assault upon that document appeared in Dumont's French version in the year 1816, at the very time when he was accepting its practical conclusions.

The schemes in which Mill was interested at this time drew Bentham's attention in other directions. In 1813 the Quaker, William Allen, who had been a close ally of Mill, induced Bentham to invest money in the New Lanark establishment. Owen, whose benevolent schemes had been hampered by his partners, bought them out, the new capital being partly provided by Allen, Bentham, and others. Bentham afterwards spoke contemptuously of Owen, who, as he said, 'began in vapour and ended in smoke,'[2] and whose disciples came in after years into sharp conflict with the Utilitarians. Bentham, however, took pleasure, it seems, in Owen's benevolent schemes for infant education, and made money by his investment, for once combining business with philanthropy successfully.[3] Probably he regarded New Lanark as a kind of Panopticon. Owen had not as yet become a prophet of Socialism.

Another set of controversies in which Mill and his friends took an active part, started Bentham in a whole series of speculations. A plan (which I shall have to mention in connection with Mill), was devised in 1815

[1] Printed in *Works*, x. 495-97.   [2] *Ibid.* x. 570.   [3] *Ibid.* x. 476.

for a 'Chrestomathic school,' which was to give a sound education of proper Utilitarian tendencies to the upper and middle classes. Brougham, Mackintosh, Ricardo, William Allen, and Place were all interested in this undertaking.[1] Bentham offered a site at Queen's Square Place, and though the scheme never came to the birth, it set him actively at work. He wrote a series of papers during his first year at Ford Abbey[2] upon the theory of education, published in 1816 as *Chrestomathia*; and to this was apparently due a further excursion beyond the limits of jurisprudence. Educational controversy in that ignorant day was complicated by religious animosity; the National Society and the 'British and Foreign' Society were fighting under the banners of Bell and Lancaster, and the war roused excessive bitterness. Bentham finding the church in his way, had little difficulty in discovering that the whole ecclesiastical system was part of the general complex of abuse against which he was warring. He fell foul of the Catechism; he exposed the abuses of non-residence and episcopal wealth; he discovered that the Thirty-nine Articles contained gross fallacies; he went on to make an onslaught upon the Apostle St Paul, whose evidence as to his conversion was exposed to a severe cross-examination; and, finally, he wrote, or supplied the materials for, a remarkable *Analysis of Natural Religion*, which was ultimately published by Grote under the pseudonym 'Philip Beauchamp,' in 1822. This procedure from the particular case of the Catechism in schools up to the general problem of the

[1] *Works*, x. 485.
[2] Bain's *James Mill*, 136.   *Church of Englandism* and *Not Paul but Jesus* were also written at Ford Abbey.

utility of religion in general, is curiously characteristic of Bentham.

Bentham's mind was attracted to various other schemes by the disciples who came to sit at his feet, and professed, with more or less sincerity, to regard him as a Solon. Foreigners had been resorting to him from all parts of the world, and gave him hopes of new fields for codifying. As early as 1808 he had been visited at Barrow Green by the strange adventurer, politician, lawyer, and filibuster, Aaron Burr, famous for the duel in which he killed Alexander Hamilton, and now framing wild schemes for an empire in Mexico. Unscrupulous, restlessly active and cynical, he was a singular contrast to the placid philosopher, upon whom his confidences seem to have made an impression of not unpleasing horror. Burr's conversation suggested to Bentham a singular scheme for emigrating to Mexico. He applied seriously for introductions to Lord Holland, who had passed some time in Spain, and to Holland's friend, Jovellanos (1749-1812), a member of the Spanish Junta, who had written treatises upon legislation (1785), of which Bentham approved.[1] The dream of Mexico was succeeded by a dream of Venezuela. General Miranda spent some years in England, and had become well known to James Mill. He was now about to start upon an unfortunate expedition to Venezuela, his native country. He took with him a draft of a law for the freedom of the press, which Bentham drew up, and he proposed that when his new state was founded, Bentham should be its legislator.[2] Miranda was betrayed to the Spanish government in 1812, and died (1816) in the hands of the Inquisition. Bolivar,

[1] *Works*, x. 433, 448.   [2] *Ibid.* x. 457-58; Bain's *James Mill*, 79.

who was also in London in 1810 and took some notice of Joseph Lancaster, applied in flattering terms to Bentham. Long afterwards, when dictator of Columbia, he forbade the use of Bentham's works in the schools, to which, however, the privilege of reading him was restored, and, let us hope, duly valued, in 1835.[1] Santander, another South American hero, was also a disciple, and encouraged the study of Bentham. Bentham says in 1830 that forty thousand copies of Dumont's *Traités* had been sold in Paris for the South American trade.[2] What share Bentham may have had in modifying South American ideas is unknown to me. In the United States he had many disciples of a more creditable kind than Burr. He appealed in 1811 to Madison, then President, for permission to construct a 'Pannomion' or complete body of law, for the use of the United States; and urged his claims both upon Madison and the Governor of Pennsylvania in 1817, when peace had been restored. He had many conversations upon this project with John Quincy Adams, who was then American minister in England.[3] This, of course, came to nothing, but an eminent American disciple, Edward Livingston (1764-1836), between 1820 and 1830 prepared codes for the State of Louisiana, and warmly acknowledged his obligations to Bentham.[4] In 1830 Bentham also acknowledges a notice of his labours, probably resulting from this, which had been made in one of General Jackson's presidential messages.[5] In his later years the United States became his ideal, and he never tired of comparing its cheap and

[1] *Works*, 553-54, 565   [2] *Ibid.* xi. 53.
[3] See *Memoirs of J. Q. Adams* (1874), iii. 511, 520, 532, 535-39, 540, 544, 560, 562-63; and Bentham's letter to Adams in *Works*, x. 554.
[4] *Works*, xi. 23.   [5] *Ibid.* xi. 40.

honest enactment with the corruption and extravagance at home.

V. CODIFICATION.

The unsettled conditions which followed the peace in various European countries found Bentham other employment. In 1809 Dumont did some codifying for the Emperor of Russia, and in 1817 was engaged to do the same service for Geneva. He was employed for some years, and is said to have introduced a Benthamite Penal Code and Panopticon, and an application of the Tactics.[1] In 1820 and 1821 Bentham was consulted by the Constitutional party in Spain and Portugal, and wrote elaborate tracts for their enlightenment. He made an impression upon at least one Spaniard. Borrow, when travelling in Spain some ten years after Bentham's death, was welcomed by an Alcalde on Cape Finisterre, who had upon his shelves all the works of the 'grand Baintham,' and compared him to Solon, Plato, and even Lope de Vega.[2] The last comparison appeared to Borrow to be overstrained. Bentham even endeavoured in 1822-23 to administer some sound advice to the government of Tripoli, but his suggestions for 'remedies against misrule' seem never to have been communicated.[3] In 1823 and 1824 he was a member of the Greek Committee; he corresponded with Mavrocordato and other leaders; and he begged Parr to turn some of his admonitions into 'Parrian' Greek for the benefit of the moderns.[4] Blaquière and Stanhope, two ardent members of the

---

[1] See correspondence upon his codification plans in Russia, America, and Geneva in *Works*, iv. 451-594.   [2] Borrow's *Bible in Spain*, ch. xxx.
[3] *Works*, viii. 555-600.
[4] *Ibid.* x. 534.   See Blaquière's enthusiastic letter to Bentham.—*Works*, x. 475.

committee, were disciples; and Stanhope carried with him to Greece Bentham's *Table of the Springs of Action*, with which he tried to indoctrinate Byron. The poet, however, thought with some plausibility that he was a better judge of human passions than the philosopher. Parry, the engineer, who joined Byron at the same time, gives a queer account of the old philosopher trotting about London in the service of the Greeks.[1] The coarse and thoughtless might laugh, and perhaps some neither coarse nor thoughtless might smile. But Bowring tells us that these were days of boundless happiness for Bentham.[2] Tributes of admiration were pouring in from all sides, and the true Gospel was spreading across the Atlantic and along the shores of the Mediterranean.

At home the Utilitarian party was consolidating itself; and the struggle which resulted in the Reform Bill was slowly beginning. The veteran Cartwright, Bentham's senior by eight years, tried in 1821 to persuade him to come out as one of a committee of 'Guardians of Constitutional Reform,' elected at a public meeting.[3] Bentham wisely refused to be drawn from his privacy. He left it to his friends to agitate, while he returned to labour in his study. The demand for legislation which had sprung up in so many parts of the world encouraged Bentham to undertake the last of his great labours. The Portuguese Cortes voted in December 1821 that he should be invited to prepare an 'all-comprehensive code'; and in 1822 he put out a curious 'Codification proposal,' offering to do the work for any nation in need of a legislator, and appending testimonials

---

[1] See, however, Bentham's reference to this story.—*Works*, xi. 66.
[2] *Works*, x. 539.   [3] *Ibid.* x. 522.

to his competence for the work. He set to work upon a 'Constitutional Code,' which occupied him at intervals during the remainder of his life, and embodied the final outcome of his speculations. He diverged from this main purpose to write various pamphlets upon topics of immediate interest; and was keenly interested in the various activities of his disciples. The Utilitarians now thought themselves entitled to enter the field of politics as a distinct body. An organ to defend their cause was desirable, and Bentham supplied the funds for the *Westminster Review*, of which the first number appeared in April 1824.

The editorship fell chiefly into the hands of Bowring (1792-1872). Bowring had travelled much upon the Continent for a commercial house, and his knowledge of Spanish politics had brought him into connection with Bentham, to whom Blaquière recommended him in 1820.[1] A strong attachment sprang up between the two. Bentham confided all his thoughts and feelings to the young man, and Bowring looked up to his teacher with affectionate reverence. In 1828 Bentham says that Bowring is 'the most intimate friend he has.'[2] Bowring complains of calumnies, by which he was assailed, though they failed to alienate Bentham. What they may have been matters little; but it is clear that a certain jealousy arose between this last disciple and his older rivals. James Mill's stern and rigid character had evidently produced some irritation at intervals; and to him it would naturally appear that Bowring was the object of a senile favouritism. In any case it is to be regretted that Bentham thus became partly alienated from his older

---

[1] *Works*, x. 516.   [2] *Ibid.* x. 591.

friends.[1] Mill was too proud to complain; and never wavered in his allegiance to the master's principles. But one result, and to us the most important, was that the new attachment led to the composition of one of the worst biographies in the language, out of materials which might have served for a masterpiece. Bowring was a great linguist, and an energetic man of business. He wrote hymns, and one of them, 'In the cross of Christ I glory,' is said to have 'universal fame.' A Benthamite capable of so singular an eccentricity judiciously agreed to avoid discussions upon religious topics with his master. To Bowring we also owe the *Deontology*, which professes to represent Bentham's dictation. The Mills repudiated this version, certainly a very poor one, of their teacher's morality, and held that it represented less Bentham than such an impression of Bentham as could be stamped upon a muddle-headed disciple.[2]

The last years of his life brought Bentham into closer connection with more remarkable men. The Radicals had despised the Whigs as trimmers and half-hearted reformers, and James Mill expressed this feeling very frankly in the first numbers of the *Westminster Review*. Reform, however, was now becoming respectable, and the Whigs were gaining the courage to take it up seriously. Foremost among the Edinburgh Reviewers was the great Henry Brougham, whose fame was at this time almost as great as his ambition could desire, and who considered himself to be the natural leader of all reform. He had shown eagerness to distinguish himself in lines fully

---

[1] A letter from Mill in the University College MSS. describes a misunderstanding about borrowed books, a fertile, but hardly adequate, cause of quarrel.
[2] Bowring's religious principles prevented him from admitting some of Bentham's works to the collective edition.

approved by Bentham. His admirers regarded him as a giant ; and his opponents, if they saw in him a dash of the charlatan, could not deny his amazing energy and his capacity as an orator. The insatiable vanity which afterwards ruined his career already made it doubtful whether he fought for the cause or the glory. But he was at least an instrument worth having. He was a kind of half-disciple. If in 1809 he had checked Mill's praise of Bentham, he was soon afterwards in frequent communication with the master. In July 1812 Bentham announces that Brougham is at last to be admitted to a dinner, for which he had been 'intriguing any time this six months,' and expects that his proselyte will soon be the first man in the House of Commons, and eclipse even Romilly.[1] In later years they had frequent communications; and when in 1827 Brougham was known to be preparing an utterance upon law reform, Bentham's hopes rose high. He offered to his disciple 'some nice little sweet pap of my own making,' sound teaching that is, upon evidence, judicial establishments and codification. Brougham thanks his 'dear grandpapa,' and Bentham offers further supplies to his 'dear, sweet little poppet.'[2] But when the orator had spoken Bentham declares (9th February 1828) that the mountain has been delivered of a mouse. Brougham was 'not the man to set up' simple and rational principles. He was the sham adversary but the real accomplice of Peel, pulling up lies by the root to plant others equally noxious.[3] In 1830 Bentham had even to hold up 'Master Peel' as a 'model good boy' to the self-styled reformer. Brougham needs a dose of jalap instead of pap, for he cannot even spell the 'greatest

[1] Works, x. 471-72.   [2] Ibid. x. 576.   [3] Ibid. x. 588.

happiness principle' properly.[1] Bentham went so far as to write what he fondly took to be an epigram upon Brougham :

'So foolish and so wise, so great, so small,
Everything now, to-morrow nought at all.'[2]

In September 1831 Brougham as Chancellor announced a scheme for certain changes in the constitution of the courts. The proposal called forth Bentham's last pamphlet, Lord Brougham displayed.[3] Bentham laments that his disciple has 'stretched out the right hand of fellowship to jobbers of all sorts.'[4] In vain had Brougham in his speech called Bentham 'one of the great sages of the law.' Bentham acknowledges his amiability and his genius ; but laments over the untrustworthy character of a man who could only adopt principles so far as they were subservient to his own vanity.

Another light of the Edinburgh Review, who at this time took Brougham at his own valuation, did an incidental service to Bentham. Upon the publication of the Book of Fallacies in 1825, Sydney Smith reviewed or rather condensed it in the Edinburgh Review, and gave the pith of the whole in his famous Noodle's Oration. The noodle utters all the commonplaces by which the stupid conservatives, with Eldon at their head, met the demands of reformers. Nothing could be wittier than Smith's brilliant summary. Whigs and Radicals for the time agreed in ridiculing blind prejudice. The day was to come when the Whigs at least would see that some principles might be worse than prejudice. All the fools, said Lord Melbourne, 'were against Catholic

[1] Works, xi. 37. Papers preserved at University College show that during Peel's law reforms at this time Bentham frequently communicated with him.
[2] Ibid. xi. 50.   [3] Ibid. v. 549.   [4] Ibid. v. 609.

Emancipation, and the worst of it is, the fools were in the right.' Sydney Smith was glad to be Bentham's mouthpiece for the moment : though, when Benthamism was applied to church reform, Smith began to perceive that Noodle was not so silly as he seemed.

One other ally of Bentham deserves notice. O'Connell had in 1828, in speaking of legal abuses, called himself 'an humble disciple of the immortal Bentham.'[1] Bentham wrote to acknowledge the compliment. He invited O'Connell to become an inmate of his hermitage at Queen's Square Place, and O'Connell responded warmly to the letters of his 'revered master.' Bentham's aversion to Catholicism was as strong as his objection to Catholic disqualifications, and he took some trouble to smooth down the difficulties which threatened an alliance between ardent believers and thorough-going sceptics. O'Connell had attacked some who were politically upon his side. 'Dan, dear child,' says Bentham, 'whom in imagination I am at this moment pressing to my fond bosom, put off, if it be possible, your intolerance.'[2] Their friendship, however, did not suffer from this discord, and their correspondence is in the same tone till the end. In one of Bentham's letters he speaks of a contemporary correspondence with another great man, whom he does not appear to have met personally. He was writing long letters, entreating the duke of Wellington to eclipse Cromwell by successfully attacking the lawyers. The duke wrote 'immediate answers in his own hand,' and took good-humouredly a remonstrance from Bentham upon the duel with Lord Winchilsea in 1829.[3] Bentham was ready to the end to

[1] Works, x. 594.   [2] Ibid. xi. 26.   [3] Ibid. xi. 13, 28.

seek allies in any quarter. When Lord Sidmouth took office in 1812, Bentham had an interview with him, and had some hopes of being employed to prepare a penal code.[1] Although experience had convinced him of the futility of expectations from the Sidmouths and Eldons, he was always on the look out for sympathy ; and the venerable old man was naturally treated with respect by people who had little enough of real interest in his doctrines.

During the last ten years of his life, Bentham was cheered by symptoms of the triumph of his creed. The approach of the millennium seemed to be indicated by the gathering of the various forces which carried Roman Catholic Emancipation and the Reform Bill. Bentham still received testimonies of his fame abroad. In 1825 he visited Paris to consult some physicians. He was received with the respect which the French can always pay to intellectual eminence.[2] All the lawyers in a court of justice rose to receive him, and he was placed at the president's right hand. On the revolution of 1830, he addressed some good advice to the country of which he had been made a citizen nearly forty years before. In 1832, Talleyrand, to whom he had talked about the Panopticon in 1792, dined with him alone in his hermitage.[3] When Bowring observed to the prince that Bentham's works had been plundered, the polite diplomatist replied, et pillé de tout le monde, il est toujours riche. Bentham was by this time failing. At eighty-two he was still, as he put it, 'codifying like any dragon.'[4] On 18th May 1832 he did his last bit of his life-long labour, upon the 'Constitutional Code.' The great

[1] Works, x. 468.   [2] Ibid. x. 551.   [3] Ibid. xi. 75.   [4] Ibid. xi. 33.

reform agitation was reaching the land of promise, but Bentham was to die in the wilderness. He sank without a struggle on 6th June 1832, his head resting on Bowring's bosom. He left the characteristic direction that his body should be dissected for the benefit of science. An incision was formally made; and the old gentleman, in his clothes as he lived, his face covered by a wax mask, is still to be seen at University College in Gower Street.

Bentham, as we are told, had a strong personal resemblance to Benjamin Franklin. Sagacity, benevolence, and playfulness were expressed in both physiognomies. Bentham, however, differed from the man whose intellect presents many points of likeness, in that he was not a man of the market-place or the office. Bentham was in many respects a child through life:[1] a child in simplicity, good humour, and vivacity; his health was unbroken; he knew no great sorrow; and after emerging from the discouragement of his youth, he was placidly contemplating a continuous growth of fame and influence. He is said to have expressed the wis that he could awake once in a century to contemplate th prospect of a world gradually adopting his principles and so making steady progress in happiness and wisdom.

No man could lead a simpler life. His chief luxuries at table were fruit, bread, and tea. He had a 'sacred teapot' called Dick, with associations of its own, and carefully regulated its functions. He refrained from wine during the greatest part of his life, and was never guilty of a single act of intemperance. In later life he took a daily half-glass of Madeira. He was scrupulously

[1] Mill's *Dissertations*, i. 354 and 392 *n*.

neat in person, and wore a Quaker-like brown coat, brown cassimere breeches, white worsted stockings and a straw hat. He walked or 'rather trotted' with his stick Dapple, and took his 'ante-prandial' and other 'circumgyrations' with absolute punctuality. He loved pets; he had a series of attached cats; and cherished the memory of a 'beautiful pig' at Hendon, and of a donkey at Ford Abbey. He encouraged mice to play in his study—a taste which involved some trouble with his cats, and suggests problems as to the greatest happiness of the greatest number. Kindness to animals was an essential point of his moral creed. 'I love everything,' he said, 'that has four legs.' He had a passion for flowers, and tried to introduce useful plants. He loved music—especially Handel—and had an organ in his house. He cared nothing for poetry: 'Prose,' he said,[1] 'is when all the lines except the last go on to the margin. Poetry is when some of them fall short of it.' He was courteous and attentive to his guests, though occasionally irritable when his favourite crotchets were transgressed, or especially if his fixed hours of work were deranged.

His regularity in literary work was absolute. He lived by a time-table, working in the morning and turning out from ten to fifteen folio pages daily. He read the newspapers regularly, but few books, and cared nothing for criticisms on his own writings. His only substantial meal was a dinner at six or half-past, to which he occasionally admitted a few friends as a high privilege. He liked to discuss the topics of which his mind was full, and made notes beforehand of particular points to

[1] *Works*, x. 442.

be introduced in conversation. He was invariably inaccessible to visitors, even famous ones, likely to distract his thoughts. 'Tell Mr. Bentham that Mr. Richard Lovell Edgeworth desires to see him.' 'Tell Mr. Richard Lovell Edgeworth that Mr. Bentham does not desire to see him' was the reply. When Mme. de Stael came to England, she said to Dumont: 'Tell Bentham I shall see nobody till I have seen him.' 'I am sorry for it,' said Bentham, 'for then she will never see anybody.' And he summed up his opinion of the famous author of *Corinne* by calling her 'a trumpery magpie.'[1] There is a simplicity and vivacity about some of the sayings reported by Bowring, which prove that Bentham could talk well, and increase our regret for the absence of a more efficient Boswell. At ten Bentham had his tea, at eleven his nightcap, and by twelve all his guests were ignominiously expelled. He was left to sleep on a hard bed. His sleep was light, and much disturbed by dreams.

Bentham was certainly amiable. The 'surest way to gain men,' he said, 'is to appear to love them, and the surest way to appear to love them is to love them in reality.' The least pleasing part of his character, however, is the apparent levity of his attachments. He was, as we have seen, partly alienated from Dumont, though some friendly communications are recorded in later years, and Dumont spoke warmly of Bentham only a few days before his death in 1829.[2] He not only cooled towards James Mill, but, if Bowring is to be trusted, spoke of him with great harshness.[3] Bowring was not a judicious reporter, indeed, and capable of taking hasty phrases too seriously. What Bentham's remarks upon these and

[1] *Works*, x. 467; xi. 79.   [2] *Ibid.* xi. 23-24.   [3] *Ibid.* x. 450.

other friends suggest is not malice or resentment, but the flippant utterance of a man whose feelings are wanting in depth rather than kindliness. It is noticeable that, after his early visit at Bowood, no woman seems to have counted for anything in Bentham's life. He was not only never in love, but it looks as if he never even talked to any woman except his cook or housemaid.

The one conclusion that I need draw concerns a question not, I think, hard to be solved. It would be easy to make a paradox by calling Bentham at once the most practical and most unpractical of men. This is to point out the one-sided nature of Bentham's development. Bentham's habits remind us in some ways of Kant; and the thought may be suggested that he would have been more in his element as a German professor of philosophies. In such a position he might have devoted himself to the delight of classifying and co-ordinating theories, and have found sufficient enjoyment in purely intellectual activity. After a fashion that was the actual result. How far, indeed, Bentham could have achieved much in the sphere of pure philosophy, and what kind of philosophy he would have turned out, must be left to conjecture. The circumstances of his time and country, and possibly his own temperament generally, turned his thoughts to problems of legislation and politics, that is to say, of direct practical interest. He was therefore always dealing with concrete facts, and a great part of his writings may be considered as raw material for acts of parliament. Bentham remained, however, unpractical, in the sense that he had not that knowledge which we ascribe either to the poet or to the man of the world. He had neither the passion nor the sympathetic imagination. The springs

of active conduct which Byron knew from experience
were to Bentham nothing more than names in a careful classification.   Any shrewd attorney or Bow Street
runner would have been a better judge of the management of convicts; and here were dozens of party
politicians, such as Rigby and Barré, who could have
explained to him beforehand those mysteries in the
working of the political machinery, which it took him
half a lifetime to discover.   In this sense Bentham was
unpractical in the highest degree, for at eighty he had
not found out of what men are really made.   And yet
by his extraordinary intellectual activity and the concentration of all his faculties upon certain problems, he
succeeded in preserving an example, and though not a
unique yet an almost unsurpassable example, of the power
which belongs to the man of one idea.

CHAPTER VI

BENTHAM'S DOCTRINE

I. FIRST PRINCIPLES

BENTHAM's position is in one respect unique.   There
have been many greater thinkers ; but there has been
hardly any one whose abstract theory has become in the
same degree the platform of an active political party.
To accept the philosophy was to be also pledged to
practical applications of Utilitarianism.   What, then,
was the revelation made to the Benthamites, and to what
did it owe its influence?   The central doctrine is
expressed in Bentham's famous formula : the test of
right and wrong is the 'greatest happiness of the
greatest number.'   There was nothing new in this
assertion.   It only expresses the fact that Bentham
accepted one of the two alternatives which have commended themselves to conflicting schools ever since
ethical speculation was erected into a separate department
of thought.   Moreover, the side which Bentham took
was, we may say, the winning side.   The ordinary
morality of the time was Utilitarian in substance.
Hutcheson had invented the sacred phrase': and Hume
had based his moral system upon 'utility.'[1]   Bentham

[1] See note under Bentham's life, *ante*, p. 178.

had learned much from Helvétius the French freethinker,
and had been anticipated by Paley the English divine.
The writings in which Bentham deals explicitly with the
general principles of Ethics would hardly entitle him to
a higher position than that of a disciple of Hume without
Hume's subtlety ; or of Paley without Paley's singular
gift of exposition.   Why, then, did Bentham's message
come upon his disciples with the force and freshness of a
new revelation?   Our answer must be in general terms
that Bentham founded not a doctrine but a method : and
that the doctrine which came to him simply as a general
principle was in his hands a potent instrument applied
with most fruitful results to questions of immediate
practical interest.

Beyond the general principle of utility, therefore, we
have to consider the 'organon' constructed by him to
give effect to a general principle too vague to be
applied in detail.   The fullest account of this is contained in the *Introduction to the Principles of Morals and
Legislation*.   This work unfortunately is a fragment, but
it gives his doctrine vigorously and decisively, without
losing itself in the minute details which become wearisome in his later writings.   Bentham intended it as an
introduction to a penal code ; and his investigation sent
him back to more general problems.   He found it
necessary to settle the relations of the penal code to the
whole body of law ; and to settle these he had to consider
the principles which underlie legislation in general.   He
had thus, he says, to 'create a new science,' and then to
elaborate one department of the science.   The 'introduction' would contain prolegomena not only for the
penal code but for the other departments of inquiry

which he intended to exhaust.[1]   He had to lay down
primary truths which should be to this science what the
axioms are to mathematical sciences.[2]   These truths
therefore belong to the sphere of conduct in general, and
include his ethical theory.

'Nature has placed mankind' (that is his opening
phrase) 'under the governance of two sovereign masters,
pain and pleasure.   It is for them alone to point out
what we ought to do, as well as to determine what we
shall do.'   There is the unassailable basis.   It had been
laid down as unequivocally by Locke,[3] and had been
embodied in the brilliant couplets of Pope's *Essay on
Man*.[4]   At the head of the curious table of universal
knowledge, given in the *Chrestomathia*, we have Eudæmonics as an all-comprehensive name of which every art
is a branch.[5]   Eudæmonics, as an art, corresponds to the
science ' ontology.'   It covers the whole sphere of human
thought.   It means knowledge in general as related to
conduct.   Its first principle, again, requires no more
proof than the primary axioms of arithmetic or geometry.
Once understood, it is by the same act of the mind seen
to be true.   Some people, indeed, do not see it.   Bentham
rather ignores than answers some of their arguments.
But his mode of treating opponents indicates his own
position.   'Happiness,' it is often said, is too vague a
word to be the keystone of an ethical system ; it varies

[1] Preface to *Morals and Legislation*.
[2] *Works*, i. ('Morals and Legislation'), ii. *n*.
[3] *Essay*, bk. ii. ch. xxi. § 39-§ 44.   The will, says Locke, is determined
by the 'uneasiness of desire.'   What moves desire ?   Happiness, and that
alone.   Happiness is pleasure, and misery pain.   What produces pleasure we
call good ; and what produces pain we call evil.   Locke, however, was not a
consistent Utilitarian.
[4] Epistle iv., opening lines.   [5] *Works*, viii. 82.

from man to man : or it is 'subjective,' and therefore gives no absolute or independent ground for morality. A morality of 'eudæmonism' must be an 'empirical' morality, and we can never extort from it that 'categorical imperative,' without which we have instead of a true morality a simple system of 'expediency.' From Bentham's point of view the criticism must be retorted. He regards 'happiness' as precisely the least equivocal of words ; and 'happiness' itself as therefore affording the one safe clue to all the intricate problems of human conduct. The authors of the *Federalist*, for example, had said that justice was the 'end of government.' 'Why not happiness?' asks Bentham. 'What happiness is every man knows, because what pleasure is, every man knows, and what pain is, every man knows. But what justice is—this is what on every occasion is the subject-matter of dispute.'[1] That phrase gives his view in a nutshell. Justice is the means, not the end. That is just which produces a maximum of happiness. Omit all reference to Happiness, and Justice becomes a meaningless word prescribing equality, but not telling us equality of what. Happiness, on the other hand, has a substantial and independent meaning from which the meaning of justice can be deduced. It has therefore a logical priority : and to attempt to ignore this is the way to all the labyrinths of hopeless confusion by which legislation has been made a chaos. Bentham's position is indicated by his early conflict with Blackstone, not a very powerful representative of the opposite principle. Blackstone, in fact, had tried to base his defence of that eminently empirical product, the British Constitution,

[1] *Works* ('Constitutional Code'), ix. 123.

upon some show of a philosophical groundwork. He had used the vague conception of a 'social contract,' frequently invoked for the same purpose at the revolution of 1688, and to eke out his arguments applied the ancient commonplaces about monarchy, aristocracy, and democracy. He thus tried to invest the constitution with the sanctity derived from this mysterious 'contract,' while appealing also to tradition or the incarnate 'wisdom of our ancestors,' as shown by their judicious mixture of the three forms. Bentham had an easy task, though he performed it with remarkable vigour, in exposing the weakness of this heterogeneous aggregate. Look closely, and this fictitious contract can impose no new obligation : for the obligation itself rests upon Utility. Why not appeal to Utility at once? I am bound to obey, not because my great-grandfather may be regarded as having made a bargain, which he did not really make, with the great-grandfather of George III. ; but simply because rebellion does more harm than good. The forms of government are abstractions, not names of realities, and their 'mixture' is a pure figment. King, Lords, and Commons are not really incarnations of power, wisdom, and goodness. Their combination forms a system the merits of which must in the last resort be judged by its working. 'It is the principle of utility, accurately apprehended and steadily applied, that affords the only clew to guide a man through these streights.'[1] So much in fact Bentham might learn from Hume ; and to defend upon any other ground the congeries of traditional arrangements which passed for the British Constitution was obviously absurd. It was in this warfare against the

[1] *Works* ('Fragment'), i. 287.

shifting and ambiguous doctrines of Blackstone that Bentham first showed the superiority of his own method : for, as between the two, Bentham's position is at least the most coherent and intelligible.

Blackstone, however, represents little more than a bit of rhetoric embodying fragments of inconsistent theories. The *Morals and Legislation* opens by briefly and contemptuously setting aside more philosophical opponents of Utilitarianism. The 'ascetic' principle, for example, is the formal contradiction of the principle of Utility, for it professedly declares pleasure to be evil. Could it be consistently carried out it would turn earth into hell. But in fact it is at bottom an illegitimate corollary from the very principle which it ostensibly denies. It professes to condemn pleasure in general ; it really means that certain pleasures can only be bought at an excessive cost of pain. Other theories are contrivances for avoiding the appeal 'to any external standard' ; and in substance, therefore, they make the opinion of the individual theorist an ultimate and sufficient reason. Adam Smith by his doctrine of 'sympathy' makes the sentiment of approval itself the ultimate standard. My feeling echoes yours, and reciprocally ; each cannot derive authority from the other. Another man (Hutcheson) invents a thing made on purpose to tell him what is right and what is wrong and calls it a 'moral sense.' Beattie substitutes 'common' for 'moral' sense, and his doctrine is attractive because every man supposes himself to possess common-sense. Others, like Price, appeal to the Understanding, or, like Clarke, to the 'Fitness of Things,' or they invent such phrases as 'Law of Nature,' or 'Right Reason' or 'Natural Justice,' or what you

please. Each really means that whatever he says is infallibly true and self-evident. Wollaston discovers that the only wrong thing is telling a lie ; or that when you kill your father, it is a way of saying that he is not your father, and the same method is applicable to any conduct which he happens to dislike. The 'fairest and openest of them all' is the man who says, 'I am of the number of the Elect'; God tells the Elect what is right : therefore if you want to know what is right, you have only to come to me.[1] Bentham is writing here in his pithiest style. His criticism is of course of the rough and ready order ; but I think that in a fashion he manages to hit the nail pretty well on the head.

His main point, at any rate, is clear. He argues briefly that the alternative systems are illusory because they refer to no 'external standard.' His opponents, not he, really make morality arbitrary. This, whatever the ultimate truth, is in fact the essential core of all the Utilitarian doctrine descended from or related to Benthamism. Benthamism aims at converting morality into a science. Science, according to him, must rest upon facts. It must apply to real things, and to things which have definite relations and a common measure. Now, if anything be real, pains and pleasures are real. The expectation of pain or pleasure determines conduct ; and, if so, it must be the sole determinant of conduct. The attempt to conceal or evade this truth is the fatal source of all equivocation and confusion. Try the

[1] *Works* ('Morals and Legislation'), i. 6-10. Mill quotes this passage in his essay on Bentham in the first volume of his *Dissertations*. This essay, excellent in itself, must be specially noticed as an exposition by an authoritative disciple.

experiment. Introduce a 'moral sense.' What is its relation to the desire for happiness ? If the dictates of the moral sense be treated as ultimate, an absolutely arbitrary element is introduced ; and we have one of the 'innate ideas' exploded by Locke, a belief summarily intruded into the system without definite relations to any other beliefs : a dogmatic assertion which refuses to be tested or to be correlated with other dogmas ; a reduction therefore of the whole system to chaos. It is at best an instinctive belief which requires to be justified and corrected by reference to some other criterion. Or resolve morality into 'reason,' that is, into some purely logical truth, and it then remains in the air—a mere nonentity until experience has supplied some material upon which it can work. Deny the principle of utility, in short, as he says in a vigorous passage,[1] and you are involved in a hopeless circle. Sooner or later you appeal to an arbitrary and despotic principle and find that you have substituted words for thoughts.

The only escape from this circle is the frank admission that happiness is, in fact, the sole aim of man. There are, of course, different kinds of happiness as there are different kinds of physical forces. But the motives to action are, like the physical forces, commensurable. Two courses of conduct can always be compared in respect of the happiness produced, as two motions of a body can be compared in respect of the energy expended. If, then, we take the moral judgment to be simply a judgment of amounts of happiness, the whole theory can be systematised, and its various theorems ranged under a single axiom or consistent set of axioms. Pain and

[1] *Works* ('Morals and Legislation '), i. 13.

pleasure give the real value of actions ; they are the currency with a definite standard into which every general rule may be translated. There is always a common measure applicable in every formula for the estimation of conduct. If you admit your Moral Sense, you profess to settle values by some standard which has no definite relation to the standard which in fact governs the normal transactions. But any such double standard, in which the two measures are absolutely incommensurable, leads straight to chaos. Or, if again you appeal to reason in the abstract, you are attempting to settle an account by pure arithmetic without reference to the units upon which your operation is performed. Two pounds and two pounds will make four pounds whatever a pound may be ; but till I know what it is, the result is nugatory. Somewhere I must come upon a basis of fact, if my whole construction is to stand.

This is the fundamental position implied in Bentham's doctrine. The moral judgment is simply one case of the judgment of happiness. Bentham is so much convinced of this that to him there appeared to be in reality no other theory. What passed for theories were mere combinations of words. Having said this, we know where to lay the foundations of the new science. It deals with a vast complicity of facts : it requires 'investigations as severe as mathematical ones, but beyond all comparison more intricate and extensive.'[1] Still it deals with facts, and with facts which have a common measure, and can, therefore, be presented as a coherent system. To present this system, or so much of it as is required for purposes of legislation, is therefore

[1] *Works* ('Morals and Legislation '), i. v.

his next task. The partial execution is the chief substance of the *Introduction*. Right and wrong conduct, we may now take for granted, mean simply those classes of conduct which are conducive to or opposed to happiness ; or, in the sacred formula, to act rightly means to promote the greatest happiness of the greatest number. The legislator, like every one else, acts rightly in so far as he is guided by the principle (to use one of the phrases coined by Bentham) of 'maximising' happiness. He seeks to affect conduct ; and conduct can be affected only by annexing pains or pleasures to given classes of actions. Hence we have a vitally important part of his doctrine— the theory of 'sanctions.' Pains and pleasures as annexed to action are called 'sanctions.' There are 'physical or natural,' 'political,' 'moral or popular,' and 'religious' sanctions. The 'physical' sanctions are such pleasures and pains as follow a given course of conduct independently of the interference of any other human or supernatural being ; the 'political' those which are annexed by the action of the legislator ; the 'moral or popular' those which are annexed by other individuals not acting in a corporate capacity ; and the 'religious' those which are annexed by a 'superior invisible being,' or, as he says elsewhere,[1] 'such as are capable of being expected at the hands of an invisible Ruler of the Universe.' The three last sanctions, he remarks, 'operate through the first.' The 'magistrate' or 'men at large' can only operate, and God is supposed only to operate, 'through the powers of nature,' that is, by applying some of the pains and pleasures which may also be natural sanctions. A man is burnt : if by his own imprudence, that is a

[1] *Works* ('Evidence '), vi. 261.

'physical' sanction ; if by the magistrate, it is a 'political' sanction ; if by some neglect of his neighbours, due to their dislike of his 'moral character,' a 'moral' sanction ; if by the immediate act of God or by distraction caused by dread of God's displeasure, it is a 'religious' sanction. Of these, as Bentham characteristically observes[1] in a later writing the political is much stronger than the 'moral' or 'religious.' Many men fear the loss of character or the 'wrath of Heaven,' but all men fear the scourge and the gallows.[2] He admits, however, that the religious sanction and the additional sanction of 'benevolence' have the advantage of not requiring that the offender should be found out.[3] But in any case, the 'natural' and religious sanctions are beyond the legislator's power. His problem, therefore, is simply this : what sanctions ought he to annex to conduct, or remembering that 'ought' means simply 'conducive to happiness,' what political sanctions will increase happiness ?

To answer this fully will be to give a complete system of legislation ; but in order to answer it we require a whole logical and psychological apparatus. Bentham shows this apparatus at work, but does not expound its origin in any separate treatise. Enough information, however, is given as to his method in the curious collection of the fragments connected with the *Chrestomathia*. A logical method upon which he constantly

[1] *Works* ('Evidence '), vii. 116.
[2] *Ibid.* ('Morals and Legislation '), i. 14, etc. ; *Ibid.* vi. 260. In *Ibid.* ('Evidence ') vii. 116, 'humanity,' and in 'Logical Arrangements,' *Ibid.* ii. 290, 'sympathy' appears as a fifth sanction. Another modification is suggested in *Ibid.* i. 14 *n.*
[3] *Ibid.* ('Morals and Legislation ') i. 67.

insisted is that of 'bipartition,'[1] called also the 'dichotomous' or 'bifurcate' method, and exemplified by the so-called 'Porphyrian Tree.' The principle is, of course, simple. Take any genus: divide it into two classes, one of which has and the other has not a certain mark. The two classes must be mutually exclusive and together exhaustive. Repeat the operation upon each of the classes and continue the process as long as desired.[2] At every step you thus have a complete enumeration of all the species, varieties, and so on, each of which excludes all the others. No mere logic, indeed, can secure the accuracy and still less the utility of the procedure. The differences may be in themselves ambiguous or irrelevant. If I classify plants as 'trees' and 'not trees,' the logical form is satisfied : but I have still to ask whether 'tree' conveys a determinate meaning, and whether the distinction corresponds to a difference of any importance. A perfect classification, however, could always be stated in this form. Each species, that is, can be marked by the presence or absence of a given difference, whether we are dealing with classes of plants or actions : and Bentham aims at that consummation though he admits that centuries may be required for the construction of an accurate classification in ethical speculations.[3] He exaggerates the efficiency of his method, and overlooks the tendency of tacit assumptions to smuggle themselves into what affects to be a mere enumeration of classes. But in any case, no one could labour more industriously to get every object of his

[1] Works ('Morals and Legislation '), i. 96 n.
[2] See especially Ibid. viii. 104, etc. ; 253, etc. ; 289, etc.
[3] Ibid. viii. 106.

thought arranged and labelled and put into the right pigeon-hole of his mental museum. To codify[1] is to classify, and Bentham might be defined as a codifying animal.

Things thus present themselves to Bentham's mind as already prepared to fit into pigeon-holes. This is a characteristic point, and it appears in what we must call his metaphysical system. 'Metaphysics,' indeed, according to him, is simply 'a sprig,' and that a small one, of the 'branch termed Logic.'[2] It is merely the explanation of certain general terms such as 'existence,' 'necessity,' and so forth.[3] Under this would apparently fall the explanation of 'reality' which leads to a doctrine upon which he often insists, and which is most implicitly given in the fragment called Ontology. He there distinguishes 'real' from 'fictitious entities,' a distinction which, as he tells us,[4] he first learned from d'Alembert's phrase Êtres fictifs, and which he applies in his Morals and Legislation. 'Real entities,' according to him,[5] are 'individual perceptions,' 'impressions,' and 'ideas.' In this, of course, he is following Hume, though he applies the Johnsonian argument to Berkeley's immaterialism.[6] A 'fictitious entity' is a name which does not 'raise up in the mind any correspondent images.'[7] Such names owe their existence to the necessities of language. Without employing such fictions, however, 'the language of man could not have risen above the language of

[1] 'Codify' was one of Bentham's successful neologisms.
[2] Works ('Logic'), viii. 220.
[3] Here Bentham coincides with Horne Tooke, to whose 'discoveries' he refers in the Chrestomathia (Works, viii. 120, 185, 188).
[4] Works, iii. 286 ; viii. 119.   [5] Ibid. ('Ontology') viii. 196 n.
[6] Ibid. viii. 197 n.   [7] Ibid. viii. 263.

brutes';[1] and he emphatically distinguishes them from 'unreal' or 'fabulous entities.' A 'fictitious entity' is not a 'nonentity.'[2] He includes among such entities all Aristotle's 'predicaments' except the first: 'substance.'[3] Quantity, quality, relation, time, place are all 'physical fictitious entities.' This is apparently equivalent to saying that the only 'physical entities' are concrete things—sticks, stones, bodies, and so forth— the 'reality' of which he takes for granted in the ordinary common-sense meaning. It is also perfectly true that things are really related, have quantity and quality, and are in time and space. But we cannot really conceive the quality or relation apart from the concrete things so qualified and related. We are forced by language to use substantives which in their nature have only the sense of adjectives. He does not suppose that a body is not really square or round ; but he thinks it a fiction to speak of squareness or roundness or space in general as something existing apart from matter and, in some sense, alongside of matter.

This doctrine, which brings us within sight of metaphysical problems beyond our immediate purpose, becomes important to his moral speculation. His special example of a 'fictitious entity' in politics is 'obligation.'[4] Obligations, rights, and similar words are 'fictitious 'entities.' Obligation in particular implies a metaphor. The statement that a man is 'obliged' to perform an act means simply that he will suffer pain if he does not perform it. The use of the word obligation, as a noun substantive, introduces the 'fictitious entity' which represents nothing

[1] Works ('Ontology'), viii. 119.   [3] Ibid. viii. 198.
[2] Ibid. viii. 199.   [4] Ibid. viii. 206, 247.

really separable from the pain or pleasure. Here, therefore, we have the ground of the doctrine already noticed. 'Pains and pleasures' are real.[1] 'Their existence,' he says,[2] 'is matter of universal and constant experience.' But other various names referring to these : emotion, inclination, vice, virtue, etc., are only 'psychological entities.' 'Take away pleasures and pains, not only happiness but justice and duty and obligation and virtue —all of which have been so elaborately held up to view as independent of them—are so many empty sounds.'[3] The ultimate facts, then, are pains and pleasures. They are the substantives of which these other words are properly the adjectives. A pain or a pleasure may exist by itself, that is without being virtuous or vicious : but virtue and vice can only exist in so far as pain and pleasure exists.

This analysis of 'obligation' is a characteristic doctrine of the Utilitarian school. We are under an 'obligation' so far as we are affected by a 'sanction.' It appeared to Bentham so obvious as to need no demonstration, only an exposition of the emptiness of any verbal contradiction. Such metaphysical basis as he needed is simply the attempt to express the corresponding conception of reality which, in his opinion, only requires to be expressed to carry conviction.

II. SPRINGS OF ACTION

Our path is now clear. Pains and pleasures give us what mathematicians call the 'independent variable.'

[1] Helvétius adds to this that the only real pains and pleasures are the physical, but Bentham does not follow him here. See Helvétius, Œuvres (1781), ii. 121, etc.   [2] Works, i. 211 ('Springs of Action').   [3] Ibid. i. 206.

Our units are (in Bentham's phrase) 'lots' of pain or pleasure. We have to interpret all the facts in terms of pain or pleasure, and we shall have the materials for what has since been called a 'felicific calculus.' To construct this with a view to legislation is his immediate purpose. The theory will fall into two parts: the 'pathological,' or an account of all the pains and pleasures which are the primary data; and the 'dynamical,' or an account of the various modes of conduct determined by expectations of pain and pleasure. This gives the theory of 'springs of action,' considered in themselves, and of 'motives,' that is, of the springs as influencing conduct.[1] The 'pathology' contains, in the first place, a discussion of the measure of pain and pleasure in general; secondly, a discussion of the various species of pain and pleasure; and thirdly, a discussion of the varying sensibilities of different individuals to pain and pleasure.[2] Thus under the first head, we are told that the value of a pleasure, considered by itself, depends upon its intensity, duration, certainty, and propinquity; and, considered with regard to modes of obtaining it, upon its fecundity (or tendency to produce other pains and pleasures) and its purity (or freedom from admixture of other pains and pleasures). The pain or pleasure is thus regarded as an entity which is capable of being in some sense weighed and measured.[3]

[1] *Works*, i. 205; and Dumont's *Traités* (1820), i. xxv, xxvi. The word 'springs of action' perhaps comes from the marginal note to the above-mentioned passage of Locke (bk. ii. chap. xxvi. § 41, 42).
[2] *Morals and Legislation*, chaps. iv., v., vi.
[3] See 'Codification Proposal' (*Works*, iv. 540), where Bentham takes money as representing pleasure, and shows how the present value may be calculated like that of a sum put out to interest. The same assumption is often made by Political Economists in regard to 'utilities.'

The next step is to classify pains and pleasures, which though commensurable as psychological forces, have obviously very different qualities. Bentham gives the result of his classification without the analysis upon which it depends. He assures us that he has obtained an 'exhaustive' list of 'simple pleasures.' It must be confessed that the list does not commend itself either as exhaustive or as composed of 'simple pleasures.' He does not explain the principle of his analysis because he says, it was of 'too metaphysical a cast,'[1] but he thought it so important that he published it, edited with considerable modifications by James Mill, in 1817, as a *Table of the Springs of Action*.[2]

J. S. Mill remarks that this table should be studied by any one who would understand Bentham's philosophy. Such a study would suggest some unfavourable conclusions. Bentham seems to have made out his table without the slightest reference to any previous psycho-

[1] *Works* ('Morals and Legislation'), i. 17 n.
[2] It is not worth while to consider this at length; but I give the following conjectural account of the list as it appears in the *Morals and Legislation* above. In classifying pain or pleasures, Bentham is, I think, following the clue suggested by his 'sanctions.' He is really classifying according to their causes or the way in which they are 'annexed.' Thus pleasures may or may not be dependent upon other persons, or if upon other persons, may be indirectly or directly caused by their pleasures or pains. Pleasures not caused by persons correspond to the 'physical sanction,' and are those (1) of the 'senses,' (2) of wealth, *i.e.* caused by the possession of things, and (3) of 'skill,' *i.e.* caused by our ability to use things. Pleasures caused by persons indirectly correspond first to the 'popular or moral sanction,' and are pleasures (4) of 'amity,' caused by the goodwill of individuals, and (5) of a 'good name,' caused by the goodwill of people in general; secondly, to 'political sanction,' namely (6) pleasures of 'power'; and thirdly, to the 'religious sanction,' or (7) pleasures of 'piety.' All these are 'self-regarding pleasures.' The pleasures caused directly by the pleasure of others are those (8) of 'benevolence,' and (9) of malevolence. We then have what is really a cross

logist. It is simply constructed to meet the requirements of his legislative theories. As psychology it would be clearly absurd, especially if taken as giving the elementary or 'simple' feelings. No one can suppose, for example, that the pleasures of 'wealth' or 'power' are 'simple' pleasures. The classes therefore are not really distinct, and they are as far from being exhaustive. All that can be said for the list is that it gives a sufficiently long enumeration to call attention from his own point of view to most of the ordinary pleasures and pains; and contains as much psychology as he could really turn to account for his purpose.

The omissions with which his greatest disciple charges him are certainly significant. We find, says Mill, no reference to 'Conscience,' 'Principle,' 'Moral Rectitude,' or 'Moral Duty' among the 'springs of action,' unless among the synonyms of a 'love of reputation,' or in so far as 'Conscience' and 'Principle' are sometimes synonymous with the 'religious' motive or the motive

division by classes of 'derivative' pleasures; these being due to (10) memory, (11) imagination, (12) expectation, (13) association. To each class of pleasures corresponds a class of pains, except that there are no pains corresponding to the pleasures of wealth or power. We have, however, a general class of pains of 'privation,' which might include pains of poverty or weakness: and to these are opposed (14) pleasures of 'relief,' *i.e.* of the privation of pains. In the *Table*, as separately published, Bentham modified this by dividing pleasures of sense into three classes, the last of which includes the two first; by substituting pleasures of 'curiosity' for pleasures of 'skill,' by suppressing pleasures of relief and pains of privation; and by adding, as a class of 'pains' without corresponding pleasures, pains (1) of labour, (2) of 'death, and bodily pains in general.' These changes seem to have been introduced in the course of writing his *Introduction*, where they are partly assumed. Another class is added to include all classes of 'self-regarding pleasures or pains.' He is trying to give a list of all 'synonyms' for various pains and pleasures, and has therefore to admit classes corresponding to general names which include other classes.

of 'sympathy.' So the sense of 'honour,' the love of beauty, and of order, of power (except in the narrow sense of power over our fellows) and of action in general are all omitted. We may conjecture what reply Bentham would have made to this criticism. The omission of the love of beauty and æsthetic pleasures may surprise us when we remember that Bentham loved music, if he cared nothing for poetry. But he apparently regarded these as 'complex pleasures,'[1] and therefore not admissible into his table, if it be understood as an analysis into the simple pleasures alone. The pleasures of action are deliberately omitted, for Bentham pointedly gives the 'pains' of labour as a class without corresponding pleasure; and this, though indicative, I think, of a very serious error, is characteristic rather of his method of analysis than of his real estimate of pleasure. Nobody could have found more pleasure than Bentham in intellectual labour, but he separated the pleasure from the labour. He therefore thought 'labour,' as such, a pure evil, and classified the pleasure as a pleasure of 'curiosity.' But the main criticism is more remarkable. Mill certainly held himself to be a sound Utilitarian; and yet he seems to be condemning Bentham for consistent Utilitarianism. Bentham, by admitting the 'conscience' into his simple springs of action, would have fallen into the very circle from which he was struggling to emerge. If, in fact, the pleasures of conscience are simple pleasures, we have the objectionable 'moral sense' intruded as an ultimate factor of human

[1] *Works*, i. 210, where he speaks of pleasures of the 'ball-room,' the 'theatre,' and the 'fine arts' as derivable from the 'simple and elementary' pleasures.

nature. To get rid of that 'fictitious entity' is precisely Bentham's aim. The moral judgment is to be precisely equivalent to the judgment: 'this or that kind of conduct increases or diminishes the sum of human pains or pleasures.' Once allow that among the pains and pleasures themselves is an ultimate conscience—a faculty not constructed out of independent pains and pleasures—and the system becomes a vicious circle. Conscience on any really Utilitarian scheme must be a derivative, not an ultimate, faculty. If, as Mill seems to say, the omission is a blunder, Bentham's Utilitarianism at least must be an erroneous system.

We have now our list both of pains and pleasures and of the general modes of variation by which their value is to be measured. We must also allow for the varying sensibilities of different persons. Bentham accordingly gives a list of thirty-two 'circumstances influencing sensibility.'[1] Human beings differ in constitution, character, education, sex, race, and so forth, and in their degrees of sensibility to all the various classes of pains and pleasures; the consideration of these varieties is of the highest utility for the purposes of the judge and the legislator.[2] The 'sanctions' will operate differently in different cases. A blow will have different effects upon the sick and upon the healthy; the same fine imposed upon the rich and the poor will cause very different pains; and a law which is beneficent in Europe may be a scourge in America.

We have thus our 'pathology' or theory of the passive sensibilities of man. We know what are the 'springs of action,' how they vary in general, and how they vary

[1] Works ('Morals and Legislation'), i. 22 etc.   [2] Ibid. i. 33.

from one man to another. We can therefore pass to the dynamics.[1] We have described the machinery in rest, and can now consider it in motion. We proceed as before by first considering action in general: which leads to consideration of the 'intention' and the 'motive' implied by any conscious action: and hence of the relation of these to the 'springs of action' as already described. The discussion is minute and elaborate; and Bentham improves as he comes nearer to the actual problems of legislation and further from the ostensible bases of pyschology. The analysis of conduct, and of the sanctions by which conduct is modified, involves a view of morals and of the relations between the spheres of morality and legislation which is of critical importance for the whole Utilitarian creed. 'Moral laws' and a 'Positive law' both affect human action. How do they differ? Bentham's treatment of the problem shows, I think, a clearer appreciation of some difficulties than might be inferred from his later utterances. In any case, it brings into clear relief a moral doctrine which deeply affected his successors.

III. THE SANCTIONS

Let us first take his definitions of the fundamental conceptions. All action of reasonable beings implies the expectation of consequences. The agent's 'intention' is defined by the consequences actually contemplated. The cause of action is the hope of the consequent pleasures or the dread of the consequent

[1] Morals and Legislation, ch. vii. to xi.

pains. This anticipated pleasure or pain constitutes the 'internal motive' (a phrase used by Bentham to exclude the 'external motive' or event which causes the anticipation).[1] The motive, or 'internal motive,' is the anticipation of pain to be avoided or pleasure to be gained. Actions are good or bad simply and solely as they are on the whole 'productive of a balance of pleasure or pain.' The problem of the legislator is how to regulate actions so as to incline the balance to the right side. His weapons are 'sanctions' which modify 'motives.' What motives, then, should be strengthened or checked? Here we must be guided by a principle which is, in fact, the logical result of the doctrines already laid down. We are bound to apply our 'felicific calculus' with absolute impartiality. We must therefore assign equal value to all motives. 'No motives,' he says,[2] are 'constantly good or constantly bad.' Pleasure is itself a good; pain is an evil: nay, they are 'the only good and the only evil.' This is true of every sort of pain and pleasure, even of the pains and pleasures of illwill. The pleasures of 'malevolence' are placed in his 'table' by the side of pleasures of 'benevolence.' Hence it 'follows immediately and incontestably, that there is no such thing as any sort of motive that is in itself a bad one.' The doctrine is no doubt a logical deduction from Bentham's assumptions, and he proceeds to illustrate its meaning. A 'motive' corresponds to one of his 'springs of action.' He shows how every one of the motives included in his table may lead either to good or to bad consequences. The desire of wealth may lead me to kill a man's enemy or to plough his field for him; the

[1] Works ('Morals and Legislation'), i. 46.   [2] Ibid. i. 48.

fear of God may prompt to fanaticism or to charity; ill-will may lead to malicious conduct or may take the form of proper 'resentment,' as, for example, when I secure the punishment of my father's murderer. Though one act, he says, is approved and the other condemned, they spring from the same motive, namely, illwill.[1] He admits, however, that some motives are more likely than others to lead to 'useful' conduct; and thus arranges them in a certain 'order of pre-eminence.'[2] It is obvious that 'goodwill,' 'love of reputation,' and the 'desire of amity' are more likely than others to promote general happiness. 'The dictates of utility,' as he observes, are simply the 'dictates of the most extensive and enlightened (that is, well advised) benevolence.' It would, therefore, seem more appropriate to call the 'motive' good; though no one doubts that when directed by an erroneous judgment it may incidentally be mischievous.

The doctrine that morality depends upon 'consequences' and not upon 'motives' became a characteristic Utilitarian dogma, and I shall have to return to the question. Meanwhile, it was both a natural and, I think, in some senses, a correct view, when strictly confined to the province of legislation. For reasons too obvious to expand, the legislator must often be indifferent to the question of motives. He cannot know with certainty what are a man's motives. He must enforce the law whatever may be the motives for breaking it; and punish rebellion, for example, even if he attributes it to misguided philanthropy. He can, in any case, punish only such crimes as are found out; and must define crimes by

[1] Works ('Morals and Legislation'), i. 56.   [2] Ibid. i. 56.

palpable 'external' marks. He must punish by such coarse means as the gallows and the gaol: for his threats must appeal to the good and the bad alike. He depends, therefore, upon 'external' sanctions, sanctions, that is, which work mainly upon the fears of physical pain; and even if his punishments affect the wicked alone, they clearly cannot reach the wicked as wicked, nor in proportion to their wickedness. That is quite enough to show why in positive law motives are noticed indirectly or not at all. It shows also that the analogy between the positive and the moral law is treacherous. The exclusion of motive justifiable in law may take all meaning out of morality. The Utilitarians, as we shall see, were too much disposed to overlook the difference, and attempt to apply purely legal doctrine in the totally uncongenial sphere of ethical speculation. To accept the legal classification of actions by their external characteristics is, in fact, to beg the question in advance Any outward criterion must group together actions springing from different 'motives' and therefore, as other moralists would say, ethically different.

There is, however, another meaning in this doctrine which is more to the purpose here. Bentham was aiming at a principle which, true or false, is implied in all ethical systems based upon experience instead of pure logic or *a priori* 'intuitions.' Such systems must accept human nature as a fact, and as the basis of a scientific theory. They do not aim at creating angels but at developing the existing constitution of mankind. So far as an action springs from one of the primitive or essential instincts of mankind, it simply proves the agent to be human, not to be vicious or virtuous, and

therefore is no ground for any moral judgment. If Bentham's analysis could be accepted, this would be true of his 'springs of action.' The natural appetites have not in themselves a moral quality: they are simply necessary and original data in the problem. The perplexity is introduced by Bentham's assumption that conduct can be analysed so that the 'motive' is a separate entity which can be regarded as the sole cause of a corresponding action. That involves an irrelevant abstraction. There is no such thing as a single 'motive.' One of his cases is a mother who lets her child die for love of 'ease.' We do not condemn her because she loves ease, which is a motive common to all men and therefore unmoral, not immoral. But neither do we condemn her merely for the bad consequences of a particular action. We condemn her because she loves ease better than she loves her child: that is, because her whole character is 'unnatural' or ill-balanced, not on account of a particular element taken by itself. Morality is concerned with concrete human beings, and not with 'motives' running about by themselves. Bentham's meaning, if we make the necessary correction, would thus be expressed by saying that we don't blame a man because he has the 'natural' passions, but because they are somehow wrongly proportioned or the man himself wrongly constituted. Passions which may make a man vicious may also be essential to the highest virtue. That is quite true; but the passion is not a separate agent, only one constituent of the character.

Bentham admits this in his own fashion. 'If 'motives' cannot be properly called good or bad, is there, he asks, nothing good or bad in the man who on a given occasion

obeys a certain motive? 'Yes, certainly,' he replies, 'his disposition.'[1] The disposition, he adds, is a 'fictitious entity, and designed for the convenience of discourse in order to express what there is supposed to be permanent in a man's frame of mind.' By 'fictitious,' as we have seen, he means not 'unreal' but simply not tangible, weighable, or measurable—like sticks and stones, or like pains and pleasures. 'Fictitious' as they may be, therefore, the fiction enables us to express real truths, and to state facts which are of the highest importance to the moralist and the legislator. Bentham discusses some cases of casuistry in order to show the relation between the tendency of an action and the intention and motives of the agent. Ravaillac murders a good king; Ravaillac's son enables his father to escape punishment, or conveys poison to his father to enable him to avoid torture by suicide.[2] What is the inference as to the son's disposition in either case? The solution (as he substantially and, I think, rightly suggests) will have to be reached by considering whether the facts indicate that the son's disposition was mischievous or otherwise; whether it indicates political disloyalty or filial affection, and so forth, and in what proportions. The most interesting case perhaps is that of religious persecution, where the religious motive is taken to be good, and the action to which it leads is yet admitted to be mischievous. The problem is often puzzling, but we are virtually making an inference as to the goodness or badness of the 'disposition' implied by the given action under all the supposed circumstances. This gives what Bentham calls the 'meritoriousness'[3] of the disposition. The 'intention' is

caused by the 'motive.' The 'disposition' is the 'sum of the intentions'; that is to say, it expresses the agent's sensibility to various classes of motives; and the merit therefore will be in proportion to the total goodness or badness of the disposition thus indicated. The question of merit leads to interesting moral problems. Bentham, however, observes that he is not here speaking from the point of view of the moralist but of the legislator. Still, as a legislator he has to consider what is the 'depravity' of disposition indicated by different kinds of conduct. This consideration is of great importance. The 'disposition' includes sensibility to what he calls 'tutelary motives'— motives, that is, which deter a man from such conduct as generally produces mischievous consequences. No motive can be invariably, though some, especially the motive of goodwill, and in a minor degree those of 'amity' and a 'love of reputation,' are generally, on the right side. The legislator has to reinforce these 'tutelary motives' by 'artificial tutelary motives,' and mainly by appealing to the 'love of ease,' that is, by making mischievous conduct more difficult, and to 'self-preservation,' that is, by making it more dangerous.[1] He has therefore to measure the force by which these motives will be opposed; or, in other words, the 'strength of the temptation.' Now the more depraved a man's disposition, the weaker the temptation which will seduce him to crime. Consequently if an act shows depravity, it will require a stronger counter-motive or a more severe punishment, as the disposition indicated is more mischievous. An act, for example, which implies deliberation proves a greater insensibility to these social

[1] *Works* ('Morals and Legislation'), i. 60.   [2] *Ibid.* i. 62.   [3] *Ibid.* i. 65.

[1] These are the two classes of 'springs of action' omitted in the *Table*.

motives which, as Bentham remarks,[1] determine the 'general tenor of a man's life,' however depraved he may be. The legislator is guided solely by 'utility,' or aims at maximising happiness without reference to its quality. Still, so far as action implies disposition, he has to consider the depravity as a source of mischief. The legislator who looks solely at the moral quality implied is wrong ; and, if guided solely by his sympathies, has no measure for the amount of punishment to be inflicted. These considerations will enable us to see what is the proper measure of resentment.[2]

The doctrine of the neutrality or 'unmorality' of motive is thus sufficiently clear. Bentham's whole aim is to urge that the criterion of morality is given by the consequences of actions. To say the conduct is good or bad is to say in other words that it produces a balance of pleasure or pain. To make the criterion independent, or escape the vicious circle, we must admit the pleasures and pains to be in themselves neutral ; to have, that is, the same value, if equally strong, whatever their source. In our final balance-sheet we must set down pains of ill-will and of goodwill, of sense and of intellect with absolute impartiality, and compare them simply in respect

of intensity. We must not admit a 'conscience' or 'moral sense' which would be autocratic ; nor, indeed, allow moral to have any meaning as applied to the separate passions. But it is quite consistent with this to admit that some motives, goodwill in particular, generally tend to bring out the desirable result, that is, a balance of pleasure for the greatest number. The pains and pleasures are the ultimate facts, and the 'disposition' is a 'fictitious entity' or a name for the sum of sensibilities. It represents the fact that some men are more inclined than others to increase the total of good or bad.

IV. CRIMINAL LAW

We have now, after a long analysis, reached the point at which the principles can be applied to penal law. The legislator has to discourage certain classes of conduct by annexing 'tutelary motives.' The classes to be suppressed are of course those which diminish happiness. Pursuing the same method, and applying results already reached, we must in the first place consider how the 'mischief of an act' is to be measured.[1] Acts are mischievous as their 'consequences' are mischievous ; and the consequences may be 'primary' or 'secondary.' Robbery causes pain to the loser of the money. That is a primary evil. It alarms the holders of money ; it suggests the facility of robbery to others ; and it weakens the 'tutelary motive' of respect for property. These are secondary evils. The 'secondary' evil may be at times the most important. The non-payment of a tax may do no

---

[1] *Works* ('Morals and Legislation '), i. 68.
[2] Here Bentham lays down the rule that punishment should rise with the strength of the temptation, a theory which leads to some curious casuistical problems. He does not fully discuss, and I cannot here consider, them. I will only note that it may conceivably be necessary to increase the severity of punishment, instead of removing the temptation or strengthening the preventive action. If so, the law becomes immoral in the sense of punishing more severely as the crime has more moral excuse. This was often true of the old criminal law, which punished offences cruelly because it had no effective system of police. Bentham would of course have agreed that the principle in this case was a bad one.

[1] *Morals and Legislation*, ch. xii.

---

appreciable harm in a particular case. But its secondary effects in injuring the whole political fabric may be disastrous and fruitful beyond calculation. Bentham proceeds to show carefully how the 'intentions' and 'motives' of the evil-doer are of the greatest importance, especially in determining these secondary consequences, and must therefore be taken into account by the legislator. A homicide may cause the same primary evil, whether accidental or malignant ; but accidental homicide may cause no alarm, whereas the intentional and malignant homicide may cause any quantity of alarm and shock to the general sense of security. In this way, therefore, the legislator has again indirectly to take into account the moral quality which is itself dependent upon utility.

I must, however, pass lightly over a very clear and interesting discussion to reach a further point of primary importance to the Utilitarian theory, as to the distinction between the moral and legal spheres.[1] Bentham has now 'made an analysis of evil.' He has, that is, classified the mischiefs produced by conduct, measured simply by their effect upon pleasures or pains, independently of any consideration as to virtue and vice. The next problem is : what conduct should be criminal ?—a subject which is virtually discussed in two chapters (xv. and xix.) 'on cases unmeet for punishment' and on 'the limits between Private Ethics and the act of legislation.' We must, of course, follow the one clue to the labyrinth. We must count all the 'lots' of pain and pleasure indifferently. It is clear, on the one hand, that the pains suffered by criminals are far less than the pains which would be

suffered were no such sanctions applied. On the other hand, all punishment is an evil, because punishment means pain, and it is therefore only to be inflicted when it excludes greater pain. It must, therefore, not be inflicted when it is 'groundless,' 'inefficacious,' 'unprofitable,' or 'needless.' 'Needless' includes all the cases in which the end may be attained 'as effectually at a cheaper rate.'[1] This applies to all 'dissemination of pernicious principles'; for in this case reason and not force is the appropriate remedy. The sword inflicts more pain, and is less efficient than the pen. The argument raises the wider question, What are the true limits of legislative interference? Bentham, in his last chapter, endeavours to answer this problem. 'Private ethics,' he says, and 'legislation' aim at the same end, namely, happiness, and the 'acts with which they are conversant are *in great measure* the same.' Why, then, should they have different spheres? Simply because the acts 'are not *perfectly and throughout* the same.'[2] How, then, are we to draw the line? By following the invariable clue of 'utility.' We simply have to apply an analysis to determine the cases in which punishment does more harm than good. He insists especially upon the cases in which punishment is 'unprofitable'; upon such offences as drunkenness and sexual immorality, where the law could only be enforced by a mischievous or impossible system of minute supervision, and such offences as ingratitude or rudeness, where the definition is so vague that the judge could not safely be entrusted with the power to punish.'[3] He endeavours to give a rather more precise distinction by

---

[1] *Morals and Legislation*, ch. xiv. (a chapter inserted from Dumont's *Traités*).

[1] *Works* ('Morals and Legislation '), i. p. 86.   [2] *Ibid.* i. 144.
[3] *Ibid.* i. 145.

sub-dividing 'ethics in general' into three classes. Duty may be to oneself, that is 'prudence'; or to one's neighbour negatively, that is 'probity'; or to one's neighbour positively, that is 'benevolence.'[1] Duties of the first class must be left chiefly to the individual, because he is the best judge of his own interest. Duties of the third class again are generally too vague to be enforced by the legislator, though a man ought perhaps to be punished for failing to help as well as for actually injuring. The second department of ethics, that of 'probity,' is the main field for legislative activity.[2] As a general principle, 'private ethics' teach a man how to pursue his own happiness, and the art of legislation how to pursue the greatest happiness of the community. It must be noticed, for the point is one of importance, that Bentham's purely empirical method draws no definite line. It implies that no definite line can be drawn. It does not suggest that any kind of conduct whatever is outside the proper province of legislator except in so far as the legislative machinery may happen to be inadequate or inappropriate.

Our analysis has now been carried so far that we can proceed to consider the principles by which we should be guided in punishing. What are the desirable properties of a 'lot of punishment'? This occupies two interesting chapters. Chapter xvi., 'on the proportion between punishments and offences,' gives twelve rules. The punishment, he urges, must outweigh the profit of the offence; it must be such as to make a man prefer a less offence to a greater—simple theft, for example, to violent robbery; it must be such that the punishment must be

---

[1] *Works* ('Morals and Legislation'), i. 143.   [2] *Ibid.* i. 147-48.

adaptable to the varying sensibility of the offender; it must be greater in 'value' as it falls short of certainty; and, when the offence indicates a habit, it must outweigh not only the profit of the particular offence, but of the undetected offences. In chapter xvii. Bentham considers the properties which fit a punishment to fulfil these conditions. Eleven properties are given. The punishment must be (1) 'variable,' that is, capable of adjustment to particular cases; and (2) equable, or inflicting equal pain by equal sentences. Thus the 'proportion' between punishment and crimes of a given class can be secured. In order that the punishments of different classes of crime may be proportional, the punishments should (3) be commensurable. To make punishments efficacious they should be (4) 'characteristical' or impressive to the imagination; and that they may not be excessive they should be (5) exemplary or likely to impress others, and (6) frugal. To secure minor ends they should be (7) reformatory; (8) disabling, *i.e.* from future offences; and (9) compensatory to the sufferer. Finally, to avoid collateral disadvantages they should be (10) popular, and (11) remittable. A twelfth property, simplicity, was added in Dumont's redaction. Dumont calls attention here to the value of Bentham's method.[1] Montesquieu and Beccaria had spoken in general terms of the desirable qualities of punishment. They had spoken of 'proportionality,' for example, but without that precise or definite meaning which appears in Bentham's Calculus. In fact, Bentham's statement, compared to the vaguer utterances of his predecessors, but still more when compared to the haphazard brutalities and inconsistencies of

---

[1] *Works* ('Morals and Legislation'), i. 406 *n.*

English criminal law, gives the best impression of the value of his method.

Bentham's next step is an elaborate classification of offences, worked out by a further application of his bifurcatory method.[1] This would form the groundwork of the projected code. I cannot, however, speak of this classification, or of many interesting remarks contained in the *Principles of Penal Law*, where some further details are considered. An analysis scarcely does justice to Bentham, for it has to omit his illustrations and his flashes of real vivacity. The mere dry logical framework is not appetising. I have gone so far in order to illustrate the characteristic of Bentham's teaching. It was not the bare appeal to utility, but the attempt to follow the clue of utility systematically and unflinchingly into every part of the subject. This one doctrine gives the touchstone by which every proposed measure is to be tested; and which will give to his system not such unity as arises from the development of an abstract logical principle, but such as is introduced into the physical sciences when we are able to range all the indefinitely complex phenomena which arise under some simple law of force. If Bentham's aim could have been achieved, 'utility' would have been in legislative theories what gravitation is in astronomical theories. All human conduct being ruled by pain and pleasure, we could compare all motives and actions, and trace out the consequences of any given law. I shall have hereafter to consider how this conception worked in different minds and was applied to different problems: what were the tenable results to which it led, and what

---

[1] *Works* ('Morals and Legislation,') i. 96 *n.*

were the errors caused by the implied oversight of some essential considerations.

Certain weaknesses are almost too obvious to be specified. He claimed to be constructing a science, comparable to the physical sciences. The attempt was obviously chimerical if we are to take it seriously. The makeshift doctrine which he substitutes for psychology would be a sufficient proof of the incapacity for his task. He had probably not read such writers as Hartley or Condillac, who might have suggested some ostensibly systematic theory. If he had little psychology he had not even a conception of 'sociology.' The 'felicific calculus' is enough to show the inadequacy of his method. The purpose is to enable us to calculate the effects of a proposed law. You propose to send robbers to the gallows or the gaol. You must, says Bentham, reckon up all the evils prevented: the suffering to the robbed, and to those who expect to be robbed, on the one hand; and, on the other, the evils caused, the suffering to the robber, and to the tax-payer who keeps the constable; then strike your balance and make your law if the evils prevented exceed the evils caused. Some such calculation is demanded by plain common sense. It points to the line of inquiry desirable. But can it be adequate? To estimate the utility of a law we must take into account all its 'effects.' What are the 'effects' of a law against robbery? They are all that is implied in the security of property. They correspond to the difference between England in the eighteenth century and England in the time of Hengist and Horsa; between a country where the supremacy of law is established, and a country still under the rule of the strong hand. Bentham's method may be applicable at a given moment, when the social structure is already consolidated and uniform. It would represent the practical arguments for establishing the police-force demanded by Colquhoun, and show the disadvantages of the old constables and watchmen. Bentham, that is, gives an admirable method for settling details of administrative and legislative machinery, and dealing with particular cases when once the main principles of law and order are established. Those principles, too, may depend upon 'utility,' but utility must be taken in a wider sense when we have to deal with the fundamental questions. We must consider the 'utility' of the whole organisation, not the fitness of separate details. Finally, if Bentham is weak in psychology and in sociology, he is clearly not satisfactory in ethics. Morality is, according to him, on the same plane with law. The difference is not in the sphere to which they apply, or in the end to which they are directed; but solely in the 'sanction.' The legislator uses threats of physical suffering; the moralist threats of 'popular' disapproval. Either 'sanction' may be most applicable to a given case; but the question is merely between different means to the same end under varying conditions. This implies the 'external' character of Bentham's morality, and explains his insistence upon the neutrality of motives. He takes the average man to be a compound of certain instincts, and merely seeks to regulate their action by supplying 'artificial tutelary motives.' The 'man' is given; the play of his instincts, separately neutral, makes his conduct more or less favourable to general happiness; and the moralist and the legislator have both to correct

his deviations by supplying appropriate 'sanctions.' Bentham, therefore, is inclined to ignore the intrinsic character of morality, or the dependence of a man's morality upon the essential structure of his nature. He thinks of the superficial play of forces, not of their intimate constitution. The man is not to be changed in either case; only his circumstances. Such defects no doubt diminish the value of Bentham's work. Yet, after all, in his own sphere they are trifles. He did very well without philosophy. However imperfect his system might be considered as a science or an ultimate explanation of society and human nature, it was very much to the point as an expression of downright common-sense. Dumont's eulogy seems to be fully deserved, when we contrast Bentham's theory of punishment with the theories (if they deserve the name) of contemporary legislators. His method involved a thoroughgoing examination of the whole body of laws, and a resolution to apply a searching test to every law. If that test was not so unequivocal or ultimate as he fancied, it yet implied the constant application of such considerations as must always carry weight, and, perhaps, be always the dominant considerations, with the actual legislator or jurist. What is the use of you? is a question which may fairly be put to every institution and to every law; and it concerns legislators to find some answer, even though the meaning of the word 'use' is not so clear as we could wish.

V. ENGLISH LAW

The practical value of Bentham's method is perhaps best illustrated by his *Rationale of Evidence*. The composition of the papers ultimately put together by

J. S. Mill had occupied Bentham from 1802 to 1812. The changed style is significant. Nobody could write more pointedly, or with happier illustrations, than Bentham in his earlier years. He afterwards came to think that a didactic treatise should sacrifice every other virtue to fulness and precision. To make a sentence precise, every qualifying clause must be somehow forced into the original formula. Still more characteristic is his application of what he calls the 'substantive-preferring principle.'[1] He would rather say, 'I give extension to an object,' than 'I extend an object.' Where a substantive is employed, the idea is 'stationed upon a rock'; if only a verb, the idea is 'like a leaf floating on a stream.' A verb, he said,[2] 'slips through your fingers like an eel.' The principle corresponds to his 'metaphysics.' The universe of thought is made up of a number of separate 'entities' corresponding to nouns-substantive, and when these bundles are distinctly isolated by appropriate nouns, the process of arranging and codifying according to the simple relations indicated by the copula is greatly facilitated. The ideal language would resemble algebra, in which symbols, each representing a given numerical value, are connected by the smallest possible number of symbols of operation, +, −, =, and so forth. To set two such statements side by side, or to modify them by inserting different constants, is then a comparatively easy process, capable of being regulated by simple general rules. Bentham's style becomes tiresome, and was often improperly called obscure. It requires attention, but the meaning is never

[1] *Works*, iii. 267.   [2] *Ibid*. x. 569

doubtful—and to the end we have frequent flashes of the old vivacity.

The *Rationale of Evidence*, as Mill remarks,[1] is 'one of the richest in matter of all Bentham's productions.' It contains, too, many passages in Bentham's earlier style, judiciously preserved by his young editor; indeed, so many that I am tempted even to call the book amusing. In spite of the wearisome effort to say everything, and to force language into the mould presented by his theory, Bentham attracts us by his obvious sincerity. The arguments may be unsatisfactory, but they are genuine arguments. They represent conviction; they are given because they have convinced; and no reader can deny that they really tend to convince. We may complain that there are too many words, and that the sentences are cumbrous; but the substance is always to the point. The main purpose may be very briefly indicated. Bentham begins by general considerations upon evidence, in which he and his youthful editor indicate their general adherence to the doctrines of Hume.[2] This leads to an application of the methods expounded in the 'Introduction,' in order to show how the various motives or 'springs of action' and the 'sanctions' based upon them may affect the trustworthiness of evidence. Any motive whatever may incidentally cause 'mendacity.' The second book, therefore, considers what securities may be taken for 'securing trustworthiness.' We have, for example, a discussion of the value of oaths (he thinks them valueless), of the advantages and disadvantages of re-

[1] *Autobiography*, p. 116.
[2] The subject is again treated in Book v. on 'Circumstantial Evidence.'

ducing evidence to writing, of interrogating witnesses, and of the publicity or privacy of evidence. Book iii. deals with the 'extraction of evidence.' We have to compare the relative advantages of oral and written evidence, the rules for cross-examining witnesses and for taking evidence as to their character. Book iv. deals with 'pre-appointed evidence,' the cases, that is, in which events are recorded at the time of occurrence with a view to their subsequent use as evidence. We have under this head to consider the formalities which should be required in regard to contracts and wills ; and the mode of recording judicial and other official decisions and registering births, deaths, and marriages. In Books v. and vi. we consider two kinds of evidence which is in one way or other of inferior cogency, namely, 'circumstantial evidence,' in which the evidence if accepted still leaves room for a process of more or less doubtful inference ; and 'makeshift evidence,' such evidence as must sometimes be accepted for want of the best, of which the most conspicuous instance is 'hearsay evidence.' Book vii. deals with the 'authentication' of evidence. Book viii. is a consideration of the 'technical' system, that namely which was accepted by English lawyers ; and finally Book ix. deals with a special point, namely, the exclusion of evidence. Bentham announces at starting[1] that he shall establish 'one theorem' and consider two problems. The problems are : 'what securities can be taken for the truth of evidence?' and 'what rules can be given for estimating the value of evidence?' The 'theorem' is that no evidence should be excluded with the pro-

[1] *Works*, vi. 204.

fessed intention of obtaining a right decision ; though some must be excluded to avoid expense, vexation, and delay. This, therefore, as his most distinct moral, is fully treated in the last book.

Had Bentham confined himself to a pithy statement of his leading doctrines, and confirmed them by a few typical cases, he would have been more effective in a literary sense. His passion for 'codification,' for tabulating and arranging facts in all their complexity, and for applying his doctrine at full length to every case that he can imagine, makes him terribly prolix. On the other hand, this process no doubt strengthened his own conviction and the conviction of his disciples as to the value of his process. Follow this clue of utility throughout the whole labyrinth, see what a clear answer it offers at every point, and you cannot doubt that you are in possession of the true compass for such a navigation. Indeed, it seems to be indisputable that Bentham's arguments are the really relevant and important arguments. How can we decide any of the points which come up for discussion? Should a witness be cross-examined? Should his evidence be recorded? Should a wife be allowed to give evidence against her husband? or the defendant to give evidence about his own case? These and innumerable other points can only be decided by reference to what Bentham understood by 'utility.' This or that arrangement is 'useful' because it enables us to get quickly and easily at the evidence, to take effective securities for its truthfulness, to estimate its relevance and importance, to leave the decision to the most qualified persons, and so forth. These points, again, can only be decided by a careful appeal to experi-

ence, and by endeavouring to understand the ordinary play of 'motives' and 'sanctions.' What generally makes a man lie, and how is lying to be made unpleasant? By rigorously fixing our minds at every point on such issues, we find that many questions admit of very plain answers, and are surprised to discover what a mass of obscurity has been dispelled. It is, however, true that although the value of the method can hardly be denied unless we deny the value of all experience and common sense, we may dispute the degree in which it confirms the general principle. Every step seems to Bentham to reflect additional light upon his primary axiom. Yet it is possible to hold that witnesses should be encouraged to speak the truth, and that experience may help us to discover the best means to that end without, therefore, admitting the unique validity of the 'greatest happiness' principle. That principle, so far as true, may be itself a deduction from some higher principle ; and no philosopher of any school would deny that 'utility' should be in some way consulted by the legislator.

The book illustrates the next critical point in Bentham's system—the transition from law to politics. He was writing the book at the period when the failure of the Panopticon was calling his attention to the wickedness of George iii. and Lord Eldon, and when the English demand for parliamentary reform was reviving and supplying him with a sympathetic audience. Now, in examining the theory of evidence upon the plan described, Bentham found himself at every stage in conflict with the existing system, or rather the existing chaos of unintelligible rules. English lawyers, he discovered, had worked out a system of rules for excluding evidence.

Sometimes the cause was pure indolence. 'This man, were I to hear him,' says the English judge, 'would come out with a parcel of lies. It would be a plague to hear him : I have heard enough already ; shut the door in his face.'[1] But, as Bentham shows with elaborate detail, a reason for suspecting evidence is not a reason for excluding it. A convicted perjurer gives evidence, and has a pecuniary interest in the result. That is excellent ground for caution ; but the fact that the man makes a certain statement may still be a help to the ascertainment of truth. Why should that help be rejected? Bentham scarcely admits of any exception to the general rule of taking any evidence you can get—one exception being the rather curious one of confession to a Catholic priest ; secrecy in such cases is on the whole, he thinks, useful. He exposes the confusion implied in an exclusion of evidence because it is not fully trustworthy, which is equivalent to working in the dark because a partial light may deceive. But this is only a part of a whole system of arbitrary, inconsistent, and technical rules worked out by the ingenuity of lawyers. Besides the direct injury they gave endless opportunity for skilful manœuvring to exclude or admit evidence by adopting different forms of procedure. Rules had been made by judges as they were wanted and precedents established of contradictory tendency and uncertain application. Bentham contrasts the simplicity of the rules deducible from 'utility' with the amazing complexity of the traditional code of technical rules. Under the 'natural' system, that of utility, you have to deal with a quarrel between your servants or children. You

[1] *Works*, vii. 391.

send at once for the disputants, confront them, take any relevant evidence, and make up your mind as to the rights of the dispute. In certain cases this 'natural' procedure has been retained, as, for example, in courts-martial, where rapid decision was necessary. Had the technical system prevailed, the country would have been ruined in six weeks.[1] But the exposure of the technical system requires an elaborate display of intricate methods involving at every step vexation, delay, and injustice. Bentham reckons up nineteen separate devices employed by the courts. He describes the elaborate processes which had to be gone through before a hearing could be obtained ; the distance of courts from the litigants ; the bandying of cases from court to court ; the chicaneries about giving notice ; the frequent nullification of all that had been done on account of some technical flaw ; the unintelligible jargon of Latin and Law-French which veiled the proceedings from the public ; the elaborate mysteries of 'special pleading' ; the conflict of jurisdictions, and the manufacture of new 'pleas' and new technical rules ; the 'entanglement of jurisdictions,' and especially the distinction between law and equity, which had made confusion doubly confounded. English law had become a mere jungle of unintelligible distinctions, contradictions, and cumbrous methods through which no man could find his way without the guidance of the initiated, and in which a long purse and unscrupulous trickery gave the advantage over the poor to the rich, and to the knave over the honest man. One fruitful source of all these evils was the 'judge-made' law, which Bentham henceforth never ceased to denounce. His

[1] *Works*, vii. 321-25. Court-martials are hardly a happy example now.

ideal was a distinct code which, when change was required, should be changed by an avowed and intelligible process. The chaos which had grown up was the natural result of the gradual development of a traditional body of law, in which new cases were met under cover of applying precedents from previous decisions, with the help of reference to the vague body of unwritten or 'common law,' and of legal fictions permitting some non-natural interpretation of the old formulæ. It is the judges, he had already said in 1792,[1] 'that make the common law. Do you know how they make it ? Just as a man makes laws for his dog. When your dog does anything you want to break him of, you wait till he does it and then beat him. This is the way you make laws for your dog, and this is the way the judges make laws for you and me.' The 'tyranny of judge-made law' is 'the most all-comprehensive, most grinding, and most crying of all grievances,'[2] and is scarcely less bad than 'priest-made religion.'[3] Legal fictions, according to him, are simply lies. The permission to use them is a 'mendacity licence.' In 'Rome-bred law . . . fiction' is a 'wart which here and there disfigures the face of justice. In English law fiction is a syphilis which runs into every vein and carries into every part of the system the principle of rottenness.'[4]

The evils denounced by Bentham were monstrous. The completeness of the exposure was his great merit ; and his reputation has suffered, as we are told on competent authority, by the very efficiency of his attack. The worst evils are so much things of the past, that we

[1] 'Truth *v*. Ashhurst' (1792), *Works*, v. 235.
[2] *Works* ('Codification Petition '), v. 442   [3] *Ibid*. vi. 11.   [4] *Ibid*. v. 92.

forget the extent of the evil and the merits of its assailant. Bentham's diagnosis of the evil explains his later attitude. He attributes all the abuses to consciously corrupt motives even where a sufficient explanation can be found in the human stupidity and honest incapacity to look outside of traditional ways of thought. He admits, indeed, the personal purity of English judges. No English judge had ever received a bribe within living memory.[1] But this, he urges, is only because the judges find it more profitable as well as safer to carry out a radically corrupt system. A synonym for 'technical' is 'fee-gathering.' Lawyers of all classes had a common interest in multiplying suits and complicating procedure : and thus a tacit partnership had grown up which he describes as 'Judge and Co.' He gives statistics showing that in the year 1797 five hundred and forty-three out of five hundred and fifty 'writs of error' were 'shams,' or simply vexatious contrivances for delay, and brought a profit to the Chief Justice of over £1400.[2] Lord Eldon was always before him as the typical representative of obstruction and obscurantism. In his *Indications respecting Lord Eldon* (1825) he goes into details which it must have required some courage to publish. Under Eldon, he says, 'equity has become an instrument of fraud and extortion.'[3] He details the proceedings by which Eldon obtained the sanction of parliament for a system of fee-taking, which he had admitted to be illegal, and which had been denounced by an eminent solicitor as leading to gross corruption. Bentham intimates that the Masters in Chancery were 'swindlers,'[4] and that Eldon was

[1] *Works*, vii. 204, 331 ; ix. 143.   [2] *Ibid*. vii. 214.
[3] *Ibid*. v. 349.   [4] *Ibid* v. 364.

knowingly the protector and sharer of their profits. Romilly, who had called the Court of Chancery 'a disgrace to a civilised nation,' had said that Eldon was the cause of many of the abuses, and could have reformed most of the others. Erskine had declared that if there was a hell, the Court of Chancery was hell.[1] Eldon, as Bentham himself thought, was worse than Jeffreys. Eldon's victims had died a lingering death, and the persecutor had made money out of their sufferings. Jeffreys was openly brutal ; while Eldon covered his tyranny under the 'most accomplished indifference.'[2]

Yet Eldon was but the head of a band. Judges, barristers, and solicitors were alike. The most hopeless of reforms would be to raise a 'thorough-paced English lawyer' to the moral level of an average man.[3] To attack legal abuses was to attack a class combined under its chiefs, capable of hoodwinking parliament and suppressing open criticism. The slave-traders whom Wilberforce attacked were comparatively a powerless excrescence. The legal profession was in the closest relations to the monarchy, the aristocracy, and the whole privileged and wealthy class. They were welded into a solid 'ring.' The king, and his ministers who distributed places and pensions ; the borough-mongers who sold votes for power ; the clergy who looked for bishoprics ; the monied men who aspired to rank and power, were all parts of a league. It was easy enough to talk of law reform. Romilly had proposed and even carried a 'reformatiuncle' or two ;[4] but to achieve a serious success required not victory in a skirmish or two, not the exposure of some abuse too palpable to be openly

[1] *Works*, v. 37'   [2] *Ibid*. v. 375.   [3] *Ibid*. vii. 188.   [4] *Ibid*. v. 370.

defended even by an Eldon, but a prolonged war against an organised army fortified and entrenched in the very heart of the country.

VI. RADICALISM

Thus Bentham, as his eyes were opened, became a Radical. The political purpose became dominant, although we always see that the legal abuses are uppermost in his mind ; and that what he really seeks is a fulcrum for the machinery which is to overthrow Lord Eldon. Some of the pamphlets deal directly with the special instruments of corruption. The *Elements of the Art of Packing* shows how the crown managed to have a permanent body of special 'jurors' at its disposal. The 'grand and paramount use'[1] of this system was to crush the liberty of the press. The obscure law of libel, worked by judges in the interest of the government, enabled them to punish any rash Radical for 'hurting the feelings' of the ruling classes, and to evade responsibility by help of a 'covertly pensioned' and servile jury. The pamphlet, though tiresomely minute and long-winded, contained too much pointed truth to be published at the time. The *Official Aptitude minimised* contains a series of attacks upon the system of patronage and pensions by which the machinery of government was practically worked. In the *Catechism* of reformers, written in 1809, Bentham began the direct application of his theories to the constitution; and the final and most elaborate exposition of these forms the *Constitutional Code*, which was the main work of his later years. This

[1] *Works*, v. 97, etc.

book excited the warmest admiration of Bentham's disciples.[1] J. S. Mill speaks of its 'extraordinary power . . . of at once seizing comprehensive principles and scheming out minute details,' and of its 'surpassing intellectual vigour.' Nor, indeed, will any one be disposed to deny that it is a singular proof of intellectual activity, when we remember that it was begun when the author was over seventy, and that he was still working at eighty-four.[2] In this book Bentham's peculiarities of style reach their highest development, and it cannot be recommended as light reading. Had Bentham been a mystical philosopher, he would, we may conjecture, have achieved a masterpiece of unintelligibility which all his followers would have extolled as containing the very essence of his teaching. His method condemned him to be always intelligible, however crabbed and elaborate. Perhaps, however, the point which strikes one most is the amazing simple-mindedness of the whole proceeding. Bentham's light-hearted indifference to the distinction between paper constitutions and operative rules of conduct becomes almost pathetic.

Bentham was clearly the victim of a common delusion. If a system will work, the minutest details can be exhibited. Therefore, it is inferred, an exhibition of minute detail proves that it will work. Unfortunately, the philosophers of Laputa would have had no more difficulty in filling up details than the legislators of England or the United States. When Bentham had settled in his 'Radical

[1] See preface to *Constitutional Code* in vol. ix.
[2] Bentham's nephew, George, who died when approaching his eighty-fourth birthday, devoted the last twenty-five years of his life with equal assiduity to his *Genera Plantarum*. See a curious anecdote of his persistence in the *Dictionary of National Biography*.

Reform Bill'[1] that the 'voting-box' was to be a double cube of cast-iron, with a slit in the lid, into which cards two inches by one, white on one side and black on the other, could be inserted, he must have felt that he had got very near to actual application : he can picture the whole operation and nobody can say that the scheme is impracticable for want of working plans of the machinery. There will, doubtless, be no difficulty in settling the shape of the boxes, when we have once agreed to have the ballot. But a discussion of such remote details of Utopia is of incomparably less real interest than the discussion in the *Rationale of Evidence* of points, which, however minute, were occurring every day, and which were really in urgent need of the light of common-sense.

Bentham's general principles may be very simply stated. They are, in fact, such as were suggested by his view of legal grievances. Why, when he had demonstrated that certain measures would contribute to the 'greatest happiness of the greatest number,' were they not at once adopted? Because the rulers did not desire the greatest happiness of the greatest number. This, in Bentham's language, is to say that they were governed by a 'sinister interest.' Their interest was that of their class, not that of the nation ; they aimed at the greatest happiness of some, not at the greatest happiness of all. A generalisation of this remark gives us the first axioms of all government. There are two primary principles : the 'self-preference' principle, in virtue of which every man always desires his own greatest happiness'; and the 'greatest happiness' principle, in virtue of which 'the right and proper end' of government is the 'greatest happiness of

[1] *Works*, iii. 573.

the greatest number.'[1] The 'actual end' of every government, again, is the greatest happiness of the governors. Hence the whole problem is to produce a coincidence of the two ends, by securing an identity of interest between governors and governed. To secure that we have only to identify the two classes or to put the government in the hands of all.[2] In a monarchy, the ruler aims at the interest of one—himself ; in a 'limited monarchy' the aim is at the happiness of the king and the small privileged class ; in a democracy, the end is the right one—the greatest happiness of the greatest number. This is a short cut to all constitutional questions. Probably it has occurred in substance to most youthful members of debating societies. Bentham's confidence in his logic lifts him above any appeal to experience ; and he occasionally reminds us of the proof given in *Martin Chuzzlewit* that the queen must live in the Tower of London. The 'monarch,' as he observes,[3] 'is naturally the very worst—the most maleficent member of the whole community.' Wherever an aristocracy differs from the democracy, their judgment will be erroneous.[4] The people will naturally choose 'morally apt agents,' and men who wish to be chosen will desire truly to become 'morally apt,' for they can only recommend themselves by showing their desire to serve the general interest.[5] 'All experience testifies to this theory,' though the evidence is 'too bulky' to be given. Other proofs,

[1] *Works*, ix. 5, 8.
[2] The theory, as Mill reminds us, had been very pointedly anticipated by Helvétius. Bentham's practical experience, however, had forced it upon his attention.
[3] *Works*, ix. 141. The general principle, however, is confirmed by the case of George III.   [4] *Ibid*. ix. 45.   [5] *Ibid*. ix. 98.

however, may at once be rendered superfluous by appealing to 'the uninterrupted and most notorious experience of the United States.'[1] To that happy country he often appeals indeed[2] as a model government. In it, there is no corruption, no useless expenditure, none of the evils illustrated by our 'matchless constitution.'

The constitution deduced from these principles has at least the merit of simplicity. We are to have universal suffrage, annual parliaments, and vote by ballot. He inclines to give a vote to women.[3] There is to be no king, no house of peers, no established church. Members of parliament are not to be re-eligible, till after an interval. Elaborate rules provide for their regular attendance and exclusive devotion to their masters' business. They are to be simply 'deputies,' not 'representatives.' They elect a prime minister who holds office for four years. Officials are to be appointed by a complex plan of competitive examination ; and they are to be invited to send in tenders for doing the work at diminished salary. When once in office, every care is taken for their continual inspection by the public and the verification of their accounts. They are never for an instant to forget that they are servants, not the masters, of the public.

Bentham, of course, is especially minute and careful in regard to the judicial organisation—a subject upon which he wrote much, and much to the purpose. The functions and fees of advocates are to be narrowly restricted, and advocates to be provided gratuitously for the poor. They are not to become judges : to make a barrister a judge is as sensible as it would be to select

_____
[1] *Works,* ix. 98.   [2] *Ibid.* ix. 38, 50, 63, 99, etc.
[3] *Ibid.* ('Plan of Parliamentary Reform,') iii. 463.

a procuress for mistress of a girls' school.[1] Judges should be everywhere accessible : always on duty, too busy to have time for corruption, and always under public supervision. One characteristic device is his quasi-jury. The English system of requiring unanimity was equivalent to enforcing perjury by torture. Its utility as a means of resisting tyranny would disappear when tyranny had become impossible. But public opinion might be usefully represented by a 'quasi-jury' of three or five, who should not pronounce a verdict, but watch the judge, interrogate, if necessary, and in case of need demand a rehearing. Judges, of course, were no longer to make law, but to propose amendments in the 'Pannomion' or universal code, when new cases arose.

His leading principle may be described in one word as 'responsibility,' or expressed in his leading rule, 'Minimise Confidence.'[2] 'All government is in itself one vast evil.'[3] It consists in applying evil to exclude worse evil. Even ' to reward is to punish,'[4] when reward is given by government. The less government, then, the better ; but as governors are a necessary evil, they must be limited by every possible device to the sole legitimate aim, and watched at every turn by the all-seeing eye of public opinion. Every one must admit that this is an application of a sound principle, and that one condition of good government is the diffusion of universal responsibility. It must be admitted, too, that Bentham's theory represents a vigorous embodiment and unflinching application of doctrines which since his time have spread and gained more general authority.

_____
[1] *Works,* ix. 594.   [2] *Ibid.* ix. 62.   [3] *Ibid.* ix. 24.   [4] *Ibid.* ix. 48.

Mill says that granting one assumption, the Constitutional Code is 'admirable.'[1] That assumption is that it is for the good of mankind to be under the absolute authority of a majority. In other words, it would justify what Mill calls the 'despotism of public opinion.' To protest against that despotism was one of the main purposes of Mill's political writings. How was it that the disciple came to be in such direct opposition to his master ? That question cannot be answered till we have considered Mill's own position. But I have now followed Bentham far enough to consider the more general characteristics of his doctrine.

I have tried, in the first place, to show what was the course of Bentham's own development; how his observation of certain legal abuses led him to attempt the foundation of a science of jurisprudence ; how the difficulty of obtaining a hearing for his arguments led him to discover the power of 'Judge and Co.' ; how he found out that behind 'Judge and Co.' were George III. and the base Sidmouth, and the whole band of obstructors entrenched within the 'matchless constitution' ; and how thus his attack upon the abuses of the penal law led him to attack the whole political framework of the country. I have also tried to show how Bentham's development coincided with that of the English reformers generally. They too began with attacking specific abuses. They were for 'reform, not revolution.' The constitution satisfied them in the main : they boasted of the palladia of their liberties, 'trial by jury' and the 'Habeas Corpus' Act, and held Frenchmen to be frog-eating slaves in danger of *lettres de cachet* and the Bastille.

_____
Dissertations, i. 377.

English public opinion in spite of many trammels had a potent influence. Their first impulse, therefore, was simply to get rid of the trammels—the abuses which had grown up from want of a thorough application of the ancient principles in their original purity. The English Whig, even of the more radical persuasion, was profoundly convinced that the foundations were sound, however unsatisfactory might be the superstructure. Thus, both Bentham and the reformers generally started —not from abstract principles, but from the assault upon particular abuses. This is the characteristic of the whole English movement, and gives the meaning of their claim to be 'practical.' The Utilitarians were the reformers on the old lines ; and their philosophy meant simply a desire to systematise the ordinary common-sense arguments. The philosophy congenial to this vein is the philosophy which appeals to experience. Locke had exploded 'innate ideas.' They denounced 'intuitions,' or beliefs which might override experience as 'innate ideas' in a new dress ; and the attempt to carry out this view systematically became the distinctive mark of the whole school. Bentham accepted, though he did little to elaborate, this doctrine. That task remained for his disciples. But the tendency is shown by his view of a rival version of Radicalism.

Bentham, as we have seen, regarded the American Declaration of Independence as so much 'jargon.' He was entirely opposed to the theory of the 'rights of man,' and therefore to the 'ideas of 1789.' From that theory the revolutionary party professed to deduce their demands for universal suffrage, the levelling of all privileges, and the absolute supremacy of the people. Yet

Bentham, repudiating the premises, came to accept the conclusion. His Constitutional Code scarcely differs from the ideal of the Jacobins', except in pushing the logic further. The machinery by which he proposed to secure that the so-called rulers should become really the servants of the people was more thoroughgoing and minutely worked out than that of any democratic constitution that has ever been adopted. How was it that two antagonist theories led to identical results ; and that the 'rights of man,' absurd in philosophy, represented the ideal state of things in practice ?

The general answer may be that political theories are not really based upon philosophy. The actual method is to take your politics for granted on the one side and your philosophy for granted on the other, and then to prove their necessary connection. But it is, at any rate, important to see what was the nature of the philosophical assumptions implicitly taken for granted by Bentham.

The 'rights of man' doctrine confounds a primary logical canon with a statement of fact. Every political theory must be based upon facts as well as upon logic. Any reasonable theory about politics must no doubt give a reason for inequality and a reason, too, for equality. The maxim that all men were, or ought to be, 'equal' asserts correctly that there must not be arbitrary differences. Every inequality should have its justification in a reasonable system. But when this undeniable logical canon is taken to prove that men actually are equal, there is an obvious begging of the question. In point of fact, the theorists immediately proceeded to disfranchise half the race on account of sex, and a third of the remainder on account of infancy. They could

only amend the argument by saying that all men were equal in so far as they possessed certain attributes. But those attributes could only be determined by experience, or, as Bentham would have put it, by an appeal to 'utility.' It is illogical, said the anti-slavery advocate, to treat men differently on account of the colour of their skins. No doubt it is illogical if, in fact, the difference of colour does not imply a difference of the powers which fit a man for the enjoyment of certain rights. We may at least grant that the burden of proof should be upon those who would disfranchise all red-haired men. But this is because experience shows that the difference of colour does not mark a relevant difference. We cannot say, *a priori*, whether the difference between a negro and a white man may not be so great as to imply incapacity for enjoyment of equal rights. The black skin might—for anything a mere logician can say— indicate the mind of a chimpanzee. The case against slavery does not rest on the bare fact that negroes and whites both belong to the class 'man,' but on the fact that the negro has powers and sensibilities which fit him to hold property, to form marriages, to learn his letters, and so forth. But that fact is undeniably to be proved, not from the bare logic, but from observation of the particular case.

Bentham saw with perfect clearness that sound political theory requires a basis of solid fact. The main purpose of his whole system was to carry out that doctrine thoroughly. His view is given vigorously in the 'Anarchical Fallacies'—a minute examination of the French Declaration of Rights in 1791. His argument is of merciless length, and occasionally so minute as to

sound like quibbling. The pith, however, is clear enough. 'All men are born and remain free and equal in respect of rights' are the first words of the Declaration. Nobody is 'born free,' retorts Bentham. Everybody is born, and long remains, a helpless child. All men born free ! Absurd and miserable nonsense ! Why, you are complaining in the same breath that nearly everybody is a slave.[1] To meet this objection, the words might be amended by substituting 'ought to be' for 'is.' This, however, on Bentham's showing, at once introduces the conception of utility, and therefore leads to empirical considerations. The proposition, when laid down as a logical necessity, claims to be absolute. Therefore it implies that all authority is bad ; the authority, for example, of parent over child, or of husband over wife ; and moreover, that all laws to the contrary are *ipso facto* void. That is why it is 'anarchical.' It supposes a 'natural right,' not only as suggesting reasons for proposed alterations of the legal right, but as actually annihilating the right and therefore destroying all government. ' *Natural rights*,' says Bentham,[2] is simple nonsense ; natural and imprescriptible rights 'rhetorical nonsense—nonsense upon stilts.' For 'natural right' substitute utility, and you have, of course, a reasonable principle, because an appeal to experience. But lay down 'liberty' as an absolute right and you annihilate law, for every law supposes coercion. One man gets liberty simply by restricting the liberty of others.[3] What Bentham substantially says, therefore, is that on this version absolute rights of individuals could mean nothing but anarchy ; or that

¹ *Works*, ii. 497.   ² *Ibid.* ii. 501.   ³ *Ibid.* ii. 503.

no law can be defended except by a reference to facts, and therefore to 'utility.'

One answer might be that the demand is not for absolute liberty, but for as much liberty as is compatible with equal liberty for all. The fourth article of the Declaration says : 'Liberty consists in being able to do that which is not hurtful to another, and therefore the exercise of the natural rights of each man has no other bounds than those which ensure to the other members of the society the enjoyment of the same rights.' This formula corresponds to a theory held by Mr. Herbert Spencer ; and, as he observes,[1] held on different grounds by Kant. Bentham's view, indicated by his criticism of this article in the 'Anarchical Fallacies,' is therefore worth a moment's notice. The formula does not demand the absolute freedom which would condemn all coercion and all government ; but it still seems to suggest that liberty, not utility, is the ultimate end. Bentham's formula, therefore, diverges. All government, he holds, is an evil, because coercion implies pain. We must therefore minimise, though we cannot annihilate, government ; but we must keep to utility as the sole test. Government should, of course, give to the individual all such rights as are 'useful' ; but it does not follow, without a reference to utility, that men should not be restrained even in 'self-regarding' conduct. Some men, women, and children require to be protected against the consequences of their own 'weakness, ignorance, or imprudence.'[2] Bentham adheres, that is, to the strictly

¹ *Justice*, p. 264 ; so Price, in his *Observations on Liberty*, lays it down that government is never to entrench upon private liberty, 'except so far as private liberty entrenches on the liberty of others.'   ² *Works*, ii. 506.

empirical ground. The absolute doctrine requires to be qualified by a reference to actual circumstances: and, among those circumstances, as Bentham intimates, we must include the capacity of the persons concerned to govern themselves. Carried out as an absolute principle, it would imply the independence of infants; and must therefore require some reference to 'utility.'

Bentham, then, objects to the Jacobin theory as too absolute and too 'individualist.' The doctrine begs the question; it takes for granted what can only be proved by experience; and therefore lays down as absolute theories which are only true under certain conditions or with reference to the special circumstances to which they are applied. That is inconsistent with Bentham's thoroughgoing empiricism. But he had antagonists to meet upon the other side: and, in meeting them, he was led to a doctrine which has been generally condemned for the very same faults—as absolute and individualist. We have only to ask in what sense Bentham appealed to 'experience' to see how he actually reached his conclusions. The adherents of the old tradition appealed to experience in their own way. The English people, they said, is the freest, richest, happiest in the world; it has grown up under the British Constitution: therefore the British Constitution is the best in the world, as Burke tells you, and the British common law, as Blackstone tells you, is the 'perfection of wisdom.' Bentham's reply was virtually that although he, like Burke, appealed to experience, he appealed to experience scientifically organised, whereas Burke appealed to mere blind tradition. Bentham is to be the founder of a new science, founded like chemistry on experiment,

and his methods are to be as superior to those of Burke as those of modern chemists to those of the alchemists who also invoked experience. The true plan was not to throw experience aside because it was alleged by the ignorant and the prejudiced, but to interrogate experience systematically, and so to become the Bacon or the Newton of legislation, instead of wandering off into the *a priori* constructions of a Descartes or a Leibniz.

Bentham thus professes to use an 'inductive' instead of the deductive method of the Jacobins; but reaches the same practical conclusions from the other end. The process is instructive. He objected to the existing inequalities, not as inequalities simply, but as mischievous inequalities. He, as well as the Jacobins, would admit that inequality required justification; and he agreed with them that, in this case, there was no justification. The existing privileges did not promote the 'greatest happiness of the greatest number.' The attack upon the 'Anarchical Fallacies' must be taken with the *Book of Fallacies*, and the *Book of Fallacies* is a sustained and vigorous, though a curiously cumbrous, assault upon the Conservative arguments. Its pith may be found in Sydney Smith's *Noodle's Oration*; but it is itself well worth reading by any one who can recognise really admirable dialectical power, and forgive a little crabbedness of style in consideration of genuine intellectual vigour. I only notice Bentham's assault upon the 'wisdom of our ancestors.' After pointing out how much better we are entitled to judge now that we have got rid of so many superstitions, and have learned to read and write, he replies to the question, 'Would you have us speak and act as if we never had any ancestors?'

'By no means,' he replies; 'though their opinions were of little value, their practice is worth attending to; but chiefly because it shows the bad consequences of their opinions.' 'From foolish opinion comes foolish conduct; from foolish conduct the severest disaster; and from the severest disaster the most useful warning. It is from the folly, not from the wisdom, of our ancestors that we have so much to learn.'[1] Bentham has become an 'ancestor,' and may teach us by his errors. Pointed and vigorous as is his exposure of many of the sophistries by which Conservatives defended gross abuses and twisted the existence of any institution into an argument for its value, we get some measure from this of Bentham's view of history. In attacking an abuse, he says, we have a right to inquire into the utility of any and every arrangement. The purpose of a court of justice is to decide litigation; it has to ascertain facts and apply rules: does it then ascertain facts by the methods most conducive to the discovery of truth? Are the rules needlessly complex, ambiguous, calculated to give a chance to knaves, or to the longest purse? If so, undoubtedly they are mischievous. Bentham had done inestimable service in stripping away all the disguises and technical phrases which had evaded the plain issue, and therefore made of the laws an unintelligible labyrinth. He proceeded to treat in the same way of government generally. Does it work efficiently for its professed ends? Is it worked in the interests of the nation, or of a special class, whose interests conflict with those of the nation? He treated, that is, of government as a man of business might investigate a commercial undertaking.

1 *Works*, ii. 401.

If he found that clerks were lazy, ignorant, making money for themselves, or bullying and cheating the customers, he would condemn the management. Bentham found the 'matchless constitution' precisely in this state. He condemned political institutions worked for the benefit of a class, and leading, especially in legal matters, to endless abuses and chicanery. The abuses everywhere imply 'inequality' in some sense; for they arise from monopoly. The man who holds a sinecure, or enjoys a privilege, uses it for his own private interest. The 'matter of corruption,' as Bentham called it, was provided by the privilege and the sinecure. The Jacobin might denounce privileges simply as privileges, and Bentham denounce them because they were used by the privileged class for corrupt purposes. So far, Bentham and the Jacobins were quite at one. It mattered little to the result which argument they preferred to use, and without doubt they had a very strong case, and did in fact express a demand for justice and for a redress of palpable evils. The difference seems to be that in one case the appeal is made in the name of justice and equality; in the other case, in the name of benevolence and utility.

The important point here, however, is to understand Bentham's implicit assumptions. J. S. Mill, in criticising his master, points out very forcibly the defects arising from Bentham's attitude to history. He simply continued, as Mill thinks, the hostility with which the critical or destructive school of the eighteenth century regarded their ancestors. To the revolutionary party history was a record of crimes and follies and of little else. The question will meet us again; and here it is

enough to ask what is the reason of his tacit implication of Bentham's position. Bentham's whole aim, as
I have tried to show, was to be described as the
construction of a science of legislation. The science,
again, was to be purely empirical. It was to rest
throughout upon the observation of facts. That aim
—an admirable aim—runs through his whole work
and that of his successors. I have noticed, indeed,
how easily Bentham took for granted that his makeshift classification of common motives amounted to a
scientific psychology. A similar assumption that a
rough sketch of a science is the same thing as its
definite constitution is characteristic of the Utilitarians
in general. A scientific spirit is most desirable; but
the Utilitarians took a very short cut to scientific
certainty. Though appealing to experience, they reach
formulæ as absolute as any 'intuitionist' could desire.
What is the logical process implied? To constitute an
empirical science is to show that the difference between
different phenomena is due simply to 'circumstances.'
The explanation of the facts becomes sufficient when
the 'law' can be stated, as that of a unit of constant properties placed in varying positions. This
corresponds to the procedure in the physical sciences,
where the ultimate aim is to represent all laws as corresponding to the changes of position of uniform atoms.
In social and political changes the goal is the same.
J. S. Mill states in the end of his *Autobiography*[1] that
one main purpose of his writing was to show that
'differences between individuals, races, or sexes' are
due to 'differences in circumstances.' In fact, this is an

[1] *Autobiography*, p. 274.

aim so characteristic from the beginning of the whole
school, that it may be put down almost as a primary
postulate. It was not, indeed, definitely formulated; but
to 'explain' a social theorem was taken to be the same
thing as to show how differences of character or conduct
could be explained by 'circumstance'—meaning by
'circumstance' something not given in the agent himself. We have, however, no more right as good
empiricists to assert than to deny that all difference
comes from 'circumstance.' If we take 'man' as a
constant quantity in our speculations, it requires at least
a great many precautions before we can assume that our
abstract entity corresponds to a real concrete unit.
Otherwise we have a short cut to a doctrine of
'equality.' The theory of 'the rights of man' lays down
the formula, and assumes that the facts will correspond.
The Utilitarian assumes the equality of fact, and of
course brings out an equally absolute formula. 'Equality,'
in some sense, is introduced by a side wind, though not
explicitly laid down as an axiom.[1] This underlying
tendency may partly explain the coincidence of results—
though it would require a good many qualifications in
detail; but here I need only take Bentham's more or less
unconscious application.

Bentham's tacit assumption, in fact, is that there is
an average 'man.' Different specimens of the race,
indeed, may vary widely according to age, sex, and so
forth; but, for purposes of legislation, he may serve as
a unit. We can assume that he has on the average
certain qualities from which his actions in the mass can

[1] Hobbes, in the *Leviathan* (chap. xiii.), has in the same way to argue for
the *de facto* equality of men.

be determined with sufficient accuracy, and we are
tempted to assume that they are mainly the qualities
obvious to an inhabitant of Queen's Square Place about
the year 1800. Mill defends Bentham against the
charge that he assumed his codes to be good for all men
everywhere. To that, says Mill,[1] the essay upon the
'Influence of Time and Place in Matters of Legislation'
is a complete answer. Yet Mill[2] admits in the same
breath that Bentham omitted all reference to 'national
character.' In fact, as we have seen, Bentham was ready
to legislate for Hindoostan as well as for his own parish;
and to make codes not only for England, Spain, and
Russia, but for Morocco. The Essay mentioned really
explains the point. Bentham not only admitted but
asserted as energetically as became an empiricist, that
we must allow for 'circumstances'; and circumstances
include not only climate and so forth, but the varying
beliefs and customs of the people under consideration.
The real assumption is that all such circumstances are
superficial, and can be controlled and altered indefinitely
by the 'legislator.' The Moor, the Hindoo, and the
Englishman are all radically identical; and the differences
which must be taken into account for the moment can
be removed by judicious means. Without pausing to
illustrate this from the Essay, I may remark that for
many purposes such an assumption is justifiable and
guides ordinary common sense. If we ask what would
be the best constitution for a commercial company, or the
best platform for a political party, we can form a fair
guess by arguing from the average of Bentham and his

[1] *Dissertations*, i. 375.
[2] I remark by anticipation that this expression implies a reference to Mill's
Ethology, of which I shall have to speak.

contemporaries—especially if we are shrewd attornies or
political wirepullers. Only we are not therefore in a
position to talk about the 'science of human nature' or
to deal with problems of 'sociology.' This, however,
gives Bentham's 'individualism' in a sense of the phrase
already explained. He starts from the 'ready-made
man,' and deduces all institutions or legal arrangements
from his properties. I have tried to show how naturally
this view fell in with the ordinary political conceptions of
the time. It shows, again, why Bentham disregards
history. When we have such a science, empirical or *a
priori*, history is at most of secondary importance. We
can deduce all our maxims of conduct from the man
himself as he is before us. History only shows how
terribly he blundered in the pre-scientific period. The
blunders may give us a hint here and there. Man was
essentially the same in the first and the eighteenth
century, and the differences are due to the clumsy
devices which he made by rule of thumb. We do not
want to refer to them now, except as illustrations of
errors. We may remark how difficult it was to count
before the present notation was invented; but when it
has once been invented, we may learn to use it without
troubling our heads about our ancestors' clumsy contrivances for doing without it. This leads to the real
shortcoming. There is a point at which the historical
view becomes important—the point, namely, where it is
essential to remember that man is not a ready-made
article, but the product of a long and still continuing
'evolution.' Bentham's attack (in the *Fragment*) upon
the 'social contract' is significant. He was, no doubt,
perfectly right in saying that an imaginary contract could

add no force to the ultimate grounds for the social union. Nobody would now accept the fiction in that stage. And yet the 'social contract' may be taken to recognise a fact; namely, that the underlying instincts upon which society alternately rests correspond to an order of reasons from those which determine more superficial relations. Society is undoubtedly useful, and its utility may be regarded as its ground. But the utility of society means much more than the utility of a railway company or a club, which postulates as existing a whole series of already established institutions. To Bentham an 'utility' appeared to be a kind of permanent and ultimate entity which is the same at all periods—it corresponds to a psychological currency of constant value. To show, therefore, that the social contract recognises 'utility' is to show that the whole organism is constructed just as any particular part is constructed. Man comes first and 'society' afterwards. I have already noticed how this applies to his statements about the utility of a law; how his argument assumes an already constituted society, and seems to overlook the difference between the organic law upon which all order essentially depends, and some particular modification or corollary which may be superinduced. We now have to notice the political version of the same method. The 'law,' according to Bentham, is a rule enforced by a 'sanction.' The imposer of the rule in the phrase which Hobbes had made famous is the 'sovereign.' Hobbes was a favourite author, indeed, of the later Utilitarians, though Bentham does not appear to have studied him. The relation is one of natural affinity. When in the *Constitutional Code* Bentham transfers the 'sovereignty' from the king to

the 'people,'[1] he shows the exact difference between his doctrine and that of the *Leviathan*. Both thinkers are absolutists in principle, though Hobbes gives to a monarch the power which Bentham gives to a democracy. The attributes remain though their subject is altered. The 'sovereign,' in fact, is the keystone of the whole Utilitarian system. He represents the ultimate source of all authority, and supplies the motive for all obedience. As Hobbes put it, he is a kind of mortal God.

Mill's criticism of Bentham suggests the consequences. There are, he says,[2] three great questions : What government is for the good of the people? How are they to be induced to obey it? How is it to be made responsible? The third question, he says, is the only one seriously considered by Bentham; and Bentham's answer, we have seen, leads to that 'tyranny of the majority' which was Mill's great stumbling-block. Why, then, does Bentham omit the other questions? or rather, how would he answer them? for he certainly assumes an answer. People, in the first place, are 'induced to obey' by the sanctions. They don't rob that they may not go to prison. That is a sufficient answer at a given moment. It assumes, indeed, that the law will be obeyed. The policeman, the gaoler, and the judge will do what the sovereign—whether despot or legislature—orders them to do. The jurist may naturally take this for granted. He does not go 'behind the law.' That is the law which the sovereign has declared to be the law. In that sense, the sovereign is omnipotent. He can, as a fact, threaten evildoers with the gallows ; and the jurist simply takes the fact for granted, and

[1] *Works*, ix. 96, 113.   [2] *Dissertations*, i. 376.

assumes that the coercion is an ultimate fact. No doubt it is ultimate for the individual subject. The immediate restraint is the policeman, and we need not ask upon what does the policeman depend. If, however, we persist in asking, we come to the historical problems which Bentham simply omits. The law itself, in fact, ultimately rests upon 'custom,'—upon the whole system of instincts, beliefs, and passions which induce people to obey government, and are, so to speak, the substance out of which loyalty and respect for the law is framed. These, again, are the product of an indefinitely long elaboration, which Bentham takes for granted. He assumes as perfectly natural and obvious that a number of men should meet, as the Americans or Frenchmen met, and create a constitution. That the possibility of such a proceeding involves centuries of previous training does not occur to him. It is assumed that the constitution can be made out of hand, and this assumption is of the highest importance, not only historically, but for immediate practice. Mill assumes too easily that Bentham has secured responsibility. Bentham assumes that an institution will work as it is intended to work—perhaps the commonest error of constitution-mongers. If the people use the instruments which he provides, they have a legal method for enforcing obedience. To infer that they will do so is to infer that all the organic instincts will operate precisely as he intends ; that each individual, for example, will form an independent opinion upon legislative questions, vote for men who will apply his opinions, and see that his representatives perform his bidding honestly. That they should do so is essential to his scheme; but that they will do so is what he takes

for granted. He assumes, that is, that there is no need for inquiring into the social instincts which lie beneath all political action. You can make your machine and assume the moving force. That is the natural result of considering political and legislative problems without taking into account the whole character of the human materials employed in the construction. Bentham's sovereign is thus absolute. He rules by coercion, as a foreign power may rule by the sword in a conquered province. Thus, force is the essence of government, and it is needless to go further. To secure the right application of the force, we have simply to distribute it among the subjects. Government still means coercion, and ultimately nothing else ; but then, as the subjects are simply moved by their own interests, that is, by utility, they will apply the power to secure those interests. Therefore, all that is wanted is this distribution, and Mill's first problem, What government is for the good of the people? is summarily answered. The question, how obedience is to be secured, is evaded by confining the answer to the 'sanctions,' and taking for granted that the process of distributing power is perfectly simple, or that a new order can be introduced as easily as parliament can pass an act for establishing a new police in London. The 'social contract' is abolished ; but it is taken for granted that the whole power of the sovereign can be distributed, and rules made for its application by the common sense of the various persons interested. Finally, the one bond outside of the individual is the sovereign. He represents all that holds society together; his 'sanctions,' as I have said, are taken to be on the same plane with the 'moral sanctions'—not dependent upon them, but other modes of applying similar motives. As the sovereign, again, is in a sense omnipotent, and yet can be manufactured, so to speak, by voluntary arrangements among the individual members of society, there is no limit to the influence which he may exercise. I note, indeed, that I am speaking rather of the tendencies of the theory than of definitely formulated conclusions. Most of the Utilitarians were exceedingly shrewd, practical people, whose regard for hard facts imposed limits upon their speculations. They should have been the last people to believe too implicitly in the magical efficacy of political contrivances, for they were fully aware that many men are knaves and most men fools. They probably put little faith in Bentham's Utopia, except as a remote ideal, and an ideal of unimaginative minds. The Utopia was constructed on 'individualist' principles, because common-sense naturally approves individualism. The whole social and political order is clearly the sum of the individuals, who combine to form an aggregate ; and theories about social bonds take one to the mystical and sentimental. The absolute tendency is common to Bentham and the Jacobins. Whether the individual be taken as a unit of constant properties, or as the subject of absolute rights, we reach equally absolute conclusions. When all the social and political regulations are regarded as indefinitely modifiable, the ultimate laws come to depend upon the absolute framework of unalterable fact. This, again, is often the right point of view for immediate questions in which we may take for granted that the average individual is in fact constant ; and, as I have said in regard to Bentham's legislative process, leads to very relevant and

important, though not ultimate, questions. But there are certain other results which require to be noticed. 'Individualism,' like other words that have become watchwords of controversy, has various shades of meaning, and requires a little more definition.

VII. INDIVIDUALISM

'Individualism' in the first place is generally mentioned in a different connection. The 'ready-made' man of whom I have spoken becomes the 'economic man.' Bentham himself contributed little to economic theory. His most important writing was the *Defence of Usury*, and in this, as we have seen, he was simply adding a corollary to the *Wealth of Nations*. The *Wealth of Nations* itself represented the spirit of business ; the revolt of men who were building up a vast industrial system against the fetters imposed by traditional legislation and by rulers who regarded industry in general, as Telford is said to have regarded rivers. Rivers were meant to supply canals, and trade to supply tax-gatherers. With this revolt, of course, Bentham was in full sympathy, but here I shall only speak of one doctrine of great interest, which occurs both in his political treatises and his few economical remarks. Bentham objected, as we have seen, to the abstract theory of equality ; yet it was to the mode of deduction rather than to the doctrine itself which he objected. He gave, in fact, his own defence ; and it is one worth notice.[1] The principle of equality is derivative, not ultimate. Equality is good

[1] *Works*, ' Civil Code' (from Dumont), i. 302, 305 ; *Ibid.* (' Principles of Constitutional Code ') ii. 271 ; *Ibid.* (' Constitutional Code ') ix. 15-18.

because equality increases the sum of happiness. Thus, as he says,[1] if two men have £1000, and you transfer £500 from one to the other, you increase the recipient's wealth by one-third, and diminish the loser's wealth by one-half. You therefore add less pleasure than you subtract. The principle is given less mathematically[2] by the more significant argument that 'felicity' depends not simply on the 'matter of felicity' or the stimulus, but also on the sensibility to felicity which is necessarily limited. Therefore by adding wealth—taking, for example, from a thousand labourers to give to one king—you are supersaturating a sensibility already glutted by taking away from others a great amount of real happiness. With this argument, which has of late years become conspicuous in economics, he connects another of primary importance. The first condition of happiness, he says, is not 'equality' but 'security.' Now you can only equalise at the expense of security. If I am to have my property taken away whenever it is greater than my neighbour's, I can have no security.[3] Hence, if the two principles conflict, equality should give way. Security is the primary, which must override the secondary, aim. Must the two principles, then, always conflict ? No ; but 'time is the only mediator.'[4] The law may help to accumulate inequalities ; but in a prosperous state there is a 'continual progress towards equality.' The law has to stand aside ; not to maintain monopolies ; not to restrain trade ; not to permit entails ; and then property will diffuse itself by a natural process, already exemplified in the growth of Europe. The 'pyramids'

[1] *Works*, i. 306 n.   [2] *Ibid.* ix. 15.
[3] *Ibid.* (' Principles of Penal Code ') i. 311.   [4] *Ibid.* i. 312.

heaped up in feudal times have been lowered, and their '*débris* spread abroad' among the industrious. Here again we see how Bentham virtually diverges from the *a priori* school. Their absolute tendencies would introduce 'equality' by force ; he would leave it to the spontaneous progress of security. Hence Bentham is in the main an adherent of what he calls[1] the '*laissez-nous faire*' principle. He advocates it most explicitly in the so-called *Manual of Political Economy*—a short essay first printed in 1798.[2] The tract, however, such as it is, is less upon political economy proper than upon economic legislation ; and its chief conclusion is that almost all legislation is improper. His main principle is 'Be quiet' (the equivalent of the French phrase, which surely should have been excluded from so English a theory). Security and freedom are all that industry requires ; and industry should say to government only what Diogenes said to Alexander, 'Stand out of my sunshine.'[3]

Once more, however, Bentham will not lay down the 'let alone' principle absolutely. His adherence to the empirical method is too decided. The doctrine 'be quiet,' though generally true, rests upon utility, and may, therefore, always be qualified by proving that in a particular case the balance of utility is the other way. In fact, some of Bentham's favourite projects would be condemned by an absolute adherent of the doctrine. The Panopticon, for example, though a 'mill to grind rogues honest' could be applied to others than rogues, and Bentham hoped to make his machinery equally effective in the case of pauperism. A system of national education is also included in his ideal constitution. It is, in

[1] *Works*, x. 440.   [2] *Ibid.* iii. 33, etc.   [3] *Ibid.* iii. 35.

fact, important to remember that the 'individualism' of Benthamism does not necessarily coincide with an absolute restriction of government interference. The general tendency was in that direction; and in purely economical questions, scarcely any exception was admitted to the rule. Men are the best judges, it was said, of their own interest; and the interference of rulers in a commercial transaction is the interference of people inferior in knowledge of the facts, and whose interests are 'sinister' or inconsistent with those of the persons really concerned. Utility, therefore, will, as a rule, forbid the action of government: but, as utility is always the ultimate principle, and there may be cases in which it does not coincide with the 'let alone' principle, we must always admit the possibility that in special cases government can interfere usefully, and, in that case, approve the interference.

Hence we have the ethical application of these theories. The individualist position naturally tends to take the form of egoism. The moral sentiments, whatever they may be, are clearly an intrinsic part of the organic social instincts. They are intimately involved in the whole process of social evolution. But this view corresponds precisely to the conditions which Bentham overlooks. The individual is already there. The moral and the legal sanctions are 'external'; something imposed by the action of others; corresponding to 'coercion,' whether by physical force or the dread of public opinion; and, in any case, an accretion or addition, not a profound modification of his whole nature. The Utilitarian 'man' therefore inclines to consider other people as merely parts of the necessary machinery. Their feelings

are relevant only as influencing their outward conduct. If a man gives me a certain 'lot' of pain or pleasure, it does not matter what may be his motives. The 'motive' for all conduct corresponds in all cases to the pain or pleasure accruing to the agent. It is true that his happiness will be more or less affected by his relations to others. But as conduct is ruled by a calculation of the balance of pains or pleasures dependent upon any course of action, it simplifies matters materially, if each man regards his neighbour's feelings simply as instrumental, not intrinsically interesting. And thus the coincidence between that conduct which maximises my happiness and that conduct which maximises happiness in general, must be regarded as more or less accidental or liable in special cases to disappear. If I am made happier by action which makes others miserable, the rule of utility will lead to my preference of myself.

Here we have the question whether the Utilitarian system be essentially a selfish system. Bentham, with his vague psychology, does not lay down the doctrine absolutely. After giving this list of self-regarding 'springs of action,' he proceeds to add the pleasures and pains of 'sympathy' and 'antipathy' which, he says, are not self-regarding. Moreover, as we have seen, he has some difficulty in denying that 'benevolence' is a necessarily moral motive: it is only capable of prompting to bad conduct in so far as it is insufficiently enlightened; and it is clear that a moralist who makes the 'greatest happiness of the greatest number' his universal test, has some reason for admitting as an elementary pleasure the desire for the greatest happiness. This comes out curiously in the *Constitutional Code*. He there lays down the 'self-preference principle'—the principle,

namely, that 'every human being' is determined in every action by his judgment of what will produce the greatest happiness to himself, 'whatsoever be the effect . . . in relation to the happiness of other similar beings, any or all of them taken together.'[1] Afterwards, however, he observes that it is 'the constant and arduous task of every moralist' and of every legislator who deserves the name to 'increase the influence of sympathy at the expense of that of self-regard and of sympathy for the greater number at the expense of sympathy for the lesser number.'[2] He tries to reconcile these views by the remark 'that even sympathy has its root in self-regard,' and he argues, as Mr. Herbert Spencer has done more fully, that if Adam cared only for Eve and Eve only for Adam—neither caring at all for himself or herself—both would perish in less than a year. Self-regard, that is, is essential, and sympathy supposes its existence. Hence Bentham puts himself through a catechism.[3] What is the 'best' government? That which causes the greatest happiness of the given community. What community? 'Any community, which is as much as to say, every community.' But *why* do you desire this happiness? Because the establishment of that happiness would contribute to *my* greatest happiness. And *how* do you prove that you desire this result? By my labours to obtain it, replies Bentham. This oddly omits the more obvious question, how can you be sure that your happiness will be promoted by the greatest happiness of all? What if the two criteria differ? I desire the general happiness, he might have replied, because my benevolence is an original or elementary instinct which can override my

self-love; or I desire it, he would perhaps have said, because I know as a fact that the happiness of others will incidentally contribute to my own. The first answer would fall in with some of his statements; but the second is, as I think must be admitted, more in harmony with his system. Perhaps, indeed, the most characteristic thing is Bentham's failure to discuss explicitly the question whether human action is or is not necessarily 'selfish.' He tells us in regard to the 'springs of action' that all human action is always 'interested,' but explains that the word properly includes actions in which the motive is not 'self-regarding.'[1] It merely means, in fact, that all conduct has motives. The statement which I have quoted about the 'self-preference' principle may only mean a doctrine which is perfectly compatible with a belief in 'altruism'—the doctrine, namely, that as a fact most people are chiefly interested by their own affairs. The legislator, he tells us, should try to increase sympathy, but the less he takes sympathy for the 'basis of his arrangements'—that is, the less call he makes upon purely unselfish motives—the greater will be his success.[2] This is a shrewd and, I should say, a very sound remark, but it implies—not that all motives are selfish in the last analysis, but—that the legislation should not assume too exalted a level of ordinary morality. The utterances in the very unsatisfactory *Deontology* are of little value, and seem to imply a moral sentiment corresponding to a petty form of commonplace prudence.[3]

Leaving this point, however, the problem necessarily presented itself to Bentham in a form in which selfishness is the predominating force, and any recognition of independent benevolence rather an incumbrance than a help. If we take the 'self-preference principle' absolutely, the question becomes how a multitude of individuals, each separately pursuing his own happiness, can so arrange matters that their joint action may secure the happiness of all. Clearly a man, however selfish, has an interest generally in putting down theft and murder. He is already provided with a number of interests to which security, at least, and therefore a regular administration of justice, is essential. His shop could not be carried on without the police; and he may agree to pay the expenses, even if others reap the benefit in greater proportion. A theory of legislation, therefore, which supposes ready formed all the instincts which make a decent commercial society possible can do without much reference to sympathy or altruism. Bentham's man is not the colourless unit of *a priori* writing, nor the noble savage of Rousseau, but the respectable citizen with a policeman round the corner. Such a man may well hold that honesty is the best policy; he has enough sympathy to be kind to his old mother, and help a friend in distress; but the need of romantic and elevated

apologue of 'Walter Wise,' who becomes Lord Mayor, and 'Timothy Thoughtless,' who ends at Botany Bay (i. 118), giving the lowest kind of prudential morality. The manuscript of the *Deontology*, now in University College, London, seems to prove that Bentham was substantially the author, though the Mills seem to have suspected Bowring of adulterating the true doctrine. He appears to have been an honest if not very intelligent editor; though the rewriting, necessary in all Bentham's works, was damaging in this case; and he is probably responsible for some rhetorical amplification, especially in the later part.

conduct rarely occurs to him; and the heroic, if he meets it, appears to him as an exception, not far removed from the silly. He does not reflect—especially if he cares nothing for history—how even the society in which he is a contented unit has been built up, and how much loyalty and heroism has been needed for the work; nor even, to do him justice, what unsuspected capacities may lurk in his own commonplace character. The really characteristic point is, however, that Bentham does not clearly face the problem. He is content to take for granted as an ultimate fact that the self-interest principle in the long run coincides with the greatest 'happiness' principle, and leaves the problem to his successors. There we shall meet it again.

Finally, Bentham's view of religion requires a word. The short reply, however, would be sufficient, that he did not believe in any theology, and was in the main indifferent to the whole question till it encountered him in political matters. His first interest apparently was roused by the educational questions which I have noticed, and the proposal to teach the catechism. Bentham, remembering the early bullying at Oxford, examines the catechism; and argues in his usual style that to enforce it is to compel children to tell lies. But this leads him to assail the church generally; and he regards the church simply as a part of the huge corrupt machinery which elsewhere had created Judge and Co. He states many facts about non-residence and bloated bishoprics which had a very serious importance; and he then asks how the work might be done more cheaply. As a clergyman's only duty is to read weekly services and preach sermons, he suggests (whether seriously may

be doubted) that this might be done as well by teaching a parish boy to read properly, and provide him with the prayer-book and the homilies.[1] A great deal of expense would be saved. This, again, seems to have led him to attack St. Paul, whom he took to be responsible for dogmatic theology, and therefore for the catechism; and he cross-examines the apostle, and confronts his various accounts of the conversion with a keenness worthy of a professional lawyer. In one of the MSS. at University College the same method is applied to the gospels. Bentham was clearly not capable of anticipating Renan. From these studies he was led to the far more interesting book, published under the name of *Philip Beauchamp*. Bentham supplied the argument in part; but to me it seems clear that it owes so much to the editor, Grote, that it may more fitly be discussed hereafter.

The limitations and defects of Bentham's doctrine have been made abundantly evident by later criticism. They were due partly to his personal character, and partly to the intellectual and special atmosphere in which he was brought up. But it is more important to recognise the immense real value of his doctrine. Briefly, I should say, that there is hardly an argument in Bentham's voluminous writings which is not to the purpose so far as it goes. Given his point of view, he is invariably cogent and relevant. And, moreover, that is a point of view which has to be taken. No ethical or political doctrine can, as I hold, be satisfactory which does not find a place for Bentham, though he was far, indeed, from giving a complete theory of his subject. And the main reason of this is that which I have already

[1] *Church of Englandism* (Catechism examined), p. 207.

indicated. Bentham's whole life was spent in the attempt to create a science of legislation. Even where he is most tiresome, there is a certain interest in his unflagging working out of every argument, and its application to all conceivable cases. It is all genuine reasoning; and throughout it is dominated by a respect for good solid facts. His hatred of 'vague generalities'[1] means that he will be content with no formula which cannot be interpreted in terms of definite facts. The resolution to insist upon this should really be characteristic of every writer upon similar subjects, and no one ever surpassed Bentham in attention to it. Classify and reclassify, to make sure that at every point your classes correspond to realities. In the effort to carry out these principles, Bentham at least brought innumerable questions to a sound test, and exploded many pestilent fallacies. If he did not succeed further, if whole spheres of thought remained outside of his vision, it was because in his day there was not only no science of 'sociology' or psychology—there are no such sciences now—but no adequate perception of the vast variety of investigation which would be necessary to lay a basis for them. But the effort to frame a science is itself valuable, indeed of surpassing value, so far as it is combined with a genuine respect for facts. It is common enough to attempt to create a science by inventing technical terminology. Bentham tried the far wider and far more fruitful method of a minute investigation of particular facts. His work, therefore, will stand, however different some of the results may appear when fitted into a different framework. And, therefore, however crudely and im-

[1] See this phrase expounded in *Works* ('Book of Fallacies'), ii. 440, etc.

perfectly, Bentham did, as I believe, help to turn speculation into a true and profitable channel. Of that, more
will appear hereafter ; but, if any one doubts Bentham's
services, I will only suggest to him to compare Bentham
with any of his British contemporaries, and to ask where
he can find anything at all comparable to his resolute
attempt to bring light and order into a chaotic infusion
of compromise and prejudice.

NOTE ON BENTHAM'S WRITINGS

THE following account of Bentham's writings may be of some use. The arrangement is intended to show what were the topics which attracted his attention at successive periods.

The collected *Works*, edited by Bowring, appeared from 1838 to 1843 in eleven volumes, the last two containing the life and an elaborate index. The first nine volumes consist partly of the works already published; partly of works published for the first time from Bentham's MSS.; and partly of versions of Dumont's redactions of Bentham. Dumont's publications were (1) *Traités de Legislation civile et pénale* (1802; second edition, revised, 1820): [vol. i. contains *Principes généraux de Legislation* and *Principes du Code civil*; vol. ii. *Principes du Code pénal*; and vol. iii. *Mémoire sur le Panoptique, De la Promulgation des Lois, De l'Influence du Temps et des Lieux*, and *Vue générale d'un Corps complet des Lois*]; (2) *Théorie des Peines et des Récompenses*, 1811, 1818, 1825; (3) *Tactiques des Assemblées déliberantes et Traité des Sophismes politiques*, 1816; (4) *Traité des Preuves judiciaires*, 1823; and (5) *De l'Organisation judiciaire et de la Codification*, 1823.

In the following I give references to the place of each work in Bowring's edition.

Bentham's first book was the *Fragment on Government*, 1776 (i. 221-295). An interesting 'historical preface,' intended for a second edition (i. 240-259), was first printed in 1828. The *Fragment*, edited by Mr. F. C. Montague, was republished in 1891.

The *Introduction to the Principles of Morals and Legislation* was published in 1789, in one vol. 4to (i. 1-154). It had been printed in 1780. A second edition, in two vols. 8vo, appeared in 1823. It was intended as an introduction to the plan of a penal code. Bentham says in his preface that his scheme would be completed by a series of works applying his principles to (1) civil law; (2) penal law; (3) procedure; (4) reward; (5) constitutional law; (6) political tactics; (7) international law; (8) finance; and (9) political economy, and by a tenth treatise giving a plan of a body of law 'considered in respect of its form,' that is, upon 'nomograpny.' He wrote more or less in the course of his life upon all these topics. Dumont's *Traités* of 1802 were based partly upon the *Introduction* and partly upon Bentham's MSS. corresponding to unfinished parts of this general scheme.

The two first sections of this scheme are represented in the *Works* by *Principles of the Civil Code* (i. 297-364) and *Principles of Penal Law* (i. 365-580). The *Principles of the Civil Code* is translated from Dumont's *Traités*, where it follows a condensed statement of 'general principles' taken from the opening chapters of the *Introduction*. An appendix 'on the levelling system' is added in the *Works* from Bentham's MSS. The *Principles of Penal Law* consists of three parts: the first and third (on 'political remedies for the evil of offences' and on 'indirect means of preventing crimes') are translated from parts 2 and 4 of Dumont's *Principes du Code pénal* (parts 1 and 3 of Dumont being adaptations from the *Introduction to Morals and Legislation*). The second part of the *Penal Law*, or *The Rationale of Punishment* is from Dumont's *Théorie des Peines et des Récompenses*. Dumont took it from a MS. written by Bentham in 1775. (See Bentham's *Works*, i. 388.) An appendix on 'Death Punishment,' addressed by Bentham to the French people in 1830, is added to Part II. in the *Works* (i. 525-532). No. 4 of Bentham's general scheme corresponds to the *Rationale of Reward*, founded upon two MSS., one in French and one in English, used by Dumont in the *Théorie des Peines et des Récompenses*. The English version in the *Works*, chiefly translated from Dumont and compared with the original manuscript, was first published in 1825 (ii. 189-266).   Richard Smith 'of the Stamps and Taxes' was the editor of this and of an edition of the *Rationale of Punishment* in 1831, and of various minor treatises.   (Bentham's *Works*, x. 548 *n.*)

The *Table of the Springs of Action* (i. 195-220), written at an early period, was printed in 1815, and published, with modifications, in 1817.   The *Vue générale* included in the *Traités* of 1802 was intended by Bentham as a sketch for his own guidance, and is translated as *View of a Complete Code of Laws* in the *Works* (iii. 154-210).   The two essays in the 1802 *Traités* on 'the promulgation of laws' and the 'influence of time and place in matters of legislation' are translated in *Works* (i. 157-194).   A fragment on *International Law*—a phrase invented by Bentham—written between 1786 and 1789, first appeared in the *Works* (ii. 535-571), with *Junctiana proposal*—a plan for a canal between the Atlantic and the Pacific —written in 1822, as an appendix.

Besides the above, all written before 1789 in pursuance of his scheme, Bentham had published in 1778 his *View of the Hard Labour Bill* (iv. 1-36); and in 1787 his *Defence of Usury* (iii. 1-29).   A third edition of the last (with the 'protest against law taxes') was published in 1816.

During the following period (1789-1802) Bentham wrote various books, more or less suggested by the French revolution. The *Essay on Political Tactics* (ii. 299-373), (corresponding to No. 6 of the scheme), was sent to Morellet in 1789, but first published by Dumont in 1816.   With it Dumont also published the substance of the *Anarchical Fallacies* (ii. 489-534), written about 1791.   A *Draught of a Code for the Organisation of the Judicial Establishment of France*, dated March 1790, is reprinted in *Works* iv. 285-406.   *Truth* v. *Ashhurst*, written in 1792 (v. 231-237), was first published in 1823.   A *Manual of Political Economy*, written by 1793 (see *Works*, iii. 73 *n.*), corresponds to No. 9 of his scheme.   A chapter appeared in the *Bibliothèque Britannique* in 1798.   It was partly used in Dumont's *Théorie des Récompenses*, and first published in English in *Works* (iii.

31-84). *Emancipate your Colonies* (iv. 407-481) was privately printed in 1793, and first published for sale in 1830. A *Protest against Law Taxes*, printed in 1793, was published in 1795 together with *Supply without Burthen, or Escheat vice Taxation*, written in 1794. To them is appended a short paper called *Tax with Monopoly* (ii. 573-600). *A Plan for saving all Trouble and Expense in the Transfer of Stock*, written and partly printed in 1800, was first published in *Works* (iii. 105-153).

During this period Bentham was also occupied with the Panopticon, and some writings refer to it. *The Panopticon, or the Inspection House* (iv. 37-172), written in 1787, was published in 1791. *The Panopticon versus New South Wales* (iv. 173-248) appeared in 1802; and *A Plea for the Constitution* (on transportation to New South Wales) (iv. 249-284), in 1803. Closely connected with these are *Poor-laws and Pauper Management* (viii. 358-461), reprinted from Arthur Young's *Annals* of September 1797 and following months; and *Observations on the Poor Bill* (viii. 440-459), written in February 1797, privately printed in 1838, and first published in the *Works*.

About 1802 Bentham returned to jurisprudence. James Mill prepared from the papers then written an *Introductory View of the Rationale of Evidence*, finished and partly printed in 1812 (see *Works*, x. 468 *n*. and Bain's *James Mill*, 105, 120). Dumont's *Traité des Preuves judiciaires* (1823) was a redaction of the original papers, and an English translation of this appeared in 1825. The parts referring to English Law were omitted. The *Rationale of Evidence* (5 vols. 8vo, 1827), edited by J. S. Mill, represents a different and fuller redaction of the same papers. It is reprinted in vols. vi. and vii. of the *Works* with the *Introductory View* (now first published) prefixed. To the same period belongs *Scotch Reform*, with a *Summary View of a Plan for a Judicatory*, 1808 (second edition 1811, v. 1-60).

After 1808 Bentham's attention was especially drawn to political questions. His *Catechism of Parliamentary Reform* (iii. 433-557), written in 1809, was first published with a long 'introduction' in the *Pamphleteer* for January 1817. Bentham's

Radical Reform Bill, with explanations (iii. 558-597) followed in December 1819. *Radicalism not dangerous* (iii. 598-622), written at the same time, first appeared in the *Works* (iii. 398-622). *Elements of the Art of Packing as applied to Special Juries, especially in Cases of Libel Law* (v. 61-186), written in 1809, was published in 1821. *Swear not at all* (v. 188-229) (referring chiefly to Oxford tests), written in 1813, was published in 1817. *The King against Edmonds* and *The King against Wolseley* (v. 239-261) were published in 1820. *Official Aptitude minimized ; Official Expense limited* (v. 263-286), is a series of papers, first collected in 1831. It contains a *Defence of Economy against Burke*, and a *Defence of Economy against George Rose*, both written in 1810, and published in the *Pamphleteer* in 1817, with *Observations* on a speech by Peel in 1825, and *Indications respecting Lord Eldou*. The two last appeared in 1825. Connected with these political writings is the *Book of Fallacies* (ii. 375-488), edited by Bingham in 1824, from the 'most unfinished of all Bentham's writings.' Allusions seem to show that the original MSS. were written from 1810 to 1819. It was partly published by Dumont with the *Tactique, etc.*

Bentham, during this period (1808-1820), was also led into various outlying questions. The *Pannomial Fragments, Nomography*, and *Appendix on Logical Arrangements employed by Jeremy Bentham* (iii. 211-295) were first published in the *Works* from MSS. written from 1813 to 1831. With the *Chrestomathia* (viii. 1-192), first published in 1816, are connected fragments upon 'Ontology,' 'Language,' and 'Universal Grammar' (viii. 193-358), first published in *Works* from fragments of MSS. of 1813 and later. George Bentham's *Outline of a New System of Logic* was partly founded upon his uncle's papers. Bentham at the Ford Abbey time (1814-1818) was also writing his *Church of Englandism and its Catechism examined*, 1818. The *Analysis of the Influence of Natural Religion upon the Temporal Happiness of Mankind*, by Philip Beauchamp, edited by George Grote, appeared in 1822 ; and *Not Paul but Jesus*, by Gamaliel

Smith, in 1823. Francis Place helped in preparing this at Ford Abbey in 1817 (Mr. Wallas's *Life of Place*, p. 83). *Mother Church of England relieved by Bleeding* (1823) and the *Book of Church Reform* (1831) are extracted from *Church of Englandism*. Bowring did not admit these works to his collection.

In his later years (1820-1832) Bentham began to be specially occupied with codification. *Papers upon Codification and Public Instruction* (iv. 451-534) consist chiefly of letters, written from 1811 to 1815, offering himself for employment in codification in America and Russia, and first published in 1817. In 1821 appeared *Three Tracts relating to Spanish and Portuguese Affairs, with a Continual Eye to English ones*; and in 1822 *Three Letters to Count Toreno on the proposed Penal Code* (in Spain) (viii. 460-554). A short tract on *Liberty of the Press* was addressed to the Spanish people in 1821 (ii. 275-299). *Codification Proposals* (iv. 535-594) appeared in 1823, offering to prepare an 'all-comprehensive code of law' for 'any nation professing liberal opinions.' *Securities against Misrule addressed to a Mahommedan State, and prepared with a special Reference to Tripoli*, written in 1822-23, was first published in the *Works* (viii. 551-600). A tract on the *Leading Principles of a Constitutional Code* (ii. 267-274) appeared in the *Pamphleteer* in 1823. The first volume of the *Constitutional Code*, printed in 1827, was published with the first chapter of the second volume in 1830. The whole book, edited by R. Doane from papers written between 1818 and 1832, was published in 1841, and forms volume ix. of the *Works*. Doane also edited *Principles of Judicial Procedure* (ii.1-188) from papers written chiefly from 1820 to 1827, though part had been written in 1802. Several thousand pages upon this subject—the third part of the original scheme—were left by Bentham at his death.

During his last years Bentham also wrote a *Commentary on Mr. Humphrey's Real Property Code*, published in the *Westminster Review* for October 1826 (v. 387-416); *Justice and Codification Petitions* (v. 437-548), printed in 1829; *Jeremy Bentham to his Fellow-Citizens in France on Houses of Peers and*

Senates (iv. 419-450), dated 15th October 1830; *Equity Dispatch Court Proposals* (iii. 297-432), first published in *Works* and written from 1829 to 1831; *Outline of a Plan of a General Register of Real Property* (v. 417-435), published in the Report of the Real Property Commission in 1832; and *Lord Brougham Displayed* (v. 549-612), 1832.

The *Deontology* or *Science of Morality* was published by Bowring in two vols. 8vo in 1834, but omitted from the *Works*, as the original edition was not exhausted. The MS. preserved at University College, London, shows that a substantial beginning had been made in 1814; most of the remainder about 1820. The second volume, made, as Bowring says, from a number of scraps, is probably more 'Bowringised' than the first.

Dumont's *Traités* were translated into Spanish in 1821, and the *Works* in 1841-43. There are also Russian and Italian translations. In 1830 a translation from Dumont, edited by F. E. Beneke, as *Grundsätze der Civil- und Criminal-Gesetzgebung*, etc., was published at Berlin. Beneke observes that Bentham had hitherto received little attention in Germany, though well known in other countries. He reports a saying attributed to Mme. de Staël that the age was that of Bentham, not of Byron or Buonaparte. The neglect of Bentham in Germany was due, as Beneke says, to the prevalence of the Kantian philosophy. Bentham, however, had been favourably noticed in the *Hermes* for 1822, and his merits since acknowledged by Mittermaier and Warnkönig in the *Zeitschrift für Rechtswissenschaft*. Beneke (1798-1854) was opposed to the Hegelian tendencies of his time, and much influenced by Herbart. See Ueberweg's *History of Philosophy* (English translation, 1874, ii. 281, etc.) and the account of Bentham in Robert von Mohl's *Staatswissenschaften*, etc. (1853), iii. 595-635.

A great mass of Bentham MSS. belongs to University College, London. They are contained in 148 boxes, which were examined and catalogued by Mr. T. Whittaker in 1892. A few of these contain correspondence, part of which was printed by Bowring. Others are the manuscripts of published works. Some are upon the same subjects as the published works, and others refer to topics not included in his publications. Besides the *Deontology* manuscripts and a fragment upon 'Political Deontology,' there is a discussion of the means of suppressing duels, an argument against the legal punishment of certain offences against decency, and a criticism of the gospel narrative similar to *Not Paul*, etc. I have not thought it necessary to examine these fragments after reading Mr. Whittaker's report. Bentham's principles are sufficiently stated in his published works; and the papers which have been reposing in the cellars of University College can have had no influence upon the world. There is another large collection of MSS. in the British Museum from the papers of Bentham and his brother, Sir Samuel. Ten folio volumes contain correspondence, much of it referring only to Sir Samuel. A long correspondence upon the acquisition of the 'Panopticon' land is included. Another volume contains many of Bentham's school and college exercises. There are also the manuscripts of the *Nomography*, *Logical Arrangements*, etc. This collection was used by Bowring and by Lady Bentham in the life of her husband.

THE ENGLISH UTILITARIANS

THE ENGLISH
UTILITARIANS

By LESLIE STEPHEN

IN THREE VOLUMES

———————

VOL. II
JAMES MILL

———————

NEW YORK
PETER SMITH
1950

Published, 1900, By
Duckworth and Co., London

Reprinted, 1950,
By Arrangement With
Gerald Duckworth and Co., Ltd.

PRINTED IN THE UNITED STATES OF AMERICA

CONTENTS

CHAPTER I
JAMES MILL

CHAPTER II
REFORM MOVEMENTS

CHAPTER III
POLITICAL THEORY

CHAPTER IV
MALTHUS

CHAPTER I

JAMES MILL

I. EARLY LIFE

BENTHAM's mantle fell upon James Mill.[1] Mill expounded in the tersest form the doctrines which in Bentham's hands spread into endless ramifications and lost themselves in minute details. Mill became the leader of Bentham's bodyguard ; or, rather, the mediator between the prophet in his 'hermitage' and the missionaries who were actively engaged on the hustings and in committee-rooms. The special characteristics of English Utilitarianism in the period of its greatest activity were thus more affected by Mill than by any other leader of opinion.

James Mill was one of the countless Scots who, having been trained at home in strict frugality and stern Puritanic principles, have fought their way to success in England. He was born 6th April 1773 in the parish of Logie Pert, Forfarshire. His father, also named James Mill, was a village shoemaker, employing two or three

---

[1] The chief authority for James Mill is *James Mill: a Biography*, by Alexander Bain, Emeritus Professor of Logic in the University of Aberdeen. London, 1882. The book contains very full materials ; and, if rather dry, deals with a dry subject.

journeymen when at the height of his prosperity. His mother, Isabel Fenton, daughter of a farmer, had been a servant in Edinburgh. Her family had some claims to superior gentility; she was fastidious, delicate in frame, and accused of pride by her neighbours. She resolved to bring up James, her eldest son, to be a gentleman, which practically meant to be a minister. He probably showed early promise of intellectual superiority. He received the usual training at the parish school, and was then sent to the Montrose Academy, where he was the school-fellow and friend of a younger lad, Joseph Hume (1777-1855), afterwards his political ally. He boarded with a Montrose shopkeeper for 2s. 6d. a week, and remained at the Academy till he was seventeen. He was never put to work in his father's shop, and devoted himself entirely to study. The usual age for beginning to attend a Scottish university was thirteen or fourteen; and it would have been the normal course for a lad in Mill's position to be sent at that age to Aberdeen. Mill's education was prolonged by a connection which was of great service to him. Sir John Stuart (previously Belches), of Fettercairn House, in Mill's neighbourhood, had married Lady Jane Leslie, and was by her father of an only child, Wilhelmina. Lady Jane was given to charity, and had set up a fund to educate promising lads for the ministry. Mill was probably recommended to her by the parish minister, as likely to do credit to her patronage. He also acted as tutor to Wilhelmina, who afterwards became the object of Scott's early passion. Mill spent much time at Fettercairn House, and appears to have won the warm regards both of the Stuarts and of their daughter, who spoke of him affectionately 'with

almost her last breath.'[1] The Stuarts passed their winters at Edinburgh, whither Mill accompanied them. He entered the university in 1790, and seems to have applied himself chiefly to Greek and to philosophy. He became so good a Greek scholar that long afterwards (1818) he had some thoughts of standing for the Greek chair at Glasgow.[2] He was always a keen student of Plato. He read the ordinary Scottish authorities, and attended the lectures of Dugald Stewart. Besides reading Rousseau, he studied Massillon, probably with a view to his future performances in the pulpit. Massillon might be suggested to him by quotations in Adam Smith's *Moral Sentiments*. There are few records of acquaintanceship with any of his distinguished contemporaries, except the chemist Thomas Thomson, who became a life-long friend. He probably made acquaintance with Brougham, and may have known Jeffrey; but he was not a member of the Speculative Society, joined by most young men of promise.

In 1794 he began his course of divinity, and on 4th October 1798 was licensed to preach. He lived in his father's house, where part of the family room was screened off to form a study for him. He delivered some sermons, apparently with little success. He failed to obtain a call from any parish; and there are vague reports of his acting as tutor in some families, and of a rebuff received at the table of the marquis of Tweeddale, father of one of his pupils, which made him resolve to seek for independence by a different career.

In 1802 Mill went to London in company with Sir John Stuart, who was about to take his seat in parlia-

[1] Wallas's *Francis Place*, p. 70 n.   [2] Bain's *James Mill*, p. 166.

ment. Stuart procured admission for him to the gallery of the House of Commons, where he attended many debates, and acquired an interest in politics. His ambition, however, depended upon his pen; and at first, it would seem, he was not more particular than other journalists as to the politics of the papers to which he contributed. He had obtained a testimonial from Thomson, on the strength of which he introduced himself to John Gifford, editor of the *Anti-Jacobin Review*.[1] This was a monthly magazine, which had adopted the name and politics of the deceased *Anti-Jacobin*, edited by William Gifford. Mill obtained employment, and wrote articles implying an interest in the philosophy, and especially in the political economy, of the time. It is noteworthy, considering his later principles, that he should at this time have taken part in a strong Tory organ. He wrote a pamphlet in 1804 (the first publication under his name) to prove the impolicy of a bounty upon the exportation of grain; and in 1807 replied in *Commerce Defended* to William Spence's *Britain independent of Commerce*. Meanwhile he had found employment of a more regular kind. He had formed a connection with a bookseller named Baldwin, for whom he undertook to help in rewriting a book called *Nature Delineated*. This scheme was changed for a periodical called the *Literary Journal*, which started at the beginning of 1803, and lived through four years with Mill as editor. At the same time apparently he

[1] Gifford's real name was John Richards Green. The identity of his assumed name with that of the more famous William Gifford has led to a common confusion between the two periodicals. 'Peter Pindar' assaulted William Gifford under the erroneous impression that he was editor of the second.

edited the *St. James's Chronicle*, also belonging to Baldwin, which had no very definite political colour. The *Journal* professed to give a systematic survey of literary, scientific, and philosophical publications. For the scientific part Mill was helped by Thomson. His own contributions show that, although clearly a rationalist, he was still opposed to open infidelity. A translation of Villers' *History of the Reformation* implies similar tendencies. Other literary hack-work during this and the next few years is vaguely indicated. Mill was making about £500 a year or something more during his editorships, and thought himself justified in marrying. On 5th June 1805 he became the husband of Harriett Burrow, daughter of a widow who kept a private lunatic asylum originally started by her husband. The Mills settled in a house in Pentonville belonging to Mrs. Burrow, for which they paid £50 a year.

The money question soon became pressing. The editorships vanished, and to make an income by periodical writing was no easy task. His son observes that nothing could be more opposed to his father's later principles than marrying and producing a large family under these circumstances. Nine children were ultimately born, all of whom survived their father. The family in his old home were an additional burthen. His mother died before his departure from Scotland. His father was paralysed, and having incautiously given security for a friend, became bankrupt. His only brother, William, died soon afterwards, and his only sister, Mary, married one of her father's journeymen named Greig, and tried to carry on the business.

The father died about 1808, and the Greigs had a hard struggle, though two of the sons ultimately set up a business in Montrose. James Mill appears to have helped to support his father, whose debts he undertook to pay, and to have afterwards helped the Greigs. They thought, it seems, that he ought to have done more, but were not unlikely to exaggerate the resources of a man who was making his way in England. Mill was resolute in doing his duty, but hardly likely to do it graciously. At any rate, in the early years, it must have been a severe strain to do anything.

In spite of all difficulties Mill, by strict frugality and unremitting energy, managed to keep out of debt. In the end of 1806 he undertook the history of British India. This was to be the great work which should give him a name, and enable him to rise above the herd of contemporary journalists. He calculated the time necessary for its completion at three years, but the years were to be more than trebled before the book was actually finished. At that period there were fewer facilities than there could now be for making the necessary researches : and we do not know what were the reasons which prompted the selection of a subject of which he could have no first-hand knowledge. The book necessarily impeded other labours ; and to the toil of writing Mill added the toil of superintending the education of his children. His struggle for some years was such as to require an extraordinary strain upon all his faculties. Mill, however, possessed great physical and mental vigour. He was muscular, well-made, and handsome ; he had marked powers of conversation, and made a strong impression upon all with whom he came

in contact. He gradually formed connections which effectually determined his future career.

II. BENTHAM'S LIEUTENANT

The most important influence in Mill's life was the friendship with Bentham. This appears to have begun in 1808. Mill speedily became a valued disciple. He used to walk from Pentonville to dine with Bentham in Queen's Square Place. Soon the elder man desired to have his new friend nearer at hand. In 1810 Mill moved to the house in Bentham's garden, which had once belonged to Milton ; when this proved unsuitable, he was obliged to move to a more distant abode at Stoke Newington ; but finally, in 1814, he settled in another house belonging to Bentham, 1 Queen's Square, close under the old gentleman's wing. Here for some years they lived in the closest intimacy. The Mills also stayed with Bentham in his country-houses at Barrow Green, and afterwards at Ford Abbey. The association was not without its troubles. Bentham was fanciful, and Mill stern and rigid. No one, however, could be a more devoted disciple. The most curious illustration of their relations is a letter written to Bentham by Mill, 19th September 1814, while they were both at Ford Abbey. Mill in this declares himself to be a 'most faithful and fervent disciple' of the truths which Bentham had the 'immortal honour' of propounding. He had fancied himself to be his master's favourite disciple. No one is so completely of Bentham's way of thinking, or so qualified by position for carrying on the propaganda. Now, however, Bentham showed that he had

taken umbrage at some part of Mill's behaviour. An open quarrel would bring discredit upon both sides, and upon their common beliefs. The great dangers to friendship are pecuniary obligation and too close intimacy. Mill has made it a great purpose of his life to avoid pecuniary obligation, though he took pride in receiving obligations from Bentham. He has confined himself to accepting Bentham's house at a low rent, and allowing his family to live for part of the year at Bentham's expense. He now proposes so to arrange his future life that they shall avoid an excessively close intimacy, from which, he thinks, had arisen the 'umbrage.' The letter, which is manly and straightforward, led to a reconciliation, and for some years the intercourse was as close as ever.[1]

Mill's unreserved adoption of Bentham's principles, and his resolution to devote his life to their propagation, implies a development of opinion. He had entirely dropped his theology. In the early years of his London life, Mill had been only a rationalist. He had by this time become what would now be called an agnostic. He thought 'dogmatic atheism' absurd, says J. S. Mill ;[2] 'but he held that we can know nothing whatever as to the origin of the world.' The occasion of the change, according to his family, was his intercourse with General Miranda, who was sitting at Bentham's feet about this time. J. S. Mill states that the turning-point in his father's mind was the study of Butler's *Analogy*. That book, he thought, as others have thought, was conclusive against the optimistic deism which it assails ; but he thought also that the argument really destroyed Butler's own standing-ground. The

evils of the world are incompatible with the theory of Almighty benevolence. The purely logical objection was combined with an intense moral sentiment. Theological doctrines, he thought, were not only false, but brutal. His son had heard him say 'a hundred times' that men have attributed to their gods every trait of wickedness till the conception culminated in the Christian doctrine of hell. Mill still attended church services for some time after his marriage, and the children were christened. But the eldest son did not remember the period of even partial conformity, and considered himself to have been brought up from the first without any religious belief. James Mill had already taken up the uncompromising position congenial to his character, although the reticence which the whole party observed prevented any open expression of his sentiments.

Mill's propaganda of Benthamism was for some time obscure. He helped to put together some of Bentham's writings, especially the book upon evidence. He was consulted in regard to all proposed publications, such as the pamphlet upon jury-packing, which Mill desired to publish in spite of Romilly's warning. Mill endeavoured also to disseminate the true faith through various periodicals. He obtained admission to the *Edinburgh Review*, probably through its chief contributor, Brougham. Neither Brougham nor Jeffrey was likely to commit the great Whig review to the support of a creed still militant and regarded with distrust by the respectable. Mill contributed various articles from 1808 to 1813, but chiefly upon topics outside of the political sphere. The *Edinburgh Review*, as I have said, had taken a condescending notice of Bentham in 1804. Mill tried to

[1] Letter in Bain's *James Mill*, pp. 136-40.   [2] *Autobiography*, p. 39.

introduce a better tone into an article upon Bexon's *Code de la Législation pénale*, which he was permitted to publish in the number for October 1809. Knowing Jeffrey's 'dislike of praise,' he tried to be on his guard, and to insinuate his master's doctrine without openly expressing his enthusiasm. Jeffrey, however, sadly mangled the review, struck out every mention but one of Bentham, and there substituted words of his own for Mill's. Even as it was, Brougham pronounced the praise of Bentham to be excessive.[1] Mill continued to write for a time, partly, no doubt, with a view to Jeffrey's cheques. Almost his last article (in January 1813) was devoted to the Lancasterian controversy, in which Mill, as we shall directly see, was in alliance with the Whigs. But the Edinburgh Reviewers were too distinctly of the Whig persuasion to be congenial company for a determined Radical. They would give him no more than a secondary position, and would then take good care to avoid the insertion of any suspicious doctrine. Mill wrote no more after the summer of 1813.

Meanwhile he was finding more sympathetic allies. First among them was William Allen (1770-1843), chemist, of Plough Court. Allen was a Quaker; a man of considerable scientific tastes; successful in business, and ardently devoted throughout his life to many philanthropic schemes. He took, in particular, an active part in the agitation against slavery. He was, as we have seen, one of the partners who bought Owen's

[1] Bain's *James Mill*, pp. 97-106. Mill appears to have said something 'extravagant' about Bentham in an article upon Miranda in the *Edinburgh Review* for January 1809. He also got some praises of Bentham into the *Annual Review* of 1809 (Bain, 92-96).

establishment at New Lanark; and his religious scruples were afterwards the cause of Owen's retirement. These, however, were only a part of his multifarious schemes. He was perhaps something of a busybody; his head may have been a little turned by the attentions which he received on all hands; he managed the affairs of the duke of Kent; was visited by the Emperor Alexander in 1814; and interviewed royal personages on the Continent, in order to obtain their support in attacking the slave-trade, and introducing good schools and prisons. But, though he may have shared some of the weaknesses of popular philanthropists, he is mentioned with respect even by observers such as Owen and Place, who had many prejudices against his principles. He undoubtedly deserves a place among the active and useful social reformers of his time.

I have already noticed the importance of the Quaker share in the various philanthropic movements of the time. The Quaker shared many of the views upon practical questions which were favoured by the free-thinker. Both were hostile to slavery, in favour of spreading education, opposed to all religious tests and restrictions, and advocates of reform in prisons, and in the harsh criminal law. The fundamental differences of theological belief were not so productive of discord in dealing with the Quakers as with other sects; for it was the very essence of the old Quaker spirit to look rather to the spirit than to the letter. Allen, therefore, was only acting in the spirit of his society when he could be on equally good terms with the Emperor Alexander or the duke of Kent, and, on the other hand, with James Mill, the denouncer of kings and autocrats.

He could join hands with Mill in assailing slavery, insisting upon prison reform, preaching toleration and advancing civilisation, although he heartily disapproved of the doctrines with which Mill's practical principles were associated. Mill, too, practised—even to a questionable degree—the method of reticence, and took good care not to offend his coadjutor.

Their co-operation was manifested in a quarterly journal called the *Philanthropist*, which appeared during the seven years, 1811-1817, and was published at Allen's expense. Mill found in it the opportunity of advocating many of his cherished opinions. He defended toleration in the name of Penn, whose life had been published by Clarkson. He attacked the slave-owners, and so came into alliance with Wilberforce, Zachary Macaulay, and others of the evangelical persuasion. He found, at the same time, opportunities for propagating the creed of Bentham in connection with questions of prison reform and the penal code. His most important article, published in 1812, was another contribution to the Lancasterian controversy. In this Mill had allies of a very different school; and his activity brings him into close connection with one of the most remarkable men of the time.[1]

This was Francis Place, the famous Radical tailor. Place, born 3rd November 1771, had raised himself from the position of a working-man to be occupant of a shop at Charing Cross, which became the centre of important political movements. Between Place and Mill there was much affinity of character. Place, like Mill, was

[1] See the very interesting Life of Francis Place, by Mr. Graham Wallas, 1898.

a man of rigid and vigorous intellect. Dogmatic, self-confident, and decidedly censorious, not attractive by any sweetness or grace of character, but thoroughly sincere and independent, he extorts rather than commands our respect by his hearty devotion to what he at least believed to be the cause of truth and progress. Place was what is now called a thorough 'individualist.' He believed in self-reliance and energy, and held that the class to which he belonged was to be raised, as he had raised himself, by the exercise of those qualities, not by invoking the direct interference of the central power, which, indeed, as he knew it, was only likely to interfere on the wrong side. He had the misfortune to be born in London instead of Scotland, and had therefore not Mill's educational advantages. He tried energetically, and not unsuccessfully, to improve his mind, but he never quite surmounted the weakness of the self-educated man, and had no special literary talent. His writing, in fact, is dull and long-winded, though he has the merit of judging for himself, and of saying what he thinks.

Place had been a member of the Corresponding Society, and was at one time chairman of the weekly committee. He had, however, disapproved of their proceedings, and retired in time to escape the imprisonment which finally crushed the committee. He was now occupied in building up his own fortunes at Charing Cross. When, during the second war, the native English Radicalism began again to raise its head, Place took a highly important share in the political agitation. Westminster, the constituency in which he had a vote, had long been one of the most important boroughs. It was one of the few large popular constituencies, and was affected by the influences naturally strongest in the metropolis. After being long under the influence of the court and the dean and chapter, it had been carried by Fox during the discontents of 1780, when the reform movement took a start and the county associations were symptoms of a growing agitation. The great Whig leader, though not sound upon the question of reform, represented the constituency till his death, and reform dropped out of notice for the time. Upon Fox's death (13th September 1806) Lord Percy was elected without opposition as his successor by an arrangement among the ruling families. Place was disgusted at the distribution of ' bread and cheese and beer,' and resolved to find a truly popular candidate. In the general election which soon followed at the end of 1806 he supported Paull, an impecunious adventurer, who made a good fight, but was beaten by Sir J. Hood and Sheridan. Place now proposed a more thorough organisation of the constituency, and formed a committee intended to carry an independent candidate. Sir Francis Burdett, a typical country gentleman of no great brains and of much aristocratic pride, but a man of honour, and of as much liberal feeling as was compatible with wealth and station, had sat at the feet of the old Radical, Horne Tooke. He had sympathised with the French revolution ; but was mainly, like his mentor, Tooke, a reformer of the English type, and a believer in Magna Charta and the Bill of Rights. He had sat in parliament, and in 1802 had been elected for Middlesex. After a prolonged litigation, costing enormous sums, the election had been finally annulled in 1806. He had subscribed £1000 towards Paull's expenses ;

but was so disgusted with his own election experiences that he refused to come forward as a candidate. Place's committee resolved therefore to elect him and Paull free of expense. Disputes between Paull and Burdett led to a duel, in which both were wounded. The committee threw over Paull, and at the election on the dissolution of parliament in the spring of 1807, Burdett and Cochrane—afterwards Lord Dundonald—were triumphantly elected, defeating the Whig candidates, Sheridan and Elliot. The election was the first triumph of the reformers, and was due to Place more than any one. Burdett retained his seat for Westminster until 1837, and, in spite of many quarrels with his party, was a leading representative of the movement, which henceforward slowly gathered strength. Place, indeed, had apparently but scanty respect for the candidate whose success he had secured. Burdett and his like aimed at popularity, while he was content to be ignored so long as he could by any means carry the measures which he approved. Place, therefore, acted as a most efficient wirepuller, but had no ambition to leave his shop to make speeches on the hustings.

The scandals about the duke of York and the Walcheren expedition gave a chance to the Radicals and to their leader in the House of Commons. Events in 1810 led to a popular explosion, of which Burdett was the hero. John Gale Jones, an old member of the Corresponding Societies, had put out a placard denouncing the House of Commons for closing its doors during a debate upon the Walcheren expedition. The House proceeded against Jones, who was more or less advised by Place in his proceedings. Burdett took the

part of Jones, by a paper published in Cobbett's *Register*, and was ultimately committed to the Tower in consequence. The whole of London was for a time in a state of excitement, and upon the verge of an outbreak. Burdett refused to submit to the arrest. Mobs collected ; soldiers filled the streets and were pelted. Burdett, when at last he was forced to admit the officers, appeared in his drawing-room in the act of expounding Magna Charta to his son. That, it was to be supposed, was his usual occupation of an afternoon. Meetings were held, and resolutions passed, in support of the martyr to liberty ; and when his imprisonment terminated on the prorogation of parliament, vast crowds collected, and a procession was arranged to convoy him to his home. Place had been active in arranging all the details of what was to be a great popular manifestation. To his infinite disgust, Burdett shrank from the performance, and went home by water. The crowd was left to expend its remaining enthusiasm upon the hackney carriage which contained his fellow-sufferer Jones. Jones, in the following December, was sentenced to twelve months' imprisonment for a libel. Cobbett, Burdett's special supporter at this time, was also imprisoned in June 1810. For a time the popular agitation collapsed. Place seems to have thought that the failure was due to Burdett's want of courage, and dropped all communication with him till a later contest at Westminster.

Place was thus at the centre of the political agitation which, for the time, represented the most energetic reforming movement. It was in 1811 or 1812 that he became acquainted with Mill.[1] In Mill he recognised a

congenial spirit, and a man able to defend and develop principles. He perhaps, as Professor Bain thinks, made advances to Mill upon the strength of the history of India ; and in 1814 he was certainly endeavouring to raise money to put Mill above the need of precarious hack-work.[1] The anticipated difficulty of persuading Mill so far to sacrifice his independence was apparently fatal to the scheme. Place was in occasional communication with Bentham, and visited him at Ford Abbey in 1817. He became intimate with the great man ; helped him in business affairs ; and was one of the disciples employed to prepare his books for publication.[2] Bentham was the source of philosophy, and Mill only his prophet. But Mill, who was capable of activity in practical affairs, was more useful to a man of the world. The first business which brought them into close connection was the Lancasterian controversy. The strong interest roused by this agitation was significant of many difficulties to come. The average mind had been gradually coming to the conclusion that the poor should be taught to read and write. Sunday schools and Hannah More's schools in Somersetshire had drawn the attention of the religious world to the subject. During the early years of the century the education question had steadily become more prominent, and the growing interest was shown by a singularly bitter and complicated controversy. The opposite parties fought under the banners of Bell and Lancaster. Andrew Bell, born at St. Andrews, 27th March 1753, was both a canny Scot and an

---

[1] Bain's *James Mill*, p. 78, and Wallas's *Francis Place*, p. 66.

[1] Wallas's *Francis Place*, p. 68.
[2] He ' put together ' the *Not Paul but Jesus* at Ford Abbey in 1817, and helped to preface the Reform *Catechism*. Wallas's *Francis Place*, p. 84.

Anglican clergyman. He combined philanthropy with business faculties. He sailed to India in 1787 with £128, 10s. in his pocket to be an army chaplain; he returned in 1796 with £25,000 and a new system of education which he had devised as superintendent of an orphan asylum. He settled in England, published an account of his plan, and did something to bring it into operation. Meanwhile Joseph Lancaster (1770-1838), a young Quaker, had set up a school in London; he devised a plan similar to that of Bell, and in 1803 published an account of his improvements in education with acknowledgments to Bell. For a time the two were on friendly terms. Lancaster set about propagating his new system with more enthusiasm than discretion. His fame rapidly spread till it reached the throne. In 1805 George III. sent for him; the royal family subscribed to his schools; and the king declared his wish that every child in his dominions should be taught to read the Bible. The king's gracious wish unconsciously indicated a difficulty. Was it safe to teach the Bible without the safeguard of authorised interpretation? Orthodox opponents feared the alliance with a man whose first principle was toleration, and first among them was the excellent Mrs. Trimmer, who had been already engaged in the Sunday-school movement. She pointed out in a pamphlet that the schismatic Lancaster was weakening the Established Church. The *Edinburgh Review* came to his support in 1806 and 1807; for the Whig, especially if he was also a Scot, was prejudiced against the Church of England. Lancaster went on his way, but soon got into difficulties, for he was impetuous, careless of money, and autocratic. William Allen, with another Quaker,

came to his support in 1808, and founded the Royal Lancasterian Society to maintain his school in the Borough Road, and propagate its like elsewhere. Lancaster travelled through the country, and the agitation prospered, and spread even to America. The church, however, was now fairly aroused. Bishop Marsh preached a sermon in St. Paul's, and followed it up by pamphlets; the cause was taken up by the *Quarterly Review* in 1811, and in the same year the National Society was founded to 'educate the poor in the principles of the Established Church.' Bell had suggested a national system, but the times were not ripe. Meanwhile the controversy became furious. The *Edinburgh* and the *Quarterly* thundered on opposite sides. Immense importance was attached by both parties to the scheme devised by Bell, and partly adopted by Lancaster. The war involved a personal element and the charges of plagiarism which give spice to a popular controversy. All parties, and certainly the Utilitarians, strangely exaggerated the value of the new method. They regarded the proposal that children should be partly taught by other children instead of being wholly taught by adults as a kind of scientific discovery which would enormously simplify and cheapen education. Believers in the 'Panopticon' saw in it another patent method of raising the general level of intelligence. But the real question was between church and dissent. Was the church catechism to be imposed or not? This, as we have seen, was the occasion of Bentham's assault upon church and catechism. On the other side, Bell's claims were supported with enthusiasm by all the Tories, and by such men as Southey and Coleridge. Southey, who had

defended Bell in the *Quarterly*,[1] undertook to be Bell's biographer[2] and literary executor. Coleridge was so vehement in the cause that when lecturing upon 'Romeo and Juliet' in 1811, he plunged by way of exordium into an assault upon Lancaster's modes of punishment.[3] De Quincey testifies that he became a positive bore upon Bell's virtues. In 1812 Lancaster had got deeply into debt to the trustees of the Society, who included besides Allen, Joseph Fox—a 'shallow, gloomy bigot' according to Place—and some other Quakers. Lancaster resented their control, and in 1812 made over his Borough Road school to them, and set up one of his own at Tooting. They continued, however, to employ him, and in 1813 formed themselves into the 'British and Foreign' School Society. Place had known Lancaster from 1804, and Mill had supported him in the press. They both became members of the committee, though Place took the most active part. He makes many grave charges against Lancaster, whom he regarded as hopelessly flighty and impracticable, if not worse. Ultimately in 1814 Lancaster resigned his position, and naturally retorted that Place was an infidel. Place, meanwhile, was ill at ease with the 'gloomy bigot,' as he calls Fox. After many quarrels, Fox succeeded in getting the upper hand, and Place finally withdrew from the committee in 1815.

Two other schemes arose out of this, in which Mill was specially interested, but which both proved abortive. Mill and Place resolved in 1813 to start a 'West

London Lancasterian Institution,' which was to educate the whole population west of Temple Bar. They were joined by Edward Wakefield, father of the Edward Gibbon Wakefield who in later years was known as an economist, and himself author of a work of considerable reputation, *An Account of Ireland, Statistical and Political* (1812). The three joined Joseph Fox, and ultimately a meeting was held in August 1813. Sir James Mackintosh was in the chair. Mill wrote the address, and motions were proposed by his friend Joseph Hume and by William Allen. Papers were circulated, headed 'Schools for all,'[1] and the institution was launched with a sufficiency of applause. But the 'gloomy bigot' was secretary. He declared that he would rather see the institution destroyed than permit it to be used for infidel purposes. The Bible was, of course, to be read in the schools, but Fox wished that the Bible alone should be read. As the committee, according to Place, included four infidels, three Unitarians, six Methodists, two Baptists, two Roman Catholics, and several members of the Established Church, it was hardly a happy family. To add to the confusion, Sir Francis Burdett, who had contributed a thousand pounds, had taken it into his head that Place was a government spy.[2] The Association, as is hardly surprising, ceased to exist in 1816, after keeping up a school of less than three hundred children, and ended in hopeless failure. The Utilitarians had higher hopes from a scheme of their

---

[1] The article of 1811 was also published separately.
[2] He wrote only the first volume. Two others were added by Cuthbert Southey.
[3] *Lectures* (Ashe, 1885), pp. 32, 61.

[1] James Mill, according to Place, wrote a 'memorable and admirable essay, "Schools for all, not schools for Churchmen only."'—Wallas's *Francis Place*, 99 *n.*
[2] This absurd suspicion was aroused by the quarrel about Burdett's arrest. See Wallas's *Place*, p. 56.

own. This was the Chrestomathic school which occasioned Bentham's writing. An association was formed in February 1814. Mackintosh, Brougham, Mill, Allen, Fox, and Wakefield were to be trustees. The school was to apply Lancasterian principles to the education of the middle classes, and Bentham was to supply them with a philosophy and with a site in his garden. There the old gentleman was to see a small version of the Panopticon building, and, for a time, he took great delight in the prospect. Gradually, however, it seems to have dawned upon him that there might be inconveniences in being overlooked by a set of even model schoolboys. There were difficulties as to funds. Ricardo offered £200 and collected subscriptions for £900, but Place thought that he might have been more liberal. About 1817 they counted upon subscriptions for £2310. Allen was treasurer, Place secretary, and the dukes of Kent and York were on the committee. Romilly was persuaded to join, and they had hopes of the £1000 given by Burdett to the West London Institution. But the thing could never be got into working order, in spite of Place's efforts and Mill's counsels; and, after painful haulings and tuggings, it finally collapsed in 1820.[1]

The efforts of the Utilitarians to effect anything directly in the way of education thus fell completely flat. One moral is sufficiently obvious. They were, after all, but a small clique, regarded with suspicion by all outsiders; and such a system as could seriously affect education could only be carried out either by

[1] Mr. Wallas gives an account of these schemes in chap. iv. of his Life of Place. I have also consulted Place's collections in Additional MSS., 27,823.

government, which was thinking of very different things, or by societies already connected with the great religious bodies. The only function which could be adequately discharged by the little band of Utilitarians was to act upon public opinion; and this, no doubt, they could do to some purpose. I have gone so far into these matters in order to illustrate their position; but, as will be seen, Mill, though consulted at every stage by Place, and doing what he could to advocate the cause, was, after all, in the background. He was still wrestling with the Indian History, which was, as he hoped, to win for him an independent position. The effort was enormous. In 1814 he told Place that he was working at the History from 5 A.M. till 11 P.M. When at Ford Abbey his regular day's work began at 6 A.M. and lasted till 11 P.M., during which time three hours were given to teaching his children, and a couple of short walks supplied him with recreation. How, with all his energy, he managed to pay his way is a mystery, which his biographer is unable fully to solve.[1]

The History at last appeared in 3 vols. 4to, at the end of 1817. Dry and stern as its author, and embodying some of his political prejudices, it was at least a solid piece of work, which succeeded at once, and soon became the standard book upon the subject. Mill argues in the preface with characteristic courage that his want of personal knowledge of India was rather an advantage. It made him impartial. A later editor[2] has shown that it led to some serious misconceptions. It is characteristic of the Utilitarian attitude to assume that a sufficient

[1] Bain's *James Mill*, p. 162.
[2] H. H. Wilson in his preface to the edition of 1840.

knowledge of fact can always be obtained from blue-books and statistics. Some facts require imagination and sympathy to be appreciated, and there Mill was deficient. He could not give an adequate picture of Hindoo beliefs and customs, though he fully appreciated the importance of such questions. Whatever its shortcomings, the book produced a remarkable change in Mill's position. He applied for a vacant office in the India House. His friends, Joseph Hume and Ricardo, made interest for him in the city. Place co-operated energetically.[1] Canning, then president of the Board of Control, is said to have supported him; and the general impression of his ability appears to have caused his election, in spite of some Tory opposition. He became Assistant to the Examiner of India Correspondence, with a salary of £800 on 12th May 1819. On 10th April 1821 he became Second Assistant, with £1000 a year; on 9th April 1823 he was made Assistant Examiner, with £1200 a year; and on 1st December 1830 Examiner, with £1900, which on 17th February 1836 was raised to £2000. The official work came in later years to absorb the greatest part of Mill's energy, and his position excluded him from any active participation in politics, had he ever been inclined for it. Mill, however, set free from bondage, was able to exert himself very effectually with his pen; and his writings became in a great degree the text-books of his sect.

During 1818 he had again co-operated with Place in a political matter. The dissolution of parliament in 1818 produced another contest at Westminster. Place and Mill were leaders in the Radical committee, which

[1] Wallas's *Francis Place*, p. 78.

called a public meeting, where Burdett and Kinnaird were chosen as candidates. They were opposed to Romilly, the old friend of Bentham and of Mill himself. Both Mill and Bentham regarded him as not sufficiently orthodox. Romilly, however, was throughout at the head of the poll, and the Radical committee were obliged to withdraw their second candidate, Kinnaird, in order to secure the election of Burdett against the government candidate Maxwell. Romilly soon afterwards dined at Bentham's house, and met Mill, with Dumont, Brougham, and Rush, on friendly terms. On Romilly's sad death on 2nd November following, Mill went to Worthing to offer his sympathy to the family, and declared that the 'gloom' had 'affected his health.' He took no part in the consequent election, in which Hobhouse stood unsuccessfully as the Radical candidate.

III. LEADER OF THE UTILITARIANS

Politics were beginning to enter upon a new phase. The period was marked by the 'Six Acts' and the 'Peterloo massacre.' The Radical leaders who upheld the cause in those dark days were not altogether to the taste of the Utilitarians. After Burdett, John Cartwright (1740-1824) and Henry (or 'Orator') Hunt (1773-1835), hero of the 'Peterloo massacre,' were the most conspicuous. They were supported by Cobbett, the greatest journalist of the time, and various more obscure writers. The Utilitarians held them in considerable contempt. Burdett was flashy, melodramatic, and vain; Hunt an 'unprincipled demagogue'; and Cartwright, the Nestor of reform, who had begun his labours in 1780, was, according to Place, wearisome, impracticable, and a mere nuisance in matters of business. The Utilitarians tried to use such men, but shared the Tory opinion of their value. They had some relations with other obscure writers who were martyrs to the liberty of the press. Place helped William Hone in the *Reformer's Register*, which was brought out in 1817. The famous trial in which Hone triumphed over Ellenborough occurred at the end of that year. Richard Carlile (1790-1843), who reprinted Hone's pamphlets, and in 1818 published Paine's works, was sentenced in 1819 to three years' imprisonment; and while in confinement began the *Republican*, which appeared from 1819 to 1826. Ultimately he passed nine years in jail, and showed unflinching courage in maintaining the liberty of speech. The Utilitarians, as Professor Bain believes, helped him during his imprisonments, and John Mill's first publication was a protest against his prosecution.[1] A 'republican, an atheist, and Malthusian,' he was specially hated by the respectable, and had in all these capacities claims upon the sympathy of the Utilitarians. One of Carlile's first employments was to circulate the *Black Dwarf*, edited by Thomas Jonathan Wooler from 1817 to 1824.[2] This paper represented Cartwright, but it also published Bentham's reform *Catechism*, besides direct contributions and various selections from his works.

The Utilitarians were opposed on principle to Cobbett, a reformer of a type very different from their own; and still more vitally opposed to Owen, who was beginning to develop his Socialist schemes. If they had

[1] Bain's *James Mill*, p. 435.   [2] *Ibid.* p. 433.

sympathy for Radicalism of the Wooler or Carlile variety, they belonged too distinctly to the ranks of respectability, and were too deeply impressed with the necessity of reticence, to allow their sympathies to appear openly. As, on the other hand, they were too Radical in their genuine creed to be accepted by Edinburgh Reviewers and frequenters of Holland House, there was a wide gap between them and the genuine Whig. Their task therefore was to give a political theory which should be Radical in principle, and yet in such a form as should appeal to the reason of the more cultivated readers without too openly shocking their prejudices.

James Mill achieved this task by the publication of a series of articles in the Supplement to the *Encyclopædia Britannica*, which appeared from 1816 to 1823, of which I shall presently speak at length. It passed for the orthodox profession of faith among the little circle of friends who had now gathered round him. First among them was David Ricardo. He had become known to Mill in 1811. 'I,' said Bentham, 'was the spiritual father of Mill, and Mill the spiritual father of Ricardo.'[1] Mill was really the disciple of Ricardo in economics; but it was Mill who induced him to publish his chief work, and Mill's own treatise upon the subject published in 1820 is substantially an exposition of Ricardo's doctrine. Mill, too, encouraged Ricardo to take a seat in parliament in 1818, and there for the short remainder of his life, Ricardo defended the characteristic Utilitarian principles with the authority derived from his reputation as an economist.[2] The two were now especially intimate. During Mill's first years in the India House, his only

[1] Bentham's *Works*, p. 498.   [2] See Cannan in *Economic Review*, 1894.

recreation was an annual visit to Ricardo at Gatcombe. Meetings at Ricardo's house in London led to the foundation of the 'Political Economy Club' in 1821. Mill drafted the rules of the club, emphasising the duty of members to propagate sound economic opinions through the press. The club took root and helped to make Mill known to politicians and men of commercial influence. One of the members was Malthus, who is said, and the assertion is credible enough, to have been generally worsted by Mill in the discussions at the club. Mill was an awkward antagonist, and Malthus certainly not conspicuous for closeness of logic. The circle of Mill's friends naturally extended as his position in the India House enabled him to live more at his ease and brought him into contact with men of political position. His old school-fellow Joseph Hume had made a fortune in India, and returned to take a seat in parliament and become the persistent and tiresome advocate of many of the Utilitarian doctrines. A younger generation was growing up, enthusiastic in the cause of reform, and glad to sit at the feet of men who claimed at least to be philosophical leaders. John Black (1783-1855), another sturdy Scot, who came from Duns in Berwickshire, had, in 1817, succeeded Perry as editor of the *Morning Chronicle*. The *Chronicle* was an opposition paper, and day by day Black walked with Mill from the India House, discussing the topics of the time and discharging himself through the *Chronicle*. The *Chronicle* declined after 1821, owing to a change in the proprietorship.[1] Albany Fonblanque (1793-1872) took to journalism at an early age, succeeded Leigh Hunt as leader-writer for

[1] See under Black in *Dictionary of National Biography*.

the *Examiner* in 1826, became another exponent of Utilitarian principles, and for some time in alliance with John Stuart Mill was among the most effective representatives of the new school in the press. John Ramsay M'Culloch (1789-1864) upheld the economic battle in the *Scotsman* at Edinburgh from 1817-1827, and edited it from 1818-1820. He afterwards devoted himself to lecturing in London, and was for many years the most ardent apostle of the 'dismal science.' He was a genial, whisky-loving Scot; the favourite object of everybody's mimicry; and was especially intimate with James Mill. Many other brilliant young men contributed their help in various ways. Henry Bickersteth (1783-1851), afterwards Lord Langdale and Master of the Rolls, had brought Bentham and Burdett into political alliance; and his rising reputation at the bar led to his being placed in 1824 upon a commission for reforming the procedure of the Court of Chancery, one of the most cherished objects of the Utilitarian creed. Besides these there were the group of young men, who were soon to be known as the 'philosophical Radicals.' John Stuart Mill, upon whom the mantle of his father was to descend, was conspicuous by his extraordinary precocity, and having been carefully educated in the orthodox faith, was employed in 1825 upon editing Bentham's great work upon evidence. George Grote (1794-1871), the future historian, had been introduced to Mill by Ricardo; and was in 1821 defending Mill's theory of government against Mackintosh, and in 1822 published the *Analysis of Revealed Religion*, founded upon Bentham's manuscripts and expressing most unequivocally the Utilitarian theory of religion. With them were associated the two Austins, John (1790-1859) who, in 1821, lived close to Bentham and Mill in Queen's Square, and who was regarded as the coming teacher of the Utilitarian system of jurisprudence; and Charles (1799-1874), who upheld the true faith among the young gentlemen at Cambridge with a vigour and ability which at least rivalled the powers of his contemporary, Macaulay. Meanwhile, Mill himself was disqualified by his office from taking any direct part in political agitations. Place continued an active connection with the various Radical committees and associations; but the younger disciples had comparatively little concern in such matters. They were more interested in discussing the applications of Utilitarianism in various directions, or, so far as they had parliamentary aspirations, were aspiring to found a separate body of 'philosophical Radicals,' which looked down upon Place and his allies from the heights of superior enlightenment.

Mill could now look forward to a successful propaganda of the creed which had passed so slowly through its period of incubation. The death of Ricardo in 1823 affected him to a degree which astonished his friends, accustomed only to his stern exterior. A plentiful crop of young proselytes, however, was arising to carry on the work; and the party now became possessed of the indispensable organ. The *Westminster Review* was launched at the beginning of 1824. Bentham provided the funds; Mill's official position prevented him from undertaking the editorship, which was accordingly given to Bentham's young disciple, Bowring, helped for a time by Henry Southern. The *Westminster* was to represent the Radicals as the two older reviews represented the Whigs and the Tories;

and to show that the new party had its philosophers and its men of literary cultivation as well as its popular agitators and journalists. It therefore naturally put forth its claims by opening fire in the first numbers against the *Edinburgh* and the *Quarterly Reviews*. The assault upon the *Edinburgh Review*, of which I shall speak presently, made an impression, and, as J. S. Mill tells us, brought success to the first number of the new venture. The gauntlet was thrown down with plenty of vigour, and refo mers were expected to rally round so thoroughgoing a champion. In later numbers Mill afterwards (Jan. 9, 1826) fell upon Southey's *Book of the Church*, and (April 1826) assailed church establishments in general. He defended toleration during the same year in a review of Samuel Bailey's *Formation of Opinions*, and gave a general account of his political creed in an article (October) on the 'State of the Nation.' This was his last contribution to the *Westminster*; but in 1827 he contributed to the *Parliamentary History and Review*, started by James Marshall of Leeds, an article upon recent debates on reform, which ended for a time his political writings.

The Utilitarians had no great talent for cohesion. Their very principles were indeed in favour of individual independence, and they were perhaps more ready to diverge than to tolerate divergence. The *Westminster Review* had made a good start, and drew attention to the rising 'group'—J. S. Mill declares that it never formed a 'school.'[1] From the very first the Mills distrusted Bowring and disapproved of some articles; the elder Mill failed to carry his disciples with him, partly

[1] *Autobiography*, p. 101.

because they were already in favour of giving votes to women; and as the *Review* soon showed itself unable to pay its way, some new arrangement became necessary. It was finally bought by Perronet Thompson, and ceased for a time to be the official organ of Benthamism.

Another undertaking occupied much of Mill's attention in the following years. The educational schemes of the Utilitarians had so far proved abortive. In 1824, however, it had occurred to the poet, Thomas Campbell, then editing the *New Monthly Magazine*, that London ought to possess a university comparable to that of Berlin, and more on a level with modern thought than the old universities of Oxford and Cambridge, which were still in the closest connection with the church. Campbell addressed a letter to Brougham, and the scheme was taken up energetically on several sides. Place[1] wrote an article, which he offered to Campbell for the *New Monthly*, who declined out of modesty to publish it in his own organ. It was then offered to Bowring for the *Westminster*, and ultimately suppressed by him, which may have been one of the causes of his differences with the Mills. Brougham took a leading part in the agitation; Joseph Hume promised to raise £100,000. George Birkbeck, founder of the Mechanics' Institution, and Zachary Macaulay, who saw in it a place of education for dissenting ministers, joined the movement, and among the most active members of the new body were James Mill and Grote. A council was formed at the end of 1825, and after various difficulties a sum of £160,000 was raised, and the university started in Gower Street in 1828. Among the first body of pro-

[1] See Place's account in Additional MSS. 27,823.

fessors were John Austin and M'Culloch, both of them sound Utilitarians. The old difficulty, however, made itself felt. In order to secure the unsectarian character of the university, religious teaching was omitted. The college was accused of infidelity. King's College was started in opposition; and violent antipathies were aroused. A special controversy raged within the council itself. Two philosophical chairs were to be founded; and philosophy cannot be kept clear of religion. After long discussions, one chair was filled by the appointment of the Reverend John Hoppus, an independent minister. Grote, declaring that no man, pledged by his position to the support of any tenets, should be appointed, resigned his place on the council.[1] The university in 1836 became a college combined with its rival King's College under the newly formed examining body called the University of London. It has, I suppose, been of service to education, and may be regarded as the one practical achievement of the Utilitarians in that direction, so far as its foundation was due to them. It must, however, be admitted that the actual body still falls very far short of the ideal present to the minds of its founders.

From 1822 James Mill spent his vacations at Dorking, and afterwards at Mickleham. He had devoted them to a task which was necessary to fill a gap in the Utilitarian scheme. Hitherto the school had assumed, rather than attempted to establish, a philosophical basis of its teaching. Bentham's fragmentary writings about the Chrestomathic school supplied all that could by courtesy

[1] G. C. Robertson, *Philosophical Remains*, p. 166; and under George Grote in *Dictionary of National Biography*.

be called a philosophy. Mill, however, had been from the first interested in philosophical questions. His reading was not wide; he knew something of the doctrines taught by Stewart and Stewart's successor, Brown. He had been especially impressed by Hobbes, to some degree by Locke and Hume, but above all by Hartley. He knew something, too, of Condillac and the French Ideologists. Of recent German speculation he was probably quite ignorant. I find indeed that Place had called his attention to the account of Kant, published by Wirgman in the *Encyclopædia Londinensis* in 1817. Mill about the same time tells Place that he has begun to read *The Critic of Pure Reason*. 'I see clearly enough,' he says, 'what poor Kant would be about, but it would require some time to give an account of him.' He wishes (December 6, 1817) that he had time to write a book which would 'make the human mind as plain as the road from Charing Cross to St. Paul's.'[1] This was apparently the task to which he applied himself in his vacations. The *Analysis* appeared in 1829, and, whatever its defects of incompleteness and one-sidedness from a philosophical point of view, shows in the highest degree Mill's powers of close, vigorous statement; and lays down with singular clearness the psychological doctrine, which from his point of view supplied the fundamental theorems of knowledge in general. It does not appear, however, to have made an impression proportionate to the intellectual power displayed, and had to wait a long time before reaching the second edition due to the filial zeal of J. S. Mill.

[1] Letters communicated by Mr. Graham Wallas. See Mr. Wallas's *Francis Place*, p. 91.

James Mill, after his articles in the *Westminster*, could take little part in political agitation. He was still consulted by Place in regard to the Reform movement. Place himself took an important part at the final crisis, especially by his circulation in the week of agony of the famous placard, 'Go for Gold.' But the Utilitarians were now lost in the crowd. The demand for reform had spread through all classes. The attack upon the ruling class carried on by the Radicals of all shades in the dark days of Sidmouth and the six Acts was now supported by the nation at large. The old Toryism could no longer support itself by appealing to the necessities of a struggle for national existence. The prestige due to the victorious end of the war had faded away. The Reform Bill of 1832 was passed, and the Utilitarians hoped that the millennium would at least begin to dawn.

Mill in 1830 removed from Queen's Square to Vicarage Place, Kensington. He kept his house at Mickleham, and there took long Sunday walks with a few of his disciples. His strength was more and more absorbed in his official duties. He was especially called upon to give evidence before the committees which from 1830 to 1833 considered the policy to be adopted in renewing the charter of the East India Company. Mill appeared as the advocate of the company, defended their policy, and argued against the demands of the commercial body which demanded the final suppression of the old trading monopoly of the Company. The abolition, indeed, was a foregone conclusion; but Mill's view was not in accordance with the doctrines of the thoroughgoing free-traders. His official experience, it seems, upon this and

other matters deterred him from the *a priori* dogmatism too characteristic of his political speculations. Mill also suggested the formation of a legislative council, which was to contain one man 'versed in the philosophy of men and government.' This was represented by the appointment of the legal member of council in the Act of 1833. Mill approved of Macaulay as the first holder of the post. It was 'very handsome' of him, as Macaulay remarks, inasmuch as the famous articles written by Macaulay himself, in which the *Edinburgh* had at last retorted upon the Utilitarians, must still have been fresh in his memory. The 'Penal Code' drawn by Macaulay as holder of the office was the first actual attempt to carry out Bentham's favourite schemes under British rule, and the influence of the chief of Bentham's disciples at the India House may have had something to do with its initiation. Macaulay's chief subordinate, it may be remarked, Charles Hay Cameron, was one of the Benthamites, and had been proposed by Grote for the chair at the London University ultimately filled by Hoppus.

After 1830 Mill wrote the severe fragment on Mackintosh, which, after a delay caused by Mackintosh's death, appeared in 1835. He contributed some articles to the *London Review*, founded by Sir W. Molesworth, as an organ of the 'philosophical Radicals,' and superintended, though not directly edited, by J. S. Mill. These, his last performances, repeat the old doctrines. It does not appear, indeed, that Mill ever altered one of his opinions. He accepted Bentham's doctrine to the end, as unreservedly as a mathematician might accept Newton's *Principia*.

Mill's lungs had begun to be affected. It was sup-

posed that they were injured by the dust imbibed on coach journeys to Mickleham. He had a bad attack of hæmorrhage in August 1835, and died peacefully on 23rd June 1836.

What remains to be said of Mill personally may be suggested by a noticeable parallel. S. T. Coleridge, born about six months before Mill, died two years before him. The two lives thus coincided for more than sixty years, and each man was the leader of a school. In all else the contrast could hardly be greater. If we were to apply the rules of ordinary morality, it would be entirely in Mill's favour. Mill discharged all his duties as strenuously as a man could, while Coleridge's life was a prolonged illustration of the remark that when an action presented itself to him as a duty he became physically incapable of doing it. Whatever Mill undertook he accomplished, often in the face of enormous difficulties. Coleridge never finished anything, and his works are a heap of fragments of the prolegomena to ambitious schemes. Mill worked his hardest from youth to age, never sparing labour or shirking difficulties or turning aside from his path. Coleridge dawdled through life, solacing himself with opium, and could only be coaxed into occasional activity by skilful diplomacy. Mill preserved his independence by rigid self-denial, temperance, and punctuality. Coleridge was always dependent upon the generosity of his friends. Mill brought up a large family, and in the midst of severe labours found time to educate them even to excess. Coleridge left his wife and children to be cared for by others. And Coleridge died in the odour of sanctity, revered by his disciples, and idolised by his children; while Mill went to the grave amidst the shrugs of respectable shoulders, and respected rather than beloved by the son who succeeded to his intellectual leadership.

The answer to the riddle is indeed plain enough ; or rather there are many superabundantly obvious answers. Had Mill defended orthodox views and Coleridge been avowedly heterodox, we should no doubt have heard more of Coleridge's opium and of Mill's blameless and energetic life. But this explains little. That Coleridge was a man of genius and, moreover, of exquisitely poetical genius, and that Mill was at most a man of remarkable talent and the driest and sternest of logicians is also obvious. It is even more to the purpose that Coleridge was overflowing with kindliness, though little able to turn goodwill to much effect ; whereas Mill's morality took the form chiefly of attacking the wicked. This is indicated by the saying attributed by Bowring to Bentham that Mill's sympathy for the many sprang out of his hatred of the oppressing few.[1] J. S. Mill very properly protested against this statement when it was quoted in the *Edinburgh Review*. It would obviously imply a gross misunderstanding, whether Bentham, not a good observer of men, said so or not. But it indicates the side of Mill's character which made him unattractive to contemporaries and also to posterity. He partook, says his son,[2] of the Stoic, the Epicurean, and the Cynic character. He was a Stoic in his personal qualities ; an Epicurean so far as his theory of morals was concerned ; and a Cynic in that he cared little for pleasure. He thought life a ' poor

[1] So Place observed that Mill ' could help the mass, but could not help the individual, not even himself or his own.'—Wallas's *Francis Place*, p. 79.
[2] *Autobiography*, p. 48.

thing ' after the freshness of youth had passed ; and said that he had never known an old man happy unless he could live over again in the pleasures of the young. Temperance and self-restraint were therefore his favourite virtues. He despised all ' passionate emotions ' ; he held with Bentham that feelings by themselves deserved neither praise nor blame ; he condemned a man who did harm whether the harm came from malevolence or from intellectual error. Therefore all sentiment was objectionable, for sentiment means neglect of rules and calculations. He shrank from showing feeling with more than the usual English reserve ; and showed his devotion to his children by drilling them into knowledge with uncompromising strictness. He had no feeling for the poetical or literary side of things ; and regarded life, it would seem, as a series of arguments, in which people were to be constrained by logic, not persuaded by sympathy. He seems to have despised poor Mrs. Mill, and to have been unsuccessful in concealing his contempt, though in his letters he refers to her respectfully. Mill therefore was a man little likely to win the hearts of his followers, though his remarkable vigour of mind dominated their understandings.

The amiable and kindly, whose sympathies are quickly moved, gain an unfair share of our regard both in life and afterwards. We are more pleased by an ineffectual attempt to be kindly, than by real kindness bestowed ungraciously. Mill's great qualities should not be overlooked because they were hidden by a manner which seems almost deliberately repellent. He devoted himself through life to promote the truth as he saw it ; to increase the scanty amounts of pleasures enjoyed by

mankind ; and to discharge all the duties which he owed to his neighbours. He succeeded beyond all dispute in forcibly presenting one set of views which profoundly influenced his countrymen ; and the very narrowness of his intellect enabled him to plant his blows more effectively.

CHAPTER II

REFORM MOVEMENTS

I. POLITICAL CHANGE

THE last years of Mill's life correspond to the period in which Utilitarianism reached, in certain respects, its highest pitch of influence. The little band who acknowledged him as their chief leader, and as the authorised lieutenant of Bentham, considered themselves to be in the van of progress. Though differing on many points from each other, and regarded with aversion or distrust by the recognised party leaders, they were in their most militant and confident state of mind. They were systematically reticent as to their religious views : they left to popular orators the public advocacy of their favourite political measures ; and the credit of finally passing such of those measures as were adopted fell chiefly to the hands of the great political leaders. The Utilitarians are ignored in the orthodox Whig legend. In the preface to his collected works, Sydney Smith runs over the usual list of changes which had followed, and, as he seems to think, had in great part resulted from, the establishment of the *Edinburgh Review*. Smith himself, and Jeffrey and Horner and, above all, ' the gigantic Brougham,' had blown the blast which brought down the towers of Jericho. Sir G. O. Trevelyan, in his *Life of Macaulay*, describes the advent of the Whigs to office in a similar sense. 'Agitators and incendiaries,' he says, 'retired into the background, as will always be the case when the country is in earnest : and statesmen who had much to lose, and were not afraid to risk it, stepped quietly and firmly to the front. The men and the sons of the men who had so long endured exclusion from office, embittered by unpopularity, at length reaped their reward.'[1] The Radical version of the history is different. The great men, it said, who had left the cause to be supported by agitators so long as the defence was dangerous and profitless, stepped forward now that it was clearly winning, and received both the reward and the credit. Mill and Place could not find words to express their contempt for the trimming, shuffling Whigs. They were probably unjust enough in detail ; but they had a strong case in some respects. The Utilitarians represented that part of the reforming party which had a definite and a reasoned creed. They tried to give logic where the popular agitators were content with declamation, and represented absolute convictions when the Whig reformers were content with tentative and hesitating compromises. They had some grounds for considering themselves to be the 'steel of the lance' ; the men who formulated and deliberately defended the principles which were beginning to conquer the world.

The Utilitarians, I have said, became a political force in the concluding years of the great war struggle. The catastrophe of the revolution had unchained a whole whirlwind of antagonisms. The original issues had

[1] *Life of Macaulay*, p. 114 (Popular Edition).

passed out of sight ; and great social, industrial, and political changes were in progress which made the nation that emerged from the war a very different body from the nation that had entered it nearly a generation before. It is not surprising that at first very erroneous estimates were made of the new position when peace at last returned.

The Radicals, who had watched on one side the growth of debt and pauperism, and, on the other hand, the profits made by stockjobbers, landlords, and manufacturers, ascribed all the terrible sufferings to the selfish designs of the upper classes. When the war ended they hoped that the evils would diminish, while the pretext for misgovernment would be removed. A bitter disappointment followed. The war was followed by widespread misery. Plenty meant ruin to agriculturists, and commercial 'gluts' resulting in manufacturers' warehouses crammed with unsaleable goods. The discontent caused by misery had been encountered during the war by patriotic fervour. It was not a time for redressing evils, when the existence of the nation was at stake. Now that the misery continued, and the excuse for delaying redress had been removed, a demand arose for parliamentary reform. Unfortunately discontent led also to sporadic riotings, to breaking of machinery and burning of ricks. The Tory government saw in these disturbances a renewal of the old Jacobin spirit, and had visions—apparently quite groundless—of widespread conspiracies and secret societies ready to produce a ruin of all social order. It had recourse to the old repressive measures, the suspension of the Habeas Corpus Act, the passage of the 'Six Acts,' and the prosecution of popular agitators.

Many observers fancied that the choice lay between a servile insurrection and the establishment of arbitrary power.

By degrees, however, peace brought back prosperity. Things settled down ; commerce revived ; and the acute distress passed away. The whole nation went mad over the wrongs of Queen Caroline ; and the demand for political reform became for the time less intense. But it soon appeared that, although this crisis had been surmounted, the temper of the nation had profoundly changed. The supreme power still belonged constitutionally to the landed interest. But it had a profoundly modified social order behind it. The war had at least made it necessary to take into account the opinions of larger classes. An appeal to patriotism means that some regard must be paid to the prejudices and passions of people at large. When enormous sums were to be raised, the moneyed classes would have their say as to modes of taxation. Commerce and manufactures went through crises of terrible difficulty due to the various changes of the war ; but, on the whole, the industrial classes were steadily and rapidly developing in wealth, and becoming relatively more important. The war itself was, in one aspect at least, a war for the maintenance of the British supremacy in trade. The struggle marked by the policy of the 'Orders in Council' on one side, and Napoleon's decrees on the other, involved a constant reference to Manchester and Liverpool and the rapidly growing manufacturing and commercial interests. The growth, again, of the press, at a time when every one who could read was keenly interested in news of most exciting and important events, implied the rapid development of a great organ of public opinion.

The effects of these changes soon became palpable. The political atmosphere was altogether different ; and an entirely new set of influences was governing the policy of statesmen. The change affected the Tory as much as the Whig. However strongly he might believe that he was carrying on the old methods, he was affected by the new ideas which had been almost unconsciously incorporated in his creed. How great was the change, and how much it took the shape of accepting Utilitarian theories, may be briefly shown by considering a few characteristic facts.

The ablest men who held office at the time were Canning, Huskisson, and Peel. They represented the conservatism which sought to distinguish itself from mere obstructiveness. Their influence was felt in many directions. The Holy Alliance had the sympathy of men who could believe that the war had brought back the pre-revolutionary order, and that its main result had been to put the Jacobin spirit in chains. Canning's accession to office in 1822 meant that the foreign policy of England was to be definitely opposed to the policy of the 'Holy Alliance.' A pithy statement of his view is given in a remarkable letter, dated 1st February 1823, to the prince who was soon to become Charles x.[1] The French government had declared that a people could only receive a free constitution as a gift from their legitimate kings. Should the English ministry, says Canning, after this declaration, support the French in their attack upon the constitutional government of Spain, it would be driven from office amid 'the execration of Tories and Whigs alike.' He thought that the doctrine

[1] Canning's *Political Correspondence*, i. 71-76.

of the sovereignty of the people was less alien to the spirit of the British Constitution than the opposite doctrine of the legitimists. In the early days, when Canning sat at the feet of Pitt, the war, if not in their eyes an Anti-Jacobin crusade, had to be supported by stimulating the Anti-Jacobin sentiment. In later days, the war had come to be a struggle against the oppression of nations by foreign despots. Canning could now accept the version of Pitt's policy which corresponded to the later phase. Englishmen in general had no more sympathy for despots who claimed a divine right than for despots who acted in the name of democracy—especially when the despots threatened to interfere with British trade. When Canning called 'the new world into existence to redress the balance of the old,'[1] he declared that English policy should resist threats from the Holy Alliance directed against some of our best customers. The general approval had special force among the Utilitarians. In the South American States Bentham had found eager proselytes, and had hoped to become a Solon. He had been consulted by the constitutionalists in Spain and Portugal; and he and his disciples, Joseph Hume in particular, had joined the Greek Committee, and tried to regenerate Athens by sound Utilitarian tracts. All English Liberals sympathised with the various movements which were more or less favoured by Canning's policy; but the Utilitarians could also see in them the opening of new fields already white for the harvest.

The foreign policy was significant. It proved that the war, whatever else it had done, had not brought back the old order; and the old British traditions in favour of

[1] 12th December 1826.

---

liberty of speech and action would revive now that they were no longer trammelled by the fears of a destructive revolution. The days of July in 1830 gave fresh importance to the reaction of foreign upon English politics.

II. LAW REFORM

Meanwhile, however, the Utilitarians had a far stronger interest in domestic problems. In the first place, in Bentham's especial province a complete change of feeling had taken place. Romilly was Bentham's earliest disciple (so Bentham said), and looked up to him with 'filial reverence.' Every 'reformatiuncle' introduced by Romilly in parliament had been first brought to Bentham, to be conned over by the two.[1] With great difficulty Romilly had got two or three measures through the House of Commons, generally to be thrown out by Eldon's influence in the Lords.[2] After Romilly's death in 1818, the cause was taken up by the Whig philosopher, Sir James Mackintosh, and made a distinct step in advance. Though there were still obstacles in the upper regions, a committee was obtained to consider the frequency of capital punishment, and measures were passed to abolish it in particular cases. Finally, in 1823,

[1] Bentham's *Works*, v. p. 370.
[2] Romilly's attempts to improve the criminal law began in 1808. For various notices of his efforts, see his *Life* (3 vols. 1860), especially vol. ii. 243-54, 309, 321, 331, 369, 371, 389-91. Romilly was deeply interested in Dumont's *Théorie des Peines Légales* (1811), which he read in MS. and tried to get reviewed in the *Quarterly* (ii. 258, 391; iii. 136). The remarks (ii. 2-3) on the 'stupid dread of innovation' and the savage spirit infused into Englishmen by the horrors of the French revolution are worth notice in this connection.

---

the reform was adopted by Peel. Peel was destined to represent in the most striking way the process by which new ideas were gradually infiltrating the upper sphere. Though still a strong Tory and a representative of the university of Oxford, he was closely connected with the manufacturing classes, and had become aware, as he wrote to Croker (23rd March 1820), that public opinion had grown to be too large for its accustomed channels. As Home Secretary, he took up the whole subject of the criminal law, and passed in the next years a series of acts consolidating and mitigating the law, and repealing many old statutes. A measure of equal importance was his establishment in 1829 of the metropolitan police force, which at last put an end to the old chaotic muddle described by Colquhoun of parish officers and constables. Other significant legal changes marked the opening of a new era. Eldon was the very incarnation of the spirit of obstruction; and the Court of Chancery, over which he presided for a quarter of a century, was thought to be the typical stronghold of the evil principles denounced by Bentham. An attack in 1823 upon Eldon was made in the House of Commons by John Williams (1777-1846), afterwards a judge. Eldon, though profoundly irritated by the personal imputations involved, consented to the appointment of a commission, which reported in 1825, and recommended measures of reform. In 1828, Brougham made a great display upon which he had consulted Bentham.[1] In a speech of six hours' length he gave a summary of existing abuses, which may still be read with interest.[2] Commissions were appointed to investigate the procedure of the Common Law Court and the law

[1] Bentham's *Works*, x. p. 574.   [2] Brougham's *Speeches* (1838), ii. 287-486.

---

of real property. Another commission, intended to codify the criminal law, was appointed in 1833. Brougham says that of 'sixty capital defects' described in his speech, fifty-five had been removed, or were in course of removal, when his speeches were collected (i.e. 1838). Another speech of Brougham's in 1828 dealt with the carrying into execution of a favourite plan of Bentham's —the formation of local courts, which ultimately became the modern county courts.[1] The facts are significant of a startling change—no less than an abrupt transition from the reign of entire apathy to a reign of continuous reform extending over the whole range of law. The Reform Bill accelerated the movement, but it had been started before Bentham's death. The great stone, so long immovable, was fairly set rolling.

Bentham's influence, again, in bringing about the change is undeniable. He was greatly dissatisfied with Brougham's speech, and, indeed, would have been dissatisfied with anything short of a complete logical application of his whole system. He held Brougham to be 'insincere,'[2] a trimmer and popularity-hunter, but a useful instrument. Brougham's astonishing vanity and self-seeking prompted and perverted his amazing activity. He represents the process, perhaps necessary, by which a philosopher's ideas have to be modified before they can be applied to practical application. Brougham, however, could speak generously of men no longer in a position to excite his jealousy. He says in the preface to his first speech that 'the age of law reform and the age of

[1] An interesting summary of the progress of law reforms and of Bentham's share in them is given in Sir R. K. Wilson's *History of Modern English Law* (1875).
[2] Bentham's *Works*, x. 571.

Jeremy Bentham' were the same thing, and declares Bentham to be the 'first legal philosopher' who had appeared in the world. As the chief advocates of Bentham he reckons Romilly, his parliamentary representative ; Dumont, his literary interpreter ; and James Mill, who, in his article upon 'jurisprudence,' had popularised the essential principles of the doctrine.

The Utilitarians had at last broken up the barriers of obstruction and set the stream flowing. Whigs and Tories were taking up their theories. They naturally exaggerated in some respects the completeness of the triumph. The English law has not yet been codified, and it was characteristic of the Benthamite school to exaggerate the facility of that process. In their hatred of 'judge-made law' they assumed too easily that all things would be arranged into convenient pigeon-holes as soon as 'Judge and Co.' were abolished. It was a characteristic error to exaggerate the simplicity of their problem, and to fail to see that 'judge-made' law corresponds to a necessary inductive process by which the complex and subtle differences have to be gradually ascertained and fitted into a systematic statement. One other remark suggests itself. The Utilitarians saw in the dogged obstructiveness of Eldon and his like the one great obstacle to reform. It did not occur to them that the clumsiness of parliamentary legislation might be another difficulty. They failed to notice distinctly one tendency of their reforms. To make a code you require a sovereign strong enough to dominate the lawyers, not a system in which lawyers are an essential part of a small governing class. Codification, in short, means centralisation in one department. Blindness to

similar results elsewhere was a characteristic of the Utilitarian thinkers.

III. ECONOMIC REFORM

In another department the Utilitarians boasted, and also with good reason, of the triumph of their tenets. Political economy was in the ascendant. Professorships were being founded in Oxford, Cambridge,[1] London, and Edinburgh. Mrs. Marcet's *Conversations* (1818) were spreading the doctrine among babes and sucklings. The Utilitarians were the sacred band who defended the strictest orthodoxy against all opponents. They spoke as recognised authorities upon some of the most vital questions of the day, of which I need here only notice Free Trade, the doctrine most closely associated with the teaching of their revered Adam Smith. In 1816 Ricardo remarks with satisfaction that the principle 'is daily obtaining converts' even among the most prejudiced classes; and he refers especially to a petition in which the clothiers of Gloucestershire[2] expressed their willingness to give up all restrictions. There was, indeed, an important set-off against this gain. The landowners were being pledged to protection. They had decided that in spite of the peace, the price of wheat must be kept up to 80s. a quarter. They would no longer be complimented as Adam Smith had complimented them on their superior liberality, and were now creating a barrier only to be stormed after a long

---

[1] In Cambridge Pryme was the first professor in 1828, but had only the title without endowment. The professorship was only salaried in 1863.
[2] Ricardo's *Works* (1888), p. 407.

struggle. Meanwhile the principle was making rapid way among their rivals. One symptom was the adoption by the London merchants in 1820 of a famous petition on behalf of free trade.[1] It was drawn up by Thomas Tooke (1774-1858), who had long been actively engaged in the Russian trade, and whose *History of Prices* is in some respects the most valuable economic treatise of the time. Tooke gives a curious account of his action on this occasion.[2] He collected a few friends engaged in commerce, who were opposed to the corn laws. He found that several of them had 'crude and confused' notions upon the subject, and that each held that his own special interests should be exempted on some pretext from the general rule. After various dexterous pieces of diplomacy, however, he succeeded in obtaining the signature of Samuel Thornton, a governor of the bank of England, and ultimately procured a sufficient number of signatures by private solicitation. He was favourably received by the Prime Minister Lord Liverpool, and Vansittart (then Chancellor of the Exchequer), and finally got the petition presented to the House of Commons by Alexander Baring (afterwards Lord Ashburton). Tooke remarks that the Liverpool administration was in advance, not only of the public generally, but of the 'mercantile community.' Glasgow and Manchester, however, followed in the same steps, and the petition became a kind of official manifesto of the orthodox doctrine. The Political Economy Club formed next year at Tooke's instigation (April 18, 1821) was

---

[1] Printed in Porter's *Progress of the Nation* and elsewhere.
[2] See sixth volume of *History of Prices* by Tooke and Newmarch, and privately printed *Minutes of Political Economy Club* (1882).

intended to hasten the process of dispersing crude and confused ideas. It was essentially an organ of the Utilitarian propaganda.

The influence of the economists upon public policy was shown by the important measures carried through chiefly by Huskisson. Huskisson (1770-1830) was a type of the most intelligent official of his time. Like his more brilliant friend Canning, he had been introduced into office under Pitt, and retained a profound reverence for his early leader. Huskisson was a thorough man of business, capable of wrestling with blue-books, of understanding the sinking-fund, and having theories about the currency; a master of figures and statistics and the whole machinery of commerce. Though eminently useful, he might at any moment be applying some awkward doctrine from Adam Smith.

Huskisson began the series of economic reforms which were brought to their full development by Peel and Gladstone. The collection of his speeches[1] incidentally brings out very clearly his relation to the Utilitarians. The most remarkable is a great speech of April 24, 1826[2] (upon the state of the silk manufacture), of which Canning declared that he had never heard one abler, or which made a deeper impression upon the House. In this he reviews his policy, going over the most important financial measures of the preceding period. They made a new era, and he dates the beginning of the movement from the London petition, and the 'luminous speech' made by Baring when presenting it. We followed public opinion, he says, and did not create it.[3] Adopting the essential principles

---

[1] *Speeches*, 3 vols. 8vo, 1831. [2] *Ibid.* ii. 465-530. [3] *Ibid.* ii. 477.

of the petition, the government had in the first place set free the great woollen trade. The silk trade had been emancipated by abolishing the Spitalfield Acts passed in the previous century, which enabled magistrates to fix the rates of wages. The principle of prohibition had been abandoned, though protective duties remained. The navigation laws had been materially relaxed, and steps taken towards removing restrictions of different kinds upon trade with France and with India. One symptom of the change was the consolidation of the custom law effected by James Deacon Hume (1774-1842), an official patronised by Huskisson, and an original member of the Political Economy Club. By a law passed in 1825, five hundred statutes dating from the time of Edward 1. were repealed, and the essence of the law given in a volume of moderate size. Finally, the removal of prohibitions was undermining the smugglers.

The measures upon which Huskisson justly prided himself might have been dictated by the Political Economy Club itself. So far as they went they were an application of the doctrines of its thoroughgoing members, of Mill, Ricardo, and the orthodox school. They indeed supported him in the press. The *Morning Chronicle*, which expressed their views, declared him to be the most virtuous minister, that is (in true Utilitarian phrase), the most desirous of national welfare who had ever lived. The praise of Radicals would be not altogether welcome. Canning, in supporting his friend, maintained that sound commercial policy belonged no more to the Whigs than to the Tories. Huskisson and he were faithful disciples of Pitt, whose treaty with

France in 1786, assailed by Fox and the Whigs, had been the first practical application of the Wealth of Nations. Neither party, perhaps, could claim a special connection with good or bad political economy ; and certainly neither was prepared to incur political martyrdom in zeal for scientific truth. A question was beginning to come to the front which would make party lines dependent upon economic theories, and Huskisson's view of this was characteristic.

The speech from which I have quoted begins with an indignant retort upon a member who had applied to him Burke's phrase about a perfect-bred metaphysician exceeding the devil in malignity and contempt for mankind. Huskisson frequently protested even against the milder epithet of theorist. He asserted most emphatically that he appealed to 'experience' and not to 'theory,' a slippery distinction which finds a good exposure in Bentham's *Book of Fallacies*.[1] The doctrine, however, was a convenient one for Huskisson. He could appeal to experience to show that commercial restrictions had injured the woollen trade, and their absence benefited the cotton trade,[2] and when he was not being taunted with theories, he would state with perfect clearness the general free trade argument.[3] But he had to keep an eye to the uncomfortable tricks which theories sometimes play. He argued emphatically in 1825[4] that analogy between manufactures and agriculture is 'illogical.' He does not

[1] Bentham's *Works*, ii. 459. We may remember how J. S. Mill in his boyhood was abashed because he could not explain to his father the force of the distinction.
[2] *Speeches*, ii. 246, 332.
[3] *Ibid.* i. 102-108 (Currency Pamphlet of 1810).
[4] *Ibid.* ii. 397.

wish to depress the price of corn, but to keep it at such a level that our manufactures may not be hampered by dear food. Here he was forced by stress of politics to differ from his economical friends. The country gentleman did not wish to pay duties on his silk or his brandy, but he had a direct and obvious interest in keeping up the price of corn. Huskisson had himself supported the Corn Bill of 1815, but it was becoming more and more obvious that a revision would be necessary. In 1828 he declared that he 'lamented from the bottom of his soul the mass of evil and misery and destruction of capital which that law in the course of twelve years had produced.'[1] Ricardo, meanwhile, and the economists had from the first applied to agriculture the principles which Huskisson applied to manufactures.[2] Huskisson's melancholy death has left us unable to say whether upon this matter he would have been as convertible as Peel. In any case the general principle of free trade was as fully adopted by Huskisson and Canning as by the Utilitarians themselves. The Utilitarians could again claim to be both the inspirers of the first principles, and the most consistent in carrying out the deductions. They, it is true, were not generally biassed by having any interest in rents. They were to be the allies or teachers of the manufacturing class which began to be decidedly opposed to the squires and the old order.

In one very important economic question, the Utilitarians not only approved a change of the law, but were

[1] *Speeches*, iii. 257.
[2] Ricardo indeed made a reservation as to the necessity of counterbalancing by a moderate duty the special burthens upon agriculture.

the main agents in bringing it about. Francis Place was the wire-puller, to whose energy was due the abolition of the Conspiracy Laws in 1824. Joseph Hume in the House of Commons, and M'Culloch, then editor of the *Scotsman*, had the most conspicuous part in the agitation, but Place worked the machinery of agitation. The bill passed in 1824 was modified by an act of 1825 ; but the modification, owing to Place's efforts, was not serious, and the act, as we are told on good authority, 'effected a real emancipation,' and for the first time established the right of 'collective bargaining.'[1] The remarkable thing is that this act, carried on the principles of 'Radical individualism' and by the efforts of Radical individualists, was thus a first step towards the application to practice of socialist doctrine. Place thought that the result of the act would be not the encouragement, but the decline, of trades-unions. The unions had been due to the necessity of combining against oppressive laws, and would cease when those laws were abolished.[2] This marks a very significant stage in the development of economic opinion.

IV. CHURCH REFORM

The movement which at this period was most conspicuous politically was that which resulted in Roman Catholic emancipation, and here, too, the Utilitarians might be anticipating a complete triumph of their principles. The existing disqualifications, indeed, were

[1] In the *History of Trades-Unionism* by Sidney and Beatrice Webb (1894), pp. 88-98. The history of Place's agitation is fully given in Mr. Graham Wallas's *Life*, chap. viii.
[2] Wallas's *Francis Place*, p. 217.

upheld by little but the purely obstructive sentiment. When the duke of York swore that 'so help him God!' he would oppose the change to the last, he summed up the whole 'argument' against it. Canning and Huskisson here represented the policy not only of Pitt, but of Castlereagh. The Whigs, indeed, might claim to be the natural representatives of toleration. The church of England was thoroughly subjugated by the state, and neither Whig nor Tory wished for a fundamental change. But the most obvious differentia of Whiggism was a dislike to the ecclesiastical spirit. The Whig noble was generally more or less of a freethinker; and upon such topics Holland House differed little from Queen's Square Place, or differed only in a rather stricter reticence. Both Whig and Tory might accept Warburton's doctrine of an 'alliance' between church and state. The Tory inferred that the church should be supported. His prescription for meeting discontent was 'more yeomanry' and a handsome sum for church-building. The Whig thought that the church got a sufficient return in being allowed to keep its revenues. On the Tory view, the relation might be compared to that of man and wife in Christian countries where, though the two are one, the husband is bound to fidelity. On the Whig view it was like a polygamous system, where the wife is in complete subjection, and the husband may take any number of concubines. The Whig noble regarded the church as socially useful, but he was by no means inclined to support its interests when they conflicted with other political considerations. He had been steadily in favour of diminishing the privileges of the establishment, and had taken part in removing the

grievances of the old penal laws. He was not prepared to uphold privileges which involved a palpable danger to his order.

This position is illustrated by Sydney Smith, the ideal divine of Holland House. The *Plymley Letters*[1] give his views most pithily. Smith, a man as full of sound sense as of genuine humour, appeals to the principles of toleration, and is keenly alive to the absurdity of a persecution which only irritates without conversion. But he also appeals to the danger of the situation. 'If Bonaparte lives,'[2] he says, 'and something is not done to conciliate the Catholics, it seems to me absolutely impossible but that we must perish.' We are like the captain of a ship attacked by a pirate, who should begin by examining his men in the church catechism, and forbid any one to sponge or ram who had not taken the sacrament according to the forms of the church of England. He confesses frankly that the strength of the Irish is with him a strong motive for listening to their claims. To talk of 'not acting from fear is mere parliamentary cant.'[3] Although the danger which frightened Smith was evaded, this was the argument which really brought conviction even to Tories in 1829. In any case the Whigs, whose great boast was their support of toleration, would not be prompted by any Quixotic love of the church to encounter tremendous perils in defence of its privileges.

Smith's zeal had its limits. He observes humorously in his preface that he had found himself after the Reform Bill engaged in the defence of the National Church against the archbishop of Canterbury and the bishop of London.

---

[1] First published in 1807-8.   [2] *Letter* iii.   [3] *Ibid.* vi.

The letters to Archdeacon Singleton, written when the Whigs were flirting with the Radicals, show how much good an old Whig could find in the establishment. This marks the difference between the true Whig and the Utilitarian. The Whig would not risk the country for the sake of church; he would keep the clerical power strictly subordinate to the power of the state, but then, when considered from the political side, it was part of a government system providing him with patronage, and to be guarded from the rude assaults of the Radical reformer. The Utilitarian, though for the moment he was in alliance with the Whig, regarded the common victory as a step to something far more sweeping. He objected to intolerance as decidedly as the Whig, for absolute freedom of opinion was his most cherished doctrine. He objected still more emphatically to persecution on behalf of the church, because he entirely repudiated its doctrines. The objection to spreading true doctrine by force is a strong one, but hardly so strong as the objection to a forcible spread of false doctrine. But, besides this, the church represented to the Utilitarian precisely the very worst specimen of the corruptions of the time. The Court of Chancery was bad enough, but the whole ecclesiastical system with its vast prizes,[1] its opportunities for corrupt patronage, its pluralism and non-residence was an evil on a larger scale. The Radical, therefore, unlike the Whig, was an internecine enemy of the whole system. The 'church of England system,' as Bentham calmly remarks, is 'ripe

---

[1] Sydney Smith put very ingeniously the advantages of what he called the 'lottery' system: of giving, that is, a few great prizes, instead of equalising the incomes of the clergy. Things look so different from opposite points of views.

for dissolution.'[1] I have already noticed his quaint proposal for giving effect to his views. Mill, in the *Westminster Review*, denounced the church of England as the worst of all churches.[2] To the Utilitarian, in short, the removal of the disqualification of dissenters and Catholics was thus one step to the consummation which their logic demanded—the absolute disestablishment and disendowment of the church. Conservatives in general anticipated the confiscation of church revenues as a necessary result of reform; and so far as the spirit of reformers was represented by the Utilitarians and their Radical allies, they had good grounds for the fear. James Mill's theory is best indicated by a later article published in the *London Review* of July 1835. After pointing out that the church of England retains all the machinery desired for supporting priests and preventing the growth of intellect and morality, he proceeds to ask what the clergy do for their money. They read prayers, which is a palpable absurdity; they preach sermons to spread superstitious notions of the Supreme Being, and perform ceremonies—baptism, and so forth—which are obviously silly. The church is a mere state machine worked in subservience to the sinister interest of the governing classes. The way to reform it would be to equalise the pay: let the clergy be appointed by a 'Minister of Public Instruction' or the county authorities; abolish the articles, and constitute a church 'without dogmas or ceremonies'; and employ the clergy to give lectures on ethics, botany, political economy, and so forth, besides holding Sunday

---

[1] *Church of Englandism*, ii. 199.
[2] See especially his review of Southey's *Book of the Church*.

meetings, dances (decent dances are to be specially invented for the purpose), and social meals, which would be a revival of the 'agapai' of the early Christians. For this purpose, however, it might be necessary to substitute tea and coffee for wine. In other words, the church is to be made into a popular London University. The plan illustrates the incapacity of an isolated clique to understand the real tone of public opinion. I need not pronounce upon Mill's scheme, which seems to have some sense in it, but one would like to know whether Newman read his article.

V. SINISTER INTERESTS

In questions of foreign policy, of law reform, of political economy, and of religious tests, the Utilitarians thus saw the gradual approximation to their most characteristic views on the part of the Whigs, and a strong infiltration of the same views among the less obstructive Tories. They held the logical creed, to which others were slowly approximating, either from the force of argument or from the great social changes which were bringing new classes into political power. The movement for parliamentary reform which for a time overshadowed all other questions might be regarded as a corollary from the position already won. Briefly, it was clear that a new social stratum was exercising a vast influence; the doctrines popular with it had to be more or less accepted; and the only problem worth consideration by practical men was whether or not such a change should be made in the political machinery as would enable the influence to be exercised by direct and constitutional means. To

the purely obstructive Tory parliamentary reform was a step to the general cataclysm. The proprietor of a borough, like the proprietor of a church patronage or commission in the army, had a right to his votes, and to attack his right was simply confiscation of private property. The next step might be to confiscate his estate. But even the more intelligent Conservative drew the line at such a measure. Canning, Huskisson, and even Peel might accept the views of the Utilitarians in regard to foreign policy, to law reform, to free trade, or the removal of religious tests, declaring only that they were obeying 'experience' instead of logic, and might therefore go just as far as they pleased. But they were all pledged to resist parliamentary reform to the utmost. Men thoroughly steeped in official life, and versed in the actual working of the machinery, were naturally alive to the magnitude of the change to be introduced. They saw with perfect clearness that it would amount to a revolution. The old system in which the ruling classes carried on business by family alliances and bargains between ministers and great men would be impracticable. The fact that so much had been done in the way of concession to the ideas of the new classes was for them an argument against the change. If the governing classes were ready to reform abuses, why should they be made unable to govern? A gradual enfranchisement of the great towns on the old system might be desirable. Such a man as Huskisson, representing great commercial interests, could not be blind to the necessity. But a thorough reconstruction was more alarming. As Canning had urged in a great speech at Liverpool, a House of Commons, thoroughly democratised, would be incompatible with

the existence of the monarchy and the House of Lords. So tremendously powerful a body would reduce the other parts of the constitution to mere excrescences, feeble drags upon the new driving-wheel in which the whole real force would be concentrated.

That this expressed, in point of fact, a serious truth, was, I take it, undeniable. The sufficient practical answer was, that change was inevitable. To refuse to adapt the constitutional machinery to the altered political forces was not to hinder their growth, but to make a revolution necessary. When, accordingly, the excluded classes began seriously to demand admission, the only question came to lie between violent and peaceable methods. The alarm with which our fathers watched the progress of the measure may seem to us exaggerated, but they scarcely overestimated the magnitude of the change. The old rulers were taking a new partner of such power, that whatever authority was left to them might seem to be left on sufferance. As soon as he became conscious of his strength, they would be reduced to nonentities. The Utilitarians took some part in the struggle, and welcomed the victory with anticipations destined to be, for the time at least, cruelly disappointed. But they were still a small minority, whose views rather scandalised the leaders of the party with which they were in temporary alliance. The principles upon which they based their demands, as formulated by James Mill, looked, as we shall see, far beyond the concessions of the moment.

One other political change is significant, though I am unable to give an adequate account of it. Bentham's denunciation of 'sinister interests'—one of his leading

topics—corresponds to the question of sinecures, which was among the most effective topics of Radical declamation. The necessity of limiting the influence of the crown and excluding 'placemen' from the House of Commons had been one of the traditional Whig commonplaces, and a little had been done by Burke's act of 1782 towards limiting pensions and abolishing obsolete offices. When English Radicalism revived, the assault was renewed in parliament and the press. During the war little was achieved, though a revival of the old complaints about placemen in parliament was among the first symptoms of the rising sentiment. In 1812 an attack was made upon the 'tellers of the Exchequer.' Romilly[1] says that the value of one of these offices had risen to £26,000 or £27,000 a year. The income came chiefly from fees, and the actual work, whatever it was, was done by deputy. The scandal was enormous at a time when the stress upon the nation was almost unbearable. One of the tellerships was held by a member of the great Grenville family, who announced that they regarded the demand for reform as a personal attack upon them. The opposition, therefore, could not muster even its usual strength, and the motion for inquiry was rejected. When the war was over, even the government began to feel that something must be done. In 1817 some acts were passed[2] abolishing a variety of sinecure offices and 'regulating certain offices in the Court of Exchequer.' The Radicals considered this as a mere delusion, because it was provided at the same time that pensions might be given to persons who had held certain great offices. The change, however, was apparently of importance as re-

[1] Romilly's *Memoirs*, iii. 33.   [2] 57 George III. caps. 60-67.

moving the chief apology for sinecures, and the system
with modifications still remains. The marquis of
Camden, one of the tellers of the Exchequer, voluntarily
resigned the fees and accepted only the regular salary
of £2500. His action is commended in the *Black Book*,[1]
which expresses a regret that the example had not been
followed by other great sinecurists. Public opinion was
beginning to be felt. During the subsequent period
the cry against sinecures became more emphatic. The
Black Book, published originally in 1820 and 1823, and
afterwards reissued, gave a list, so far as it could be
ascertained, of all pensions, and supplied a mass of information for Radical orators. The amount of pensions
is stated at over £1,000,000, including sinecure offices
with over £350,000 annually;[2] and the list of offices
(probably very inaccurate in detail) gives a singular
impression of the strange ramifications of the system.
Besides the direct pensions, every new department of
administration seems to have suggested the foundation
of offices which tended to become sinecures. The cry
for 'retrenchment' was joined to the cry for reform.[3]
Joseph Hume, who first entered parliament in 1818,
became a representative of the Utilitarian Radicalism,
and began a long career of minute criticism which won
for him the reputation of a stupendous bore, but helped
to keep a steady pressure upon ministers.[4] Sir James

[1] Edition of 1828, p. 24.   [2] *Ibid.* p. 10.
[3] A Mr. Gray proposed at a county meeting in 1816 that the cry of
'retrenchment and reform' should be raised in every corner of the island
(Henry Jephson's *Platform*, p. 378). I do not know whether this was the first
appearance of the formula.
[4] Hume had been introduced to Place by James Mill, who thought him
worth 'nursing.' Place found him at first 'dull and selfish,' but 'nursed him'
so well that by 1836 he had become the 'man of men.'—Wallas's *Francis
Place*, p. 181, 182.

Graham (1792-1861) was at this time of Radical tendencies, and first made himself conspicuous by demanding
returns of pensions.[1] The settlements of the civil lists of
George IV., William IV., and Victoria, gave opportunities
for imposing new restrictions upon the pension system.
Although no single sweeping measure was passed, the
whole position was changed. By the time of the Reform
Bill, a sinecure had become an anachronism. The presumption was that whenever an opportunity offered, it
would be suppressed. Some of the sinecure offices in
the Court of Chancery, the 'Keeper of the Hanaper,'
the 'Chaffwax,' and so forth, were abolished by an act
passed by the parliament which had just carried the
Reform Bill.[2] In 1833 a reform of the system of naval
administration by Sir James Graham got rid of some
cumbrous machinery; and Graham again was intrusted
in 1834 with an act under which the Court of Exchequer
was finally reformed, and the 'Clerk of the Pells' and
the 'Tellers of the Exchequer' ceased to exist.[3] Other
offices seem to have melted away by degrees, whenever
a chance offered.

Many other of the old abuses had ceased to require
any special denunciations from political theorists. The
general principle was established, and what remained was
to apply it in detail. The prison system was no longer
in want of a Howard or a Bentham. Abuses remained
which occupied the admirable Mrs. Fry; and many
serious difficulties had to be solved by a long course of
experiment. But it was no longer a question whether

[1] Torrens's *Life of Graham*, i. 250-72, where his great speech of 14th May
1830 is given.
[2] 2 and 3 William IV. cap. 111 (passed 15 August 1832).
[3] 4 and 5 William IV. cap. 15.

anything should be doing, but of the most efficient means
of bringing about an admittedly desirable end. The
agitation for the suppression of the slave-trade again had
been succeeded by the attack upon slavery. The system
was evidently doomed, although not finally abolished till
after the Reform Bill; and ministers were only considering
the question whether the abolition should be summary or
gradual, or what compensation might be made to vested
interests. The old agitation had been remarkable, as I
have said, not only for its end but for the new kind of
machinery to which it had applied. Popular agitation[1]
had taken a new shape. The county associations formed
in the last days of the American war of independence,
and the societies due to the French revolution had set
a precedent. The revolutionary societies had been
suppressed or had died out, as opposed to the general
spirit of the nation, although they had done a good deal
to arouse political speculation. In the period of distress
which followed the war the Radical reformers had again
held public meetings, and had again been met by repressive measures. The acts of 1817 and 1819[2] imposed
severe restrictions upon the right of public meeting.
The old 'county meeting,' which continued to be common
until the reform period, and was summoned by the lord-
lieutenant or the sheriff on a requisition from the freeholders, had a kind of constitutional character, though
I do not know its history in detail.[3] The extravagantly
repressive measures were an anachronism, or could only
be enforced during the pressure of an intense excitement.

[1] *The Platform, its Origin and Progress*, by Henry Jephson (1892), gives a
very interesting historical account of the process.
[2] 57 George III. cap. 19, and 60 George III. cap. 6.
[3] See Jephson's *Platform*, pp. 167-70.

In one way or other, public meetings were soon being
held as frequently as ever. The trial of Queen Caroline
gave opportunity for numerous gatherings, and statesmen
began to find that they must use instead of suppressing
them. Canning[1] appears to have been the first minister
to make frequent use of speeches addressed to public
meetings; and meetings to which such appeals were
addressed soon began to use their authority to demand
pledges from the speakers.[2] Representation was to be
understood more and more as delegation. Meanwhile
the effect of public meetings was enormously increased
when a general organisation was introduced. The great
precedent was the Catholic Association, founded in 1823
by O'Connell and Sheil. The peculiar circumstances of
the Irish people and their priests gave a ready-made
machinery for the agitation which triumphed in 1829.
The Political Union founded by Attwood at Birmingham
in the same year adopted the method, and led to the
triumph of 1832. Political combination henceforth took
a different shape, and in the ordinary phrase, 'public
opinion' became definitely the ultimate and supreme
authority. This enormous change and the corresponding
development of the power of the press, which affected to
mould and, at any rate, expressed public opinion, entirely
fell in with Utilitarian principles. Their part in bringing
about the change was of no special importance except in
so far as they more or less inspired the popular orators.
They were, however, ready to take advantage of it.
They had the *Westminster Review* to take a place beside
the *Edinburgh* and *Quarterly Reviews*, which had raised

[1] See Jephson's *Platform*, i. 348, 455, 517.
[2] See *Ibid.* ii. 129-40 for some interesting passages as to this.

periodical writing to a far higher position than it had ever occupied, and to which leading politicians and leading authors on both sides had become regular contributors. The old contempt for journalism was rapidly vanishing. In 1825 Canning expresses his regret for having given some information to a paper of which an ill use had been made. He had previously abstained from all communication with 'these gentry,' and was now resolved to have done with *hoc genus omne* for good and all.[1] In 1839 we find his former colleague, Lord Lyndhurst, seeking an alliance with Barnes, the editor of the *Times*, as eagerly as though Barnes had been the head of a parliamentary party.[2]

The newspapers had probably done more than the schools to spread habits of reading through the country. Yet the strong interest which was growing up in educational matters was characteristic. Brougham's phrase, ' the schoolmaster is abroad' (29th January 1821), became a popular proverb, and rejoiced the worthy Bentham.[3] I have already described the share taken by the Utilitarians in the great Bell and Lancaster controversy. Parliament had as yet done little. A bill brought in by Whitbread had been passed in 1807 by the House of Commons, enabling parishes to form schools on the Scottish model, but according to Romilly,[4] it was passed in the well-grounded confidence that it would be thrown out by the peers. A committee upon education was obtained by Brougham after the peace, which reported in 1818, and which led to a commission upon school endowments.

[1] *Official Correspondence* (1887), 308.
[2] Greville's *George IV. and William IV.*, iii. 155, 167-69, 171.
[3] Bentham's *Works*, x. 571.
[4] Romilly's *Memoirs*, ii. 67, 222.

Brougham introduced an education bill in 1820, but nothing came of it. The beginning of any participation by government in national education was not to take place till after the Reform Bill. Meanwhile, however, the foundation of the London University upon unsectarian principles was encouraging the Utilitarians; and there were other symptoms of the growth of enlightenment. George Birkbeck (1776-1841) had started some popular lectures upon science at Glasgow about 1800, and having settled as a physician in London, started the 'Mechanics' Institution' in 1824. Brougham was one of the first trustees; and the institution, though exposed to a good deal of ridicule, managed to take root and become the parent of others. In 1827 was started the Society for the Diffusion of Useful Knowledge, of which Brougham was president, and the committee of which included James Mill. In the course of its twenty years' existence it published or sanctioned the publication by Charles Knight of a great mass of popular literature. The *Penny Magazine* (1832-1845) is said to have had two hundred thousand subscribers at the end of its first year of existence. Crude and superficial as were some of these enterprises, they clearly marked a very important change. Cobbett and the Radical orators found enormous audiences ready to listen to their doctrine. Churchmen and Dissenters, Tories and Radicals were finding it necessary both to educate and to disseminate their principles by writing; and as new social strata were becoming accessible to such influences, their opinions began to exercise in turn a more distinct reaction upon political and ecclesiastical affairs.

No party felt more confidence at the tendency of this

new intellectual fermentation than the Utilitarians. They had a definite, coherent, logical creed. Every step which increased the freedom of discussion increased the influence of the truth. Their doctrines were the truth, if not the whole truth. Once allow them to get a fulcrum and they would move the world. Bit by bit their principles of legislation, of economy, of politics were being accepted in the most different quarters; and even the more intelligent of their opponents were applying them, though the application might be piecemeal and imperfect. It was in vain that an adversary protested that he was not bound by logic, and appealed to experience instead of theory. Let him justify his action upon what grounds he pleased, he was, in point of fact, introducing the leaven of true doctrine, and it might be trusted to work out the desirable results.

I must now deal more in detail with the Utilitarian theories. I will only observe in general terms that their triumph was not likely to be accepted without a struggle. Large classes regarded them with absolute abhorrence. Their success, if they did succeed, would mean the destruction of religious belief, of sound philosophy, of the great important ecclesiastical and political institutions, and probably general confiscation of property and the ruin of the foundations of society. And, meanwhile, in spite of the progress upon which I have dwelt, there were two problems, at least, of enormous importance, upon which it could scarcely be said that any progress had been made. The church, in the first place, was still where it had been. No change had been made in its constitution; it was still the typical example of corrupt patronage; and the object of the hatred of

all thoroughgoing Radicals. And, in the second place, pauperism had grown to appalling dimensions during the war; and no effectual attempt had been made to deal with it. Behind pauperism there were great social questions, the discontent and misery of great masses of the labouring population. Whatever reforms might be made in other parts of the natural order, here were difficulties enough to task the wisdom of legislators and speculators upon legislative principles.

CHAPTER III

POLITICAL THEORY

I. MILL ON GOVERNMENT

I now turn to the general political theory of which Mill was the authoritative exponent. The *Encyclopædia* article upon 'Government' (1820) gives the pith of their doctrine. It was, as Professor Bain[1] thinks, an 'impelling and a guiding force' in the movement which culminated in the Reform Bill. The younger Utilitarians regarded it, says J. S. Mill, as 'a masterpiece of political wisdom';[2] while Macaulay[3] taunts them for holding it to be 'perfect and unanswerable.' This famous article is a terse and energetic summary of the doctrine implied in Bentham's *Works*, but there obscured under elaboration of minute details. It is rather singular, indeed, that so vigorous a manifesto of Utilitarian dogma should have been accepted by Macvey Napier—a sound Whig —for a publication which professed scientific impartiality. It has, however, in the highest degree, the merits of clearness and condensation desirable in a popular exposition. The reticence appropriate to the place excuses the omission of certain implicit conclusions. Mill has to give a complete theory of politics in thirty-two 8vo

[1] Bain's *James Mill*, p. 215.   [2] *Autobiography*, p. 104.
[3] *Miscellaneous Works* (Popular Edition), p. 131.

pages. He has scanty room for qualifying statement or historical illustration. He speaks as from the chair of a professor laying down the elementary principles of a demonstrated science.[1]

Mill starts from the sacred principle. The end of government, as the end of all conduct, must be the increase of human happiness. The province of government is limited by another consideration. It has to deal with one class of happiness, that is, with the pains and pleasures 'which men derive from one another.' By a 'law of nature' labour is requisite for procuring the means of happiness. Now, if 'nature' produced all that any man desired, there would be no need of government, for there would be no conflict of interest. But, as the material produced is finite, and can be appropriated by individuals, it becomes necessary to insure to every man his proper share. What, then, is a man's proper share? That which he himself produces; for, if you give to one man more than the produce of his labour, you must take away the produce of another man's labour. The greatest happiness, therefore, is produced by 'assuring to every man the greatest possible quantity of the produce of his own labour.' How can this be done? Will not the strongest take the share of the weakest? He can be prevented in one and apparently only in one way. Men must unite and delegate to a few the power necessary for protecting all. 'This is government.'[2]

[1] The articles from the *Encyclopædia* upon Government, Jurisprudence, Liberty of the Press, Prisons and Prison Discipline, Colonies, Law of Nations, Education, were reprinted in a volume 'not for sale,' in 1825 and 1828. I quote from a reprint not dated.
[2] 'Government,' pp. 3-5.

The problem is now simple. Government is essentially an association of men for the protection of property. It is a delegation of the powers necessary for that purpose to the guardians, and 'all the difficult questions of government relate to the means' of preventing the guardians from themselves becoming plunderers.

How is this to be accomplished? The power of protection, says Mill, following the old theory, may be intrusted to the whole community, to a few, or to one; that is, we may have a democracy, an aristocracy, or a monarchy. A democracy, or direct government of all by all, is for the ordinary reasons pronounced impracticable. But the objections to the other systems are conclusive. The need of government, he has shown, depends upon 'the law of human nature'[1] that 'a man, if able, will take from others anything which they have and he desires.' The very principle which makes government necessary, therefore, will prompt a government to defeat its own proper end. Mill's doctrine is so far identical with the doctrine of Hobbes; men are naturally in a state of war, and government implies a tacit contract by which men confer upon a sovereign the power necessary for keeping the peace. But here, though admitting the force of Hobbes's argument, he diverges from its conclusion. If a democracy be impossible, and an aristocracy or monarchy necessarily oppressive, it might seem, he admits, as it actually seemed to Hobbes and to the French economists, that the fewer the oppressors the better, and that therefore an absolute monarchy is the best. Experience, he thinks, is 'on the surface' ambiguous. Eastern despots

[1] 'Government,' p. 8.

and Roman emperors have been the worst scourges to mankind; yet the Danes preferred a despot to an aristocracy, and are as 'well governed as any people in Europe.' In Greece, democracy, in spite of its defects, produced the most brilliant results.[1] Hence, he argues, we must go 'beyond the surface,' and 'penetrate to the springs within.' The result of the search is discouraging. The hope of glutting the rulers is illusory. There is no 'point of saturation'[2] with the objects of desire, either for king or aristocracy. It is a 'grand governing law of human nature' that we desire such power as will make 'the persons and properties of human beings subservient to our pleasures.'[3] This desire is indefinitely great. To the number of men whom we would force into subservience, and the degree in which we would make them subservient, we can assign no limits. Moreover, as pain is a more powerful instrument for securing obedience than pleasure, a man will desire to possess 'unlimited power of inflicting pain upon others.' Will he also desire, it may be asked, to make use of it? The 'chain of inference,' he replies, in this case is close and strong 'to a most unusual degree.' A man desires the actions of others to be in correspondence with his own wishes. 'Terror' will be the 'grand instrument.'[4] It thus follows that the very principle upon which government is founded leads, in the absence of checks, 'not only to that degree of plunder which leaves the members (of a community) . . . the bare means of subsistence, but to that degree of cruelty which is necessary to keep in existence the most intense terror.' An English gentleman, he says, is a favourable specimen of civilisation,

[1] 'Government,' p. 9.   [2] *Ibid.* p. 11.   [3] *Ibid.* p. 9.   [4] *Ibid.* p. 12.

and yet West Indian slavery shows of what cruelty he could be guilty when unchecked. If equal cruelty has not been exhibited elsewhere, it is, he seems to think, because men were not 'the same as sheep in respect to their shepherd,'[1] and may therefore resist if driven too far. The difficulty upon this showing is to understand how any government, except the most brutal tyranny, ever has been, or ever can be, possible. What is the combining principle which can weld together such a mass of hostile and mutually repellent atoms? How they can even form the necessary compact is difficult to understand, and the view seems to clash with his own avowed purpose. It is Mill's aim, as it was Bentham's, to secure the greatest happiness of the greatest number; and yet he seems to set out by proving as a 'law of human nature' that nobody can desire the happiness of any one except himself. He quotes from Montesquieu the saying, which shows an 'acute sense of this important truth,' 'that every one who has power is led to abuse it.'[2] Rather it would seem, according to Mill, all power implies abuse in its very essence. The problem seems to be how to make universal cohesion out of universal repulsion.

Mill has his remedy for this deeply seated evil. He attacks, as Bentham had already done, the old-fashioned theory, according to which the British Constitution was an admirable mixture of the three 'simple forms.' Two of the powers, he argues, will always agree to 'swallow up the third.'[3] 'The monarchy and aristocracy have all

[1] 'Government,' p. 9.
[2] C'est une expérience éternelle que tout homme qui a du pouvoir est porté à en abuser; il va jusqu'à ce qu'il trouve des limites.—Esprit des Lois, Bk. xi. chap. 4.   [3] 'Government,' p. 15.

possible motives for endeavouring to obtain unlimited power over the persons and property of the community,' though the democracy, as he also says, has every possible motive for preventing them. And in England, as he no doubt meant his readers to understand, the monarchy and aristocracy had to a great extent succeeded. Where, then, are we to look? To the 'grand discovery of modern times,' namely, the representative system. If this does not solve all difficulties we shall be forced to the conclusion that good government is impossible. Fortunately, however, the representative system may be made perfectly effective. This follows easily. It would, as he has said,[1] be a 'contradiction in terms' to suppose that the community at large can 'have an interest opposite to its interest.' In the Bentham formula, it can have 'no sinister interest.' It cannot desire its own misery. Though the community cannot act as a whole, it can act through representatives. It is necessary to intrust power to a governing body; but that body can be prevented by adequate checks from misusing its powers. Indeed, the common theory of the British Constitution was precisely that the House of Commons was 'the checking body.'[2] The whole problem is to secure a body which shall effectively discharge the function thus attributed in theory to the House of Commons. That will be done when the body is chosen in such a way that its interests are necessarily coincident with those of the community at large. Hence there is of course no difficulty in deducing the actual demands of reformers. Without defining precise limits, he shows that representatives must be elected for brief periods, and that the

[1] 'Government,' p. 7.   [2] Ibid. p. 18.

right to a vote must at least be wide enough to prevent the electoral body from forming a class with 'sinister interests.' He makes some remarkable qualifications, with the view apparently of not startling his readers too much by absolute and impracticable claims. He thinks that the necessary identity of interest would still be secured if classes were unrepresented whose interests are 'indisputably included in those of others.' Children's interests are involved in those of their parents, and the interests of 'almost all women' in those of their fathers or husbands.[1] Again, all men under forty might be omitted without mischief, for 'the great majority of old men have sons whose interests they regard as an essential part of their own. This is a law of human nature.'[2] There would, he observes, be no danger that men above forty would try to reduce the 'rest of the community to the state of abject slaves.' Mill, as his son tells us,[3] disowned any intention of positively advocating these exclusions. He only meant to say that they were not condemned by his general principle. The doctrine, however, about women, even as thus understood, scandalised his younger followers.

Mill proceeds to argue at some length that a favourite scheme of some moderate reformers, for the representation of classes, could only lead to 'a motley aristocracy,' and then answers two objections. The first is that his scheme would lead to the abolition of the monarchy and the House of Lords. The reply is simple and significant. It would only lead to that result if a monarchy or a House of Lords were favourable to bad government. He does not inquire whether they are so in fact. The second

[1] 'Government,' p. 21.   [2] Ibid. p. 22.   [3] Autobiography, p. 104.

objection is that the people do not understand their own interest, and to this his answer is more remarkable. If the doctrine be true, he says, we are in a 'deplorable' position: we have to choose between evils which will be designedly produced by those who have both the power to oppress and an interest in oppression; and the evils which will be accidentally produced by men who would act well if they recognised their own interests.[1] Now the first evil is in any case the worst, for it supposes an 'invariable' evil; while in the other case, men may at least act well by accident. A governing class, that is with interests separate from those of the government, *must* be bad. If the interests be identical, the government *may* be bad. It will be bad if ignorant, but ignorance is curable. Here he appeals for once to a historical case. The priesthood at the Reformation argued on behalf of their own power from the danger that the people would make a bad use of the Bible. The Bible should therefore be kept for the sacred caste. They had, Mill thinks, a stronger case in appearance than the Tories, and yet the effect of allowing the people to judge for themselves in religious matters has been productive of good effects 'to a degree which has totally altered the condition of human nature.'[2] Why should not the people be trusted to judge for themselves in politics? This implies a doctrine which had great influence with the Utilitarians. In the remarkable essay upon 'Education,' which is contained in the volume of reprints, Mill discusses the doctrine of Helvétius that all the differences between

[1] 'Government,' p. 28.
[2] Ibid. p. 30. Mill especially refers to the exposure of clerical artifices in Father Paul's Council of Trent.

men are due to education. Without pronouncing positively upon the differences between individuals, Mill observes that, at any rate, the enormous difference between classes of men is wholly due to education.[1] He takes education, it must be observed, in the widest possible sense, as meaning what would now be called the whole action of the 'environment' upon the individual. This includes, as he shows at length, domestic education, all the vast influence exercised upon a child in his family, 'technical education,' by which he means the ordinary school teaching, 'social education,' that is the influences which we imbibe from the current opinions of our neighbours, and finally, 'political education,' which he calls the 'keystone of the arch.' The means, he argues, by which the 'grand objects of desire may be attained, depend almost wholly upon the political machine.'[2] If that 'machine' be so constituted as to make the grand objects of desire the 'natural prizes of just and virtuous conduct, of high services to mankind and of the generous and amiable sentiments from which great endeavours in the service of mankind naturally proceed, it is natural to see diffused among mankind a generous ardour in the acquisition of those admirable qualities which prepare a man for admirable action, great intelligence, perfect self-command, and over-ruling benevolence.' The contrary will be the case where the political machine prompts to the flattery of a small ruling body.

This characteristic passage betrays an enthusiasm which really burned under Mill's stern outside. He confines himself habitually to the forms of severe logic, and scorns anything like an appeal to sentiment. The trammels of his

[1] 'Education,' p. 20   [2] Ibid. p. 45.

scientific manner impede his utterance a little, even when he is speaking with unwonted fervour. Yet the prosaic Utilitarian who has been laying down as a universal law that the strong will always plunder the weak, and that all rulers will reduce their subjects to abject slavery, is absolutely convinced, it seems, of the possibility of somehow transmuting selfishness into public spirit, justice, generosity, and devotion to truth. Equally characteristic is the faith in the 'political machine.' Mill speaks as if somebody had 'discovered' the representative system as Watt (more or less) discovered the steam-engine; that to 'discover' the system is the same thing as to set it to work; and that, once at work, it will be omnipotent. He is not less certain that a good constitution will make men virtuous, than was Bentham that he could grind rogues honest by the Panopticon. The indefinite modifiability of character was the ground upon which the Utilitarians based their hopes of progress; and it was connected in their minds with the doctrine of which his essay upon education is a continuous application. The theory of 'association of ideas' appeared to him to be of the utmost importance in education and in politics, because it implied almost unlimited possibilities of moulding human beings to fit them for a new order. In politics this implied, as J. S. Mill says,[1] 'unbounded confidence' in the influence of 'reason.' Teach the people and let them vote freely, and everything would follow.

This gives Mill's answer to one obvious objection. The Conservative who answered him by dwelling upon the ignorance of the lower classes was in some respects

[1] Autobiography, p. 106.

preaching to a convert. Nobody was more convinced than Mill of the depths of popular ignorance or, indeed, of the stupidity of mankind in general. The labourers who cheered Orator Hunt at Peterloo were dull enough; but so were the peers who cheered Eldon in the House of Lords; and the labourers at least desired general prosperity, while the peers were content if their own rents were kept up. With general education, however, even the lower orders of the people would be fit for power, especially when we take into account one other remarkable conclusion. The 'wise and good,' he says, 'in any class of men do, for all general purposes, govern the rest.'[1] Now, the class in which wisdom and virtue are commonest is not the aristocracy, but the middle rank. Another truth follows 'from the principles of human nature in general.' That is the rather surprising truth that the lower orders take their opinions from the middle class; apply to the middle class for help in sickness and old age; hold up the same class as a model to be imitated by their children, and 'account it an honour' to adopt its opinions. Consequently, however far the franchise were extended, it is this class which has produced the most distinguished ornaments of art, science, and even of legislation, which will ultimately decide upon political questions. 'The great majority of the people,' is his concluding sentence, 'never cease to be guided by that rank; and we may with some confidence challenge the adversaries of the people to produce a single instance to the contrary in the history of the world.'

This article upon 'Government' gives the very essence of Utilitarian politics. I am afraid that it also suggests

[1] 'Government,' p. 31.

that the political theory was chiefly remarkable for a simple-minded audacity. Good political treatises are rare. They are apt to be pamphlets in disguise, using 'general principles' for showy perorations, or to be a string of platitudes with no definite application to facts. They are fit only for the platform, or only for the professor's lecture-room. Mill's treatise, according to his most famous antagonist, was a mere bundle of pretentious sophistry.

Macaulay came forth like a Whig David to slay the Utilitarian Goliath. The Encyclopædia articles, finished in 1824, were already in 1825,[1] as Mill says, text-books of the young men at the Cambridge Union. Macaulay, who won his Trinity fellowship in 1824, had there argued the questions with his friend Charles Austin, one of Bentham's neophytes. In the next year Macaulay made his first appearance as an Edinburgh Reviewer; and in 1829 he took the field against Mill. In the January number he attacked the essay upon 'Government'; and in two articles in the succeeding numbers of the Review replied to a defence made by some Utilitarian in the Westminster. Mill himself made no direct reply; and Macaulay showed his gratitude for Mill's generosity in regard to the Indian appointment by declining to republish the articles.[2] He confessed to have treated his opponent with a want of proper respect, though he retracted none of his criticisms. The offence had its excuses. Macaulay was a man under thirty, in the full flush of early success; nor was Mill's own treatment of antagonists conciliatory. The dogmatic arrogance of

[1] Bain's James Mill, p. 292.
[2] They were reprinted in the Miscellaneous Works after Macaulay's death. I quote from the 'popular edition' of that work (1875).

the Utilitarians was not unnaturally met by an equally
arrogant countercheck.   Macaulay ridicules the Utilitarians for their claim to be the defenders of the true
political faith.   He is afraid not of them but of the
'discredit of their alliance'; he wishes to draw a broad
line between judicious reformers and a 'sect which having
derived all its influence from the countenance which they
imprudently bestowed upon it, hates them with the
deadly hatred of ingratitude.'   No party, he says, was
ever so unpopular.   It had already disgusted people with
political economy; and would disgust them with parliamentary reform, if it could associate itself in public
opinion with the cause.[1]   This was indeed to turn the
tables.   The half-hearted disciple was insulting the
thoroughbred teacher who had borne the heat and
burthen of the day, and from whom he had learned his
own doctrine.   Upon this and other impertinences—the
assertion, for example, that Utilitarians were as incapable
of understanding an argument as any 'true blue baronet
after the third bottle at a Pitt Club'—it is needless to
dwell.   They illustrate, however, the strong resentment
with which the Utilitarians were regarded by the classes
from whom the Whigs drew their most cultivated supporters.   Macaulay's line of argument will show what
was the real conflict of theory.

His view is, in fact, a long amplification of the charge
that Mill was adopting a purely *a priori* method.   Mill's
style is as dry as Euclid, and his arguments are presented
with an affectation of logical precision.   Mill has inherited
the 'spirit and style of the Schoolmen.   He is an Aristotelian of the fifteenth century.'   He writes about

[1] *Miscellaneous Works*, p. 166.

government as though he was unaware that any actual
governments had ever existed.   He deduces his science
from a single assumption of certain 'propensities of
human nature.'[1]   After dealing with Mill's arguments,
Macaulay winds up with one of his characteristic purple
patches about the method of induction.   He invokes the
authority of Bacon—a great name with which in those
days writers conjured without a very precise consideration
of its true significance.   By Bacon's method we are to
construct in time the 'noble science of politics,' which is
equally removed from the barren theories of Utilitarian
sophists and the petty craft of intriguing jobbers.   The
Utilitarians are schoolmen, while the Whigs are the true
followers of Bacon and scientific induction.   J. S. Mill
admitted within certain limits the relevancy of this criticism,
and was led by the reflections which it started to a theory
of his own.   Meanwhile, he observes that his father ought
to have justified himself by declaring that the book was
not a 'scientific treatise on politics,' but an 'argument
for parliamentary reform.'[2]   It is not quite easy to see
how James Mill could have made such a 'justification'
and distinguished it from a recantation.

If Mill really meant what Macaulay took him to mean,
it would be superfluous to argue the question gravely.
The reasoning is only fit, like the reasoning of all
Macaulay's antagonists, for the proverbial schoolboy.
Mill, according to Macaulay, proposes to discover what
governments are good ; and, finding that experience gives
no clear answer, throws experience aside and appeals
to absolute laws of human nature.   One such 'law'
asserts that the strong will plunder the weak.   There-

[1] *Miscellaneous Works*, p. 132.   [2] Mill's *Autobiography*, p. 158.

fore all governments except the representative must
be oppressive, and rule by sheer terror.   Mill's very
reason for relying upon this argument is precisely that the
facts contradict it.   Some despotisms work well, and some
democracies ill ; therefore we must prove by logic that all
despotisms are bad, and all democracies good.   Is this
really Mill's case ?

An answer given by Mill's champion, to which
Macaulay replies in his last article, suggests some
explanation of Mill's position.   Macaulay had paid
no attention to one highly important phrase.   The
terrible consequences which Mill deduces from the
selfishness of rulers will follow, he says, 'if nothing
checks.'[1]   Supplying this qualification, as implied throughout, we may give a better meaning to Mill's argument.
A simple observation of experience is insufficient.   The
phenomena are too complex ; governments of the
most varying kinds have shown the same faults ; and
governments of the same kind have shown them in the
most various degrees.   Therefore the method which
Macaulay suggests is inapplicable.   We should reason
about government, says Macaulay,[2] as Bacon told us
to reason about heat.   Find all the circumstances in
which hot bodies agree, and you will determine the
principle of heat.   Find all the circumstances in which
good governments agree, and you will find the principles
of good government.   Certainly ; but the process, as
Macaulay admits, would be a long one.   Rather, it would
be endless.   What 'circumstances' can be the same in
all good governments in all times and places?   Mill
held in substance, that we could lay down certain broad

[1] 'Government,' p. 12.   [2] *Miscellaneous Works*, p. 169.

principles about human nature, the existence of which is
of course known from 'experience,' and by showing how
they would work, if restrained by no distinct checks,
obtain certain useful conclusions.   Mill indicates this line
of reply in his own attack upon Mackintosh.[1]   There he
explains that what he really meant was to set forth a
principle recognised by Berkeley, Hume, Blackstone, and,
especially, in Plato's *Republic*.   Plato's treatise is a development of the principle that 'identity of interests
affords the only security for good government.'   Without
such identity of interest, said Plato, the guardians of the
flock become wolves.   Hume[2] had given a pithy expression of the same view in the maxim 'established,' as
he says, 'by political writers,' that in framing the 'checks
and controls of the constitution, every man ought to be
supposed a knave and to have no other end in his actions
than private interest.'   Mill points this by referring to
the 'organs of aristocratical opinion' for the last fifty
years.   The incessant appeal has been for 'confidence in
public men,' and confidence is another name for scope for
misrule.[3]   This, he explains, was what he meant by the
statement (which Mackintosh considered to have been
exploded by Macaulay) that every man pursued his own
interest.[4]   It referred to the class legislation of the great
aristocratic ring : kings, nobles, church, law, and army.
Utilitarianism, in its political relations, was one continuous
warfare against these sinister 'interests.'   The master-evil
of the contemporary political state undoubtedly implied a
want of responsibility.   A political trust was habitually

[1] *Fragment on Mackintosh* (1870), pp. 275-94.
[2] Essay on the 'Independency of Parliament.'
[3] *Fragment*, p. 292.   [4] *Ibid.* p. 276.

confounded with private property. Moreover, whatever else may be essential to good government, one essential is a strong sense of responsibility in the governors. That is a very sound principle, though not an axiom from which all political science can be deduced. If the essay on 'Government' was really meant as a kind of political Euclid—as a deduction of the best system of government from this single principle of responsibility—it was as grotesque as Macaulay asserted. Mill might perhaps have met the criticism by lowering his claims as his son suggests. He certainly managed to express his argument in such terms that it has an uncomfortable appearance of being intended for a scientific exposition.

This deserves notice because the position is characteristic of the Utilitarians' method. Their appeals to experience always end by absolute assertions. We shall find the same difficulty in their economic inquiries. When accused, for example, of laying down absolute principles in such cases, they reply that they are only speaking of 'tendencies,' and recognise the existence of 'checks.' They treat of what would be, if certain forces acted without limit, as a necessary step towards discovering what is when the limits exist. They appear to their opponents to forget the limits in their practical conclusions. This political argument is an instance of the same method. The genesis of his theory is plain. Mill's 'government,' like Bentham's, is simply the conception of legal 'sovereignty' transferred to the sphere of politics. Mill's exposition is only distinguished from his master's by the clearness with which he brings out the underlying assumptions. The legal sovereign is omnipotent, for what he declares to be the law is therefore the law.

The law is his commands enforced by 'sanctions,' and therefore by organised force. The motives for obedience are the fear of the gallows on one side, and, on the other, the desire of protection for life and property. Law, again, is the ultimate social bond, and can be made at will by the sovereign. He thus becomes so omnipotent that it is virtually assumed that he can even create himself. Not only can the sovereign, once constituted, give commands enforced by coercive sanctions upon any kind of conduct, but he can determine his own constitution. He can at once, for example, create a representative system in practice, when it has been discovered in theory, and can by judicious regulations so distribute 'self-interest' as to produce philanthropy and public spirit. Macaulay's answer really makes a different assumption. He accepts the purely 'empirical' or 'rule of thumb' position. It is idle, he says, to ask what would happen if there were no 'checks.' It is like leaving out the effect of friction in a problem of mechanics. The logic may be correct, but the conclusions are false in practice.[1] Now this 'friction' was precisely the favourite expedient of the Utilitarians in political economy. To reason about facts, they say, you must analyse, and therefore provisionally disregard the 'checks,' which must be afterwards introduced in practical applications. Macaulay is really bidding us take 'experience' in the lump, and refrains from the only treatment which can lead to a scientific result. His argument, in fact, agrees with that of his famous essay on Bacon, where we learn that philosophy applied to moral questions is all nonsense, and that science is simply crude common-sense. He is really saying that all political

[1] *Miscellaneous Works*, p. 170.

reasoning is impossible, and that we must trust to unreasoned observation. Macaulay, indeed, has good grounds of criticism. He shows very forcibly the absurdity of transferring the legal to the political sovereignty. Parliament might, as he says, make a law that every gentleman with £2000 a year might flog a pauper with a cat-of-nine-tails whenever he pleased. But, as the first exercise of such a power would be the 'last day of the English aristocracy,' their power is strictly limited in fact.[1] That gives very clearly the difference between legal and political sovereignty. What parliament makes law is law, but is not therefore enforceable. We have to go behind the commands and sanctions before we understand what is the actual power of government. It is very far from omnipotent. Macaulay, seeing this, proceeds to throw aside Mill's argument against the possibility of a permanent division of power. The *de facto* limitation of the sovereign's power justifies the old theory about 'mixed forms of government.' 'Mixed governments' are not impossible, for they are real. All governments are, in fact, 'mixed.' Louis xiv. could not cut off the head of any one whom he happened to dislike. An oriental despot is strictly bound by the religious prejudices of his subjects. If 'sovereignty' means such power it is a chimera in practice, or only realised approximately when, as in the case of negro slavery, a class is actually ruled by force in the hands of a really external power. And yet the attack upon 'mixed governments,' which Bentham had expounded in the *Fragment*, has a real force which Macaulay seems to overlook. Mill's argument against a possible 'balance' of power was, as

[1] *Miscellaneous Works*, p. 173.

Macaulay asserted, equally applicable to the case of independent sovereigns; yet France might be stronger at Calais and England at Dover.[1] Mill might have replied that a state is a state precisely because, and in so far as, there is an agreement to recognise a common authority or sovereign. Government does not imply a 'mixture,' but a fusion of power. There is a unity, though not the abstract unity of the Utilitarian sovereign. The weakness of the Utilitarians is to speak as though the sovereign, being external to each individual, could therefore be regarded as external to the whole society. He rules as a strong nation may rule a weak dependency. When the sovereign becomes also the society, the power is regarded as equally absolute, though now applied to the desirable end of maximising happiness. The whole argument ignores the simple consideration that the sovereign is himself in all cases the product of the society over which he rules, and his whole action, even in the most despotic governments, determined throughout by organic instincts, explaining and not ultimately explicable by coercion. Macaulay's doctrine partially recognises this by falling back upon the Whig theory of checks and balances, and the mixture of three mysterious entities, monarchy, aristocracy, and democracy. But, as Bentham had sufficiently shown in the *Fragment*, the theory becomes hopelessly unreal when we try to translate it into facts. There are not three separate forces, conflicting like three independent forces, but a complex set of social institutions bound together into a whole. It is impossible really to regard government as a permanent balance of antagonistic forces, confronting each other

[1] *Miscellaneous Works*, p. 138.

like the three duellists in Sheridan's *Critic*. The practical
result of that theory is to substitute for the 'greatest
happiness' principle the vague criterion of the preservation of an equilibrium between indefinable forces; and to
make the ultimate end of government the maintenance as
long as possible of a balance resting on no ulterior
principle, but undoubtedly pleasant for the comfortable
classes. Nothing is left but the rough guesswork, which,
if a fine name be wanted, may be called Baconian induction. The 'matchless constitution,' as Bentham calls it,
represents a convenient compromise, and the tendency is
to attach exaggerated importance to its ostensible terms.
When Macaulay asserted against Mill[1] that it was
impossible to say which element—monarchy, aristocracy,
or democracy—had gained strength in England in the last
century, he is obviously looking at the formulæ and not
at the social body behind.

This leads to considerations really more important than
the argumentation about *a priori* and inductive methods.
Mill in practice knew very well the qualifications necessary
before his principles applied. He showed it in his Indian
evidence; and Place could have told him, had it required
telling, that the actual political machinery worked by
very strange and tortuous methods. Yet he was content
to override such considerations when he is expounding
his theory, and laid himself open to Macaulay's broad
common-sense retort. The nation at large cannot, he says,
have a 'sinister interest.' It must desire legislation which
is beneficial to the whole. This is to make the vast
assumption that every individual will desire what is good
for all, and will be a sufficient judge of what is good.

[1] *Miscellaneous Works*, pp. 135-40.

But is it clear that a majority will even desire what is
good for the whole? May they not wish to sacrifice
both other classes and coming generations to their own
instantaneous advantages? Is it plain that even enlightenment of mind would induce a poor man to see his own
advantage in the policy which would in the long run be
best for the whole society? You are bound, said
Macaulay, to show that the poor man will not believe
that he personally would benefit by direct plunder of the
rich; and indeed that he would not be right in so
believing. The nation, no doubt, would suffer, but in
the immediate period which alone is contemplated by a
selfish pauper, the mass of the poor might get more
pleasure out of confiscation. Will they not, on your
own principles, proceed to confiscation? Shall we not
have such a catastrophe as the reign of terror?

The Westminster Reviewer retorted by saying that
Macaulay prophesied a reign of terror as a necessary
consequence of an extended franchise. Macaulay, skilfully enough, protested against this interpretation. 'We
say again and again,' he declares, 'that we are on the
defensive. We do not think it necessary to prove that
a quack medicine is poison. Let the vendor prove it to
be sanative. We do not pretend to show that universal
suffrage is an evil. Let its advocates show it to be a
good.'[1] Mill rests his whole case upon the selfishness of
mankind. Will not the selfishness lead the actual majority
at a given moment to plunder the rich and to disregard
the interests of their own successors?

Macaulay's declaration that he was only 'upon the
defensive' might be justifiable in an advocate. His real

[1] *Miscellaneous Works*, p. 158, and see pp. 143-47.

thought may be inferred from a speech on the charter
made in 1842. The chartists' petition of that year had
asked for universal suffrage. Universal suffrage, he
replies, would be incompatible with the 'institution of
property.'[1] If the chartists acted upon their avowed
principles, they would enforce 'one vast spoliation.'
Macaulay could not say, of course, what would actually
result, but his 'guess' was that we should see 'something
more horrible than can be imagined—something like the
siege of Jerusalem on a far larger scale.' The very best
event he could anticipate—'and what must the state of
things be, if an Englishman and a Whig calls such an
event the very best?'—would be a military despotism,
giving a 'sort of protection to a miserable wreck of all
that immense glory and prosperity.'[2] So in the criticism
of Mill he had suggested that if his opponent's principles
were correct, and his scheme adopted, 'literature, science,
commerce, manufactures' would be swept away, and that
a 'few half-naked fishermen would divide with the owls
and foxes the ruins of the greatest of European cities.'[3]

Carefully as Macaulay guards himself in his articles
upon Mill, the speech shows sufficiently what was his
'guess'; that is, his real expectation. This gives the
vital difference. What Macaulay professes to deduce
from Mill's principles he really holds himself, and he holds
it because he argues, as indeed everybody has to argue,
pretty much on Mill's method. He does not really
remain in the purely sceptical position which would correspond to his version of 'Baconian induction.' He
argues, just as Mill would have argued, from general

[1] *Speeches* (Popular Edition), p. 125.   [2] *Ibid.* p. 128.
[3] *Miscellaneous Works*, p. 146.

rules about human nature. Selfish and ignorant people
will, he thinks, be naturally inclined to plunder; therefore, if they have power, they will plunder. So Mill
had argued that a selfish class would rule for its own
sinister interests and therefore not for the happiness of
the greatest number. The argument is the same, and
it is the only line of argument which is possible till, if
that should ever happen, a genuine science of politics
shall have been constituted. The only question is whether
it shall take the pomp of *a priori* speculation or conceal
itself under a show of 'Baconian induction.'

On one point they agree. Both Mill and Macaulay
profess unbounded confidence in the virtue and wisdom
of the middle, that is, of their own class. Macaulay
hopes for a reform bill which will make the votes of the
House of Commons 'the express image of the opinion
of the middle orders of Britain.'[1] Mill holds that the
middle class will retain this moral authority, however
widely the franchise be extended; while Macaulay fears
that they will be swamped by its extension to the
masses. The reform bill which they joined in supporting
was regarded by the Radicals as a payment on account;
while the Whig hoped that it would be a full and final
discharge. The Radical held that no barriers against
democracy were needed; he took for granted that a
democracy would find its natural leaders in the educated
and intelligent. The Whig, to whom such confidence
appeared to be altogether misplaced, had to find some
justification for the 'checks' and 'balances' which he
thought essential.

[1] *Miscellaneous Works*, p. 183.

II. WHIGGISM

I have spoken of Macaulay's articles because they represent the most pointed conflict between the Utilitarian and the Whig. Macaulay belongs properly to the next generation, but he appeared as the mouthpiece of the earlier group of writers who in Mill's time delivered through the *Edinburgh Review* the true oracles of the Whig faith. Upon that ground Mill had assailed them in his article. Their creed, he said, was a 'see-saw.' The Whigs were aristocrats as much as the Tories. They were simply the 'outs' who hoped to be the 'ins.' They trimmed their sails to catch public opinion, but were careful not to drift into the true popular currents. They had no desire to limit the power which they hoped one day to possess. They would attack abuses—the slave-trade or the penal laws—to gain credit for liberality and enlightenment, when the abuses were such as could be removed without injuring the power of the aristocracy. They could use 'vague generalities' about liberty and so forth, but only to evade definite applications. When any measure was proposed which really threatened the power of the privileged classes, they could bring out a contradictory set of fine phrases about Jacobinism and democracy. Their whole argument was a shuffle and they themselves mere selfish trimmers.[1] To this Jeffrey replied (in December 1826) by accepting the position.[2] He pleaded guilty to a love of 'trimming,' which meant a love of the British Constitution. The constitution was a compromise—a balance of opposing forces—and the

[1] A full analysis of this article is in Bain's *James Mill*, pp. 265-75.
[2] Article upon Sheridan, reprinted in Jeffrey's *Essays*, iv. (1844).

only question could be whether they were properly balanced. The answer was fair enough. Mill was imputing motives too easily, and assuming that the Reviewers saw the abuses in the same light as he did, and were truckling to public robbers in hopes of sharing the plunder. He was breaking a butterfly upon a wheel. The Edinburgh Reviewers were not missionaries of a creed. They were a set of brilliant young men, to whom the *Review* was at first a mere pastime, occupying such leisure as was allowed by their professional pursuits. They were indeed men of liberal sympathies, intelligent and independent enough to hold by a party which was out of power. They had read Hume and Voltaire and Rousseau; they had sat at the feet of Dugald Stewart; and were in sympathy with intellectual liberalism. But they were men who meant to become judges, members of parliament, or even bishops. Nothing in their social atmosphere had stimulated the deep resentment against social injustice which makes the fanatic or the enthusiast. We may take as their interpreter the Whig philosopher James Mackintosh (1765-1832), a man of wide reading, both in history and philosophy, an eloquent orator, and a very able writer. Mackintosh, said Coleridge,[1] is the 'king of the men of talent'; by which was intimated that, as a man of talent, he was not, like some people, a man of genius. Mackintosh, that is, was a man to accept plausible formulæ and to make them more plausible; not a man to pierce to the heart of things, or reveal fruitful germs of thought. His intellect was judicial; given to compromises, affecting a judicious *via media*, and endeavouring to reconcile antagonistic tendencies.

[1] *Table-Talk*, 27th April 1823.

Thoroughgoing or one-sided thinkers, and Mill in particular, regarded him with excessive antipathy as a typical representative of the opposite intellectual tendencies. Mackintosh's political attitude is instructive. At the outbreak of the French revolution he was a struggling young Scot, seeking his fortune in London, just turning from medicine to the bar, and supporting himself partly by journalism. He became secretary to the Society of the 'Friends of the People,' the Whig rival of the revolutionary clubs, and in April 1791 sprang into fame by his *Vindiciæ Gallicæ*. The Whigs had not yet lost the fervour with which they had welcomed the downfall of the Bastille. Burke's *Reflections*, the work of a great thinker in a state of irritation bordering upon frenzy, had sounded the note of alarm. The revolution, as Burke maintained, was in fact the avatar of a diabolic power. It meant an attack upon the very organic principles of society. It therefore implied a complete breach of historical continuity, and a war against the reverence for 'prescription' and tradition which is essential to all healthy development. To his extreme opponents the same theory afforded the justification of the revolution. It meant that every institution was to be thrown into the crucible, and a new world to arise governed only by reason. The view very ably defended by Mackintosh was opposed to both. He looks upon the French revolution as a more complete application of the principles of Locke and the English Whigs of 1688. The revolutionists are, as he urges,[1] applying the principles which had been worked out by the 'philosophers of Europe' during the preceding century. They were not,

[1] *Vindiciæ Gallicæ*, in *Miscellaneous Works*, iii. (1846), p. 57.

as Burke urged, rejecting experience for theory. The relation between their doctrine and politics is analogous to the relation between geometry and mechanics.[1] We are now in the position of a people who should be familiar with Newton, but in shipbuilding be still on a level with the Esquimaux. The 'rights of man' appear to him to mean, not, as Burke and Bentham once agreed, a set of 'anarchical fallacies,' but a set of fundamental moral principles; and the declaration of them a most wise and 'auspicious' commencement of the 'regenerating labours' of the new legislators. The French revolution represented what Somers would now approve if he had our advantages.[2] A thoroughgoing change had become necessary in France. The church, army, and law were now 'incorrigible.'[3] Burke had seen, in the confiscation of church property, an attempt to abolish Christianity. To Mackintosh it seemed to be a reform justifiable in principle, which, though too roughly carried out, would reduce 'a servile and imperious priesthood to humble utility.'[4] A poor priesthood, indeed, might incline to popular superstition. We could console ourselves by reflecting that the power of the church, as a corporation, was broken, and that toleration and philosophy would restrain fanaticism.[5] The assignats were still 'almost at par.'[6] The sale of the national property would nearly extinguish the debt. France had 'renounced for ever the idea of conquest,'[7] and had no

[1] Mackintosh thinks it necessary to add that this parallel was suggested to him by William Thomson (1746-1837), a literary gentleman who continued Watson's *Philip III.*, and may, for anything I know, deserve Mackintosh's warm eulogy.
[2] *Vindiciæ Gallicæ*, p. 59.
[3] *Ibid.* p. 51.
[4] *Ibid.* p. 148.
[5] *Ibid.* p. 68.
[6] *Ibid.* p. 72.
[7] *Ibid.* p. 125.

temptations to war, except her colonies. Their commercial inutility and political mischievousness had been so 'unanimously demonstrated,' that the French empire must soon be delivered from 'this cumbrous and destructive appendage.' An armed people, moreover, could never be used like a mercenary army to suppress liberty. There was no danger of military despotism, and France would hereafter seek for a pure glory by cultivating the arts of peace and extending the happiness of mankind.[1]

No wonder that Mackintosh, with these views, thought that the history of the fall of the Bastille would 'kindle in unborn millions the holy enthusiasm of freedom'; [2] or that, in the early disorders, he saw temporary aberrations of mobs, destined to be speedily suppressed by the true leaders of the revolution. Mackintosh saw, I take it, about as far as most philosophers, that is, about as far as people who are not philosophers. He observes much that Burke ought to have remembered, and keeps fairly to the philosophical principle which he announces of attributing the revolution to general causes, and not to the schemes of individuals.[3] When assignats became waste paper, when the guillotine got to work, when the religion of reason was being set up against Christianity, when the French were conquering Europe, when a military despotism was arising, when, in short, it became quite clear that the French revolution meant something very different from a philosophical application of the principles of Locke and Adam Smith, Mackintosh began to see that Burke had not so far missed the mark. Burke, before dying, received

[1] *Vindiciæ Gallicæ*, p. 128.   [2] *Ibid.* p. 84.   [3] *Ibid.* p. 30.

his penitent opponent at Beaconsfield; and in 1800 Mackintosh took the opportunity of publicly declaring that he 'abhorred, abjured, and for ever renounced the French revolution, with its sanguinary history, its abominable principles, and its ever execrable leaders.' He hoped to 'wipe off the disgrace of having been once betrayed into that abominable conspiracy against God and man.'[1] In his famous defence of Peltier (1803), he denounced the revolution in a passage which might have been adopted from Burke's *Letters on a Regicide Peace*.[2]

In a remarkable letter to Windham[3] of 1806, Mackintosh gives his estimate of Burke, and takes some credit to himself for having discovered, even in the time of his youthful errors, the consistency of Burke's principles, as founded upon an abhorrence of 'abstract politics.'[4] Politics, he now thought, must be made scientific by recognising with Burke the supreme importance of prescription and historic continuity, and by admitting that the philosophers had not yet constructed a science bearing to practical politics the same relation as geometry to mechanics. He applied his theory to the question of parliamentary reform in the *Edinburgh Review*.[5] Here he accepts the doctrine, criticised by James Mill, that a proper representative system must be judged, not, as Mill maintained, solely by the identity of its interest with that of the community at large, but by its fitness to give power to different classes. It follows that the landowners, the professional classes, and the populace should

[1] *Life of Mackintosh*, i. 125.   [2] *Miscellaneous Works*, iii. 261-65.
[3] *Life*, i. 309-16.   [4] See *Miscellaneous Works*, iii. 3.
[5] *Ibid.* iii. 203-38 (an article highly praised by Bagehot in his *Parliamentary Reform*).

all be represented. And he discovers that the variety of the English system was calculated to secure this end. Though it was only in a few constituencies that the poorest class had a voice, their vote in such places represented the same class elsewhere. It was as well that there should be some extreme Radicals to speak for the poorest. But he thinks that any uniform suffrage would be bad, and that universal suffrage would be the most mischievous of all systems.[1] That would mean the swamping of one class by all—a 'tyranny more oppressive, perhaps, than any other tyranny. If one class alone were to be represented, it should be the favourite middle class, which has the 'largest share of sense and virtue,' and is most connected in interest with other classes.[2] A legitimate aim of the legislator is, therefore, to prevent an excess of democracy. With Mackintosh it seems essential not simply to suppress 'sinister interests,' but to save both the aristocracy and the middle class from being crushed by the lower classes. The opposition is vital; and it is plain that the argument for the aristocracy, that is, for a system developed from all manner of historical accidents and not evolved out of any simple logical principles, must be defended upon empirical grounds.

Mackintosh was in India during the early period of the *Edinburgh Review*. Jeffrey, as editor for its first quarter of a century, may be taken more fully to repre-

[1] *Miscellaneous Works*, iii. 215-16.
[2] *Ibid.* iii. 226. Mackintosh in this article mentions the 'caucus,' and observes that the name implies that combinations have been already formed upon 'which the future government of the confederacy may depend more than on the forms of election, or the letter of the present laws.' He inclines to approve the system as essential to party government.

sent its spirit. Jeffrey's trenchant, if not swaggering style, covered a very timid, sensitive, and, in some respects, a very conservative temperament. His objection to the 'Lake Poets' was the objection of the classical to the romantic school. Jeffrey's brightness of intellect may justify Carlyle's comparison of him to Voltaire,—only a Voltaire qualified by dislike to men who were 'dreadfully in earnest.' Jeffrey was a philosophical sceptic; he interpreted Dugald Stewart as meaning that metaphysics, being all nonsense, we must make shift with common-sense; and he wrote a dissertation upon taste, to prove that there are no rules about taste whatever. He was too genuine a sceptic to sacrifice peace to the hopeless search for truth. One of the most striking passages in his *Essays*[1] is an attack upon 'perfectibility.' He utterly disbelieves that progress in knowledge will improve morals or diminish war, or cure any of the evils that flesh is heir to. Such a man is not of the material of which enthusiastic reformers are made. Throughout the war he was more governed by his fear than by his zeal. He was in constant dread of failure abroad and ruin at home. The *Review* provoked the Tories, and induced them to start its rival, not by advocacy of political principles, but by its despairing view of the war.[2] He was still desiring at that time (1808) to avoid 'party politics' in the narrower sense.

[1] *Essays* (1844), i. 84-106.
[2] The famous 'Cevallos' article of 1808, said to be written by Jeffrey and Brougham (Macvey Napier's *Correspondence*, p. 308), gave the immediate cause of starting the *Quarterly*; and, according to Brougham, first gave a distinctly Liberal character to the *Edinburgh*. For Jeffrey's desire to avoid 'party politics,' see Lockhart's *Life of Scott*, M. Napier's *Correspondence*, p. 435, and Horner's *Memoirs* (1853), i. 464.

The political view corresponding to this is given in the articles, some of which (though the authorship was not yet avowed) were assailed by Mill in the *Westminster*. In an early article[1] he defends the French philosophers against the imputation of responsibility for the reign of terror. Their excellent and humane doctrines had been misapplied by the 'exasperation' and precipitation of inexperienced voters. His most characteristic article is one published in January 1810. The failure of the Walcheren expedition had confirmed his disbelief in our military leaders; the rise of English Radicalism, led by Burdett in the House of Commons, and Cobbett in the press, the widely spread distress and the severity of oppressive measures, roused his keenest alarm.[2] We are, he declared, between two violent and pernicious factions—the courtiers of arbitrary power and the democrats. If the Whig leaders did not first conciliate and then restrain the people, the struggle of the extreme parties would soon sweep away the constitution, the monarchy, and the Whig aristocracy by which that monarchy 'is controlled, confirmed, and exalted above all other forms of polity.' Democracy, it was plain, was increasing with dangerous rapidity. A third of every man's income was being taken by taxes, and after twenty years' boastful hostility we were left without a single ally. Considering all this, it seems as though 'the wholesome days of England were numbered,' and we are on the 'verge of the most dreadful of all calamities' —a civil war.

[1] April 1805; reprinted in *Essays*, ii. 38, etc., to show, as he says, how early he had taken up his view of the French revolution.
[2] Sydney Smith complains in his correspondence of this article as exaggerating the power of the aristocracy.

Jeffrey has learned from Hume that all government is ultimately founded upon opinion. The great thing is to make the action of public opinion regular and constituted. The whole machinery of the constitution, he says, is for the express purpose of 'preventing the kingly power from dashing itself to pieces against the more radical power of the people.'[1] The merit of a representative body is not to be tested simply by the goodness of its legislation, but by its diminishing the intensity of the struggle for the supreme power. Jeffrey in fact is above all preoccupied with the danger of revolution. The popular will is, in fact, supreme; repression may force it into explosion; but by judicious management it may be tamed and tempered. Then we need above all things that it should, as he says in his reply to Mill (December 1826), give their 'natural and wholesome influence to wealth and rank.' The stability of the English Constitution depends, as he said in 1810, upon the monarchy and aristocracy, and their stability on their being the natural growth of ages and having 'struck their roots deep into every stratum of the political soil.'

The Whigs represent the view implied in Macaulay's attack upon Mill—the view of cultivated men of sense, with their eyes open to many difficulties overlooked by zealots, but far too sceptical and despondent to rouse any enthusiasm or accept any dogmas absolutely. By the time of the Reform Bill the danger was obviously on the side of dogged obstructionism, and then the 'middle party,' as Jeffrey calls it, inclined towards the Radical side and begged them to join its ranks and abandon the attempt to realise extreme views. They

[1] *Essays*, iv. 29.

could also take credit as moderate men do for having all along been in the right. But to both extremes, as Jeffrey pathetically complains, they appeared to be mere trimmers.[1]

The Utilitarian held the Whig to be a 'trimmer'; the Whig thought the Utilitarian a fanatic; they agreed in holding that the Tory was simply stupid. And yet, when we look at the Tory creed, we shall find that both Whig and Utilitarian overlooked some very vital problems. The Tories of course represent the advocates of strong government; and, as their opponents held, had no theories—only prejudices. The first article of the creed of an Eldon or a Sidmouth was, 'I believe in George III.';—not a doctrine capable of philosophical justification. Such Toryism meant the content of the rich and powerful with the system by which their power and wealth were guaranteed. Their instincts had been sharpened by the French revolution; and they saw in any change the removal of one of the safeguards against a fresh outburst of the nether fires. The great bulk of all political opinion is an instinct, not a philosophy; and the obstructive Tories represented little more than class prejudice and the dread of a great convulsion. Yet intelligent Tories were being driven to find some reasons for their creed, which the Utilitarians might have considered more carefully.

[1] I need not speak of Brougham, then the most conspicuous advocate of Whiggism. He published in 1843 a *Political Philosophy*, which, according to Lord Campbell, killed the 'Society for the Diffusion of Useful Knowledge.' No such hypothesis is necessary to account for the death of a society encumbered by a 'Dictionary of Universal Biography.' But the book was bad enough to kill, if a collection of outworn platitudes can produce that effect.

III. CONSERVATISM

A famous man of letters represents certain tendencies more clearly than the average politician. Robert Southey (1777-1843), the 'ultra servile sack-guzzler,' as Bentham pleasantly calls him in 1823,[1] was probably the best abused man, on his own side at least, among Mill's contemporaries. He was attacked by Mill himself, and savagely denounced by Byron and Hazlitt. He was not only a conspicuous writer in the *Quarterly Review*, but, as his enemies thought, a renegade bought by pensions. It is, I hope, needless to defend him against this charge. He was simply an impatient man of generous instincts and no reflective power, who had in his youth caught the revolutionary fever, and, as he grew up, developed the patriotic fever.

Later views are given in the *Colloquies on the Progress and Prospects of Society* (1829), chiefly known to modern readers by one of Macaulay's essays. Southey was as assailable as Mill. His political economy is a mere muddle; his political views are obviously distorted by accidental prejudices; and the whole book is desultory and disjointed. In a dialogue with the ghost of Sir Thomas More, he takes the opportunity of introducing descriptions of scenery, literary digressions, and quaint illustrations from his vast stores of reading to the confusion of all definite arrangement. Southey is in the awkward position of a dogmatist defending a compromise. An Anglican claiming infallibility is necessarily inconsistent. His view of toleration, for example, is oddly obscure. He would apparently like to persecute

[1] Bentham's *Works*, x. 536.

infidels;[1] and yet he wishes to denounce the Catholic church for its persecuting principles. He seems to date the main social evils to the changes which began at the Reformation, and yet he looks back to the period which succeeded the Reformation as representing the ideal state of the British polity. His sympathy with the literature of the sixteenth and seventeenth centuries predisposed him to this position. He would have been more intelligible if he had been more distinctly reactionary. For all that, his views show the presence of a leaven which was materially to affect the later development of English opinions. That Jacobinism meant anarchy, and that anarchy led irresistibly to military despotism were propositions which to him, as to so many others, seemed to be established by the French revolution. What, then, was the cause of the anarchy? Sir Thomas More comes from the grave to tell us this, because he had witnessed the past symptoms of the process. The transition from the old feudal system to the modern industrial organisation had in his day become unmistakably developed. In feudal times, every man had his definite place in society; he was a member of a little group; supported, if controlled and disciplined, by an elaborate system of spiritual authority. The Reformation was the period at which the 'masterless man' made his appearance. The conversion of pastures into arable land, the growth of commerce and of pauperism, were marks of the coming change. It proceeded quietly for some generations; but the development of the modern manufacturing system represents the operation of the same process on a far larger scale, and with far greater in-

[1] *Colloquies*, i. 253.

tensity. The result may be described by saying that we have instead of a legitimate development a degeneration of society. A vast populace has grown up outside of the old order. It is independent indeed, but at the heavy price of being rather an inorganic mass than a constituent part of the body politic. It is, briefly, to the growth of a huge 'proletariate' outside the church, and hostile to the state, that Southey attributes all social evils.

The view has become familiar enough in various shapes; and in the reproaches which Southey brings against the manufacturing system we have an anticipation of other familiar lamentations. Our manufacturing wealth is a 'wen,' a 'fungous excrescence from the body politic';[1] it is no more a proof of real prosperity than the size of a dropsical patient is a proof of health;[2] the manufacturer worships mammon instead of Moloch;[3] and wrings his fortune from the degradation of his labourers as his warlike ancestors wrung wealth from their slaves; he confines children in a tainted atmosphere, physical and moral, from morning till night, and a celebrated minister (Pitt) boasts of this very evil;[4] he treats his fellow-creatures as machines,[5] and wealth, though accumulated, is not diffused; the great capitalists, 'like pikes in a fishpond,' devour the weaker fish;[6] competition is not directed to providing the best goods, but the cheapest;[7] every man oppresses his neighbour; the landlord racks his tenant, the farmer grinds the labourer; all the little centres of permanent life are broken up;

[1] *Colloquies*, i. 171   [2] *Ibid.* i. 178.   [3] *Ibid.* i. 169.
[4] *Ibid.* i. 167.   [5] *Ibid.* i. 170.   [6] *Ibid.* i. 194.
[7] *Ibid.* ii. 247.

not one man in a thousand is buried with his fathers, and the natural ties and domestic affections are prematurely dissolved.[1]

Here, too, is to be found the source of the infidel opinions which call for suppression. London is a hotbed of corruption;[2] a centre of wealth; and yet, in spite of poor-laws, a place where wretches are dying of starvation, and which could collect a mob capable of producing the most appalling catastrophes. In such a place, men become unbelievers like savages, because removed from all humanising influences, and booksellers can carry on a trade in blasphemy. Infidelity is bred in 'the filth and corruption of large towns and manufacturing districts.'[3] The disappearance of clerical influence has led to 'a mass of ignorance, vice, and wretchedness which no generous heart can contemplate without grief.'[4] It is not surprising that, in Southey's opinion, it is doubtful whether the bulk of the people has gained or lost in the last thousand years.[5] Macaulay takes all this as mere sentimentalism and preference of a picturesque outside to solid comfort. But whatever Southey's errors of fact, they show at least a deeper insight than his opponent into some social evils. His proposed remedies explain his diagnosis of the evil. In the first place, it is not surprising, though it surprised Macaulay, that he had many sympathies with the socialist, Robert Owen. He saw Owen in 1816,[6] and was much impressed by his views. In the *Colloquies*,[7] Owen is called the 'happiest, most beneficent, and most practical of all enthusiasts'; an

[1] *Colloquies*, ii. 259.   [2] *Ibid.* i. 109.   [3] *Ibid.* ii. 105-7.
[4] *Ibid.* i. 106.   [5] *Ibid.* i. 47.
[6] *Life and Correspondence*, iv. 195; *Selections*, iii. 45.   [7] *Colloquies*, i. 62.

account is given of one of the earliest co-operative schemes,[1] and Southey believes in the possibility of the plan. He makes, however, one significant remark. Owen, he thinks, could not succeed without enlisting in his support some sectarian zeal. As Owen happened to object to all religious sects, this defect could not be remedied.

Southey, in fact, held that the absence of religious discipline was at the root of the whole evil. Religion, he declares, much to the scorn of Macaulay, 'is the basis upon which civil government rests.'[2] There must, as he infers, be an established religion, and the state which neglects this duty is preparing its own ruin. 'Nothing,' he declares, 'in abstract science can be more certain than these propositions,' though they are denied by 'our professors of the arts babblative and scribblative'—that is, by Benthamites and Whigs. For here, in fact, we come to the irreconcilable difference. Government is not to be a mere machinery for suppressing violence, but an ally of the church in spreading sound religion and morality. The rulers, instead of merely reflecting the popular will, should lead and direct all agencies for suppressing vice and misery. Southey, as his son takes pains to show,[3] though he was for upholding authority by the most stringent measures, was convinced that the one way to make government strong was to improve the condition of the people. He proposed many measures of reform; national education on the principles, of course, of Dr. Bell; state-aided colonisation and the

[1] *Colloquies*, i. 135.
[2] *Ibid.* ii. 147. Southey is here almost verbally following Burke's *Reflections*.
[3] *Life and Correspondence*, v. 4-6.

cultivation of waste lands at home ; Protestant sister-hoods to reproduce the good effects of the old order which he regretted and yet had to condemn on Anglican principles. The English church should have made use of the Wesleyans as the church of Rome had used the Franciscans and Dominicans ; and his *Life of Wesley* was prompted by his fond belief that this might yet be done. Government, he said, ought to be 'paternal' ;[1] and his leading aspirations have been adopted by Socialists on the one hand, and the converts to Catholicism on the other.

For his philosophy, Southey was in the habit of referring to Coleridge ; and Coleridge's *Constitution of Church and State* is perhaps the book in which Coleridge comes nearest to bringing an argument to a conclusion. Though marked by his usual complexities of style, his parentheses and irrelevant allusions and glances at wide metaphysical discussions, he succeeds in laying down a sufficient sketch of his position. The book was originally published in 1830, and refers to the Catholic emancipation of the previous year. Unlike Southey, he approves of the measure, only regretting the absence of certain safe-guards ; and his general purpose may be said to be to give such a theory of the relations of church and state as may justify an establishment upon loftier grounds than those of the commonplace Tory.

His method, as he explains, is to find the true 'idea' of a constitution and a national church. The 'idea,' he explains, does not mean the conscious aim of the persons who founded or now constitute the bodies in question. An 'idea' is the subjective counterpart of an objective

[1] *Colloquies*, i. 105.

law.[1] It corresponds to the vital force which moulds the structure of the social organism, although it may never have been distinctly formulated by any one of the actors. In this sense, therefore, we should have to proceed by a historical method. We should study the constitution as we study the physiology of a physical body ;[2] and he works out the analogy at some length. So far, Coleridge is expressing the characteristic view that Nature in general is to be regarded as an evolution ; only that evolution is to be understood in the sense of Schelling not in the sense of either Darwin. Of course, when Coleridge professes to find the 'idea' of the church and state, what he really finds is not the idea so much as his idea of the idea—which may be a very different thing. His theory of 'evolution' is compatible with assuming that evolutions are illegitimate whenever he happens to dislike them.

He coincides rather curiously with James Mill in asserting that the 'social bond' was originally formed to protect property, not to protect life.[3] He discovers accordingly that the ancient races, Jews, Goths, and Kelts alike, divided the land into two parts, one to be inherited by separate families, the other to be set apart for the nation. From the latter or the 'nationalty' springs the church establishment. This property belongs rightfully and inalienably to the nation itself. It is held by what he calls the 'clerisy.' Its functions are, in the first place, to provide a career by which the poorest classes may rise to a higher position ; and secondly, to provide for the

[1] *On the Constitution of Church and State, according to the idea of each*, 1852 (fourth edition).
[2] *Church and State*, p. 100.   [3] *Ibid*. p. 97.

development of all the qualities which distinguish the civilised man from the savage.[1] Briefly, then, the church is that part of the national organism which is devoted to educating the people to be 'obedient, free, useful organisable subjects, citizens, and patriots, living to the benefit of the estate, and prepared to die for its defence.' Henry VIII. would have surpassed Alfred if he had directed the 'nationalty' to its true purposes ; that is, especially to the maintenance of universities, of a parochial clergy, and of schools in every parish. Un-luckily, Henry VIII.'s 'idea' of a national church was vague. Ideas were not his strong point. Coleridge appears to be especially troubled to work the principles into conformity with his views of Catholic emancipation. The peculiarity of the theory is that the church, according to him, seems to be simply a national institution. It might exist, and in fact, did exist before Christianity, as is proved not only by the Jewish but by the Druidical church.[2] That it should be Christian in England is a 'blessed accident,' or 'providential boon '—or, as he puts it, 'most awfully a godsend.' Hence it follows that a primary condition of its utility is that the clerisy should contribute to the support of the other organs of the community. They must not be the subjects of a foreign power, nor, as he argues at length, subject to the desocialising influence of celibacy. It follows that the Roman church is unfitted to be ever a national church, although, if that danger be sufficiently obviated, no political disqualifications should be imposed upon Romanists. And thus, too, the Church Catholic is essentially a body which has no relations to any par-

[1] *Church and State*, p. 85.   [2] *Ibid*. p. 67.

ticular state. It is opposed to the world, not to the nation, and can have no visible head or 'personal centre of unity.'[1] The church which makes such claims is the revelation of Antichrist.

We need not inquire into the prophecies. It is enough to say that to Coleridge as to Southey the preservation of an established church seemed to be an essential condition of morality and civilisation. They differed from the ordinary Tory, who was content to defend any of the abuses by the cry of sacrilege and confiscation. The church was to be made worthy of its position, and rendered capable of discharging its high functions effectually. Coleridge, it may be said, would fully admit that an organ which had ceased to correspond to its idea must die. It could not continue to preserve itself by mere force of obstruction, but must arouse, throw off its abuses, and show itself to be worthy of its high claims. Meanwhile, however, he was perhaps more anxious to show the Utilitarians that in assailing the institution on account of its abuses, they were really destroying the most essential guarantee of progress. He sums up, in a curious passage, the proofs of modern degradation.[2] The wicked eighteenth century is of course responsible for everything. The 'mechanic corpuscular theory' ; the consequent decay of philosophy, illustrated by such phrases as an excellent 'idea' of cooking ; 'the ourang-outang theology of the origin of the human species substituted for the first ten chapters of the book of Genesis ; rights of nature for the duties and privileges of citizens ; idealess facts, misnamed proofs from history, for principles and the insight derived from

[1] *Church and State*, p. 142.   [2] *Ibid*. pp. 75-79.

them': all these and other calamitous results of modern philosophy are connected with a neglect of the well-being of the people, the mistaking of a large revenue for prosperity, and the consumption of gin by paupers to the 'value of eighteen millions yearly.' He appeals pathetically to the leaders of the Utilitarians. They will scorn him for pronouncing that a 'natural clerisy' is 'an essential element of a rightly constituted nation.' All their tract societies and mechanics' institutes and 'lecture bazaars under the absurd name of universities' are 'empiric specifics' which feed the disease. Science will be plebified, not popularised. The morality necessary for a state 'can only exist for the people in the form of religion. But the existence of a true philosophy, or the power and habit of contemplating particulars in the unity and fontal mirror of the idea,—this in the rulers and teachers of a nation is indispensable to a sound state of religion in all classes. In fact, religion, true or false, is and ever has been the centre of gravity in a realm to which all other things must and will accommodate themselves.'

The existence of the eighteenth century always remained a hopeless puzzle for Coleridge and his followers. Why at that period everything went wrong in the higher regions of thought remained a mystery. 'God is above,' says Sir Thomas More to Southey,[1] 'but the devil is below; evil principles are in their nature more active than good.' The devil seemed to have got into the upper air, and was working with his allies, Bentham and Mill and Paine and Cobbett, with remarkable success. But, whatever the theories of conservatives in church and

[1] *Colloquies*, i. 37.

state, the fact that the theories were held is important. The diametrical opposition between two schools, one of which regarded the church as a simple abuse, and its doctrines as effete superstitions, while the other looked to the church and its creed as giving the sole hope for suppressing the evil principle, was a critical point in later movements, political as well as religious.

IV. SOCIALISM

I have spoken of Southey's sympathy for Robert Owen. Owen (1771-1858) is one of the characteristic figures of the time. He was the son of a village tradesman in Wales, and had risen to prosperity by the qualities of the virtuous apprentice. Industry, patience, an imperturbably good temper, and sagacity in business matters had raised him to high position as a manufacturer at the time of the rapid advance of the cotton trade. Many poor men have followed the same path to wealth. Owen's peculiarity was that while he became a capitalist he preserved his sympathy with the working classes. While improving machinery, he complained that the 'living machinery' was neglected. One great step in his career was his marriage to the daughter of David Dale of New Lanark, a religious and worthy manufacturer.[1] Dale had employed a number of pauper children who were in that day to be disposed of by their parishes; and had done his best to make their position more tolerable. Owen took up this scheme, and carried it out more systematically. New Lanark, in his hands, became a model village; he

[1] See an early account of Dale (in 1798) in Sydney Smith's *Life and Letters*, i. 35, and another in Wilberforce's *Correspondence* (1840), i. 137 (in 1796).

provided in various ways for the encouragement of sobriety, industry, and honesty among his workmen, set up stores to supply cheap and good provisions, and especially provided infant schools and a systematic education. 'The children,' he declares, 'were the happiest human beings he ever saw.' When his partners interfered with his plans, Owen bought them out and started the company to which Bentham and Allen belonged. New Lanark rapidly became famous. It was visited by all the philanthropists of the day. The royal dukes not only of England but of Russia were interested; and Owen even believed that he had converted Napoleon at Elba. So far, Owen was a benevolent capitalist, exercising a paternal sway over his people. He became convinced, however, that he had discovered the key to the great social problems of the day. When the distresses followed the peace, he was prepared to propound his remedy, and found many willing hearers in all classes. Liverpool and Sidmouth listened to him with favour, and the duke of Kent became president of a committee started to carry out his views. He gave the impetus to the movement by which the Factory Act of 1819 was carried, although it was far from embodying his proposals in their completeness.

Owen's diagnosis of the social disease explains Southey's partiality. Like Southey, he traced the evil to the development of the manufacturing system. That system involved, as he held, what later Socialists have called the 'exploitation' of the labouring classes by the capitalists. With singularly crude notions of political economy, Owen assumed that the 'dead machinery' was in competition with the 'living machinery.' He made startling calcula-

tions as to the amount of human labour represented by steam-engines; and took for granted that the steam-engine displaced an equal number of workmen. His remedy for poverty was to set up a number of communities, which should maintain themselves by cultivating the soil with the spade, and in which every man should labour for all. Thus New Lanarks were to be spread over the country, with the difference that the employer was to be omitted. Owen, in short, became properly a Socialist, having been simply a paternal philanthropist. For a time Owen met with considerable support. A great meeting was held in London in 1817, and a committee was started two years afterwards, of which Ricardo was a member. Ricardo, indeed, took pains to let it be known that he did not believe in the efficacy of Owen's plans. Meanwhile Owen was breaking off his connection with New Lanark, and becoming the apostle of a new social creed. His missionary voyages took him to Ireland, to the United States and Mexico, and attempts were made to establish communities in Scotland and in the State of Illinois.

Owen and his followers became natural antagonists of the Utilitarians. He agreed with Southey in tracing distress to the development of the great manufacturing system, though he went much further. The principles essentially involved in the whole industrial system were, according to him, pernicious. He held the essential doctrine of his modern successors that property is theft. Between such a man and the men who took the *Wealth of Nations* for their gospel, and Ricardo as its authorised commentator, there was an impassable gulf. On the other hand, Owen was equally far from the Tory view of religious principles. Southey's remark that he could only succeed by allying himself with some religious fanaticism was just to the point.

Owen was a man of very few ideas, though he held such as he had with extraordinary tenacity, and enforced them by the effective if illogical method of incessant repetition. Among them was the idea which, as he declares, had occurred to him before he was ten years old that there was something radically wrong in all religions. Whether this opinion had come to him from the diffused rationalism of his time, or was congenial to the practical and prosaic temperament which was disquieted by the waste of energy over futile sectarian squabbles, or was suggested by his early study of Seneca —the only author of whom he speaks as having impressed him in early years—it became a fixed conviction. He had been an early supporter of Lancaster and 'unsectarian' education. When his great meeting was to be held in 1817 it occurred to him that he might as well announce his views. He accordingly informed his hearers that the religions of the world were the great obstacles to progress. He expected, as he assures us, that this candid avowal would cause him to be 'torn in pieces.' It provoked on the contrary general applause, and Owen congratulated himself rather hastily on having struck the deathblow of superstition.

Owen's position, at any rate, was a significant symptom. It showed that the Socialist movement sprang from motives outside the sphere of the churches. Owen's personal simplicity and calmness seems to have saved him from any bitter animosity. He simply set aside Christianity as not to the purpose, and went on calmly

asserting and re-asserting his views to Catholics and Protestants, Whigs, Radicals, and Tories. They agreed in considering him to be a bore, but were bored rather than irritated. Owen himself, like later Socialists, professed indifference to the political warfare of Whigs and Tories. When, at the height of the Reform movement, he published a paper called the *Crisis*, the title referred not to the struggle in which all the upper classes were absorbed, but to the industrial revolution which he hoped to bring about. He would have been equally ready to accept help from Whig, Tory, or Radical; but his position was one equally distasteful to all. The Tory could not ally himself with the man who thought all religions nonsense; nor any of the regular parties with the man who condemned the whole industrial system and was opposed to all the cherished prejudices of the respectable middle classes.

Owen's favourite dogma is worth a moment's notice. He was never tired of repeating that 'character is formed by circumstances'; from which he placidly infers that no man deserves praise or blame for his conduct. The inference, it must be admitted, is an awkward one in any ethical system. It represents, probably, Owen's most serious objection to the religions of the world. The ultimate aim of the priest is to save men's souls; and sin means conduct which leads to supernatural punishment. Owen, on the contrary, held that immorality was simply a disease to be cured, and that wrath with the sinner was as much out of place as wrath with a patient. In this sense Owen's view, as I at least should hold, defines the correct starting-point of any social reformer. He has to consider a scientific problem, not to be an agent of

a supernatural legislator. He should try to alter the general conditions from which social evils spring, not to deal in pardons or punishment. Owen was acting with thoroughly good sense in his early applications of this principle. The care, for example, which he bestowed upon infant education recognised the fact that social reform implied a thorough training of the individual from his earliest years. Owen's greatest error corresponds to the transformation which this belief underwent in his mind. Since circumstances form character, he seems to have argued, it is only necessary to change the circumstances of a grown-up man to alter his whole disposition. His ambitious scheme in America seemed to suppose that it was enough to bring together a miscellaneous collection of the poor and discontented people, and to invite them all to behave with perfect unselfishness. At present I need only remark that in this respect there was a close coincidence between Owen and the Utilitarians. Both of them really aimed at an improvement of social conditions on a scientific method; and both justified their hopes by the characteristic belief in the indefinite modifiability of human nature by external circumstances.

I turn to a man who was in some ways the most complete antithesis to Owen. William Cobbett (1762-1835), unlike Owen, took a passionate and conspicuous part in the political struggles of the day. Cobbett, declares the *Edinburgh Review* in July 1807, has more influence than all the other journalists put together. He had won it, as the reviewer thought, by his force of character, although he had changed his politics completely 'within the last six months.' The fact was more significant than was then apparent. Cobbett, son of a

labourer who had risen to be a small farmer, had in spite of all obstacles learned to read and write and become a great master of the vernacular. His earliest model had been Swift's *Tale of a Tub*, and in downright vigour of homely language he could scarcely be surpassed even by the author of the *Drapier's Letters*. He had enlisted as a soldier, and had afterwards drifted to America. There he had become conspicuous as a typical John Bull. Sturdy and pugnacious in the highest degree, he had taken the English side in American politics when the great question was whether the new power should be bullied by France or by England. He had denounced his precursor, Paine, in language savouring too much, perhaps, of barrack-rooms, but certainly not wanting in vigour. He defied threats of tar and feathers; put a portrait of George III. in his shop-window; and gloried in British victories, and, in his own opinion, kept American policy straight. He had, however, ended by making America too hot to hold him; and came back to declare that republicanism meant the vilest and most corrupt of tyrannies, and that, as an Englishman, he despised all other nations upon earth. He was welcomed on his return by Pitt's government as likely to be a useful journalist, and became the special adherent of Windham, the ideal country-gentleman and the ardent disciple of Burke's principles. He set up an independent paper and heartily supported the war. On the renewal of hostilities in 1803 Cobbett wrote a manifesto[1] directed by the government to be read in every parish church in the kingdom, in order to rouse popular feeling. When Windham came into office in 1806, Cobbett's friends supposed that his fortune

[1] Printed in *Political Works*, i. 302.

was made. Yet at this very crisis he became a reformer. His conversion was put down, of course, to his resentment at the neglect of ministers. I do not think that Cobbett was a man to whose character one can appeal as a conclusive answer to such charges. Unfortunately he was not free from weaknesses which prevent us from denying that his political course was affected by personal motives. But, in spite of weaknesses and of countless inconsistencies, Cobbett had perfectly genuine convictions and intense sympathies which sufficiently explain his position, and make him more attractive than many less obviously imperfect characters. He tells us unconsciously what were the thoughts suggested to a man penetrated to the core by the strongest prejudices—they can hardly be called opinions—of the true country labourer.

The labourer, in the first place, if fairly represented by Cobbett, had none of the bitter feeling against the nobility which smouldered in the French peasantry. Cobbett looked back as fondly to the surroundings of his youth as any nobleman could look back to Eton or to his country mansion. He remembered the 'sweet country air' round Crooksbury Hill, the song of birds, and the rambles through heather and woodland. He loved the rough jovial sports; bull-baiting and prize-fighting and single-stick play. He had followed the squire's hounds on foot, and admired without jealousy the splendid gardens of the bishop's palace at Farnham. Squire and parson were an intrinsic part of the general order of things. The state of the English working classes was, he often declares, the happiest that could be imagined,[1] and he appeals in confirmation to his own

[1] *Political Works*, v. 313 ; vi. 579.

memories. Although, upon enlisting, he had found the army corrupt, he not only loved the soldier for the rest of his life, but shared to the full the patriotic exultation which welcomed the 1st of June and the Nile. Even to the last, he could not stomach the abandonment of the title 'King of France'; for so long as it was retained, it encouraged the farmer to tell his son the story of Crecy and Agincourt.[1]

What, then, alienated Cobbett? Briefly, the degradation of the class he loved. 'I wish,' he said, 'to see the poor men of England what the poor men of England were when I was born, and from endeavouring to accomplish this task, nothing but the want of means shall make me desist.'[2] He had a right to make that boast, and his ardour in the cause was as unimpeachable as honourable. It explains why Cobbett has still a sympathetic side. He was a mass of rough human nature; no prig or bundle of abstract formulæ, like Paine and his Radical successors. Logic with him is not in excess, but in defect. His doctrines are hopelessly inconsistent, except so far as they represent his stubborn prejudices. Any view will serve his purpose which can be made a weapon of offence in his multitudinous quarrels. Cobbett, like the Radicals of the time, was frightened by the gigantic progress of the debt. He had advocated war ; but the peasant who was accustomed to reckon his income by pence, and had cried like a child when he lost the price of a red herring, was alarmed by the reckless piling up of millions of indebtedness. In 1806 he calmly proposed to his patron Windham to put matters straight by repudiating the interest. 'The nation must

[1] *Political Works*, i. 473 ; v. 319.   [2] *Ibid.* ii. 285.

destroy the debt, or the debt will destroy the nation,' as he argued in the *Register*.[1] The proposal very likely caused the alienation of a respectable minister, though propounded with an amusing air of philosophical morality. Cobbett's alarm developed until it became to him a revelation of the mystery of iniquity. His Radical friends were denouncing placemen and jobbery, and Cobbett began to perceive what was at the bottom of the evil. The money raised to carry on the war served also to support a set of bloodsuckers, who were draining the national strength. Already, in 1804, he was lamenting a change due to Pitt's funding system. The old families, he said, were giving way to 'loanjobbers, contractors, and nabobs'; and the country people amazed to find that their new masters had been 'butchers, bakers, bottle-corkers, and old-clothesmen.'[2] Barings and Ricardos and their like were swallowing up the old country gentry wholesale ; and in later years he reckons up, as he rides, the changes in his own neighbourhood.[3] His affection for the old country-gentleman might be superficial ; but his lamentations over the degradation of the peasantry sprang from his heart. It was all, in his eyes, part of one process. Paper money, he found out, was at the bottom of it all ; for paper money was the outward and visible symbol of a gigantic system of corruption and jobbery. It represented the device by which the hard-earned wages of the labourer were being somehow conjured away into the pockets of Jews and stockjobbers. The classes which profited by this atrocious system formed what he called the 'Thing'—the huge,

[1] *Political Works*, ii. 28 ; iv. 388.   [2] *Ibid.* i. 443.
[3] *Rural Rides* (1853), p. 311.

intricate combination of knaves which was being denounced by the Radicals—though with a difference. Cobbett could join the reformers in so far as, like them, he thought that the rotten boroughs were a vital part of the system. He meets a miserable labourer complaining of the 'hard times.' The harvest had been good, but its blessings were not for the labourer. That 'accursed hill,' says Cobbett, pointing to old Sarum, 'is what has robbed you of your supper.'[1] The labourer represented the class whose blood was being sucked.

So far, then, as the Radicals were assailing the boroughmongers, Cobbett could be their cordial ally. Two years' imprisonment for libel embittered his feelings. In the distress which succeeded the peace, Cobbett's voice was for a time loudest in the general hubbub. He reduced the price of his *Register*, and his 'two-penny trash' reached a circulation of 25,000 or 30,000 copies. He became a power in the land, and anticipated the immediate triumph of reform. The day was not yet. Sidmouth's measures of repression frightened Cobbett to America (March 1819), where he wrote his history of the 'last hundred days of English liberty.' He returned in a couple of years, damaged in reputation and broken in fortune ; but only to carry on the war with indomitable energy, although with a recklessness and extravagance which alienated his allies and lowered his character. He tried to cover his errors by brags and bombast, which became ridiculous, and which are yet not without significance.

Cobbett came back from America with the relics of Paine. Paine, the object of his abuse, had become his

[1] *Rural Rides*, p. 386.

idol, not because Cobbett cared much for any abstract political theories, or for religious dogmas. Paine's merit was that he had attacked paper money. To Cobbett, as to Paine, it seemed that English banknotes were going the way of French assignats and the provincial currency of the Americans. This became one main topic of his tirades, and represented, as he said, the 'Alpha and Omega' of English politics. The theory was simple. The whole borough-mongering system depended upon the inflated currency. Prick that bubble and the whole would collapse. It was absolutely impossible, he said, that the nation should return to cash payments and continue to pay interest on the debt. Should such a thing happen, he declared, he would 'give his poor body up to be broiled on one of Castlereagh's widest-ribbed gridirons.'[1] The 'gridiron prophecy' became famous; a gridiron was for long a frontispiece to the *Register*; and Cobbett, far from retracting, went on proving, in the teeth of facts, that it had been fulfilled. His inference was, not that paper should be preserved, but that the debt should be treated with a 'sponge.'

Cobbett, therefore, was an awkward ally of political economists, whose great triumph was the resumption of cash payments, and who regarded repudiation as the deadly sin. The burthen of the debt, meanwhile, was so great that repudiation was well within the limits of possibility.[2] Cobbett, in their eyes, was an advocate of the grossest dishonesty, and using the basest incentives. Cobbett fully retorted their scorn. The economists belonged to the very class whom he most hated. He

[1] *Political Works*, v. 436 (22nd July 1819).
[2] Even M'Culloch had recommended a partial repudiation.

was never tired of denouncing Scottish 'feelosophers'; he sneers at Adam Smith,[1] and Ricardo was to him the incarnation of the stock-jobbing interest. Cobbett sympathised instinctively with the doctrine of the French economists that agriculture was the real source of all wealth. He nearly accepts a phrase, erroneously attributed to Windham, 'Perish Commerce'; and he argues that commerce was, in fact, of little use, and its monstrous extension at the bottom of all our worst evils.[2] Nobody could be more heartily opposed to the spirit which animated the political economists and the whole class represented by them. At times he spoke the language of modern Socialists. He defines Capital as 'money taken from the labouring classes, which, being given to army tailors and suchlike, enables them to keep foxhounds and trace their descent from the Normans.'[3]

The most characteristic point of his speculations is his view of the poor-laws. Nobody could speak with more good sense and feeling of the demoralisation which they were actually producing, of the sapping of the spirit of independence, and of all the devices by which the agricultural labourer was losing the happiness enjoyed in early years. But Cobbett's deduction from his principles is peculiar. 'Parson Malthus' is perhaps the favourite object of his most virulent abuse. 'I have hated many men,' he says, 'but never any one so much as you.' 'I call you parson,' he explains, 'because that word includes "boroughmonger" among other meanings, though no single word could be sufficient.'[4] Cobbett

[1] *Political Works*, iv. 237.
[2] *Ibid.* ii. 19, 107, 250, 346; and iii. 423. See *Parliamentary History*, xxx., where the first use of the phrase by Hardinge is reported.
[3] *Political Works*, vi. 176.   [4] *Ibid.* 395.

rages against the phrase 'redundant population.' There would be plenty for all if the boroughmongers and stockjobbers could be annihilated, taxes abolished, and the debt repudiated. The ordinary palliatives suggested were little to the taste of this remarkable Radical. The man who approved bull-fighting and supported the slave-trade naturally sneered at 'heddekashun,' and thought savings-banks a mean device to interest the poor in the keeping up of the funds. His remedy was always a sponge applied to the debt, and the abolition of taxes.

This leads, however, to one remarkable conclusion. Cobbett's attack upon the church establishment probably did more to cause alarm than any writings of the day. For Paine's attacks upon its creed he cared little enough. 'Your religion,' said a parson to him, 'seems to be altogether political.' It might well be, was Cobbett's retort, since his creed was made for him by act of parliament.[1] In fact, he cared nothing for theology, though he called himself a member of the church of England, and retained an intense dislike for Unitarians, dissenters in general, 'saints' as he called the Evangelical party, Scottish Presbyterians, and generally for all religious sects. He looked at church questions solely from one point of view. He had learned, it seems, from a passage in Ruggles's *History of the Poor*,[2] that the tithes had been originally intended to support the poor as well as the church. Gradually, as he looked back upon the 'good old times,' he developed the theory expounded in his *History of the Reformation*. It is a singular performance,

[1] *Rural Rides*, p. 446.
[2] He complains bitterly that Ruggles had suppressed this in a second edition. *Protestant Reformation* (1850), ii., Introduction.

written at the period of his most reckless exasperation (1824-27), but with his full vigour of style. He declares[1] in 1825 that he has sold forty-five thousand copies, and it has been often reprinted. The purpose is to show that the Reformation was 'engendered in beastly lust, brought forth in hypocrisy, and cherished and fed by plunder and devastation, and by rivers of English and Irish blood.'[2] Briefly, it is the cause of every evil that has happened since, including 'the debt, the banks, the stockjobbers, and the American revolution.'[3] In proving this, Cobbett writes in the spirit of some vehement Catholic bigot, maddened by the penal laws. Henry VIII., Elizabeth, and William III. are his monsters; the Marys of England and Scotland his ideal martyrs. He almost apologises for the massacre of St. Bartholomew and the Gunpowder Plot; and, in spite of his patriotism, attributes the defeat of the Armada to a storm, for fear of praising Elizabeth. The bitterest Ultramontane of to-day would shrink from some of this Radical's audacious statements. Cobbett, in spite of his extravagance, shows flashes of his usual shrewdness. He remarks elsewhere that the true way of studying history is to examine acts of parliament and lists of prices of labour and of food;[4] and he argues upon such grounds for the prosperity of the agricultural labourer under Edward III., 'when a dung-cart filler could get a fat goose and a half for half a day's work.' He makes some telling hits, as when he contrasts William of Wykeham with Brownlow North, the last bishop of Winchester. Protestants condemned celibacy. Well,

[1] *Political Register*, 29th Jan. 1825.   [2] *Protestant Reformation*, p. 13.
[3] *Ibid.* p. 262.   [4] *Advice to Young Men*, p. 8.

had William been married, we should not have had Winchester school, or New College ; had Brownlow North been doomed to celibacy, he would not have had ten sons and sons-in-law to share twenty-four rich livings, besides prebends and other preferments ; and perhaps he would not have sold small beer from his episcopal palace at Farnham. Cobbett's main doctrine is that when the Catholic church flourished, the population was actually more numerous and richer, that the care of the priests and monks made pauperism impossible, and that ever since the hideous blunder perpetrated by the reformers everything has been going from bad to worse. When it was retorted that the census proved the population to be growing, he replied that the census was a lie. Were the facts truly stated, he declares, we should have a population of near twenty-eight million in England by the end of this century,[1] a manifest *reductio ad absurdum*. If it were remarked that there was a Catholic church in France, and that Cobbett proves his case by the superiority of the English poor to the French poor, he remarked summarily that the French laws were different.[2]

Thus, the one monster evil is the debt, and the taxes turn out to have been a Protestant invention made necessary by the original act of plunder. That was Cobbett's doctrine, and, however perverse might be some of his reasonings, it was clearly to the taste of a large audience. The poor-law was merely a partial atonement for a vast and continuous process of plunder. Corrupt

[1] *Political Works*, v. 405. If our census be not a lie, there were twenty-seven million Englishmen in 1891.
[2] *Protestant Reformation*, i. 311.

as might be its actual operation, it was a part of the poor man's patrimony, extorted by fear from the gang of robbers who fattened upon their labours.

Cobbett's theories need not be discussed from the logical or historical point of view. They are the utterances of a man made unscrupulous by his desperate circumstances, fighting with boundless pugnacity, ready to strike any blow, fair or foul, so long as it will vex his enemies, and help to sell the *Register*. His pugnacity alienated all his friends. Not only did Whigs and Tories agree in condemning him, but the Utilitarians hated and despised him, and his old friends, Burnett and Hunt, were alienated from him, and reviled by him. His actual followers were a small and insignificant remnant. Yet Cobbett, like Owen, represented in a crude fashion blind instincts of no small importance in the coming years. And it is especially to be noted that in one direction the philosophic Coleridge and the keen Quarterly Reviewer Southey, and the Socialist Owen and the reactionary Radical Cobbett, were more in agreement than they knew. What alarmed them was the vast social change indicated by the industrial revolution. In one way or another they connected all the evils of the day with the growth of commerce and manufactures, and the breaking up of the old system of domestic trade and village life.[1] That is to say, that in a dumb and inarticulate logic, though in the loudest tones of denunciation, Tories and Socialists, and nondescript Radicals were raging against the results of the great

[1] Coleridge in a letter to Allsop (*Conversations*, etc., i. 20) approves one of Cobbett's articles, because it popularises the weighty truth of the 'hollowness of commercial wealth.' Cobbett, he sadly reflects, is an overmatch for Liverpool. See Cobbett's *Political Works*, v. 466 n.

social change, which the Utilitarians regarded as the true line of advance of the day. This gives the deepest line of demarcation, and brings us to the political economy, which shows most fully how the case presented itself to the true Utilitarian.

CHAPTER IV

MALTHUS

I. MALTHUS'S STARTING-POINT

THE political movement represented the confluence of many different streams of agitation. Enormous social changes had generated multifarious discontent. New wants and the new strains and stresses between the various parts of the political mechanism required new adaptations. But, if it were inquired what was the precise nature of the evils, and how the reform of parliament was to operate, the most various answers might be given. A most important line of division did not coincide with the line between the recognised parties. One wing of the Radicals agreed with many Conservatives in attributing the great evils of the day to the industrial movement and the growth of competition. The middle-class Whigs and the Utilitarians were, on the contrary, in thorough sympathy with the industrial movement, and desired to limit the functions of government, and trust to self-help and free competition. The Socialistic movement appeared for the present to be confined to a few dreamers and demagogues. The Utilitarians might approve the spirit of the Owenites, but held their schemes to be chimerical. Beneath the political controversies there was therefore a set of problems to be answered ; and the Utilitarian answer defines their distinction from Radicals of a different and, as they would have said, unphilosophical school.

What, then, was the view really taken by the Utilitarians of these underlying problems ? They not only had a very definite theory in regard to them, but in working it out achieved perhaps their most important contribution to speculation. Beneath a political theory lies, or ought to lie, what we now call a ' sociology '—a theory of that structure of society which really determines the character and the working of political institutions. The Utilitarian theory was embodied in their political economy. I must try to define as well as I can what were the essential first principles implied, without going into the special problems which would be relevant in a history of political economy.

The two leading names in the literature of political economy during the first quarter of this century were undoubtedly Malthus and Ricardo. Thomas Robert Malthus[1] (1766-1834) was not one of the Utilitarian band. As a clergyman, he could not share their opinion of the Thirty-nine Articles. Moreover, he was a Whig, not a Radical ; and he was even tainted with some economic heresy. Still, he became one of the prophets, if not the leading prophet, of the Utilitarians. Belief in the Malthusian theory of population was the most essential article of their faith, and marked the line of cleavage between the two wings of the Radical party.

Malthus was the son of a country gentleman in Surrey.

[1] Mr. James Bonar's *Malthus and his Work* (1885) gives an admirable account of Malthus. The chief original authorities are a life by Bishop Otter, prefixed to a second edition of the *Political Economy* (1831), and an article by Empson, Malthus's colleague, in the *Edinburgh Review* for January 1837.

His father was a man of studious habits, and one of the enthusiastic admirers of Rousseau. His study of *Émile* probably led to the rather desultory education of his son. The boy, after being taught at home, was for a time a pupil of R. Graves (1715-1804), author of the *Spiritual Quixote*, a Whig clergyman who was at least orthodox enough to ridicule Methodism. Malthus was next sent to attend Gilbert Wakefield's lectures at the Warrington ' Academy,' the Unitarian place of education, and in 1784 went to Jesus College, Cambridge, of which Wakefield had been a fellow. For Wakefield, who had become a Unitarian, and who was afterwards a martyr to political Radicalism, he appears to have retained a strong respect. At Jesus, again, Malthus was under Frend, who also was to join the Unitarians. Malthus was thus brought up under the influences of the modified rationalism which was represented by the Unitarians outside the establishment and by Paley within. Coleridge was at Jesus while Malthus was still a fellow, and there became an ardent admirer of Priestley. Malthus remained within the borders of the church. Its yoke was light enough, and he was essentially predisposed to moderate views. He took his degree as ninth wrangler in 1788, became a fellow of his college in 1793, took orders, and in 1798 was curate of Albury, near his father's house in Surrey. Malthus's home was within a walk of Farnham, where Cobbett had been born and passed his childhood. He had, therefore, before his eyes the same agricultural labourer whose degradation excited Cobbett to Radicalism. Very different views were suggested to Malthus. The revolutionary doctrine was represented in England by the writings of Godwin, whose

Political Justice appeared in 1793 and *Enquirer* in 1797. These books naturally afforded topics for discussion between Malthus and his father. The usual relations between senior and junior were inverted ; the elder Malthus, as became a follower of Rousseau, was an enthusiast ; and the younger took the part of suggesting doubts and difficulties. He resolved to put down his arguments upon paper, in order to clear his mind ; and the result was the *Essay upon Population*, of which the first edition appeared anonymously in 1798.

The argument upon which Malthus relied was already prepared for him. The dreams of the revolutionary enthusiasts supposed either a neglect of the actual conditions of human life or a belief that those conditions could be radically altered by the proposed political changes. The cooler reasoner was entitled to remind them that they were living upon solid earth, not in dreamland. The difficulty of realising Utopia may be presented in various ways. Malthus took a point which had been noticed by Godwin. In the conclusion of his *Political Justice*,[1] while taking a final glance at the coming millennium, Godwin refers to a difficulty suggested by Robert Wallace. Wallace had[2] said that all the evils under which mankind suffers might be removed by a community of property, were it not that such a state of things would lead to an ' excessive population.' Godwin makes light of the difficulty. He thinks that there is some ' principle in human society by means of which everything tends to find its own level and proceed in

[1] *Political Justice* (3rd edition, 1798), ii. bk. viii. chap. ix., p. 514.
[2] Wallace wrote in answer to Hume, *A Dissertation on the Numbers of Mankind in Ancient and Modern Times* (1753), and *Various Prospects of Mankind, and Nature and Providence* (1761). Godwin refers to the last.

the most auspicious way, when least interfered with by the mode of regulation.' Anyhow, there is plenty of room on the earth, at present. Population may increase for ' myriads of centuries.' Mind, as Franklin has said, may become ' omnipotent over matter ' ;[1] life may be indefinitely prolonged ; our remote descendants who have filled the earth ' will probably cease to propagate ' ;[2] they will not have the trouble of making a fresh start at every generation ; and in those days there will be ' no war, no crimes, no administration of justice ' ; and moreover, ' no disease, anguish, melancholy, or resentment.' Briefly, we shall be like the angels, only without the needless addition of a supreme ruler. Similar ideas were expressed in Condorcet's famous *Tableau historique des progrès de l'esprit humain*,[3] written while he was in daily fear of death by the guillotine, and so giving the most striking instance on record of the invincibility of an idealist conviction under the hardest pressure of facts.

The argument of Malthus is a product of the whole previous course of speculation. The question of population had occupied the French economists. The profound social evils of France gave the starting-point of their speculations ; and one of the gravest symptoms had been the decay of population under the last years of Louis xiv. Their great aim was to meet this evil by encouraging agriculture. It could not escape the notice of the simplest observer that if you would have more mouths you must provide more food, unless, as some pious people assumed, that task might be left to Providence.

[1] *Political Justice*, ii. 520.　　[2] *Ibid.* ii. 528.
[3] First published in 1795, after the first edition, as Godwin remarks, of the *Political Justice*.

Quesnay had laid it down as one of his axioms that the statesman should aim at providing sustenance before aiming simply at stimulating population. It follows, according to Gulliver's famous maxim, that the man who makes two blades of grass grow where one grew before deserves better of his country than the 'whole race of politicians put together.' Other writers, in developing this thesis, had dwelt upon the elasticity of population. The elder Mirabeau, for example, published his *Ami des hommes ou traité de la population* in 1756. He observes that, given the means of subsistence, men will multiply like rats in a barn.[1] The great axiom, he says,[2] is 'la mesure de la subsistance est celle de la population.' Cultivate your fields, and you will raise men. Mirabeau replies to Hume's essay upon the 'Populousness of ancient nations' (1752), of which Wallace's first treatise was a criticism. The problem discussed by Hume and Wallace had been comparatively academical; but by Malthus's time the question had taken a more practical shape. The sentimentalists denounced luxury as leading to a decay of the population. Their prevailing doctrine is embodied in Goldsmith's famous passage in the *Deserted Village* (1770):

> 'Ill fares the land, to hastening ills a prey,
> Where wealth accumulates and men decay.'

The poetical version only reflected the serious belief of Radical politicians. Although, as we are now aware, the population was in fact increasing rapidly, the belief prevailed among political writers that it was actually declining. Trustworthy statistics did not exist. In 1753 John Potter, son of the archbishop, proposed to the

---

[1] *Ami des hommes* (reprint of 1883), p. 15.   [2] *Ami des hommes*, p. 26.

House of Commons a plan for a census. A violent discussion arose,[1] in the course of which it was pointed out that the plan would inevitably lead to the adoption of the 'canvas frock and wooden shoes.' Englishmen would lose their liberty, become French slaves, and, when counted, would no doubt be taxed and forcibly enlisted. The bill passed the House of Commons in spite of such reasoning, but was thrown out by the House of Lords. Till the first census was taken in 1801—a period at which the absolute necessity of such knowledge had become obvious—the most elementary facts remained uncertain. Was population increasing or decreasing? That surely might be ascertainable.

Richard Price (1723–1791) was not only a distinguished moralist and a leading politician, but perhaps the best known writer of his time upon statistical questions. He had the credit of suggesting Pitt's sinking fund,[2] and spoke with the highest authority upon facts and figures. Price argued in 1780[3] that the population of England had diminished by one-fourth since the revolution of 1688. A sharp controversy followed upon the few ascertainable data. The vagueness of the results shows curiously how much economists had to argue in the dark. Malthus

---

[1] See the curious debate in *Parl. Hist.* xiv. 1318-1365.

[2] The seventh edition of Price's *Observations on Reversionary Payments*, etc. (1812), contains a correspondence with Pitt (i. 216, etc.). The editor, W. Morgan, accuses Pitt of adopting Price's plans without due acknowledgment and afterwards spoiling them.

[3] *Essay on Population*, p. 18. In *Observations*, ii. 141, he estimates the diminution at a million and a half. Other books referring to the same controversy are Howlett's *Examination of Dr. Price's Essay* (1781); *Letter to Lord Carlisle*, by William Eden (1744-1814), first Lord Auckland; William Wales's *Enquiry into Present State of Population*, etc. (1781); and Geo. Chalmers's *Estimate of the Comparative Strength of Great Britain* (1782 and several later editions).

observes in his first edition that he had been convinced by reading Price that population was restrained by 'vice and misery,' as results, not of political institutions, but of 'our own creation.'[1] This gives the essential point of difference. Mirabeau had declared that the population of all Europe was decaying. Hume's essay, which he criticises, had been in answer to a similar statement of Montesquieu. Price had learned that other countries were increasing in number, though England, he held, was still declining. What, then, was the cause? The cause, replied both Price and Mirabeau, was 'luxury,' to which Price adds the specially English evils of the 'engrossment of farms' and the enclosure of open fields. Price had to admit that the English towns had increased; but this was an additional evil. The towns increased simply by draining the country; and in the towns themselves the deaths exceeded the births. The great cities were the graves of mankind. This opinion was strongly held, too, by Arthur Young, who ridiculed the general fear of depopulation, and declared that if money were provided, you could always get labour, but who looked upon the towns as destructive cancers in the body politic.

The prevalence of this view explains Malthus's position. To attribute depopulation to luxury was to say that it was caused by the inequality of property. The rich man wasted the substance of the country, became demoralised himself, and both corrupted and plundered his neighbours. The return to a 'state of nature,' in Rousseau's phrase, meant the return to a state of things in which this misappropriation should become impossible. The whole industry of the nation would then be devoted to supporting

---

[1] *Essay* (first edition), p. 339.

millions of honest, simple peasants and labourers, whereas it now went to increasing the splendour of the great at the expense of the poor. Price enlarges upon this theme, which was, in fact, the contemporary version of the later formula that the rich are growing richer and the poor poorer. The immediate effect of equalising property, then, would be an increase of population. It was the natural retort, adopted by Malthus, that such an increase would soon make everybody poor, instead of making every one comfortable. Population, the French economists had said, follows subsistence. Will it not multiply indefinitely? The rapid growth of population in America was noticed by Price and Godwin; and the theory had been long before expanded by Franklin, in a paper which Malthus quotes in his later editions. 'There is no bound,' said Franklin in 1751,[1] 'to the prolific nature of plants and animals but what is made by their crowding and interfering with each other's means of subsistence.' The whole earth, he infers, might be overspread with fennel, for example, or, if empty of men, replenished in a few ages with Englishmen. There were supposed to be already one million of Englishmen in North America. If they doubled once in twenty-five years, they would in a century exceed the number of Englishmen at home. This is identical with Mirabeau's principle of the multiplying of rats in a barn. Population treads closely on the heels of subsistence. Work out your figures and see the results.[2]

---

[1] *Memoirs*, etc. (1819), ii. 10.

[2] So Sir James Stewart, whose light was extinguished by Adam Smith, begins his *Enquiry into the Principles of Political Economy* (1767) by discussing the question of population, and compares the 'generative faculty' to a spring loaded with a weight, and exerting itself in proportion to the diminution of

Malthus's essay in the first edition was mainly an application of this retort, and though the logic was effective as against Godwin, he made no elaborate appeal to facts. Malthus soon came to see that a more precise application was desirable. It was clearly desirable to know whether population was or was not actually increasing, and under what conditions. I have spoken of the contemporary labours of Sinclair, Young, Sir F. Eden, and others. To collect statistics was plainly one of the essential conditions of settling the controversy. Malthus in 1799 travelled on the continent to gather information, and visited Sweden, Norway, Russia, and Germany. The peace of Amiens enabled him in 1802 to visit France and Switzerland. He inquired everywhere into the condition of the people, collected such statistical knowledge as was then possible, and returned to digest it into a more elaborate treatise. Meanwhile, the condition of England was giving a fresh significance to the argument. The first edition had been published at the critical time when the poor-law was being relaxed, and disastrous results were following war and famine. The old complaint that the poor-law was causing depopulation was being changed for the complaint that it was stimulating pauperism. The first edition already discussed this subject, which was occupying all serious thinkers; it was now to receive a fuller treatment. The second edition, greatly altered,

resistance (*Works*, 1805, i. 22). He compares population to 'rabbits in a warren.' Joseph Townsend, in his *Journey Through Spain* (1792), to whom Malthus refers, had discussed the supposed decay of the Spanish population, and illustrates his principles by a geometric progression: see ii. 213-56, 386-91. Eden, in his book on the poor (i. 214), quotes a tract attributed to Sir Matthew Hale for the statement that the poor increase on 'geometrical progression.'

appeared in 1803, and made Malthus a man of authority. His merits were recognised by his appointment in 1805 to the professorship of history and political economy at the newly founded East India College at Haileybury. There he remained till the end of his life, which was placid, uneventful, and happy. He made a happy marriage in 1804; and his calm temperament enabled him to bear an amount of abuse which might have broken the health of a more irritable man. Cobbett's epithet, 'parson Malthus,' strikes the keynote. He was pictured as a Christian priest denouncing charity, and proclaiming the necessity of vice and misery. He had the ill luck to be the centre upon which the antipathies of Jacobin and anti-Jacobin converged. Cobbett's language was rougher than Southey's; but the poet-laureate and the author of 'two-penny trash' were equally vehement in sentiment. Malthus, on the other hand, was accepted by the political economists, both Whig and Utilitarian. Horner and Mackintosh, lights of the Whigs, were his warm friends as well as his disciples. He became intimate with Ricardo, and he was one of the original members of the Political Economy Club. He took abuse imperturbably; was never vexed 'after the first fortnight' by the most unfair attack; and went on developing his theories, lecturing his students, and improving later editions of his treatise. Malthus died on 23rd December 1834.

II. THE RATIOS

The doctrine marks a critical point in political economy. Malthus's opponents, as Mr. Bonar remarks,[1] attacked him alternately for propounding a truism and

[1] *Malthus and his Work*, p. 85.

for maintaining a paradox. A 'truism' is not useless so long as its truth is not admitted. It would be the greatest of achievements to enunciate a law self-evident as soon as formulated, and yet previously ignored or denied. Was this the case of Malthus? Or did he really startle the world by clothing a commonplace in paradox, and then explain away the paradox till nothing but the commonplace was left?

Malthus laid down in his first edition a proposition which continued to be worried by all his assailants. Population, he said, when unchecked, increases in the geometrical ratio; the means of subsistence increase only in an arithmetical ratio. Geometrical ratios were just then in fashion.[1] Price had appealed to their wonderful ways in his arguments about the sinking fund; and had pointed out that a penny put out to 5 per cent. compound interest at the birth of Christ would, in the days of Pitt, have been worth some millions of globes of solid gold, each as big as the earth. Both Price and Malthus lay down a proposition which can easily be verified by the multiplication-table. If, as Malthus said, population doubles in twenty-five years, the number in two centuries would be to the present number as 256 to 1, and in three as 4096 to 1. If, meanwhile, the quantity of subsistence increased in 'arithmetical progression,' the multipliers for it would be only 9 and 13. It follows that, in the year 2003, two hundred and fifty-six persons will have to live upon what now supports nine. So far,

[1] Voltaire says in the *Dictionnaire Philosophique* (art. 'Population'): 'On ne propage point en Progression Géométrique. Tous les calculs qu'on a faits sur cette prétendue multiplication sont des chimères absurdes.' They had been used to reconcile the story of the deluge with the admitted population of the world soon afterwards.

the case is clear. But how does the argument apply to facts? For obvious reasons, Price's penny could not become even one solid planet of gold. Malthus's population is also clearly impossible. That is just his case. The population of British North America was actually, when he wrote, multiplying at the assigned rate. What he pointed out was that such a rate must somehow be stopped; and his question was, how precisely will it be stopped? The first proposition, he says[1] (that is, that population increased geometrically), 'I considered as proved the moment that the American increase was related; and the second as soon as enunciated.' To say that a population increases geometrically, in fact, is simply to say that it increases at a fixed rate. The arithmetical increase corresponds to a statement which Malthus, at any rate, might regard as undeniable; namely, that in a country already fully occupied, the possibility of increasing produce is restricted within much narrower limits. In a 'new country,' as in the American colonies, the increase of food might proceed as rapidly as the increase of population. Improved methods of cultivation, or the virtual addition of vast tracts of fertile territory by improved means of communication, may of course add indefinitely to the resources of a population. But Malthus was contemplating a state of things in which the actual conditions limited the people to an extraction of greater supplies from a strictly limited area. Whether Malthus assumed too easily that this represented the normal case may be questionable. At any rate, it was not only possible but

[1] *Essay* (1826), ii. 453 n. I cite from this, the last edition published in Malthus's lifetime, unless otherwise stated.

actual in the England of the time. His problem was very much to the purpose. His aim was to trace the way in which the population of a limited region is prevented from increasing geometrically. If the descendants of Englishmen increase at a certain rate in America, why do they not increase equally in England? That, it must be admitted, is a fair scientific problem. Finding that two races of similar origin, and presumably like qualities, increase at different rates, we have to investigate the causes of the difference.

Malthus answered the problem in the simplest and most consistent way in his first edition. What are the checks? The ultimate check would clearly be starvation. A population might multiply till it had not food. But before this limit is actually reached, it will suffer in various ways from scarcity. Briefly, the checks may be distinguished into the positive, that is, actual distress, and the preventive, or 'foresight.' We shall actually suffer unless we are restrained by the anticipation of suffering. As a fact, however, he thinks that men are but little influenced by the prudence which foresees sufferings. They go on multiplying till the consequences are realised. You may be confined in a room, to use one of his illustrations,[1] though the walls do not touch you; but human beings are seldom satisfied till they have actually knocked their heads against the wall. He sums up his argument in the first edition in three propositions.[2] Population is limited by the means of subsistence; that is obvious; population invariably increases when the means of subsistence are increased; that is shown by experience to be practically true; and therefore, finally,

[1] *Essay*, ii. 251 (bk. iii. ch. xiv.).   [2] *Ibid.* (1798), p. 141.

the proportion is maintained by 'misery and vice.' That is the main conclusion which not unnaturally startled the world. Malthus always adhered in some sense to the main doctrine, though he stated explicitly some reserves already implicitly involved. A writer must not be surprised if popular readers remember the unguarded and dogmatic utterances which give piquancy to a theory, and overlook the latent qualifications which, when fully expressed, make it approximate to a commonplace. The political bearing of his reasoning is significant. The application of Godwin's theories of equality would necessarily, as he urges, stimulate an excessive population. To meet the consequent evils, two measures would be obviously necessary; private property must be instituted in order to stimulate prudence; and marriage must be instituted to make men responsible for the increase of the population. These institutions are necessary, and they make equality impossible. Weak, then, as foresight may be with most men, the essential social institutions have been developed by the necessity of enabling foresight to exercise some influence; and thus indirectly societies have in fact grown in wealth and numbers through arrangements which have by one and the same action strengthened prudence and created inequality. Although this is clearly implied, the main impression produced upon Malthus's readers was that he held 'vice and misery' to be essential to society; nay, that in some sense he regarded them as blessings. He was accused, as he tells us,[1] of objecting to vaccination, because it tended to prevent deaths from small-pox, and has to protest against some one who had declared his principles

[1] *Essay*, ii. 449 (Appendix).

to be favourable to the slave trade.[1] He was represented, that is, as holding depopulation to be good in itself. These perversions were grotesque, but partly explain the horror with which Malthus was constantly regarded; and we must consider what made them plausible.

I must first notice the maturer form of his doctrine. In the second edition he turns to account the result of his later reading, his personal observations, and the statistical results which were beginning to accumulate. The remodelled book opens with a survey of the observed action of the checks; and it concludes with a discussion of the 'moral restraint' which is now added to 'vice and misery.' Although considerable fragments of the old treatise remained to the last, the whole book was altered both in style and character. The style certainly suffers, for Malthus was not a master of the literary art; he inserts his additions with little care for the general effect. He tones down some of the more vivid phrases which had given offence, though he does not retract the substance. A famous passage[2] in the second edition, in which he speaks of 'nature's mighty feast,' where, unluckily, the 'table is already full,' and therefore unbidden guests are left to starve, was suppressed in the later editions. Yet the principle that no man has a claim to subsistence as of right remains unaltered. The omission injures the literary effect without altering the logic; and I think that, where the argument is amended, the new element is scarcely worked into the old so as to gain thorough consistency.

[1] *Essay*, ii. 473 (Appendix).
[2] *Ibid.* (Second Edition), p. 400. The passage is given in full in *Malthus and his Work*, p. 307.

Malthus's survey of different countries showed how various are the 'checks' by which population is limited in various countries. We take a glance at all nations through all epochs of history. In the South Sea we find a delicious climate and a fertile soil, where population is mainly limited by vice, infanticide, and war; and where, in spite of these influences, the population multiplies at intervals till it is killed off by famine. In China, a vast and fertile territory, inhabited by an industrious race, in which agriculture has always been encouraged, marriage stimulated, and property widely diffused, has facilitated the production of a vast population in the most abject state of poverty, driven to expose children by want, and liable at intervals to destructive famines. In modern Europe, the checks appear in the most various forms; in Switzerland and Norway a frugal population in small villages sometimes instinctively understands the principle of population, and exhibits the 'moral restraint,' while in England the poor-laws are producing a mass of hopeless and inert pauperism. Consideration of these various cases, and a comparison of such records as are obtainable of the old savage races, of the classical states of antiquity, of the Northern barbarians and of the modern European nations, suggests a natural doubt. Malthus abundantly proves what can hardly be denied, that population has everywhere been found to press upon the means of subsistence, and that vice and misery are painfully abundant. But does he establish or abandon his main proposition? He now asserts the 'tendency' of population to outrun the means of subsistence. Yet he holds unequivocally that the increase of population has been accompanied by an increased comfort; that want has diminished although population has increased; and that the 'preventive' check is stronger than of old in proportion to the positive check. Scotland, he says,[1] is 'still overpeopled, but not so much as when it contained fewer inhabitants.' Many nations, as he points out in general terms, have been most prosperous when most populous.[2] They could export food when crowded, and have ceased to import it when thinned. This, indeed, expresses his permanent views, though the facts were often alleged by his critics as a disproof of them. Was not the disproof real? Does not a real evasion lurk under the phrase 'tendency'? You may say that the earth has a tendency to fall into the sun, and another 'tendency' to move away from the sun. But it would be absurd to argue that we were therefore in danger of being burnt or of being frozen. To explain the law of a vital process, we may have to analyse it, and therefore to regard it as due to conflicting forces; but the forces do not really exist separately, and in considering the whole concrete phenomenon we must take them as mutually implied. A man has a 'tendency' to grow too fat; and another 'tendency' to grow too thin. That surely means that on the whole he has a 'tendency' to preserve the desirable mean. The phrase, then, can only have a distinct meaning when the conflicting forces represent two independent or really separable forces. To use an illustration given by Malthus, we might say that a man had a 'tendency' to grow upwards; but was restrained by a weight on his head. The man has the 'tendency,' because we may regard the weight as a separable accident. When both forces are of

[1] *Essay*, i. 469 (bk. ii. ch. x.). Eden had made the same remark.
[2] *Ibid*. ii. 229 (bk. iii. ch. xiv.).

the essence, the separate 'tendencies' correspond merely to our way of analysing the fact. But if one can be properly regarded as relatively accidental, the 'tendency' means the way in which the other will manifest itself in actual cases.

In 1829, Senior put this point to Malthus.[1] What, he asked, do you understand by a 'tendency' when you admit that the tendency is normally overbalanced by others? Malthus explains his meaning to be that every nation suffers from evils 'specifically arising from the pressure of population against food.' The wages of the labourer in old countries have never been sufficient to enable him to maintain a large family at ease. There is overcrowding, we may say, in England now as there was in England at the Conquest; though food has increased in a greater proportion than population; and the pressure has therefore taken a milder form. This, again, is proved by the fact that, whenever a relaxation of the pressure has occurred, when plagues have diminished population, or improvements in agriculture increased their supply of food, the gap has been at once filled up. The people have not taken advantage of the temporary relaxation of the check to preserve the new equilibrium, but have taken out the improvement by a multiplication of numbers. The statement then appears to be that at any given time the population is in excess. Men would be better off if they were less numerous. But, on the other hand, the tendency to multiply does not represent a constant force, an irresistible instinct which will always bring men down to the same level, but something which, in fact, may vary materially. Malthus admits, in fact, that

[1] Correspondence in Senior's *Three Essays on Population* (1829).

the 'elasticity' is continually changing; and therefore repudiates the interpretation which seemed to make all improvement hopeless. Why, then, distinguish the 'check' as something apart from the instinct? If, in any case, we accept this explanation, does not the theory become a 'truism,' or at least a commonplace, inoffensive but hardly instructive? Does it amount to more than the obvious statement that prudence and foresight are desirable and are unfortunately scarce?

III. MORAL RESTRAINT

The change in the theory of 'checks' raises another important question. Malthus now introduced a modification upon which his supporters laid great stress. In the new version the 'checks' which proportion population to means of subsistence are not simply 'vice and misery,' but 'moral restraint, vice, and misery.'[1] How, precisely, does this modify the theory? How are the different 'checks' related? What especially is meant by 'moral' in this connection? Malthus takes his ethical philosophy pretty much for granted, but is clearly a Utilitarian according to the version of Paley.[2] He agrees with Paley that 'virtue evidently consists in educing from the materials which the Creator has placed under our guidance the greatest sum of human happiness.'[3] He adds to this that our 'natural impulses are, abstractedly considered, good, and only to be distinguished by their consequences.'

[1] *Essay*, i. 234 (bk. i. ch. ii.).
[2] Mr. Bonar thinks (*Malthus and his Work*, p. 324) that Malthus followed Paley's predecessor, Abraham Tucker, rather than Paley. The difference is not for my purpose important. In any case, Malthus's references are to Paley.
[3] *Essay*, ii. 266 (bk. iv. ch. i.).

Hunger, he says, as Bentham had said, is the same in itself, whether it leads to stealing a loaf or to eating your own loaf. He agrees with Godwin that morality means the 'calculation of consequences,'[1] or, as he says with Paley, implies ·the discovery of the will of God by observing the effect of actions upon happiness. Reason then regulates certain innate and practically unalterable instincts by enabling us to foretell their consequences. The reasonable man is influenced not simply by the immediate gratification, but by a forecast of all the results which it will entail. In these matters Malthus was entirely at one with the Utilitarians proper, and seems to regard their doctrine as self-evident.

He notices briefly one logical difficulty thus introduced. The 'checks' are vice, misery, and moral restraint. But why distinguish vice from misery? Is not conduct vicious which causes misery,[2] and precisely because it causes misery? He replies that to omit 'vice' would confuse our language. Vicious conduct may cause happiness in particular cases; though its general tendency would be pernicious. The answer is not very clear; and Malthus, I think, would have been more logical if he had stuck to his first theory, and regarded vice as simply one form of imprudence. Misery, that is, or the fear of misery, and the indulgence in conduct which produces misery are the 'checks' which limit population; and the whole problem is to make the ultimate sanction more operative upon the immediate conduct. Man becomes more virtuous simply as he becomes more prudent, and is therefore governed in his conduct by recognising the wider and more remote series of consequences. There

[1] *Essay* (first edition), p. 212. [2] *Ibid*. i. 16 *n*. (bk. i. ch. ii.).

is, indeed, the essential difference that the virtuous man acts (on whatever motives) from a regard to the 'greatest happiness of the greatest number,' and not simply from self-regard. Still the ultimate and decisive criterion is the tendency of conduct to produce misery; and if Malthus had carried this through as rigorously as Bentham, he would have been more consistent. The 'moral check' would then have been simply a department of the prudential; including prudence for others as well as for ourselves. One reason for the change is obvious. His assumption enables him to avoid coming into conflict with the accepted morality of the time. On his exposition 'vice' occasionally seems not to be productive of misery but an alternative to misery; and yet something bad in itself. Is this consistent with his Utilitarianism? The vices of the South Sea Islanders, according to him, made famine less necessary; and, if they gave pleasure at the moment, were they not on the whole beneficial? Malthus again reckons among vices practices which limit the population without causing 'misery' directly.[1] Could he logically call them vicious? He wishes to avoid the imputation of sanctioning such practices, and therefore condemns them by his moral check; but it would be hard to prove that he was consistent in condemning them. Or, again, there is another familiar difficulty. The Catholic church encourages marriage as a remedy for vice; and thereby stimulates both population and poverty. How would Malthus solve the problem: is it better to encourage chastity and a superabundance of people, or to restrict marriage at the cost of increasing temptation to vice? He

[1] See e.g. his remarks upon Condorcet in Essay, ii. 8 (bk. iii. ch. i.); and Owen in Ibid. ii. 48 (bk. iii. ch. ii.).

seems to evade the point by saying that he recommends both chastity and abstinence from marriage. By 'moral restraint,' as he explains, he means 'restraint from marriage from prudential motives, with a conduct strictly moral during the period of this restraint.' 'I have never,' he adds, 'intentionally deviated from this sense.'[1] A man, that is, should postpone taking a wife, and should not console himself by taking a mistress. He is to refrain from increasing the illegitimate as well as from increasing the legitimate population. It is not surprising that Malthus admits that this check has 'in past ages operated with inconsiderable force.'[2] In fact Malthus, as a thoroughly respectable and decent clergyman, manages by talking about the 'moral restraint' rather to evade than to answer some awkward problems of conduct; but at the cost of some inconsequence.

But another result of this mode of patching up his argument is more important. The 'vices of mankind,' he says in an unusually rhetorical summary of his historical inquiry,[3] 'are active and able ministers of depopulation. They are the precursors in the great army of destruction, and often finish the dreadful work themselves. But should they fail in the war of extermination, sickly seasons, epidemics, pestilence, and plague advance in terrific array, and sweep off their thousands and ten thousands. Should success still be incomplete, gigantic inevitable famine stalks in the rear, and at one mighty blow levels the population with the food of the world.' The life of the race, then, is a struggle with misery; its

[1] Essay, i. 15 n. (bk. i. ch. ii.); and see Ibid. (edit. of 1807) ii. 128.
[2] Ibid. (1807) ii. 128.
[3] Ibid. (1807) ii. 3 (bk. ii. ch. ii.). (Omitted in later editions.)

expansion is constantly forcing it upon this array of evils; and in proportion to the elasticity is the severity of the evils which follow. This is not only a 'gloomy view,' but again seems to suggest that 'vice' is an alternative to 'misery.' Vices are bad, it would seem, but at least they obviate the necessity for disease and famine. Malthus probably suppressed the passage because he thought it liable to this interpretation. It indicates, however, a real awkwardness, if not something more, in his exposition. He here speaks as if there was room for a fixed number of guests at his banquet. Whatever, therefore, keeps the population to that limit must be so far good. If he had considered his 'moral check' more thoroughly, he might have seen that this does not correspond to his real meaning. The 'moral' and the prudential checks are not really to be contrasted as alternative, but co-operative. Every population, vicious or virtuous, must of course proportion its numbers to its means of support. That gives the prudential check. But the moral check operates by altering the character of the population itself. From the purely economic point of view, vice is bad because it lowers efficiency. A lazy, drunken, and profligate people would starve where an industrious, sober, and honest people would thrive. The check of vice thus brings the check of misery into play at an earlier stage. It limits by lowering the vitality and substituting degeneration for progress. The check, therefore, is essentially mischievous. Though it does not make the fields barren, it lowers the power of cultivation. Malthus had recognised this when he pointed out, as we have seen, that emergence from the savage state meant the institution of marriage and property and,

we may infer, the correlative virtues of chastity, industry, and honesty. If men can form large societies, and millions can be supported where once a few thousands were at starvation point, it is due to the civilisation which at every stage implies 'moral restraint' in a wider sense than Malthus used the phrase. An increase of population by such means was, of course, to be desired. If Malthus emphasises this inadequately, it is partly, no doubt, because the Utilitarian view of morality tended to emphasise the external consequences rather than the alteration of the man himself. Yet the wider and sounder view is logically implied in his reasoning—so much so that he might have expressed his real aim more clearly if he had altered the order of his argument. He might have consistently taken the same line as earlier writers and declared that he desired, above all things, the increase of population. He would have had indeed to explain that he desired the increase of a sound and virtuous population; and that hasty and imprudent increase led to misery and to a demoralisation which would ultimately limit numbers in the worst way. We shall see directly how nearly he accepts this view. Meanwhile, by insisting upon the need of limitation, he was led to speak often as if limitation by any means was good and the one thing needful, and the polemic against Godwin in the first edition had given prominence to this side of the question. Had he put his views in a different shape, he would perhaps have been so edifying that he would have been disregarded. He certainly avoided that risk, and had whatever advantage is gained by stating sound doctrine paradoxically.

We shall, I think, appreciate his real position better by

considering his approximation to the theory which, as we
know, was suggested to Darwin by a perusal of Malthus.[1]
There is a closer resemblance than appears at first. The
first edition concludes by two chapters afterwards omitted,
giving the philosophical application of his theory. He
there says that the 'world is a mighty process of God
not for the trial but for the creation and formation of
the mind.'[2] It is not, as Butler thought, a place of
'probation,' but a scene in which the higher qualities are
gradually developed. Godwin had quoted Franklin's
view that 'mind' would become 'omnipotent over
matter.' Malthus holds that, as he puts it, 'God is
making matter into mind.' The difference is that Malthus
regards evil in general not as a sort of accident of which
we can get rid by reason; but as the essential stimulus
which becomes the efficient cause of intellectual activity.
The evils from which men suffer raise savage tribes from
their indolence, and by degrees give rise to the growth
of civilisation. The argument, though these chapters
were dropped by Malthus, was taken up by J. B. Sumner,
to whom he refers in later editions.[3] It is, in fact, an

[1] Mr. A. R. Wallace, Darwin's fellow-discoverer of the doctrine, also
learned it from Malthus. See Clodd's *Pioneers of Evolution.* Malthus uses
the phrase 'struggle for existence' in relation to a fight between two savage
tribes in the first edition of his *Essay,* p. 48. In replying to Condorcet,
Malthus speaks (*Essay,* ii. 12, bk. iii. ch. i.) of the possible improvement of
living organisms. He argues that, though a plant may be improved, it
cannot be indefinitely improved by cultivation. A carnation could not be
made as large as a tulip. It has been said that this implies a condemnation
by anticipation of theories of the development of species. This is hardly
correct. Malthus simply urges against Condorcet that our inability to fix
limits precisely does not imply that there are no limits. This, it would seem,
must be admitted on all hands. Evolution implies definite though not precisely
definable limits. Life may be lengthened, but not made immortal.
[2] *Essay* (first edition), 353.   [3] *Ibid.* ii. 42 *n.* (bk. iii. ch. iii.).

imperfect way of stating a theory of evolution. This
appears in his opening chapters upon the 'moral restraint.'[1] He explains that moral and physical evils are
'instruments employed by the Deity' to admonish us
against such conduct as is destructive of happiness.
Diseases are indications that we have broken a law of
nature. The plague of London was properly interpreted
by our ancestors as a hint to improve the sanitary conditions of the town. Similarly, we have to consider the
consequences of obeying our instincts. The desire of
food and necessaries is the most powerful of these instincts, and next to it the passion between the sexes.
They are both good, for they are both natural; but they
have to be properly correlated. To 'virtuous love' in
particular we owe the 'sunny spots' in our lives, where
the imagination most loves to bask. Desire of necessaries gives us the stimulus of the comfortable fireside;
and love adds the wife and children, without whom the
fireside would lose half its charm. Now, as a rule, the
sexual passion is apt to be in excess. The final cause
of this excess is itself obvious. We cannot but conceive that it is an object of 'the Creator that the
earth should be replenished.'[2] To secure that object, it
is necessary that 'there should be a tendency in the

[1] *Essay,* ii. 301-36 (bk. iv. ch. i. and ii.). Sumner's *Treatise on the
Records of the Creation, and on the Moral Attributes of the Creator: with Particular Reference to the Jewish History and the Consistency of the Principle of
Population with the Wisdom and Goodness of the Creator* (1815), had gained the
second Burnett prize. It went through many editions; and shows how Cuvier
confirms Genesis, and Malthus proves that the world was intended to involve
a competition favourable to the industrious and sober. Sumner's view of
Malthus is given in Part II., chaps. v. and vi. In previous chapters he has
supported Malthus's attack on Godwin and Condorcet.
[2] *Essay,* ii. 266 (bk. iv. ch. i.).

population to increase faster than food.' If the two
instincts were differently balanced, men would be content
though the population of a fertile region were limited
to the most trifling numbers. Hence the instinct has
mercifully been made so powerful as to stimulate population, and thus indirectly and eventually to produce a
population at once larger and more comfortable. On
the one hand, 'it is of the very utmost importance to
the happiness of mankind that they should not increase
too fast,'[1] but, on the other hand, if the passion were
weakened, the motives which make a man industrious
and capable of progress would be diminished also. It
would, of course, be simpler to omit the 'teleology'; to
say that sanitary regulations are made necessary by the
plague, not that the plague is divinely appointed to encourage sanitary regulations. Malthus is at the point of
view of Paley which becomes Darwinism when inverted;
but the conclusion is much the same. He reaches elsewhere, in fact, a more precise view of the value of the
'moral restraint.' In a chapter devoted for once to an
ideal state of things,[2] he shows how a race thoroughly imbued with that doctrine would reconcile the demands of
the two instincts. Population would in that case increase,
but, instead of beginning by an increase, it would begin
by providing the means of supporting. No man would
become a father until he had seen his way to provide for
a family. The instinct which leads to increasing the
population would thus be intrinsically as powerful as it
now is; but when regulated by prudence it would impel
mankind to begin at the right end. Food would be
ready before mouths to eat it.

[1] *Essay,* ii. 268 (bk. iv. ch. i.).   [2] *Ibid.* (bk. iv. ch. ii.).

IV. SOCIAL REMEDIES

This final solution appears in Malthus's proposed
remedies for the evils of the time. Malthus[1] declares
that 'an increase of population when it follows in its
natural order is both a great positive good in itself, and
absolutely necessary' to an increase of wealth. This
natural order falls in, as he observes, with the view to
which Mirabeau had been converted, that 'revenue was
the source of population,' and not population of revenue.[2]
Malthus holds specifically that, 'in the course of some
centuries,' the population of England might be doubled
or trebled, and yet every man be 'much better fed and
clothed than he is at present.'[3] He parts company with
Paley, who had considered the ideal state to be 'that of
a laborious frugal people ministering to the demands
of an opulent luxurious nation.'[4] That, says Malthus, is
'not an inviting prospect.' Nothing but a conviction
of absolute necessity could reconcile us to the 'thought of
ten millions of people condemned to incessant toil, and to
the privation of everything but absolute necessaries, in
order to minister to the excessive luxuries of the other
million.' But he denies that any such necessity exists.
He wishes precisely to see luxury spread among the
poorer classes. A desire for such luxury is the best of
all checks to population, and one of the best means of
raising the standard. It would, in fact, contribute to his
'moral restraint.' So, too, he heartily condemns the

[1] *Essay,* ii. 241 (bk. iii. ch. xiv.).
[2] *Ibid.* ii. 241 (bk. iii. ch. xiv.).   [3] *Ibid.* ii. 293 (bk. iv. ch. iv.).
[4] *Ibid.* ii. 425 (bk. iv. ch. xiii.). Malthus expresses a hope that Paley had
modified his views upon population, and refers to a passage in the *Natural
Theology.*

hypocrisy of the rich, who professed a benevolent desire to better the poor, and yet complained of high wages.[1] If, he says elsewhere,[2] a country can 'only be rich by running a successful race for low wages, I should be disposed to say, Perish such riches!' No one, in fact, could see more distinctly than Malthus the demoralising influence of poverty, and the surpassing importance of raising the people from the terrible gulf of pauperism. He refers to Colquhoun's account of the twenty thousand people who rose every morning in London without knowing how they were to be supported; and observes that 'when indigence does not produce overt acts of vice, it palsies every virtue.'[3] The temptations to which the poor man is exposed, and the sense of injustice due to an ignorance of the true cause of misery, tend to 'sour the disposition, to harden the heart, and deaden the moral sense.' Unfortunately, the means which have been adopted to lessen the evil have tended to increase it. In the first place, there was the master-evil of the poor-laws. Malthus points out the demoralising effects of these laws in chapters full of admirable common sense, which he was unfortunately able to enforce by fresh illustrations in successive editions. He attends simply to the stimulus to population. He thinks that if the laws had never existed, the poor would now have been much better off.[4] If the laws had been fully carried out, every labourer might have been certain that all his children would be supported, or, in other words, every check to population would have been removed.[5] Happily,

1 *Essay*, ii. 292 (bk. iv. ch. iv.).   2 *Political Economy* (1836), p. 214.
3 *Essay*, ii. 298 (bk. iv. ch. iv.).   4 *Ibid.* ii. 86 (bk. iii. ch. vi.).
5 *Ibid.* ii. 87 (bk. iii. ch. vi.).

the becoming pride of the English peasantry was not quite extinct; and the poor-law had to some extent counteracted itself, or taken away with one hand what it gave with the other, by placing the burthen upon the parishes.[1] Thus landlords have been more disposed to pull down than to build cottages, and marriage has been checked. On the whole, however, Malthus could see in the poor-laws nothing but a vast agency for demoralising the poor, tempered by a system of petty tyrannical interference. He proposes, therefore, that the poor-law should be abolished. Notice should be given that no children born after a certain day should be entitled to parish help; and, as he quaintly suggests, the clergyman might explain to every couple, after publishing the banns, the immorality of reckless marriage, and the reasons for abolishing a system which had been proved to frustrate the intentions of the founders.[2] Private charity, he thinks, would meet the distress which might afterwards arise, though humanity imperiously requires that it should be 'sparingly administered.' Upon this duty he writes a sensible chapter.[3] To his negative proposals Malthus adds a few of the positive kind. He is strongly in favour of a national system of education, and speaks with contempt of the 'illiberal and feeble' arguments opposed to it. The schools, he observes, might confer 'an almost incalculable benefit' upon society, if they taught 'a few of the simplest principles of political economy.'[4] He had been disheartened by the prejudices of the ignorant labourer, and felt the incompatibility of a free government with such ignorance. A real education,

1 *Essay*, ii. 90 (bk. iii. ch. vi.).   2 *Ibid.* ii. 338 (bk. iv. ch. viii.).
3 *Ibid.* ii. (bk. iv. ch. x.).   4 *Ibid.* ii. 353 (bk. iv. ch. ix.).

such as was given in Scotland, would make the poor not, as alarmists had suggested, more inflammable, but better able to detect the sophistry of demagogues.[1] He is, of course, in favour of savings banks,[2] and approves friendly societies, though he is strongly opposed to making them compulsory, as they would then be the poor-law in a new form.[3] The value of every improvement turns upon its effect in encouraging the 'moral restraint.' Malthus's ultimate criterion is always, Will the measure make people averse to premature marriage? He reaches the apparently inconsistent result that it might be desirable to make an allowance for every child beyond six.[4] But this is on the hypothesis that the 'moral restraint' has come to be so habitual that no man marries until he has a fair prospect of maintaining a family of six. If this were the practical code, the allowance in cases where the expectation was disappointed would not act as an encouragement to marriage, but as a relief under a burthen which could not have been anticipated. Thus all Malthus's teaching may be said to converge upon this practical point. Add to the Ten Commandments the new law, 'Thou shalt not marry until there is a fair prospect of supporting six children.' Then population will increase, but sufficient means for subsistence will always be provided beforehand. We shall make sure that there is a provision for additional numbers before, not after, we add to our numbers. Food first and population afterwards gives the rule; thus we achieve the good end without the incidental evils.

Malthus's views of the appropriate remedy for social

1 *Essay*, ii. 356 (bk. iv. ch. ix.).   2 *Ibid.* ii. 407 (bk. iv. ch. xii.).
3 *Ibid.* ii. 375 (bk. iv. ch. xi.).   4 *Ibid.* ii. 429 (bk. iv. ch. xiii.).

evils undoubtedly show an imperfect appreciation of the great problems involved. Reckless propagation is an evil; but Malthus regards it as an evil which can be isolated and suppressed by simply adding a new article to the moral code. He is dealing with a central problem of human nature and social order. Any modification of the sexual instincts or of the constitution of the family involves a profound modification of the whole social order and of the dominant religious and moral creeds. Malthus tacitly assumes that conduct is determined by the play of two instincts, unalterable in themselves, but capable of modification in their results by a more extensive view of consequences. To change men's ruling motives in regard to the most important part of their lives is to alter their whole aims and conceptions of the world, and of happiness in every other relation. It supposes, therefore, not a mere addition of knowledge, but a transformation of character and an altered view of all the theories which have been embodied in religious and ethical philosophy. He overlooks, too, considerations which would be essential to a complete statement. A population which is too prudent may suffer itself to be crowded out by more prolific races in the general struggle for existence; and cases may be suggested such as that of the American colonies, in which an increase of numbers might be actually an advantage by facilitating a more efficient organisation of labour.

The absence of a distinct appreciation of such difficulties gives to his speculation that one-sided character which alienated his more sentimental contemporaries. It was natural enough in a man who was constantly confronted by the terrible development of pauperism in England,

and was too much tempted to assume that the tendency to reckless propagation was not only a very grave evil, but the ultimate source of every evil. The doctrine taken up in this unqualified fashion by some of his disciples, and preached by them with the utmost fervour as the one secret of prosperity, shocked both the conservative and orthodox whose prejudices were trampled upon, and such Radicals as inherited Godwin's or Condorcet's theory of perfectibility. Harsh and one-sided as it might be, however, we may still hold that it was of value, not only in regard to the most pressing difficulty of the day, but also as calling attention to a vitally important condition of social welfare. The question, however, recurs whether, when the doctrine is so qualified as to be admissible, it does not also become a mere truism.

An answer to this question should begin by recognising one specific resemblance between his speculations and Darwin's. Facts, which appear from an older point of view to be proofs of a miraculous interposition, become with Malthus, as with Darwin, the normal results of admitted conditions. Godwin had admitted that there was some 'principle which kept population on a level with subsistence.' 'The sole question is,' says Malthus,[1] 'what is this principle? Is it some obscure and occult cause? a mysterious interference of heaven,' inflicting barrenness at certain periods? or 'a cause open to our researches and within our view?' Other writers had had recourse to the miraculous. One of Malthus's early authorities was Süssmilch, who had published his

[1] *Essay of* 1807 (bk. iii. ch. ii., and vol. ii. p. 111). The phrases quoted are toned down in later editions.

Göttliche Ordnung in 1761, to show how Providence had taken care that the trees should not grow into the sky. The antediluvians had been made long-lived in order that they might have large families and people an empty earth, while life was divinely shortened as the world filled up. Süssmilch, however, regarded population as still in need of stimulus. Kings might help Providence. A new Trajan would deserve to be called the father of his people, if he increased the marriage-rate. Malthus replies that the statistics which the worthy man himself produced showed conclusively that the marriages depended upon the deaths. The births fill up the vacancies, and the prince who increased the population before vacancies arose would simply increase the rate of mortality.[1] If you want to increase your birth-rate without absolutely producing famine, as he remarks afterwards,[2] make your towns unhealthy, and encourage settlement by marshes. You might thus double the mortality, and we might all marry prematurely without being absolutely starved. His own aim is not to secure the greatest number of births, but to be sure that the greatest number of those born may be supported.[3] The ingenious M. Muret, again, had found a Swiss parish in which the mean life was the highest and the fecundity smallest known. He piously conjectures that it may be a law of God that 'the force of life in each country should be in the inverse ratio of its fecundity.' He needs not betake himself to a miracle, says Malthus.[4] The case is simply that in a small and healthy village, where people had become aware of the importance of the 'preventive

[1] *Essay,* i. 330 (bk. ii. ch. iv.).   [2] *Ibid.* ii. 300 (bk. iv. ch. v.).
[3] *Ibid.* ii. 405 (bk. iv. ch. xiii.).   [4] *Ibid.* i. 343 (bk. ii. ch. v.).

check,' the young people put off marriage till there was room for them, and consequently both lowered the birth-rate and raised the average duration of life.

Nothing, says Malthus very forcibly, has caused more errors than the confusion between 'relative and positive, and between cause and effect.'[1] He is here answering the argument that because the poor who had cows were the most industrious, the way to make them industrious was to give them cows. Malthus thinks it more probable that industry got the cow than that the cow produced industry. This is a trifling instance of a very general truth. People had been content to notice the deaths caused by war and disease, and to infer at once that what caused death must diminish population. Malthus shows the necessity of observing other collateral results. The gap may be made so great as to diminish population; but it may be compensated by a more rapid reproduction; or, the rapidity of reproduction may itself be the cause of the disease; so that to remove one kind of mortality may be on some occasion to introduce others. The stream is dammed on one breach to flow more strongly through other outlets.[2]

This is, I conceive, to say simply that Malthus was introducing a really scientific method. The facts taken in the true order became at once intelligible instead of suggesting mysterious and irregular interferences. Earlier writers had been content to single out one particular set of phenomena without attending to its place in the more general and complex processes, of which they formed an integral part. Infanticide, as Hume had pointed out, might tend to increase popula-

[1] *Essay,* ii. 424 (bk. iv. ch. xiii.).   [2] *Ibid.* ii. 304 (bk. iv. ch. v.).

tion.[1] In prospect, it might encourage people to have babies; and when babies came, natural affection might prevent the actual carrying out of the intention. To judge of the actual effect, we have to consider the whole of the concrete case. It may be carried out, as apparently in the South Sea Islands, so generally as to limit population; or it may be, as in China, an indication that the pressure is so great that a number of infants become superfluous. Its suppression might, in the one case, lead to an increase of the population; in the other, to the increase of other forms of mortality. Malthus's investigations illustrate the necessity of referring every particular process to its place in the whole system, of noting how any given change might set up a set of actions and reactions in virtue of the general elasticity of population, and thus of constantly referring at every step to the general conditions of human life. He succeeded in making many points clear, and of showing how hastily many inferences had been drawn. He explained, for example, why the revolutionary wars had not diminished the population of France, in spite of the great number of deaths,[2] and thus gave an example of a sound method of inquiry which has exercised a great influence upon later observers. Malthus was constantly misunderstood and misrepresented, and his opponents often allege as fatal objections to his doctrine the very facts by which it was really supported. But we may, I think, say that since his writing no serious economical writer has adopted the old hasty guesses, or has ventured to propose a theory without regard to the principles of which he first brought out the full significance.

[1] *Essay,* i. 75 (bk. i. ch. v.).   [2] *Ibid.* (bk. ii. ch. vi.).

V. POLITICAL APPLICATION

This I take to indicate one real and permanent value of Malthus's writings. He introduced a new method of approaching the great social problems. The value of the method may remain, however inaccurate may be the assumptions of facts. The 'tendency,' if interpreted to mean that people are always multiplying too rapidly, may be a figment. If it is taken as calling attention to one essential factor in the case, it is a most important guide to investigation. This brings out another vital point. The bearing of the doctrine upon the political as well as upon the economical views of the Utilitarians is of conspicuous importance. Malthus's starting-point, as we have seen, was the opposition to the doctrine of 'perfectibility.' Hard facts, which Godwin and Condorcet had neglected, were fatal to their dreams. You have, urged Malthus, neglected certain undeniable truths as to the unalterable qualities of human nature, and, therefore, your theories will not work. The revolutionists had opposed an ideal 'state of nature' to the actual arrangements of society. They imagined that the 'state of nature' represented the desirable consummation, and that the constitution of the 'natural' order could be determined from certain abstract principles. The equality of man, and the absolute rights which could be inferred by a kind of mathematical process, supplied the necessary dogmatic basis. The antithesis to the state of nature was the artificial state, marked by inequality, and manifesting its spirit by luxury. Kings, priests, and nobles had somehow established this unnatural order; and to sweep them away summarily was the way of bringing the natural order into full activity. The ideal system was already potentially in existence, and would become actual when men's minds were once cleared from superstition, and the political made to correspond to the natural rights of man. To this Malthus had replied, as we have seen, that social inequality was not a mere arbitrary product of fraud and force, but an expedient necessary to restrain the primitive instincts of mankind. He thus coincides with Bentham's preference of 'security' to 'equality,' and illustrates the real significance of that doctrine. Property and marriage, though they involve inequality, were institutions of essential importance. Godwin had pushed his theories to absolute anarchy; to the destruction of all law, for law in general represented coercion or an interference with the state of nature. Malthus virtually asserted that the metaphysical doctrine was inapplicable because, men being what they are, these conclusions were incompatible with even the first stages of social progress. This means, again, that for the metaphysical method Malthus is substituting a scientific method. Instead of regarding all government as a kind of mysterious intervention from without, which has somehow introduced a fatal discord into the natural order, he inquires what are the facts; how law has been evolved; and for what reason. His answer is, in brief, that law, order, and inequality have been absolutely necessary in order to limit tendencies which would otherwise keep men in a state of hopeless poverty and depression.

This gives the 'differentia' of the Utilitarian considered as one species of the genus 'Radical.' Malthus's criticism of Paine is significant.[1] He agrees with Paine

[1] _Essay_, ii. 318 (bk. iv. ch. vi.).

that the cause of popular risings is 'want of happiness.' But Paine, he remarks, was 'in many important points totally ignorant of the structure of society'; and has fallen into the error of attributing all want of happiness to government. Consequently, Paine advocates a plan for distributing taxes among the poorest classes, which would aggravate the evils a hundredfold. He fully admits with Paine that man has rights. The true line of answer would be to show what those rights are. To give this answer is not Malthus's present business; but there is one right, at any rate, which a man does not and cannot possess: namely, the 'right to subsistence when his labour will not fairly purchase it.' He does not possess it because he cannot possess it; to try to secure it is to try to 'reverse the laws of nature,' and therefore to produce cruel suffering by practising an 'inhuman deceit.' The Abbé Raynal had said that a man had a right to subsist 'before all social laws.' Man had the same right, replied Malthus, as he had to live a hundred or a thousand years. He may live, _if he can_ without interfering with others. Social laws have, in fact, enlarged the power of subsistence; but neither before nor after their institution could an unlimited number subsist. Briefly, the question of fact comes before the question of right, and the fault of the revolutionary theorists was to settle the right without reference to the possibility of making the right correspond to the fact.

Hence Malthus draws his most emphatic political moral. The admission that all evil is due to government is the way to tyranny. Make men believe that government is the one cause of misery, and they will inevitably throw the whole responsibility upon their rulers; seek for redress by cures which aggravate the disease; and strengthen the hands of those who prefer even despotism to anarchy. This, he intimates, is the explanation of the repressive measures in which the country-gentlemen had supported Pitt. The people had fancied that by destroying government they would make bread cheap; government was forced to be tyrannical in order to resist revolution; while its supporters were led to 'give up some of the most valuable privileges of Englishmen.'[1] It is then of vital importance to settle what is and what is not to be set down to government. Malthus, in fact, holds that the real evils are due to underlying causes which cannot be directly removed, though they may be diminished or increased, by legislators. Government can do something by giving security to property, and by making laws which will raise the self-respect of the lower classes. But the effect of such laws must be slow and gradual; and the error which has most contributed to that delay in the progress of freedom, which is 'so disheartening to every liberal mind,'[2] is the confusion as to the true causes of misery. Thus, as he has already urged, professed economists could still believe, so long after the publication of Adam Smith's work, that it was 'in the power of the justices of the peace or even of the omnipotence of parliament to alter by a _fiat_ the whole circumstances of the country.'[3] Yet men who saw the absurdity of trying to fix the price of provisions were ready to propose to fix the rate of wages. They did not see that one term of the proportion implied the other. Malthus's whole criticism of the poor-law, already noticed, is a commentary upon

[1] _Essay_, ii. 315 (bk. iv. ch. v.). [2] _Ibid._ ii. 326 (bk. iv. ch. vi.).
[3] _Ibid._ ii. 78 (bk. iii. ch. v.).

this text. It is connected with a general theory of human nature. The author of nature, he says, has wisely made 'the passion of self-love beyond expression stronger than the passion of benevolence.'[1] He means, as he explains, that every man has to pursue his own welfare and that of his family as his primary object. Benevolence, of course, is the 'source of our purest and most refined pleasures,' and so forth; but it should come in as a supplement to self-love. Therefore we must never admit that men have a strict right to relief. That is to injure the very essential social force. 'Hard as it may seem in individual instances, dependent poverty ought to be held disgraceful.'[2] The spirit of independence or self-help is the one thing necessary. 'The desire of bettering our condition and the fear of making it worse, like the *vis medicatrix* in physics, is the *vis medicatrix naturae* in politics, and is continually counteracting the disorders arising from narrow human institutions.'[3] It is only because the poor-laws have not quite destroyed it, that they have not quite ruined the country. The pith of Malthus's teaching is fairly expressed in his last letter to Senior.[4] He holds that the improvement in the condition of the great mass of the labouring classes should be considered as the main interest of society. To improve their condition, it is essential to impress them with the conviction that they can do much more for themselves than others can do for them, and that the *only* source of permanent improvement is the improvement of their moral and religious habits. What government can do, therefore, is to maintain such institutions as may

---

[1] *Essay*, ii. 454 (Appendix).
[2] *Ibid.* ii. 82 (bk. iii. ch. vi.).
[3] *Ibid.* ii. 90 (bk. iii. ch. vi.).
[4] Senior's *Three Lectures*, p. 86.

strengthen the *vis medicatrix*, or 'desire to better our condition,' which poor-laws had directly tended to weaken. He maintains in his letter to Senior, that this desire is 'perfectly feeble' compared with the tendency of the population to increase, and operates in a very slight degree upon the great mass of the labouring class.[1] Still, he holds that on the whole the 'preventive checks' have become stronger relatively to the positive,[2] and, at any rate, all proposals must be judged by their tendency to strengthen the preventive.

Malthus was not a thoroughgoing supporter of the 'do-nothing' doctrine. He approved of a national system of education, and of the early factory acts, though only as applied to infant labour. So, as we shall see, did all the Utilitarians. The 'individualism,' however, is not less decided; and leads him to speak as though the elasticity of population were not merely an essential factor in the social problem, but the sole principle from which all solutions must be deduced. He is thus led, as I have tried to show, to a narrow interpretation of his 'moral check.' He is apt to take 'vice' simply as a product of excessive pressure, and, in his general phrases at least, to overlook its reciprocal tendency to cause pressure. The 'moral check' is only preventive or negative, not a positive cause of superior vigour. A similar defect appears in his theory of the *vis medicatrix*. He was, I hold, perfectly right in emphasising the importance of individual responsibility. No reform can be permanent which does not raise the morality of the individual. His insistence upon this truth was of the highest importance, and it is to be wished that its

---

[1] Senior's *Three Lectures*, p. 60.
[2] *Essay*, i. 534 (bk. ii. ch. xiii.).

importance might be more fully recognised to-day. The one-sidedness appears in his proposal to abolish the poor-law simply. That became the most conspicuous and widely accepted doctrine. All men of 'sense,' said Sydney Smith—certainly a qualified representative of the class—in 1820, agree, first, that the poor-law must be abolished; and secondly, that it must be abolished very gradually.[1] That is really to assume that by refusing to help people at all, you will force them to help themselves. There is another alternative, namely, that they may, as Malthus himself often recognises, become demoralised by excessive poverty. To do simply nothing may lead to degeneration instead of increased energy. The possibility of an improved law, which might act as a moral discipline instead of a simply corrupting agency, is simply left out of account; and the tendency to stimulate reckless population is regarded not only as one probable consequence, but as the very essence of all poor-laws. Upon Malthus's assumptions, the statement that sound political and social theories must be based upon systematic inquiry into facts, meant that the individual was the ultimate unalterable unit, whose interest in his own welfare gave the one fulcrum for all possible changes. The ideal 'state of nature' was a fiction. The true basis of our inquiries is the actual man known to us by observation. The main fault of this being was the excess of the instinct of multiplication, and the way to improve him was to show how it might conflict with the instinct of self-preservation. In this shape the doctrine expressed the most characteristic tendency of the Utilitarians, and divided them from the Socialists or believers in abstract rights of man.

---

[1] Smith's *Works* (1859), i. 295.

VI. RENT

Here, then, we are at a central point of the Utilitarian creed. The expansive force of population is, in a sense, the great motive power which moulds the whole social structure; or, rather, it forces together the independent units, and welds them into an aggregate. The influence of this doctrine upon other economical speculations is of the highest importance. One critical stage in the process is marked by the enunciation of the theory of rent, which was to become another essential article of the true faith. The introduction of this doctrine is characteristic, and marks the point at which Ricardo superseded Malthus as chief expositor of the doctrine.

Malthus's views were first fully given in his *Inquiry into Rent*, the second of three pamphlets which he published during the corn-law controversy of 1814-15.[1] The opinions now stated had, he says, been formed in the course of his lecturing at Haileybury; and he made them public on account of their bearing upon the most absorbing questions of the time. The connection of the theory with Malthus's speculations and with the contemporary difficulties is indeed obvious. The landlord had clearly one of the reserved seats at the banquet of nature. He was the most obvious embodiment of 'security' as opposed to equality. Malthus, again, had been influenced by the French economists and their theory of the 'surplus fund,' provided by agriculture. According to them, as

---

[1] *Observations on the Effects of the Corn-laws*, 1814; *Inquiry into the Nature and Progress of Rent*, 1815; and *The Grounds of an Opinion on the Policy of restricting the Importation of Foreign Corn*, intended as an appendix to the *Observations on the Corn-laws*, 1815.

he says,[1] this fund or rent constitutes the whole national wealth. In his first edition he had defended the economists against some of Adam Smith's criticisms ; and though he altered his views and thought that they had been led into preposterous errors, he retained a certain sympathy for them. Agriculture has still a certain ' pre-eminence.' God has bestowed upon the soil the ' inestimable quality of being able to maintain more persons than are necessary to work it.'[2] It has the special virtue that the supply of necessaries generates the demand. Make more luxuries and the price may fall ; but grow more food and there will be more people to eat it. This, however, seems to be only another way of stating an unpleasant fact. The blessing of 'fertility' counteracts itself. As he argues in the essay,[3] an equal division of land might produce such an increase of population as would exhaust any conceivable increase of food. These views—not, I think, very clear or consistently worked out—lead apparently to the conclusion that the fertility is indeed a blessing, but on condition of being confined to a few. The result, in any case, is the orthodox theory of rent. The labourer gets less than he would if the products of the soil were equally distributed. Both wages and profits must fall as more is left to rent, and that this actually happens, he says, with unusual positiveness, is an ' incontrovertible truth '[4] The fall enables the less fertile land to be cultivated, and gives an excess of produce on the more fertile. ' This excess is rent.'[5] He proceeds to expound his doctrine by comparing land to a set of machines for making corn.[6]

[1] *Inquiry into Rent*, p. 1. [2] *Ibid.* p. 16.
[3] *Essay*, ii. 35 (bk. iii. ch. ii.). [4] *Inquiry into Rent*, p. 20.
[5] *Ibid.* p. 18. [6] *Ibid.* p. 38.

If, in manufacture, a new machine is introduced every one adopts it. In agriculture the worst machines have still to be used ; and those who have the best and sell at the same price, can appropriate the surplus advantage. This, he declares, is a law ' as invariable as the action of the principle of gravity. '[1] Yet Smith and others have overlooked a ' principle of the highest importance '[2] and have failed to see that the price of corn, as of other things, must conform to the cost of production. The same doctrine was expounded in the same year by Sir Edward West ;[3] and, as it seems to me, more clearly and simply. West, like Malthus, says that he has to announce a principle overlooked by Adam Smith. This is briefly that ' each equal additional quantity of work bestowed on agriculture yields an actually diminished return.' He holds that profits fall as wealth increases, but he denies Adam Smith's view that this is a simple result of increased competition.[4] Competition would equalise, but would not lower profits, for ' the productive powers of manufactures are constantly increasing.' In agriculture the law is the opposite one of diminishing returns. Hence the admitted fall of profits shows that the necessity of taking inferior soils into cultivation is the true cause of the fall.

Such coincidences as that between Malthus and West are common enough, for very obvious reasons. In this case, I think, there is less room for surprise than usual. The writer generally credited with the discovery of the rent doctrine is James Anderson, who had stated it as

[1] *Inquiry into Rent*, p. 20. [2] *Ibid.* p. 37.
[3] *Essay on the Application of Capital to Land, by a Fellow of University College, Oxford*, 1815. [4] *Essay*, p. 19.

early as 1777.[1] The statement, however, did not attract attention until at the time of West and Malthus it was forced upon observers by the most conspicuous facts of the day. Adam Smith and other economists had, as Malthus notices, observed what is obvious enough, that rent in some way represented a ' net produce '—a something which remained after paying the costs of production. So much was obvious to any common-sense observer. In a curious paper of December 1804,[2] Cobbett points out that the landlords will always keep the profits of farmers down to the average rate of equally agreeable businesses. This granted, it is a short though important step to the theory of rent. The English system had, in fact, spontaneously analysed the problem. The landlord, farmer, and labourer represented the three interests which might elsewhere be combined. Prices raised by war and famine had led to the enclosure of wastes and the breaking up of pastures. The ' margin of cultivation ' was thus illustrated by facts. Farmers were complaining that they could not make a profit if prices were lowered. The landed classes were profiting by a rise of price raised, according to a familiar law, in greater proportion than the deficiency of the harvest. Facts of this kind were, one must suppose, familiar to every land-agent ; and to discover the law of rent, it was only necessary for

[1] In *An Inquiry into the Nature of the Corn-laws*, and again (1801) in *Observations on Agriculture*, etc., vol. v. 401-51.
[2] *Political Works*, i. 485, etc. In this paper, I may add, Cobbett, not yet a Radical, accepts Malthus's view of the tendency of the human species to multiply more quickly than its support. He does not mention Malthus, but speaks of the belief as universally admitted, and afterwards illustrates it amusingly by saying that, in his ploughboy days, he used to wonder that there was always just enough hay for the horses and enough horses for the hay.

Malthus and West to put them in their natural order. The egg had only to be put on its end, though that, as we know, is often a difficult task. When the feat was accomplished consequences followed which were fully developed by Ricardo.

CHAPTER V

RICARDO

I. RICARDO'S STARTING-POINT

DAVID RICARDO,[1] born 19th April 1772, was the son of a Dutch Jew who had settled in England, and made money upon the Stock Exchange. Ricardo had a desultory education, and was employed in business from his boyhood. He abandoned his father's creed, and married an Englishwoman soon after reaching his majority. He set up for himself in business, and, at a time when financial transactions upon an unprecedented scale were giving great opportunities for speculators, he made a large fortune, and about 1814 bought an estate at Gatcombe Park, Gloucestershire. He withdrew soon afterwards from business, and in 1819 became member of parliament. His death on 11th September 1823 cut short a political career from which his perhaps too sanguine friends anticipated great results. His influence in his own department of inquiry had been, meanwhile, of the greatest importance. He had shown in his youth

---

[1] A life of Ricardo by M'Culloch is prefixed to his *Works*. I cite the edition of 1880. Ricardo's letters to Malthus were published by Mr. Bonar in 1887; his letters to M'Culloch, edited by Mr. Hollander for the American Economic Association, in 1895; and his letters to H. Trower, edited by Mr. Bonar and Mr. Hollander, have just appeared (1900).

some inclination for scientific pursuits; he established a laboratory, and became a member of scientific societies. The perusal of Adam Smith's *Wealth of Nations* in 1799 gave him an interest in the application of scientific methods to the questions with which he was most conversant. Accepting Adam Smith as the leading authority, he proceeded to think out for himself certain doctrines, which appeared to him to have been insufficiently recognised by his teacher. The first result of his speculations was a pamphlet published in 1809 upon the depreciation of the currency. Upon that topic he spoke as an expert, and his main doctrines were accepted by the famous Bullion Committee. Ricardo thus became a recognised authority on one great set of problems of the highest immediate interest. Malthus's *Inquiry into Rent* suggested another pamphlet; and in 1817, encouraged by the warm pressure of his friend, James Mill, he published his chief book, the *Principles of Political Economy and Taxation*. This became the economic Bible of the Utilitarians. The task of a commentator or interpreter is, for various reasons, a difficult one.

There is a certain analogy between Ricardo and a very different writer, Bishop Butler. Each of them produced a great effect by a short treatise, and in each case the book owed very little to the ordinary literary graces. Ricardo's want of literary training, or his natural difficulty of utterance, made his style still worse than Butler's; but, like Butler, he commands our respect by his obvious sincerity and earnestness. He is content when he has so expressed his argument that it can be seized by an attentive reader. He is incapable of, or indifferent to, clear and orderly exposition of principles. The logic is

there, if you will take the trouble to look for it. Perhaps we ought to be flattered by this tacit reliance upon our patience. 'You,' Ricardo, like Butler, seems to say to us, 'are anxious for truth:' you do not care for ornament, and may be trusted to work out the full application of my principles.' In another respect the two are alike. Butler's argument has impressed many readers as a demolition of his own case. It provokes revolt instead of adhesion. Ricardo, an orthodox economist, laid down principles which were adopted by Socialists to upset his own assumptions. Such a God as you worship, said Butler's opponents, is an unjust being, and therefore worse than no God. Such a system as you describe, said Ricardo's opponents, is an embodiment of injustice, and therefore to be radically destroyed. Admitting the logic, the argument may be read as a *reductio ad absurdum* in both cases.

Ricardo has involved himself in certain special difficulties. In the first place, he presupposes familiarity with Adam Smith. The *Principles* is a running comment upon some of Smith's theories, and no attempt is made to reduce them to systematic order. He starts by laying down propositions, the proof of which comes afterwards, and is then rather intimated than expressly given. He adopts the terminology which Smith had accepted from popular use,[1] and often applies it in a special significance, which is at least liable to be misunderstood by his readers, or forgotten by himself. It is difficult, again, to feel sure whether some of his

---

[1] He remarks upon this difficulty in the case of Smith's treatment of rent, and gives a definition to which he scarcely adheres.—*Works*, p. 34 ('Principles,' ch. ii., 1888).

statements are to be taken as positive assertions of fact, or merely as convenient assumptions for the purposes of his argument. Ricardo himself, as appears in his letters, was painfully aware of his own awkwardness of expression, and upon that point alone all his critics seem to be in tolerable agreement. Happily, it will be enough for my purpose if I can lay down his essential premises without following him to the remoter deductions.

Ricardo's pamphlet upon Malthus (1815) gives a starting-point. Ricardo cordially adopts Malthus's theory of rent, but declares that it is fatal to some of Malthus's conclusions. Malthus, we have seen, wished to regard rent as in some sense a gift of Providence —a positive blessing due to the fertility of the soil. Ricardo maintains, on the contrary, that 'the interest of the landlord is necessarily opposed to the interest of every other class in the community.'[1] The landlord is prosperous when corn is scarce and dear; all other persons when it is plentiful and cheap. This follows upon Malthus's own showing. As men are forced to have recourse to inferior soils, the landlord obtains a larger share of the whole produce; and, moreover, since corn also becomes more valuable, will have a larger share of a more valuable product. The question apparently in dispute—whether we should be glad that some land is better than the worst, or sorry because all is not equal to the best—seems rather idle. The real question, however, is whether rent, being a blessing, should be kept up

---

[1] *Works*, p. 378. Ricardo, it should be said, complained when Malthus interpreted him to mean that this opposition of interests was permanent and absolute.

by protection,[1] or, being a curse, should be brought down by competition? What is the real working of the system? Set the trade free, says Ricardo, and the capital will be withdrawn from the poor land and employed upon manufactures, to be exchanged for the corn of other countries.[2] The change must correspond to a more advantageous distribution of capital, or it would not be adopted. The principle involved in this last proposition is, he adds, one of the 'best established in the science of political economy, and by no one is more readily admitted than by Mr. Malthus.' To enforce protection would be, on Malthus's illustration, to compel us to use the 'worst machines, when, at a less expense, we could hire the very best from our neighbours.'[3] Briefly, then, the landlord's interest is opposed to the national interest, because it enforces a worse distribution of capital. He compels us to get corn from his worst land, instead of getting it indirectly, but in greater quantity, from our spinning-jennies.

For Ricardo, as for Malthus, the ultimate driving force is the pressure of population. The mass of mankind is always struggling to obtain food, and is able to multiply so rapidly as to exhaust any conceivable increase of supplies. The landlord class alone profits. The greater the struggle for supply the greater will be the share of the whole produce which must be surrendered to it. Beyond this, however, lies the further problem which specially

---

[1] Malthus admits the general principle of free trade, but supports some degree of protection to corn, mainly upon political grounds. He holds, however, with Adam Smith, that 'no equal quantity of productive labour employed in manufactures could ever occasion so great a reproduction as in agriculture' (*Grounds of an Opinion, etc.*, p. 35)—a relic of the 'physiocrat' doctrine.   [2] *Works*, p. 385.   [3] *Ibid.* p. 386.

occupied Ricardo. How will the resulting strain affect the relations of the two remaining classes, the labourers and the capitalists? The ultimate evil of protection is the bad distribution of capital. But capital always acts by employing labour. The farmer's capital does not act by itself, but by enabling his men to work. Hence, to understand the working of the industrial machinery, we have to settle the relation of wages and profits. Ricardo states this emphatically in his preface. Rent, profit, and wages, he says, represent the three parts into which the whole produce of the earth is divided. 'To determine the laws which regulate this distribution is the principal problem in political economy'; and one, he adds, which has been left in obscurity by previous writers.[1] His investigations are especially directed by the purpose thus defined. He was the first writer who fairly brought under distinct consideration what he held, with reason, to be the most important branch of economical inquiry.

There was clearly a gap in the economic doctrine represented by the *Wealth of Nations*. Adam Smith was primarily concerned with the theory of the 'market.' He assumes the existence of the social arrangement which is indicated by that phrase. The market implies a constitution of industrial agencies such that, within it, only one price is possible for a given commodity, or, rather, such that a difference of price cannot be permanent. According to the accepted illustration, the sea is not absolutely level, but it is always tending to a level.[2] A

---

[1] See also *Letters to Malthus*, p. 175.

[2] 'Your modern political economists say that it is a principle in their science that all things find their level; which I deny, and say, on the contrary, that it is the true principle that all things are finding their level, like water in a storm.'—Coleridge's *Table-Talk*, 17th May 1833.

permanent elevation at one point is impossible. The agency by which this levelling or equilibrating process is carried out is competition, involving what Smith called the 'higgling of the market.' The momentary fluctuation, again, supposes the action of 'supply and demand,' which, as they vary, raise and depress prices. To illustrate the working of this machinery, to show how previous writers had been content to notice a particular change without following out the collateral results, and had thus been led into fallacies such as that of the 'mercantile system,' was Smith's primary task.

Beyond or beneath these questions lie difficulties, which Smith, though not blind to their existence, treated in a vacillating and inconsistent fashion. Variations of supply and demand cause fluctuations in the price; but what finally determines the point to which the fluctuating prices must gravitate? We follow the process by which one wave propagates another; but there is still the question, What ultimately fixes the normal level? Upon this point Ricardo could find no definite statement in his teacher. 'Supply and demand' was a sacred phrase which would always give a verbal answer, or indicate the immediate cause of variations on the surface. Beneath the surface there must be certain forces at work which settle why a quarter of corn 'gravitates' to a certain price; why the landlord can get just so many quarters of corn for the use of his fields; and why the produce, which is due jointly to the labourer and the farmer, is divided in a certain fixed proportion. To settle such points it is necessary to answer the problem of distribution, for the play of the industrial forces is directed by the constitution of the classes which co-operate in the result.

Ricardo saw in Malthus's doctrines of rent and of population a new mode of approaching the problem. What was wanted, in the first place, was to systematise the logic adopted by his predecessors. Rent, it was clear, could not be both a cause and an effect of price, though at different points of his treatise Smith had apparently accepted each view of the relation. We must first settle which is cause and which effect; and then bring our whole system into the corresponding order. For the facts, Ricardo is content to trust mainly to others. The true title of his work should be that which his commentator, De Quincey, afterwards adopted, the *Logic of Political Economy*. This aim gives a partial explanation of the characteristic for which Ricardo is most generally criticised. He is accused of being abstract in the sense of neglecting facts. He does not deny the charge. 'If I am too theoretical (which I really believe to be the case) you,' he says to Malthus, 'I think, are too practical.'[1] If Malthus is more guided than Ricardo by a reference to facts, he has of course an advantage. But so far as Malthus or Adam Smith theorised—and, of course, their statement of facts involved a theory—they were at least bound to be consistent. It is one thing to recognise the existence of facts which your theory will not explain, and to admit that it therefore requires modification. It is quite another thing to explain each set of facts in turn by theories which contradict each other. That is not to be historical but to be muddle-

---

[1] *Letters to Malthus*, p. 96; and see the frequently quoted passage where he complains that Malthus has taken his book as more 'practical' than he had intended it to be, and speaks of his method of imagining 'strong cases.'—*Ibid.* p. 167.

headed. Malthus and Smith, as it seemed to Ricardo, had occasionally given explanations which, when set side by side, destroyed each other. He was therefore clearly justified in the attempt to exhibit these logical inconsistencies and to supply a theory which should be in harmony with itself. He was so far neither more nor less 'theoretical' than his predecessors, but simply more impressed by the necessity of having at least a consistent theory.

There was never a time at which logic in such matters was more wanted, or its importance more completely disregarded. Rash and ignorant theorists were plunging into intricate problems and propounding abstract solutions. The enormous taxation made necessary by the war suggested at every point questions as to the true incidence of the taxes. Who really gained or suffered by the protection of corn? Were the landlords, the farmers, or the labourers directly interested? Could they shift the burthen upon other shoulders or not? What, again, it was of the highest importance to know, was the true 'incidence' of tithes, of a land-tax, of the poor-laws, of an income-tax, and of all the multitudinous indirect taxes from which the national income was derived? The most varying views were held and eagerly defended. Who really paid? That question interested everybody, and occupies a large part of Ricardo's book. The popular answers involved innumerable inconsistencies, and were supported by arguments which only required to be confronted in order to be confuted. Ricardo's aim was to substitute a clear and consistent theory for this tangle of perplexed sophistry. In that sense his aim was in the highest degree 'practical,' although he left to others the

detailed application of his doctrines to the actual facts of the day.

II. THE DISTRIBUTION PROBLEM

The rent doctrine gives one essential datum. A clear comprehension of rent is, as he was persuaded, 'of the utmost importance to political economy.'[1] The importance is that it enables him to separate one of the primary sources of revenue from the others. It is as though, in the familiar illustration, we were considering the conditions of equilibrium of a fluid; and we now see that one part may be considered as a mere overflow, resulting from (not determining) the other conditions. The primary assumption in the case of the market is the level of price. When we clearly distinguish rent on one side from profits and wages on the other, we see that we may also assume a level of profits. There cannot, as Ricardo constantly says, 'be two rates of profit,' that is, at the same time and in the same country. But so long as rent was lumped with other sources of revenue it was impossible to see, what Malthus and West had now made clear, that in agriculture, as in manufactures, the profits of the producer must conform to the principle. Given their theory, it follows that the power of land to yield a great revenue does not imply a varying rate of profit or a special bounty of nature bestowed upon agriculture. It means simply that, since the corn from the good and bad land sells at the same price, there is a surplus on the good. But as that surplus constitutes rent, the farmer's rate of profit will still be uniform. Thus we have got rid of one complication, and we are

[1] *Works*, p. 40 n. (ch. ii.).

left with a comparatively simple issue. We have to consider the problem, What determines the distribution as between the capitalist and the labourer? That is the vital question for Ricardo.

Ricardo's theory, in the first place, is a modification of Adam Smith's. He accepts Smith's statement that wages are determined by the 'supply and demand of labourers,' and by the 'price of commodities on which their wages are expended.'[1] The appeal to 'supply and demand' implies that the rate of wages depends upon unchangeable economic conditions. He endorses[2] Malthus's statement about the absurdity of considering 'wages' as something which may be fixed by his Majesty's 'Justices of the Peace,' and infers with Malthus that wages should be left to find their 'natural level.' But what precisely is this 'natural level?' If the Justice of the Peace cannot fix the rate of wages, what does fix them? Supply and demand? What, then, is precisely meant in this case by the supply and demand? The 'supply' of labour, we may suppose, is fixed by the actual labouring population at a given time. The 'demand,' again, is in some way clearly related to 'capital.' As Smith again had said,[3] the demand for labour increases with the 'increase of revenue and "stock,"' and cannot possibly increase without it.' Ricardo agrees that 'population regulates itself by the funds which are to employ it, and therefore always increases or diminishes with the increase or diminution of capital.'[4] It was indeed a

[1] *Works*, p. 53 (ch. v.), and p. 124 (ch. xvi.), where he quotes from the *Wealth of Nations* (M'Culloch), p. 390 (bk. v. ch. ii. art. 3).
[2] *Works*, p. 131.
[3] *Wealth of Nations* (M'Culloch), p. 31 (bk. i. ch. viii.).
[4] *Works*, p. 41 (ch. ii.).

commonplace that the increase of capital was necessary to an increase of population, as it is obvious enough that population must be limited by the means of subsistence accumulated. Smith, for example, goes on to insist upon this in one of the passages which partly anticipates Malthus.[1] But this does not enable us to separate profit from wages, or solve Ricardo's problem. When we speak of supply and demand as determining the price of a commodity, we generally have in mind two distinct though related processes. One set of people is growing corn, and another working coal mines. Each industry, therefore, has a separate existence, though each may be partly dependent upon the other. But this is not true of labour and capital. They are not products of different countries or processes. They are inseparable constituents of a single process. Labour cannot be maintained without capital, nor can capital produce without labour. Capital, according to Ricardo's definition, is the 'part of the wealth of a country which is employed in production, and consists of food, clothing, raw materials, machinery, etc., necessary to give effect to labour.'[2] That part, then, of capital which is applied to the support of the labourer—his food, clothing, and so forth—is identical with wages. To say that, if it increases, his wages increase is to be simply tautologous. If, on the other hand, we include the machinery and raw materials, it becomes difficult to say in what sense 'capital' can be taken as a demand for labour. Ricardo tells Malthus that an accumulation of profit does not, as Malthus had said, necessarily raise wages[3]; and he ultimately decided, much

[1] *Wealth of Nations* (M'Culloch), p. 36.　　[2] *Works*, p. 51 (ch. v.).
[3] *Letters to Malthus*, p. 98.

to the scandal of his disciple, M'Culloch, that an increase of 'fixed capital' or machinery might be actually prejudicial, under certain circumstances, to the labourer. The belief of the labouring class that machinery often injures them is not, he expressly says, 'founded on prejudice and error, but is conformable to the correct principles of political economy.'[1] The word 'capital,' indeed, was used with a vagueness which covered some of the most besetting fallacies of the whole doctrine. Ricardo himself sometimes speaks as though he had in mind merely the supply of labourers' necessaries, though he regularly uses it in a wider sense. The generalities, therefore, about supply and demand, take us little further.

From these difficulties Ricardo escapes by another method. Malthus's theory of population gives him what he requires. The 'natural price of labour' (as distinguished from its 'market price') is, as he asserts, 'that price which is necessary to enable the labourers, one with another, to subsist and perpetuate their race without either increase or diminution.'[2] This is the true 'natural price,' about which the 'market price' oscillates. An increase of capital may raise wages for a time above the natural price, but an increase of population will bring back the previous rate. Ricardo warns us, indeed, that this natural price of labour is not to be regarded as something 'absolutely fixed and constant.'[3] It varies in different times and countries, and even in the same country at different times. An English cottager now possesses what would once have been luxuries. Ricardo admits again[4] that the wages of different classes of

[1] *Works*, p. 239 (ch. xxxi., added in third edition, 1821).
[2] *Ibid.* p. 50 (ch. v.).   [3] *Ibid.* p. 52.   [4] *Ibid.* p. 15 (ch. i. sec. ii.).

labourers may be different, although he does not consider that this fact affects his argument. We may allow for it by considering the skilled labourer as 2 or $1\frac{1}{2}$ labourers rolled into one. The assumption enables him to get out of a vicious circle. He is seeking to discover the proportions in which produce will be divided between the two classes, and which co-operate in the production. The 'demand and supply' principle may show that an increase of capital will tend to increase wages, but even that tendency, as he carefully points out, can only be admitted subject to certain important reservations. In any case, if it explains temporary fluctuations, it will not ascertain the point round which the fluctuations take place. But the two variables, wages and profit, are clearly connected, and if we can once assume that one of these variables is fixed by an independent law, we may explain in what way the other will be fixed. Having got rid of 'rent,' the remaining produce has to be divided between wages and profit. If the produce be fixed, the greater the share of the labourer the less will be the share of the capitalist, and *vice versa*. But the labourer's share again is determined by the consideration that it must be such as to enable him to keep up the population. The capitalist will get the surplus produce after allowing to the labourer the share so determined. Everything turns ultimately upon this 'natural price'—the constant which underlies all the variations.

One other point is implied. The population is limited, as we see, by the necessity of raising supplies of food from inferior soils. Moreover, this is the sole limit. A different view had been taken which greatly exercised the orthodox economists. It was generally admitted that

in the progress of society the rate of profit declined. Adam Smith explained this by arguing that, as capital increased, the competition of capitalists lowered the rate. To this it was replied (as by West) that though competition equalised profits, it could not fix the rate of profit. The simple increase of capital does not prove that it will be less profitably employed. The economists had constantly to argue against the terrible possibility of a general 'glut.' The condition of things at the peace had suggested this alarm. The mischief was ascribed to 'over-production' and not to misdirected production. The best cure for our evils, as some people thought, would be to burn all the goods in stock. On this version of the argument, it would seem that an increase of wealth might be equivalent to an increase of poverty. To confute the doctrine in this form, it was only necessary to have a more intelligent conception of the true nature of exchange. As James Mill had argued in his pamphlet against Spence, every increase of supply is also an increase of demand. The more there is to sell, the more there is to buy. The error involved in the theory of a 'glut' is the confusion between a temporary dislocation of the machinery of exchange, which can and will be remedied by a new direction of industry, and the impossible case of an excess of wealth in general.[1] Malthus never quite

[1] There is, indeed, a difficulty which I happily need not discuss. Undoubtedly the doctrine of gluts was absurd. There is, of course, no limit to the amount of wealth which can be used or exchanged. But there certainly seems to be a great difficulty in effecting such a readjustment of the industrial system as is implied in increased production of wealth; and the disposition to save may at a given time be greater than the power of finding profitable channels for employing wealth. This involves economical questions beyond my ability to answer, and happily not here relevant.

cleared his mind of this error, and Ricardo had to argue the point with him. Abundance of capital cannot by itself, he says, 'make capital less in demand.' The 'demand for capital is infinite.'[1] The decline in the rate of profit, therefore, depends upon another cause. 'If, with every accumulation of profit, we could tack a piece of fresh fertile land to our Island, profits would never fall.'[2] Fertile land, however, is limited. We have to resort to inferior soil, and therefore to employ capital at a less advantage. In the *Principles* he enforces the same doctrine with the help of Say, who had shown 'most satisfactorily' that any amount of capital might be employed.[3] If, in short, labour and capital were always equally efficient, there would be no limit to the amount producible. If the supply of food and raw materials can be multiplied, wealth can be multiplied to any amount. The admitted tendency of profits to fall must therefore be explained simply and solely by the growing difficulty of producing the food and the raw material.

Ricardo's doctrine, then, is Malthus carried out more logically. Take a nation in a state of industrial equilibrium. The produce of the worst soil just supports the labourer, and leaves a profit to the capitalist. The labourer gets just enough to keep up his numbers to the standard; the capitalist just enough profit to induce him to keep up the capital which supports the labourer. Since there can be only one rate of wages and only one rate of profit, this fixes the shares into which the whole produce of the nation is divided, after leaving to the landlord the surplus produce of the more fertile soils.

[1] *Letters to Malthus*, p. 101.   [2] *Ibid.* p. 52.
[3] *Works*, p. 174 (ch. xxi.).

Accepting this scheme as a starting-point, we get a method for calculating the results of any changes. We can see how a tax imposed upon rents or profits or wages will affect the classes which are thus related; how improvements in cultivation or machinery, or a new demand for our manufactures, will act, assuming the conditions implied in this industrial organisation; how, in short, any disturbance of the balance will work, so as to produce a new equilibrium. Ricardo exerts all his ingenuity in working out the problem which, with the help of a few assumptions, becomes mathematical. The arithmetical illustrations which he employed for the purpose became a nuisance in the hands of his disciples. They are very useful as checks to general statements, but lend themselves so easily to the tacit introduction of erroneous assumptions as often to give a totally false air of precision to the results. Happily I need not follow him into that region, and may omit any consideration of the logical value of his deductions. I must be content to say that, so far as he is right, his system gives an economic calculus for working out the ultimate result of assigned economic changes. The pivot of the whole construction is the 'margin of cultivation'—the point at which the food for a pressing population is raised at the greatest disadvantages. 'Profits,' as he says,[1] 'depend on high and low wages; wages on the price of necessaries; and the price of necessaries chiefly on the price of food, because all other requisites may be increased almost without limit.'

Ricardo takes the actual constitution of society for granted. The threefold division into landowners, capital-

[1] *Works*, p. 66 (ch. vi.).

ists, and labourers is assumed as ultimate. For him that is as much a final fact as to a chemist it is a final fact that air and water are composed of certain elements. Each class represents certain economic categories. The landlord sits still and absorbs the overflow of wealth created by others. The labourer acts a very important but in one respect a purely passive part. His whole means of subsistence are provided by the capitalist, and advanced to him in the shape of wages. His share in the process is confined to multiplying up to a fixed standard. The capitalist is the really active agent. The labourer is simply one of the implements used in production. His wages are part of the capitalist's 'costs of production.' The capitalist virtually raises labourers, one may say, so long as raising them is profitable, just as he raises horses for his farm. Ricardo, in fact, points out that in some cases it may be for the farmer's interest to substitute horses for men.[1] If it be essential to any product that there should be a certain number of labourers or a certain number of horses, that number will be produced. But when the expense becomes excessive, and in the case of labourers that happens as worse soils have to be broken up for food, the check is provided through its effect upon the accumulation of capital. That, therefore, becomes the essential point. The whole aim of the legislator should be to give facilities for the accumulation of capital, and the way to do that is to abstain from all interference with the free play of the industrial forces. The test, for example, of the goodness of a tax—or rather of its comparative freedom from the evils of every tax —is that it should permit of accumulation by interfering as

[1] *Works*, p. 240 (ch. xxxi.).

little as possible with the tendency of the capital to distribute itself in the most efficient way.

III. VALUE AND LABOUR

To solve the distribution problem, then, it is necessary to get behind the mere fluctuations of the market, and to consider what are the ultimate forces by which the market is itself governed. What effect has this upon the theory of the market itself? This leads to a famous doctrine.

According to his disciple, M'Culloch, Ricardo's great merit was that he 'laid down the fundamental theorem of the science of value.' He thus cleared up what had before been an 'impenetrable mystery,' and showed the true relations of profit, wages, and prices.[1] Ricardo's theory of value, again, was a starting-point of the chief modern Socialist theories. It marked, as has been said,[2] the point at which the doctrine of the rights of man changes from a purely political to an economical theory. Ricardo remarks in his first chapter that the vagueness of theories of value has been the most fertile source of economic errors. He admitted to the end of his life that he had not fully cleared up the difficulty. Modern economists have refuted and revised and discussed, and, let us hope, now made everything quite plain. They have certainly shown that some of Ricardo's puzzles implied confusions singular in so keen a thinker. That may serve as a warning against dogmatism. Boys in the next generation will probably be asked by examiners to expose the palpable fallacies of what to us seem to be

[1] Ricardo, *Works*, p. xxiv.
[2] Menger's *Das Recht auf den vollen Arbeitsertrag* (1891), p. 38.

demonstrable truths. At any rate, I must try to indicate the critical point as briefly as possible.

The word 'value,' in the first place, has varying meanings, which give an opportunity for writers of text-books to exhibit their powers of lucid exposition. The value of a thing in one sense is what it will fetch; the quantity of some other thing for which it is actually exchanged in the market. In that sense, as Ricardo incidentally observes,[1] the word becomes meaningless unless you can say what is the other thing. It is self-contradictory to speak as if a thing by itself could have a constant or any value. Value, however, may take a different sense. It is the economic equivalent of the 'utility' of Bentham's 'felicific calculus.' It means the 'lot of pleasure' which causes a thing to be desirable. If we could tell how many units of utility it contained we could infer the rate of exchange for other things. The value of anything 'in use' will correspond to the number of units of utility which it contains; and things which have the same quantity of 'utilities' will have the same 'exchangeable value.' Ricardo can thus consider the old problem of finding 'an invariable measure of value.' He points out the difficulty of finding any particular thing which will serve the purpose, inasmuch as the relations of everything to everything else are constantly varying. He therefore proposes to make use of an imaginary measure. If gold were always produced under exactly the same circumstances, with the same labour and the same capital, it would serve approximately for a standard. Accordingly he gives notice that, for the purposes of his book, he will assume this

[1] *Works*, p. 228 (ch. xxviii.).

to be the case, and money to be 'invariable in value.'[1] We can thus, on the one hand, compare values at different periods. A thing has the same value at all times which at all times requires 'the same sacrifice of toil and labour to produce it.'[2] The 'sacrifice' measures the 'utility,' and we may assume that the same labour corresponds in all ages to the same psychological unit. But, on the other hand, at any given period things will exchange in proportion to the labour of producing them. This follows at once from Ricardo's postulates. Given the single rate of wages and profits, and assuming the capital employed to be in the same proportion, things must exchange in proportion to the quantity of labour employed ; for if I got the same value by employing one labourer as you get by employing two, my profits would be higher. Ricardo, indeed, has to allow for many complexities arising from the fact that very different quantities of capital are required in different industries ; but the general principle is given by the simplest case. Hence we have a measure of value, applicable at any given time and in comparing different times. It implies, again, what M'Culloch sums up as the 'fundamental theorem,' that the value of 'freely produced commodities' depends on the quantity of labour required for their 'production.' What is made by two men is worth twice what is made by one man. That gives what M'Culloch calls the 'clue to the labyrinth.'

The doctrine leads to a puzzle. If I can measure the 'sacrifice,' can I measure the 'utility' which it gains ? The 'utility' of an ounce of gold is not something 'objective' like its physical qualities, but varies with the

varying wants of the employer. Iron or coal may be used for an infinite variety of purposes and the utility will be different in each. The thing may derive part of its 'utility' from its relation to other things. The utility of my food is not really separate from the utility of my hat ; for unless I eat I cannot wear hats. My desire for any object, again, is modified by all my other desires, and even if I could isolate a 'desire' as a psychological unit, it would not give me a fixed measure. Twice the article does not give twice the utility ; a double stimulus may only add a small pleasure or convert it into agony. These and other difficulties imply the hopelessness of searching for this chimerical unit of 'utility' when considered as a separate thing. It shifts and escapes from our hands directly we grasp it. Ricardo discusses some of these points in his interesting chapter on 'Value and Riches.' Gold, he says, may cost two thousand times more than iron, but it is certainly not two thousand times as useful.[1] Suppose, again, that some invention enables you to make more luxuries by the same labour, you increase wealth but not value. There will be, say, twice as many hats, but each hat may have half its former value. There will be more things to enjoy, but they will only exchange for the same quantity of other things. That is, he says, the amount of 'riches' varies, while the amount of value is fixed. This, according to him, proves that value does not vary with 'utility.' 'Utility,' as he declares in his first chapter, is 'absolutely essential to value,' but it is 'not the measure of exchangeable value.'[2] A solution of these puzzles may be sought in any modern text-book. Ricardo

[1] *Works*, pp. 29, 60.   [2] *Ibid.* p. 166.

[1] *Works*, p. 170 (ch. xx.).   [2] *Ibid.* p. 7.

escapes by an apparently paradoxical conclusion. He is undertaking an impossible problem when he starts from the buyers' desire of an 'utility.' Therefore he turns from the buyers to the sellers. The seller has apparently a measurable and definable motive—the desire to make so much per cent. on his capital.[1] Ricardo, unfortunately, speaks as though the two parties to the bargain somehow represented mutually exclusive processes. 'Supply and demand' determine the value of 'monopolised articles,' but the cost of other articles depends *not* 'on the state of demand and supply,' *but* 'on the increased or diminished cost of their production.'[2] Why 'not' and 'but'? If supply and demand corresponds to the whole play of motives which determines the bargain, this is like saying, according to the old illustration, that we must attribute the whole effect of a pair of scissors to one blade and not to the other. His view leads to the apparent confusion of taking for the cause of value not our desire for a thing, but the sacrifice we must make to attain it. Bentham[3] said, for example, that Ricardo confused 'cost' with 'value.' The denial that utility must in some sense or other determine value perplexes an intelligible and consistent meaning. It is clearly true, upon his postulates, that the value of goods, other than 'monopolised,' must conform to the cost of production. He speaks as if he confounded a necessary condition with an 'efficient cause,' and as if one of two correlative processes could be explained without the other.

[1] So he tells Malthus (*Letters*, pp. 173, 174) that the buyer has 'the least to do in the world' with the regulation of prices. It is all the competition of the sellers. 'Demand' influences price for the moment, but 'supply follows close upon its heels, and takes up the regulation of price.'

[2] *Works*, p. 234.   [3] Bentham's *Works*, x. 498.

But the fact that there is a conformity, however brought about, was enough for his purpose. The demand of buyers, he would say, determines the particular direction of production : it settles whether hats should be made of silk or beaver ; whether we should grow corn or spin cotton. But the ultimate force is the capitalist's desire for profit. So long as he can raise labourers' necessaries by employing part of his capital, he can employ the labour as he chooses. He can always produce wealth ; all the wealth produced can be exchanged, and the demand always be equal to the supply, since the demand is merely the other side of the supply. The buyer's tastes decide how the capital shall be applied, but does not settle how much wealth there shall be, only what particular forms it shall take. Somehow or other it must always adjust itself so that the value of each particular kind shall correspond to the 'cost of production.' The cost of production includes the tools and the raw materials, which are themselves products of previous labour. All capital itself is ultimately the product of labour, and thus, as Ricardo incidentally says, may be regarded as 'accumulated labour.'[1]

This phrase sums up the doctrine which underlies his theory of value and indicates its connection with the theory of distribution. Ricardo had perceived that the supply and demand formula which would serve sufficiently in problems of exchange, or the fluctuations of market-price, could not be made to solve the more fundamental problem of distribution. We must look beneath the superficial phenomena and ask what is the nature of the structure itself : what is the driving force or the main-

[1] *Works*, p. 250 (ch. xxxii.).

spring which works the whole mechanism. We seem, indeed, to be inquiring into the very origin of industrial organisation. The foundation of a sound doctrine comes from Adam Smith. Smith had said that in a primitive society the only rule would be that things should exchange in proportion to the labour of getting them. If it cost twice as much labour to kill a beaver as to kill a deer, one beaver would be worth two deer. In accepting this bit of what Smith's commentator, Dugald Stewart,[1] calls 'theoretical' or 'conjectural' history, Ricardo did not mean to state a historical fact. He was not thinking of actual Choctaws or Cherokees. The beaver was exchanged for the deer about the time when the primitive man signed the 'social contract.' He is a hypothetical person used for purposes of illustration and simplification. Ricardo is not really dealing with the question of origins; but he is not the less implying a theory of structure. It did not matter that the 'social contract' was historically a figment; it would serve equally well to explain government. It did not matter that actual savages may have exchanged beavers and deer by the help of clubs instead of competition in the market. The industrial fabric is what would have been had it been thus built up. It can be constructed from base to summit by the application of his formula. As in the imaginary state of deer and beaver, we have a number of independent persons making their bargains upon this principle of the equivalence of labour; and that principle is supposed to be carried out so that the most remote processes of the industrial machinery can be analysed into results of this principle. This gives a sufficient clue to

[1] Stewart's *Works*, x. 34.

the whole labyrinth of modern industry, and there is no need of considering the extinct forms of social structure, which we know to have existed, and under which the whole system of distribution took place under entirely different conditions.[1] A great change has taken place since the time of the deer and beaver: the capitalist has been developed, and has become the motive power. The labourer's part is passive; and the 'value' is fixed by the bargaining between the proprietors of 'accumulated labour,' forced by competition to make equal profits, instead of being fixed by the equitable bargain between the two hunters exchanging the products of their individual labour. Essentially, however, the principle is the same. In the last as in the first stage of society, things are exchanged in proportion to the labour necessary to produce them. Now it is plain enough that such a doctrine cannot lead to a complete solution of the problem of distribution. It would be a palpably inadequate account of historical processes which have determined the actual relation of classes. The industrial mechanism has been developed as a part of the whole social evolution; and, however important the economic forces, they have been inextricably blended with all the other forces by which a society is built up. For the same reason, Ricardo's theorem would be inadequate 'sociologically,' or as a formula which would enable us to predict the future distribution of wealth. It omits essential factors in the process, and therefore supposes forces to act automatically and invariably which will in fact be profoundly modified in societies differently

[1] See Bagehot's remarks upon J. S. Mill's version of this doctrine in *Economic Studies*: chapter on 'Cost of Production.'

organised and composed of individuals differing in character. The very fundamental assumptions as to the elasticity of population, and the accumulation of capital as wages and profits fluctuate, are clearly not absolute truths. An increase of the capitalist's share, for example, at the expense of wages, may lead to the lowered efficiency of the labourer; and, instead of the compensating process supposed to result from the stimulus to accumulation, the actual result may be a general degeneration of the industry. Or, again, the capacity of labourers to combine both depends and reacts upon their intelligence and moral character, and will profoundly modify the results of the general competition.[1] Such remarks, now familiar enough, are enough to suggest that a full explanation of the economic phenomena would require reference to considerations which lie beyond the proper sphere of the economist. Yet the economist may urge that he is making a fair and perhaps necessary abstraction. He may consider the forces to be constant, although he may be fully aware that the assumption requires to be corrected when his formulæ are applied to facts. He may consider what is the play at any given time of the operations of the market, though the market organisation is itself dependent upon the larger organisation of which it is a product. He does not profess to deal in 'sociology,' but 'pure political economy.' In that

[1] Another illustration of the need of such considerations is given, as has been pointed out, in Adam Smith's famous chapter upon the variation in the rate of wages. He assumes that the highest wages will be paid for the least agreeable employments, whereas, in fact, the least agreeable are generally the worst paid. His doctrine, that is, is only true upon a tacit assumption as to the character and position of the labourer, which must be revised before the rule can be applied.

more limited sphere he may accept Ricardo's postulates. The rate of wages is fixed at any given moment by the 'labour market.' That is the immediate organ through which the adjustment is effected. Wages rise and fall like the price of commodities, when for any reason the number of hirers or the number of purchasers varies. The 'supply and demand' formula, however, could not, as Ricardo saw, be summarily identified with labour and capital. We must go behind the immediate phenomena to consider how they are regulated by the ultimate moving power. Then, with the help of the theories of population and rent, we find that the wages are one product of the whole industrial process. We must look beyond the immediate market fluctuation to the effect upon the capitalists who constitute the market. The world is conceived as one great market, in which the motives of the capitalist supply the motive power; and the share which goes to the labourer is an incidental or collateral result of the working of the whole machinery. Now, though the sociologist would say that this is quite inadequate for his purpose, and that we must consider the whole social structure, he may also admit that the scheme has a validity in its own sphere. It describes the actual working of the mechanism at any given time; and it may be that in Ricardo's time it gave an appproximate account of the facts. To make it complete, it requires to be set, so to speak, in a more general framework of theory; and we may then see that it cannot give a complete solution. Still, as a consistent scheme which corresponds to the immediate phenomena, it helps us to understand the play of the industrial forces which immediately regulate the market.

Ricardo's position suggested a different line of reply. The doctrines that capital is 'accumulated labour' and that all value is in proportion to the labour fell in with the Socialist theory. If value is created by labour, ought not 'labour' to possess what it makes? The right to the whole produce of labour seemed to be a natural conclusion. Ricardo might answer that when I buy your labour, it becomes mine. I may consider myself to have acquired the rights of the real creator of the wealth, and to embody all the labourers, whose 'accumulated labour' is capital. Still, there is a difficulty. The beaver and deer case has an awkward ethical aspect. To say that they are exchanged at such a rate seems to mean that they ought to be exchanged at the rate. This again implies the principle that a man has a right to what he has caught; that is, to the whole fruits of his labour. James Mill, as we have seen, starts his political treatise by assuming this as obvious.[1] He did not consider the possible inferences; for it is certainly a daring assumption that the principle is carried out by the economic system. According to Ricardo rent is paid to men who don't labour at all. The fundholder was a weight upon all industry, and as dead a weight as the landlord. The capitalist, Ricardo's social mainspring, required at least cross-examination. He represents 'accumulated labour' in some fashion, but it is not plain that the slice which he takes out of the whole cake is proportioned accurately to his personal labour. The right and the fact which coincided in the deer and beaver period have somehow come to diverge.

[1] J. S. Mill, too, in his *Political Economy* makes the foundation of private property 'the right of producers to what they themselves have produced.' (Bk. ii. ch. ii. § 1.)

Here, then, we are at a point common to the two opposing schools. Both are absolute 'individualists' in different senses. Society is built up, and all industrial relations determined, by the competition of a multitude of independent atoms, each aiming at self-preservation. Malthus's principle applies this to the great mass of mankind. Systematically worked out, it has led to Ricardo's identification of value with quantities of labour. Keeping simply to the matter of fact, it shows how a small minority have managed to get advantages in the struggle, and to raise themselves upon the shoulders of the struggling mass. Malthus shows that the resulting inequality prevents the struggle from lowering every one to starvation point. But the advantage was not obvious to the struggling mass which exemplified the struggle for existence. If equality meant not the initial facts but the permanent right, society was built upon injustice. Apply the political doctrine of rights of man to the economic right to wealth, and you have the Socialist doctrine of right to the whole produce of labour. It is true that it is exceedingly difficult to say what each man has created when he is really part of a complex machinery; but that is a problem to which Socialists could apply their ingenuity. The real answer of the political economists was that although the existing order implied great inequalities of wealth it was yet essential to industrial progress, and therefore to an improvement in the general standard of comfort. This, however, was the less evident the more they insisted upon the individual interest. The net result seemed to be that by accident or inheritance, possibly by fraud or force, a small number of persons have got a much larger share of wealth than their rivals.

Ricardo may expound the science accurately; and, if so, we have to ask, What are the right ethical conclusions?

For the present, the Utilitarians seem to have considered this question as superfluous. They were content to take the existing order for granted; and the question remains how far their conclusions upon that assumption could be really satisfactory.

IV. THE CLASSICAL POLITICAL ECONOMY.

Ricardo had worked out the main outlines of the 'Classical Political Economy': the system which to his disciples appeared to be as clear, consistent, and demonstrable as Euclid; and which was denounced by their opponents as mechanical, materialistic, fatalistic, and degrading. After triumphing for a season, it has been of late years often treated with contempt, and sometimes banished to the limbo of extinct logomachies. It is condemned as 'abstract.' Of all delusions on the subject, replies a very able and severe critic,[1] there is none greater than the belief that it was 'wholly abstract and unpractical.' Its merits lay in its treatment of certain special questions of the day; while in the purely scientific questions it was hopelessly confused and inconsistent. Undoubtedly, as I have tried to point out, Malthus and Ricardo were reasoning upon the contemporary state of things. The doctrine started from observation of facts; it was too 'abstract' so far as it neglected elements in the concrete realities which were really relevant to the conclusions. One cause of confusion was the necessity of starting from the classification implied in ordinary phrases. It is exemplified by the vague use

[1] Mr. Edwin Cannan, in *Production and Distribution* (1894), p. 383.

of such words as 'capital,' 'value,' 'supply and demand.' Definitions, as is often remarked,[1] come at the end of an investigation, though they are placed at the beginning of an exposition. When the primary conceptions to be used were still so shifting and contradictory as is implied in the controversies of the day, it is no wonder that the formulæ should be wanting in scientific precision. Until we have determined what is meant by 'force' we cannot have a complete science of dynamics. The economists imagined that they had reached the goal before they had got rid of ambiguities hidden in the accepted terminology. Meanwhile it will be enough if I try to consider broadly what was the nature of the body of statements which thus claimed to be an elaborated science.

Ricardo's purpose was to frame a calculus, to give a method of reasoning which will enable us to clinch our economic reasoning. We are to be sure that we have followed out the whole cycle of cause and effect. Capitalists, landowners, labourers form parts of a rounded system, implying reciprocal actions and reactions. The imposition of a tax or a tariff implies certain changes in existing relations: that change involves other changes; and to trace out the total effect, we must understand what are the ultimate conditions of equilibrium, or what are the processes by which the system will adjust itself to the new conditions. To describe, again, the play of a number of reciprocal forces, we have to find what mathematicians call an 'independent variable': some one element in the changes on which all other changes will

[1] A definition, says Burke in his essay on the 'Sublime and Beautiful' (introduction) 'seems rather to follow than to precede our inquiry, of which it ought to be considered as the result.'

depend. That element, roughly speaking, ultimately comes out to be 'labour.' The simplicity of the system gave an impression both of clearness and certainty, which was transferred from the reasoning to the premises. The facts seemed to be established, because they were necessary to the system. The first step to an estimate of the value of the doctrine would be to draw up a statement of the 'postulates' implied. Among them, we should have such formulæ as the single rate of profits and wages; which imply the 'transferability' of labour and capital, or the flow of either element to the best-paid employment. We should have again the Malthusian doctrine of the multiplication of labour up to a certain standard; and the fact that scarcity means dearness and plenty cheapness. These doctrines at least are taken for granted; and it may perhaps be said that they are approximations which only require qualifications, though sometimes very important qualifications, to hold good of the society actually contemplated.

They were true enough to give the really conclusive answer to many popular fallacies. The type of sophistry which Ricardo specially assailed was that which results from neglecting the necessary implications of certain changes. The arguments for the old 'mercantile theory'—for 'protection' of industry, for the poor-law, for resisting the introduction of machinery, the fear of 'gluts' and all manner of doctrines about the currency—were really exposed by the economists upon the right grounds. It was absurd to suppose that by simply expanding the currency, or by making industry less efficient, or forcing it to the least profitable employments, you were increasing the national wealth; or to overlook the demoralising effects of a right to support

because you resolved only to see the immediate benefits of charity to individuals. It is true, no doubt, that in some cases there might be other arguments, and that the economists were apt to take a narrow view of the facts. Yet they decisively exploded many bad arguments, and by the right method of enforcing the necessity of tracing out the whole series of results. It was partly to their success in confuting absurd doctrines that their confidence was due; though the confidence was excessive when it was transferred to the axioms from which they professed to start. A doctrine may be true enough to expose an error, and yet not capable of yielding definite and precise conclusions. If I know that nothing can come out of nothing, I am on the way to a great scientific principle and able to confute some palpable fallacies; but I am still a very long way from understanding the principle of the 'conservation of energy.' The truth that scarcity meant dearness was apparently well known to Joseph in Egypt, and applied very skilfully for his purpose. Economists have framed a 'theory of value' which explains more precisely the way in which this is brought about. A clear statement may be valuable to psychologists; but for most purposes of political economy Joseph's knowledge is quite sufficient. It is the doctrine which is really used in practice whatever may be its ultimate justification.

The postulates, however, were taken by the economists to represent something more than approximate statements of the fact. They imply certain propositions which might be regarded as axioms. Men desire wealth and prefer their own interests. The whole theory might then be regarded as a direct deduction from the axioms.

It thus seemed to have a kind of mathematical certainty. When facts failed to conform to the theory the difficulty could be met by speaking, as Malthus spoke, of 'tendencies,' or by appealing to the analogy of 'friction' in mechanics. The excuse might be perfectly valid in some cases, but it often sanctioned a serious error. It was assumed that the formula was still absolutely true of something, and that the check or friction was a really separable and accidental interference. Thus it became easy to discard, as irrelevant, objections which really applied to the principle itself, and to exaggerate the conformity between fact and theory. The economic categories are supposed to state the essential facts, and the qualifications necessary to make them accurate were apt to slip out of sight. Ricardo,[1] to mention a familiar instance, carefully points out that the 'economic rent,' which clearly represents an important economic category, is not to be confounded, as in 'popular' use, with the payments actually made, which often include much that is really profit. The distinction, however, was constantly forgotten, and the abstract formula summarily applied to the concrete fact.

The economists had constructed a kind of automaton which fairly represented the actual working of the machinery. But then, each element of their construction came to represent a particular formula, and to represent nothing else. The landlord is simply the receiver of surplus value; the capitalist the one man who saves, and who saves in proportion to profit; and the labourer simply the embodiment of Malthus's multi-

plying tendency. Then the postulates as to the ebb and flow of capital and labour are supposed to work automatically and instantaneously. Ricardo argues that a tax upon wages will fall, not, as Buchanan thought, upon the labourer, nor, as Adam Smith thought, upon rent, but upon profits; and his reason is apparently that if wages were 'lowered the requisite population would not be kept up.'[1] The labourer is able to multiply or diminish so rapidly that he always conforms at once to the required standard. This would seem to neglect the consideration that, after all, some time is required to alter the numbers of a population, and that other changes of a totally different character may be meanwhile set up by rises and falls of wages. Ricardo, as his letters show,[2] was well aware of the necessity of making allowance for such considerations in applying his theorems. He simplified the exposition by laying them down too absolutely; and the doctrine, taken without qualification, gives the 'economic man,' who must be postulated to make the doctrine work smoothly. The labourer is a kind of constant unit—absolutely fixed in his efficiency, his wants, and so forth; and the same at one period as at another, except so far as he may become more prudent, and therefore fix his 'natural price' a little higher. An 'iron law' must follow when you have invented an iron unit. In short, when society is represented by this hypothetical mechanism, where each man is an embodiment of the required formula, the theory becomes imperfect so far as society is made up of living beings, varying, though

---

[1] *Works*, p. 34 (chap. ii.). Rent is there defined as the sum paid for the original and indestructible powers of the soil.

[1] *Works*, p. 132 (chap. xvii.). He admits (*Ibid.* p. 210 *n.*) that the labourer may have a little more than what is absolutely necessary, and that his inference is therefore 'expressed too strongly.'
[2] See *Letters to M'Culloch*, p. xxi.

gradually, in their whole character and attributes, and forming part of an organised society incomparably too complex in its structure to be adequately represented by the three distinct classes, each of which is merely a formula embodied in an individual man. The general rules may be very nearly true in a great many cases, especially on the stock-exchange ; but before applying them to give either a history or a true account of the actual working of concrete institutions, a much closer approximation must be made to the actual data.

I need not enlarge, however, upon a topic which has been so often expounded. I think that at present the tendency is rather to do injustice to the common-sense embodied in this system, to the soundness of its aims, and to its value in many practical and immediate questions, than to overestimate its claim to scientific accuracy. That claim may be said to have become obsolete.

One point, however, remains. The holders of such a doctrine must, it is said, have been without the bowels of compassion. Ricardo, as critics observe with undeniable truth, was a Jew and a member of the stock-exchange. Now Jews, in spite of Shylock's assertions, and certainly Jewish stockbrokers, are naturally without human feeling. If you prick them, they only bleed banknotes. They are fitted to be capitalists, who think of wages as an item in an account, and of the labourer as part of the tools used in business. Ricardo, however, was not a mere money-dealer, nor even a walking treatise. He was a kindly, liberal man, desirous to be, as he no doubt believed himself to be, in sympathy with the leaders of political and scientific thought, and fully sharing their aspirations. No doubt he, like his friends, was more

conspicuous for coolness of head than for impulsive philanthropy. Like them, he was on his guard against 'sentimentalism' and 'vague generalities,' and thought that a hasty benevolence was apt to aggravate the evils which it attacked. The Utilitarians naturally translated all aspirations into logical dogmas ; but some people who despised them as hard-hearted really took much less pains to give effect to their own benevolent impulses. Now Ricardo, in this matter, was at one with James Mill and Bentham, and especially Malthus.[1] The essential doctrine of Malthus was that the poor could be made less poor by an improved standard of prudence. In writing to Malthus, Ricardo incidentally remarks upon the possibility of raising the condition of the poor by 'good education' and the inculcation of foresight in the great matter of marriage.[2] Incidental references in the *Principles* are in the same strain. He accepts Malthus's view of the poor-laws, and hopes that, by encouraging foresight, we may by degrees approach 'a sounder and more healthful state.'[3] He repudiates emphatically a suggestion of Say that one of his arguments implies 'indifference to the happiness' of the masses,[4] and holds that 'the friends of humanity' should encourage the poor to raise their standard of comfort and enjoyment. The labourers, as he elsewhere incidentally observes, are 'by far the most important class in society.'[5] How should they not be if the greatest happiness of the greatest number be the legitimate aim of all legislation ?

[1] 'The assaults upon Malthus's "great work,"' he says (*Works*, p. 243, ch. xxxii.), 'have only served to prove its strength.'
[2] *Letters to Malthus*, p. 226.   [3] *Works*, p. 58 (ch. v.).
[4] *Ibid.* p. 211 *n.* (ch. xxvi.).   [5] *Ibid.* p. 258 (ch. xxxii.).

It is true that in his argument Ricardo constantly assumes that his 'natural price' will also be the real price of labour. The assumption that the labourers' wages tend to a minimum is a base for his general arguments. The inconsistency, if there be one, is easily intelligible. Ricardo agreed with Malthus that, though the standard might be raised, and though a rise was the only way to improvement, the chances of such a rise were not encouraging. Improved wages, as he says,[1] might enable the labourer to live more comfortably if only he would not multiply. But 'so great are the delights of domestic society, that in practice it is invariably found that an increase of population follows an amended condition of the labourer,' and thus the advantage is lost as soon as gained.

I have tried to show what was the logical convenience of the assumption. Ricardo, who has always to state an argument at the cost of an intellectual contortion, is content to lay down a rule without introducing troublesome qualifications and reserves. Yet he probably held that his postulate was a close approximation to the facts. Looking at the actual state of things at the worst time of the poor-law, and seeing how small were the prospects of stirring the languid mind of the pauper to greater forethought, he thought that he might assume the constancy of an element which varied so slowly. The indifference of the Ricardo school generally to historical inquiry had led them no doubt to assume such constancy too easily. Malthus, who had more leaning to history, had himself called attention to many cases in which the 'prudential check' operated more strongly than it did among the English poor. Probably Ricardo was in this, as in other

[1] *Works*, p. 248 (ch. xxii.).

cases, too hasty in assuming facts convenient for his argument. The poor man's character can, it is clear, be only known empirically ; and, in fact, Ricardo simply appeals to experience. He thinks that, as a fact, men always do multiply in excess. But he does not deny that better education might change their character in this respect. Indeed, as I have said, an even excessive faith in the possible modification of character by education was one of the Utilitarian tenets. If Ricardo had said broadly that a necessary condition of the improvement of the poor was a change of the average character, I think that he would have been saying what was perfectly true and very much to the purpose both then and now. The objection to his version of a most salutary doctrine is that it is stated in too narrow terms. The ultimate unit, the human being, is indeed supposed to be capable of great modification, but it is solely through increasing his foresight as to the effects of multiplication that the change is supposed to be attainable. The moral thus drawn implied a very limited view of the true nature and influence of great social processes, and in practice came too often to limiting possible improvement to the one condition of letting things alone. Let a man starve if he will not work, and he will work. That, as a sole remedy, may be insufficient ; though, even in that shape, it is a doctrine more likely to be overlooked than overvalued. And meanwhile the acquiescence in the painful doctrine that, as a matter of fact, labourers would always multiply to starvation point, was calculated to produce revolt against the whole system. Macaulay's doctrine that the Utilitarians had made political economy unpopular was so far true that the average person resented the unpleasant doctrines thus obtruded upon him in their most unpleasant shape ; and, if he was told that they were embodied logic, revolted against logic itself.

V. THE RICARDIANS

It will be quite sufficient to speak briefly of the minor prophets who expounded the classical doctrine; sometimes falling into fallacies, against which Ricardo's logical instinct had warned him; and sometimes perhaps unconsciously revealing errors which really lurked in his premises. When Ricardo died, James Mill told M'Culloch that they were ' the two and only genuine disciples' of their common friend.[1] Mill wrote what he intended for a Schoolbook of Political Economy.[2] Brief, pithy, and vigorous, it purports to give the essential principles in their logical order ; but, as his son remarks,[3] had only a passing importance. M'Culloch took a more important place by his writings in the *Edinburgh Review* and elsewhere, and by his lectures at Edinburgh and at London. He was one of the first professors of the new university. His *Principles of Political Economy*[4] became a text-book, to be finally superseded by John Stuart Mill. Other works statistical and bibliographical showed great industry, and have still their value. He was so much the typical economist of the day that he has been identified with Carlyle's *M'Crowdy*, the apostle of the dismal science.[5] He writes, however, with enough vivacity and

[1] Bain's *James Mill*, p. 211.   [2] Editions in 1821, 1824, and 1826.
[3] *Autobiography*, p. 204.
[4] The first edition, an expanded version of an article in the *Encyclopædia Britannica*, appeared in 1825.
[5] *Latter-day Pamphlets* (New Downing Street). M'Crowdy is obviously a type, not an individual.

fervour of belief in his creed to redeem him from the charge of absolute dulness. An abler thinker was Colonel (Robert) Torrens (1780-1864).[1] He had served with distinction in the war ; but retired on half-pay, and was drawn by some natural idiosyncrasy into the dry paths of economic discussion. He was already confuting the French economists in 1808 ; and was writing upon the Bank-charter Act and the Ten Hours' Bill in 1844. Torrens held himself, apparently with justice, to be rather an independent ally than a disciple of Ricardo. His chief works were an essay upon the 'External Corn-trade' (1815)[2] and an 'Essay on the Production of Wealth' (1821). Ricardo pronounced his arguments upon the Corn-trade to be 'unanswered and unanswerable,'[3] and he himself claimed to be an independent discoverer of the true theory of rent.[4] He was certainly a man of considerable acuteness and originality. In these writings we find the most sanguine expressions of the belief that political economy was not only a potential, but on the verge of becoming an actual, science. Torrens observes that all sciences have to pass through a period of controversy ; but thinks that economists are emerging from this stage, and rapidly approaching unanimity. In twenty years, says this hopeful prophet, there will scarcely exist a ' doubt of its' (Political Economy's) 'fundamental principles.'[5] Torrens thinks that Ricardo has generalised too

[1] See Mr. Hewins's life of him in *Dictionary of National Biography*.
[2] Fourth edition in 1827.   [3] Ricardo's *Works*, p. 164 *n*.
[4] *External Corn-trade*, preface to fourth edition. J. S. Mill observes in his chapter upon 'International Trade' that Torrens was the earliest expounder of the doctrine afterwards worked out by Ricardo and Mill himself. For Ricardo's opinion of Torrens, see *Letters to Trower*, p. 39.
[5] *Production of Wealth* (Preface).

much, and Malthus too little ; but proposes, with proper professions of modesty, to take the true *via media*, and weld the sound principles into a harmonious whole by a due combination of observation and theory. The science, he thinks, is 'analogous to the mixed mathematics.'[1] As from the laws of motion we can deduce the theory of dynamics, so from certain simple axioms about human nature we can deduce the science of Political Economy. M'Culloch, at starting, insists in edifying terms upon the necessity of a careful and comprehensive induction, and of the study of industrial phenomena in different times and places, and under varying institutions.[2] This, however, does not prevent him from adopting the same methods of reasoning. 'Induction' soon does its office, and supplies a few simple principles, from which we may make a leap to our conclusions by a rapid, deductive process.

The problems appear to be too simple to require long preliminary investigations of fact. Torrens speaks of proving by 'strictly demonstrative evidence' or of ' proceeding to demonstrate' by strict analysis.[3] This is generally the preface to one of those characteristic arithmetical illustrations to which Ricardo's practice gave a sanction. We are always starting an imaginary capitalist with so many quarters of corn and suits of clothes, which he can transmute into any kind of product, and taking for granted that he represents a typical case. This gives a certain mathematical air to the reasoning, and too often hides from the reasoner that he may be begging the question in more ways than one by the arrangement of

[1] *Production of Wealth* (Preface).   [2] *Political Economy* (1825), p. 21.
[3] *External Corn-trade*, pp. xviii, 109, 139 ; *Production of Wealth*, p. 375.

his imaginary case. One of the offenders in this kind was Nassau Senior (1790-1864), a man of remarkable good sense, and fully aware of the necessity of caution in applying his theories to facts. He was the first professor of Political Economy at Oxford (1825-1830), and his treatise[1] lays down the general assumption of his orthodox contemporaries clearly and briefly. The science, he tells us, is deducible from four elementary propositions : the first of which asserts that every 'man desires to obtain additional wealth with as little sacrifice as possible' ; while the others state the first principles embodied in Malthus's theory of population, and in the laws corresponding to the increasing facility of manufacturing and the decreasing facility of agricultural industry.[2] As these propositions include no reference to the particular institutions or historical development of the social structure, they virtually imply that a science might be constructed equally applicable in all times and places ; and that, having obtained them, we need not trouble ourselves any further with inductions. Hence it follows that we can at once get from the abstract ' man' to the industrial order. We may, it would seem, abstract from history in general. This corresponds to the postulate explicitly stated by M'Culloch. ' A state,' he tells us, ' is nothing more than an aggregate of individuals' : men, that is, who 'inhabit a certain tract of country.'[3] He infers that 'whatever is most advantageous to them' (the individuals) 'is most advantageous to the state.' Self-interest, therefore, the individual's desire of

[1] Originally in the *Encyclopædia Metropolitana*, 1836.
[2] Senior's *Political Economy* (1850), p. 26.
[3] *Ibid.* (1825), pp. 55, 129 131.

adding to his 'fortune,' is the mainspring or *causa causans* of all improvement.[1] This is, of course, part of the familiar system, which applies equally in ethics and politics. M'Culloch is simply generalising Adam Smith's congenial doctrine that statesmen are guilty of absurd presumption when they try to interfere with a man's management of his own property.[2] This theory, again, is expressed by the familiar maxim *pas trop gouverner*, which is common to the whole school, and often accepted explicitly.[3]

It will be quite enough to notice one or two characteristic results. The most important concern the relation between the labourer and the capitalist. Malthus gives the starting-point. Torrens, for example, says that the 'real wages of labour have a constant tendency to settle down' to the amount rendered necessary by 'custom and climate' in order to keep up his numbers.[4] Mill observes in his terse way that the capitalist in the present state of society 'is as much the owner of the labour' as the manufacturer who operates with slaves. The only 'difference is in the mode of purchasing.'[5] One buys a man's whole labour ; the other his labour for a day. The rate of wages can therefore be raised, like the price of slaves, only by limiting the supply. Hence the 'grand practical problem is to find the means of limiting the number of births.'[6] M'Culloch is equally clear, and

[1] Senior's *Political Economy* (150), p. 125.
[2] *Ibid.* p. 135. M'Culloch admits the possibility that a man may judge his own interests wrongly, but thinks that this will not happen in one case out of twenty (*Ibid.* p. 15).
[3] See Torrens's *Production of Wealth*, p. 208 ; and M'Culloch's *Political Economy* (1843), p. 294, where he admits some exceptions.
[4] *External Corn-trade*, p. 87, etc.
[5] *Political Economy* (second edition), pp. 21, 22.   [6] *Ibid.* p. 67.

infers that every scheme 'not bottomed on' the principle of proportioning labour to capital must be 'completely nugatory and ineffectual.'[1]

The doctrine common to the whole school led M'Culloch to conclusions which became afterwards notorious enough to require a word of notice. Torrens, like Ricardo, speaks of capital as 'accumulated labour,' but makes a great point of observing that, although this is true, the case is radically changed in a developed state of society. The value of things no longer depends upon the labour, but upon the amount of capital employed in their production.[2] This, indeed, may seem to be the most natural way of stating the accepted principle. M'Culloch replies that the change makes no difference in the principle,[3] inasmuch as capital being 'accumulated labour,' value is still proportioned to labour, though in a transubstantiated shape. M'Culloch supposed that by carrying out this principle systematically he was simplifying Ricardo and bringing the whole science into unity. All questions, whether of value in exchange, or of the rate of wages, can then be reduced to comparing the simple unit called labour. Both Mill and M'Culloch regard capital as a kind of labour, so that things may be produced by capital alone, 'without the co-operation of any immediate labour'[4]—a result which can hardly be realised with the discovery of a perpetual motion. So, again, the value of a joint product is the 'sum' of these two values.[5] All value, therefore, can be regarded as pro-

[1] *Political Economy* (1825), p. 329.
[2] *Production of Wealth*, p. 34, etc.   [3] *Political Economy* (1825), p. 318.
[4] Mill's *Political Economy* (second edition), p. 102 ; M'Culloch's *Political Economy* (1825), pp. 289-291.   [5] M'Culloch's *Political Economy*, p. 290.

portioned to labour in one of its two states. M'Culloch advanced to an unfortunate conclusion, which excited some ridicule. Though Ricardo and Torrens[1] rejected it, it was accepted by Mill in his second edition.[2] Wine kept in a cask might increase in value. Could that value be ascribed to 'additional labour actually laid out'? M'Culloch gallantly asserted that it could, though 'labour' certainly has to be interpreted in a non-natural sense.[3] Not only is capital labour, but fermentation is labour, or how can we say that all value is proportioned to labour? This is only worth notice as a pathetic illustration of the misfortunes of a theorist ridden by a dogma of his own creation. Another conclusion is more important. The 'real value' of anything is measured by the labour required to produce it. Nothing 'again is more obvious' than that equal labour implies the 'same sacrifice' in all states of society.[4] It might seem to follow that the value of anything was measured by the labour which it would command. This doctrine, however, though maintained by Malthus, was, according to M'Culloch, a pestilent heresy, first exploded by Ricardo's sagacity.[5] Things exchange, as he explains, in proportion to the labour which produces them, but the share given to the labourer may vary widely. The labourer, he says, 'gives a constant, but receives a variable quantity in its stead.' He makes the same sacrifice when he works for a day, but may get for it what he

[1] Preface to *External Corn-trade*.   [2] *Ibid.* p. 95.
[3] *Political Economy* (1825), pp. 313-18. This argument disappears in later editions.   [4] *Ibid.* p. 217.
[5] *Political Economy*, p. 221. De Quincey makes a great point of this doctrine, of which it is not worth while to examine the meaning.

produces in ten hours, or only in one. In every case, however, he gets less than he produces, for the excess 'constitutes profits.'[1] The capitalist must get his interest, that is, the wages of the accumulated labour. Here we come again to the Socialist position, only that the Socialist infers that the labourer is always cheated by the capitalist, and does not consider that the machine can ask for 'wages' on the pretext that it is accumulated labour. What, however, determines the share actually received? After all, as a machine is not actually a labourer, and its work not a separable product, we cannot easily see how much wages it is entitled to receive. M'Culloch follows the accepted argument. 'No proposition,' he says, 'can be better established than that the market rate of wages . . . is exclusively determined by the proportion between capital and population.'[2] We have ultimately here, as elsewhere, 'the grand principle to which we must always come at last,' namely, 'the cost of production.'[3] Wages must correspond to the cost of raising the labourer. This leads to a formula, which afterwards became famous. In a pamphlet[4] devoted to the question, he repeats the statement that wages depend upon the proportion between population and capital ; and then, as if the phrase were identical, substitutes that portion of capital which is required for the labourer's consumption. This is generally cited as the first statement of the 'wage-fund' theory, to which I shall have to return.

[1] *Political Economy*, p. 221 *n.*   [2] *Ibid.* p. 336.   [3] *Ibid.* p. 337.
[4] 'Essay upon the Circumstances which determine the Rate of Wages' (1826), p. 113. This was written for Constable's *Miscellany*, and is mainly repetition from the *Political Economy*. It was republished, with alterations, in 1851.

I need not pursue these illustrations of the awkward results of excessive zeal in a disciple. It is worth noticing, however, that M'Culloch's practical conclusions are not so rigid as might be inferred. His abstract doctrines do not give his true theory, so much as what he erroneously took to be his theory, The rules with which he works are approximately true under certain conditions, and he unconsciously assumes the conditions to be negligible, and the rules therefore absolute. It must be added that he does not apply his conclusions so rigidly as might be expected. By the help of 'friction,' or the admission that the rule is only true in nineteen cases out of twenty, he can make allowance for many deviations from rigid orthodoxy. He holds, for example, that government interference is often necessary. He wishes in particular for the establishment of a 'good system of public education.'[1] He seems to have become more sentimental in later years. In the edition of 1843 he approves the Factory Acts, remarking that the last then passed 'may not, in some respects, have gone far enough.'[2] He approves a provision for the 'impotent poor,' on the principle of the Elizabethan act, though he disapproves the centralising tendency of the new poor-law. Though he is a good Malthusian,[3] and holds the instinct of population to be a 'constant quantity,'[4] he does not believe in the impossibility of improvement. The 'necessary' rate of wages fixes only a minimum :

[1] Political Economy, pp. 359-61.
[2] Ibid. (1843), p. 178. And see his remarks on the unfavourable side of the Factory System, p. 186 seq.
[3] 'Wherever two persons have the means of subsisting,' as he quaintly observes, 'a marriage invariably takes place' (Political Economy, p. 154).
[4] Political Economy, p. 206.

an increase of population has been accompanied by an increase of comfort.[1] Wages rise if the standard of life be raised, and a rise of wages tends to raise the standard. He cordially denounces the benevolent persons who held that better wages only meant more dissipation. Better wages are really the great spur to industry and improvement.[2] Extreme poverty causes apathy ; and the worst of evils is the sluggishness which induces men to submit to reductions of wages. A sense of comfort will raise foresight ; and the vis medicatrix should be allowed to act upon every rank of society. He is no doubt an individualist, as looking to the removal of restrictions, such as the Conspiracy Laws,[3] rather than to a positive action of the government ; but it is worth notice that this typical economist is far from accepting some of the doctrines attributed to the school in general.

The classical school blundered when it supposed that the rules which it formulated could be made absolute. To give them that character, it was necessary to make false assumptions as to the ultimate constitution of society ; and the fallacy became clear when the formulæ were supposed to give a real history or to give first principles, from which all industrial relations could be deduced. Meanwhile, the formulæ, as they really expressed conditional truths, might be very useful so long as, in point of fact, the conditions existed, and were very effective in disposing of many fallacies. The best illustration would probably be given by the writings of Thomas Tooke (1774-1858),[4]

[1] Political Economy, p. 344.   [2] Ibid. pp. 349-52.
[3] See pamphlet on the rate of wages, pp. 178-204.
[4] Tooke's Thoughts and Details on the High and Low Prices of the last Thirty Years appeared in 1823 (second edition 1824). This was rewritten and embodied in the History of Prices, the first two volumes of which appeared in 1838. Four later volumes appeared in 1839, 1848, and 1857.

one of the founders of the Political Economy Club. The History of Prices is an admirable explanation of phenomena which had given rise to the wildest theories. The many oscillations of trade and finance during the great struggle, the distress which had followed the peace, had bewildered hasty reasoners. Some people, of course, found consolation in attributing everything to the mysterious action of the currency ; others declared that the war-expenditure had supplied manufacturers and agriculturists with a demand for their wares, apparently not the less advantageous because the payment came out of their own pockets.[1] Tooke very patiently and thoroughly explodes these explanations, and traces the fluctuations of price to such causes as the effect of the seasons and the varying events of the war which opened or closed the channels of commerce. The explanation in general seems to be thoroughly sound and conclusive, and falls in, as far as it goes, with the principles of his allies. He shows, for example, very clearly what were the conditions under which the orthodox theory of rent was really applicable ; how bad seasons brought gain instead of loss to the 'agricultural interest,' that is, as Tooke explains, to the landlord and farmer ; how by a rise of price out of proportion to the diminution of supply, the farmer made large profits ; how rents rose, enclosure bills increased, and inferior land was brought under the plough. The landlord's interest was for the time clearly opposed to that of all other classes, however

[1] The popular view is given by Southey. The Radicals, he says in 1823, desire war because they expect it to lead to revolution. 'In this they are greatly deceived, for it would restore agricultural prosperity, and give a new spur to our manufactures' (Selections from Southey's Letters, iii. 382. See also Life and Correspondence, iv. 228, 386).

inadequate the doctrine might become when made absolute by a hasty generalisation. I need not dwell upon the free-trade argument which made the popular reputation of the economists. It is enough to note briefly that the error as to the sphere of applicability of the doctrine did not prevent many of the practical conclusions from being of the highest value.

CHAPTER VI

ECONOMIC HERETICS

I. THE MALTHUSIAN CONTROVERSY

THE Economic theory became triumphant. Expounded from new university chairs, summarised in textbooks for schools, advocated in the press, and applied by an energetic party to some of the most important political discussions of the day, it claimed the adhesion of all enlightened persons. It enjoyed the prestige of a scientific doctrine, and the most popular retort seemed to be an involuntary concession of its claims. When opponents appealed from 'theorists' to practical men, the Utilitarians scornfully set them down as virtually appealing from reason to prejudice. No rival theory held the field. If Malthus and Ricardo differed, it was a difference between men who accepted the same first principles. They both professed to interpret Adam Smith as the true prophet, and represented different shades of opinion rather than diverging sects. There were, however, symptoms of opposition, which, at the time, might be set down as simple reluctance to listen to disagreeable truths. In reality, they were indications of a dissatisfaction which was to become of more importance and to lead in time to a more decided revolt. I must indicate some of them,

though the expressions of dissent were so various and confused that it is not very easy to reduce them to order.

Malthus's doctrine was really at the base of the whole theory, though it must be admitted that neither Malthus himself nor his opponents were clear as to what his doctrine really was. His assailants often attacked theories which he disavowed, or asserted principles which he claimed as his own.[1] I mention only to set aside some respectable and wearisome gentlemen such as Ingram, Jarrold, Weyland, and Grahame, who considered Malthus chiefly as impugning the wisdom of Providence. They quote the divine law, 'Increase and multiply'; think that Malthus regards vice and misery as blessings, and prove that population does not 'tend' to increase too rapidly. Jarrold apparently accepts the doctrine which Malthus attributes to Süssmilch, that lives have been shortened since the days of the patriarchs, and the reproductive forces diminished as the world has grown fuller. Grahame believes in a providential 'ordeal,' constituted by infant mortality, which is not, like war and vice, due to human corruption, but a beneficent regulating force which correlates fertility with the state of society. This might be taken by Malthus as merely amounting to another

[1] The discussions of population most frequently mentioned are:—W. Godwin, *Thoughts occasioned by Dr. Parr's Spital Sermon*, etc., 1801; R. Southey, in (Aikin's) *Annual Review for 1803*, pp. 292-301; Thomas Jarrold, *Dissertations on Man*, etc., 1806; W. Hazlitt, *Reply to the Essay on Population*, 1807; A. Ingram, *Disquisitions on Population*, 1808; John Weyland, *Principles of Population*, etc., 1806; James Grahame, *Inquiry into the Principle of Population*, 1816; George Ensor, *Inquiry concerning the Population of Nations*, 1818; W. Godwin, *On Population*, 1820; Francis Place, *Principles of Population*, 1822; David Booth, *Letter to the Rev. T. R. Malthus*, 1823; M. T. Sadler, *Law of Population*, 1830; A. Alison, *Principles of Population*, 1840; T. Doubleday, *True Law of Population*, 1842.

version of his checks. Such books, in fact, simply show, what does not require to be further emphasised, that Malthus had put his version of the struggle for existence into a form which seemed scandalous to the average orthodox person. The vagueness of Malthus himself and the confused argument of such opponents makes it doubtful whether they are really answering his theories or reducing them to a less repulsive form of statement.

In other directions, the Malthusian doctrine roused keen feeling on both sides, and the line taken by different parties is significant. Malthus had appeared as an antagonist of the revolutionary party. He had laid down what he took to be an insuperable obstacle to the realisation of their dreams. Yet his views were adopted and extended by those who called themselves thorough Radicals. As, in our days, Darwinism has been claimed as supporting both individualist and socialist conclusions, the theory of his predecessor, Malthus, might be applied in a Radical or a Conservative sense. In point of fact, Malthus was at once adopted by the Whigs, as represented by the *Edinburgh Review*. They were followers of Adam Smith and Dugald Stewart; they piqued themselves, and, as even James Mill admitted, with justice, upon economic orthodoxy. They were at the same time predisposed to a theory which condemned the revolutionary Utopias. It provided them with an effective weapon against the agitators whom they especially dreaded. The Tories might be a little restrained by orthodox qualms. In 1812 Southey was permitted to make an onslaught upon Malthus in the *Quarterly*;[1] but more complimentary

[1] *Quarterly Review*, Dec. 1812 (reprinted in Southey's *Moral and Political Essays*, 1832).

allusions followed, and five years later the essay was elaborately defended in an able article.[1] An apology was even insinuated for the previous assault, though the blame was thrown upon Malthus for putting his doctrines in an offensive shape. A reference to Owen suggests that the alarm excited by Socialism had suggested the need of some sound political economy.

Another controversy which was being carried on at intervals indicates the line of cleavage between the capitalist and the landed interest. James Mill's early pamphlet, *Commerce Defended* (1808), and Torrens's pamphlet, *Economists Refuted*, were suggested by this discussion. Although the war was partly in defence of British trade, its vicissitudes produced various commercial crises; and the patriotic Tories were anxious to show that we could thrive even if our trade was shut out from the Continent. The trading classes maintained that they really supplied the sinews of war, and had a right to some control of the policy. The controversy about the orders in council and Berlin decrees emphasised these disputes, and called some attention to the questions involved in the old controversy between the 'mercantile' and the 'agricultural' systems. A grotesque exaggeration of one theory was given by Mill's opponent, William Spence[2] (1783-1860), in his *Britain independent of Commerce*, which went through several editions in 1808, and refurbished or perverted the doctrine of the French economists. The argument, at least, shows what fallacies then needed

[1] *Quarterly Review*, July 1817, by (Archbishop) Sumner, Malthus's commentator in the *Records of Creation*. Ricardo's *Letters to Trower*, p. 47.

[2] Spence's *Tracts on Political Economy* were collected with a preface in 1822. Spence is better known as an entomologist, and collaborated with William Kirby.

confutation by the orthodox. In the preface to his collected tracts, Spence observes that the high price of corn was the cause of 'all our wealth and prosperity during the war.' The causes of the high price ('assisted,' he admits, ' by occasional bad seasons ') were the 'national debt, in other words, taxation,' which raised the price, first, of necessaries, and then of luxuries (thus, he says, ' neutralising its otherwise injurious effects '), and the virtual monopoly by the agriculturist of the home market.[1] All our wealth, that is, was produced by taxation aided by famine, or, in brief, by the landowner's power of squeezing more out of the poor. Foreign trade, according to Spence, is altogether superfluous. Its effect is summed up by the statement that we give hardware to America, and, in return, get only ' the vile weed, tobacco.'[2] Spence's writings only show the effect of strong prejudices on a weak brain. A similar sentiment dictated a more noteworthy argument to a much abler writer, whose relation to Malthus is significant—Thomas Chalmers (1780-1847),[3] probably best remembered at present for his leadership of the great disruption of 1843. He had a reputation for eloquence and philosophic ability not fully intelligible at the present day. His appearance was uncouth, and his written style is often clumsy. He gave an impression at times of indolence and of timidity. Yet his superficial qualities concealed an ardent temperament and cordial affections. Under a sufficient stimulus he could blaze out in stirring speech and vigorous action. His intellectual training was limited. He had, we are

[1] *Tracts* (1822), p. xiii.   [2] *Ibid.* p. 59.
[3] Chalmers's *Works* were published in twenty-five volumes in 1841-42.

told, been much influenced in his youth by the French philosophers of the time, and had appeared on the side of the more freethinking party in the famous Leslie controversy. Soon afterwards, however, he was converted to ' evangelical ' views. He still accepted Thomas Brown as a great metaphysician,[1] but thought that in moral questions Brown's deistical optimism required to be corrected by an infusion of Butler's theory of conscience. He could adapt Butler's *Analogy*, and write an edifying Bridgewater Treatise. I need only say, however, that, though his philosophy was not very profound, he had an enthusiasm which enables him at times to write forcibly and impressively.

Chalmers was from 1803 to 1815 minister of Kilmany, Fifeshire, and his attention had already been drawn to the question of pauperism. He took part in the Spence controversy, by an essay upon the *Extent and Stability of National Resources*.[2] In this he expounds a doctrine which is afterwards given in his *Political Economy in Connection with the Moral State and Moral Aspects of Society*.[3] The main purpose of his early book is the patriotic. It is meant, like Spence's pamphlet, to prove that Napoleon could do us no vital injury. Should he succeed, he would only lop off superfluous branches, not hew down the main trunk. Chalmers's argument to show the ease with which a country may recover the effects of a disastrous war is highly praised by J. S. Mill[4] as the first sound explanation of the facts. Chalmers's position, however, is radically different from

[1] Chalmers's *Works*, i. 237.
[2] This essay is not in his collected *Works*, though in vol. xxi. it is promised for the next volume.   [3] *Works*, xix. and xx.
[4] Mill's *Political Economy*, bk. i. ch. v. § 7 and 8. See Chalmers, xix. 140.

the position of either James or J. S. Mill. Essentially it is the development of the French economists' theory, though Chalmers is rather unwilling to admit his affinity to a discredited school.[1] He has reached some of their conclusions, he admits, but by a different path.[2] He coincides, in this respect, with Malthus, who was equally impressed by the importance of ' subsistence,' or of the food-supply of the labourer. The great bulk of the food required must be raised within our own borders. As Chalmers says, in 1832, the total importation of corn, even in the two famine years, 1800 and 1801, taken together, had only provided food for five weeks,[3] and could normally represent a mere fringe or superfluous addition to our resources. His main argument is simple. The economists have fallen into a fatal error. A manufacturer, he observes, only makes his own article.[4] The economists somehow imagine that he also supports himself. You see a prosperous ' shawl-making village.' You infer that its ruin would cause the destitution of so many families. It would only mean the loss of so many shawls. The food which supports the shawl-makers would still be produced, and would be only diverted to support makers of some other luxury.[5] There would be a temporary injury to individuals, but no permanent weakening of national resources. Hence we have his division of the population. The agriculturists, and those who make the ' second necessaries ' (the cottages, ploughs, and so forth, required by the agriculturist), create the great wealth of the country. Besides these we have the ' dis-

[1] *National Resources* (Appendix).   [2] *Works*, xix. 306.
[3] *Ibid.* xix. 226, 233.   [4] *National Resources*, p. 48.
[5] *Works*, xix. 64.

posable' population, which is employed in making luxuries for the landowners, and, finally, the ' redundant ' or what he calls in his later book the ' excrescent ' or ' superinduced ' population,[1] which is really supported by foreign trade. Commerce, then, is merely ' the efflorescence of our agriculture.'[2] Were it annihilated this instant, we should still retain our whole disposable population. The effect of war is simply to find a different employment for this part of the nation. Napoleon, he says, is ' emptying our shops and filling our battalions.'[3] All the ' redundant ' population might be supported by simply diminishing the number of our cart-horses.[4] Similarly, the destruction of the commerce of France ' created her armies.' It only transferred men from trade to war, and ' millions of artisans ' were ' transformed into soldiers.'[5] Pitt was really strengthening when he supposed himself to be ruining his enemy. 'Excrescence' and ' efflorescence ' are Chalmers's equivalent for the ' sterility ' of the French economists. The backbone of all industry is agriculture, and the manufacturers simply employed by the landowner for such purposes as he pleases. Whether he uses them to make his luxuries or to fight his battles, the real resources of the nation remain untouched. The Ricardians insist upon the vital importance of ' capital.' The one economic end of the statesmen, as the capitalist class naturally thinks, should be to give every facility for its accumulation, and consequently for allowing it to distribute itself in the most efficient way. Chalmers, on the contrary, argues that we

[1] *Works*, xix. 226.   [2] *Ibid.* xix. 235.
[3] *National Resources*, p. 158.   [4] *Ibid.* p. 160.   [5] *Works*, xix. 262.

may easily have too much capital. He was a firm believer in gluts. He admits that the extension of commerce was of great good at the end of the feudal period, but not as the 'efficient cause' of wealth, only as 'unlocking the capabilities of the soil.'[1] This change produced the illusion that commerce has a 'creative virtue,' whereas its absolute dependence upon agriculture is a truth of capital importance in political economy. More Malthusian than Malthus, Chalmers argues that the case of capital is strictly parallel to the case of population.[2] Money may be redundant as much as men, and the real causes of every economic calamity are the 'over-speculation of capitalists,' and the 'over-population of the community at large.'[3] In this question, however, Chalmers gets into difficulties, which show so hopeless a confusion between 'capital,' income, and money, that I need not attempt to unravel his meaning.[4] Anyhow, he is led to approve the French doctrine of the single tax. Ultimately, he thinks, all taxes fall upon rent.[5] Agriculture fills the great reservoir from which all the subsidiary channels are filled. Whether the stream be tapped at the source or further down makes no difference. Hence he infers that, as the landlords necessarily pay the taxes, they should pay them openly. By an odd coincidence, he would tax rents like Mill,

---

[1] *Works*, xix. 75.   [2] *Ibid.* xix. 118-47.   [3] *Ibid.* xix. 343.
[4] See *Ibid.* xix. 171. J. S. Mill speaks of Chalmers's speculations with a respect which it is difficult to understand.
[5] Chalmers holds that the Ricardian doctrine of rent inverts the true order. Fertile lands do not pay rent because poor lands are brought into cultivation, but poor lands are cultivated because fertile lands pay rent. He apparently wishes, like Malthus, to regard rent as a blessing, not a curse. The point is not worth arguing. See *Works*, xix. 320.

though upon opposite grounds. He holds that the interest of the landowners is not opposed to, but identical with, the interest of all classes. Politically, as well as economically, they should be supreme. They are, 'naturally and properly, the lords of the ascendant,' and, as he oddly complains in the year of the Reform Bill, not 'sufficiently represented in parliament.'[1] A 'splendid aristocracy' is, he thinks, a necessary part of the social edifice;[2] the law of primogeniture is necessary to support them; and the division of land will cause the decay of France. The aristocracy are wanted to keep up a high standard of civilisation and promote philosophy, science, and art.[3] The British aristocracy in the reign of George IV. scarcely realised this ideal, and would hardly have perceived that to place all the taxes upon their shoulders would be to give them a blessing in disguise. According to Chalmers, however, an established church represents an essential part of the upper classes, and is required to promote a high standard of life among the poor.[4] In connection with this, he writes a really forcible chapter criticising the economical distinction of productive and unproductive labour, and shows at least that the direct creation of material wealth is not a sufficient criterion of the utility of a class.

Chalmers's arguments are of interest mainly from their bearing upon his practical application of the Malthusian problem. His interest in the problem of pauperism had been stimulated by his residence in Glasgow, where from 1815 to 1823 he had been actively engaged in parochial duties. In 1819 he had set up an organised system of

---

[1] *Works*, xix. 304-5.   [2] *Ibid.* xix. 370.
[3] *Ibid.* xix. 366.   [4] *Ibid.* xix. 322.

charity in a poor district, which both reduced the expenditure and improved the condition of the poor. The experiment, though dropped some years later, became famous, and in later years Chalmers successfully started a similar plan in Edinburgh. It was this experience which gave shape to his Malthusian theories. He was, that is, a Malthusian in the sense of believing that the great problem was essentially the problem of raising the self-respect and spirit of independence of the poor. The great evil which confronted him in Glasgow was the mischief connected with the growth of the factory system. He saw, as he thought, the development of wealth leading to the degradation of the labourer. The great social phenomenon was the tendency to degeneration, the gradual dissolution of an organism, and corruption destroying the vital forces. On the one hand, this spectacle led him, as it led others, to look back fondly to the good old times of homely food and primitive habits, to the peasantry as represented in Burns's *Cotter's Saturday Night* or Scott's *Heart of Midlothian*, when the poor man was part of a social, political, and ecclesiastical order, disciplined, trained, and self-respecting, not a loose waif and stray in a chaotic welter of separate atoms. These were the facts which really suggested his theory of the 'excrescent' population, produced by the over-speculation of capitalists. The paupers of Glasgow were 'excrescent,' and the 'gluts' were visible in the commercial crises which had thrown numbers of poor weavers out of employment and degraded them into permanent paupers. The facts were before his eyes, if the generalisation was hasty and crude. He held, on the other hand, that indiscriminate charity, and still more the

establishment by poor-laws of a legal right to support, was stimulating the evil. The poor-law had worked incalculable mischiefs in England,[1] and he struggled vigorously, though unavailingly, to resist its introduction into Scotland. Chalmers, however, did not accept the theory ascribed to the Utilitarians, that the remedy for the evils was simply to leave things alone. He gives his theory in an article upon the connection between the extension of the church and the extinction of pauperism. He defends Malthus against the 'execrations' of sentimentalism. Malthus, he thinks, would not suppress but change the direction of beneficence. A vast expenditure has only stimulated pauperism. The true course is not to diminish the rates but to make them 'flow into the wholesome channel of maintaining an extended system of moral and religious instruction.'[2] In other words, suppress workhouses but build schools and churches; organise charity and substitute a systematic individual inspection for reckless and indiscriminate almsgiving. Then you will get to the root of the mischief. The church, supported from the land, is to become the great civilising agent. Chalmers, accordingly, was an ardent advocate of a church establishment. He became the leader of the Free Church movement not as objecting to an establishment on principle, but because he thought that the actual legal fetters of the Scottish establishment made it impossible to carry out an effective reorganisation and therefore unable to discharge its true functions.

Here Chalmers's economical theories are crossed by various political and ecclesiastical questions with which

---

[1] *Works*, xx. 247, 296.   [2] *Ibid.* xx. 290.

I am not concerned. His peculiarities as an economist bring out, I think, an important point. He shows how Malthus's views might be interpreted by a man who, instead of sharing, was entirely opposed to the ordinary capitalist prejudices. It would be idle to ask which was the more logical development of Malthus. When two systems are full of doubtful assumptions of fact and questionable logic and vague primary conceptions, that question becomes hardly intelligible. We can only note the various turns given to the argument by the preconceived prejudices of the disputants. By most of them the Malthusian view was interpreted as implying the capitalist as distinguished from the landowning point of view.

To Southey as to Chalmers the great evil of the day was the growth of the disorganised populace under the factory system. The difference is that while Chalmers enthusiastically adopted Malthus's theory as indicating the true remedy for the evil, Southey regards it with horror as declaring the evil to be irremediable. Chalmers, a shrewd Scot actively engaged in parochial work, had his attention fixed upon the reckless improvidence of the 'excrescent' population, and welcomed a doctrine which laid stress upon the necessity of raising the standard of prudence and morality. He recognised and pointed out with great force the inadequacy of such palliatives as emigration, home-colonisation, and so forth.[1] Southey, an ardent and impulsive man of letters, with no practical experience of the difficulties of social reform, has no patience for such inquiries. His remedy, in all cases, was a 'paternal government' vigorously regulating

[1] *Works*, xix. 380.

society; and Malthus appears to him to be simply an opponent of all such action. Southey had begun the attack in 1803 by an article in the *Annual Review* (edited by A. Aikin) for which the leading hints were given by Coleridge, then with Southey at Keswick.[1] In his letters and his later articles he never mentions Malthus without abhorrence.[2] Malthus, according to his article in the *Annual Review*, regards 'vice' and 'misery' as desirable; thinks that the 'gratification of lust' is a 'physical necessity'; and attributes to the 'physical constitution of our nature' what should be ascribed to the 'existing system of society.' Malthus, that is, is a fatalist, a materialist, and an anarchist. His only remedy is to abolish the poor-rates, and starve the poor into celibacy. The folly and wickedness of the book have provoked him, he admits, to contemptuous indignation; and Malthus may be a good man personally. Still, the 'farthing candle' of Malthus's fame as a political philosopher must soon go out. So in the *Quarterly Review* Southey attributes the social evils to the disintegrating effect of the manufacturing system, of which Adam Smith was the 'tedious and hard-hearted' prophet. The excellent Malthus indeed becomes the 'hard-hearted' almost as Hooker was the 'judicious.' This sufficiently represents the view of the sentimental Tory. Malthus, transformed into a monster, deserves the 'execrations' noticed by Chalmers. There is a thorough coincidence between this view and that of the sentimental Radicals. Southey observes that Malthus (as interpreted by him) does not

[1] The copy of Malthus's second edition with Coleridge's notes used by Southey is in the British Museum.
[2] See Southey's *Political*.

really answer Godwin. Malthus argues that 'perfectibility' gives an impossible end because equality would lead to vice and misery. But why should we not suppose with Godwin a change of character which would imply prudence and chastity? Men as they are may be incapable of equality because they have brutal passions. But men as they are to be may cease to be brutal and become capable of equality. This, indeed, represents a serious criticism. What Malthus was really concerned to prove was that the social state and the corresponding character suppose each other; and that real improvement supposes that the individual must somehow acquire the instincts appropriate to an improved state. The difference between him and his opponents was that he emphasised the mischief of legislation, such as that embodied in the poor-law, which contemplated a forcible change, destroying poverty without raising the poor man's character. Such a rise required a long and difficult elaboration, and he therefore dwells mainly upon the folly of the legislative, unsupported by the moral, remedy. To Godwin, on the other hand, who professed an unlimited faith in the power of reason, this difficulty was comparatively unimportant. Remove political inequalities and men will spontaneously become virtuous and prudent.

Godwin accordingly, when answering Dr. Parr and Mackintosh,[1] in 1801, welcomed Malthus's first version of the essay. He declares it to be as 'unquestionable an addition to the theory of political economy' as has been made by any writer for a century past'; and 'admits

[1] *Thoughts occasioned by Dr. Parr's Spital Sermon.* A copy annotated by Coleridge is in the British Museum.

the ratios to their full extent.'[1] In this philosophical spirit he proceeds to draw some rather startling conclusions. He hopes that, as mankind improves, such practices as infanticide will not be necessary; but he remarks that it would be happier for a child to perish in infancy than to spend seventy years in vice and misery.[2] He refers to the inhabitants of Ceylon as a precedent for encouraging other practices restrictive of population. In short, though he hopes that such measures may be needless, he does not shrink from admitting their possible necessity. So far, then, Godwin and Malthus might form an alliance. Equality might be the goal of both; and both might admit the necessity of change in character as well as in the political framework; only that Malthus would lay more stress upon the evil of legislative changes outrunning or independent of moral change. Here, however, arose the real offence. Malthus had insisted upon the necessity of self-help. He had ridiculed the pretensions of government to fix the rate of wages; and had shown how the poor-laws defeated their own objects. This was the really offensive ground to the political Radicals. They had been in the habit of tracing all evils to the selfishness and rapacity of the rulers; pensions, sinecures, public debts, huge armies, profligate luxuries of all kinds, were the fruits of bad government and the true causes of poverty. Kings and priests were the harpies who had settled upon mankind, and were ruining their happiness. Malthus, they thought, was insinuating a base apology for rulers when he attributed the evil to the character of the subjects instead of attributing it to the

[1] *Thoughts*, etc., pp. 56, 61, 62.
[2] *Ibid.* p. 71.

wickedness of their rulers.   He was as bad as the old Tory, Johnson,[1] exclaiming :—

> ' How small of all that human hearts endure
>   That part which kings and laws can cause or cure ! '

He was, they held, telling the tyrants that it was not their fault if the poor were miserable.   The essay was thus an apology for the heartlessness of the rich.   This view was set forth by Hazlitt in an attack upon Malthus in 1807.[2]   It appears again in the *Enquiry* by G. Ensor (1769-1843)—a vivacious though rather longwinded Irishman, who was known both to O'Connell and to Bentham.[3]   Godwin himself was roused by the appearance of the fifth edition of Malthus's *Essay* to write a reply, which appeared in 1820.   He was helped by David Booth (1766-1846),[4] a man of some mathematical and statistical knowledge.   Hazlitt's performance is sufficiently significant of the general tendency.   Hazlitt had been an enthusiastic admirer of Godwin, and retained as much of the enthusiasm as his wayward prejudices would allow.   He was through life what may be called a sentimental Radical, so far as Radicalism was compatible with an ardent worship of Napoleon.   To him Napoleon meant the enemy of Pitt and Liverpool and Castlereagh and the Holy Alliance.   Hazlitt could forgive any policy which meant the humiliation of the men whom he most heartily hated.   His attack upon Malthus was such as

[1] Lines added to Goldsmith's *Traveller*.
[2] *Reply to the Essay on Population*, etc., 1807.   The book was anonymous. The first three letters had appeared in Cobbett's *Register*.   Two others with an appendix are added.
[3] Bentham's *Works*, x. 603, 604 ; and *Dictionary of National Biography*.
[4] See *Dictionary of National Biography*.

might satisfy even Cobbett, whose capacity for hatred, and especially for this particular object of hatred, was equal to Hazlitt's.   The personal rancour of which Hazlitt was unfortunately capable leads to monstrous imputations.   Not only does Malthus's essay show the ' little low rankling malice of a parish beadle . . . disguised in the garb of philosophy,' and bury ' false logic ' under ' a heap of garbled calculations,'[1] and so forth ; but he founds insinuations upon Malthus's argument as to the constancy of the sexual passion.   Malthus, he fully believes, has none of the ordinary passions, anger, pride, avarice, or the like, but declares that he must be a slave to an ' amorous complexion,' and believe all other men to be made ' of the same combustible materials.'[2]   This foul blow is too characteristic of Hazlitt's usual method ; but indicates also the tone which could be taken by contemporary journalism.

The more serious argument is really that the second version of Malthus is an answer to his first.   Briefly, the ' moral check ' which came in only as a kind of afterthought is a normal part of the process by which population is kept within limits, and prevents the monstrous results of the ' geometrical ratio.'   Hazlitt, after insisting upon this, admits that there is nothing in ' the general principles here stated that Mr. Malthus ' at present disposed to deny, or that he has not himself expressly insisted upon in some part or other of his various works.'[3]   He only argues that Malthus's concessions are made at the cost of self-contradiction.   Why then, it may be asked, should not Hazlitt take the position of an improver and harmoniser of the doctrine

[1] Hazlitt's *Reply*, p. 19.   [2] *Ibid*. pp. 139-41.   [3] *Ibid*. p. 117.

rather than of a fierce opponent?   The answer has been already implied.   He regards Malthus as an apologist for an unjust inequality.   Malthus, he says, in classifying the evils of life, has ' allotted to the poor all the misery, and to the rich as much vice as they please.'[1]   The check of starvation will keep down the numbers of the poor ; and the check of luxury and profligacy will restrain the multiplication of the rich. ' The poor are to make a formal surrender of their right to provoke charity or parish assistance that the rich may be able to lay out all their money on their vices.'[2]   The misery of the lower orders is the result of the power of the upper.   A man born into a world where he is not wanted has no right, said Malthus, to a share of the food. That might be true if the poor were a set of lazy supernumeraries living on the industrious.   But the truth is that the poor man does the work, and is forced to put up in return with a part of the produce of his labour.[3]   The poor-laws recognise the principle that those who get all from the labour of others should provide from their superfluities for the necessities of those in want.[4]   The ' grinding necessity ' of which Malthus had spoken does not raise but lower the standard ; and a system of equality would lessen instead of increasing the pressure. Malthus, again, has proposed that parents should be responsible for their children.   That is, says Hazlitt, Malthus would leave children to starvation, though he professes to disapprove infanticide.   He would ' extinguish every spark of humanity . . . towards the children of others ' on pretence of preserving the ' ties of parental affection.'   Malthus tries to argue that the ' iniquity of

[1] *Reply*, p. 263.   [2] *Ibid*. p. 344.   [3] *Ibid*. p. 284.   [4] *Ibid*. p. 287.

government ' is not the cause of poverty.   That belief, he says, has generated discontent and revolution.   That is, says Hazlitt, the way to prevent revolutions and produce reforms is to persuade people that all the evils which government may inflict are their own fault. Government is to do as much mischief as it pleases, without being answerable for it.[1]   The poor-laws, as Hazlitt admits, are bad, but do not show the root of the evil.   The evils are really due to increasing tyranny, dependence, indolence, and unhappiness due to other causes.   Pauperism has increased because the government and the rich have had their way in everything.   They have squandered our revenues, multiplied sinecures and pensions, doubled salaries, given monopolies and encouraged jobs, and depressed the poor and industrious. The ' poor create their own fund,' and the necessity for it has arisen from the exorbitant demands made by the rich.[2]   Malthus is a Blifil,[3] hypocritically insinuating arguments in favour of tyranny under pretence of benevolence.

Hazlitt's writing, although showing the passions of a bitter partisan, hits some of Malthus's rather cloudy argumentation.   His successor, Ensor, representing the same view, finds an appropriate topic in the wrongs of Ireland.   Irish poverty, he holds, is plainly due not to over-population but to under-government,[4] meaning, we must suppose, misgovernment.   But the same cause explains other cases.   The ' people are poor and are growing poorer,'[5] and there is no mystery about it.   The expense of a court, the waste of the profits and money

[1] *Reply*, p. 351.   [2] *Ibid*. pp. 362-64.   [3] *Ibid*. p. 352.
[4] Ensor's *Enquiry*, p. 294.   [5] *Ibid*. p. 441.

in the House of Commons, facts which are in striking contrast to the republican virtues of the United States, are enough to account for everything ; and Malthus's whole aim is to ' calumniate the people.' Godwin in 1820 takes up the same taunts. Malthus ought, he thinks, to welcome war, famine, pestilence, and the gallows.[1] He has taught the poor that they have no claim to relief, and the rich that, by indulging in vice, they are conferring a benefit upon the country. The poor-laws admit a right, and he taunts Malthus for proposing to abolish it, and refusing food to a poor man on the ground that he had notice not to come into the world two years before he was born.[2]

Godwin, whose earlier atheism had been superseded by a vague deism, now thinks with Cobbett that the poor were supported by the piety of the mediæval clergy, who fed the hungry and clothed the naked from their vast revenues, while dooming themselves to spare living.[3] He appeals to the authority of the Christian religion, which indeed might be a fair *argumentum ad hominem* against ' Parson Malthus.' He declares that Nature takes more care of her work than such irreverent authors suppose, and ' does not ask our aid to keep down the excess of population.'[4] In fact, he doubts whether population increases at all. Malthus's whole theory, he says, rests upon the case of America ; and with the help of Mr. Booth and some very unsatisfactory statistics, he tries to prove that the increase shown in the American census has been entirely due to immigration. Malthus safely declined to take any notice of a production which

[1] Godwin on *Population*, p. 506.   [2] *Ibid.* p. 553.
[3] *Ibid.* p. 558.   [4] Godwin, p. 219.

in fact shows that Godwin had lost his early vigour. The sound Utilitarian, Francis Place, took up the challenge, and exploded some of Godwin's statistics. He shows his Radicalism by admitting that Malthus, to whose general benevolence he does justice, had not spoken of the poor as one sprung like himself from the poor would naturally do; and he accepts modes of limiting the population from which Malthus himself had shrunk. For improvement, he looks chiefly to the abolition of restrictive laws.

II. SOCIALISM

The arguments of Hazlitt and his allies bring us back to the Socialist position. Although it was represented by no writer of much literary position, Owen was becoming conspicuous, and some of his sympathisers were already laying down principles more familiar to-day. Already, in the days of the Six Acts, the government was alarmed by certain ' Spencean Philanthropists.' According to Place they were a very feeble sect, numbering only about fifty, and perfectly harmless. Their prophet was a poor man called Thomas Spence (1750-1815),[1] who had started as a schoolmaster, and in 1775 read a paper at Newcastle before a ' Philosophical Society.'[2] He proposed that the land in every village should belong to all the inhabitants—a proposal which Mr. Hyndman regards as a prophecy of more thoroughgoing schemes of Land Nationalisation. Spence drifted to London, picked up a precarious living, partly by selling books of a revolutionary kind, and died

[1] See account of him reprinted from Mackenzie's *History of Newcastle* and *Dictionary of National Biography*.
[2] Reprinted by Mr. Hyndman in 1822, with a preface.

in 1815, leaving, it seems, a few proselytes. A writer of higher literary capacity was Charles Hall, a physician at Tavistock, who in 1805 published a book on *The Effects of Civilisation*.[1] The effects of civilisation, he holds, are simply pernicious. Landed property originated in violence, and has caused all social evils. A great landlord consumes unproductively as much as would keep eight thousand people.[2] He gets everything from the labour of the poor ; while they are forced to starvation wages by the raising of rents. Trade and manufactures are equally mischievous. India gets nothing but jewellery from Europe, and Europe nothing but muslin from India, while so much less food is produced in either country.[3] Manufactures generally are a cause and sign of the poverty of nations.[4]

Such sporadic protests against the inequalities of wealth may be taken as parts of that ' ancient tale of wrong' which has in all ages been steaming up from the suffering world, and provoking a smile from epicurean deities. As Owenism advanced, the argument took a more distinct form. Mill[5] mentions William Thompson of Cork as a ' very estimable man,' who was the ' principal champion' of the Owenites in their debates with the Benthamites. He published in 1824 a book upon the distribution of

[1] See *Dictionary of National Biography*. Hall's book was reprinted by J. M. Morgan in the ' Phœnix Library,' 1850. See Anton Menger's *Das Recht auf den vollen Arbeitsertrag* (second edition, 1891), for notices of Hall, Thompson, and others.
[2] *Effects of Civilisation* (1850), p. 86.   [3] *Ibid.* p. 71.   [4] *Ibid.* p. 115.
[5] *Autobiography*, p. 125. See Holyoake's *History of Co-operation*, i. 16, 109, 278-83, 348, for some interesting notices of Thompson. Menger (*Recht auf den vollen Arbeitsertrag*, p. 100 n.) holds that Thompson not only anticipated but inspired Marx: Rodbertus, he says, drew chiefly upon St. Simon and Proudhon.

wealth.[1] It is wordy, and is apt to remain in the region of ' vague generalities' just at the points where specific statements would be welcome. But besides the merit of obvious sincerity and good feeling, it has the interest of showing very clearly the relation between the opposing schools. Thompson had a common ground with the Utilitarians, though they undoubtedly would consider his logic to be loose and overridden by sentimentalism. In the first place, he heartily admired Bentham : ' the most profound and celebrated writer on legislation in this or any other country.'[2] He accepts the ' greatest happiness principle' as applicable to the social problem. He argues for equality upon Bentham's ground. Take a penny from a poor man to give it to the rich man, and the poor man clearly loses far more happiness than the rich man gains. With Bentham, too, he admits the importance of ' security,' and agrees that it is not always compatible with equality. A man should have the fruits of his labour ; and therefore the man who labours most should have most. But, unlike Bentham, he regards equality as more important than security. To him the main consideration is the monstrous mass of evil resulting from vast accumulations of wealth in a few hands. In the next place, he adapts to his own purpose the Ricardian theory of value. All value whatever, he argues, is created by labour. The labourer, he infers, should have the value which he creates. As things are, the labourer parts with most of it to the capitalist or the owner of rents. The capitalist claims a right to the

[1] *An Inquiry into the Principles of the Distribution of Wealth most conducive to Human Happiness; applied to the Newly Proposed System of Voluntary Equality of Wealth.*—1824.   [2] *Distribution of Wealth*, p. 327.

whole additional production due to the employment of capital. The labourer, on the other hand, may claim a right to the whole additional production, after replacing the wear and tear and allowing to the capitalist enough to support him in equal comfort with the productive labourers.[1] Thompson holds that while either system would be compatible with 'security,' the labourer's demand is sanctioned by 'equality.' In point of fact, neither system has been fully carried out; but the labourer's view would tend to prevail with the spread of knowledge and justice. While thus anticipating later Socialism, he differs on a significant point. Thompson insists upon the importance of 'voluntary exchange' as one of his first principles. No one is to be forced to take what he does not himself think a fair equivalent for his labour. Here, again, he would coincide with the Utilitarians. They, not less than he, were for free trade and the abolition of every kind of monopoly. But that view may lead by itself to the simple adoption of the do-nothing principle, or, as modern Socialists would say, to the more effectual plunder of the poor. The modern Socialist infers that the means of production must be in some way nationalised. Thompson does not contemplate such a consummation. He denounces, like all the Radicals of the day, monopolies and conspiracy laws. Sinecures and standing armies and State churches are the strongholds of tyranny and superstition. The 'hereditary possession of wealth' is one of the master-evils, and with sinecures will disappear the systems of entails and unequal distribution of inheritance.[2] Such institutions have encouraged the use of fraud and force,

[1] *Distribution of Wealth*, p. 167, etc.   [2] *Ibid.* p. 310.

and indirectly degraded the labourer into a helpless position. He would sweep them all away, and with them all disqualifications imposed upon women.[1] This once done, it will be necessary to establish a universal and thoroughgoing system of education. Then the poor man, freed from the shackles of superstition and despotism, will be able to obtain his rights as knowledge and justice spread through the whole community. The desire to accumulate for selfish purposes will itself disappear. The labourer will get all that he creates; the aggregate wealth will be enormously multiplied, though universally diffused; and the form taken by the new society will, as he argues at great length, be that of voluntary co-operative associations upon Owen's principles.

The economists would, of course, reject the theory that the capitalists should have no profits; but, in spite of this, they might agree to a great extent with Thompson's aspirations. Thompson, however, holds the true Socialist sentiment of aversion to Malthus. He denies energetically what he takes to be the Malthusian doctrine: that increased comfort will always produce increased numbers.[2] This has been the 'grand scarecrow to frighten away all attempts at social improvement.' Thompson accordingly asserts that increased comfort always causes increased prudence ultimately; and looks forward to a stationary state in which the births will just balance the deaths. I need not inquire here which theory puts the cart before the horse. The opposition possibly admits of reconciliation; but here I only

[1] He wrote, as J. S. Mill observes, an *Appeal* [1825] against James Mill's views on this matter—a fact which no doubt commended him to the son.
[2] *Distribution of Wealth*, pp. 425, 535, etc.

remark once more how Malthus stood for the appeal to hard facts which always provoked the Utopians as much as it corresponded to the stern Utilitarian view.

Another writer, Thomas Hodgskin, honorary secretary of the Birkbeck Institution, who published a tract called *Labour defended against the Claims of Capital, or the Unproductiveness of Capital proved* (1825), and afterwards gave some popular lectures on political economy, has been noticed as anticipating Socialist ideas. He can see, he says, why something should go to the maker of a road and something be paid by the person who gets the benefit of it. But he does not see why the road itself should have anything.[1] Hodgskin writes without bitterness, if without much logic. It is not for me to say whether modern Socialists are well advised in admitting that these crude suggestions were anticipations of their own ideas. The most natural inference would be that vague guesses about the wickedness of the rich have been in all ages current among the poor, and now and then take more pretentious form. Most men want very naturally to get as much and to work as little as they can, and call their desire a first principle of justice.

Perhaps, however, it is fairer to notice in how many points there was unconscious agreement; and how by converting very excellent maxims into absolute dogmas, from which a whole system was deducible, the theories appeared to be mutually contradictory, and, taken separately, became absurd. The palpable and admitted evil was the growth of pauperism and demoralisation of the labourer. The remedy, according to the Utilitarians, is to raise the sense of individual responsibility, to make

[1] *Labour Defended*, p. 16.

a man dependent upon his own exertions, and to give him security that he will enjoy their fruit. Let government give education on one hand and security on the other, and equality will follow in due time. The sentimental Radical naturally replies that leaving a man to starve does not necessarily make him industrious; that, in point of fact, great and growing inequality of wealth has resulted; and that the rights of man should be applied not only to political privilege, but to the possession of property. The Utilitarians have left out justice by putting equality in the background. Justice, as Bentham replied, has no meaning till you have settled by experience what laws will produce happiness; and your absolute equality would destroy the very mainspring of social improvement. Meanwhile the Conservative thinks that both parties are really fostering the evils by making individualism supreme, and that organisation is necessary to improvement; while one set of Radicals would perpetuate a mere blind struggle for existence, and the other enable the lowest class to enforce a dead level of ignorance and stupidity. They therefore call upon government to become paternal and active, and to teach not only morality but religion; and upon the aristocracy to discharge its functions worthily, in order to stamp out social evils and prevent a servile insurrection. But how was the actual government of George iv. and Sidmouth and Eldon to be converted to a sense of its duties? On each side appeal is made to a sweeping and absolute principle, and amazingly complex and difficult questions of fact are taken for granted. The Utilitarians were so far right that they appealed to experience, as, in fact, such questions have to be settled by the slow co-operation of many minds in many generations. Unfortunately the Utilitarians had, as we have seen, a very inadequate conception of what experience really meant, and were fully as rash and dogmatic as their opponents. I must now try to consider what were the intellectual conceptions implied by their mode of treating these problems.

CHAPTER VII

PSYCHOLOGY

I. THOMAS BROWN

THE politicians and economists, of whom I have spoken, took first principles for granted. The intellectual temperament, which made certain methods congenial to them, would no doubt have led them to an analogous position in philosophy. Bentham had touched upon philosophical points in a summary way, and James Mill, as we shall see, gave a more explicit statement. But such men as Ricardo and Malthus had no systematic philosophy, though a certain philosophy was congenial to their methods. Desire to reach a solid groundwork of fact, hearty aversion to mere word-juggling, and to effeminate sentimentalism, respect for science and indifference to, if not contempt for, poetry, resolution to approve no laws or institutions which could not be supported on plain grounds of utility, and to accept no theory which could not be firmly based on verifiable experience, imply moral and intellectual tendencies, in which we may perhaps say that the Utilitarians represent some of the strongest and most valuable qualities of the national character. Taking these qualities for granted, let us consider how the ultimate problems presented themselves to the school thus distinguished.

I have already observed that the Scottish philosophy, taught by Reid and Dugald Stewart, represented the only approach to a living philosophical system in these islands at the beginning of the century. It held this position for a long period. Mill, who had heard Dugald Stewart's lectures, knew nothing of German thought. He was well read in French philosophers, and in harmony with one leading sect. The so-called *idéologues*,[1] who regarded Condillac as representing the true line of intellectual progress, were in France the analogues of the English Utilitarians. Destutt de Tracy and Cabanis were their most conspicuous leaders in this generation. The philosophy of Reid and Stewart crossed the channel, and supplied the first assailants of the *idéologues* with their controversial weapons. Thus, until the German influence came to modify the whole controversy, the vital issue seemed to lie between the doctrine of Reid or 'intuitionism' on the one hand, and the purely 'experiential' school on the other, whether, as in France, it followed Condillac, or, as in England, looked back chiefly to Hartley. Both sections traced their intellectual ancestry to Locke and Hobbes, with some reference to Bacon, and, by the French writers, to Descartes. Stewart, again, as I have said, was the accepted Whig philosopher. It is true that the Whig sat habitually in the seat of Gallio. Jeffrey, whether he fully realised the fact or not, was at bottom a sceptic in philosophy as in politics. John Allen, the prophet of Holland House, was a thorough sceptic, and says[2] that Horner, one of Stewart's personal

---

[1] For an account of these writers and their relation to the pre-revolutionary schools, see *Les Idéologues* by F. Picavet (1891).
[2] Macvey Napier's *Correspondence*, p. 424.

admirers, was really a follower of Hume. The Whigs were inclined to Shaftesbury's doctrine that sensible men had all one religion, and that sensible men never said what it was. Those who had a more definite and avowable creed were content to follow Stewart's amiable philosophising. Brougham professed, let us hope, sincerely, to be an orthodox theist, and explained the argument from design in a commentary upon Paley. Sydney Smith expounded Reid and Stewart in lectures which showed at least that he was still a wit when talking 'philosophy' at the Royal Institution; and, though he hated 'enthusiasm' in dissenters, evangelicals, and tractarians, and kept religion strictly in its place— a place well outside of practical politics—managed to preach a wholesome, commonplace morality in terms of Christian theology. The difference between the Whig and the Radical temper showed itself in philosophical as in political questions. The Radical prided himself on being logical and thoroughgoing, while the Whig loved compromise, and thought that logic was very apt to be a nuisance. The systematic reticence which the Utilitarians held to be necessary prevented this contrast from showing itself distinctly on the surface. The Utilitarians, however, though they avoided such outspoken scepticism as would startle the public, indicated quite sufficiently to the initiated their essential position. It implied what they fully recognised in private conversation—a complete abandonment of theology. They left the obvious inferences to be drawn by others. In philosophy they could speak out in a well-founded confidence that few people were able to draw inferences. I will begin by considering the doctrine against which they protested;

for the antagonism reveals, I think, the key to their position.

When Stewart was obliged by infirmity to retire from the active discharge of his duties, he was succeeded by Thomas Brown (1778-1820). Brown had shown early precocity, and at the age of fifteen had attracted Stewart's notice by some remarks on a psychological point. He published at twenty a criticism of Darwin's *Zoonomia*, and he became one of the *Edinburgh Review* circle. When the *Review* was started he contributed an article upon Kant. In those happy days it was so far from necessary to prepare oneself for such a task by studying a library of commentators that the young reviewer could frankly admit his whole knowledge to be derived from Villers' *Philosophie de Kant* (1801).[1] Soon afterwards he took an important share in a once famous controversy. John Leslie, just elected to the mathematical chair at Edinburgh, was accused of having written favourably of Hume's theory of causation. Whigs and Tories took this up as a party question,[2] and Brown undertook to explain in a pamphlet what Hume's theory was, and to show that it did not lead to atheism. Leslie's friends triumphed, though it does not appear how far Brown's arguments contributed to their success. The pamphlet was rewritten and enlarged, and a third

[1] Charles François Dominique de Villers (1767-1815) was a French officer, who emigrated in 1792, and took refuge at Lübeck. He became profoundly interested in German life and literature, and endeavoured to introduce a knowledge of German speculation to his countrymen. His chief books were this exposition of Kant and an essay upon the *Reformation of Luther* (1803), which went through several editions, and was translated by James Mill in 1805. An interesting account of Villers is in the *Biographie Universelle*.

[2] See Cockburn's *Memorials* for a good notice of this.

edition of 1818 gives a full exposition of his theory. Brown had meanwhile become Stewart's leading disciple, and in 1810 was elected to be his colleague. Brown held the position, doing all the active duties, until his premature death in 1820. Brown, according to his biographer, wrote his lectures immediately before delivery, and completed them during his first two years of office. His theories, as well as his words, were often, according to the same authority, extemporised. Brown found that he could not improve what he had written under 'very powerful excitement.' Moreover, he had an unlucky belief that he was a poet. From 1814 till 1819 he brought out yearly what he supposed to be a poem. These productions, the *Paradise of Coquets* and the rest, are in the old-fashioned taste, and have long passed into oblivion.

The lectures, published posthumously, became a text-book for students, and reached a nineteenth edition in 1851. Their faults, considered as philosophical treatises, are palpable. They have the wordiness of hasty composition, and the discursive rhetoric intended to catch the attention of an indolent audience. Brown does not see that he is insulting his hearers when he apologises for introducing logic into lectures upon metaphysics, and indemnifies them by quotations from Akenside and the *Essay on Man*. Brown, however, showed great acuteness and originality. He made deviations, and took pains to mark his deviations, from Reid, though he spoke more guardedly of his own friend, Stewart. Stewart, who had strongly supported Brown's election, was shocked when, on the publication of the lectures, he came to discover that his colleague had been preaching

heresy, and wrote with obvious annoyance of Brown's hastiness and dangerous concessions to the enemy.[1] Brown, however, impressed his contemporaries by his ability. Sydney Smith is probably reporting the current judgment of his own circle when he says[2] that in metaphysics Stewart was a 'humbug' compared with Brown. I certainly think that Stewart, whom I should be sorry to call a humbug, shows less vigour and subtlety. Brown, at any rate, impressed both the Mills, and his relation to them is significant.

Brown's essay upon Causation indicates this relation. In this, indeed, there is little, if any, divergence from Stewart, though he attacks Reid with considerable asperity. He urges that Reid, while really agreeing with Hume, affected to answer him under cover of merely verbal distinctions.[3] The main point is simple. Hume had asserted that all events seem to be 'entirely loose and separate,' or, in other words, 'conjoined but never connected.' Yet he points out that, in fact, when we have found two events to be 'conjoined,' we call one cause and the other effect, and assume a 'necessary connection' between them. He then asks, What is the origin of this belief, and what, therefore, is the logical warrant for its validity? Brown entirely accepts Hume's statement of the facts. The real meaning of our statements is evaded by appealing to the conception of 'power.' When the loadstone (in his favourite illustration) attracts the iron, we say it has a 'power' of attracting iron. But to speak thus of

[1] Stewart's *Works*, iv. 345.   [2] Lady Holland's *Life of Smith*, ii. 388.
[3] *Inquiry into the Relations of Cause and Effect* (third edition), pp. 178, 180, and part iv. sec. 6.

a power is simply to describe the same facts in other words. We assert this, and nothing more than this, that when the loadstone comes near the iron, each moves towards the other. 'Power' is a word which only covers a statement of 'invariable antecedence.' Brown traces the various confusions which have obscured the true nature of this belief. He insists especially that we can no more discover power in mental than in physical sequences. The will had been supposed to be the type of causal power; but volition, according to Brown, reveals simply another succession of desires and bodily actions. The hypothesis of 'power' has been really the source of 'illusion.' The tendency to personify leads us to convert metaphor into fact, to invent a subject of this imaginary 'power,' and thus to create a mythology of beings to carry on the processes of nature. In other words, Brown here follows Hume or even anticipates Comte. As J. S. Mill remarks,[1] this erroneous identification of 'power' with 'will' gives the 'psychological rationale of Comte's great historical generalisation'; and, so far, Brown, as a follower of Hume, is clearly on the way to positivism.

The world, then, is a vast aggregate of 'loose' phenomena. A contemplation of things reveals no reason for one order rather than another. You may look at your loadstone as long as you please, but you will find no reason for its attracting iron. You may indeed interpolate a number of minute intervening sequences, and the process often suggests a vague something more than sequence; but this is a mere illusion.[2]

[1] *Examination of Hamilton* (fourth edition), p. 379.
[2] *Cause and Effect*, pp. 184-87.

Could we, in fact, see all the minute changes in bodies we should actually perceive that cause means nothing but 'the immediate invariable antecedence of an event.'[1] Brown especially argues against the attempts of d'Alembert and Euler to deduce the first laws of motion from the principle of 'sufficient reason.'[2] That, as he argues in detail, is merely begging the question, by introducing the principle of causation under an alias.

What, then, is the principle? We believe, he says,[3] that 'every event must have a cause,' and that circumstances exactly 'similar must have results exactly similar.' This belief, though applicable to all events, does not give us the 'slightest aid' to determining, independently of experience, any particular event. We observe that B follows A, but, for all we can say, it might as well follow any other letter of the alphabet. Yet we are entitled to say in general that it does uniformly follow some particular letter. The metaphor which describes cause and effect as a 'bond' tying A and B together is perfectly appropriate if taken to express the bare fact of sequence;[4] but we fall into error if we fancy there is really any bond whatever beside the events themselves.

The belief, then, in causation has precisely the same import according to Hume and Brown; and both agree that it is not produced by 'reasoning.' The proposition 'B has once succeeded A,' or 'has succeeded A a thousand times,' is entirely different from the proposition 'B will for ever succeed A.'[5] No process of logical inference can extract one from the other. Shall we, then, give up a belief in causation? The belief in

[1] *Cause and Effect*, p. 197.
[2] *Ibid.* p. 239 seq.
[3] *Ibid.* p. 244.
[4] *Ibid.* p. 150.
[5] *Ibid.* p. 357.

any case exists as a fact. Hume explains it by custom or association. Brown argues, and I think with much force, that Hume's explanation is insufficient. Association may explain (if it does more than restate) the fact that one 'idea' calls up another idea, but such association may and often does occur without suggesting any belief. The belief, too, precedes the association. We begin by believing too much, not too little, and assume a necessary connection of many phenomena which we afterwards find to be independent. The true answer is therefore different. There are three sources of belief, 'perception,' 'reasoning,' and 'intuition.'[1] Now, we cannot 'perceive' anything but a present coincidence; neither can we establish a connection by any process of 'reasoning,' and therefore the belief must be an 'intuition.' This, accordingly, is Brown's conclusion. 'There are principles,' he says, 'independent of reasoning, in the mind which save it from the occasional follies of all our ratiocinations';[2] or rather, as he explains, which underlie all reasoning. The difference, then, between Hume and Brown (and, as Brown argues, between Hume and Reid's real doctrine) is not as to the import, but as to the origin, of the belief. It is an 'intuition' simply because it cannot be further analysed. It does not allow us to pass a single step beyond experience; it merely authorises us to interpret experience. We can discover any actual law of connection between phenomena only by observing that they occur in succession.

[1] *Cause and Effect*, p. 313.
[2] *Cause and Effect*, p. 482. Brown thinks that we can logically disprove the existence of motion by the hare and tortoise argument, and should therefore disregard logic.

We cannot get beyond or behind the facts—and therefore intuitionism in this sense is not opposed to empiricism, but a warrant for empirical conclusions. An 'intuition,' briefly, is an unanalysable belief. Brown asserts that a certain element of thought has not been explained, and assumes it to be therefore inexplicable or ultimate. Brown's account of causation had a great influence upon both the Mills, and especially affected the teaching of the younger Mill.

Another point is important. Reid, as I have said, had specially prided himself upon his supposed overthrow of Berkeley's idealism. He was considered to have shown, in spite of sceptics, that the common belief in an external world was reasonable. Brown in his lectures ridiculed Reid's claim. This 'mighty achievement,' the 'supposed overthrow of a great system,' was 'nothing more than the proof that certain phrases are metaphorical, which were intended by their authors to be understood *only* as metaphors.'[1] The theory was dead before Reid slew it, though the phrases were still used as a mere 'relic,' or survival of an obsolete doctrine.[2] The impossibility of constructing extension out of our sensations is the *experimentum crucis* upon which Reid was ready to stake his case. If the attempt at such a construction could succeed, he would 'lay his hand upon his mouth' and give up the argument.[3] Brown takes up the

[1] Brown's *Lectures*, (1851), p. 167, Lect. xxvi.
[2] Lecture xxv. This question as to whether Brown had or had not grossly misrepresented Reid and other philosophers, led to an entangled argument, in which Mill defended Brown against Hamilton. I will not ask whether Reid was a 'natural realist' or a 'cosmothetic idealist,' or what Descartes or Arnauld thought about the question.
[3] Reid's *Works*, p. 128.

challenge thus thrown out. He holds that our knowledge of an external world is derived from a source which Reid overlooked. He modifies the Scottish psychology by introducing the muscular senses. His theory is that the infant which has learned to move discovers that on some occasions its movements are modified by a sense of 'impeded effort.'[1] The sudden interruption to a well-known series excites in its mind the notion of 'a cause which is not in itself.' This is the source of our belief in an external world. That belief is essentially the belief in some cause which we know to be other than our own mental constitution or the series of 'internal' phenomena, and of which we can know nothing else. It is enough to indicate a theory which has been elaborated by later psychologists, and plays a great part (for example) in the theories of Mill, Bain, and Mr. Herbert Spencer. It shows the real tendency of Brown's speculations. In the first place, it must be noticed that the theory itself had been already emphatically stated by Destutt de Tracy. Hamilton accuses Brown of plagiarism.[2] Whether his accusation be justifiable or not, it is certainly true that Brown had in some way reached the same principles which had been already set forth by a leading 'ideologist.' Brown, that is, though the official exponent of the Scottish philosophy,

[1] *Lectures*, pp. 150, 158-59.
[2] *Dissertations*, p. 98. Compare Brown's Twenty-fourth Lecture with Tracy's *Idéologie*, ch. vii., and the account of the way in which the infant learns from resistance to infer a cause, and make of the cause *un être qui n'est pas moi*. The resemblance is certainly close. Brown was familiar with French literature, and shows it by many quotations, though he does not, I think, refer to Tracy. Brown, it must be noticed, did not himself publish his lectures, and a professor is not bound to give all his sources in popular

was in this philosophical tenet at one with the school which they regarded as materialistic or sceptical. The path by which he reaches his conclusions is also characteristic.

Brown has reversed the interpretation of Reid's *experimentum crucis*. I will give up my case, says Reid, if you can make the external world out of sensations. That, replies Brown, is precisely what we can do. How from sensations do we get what Berkeley called 'outness'? We get it, says Brown, from the sense of resistance or 'impeded effort.' That reveals to us the fact that there is something independent of ourselves, and the belief in such a something is precisely what we mean, and all that we mean, by the belief in an external world. Consistently with this, Brown rejects Reid's distinction between the primary and secondary qualities. The distinction corresponds no doubt to some real differences, but there is no difference of the kind suggested by Reid. 'All [the qualities] are relative and equally relative—our perception of extension and resistance as much as our perception of fragrance and bitterness.'[1] We ascribe the sensations to 'external objects,' but the objects are only known by the 'medium' of our sensations. In other words, the whole world may be regarded as a set of sensations, whether of sight, smell, touch, or resistance

lectures. An explanation would have been due in a treatise. Picavet quotes Rhétoré's *Philosophie de Thomas Brown* (a book which I have not seen) for the statement that Brown's lectures often read like a translation of Laromiguière, with whom Brown was 'perhaps' acquainted. As, however, the *Leçons*, to which reference is apparently made, did not appear till 1815 and 1818, when Brown's lectures were already written, this seems to be impossible. The coincidence, which to me seems to be exaggerated by the statement, is explicable by a common relation to previous writers.

[1] *Lectures*, p. 166 (Lect. xxvi.).

to muscular movement, accompanied by the belief that they are caused by something not ourselves, and of which something we can only say that it is not ourselves.

Once more, the analysis of the process by which the belief is generated is significant. From resistance, or the sensation produced when something 'resists our attempts to grasp it,' we get the 'outness.' Then perception is 'nothing more than the association of this complex notion with our other sensations—the notion of something extended and resisting, suggested by these sensations, when the suggestions themselves have previously arisen, and suggested in the same manner and on the same principle as any other associate feeling suggests any other associate feeling.'[1] The odour or colour of a rose recalls the sensation of touching and of resistance to our grasp. Thus we regard the whole group of sensations as due to the external cause which produces the sensation of resistance. Brown seems to hesitate a little as to whether he shall appeal to an 'intuition' or to 'association,' but 'as I rather think,' he says, the belief is founded 'on associations as powerful as intuition.'[2]

Whatever, then, may be the origin of the belief—'intuition' or 'association'—it is clear that it can give us no knowledge except such as is derived from sensations. Moreover, Brown is thus led, as in the doctrine of causation, to accept a really sceptical position. He declares that he is in this respect at one with both Reid and Hume. They both accept two propositions: first, that we cannot 'by mere reasoning' prove the existence of an external world; secondly, that it is 'absolutely

[1] *Lectures*, p. 158 (Lect. xxv.).　　　[2] *Ibid.* p. 151 (Lect. xxiv.).

impossible for us not to believe' in its existence. Hume, he says, pronounces the first proposition in a 'loud tone of voice' and 'whispers' the second. Reid, conversely, passes over the first rapidly and 'dwells on the second with a tone of confidence.'[1] Brown accepts both statements. He has already said that there is no argument against Berkeley's denial of matter any more than against the 'infinite divisibility of matter.' But he adds, it is 'physically impossible' for us to admit the conclusion, at least without 'an instant dissent from a momentary logical admission.'[2] This, indeed, is but a version of Hume's familiar statement that Berkeley's arguments admit of no reply and produce no conviction.

Another essential doctrine of the Mills, the 'association' theory, is treated differently by Brown. Brown, as we have seen, both in his theory of causation and in his theory of our belief in an external world, speaks of principles in the mind which somehow override 'ratiocination.' In the first case, he speaks of 'intuition,' but in the other, as I have said, he seems to prefer association. The difference is remarkable because the belief in an external world is upon his showing simply a case of causation. It means essentially the reference of our sensations as to an external cause. Now, in the argument upon causation, he has insisted upon the insufficiency of association to generate the belief; and he would have found it difficult to meet his own arguments if applied to the belief in an external world. Yet it does not seem to occur to him that there is any difficulty in explaining this belief in an external

[1] *Lectures*, p. 177 (ch. xxviii.). Brown made the same remark to Mackintosh in 1812. (Mackintosh's *Ethical Philosophy*, 1872, 236 *n*.)

[2] *Ibid.* p. 154 (Lect. xxiv.).

world as a case of what Mill called 'indissoluble association.' Brown, as Mill thought, was not sufficiently aware of the power of this principle, and the difference between them is marked by this divergence. Brown had a great deal to say about association, though he chose generally to substitute the word 'suggestion,' previously familiar to Reid and Berkeley.[1] He considers it, however, mainly in another relation. He proposes to trace the order in which 'trains' of ideas succeed each other in our minds. He does not dwell upon the influence of association in producing belief. His question is not primarily as to the logic, but as to the actual succession of our thoughts. He explains that he uses the word 'suggestion' in order to avoid the hypothesis that the sequence of two ideas necessarily implies a previous state of mind in which they were brought together; and endeavours to explain various cases (as, for example, association by 'contrast' as well as by 'likeness' or 'continuity') by a more 'subtle' analysis.[2] He then works out an elaborate theory of 'simple' and 'relative' suggestion. Simple 'suggestion'[3] corresponds mainly to ordinary association, as when a friend's name or his book calls up the thought of the man himself. 'Relative suggestion' arises when two or more objects are perceived and suggest various relations of likeness and so forth.[4] This provides a scheme for working out the whole doctrine of the sequences of ideas so far as the sequences depend upon the mind itself and not upon external causes. It thus leads to problems of abstraction and

[1] See Hamilton's note to Reid's *Works*, p. 111.

[2] *Lectures*, p. 255 (Lect. xl.).　　　[3] *Ibid.* (Lect. xxxiii. and following).

[4] *Ibid.* p. 214-15 (Lect. xxxiii.). The phrase is revived by Professor Stout in his *Analytic Psychology*.

generalisation and to his whole theory of what he calls the 'intellectual states.' He again closely coincides with the French ideologists. He starts by examining Locke and Condillac. He of course professes to hold that Condillac's version of Locke is illegitimate, and ridicules the famous formula *penser c'est sentir*. He is, however, equally unwilling to admit Reid's 'variety of powers.'[1] In fact, his criticism of Condillac shows more affinity than contrast. Condillac erred, he says, in holding that thoughts are 'transformed sensations.' This was a false simplification into which he considers Condillac to have been led partly by the ambiguity of the word *sentir*.[2] Condillac applied to the mind the theory, true in 'the chemistry of the material chemists,' that the 'compounds are the elements themselves.'[3] He errs when he infers from the analogy that a feeling which arises out of others can be resolved into them. 'Love and hate' and other emotions are fundamentally different from the sensations by which they are occasioned, not mere 'transformations' of those sensations. We, on the other hand (that is to say, Reid and Stewart), have erred by excessive amplification. Instead of identifying different things, we have admitted a superfluous number of 'ultimate principles.'

The result is that besides the original sensations, we have to consider a number of feelings, which, while essentially different, are 'suggested' or caused by them. These are parts of the whole intellectual construction, and, though not transformed sensations, are still 'feelings' arising in consequence of the sensations. They are parts

[1] *Lectures*, p. 213 (Lect. xxxiii.).
[2] This is one of the coincidences with Laromiguière (*Leçons* (1837), i. 103).
[3] *Lectures*, p. 210.

of the 'trains' or sequences of 'ideas.' It is accordingly characteristic of Brown that he habitually describes an intellectual process as a 'feeling.' The statement of a mathematical proportion, for example, is a case of 'relative suggestion.' When we consider two numbers together we have a '*feeling* of the relation of proportion.'[1] The 'profoundest reasonings' are 'nothing more than a continued analysis of our thought,' by which we resolve the 'complex *feelings* of our minds' into the simpler conceptions out of which they were constructed.[2] In other words, Brown, it would seem, really accepts the *penser c'est sentir*, only that he regards the *sentir* as including separate classes of feeling, which cannot be regarded as simple 'transformations' of sensation. They are 'states of the mind' caused by, that is, invariably following upon, the simpler states, and, of course, combining in an endless variety of different forms. Reasoning is nothing more than a series of relative 'suggestions of which the separate subjects are felt by us to be mutually related.'[3] Hence, too, arises his theory of generalisation. He is, he says, not a 'nominalist' but a 'conceptualist,' and here, for once, agrees with Reid as against Stewart.[4] The 'general term,' according to him, expresses the 'feeling or general notion of resemblance,' which arises upon a contemplation of two objects. 'In Nature,' as he observes elsewhere,[5] 'there are no classes,' but the observation of a number of

[1] *Lectures*, p. 315 (Lect. xlviii.).　　[2] *Ibid*. p. 314.
[3] *Lectures*, p. 335 (Lect. li.). See Lect. xi. for a general explanation. The mind is nothing but a 'series of feelings'; and to say that 'I am conscious of feeling' is simply to say 'I feel.' The same phrase often occurs in James Mill.
[4] *Ibid*. p. 298 (Lect. xlvi.).　　[5] *Ibid*. p. 498 (Lect. lxxiv.).

particular cases and a certain feeling to which we give a name. Here, again, Brown's view coincides with that of his French contemporaries.

We may then say briefly that Brown carries out in his own fashion the conception of psychology which makes it an inductive science parallel to the physical sciences, and to be pursued by the same methods. We have to do with 'feelings' instead of atoms, and with mental instead of 'material' chemistry. Our sole method is still an analysis such as guides us in unravelling complex physical phenomena. We have, indeed, to admit certain first truths—the belief in our own identity is one of them—which are necessary to our very existence, although the assertion of such principles was carried to an extravagant and ridiculous length 'by Reid and some of his friends.' When, however, we come to ask what these principles are, it must be admitted that they are very innocent. They are not dangerous things, like 'innate ideas,' capable of leading us to a transcendental world, but simply assertions that we are warranted in trusting our sensations and applying a thoroughly inductive and empirical method. They are the cement which joins the feelings, and which, as Mill thought, could be supplanted by 'indissoluble associations.' The indefinite power thus attributed to association became, as we shall see, Mill's most characteristic doctrine. Meanwhile, I will only mention one inference which illustrates Brown's philosophical tendencies. Stewart had spoken doubtfully of the ontological argument for theology. Brown throws it over altogether. He does not even change it into an 'intuition.' He has always, he says, regarded it as 'absolutely void of force' unless it tacitly assumes the

'physical argument.' Nay, it is one proof of the force of this physical argument that it has saved us from doubts which would be rather strengthened than weakened by the 'metaphysical arguments.'[1] The 'physical argument' means the argument from design, which thus becomes the sole support of theology.

Hamilton naturally regards Brown as a mere sceptic in disguise. His theory of perception destroys his theory of personal identity. He has refused to accept our intuitive belief in one case, and cannot appeal to it in the other. He leaves no room for 'liberty of will,' and advances 'no argument in support of this condition of our moral being.'[2] Indeed, as Stewart complained, Brown, by identifying 'will' and 'desire,' has got rid of the will altogether. It is only natural that a man who is making a scientific study of the laws of human nature should find no room for an assertion that within a certain sphere there are no laws. A physiologist might as well admit that some vital processes are uncaused.

Brown thus illustrates the gravitation of the 'common-sense' philosophy to pure empiricism. He was the last in the genuine line of Scottish common-sense philosophers. When after what may be called the unphilosophical interregnum which followed Brown's death, Hamilton became professor, the Scottish tradition was blended with the very different theories derived from Kant. Upon Brown's version, the Scottish philosophy had virtually declared itself bankrupt. The substance of his teaching was that of the very school which his predecessors had attempted to confute, carefully as the fact might be hidden by dexterous rhetoric and manipulation of

[1] *Lectures*, p. 622 (Lect. xciii.).　　[2] *Dissertations*, p. 98.

technical terms. He agrees with Hume's premises, and adopts the method of Condillac. This was perceived by his most remarkable hearer. Carlyle went to Edinburgh at the end of 1809. Brown, 'an eloquent, acute little gentleman, full of enthusiasm about simple suggestions, relative, etc.,' was 'utterly unprofitable' to him, dis-spiriting 'as the autumn winds among withered leaves.'[1] In *Signs of the Times* (1829) Carlyle gave his view of the Scottish philosophy generally. They had, he says, started from the 'mechanical' premises suggested by Hume. 'They let loose instinct as an indiscriminatory bandog to guard them against (his) conclusions' : 'they tugged lustily at the logical chain by which Hume was so coldly towing them and the world into bottomless abysses of Atheism and Fatalism. But the chain somehow snapped between them, and the issue has been that nobody now cares about either—any more than about Hartley's, Darwin's, or Priestley's contemporaneous doings in England.'[2] The judgment goes to the root of the matter. The method of Reid inevitably led to this result. Consider the philosophy as based upon, if not identical with, an inductive science of psychology, and the end is clear. You may study and analyse the phenomena as carefully as you please ; and may, as the Scottish professors did, produce, if not a scientific psychology, yet a mass of acute prolegomena to a science. But the analysis can only reveal the actual combinations,

[1] Froude's *Carlyle*, p. 25.
[2] *Miscellanies* (1858), ii. 104. See, too, *Miscellanies*, i. 60, on German Literature, where he thinks that the Germans attacked the centre instead of the outworks of Hume's citadel. Carlyle speaks with marked respect of Dugald Stewart, who, if he knew what he was about, would agree with Kant.

chemical or mechanical, of thought. The ultimate principles which the teachers profess to discover are simply provisional ; products not yet analysed, but not therefore incapable of analysis. It was very desirable to point them out : an insistence upon the insufficiency of Hume's or Condillac's theories was a most valuable service ; but it was valuable precisely because every indication of such an unresolved element was a challenge to the next comer to resolve it by closer analysis. And thus, in fact, the intuitions, which had played so great a part with Reid, come in Brown's hands to be so clearly limited to the materials given by sensation or experience that any show of 'philosophy,' meaning an independent theory of the universe, was an illusory combination of fine phrases.[1]

II. JAMES MILL'S 'ANALYSIS'

James Mill's *Analysis of the Phenomena of the Human Mind* is on the one hand an exposition of the principles implied in Bentham's writings, and, on the other hand, a statement of the position from which the younger Mill started. J. S. Mill discussed the book with his father during its composition, and in 1869 he published a new edition, with elaborate notes by himself, George Grote, Professor Bain, and Andrew Findlater.[2] The com-

[1] In Caroline Fox's *Memories of Old Friends* (second edition), ii. 314, is a letter from J. S. Mill, expressing a very high opinion of Brown, whom he had just been re-reading (1840) with a view to the *Logic*. Brown's 'analysis in his early lectures of the amount of what we can learn of the phenomena of the world seems to me perfect, and his mode of inquiry into the mind is strictly founded upon that analysis.'
[2] I quote from this edition. Andrew Findlater (1810-1885), a Scottish school-master, and editor of Chambers's *Cyclopædia*, was a philologist (*Dictionary of National Biography*), and his notes chiefly concern Mill's adaptations of Horne Tooke.

mentary is of great importance in defining the relation between the two successors to the throne of Bentham.

Mill's *Analysis*, though not widely read, made a deep impression upon Mill's own disciples. It is terse, trenchant, and uncompromising. It reminds us in point of style of the French writers, with whom he sympathised, rather than of the English predecessors, to whom much of the substance was owing. The discursive rhetoric of Brown or Stewart is replaced by good, hard, sinewy logic. The writer is plainly in earnest. If over con-fident, he has no petty vanity, and at least believes every word that he says. Certain limitations are at once obvious. Mill, as a publicist, a historian, and a busy official, had not had much time to spare for purely philosophic reading. He was not a professor in want of a system, but an energetic man of business, wishing to strike at the root of the superstitions to which his political opponents appealed for support. He had heard of Kant, and seen what 'the poor man would be at.' Later German systems, had he heard of them, would have been summarily rejected by him as so much transcendental moonshine. The problem of philosophy was, he held, a very simple one, if attacked in a straight-forward, scientific method.

Mill, like his Scottish rivals, applies 'Baconian' prin-ciples. The inductive method, which had already been so fruitful in the physical sciences, will be equally effective in philosophy, and ever since Locke, philosophy had meant psychology. The 'philosophy of the mind' and the philosophy of the body may be treated as co-ordinate and investigated by similar methods. In the physical sciences we come ultimately to the laws of movement of

their constituent atoms. In the moral sciences we come in the same way to the study of 'ideas.' The questions, How do ideas originate? and how are they combined so as to form the actual state of consciousness? are therefore the general problems to be solved. Hume had definitely proposed the problem. Hartley had worked out the theory of association of ideas which Hume had already compared[1] to the universal principle of gravitation in the physical world ; and had endeavoured to show how this might be connected with physiological principles. Hartley's followers had been content to dwell upon the power of association. Abraham Tucker, Priestley, Erasmus Darwin, and Belsham represented this tendency, and were the normal antagonists of Reid and Stewart. In France the 'ideologists' mainly followed Condillac, and apparently knew nothing of Hartley. Mill, as his son testifies, had been profoundly influenced by Hartley's treatise—the 'really master-production,' as he esteemed it, 'in the philosophy of mind.'[2] Hartley's work, as the younger Mill thought, and the elder apparently agreed, was very superior to the 'merely verbal generalisation of Condillac.' James Mill, however, admired Condillac and his successors. In his article upon education, Mill traces the association theory to Hobbes, Locke, and Hume, the last of whom, he says, was succeeded by the two 'more sober-minded' philosophers, Condillac and Hartley ; while he especially praises Erasmus Darwin, Helvétius, and Cabanis. Mill, therefore, may be regarded as an inde-pendent ally of the ideologists whose influence upon Brown has been already noticed. Mill had not read Brown's *Lectures* when he began his *Analysis*, and after

[1] *Treatise* (bk. i. pt. i. sec. iv.). [2] J. S. Mill's *Autobiography*, p. 68.

reading them thought Brown 'but poorly read in the doctrine of association.'[1] He had, however, read the essay upon causation, which he rather oddly describes as 'one of the most valuable contributions to science for which we are indebted to the last generation.'[2] He accepted Brown's view *minus* the 'intuition.'

The pith of Mill's book is thus determined. His aim is to give a complete analysis of mental phenomena, and therefore to resolve those phenomena into their primitive constituent atoms. Here we have at once a tacit assumption which governs his method. Philosophy, speaking roughly, is by some people supposed to start from truths, and thus to be in some way an evolution of logic. According to Mill it must start from facts, and therefore from something not given by logic. To state clearly, indeed, the relation between truth and fact may suggest very intricate problems. Mill, at any rate, must find a basis in fact, and for him the ultimate facts must be feelings. The reality at least of a feeling is undeniable. The *Penser c'est sentir*, or the doctrine that all 'ideas' are transformed sensations is his starting-point. The word 'feeling,' according to him, includes every 'phenomenon of the mind.' 'Think,' he says elsewhere,[3] does not include all our experience, but 'there is nothing to which we could not extend the term "I feel."' He proceeds to infer that our experience is either a knowledge of the feelings separately, or 'a knowledge of the order in which they follow each other; and this is all.' We may add that the knowledge is the

feeling. Reid, Kant, and the Germans have indeed tried to show that there are feelings not derived from the sensations, but this, as Hartley and Condillac have shown, is a mistake. This is his first principle in a nutshell, and must give a clue to the various applications.

The next step is familiar. Hume had distinguished impressions and ideas. 'Ideas' are copies of previous 'impressions.' It is for psychology to say what are the laws by which they are related to their originals. The ultimate origin cannot be explained by psychology alone. Impressions are caused by the outward world acting in some way upon the mind; and the psychologist can only classify the various modes in which they present themselves. Mill therefore begins by the usual account of the five senses, through which comes all knowledge of the external world. He adds to Reid's list muscular sensations, and those derived from the internal organs, to which last Cabanis in particular had called attention. So far he is following the steps of his predecessors. He is, he says, simply asserting an 'indisputable' fact.[1] We have sensations and we have ideas, which are 'copies of sensations.' We may then consider how far these facts will enable us to explain the whole series of mental phenomena. 'Ideation,' which he suggests as a new word—the process by which a continuous series of thoughts goes on in our minds—is the general phenomenon to be considered. Without, as yet, pronouncing that sensations and copies of sensations will turn out to form the whole contents of our consciousness, he tries to show for what part of those contents they will account.

[1] *Fragment on Mackintosh*, p. 314.
[2] *Analysis*, ii. 42. 'Odd,' because Brown was six years younger than Mill.
[3] 'Education,' p. 6.

[1] *Analysis*, i. 52.

Here we come to the doctrine which for him and his school gave the key to all psychological problems. It was James Mill's real merit, according to his son, that he carried the principle of association of ideas further than it had been carried by Hartley or other predecessors.[1] The importance of the doctrine, indeed, is implied in the very statement of the problem. If it be true, or so far as it is true, that our consciousness reveals to us simply a series of 'sensations' and 'ideas,' the question must be how they are combined. 'Thought succeeds thought, idea follows idea incessantly,'[2] says Mill; and this phrase assumes 'thoughts' and ideas' to be separable atoms. How, then, do they come to coalesce into an apparently continuous stream? The mind is a stream of 'ideas.' If the stream is composed of drops, we must, of course, consider the drops as composing the stream. The question is, What laws can we assign which will determine the process of composition? The phrase 'association' admittedly expresses some general and very familiar truths. Innumerable connections may be established when there is no assignable ground of connection in the ideas themselves other than the fact of a previous contact. One idea not only calls up the other, but in some way generates a belief in an independent connection. We hear thunder, for example, and think of lightning. The two ideas are entirely distinct and separate, for they are due to different senses. Yet we not only think of lightning when we hear thunder, but we have no doubt that there is a causal connection. We believe in this connection, again, though no further explanation can be given of the fact. Thunder

and lightning have occurred together, and we infer that they will, and even must, occur together. When we examine our whole structure of belief, we find such 'arbitrary' associations pervade it in every direction. Language itself is learned simply by association. There is no connection whatever between the sound of the word 'man' and the 'ideas' which the word excites, beyond the fact that the sound has been previously heard when the ideas were excited. Here, then, is a phenomenon to be explained or generalised. We have in countless cases a certain connection established for which no further reason can be assigned than the fact of its previous occurrence. On such a ground, we believe that fire burns, that bread is wholesome, that stones fall; and but for such beliefs could know nothing of the outside world. 'Contingent' truth, therefore, or truth derived from mere contact, pervades, if it does not constitute, the whole fabric of our whole knowledge. To prove that all our knowledge is derived from experience is, according to Mill, to prove that in some sense or other association of ideas lies at the base of all intellectual processes. When Locke introduced a chapter upon 'Association of Ideas' into the fourth edition of his essay, he treated it as the exceptional case. Some ideas had a connection traceable by reason; others were only connected by 'chance and custom.' Association does not explain reasoning, only the deviations from reasoning. But with Hume and Hartley the relation is inverted. The principle, instead of being an exceptional case, is simply the universal rule from which logical connection may be deduced as a special case.

The facts upon which Mill relied, and the account of

[1] *Analysis*, i. xvii.   [2] *Ibid.* i. 70.

them which he gave, require notice and embodiment in any sound psychology. In some shape or other they form the starting-point of all later systems. Mill's vigorous application of his principle, worked out with imperfect appreciation and with many oversights, had therefrom, at least, the merit of preparing the ground for a more scientific method. In any case, however, his conclusions, so far as sound, must be placed in a different framework of theory. It becomes necessary to dwell chiefly upon the curious defects of his theory, if taken as he wished it to be taken, for an ultimate scientific statement. The fact that there is a synthesis and an analysis is expressed by 'association.' But what more can we say? What are the 'laws' of association? Unless some rule can be given, we shall get nothing that can be called a theory. One idea is not suggested by the other through any logical process. They are still 'conjoined' but not 'connected.' The connection, therefore, must be given by something different from the ideas themselves. Now the order of the original 'sensations' depends upon the 'objects of nature,' and is therefore left to 'physical philosophy.'[1] They occur, however, either in 'synchronous' or in 'successive' order. Then 'ideas' spring up in the order of 'sensations,' and this is the 'general law of association of ideas.'[2] The synchronous sensations produce synchronous ideas and the successive sensations successive ideas. Finally, the strength of the association between the ideas depends upon 'the vividness of the associated feelings, and the frequency of the association.'[3] Hume had said that association depended upon three

[1] *Analysis*, i. 71.   [2] *Ibid.* i. 78.   [3] *Ibid.* i. 83.

principles, 'contiguity in time and place,' 'causation,' and 'resemblance.' Contiguity in time corresponds to the successive, and contiguity in place to the synchronous, order. Causation, as Brown had finally proved,[1] means simply antecedence and consequence. 'Resemblance' remains and is, as Mill afterwards says,[2] a most important principle; but in an unlucky moment he is half inclined to reduce even 'resemblance' to 'contiguity.'[3] Resemblance is, he even suggests, merely 'a case of frequency,' because we generally see like things together. When we see one tree or sheep, we generally see several trees or sheep. J. S. Mill mildly remarks upon this quaint suggestion as the 'least successful simplification' in the book. He argues the point gravely. Sheep, it is clear, are not seen to be like because they often compose a flock, but are considered to be a flock because they are seen to be like. To do James Mill justice, he drops the argument as soon as he has struck it out. It is only worth notice as showing his aim. 'Likeness' seems to imply a relation dependent on the ideas themselves; not purely external and arbitrary. If we could get rid of likeness, all association would ultimately be 'contiguity.' 'The fundamental law of association,' as he says elsewhere,[4] 'is that when two things have been frequently found together, we never perceive or think of the one without thinking of the other.' The two ideas are associated as two balls are associated when they are in the same box. So far as they are themselves concerned, they might be separated without any alteration in their own properties. What, then, corresponds to the 'box'? Association depends upon relations of time and space.

[1] *Analysis*, ii. 42.   [2] *Ibid.* i. 270.   [3] *Ibid.* i. 111.   [4] *Ibid.* i. 362.

Things are associated by occurring in succession or together; the red colour of a rose is in the same place with the shape of the leaf; the scent is perceived at the same time with the colour. The thunder follows the lightning. What, then, he might ask, are 'time' and 'space'? Are they 'ideas' or 'sensations' or qualities of the objects? or, in any case, as supplying the ultimate principle of association, do they not require investigation? Before coming to that problem, however, we have to settle other knotty points. We must clear away illusions which seem to introduce something more than association. Elements of thought not at first sight expressible simply in terms of sensations and ideas must be analysed to show that they are only disguises for different combinations of the facts. Reasoning, according to most logicians, supposes, first, concepts, and therefore some process of classification of the objects of thought; and, secondly, some process of combining these concepts to bring out hitherto unknown truths. What, then, is the meaning of the general or abstract symbols employed in the process? Mill's provision of raw materials consists so far of sensations and ideas, which are worked up so as to form 'clusters' (the word is taken from Hartley) and 'trains.' This corresponds to synchronous and successive associations. How does the logical terminology express these 'clusters' and 'trains'? Mill answers by a theory of 'naming.' Language fulfils two purposes; it is required in order to make our ideas known to others; and in order to fix our own ideas. Ideas are fluctuating, transitory, and 'come into the mind unbidden.' We must catch and make a note of these shifting crowds of impal-

pable entities. We therefore put marks upon the simple sensations or upon the 'clusters.' We ticket them as a tradesman tickets bundles of goods in his warehouse, and can refer to them for our own purposes or those of others. As the number of objects to be marked is enormous, as there are countless ideas and clusters and clusters of clusters of endless variety to be arranged in various ways, one main object of naming is economy. A single word has to be used to mark a great number of individuals. This will account for such general names as are represented by noun-substantives: man, horse, dog, and so forth. Mill then proceeds, with the help of Horne Tooke, to explain the other grammatical forms. An adjective is another kind of noun marking a cross division. Verbs, again, are adjectives marking other sets of facts, and enabling us to get rid of the necessity of using a new mark for every individual or conceivable combination into clusters. J. S. Mill remarks that this omits the special function of verbs— their 'employment in predication.'[1] James Mill, however, has his own view of 'predication.' 'Man' is a mark of John, Peter, Thomas, and the rest. When I say 'John is a man,' I mean that 'man is another mark to that idea of which John is a mark.'[2] I am then able to make a statement which will apply to all the individuals, and save the trouble of repeating the assertion about each. 'Predication,' therefore, is simply a substitution of one name for another. So, for example, arithmetic is simply naming. What I call two and two, I also call four. The series of thoughts in this case is merely 'a series of names applicable to the same thing and meaning the

[1] *Analysis*, i. 154 *n.*   [2] *Ibid.* i. 161.

same thing.'[1] This doctrine, as J. S. Mill remarks, is derived from Hobbes, whom Leibniz in consequence called *plus quam nominalis*.[2] My belief that two and two make four explains why I give the same name to certain numbers ; but the giving the name does not explain the belief. Meanwhile, if a class name be simply the mark which is put upon a bundle of things, we have got rid of a puzzle. Mill triumphs over the unfortunate realists who held that a class meant a mysterious entity, existing somewhere apart from all the individuals in which it is embodied. There is really nothing mysterious ; a name is first the mark of an individual, the individual corresponding to a ' cluster ' or a set of ' simple ideas, concreted into a complex idea.'[3] Then the name and the complex idea are associated reciprocally ; each ' calls up ' the other. The complex idea is ' associated ' with other resembling ideas. The name becomes a talisman calling up the ideas of an indefinite number of resembling individuals, and the name applied to one in the first instance becomes a mark which calls up all, or, as he says, is the ' name of the whole combination.' Classification, therefore, ' is merely a process of naming, and is all resolvable into association.'[4] The peculiarity of this theory, as his commentators again remark, is that it expressly omits any reference to abstraction. The class simply means the aggregate of resembling individuals without any selection of the common attributes which are, in J. S. Mill's phrase, ' connoted ' by the class-name. Abstraction, as James Mill explains, is a subsidiary process, corresponding to the ' formation of *sub-species*.'[5]

[1] *Analysis*, i. 189.   [2] *Ibid*. i. 163 *n*.   [3] *Ibid*. i. 266.
[4] *Ibid*. i. 269.   [5] *Ibid*. i. 295.

Mill has now shown how the various forms of language correspond to ideas, formed into clusters of various orders by the principle of association. The next step will naturally be to show how these clusters are connected in the process of reasoning. Here the difficulty about predication recurs. J. S. Mill[1] remarks that his father's theory of predication consistently omits ' the element Belief.' When I say, ' John is a man,' I make an affirmation or assert a belief. I do not simply mean to call up in the mind of my hearer a certain ' cluster ' or two coincident clusters of ideas, but to convey knowledge of truths. The omission of reference to belief is certainly no trifle. Mill has classified the various ideas and combinations of ideas which are used in judgment, but the process of judgment itself seems to have slipped out of account. He may have given us, or be able to give us, a reasoned catalogue of the contents of our minds, but has not explained how the mind itself acts. It is a mere passive recipient of ideas, or rather itself a cluster of ideas cohering in various ways, without energy of its own. One idea, as he tells us, calls up another ' by its own associating power.'[2] Ideas are things which somehow stick together and revive each other, without reference to the mind in which they exist or which they compose. This explains his frequent insistence upon one assertion. As we approach the question of judgment he finds it essential. ' Having a sensation and having a feeling,' he says, ' are not two things.' To ' feel an idea and be conscious of that feeling are not two things ; the feeling and the consciousness are but two names for the same thing.'[3] So, again, ' to have a sensation and to believe

[1] *Analysis*, i. 162 *n*., 187 *n*.   [2] *Ibid*. ii. 21.   [3] *Ibid*. i. 224-25.

that we have it, are not distinguishable things.'[1] Locke's reflection thus becomes nothing but simple consciousness, and having a feeling is the same as attending to it.[2] The point is essential. It amounts to saying that we can speak of a thought as though it were simply a thing.

Thus belief not only depends upon, but actually *is* association. ' It is not easy,' he says, ' to treat of memory, belief, and judgment separately.'[3] As J. S. Mill naturally asks, ' How is it possible to treat of belief without including in it memory and judgment?' Memory is a case of belief, and judgment an ' act of belief.'[4] To James Mill, however, it appears that as these different functions all involve association, they may be resolved into varying applications of that universal power. Memory involves ' an idea of my present self ' and an ' idea of my past self,' and to remember is to ' run over the intervening states of consciousness called up by association.'[5] Belief involves association at every step. The belief in external objects is, as ' all men admit ' . . . ' wholly resolvable into association.'[6] ' That a cause means and can mean nothing to the human mind but constant antecedence ' (and therefore ' inseparable association,' as he thinks) ' is no longer a point in dispute.'[7] Association, it is true, may produce wrong as well as right beliefs ; right beliefs when ' in conformity with the connections of things,'[8] and wrong beliefs when not in conformity. In both cases the belief is produced by ' custom,' though, happily, the right custom is by far the

[1] *Analysis*, i. 342.   [2] *e.g. Ibid*. ii. 176.   [3] *Ibid*. i. 341.
[4] *Ibid*. i. 342 *n*.   [5] *Ibid*. i. 331.   [6] *Ibid*. i. 345.
[7] *Ibid*. i. 352.   [8] *Ibid*. i. 381.

commonest. The ' strength of the association follows the frequency.' The crow flies east as well as west ; but the stone always falls downwards.[1] Hence I form an ' inseparable association ' corresponding to a belief in gravitation, but have no particular belief about the direction of a crow's flight.

This gives the doctrine of ' indissoluble association ' —the pivot of the whole scheme—the doctrine, says J. S. Mill, which, ' if it can be proved, is the greatest of all the triumphs of the Association Philosophy.'[2] The younger Mill always insisted upon the vast importance of the principle ; but he here admits a difficulty. In a long note[3] upon James Mill's chapter on ' Belief,' conspicuous for his usual candour, he confesses the inadequacy of his father's view. The comment indicates the point of divergence and yet shows curiously the ground common to both. James Mill's theory states facts in some sense undeniable. Our ' ideas ' cohere and combine to form a tissue : an imagery or series of pictures which form the content and are somehow the ground of our beliefs. The process of formation clearly involves ' association.' The scent of the rose is associated with the colour : both with the visible form and so forth. But is this process the same thing as believing, or have we to explain the belief by some mental activity different from, however closely connected with, the imagination, or in his phrase the ' ideation ' ? Here J. S. Mill finds a difficulty. The statement, ' I believe that thunder will follow lightning,' is something more than the statement, ' the sight suggests or calls up the sound.' The mental picture considered by itself may be described as a fact,

[1] *Analysis*, i. 363.   [2] *Ibid*. i. 402.   [3] *Ibid*. i. 402-23.

without considering what belief, or whether any belief, is implied. J. S. Mill therefore makes a distinction intended to clear up his father's confusion. There is a difference, he says, between remembering 'a real fact' and remembering a 'thought.'[1] He illustrates this by the difference between the idea of Lafayette and the idea of Falstaff. Lafayette was real, and had been seen by the rememberer. Falstaff is a figment who, having never existed, can never have been seen. Yet the idea of Falstaff may be quite as vivid as the idea of Lafayette. What, then, is the difference between the two states of mind? One, says J. S. Mill, is a belief about 'real facts'; the other about 'thoughts.' This, he observes, corresponds to James Mill's distinction between a 'sensation' and an 'idea,'[2] a difference which he had admitted to be 'primordial.' Then, says J. S. Mill, we may as well admit that there is an 'element' in the remembrance of a real fact not implied in the remembrance of a thought and not dependent on any difference in the 'ideas' themselves. It, too, may be taken as 'primordial,' or incapable of further analysis. This doctrine becomes important in some of Mill's logical speculations,[3] and is connected with his whole theory of belief in an external world. It has an uncomfortable likeness to Reid's 'common-sense' view, and even to the hated 'intuitionism'; and Mill deserves the more credit for his candour.

Meanwhile it seems clear that the criticism implies an important confusion. The line of distinction is drawn in

[1] *Analysis*, i. 423.   [2] *Ibid.* i. 413, 419.
[3] See especially his account of definition, *Logic*, bk. i. ch. viii., and the problem about the serpent and the dragon.

the wrong place. So far as the simple 'imagination' is concerned, there may be no question of belief or disbelief. The picture of Falstaff or of Lafayette, a horse or a centaur, arises equally, and is put together, let us suppose, by simple association. But as soon as I think about either I believe or disbelieve, and equally whether I judge the object to be a thought or to be a 'real fact,' whether I say that I could have seen Lafayette, or that I could not have seen Falstaff. It is not a question between reality and unreality, but between two classes of reality. A dream is a real dream, just as a man is a real man. The question is simply where or how it exists, not whether it exists. The picture is, in one case, put together by my mind; in the other, due to a stimulus from without; but it exists in both cases; and belief is equally present whether I put it in one class of reality or the other: as we form a judgment equally when we pronounce a man to be lying, and when we pronounce him to be speaking the truth. J. S. Mill seems to suppose that association can explain the imagination of a centaur or a Falstaff, but cannot explain the belief in a horse or Lafayette. The imagination or 'ideation,' he should have said, accounts in both cases for the mere contents of the thought; but in neither case can it by itself explain the judgment as to 'reality.' That is to say, James Mill may have described accurately a part of the process by which the mental picture is constructed, but has omitted to explain the action of the mind itself. Belief, we may agree, is a 'primordial' or ultimate faculty; but we must not interpret it as belief in a 'real fact' as distinguished from belief in 'a thought': that is a secondary and incidental distinction.

This confusion, as I have said, apparently prevents J. S. Mill from seeing how deeply his very frank admissions cut into the very structure of his father's system. He has, as I have said, remarked upon the singular absence of any reference to 'belief,' 'abstraction,' and so forth; but he scarcely observes how much is implied by the omission. His criticism should have gone further. James Mill has not only omitted a faculty which enables us to distinguish between 'thoughts' and 'things,' images of fancy and pictures of reality, but also the faculty which is equally present whenever we properly think instead of simply seeing images passively; and equally whether we refer an image to fact or fancy. His 'analysis of the mind' seems to get rid of the mind itself.

The omission becomes important at the next step. 'Under the modest title of an explanation of the meaning of several names,' says his son, James Mill discusses 'some of the deepest and most intricate questions in all metaphysics.' A treatise on chemistry might almost as well be 'described as an explanation of the names, air, water, potass, sulphuric acid, and so forth.'[1] Why does the chapter come in this place and in this peculiar form? Probably because James Mill was partly conscious of the inadequacy of his previous chapters. The problems which he has been considering could not be adequately treated by regarding ideas as 'things' bound together by association. What, after all, is a proposition? What is meant by 'true' or 'false,' as distinguished from real and unreal? If an association actually *is* a truth, what is the difference between right and wrong associations? Both

[1] *Analysis*, ii. 2.

are facts, and the very words 'right' and 'wrong,' that is, true and false, apply not to facts but to propositions.[1] The judgment is tested in some way by correspondence to the 'order of Nature,' or of our sensations and ideas. What precisely is meant by this order? So far as we have gone, it seems as if ideas might be combined in any order whatever, and the most various beliefs generated in different minds. Perhaps, however, the principle of association itself may reveal something as to the possible modes of coalescence. Mill makes contiguity an ultimate ground of association; and contiguity implies that things have certain relations expressible in terms of space and time and so forth. These primitive relations now come up for consideration, and should enable us to say more precisely what kind of order is possible. In fact, Mill now endeavours to analyse the meanings of such words as relation in general, time, space, number, likeness, personal identity and others. The effect of his analysis is that the principles, whatever they may be, which might be supposed to underlie association appear to be products of association. He begins by asking what is the meaning of 'relative terms.' Their peculiarity is that they 'always exist in pairs,' such as 'father and son,' 'high and low,' 'right and left.' 'If it is asked, Why do we give names in pairs? the general answer immediately suggests itself; it is because the things named present themselves in pairs, that is, are joined by association.'[2] J. S. Mill thinks that no part of the

[1] This point puzzles Destutt de Tracy. All error, he says, arises in judgments: 'Cependant les jugements, les perceptions de rapports, en tant que perceptions que nous avons actuellement, sont aussi certaines et aussi réelles que toutes les autres.'—*Éléments d'Idéologie* (1865), iii. 449.
[2] *Analysis*, ii. 6, 7.

Analysis is more valuable than the 'simple explanation' which follows. There is no 'mystical bond called a relation' between two things, but 'a very simple peculiarity in the concrete fact' marked by the names. In 'ordinary names of objects, the fact connoted by a name . . . concerns one object only'; in the case of relative names, 'the fact connoted concerns two objects, and cannot be understood without thinking of them both.' A 'fact concerning an object' is a curiously awkward expression; but one point is clear. If the two objects concerned are the same, whether considered apart or together, the 'relation' must be something more than the facts, and therefore requires to be specified. If they are, in fact, one thing, or parts of a continuous process, we must ask how they come to be distinguished, and what ground there is for speaking of association. James Mill, by considering the problem as a mere question of 'names,' seems to intimate that the relation is a mere figment. In fact, as J. S. Mill perceives, the 'explanations' become nugatory. They simply repeat the thing to be explained. He begins with 'resemblance.' To feel two things to be alike is, he says, the same thing as to have the two feelings. He means to say, apparently, that when there are two 'ideas' there is not also a third idea of 'likeness.' That would be what Bentham called a 'fictitious entity.' But this cannot 'explain' the likeness of the ideas. 'Their being alike,' as his son interprets, 'is nothing but their being felt to be alike— which does not help us.'[1] So 'antecedence and consequence' are 'explained' by saying that one of two feelings calls up the other; or, as the son again remarks,

[1] *Analysis*, ii. 18 n.

antecedence is explained by antecedence, and succession by succession. Antecedence and consequence, like likeness and unlikeness, must therefore, according to J. S. Mill, be 'postulated as universal conditions of Nature, inherent in all 'our feelings whether of external or internal consciousness.'[1] In other words, apparently, time is an ultimate form of thought. Time and space, generally, as James Mill thinks, are the 'abstract names' respectively of successive and simultaneous order, which become 'indissolubly associated with the idea of every object.'[2] Space, of course, is said to be a product of touch and muscular sensations, and the problem as to how these varying sensations and these alone give rise to apparently necessary and invariable beliefs is not taken into consideration. Mill is here dealing with the questions which Kant attempted to answer by showing how the mind imposes its forms upon sense-given materials, forms them into concepts, and combines the concepts into judgments and reasoning. Mill evades the mysterious and transcendental at the cost of omitting reason altogether. He represents the result of accepting one horn of a dilemma, which presses upon philosophies of loftier pretensions. Those who accept the other horn speak of a 'fact' as though it were a truth, and argue as though the world could be spun out of pure logic, or a tissue be made of relations without any things to be related. Mill, with scarcely a glance at such doctrines, tries systematically to speak of a truth as if it were a fact. The world for him is made up of ideas sticking together; and nothing else exists. The relation is the fact; belief is the association; consciousness and reflection, considered

[1] *Analysis*, ii. 24 n.   [2] *Ibid.* ii. 132-33.

apart, are nothing but the sensations, ideas, clusters, and trains. The attempt to base all truth upon experience, to bring philosophy into harmony with science was, as I hold, perfectly right. Only, upon these assumptions it could not be carried out. Mill had the merit which is implied even by an unsuccessful attempt to hold by fact. He raises a number of interesting questions; and I think that it is more remarkable that so many of his observations have still an interest for psychologists than that so much is obviously wrong. Mill, it may be said, took an essay upon association for a treatise upon psychology in general. He was writing what might be one important chapter in such a treatise, and supposes that he has written the whole, and can deduce 'philosophy' from it, if, indeed, any philosophy can be said to remain. Meanwhile, I may observe, that by pushing his principles to extremes, even his 'association' doctrine is endangered. His *Analysis* seems to destroy even the elements which are needed to give the simplest laws of association. It is rather difficult to say what is meant by the 'contiguity,' 'sequence,' and 'resemblance,' which are the only conditions specified, and which he seems to explain not as the conditions but as the product of association. J. S. Mill perceived that something was wanting which he afterwards tried to supply. I will just indicate one or two points, which may show what problems the father bequeathed to the son. James Mill, at one place, discusses the odd problem 'how it happens that all trains of thought are not the same.'[1] The more obvious question is, on his hypothesis, how it happens that any two people have the same beliefs, since the beliefs are made of the most

[1] *Analysis*, ii. 67-69.

varying materials. If, again, two ideas when associated remain distinct, we have Hume's difficulty. Whatever is distinguishable, he argued, is separable. If two ideas simply lie side by side, as is apparently implied by 'contiguity,' so that each can be taken apart without change, why should we suppose that they will never exist apart, or, indeed, that they should ever again come together? The contiguity does not depend upon them, but upon some inscrutable collocation, of which we can only say that it exists now. This is the problem which greatly occupied J. S. Mill.

The 'indissoluble' or 'inseparable' association, which became the grand arcanum of the school, while intended to answer some of these difficulties, raises others. Mill seems to insist upon splitting a unit into parts in order that it may be again brought together by association. So J. S. Mill, in an admiring note, confirms his father's explanation ('one of the most important thoughts in the whole treatise') of the infinity of space.[1] We think space infinite because we always 'associate' position with extension. Surely space is extension; and to think of one without the other implies a contradiction. We think space infinite, because we think of a space as only limited by other space, and therefore indefinitely extensible. There is no 'association,' simply repetition. Elsewhere we have the problem, How does one association exclude another? Only, as J. S. Mill replies, when one idea includes the idea of the absence of the others.[2] We cannot combine the ideas of a plane and a convex surface. Why? Because we have never had both sets of sensations together. The 'commencement' of one set has

[1] *Analysis*, ii. 113 n.   [2] *Ibid.* i. 97 n.

always been 'simultaneous with the cessation of another set,' as, for instance, when we bend a flat sheet of paper. The difficulty seems to be that one fact cannot be contradictory of another, since contradiction only applies to assertions. When I say that A is above B, however, I surely assert that B is below A ; and I cannot make both assertions about A and B at the same time without a contradiction. To explain this by an association of simultaneous and successive sensations seems to be a curiously roundabout way of 'explaining.' Every assertion is also a denial ; and, if I am entitled to say anything, I am enabled without any help from association to deny its contradictory. On Mill's showing, the assertion and the denial of its contradiction, instead of being identical, are taken to be two beliefs accidentally associated. Finally, I need only make one remark upon the fundamental difficulty. It is hard to conceive of mere loose 'ideas' going about in the universe at large and sticking accidentally to others. After all, the human being is in true sense also an organised whole, and his constitution must be taken into account in discovering the laws of 'ideation.' This is the point of view to which Mill, in his anxiety to get rid of everything that had a savour of *a priori* knowledge about it, remains comparatively blind. It implies a remarkable omission. Mill's great teacher, Hartley, had appealed to physiology in a necessarily crude fashion. He had therefore an organism : a brain or a nervous system which could react upon the external world and modify and combine sensations. Mill's ideas would have more apparent connection if they could be made to correspond to 'vibratiuncles' or physical processes of some kind. But this part of Hartley's hypothesis had been dropped :

and all reality is therefore reduced to the whirl of vagrant and accidentally cohering ideas in brains and clusters. His one main aim is to get rid of everything that can be called mystical and to trace all mental processes to 'experience,' as he understands experience—to show that we are never entitled to assert that two ideas may not be joined in any way whatever.

The general tendency of the 'Association Philosophy' is sufficiently clear. It may be best appreciated by comparing it to the method of the physical sciences, which it was intended to rival. The physicist explains the 'laws of nature' by regarding a phenomenon as due to the varying arrangements of an indefinite multitude of uniform atoms. I need not ask whether these atoms are to be regarded as realities, even the sole realities, or, on the other hand, as a kind of logical scaffolding removable when the laws are ascertained. In any case, the assumption is necessary and most fruitful in the search for accurate and quantitative formulæ. Mill virtually assumes that the same thing can be done by breaking up the stream of consciousness into the ideas which correspond to the primitive atoms. What precisely these atoms may be, how the constantly varying flow of thought can be resolved into constituent fractions, is not easy to see. The physicist at least supposes his atoms to have definite space relations, but there is nothing clearly corresponding to space in the 'ideas.' They are capable of nothing but co-existence, sequence, and likeness ; but the attempt to explain the meaning of those words ends in nothing but repeating them. One result is the curious combination of the absolute and the indefinitely variable. We get absolute statements because the ultimate constituents are

taken to be absolutely constant. We have indefinite variability because they may be collocated in any conceivable or inconceivable way. This becomes evident when we have to do with organisms of any kind : with characters or societies an organism varies, but varies along definite lines. But, on Mill's showing, the organic relations correspond to the indefinitely variable. Education is omnipotent ; state constitutions can be manufactured at will, and produce indefinite consequences. And yet he can lay down laws of absolute validity, because he seems to be deducing them from one or two formulæ corresponding to the essential and invariable properties of the ultimate unit—whether man or ideas. From this follows, too, the tendency to speak as if human desires corresponded to some definite measurable things, such as utility in ethics, value in political economy, and self-interest in politics. This point appears in the application of Mill's theories to the moral sciences.

III. JAMES MILL'S ETHICS

James Mill in his ethical doctrine follows Bentham with little variation ; but he shows very clearly what was the psychology which Bentham virtually assumed. I may pass very briefly over Mill's theory of conduct[1] in general. The 'phenomena of thought,' he says, may be divided into the 'intellectual' and the 'active' powers. Hitherto he has considered 'sensations' and 'ideas' merely as existing ; he will now consider them as 'exciting to action.'[2] The phenomena consist in

---

[1] Professor Bain points out that Mill is occasionally confused by his ignorance of the triple division, intellect, feelings : and will, introduced in the next generation.—*Analysis*, ii. 180 *n*.   [2] *Analysis*, ii. 181-83.

both cases of sensations and ideas, combined into 'clusters,' and formed into trains 'according to the sense laws.' We have now to consider the ideas as active, and 'to demonstrate the simple laws into which the phenomena of human life, so numerous and apparently so diversified, may all be easily resolved.'

A desire is an 'idea' of a pleasant sensation ; an 'aversion' an idea of painful sensation. The idea and the sensation are not two things, but two names for the same thing. Desire, again, has a 'tacit reference to future time' when applied to a given case. We associate these pains and pleasures with the causes ; and in the important case our own actions are the causes. Thus the association produces the motive, and the readiness to obey the motive is, as Bentham says, the 'disposition.' Then, following Hartley, Mill explains the will. Bodily actions are muscular contractions, which are slowly coordinated by habit—association, of course, acting at every stage of the process. Now, it is a plain fact that muscular contractions follow 'ideas.' It is easy, then, to see how the 'idea of a pleasure should excite the idea of the action which is the cause of it ; and how, when the idea exists, the action should follow.'[1] An 'end' is a pleasure desired, and gives the 'motive.' When we start from the motive and get the pleasure the same association is called 'will.' 'Free-will' is of course nonsense. We have a full account of the human mechanism, and can see that it is throughout worked by association, admitting the primary fact of experience that the idea causes the muscular contraction.

This, and the ethical conclusions which follow, sub-

---

[1] *Analysis*, ii. 351.

stantially coincide with Bentham's doctrine, or supply the first principles from which Bentham might be deduced. A fuller exposition of the ethics is given in the *Fragment on Mackintosh*. Mackintosh, in 1829, wrote a Dissertation upon 'Ethical Philosophy,' for the *Encyclopædia Britannica*.[1] The book stirred Mill's 'indignation against an evil-doer.'[2] He wrote a *Fragment on Mackintosh*, which was suppressed for a time in consequence of his antagonist's death in 1832, but published in the year of his own death, 1835.[3] According to Professor Bain, the book was softened in consequence of remonstrances from Bickersteth. It would be curious to see the previous version. Professor Bain says that there are 'thousands' of books which contain 'far worse severities of language.' I confess that I cannot remember quite 'a thousand.' It is at least difficult to imagine more unmitigated expressions of contempt and aversion. Mackintosh, says Mill, uses 'macaroni phrases,' 'tawdry talk,' 'gabble'; he gets 'beyond drivelling' into something more like 'raving'; he 'deluges' us with 'unspeakable nonsense.' 'Good God!' sums up the comment which can be made upon one sentence.[4] Sir James, he declares, 'has got into an intellectual state so thoroughly depraved that I doubt whether a parallel to it is possible to be found.'[5] There is scarcely a mention of Mackintosh without an insult. A partial explanation of Mill's wrath may be suggested by the chapter upon Bentham. Mackintosh there accused the Utilitarians generally of

[1] Also privately printed in 1830. Later editions, edited by Whewell, appeared in 1836, 1862, 1873. I quote the last. See M. Napier's *Correspondence*, pp. 57-59, for the composition.
[2] Mill's *Fragment* (Preface).   [3] See Bain's *James Mill*, pp. 374, 415-18.
[4] *Fragment*, pp. 190, 192, 213, 298, 307, 326.   [5] *Ibid*. p. 210.

'wantonly wounding the most respectable feelings of mankind'; of 'clinging to opinions because they are obnoxious'; of taking themselves to be a 'chosen few,' despising the multitude, and retorting the dislike which their arrogance has provoked by using still more exasperating language.[1] He suggested that they should do more justice to 'the Romillys and the Broughams,' who had been the real and judicious reformers; and he illustrated the errors of Bentham by especial reference to Mill's arguments upon government and education. There had long been an antipathy. Mackintosh, said Mill in 1820, 'lives but for London display; *parler et faire parler de lui* in certain circles is his heaven.'[2]

Mackintosh would have been most at home in a professorial chair. He was, indeed, professor at Haileybury from 1818 to 1824, and spoken of as a probable successor to Brown at Edinburgh. But he could never decidedly concentrate himself upon one main purpose. Habits of procrastination and carelessness about money caused embarrassment which forced him to write hastily. His love of society interfered with study, and his study was spread over an impossible range of subjects. His great abilities, wasted by these infirmities, were seconded by very wide learning. Macaulay describes the impression which he made at Holland House.[3] He passed among his friends as the profound philosopher; the man of universal knowledge of history; of ripe and most impartial judgment in politics; the oracle to whom all men might appeal with confidence, though a little too apt to find out that all sides were in the right. When he went to India

[1] *Ethical Philosophy* (1873), pp. 188, 193.
[2] M. Napier's *Correspondence*, p. 25.   [3] *Essay on Sir J. Mackintosh*.

he took with him some of the scholastic writers and the works of Kant and Fichte, then known to few Englishmen. One of Macaulay's experiences at Holland House was a vision of Mackintosh verifying a quotation from Aquinas.[1] It must have been delightful. The ethical 'dissertation,' however, had to be shortened by omitting all reference to German philosophy, and the account of the schoolmen is cursory. It is easy to see why the suave and amiable Mackintosh appeared to Mill to be a 'dandy' philosopher, an unctuous spinner of platitudes to impose upon the frequenters of Holland House, and hopelessly confused in the attempt to make compromises between contradictory theories. It is equally easy to see why to Mackintosh the thoroughgoing and strenuous Mill appeared to be a one-sided fanatic, blind to the merits of all systems outside the narrow limits of Benthamism, and making even philanthropy hateful. Had Mackintosh lived to read Mill's *Fragment*, he would certainly have thought it a proof that the Utilitarians were as dogmatic and acrid as he had ever asserted.

Mackintosh's position in ethics explains Mill's antagonism. Neither Aquinas nor Kant nor Fichte influenced him. His doctrine is the natural outcome of the Scottish philosophy. Hutcheson had both invented Bentham's sacred formula, and taught the 'Moral Sense' theory which Bentham attacked. To study the morality from the point of view of 'inductive psychology' is to study the moral faculty, and to reject the purely 'intellectual' system. To assign the position of the moral faculty in the psychological system is to show its utility. On the other hand, it was the very

[1] *Essay on Lord Holland*.

aim of the school to avoid the sceptical conclusions of Hume in philosophy, and in ethics to avoid the complete identification of morality with utility. There must be a distinction between the judgments, 'this is right,' and 'this is useful'; even 'useful to men in general.' Hence, on the one hand, morality is immediately dictated by a special sense or faculty, and yet its dictates coincide with the dictates of utility. I have spoken of this view as represented by Dugald Stewart; and Brown had, according to his custom, moved a step further by diminishing the list of original first principles, and making 'virtue' simply equivalent to 'feelings' of approval and disapproval.[1] Virtue, he said, is useful; the utility 'accompanies our moral approbation; but the perception of that utility does not constitute our moral approbation, nor is it necessarily presupposed by it.'[2] He compares the coincidence between virtue and utility to Leibniz's pre-established harmony.[3] The position is familiar. The adaptation of an organism to its conditions may be taken either as an explanation of its development or as a proof of a creative purpose.

Mackintosh takes nearly the same position. Ethical inquiries, he says, relate to 'two perfectly distinct subjects.' We have the problem of the 'criterion' (What is the distinction between right and wrong?) and the problem of the 'moral sentiments' (What are the feelings produced by the contemplation of right and wrong?). In treating of the feelings, again, we must avoid the confusion caused in the older philosophy by

[1] *Lectures*, p. 500 (Lect. lxxv.).   [2] *Ibid*. p. 519 (Lect. lxxvii.).
[3] *Ibid*. p. 522 (Lect. lxxviii.).

the reduction of 'feeling' to 'thought.'[1]   Reason and
sensation are distinct though inseparably combined ; and
hence, he argues, it is a fallacy to speak with Clarke as
if reason could by itself be a motive.   An argument to
influence conduct must always be in the last resort an
appeal to a 'feeling.'[2]   It is idle to tell a man that
conduct is infamous unless he *feels* infamy to be painful.
We have then to ask what are the feelings which prompt
to morality.   So far as the criterion is concerned, Mackintosh fully agrees with Hume, whose theory that
'general utility constitutes a general ground of moral
distinctions can never be impugned until some example
can be produced of a virtue generally pernicious or a vice
generally beneficial.'[3]   Hume, however, overlooks the
'rightful supremacy of the moral faculty over every other
principle of human action.'   Mackintosh thought that
his best service, as he told Macvey Napier,[4] had been his
'endeavour to slip in a foundation under Butler's doctrine
of the supremacy of the conscience, which he left baseless.'
To slip in a foundation is a very delicate operation in
logical as in material architecture ; and the new foundation seems here to be in danger of inverting the edifice.
The 'supremacy of conscience'[5] means with him that
the 'moral sentiments' form a separate class.   They are
the feelings with which we contemplate voluntary actions
in general, and therefore those aroused by the character
and conduct of the agent.   Mackintosh thus takes an
æsthetic view of morality.   We have a 'moral taste' or
perception of beauty.   The same qualities which make
a horse beautiful make him also swift and safe, but we

[1] *Ethical Philosophy* (Hobbes), pp. 62-64.   [2] *Ibid.* p. 85.
[3] *Ibid.* p. 145.   [4] *Ibid.* p. 9.   [5] *Ibid.* p. 120.

perceive the beauty without thinking of the utility, or
rather when we do not think of it.   So we admire a hero
or martyr for the beauty of his character without reference
to his services to us.[1]   This moral taste, though not
identical with the conscience, becomes 'absorbed into it.'
The conscience differs from the 'moral taste' because it
acts upon the will.   But its supremacy seems to be this
quality which it shares with or derives from the taste—
its immediate and spontaneous operation.   It is, he seems
to mean, a direct perception of beauty in character applied
to the regulation of conduct.   Virtue corresponds to an
instinctive and so far ultimate appreciation of beauty of
character.   Mackintosh insists upon this intrinsic charm
of virtue in the language which struck Mill as simply
foppish affectation.   The pleasure of 'benevolence'
itself, says Mackintosh, is infinitely superior to the
pleasures to which it may lead.   Could it become
'lasting and intense,' it would convert the heart into
a heaven.[2]   To love virtue, you must love it 'for its
own sake.'[3]   The delights of being virtuous (as he
interprets the phrase) are greater than any delight from
the consequences of virtue.   And he holds up as a model
Fletcher of Saltoun, who would 'lose his life to serve his
country, but would not do a base thing to save it.'[4]

How, then, is this view to be reconciled with the
unreserved admission of 'utility' as the 'criterion' of
right and wrong ?   One answer is that Mackintosh fully
accepts Hartley's doctrine of association.   He even
criticises previous philosophers for not pushing it far
enough.   He says that association, instead of merely

[1] *Ethical Philosophy*, pp. 14, 170.   [2] *Ibid.* p. 197.
[3] *Ibid.* p. 248.   [4] *Ibid.* p. 204.

combining a 'thought' and a 'feeling,' 'forms them into
a new compound, in which the properties of the component parts are no longer discoverable, and which may
itself become a substantive principle of human virtue.'[1]
The question of origin, therefore, is different from the
question of nature.   He follows Hartley in tracing the
development of various desires, and in showing how the
'secondary desires' are gradually formed from the
primitive by transference to different objects.[2]   We must
start from feelings which lie beneath any intellectual
process, and thus the judgment of utility is from the
first secondary.   We arrive at the higher feelings which
are 'as independent as if they were underived,'[3] and yet,
as happiness has been involved at every stage as an end
of each desire, it is no wonder that the ultimate result
should be to make the general happiness the end.   The
coincidence, then, of the criterion with the end of the
moral sentiments is 'not arbitrary,' but arises necessarily
from 'the laws of human nature and the circumstances
in which mankind are placed.'[4]   Hence we reach the
doctrine which 'has escaped Hartley as well as every
other philosopher.'[5]   That doctrine is that the moral
faculty is one ; it is compound, indeed, in its origin ; but
becomes an independent unit, which can no longer be
resolved even in thought into its constituent elements.

The doctrine approximates, it would seem, to Mill's ;
but was all the more unpalatable to him on that account.
The agreement implies plagiarism, and the difference
hopeless stupidity.   To Mill Bentham was the legitimate
development of Hartley, while to Mackintosh Bentham

[1] *Ethical Philosophy* p. 242.   [2] *Ibid.* p. 251.   [3] *Ibid.* p. 262.
[4] *Ibid.* p. 264.   [5] *Ibid.* p. 169.

was the plausible perverter of Hartley.   Mill regarded
Mackintosh as a sophist, whose aim was to mislead
honest Utilitarians into the paths of orthodoxy, and who
also ignored the merits of Mill himself.   'It was Mr.
Mill,' he says, 'who first made known the great importance of the principle of the indissoluble association' ;[1]
'Mr. Mill' who had taken up Hartley's speculations
and 'prosecuted the inquiry to its end.' ;[2] 'Mr. Mill'
who explained affections and motives and dispositions ;[3]
and 'Mr. Mill' who had cleared up mistakes about classification which 'had done more to perpetuate darkness
on the subject of mind than any other cause, perhaps than
all other causes taken together.'[4]   Sir James blundered
because he had not read Mill's book, as he pretended
to have done.   Mill does not say all this from vanity ;
he is simply stating an obvious matter of fact.

Mill's polemic against the Moral Sense theory, even
against a moral sense produced by association, reveals
the really critical points of the true Utilitarian doctrine.
Mill would cut down the moral sense root and branch.
The 'moral sense' means a 'particular faculty' necessary
to discern right and wrong.   But no particular faculty
is necessary to discern 'utility.'[5]   Hence the distinction
between the 'criterion' and the 'moral sentiments' is
absurd.   The utility is not the 'criterion' of the morality
but itself constitutes the morality.   To say that conduct
is right, according to the Utilitarians, is the same thing
as to say that it produces happiness.   If the moral sense
orders conduct opposed to the criterion, it is so far bad.

[1] *Fragment*, p. 173.   [2] *Ibid.* p. 323.   [3] *Ibid.* p. 221.
[4] *Fragment*, p. 247. Mackintosh quotes Mill's *Analysis* at p. 197. It had
only just appeared.   [5] *Fragment*, p. 11.

If it never orders such conduct, it is superfluous.
Happiness, as with Bentham, is a definite thing—a
currency of solid bullion; and 'virtue' means nothing
except as calculated in this currency. Mill, again, like
Bentham, regards the 'utility' principle as giving the sole
'objective' test. The complaint that it sanctions 'expediency' is a simple fallacy.

If you do not love virtue 'for its own sake,' said
Mackintosh, you will break a general law wherever the
law produces a balance of painful consequences. Mill
replies with great vigour.[1] All general rules, it is true,
imply exceptions, but only when they conflict with the
supreme rule. 'There is no exception to a rule of
morality,' says Mill, 'but what is made by a rule of
morality.'[2] There are numerous cases in which the
particular laws conflict; and one law must then be
broken. The question which to break must then be
decided by the same unequivocal test, 'utility.' If a
rule for increasing utility diminishes utility in a given
case, it must be broken in that case. Mackintosh's
Fletcher of Saltoun illustrates the point.[3] What is the
'base' thing which Fletcher would not do to save his
country? Would he not be the basest of men if he did
not save his country at any cost? To destroy half a
population and reduce the other half to misery has been
thought a sacrifice not too great for such an end. Would
not Mackintosh himself allow Fletcher, when intrusted
with an important fortress, to sacrifice the lives and properties of innocent people in defence of his position?[4]

[1] *Fragment*, p. 246, etc.   [2] *Ibid.* p. 246.   [3] *Ibid.* pp. 269, 270.
[4] Cf. Newman's *Apologia*. 'The Catholic Church holds it better for the
sun and moon to drop from heaven, for the earth to fail, and for all the
millions on it to die of starvation in extremest agony, so far as temporal

What, then, does the love of virtue 'for its own sake'
come to? If you refuse to save your country, because
you think the means base, your morality is mischievous,
that is, immoral. If, on the other hand, you admit that
the means cease to be base, the supposed supremacy is
an empty brag. The doctrine is then verbally maintained,
but interpreted so as to conform to the criterion of utility.
In other words, Mackintosh cannot reconcile his admission of utility as a 'criterion' with his support of a moral
sense entitled to override the criterion. Mackintosh's
moral sense is meant to distinguish the moral motive
from 'expediency.' To this, again, Mill has a very
forcible answer. A man is blameable who makes exceptions to laws in his own private interest. But if a man
consistently and invariably acted for the 'greatest happiness
of the greatest number,' and paid no more attention to
his own happiness than to other people's, he would certainly have a very lofty and inflexible test, assuming—as
we must allow Mill to assume—that we can calculate the
effect of conduct upon happiness at large. Again, upon
the assumption that 'moral' is equivalent to 'felicific,' we
get a general rule entitled to override any individual
tastes or fancies, such as Mill supposes to be meant by
the 'Moral Sense.' The rule is derived from the interests
of all, and gives an ultimate 'objective criterion.' J. S.
Mill, describing his father's system, observes that the
teaching of such a man was not likely to err on 'the side

affliction goes, than that one soul,—I will not say should be lost, but should
commit one single venial sin, tell one wilful untruth, or should steal one poor
farthing without excuse.' I should steal the farthing and assume the 'excuse.'
I confess that I would not only lie, but should think lying right under the
supposed circumstances.

of laxity or indulgence.'[1] It certainly did not. And, in
fact, his criterion, however obtained, had in his eyes the
certainty of a scientific law. This or that is right as
surely as this or that food is wholesome. My taste has
nothing to do with it. And, moreover, the criterion
certainly gives a moral ground. If I know that any
conduct will produce more happiness than misery that is
a moral reason for adopting it. A 'moral sense' which
should be radically inconsistent with that criterion, which
should order me to inflict suffering as suffering, or without some ulterior reason, would be certainly at fault.
Mackintosh indeed would have agreed to this, though,
if Mill was right, at the expense of consistency.

Mill, however, deduces from his criterion doctrines
which involve a remarkable paradox. The mode in
which he is led to them is characteristic of the whole
method. Mill, like Bentham, puts morality upon the
same plane with law. Conduct is influenced either by
the 'community in its conjunct capacity'—that is, by law;
or by 'individuals in their individual capacity'—that
is, by morality.[2] The sanction of one, we may infer,
is force; of the other, approval and disapproval. With
this we must take another Benthamite doctrine, of which
I have already spoken.[3] 'Mr. Bentham demonstrated,'
says Mill, 'that the morality of an act does not depend
upon the motive,' and, further, that it 'is altogether
dependent on the intention.'[4] Upon this he constantly
insists. Mackintosh's view that virtue depends upon
motive will be 'scorned by every man who has any
knowledge of the philosophy of the human mind. . . .

[1] *Autobiography*, p. 51.   [2] *Fragment*, p. 251.
[3] Vol. i. p. 257.   [4] *Fragment*, p. 161.

The virtue does not depend upon the motive. There is
no bad motive. Every motive is the desire of good;
to the agent himself or to some one else.'[1] He gives
an analysis of action to put the point beyond doubt.
Action supposes a 'motive,' a 'volition,' and an 'external
act' or muscular contraction. So far there is nothing
moral. But then an act has consequences, good or bad,
to human beings, which constitute its utility. To make it
moral, the agent must anticipate 'beneficial consequences,'
and must have no reason to anticipate a balance of evil
consequences. Intention means the calculation of consequences, and without that calculation there can be no
morality.[2] Hence the morality is equivalent to a
'conviction of the general utility' of the action.[3] 'All
this,' he concludes, 'is settled by universal consent. It is
vain, therefore, to think of disputing it.' One may,
however, ask what it means. I have already observed
that the view of the non-moral character of motive was a
natural corollary from the purely legal point of view. I
must now consider the results of applying it unreservedly
in the inappropriate sphere of ethics.

In the first place, the denial of any moral quality in
motive seems to be inconsistent with Mill's own principles.
The Utilitarian, according to him, holds that the moral law
is essentially the statement that certain conduct produces
general happiness. If, then, we ask, Who is a good man?
we first reply that he is a man whose conduct produces
happiness. Another conclusion is obviously necessary, and
is implied in Mill's statement that the 'intention' is
essential to morality. The man, that is, must foresee that
his conduct will produce happiness. The 'calculation' is

[1] *Fragment*, pp. 315-16.   [2] *Ibid.* p. 164.   [3] *Ibid.* pp. 320-22.

precisely what makes an action moral as well as accidentally useful. In other words, the man is good to whom the knowledge that an act will produce happiness is the same thing as a command to perform the act. The 'intention' could not affect conduct without the corresponding motive, and Mill can at times recognise the obvious consequence. The 'physical law' (meaning the law enforced by physical coercion), he says incidentally, has 'extrinsic' sanctions;[1] the moral law is different, because it sanctions good actions for their goodness. 'Moral approval' must therefore include approval of character. A man, to be moral, must be one who does useful things simply because they are useful. He must then, it would seem, be at least benevolent. The same thing is implied by the doctrine of 'intention' or 'calculation' An action may be useful or the reverse without being moral when the consequences are unknown to the agent. To make it moral he must know the consequences—for otherwise he is merely acting at random; and the foreseen consequences constitute the 'intention.' To this Mill adds that he must have taken into account the consequences which 'might have been foreseen.'[2] Otherwise we should have to excuse a man because he had neglected to calculate, whereas to calculate is the very essence of virtue. A man who fired a gun down a crowded street would not be excusable because he had not thought of the result. He 'ought' to have thought of it. The question of moral approval of any given action turns upon these questions. Did a man foresee evil consequences and disregard them? He is then cruel. Did he neglect to consider them? He is

[1] *Fragment*, p. 102. [2] *Ibid.* p. 162.

then culpably careless, though not actually malignant. Were the consequences altogether beyond the powers of reasonable calculation? Then he may be blameless. The whole moral question, therefore, depends upon the character indicated; that is, upon the motives which induce a man to calculate consequences and which determine his conduct when the calculation is made.

The truth is, I think, and it is characteristic of Mill's modes of analysis, that he is making an impossible abstraction. He is separating parts of a single process and treating them as independent. If actions are bad because they have bad consequences, motives are bad because they are causes of bad actions. You cannot suppress the effect without suppressing the cause, and therefore the cause of the cause. Mill relies chiefly upon one argument. The same conduct will produce the same consequences whatever the motives. That is undeniable. It is the same to me whether I am burnt because the persecutor loves my soul or because he hates me as a rebel to his authority. But when is conduct 'the same'? If we classify acts as the legislator has to classify them by 'external' or 'objective' relations, we put together the man who is honest solely from fear of the gallows and the man who is honest from hatred of stealing. So long as both act alike, the 'consequences' to their neighbours are alike. Neither is legally punishable. But if acts are classified by their motives, one is a rogue and the other virtuous; and it is only then that the question of morality properly arises. In that case, it is idle to separate the question of motive and consequences, because the character determines the motive and therefore the action. Nobody should have seen this more clearly than Mill as a good

'determinist.' Conduct and character are related as the convex and concave of the curve; conduct is simply the manifestation of character, and to separate them is absurd.

Why did he not see this? For reasons, I think, which illustrate his whole method. From a scientific point of view, the ethical problem raises the wide questions, What are the moral sentiments? and, What functions do they discharge in regard to the society or to its individual members? We might hold that morality is justified by 'utility' in the sense that the moral rules and the character which they indicate are essential to the welfare of the race or its individual constituents. But to Mill this proposition is interpreted as identical with the proposition that conduct must be estimated by its 'consequences.' We are to consider not the action itself, but its effects; and the effects are clearly independent of the motive when once the action has been done. We may therefore get a calculus of 'utility': general rules stating what actions will be useful considered abstractedly from their motives. The method, again, might be plausible if we could further assume that all men were the same and differed only in external circumstances. That is the point of view to which Mill, like Bentham, is always more or less consciously inclining. The moral and the positive law are equally enforced by 'sanctions'; by something not dependent upon the man himself, and which he is inclined to suppose will operate equally upon all men. Such language could be justifiable only of an average and uniform 'man,' a kind of constant unit, whose varying behaviour must always be explained by difference in circumstance. We have sufficiently seen the results elsewhere, and in this ethical doctrine they are especially manifest.

Mackintosh recognised the fact that morality is essentially a function of character. Mill cannot fully admit that, because he virtually assumes all character to be the same. Regarding morality as something co-ordinate with law, he does not perceive that the very possibility of law implies the moral instincts, which correspond to the constitution of character, and belong to a sphere underlying, not on the same plane with, the legislative sphere. They are the source of all order; not themselves the product of the order. It is impossible to deduce them, therefore, from the organisation which presupposes them. Now, in one direction, Mill's theory leads, as his son remarked, not to laxity but to excessive strictness. The 'criterion' is laid down absolutely. The 'moral sense' is rejected because it means an autocratic faculty, entitled to override the criterion by its own authority. To appeal to 'motives' is to allow the individual to make his own feeling the ultimate test of right and wrong. If we follow Mill in this we are not really assuming the moral neutrality of motive or the indifference, but an impossible profession of character. Men are not governed by abstract principles but by their passions and affections. The emotions, as Mackintosh rightly said, cannot be resolved into the mere logic. Utility may give the true criterion of morality, but it does not follow that the perception of utility is implied in moral conduct. The motives are good which in fact produce useful conduct, though the agent does not contemplate the abstract principle. It is impossible that men should be moved simply by a desire for the 'greatest happiness of the greatest number.' What does and always must guide men is their personal relation to the little circle which they actually influence. The good man is the man so constituted that he will spontaneously fulfil his duties. The moral law, that is, will be also the law of his character and conduct. The mother is good because she loves her child, not because she sees that care of her child is dictated by the general maxim of utility. The 'utility' of character means the fitness of the agent to be an efficient member of the social structure to which he belongs. In particular cases this may lead to such problems as that of Fletcher of Saltoun. His sense of honour and his general benevolence, though both useful, might come into collision; and the most difficult of all questions of casuistry arise from such conflicts between private and public affections. Mill is justified in holding that a sense of honour cannot give an ultimate and autocratic decision. Under some pretext or other, we shall have to ask the Utilitarian question whether on the whole it may not be causing more misery than the virtuous action is worth. But that only means that the character must be so balanced as to give due weight to each motive; not that we can abstract from character altogether, as though human beings could be mere colourless and uniform atoms, embodying abstract formulæ.

Mill is following Bentham, and only brings out more clearly the psychological assumptions. A man, he says, acts from the 'same motive' whether he steals five shillings or earns it by a day's labour. The motive, in this sense, regards only one consequence, whereas the 'intention' regards all. The 'motive,' that is, is only one of the motives or a part of the character, and this way of speaking is one of the awkward results

of turning 'motives' into 'things.' The obvious answer is that which Mill himself makes to Mackintosh. Mackintosh and Butler, he thinks, personify particular 'appetites.'[1] It is not really the 'conscience' which decides, but the man. That is quite true, and similarly it is the whole man who steals or works, not the 'personified' motive; and it is accordingly from the whole character that we judge. We have to consider the relation of the love of five shillings to the other qualities of industry and honesty. The same view appears in Mill's characteristic dislike of 'sentimentalism.' Wishing to attack Mackintosh's rhetoric about the delight of virtuous feeling, he for once quotes a novel to illustrate this point. When Parson Adams defined charity as a 'generous disposition to relieve the distressed,' Peter Pounce approved; 'it is, as you say, a disposition, and does not so much consist in the act as in the disposition to do it.'[2] When, therefore, Mackintosh says that he finds it difficult to separate the virtue from the act, Mill replies that nothing is easier. The virtue is 'in the act and its consequences'; the feeling a mere removable addition. Apparently he would hold that the good Samaritan and the Pharisee had the same feeling, though it prompted one to relieve the sufferer and the other to relieve himself of the sight of the sufferer. They had, of course, a feeling in common, but a feeling which produced diametrically opposite effects, because entering into totally different combinations.

If Mill's doctrine leads to an impossible strictness in one direction, it leads to less edifying results in another. We have omitted 'motive' and come to the critical

[1] *Analysis*, p. 73.   [2] *Fragment*, p. 209.

question, How, after all, is the moral code to be enforced? By overlooking this question and declaring 'motive' to be irrelevant, we get the paradox already accepted by Bentham. His definition of virtue is action for the good of others as well as of ourselves. In what way is the existence of such action to be reconciled with this doctrine? What are the motives which make men count the happiness of others to be equally valuable with their own? or, in the Utilitarian language, What is the 'sanction' of morality? After all Bentham's insistence upon the 'self-preference principle' and Mill's account of selfishness in his political theory, we are suddenly told that morality means a lofty and rigid code in which the happiness of all is the one end. Here again Mill is entangled by the characteristic difficulty of his psychology. To analyse is to divide objects into separate units. When he has to do with complex objects and relations apparently reciprocal, he is forced to represent them by a simple sequence. The two factors are not mutually dependent but distinct things somehow connected in time. One result is his account of 'ends' or 'motives' (the two, as he observes, are synonymous).[1] The end is something to be gained by the act, the 'association' of which with the act constitutes a 'desire.' This, we have seen, always refers to the future.[2] In acting, then, I am always guided by calculations of future pleasures or pains. I believe this to be one of the most unfortunate because one of the most plausible of

[1] *Fragment*, p. 316.
[2] At one point, as J. S. Mill notes, he speaks of an 'unsatisfied desire' as a motive, which seems to indicate a present feeling; but this is not his usual view.—*Analysis*, ii. 361, 377 *n*.

Utilitarian fallacies. If we are determined by pains and pleasures, it is in one sense as contradictory to speak of our being determined by future pains and pleasures as to speak of our being nourished to-day by to-morrow's dinner. The 'future pleasure' does not exist; the anticipated pleasure acts by making the present action pleasant; and we then move (as it is said) along the line of least resistance. Certain conduct is intrinsically pleasurable or painful, and the future pleasure only acts through the present foretaste. When, however, we regard the pleasure as future and as somehow a separable thing, we can only express these undeniable facts by accepting a purely egoistic conclusion. We are, of course, moved by our own feelings, as we breathe with our own lungs and digest with our own stomachs. But when we accept the doctrine of 'ends' this harmless and self-evident truth is perverted into the statement that our 'end' must be our own pleasure; that we cannot be really or directly unselfish. The analysis, indeed, is so defective that it can hardly be applied intelligibly. Hume observes that no man would rest his foot indifferently upon a stool or a gouty toe. The action itself of giving pain would be painful, and cannot be plausibly resolved into an anticipation of an 'end.' This, again, is conspicuously true of all the truly social emotions. Not only the conscience, but the sense of shame or honour, or pride and vanity act powerfully and instantaneously as present motives without necessary reference to any future results. The knowledge that I am giving pain or causing future pain is intrinsically and immediately painful to the normal human being, and the supposed 'analysis' is throughout a fiction. Mill, however, like

Bentham, takes it for granted, but perceives more clearly than Bentham the difficulty to which it leads. How, from a theory of pure selfishness, are we to get a morality of general benevolence? The answer is given by the universal 'association.' We are governed, he holds, by our own emotions; our end is our own pleasure, and we have to consider how this end dictates a desire for general happiness. He expounds with great vigour the process by which the love of friends, children and parents and country may be gradually developed through the association of our pleasures with the fellow-creatures who caused them. J. S. Mill regards his exposition as 'almost perfect,'[1] and says that it shows how the 'acquired senti-ments'—the moral sentiments and so forth—may be gradually developed; may become 'more intense and powerful than any of the elements out of which they may have been formed, and may also in their maturity be perfectly disinterested.' James Mill declares that the analysis does not affect the reality of the sentiments analysed. Gratitude remains gratitude, and generosity generosity, just as a white ray remains white after Newton had decomposed it into rays of different colours.[2] Here once more we have the great principle of indissoluble association or mental chemistry.

Granting that the emotions so generated may be real, we may still ask whether the analysis be sufficient. James Mill's account of the way in which they are generated leaves a doubt. Morality is first impressed upon us by authority. Our parents praise and blame, reward

[1] *Analysis*, ii. 233 *n.* Mill adds that though his father explains the 'intellectual,' he does not explain the 'animal' element in the affections. This, however, is irrelevant for my purpose. [2] *Fragment*, pp. 51-52.

and punish. Thus are formed associations of praise and blame with certain actions. Then, we form further associations with the causes of praise and blame and thus acquire the sentiments of 'praiseworthiness' and 'blameworthiness.' The sensibility to praise and blame generally forms the 'popular sanction,' and this, when praiseworthiness is concerned, becomes the moral sanction.[1] Here we see that morality is regarded as somehow the product of a 'sanction'; that is, of the action of praise and blame with their usual consequences upon the indi-vidual. His sensibility causes him through association to acquire the habits which generally bring praise and blame; and ultimately these qualities become attractive for their own sake. The difficulty is to see where the line is crossed which divides truly moral or altruistic conduct from mere prudence. Admitting that association may impel us to conduct which involves self-sacrifice, we may still ask whether such conduct is reasonable. Associa-tion produces belief in error as well as in truth. If I love a man because he is useful and continue to love him when he can no longer be useful, am I not mis-guided? If I wear a ragged coat, because it was once smart, my conduct is easily explained as a particular kind of folly. If I am good to my old mother when she can no longer nurse me, am I not guilty of a similar folly? In short, a man who inferred from Mill's principles that he would never do good without being paid for it, would be hardly inconsistent. Your associations, Mill would say, are indissoluble. He might answer, I will try—it is surely not so hard to dissolve a tie of gratitude! Grant-

[1] *Analysis*, ii. 292-300; *Fragment*, pp. 247-65. Note Mill's interpretation of this theory of 'praiseworthiness.'—*Analysis*, ii. 298 *n.*

ing, in short, that Mill gives an account of such virtue as may be made of enlightened self-interest, he does not succeed in making intelligible the conduct which alone deserves the name of virtuous. The theory always halts at the point where something more is required than an external sanction, and supposes a change of character as well as a wider calculation of personal interest.

The imperfection of this theory may be taken for granted. It has been exposed by innumerable critics. It is more important to observe one cause of the imperfection. Mill's argument contains an element of real worth. It may be held to represent fairly the historical development of morals. That morality is first conceived as an external law deriving its sanctity from authority; that it is directed against obviously hurtful conduct; and that it thus serves as a protection under which the more genuine moral sentiments can develop themselves, I believe to be in full accordance with sound theories of ethics. But Mill was throughout hampered by the absence of any theory of evolution. He had to represent a series of changes as taking place in the indi-vidual which can only be conceived as the product of a long and complex social change. He is forced to repre-sent the growth of morality as an accretion of new 'ends' due to association, not as an intrinsic development of the character itself. He has to make morality out of atomic sensations and ideas collected in clusters and trains without any distinct reference to the organic constitution of the individual or of society, and as somehow or other deducible from the isolated human being, who remains a constant, though he collects into groups governed by external sanctions. He sees that morality is formed

somehow or other, but he cannot show that it is either reasonable or an essential fact of human nature. Here, again, we shall see what problem was set to his son. Finally, if Mill did not explain ethical theory satisfactorily, it must be added in common justice that he was himself an excellent example of the qualities for which he tried to account. A life of devotion to public objects and a conscientious discharge of private duties is just the pheno-menon for which a cluster of 'ideas' and 'associations' seems to be an inadequate account. How, it might have been asked, do you explain James Mill? His main purpose, too, was to lay down a rule of duty, almost mathematically ascertainable, and not to be disturbed by any sentimentalism, mysticism, or rhetorical foppery. If, in the attempt to free his hearers from such elements, he ran the risk of reducing morality to a lower level and made it appear as unamiable as sound morality can appear, it must be admitted that in this respect too his theories reflected his personal character.

CHAPTER VIII
RELIGION

I. PHILIP BEAUCHAMP

THE application of Mill's *Analysis* to the views of orthodox theologians required, one might have supposed, as little interpretation as a slap in the face. But a respectable philosopher may lay down what premises he pleases if he does not avowedly draw his conclusions. Mill could argue in perfect safety against the foundations of theology, while Richard Carlile was being sent to gaol again and again for attacking the superstructure. The Utilitarians thought themselves justified in taking advantage of the illogicality of mankind. Whether it was that the ruling powers had no philosophical principles themselves, or that they did not see what inferences would follow, or that they thought that the average person was incapable of drawing inferences, they drew the line at this point. You may openly maintain doctrines inconsistent with all theology, but you must not point out the inconsistency. The Utilitarians contented themselves with sapping the fort instead of risking an open assault. If its defenders were blind to the obvious consequences of the procedure, so much the better. In private, there was obviously no want of plain speaking.

In Bentham's MSS. the Christian religion is nicknamed 'Jug' as the short for 'Juggernaut.' He and his friends were as anxious as Voltaire to crush the 'infamous,' but they would do it by indirect means. They argued resolutely for more freedom ; and Samuel Bailey's essay upon the formation of opinions—a vigorous argument on behalf of the widest possible toleration—was enthusiastically praised by James Mill in the *Westminster Review.* For the present they carefully abstained from the direct avowal of obnoxious opinions, which were still legally punishable, and which would undoubtedly excite the strongest hostility. Bentham, as we have seen, had ventured, though anonymously, to assail the church catechism and to cross-examine St. Paul. One remarkable manifesto gave a fuller utterance to his opinions. A book called *The Analysis of the Influence of Natural Religion on the Temporal Happiness of Mankind,* by 'Philip Beauchamp,' appeared in 1822. The publisher was Richard Carlile, who was then 'safe in Dorchester gaol.' No legal notice was taken of 'Philip Beauchamp.' The reason may have been that the book excited very little attention in general. Yet it is probably as forcible an attack as has often been written upon the popular theology. The name of 'Philip Beauchamp' covered a combination of Bentham and George Grote.[1] The book, therefore, represents the view of representative Utilitarians of the first and third generation, and clearly expressed the real opinions

---

[1] See *Dictionary of National Biography,* under 'George Grote.' Bentham's MS. is in the British Museum, and shows, I think, that Grote's share in the work was a good deal more than mere editing. I quote from a reprint by Truelove (1875). It was also privately reprinted by Grote himself in 1866.

of the whole party. In his posthumous essays J. S. Mill speaks of it as the only explicit discussion known to him of the question of the utility, as distinguished from the question of the truth, of religion. Obviously, it was desirable to apply the universal test to religious belief, and this very pithy and condensed statement shows the result.

A short summary may indicate the essence of the argument. It is only necessary to observe that the phrase 'natural religion' is part of the disguise. It enables the author to avoid an explicit attack upon revelation ; but it is superabundantly obvious that the word 'natural' is superfluous. Revelation is really a fiction, and all religions are 'natural.' A religion is called a 'superstition,' as 'Philip Beauchamp' remarks at starting, when its results are thought to be bad ; and allowed to be a religion only when they are thought to be good.[1] That device covers the familiar fallacy of distinguishing between uses and abuses, and, upon that pretence, omitting to take bad consequences into account. We must avoid it by defining religion and then tracing all the consequences, good or bad. Religion is accordingly taken to mean the belief in the existence of 'an Almighty Being, by whom pains and pleasures will be dispensed to mankind during an infinite and future state of existence.' The definition is already characteristic. 'Religion' may be used in a far wider sense, corresponding to a philosophy of the universe, whether that philosophy

does or does not include this particular doctrine. But 'Philip Beauchamp's' assumption is convenient because it gives a rational reasoning to the problem of utility. Religion is taken to be something adventitious or superimposed upon other beliefs, and we can therefore intelligibly ask whether it does good or harm. Taking this definition for granted, let us consider the results.

The first point is that we are of necessity in absolute ignorance as to a posthumous state. Now, fear is from our earliest infancy the 'never-failing companion and offspring of ignorance.' Knowledge alone can rescue us from perpetual suffering, because all security depends upon knowledge. Pain, moreover, is far more 'pungent' and distinct than pleasure. 'Want and pain are natural ; satisfaction and pleasure artificial and invented.' Pain, therefore, as the strongest, will dictate our anticipations. The hope of immortality is by the orthodox described as a blessing ; but the truth, deducible from these principles of human nature and verified by experience, is that natural religion, instead of soothing apprehensions, adds fresh grounds of apprehension. A revelation, as 'Philip Beauchamp' admits, might conceivably dispel our fears ; but he would obviously say that the religion which is taken to be revealed gives a far more vivid picture of hell than of heaven.[1] In the next place, it is 'obvious at first sight' that natural religion can properly give 'no rule of guidance.' It refers us to a region of 'desperate and unfathomable' darkness.[2] But it nevertheless indirectly suggests a pernicious rule. It rests entirely upon conjectures as to the character of the invisible Being who apportions pain or pleasure for

---

[1] Cf. Hobbes's definition : 'Fear of power invisible feigned by the mind, or imagined from tales publicly allowed, [is] RELIGION : not allowed, SUPERSTITION. And when the power imagined is truly such as we imagine, TRUE RELIGION.'—*Works* (Molesworth), iii. 45.

[1] 'Philip Beauchamp,' ch. ii. pp. 11-15.   [2] *Ibid.* p. 17.

inscrutable reasons. Will this Being be expected to approve useful or pernicious conduct? From men's language we might suppose that he is thought to be purely benevolent. Yet from their dogmas it would seem that he is a capricious tyrant. How are we to explain the discrepancy? The discrepancy is the infallible result of the circumstances already stated.[1] The Deity has limitless power, and therefore is the natural object of our instinctive fears. The character of the Deity is absolutely incomprehensible, and incomprehensibility in human affairs is identical with caprice and insanity.[2] The ends and the means of the Deity are alike beyond our knowledge; and the extremes both of wisdom and of folly are equally unaccountable. Now, we praise or blame human beings in order to affect their conduct towards us, to attract favours or repel injuries. A tyrant possessed of unlimited power considers that by simple abstinence from injury he deserves boundless gratitude. The weak will only dare to praise, and the strong will only blame. The slave-owner never praises and the slave never blames, because one can use the lash while the other is subject to the lash. If, then, we regard the invisible Being as a capricious despot, and, moreover, as a despot who knows every word we utter, we shall never speak of him without the highest eulogy, just because we attribute to him the most arbitrary tyranny. Hence, the invisible despot will specially favour the priests whose lives are devoted to supporting his authority, and, next to priests, those who, by the practice of ceremonies painful or useless to themselves, show that their sole aim is to give him pleasure. He

1 'Philip Beauchamp,' p. 21.   2 *Ibid.* pp. 22 and 104.

will specially detest the atheists, and, next to atheists, all who venture to disregard his arbitrary laws. A human judge may be benevolent, because he is responsible to the community. They give and can take away his power. But the invisible and irresponsible ruler will have no motives for benevolence, and approve conduct pernicious to men because it is the best proof of a complete subservience to himself.[1] In spite of this, it has been generally asserted that religion supplies a motive, and the only adequate motive, to moral conduct. But the decay of religion would leave the sources of pain and pleasure unchanged. To say, then, that the conduct prescribed by religion would disappear if the religious motives were removed is virtually to admit that it produces no 'temporal benefit.' Otherwise, the motives for practising such conduct would not be affected. In fact, morality is the same in all countries, though the injunctions of religion are various and contradictory. If religion ordered only what is useful, it would coincide with human laws, and be at worst superfluous. As a fact, it condemns the most harmless pleasures, such as the worst of human legislators have never sought to suppress. People have become tolerant, that is, they have refused to enforce religious observances, precisely because they have seen that such observances cannot be represented as conducive to temporal happiness.

Duty, again, may be divided into duty to God and duty to man. Our 'duty to God' is a 'deduction from the pleasures of the individual without at all benefiting the species.' It must therefore be taken as a tax paid for the efficacy supposed to be communicated to the other

1 'Philip Beauchamp,' ch. iii.

branch—the 'duty to man.'[1] Does religion, then, stimulate our obedience to the code of duty to man? 'Philip Beauchamp' admits for once that, in certain cases, it 'might possibly' be useful. It might affect 'secret crimes,' that is, crimes where the offender is undiscoverable. That, however, is a trifle. These cases, he thinks, would be 'uncommonly rare' under a well-conceived system. The extent of evil in this life would therefore be trifling were superhuman inducements entirely effaced from the human bosom, and if 'human institutions were ameliorated according to the progress of philosophy.'[2] On the other hand, the imaginary punishments are singularly defective in the qualities upon which Bentham had insisted in human legislation. They are remote and uncertain, and to make up for this are represented as boundless in intensity and durability. For that reason, they precisely reverse the admitted principle that punishment should be so devised as to produce the greatest possible effect by the smallest infliction of pain. Supernatural sanctions are supposed to maximise pain with a minimum of effect. The fear of hell rarely produces any effect till a man is dying, and then inflicts great suffering, though it has been totally inefficient as a preventive at the time of temptation. The influence of supernatural penalties is therefore in 'an inverse ratio to the demand for it.'[3] In reality, the efficacy of the sanctions is due to their dependence upon public opinion. Our real motive for acting rightly is our desire for the praise of our fellows and our interest in their good conduct. We conceal this motive even from ourselves, because we wish to have the credit of serving the Deity exclusively. This is con-

1 'Philip Beauchamp,' ch. iv.   2 *Ibid.* p. 45, ch. v.   3 *Ibid.* p. 52, ch. vi.

firmed by the familiar instances of a conflict between public opinion and religious sanctions. Duelling, fornication, and perjury are forbidden by the divine law, but the prohibition is ineffectual whenever the real sentiment of mankind is opposed to it. The divine law is set aside as soon as it conflicts with the popular opinion. In exceptional cases, indeed, the credit attached to unreasonable practices leads to fanaticism, asceticism, and even insanity; but superhuman terrors fail at once when they try to curb the action of genuine substantial motives. Hence we must admit that they are useless in the case even of 'secret crimes.' Religion, in short, prescribes mischievous practices, becomes impotent except for the production of misery, and is really, though not avowedly, dependent on the popular sanction.[1]

We can now classify the evils actually produced. Religion injures individuals by prescribing useless and painful practices: fasting, celibacy, voluntary self-torture, and so forth. It suggests vague terrors which often drive the victim to insanity, and it causes remorse for harmless enjoyments.[2] Religion injures society by creating antipathies against unbelievers, and in a less degree against heretics and nonconformists. It perverts public opinion by making innocent actions blameable; by distorting the whole science of morality and sanctioning the heterogeneous dictates of a certain blind and unaccountable impulse called the 'moral instinct or conscience.'[3] Morality becomes a 'mere catalogue of reigning sentiments,' because it has cast away the standard of utility. A special aversion to improvement is generated, because

1 'Philip Beauchamp,' ch. viii.   2 *Ibid.* part ii. ch. i.
3 *Ibid.* p. 80, part ii. ch. ii.

whatever changes our conceptions of the 'sequences of phenomena' is supposed to break the divine 'laws of nature.' 'Unnatural' becomes a 'self-justifying' epithet forbidding any proposed change of conduct, which will counteract the 'designs of God.' Religion necessarily injures intellectual progress. It disjoins belief from its only safe ground, experience. The very basis, the belief in an inscrutable and arbitrary power, sanctions supernatural or 'extra-experimental' beliefs of all kinds. You reject in the case of miracles all the tests applicable to ordinary instruction, and appeal to trial by ordeal instead of listening to witnesses. Instead of taking the trouble to plough and sow, you expect to get a harvest by praying to an inscrutable Being. You marry without means, because you hold that God never sends a child without sending food for it to eat. Meanwhile you suborn 'unwarranted belief' by making belief a matter of reward and penalty. It is made a duty to dwell upon the arguments upon one side without attending to those upon the other, and 'the weaker the evidence the greater the merit in believing.'[1] The temper is depraved not only by the antipathies generated, but by the 'fitful and intermittent character' of the inducements to conduct.[2]

The final result of all this is still more serious. It is that religion, besides each separate mischief, 'subsidises a standing army for the perpetuation of all the rest.'[3] The priest gains power as a 'wonder-worker,' who knows how to propitiate the invisible Being, and has a direct interest in 'depraving the intellect,' cherishing supersti-

[1] 'Philip Beauchamp,' pp. 97, 99.   [2] Ibid. p. 101.
[3] Ibid. p. 103.

tion, surrounding himself with mysteries, representing the will of the Deity as arbitrary and capricious, and forming an organised 'array of human force and fraud.'[1] The priesthood sets up an infallible head, imposes upon the weak and dying, stimulates antipathy, forms the mass of 'extra-experimental' beliefs into the likeness of a science, and allies itself with the state. Heresy becomes a crime. The ruler helps the priests to raise a tax for their own comfort, while they repay him by suppressing all seditious opinions. Thus is formed an unholy alliance between the authorities of 'natural religion' and the 'sinister interests of the earth.' The alliance is so complete that it is even more efficient than if it had been openly proclaimed. 'Prostration and plunder of the community is indeed the common end of both' (priests and rulers). The only chance of dissension is about the 'partition of the spoil.'[2]

The book is as characteristic of the Utilitarians in style as in spirit. It is terse, vigorous reasoning, with no mere rhetorical flourishes. The consequences of the leading principle are deduced without flinching and without reserve. Had the authors given their names, they would no doubt have excited antipathies injurious to the propaganda of Utilitarianism. They held, for that reason presumably, that they were not bound to point out the ultimate goal of their speculations. No intelligent reader of their other writings could fail to see what that goal must be; but an 'open secret' is still for many purposes a real secret. Whatever might be the suspicions of their antagonists, they could only be accused of a tendency. The book amounts to an

[1] 'Philip Beauchamp, p. 163.   [2] Ibid. p. 122.

admission that the suspicions were well founded. Utilitarianism, the Utilitarians clearly recognised, logically implied the rejection of all theology. Religion—on their understanding of the word—must, like everything else, be tested by its utility, and it was shown to be either useless or absolutely pernicious. The aim of the Utilitarians was, in brief, to be thoroughly scientific. The man of science must be opposed to the belief in an inscrutable agent of boundless power, interfering at every point with the laws of nature, and a product of the fancy instead of the reason. Such a conception, so far as accepted, makes all theory of human conduct impossible, suggests rules conflicting with the supreme rule of utility, and gives authority to every kind of delusion, imposture, and 'sinister interest.'

It would, I think, be difficult to mention a more vigorous discussion of the problem stated. As anonymous, it could be ignored instead of answered; and probably such orthodox persons as read it assumed it to be a kind of reductio ad absurdum of the Utilitarian creed. It might follow, they could admit, logically from the Utilitarian analysis of human nature, but it could only prove that the analysis was fundamentally wrong. Yet its real significance is precisely its thorough applicability to the contemporary state of opinion. Beauchamp's definition coincides with Paley's. The coincidence was inevitable. Utilitarians both in ethical and philosophical questions start from the same assumptions as Paley, and the Paley doctrine gave the pith of the dominant theology. I have observed that the Scottish philosophers had abandoned the a priori argument, and laid the whole stress of their theological doctrine

upon Paley's argument from final causes. The change of base was an inevitable consequence of their whole system. They appealed to experience, to 'Baconian' methods, and to 'inductive psychology.' The theory of 'intuitions,' effective where it fell in with admitted beliefs, was idle against an atheist, who denied that he had the intuition. The 'final causes' argument, however, rested upon common ground, and supplied a possible line of defence. The existence of the Deity could perhaps be proved empirically, like the existence of the 'watchmaker.' Accordingly, this was the argument upon which reliance was really placed by the average theologian of the time. Metaphysical or ontological reasoning had been discarded for plain common-sense. The famous Bridgewater Treatises are the characteristic product of the period. It had occurred to the earl of Bridgewater, who died in 1829, that £8000 from his estate might be judiciously spent in proving the existence of a benevolent creator. The council of the Royal Society employed eight eminent men of science to carry out this design.[1] They wrote some interesting manuals of popular science, interspersed with proper theological applications. The arguments were sincere enough, though they now seem to overlook with singular blindness the answer which would be suggested by the 'evolutionist.' The logical result is, in any case, a purely empirical theology. The religion which emerges is not a philosophy or theory of the world in general, but corresponds to a belief in certain matters of fact (or

[1] The writers were Chalmers, Kidd, Whewell, Sir Charles Bell, Roget, Buckland, Kirby, and Prout. The essays appeared from 1833 to 1835. The versatile Brougham shortly afterwards edited Paley's Natural Theology.

fiction). The existence of the Deity is to be proved, like the existence of Caesar, by special evidence.

The main results are obvious. The logical base of the whole creed is 'natural theology,' and 'natural theology' is simply a branch of science, amenable to the ordinary scientific tests. It is intended to prove the existence of an agent essential to the working of the machinery, as from the movements of a planet we infer the existence of a disturbing planet. The argument from design, in this acceptation, is briefly mentioned by 'Philip Beauchamp.' It is, he argues, 'completely extra-experimental'; for experience only reveals design in living beings: it supposes a pre-existing chaos which can never be shown to have existed, and the 'omnipotent will' introduced to explain the facts is really no explanation at all, but a collection of meaningless words.[1] The argument is briefly dismissed as concerning the truth, not the utility, of religion, but one point is sufficiently indicated. The argument from 'design' is always plausible, because it applies reasoning undeniably valid when it is applied within its proper sphere. The inference from a watch to a watchmaker is clearly conclusive. We know sufficiently what is meant by the watchmaker and by 'making.' We therefore reason to a *vera causa*—an agent already known. When the inference is to the action of an inconceivable Being performing an inconceivable operation upon inconceivable materials, it really becomes illusory, or amounts to the simple assertion that the phenomenon is inexplicable. Therefore, again, it is essentially opposed to science though claiming to be scientific. The action of the

[1] 'Philip Beauchamp,' p. 88.

creator is supposed to begin where the possibility of knowledge ends. It is just the inexplicable element which suggests the creative agency. Conversely, the satisfactory explanation of any phenomenon takes it out of the theological sphere. As soon as the process becomes 'natural' it ceases to demand the supernatural artificer. 'Making,' therefore, is contradistinguished from 'growing.' If we see how the eye has come into existence, we have no longer any reason to assume that it was put together mechanically. In other words, 'teleology' of this variety is dispelled by theories of evolution. The hypothesis of interference becomes needless when we see how things came to be by working out perfectly natural processes. As science, therefore, expands, theology recedes. This was to become more evident at a later period. For the present, the teleological argument in the Paley form, triumphantly set forth in Bridgewater Treatises and the like, rested the defence of theology on the proofs of the discontinuity of the universe and the consequent necessity for admitting supernatural interference. Science was therefore invoked to place absolute limits on its own progress.

But other vital difficulties were already felt. The argument from contrivance naturally implies limitation. The maker of a machine is strictly limited by the properties of the matter upon which he works. The inference might be verbally saved by saying that the maker was 'potentially' omnipotent; but the argument, so far as it goes, is more easily satisfied by the hypothesis of a Being of great but still limited powers. The Deity so proved, if the proof be valid, is not himself the ground of the universe, the source from which nature itself emanates,

as well as the special laws of nature, but a part of the whole system; interfering, guiding, and controlling, but still only one of the powers which contribute to the formation of the whole. Hence arise questions which theologians rather evaded than attempted to answer. If with the help of Paley we can prove the existence of an invisible Being—potentially omnipotent, though always operating as though limited—there would still remain the question as to his attributes. He is skilful, we may grant, but is he benevolent or is he moral? The benevolence could of course be asserted by optimists, if facts were amenable to rhetoric. But a theory which is essentially scientific or empirical, and consistently argues from the effect to the cause, must start from an impartial view of the facts, and must make no presupposition as to the nature of the cause. The cause is known only through the effects, and our judgment of them cannot be modified by simply discovering that they are caused. If, then, contrivance is as manifest in disease as in health, in all the sufferings which afflict mankind as well as in the pleasures which solace him, we must either admit that the creator is not benevolent, or frankly admit that he is not omnipotent and fall into Manichæism. Nature, we are frequently told, is indifferent if not cruel; and though Paley and his followers choose to shut their eyes to ugly facts, it could be only by sacrificing their logic. They were bound to prove from observation that the world was so designed as to secure the 'greatest happiness' before they could logically infer a purely benevolent designer. It was of the very essence of their position that observed facts should be the ultimate basis of the whole theory;

and to alter the primary data by virtue of deductions drawn from them could obviously not be logically justifiable.

Such reflections, though sufficiently obvious, might be too far from practical application to have much immediate effect. But the question of the moral bearing of theology was of more interest; and, here, the coincidence of the Utilitarianism with the accepted theology of the day is especially important. The Deity regarded as the artificer appears to be far from purely benevolent. In respect to morality, is he not simply indifferent? Does he not make men fragile and place them amidst pitfalls? Does he not constantly slay the virtuous and save the wicked? How, indeed, from the purely empirical or scientific base, do you deduce any moral attributes whatever? 'Natural theology,' as it was called, might reveal a contriver, but could it reveal a judge or a moral guide? Here the difficulty of a purely matter-of-fact theology made itself felt on many sides. The remarkable influence of Butler upon many minds was partly due to a perception of this omission. Butler avowedly appeals to the conscience, and therefore at least recognises God as directly revealed in a moral character. That seemed to supply a gap in the ordinary theology. But in the purely empirical view Butler's argument was untenable. It appealed to one of the 'intuitions' which were incompatible with its fundamental assumptions. The compunctions of conscience were facts to be explained by 'association,' not to be regarded as intimations of wrath. Butler's view might be inverted. The 'conscience' does, in truth, suggest the divine wrath; but that only means that it suggests the quack remedies upon which 'wonder-working' priests establish their power. Instead of proving the truth of the religion, it explains the origin of superstition. To James Mill, as we have seen, Butler's argument would logically prove not a righteous governor but a cruel creator. Theologians, again, of the Paley school, were bound in consistency to the empirical or Utilitarian view of morality. Paley accepted the consequences unreservedly; and if such philosophers as Brown and Mackintosh persisted in regarding the coincidence between morality and happiness as indicative of a pre-established harmony, not of an identification of morality with the pursuit of general happiness, they still admitted that 'utility' was the 'criterion' of morality. The moral law, that is, coincides in its substance with the law, 'maximise happiness,' and happiness means, as 'Philip Beauchamp' calls it, 'temporal' happiness—the happiness of actual men living in this world and knowing nothing of any external world. How, then, is the moral law related to theology? To know what is moral, we must appeal to experience and 'utility.' We must discover what makes for happiness, just as in medicine we must discover what makes for health or pleasure, by the ordinary methods of observation. What place is left for any supernatural intervention? The ostensible answer was that though the moral code could be deduced from its utility, the motives by which it was to be enforced required some supernatural agency. The natural man might see what was right, but need not therefore do what was right. Here 'Philip Beauchamp' comes to a direct issue with the theologians. He denies that the supernatural motive will be on the side of morality. When J. S. Mill remarked that there had been few discussions of the 'utility' as distinguished

from the truth of religion, he scarcely recognises one conspicuous fact. The great argument of divines had always been the absolute necessity of religion to morality; and if morality be understood to mean utility, this is simply an argument from utility. The point, indeed, was often taken for granted; but it certainly represents one of the strongest persuasives, if not one of the strongest reasons. The divines, in fact, asserted that religion was of the highest utility as supplying the motive for moral conduct. What motives, then, can be derived from such knowledge of the Deity as is attainable from the 'Natural theology' argument? How can we prove from it that he who puts the world together is more favourable to the virtues than to the vices which are its results; or, if more favourable, that he shows any other favour than can be inferred from experience? He has, it is agreed, put men, as Bentham had said, under the command of two sovereign masters, Pleasure and Pain; and has enabled them to calculate consequences, and therefore to seek future pleasure and avoid future pain. That only proves that we can increase our happiness by prudence; but it suggests no additional reasons either for seeking happiness or for altering our estimate of happiness. As 'Philip Beauchamp' argues, we cannot from the purely empirical ground get any motive for taking into account anything beyond our 'temporal' or secular interests. This, again, was in fact admitted by Paley. His mode of escape from the dilemma is familiar. The existence of a supreme artificer is inferred from the interventions in the general order of nature. The existence of a moral ruler, or the fact that the ruler approves morality, is inferred from his interference by the par-

ticular manifestations of power which we call miraculous. We know that actions will have other consequences than those which can be inferred from our own experience, because some two thousand years ago a Being appeared who could raise the dead and heal the sick. If sufficient evidence of the fact be forthcoming, we are entitled to say upon his authority that the wicked will be damned and the virtuous go to heaven. Obedience to the law enforced by these sanctions is obviously prudent, and constitutes the true *differentia* of moral conduct. Virtue, according to the famous definition, is doing good 'for the sake of everlasting happiness.' The downright bluntness with which Paley announced these conclusions startled contemporaries, and yet it must be admitted that they were a natural outcome of his position.

In short, the theological position of the Paley school and the Utilitarian position of 'Philip Beauchamp' start from the common ground of experience. Religion means the knowledge of certain facts, which are to be inferred from appropriate evidence. It does not modify the whole system of thought, but simply adds certain corollaries; and the whole question is whether the corollaries are or are not proved by legitimate reasoning. Can we discover heaven and hell as we discovered America? Can observation of nature reveal to us a supernatural world?' The first difficulty is that the argument for natural theology has to rest upon interference, not upon order, and therefore comes into conflict with the first principles of scientific procedure. The Deity is revealed not by the rational but by the arbitrary; and the more the world is explained, the less the proof that he exists, because the

narrower the sphere of his action. Then, as such a Deity, even if proved, is not proved to be benevolent or moral, we have to rely for the moral element upon the evidence of 'miracles,' that is, again, of certain interruptions of order. The scientific tendency more or less embodied in Protestantism, so far as it appealed to reason or to 'private judgment,' had, moreover, made it necessary to relegate miracles to a remote period, while denying them at the present. To prove at once that there are no miracles now, and that there were a few miracles two thousand years ago, was really hopeless. In fact, the argument had come to be stated in an artificial form which had no real relation to the facts. If the apostles had been a jury convinced by a careful legal examination of the evidence; if they had pronounced their verdict, in spite of the knowledge that they would be put to death for finding it, there would have been some force in Paley's argument. But then they had not. To assume such an origin for any religion implied a total misconception of the facts. Paley assumed that the apostles resembled twelve respectable deans of Carlisle solemnly declaring, in spite of the most appalling threats, that John Wesley had been proved to have risen from the dead. Paley might plausibly urge that such an event would require a miracle. But, meanwhile, his argument appeared to rest the whole case for morality and religion upon this narrow and perilous base. We can only know that it is our interest to be moral if we know of heaven and hell; and we only know of heaven and hell if we accept the evidence of miracles, and infer that the worker of miracles had supernatural sources of information. The moral difficulty which emerges is obvious. The Paley conception of the Deity is, in fact, coincident with Bentham's conception of the sovereign. He is simply an invisible sovereign, operating by tremendous sanctions. The sanctions are 'external,' that is to say, pains and pleasures, annexed to conduct by the volition of the sovereign, not intrinsic consequences of the conduct itself. Such a conception, thoroughly carried through, makes the relation between religion and morality essentially arbitrary. Moreover, if with 'Philip Beauchamp' we regard the miracle argument as obviously insufficient, and consider what are the attributes really attributed to the sovereign, we must admit that they suggest such a system as he describes rather than the revelation of an all-wise and benevolent ruler. It is true, as 'Philip Beauchamp' argues, that the system has all the faults of the worst human legislation ; that the punishment is made atrociously—indeed infinitely—severe to compensate for its uncertainty and remoteness ; and that (as he would clearly add), to prevent it from shocking and stunning the intellect, it is regarded as remissible in consideration of vicarious suffering. If, then, the religion is really what its dogmas declare, it is easier to assume that it represents the cunning of a priesthood operating upon the blind fears and wild imaginations of an inaccessible world ; and the ostensible proofs of a divine origin resting upon miraculous proofs are not worth consideration. It professes to be a sanction to all morality, but is forced to construct a mythology which outrages all moral considerations. Taken as a serious statement of fact, the anthropomorphism of the vulgar belief was open to the objections which Socrates brought against the Pagan mythology. The

supreme ruler was virtually represented as arbitrary, cruel, and despotic.

If we ask the question, whether in point of fact the religion attacked by 'Philip Beauchamp' fairly represented the religion of the day, we should have, of course, to admit that it was in one sense a gross caricature. If, that is, we asked what were the real roots of the religious zeal of Wilberforce and the Evangelicals, or of the philanthropists with whom even James Mill managed to associate on friendly terms, it would be the height of injustice to assume that they tried to do good simply from fear of hell and hope of heaven, or that their belief in Christianity was due to a study of Paley's *Evidences*. Their real motives were far nobler : genuine hatred of injustice and sympathy for suffering, joined to the conviction that the sects to which they belonged were working on the side of justice and happiness ; while the the creeds which they accepted were somehow congenial to their best feelings, and enabled them to give utterance to their deepest emotions. But when they had to give a ground for that belief they could make no adequate defence. They were better than their ostensible creed, because the connection of their creed with their morality was really arbitrary and traditional. We must always distinguish between the causes of strong convictions and the reasons officially assigned for them. The religious creed, as distinguished from the religious sentiment, was really traditional, and rested upon the simple fact that it was congenial to the general frame of mind. Its philosophy meanwhile had become hopelessly incoherent. It wished to be sensible, and admitted in principle the right of 'private judgment' or rationalism so far as con-

sistent with Protestantism. The effect had been that in substance it had become Utilitarian and empirical ; while it had yet insisted upon holding on to the essentially irrational element.

The religious tradition was becoming untenable in this sense at the same time as the political tradition. If radicalism in both were to be effectually resisted, some better foundation must be found for conservatism. I should be tempted to say that a critical period was approaching, did I not admit that every period can always be described as critical. In fact, however, thoughtful people, perceiving on the one hand that the foundations of their creed were shaking, and yet holding it to be essential to their happiness, began to take a new position. The 'Oxford movement,' started soon afterwards, implied a conviction that the old Protestant position was as untenable as the radical asserted. Its adherents attempted to find a living and visible body whose supernatural authority might maintain the old dogmatic system. Liberal thinkers endeavoured to spiritualise the creed and prove its essential truths by philosophy, independently of the particular historical evidence. The popular tendency was to admit in substance that the dogmas most assailed were in fact immoral : but to put them into the background, or, if necessary, to explain them away. The stress was to be laid not upon miracles, but upon the moral elevation of Christianity or the beauty of character of its founder. The 'unsectarian' religion, represented in the most characteristic writings of the next generation, in Tennyson and Browning, Thackeray and Dickens, reflects this view. Such men detested the coarse and brutalising

dogmas which might be expounded as the true 'scheme of salvation' by ignorant preachers seeking to rouse sluggish natures to excitement ; but they held to religious conceptions which, as they thought, really underlay these disturbing images, and which, indeed, could hardly be expressed in any more definite form than that of a hope or a general attitude of the whole character. The problem seemed to be whether we shall support a dogmatic system by recognising a living spiritual authority, or frankly accept reason as the sole authority, and, while explaining away the repulsive dogmas, try to retain the real essence of religious belief.

II. CONTEMPORARY THOUGHT

If I were writing a general history of opinion, it would be necessary to discuss the views of Mill's English contemporaries ; to note their attitude in regard to the Utilitarian position, and point out how they prepared the way for the later developments of thought. The Utilitarians were opposed to a vague sentiment rather than to any definite system. They were a small and a very unpopular sect. They excited antipathy on all sides. As advocating republicanism, they were hardly more disliked by the Tories, who directly opposed them, than by the Whigs, who might be suspected of complicity. As enthusiastic political economists, they were equally detested by sentimental Radicals, Socialists, and by all who desired a strong government, whether for the suppression of social evils or the maintenance of social abuses. And now, as suspected of atheism, they were hated by theologians. But though the Utilitarians were on all sides condemned and denounced, they were met by no definite and coherent scheme of philosophy. The philosophy of Stewart and Brown had at least a strong drift in their direction. Though 'political economy' was denounced in general terms, all who spoke with authority accepted Adam Smith. Their political opponents generally did not so much oppose their theories as object to theory in general. The Utilitarian system might be both imperfect and dogmatic; but it had scarcely to contend with any clear and assignable rival. The dislike of Englishmen to any systematic philosophy, whether founded upon the national character or chiefly due to special conditions, was still conspicuous outside of the small Utilitarian camp.

To discover, therefore, the true position of contemporary opinion, we should have to look elsewhere. Instead of seeking for the philosophers who did not exist, we should have to examine the men of letters who expressed the general tendencies. In Germany, philosophical theories may be held to represent the true drift of the national mind, and a historian of German thought would inquire into the various systems elaborated by professors of philosophy. He would at least be in no want of materials for definite logical statements. In England, there was no such intellectual movement. There we should have to consider poetry and literature; to read Wordsworth and Coleridge, Scott and Byron and Shelley, if we would know what men were really thinking and feeling. The difficulty is, of course, that none of these men, unless Coleridge be an exception, had any conscious or systematic philosophy. We can only ask,

therefore, what they would have said if they had been requested to justify their views by abstract reasoning; and that is a rather conjectural and indefinite enterprise. It lies, fortunately, outside of my field; and it will be enough if I try to suggest one or two sufficiently vague hints. In the first place, the contrast between the Utilitarians and their opponents may almost be identified with the contrast between the prosaic and the poetical aspects of the world in general. Bentham frankly objected to poetry in general. It proved nothing. The true Utilitarian was the man who held on to fact, and to nothing but the barest, most naked and unadorned fact. Poetry in general came within the sweep of his denunciations of 'sentimentalism' and 'vague generalities.' It was the 'production of a rude age'; the silly jingling which might be suitable to savages, but was needless for the grown-up man, and was destined to disappear along with the whole rubbish of mythology and superstition in whose service it had been enlisted. There is indeed a natural sympathy between any serious view of life and a distrust of the æsthetic tendencies. Theologians of many different types have condemned men for dallying with the merely pleasurable, when they ought to be preoccupied with the great ethical problems or the safety of their souls. James Mill had enough of the old Puritan in him to sympathise with Carlyle's aspiration, 'May the devil fly away with the fine arts!' To such men it was difficult to distinguish between fiction and lying; and if some concession might be made to human weakness, poets and novelists might supply the relaxations and serve to fill up the intervals of life, but must be sternly excluded if they tried to intrude

into serious studies. Somehow love of the beautiful only interfered with the scientific investigation of hard facts.

Poets, indeed, may take the side of reform, or may perhaps be naturally expected to take that side. The idealist and the dreamer should be attracted most powerfully by the visions of a better world and the restoration of the golden age. Shelley was among the most enthusiastic prophets of the coming era. His words, he hoped, were to be 'the trumpet of a prophecy' to 'unawakened earth.' Shelley had sat at the feet of Godwin, and represented that vague metaphysical dreaming to which the Utilitarians were radically hostile. To the literary critic, Shelley's power is the more remarkable because from a flimsy philosophy he span an imaginative tissue of such magical and marvellous beauty. But Shelley dwelt in an ethereal region, where ordinary beings found breathing difficult. There facts seemed to dissolve into thin air instead of supplying a solid and substantial base. His idealism meant unreality. His 'trumpet' did not in fact stimulate the mass of mankind, and his fame at this period was confined to a few young gentlemen of literary refinement. The man who had really stirred the world was Byron; and if the decline of Byron's fame has resulted partly from real defects, it is partly due also to the fact that his poetry was so admirably adapted to his contemporaries. Byron at least could see facts as clearly as any Utilitarian, though fact coloured by intense passion. He, like the Utilitarians, hated solemn platitudes and hypocritical conventions. I have noticed the point at which he came into contact with Bentham's disciples. His pathetic death shortly after-

wards excited a singularly strong movement of sympathy. 'The news of his death,' said Carlyle at the time, 'came upon my heart like a mass of lead; and yet the thought of it sends a painful twinge through all my being, as if I had lost a brother.' At a later time he defines Byron as 'a dandy of sorrows and acquainted with grief.'[1] That hits off one aspect of Byronism. Byron was the Mirabeau of English literature, in so far as he was at once a thorough aristocrat and a strong revolutionist. He had the qualification of a true satirist. His fate was at discord with his character. He was proud of his order, and yet despised its actual leaders. He was ready alternately to boast of his vices and to be conscious that they were degrading. He shocked the respectable world by mocking 'Satanically,' as they held, at moral conventions, and yet rather denounced the hypocrisy and the heartlessness of precisians than insulted the real affections. He covered sympathy with human suffering under a mask of misanthropy, and attacked war and oppression in the character of a reckless outlaw. Full of the affectation of a 'dandy,' he was yet rousing all Europe by a cry of pure sentimentalism. It would be absurd to attribute any definite doctrine to Byron. His scepticism in religious matters was merely part of a general revolt against respectability. What he illustrates is the vague but profound revolutionary sentiment which indicated a belief that the world seemed to be out of joint, and a vehement protest against the selfish and stolid conservatism which fancied that the old order could be preserved in all its fossil institutions and corresponding dogmas.

[1] Froude's Carlyle, i. 215; ii. 93.

What was the philosophy congenial to Conservatism? There is, of course, the simple answer, None. Toryism was a 'reaction' due to the great struggle of the war and the excesses of the revolution. A 'reaction' is a very convenient phrase. We are like our fathers; then the resemblance is only natural. We differ; then the phrase 'reaction' makes the alteration explain itself. No doubt, however, there was in some sense a reaction. Many people changed their minds as the revolutionary movement failed to fulfil their hopes. I need not argue now that such men were not necessarily corrupt renegades. I can only try to indicate the process by which they were led towards certain philosophical doctrines. Scott, Wordsworth, and Coleridge represent it enough for my purpose. When Mill was reproaching Englishmen for their want of interest in history, he pointed out that Thierry, 'the earliest of the three great French historians' (Guizot and Michelet are the two others), ascribed his interest in his subject to *Ivanhoe*.[1] Englishmen read *Ivanhoe* simply for amusement. Frenchmen could see that it threw a light upon history, or at least suggested a great historical problem. Scott, it is often said, was the first person to teach us that our ancestors were once as much alive as ourselves. Scott, indeed, the one English writer whose fame upon the Continent could be compared to Byron's, had clearly no interest in, or capacity for, abstract speculations. An imaginative power, just falling short of the higher poetical gift, and a masculine common-sense were his most conspicuous faculties. The two qualities were occasionally at issue: his judgment struggled with his prejudices, and he

[1] Mill's *Dissertations*, i. 235; ii. 130.

sympathised too keenly with the active leaders and concrete causes to care much for any abstract theory. Yet his influence upon thought, though indirect, was remarkable. The vividness of his historical painting—inaccurate, no doubt, and delightfully reckless of dates and facts—stimulated the growing interest in historical inquiries even in England. His influence in one direction is recognised by Newman, who was perhaps thinking chiefly of his mediævalism.[1] But the historical novels are only one side of Scott. Patriotic to the core, he lived at a time when patriotic feeling was stimulated to the utmost, and when Scotland in particular was still a province, and yet in many ways the most vigorous and progressive part of a great empire. He represents patriotism stimulated by contact with cosmopolitan movements. Loving every local peculiarity, painting every class from the noble to the peasant, loving the old traditions, and yet sharing the great impulses of the day, Scott was able to interest the world at large. While the most faithful portrayer of the special national type, he has too much sense not to be well aware that picturesque cattle-stealers and Jacobite chiefs were things of the past; but he loves with his whole heart the institutions rooted in the past and rich in historical associations. He transferred to poetry and fiction the political doctrine of Burke. To him, the revolutionary movement was simply a solvent, corroding all the old ties because it sapped the old traditions, and tended to substitute a mob for a nation. The continuity of national life seemed to him the essential condition; and a nation was not a mere aggregate of

[1] George Borrow's vehement dislike of Scott as the inventor of Puseyism and modern Jesuitism of all kinds is characteristic.

separate individuals, but an ancient organism, developing on an orderly system—where every man had his rightful place, and the beggar, as he observes in the *Antiquary*, was as ready as the noble to rise against foreign invasion. To him, the kings or priests who, to the revolutionist, represented simple despotism, represented part of a rough but manly order, in which many virtues were conspicuous and the governing classes were discharging great functions. Though he did not use the phrase, the revolutionary or radical view was hateful to him on account of its 'individualism.' It meant the summary destruction of all that he cherished most warmly in order to carry out theories altogether revolting to his common-sense. The very roots of a sound social order depend upon the traditions and accepted beliefs which bind together clans or families, and assign to every man a satisfactory function in life. The vivid realisation of history goes naturally with a love—excessive or reasonable—of the old order; and Scott, though writing carelessly to amuse idle readers, was stimulating the historical conceptions, which, for whatever reason, were most uncongenial to the Utilitarian as to all the revolutionists.

The more conscious philosophical application is illustrated by Wordsworth and Coleridge. Both of them had shared the truly revolutionary enthusiasm, and both came in time to be classed with the Tories. Both, as will be seen, had a marked influence upon J. S. Mill. Wordsworth has written in the *Prelude* one of the most remarkable of intellectual autobiographies. He was to be, though he never quite succeeded in being, a great philosophical poet. He never succeeded, because, in

truth, he was not a great philosopher. But no one has more clearly indicated the history of his mental evolution. His sympathy with the revolution was perfectly genuine, but involved a vast misconception. A sturdy, independent youth, thoroughly imbued with the instincts of his northern dalesmen, he had early leaned to a republican sentiment. His dislike of the effete conventionalism of the literary creed blended with his aversion to the political rule of the time. He caught the contagion of revolutionary enthusiasm in France, and was converted by the sight of the 'hunger-bitten' peasant girl—the victim of aristocratic oppression. 'It is against that,' said his friend, 'that we are fighting,' and so far Wordsworth was a convert. The revolution, therefore, meant to him the restoration of an idyllic state, in which the homely virtues of the independent peasant should no longer be crushed and deprived of reward by the instruments of selfish despotism. The outbreak of war put his principles at issue with his patriotism. He suffered keenly when called upon to triumph over the calamities of his countrymen. But gradually he came to think that his sympathies were misplaced. The revolution had not altered human nature. The atrocities disturbed him, but for a time he could regard them as a mere accident. As the war went on, he began to perceive that the new power could be as tyrannical and selfish as the old. Instead of reconstructing a simple social ideal, it was forming a military despotism. When the French armies put down the simple Swiss peasantry, to whom he had been drawn by his home-bred sympathies, he finally gave up the revolutionary cause. He had gone through a mental agony, and his distracted sympathies ultimately determined a change which corresponded to the adoption of a new philosophy. Wordsworth, indeed, had little taste for abstract logic. He had imbibed Godwin's doctrine, but when acceptance of Godwin's conclusions involved a conflict with his strongest affections—the sacrifice not only of his patriotism but of the sympathies which bound him to his fellows—he revolted. Godwin represents the extreme of 'individualism,' the absolute dissolution of all social and political bonds. Wordsworth escaped, not by discovering a logical defect in the argument, but by yielding to the protest of his emotions. The system, he thought, was fatal to all the affections which had made life dear to him ; to the vague 'intimations' which, whatever else they might be, had yet power to give harmony to our existence.

By degrees he adopted a new diagnosis of the great political evils. On one side, he sympathised with Scott's sense of the fatal effects upon the whole social organism. Among his noblest poems are the 'Brothers' and 'Michael,' to which he specially called the attention of Fox. They were intended, he explained, to show the surpassing value of the domestic affections conspicuous among the shepherds and 'statesmen' of the northern dales. He had now come to hold that the principles of Godwin and his like were destructive to the most important elements of human welfare. The revolutionists were not simply breaking the fetters of the simple peasant, but destroying the most sacred ties to which the peasant owed whatever dignity or happiness he possessed. Revolution, in short, meant anarchy. It meant, therefore, the destruction of all that gives real value to life. It was, as he held, one product of the worship of the

'idol proudly named the "wealth of nations," '[1] selfishness and greed replacing the old motives to 'plain living and high thinking.' Wordsworth, in short, saw the ugly side of the industrial revolution, the injury done to domestic life by the factory system, or the substitution of a proletariate for a peasantry, and the replacement of the lowest social order by a vast inorganic mob. The contemporary process, which was leading to pauperism and to the evils of the factory system, profoundly affected Wordsworth, as well as the impulsive Southey ; and their frequent denunciations gave colour to the imputations that they were opposed to all progress. Certainly they were even morbidly alive to the evil aspects of the political economy of Malthus and Ricardo, which to them seemed to prescribe insensibility and indifference to most serious and rapidly accumulating evils.

Meanwhile, Wordsworth was also impressed by the underlying philosophical difficulties. The effect of the revolutionary principles was to destroy the religious sentiment, not simply by disproving this or that historical statement, but by making the whole world prosaic and matter-of-fact. His occasional outbursts against the man of science—the 'fingering slave' who would 'peep and botanise upon his mother's grave'—are one version of his feeling. The whole scientific method tended to materialism and atomism ; to a breaking up of the world into disconnected atoms, and losing the life in dissecting the machinery. His protest is embodied in the pantheism of the noble lines on Tintern Abbey, and his method of answering might be divined from the ode on

[1] *Prelude*, bk. xiii.

the 'Intimations of Immortality.' Somehow or other the world represents a spiritual and rational unity, not a mere chaos of disconnected atoms and fragments. We 'see into the heart of things' when we trust to our emotions and hold by the instincts, clearly manifested in childhood, but clouded and overwhelmed in our later struggles with the world. The essential thing is the cultivation of our 'moral being,' the careful preservation and assimilation of the stern sense of duty, which alone makes life bearable and gives a meaning to the universe.

Wordsworth, it is plain, was at the very opposite pole from the Utilitarians. He came to consider that their whole method meant the dissolution of all that was most vitally sacred, and to hold that the revolution had attracted his sympathies on false pretences. Yet it is obvious that, however great the stimulus which he exerted, and however lofty his highest flights of poetry, he had no distinct theory to offer. His doctrine undoubtedly was congenial to certain philosophical views, but was not itself an articulate philosophy. He appeals to instincts and emotions, not to any definite theory. In a remarkable letter, Coleridge told Wordsworth why he was disappointed with the *Excursion*.[1] He had hoped that it would be the 'first and only true philosophical poem in existence.' Wordsworth was to have started by exposing the 'sandy sophisms of Locke,' and after exploding Pope's *Essay on Man*, and showing the vanity of (Erasmus) Darwin's belief in an 'ourangoutang state,' and explaining the fall of man and the 'scheme of redemption,' to have concluded by 'a grand

[1] Coleridge's *Letters* (1890), pp. 643-49.

didactic swell on the identity of a true philosophy with true religion.' He would show how life and intelligence were to be substituted for the 'philosophy of mechanism.' Facts would be elevated into theory, theory into laws, and laws into living and intelligent powers—true idealism necessarily perfecting itself in realism, and realism refining itself into idealism.'

The programme was a large one. If it represents what Coleridge seriously expected from Wordsworth, it also suggests that he was unconsciously wandering into an exposition of one of the gigantic but constantly shifting schemes of a comprehensive philosophy, which he was always proposing to execute. To try to speak of Coleridge adequately would be hopeless and out of place. I must briefly mention him, because he was undoubtedly the most conspicuous representative of the tendencies opposed to Utilitarianism. The young men who found Bentham exasperating imbibed draughts of mingled poetry and philosophy from Coleridge's monologues at Hampstead. Carlyle has told us, in a famous chapter of his *Life of Sterling*, what they went out to see : at once a reed shaken by the wind and a great expounder of transcendental truth. The fact that Coleridge exerted a very great influence is undeniable. To define precisely what that influence was is impossible. His writings are a heap of fragments. He contemplated innumerable schemes for great works, and never got within measurable distance of writing any. He poured himself out indefinitely upon the margins of other men's books ; and the piety of disciples has collected a mass of these scattered and incoherent jottings, which announce conclusions without giving the premises, or suggest difficulties without attempting to solve them. He seems to have been almost as industrious as Bentham in writing; but whereas Bentham's fragments could be put together as wholes, Coleridge's are essentially distracted hints of views never really elaborated. He was always thinking, but seems always to be making a fresh start at any point that strikes him for the moment. Besides all this, there is the painful question of plagiarism. His most coherent exposition (in the *Biographia Literaria*) is simply appropriated from Schelling, though he ascribes the identity to a 'genial coincidence' of thought. I need make no attempt to make out what Coleridge really thought for himself, and then to try to put his thoughts together,—and indeed hold the attempt to be impossible. The most remarkable thing is the apparent disproportion between Coleridge's definite services to philosophy and the effect which he certainly produced upon some of his ablest contemporaries. That seems to prove that he was really aiming at some important aspect of truth, incapable as he may have been of definitively reaching it. I can only try to give a hint or two as to its general nature. Coleridge, in the first place, was essentially a poet, and, moreover, his poetry was of the type most completely divorced from philosophy. Nobody could say more emphatically that poetry should not be rhymed logic; and his most impressive poems are simply waking dreams. They are spontaneous incarnations of sensuous imagery, which has no need of morals or definite logical schemes. Although he expected Wordsworth to transmute philosophy into poetry, he admitted that the achievement would be unprecedented. Even in Lucretius, he said, what was poetry was not philosophy, and what was philosophy was not

poetry. Yet Coleridge's philosophy was essentially the philosophy of a poet. He had, indeed, great dialectical ingenuity—a faculty which may certainly be allied with the highest imagination, though it may involve certain temptations. A poet who has also a mastery of dialectics becomes a mystic in philosophy. Coleridge had, it seems, been attracted by Plotinus in his schooldays. At a later period he had been attracted by Hartley, Berkeley, and Priestley. To a brilliant youth, anxious to be in the van of intellectual progress, they represented the most advanced theories. But there could never be a full sympathy between Coleridge and the forefathers of English empiricism; and he went to Germany partly to study the new philosophy which was beginning to shine— though very feebly and intermittently—in England. When he had returned he began to read Kant and Schelling, or rather to mix excursions into their books with the miscellaneous inquiries to which his versatile intellect attracted him.

Now, it is abundantly clear that Coleridge never studied any philosophy systematically. He never acquired a precise acquaintance with the technical language of various schemes, or cared for their precise logical relations to each other. The 'genial coincidence' with Schelling, though an unlucky phrase, represents a real fact. He dipped into Plotinus or Behmen or Kant or Schelling, or any one who interested him, and did not know whether they were simply embodying ideas already in his own mind, or suggesting new ideas; or, what was probably more accurate, expressing opinions which, in a general way, were congenial to his own way of contemplating the world. His power of stimulating other minds proves

sufficiently that he frequently hit upon impressive and suggestive thoughts. He struck out illuminating sparks, but he never diffused any distinct or steady daylight. His favourite position, for example, of the distinction between the Reason and the Understanding is always coming up and being enforced with the strongest asseverations of its importance. That he had adopted it more or less from Kant is obvious, though I imagine it to be also obvious that he did not clearly understand his authority.[1] To what, precisely, it amounts is also unintelligible to me. Somehow or other, it implies that the mind can rise into transcendental regions, and, leaving grovelling Utilitarians and the like to the conduct of the understanding in matters of practical expediency, can perceive that the universe is in some way evolved from the pure reason, and the mind capable of ideas which correspond to stages of the evolution. How this leads to the conclusions that the Christian doctrines of the Logos and the Trinity are embodiments of pure philosophy is a problem upon which I need not touch. When we have called Coleridge a mystic, with flashes of keen insight into the weakness of the opposite theory, I do not see how we are to get much further, or attribute to him any articulate and definite scheme.

Hopelessly unsystematic as Coleridge may have been, his significance in regard to the Utilitarians is noteworthy. It is indicated in a famous article which J. S. Mill con-

[1] Mr. Hutchison Stirling insists upon this in the *Fortnightly Review* for July 1867. He proves, I think, that Coleridge's knowledge of the various schemes of German philosophy and of the precise relation of Kant, Fichte, and Schelling was altogether desultory and confused. How far this is important depends upon whether we attach much or little importance to precise combinations of words used by these philosophers.

tributed to the *Westminster Review* in March 1840.[1] Mill's concessions to Coleridge rather scandalised the faithful; and it is enough to observe here that it marks the apogee of Mill's Benthamism. Influences, of which I shall have to speak, had led him to regard his old creed as imperfect, and to assent to great part of Coleridge's doctrine. Mill does not discuss the metaphysical or theological views of the opposite school, though he briefly intimates his dissent. But it is interesting to observe how Coleridge impressed a disciple of Bentham. The 'Germano-Coleridgian doctrine,' says Mill, was a reaction against the philosophy of the eighteenth century: 'ontological,' 'conservative,' 'religious,' 'concrete and historical,' and finally 'poetical,' because the other was 'experimental,' 'innovative,' 'infidel,' 'abstract and metaphysical,' and 'matter-of-fact and prosaic.' Yet the two approximate, and each helps to restore the balance and comes a little nearer to a final equilibrium. The error of the French philosophers had been their negative and purely critical tendency. They had thought that it was enough to sweep away superstition, priestcraft, and despotism, and that no constructive process was necessary. They had not perceived the necessity of social discipline, of loyalty to rulers, or of patriotic feeling among the subjects. They had, therefore, entirely failed to recognise the historical value of old creeds and institutions, and had tried to remodel society 'without the binding forces which hold society together.'[2] Hence, too, the *philosophes* came to despise history; and D'Alembert is said to have wished that all record of past events could be blotted out. Their theory, in its popular version at

[1] *Dissertations*, i. 392-474.   [2] *Ibid.* i. 424.

least, came to be that states and churches had been got up 'for the sole purpose of picking people's pockets.'[1] This had become incredible to any intelligent reasoner, and any Tory could prove that there was something good in the past. The peculiarity of the 'Germano-Coleridgian' school was that they saw beyond the immediate controversy. They were the first to inquire with any power into 'the inductive laws of the existence and growth of human society'; the first to recognise the importance of the great constructive principles; and the first to produce not a piece of party advocacy, but 'a philosophy of society in the only form in which it is yet possible, that of a philosophy of history.' Hence arose that 'series of great writers and thinkers, from Herder to Michelet,' who have given to past history an intelligible place in the gradual evolution of humanity.[2] This very forcible passage is interesting in regard to Mill, and shows a very clear perception of some defects in his own philosophy. It also raises an important question.

Accepting Mill's view, it is remarkable that the great error of his own school, which professed to be based upon experience, was the rejection of history; and the great merit of the *a priori* and 'intuitionist' school was precisely their insistence upon history. To this I shall have to return hereafter. Meanwhile, Mill proceeds to show how Coleridge, by arguing from the 'idea' of church and state, had at least recognised the necessity of showing that political and social institutions must have a sufficient reason, and be justified by something more than mere obstinate prejudice. Men like Pitt and Sir Robert Peel, if they accepted Coleridge's support, would have to alter their

[1] *Dissertations*, i. 437.   [2] *Ibid.* i. 425-27.

---

whole position. Coleridge's defence of his ideal church was at once the severest satire upon the existing body and a proof, as against Bentham and Adam Smith, of the advantages of an endowed class for the cultivation and diffusion of learning. Coleridge, moreover, though he objected to the Reform Bill, showed himself a better reformer than Lord John Russell. He admitted what the Whigs refused to see, the necessity of diminishing the weight of the landowner interest. Landowners were not to be ultimate sources of power, but to represent one factor in a reasoned system. In short, by admitting that all social arrangements in some sense were embodiments of reason, he admitted that they must also be made to conform to reason.

Coleridge and Bentham, then, are not really enemies but allies, and they wield powers which are 'opposite poles of one great force of progression.'[1] The question, however, remains, how the philosophy of each leader is really connected with his practical conclusions. Mill's view would apparently be that Coleridge somehow managed to correct the errors or fill the gaps of the Utilitarian system—a very necessary task, as Mill admits —while Coleridge would have held that those errors were the inevitable fruit of the whole empirical system of thought. The Reason must be restored to its rightful supremacy over the Understanding, which had been working its wicked will since the days of Locke and the eighteenth century. The problem is a wide one. I must be content to remark the inevitable antithesis. Whether enemies or allies, the Utilitarians and their 'antagonists were separated by a gulf which could not be bridged for the

[1] *Dissertations*, i. 437.

---

time. The men of common-sense, who had no philosophy at all, were shocked by the immediate practical applications of Utilitarianism, its hostility to the old order which they loved, its apparent helplessness in social questions, its relegation of all progress to the conflict of selfish interests, its indifference to all the virtues associated with patriotism and local ties. By more reflective minds, it was condemned as robbing the world of its poetry, stifling the religious emotions, and even quenching sentiment in general. The few who wished for a philosophy found the root of its errors in the assumptions which reduced the world to a chaos of atoms, outwardly connected and combined into mere dead mechanism. The world, for the poet and the philosopher alike, must be not a congeries of separate things, but in some sense a product of reason. Thought, not fact, must be the ultimate reality. Unfortunately or otherwise, the poetical sentiment could never get itself translated into philosophical theory. Coleridge's random and discursive hints remained mere hints—a suggestion at best for future thought. Mill's criticism shows how far they could be assimilated by a singularly candid Utilitarian. To him, we see, they represented mainly the truth that his own party, following the general tendency of the eighteenth century, had been led to neglect the vital importance of the constructive elements of society; that they had sacrificed order to progress, and therefore confounded progress with destruction, and failed to perceive the real importance in past times even of the institutions which had become obsolete. Social atomism or individualism, therefore, implied a total misconception of what Mill calls the 'evolution of humanity.' This marks a critical point. The 'Germano-Coleridgians' had a theory

---

of evolution. By evolution, indeed, was meant a dialectical evolution; the evolution of 'ideas' or reason, in which each stage of history represents a moment of some vast and transcendental process of thought. Evolution, so understood, seemed rightly or wrongly to be mere mysticism or intellectual juggling. It took leave of fact, or managed by some illegitimate process to give to a crude generalisation from experience the appearance of a purely logical deduction. In this shape, therefore, it was really opposed to science, although the time was to come in which evolution would present itself in a scientific form.[1] Meanwhile, the concessions made by J. S. Mill were not approved by his fellows, and would have been regarded as little short of treason by the older Utilitarians. The two schools, if Coleridge's followers could be called a school, regarded each other's doctrines as simply contradictory. In appealing to experience and experience alone, the Utilitarians, as their opponents held, had reduced the world to a dead mechanism, destroyed every element of cohesion, made society a struggle of selfish interests, and struck at the very roots of all order, patriotism, poetry, and religion. They retorted that their critics were blind

[1] Coleridge's *Hints towards the Formation of a more Comprehensive Theory of Life*, edited by S. B. Watson, in 1848, is a curious attempt to apply his evolution doctrine to natural science. Lewes, in his *Letters on Comte's Philosophy of the Sciences*, says that it is a 'shameless plagiarism' from Schelling's *Erster Entwurf*, etc. It seems, as far as I can judge, that Coleridge's doctrines about magnetism, reproduction, irritability, sensibility, etc., are, in fact, adapted from Schelling. The book was intended, as Mr. E. H. Coleridge tells me, for a chapter in a work on Scrophula, projected by Gillman. As Coleridge died long before the publication, he cannot be directly responsible for not acknowledging obligations to Schelling. Unfortunately he cannot claim the benefit of a good character in such matters. Anyhow, Coleridge's occasional excursions into science can only represent a vague acceptance of the transcendental method represented, as I understand, by Oken.

adherents of antiquated prejudice, and sought to cover superstition and despotism either by unprovable dogmatic assertions, or by taking refuge in a cloudy mystical jargon, which really meant nothing.

They did not love each other.

THE ENGLISH UTILITARIANS

THE ENGLISH UTILITARIANS

By LESLIE STEPHEN

IN THREE VOLUMES

VOL. III

JOHN STUART MILL

NEW YORK

PETER SMITH

1950

CONTENTS

CHAPTER I

JOHN STUART MILL'S LIFE

CHAPTER II

MILL'S LOGIC

CHAPTER III

POLITICAL ECONOMY

CHAPTER I

JOHN STUART MILL'S LIFE [1]

I. CHILDHOOD

WHEN James Mill died, the spirit of his followers was
entering upon a new phase. A certain chill was creeping
over the confidence of previous years. The Reform Bill
had been hailed as inaugurating a new era ; the Utilitarians thought that they had made a solid lodgment in the
fortress, and looked forwards to complete occupation.
The world was going their way ; their doctrines were
triumphing ; and if those who accepted their conclusions
claimed the credit of originating the movement, the true
faith was advancing. Triumph by other hands should
be a sufficient reward for preachers who preferred solid
success to personal glory. Opinions long regarded with
horror might now be openly avowed, and might be
expected to spread when the incubus of the old repressive
system was removed. The position, to compare small

[1] Mill's *Autobiography* (1873) is the main authority. Professor Bain's *John
Stuart Mill: a Criticism, with Personal Recollections* (1882), is a necessary
supplement, and gives an excellent summary. The most interesting later
publications are the correspondence with Gustave d'Eichthal (1898) and the
correspondence with Comte. Comte's letters were published by the Positivist
Society in 1877, and the whole edited by M. Lévy-Bruhl in 1899. The
Memories of Old Friends, by Caroline Fox (1882), gives some interesting
accounts of Mill's conversation in 1840, etc.

things with great, resembled that in which Protestantism seemed to be definitely triumphing over the Papacy ; and, as in that case, the latent strength of the old order was as yet underestimated. The party which had been so hopeful when bound together by external pressure seemed to lose its energy at the moment of its greatest triumph ; its disciples became languid ; its cherished plans were rejected or emasculated ; and many of the little band of enthusiasts abandoned or materially modified their doctrine. The change, indeed, meant that many of the principles for which they contended had won general acceptance ; but, for that reason, they had no longer a common war-cry. The consequences are illustrated in the career of John Stuart Mill, who succeeded to the leadership of the sect. In certain respects, as we shall see, Mill's great aim was to soften and qualify the teaching of his predecessors. At the same time he adhered, even more strictly than he was himself conscious of adhering, to their fundamental tenets ; and as a philosopher he gained in the later years of his life a far wider authority than had ever been exercised by his predecessors. The early disciples of Bentham and of James Mill were few, and felt even painfully their isolation. But in his later years John Stuart Mill had emerged. He had become the most prominent of English thinkers ; the political liberals referred to him as the soundest expounder of their principles ; and even in the English universities, the strongholds in his youth of all ancient prejudices, he had probably more followers than any other teacher. In the following chapters I must trace the history of the intellectual change. I begin by considering Mill's personal

history. No complete biography has appeared, nor were the external events of his career of special interest. Mill, however, left an autobiography which was intended to supply what is of most importance for us, the history of his intellectual and moral development. In that respect the book is eminently deserving of study. I must indicate what appear to me to be the most important of the influences there described.

John Stuart Mill, born 20th May 1806, was twenty-six at the death of Bentham and thirty at the death of his father. He was therefore old enough to be deeply affected by their personal influence ; and his precocity had made the relation to his elders far more intimate than is often possible. James Mill and Bentham looked upon him from early years as their spiritual heir. In 1812 his father writes to Bentham [1] : 'Should I die,' says James Mill, ' one thought that would pinch me most sorely ' would be leaving the poor boy's ' mind unmade.' Therefore, ' I take your offer quite seriously '—an offer apparently to be John's guardian—' and then we may perhaps leave him a successor worthy of both of us.' John lived till his manhood almost exclusively in their little circle ; and no child was ever more elaborately and strenuously indoctrinated with the views of a sect. Had James Mill adhered to his early creed his son would probably have become a fit subject for one of those edifying tracts which deal with infantile conversions. From the earliest dawn of intellect until the age of fourteen he was the subject of one of the most singular educational experiments on record.

He gives in his *Autobiography* an account of his

[1] Bentham's *Works*, x. 472.

course of study.[1] His memory did not go back to the time at which he began Greek ; but he was told that he was then three years old. By his eighth year (1814) he had read all Herodotus, Xenophon's *Cyropædia* and *Memorabilia*, part of Lucian, and six Dialogues of Plato, including the *Theætetus*, which, he ' ventures to think,' might have been better omitted, as it ' was totally impossible that he could understand it.' In the next three years he had read Homer, Thucydides, parts of the plays of Sophocles, Euripides, and Aristophanes, Demosthenes, Æschines, and Lysias, Theocritus, Anacreon, and the *Anthology*, and (in 1817) Aristotle's *Rhetoric*, the first ' scientific treatise on any moral or psychological subject ' which he carefully analysed and tabulated. He did not begin Latin till his eighth year, when he read Cornelius Nepos and Cæsar's *Commentaries*. By his twelfth year he had read much of Virgil, Horace, Livy, Sallust, Ovid's *Metamorphoses*, Terence, Lucretius, and a great deal of Cicero. He had learned a little arithmetic by his eighth year, and had afterwards gone on to conic sections and trigonometry, and had begun the differential calculus. His father's ignorance of the higher mathematics left him to struggle by himself with the difficulties of his later studies ; but he was far in advance of most boys of his age. He read, too, some books upon the experimental sciences, especially chemistry, but had no opportunity of seeing actual experiments. In English he had read histories, making notes, and discussing the results with his father in morning walks through the green lanes near Hornsey. He had read Hume, Robertson, and Gibbon ; Watson's *Philip II. and III.*,

[1] Cf. letter of 30th July 1819 in Bain's *J. S. Mill*, pp. 6 to 9.

which particularly charmed him by the accounts of the revolts in the Netherlands ; Rollin's *Ancient History*, Hooke's *History of Rome*, Langhorne's *Plutarch*, Burnet's *Own Time*, the *Annual Register*, and Millar's *English Government*, besides Mosheim, M'Crie's *Knox*, and Sewell's *Quakers*. His father liked, he says, to put into his hands books illustrative of the struggles of energetic men. He read Anson and other voyages for this purpose. In a purely imaginative direction he was allowed more scanty fare. He was, however, devoted to *Robinson Crusoe*, read the *Arabian Nights* and *Don Quixote*, Miss Edgeworth, and Brooke's *Fool of Quality* ; admired Joanna Baillie's plays, and was fascinated by Pope's *Homer*. He was attracted by Scott's lays, and some of Campbell's lyrics, but cared little for Shakespeare, and could make nothing of Spenser's *Faery Queen*. He attempted little Latin and no Greek composition ; but he wrote a few childish ' histories,' and a little English verse. In purely literary training he was hardly above the average of clever boys. This gives his intellectual state at the age of twelve. During his thirteenth and fourteenth years he was initiated in philosophical studies. He continued to read classical literature, but was now expected to understand the thought as well as the words. He began logic by reading Aristotle, some of the scholastic treatises, and especially Hobbes's *Computatio sive Logica*. His father lectured him upon the utility of the syllogism. He made a careful study of Demosthenes, Tacitus, Juvenal, and Quintilian, and then advanced to Plato. To Plato, as he considered, he owed an especial debt, being greatly impressed by the logical method, though caring little for the more mystical or poetical doctrines congenial to those who are generally called Platonists. His faculties were also stimulated by helping his father in the proofs of the *History of India*, with whom also in the year 1819 he 'went through a complete course of political economy,' first reducing to writing his father's oral expositions, and then carefully reading Ricardo and Adam Smith.

This, he says, ended what could properly be called his lessons. The whole narrative is curiously characteristic of father and son. No one could have devoted himself more unreservedly to the education of a son. While working hard for the support of himself and his family, James Mill spared no trouble to do also the whole work of a schoolmaster. The boy prepared his lessons in the room in which the father was writing, and was constantly interrupting him for help. The father submitted, but unfortunately could not submit good-humouredly. He was 'the most impatient of men,' and the most rigorous of martinets. He did not, it seems, employ the birch, but found an equivalent in sarcastic reproaches. He was angry when his pupil failed to understand him for want—not of industry but—of knowledge, and guarded against cherishing conceit by humiliating language. When John was to leave the family, the father thought it necessary to explain that he would find himself to have learned more than other lads. But, he said, you are not to be proud of it; for it would be the deepest disgrace if you had not profited by the unusual advantage of a father willing and able to teach you. Education, like other things, was evidently a matter of sanctions; and the one sanction upon which the teacher relied was the dread of his disapproval. The child was

driven, rather than attracted by sympathetic encouragement. John Mill had also to teach his younger brothers and sisters, both at this and till a much later period. Mill records his conviction that their plan (suggested probably by the Lancasterian system, in which the father was so much interested) was both inefficient and a bad moral discipline for teacher and taught. When Place went to visit Bentham and the Mills at Ford Abbey in 1814, he found the system at work. The children were regularly kept at their lessons from six to nine, and from ten to one. Their dinner had been delayed one day till six, because the girls had mistaken a word, and John, their teacher, had not detected the mistake. Place thinks that John is a 'prodigy,' but fears that he will grow up 'morose and selfish.'[1] That anticipation was happily not verified. The health of the other children, however, appears to have suffered; and, although John speaks with the warmest appreciation of his father's character, it is evident that he felt more respect than filial affection, and that, in spite of close intellectual intercourse, there was a want of such personal confidence as gives a charm to the relation in happier cases. If I cannot say that I, like his younger children, 'loved him tenderly,' says John, 'I was always loyally devoted to him.'[2] That loyalty is shown unmistakably by every reference, and the references are very frequent, that Mill made to his father in his writings. Mill's own estimate of the result of his education is noteworthy. The experiment proves, he says, the possibility of instilling into a child an amount of knowledge such as is rarely acquired before manhood. He

[1] Given in *Dictionary of National Biography*.
[2] *Autobiography*, p. 52.

was, he considers, rather below than above par in quickness of apprehension, retentiveness of memory, and energy of character. What he did, therefore, could be done by any child of average health and capacity. His later achievements, he thinks, were due to the fact that, among other favourable circumstances, his father's training had given him the start of his contemporaries by 'a quarter of a century.'[1] His opinion is probably coloured by his tendency to set down all differences between men as due to external circumstances. He and his father, as Professor Bain notes, inclined to the doctrine of Helvétius that children all start alike.[2] Mill, by those who dissent from this view, will probably be held to have been endowed by nature with an extraordinary power of acquiring and assimilating knowledge, and presumably had from infancy whatever intellectual qualities are implied in that gift. His experience in teaching his own family might have taught him that the gift is not shared by the average child. So far, however, as Mill's judgment refers to his own case, it asserts what I take to be a truth not always admitted. He is sometimes noticed as an example of the evils done by excessive instruction. Yet, after all, he certainly became one of the leading men of his generation, and, if this strenuous education was not the sole cause, it must be reckoned as having been one main condition of his success. His father's teaching had clearly one, and that the highest, merit. The son had been taught really to use his mind; he had been trained to argue closely; to test conclusions instead of receiving them passively, and to systematise his knowledge as he acquired it. The course of strenuous mental

[1] *Autobiography*, p. 30.   [2] Bain's *J. S. Mill*, p. 84.

gymnastics qualified him to appear in early youth as a vigorous controversialist, and to achieve an immense quantity of valuable work before he passed middle age. It seems improbable that more could have been made of his faculties by any other system; and he gave a rarely approached instance of a life in which the waste of energy is reduced to a minimum.

Mill's verdict must, however, be qualified upon another ground, which he might have been expected to recognise. No one was more anxious to assert in general that an education is good in proportion as it stimulates the faculties instead of simply storing the mind with facts. Undoubtedly Mill's knowledge was of use to him. He became widely read and interested in a large circle of subjects. But we cannot hold that the mere knowledge gave him a 'quarter of a century' start. The 'knowledge' which can be acquired by a child of fourteen is necessarily crude; the *Theaetetus* or the history of Thucydides could not represent real thought for him; and one would rather say that a year's activity at twenty would have enabled him, if he had read only a quarter as much by fourteen, to make up the deficiency. The knowledge was no doubt a useful foundation; but, so far as it was acquired at the cost of excessive strain, the loss would greatly overbalance the gain. It seems clear that Mill's health did in fact suffer; and a loss of energy was far more serious than any childish knowledge could compensate. I cannot help thinking, with the so-called 'Philistine,' that a little cricket would have been an excellent substitute for half the ancient literature instilled into a lad who was not prepared really to appreciate either the thought or the literary charm.

The system had further and permanent results. Mill saw little of other boys. His father was afraid of his being corrupted or at least vulgarised by association with the average schoolboy. He had leisure enough, he declares, though he was never allowed a holiday ; but his leisure was dedicated to quiet and 'even bookish' amusements. He was unready and awkward ; untrained in the ordinary accomplishments which come from the society of contemporaries. The result was—besides the trifling loss of mere physical accomplishments—that Mill was a recluse even in childhood. There was another special reason for this isolation. Mill himself says that he was brought up without any religious instruction ; and though Professor Bain tells us that the boy went to church in his infancy, it must have been at so early a period as to leave no mark upon his memory.[1] Up to the age of fourteen, therefore, Mill, while kept apart from the ordinary influences, was imbibing with astonishing rapidity a vast amount of knowledge, and inevitably taking for granted the general opinions of his father's party.

At the end of his fourteenth year Mill went to the south of France, and stayed for a year with Sir Samuel, the brother of Jeremy, Bentham. There he learned French, attended various courses of lectures, and carried on his study of mathematics and of political economy. His intellectual appetite was still voracious and his hours of study were probably excessive. The period, however, was chiefly remarkable for the awakening of other tastes. The lessons of fencing and riding masters seem to have been thrown away ; but he learned something of botany

[1] Mill's *Autobiography*, p. 43 ; Bain's *James Mill*, p. 90.

from George, the son of Sir Samuel, afterwards eminently distinguished in the science. Mill's taste, though it did not develop into a scientific study, made him a good field botanist, and provided him with almost his only recreation. It encouraged the love of walking, which he shared with his father ; and in a tour in the Pyrenees he learned to enjoy grand natural scenery. He appears, too, to have lost some of his boyish awkwardness in the new society. The greatest advantage, however, according to himself, was his 'having breathed for a whole year the free and genial atmosphere of continental life.'[1] His comments upon this are remarkable. He could not then, as he remarks, know much of English society. He did not know its 'low moral tone,' the 'absence of high feelings' and 'sneering depreciation of all demonstrations of them,' nor, therefore, perceive the contrast with the French, who cultivate sentiments elevated by comparison at least, and who, by the habitual exercise of the feelings, encourage also a culture of the understanding, descending to the less educated classes.[2] Still, he was impressed by French amiability and sociability, and the English habit of 'acting as if everybody else was either an enemy or a bore.'

I do not venture to pronounce any opinion upon this estimate of the contrast between English and French society. Whatever truth it contains would be intensified for Mill by the fact that a large class of Englishmen clearly regarded the Utilitarians as 'enemies,' and all

[1] *Autobiography*, p. 58.
[2] Mill does not here make especial reference to his father, of whom, however, he had said before that he shared the ordinary English weakness of starving the feelings from dislike of expressing them. One would be inclined to guess that James Mill exaggerated rather than shared that feeling.

men felt them to be bores. The 'practical' Briton no doubt treated the views of the philosophical Radical with an application of what he meant for humour and Mill received as brutality. But the estimate is characteristic. Mill's Spartan discipline was already rousing him to a dumb sense of the value of the emotions. Though he, with his school, was bound to denounce 'sentimentalism,' he was beginning to see that there was another side to the question. And, in the next place, Mill's appreciation of French courtesy fell in with a marked tendency of his thought. He had, of course, at this time only laid the foundation of an acquaintance with France and Frenchmen, which, however, became much closer in the following years. He acquired a cordial sympathy with the French liberals ; he grew to be thoroughly familiar with French politics, and followed the later history of his friends with sympathy and admiration. In his early essays, he is constantly insisting upon the merits of French writers and lamenting the scandalous ignorance of their achievements prevalent in England ; the French *philosophes* of the eighteenth century became his model ;[1] and he pushed his zeal, as he thinks, even to excess ; while, as we shall afterwards see, some contemporary French writers exercised an influence upon his own views of the highest importance. He did not learn German till some time later ; and never became a profound student of German literature and philosophy. But France was a kind of second country to him ; and excited what may almost be called a patriotic sentiment. Patriotism, indeed, was scarcely held to be a virtue by the Utilitarians. It meant for them the state of mind of the country squire or his

[1] *Autobiography*, p. 108.

hanger-on the parson ; and is generally mentioned as giving a sufficient explanation of unreasoning prejudice. Mill's development, I doubt not, was furthered by this enthusiasm ; it gave him a wider outlook, and stimulated many impulses which had been hampered by the narrowness of his party. For many years, however, it contributed to make him something of an alien ; and I do not think that incapacity to sympathise even with the stupid prejudices of one's countrymen is an unmixed advantage.

Mill returned to England in July 1821. He took up his old studies, taught his brothers and sisters, read Condillac and a history of the French revolution, of which, in spite of his previous stay in France, he had known very little, and decided that it would be 'transcendent glory' to be 'a Girondist in an English convention.' Meanwhile, a profession had to be chosen. He was intended for the bar, and began to study Roman law under John Austin. He set to work upon Bentham, and the reading of Dumont's *Traités de Législation* formed an epoch in his life. His botanical studies had fostered his early taste for classification, already awaked by his early logical studies. He was now delighted to find that human actions might be classified as well as plants, and, moreover, classified by the principle of utility, that is to say, by reference to a guiding rule for all known conduct. 'Utility' took its place as 'the keystone which held together the detached and fragmentary parts of his knowledge and beliefs.'[1] He had now a philosophy and even, 'in one of the best senses of the word, a religion, the inculcation and diffusion of which could be made the principal outward purpose of a life.' The very modera-

[1] *Autobiography*, p. 66.

tion of the creed was among its claims. Mill was not roused, like Shelley, to an enthusiastic vision of an abrupt regeneration of man. His religion was strictly scientific; it recognised the necessity of slow elaboration, but offered a sufficiently wide vista of continuous improvement to be promoted by unremitting labour. He now enlarged his philosophical reading; he studied Locke, Helvétius, and Hartley, Berkeley, and Hume's *Essays*, besides Reid, Dugald Stewart, and Brown's essay upon Cause and Effect. These studies were carried on while he was reading his father's *Analysis* in manuscript, and no doubt discussing with his father the points raised by the argument. The last book which he mentions as affecting his early development is 'Philip Beauchamp's' treatise upon the utility of religion. The 'searching character of its analysis,' he says, produced a great effect upon him, of which some results will appear hereafter.

II. EARLY PROPAGANDISM

In 1822—at the age, that is, of sixteen—Mill began to compose 'argumentative' essays, which were apparently crude enough, but which were profitable exercises. Already, too, he was beginning to take a position in the Utilitarian circle. John Austin (1790-1859), his tutor, a man of lofty, if over-fastidious character, encouraged the boy by his kind interest. Another important friend was George Grote, who, as I have said, had already become a writer in the cause. To both these men, his seniors by sixteen and twelve years respectively, a boy of sixteen or seventeen would naturally look up with respectful admiration. With Grote, as with John Austin, he held much

'sympathetic communion,' but his first ally among men whom he could feel to be contemporaries was Austin's younger brother Charles. He was a man who gave the impression, according to Mill, of 'boundless strength,' with talents and will which seemed capable of 'dominating the world.' Instead of being, like his brother John, incapacitated for life by over-refinement, he made a fortune at the bar; and his energy was, after a time, entirely diverted from the Utilitarian propaganda. For the present, however, he was defending the true faith in an uncongenial atmosphere. He was, says Mill, the 'really influential mind among these intellectual gladiators'—the young Cambridge orators. James Mill, as I have said, had been encouraged by hearing that the cause of Utilitarianism was being upheld even in one of the universities, which he took to be the natural centres of obscurantism. John Mill visited Austin at Cambridge in 1822, and the boy of sixteen greatly impressed the undergraduates by his conversational power. The elder Mill was urged to send his son to Trinity College. He would no doubt have feared to expose the youth to such contagion.[1] John Mill himself long held the universities to be mere institutions for supporting the established creed. 'We regard the system of these institutions,' he said in 1836, 'as administered for two centuries past, with sentiments little short of utter abhorrence.'[2] It is

---

[1] It was not necessary at this time for an undergraduate to sign the Thirty-nine Articles as Bain supposes. From 1773 a graduate had to make the declaration that he was a '*bona fide* member of the church of England,' whatever that may mean; but any one might be a member of the University and pass the examinations. Sylvester, for example, though a Jew, was second wrangler in 1837.

[2] *Dissertations*, i. 193.

idle to ask whether closer contact with the average English youth would or would not have been beneficial, but the sentiment marks the degree in which Mill was an alien among men of his own class in English society. Meanwhile, he formed, in the winter of 1822-23, a little society of his own. He called it the Utilitarian Society, adopting the title which had been cursorily used by Bentham[1] from Galt's *Annals of the Parish*. He mentions among its members, which never amounted to ten, William Eyton Tooke, son of Thomas Tooke, the economist, who died young; William Ellis (1800-1881), known, says Mill, for his 'apostolic exertions for the improvement of education,' chiefly in the direction of promoting the study of political economy in schools; George John Graham, afterwards an official in the Bankruptcy Court; and Graham's special friend, John Arthur Roebuck (1801-1879), who was to become one of the most thoroughgoing Radicals of the following period, though in later years the faithful Abdiel became an Ishmael, and finally a Tory. With these youths, all apparently Mill's seniors by a few years, he discussed the principles of the sect, and became, as he says, 'a sort of leader.' He tried hard to enlist recruits, and soon became an effective combatant in the actual warfare of the time. The society was broken up in 1826.

Mill had already received the appointment which decided the future course of his life. He was appointed to a clerkship in the India House, 21st May 1823,

---

[1] The name soon became popular. Southey, writing to Henry Taylor (12th April 1827), calls them 'Futilitarians' (*Life and Correspondence*). Taylor was on friendly terms with the set, and gives some account of them and the later debating society. See *Autobiography*, i. 77-95; and *Correspondence*, pp. 30, 72.

having just finished his seventeenth year. He received successive promotions, till in 1856 he became chief of the office with a salary of £2000 a year. Mill gives his own view of the advantages of the position, which to a man of his extraordinary power of work were unmistakable. He was placed beyond all anxiety as to bread-winning. He was not bound to make a living by his pen, and could devote himself to writing of permanent value. He was at the same time brought into close relation with the conduct of actual affairs; forced to recognise the necessity of compromise, and to study the art of instilling his thoughts into minds not specially prepared for their reception. Mill's books show how well he acquired this art. Whatever their other merits or defects, they reconcile conditions too often conflicting; they are the product of mature reflection, and yet presented so as to be intelligible without special initiation. He is unsurpassable as an interpreter between the abstract philosopher and the man of common-sense. The duties were not such as to absorb his powers. Though his holidays were limited to a month, he could enjoy Sunday rambles in the country and pedestrian tours at home and abroad; and though conscientiously discharging his official duties, he managed to turn out as much other work as might have occupied the whole time of average men. The Utilitarians were beginning to make themselves felt in the press. Mill's first printed writings were some letters in the *Traveller* in 1822, defending Ricardo and James Mill against some criticism by Torrens. He then contributed three letters to the *Morning Chronicle*, denouncing the prosecution of Carlile, which then excited the rightful wrath of the Utilitarians. Two letters in continuation were too outspoken to be published.[1] Mill contributed to the *Westminster Review* from its start in the spring of 1824, helping his father's assault upon the *Edinburgh*. He was, he says, the most frequent writer of all, and between the second and eighteenth number contributed thirteen reviews. They show that he was reading widely. An article upon Scott's *Napoleon* in 1828 shows that he had fully made up his deficiencies as to the history of the French revolution. He had not, however, as yet attained his full powers of expression; and neither the style nor the arrangement of the matter has the merits of his later work.[2] The most remarkable by far is the review of Whately's *Logic* in January 1828. It shows some touches of youthful arrogance, though exceedingly complimentary to the author reviewed. But the knowledge displayed and the vigour of the expression are surprising in a youth of twenty-one; and it proves that Mill was already reflecting to some purpose upon the questions treated in his *Logic*.

While thus serving an apprenticeship to journalism,

[1] About this period, Mill, then aged seventeen or eighteen, took part with some friends in distributing a pamphlet called 'What is Love?' advocating what are now called Neo-Malthusian principles. The police interfered, and some scandal was caused. An allusion to this performance—which shows Mill's enthusiasm and honesty, if not his discretion—appeared in an article by Abraham Hayward upon Mill's death. Hayward was attacked by W. D. Christie in an indignant pamphlet, which gives a sufficient statement of the facts. See Cobbett's *Political Works*, vi. 421 (August 1824), for a reference to this affair.

[2] Bain thinks that J. S. Mill wrote the article in the Review upon the Carlile prosecutions in July 1824. I cannot admit this opinion. If so, Mill was a more capable journalist than the other articles would imply. But—apart from questions of style—I cannot think that Mill would have gone out of his way to avow a belief in Christianity, as is done by the writer of the article.

Mill was going through a remarkable mental training. About the beginning of 1825 he undertook to edit Bentham's *Rationale of Evidence*. He says that this work 'occupied nearly all his leisure for about a year.' That such a task should have been accomplished by a youth of twenty in a year would seem marvellous even if he had been exclusively devoted to it. He had to condense large masses of Bentham's crabbed manuscript into a continuous treatise; to 'unroll' his author's involved and parenthetic sentences; to read the standard English text-books upon evidence; to reply to reviewers of previous works of Bentham, and to add comments especially upon some logical points. Finally, he had to see 'five large volumes through the press.'[1] That this was admirable practice, and that Mill's style became afterwards 'markedly superior' to what it had been before, may be well believed. It is impossible, however, not to connect the fact that Mill had gone through this labour in 1825 with the singular mental convulsion which followed in 1826.

He was, he says, in a 'dull state of nerves' in the autumn of that year. It occurred to him to ask whether he would be happy supposing that all his objects in life could be realised. 'An irrepressible consciousness distinctly answered "No."' The cloud would not pass away. He could think of no physician of the mind who could 'raze out the rooted trouble of the brain.' His father had no experience of such feeling, nor could he

[1] In the collective edition of Bentham's *Works* the treatise occupies about 900 double-column pages of some 500 words to a column. If 300 days were given to the task, this would mean an average output of 1500 words a day.

give the elder man the pain of thinking that all the educational plans had failed. The father's philosophy, indeed, both explained, and showed the hopelessness of, the evil. Feelings depend upon association. Analysis tends to destroy the associations, and therefore to 'wear away the feelings.' Happiness has for its main source the pleasure of sympathy with others. But the knowledge that the feeling would give happiness could not suffice to restore the feeling itself. It seemed to be impossible to set to work again and create new associations. Mill dragged on mechanically through the winter of 1826-27, and the gloom only gathered. He made up his mind that he could not bear life for more than a year. The first ray of hope came from a passage in which Marmontel describes his father's death and his resolution to make up the loss to his family. Gradually he recovered, though he suffered several relapses. He learned, he says, two lessons: first, that though happiness must be the end, it must not be the immediate or conscious end, of life. Ask whether you are happy and you will cease to be happy. Fix upon some end external to happiness, and happiness will be 'inhaled with the air you breathe.' And in the second place, he learned to make the 'cultivation of the feelings one of the cardinal points in his ethical and philosophical creed.' He could not, however, for some time apply his new doctrine to practice. He mentions as a quaint illustration of this period one ingenious mode of self-torment. He had from childhood taken pleasure in music. During the period of depression even music had lost its charm. As he revived, the charm gradually returned. Yet he teased himself by the reflection that, as the number of musical notes is limited, there must

come a time when new Mozarts and Webers would no longer be possible. This, he says, was like the fear of the Laputans that the sun would in time be burnt out, a fear, it may be remarked, which modern science has not diminished. He might have noticed that, as the number of combinations of twenty-six letters is finite, new Shakespeares and Dantes will become impossible. He observes, however, that this was connected with the 'only good point in his very unromantic and in no way honourable distress.' It showed an interest in the fortunes of the race as well as in his own, and therefore gave hopes that if he could see his way to better prospects of human happiness his depression might be finally removed. This state of mind made his reading of Wordsworth's *Excursion* in the autumn of 1828 an important event in his life. He could make nothing of Byron, whom he also studied for the first time. But Wordsworth appealed to the love of scenery, which was already one of his passions, and thus revealed to him the pleasure of tranquil contemplation and of an interest in the common feelings and destiny of human beings. From the famous *Ode*, too, he inferred that Wordsworth had gone through an experience like his own, had regretted the freshness of early life, and had found compensation by the path along which he could guide his reader.

The effect upon Mill of Wordsworth's poetry is remarkable, though I cannot here discuss the relation. Readers of the fourth book of the *Excursion* (called 'Despondency corrected') may note how directly the poet applies his teaching to the philosopher. He asks, for example, whether men of science and those who have 'analysed the thinking principle' are to become a 'degraded race,' and declares that it could never be intended by nature

> 'That we should pore, and dwindle as we pore,
> Viewing all objects unremittingly
> In disconnexion dead and spiritless ;
> And still dividing, and dividing still,
> Break down all grandeur, still unsatisfied
> With the perverse attempt, while littleness
> May yet become more little ; waging thus
> An impious warfare with the very life
> Of our own souls ! '

This is the precise equivalent of Mill's doctrine about the danger of the habit of analysis, and James Mill, if Wordsworth had ever read him, would have made an admirable example for the excellent pedlar.

It is characteristic of Mill that he does not explicitly attribute this mental crisis to the obvious physical cause. As Professor Bain tells us, he would never admit that hard work could injure anybody. Disbelief in that danger is only too common with hard workers. Mill intimates that his dejection was occasioned by a 'low state of nerves,' but adds that this was one of the accidents to which every one is occasionally liable.[1] A man would at least be more liable to it who, like Mill, had been kept in a state of severe intellectual tension from his earliest infancy, and who had gone through such labours as the editing Bentham's *Rationale of Evidence*. That his health was permanently affected seems to be clear. Ten years later (1836) he was 'seized with an obstinate derangement of the brain.' One symptom was a 'ceaseless spasmodic twitching over one eye,' which never left him. In 1839 another illness forced him to take a month's holiday, which he spent in Italy. It left permanent weakness in the lungs and the stomach. An accident in

[1] *Autobiography*, p. 133.

1848 led to a long illness and prostration of the nervous system ; and in 1854 another serious illness, which he met by an eight months' tour in Italy, Sicily, and Greece, led to the 'partial destruction of one lung' and great 'general debility.'[1] In spite of these illnesses, Mill continued to labour as strenuously as before, and until the illness of 1848 at least showed no signs of any decline of intellectual energy. They must be remembered if we would do full justice to his later career.

It is, meanwhile, remarkable that his energetic course of self-education seems hardly to have been interrupted by the period of dejection. In the year 1825, while, one might have supposed, fairly drowned in Bentham's manuscript, he contributed an article upon Catholic Emancipation to a *Parliamentary History*, started by Mr. Marshall of Leeds. He wrote others upon the commercial crisis and upon the currency and upon reciprocity in commerce for the two subsequent annual issues. He thinks that his work had now ceased to be 'juvenile,' and might be called original, so far as it applied old ideas in a new connection. At the same time he learned German, forming a class for the purpose. He also set up a society which met two days a week at Grote's house in Threadneedle Street and discussed various topics from half-past 8 till 10 A.M. These meetings lasted till 1830. The young men discussed in succession political economy, logic, and pyschology. Their plan was to take some text-book, and to discuss every point raised thoroughly— sometimes keeping to a single question for weeks—until every one was satisfied with at least his own solution of the question. Ricardo, James Mill, and their like supplied the chief literature ; but in logic they went further, and,

[1] Bain's *J. S. Mill*, pp. 43, 45, 90, 95.

---

being disgusted with Aldrich, reprinted the *Manuductio ad Logicam* of the Jesuit Du Trieu. The result of these arguments appears in the review of Whately. Mill, helped by Graham and Ellis (his old allies in the Utilitarian Society), started 'most of the novelties'; while Grote and the others formed a critical tribunal. The results formed the materials of several of Mill's writings. These occupations might have been enough for a youth of twenty, but another field for discussion offered itself. The followers of Owen were starting weekly public discussions in 1825. The Utilitarians, headed by Charles Austin, went in a body, and a series of friendly but very energetic debates went on for three months. This led to the foundation of a debating society, upon the model of the 'Speculative Society' of Edinburgh. After a failure at starting, the society became active, and until 1829 Mill took part in nearly every debate. Besides the Utilitarians, it included Macaulay, Thirlwall, Praed, the Bulwers, Fonblanque, and others. Charles Buller and Cockburn came in as Radicals, and the Tories, of whom there had been a lack in those days of reforming zeal, were reinforced by Shee (afterwards judge) and A. Hayward. Maurice and Sterling were representatives of a liberalism widely differing from Utilitarianism, and accepting Coleridge in place of Bentham as intellectual guide. Mill learned to speak fluently, if not gracefully, and improved his style by preparing written speeches. It is not strange that, with all these occupations, he felt it a relief when, in 1828, he was released from contributing to the *Westminster*. Bowring, the editor, had made arrangements with Perronet Thompson, and it was no longer an organ of the orthodox

---

Utilitarians. In 1829 Mill gave up the Speculative Society and resolved to devote himself to private studies and prepare for more elaborate work. New thoughts were being suggested from various quarters. Macaulay's attack upon his father's political theory led him to recognise the inadequacy of the Utilitarian system, and forced him to consider the logical problems involved. He came under the influence of the St. Simonians at the same period. An enthusiastic disciple of the school, Gustave d'Eichthal, two years senior to Mill, was taken by young Tooke to the debating society in May 1828, and was surprised by Mill's skilful and comprehensive summing up of a discussion. He endeavoured to make proselytes of the pair, then full of the enthusiasm and expecting the triumph of their party. Tooke, apparently Mill's warmest friend at the time, committed suicide early in 1830, in an access of excitement produced by fever ascribed to overwork and tension of mind. Mill became a half-convert. He was greatly impressed by the St. Simonian doctrine of the alternation of 'critical' and 'constructive' periods. He admitted the necessity of something better than the negative or 'critical philosophy' of the eighteenth century.[1] He desired the formation of a spiritual· power. He protested, however, against the excessive spirit of system and against premature attempts to organise such a power. Yet by degrees he modified his objections, and on 30th November 1831 declares his belief that the St. Simonian ideal will be the final state of the human race. Were England ripe for an 'organic view,' which it certainly is not, he might renounce everything in the world

[1] D'Eichthal, *Correspondence*, p. 30.

to become—not one of them, but—like them. Mill
kept, as he says, a bureau of St. Simonianism for a
time, and suggested to d'Eichthal the names of many
persons to whom the publications of the party might be
sent. Bulwer, Sterling, Whately, Blanco White, W. J.
Fox, and Dr. Arnold were among them.[1] Meanwhile,
his speculations caused him to be much troubled
by the doctrine of Philosophical Necessity; and he
worked out a solution which was ultimately published in
the *Logic*. While his mind was thus fermenting with
many new thoughts, often, as he says,[2] new only to him,
he was profoundly moved by the French revolution of
July 1830. He went at once to Paris with Roebuck
and Graham; was introduced to Lafayette, made friends
with other popular leaders, and came back prepared to
take an active part as a writer on behalf of the Reform
agitation. For some years he was an active journalist,
contributing to the *Examiner* under Fonblanque. A
series of articles called 'The Spirit of the Age' in this
paper led to his acquaintance with Carlyle, who took
him to be a 'new Mystic.'[3] In 1830 and 1831 he wrote
his essays on *Some Unsettled Questions of Political Economy*,
the fruit of the discussions with Graham (not published
till 1844), and in 1832 wrote articles upon foundations

[1] D'Eichthal, *Correspondence*, p. 147. The St. Simonians excited some
interest in England at the time. See, *e.g.*, Carlyle's *Sartor Resartus*, book iii.
ch. 12; Carlyle's *Correspondence with Goethe*, 214, 226, 258; *Tennyson's Life*,
i. 99; Tedhunter's *Whewell*, i. 240; Hodder's *Shaftesbury*, i. 126. Shaftesbury's notice was called to St. Simonianism by Southey, who wrote an article
upon it in the *Quarterly* for July 1831—a mere shriek of alarm.

[2] *Autobiography*, p. 168.

[3] Seven articles appeared from January to May 1831. As Mill says in his
Autobiography (p. 175) they are 'lumbering in style,' and of no great interest
in substance, except as showing the St. Simonian influence.

and upon the 'currency juggle,' which are the first of his
collected dissertations.

I have now followed Mill's mental history until the
period at which the follower was fully competent to
become the guide. It would be difficult to mention any
thinker who has gone through a more strenuous and
continuous discipline. From his earliest infancy till the
full development of his powers he had been going
through a kind of logical mill. No student in the old
schools employing every waking hour in 'syllogising'
could have been more assiduously trained to the use of
his weapons. If his boyish years had been passed in
a kind of intellectual gymnasium, he had as a youth
proved and perfected his skill in the open arena. His
official position was making him familiar with business
and with the ordinary state of mind of the commonplace
politician. He had been interested in fresh lines of
thought through the writings of French Liberals, and
especially the St. Simonians, and through his arguments
with the Socialists who followed Owen, and with the
young men who looked up to Coleridge as their great
teacher. His own experience had brought home to him
the sense of a certain narrowness and rigidity in the
Utilitarians; his friendly controversies had led him to
regard opponents with more toleration than his party
generally displayed, and he was sincerely anxious to
widen the foundations of his creed, and to assimilate
whatever was valuable in conflicting doctrines. Meanwhile his practice as a writer had by this time enabled
him to express himself with great clearness and vigour;
and young as he still was, he was better qualified than any
of his contemporaries to expound the views of his party.

One point, however, must be marked. Mill's training
left nothing to be desired as a system of intellectual
gymnastics. It was by no means so well calculated
to widen the mental horizon. His philosophical reading was not to be compared to that, for example,
of Sir William Hamilton, who was at this time
accumulating his great stores of knowledge. He
learned German, as people were beginning to learn
it, but he did not make himself familiar with German
thought. On 13th March 1843, having just sent
a copy of his *Logic* to Comte, he observes that he
owes much to German philosophy as a corrective to
his exclusive Benthamism. He has not, he adds, read
Kant, Hegel, or any chief of the school, but knows of
them from their French and English interpreters—
presumably Cousin, Coleridge, and Sir W. Hamilton.
He tried some of the originals afterwards, but found
that he had got all that was useful in them, and the
remainder was so *fastidieux* that he could not go on
reading.[1] Considering all his occupations, his official
duties, his editing of Bentham, his many contributions
to journalism, and the time taken up by the little societies
of congenial minds, the wonderful thing is that he read
so much else. He kept himself well informed on the
intellectual movement of France; he had made a special
study of the French revolution; and was fairly familiar
with many other provinces of historical inquiry. It was
impossible, however, that he should become learned in
the strict sense. His studies, that is, were more remarkable for intensity than for extent. The vigorous discussions with his friends upon political economy, logic,

[1] *Correspondence with Comte*, pp. 169-70.

and psychology, while implying an admirable training,
implied also a limitation of study; they did not get
beyond the school of Ricardo in political economy, nor
beyond the school of James Mill in psychology, nor
beyond a few textbooks in formal logic. They argued
the questions raised thoroughly, and until they had fully
settled their own doubts. But it would be an inevitable
result that they would generally be satisfied when they
had discovered not so much a thorough solution as the
best solution which could be given from the Utilitarian
point of view. The more fundamental questions as to
the tenability of that view would hardly be raised.
Therefore, though Mill deserves all the credit which he
has received for candour, and was, in fact, most anxious
to receive light from outside, it is not surprising that he
will sometimes appear to have been blind to arguments
familiar to thinkers of a different school. The fault is
certainly not peculiar to Mill; indeed, it is his genuine
desire to escape from it which makes it necessary to ask
why the escape was not more complete. Briefly, at any-
rate, Mill, like most other people, continued through
life to be penetrated by the convictions instilled in early
youth.

III. THE PHILOSOPHICAL RADICALS

The period which followed the Reform Bill showed a
great change in Mill's personal position. The Utilitarians
had taken their part in the agitation, and expected to
share in the fruits of victory. Several of them were
members of the first reformed parliament, especially
Grote and Roebuck, who now entered the House for the
first time. Charles Buller (1806-1848) and Sir William

Molesworth (1810-1855) were also new members, and both were among the youngest recruits of the Utilitarian party. Buller had been a pupil of Carlyle, and afterwards one of the Cambridge orators. He was evidently a man of very attractive nature, though he seems to have been too fond of a joke—the only Utilitarian, probably, liable to that imputation—and was gaining a high reputation by the time of his early death. Molesworth, after a desultory education, which included a brief stay at Cambridge about Buller's time, and some study on the Continent, became a friend of Grote upon entering parliament. He was a man of many intellectual interests, and an ardent Utilitarian. These and a few more formed the party known as 'the philosophical Radicals.' Mill, whose position was incompatible with parliamentary ambition, was to be the exponent of their principles in the press. Whatever their failings, they certainly formed an important section of the most intelligent politicians of the time. Mill became their chief exponent in the press, and began operations by articles in the *Examiner* and the *Monthly Repository* (edited by W. J. Fox). He says[1] that his writings between 1832 and 1834 would fill a large volume. Molesworth then proposed to start a new quarterly, to be called the *London Review*, which should represent the true creed more faithfully than the recreant *Westminster*. He stipulated that Mill should be the virtual, though he could not, on account of his official position, be the ostensible, editor. The first number of the *London* accordingly appeared in April 1835. A year later Molesworth bought the *Westminster*, and the review was now called the *London and Westminster*.

[1] *Autobiography*, p. 198.

Molesworth, having become tired of carrying on a review which did not pay, handed it over to Mill in 1837, who continued it till 1840, when he transferred it to Mr. Hickson.[1] The vitality of unprofitable reviews is one of the mysteries of literature. Mill lost money and spent much time in this discouraging work; but he would doubtless have grudged neither had he succeeded in doing a real service to his party.

The 'philosophical' Radicals, however, were doomed to failure. One among many obvious reasons is suggested by the name. Philosophical in English is synonymous with visionary, unpractical, or perhaps, simply foolish. The philosophers seemed to be men of crotchets, fitter for the study than the platform. They had, as Mill says, little enterprise or activity, and left the lead to the 'old hands,' Hume and O'Connell. About 1838, indeed, Mill appears to have become quite alienated from them. He thought them 'craven,' and they thought him 'mad.'[2] He admits, indeed, that the men were less to blame than the times. Mill, however, held then, and seems to have always believed, that what was wanting was mainly a worthy leader. His father, he thinks, might have forced the Whigs to accept the Radical policy had he been in parliament. For want of such a leader, the philosophical Radicals became a mere left wing of the Whigs. For a time, Mill had some hopes of Lord Durham, who represented Radical leanings in the upper sphere. Durham's death in 1840

[1] *Autobiography*, pp. 199, 206, 220; Bain's *J. S. Mill*, p. 58. Mill at first supervised rather than edited the *Review*. His sub-editors were Thomas Falconer and afterwards John Robertson.

[2] Bain's *J. S. Mill*, p. 160 (quotation from Fonblanque). See also pp. 56, 82.

put an end to any such hopes; and the philosophical Radicals had pretty well ceased by that time to represent any real political force. In truth, however, it is difficult to believe that any leader could have made much out of the materials at his disposal. The Reform Bill had transferred power to the middle classes. They had resented their own exclusion from influence, and it had been impossible to prevent the great towns from acquiring a share in the representation without risk of violent revolution. But it did not at all follow that the majority of the new constituents accepted the programme of the extreme reformers. They had forced the doors for themselves, but had no desire to admit the crowd still left outside. Only a small minority desired the measures which the Radicals had contemplated, which involved organic constitutional changes, and would possibly lead to confiscation. When the Chartists proposed a sweeping reform the middle classes were frightened by the prospect of revolution. They were quite willing to leave the old aristocratic families in power, if only the policy were modified so as to be more congenial to the industrial interests. Statesmen brought up under the old system were still the office holders, and were only anxious to steer a middle course. All this is now obvious enough; and it meant at the time that the philosophical Radicals found themselves, to their surprise, without any great force behind them, and were only able to complain of the half-hearted policy of the Whigs, and to weaken the administration until the Conservatives under Peel could take advantage of a situation which had become intolerable. The favourite measure of the philosophical Radicals was the ballot. They

attributed the slackening of zeal for Radicalism to the fact that the aristocracy were trying to maintain their old power by bribery and intimidation. The ballot would be the most obvious check to this policy.

Under these conditions Mill's position is characteristic. He wrote much and forcibly. Some of his articles of this period in the *Westminster* are collected in the first volume of the *Dissertations*. He omitted others which refer to matters of more ephemeral interest. They show great power, but they also indicate the real difficulty. Mill writes as a philosopher and an expounder of general ideas. But he also writes as a partisan—insisting, for example, upon the ballot of which he afterwards came to disapprove—and it is always a very difficult matter to reconcile the requirements imposed by these different points of view. Mill was scarcely immersed enough in the current of political agitation to plant telling personal blows; and, on the other hand, his theories seem to be cramped by the necessity of supporting a platform. He aimed, he says, at two points. He tried, and, he thinks, with partial success, to supply a philosophy of Radicalism, wider than Bentham's, and yet including what was permanently valuable in Bentham. He tried also, and this aim was 'from the first chimerical,' to rouse the Radicals to the formation of a powerful party. The articles upon Durham were partly prompted by this purpose; and, though unsuccessful in that respect, he spoke, he thinks, the 'word in season,' which at a critical moment directed public opinion towards the concession of self-government to the Colonies.[1]

The articles in the *Westminster* show, now that we can

[1] *Autobiography*, pp. 214-17.

see later developments, how clearly he saw the real difficulty, and yet how far he was from estimating its full significance. They are of essential importance to an understanding of his whole career.[1] In the article which was his farewell to politics for the time, he elaborately states the problem. He considers what are a man's 'natural' politics. He claims more than the usual faith in the influence of reason and virtue over men's minds ; but then it is in the influence ' of the reason and virtue upon their own side of the question.' A man is made a Liberal or a Conservative on the average by his position ; he is made a Liberal or a Conservative of a particular kind by his 'intellect and heart.' In other words, parties, in the main, represent classes ; and the fundamental opposition is between the ' privileged ' and the ' disqualified ' classes. The line, then, as with the old Radicals, is drawn between the privileged, who are chiefly the land-owners and their adherents, clerical, legal, and military, and the 'disqualified,' who are chiefly the lower middle classes and the working classes. Now, the Radical party ought to combine the whole strength of the disqualified against the privileged. Why do they not? Among the superficial reasons is that want of a leader, which Mill hoped to supply by Durham. Another personal reason is that, as he complains rather bitterly,[2] the Radicals never spoke so as to secure the sympathy of the working classes. This points to the real difficulty. There was a gulf between the middle and the working classes, as well as between the ' privileged ' and the ' disqualified.'

[1] See articles in *Westminster Review* : Oct. 1837, ' Parties and the Ministry ' ; Jan. 1838, ' Radicalism in Canada ' ; April 1839, ' Reorganisation of the Radical party.'   [2] ' Parties and the Ministry.'

The real aim of Mill's articles is to show how this gulf could be surmounted. All the ' disqualified ' might be brought into line if only the philosophical Radicals could be got to attract the working classes, and the working classes to follow the Radicals. Mill therefore endeavours to prove that the Radical measures were in fact intended for the benefit of the working classes, and might consequently be made attractive. The position was in fact precisely this. The Chartist agitation was becoming conspicuous, and the Chartists had broken off from the Radicals. Mill had to persuade them that they did not know their true friends. His sincerity and the warmth of his sympathy are unmistakable, but so is the difficulty of the task.

In the first place, he repudiates universal suffrage (one of the six points). He thinks it bad in point of policy, because to propose it would alienate the whole middle class at once, who would see in it a direct attack upon property. But universal suffrage was also bad in itself, because the mass of the very lowest class was ignorant, degraded, and utterly unfit for power. The intelligent working man ought to recognise the fact, and therefore not to grant the suffrage to the lowest class. What, then, was to be done? The answer, given emphatically in his last article, is that we should govern for the working classes by means of the middle classes. That, he says, should be the motto of every Radical. The ideal is a government which should adopt such a policy as would be adopted under universal suffrage in a country where the masses were educated so as to be fit for it. In other words, the great aim of Radicals should be to redress practical grievances.

Did, then, the Radical platform aim at such redress? Mill's proof that it did is significant. The Radicals were unanimous against the Corn-laws ; and the Corn-laws, as he argues,[1] injure the poor man because they lower the rate of profit, and are ruining the small capitalist and destroying our trade. The philosophical Radicals were supporters of the new Poor-law. It had often been said that the sinecurists were in fact rich paupers living on other men's labours. Mill inverts the argument by saying that the paupers under the old system were poor sinecurists, equally living upon other men's labours. To say nothing of some smaller grievances, such as taxes on articles consumed by the poor, flogging in the army, and enclosure of commons, which were attacked by the Radicals, the Radicals also wished to discharge ' one of the highest duties of government' by setting up a system of national education. It is now easy to see why these proposals failed to satisfy the class to whom the Radicals were to appeal. A great part of them, he says, were ' Owenites ' or, in other words, inclined to Socialism. They had, as Mill regretfully admits, crude views upon political economy. Thus, the Chartists were not hearty, even in the anti-Corn-law agitation. They did not see that a rise of profits was at all for their benefit. They held, as Mill observes, that whatever profit was gained would go to their masters. On the other hand, they did not admire the new Poor-law. They thought that, as Cobbett had told them, it robbed them of their rights, and did not object to having small sinecures. National education, however desirable, did not seem worth a struggle till they

[1] ' Ministers and Parties.'

had got higher wages. Then, as Mill again admits, they would not see that the competition which injured them was their own competition, and due to their disregard of Malthus. They objected to competition in general, which meant, as they thought, the grinding down of their class by the wicked capitalist. Mill remarks that Owen was not really opposed to rights of property ; and one of his recommendations is that the law of partnership should be reformed so as to facilitate the growth of co-operative societies. Even if this failed, it would tend to educate the poor in sound economic principles. Meanwhile, however, the principles of their actual leaders were anything but ' sound.' Mill incidentally speaks of the ' Oastlers and Stephenses ' as representing only the worst class of the ' operative Radicals.' Oastler was at this time conspicuous for his support of the factory legislation. He was allied with Lord Ashley, and represented the alliance of Socialism with Toryism or ' New Englandism.' Now the factory legislation, which naturally seemed to the working classes the greatest step towards a recognition of their interest, is not mentioned by Mill, and for the good reason that he and his school were opposed to it on principle. He refers incidentally to measures such as the Eight Hours Bill as belonging to the quack schemes of reform.[1]

Briefly, the difficulty was that the working classes were already looking in the direction of Socialism, and that Mill remained a thorough individualist. With his sanguine belief in the power of education, he thought, with a certain simplicity, that the Owenites, with whose ultimate views he fully sympathised, might be taught to

[1] See ' Claims of Labour ' in *Dissertations*, ii. 192.

give up their crude political economy. Their education required more time and labour than he imagined.

This indicates a critical point. The classes which had been disappointed by the Reform Bill, and had hoped for great social changes, were discontented, but looked for remedies of a very different kind from Mill's. They could not see a philanthropy which was hidden behind Malthus and Ricardo, and which proposed to improve their position by removing privileges, indeed, but not by diminishing competition. If this applied to Mill, it applied still more to his friends. They represented rather intellectual scorn for old prejudices and clumsy administration than any keen sympathy with the sufferings of the poor. The harsher side of the old Utilitarianism was, therefore, emphasised by them, and Mill's attempts to enlarge and soften its teaching were regarded by his allies with a certain suspicion. They thought that his sympathy with the Socialist ends implied a tendency to look too favourably upon its means. The articles upon Bentham and Coleridge,[1] in which he tried to inculcate a wider sympathy with his opponents, scandalised such friends as Grote, and he ceased to represent even his own allies. Philosophical Radicalism died out. Its adherents became Whigs, or joined the Cobden form of Radicalism, which was the very antithesis of Socialism. Their philosophy suited neither party. To the class which still retained the leading position in politics, they appeared as destructives; and to the classes which were turning towards Chartism, they appeared as the most chilling critics of popular aspiration. The Free-trade movement, which was gathering strength as the manufacturing

[1] August 1838, and March 1840.

interest grew stronger, had no doubt an affinity for one important part of their teaching. But such men as Cobden and Bright, though they accepted the political economy of the Utilitarians, could not be counted as products or adherents of the Utilitarian philosophy. The agreement was superficial in other respects, though complete in regard to one important group of measures. This marks an essential point in Mill's political and social doctrine. For the present, it is enough to note that the philosophical Radicals who had expected to lead the van had been left on one side in the political warfare, and by 1840 were almost disbanded. Grote, the ablest of Mill's friends, retired from parliament to devote himself to his *History of Greece* about the same time as Mill set to work upon the completion of his *Logic*.

One characteristic of Mill as an editor may be noted before proceeding. Under his management, a large number of distinguished contributors were enlisted. Professor Bain mentions Bulwer, Charles Buller, Roebuck, James and Harriet Martineau, W. J. Fox, Mazzini, and others. The independent authorship of many articles was indicated by appending letters, although Mill could not introduce the more modern plan of full signatures. He occasionally attaches notes to express his personal dissent from some of the opinions advocated, and aims at representing various shades of thought. He was especially anxious to help rising men of genius. In the *London Review* in 1835 he wrote one of the first appreciations of Tennyson, and answered some depreciatory criticisms of the *Quarterly Review* and *Blackwood*.[1]

[1] Browning believed that he had written in 1833 a review of *Pauline* for *Tait's Magazine*, where, however, it was supplanted by a less favourable notice.—Mrs. Orr's *Life of Browning*, p. 59.

On the publication of Carlyle's *French Revolution* he called attention to its merits in an article (July 1837), which, though rather clumsy in form, shows no want of generous appreciation of Carlyle's historical powers; and in a later number (October 1839) admitted, with a note to explain his personal reservations, an exposition of Carlyle by Sterling. To his review of Carlyle's book, as to the Durham article, he attributes considerable success.[1] It set people right, he thinks, in regard to a writer who had set commonplace critics at defiance. From a letter quoted by Professor Bain,[2] he reckoned at the time as a third success the result of his constant 'dinning into people's ears' that Guizot was 'a great thinker and writer.' His opinion of Guizot was to change; but the article republished in the *Dissertations* from the *Edinburgh Review* of 1845 shows that he retained a high admiration for Guizot's work. Other articles upon Carrel, A. de Vigny, and Michelet in the same collection show his constant desire to rouse Englishmen to an appreciation of French literature. Tocqueville's *Democracy in America* was twice reviewed by him, and had an important influence upon his thought.[3] The rigid Utilitarianism of Grote was a little scandalised by the width of Mill's sympathies even with his opponents. The orthodoxy of a man who could see and even insist upon the good side of Coleridge and Carlyle was precarious. In any case, we may admit that Mill showed the generous desire to meet and encourage whatever seemed good in others, which is one of his strong claims upon our personal respect.

[1] *Autobiography*, p. 217.   [2] Bain's *J. S. Mill*, p. 59.
[3] *Autobiography*, p. 191.

For many years Mill's relation to Carlyle, who represented a Radicalism of a very different type, was significant. The first personal acquaintance began in 1831, when Carlyle came to London, and desired to see the author of the articles upon the 'Spirit of the Age.' For a time there was a warm liking on both sides. Mill appeared as a candid and eager disciple, and Carlyle hoped that he would become a 'mystic.' During Carlyle's subsequent retirement at Craigenputtock, they carried on an intimate correspondence.[1] Mill's letters, of which Froude gives an interesting summary, show Mill's characteristic candour and desire to profit by a new light. Though he speaks with the deference becoming to the younger man, and to one who admits his senior's superiority as a poet, if not as a mere logician, he confesses with a certain shyness to a radical dissent upon very vital points. But the most remarkable characteristic is Mill's conviction that he has emerged from the old dry Benthamism into some higher creed. What precisely that may be is not so obvious. When in 1834 Carlyle finally settled in London, the intercourse became frequent. Mill supplied Carlyle with books on the French revolution, and was responsible for the famous destruction of the manuscript of the first volume. The review in the *Westminster* was perhaps prompted partly by remorse for this catastrophe, though mainly, no doubt, by a generous desire to help his friend. At one time Carlyle hoped to be under-editor to the newly started *London Review*; and, as the old tutor of Charles

[1] Froude's *Carlyle: First Forty Years*, ii. 360. The letters are in existence, but have not been published. Mr. A. Carlyle has kindly allowed me to read them.

Buller, he was naturally acquainted with the Utilitarian circle. The divergence of the whole creed and ways of thought of the men was certain to cool the alliance. Carlyle expresses respect for the honesty of the Utilitarians, and considered them as allies in the war against cant. But his 'mysticism' implied the conviction that their negative attitude in regard to religion was altogether detestable; while, in political theories, he was at the very opposite pole. Mill sympathised with his *Chartism* (1839) and *Past and Present* (1843), published at this period, as remonstrances against the sins of the governing classes; but altogether rejects what he took to be the reactionary tendency of the Carlylese gospel. Ultimately, when Carlyle attacked the anti-slavery agitators in 1849, Mill made an indignant reply,[1] and all intercourse ceased.[2] Mill's judgment of Carlyle, as given in his *Autobiography*, shows the vital difference. Carlyle was a poet, he says, and a man of intuitions; and Mill was neither. Carlyle saw at once many things which Mill could only 'hobble after and prove' when pointed out. 'I knew that I could not see round him, and could never be certain that I saw over him, and I never presumed to judge him with any definiteness until he was interpreted to me by one greatly superior to us both, who was more a poet than he and more a thinker than I, whose own mind and nature included his and infinitely more'[3]; in short, by Mrs. Taylor, of whom I shall speak directly. Carlyle's aversion to scepticism (in some sense), to Utilitarianism, to logic, and to political economy—the

[1] 'Negro Question' in *Fraser's Magazine*, Feb. 1849.
[2] A friendly message, as the Carlyle letters show, passed between them in 1869.   [3] *Autobiography*, pp. 175-76.

'dismal science'—was indeed too inveterate to allow of any real alliance; and though Mill did his best to appreciate Carlyle, he learned from him only what one learns from an antagonist, that is, to be more confident in one's own opinions.

IV. PHILOSOPHIC LEADERSHIP

As philosophical Radicalism sank into impotence, Mill's occupation as its advocate was gone. He now again became a recluse. For many years he withdrew altogether from London society. This was obviously due in part to the connection to which he ascribed the greatest possible importance. The 'most valuable friendship of his life,' as he calls it, had been formed in 1830 with Mrs. Taylor, who was two years his junior. Her husband was a man in business,[1] a 'most upright, brave, and honourable man,' according to Mill, and regarded by her with the 'strongest affection' through life.[2] Taylor was, however, without the tastes which would have qualified him to be a worthy intellectual companion for his wife. In this respect Mill was greatly his superior; and his intimacy with Mrs. Taylor rapidly developed. He dined with her twice a week, her husband dining elsewhere. She was an invalid for many years, and had to live in country lodgings apart from her husband. He travelled with her on the Continent during her illness of 1836. Although Taylor himself behaved with singular generosity, and Mill himself states that his own relation to Mrs. Taylor was one of 'strong affection and confidential

[1] A 'drysalter' or 'wholesale druggist in Mark Lane,' according to Bain, 164 n.   [2] *Autobiography*, p. 185.

intimacy only,' the connection naturally provoked censure. His father bluntly condemned him for being in love with another man's wife. His mother and sisters disapproved, and were finally estranged by his marriage in later years.[1] Mrs. Grote gave him up, apparently upon this ground, although he continued his intercourse with Grote. Roebuck states that a remonstrance which he imprudently made to Mill led to the cessation of their friendship, which Mill attributes (with less probability) to differences of opinion as to Byron and Wordsworth.[2] Mill, who worshipped Mrs. Taylor as an embodiment of all that was excellent in human nature, resented such disapproval bitterly; any reference to Mrs. Taylor produced excitement, and he avoided collisions with possible censors by retiring from the world altogether. On giving up the *Westminster Review*, he could, as he put it,[3] indulge the inclination, 'natural to thinking persons when the age of boyish vanity is once past, for limiting his own society to very few persons.' Englishmen, as he says in his customary tone of disapproval, consider serious discussion as 'ill-bred,' and have not the French art of talking agreeably on trifles. Men of mental superiority are 'almost without exception greatly deteriorated' if they condescend to join in such society. The 'tone of the feelings is lowered,' and they adopt the low modes of judgment which alone can meet with sympathy. When the character, moreover, is once formed, agreement on cardinal points is felt to be a necessary condition of 'anything worthy the name of friendship.'

[1] Bain's *J. S. Mill*, p. 172.
[2] Leader's *Roebuck*, p. 39; and Mill's *Autobiography*, p. 150.
[3] *Autobiography*, p. 227.

Mill accordingly shut himself up in his office, and except occasional intercourse with Grote, Professor Bain, and a few others, lived as a solitary or sat at the feet of his Egeria. His admirers, who were soon to be a rapidly increasing class, heard generally that a sight of him was a rare privilege, scarcely to be enjoyed except at meetings of the Political Economy Club. There the conversation turned upon sufficiently solid topics. Whether a life of seclusion be really wise is a topic for an essay. Mill's unequivocal condemnation of the society of which he had so little experience may appear to be censorious. A philosopher may be as austere as a religious Puritan; and Mill might have been a wiser man had he been able to drop his dignity, indulge in a few amusements, and interpret a little more generously the British contempt for high-flown sentiment. His incapacity for play, as he admitted to Comte, was a weak side of his character. Sydney Smith was for a short time (1841-43) a member of the Political Economy Club, and there met Mill on two or three occasions. One would like to know what impression they made upon each other, and especially what Mill thought of the jovial, life-enjoying, and sociable parson. Probably, one fears, he would have taken the superabundant fun of the canon as one more proof of the frivolity of British society, and set his colleague down as a mere sycophant and buffoon. I will not compare the merits of such opposite types. If Mill's retirement is indicative of some weakness, it must also be admitted that it was also dictated by a devotion to great tasks requiring and displaying remarkable strength. He now set to work vigorously, and in the course of the next few years produced his most elaborate and important works.

Both of them were the outcome of his early training. The discussions at Grote's house had suggested to him the plan of a book upon logic. The end, speaking roughly, was to set forth articulately the theory of knowledge implicitly assumed in the writings of his school. Fully accepting the main principles of Bentham and James Mill, and regarding them as satisfactory, after close investigation, he had yet become aware of certain difficulties which might be solved by a more thorough inquiry. He was afterwards stimulated by the controversy between his father and Macaulay ; and this led him, as he thought, to perceiving the true logical method of political philosophy. About 1832 he took up the subject again, and tried to solve the 'great paradox of the discovery of new truths by general reasoning.' This led to his theory of the syllogism, given in the second book of his *Logic*. He now felt that he could produce a valuable work, and wrote the first book. He was stopped by fresh difficulties, and made a halt which lasted for five years. He 'could make nothing satisfactory of induction.' In 1837, while weighted by the *Review*, he received a fresh impulse. Whewell's *History of the Inductive Sciences* and Herschel's *Discourse on the Study of Natural Philosophy* provided him with materials which had before been lacking. In two months, during intervals snatched from other works, he had written a third, 'the most difficult third,' of the book. This included the remainder 'of the doctrine of reasoning' and the greater part of the book upon induction. He had now 'untied all the really hard knots,' and completion was only a question of time. Comte's *Philosophie Positive* now became known to him and greatly stimulated him,

though he owed little of definite result to it. In July and August 1838 he managed to finish his third book ; and his doctrine of 'real kinds' enabled him to turn the difficulty which had caused the five years' halt. Other chapters on 'language and classification' and upon fallacies were added in the same autumn, and the remainder of the work in the summer and autumn of 1840. Finally, the whole book was rewritten between April 1841 and the end of the year, much matter being introduced in the process which had been suggested by Whewell's *Philosophy of the Inductive Sciences* and by Comte's treatise.[1] He offered the finished book to Murray, who declined it ; and it was finally accepted by Parker, who published it in the spring of 1843.

The significance of these dates will appear hereafter. It is here enough to say that the book was the product of strenuous, long-continued thought, and of influences from various quarters. The success greatly exceeded his anticipations. No one since Locke had approached him in the power of making the problems of philosophy interesting to the laity. One remark which he makes is important. He held that the philosophy which he assailed was the great support of all deep-seated and antiquated prejudice. He was therefore attacking false philosophy in its stronghold ; and so far as he succeeded, not merely exposing philosophical fallacies, but essentially contributing to the triumph of reason. Though retiring from active politics, he was elucidating the principles which underlie all political theory.

The *Logic*, in short, was intended not merely as a discussion of abstruse problems, but as indirectly bearing

[1] *Autobiography*, pp. 122, 159, 181, 209, 221.

upon the purposes to which his life was devoted. He was led by the course of his speculation to propose the formation of a new science to be called 'ethology.' This ethology (of which I shall have to speak in its place) is described by Mill as the Science which corresponds to the Art of Education.[1] Education is to be taken in the widest sense of the word : as the training given by the whole system of institutions which mould the character and the thought of mankind. Mill had recognised the immense difficulties in the way of all his schemes of reform which resulted from the ignorance and stupidity of the classes to whom power was inevitably passing. Whether that transition would be beneficial or the reverse depended essentially upon the degree in which men could be prepared for their new duties. Believing that such a preparation was possible, he desired to determine the general principles applicable ; to give, as he says, the science corresponding to the art.

This scheme is noticed in the remarkable correspondence with Comte, which began in 1841 during the final stage of the composition of the *Logic*, and lasted until 1846. Some knowledge of Comte's doctrines was spreading in England.[2] Mill had read an early work of Comte's (the *Traité de Politique Positive*, 1822), and

[1] *Logic*, bk. vi. ch. v. § 4.
[2] Bain's *J. S. Mill*, p. 70. There was a review of Comte by Brewster in the *Edinburgh Review* for August 1838, and an article by William Smith, author of *Thorndale*, in *Blackwood* for March 1843. G. H. Lewes spoke favourably of Comte (to whom he had been personally introduced by Mill) in an article upon 'Modern French Philosophy' in the *Foreign Quarterly* in 1843. His later accounts of Comte in the *Biographical History of Philosophy* (1st edition, 1845-46), and in letters published in the *Leader* in 1852, and afterwards collected as *Comte's Philosophy of the Sciences*, are also noticeable. Miss Martineau's abridged translation appeared in 1853.

criticised it sharply in his letters to d'Eichthal in 1828, though preferring it to other works of the St. Simonians. On taking up in 1837 the two first volumes of Comte's *Philosophie Positive* (all then published), he had been deeply impressed ; he read their successors, and in November 1841 he wrote to Comte as an unknown admirer, and indeed in the tone of an ardent disciple. He has, as he says, definitively left the 'Benthamist section of the revolutionary school,' though he regards it as the best preparation for true positivist doctrine. He accepts Comte's main positions, though on some 'secondary' questions he has doubts which may disappear.[1] He had even thought of postponing the publication of his *Logic* until he had seen the completion of Comte's treatise ; and, had he been able to see the whole in time, would perhaps have translated it instead of writing a new book.[2] Two-thirds, however, of the *Logic* was substantially finished before he had read Comte, and it is adapted to the backward state of English opinion. Mill holds, as he held when writing to d'Eichthal, that a constructive should succeed to a critical philosophy, and sees the realisation of his hopes in the new doctrine. He holds with Comte that a 'spiritual power' should be constituted, which cannot be reached through simple liberty of discussion ;[3] and believes in a religion of humanity, destined to replace theology.[4] It is not surprising that Comte took Mill for a thorough convert. A discord presently showed itself. 'You frighten me,' Mill said to Comte, 'by the unity and completeness of your convictions,' which seem

[1] *Correspondence*, pp. 2, 3.   [2] *Ibid.* p. 77.
[3] *Ibid.* p. 29, cf. 414.   [4] *Ibid.* p. 135.

to need no confirmation from any other intelligence. Comte, in fact, had a rounded and definitive scheme. He had ceased to read other speculations as a mathematician might decline to read the vagaries of circle-squarers. His whole system was demonstrated, once for all. In 1843 Mill began an argument as to the equality of the sexes, which lasted for some months, and ended characteristically. Comte said[1] that further argument would be useless, as Mill was not yet prepared to accept 'fundamental truths.' Mill agreed to drop the discussion, and added that his own opinions had only been confirmed. The supposed convert announced himself as an independent, though respectful, junior colleague, with a right to differ. Mill, according to Bain, became 'dissatisfied with the concessions which he had made.' In truth, the divergence was hopeless, and implied a difference of first principles. Meanwhile, the misunderstanding had further consequences. When Comte was expecting to be dismissed from his post, Mill generously declared (June 1843) that, so long as he lived, he would share his last *sou* with his friend.[2] Mill was at this time in anxiety caused by the repudiation of American bonds, in which he had invested some of his own money and some of his father's, for which he was responsible. Comte declined to take money from a fellow-thinker, but afterwards, when he actually lost his post in July 1844, accepted help from Mill's richer friends, Grote, Molesworth, and Raikes Currie. Comte took their gift to be a tribute from disciples, and was offended when, after the first year, they declined to continue the subsidy. Instead of being disciples, they

[1] *Correspondence*, p. 273.   [2] *Ibid.* p. 206.

were simply persons interested in a philosopher, many of whose tenets they utterly repudiated, and thought that they had done quite enough to show their respect. Mill, as the mediator in an awkward position, acted with all possible frankness and delicacy, but the divergence was growing. When, in 1845, Comte proposed to start a review to propagate his doctrine, Mill had to point out that he and his friends were partial allies, not subjects, and that positivism was not yet sufficiently established to set up as a school.[1] Gradually the discord developed, and the correspondence dropped. Comte's last letter is dated 3rd September 1846, and a letter from Mill of 17th May 1847, speaking of the Irish famine, produced no reply. Mill recognised the hopeless differences, and came to think that Comte's doctrine of the spiritual power implied a despotism of the worst kind. He expressed his disapproval in his final criticism of Comte, and in the later editions of the *Logic* considerably modified some of his early compliments.[2]

On 3rd April 1844 Mill informs Comte that he has put aside the Ethology, his ideas being not yet ripe, and has resolved to write a treatise upon Political Economy. He is aware of Comte's low opinion of this study, and explains that he only attaches a provisional value to its sociological bearing. The book, he explains, will only take a few months to write. The subject, indeed, had been never far from his thoughts since his father had in early days expounded to him the principles of Ricardo. He had discussed economic questions with the meetings at Grote's house ; he had written his *Essays upon*

[1] *Correspondence*, p. 402.
[2] See Bain's *J. S. Mill*, p. 72, for an account of the changes.

Unsettled Questions ; and had been taking a part by his reviews and articles in controversies upon such topics as the Corn-laws, the currency, and the Poor-law. He thus had only to expound opinions already formed, and the book was written far more rapidly than the *Logic*. Begun in the autumn of 1845, it was finished by the end of 1847. Six months out of this were spent in writing an elaborate series of articles in the *Morning Chronicle* during the disastrous winter of 1846-47, urging the formation of peasant properties on the waste lands of Ireland.[1] The articles, of which four or five often appeared in a week, were remarkable in the journalism of the day ; but his proposals failed to attract attention from English stupidity and prejudice. He tells Comte in his last letter that the English wish to help Ireland ; but, from their total ignorance of Continental systems, can only think of enabling the population to live as paupers, instead of introducing the one obvious remedy. His friend and colleague in the India House, W. T. Thornton, was writing about the same time his *Plea for Peasant Proprietors*.[2] Thornton was one of the few who from this period saw much of Mill ; and his influence at a later time was remarkable. The *Political Economy* represents essentially a development of the Ricardo doctrine. One point requires notice here. Mill tells us that he had turned back from his 'reaction against Benthamism.'[3] At the height of that reaction he had

[1] *Autobiography*, p. 235. Mill, as we have seen, spoke of the *Political Economy* to Comte in April 1844. Possibly, therefore, some preparation may have been made for it in the interval before the autumn of 1845.
[2] Published in 1848 before the appearance of Mill's *Political Economy*. Mill read the proofs of his friend's book. Bain's *J. S. Mill*, p. 86 n.
[3] *Autobiography*, p. 231. The dates of these changes are rather vaguely indicated.

become more tolerant of compromise with current opinions. By degrees, however, he had become more than ever opposed to the established principles. He was less of a democrat, indeed, because more convinced of the incapacity of the masses ; but more of a Socialist, in the sense that he looked forward to a complete, though distant, revolution in the whole structure of society. In the first edition of the *Political Economy* he had spoken decidedly against the possibility of Socialism. The events of 1848 seemed to open new possibilities for the propagation of novel doctrines. He accordingly modified this part of his book, and the second edition (1849) represented a 'more advanced opinion.'[1] How far Mill could be called a Socialist will have to be considered hereafter. This tendency, at any rate, marks one characteristic. Mill points out, as one condition of its very remarkable success, that he regarded political economy, not as a 'thing by itself, but as part of a greater whole.' Its conclusions, he held, were valid only as conditioned by principles of 'social philosophy' in general ;[2] and the book, instead of being ostensibly a compendium of abstract scientific principles, is therefore written with constant reference to wider topics and to the application of the doctrines to concrete facts. How far Mill succeeded in giving satisfactory theories is another question, but one thing at least he achieved. The *Political Economy* became popular in a sense in which no work upon the same topic had been popular since the *Wealth of Nations* ; and it owed its success in a great degree to the constant endeavour to trace the bearings of merely abstract formulæ upon the general questions of

[1] *Autobiography*, p. 235.   [2] *Ibid.* p. 236.

social progress. He stimulated the rising interest in
those important problems, and even if his solutions did
not carry general conviction, they brought to him in
later years a following of reverent disciples.

These two books, the *Logic* and the *Political Economy*,
contain in fact a nearly complete statement of Mill's
leading position. Although in later years he was to
treat of political, ethical, and philosophical topics, his
leading doctrines were now sufficiently expounded ; and
the later writings were rather deductions or applications
than a breaking of new ground. None of them involved
so strenuous and long-continued a process of mental
elaboration. The success of these two books gave him
a position at the time unrivalled. He was accepted
as the Liberal philosopher ; and could speak as one
of unquestioned authority.

Professor Bain thinks that Mill's energy was henceforth less than it had been. The various attacks from
which he had suffered had probably weakened his constitution. It must be noticed, however, as Professor
Bain also remarks, that there were sufficient causes for
some decline of literary activity, and he certainly did an
amount of work in the remaining twenty-five years of his
life which would have been enough to absorb the powers
of most men even of high ability. The publication of
new editions of his great books, which involved revision
and replies to criticism, and the composition of occasional
review articles, occupied some of the leisure from his
official duties. The severe illness of 1854 made necessary a long foreign tour. In 1856 he became head of
his department, and more work was thrown upon him.
On the extinction of the East India Company in 1857,

he drafted a petition to parliament on their behalf. It
is remarkable that, like his father in 1833, he became
the apologist of a system generally condemned by the
Liberals of the day. His belief—whatever its value—
was that the government of India could not be efficiently
carried on by the English parliament ; that Indian
appointments would become prizes to be won by
jobbery ; and that the direct rule of English public
opinion would imply a disregard of native opinions and
feelings. The company, however, came to an end ;
and Mill, refusing to accept a place on the new Councils,
retired at the beginning of 1858 on a pension of £1500
a year.

V. MINOR WRITINGS

A great change was now to take place in his life.
Mr. Taylor had died in July 1849 ; and in April 1851
his widow became Mill's wife. They co-operated in
one remarkable work, which is to be connected with
the development of his opinions at the time. Mill had
welcomed the French revolution of 1848 with enthusiasm.
He saw in it the victory of the party to which he had been
most attached from his youth ; and in 1849 he wrote a
vigorous vindication of its leaders against the criticisms
of Brougham.[1] He spoke with much sympathy even of
the Socialism of Louis Blanc, though, of course, admitting
that it contained many grave errors. The 'success of an
unprincipled adventurer in December 1851' put an end
to his hopes for the immediate future. He felt painfully
that even the recognition of many opinions for which he
had contended in his youth had brought less benefit than

[1] Article in *Dissertations*, ii., republished from *Westminster Review* of
April 1849.

he had anticipated. He became convinced that a great
change in the 'fundamental conditions of (men's) modes
of thought' was essential to any great improvement
in their lot.[1] During 1854 he had planned an essay
upon *Liberty*, which was essentially an attempt to point
out certain conditions of such improvements. During
the last two years of his official life, he went over this
elaborately with his wife. After being twice written, he
tells us, every sentence was carefully weighed and criticised
by them both. He intended to make a final revision
during the winter of 1858-59. That was not to be given.
The book, however, is not only characteristic, but is, from
a purely literary point of view, the best of Mill's writings.
Mrs. Mill died at Avignon from a sudden attack of con-
gestion of the lungs. The blow was crushing. Mill felt
that 'the spring of his life was broken.' He withdrew
for a time into complete isolation, though he soon found
some solace in work. He bought a house at Avignon,
and spent half his time there to be near his wife's grave.
The rest of his time was spent at Blackheath. His stepdaughter, Miss Taylor, lived with him, and he expresses
his gratitude for having drawn two such prizes in 'the
lottery of life.' Other friends and disciples were to
gather round him in later years.

It is necessary to say something of the woman to
whom Mill was thus devoted. Yet it is very difficult
to speak without conveying some false impression. It
is impossible, on the one hand, to speak too respectfully
of so deep and enduring a passion. Mill's love of his
wife is a conclusive answer to any one who can doubt the
tenderness of his nature. A man who could love so

[1] *Autobiography*, p. 238.

deeply must have been lovable himself. On the other
hand, it is necessary to point out plainly certain peculiarities which it reveals. Mill speaks of his wife's
excellences in language so extravagant as almost to
challenge antagonism.[1] I have already quoted the passage in which he says that her qualities included Carlyle's
and his own and 'infinitely more.' In other passages, he
seems to be endeavouring to outdo this statement : her
judgment, he declares, was 'next to infallible' ; 'the
highest poetry, philosophy, oratory, and art seemed
trivial by the side of her, and equal only to expressing
some part of her mind' ; and he prophesies that 'if
mankind continue to improve, their spiritual history for
ages to come will be the progressive working out of her
thoughts and realisation of her conceptions.' 'Only
John Mill's reputation,' said Grote, 'could survive such
displays.'[2] The truth seems to be that in Mill's grief
one exquisite pang came from the thought that his wife
had left nothing by which her excellence could be made
manifest to others. The only article which he could
call hers was that upon the 'enfranchisement of women,'
the prefatory note to which includes the phrases cited.
He feels that it would hardly justify his words ; and has
to add that she would, had she pleased, have excelled
it in eloquence and profundity. Even that has to be
qualified by saying that she could have written nothing
on a single subject which would have adequately shown
'the depth and compass of her mind.' His readers,
therefore, have to take his statements on faith, and he

[1] See reference to Mrs. Mill in the suppressed dedication of the *Political
Economy* given in Bain's *J. S. Mill*, p. 175 ; the dedication of the *Liberty* ;
the note in *Dissertations*, ii. 412 ; and *Autobiography*, pp. 184-90 and 240-42.
[2] Bain's *J. S. Mill*, p. 167.

tries to make up for the want of proof by vehemence of asseveration. The only way of accepting such utterances fairly is to regard them as a cry of poignant anguish, not as a set of statements to be logically criticised. The accumulation of superlatives, meanwhile, has the disadvantage that it leaves us without any distinctive characteristic. The figure invested with such a blaze of light has neither distinct form nor colouring. Mill was, I think, always at his feeblest in describing character, and that was a natural weakness of one who, with all his perspicacity, was essentially a bad judge of men.

Apart from the revelation of Mill's character, the only question is whether any intellectual influence is to be attributed to Mrs. Mill. It is easy to suggest that he admired her because she was skilful in echoing his own opinions. To this Professor Bain replies that Mill generally liked intelligent opposition, and holds that in fact Mrs. Mill did set his mind to work by stimulating conversation.[1] This may be true within limits. Mill, however, himself assigns coincidence on cardinal points of opinion as a necessary condition of friendship.[2] It is plain that such an agreement existed between himself and his wife. That he could detect no error in her proves simply that she held what he thought to be true, that is, his own opinions. He has indeed said enough to explain the general relation. She had nothing to do with the *Logic*, except as to the minuter matters of composition; he had already come to believe in woman's rights before he knew her; she did not affect the logical framework of the *Political Economy*, but she suggested the chapter to which he attributes most influence upon

[1] Bain's *J. S. Mill*, p. 173.   [2] *Autobiography*, p. 229.

the future of the labouring classes; and gave to the book 'the general tone by which it is distinguished from previous treatises.' 'What was abstract and purely scientific,' he says by way of summary, 'was generally mine; the properly human element came from her.'[1] In other words, her influence was rather upon his emotions than upon his intellect, and led him to apply his abstract principles to the actual state of society and to estimate their bearing upon human interests and sympathies more clearly and widely than he would otherwise have done. Undoubtedly we may gladly admit the importance of this element in Mill's life; we can fully believe that this, the one great affection of his life, had enabled him to breathe a more genial atmosphere and helped to save him from the rigidity and dryness of some of his allies. It is, however, impossible to attribute to Mrs. Mill any real share in framing his philosophical doctrines; and the impossibility will be the more evident when we have noticed to what an extent they were simply the development of the creed which he had been imbibing from his earliest years. Mill was essentially formed by Bentham, James Mill, and Ricardo; while the relation to Mrs. Mill encouraged him to a more human version of the old Utilitarian gospel. The attribution of all conceivable excellences to his wife shows that he loved, if I may say so, with his brain. The love was perfectly genuine and of most unusual strength; but he interpreted it into terms of reason, and speaks of an invaluable sympathy as if it implied a kind of philosophical inspiration.

Mill, now released from his official labours, settled

[1] *Autobiography*, p. 244-47.

down as he expected 'for the remainder of his existence into a purely literary life.'[1] For six or seven years (end of 1858 to summer of 1865) he carried out this design, and wrote much both on political and philosophical topics. He first published the *Liberty*, in which, after the death of his wife, he resolved to make no further alterations. He gave the weight of his approval to the congenial work of his friend, Professor Bain, by a review in the *Edinburgh* of October 1859. He put together, from previously written papers, his short treatise upon *Utilitarianism*.[2] In October 1863 he reviewed in the *Edinburgh* the recently published lectures of his old friend, John Austin, the representative Utilitarian jurist. Two articles upon Comte[3] in 1864 gave his final judgment of one of the thinkers to whom he owed most outside of the Utilitarian circle. His most elaborate performance, however, was his examination of Sir William Hamilton's philosophy. This was suggested by the recent publication of Hamilton's *Lectures*, which he at first intended only to review. The work swelled upon his hands; he read all Hamilton's writings three times over, and much other literature; he completed the book in the autumn of 1864, and published it in the following spring. It involved him in some very sharp controversies, and contained his final and most elaborate protest against the Intuitionist school. This, too, with the three posthumous essays,[4] gives his position upon

[1] *Autobiography*, p. 262.
[2] First in *Fraser's Magazine* in 1861; republished in 1863.
[3] First in the *Westminster* for 1864; reprinted separately in 1865.
[4] The essays upon *Nature* and *The Utility of Religion* are stated to have been written between 1850 and 1858; that upon *Theism* between 1868 and 1870.

the general philosophical questions which were not treated in the *Logic*. In his earlier books he had been systematically reticent to a degree of which he afterwards disapproved.[1] The intelligent reader, indeed, could perceive to what conclusions his principles led; but the intelligent reader is a rarity. When, in 1865, his political opponents tried to turn his unpopular opinions to account, the only phrase upon which they could fix was the really very orthodox sentiment (in the examination of Hamilton) that he would go to hell rather than worship an unjust God. He had intended, it may be noticed, to publish the essay upon *Nature* himself; but the others were to be still held back. These last utterances, however, taken together, give a sufficient account of Mill's final position in philosophy.

VI. POLITICAL ACTIVITY

Meanwhile, he had been again drawn to politics. After the long period of indifference which followed the final decay of the philosophical Radicals, the English democracy was showing many symptoms of revived animation. The new Reform Bill was becoming the object of practical political agitation; and it seemed that the hopes entertained of the Reform Bill of 1832 had now at last a prospect of realisation. Mill thought in 1861 that there was 'a more encouraging prospect of the mental emancipation of England,' and that things were looking better for the general advance of Europe.[2] The surviving Utilitarians had declined from the true faith. John

[1] *Autobiography*, p. 230. He defends this reticence in a letter to Comte of 18th December 1841.—*Correspondence*, p. 12.
[2] *Autobiography*, p. 240.

Austin before his death had become distinctly Conservative ; and the sacred fire of Benthamism was nearly extinct. Mill himself had changed in some respects. While more awake to certain dangers of democracy, he was the more strongly convinced of the possibility of meeting them by appropriate remedies. Meanwhile Radicalism in various forms was raising its head, and willing to accept Mill, now a writer of the first celebrity, as its authorised interpreter. He wrote much at this period, which defines his position and shows his relation to the new parties. His first publication was a pamphlet on *Parliamentary Reform*, suggested by the futile Reform Bill of Lord Derby and Disraeli in 1859. He now objected to the ballot, the favourite nostrum of the philosophical Radicals to which Grote still adhered, but his main suggestions were in harmony with the scheme proposed by Mr. Hare. After the publication of his own pamphlet, he became acquainted with this scheme, of which he immediately became an ardent proselyte. In 1860 and 1861 he wrote two treatises. He expounded his whole political doctrine in his *Considerations on Parliamentary Government* (1861), and he wrote for future publication—'at the time when it should seem most likely to be useful'—his *Subjection of Women*.[1] In this, as he intimates, 'all that is most striking and profound belongs to his wife'; while it appears that his stepdaughter had also some share in the composition. The outbreak of the civil war in America led him to pronounce himself strongly in support of Bright and other sympathisers with the cause of union.[2] Although his opinions were opposed to those commonest among the

[1] Published in 1869.   [2] Article in *Fraser's Magazine*, January 1862.

English upper classes, they fell in with those of the Radicals, and made him at once a representative of a great current of opinion. His occupation with Hamilton now withdrew him for a time to another department of thought.

In the beginning of 1865 Mill published popular editions of his *Political Economy*, his *Liberty*, and his *Representative Government*. At the general election of that year he was invited to stand for Westminster. Mill accepted the invitation, though upon terms which showed emphatically that he would make no sacrifice of his principles. He declined to incur any expense. He would not canvass, although he attended a few public meetings in the week preceding the nomination. He declared that he would answer no questions about his religious beliefs, but upon all other topics would answer frankly and briefly. 'Did you,' he was asked at one meeting, 'declare that the English working classes, though differing from some other countries in being ashamed of lying, were yet "generally liars"?' His answer, 'I did,' produced, he says, 'vehement applause.' It certainly deserved the applause. Upon some points, too, of the Radical creed, Mill's views were not acceptable. His condemnation of the ballot, and his adherence to women's suffrage and to minority representation marked his opposition to some democratic tendencies. These opinions, however, referred to questions not prominent enough at the time to be important as disqualifications in a candidate. His election by a considerable majority roused great interest. He came in upon a wave of enthusiasm, which accompanied the beginning of a new political era. The Radicalism which was to succeed was, indeed, very unlike the old Radi-

calism of 1832 ; but, for the time at least, it believed itself to be simply continuing the old movement, and was willing to accept the most distinguished representative of the creed for one of its leaders.

In his *Autobiography* Mill shows a certain self-complacency in describing his proceedings in the new parliament, which is not unnatural in a man called from his study by the strong demand from practical politicians. The voice which had been crying in the wilderness was now to be heard in the senate, and philosophy to be married to practice. Mill took up his duties with his usual assiduity ; he watched business as closely as the most diligent of partisans, and was as regular in the House as he had been in his office. The scenes in which he appeared as an orator were remarkable. His figure was spare and slight, his voice weak ; a constant twitching of the eyebrow betrayed his nervous irritability ; he spoke with excessive rapidity, and at times lost the thread of his remarks, and paused deliberately to regain self-possession.[1] But he poured out continuous and thoroughly well-arranged essays—lucid, full of thought, and frequently touching the point epigrammatically. His old practice at debating societies and the Political Economy Club had qualified him to give full expression to his thoughts. A general curiosity to see so strange a phenomenon as a philosopher in parliament was manifest, and Mill undoubtedly introduced an order of considerations far higher than those of the average politician. The tone of the debates, as was said by competent witnesses, was perceptibly raised by his

[1] I heard some of his first speeches from the press gallery of the House of Commons.

speeches. The accepted leaders, such as Bright and Gladstone, welcomed him cordially, and were doubtless pleased to find that they had been talking so much philosophy without knowing it. The young men who were then entering public life looked up to him with reverence; and, for a time, even the squires, the embodiments of Tory prejudice, were favourably impressed. That could not be for long. One of the hits to which Mill refers with some glee in the *Autobiography*[1] gave the nickname of the 'stupid party' to the Conservatives. It expressed his real view a little too clearly. Between him and the typical 'John Bull' a great gulf was fixed. He could never contrive, though he honestly tried, to see anything in the class which most fully represents that ideal, except the embodiment of selfish stupidity generated by class prejudice. And the country-gentlemen naturally looked upon him as their ancestors would have looked upon Sieyes, could the Frenchman have been substituted for Charles Fox. They could dimly understand Whiggism, embodied in a genial, hearty member of their own class; but the flavour of the French philosophy, or its English correlative, was thin, acid, and calculated to set their teeth on edge. They showed the feeling after a time, and Mill retorted by some irritability as well as scorn. He did not, I fancy, obtain that kind of personal weight which is sometimes acquired by a man who, though he preaches equally offensive doctrines, is more obviously made of the same flesh and blood as his adversaries.[2]

[1] *Autobiography*, p. 289.
[2] Disraeli is said to have summed up the impression made upon practical politicians by calling him a 'political finishing governess.'

Mill took a part in various parliamentary proceedings. He helped to pass the Reform Bill of 1867 ; he acted as a mediator between the ministers and the Radicals who were responsible for the famous meeting in Hyde Park ; and he made a weighty protest on behalf of a generous and thoroughgoing Irish policy. He thought that a separation would be mischievous to both parties ; but he advocated a scheme for giving a permanent tenure to existing tenants, with a due regard to vested interests.[1] He obtained little support for a policy which, at least, went to the root of the great difficulty ; but the wisdom of his view, whatever its shortcomings, is more likely to be recognised now. The main peculiarity of Mill's position, however, is all that I am able to notice. In spite of his philosophy, he appeared to be a thorough party man. He fully adopted, that is to say, the platform of the Radical wing, and voted systematically with them on all points. His philosophy led him, as he says,[2] to advocate some measures not popular with the bulk of the Liberal party. Of these the most important were the extension of the suffrage to women and the provision of representation for minorities. Many people, he observes, took these to be 'whims of his own.' Mill, in fact, was contributing to the advance of democracy. In his eyes, these measures were of vital importance as safeguards against democratic tyranny. The democrat was, of course, content to accept his alliance, and to allow him to amuse himself with fanciful schemes, which for the time could make no difference. Mill, on the other hand, thought that by helping the democrat's immediate purposes, he was also gaining ground for the popularisa-

[1] See his pamphlet, *England and Ireland*, 1869.   [2] *Autobiography*, p. 286.

tion of these subsidiary though essential changes. The relation is significant ; for, whatever may be the value of Mill's proposals, there can be no doubt that in many ways the democratic changes which he advocated have led to results which he would have thoroughly disapproved. The alliance, that is, for the time, covered very deep differences, and Mill was virtually helping Demos to get into power, in the expectation that, when in power, Demos would consent to submit to restrictions, not yet, if they ever will be, realised. There is the further question, not here debatable, whether, if realised, they would act as Mill supposed. Anyhow, for the present, the philosopher was really the follower of the partisan. Mill made himself unpopular with a class wider than that which constituted the 'stupid party.' He took a very active part in the agitation provoked by Governor Eyre's action in the Jamaica insurrection. That he was right in demanding a thorough investigation seems to be undeniable. It seems also that a more judicial frame of mind would have restrained him from apparently assuming that such an investigation could have but one result. People of a high moral tone are too apt to show their virtue by assuming that a concrete case comes under a simple moral law, when in fact most such cases are exceedingly complex. Mill, at any rate, and his committee impressed many people besides their strongest opponents as allowing their indignation to swamp their sense of fairplay. Governor Eyre appeared to be a victim of persecution instead of a criminal, and there was, though Mill could not see it, a generous element in the feeling that allowance should be made for a man placed in a terribly critical position.

After the dissolution of parliament, Mill incurred further odium by subscribing to the election expenses of Bradlaugh. Nothing could be more in harmony with his principles than the support of an honest and straightforward man, attacked by the bitterest theological prejudice. His seat, however, for Westminster was lost (1868), and, refusing some other offers, he was glad to retire once more to private life, and to literary and philosophical pursuits. His strength was apparently failing, and he achieved little more. His parliamentary activity had enlarged his circle of acquaintance, and during these years he became far more sociable. Admiring friends gathered round him ; his old allies, such as Hare and W. T. Thornton, the economist Cairnes, and such rising politicians as Henry Fawcett, Mr. Courtney, and Mr. Morley, looked up to him, and had frequent meetings with him. One characteristic point must be noticed, his withdrawal of the 'wage fund' theory when impugned by W. T. Thornton in 1869. The candour which he showed on this occasion, and his generous appreciation of his friend, was eminently characteristic. In the same year appeared his edition of his father's *Analysis*, which, he says,[1] 'ought now to stand at the head of the systematic works on Analytic Psychology.' He was preparing for other writings, but his task was done. He died at Avignon, 8th May 1873, of a sudden attack, having three days before walked fifteen miles on a botanical excursion.

The impression made upon T. H. Green[2] by some of Mill's letters was that he must have been an 'extra-

[1] *Autobiography*, p. 308.
[2] Green's *Miscellaneous Works*, iii. cxliv.

ordinarily good man.' The remark came from a philosophical opponent, and might be echoed by many admirers and generous adversaries. The reverence of his personal friends is sufficiently indicated by the articles of Mr. John Morley,[1] written at the time of their loss. Mill's moral excellence, indeed, is in some directions beyond all dispute. No human being ever devoted himself more unreservedly to a worthy end from his earliest to his latest years ; the end was the propagation of truths of the highest importance to mankind, and the devotion implied entire freedom from all meaner or subsidiary ambitions. A man of whom that can be said without fear of contradiction has certainly extraordinary goodness. When we add that he was singularly candid, fair in argument, most willing to recognise merits in others, and a staunch enemy of oppression in every form, we may say that Mill possessed in an almost unsurpassable degree the virtues peculiarly appropriate to a philosopher. A complete judgment, however, must take other characteristics into account. One remark is obvious. Mill observes[2] that the description of a Benthamite as 'a mere reasoning machine,' though untrue of many of his friends, was true of himself during 'two or three years'—before, that is, he had learned to appreciate the value of the emotions. Many readers thought it true of him to the last. Though the phrase may be understood so as to imply the very contradictory of the truth, I take it to imply one aspect of his character which cannot be neglected. The *Autobiography*, though a very interesting, is to many readers far from an attractive, work ; and its want of

[1] *Miscellanies* (second series).   [2] *Autobiography*, p. 109.

charm is, I think, significant of the weakness which is caricatured by the epithet 'reasoning machine.' Omitting the pages about his wife, there is a singular absence of the qualities which make so many autobiographies interesting : there is no tender dwelling upon early days and associations ; his father is incidentally revealed as an object of profound respect, but without illusion as to his harsher qualities ; hardly any reference is made to his mother or his brothers and sisters ; his friends are briefly noticed and their intellectual merits duly set forth, but there is no warm expression of personal feeling towards any one of them ; his remarks upon his countrymen in general are contemptuous ; and, though he is desirous of the welfare of the species, he is as fully convinced as Carlyle, that men are 'mostly fools.' Old institutions awake no thrill ; they are simply embodiments of prejudice ; and the nation is divided between those who have a 'sinister interest' in abuses, and the masses who are still too brutalised to be trusted. At the bottom of his heart he seems to prefer a prig, a man of rigid formulæ, to the vivid and emotional character, whose merits he recognises in theory. He complains frequently of the general decay of energy, and yet his ideal would seem to be the thoroughly drilled thinker, who is the slave of abstract theories. His 'zeal for the good of mankind' was really to the last what he admits it to have been at the early period, a 'zeal for speculative opinions.' The startling phrases about his wife are in contrast to this coolness, but they are so hysterical as to check full sympathy. From such remarks, some people have inferred that Mill was really a frigid thinker, a worthy prophet of the dismal science, which leaves out

of account all that is deepest and most truly valuable in human nature.

A reply even to an unjust estimate should admit what there is of truth in it. In the first place, of course, Mill was not, and never took himself to be, a poet. He had no vivid pictures of concrete facts ; he was not, as he puts it in contrasting himself with Carlyle, a man of intuitions, and he formed his judgments of affairs by analysing and reflecting and expressing the result in abstract formulæ. That is only to say that his predominant faculty was logical, and that the imagination was comparatively feeble. He was sensitive to some poetry, to Shelley as well as to Wordsworth ; but he is more impressed by its philosophical than its direct æsthetical value. He was certainly less deficient than James Mill in this direction ; but in another quality the contrast with his father is significant. James Mill, whatever his faults, was a man, and born to be a leader of men. He was rigid, imperative, and capable of controlling and dominating. John Stuart Mill was far weaker in that sense, and weaker because he had less virility. Mill never seems fully to appreciate the force of human passions ; he fancies that the emotions which stir men to their depths can be controlled by instilling a few moral maxims or pointing out considerations of utility. He has in that respect less 'human nature' in him than most human beings ; and has not, like Carlyle's favourite Ram Dass, fire enough in his inside to burn up the sins of the world. One effect is obvious even in his philosophy. A philosopher, I think, owes more than is generally perceived to the moral quality which goes into masculine vigour. To accept, as well as to announce,

a doctrine which clashes with the opinions accepted in his class requires an amount of vigour and self-reliance which is only possessed by the few. Mill held very unpopular opinions, but they had been instilled into him from childhood ; they were those of the whole world in which he lived, and it would have required more vigour to abandon than to maintain them. It is impossible to read the *Autobiography* without wondering whether a different education might not have made him a Coleridgean instead of a Benthamite. If he disbelieved in innate principles and in the boundless power of 'association,' it was partly because the influence of his own idiosyncrasy was so slightly marked in his intellectual development. He was one of the most remarkable instances of the power of education to mould the intellect, because few intellects so powerful have been so amenable.

The want of the qualities which make a man self-assertive and original implies, however, no coldness of the affections. Mill was a man of great emotional sensibility, and of very unusual tenderness. Besides his great attachment, he was deeply devoted to a few friends, and, in certain cases, greatly overestimated their qualities. His devotion to speculative pursuits made most of his attachments the product of intellectual sympathy ; and he either did not form, or could not keep up, intimacies formed with persons incapable of such sympathy. Unless he could talk upon serious matters with man or woman, he would have no common bond with them ; and he was too sincere to express it. His feelings, however, were, I take it, as tender as a woman's. They were wanting, not in keenness, but in the massiveness which implies more masculine fibre.

And this, indeed, is what seems to indicate the truth. Mill could never admit any fundamental difference between the sexes. That is, I believe, a great but a natural misconception for one who was in character as much feminine as masculine. He had some of the amiable weaknesses which we at present—perhaps on account of the debased state of society—regard as especially feminine. The most eminent women, hitherto at least, are remarkable rather for docility than originality. Mill was especially remarkable, as I have said, for his powers of assimilation. No more receptive pupil could ever be desired by a teacher. Like a woman, he took things—even philosophers—with excessive seriousness ; and shows the complete want of humour often—unjustly perhaps—attributed to women. Prejudices provoke him, but he does not see the comic side of prejudice or of life in general. When Carlyle, in his hasty wrath, denounces 'shams' with a huge guffaw, Mill patiently unravels the sophistry, and tries to discover the secret of their plausibility. Mill's method no doubt leads as a rule to safer and more sober results. The real candour, too, and desire of light from all sides is most genuine and admirable. It may lead him rather to develop and widen the philosophy in which he was immersed than to strike out new paths. One misses at times the flashes of intuition of keener philosophers, and still more the downright protests of rough common-sense, which can sweep away cobwebs without trying elaborately to pick them to pieces.

On the other hand, he has in the highest degree the power of single-minded devotion, which is pre-eminently, though not exclusively, a feminine quality. His intellect fitted him for abstract speculation, rather than for immediate practical applications. But he was from his youth upwards devoted to the spread of principles which he held to be essential to human happiness. No philanthropist or religious teacher could labour more energetically and unremittingly for the good of mankind. He never forgets the bearing of his speculations upon this ultimate end. Whatever his limitations, he brought the whole energy of a singularly clear, comprehensive, and candid intellect to bear upon the greatest problems of his time ; and worked at them with unflagging industry for many years. He was eminently qualified to bring out the really strong points of his creed ; while his perfect intellectual honesty forced him frankly to display its weaker side. Through Mill English Utilitarianism gave the fullest account of its method and its presuppositions. In summarising his work, I must dwell less than I have hitherto done upon surrounding conditions ; and take his books, nearly in the order of publication, as representing the final outcome of Utilitarianism. He virtually answers in the *Logic* the question, what are the ultimate principles by which the Utilitarians had more or less unconsciously been guided. I shall first deal with this. I shall then take his *Political Economy*, as showing how these principles applied to sociology, which ought, upon his showing, to be the crowning science. Then I shall take the political speculations, which are a further application of the same principles ; and, finally, deal with his views in ethics and in philosophy generally.

CHAPTER II
MILL'S LOGIC

I. INTUITIONISM AND EMPIRICISM

MILL'S *System of Logic* may be regarded as the most important manifesto of Utilitarian philosophy. It lays down explicitly and in their ripest form the principles implicitly assumed by Bentham and the elder Mill. It modifies as well as expounds. It represents the process by which J. S. Mill, on becoming aware of certain defects in the Utilitarians' philosophy, endeavoured to restate the first principles so as to avoid the erroneous conclusions. The coincidence with his predecessors remains far closer than the divergence. The fundamental tenets are developed rather than withdrawn. The *Logic* thus most distinctly raises the ultimate issues. It has the impressiveness which belongs in some degree to every genuine exertion of a powerful mind. Mill is struggling with real difficulties ; not trying to bolster up a theory commended to him by extraneous considerations. He is doing his best to give an answer to his problem ; not to hide an evasion. His honourable candour incidentally reveals the weakness as frankly as the strength of his position. He neither shirks nor hides difficulties, and if we are forced to admit that some of his reasoning is

fallacious, the admission scarcely adds to the statement that he is writing a treatise upon philosophical problems. His frankness has made the task of critics comparatively easy. It takes so many volumes to settle what some philosophers have meant that we scarcely reach the question whether their meaning, or rather any of their many possible meanings, was right. In the case of Mill, that preparatory labour is not required. His book, too, has been sufficiently tested by time to enable us to mark the points at which his structure has failed to stand the wear and tear of general discussion. I must try to bring out the vital points of the doctrine.

Mill, I have said, had a very definite purpose beyond the purely philosophical. 'Bad institutions,' he says,[1] are supported by false philosophy. The false philosophy to which he refers is that of the so-called 'intuitionist school.' Its 'stronghold,' he thought, lay in appeals to the mathematical and physical sciences. To drive it from this position was to deprive it of 'speculative support' ; and, though it could still appeal to prejudice, the destruction of this support was an indispensable step to complete victory. Mill wished to provide a logical armoury for all assailants of established dogmatism, and his success as a propagandist surprised him. The book was read, to his astonishment, even in the universities. Indeed, I can testify from personal observation that it became a kind of sacred book for students who claimed to be genuine Liberals. It gave the philosophical creed of an important section of the rising generation, partly biassed, it may be, by the application to 'bad institutions.' Mill's logic, that is,

[1] *Autobiography*, p. 226.

fell in with the one main current of political opinion. His readings in logic with Grote and other friends enabled him to fashion the weapons needed for the assault. Thus in its origin and by its execution the task was in fact an attempt to give an organised statement of sound philosophy in a form applicable to social and political speculations.

Mill considered that the school of metaphysicians which he attacked had long predominated in this country.[1] When Taine called his view specially English, Mill protested. The Scottish reaction against Hume, he said, which 'assumed long ago the German form,' had ended by 'prevailing universally' in this country. When he first wrote he was almost alone in his opinions, and there were still 'twenty *a priori* and spiritualist philosophers for every partisan of the doctrine of Experience.'[2] The philosophical world, he says elsewhere,[3] is 'bisected' by the line between the 'Intuitional' and the 'Experiential' schools. Mill's conviction that a majority of Englishmen were really 'intuitionists' in any shape is significant, I think, of his isolated position. Undoubtedly most Englishmen disliked Utilitarians, and respectable professors of philosophy were anxious to disavow sympathy with covert atheism. Yet the general tendency of thought was, I suspect, far more congenial to Mill's doctrine than he admitted. Englishmen were practically, if not avowedly, predisposed to empiricism. In any case, he was carrying on the tradition which Taine rightly,

[1] *Logic*, p. 369 (bk. iii. ch. xxi. § 1). I quote from the popular edition of 1898. Book, chapter, and section are generally applicable to former editions.
[2] See letter in note to chapter upon Mill in Taine's *History of English Literature*.
[3] James Mill's *Analysis*, i. 352 n.

as I should say, regarded as specifically English. Its adherents traced its origin back through James Mill to Hartley, Hume, Locke, Hobbes, and Francis Bacon, and perhaps it might even count among its remoter ancestors such men as William of Ockham and Roger Bacon. The series of names suggests some permanent congeniality to the national character.[1] Although, moreover, this tradition had in later times been broken by Reid and his followers, their condemnation did not really imply so fundamental an antithesis of thought as Mill supposed. They and the empiricists had, in their own opinion at least, a common ancestor in Bacon, if not in Locke. But, however this may be, the Scottish school had maintained the positions which Mill thought himself concerned to attack; and for him represented the rejection of 'experience.'

Experience is a word which requires exposition; but in a general way the aim of the Utilitarians is abundantly clear. They attacked 'intuitions' as Locke had attacked 'innate ideas.' The great error of philosophy, according to them, as according to Locke, has been the attempt to transcend the limits of human intelligence, and so to wander into the regions of mysticism; to seek knowledge by spinning logical structures which, having no base in fact, ended in mere scholastic logomachy; or to override experience by claiming absolute authority for theories which dispense with further proof for the simple reason that no proof of them can be given. To limit speculation and to make it fruitful by forcing it from the first to deal with facts; to trace all its evidence to

[1] See an interesting article in G. Croom Robertson's *Philosophical Remains* (1894), pp. 28-45.

experience or the observation of facts; and to insist upon its verification by comparison with facts, is the main and surely the legitimate purpose of the Utilitarians as of all their philosophical congeners. The gulf between the world of speculation and the world of fact is the great opprobrium of philosophy. The necessity for finding a basis of fact was emphasised at this time by the rapid development of the sciences which may be called purely empirical, and which had sprung, in any case, from methods of direct observation. This development suggested the elaborate treatise written from a different point of view by Whewell. The great ambition of the Benthamites had been to apply scientific methods to all the problems of legislation, jurisprudence, economics, ethics, and philosophy. Mill could now show, with the involuntary help of Whewell, what those methods really implied. The questions remain: What are facts? and, What is experience? and, What are the consequent conditions of reasoning about facts? Admitting that, somehow or other, a vast and rapidly growing body of knowledge has been attained in the physical sciences, we may ask how it has been gained, and proceed to apply the methods in what have been called the moral sciences. Kant's famous problem was, How is *a priori* synthetic knowledge possible? Mill denies that any such knowledge exists. His problem is therefore, How can knowledge be explained without *a priori* elements? When this can be satisfactorily done, we shall be able to show how both moral and physical science can be fairly based upon experience.

Mill's view of the proper limits of his inquiry is characteristic. He accepts Bacon's account of logic.

It 'is the *ars artium*, the science of science itself.'[1] It implies an investigation into the processes of inference generally. It is not limited to the old formal logic, but includes every operation by which knowledge is extended. It is thus, as he afterwards puts it, the 'theory of proof.'[2] The book, indeed, owes its interest to the width of the field covered. It has not the repulsive dryness of formal logic, but would lead to a natural history of the whole growth of knowledge, and makes constant reference to the actual development of thought. On the other hand, Mill gives notice that he has no more to do with metaphysics than with any of the special sciences. Logic, he declares, is common ground for all schools of philosophy. It is, he says, the office of metaphysics to decide what are ultimate facts, but for the logician it is needless to go into this analysis.[3] Accordingly, he often in the course of the book considers himself entitled to hand over various problems to the metaphysicians.[4] The possibility of really keeping to this distinction is doubtful. Since Mill's very aim is to show that all knowledge comes from observation of 'facts,' it is apparently relevant to inquire

[1] *Logic*, Introduction, § 5.
[2] *Ibid.* p. 29 (bk. i. ch. iii. § 1).
[3] *Ibid.* p. 8 § 7.
[4] See John Grote's *Exploratio Philosophica* (1865), p. 209 *n*. This book is, I think, by far the most interesting contemporary discussion of Mill, Hamilton, and Whewell. It was, unfortunately, desultory and unfinished, but it is full of acute criticism, and charmingly candid and modest. Mill's *Logic* is especially discussed in chapters viii. and ix. Grote holds, and I think truly, that Mill's attempt to divide metaphysics from logic leads to real confusion, and especially to an untenable mode of conceiving the relation between 'things' and thoughts. I cannot discuss Grote's views; but the book is full of interesting suggestions, though the results are rather vague. See the excellent account of Grote by the late Croom Robertson in the *Dictionary of National Biography*.

what are these 'ultimate facts.' Indeed, his statement, though made in all sincerity, almost suggests a controversial artifice. Logic, as Mill of course admits, affects metaphysics as it affects all sciences; but in one way it affects them very differently. It justifies astronomy, but it apparently makes metaphysics superfluous. Inquiry into the 'ultimate facts' turns out to be either hopeless or meaningless. Mill does not directly assert that all 'ontological' speculations are merely cobwebs of the brain. But he tries to show that, whatever they may be, they are strictly irrelevant in reasoning. All metaphysicians are expected to grant him certain postulates. These once granted, he will be able to account for the whole structure of knowledge. 'Intuitions,' transcendental speculations, and ontology will then be deprived of the whole conditions under which they thrive. I do not now assert, he virtually says, that your doctrine is wrong, but I shall show that it is thrown away. It is a pretence of explaining something which lies altogether beyond the limits of real knowledge, and therefore admits of no explanation.

Mill starts from the classification given in old logical textbooks, to which, different as are his conclusions, he attached a very high value.[1] The schoolmen had by their elaborate acuteness established a whole system of logical distinctions and definitions which are both

[1] Mill, in his review of Whately, refers to Du Trieu (whose treatise had been privately printed by him and his friends), Crakenthorpe, and Burgersdyk; and in the *Examination of Hamilton's Philosophy* (ch. xxii.) quotes also Sanderson, Wallis, Aldrich, Keckermann, Bartholinus, and Du Hamel as the 'authorities nearest at hand.' There is nothing, as I am told by the learned, exceptionally interesting in Du Trieu; and the selection was probably accidental.

important and accurate, however sterile the inquiries in which they were used. The machinery was excellent, though its contrivers forgot that a mill cannot grind out flour if you put in no grain. Mill begins accordingly by classifying the various kinds of words in the light afforded by previous logical systems.

He is to give a theory of proof. That which is to be proved is a proposition; and a proposition deals with names, and moreover with the names of 'things,' not merely with the names 'of our ideas of things.'[1] That, in some sense, reasoning has to do with things is of course his essential principle; and the problem consequently arises, What are empirical 'things'?[2] Though we cannot ask what are 'ultimate things,' the logician must enumerate the various kinds of things to which reference may be made in predication. Mill makes out a classification which he proposes to substitute, provisionally at any rate, for the Aristotelian categories.[3] The first and simplest class of nameable things corresponds to things 'in the mind,' that is, 'feelings,' or 'states of consciousness,' sensations, emotions, thoughts, and volitions. The second class corresponds to things 'external to the mind':[4] and these are either 'substances' or 'attributes.' Here our task is lightened by a welcome discovery. All philosophers, it appears, are now agreed upon one point. Sir W. Hamilton, Cousin, Kant, nay, according to Hamilton—though that is too good to be true—nearly all previous philosophers admit one truth.[5] We know, as they agree, nothing about 'objects' except the sensations which they give

[1] *Logic*, p. 15 (bk. i. ch. ii. § 1).
[2] *Ibid.* p. 29 (bk. i. ch. iii. § 1).
[3] *Ibid.* p. 49 (bk. i. ch. iii. § 15).
[4] *Ibid.* p. 35 (bk. i ch. iv. § 6).
[5] *Ibid.* p. 38 (bk. i. ch. iv. § 7).

us and the order of those sensations. Hence the two 'substances,' body and mind, remain unknowable 'in themselves.' Body is the 'hidden external cause' to which we refer our sensations;[1] and as body is the 'mysterious something which excites the mind to feel, so mind is the mysterious something which feels and thinks.' The mind is, as he says in language quoted from his father, 'a thread of consciousness,' a series of 'feelings': it is the 'myself' which is conceived as distinct from the feelings but of which I can yet know nothing except that it has the feelings.

Thus, although we know nothing of minds and of bodies 'in themselves,' we do know their existence. That is essential to his position. The 'thread of consciousness' is a 'final inexplicability' with him, but it corresponds to some real entity. And, on the other side, we must believe, in some sense, in things. The thing, though known only through the sensations which it excites, must be something more than a mere sensation, for the whole of his logic defends the thesis that in some way or other thought has to conform to facts or to the relations between 'things.' Knowledge, however, is confined entirely to the sensations and the attributes; and the two are at bottom one. The 'verbal' distinction between a property of things and the sensation which we receive from it, is made, he says, for convenience of discourse rather than from any difference in the nature of the thing denoted.[2] This brings us to a critical point. Attributes, he says, following the old distribution, are of Quality, Quantity, and Relation. Now Quality and

[1] *Logic*, p. 40 (bk. i. ch. iv. § 8).
[2] *Ibid.* p. 41 (bk. i. ch. iii. § 9).

Quantity mean simply the sensations excited by bodies. To say that snow is white, or that there is a gallon of water, means simply that certain sensations of colour or size are excited in us by snow or a volume of water. The attribute called 'Relation' introduces a different order of feelings. A 'relation' supposes that two things are involved in some one fact or series of facts.[1] But it is still an 'attribute' or a 'state of consciousness.' It is a feeling different from other feelings by the circumstance that two 'things' instead of one are involved. This is the explanation which, as we have seen, he praises so warmly in his father's *Analysis*, and now adopts for his own purposes. It enables him to classify predications. All predication is either an assertion of simple existence or an assertion of 'relations.' By classifying the possible relations, therefore, we obtain the possible forms of predication. It turns out accordingly that we can make five possible predications: we can predicate, *first*, simple existence; or *secondly*, 'coexistence'; or *thirdly*, 'sequence' (these two being equivalent, as he adds, to 'order in place' and 'order in time'); or *fourthly*, we may predicate 'resemblance'; or *fifthly*, and this is only to be stated provisionally, we may predicate 'causation.'[2]

So far, Mill's view corresponds to the psychology of the *Analysis*, which gives a similar account of the various terms employed. J. S. Mill has now the standing ground from which he can explain the whole development of knowledge. At this point, however, he has to diverge from his father's extreme nominalism. Predica-

[1] *Logic*, p. 43 (bk. i. ch. iv. § 10).
[2] *Ibid.* p. 68 (bk. i. ch. v. § 6).

tion, according to the elder, is a process of naming. A predicate is a name of the same thing of which the subject is a name; and to predicate is simply to assert this identity of names. This doctrine, as Mill thinks, is equally implied in the *dictum de omni et nullo* which is taken as the explanation of the syllogism. We have arbitrarily put a number of things in a class, and to 'reason' is simply to repeat of each what we have said of all. This is to put the cart before the horse, or to assume that the classification precedes the reason for classification, though probably the theory 'thus nakedly stated' would not be granted by any one.[1] What, then, is the true theory? That is explained by the distinction between 'connotation' and 'denotation,' which Mill accepted (though inverting the use of the words) from his father. A general name such as 'man' *de*notes John, Thomas, and other individuals. It *con*notes certain 'attributes,' such as rationality and a certain shape. When, therefore, I say that John is a man, I say that he has the attributes 'connoted'; and when I say that all men are mortal, I assert that along with the other attributes of man goes the attribute of mortality.[2] Predication, then, in general, involves the attribute of 'relation.' We may assert the simple existence of a 'quality,' or, which is the same thing, of a 'sensation'; but to say that John is a man, or that men are mortal, or to make any of the general propositions which constitute knowledge, is to assert some of those 'relations' which are perceived when we consider two or more things together.

[1] *Logic*, p. 61 (bk. i. ch. v. § 3).
[2] *Ibid.* p. 63 (bk. i. ch. v. § 4).

'Things,' then, so far as knowable are clusters (in Hartley's language) of 'attributes'; and the attributes may be equally regarded as 'feelings.' To predicate is to refer a thing to one of the clusters, and therefore to assert its possession of the attributes connoted. I will only note in passing that by declining to go into the metaphysical question as to the difference between 'attributes' and 'sensations,' or thoughts and things, Mill leaves an obscurity at the foundation of his philosophy. But leaving this for the present, it is enough to say that we have our five possible types of predication.[1] All propositions may be reduced to one of the forms. Things exist or coexist or follow or resemble or are cause or effect.[2] The next problem, therefore, is, How are these propositions to be proved? or, by what tests is our belief to be justified?

What may be the nature of belief itself is a question which Mill leaves to the analytical psychologist,[3] who, as he admits, will probably find it puzzling, if not hopeless. But as we all agree that somehow or other we

[1] It would be interesting to compare this part of Mill with the corresponding part of Hume's *Treatise*. Hume, like Mill, begins by accepting causation as one of the relations involved, and then explains it as merely derivative. His treatment of relations generally, especially the division of relations into the two classes, which do or do not depend upon the 'ideas' themselves,* has a bearing upon Mill's doctrine too intricate to be considered here. I do not think that Mill was very familiar with Hume's writings. A note to the concluding chapter of the *Examination of Hamilton* seems to imply that he was not acquainted with the *Treatise*; nor does he appear from his posthumous *Essays* to have studied Hume's writings upon theology. Whether T. H. Green was right in holding that Hume had a more distinct view than his successor of some metaphysical difficulties, I need not inquire.
  * *Treatise of Human Nature*, pt. vi. sec. 1.

[2] *Logic*, p. 70 (bk. i. ch. v. § 7).
[3] *Ibid.* p. 434 (bk. iv. ch. iii. § 2 n.).

attain knowledge, we may inquire what is implied in the process. Now, some part of our knowledge obviously depends upon 'experience.' We know of any particular fact from the testimony of our senses. We know that London Bridge exists because we have seen and touched it; and it would be obviously hopeless to try to deduce its existence from the principle of the excluded middle. London Bridge would then be something independent of time and place. But do we not want something more than bare experience when we lay down a general rule as a law of nature? Then we not only say 'is,' but 'must be'; and this, according to the Intuitionist, marks the introduction of something more than an appeal to 'experience.' There are truths, he says, which represent 'laws of thought'; which are self-evident, or perceived by 'intuition'; or the contrary of which is 'inconceivable.' Without some such laws, we could not bind together the shifting data of experience, or advance from 'is' to 'must be,' or even to 'will be.' We lose all certainty, and fall into the scepticism of Hume, which makes belief a mere 'custom,' regards all things as distinct atoms conjoined but not connected, and holds that 'anything may be the cause of anything.' Mill's aim is to explode the intuitions without falling into the scepticism. Necessary truths, he holds, are mere figments. All knowledge whatever is of the empirical type. 'This has been' justifies 'this will be.' Empirical truths clearly exist, and are held undoubtingly, although they have no foundation except experience. Nobody ever doubted that all men die; yet no 'proof' of the fact could be ever suggested, before physiology was created, except the bare fact that all men have died. If

physiology has made the necessity more evident, it has not appreciably strengthened the conviction. We all believe even now that thunder will follow lightning, though nobody has been able to show why it should follow. The ultimate proof in countless cases, if not in all, is simply that some connection has been observed, and, in many such cases, the belief reaches a pitch which excludes all perceptible doubt. As a fact, then, belief of the strongest kind can be generated from simple experience. The burthen of proof is upon those who assume different origins for different classes of truth.[1]

II. SYLLOGISM AND DEFINITION

This main thesis leads to two lines of argument. First of all, Mill seeks to show that the methods of proof expounded by his adversaries do not really take us beyond experience; and, secondly, he seeks to show that experience gives us a sufficient basis of knowledge. Let us first notice, then, how the ground is cleared by examining previous accounts of the process of inference. The old theory of reasoning depends upon the syllogism. That gives the type of the whole process by which knowledge is extended. All men are mortal; Socrates is a man, therefore Socrates is mortal. Stewart and Brown had both attacked the syllogism on the familiar ground that it is tautologous. The major has already asserted the minor. To say that one man is mortal when you have already said that all men are mortal, is merely to repeat yourself. There can be no

[1] *Logic*, p. 152 (bk. ii. ch. v. § 4).

real inference, and no advance to new knowledge. So long as the syllogism is to be explained on the old terms, Mill thinks this criticism fatal; but he holds, too, that by a different interpretation we may assign a real and vitally important meaning to this venerable form of argument. In several places[1] he gives a view which seems to be much to the purpose. The syllogism, it would seem, corresponds really, not to a mode of reasoning, but to a system of arguing. When a disputant bases some statement upon an inference, we may challenge either the truth of the rule or the statement of fact. The cogency of the argument depends upon the applicability of the rule to the fact. If men be not mortal, or, again, if Socrates be not a man, the inference is not valid; and these two distinct issues, the issue of law and the issue of fact, may be raised in any case.[2] The value of the syllogism is that it raises these issues distinctly. The argument is thus put in such a form as to be absolutely conclusive if the premises be themselves granted. It therefore provides a test of the validity of the logic. Granting the premises, a denial of the inference must involve a contradiction. That is the only test in pure logic. The syllogism must, therefore, be in a sense tautologous, for otherwise it could not be conclusive. Acceptance of the premises must be shown from the form of statement to necessitate the admission of the inference. This follows, and the logical link is complete and irrefragable, if the

[1] Especially the early review of Whately.
[2] This suggests a parallel to the old English system of pleading—as a preparatory process for bringing out the issues really involved in a dispute—which is said to have been thoroughly logical, though it became excessively cumbrous and technical.

middle term be identical in both premises, and not otherwise. This is what Mill indicates by saying that ' the rules of the syllogism are rules for compelling a person to be aware of the whole of what he must undertake to defend if he persists in maintaining his conclusion.'[1] Ratiocination, as he sums up his view elsewhere, ' does not *consist* of syllogisms'; but the syllogism is a useful formula into which it can ' translate its reasonings,' and so guarantee their correctness.[2]

If this be granted, we must consider the essential step of inference to be embodied in, but not created by, the syllogism. Correct reasoning can always be thrown into this form. The syllogism emerges when the reasoning is complete. ' The use of the syllogism is no other,' says Mill, ' than the use of general propositions in reasoning.' It is a security for correct generalisation.[3] We have, then, still to ask what is the reasoning process for which the syllogism provides a test. Generalisation implies classification. Our general rule or major premise states some property of a class to which the individual belongs. The question is how this reference to a class enables us to draw inferences which we could not draw from the individual case. To this Mill gives a simple answer, which is already implied in his theory of predication. When I say that Socrates is a man, I say that he has the attributes connoted by the name. He is a rational, featherless biped, for example. But I already know by observation that

¹ *Logic*, p. 527 (bk. v. ch. vi. § 3). So in *Examination of Hamilton*, ch. xxii., ' The syllogism is not the form in which we necessarily reason, but a test of reasoning.'
² James Mill's *Analysis*, ii. 427.
³ *Logic*, p. 131 (bk. ii. ch. iii. § 5).

with these attributes goes the attribute of mortality. The essence of the reasoning process is therefore that, from the possession of certain attributes, I infer the possession of another attribute which has coexisted with them previously. That I do, in fact, reason in this way in countless cases is undeniable. I know that a certain quality, say malleability, goes along with other qualities of colour, shape, and so forth, by which I recognise a substance as gold. I can, it may be, give no other reason for believing the future conjunction of those qualities than the fact of their previous conjunction. The belief, that is, is as a matter of fact generated simply by the previous coincidence or corresponds to constant association. Whether this exhausts the whole logical significance may still be disputed; but, at any rate, upon these terms we can escape from the charge of tautology. The rule in the major premise registers a number of previous experiences of coexistence. When we notice some of the attributes in a given case, we make an addition to our knowledge by applying the rule, that is, by inferring that another attribute may be added to the observed attributes. This, then, gives a rational account of the advance in knowledge made through the syllogism in the case where the class can be defined as a simple sum of attributes.

But is this an adequate account of the reasoning process in general? There is another view which suggested difficulties to Mill. His solution of these difficulties, marked, as we learn from the *Autobiography*, an essential stage in the development of his doctrine. Reference to a class is, upon his interpretation, implied in the syllogism; and classification implies definition.

A class means all things which have a certain list of attributes stated in the definition. May we not then infer other properties from the definition? May not mortality, for example, be deducible from the other attributes of man? The assumption that we can do so is connected with the fallacy most characteristic of the misuse of the syllogism. It is plain that we may create as many classes as we please, and make names for combinations of attributes which have no actual, or even no possible, existence. Any inferences which we make on the strength of such classification must be nugatory or simply tautologous. I show that a certain proposition follows from my definition; but that gives no guarantee for its conformity to the realities behind the definition. Your ' proof' that a man is mortal means simply that if he is not mortal you don't call him a man. The syllogism treated on that system becomes simply an elaborate series of devices for begging the question. From such methods arise all the futilities of scholasticism, and the doctrine of essences which, though Locke confuted it,[1] has ' never ceased to poison philosophy.'[2] It may, I suppose, be taken for granted that the syllogism was constantly applied to cover such fallacies, and so far Mill is on safe ground. The theory, however, leads him to a characteristic point. Already in the early review (January 1828), he had criticised Whately's account of definition. A ' real definition,' as Whately had said, ' explains and unfolds " the nature " of the thing defined, whereas a " nominal definition " only explains the name.' Whately goes on

¹ *Logic*, p. 72 (bk. i. ch. vi. § 2).
² *Ibid.* p. 115 (bk. ii. ch. ii. § 2).

to point out that the only real definitions in this sense are the mathematical definitions. It is impossible to discover the properties of a thing, a man, or a plant from the definition. If it were possible, we might proceed to ' evolve a camel from the depths of our consciousness,' and nobody now professes to be equal to that feat. When, however, we ' define' a circle or a line and so forth, we make assertions from which we can deduce the whole theory of geometry. A geometrical figure represents a vast complex of truths, mutually implying each other, and all deducible from a few simple definitions. The middle term is not the name of a simple thing, or of a thing which has a certain set of coexisting attributes, but a word expressive of a whole system of reciprocal relations. If one property entitles me to say that a certain figure is a circle, I am virtually declaring that it has innumerable other properties, and I am thus able to make inferences which, although implicitly given, are not perceived till explicitly stated. By assigning a thing to a class, I say in this case that I may make any one of an indefinite number of propositions about it, all mutually implying each other, and requiring the highest faculties for combining and evolving. Pure mathematics give the one great example of a vast body of truths reached by purely deductive processes. They appear to be evolved from certain simple and self-evident truths. Can they, then, be explained as simply empirical? Do we know the properties of a circle as we know the properties of gold, simply by combining records of previous experience? Or can we admit that this great system of truth is all evolved out of ' definitions'?

Mill scents in Whately's doctrine a taint of *a priori* assumption, and accordingly meets it by a direct contradiction. A geometrical definition, he says, is no more a 'real' definition than the definition of a camel. No definition whatever can 'unfold the nature' of a thing. He states this in his review, though it was at a later period,[1] when meditating upon a passage of Dugald Stewart, that he perceived the full consequences of his own position. In answering Whately, he had said that all definitions were 'nominal.' A 'real definition' means that to the definition proper we add the statement that there is a thing corresponding to the name.[2] The definition itself is a 'mere identical proposition,' from which we can learn nothing as to facts. But it may be accompanied by a postulate which 'covertly asserts a fact,' and from the fact may follow consequences of any degree of importance. This distinction between the definition and the postulate may be exhibited, as he remarks, by substituting 'means' for 'is.' If we say : a centaur 'means' a being half man and half horse, we give a pure definition. If we say : a man 'is' a featherless biped, our statement includes the definition—man 'means' featherless biped ; but if we said no more, no inference could be made as to facts. If we are really to increase our knowledge by using this definition, we must add the

---

[1] *Autobiography*, p. 181. The passage to which Mill refers is apparently that in Stewart's *Works*, iii. 24-36 and 113-52. Stewart quotes a passage from Dr. Beddoes' *Observations on the Nature of Demonstrative Evidence* (1793), which anticipates Mill's view that the 'mathematical sciences are sciences of experiment and observation, founded solely on the induction of particular facts.' Stewart professes to follow Locke (see Locke's *Essay*, bk. iv. ch. xii. § 15), and gives some references to other discussions on the questions.

[2] *Logic*, p. 94 (bk. i. ch. viii. § 5).

'covert' assertion that such featherless bipeds exist. The mathematical case is identical. Stewart had argued that geometrical propositions followed, not from the axioms but, from the definitions. From the bare axiom that if equals be added to equals the wholes are equal, you can infer nothing. You must also perceive the particular figures which are compared. Of course the truth of the axioms must be admitted ; but they do not specify the first principles from which geometry is evolved. In other words, geometry implies 'intuition,' not the *a priori* 'intuitions' to which Mill objected, but the direct perception of the spatial relations. We must see the figure as well as admit the self-evident axiom. Mill, on considering this argument, thought that Stewart had stopped at a half truth.[1] He ought to have got rid of the definitions as well as the axioms. Every demonstration in Euclid, says Mill, might be carried on without them. When we argue from a diagram in which there is a circle, we do not really refer to circles in general, but only to the particular circle before us. If its radii be equal or approximately equal, the conclusions are true. We afterwards extend our reasoning to similar cases ; but only one instance is demonstrated. The definition is merely a 'notice to ourselves and others,' stating what assumptions we think ourselves entitled to make ; and in this way it resembles the major in the syllogism. The demonstration does not 'depend upon' it, though if we deny it, the demonstration fails. By this argument, Mill conceives that the case of mathematics is put on a level with other cases. We always argue from facts, and moreover from 'particular facts,' not from defini-

---

[1] *Logic*, p. 125 (bk. ii. ch. iii. § 3).

tions. We start from an observation of this particular circle—a sensible 'thing' or object, as in arguing about natural history we start from observation of the camel. Hence we may lay down the general proposition, applicable to geometry as well as to all ordinary observation, that 'all inference is from particulars to particulars.'[1] This is the 'foundation' both of Induction, which is 'popularly said' to reason from particulars to generals, and of Deduction, which is supposed to reason from generals to particulars.[2] This sums up Mill's characteristic position.

III. MATHEMATICAL TRUTHS

This attempt to bring all reasoning to the same type forces Mill to ignore what to others seems to be of the essence of the case. There are, he says, two statements : 'There may exist a figure bounded by three straight lines' ; that is the fruitful statement of facts. 'This figure is called a triangle' ; that is the merely nominal definition or explanation of words. Moreover, as he says, we may drop the definition by substituting the equivalent words or simply looking at the thing. It does not follow that we can dispense with the mode of apprehension implied by the definition. Whether we use the word triangle, or the words, 'three lines enclosing a space,' or no words at all, we must equally have the conceptions or intuitions of lines and space. All demonstration in geometry consists in mentally rearranging a combination of lines and angles so as to show that one figure may be made to coincide absolutely with

---

[1] *Logic*, p. 126 (bk. ii. ch. iii. § 4).   [2] *Ibid.* p. 107 (bk. ii. ch. i. § 3).

another figure. The original fact remains unaltered, but the ways of apprehending the fact are innumerable. Newton and his dog Diamond might both see the same circular thing ; but to Diamond the circle was a simple round object ; to Newton it was also a complex system of related lines, capable of being so regarded as to embody a vast variety of elaborate formulæ.[1] Geometry, as Mill undeniably says, deals with facts. Newton and Diamond have precisely the same fact before them. It remains the same, whether we stop at the simplest stage or proceed to the most complex evolution of geometry. The difference between the observers is not that Newton has seen new facts, but that he sees more in the same fact. The change is not in the things but in the mind, which, by grouping the things in the way pointed out by the definitions, is able to discover countless new relations involved in the same perception. This again may suggest that even the fact revealed to simple perception is not a bare 'fact,' something, as Mill puts it, 'external to the mind,' but is in some sense itself constituted by the faculty of perception. It contains already the germ of the whole intellectual evolution. The change is not in the thing perceived, but in the mode of perceiving. And, therefore, again, we do not acquire new knowledge, as we acquire it in the physical sciences, by observing new facts, discovering resemblances and differences, and generalising from the properties common to all ; but by contemplating the same fact. All geometry is in any

---

[1] Whiston (*Memoirs*, i. 35) reports that Newton saw by intuition, or previously to formal demonstration, the equality of all parallelograms described about the conjugate diameters of an ellipse. Most of us can only learn the fact by painful construction.

particular space—if only we can find it. We do not proceed by comparing a number of different regions of spaces, and inquire whether French triangles have the same properties as English triangles. To Mill, however, the statement that geometry deals with fact leads to another conclusion. We must deal with these facts as with other facts, and follow the method of other natural sciences. We really proceed in the same way whether we are investigating the properties of an ellipse or a camel. In either case we must discover truth by experience.

What, then, is really implied in the doctrine that all knowledge rests upon experience? One of Mill's intellectual ancestors lays down the fundamental principle. It is absurd, says Hume,[1] to try to demonstrate *matter of fact* by *a priori* arguments. 'Nothing is demonstrable unless the contrary implies a contradiction. Nothing that is distinctly conceivable implies a contradiction. Whatever we conceive as existent we can also conceive as non-existent. There is no being, therefore, whose non-existence implies a contradiction.' 'Matter of fact,' then, must be proved by experience; but, given a 'fact' we may deduce necessary consequences. All necessity may be hypothetical; there is an 'if' to every 'must,' but remembering the 'if' the 'must' will be harmless. It can never take us beyond experience. The existence of space itself cannot be called necessary; but space once given, all geometry may 'necessarily' follow, and imply relations running through the whole fabric of scientific knowledge. Mill agrees that a 'hypothetical' necessity

[1] Hume's *Works* (Grose and Green), ii. 432 and iv. 134. Hume's statement is criticised by G. H. Lewes in his *Problems*, etc., i. 391, but, I think, on an erroneous interpretation.

of this kind belongs to geometry; and adds, that in any science whatever, we might, by making hypotheses, arrive at an equal necessity.[1] But then, he goes on to urge, the hypotheses of geometry are not 'absolute truths,' but 'generalisations from observation,' or 'inductions from the evidence of our senses,'[2] which, therefore, are not necessarily true. This led to his keenest controversies, and, in my opinion, to his least successful answers. He especially claims credit in his *Autobiography* for having attacked the 'stronghold' of the intuitionists by upsetting belief in the *a priori* certainty of mathematical aphorisms. In fact, his opponents constantly appealed to the case of mathematics, and Mill assumes that they can be met only by reducing such truths to the case of purely empirical truths. He argues boldly that the 'character of necessity ascribed to the truths of mathematics' is 'an illusion.'[3] Geometry and arithmetic are both founded upon experience or observation. He goes indeed still further at times. At one place he even holds that the principle of contradiction itself is simply 'one of our first and most familiar generalisations from experience.' We know, 'by the simplest observation of our own minds,' that belief and disbelief exclude each other, and that when light is present darkness is absent.[4] Mill thought himself

[1] *Logic*, p. 149 (bk. ii. ch. v. § 1).   [2] *Ibid.* p. 151 (bk. ii. ch. v. § 4).
[3] *Ibid.* p. 147 (bk. ii. ch. v. § 1).
[4] *Ibid.* p 183 (bk. ii. ch. vii. § 5). In the *Examination of Hamilton* he is less confident. It is 'not only inconceivable to us, but inconceivable that it should be made conceivable' that the same statement should be both true and false (ch. vi. p. 67). Afterwards (ch. xxi. p. 418) he will only decide that such laws are now 'invincibly' laws of thought, though they may or may not be 'capable of alteration by experience.'

bound, we see, to refer to experience not only our knowledge of facts, but even the capacities, which are said by another school to be the conditions of perceiving and thus acquiring experience. If he had studied Kant, he might have reached a better version of his own view. As it was, he was led to accepting paradoxes which he was not really concerned to maintain. He had to choose between a theory of 'intuitions'—so understood as to entitle us to assert matter of fact independently of experience—and a theory which seems to make even the primary intellectual operations mere statements of empirical fact. Since necessary statements about matters of fact must be impossible, he argues that we cannot even draw necessary inferences from observed fact. Not content with saying that all necessity is hypothetical, he argues that all necessity, even the logical necessity of contradiction, is a figment. If he does not carry out a theory which would seem to make all reasoning unsatisfactory, he maintains, at least, that the hypotheses or assumptions involved in geometry, and even in arithmetic, are generalised from experience, and 'seldom, if ever, exactly true.' If the assumptions are inaccurate or uncertain, the whole superstructure of science must also be uncertain.

The nature of his argument follows from his previous positions. He treats space and number as somehow qualities of the 'things,' or as attributes which we observe without in any sense supplying them. His argument upon geometry begins by asserting that there are no such 'real things' as points or lines or circles. Nay, they are not even possible, so far as we can see, consistently with the actual constitution of the universe. It

is 'customary' to answer that such lines only exist in our minds, and have therefore nothing to do with outward experience.[1] This, however, is incorrect psychologically, because our ideas are copies of the realities. A line without breadth is 'inconceivable,' and therefore does not exist even in the mind. Hence we must suppose that geometry deals either with 'non-entities' or with 'natural objects.'[1] Arithmetic fares little better. When we say that two and one make three, we assert that the same pebbles may, 'by an alteration of place and arrangement' — that is, by being formed into one parcel or two—be made to produce either set of sensations.[2] Each of the numbers, 2, 3, 4, etc., he says elsewhere, 'denotes physical phenomena and connotes a physical property of those phenomena.'[3] Arithmetic owes its position to the 'fortunate applicability' to it of the 'inductive truth' that the sums of equals 'are equal.'[4] It is obvious to remark that this is only true of certain applications of arithmetic. When we speak of the numbers of a population, we imply, as Mill admits, no equality except that each person is a unit.[5] We may speak with equal propriety of a number of syllogisms or of metaphors, in which we have nothing to do with 'equality' or 'physical properties' at all. Further, as he observes,[6] it is the peculiarity of the case that counting one thing is to count all things. When I see that four pebbles are two pairs of pebbles, I see the same truth for all cases, including, for example, syllogisms. Mill admits, accordingly, that 'in questions

[1] *Logic*, p. 148 (bk. ii. ch. v. § 1).   [2] *Ibid.* p. 168 (bk. ii. ch. vi. § 2).
[3] *Ibid.* p. 400 (bk. iii. ch. xxiv. § 5).   [4] *Ibid.* p. 401 (bk. iii. ch. xxiv. § 5).
[5] *Ibid.* p. 170 (bk. ii. ch. vi. § 3).   [6] *Ibid.* p. 167 (bk. ii. ch. vi. § 2).

of pure number'—though only in such questions—
the assumptions are 'exactly true,' and apparently
holds that we may deduce exactly true conclusions.
That ought to have been enough for him.   He had
really no sufficient reason for depriving us of our
arithmetical faith.   He can himself point out its harm-
lessness.   As he truly says, 'from laws of space and
number alone nothing can be deduced but laws of space
and number.'[1]   We can never get outside of the world
of experience and observation by applying them.   If
we count, we do not say that there must be four things,
but that wherever there are four things there are also
two pairs of things.   The unlucky 'pebble' argument
illustrates one confusion.   'Two and two *are* four' is
changed into 'two and two *make* four.'   The statement
of a constant relation is made into a statement of an
event.   Two pebbles added to two might produce a
fifth, but the original two pairs would still be four.
The space-problem suggests greater difficulties.   Space,
he argues, must either be a property of things or an
idea in our minds, and therefore a 'non-entity.'   If we
consider it, however, to be a form of perception, the
disjunction ceases to be valid.   The space-perceptions
mark the border-line between 'object' and 'subject,' and
we cannot place its product in either sphere exclusively.
The space-relations are 'subjective,' because they imply
perception by the mind, but objective because they imply
the action of the mind as mind, and do not vary from
one person or 'subject' to another.   To say whether
they were objective or subjective absolutely we should
have to get outside of our minds altogether—which is an

[1] *Logic*, p. 212 (bk. iii. ch. v. § 1).

impossible feat.   Therefore, again, it is not really to the
purpose to allege that such a 'thing' as a straight line or
a perfect circle never exists.   Whether we say that a
curve deviates from or conforms to perfect circularity,
we equally admit the existence of a perfect circle.   We
may be unable to mark it with finger or micrometer, but
it is there.   If no two lines are exactly equal, that must
be because one has more space than the other.   Mill's
argument seems to involve the confusion between the
statement that things differ in space and the statement,
which would be surely nonsense, that the space itself
differs.   It is to transfer the difference from the
things measured to the measure itself.   It is just the
peculiarity of space that it can only be measured by
space ; and that to say one space is greater than
another, is simply to say, 'there is more space.'
As in the case of number, he is really making an
illegitimate transfer from one sphere to another.   A
straight line is a symmetrical division of space, which
must be taken to exist, though we cannot make a perfectly straight line.   Our inability does not tend to
prove that the 'space' itself is variable.   In applying a
measure we necessarily assume its constancy ; and it is
difficult even to understand what 'variability' means,
unless it is variability in reference to some assumed
standard.   If, as Mill seems to think, space is a property
of things, varying like other properties, we have to ask,
In what, then, does it vary ?   All other properties vary
in respect of their space-relations ; but, if space itself be
variable, we seem to be reduced to hopeless incoherence.

Thus, to ascribe necessity to geometry as well as to
arithmetic is not to ascribe 'necessity' to propositions

(to use Hume's language again) about 'matters of fact.'
The 'necessity' is implied in a peculiarity which Mill
himself puts very forcibly,[1] and which seems to be all
that is wanted.   An arithmetical formula of the simplest
or most complex kind is an assertion that two ways of
considering a fact are identical.   When I say that two
and two make four, or lay down some algebraical
formula, such as Taylor's theorem, I am asserting the
precise equivalence of two processes.   I do not even
say that two and two must make four, but that, if they
make four, they cannot also or ever make five.   The
number is the same in whatever order we count, so
long as we count all the units, and count them correctly.
So much is implied in Mill's observation that counting
one set of things is counting all things.   The concrete
circumstances make no difference.   The same is true of
geometry.   The complex figure may be also regarded as
a combination of simpler figures.   It remains precisely
the same, though we perceive that besides being one
figure it is also a combination of figures.   This runs
through all mathematical truths, and, I think, indicates
Mill's precise difficulty.   He says quite truly that to
know the existence of a fact you must always have something given by observation or experience.   The most
complex mathematical formulæ may still be regarded as
equating different statements of the same experience.
The difference is only that the experience is evolved
into more complex forms, not by any change in the data
supplied, but by an intellectual operation which consists
essentially in organising the data in various ways.   The
reasoner does not for an instant desert fact ; he only

[1] *Logic*, p. 402 (bk. iii. ch. xxiv. § 6).

perceives that it may be contemplated in different ways,
and that very different statements assert the very same
fact or facts.   Our experience may be increased, either
by the entrance of new objects into our field of observation, or by the different methods of contemplation.
The mathematician deals with propositions which remain
equally true if we suppose no change whatever to
take place in the world, or, as Mill puts it, 'if all the
objects of the universe were unchangeably fixed.'[1]   His
theories, in short, construct a map on which he can
afterwards lay down the changes which involve time.
The filling up of the map depends entirely upon observation and experience ; but to make the map itself a mere
bundle of accidental coexistences is to destroy the conditions of experience.   The map is our own faculty of
perception.

'There is something which seems to require explanation,' says Mill,[2] 'in the fact that an immense multitude
of mathematical truths . . . can be elicited from so small
a number of elementary laws.'   It is puzzling when you
identify Newton with Diamond on the ground that they
both see the same 'fact.'   But it is no more puzzling
than anything else, as indeed Mill proceeds to show,
when we observe the method by which in arithmetic,
for example, an indefinite number of relations is implied
by the simple process of counting.   The fact is the same
for all observers, in so far as they have the same data ;
but to perceive the data already implies the germ of
thought from which all the demonstrative sciences are

[1] *Logic*, fourth edition, i. 356 (bk. iii. ch. v. § 1).   This phrase is omitted
in the last edition (p. 211), but the meaning is apparently not altered.
[2] *Ibid.* p. 399 (bk. iii. ch. xxiv. § 5).

evolved. The knowledge can be transformed and complicated to an indefinite degree by simply identifying different ways of combining the data. Mill, in his anxiety to adhere to facts and experience, fails to recognise adequately the process by which simple observation is evolved into countless modifications. The difficulty appears in its extreme form in the curious suggestion that even the principle of contradiction is a product of experience. Mill is so resolved to leave nothing for the mind to do, that he supposes a primitive mind which is not even able to distinguish 'is not' from 'is.' It is hard to understand how such a 'mind,' if it were a 'mind,' could ever acquire any 'experience' at all. So when Mill says that the burthen of proof rests with the intuitionist, he is, no doubt, quite right in throwing the burthen of proof upon thinkers who suppose particular doctrines to have been somehow inserted into the fabric of knowledge without any relation to other truths; but it is surely not a gratuitous assumption that the mind which combines experience must have some kind of properties as well as the things combined. If it knows no 'truths' except from experience, it is at least possible that it may in some way react upon the given experience. This, at any rate, should be Mill's view, who takes 'mind' and 'body' to be unknowable, and all knowledge of fact to be a combination of 'sensations.' He only requires to admit that knowledge may be increased either by varying the data or by varying the mind's action upon fixed data. In neither case do we get beyond 'experience.' In many places, Mill seems to interpret his view in consistency with this doctrine. His invariable candour leads him to make admissions, some

of which I have noticed. Yet his prepossessions lead him to the superfluous paradoxes which, for the rest, he maintains with remarkable vigour and ingenuity.

One other device of the enemy raised the troublesome question of inconceivability as a test of truth, which brought Mill into conflict not only with Whewell and Hamilton, but with Mr. Herbert Spencer. I will only notice the curious illustration which it affords of Mill's tendency to confound statements of fact with the purely logical assertion that two modes of stating a fact are precisely equivalent. The existence of Antipodeans, in his favourite illustration,[1] was declared to be 'inconceivable.' Disbelief in their existence involved the statement of fact : gravity acts here and at the Antipodes in the same direction. That statement could of course be disproved by evidence ; and there is no reason to suppose that the truth, once suggested, would be less 'conceivable' to Augustine or, say, to Archimedes, than to Newton. It also involved the assertion : men (if the direction of gravity were constant) would drop off the earth at the Antipodes as they here drop off the ceiling. The denial of that statement is still 'inconceivable,' though the statement ceases to be applicable. Mill, however, infers that, as an 'inconceivability' has been surmounted, 'inconceivability' in general is no test of truth. 'There is,' he says,[2] 'no proposition of which it can be asserted that every human mind must eternally and irrevocably believe it,' and he tries, as I have said, to apply this even to the principle of contradiction. In other words, because our logic requires a basis in fact, and the fact must be given by experience,

[1] See *Logic*, p. 177 (bk. ii. ch. vii. § 3), and p. 493 (bk. v. ch. iii. § 3).
[2] *Ibid.* p. 370 (bk. iii. ch. xxi. § 1).

the logic is itself dependent upon experience. If 'inconceivable' be limited, as I think it should be limited in logic, to the contradictory, an inconceivable proposition is incredible because it is really no proposition at all. We may, no doubt, believe statements which are implicitly contradictory ; but when the contradiction is made explicit, the belief becomes impossible. Similarly we may disbelieve statements which appear to be contradictory ; and when the error is exposed, we may believe what was once 'inconceivable.' That only shows that our thoughts are often in a great muddle, and in great need of logical unification. It does not prove any incoherence in the logical process itself.

IV. CAUSATION

We can now proceed to what may be called the constructive part of the logic. We have got rid of proofs from intuitions, from definitions, and from inconceivabilities, and the question remains how we can prove anything. All knowledge is inductive. It is all derived from facts; it proceeds from particulars to particulars ; the previous coexistence of sequences which have been observed constitute our whole raw material. What, then, serves to bind facts together ? or how are we to know that facts are bound together, or that any two given facts have this relation ? The fundamental postulate of science is the so-called 'uniformity of nature.' But Nature, as it is seen by the unscientific mind, is anything but uniform. There are, it is true, certain simple uniformities which frequently recur. Fire burns, water drowns, stones thrown up fall down ; and

such observations are the germs of what we afterwards call scientific 'laws.' But things are constantly happening of which we can give no account. Catastrophes occur without any assignable 'antecedent' ; storm and sunshine seem to come at random ; and the same combination of events never recurs in all its details. Variety is as manifest as uniformity. How can cosmos be made out of chaos ? How do we come to trace regularity in this bewildering world of irregularities ? From any fact taken by itself, as Hume had fully shown, we can deduce no necessity for any other fact. The question is, whether we are to account for the belief in uniformity by an 'intuition' or by James Mill's universal solvent of 'association of ideas.' J. S. Mill was fully convinced of the efficacy of this panacea, but he sees difficulties over which his father had passed. If association explains everything, the tie between ideas ought to be stronger, it might be supposed, in proportion to the frequency of their association. The oftener two facts have been joined, the more confidently we should expect a junction hereafter. But this does not hold true universally. A chemist, as Mill observes, analyses a substance; and assuming the accuracy of his results, we at once infer a general law of nature from 'a single instance.' But if any one from the beginning of the world has seen that crows are black, and a single credible witness says that he has seen a grey crow, we abandon at once a conjunction which seemed to rest upon invariable and superabundant evidence. Why is a 'single instance' sufficient in one case, and any number of instances insufficient in the other ? 'Whoever can answer this question,' says Mill, 'knows more of the philosophy of logic than the wisest of the ancients, and has solved the problem of induction.'[1]

Here Mill again professes to set metaphysics aside. He has nothing to do with 'ontology.' He deals with 'physical,' not 'efficient,' causes. He does not ask whether there be or be not a 'mysterious' tie lying behind the phenomena and actually producing them.[2] He is content to lay down as his statement of the 'law of causation' that there is an invariable succession between 'every fact in nature' and 'some other fact which has preceded it.' This, he assumes, is a truth, whatever be the nature of things in themselves. The true account is rather that he will show that 'ontology' is a set of meaningless phrases. He can answer his problem without it. Causation is, in fact, conceived by him as it was conceived by all the psychologists, including Brown; and he has simply to show that Brown's supposed 'intuition' is a superfluity. His treatment of the question gives the really critical part of his philosophy. It leads to some of the results which have been most highly and, as I think, most deservedly praised. It also leads to some of his greatest errors, and shows the weak point of his method.

Mathematical knowledge, as Mill remarks, has nothing to do with causation. Every geometrical or arithmetical formula is true without supposing change. One theorem does not 'cause' the others; it 'implies' them. The most complex and the most simple are mutually involved in the single perception, though our knowledge of one may be the cause of our knowing the others. Their necessity

[1] *Logic*, p. 206 (bk. iii. ch. iii. § 3).
[2] *Ibid.* p. 213 (bk. iii. ch. v. § 2).

is another way of stating this implication. We can show that to deny one theorem while admitting another is to be contradictory. The whole of physical science, however, from first to last, is a process of stating the changes of phenomena in terms of time and place, and therefore brings them all within the range of mathematical methods. Science is not fully constituted till it becomes quantitative or can speak in terms of definite relations of magnitudes. How, then, are its laws necessary? It is contradictory to say that the same thing has different space-relations at the same time; but there is no contradiction in saying that it is here now and somewhere else to-morrow. The formula of the 'uniformity of nature,' whatever may be its warrant, transfers the necessity of the geometrical theorem to the laws of phenomena. We assume that things are continuous or retain identity in change. We are no more permitted to say that the combination of the same elements may produce a compound of different properties, than to say that the product of two numbers may sometimes give one result and sometimes another. Every change is regarded as regular, or as having a 'sufficient reason.' The same series of changes therefore must take place under the same conditions, or every difference implies a difference in the conditions. So far as we carry out this assumption, we resolve the shifting and apparently irregular panorama into a system of uniform laws. Each law may be, and if it be really a law must be, absolutely true, not in the sense that it states a fact unconditionally, but that it is stated so that the conditions under which it is absolutely true are fully specified. If we could reach a complete science of all physical phenomena, we should have a system of con-

nected laws as infallible and mutually consistent as those of geometry or arithmetic. But in order thus to organise our knowledge, we have to alter—not the facts—but the order of grouping and conceiving them. We have to see identities where there were apparent differences, and differences in apparent identities, and to regard the whole order of nature from a fresh point of view. The fact remains just as it was; but the laws—that is, the formulæ which express them—are grouped upon a new system. The questions remain, What is the precise nature of the scientific view? and What is our guarantee for a postulate which it everywhere implies?

The chapter upon causation[1] is a vigorous assertion of Mill's position. He accepts the traditional view of his school, that cause means invariable sequence; but he makes two very important amendments to the previous statements. A simple sequence of two events is not a sufficient indication, however often repeated, that they are cause and effect. We speak, he says, of a particular dish 'causing' death; but to be accurate we must also include, as part of the cause, all the other phenomena present, the man as well as the food, the man's state of health at the time, and possibly even the state of the atmosphere or the planet. The real cause must include all the relevant phenomena. The cause, therefore, is, 'philosophically speaking,' the 'sum total of the conditions,' positive and negative, 'taken together, the whole of the contingencies of every description, which, being realised, the consequent invariably follows.'[2] Mill's second amendment is made by saying that the cause does not signify simply 'invariable antecedence,'

[1] *Logic*, bk. iii. ch. v.   [2] *Ibid.* p. 217 (bk. iii. ch. v. § 3).

but also 'unconditional' sequence. There may be 'invariable' sequences, such as day and night—a case often alleged by Reid and others, which are not 'unconditional.' The sun, for anything we can say, might not rise, and then day would not follow night. The real condition, therefore, is the presence of a luminous body without the interposition of an opaque screen.[1] These are undoubtedly material improvements upon previous statements; and this view being admitted, it follows, as Mill says, that the state of the whole universe is the consequence of its state at the previous instant. Knowing all the facts and all the laws at any time we could predict all the future history of the universe.[2] Some curious confusions, it must be noticed, result apparently from Mill's use of popular language. The most singular is implied in his discussion of the question whether cause and effect can ever be simultaneous. Some 'causes,' he says, leave permanent effects; a sword runs a man through, but it need not remain in his body in order that he may 'continue dead.'[3] The 'cause' here is taken to mean the 'thing' which was once a part of a set of things, and has clearly ceased to mean the sum of all the conditions. 'Most things,' he continues, once produced, remain as they are till something changes them. Other things require the continual presence of the agencies which produced them. But since all change, according to him, supposes a cause, it is clear that not only 'most things' but all things must remain as they are till something changes them. Persistence is implied in causation as much as change, for it is merely the other side of the

[1] *Logic*, p. 221 (bk. iii. ch. v. § 5).   [2] *Ibid.* p. 227 (bk. iii. ch. v. § 8).
[3] *Ibid.* p. 224 (bk. iii. ch. v. § 7).

same principle. Inertia is as much assumed in mechanics as mobility; for it is the same thing to say that a body remains in one place when there is no moving force, as to say that whenever it ceases to remain there is a moving force. The difference which Mill means to point out is that some changes alter permanent conditions of other changes, as when a man cuts his throat and all vital processes cease; while sometimes the change leaves permanent conditions unaffected, as when a man shaves himself, and his vital processes continue. But in no case is the effect produced, as he says, after the cause has ceased; it is always produced through the actually present conditions, which may have come into their present state through a change at some more or less remote period. Each link in a chain, according to the common metaphor, depends upon all the previous links and may be said to hang from them; but the distant link can only act through the intermediate links.

These slips imply a vagueness which leads to more serious results. Mill's aim is to construct a kind of logical machinery—a sieve, if I may say so, through which we pass all the phenomena of the universe in order to find out which are really loose and which are connected by the ties of causation. We are unweaving the complex web of nature by discovering what is the hidden system of connections in virtue of which one event or thing is somehow fastened to another. Everything, we may say, which appears is called up by something else—the thunder by the lightning, the death by the poison, and so forth. In every case we can reduce a statement of causation to the form of an asser-

tion of sequence or coexistence. Here, as he observes, we meet one difficulty. Everything is connected with some other thing. But then it may or must be also connected with a third. The two connections may interfere, and we have to consider how they can be disentangled. This leads to a distinction to which he attaches, very rightly, I think, the highest importance. In some cases, the correct version of the facts can be obtained by simply superposing the laws of simpler cases. A body moves to the north under certain conditions; but other conditions force it to move also east or south. We then have only to combine the two 'laws,' and to say that it is moving both north and east, that is, north-east, or perhaps to interpret rest as an equal movement to both north and south. This, as he remarks, represents the general case in regard to mechanical phenomena. We have simply to combine two rules to get what is called in dynamics 'the composition of forces'; and, in accordance with this phase, he uses the general phrase, 'the composition of causes.'[1] But, as he observes, this principle is in many cases not applicable. In chemical combinations, in particular, we cannot infer the properties of the compound from the properties of the components. The laws of simple substances will not give us the laws of the product, and we can only learn these derivative laws by experiment. This holds, still more conspicuously, of organised bodies. From considering the properties of its chemical constituents separately you cannot deduce the properties of the human body. We thus come to a kind of knot in the web; we are at a deadlock, because the laws from which we

[1] *Logic*, p. 243 (bk. iii. ch. vi. § 1).

start are superseded by an entirely different set of laws. Mill marks this by speaking of 'heteropathic laws.'[1] Such laws are not analysable into simple laws. He thinks, indeed, that 'heteropathic laws' are—at least 'in some cases may be—derived from the separate laws, according to a fixed principle.' The fact to which he calls attention is undeniable. We discover countless laws as to the properties of bodies which it is impossible at present either to resolve into simpler laws, or to deduce from the laws of the constituent elements. Such laws are properly 'empirical.' The observation of the facts asserted is the sole guarantee for our belief in their truth; and they can be reduced under no more general formula. Is this, however, simply a challenge to the man of science to inquire further, or does it oppose an insuperable obstacle to further scientific researches? Mill avowedly limits himself to 'our present state of knowledge.' He recognised that Grove, in his *Correlation of Forces*,[2] made out a strong, though still only a probable, case for believing that a 'heteropathic law' may represent a complete transformation of one set of forces into another. Heat, light, and magnetism may be all different manifestations of a single force—not so much causes of one another as 'convertible into one another.'[3] Grove, as Mill adds, is not, as might be supposed, deviating into ontology, but giving a strictly

[1] *Logic*, p. 245 (bk. iii. ch. vi. § 2).
[2] Grove's work was first published in 1846, *i.e.* after the first edition of the *Logic*.
[3] *Logic*, fourth edition, p. 477 (bk. iii. ch. x. § 4). In the eighth edition this passage was suppressed, and Mill discusses the theory of 'conservation or persistence of force,' as he calls it, in an earlier section.—*Logic*, p. 228 (bk. iii. ch. v. § 10).

philosophical statement. Mill is here speaking of a great principle, imperfectly known at the time, which has been accepted by modern science, and he is quite ready to welcome it. It is, however, noticeable that he still guards himself against admitting any intrusion of 'necessity.' He will not allow that the dependence of the properties of compounds upon these elements must result in all cases 'according to a fixed principle.' The meaning of this may appear from his later assault upon the doctrine that 'like produces like.' This he reckons among the fallacies which he discovers in all manner of pestilent *a priori* philosophising. Descartes, Spinoza, Leibniz, and Coleridge have all been guilty of it in various forms.[1] We are therefore under no obligation to go further when we come to totally disparate phenomena in our series. We have unravelled our web sufficiently when we find laws disappearing and being superseded by a totally different set of laws, not describable even in the same language. That we may be forced to be content with such a result is undeniable. But it is equally true that one main end of scientific theorists is to get round this difficulty. Without inquiring in what sense the axiom that 'like produces like' may be fallacious, we must at least admit that to give a scientific law—that is, a rule by which one set of events is deducible from another—we must be able to express it in terms of some single measure. Till we can get such a statement, we have not the complete formula. There is a breach of continuity in our theories, which we try to remove by reducing all the forces to measures assignable in terms of space and number. The hypothesis of an ether and

[1] *Logic*, p. 501 (bk. v. ch. iii. § 8).

vibrating atoms enables us to regard phenomena as corresponding in some way to the laws which, as Mill says, can be compounded by simple superposition, without introducing heterogeneous terms. Though he does not condemn this hypothesis, Mill regards it with a certain suspicion as an attempt to wander into ontology, and the search for what is in its nature inaccessible.[1] At any rate, it does not appear to him that further inquiry is necessary when we come to an irreducible breach of continuity; to a case in which one set of phenomena is simply superseded by another, instead of being transformable into it. If a compound is made of certain elements exclusively, a physicist would clearly infer that its properties *must* be a result of the properties of the elements according to 'some fixed principle.' Mill is only prepared to admit that this *may* be the case. The physicist, again, seeks for a mode of stating the principle in theorems capable of being combined and superposed, whereas Mill holds that our knowledge may have come to an ultimate insuperable end.

V. PLURALITY OF CAUSES

It is in the applications of this view that we come to what must be regarded as downright fallacies. If, as Mill holds, an effect may be something absolutely disparate from the cause—a new thing which starts into existence when its antecedent occurs—we are led to another result. There is, then, no apparent reason why the same thing should not spring up in answer to different summonses.

[1] See, for example, his criticism of a 'luminiferous ether' in answer to Whewell, *Logic*, p. 328 (bk. iii. ch. xiv. § 6). He agrees here with Comte (*Phil. Positive*, ii. 639), whom he perhaps follows.

Not only is this possible, but, as Mill thinks, it constantly occurs. This is his doctrine of the 'Plurality of Causes.' A given cause, he holds, can only produce one effect. But a given effect may follow various causes. So long as the relation is merely one of arbitrary succession, not of continuity, this is obviously possible. The fully scientific view, I take it, would be that when we speak of 'cause and effect' we are really thinking of a single process regarded in different ways. We may analyse the process differently for different purposes, and infer the past from the future or the future from the past; but we assume that, if we could perfectly understand the whole process, there would be thorough continuity, and no abrupt supersession of one thing or one set of 'laws' by another. This continuity is precisely what Mill systematically denies. A cause, he holds, means an absolute beginning of a new effect.[1] The process becomes a series of distinct terms—a set of 'links' in a chain, not a flow of a stream. One remarkable case is enough to illustrate the point. When Bacon's claims to have founded a truly scientific theory are considered, it is generally said that his guess as to the nature of heat is a point in his favour.[2] Mill, however, takes this particular case as an instance of Bacon's errors. Bacon, he says,[3] 'entirely overlooked the Plurality of Causes. All his rules imply the assumption, so contrary to what we now know of nature, that a phenomenon

[1] See especially the chapter on causation in the *Examination of Hamilton*.
[2] Tyndall, *e.g.*, in his *Heat as a Mode of Motion*, quotes Bacon's anticipation. It is summed up by Whewell (*Phil. Ind.* ii., *Sciences*, ii. 239) in the statement that the 'form of heat is an expansive, restrained motion, modified in certain ways, and exerted in the smaller particles of the body.'
[3] *Logic*, p. 500 (bk. v. ch. iii. § 7).

cannot have more than one cause.' Bacon was misguided enough to apply this to heat. Now, as Mill had already argued, heat may have several causes: the 'sun,' or 'friction,' or 'percussion,' or 'electricity,' or 'chemical action.'[1] Consequently, the attempt to find a single cause is doomed to failure. We shall find, not that one antecedent but, that one of several antecedents is always present. Clearly the 'sun' is not 'friction,' nor is 'percussion' 'electricity.' Each of those phrases indicates concrete facts involving various processes. Heat, as a 'mode of motion,' occurs in them all, because all involve particular phases of movement. From the 'raw' fact, as it presents itself—'This body is hot'—I cannot say which of various laws represents the true antecedents in that case. The heat may have been caused by exposure to fire or by friction. In that sense, undoubtedly, one effect may really have any number of 'causes.' But replace all the conditions, and it is evident that there can be only one true analysis of the whole process. Mill's insistence upon this imaginary 'plurality of causes' is significant. It indicates the precise stage in the development of the idea of cause to which his doctrine corresponds. Taking what we may call the popular sense of causation, the 'plurality' expresses an obvious truth; and we can understand its plausibility. We take, in fact, two concrete events which follow each other, and call them cause and effect. We use a tool—a knife to cut bread, for example; we are forced to attend to the fact that every difference in the knife will have an effect on the result. The work is better or worse, as the knife is sharper or blunter. If we did not recognise this in

[1] *Logic*, p. 288 (bk. iii. ch. x. § 3).

every purposeful action, all action would be intrinsically uncertain. We are, therefore, impressed with the necessity of admitting that the effect is determined by the cause. But, on the other hand, the knife is there. It may have been made by fifty different methods, and yet be the same. The handle may have been first made and then the blade, or *vice versa*, and so forth. Therefore we believe, and in this sense of cause believe correctly, that one effect may be the product of any number of different 'causes.' In order to reach the more scientific sense of causation, we have to take into account all that we have neglected. The knife is one product of an indefinite multitude of processes, and is therefore not the total 'effect' of the concrete antecedent, but only a part of it arbitrarily singled out. We do not attend to all these collateral results, because for us at the moment they have no interest; but when we systematically carry out the 'uniformity of nature' principle, it is obvious that they must be taken into account. We then see that although precisely similar products appear in an infinite variety of concrete processes, they correspond only to a part of those processes, and may always be analysed into identical elements. The effect can no more have two causes than a cause two effects, for cause and effect are distinguished by observing the same process in a different order. It was just because men of science held that the one effect must have one cause that they could make a coherent theory of heat. Mill, however goes a step further. Bacon's error was the assumption that there was only one 'form' of heat. Now it is specially futile, says Mill, to seek for the causes of 'sensible qualities of objects. . . . In regard to scarcely any of them has it been found possible to trace any unity of cause.' Bacon, therefore, was seeking for 'what did not exist,' and to this Mill adds the surprising statement that 'the phenomenon of which he sought for the one cause has oftenest no cause at all, and, when it has, depends (as far as hitherto ascertained) on an unassignable variety of causes.'[1]

To explain this rather startling assertion we must take one more of Mill's theories. How from the doctrine, which he fully admits, that every event has a cause can he reach the conclusion that some things have 'no cause at all'? Once more we have, I think, the misapplication of an undeniable truth. A 'law' of causation, taken by itself, will obviously not fully account for a single fact. It cannot lead to the conclusion : 'this fact must exist,' but only to the conclusion : this fact must exist if certain previous facts existed. We somewhere assume an initial stage. However far back we can go, we may still repeat the question. Given a single state of facts and the 'laws of causation,' we can go indefinitely backwards or forwards in time. Given the sun, the planets, and gravitation, we can trace the whole past and future history of the solar system ; but the facts at some period must be 'given.' We cannot say that they must, but only that they do exist. Mill himself puts this[2] with all desirable clearness. He expresses it by saying that

[1] *Logic*, p. 500 (bk. v. ch. iii. § 7). It may be noticed that Whewell (in 1847) equally regards Bacon's theory as a complete failure. He thinks more favourably of an 'imponderable fluid.' Mill, therefore, had good authority as to the failure. The modern doctrine, says Lord Kelvin (*Encycl. Britannica*), was established about 1851. See Huxley on the 'Progress of Science' (*Essays*, i. 86) for Whewell's treatment of Bacon's guess.
[2] *Logic*, p. 226 (bk. iii. ch. v. § 7).

besides 'causation' there is 'collocation,' a word, he says, suggested by Chalmers.[1] To know the 'collocation,' therefore, is essential. A 'law' does not tell us that there 'must' be plums and suet, but only that if there are such things in certain 'collocations' a plum pudding 'must' be the result. All statements of fact have thus an empirical basis. This, however, takes a peculiar turn in his exposition, and one which is characteristic of a Utilitarian failing. He makes the distinction of relations correspond to a distinction of things. Instead of saying that both causation and collocation are implied in all phenomena, he speaks of some 'uniformities' as dependent upon causation and others as dependent upon collocation. He therefore writes a chapter on 'uniformities of coexistence not dependent on causation.'[2] This, however, is closely connected with, and must be explained by, another doctrine to which he attached the highest importance. After telling us how he was started afresh by Stewart's account of axioms, he adds that he came to 'inextricable difficulties' in regard to induction. He had come to the 'end of his tether,' and 'could make nothing satisfactory of the subject.' When, after five years' halt, he again set to work, he introduced his 'theory of kinds,' which, as he intimates, got round the difficulty. He felt, as we may conjecture, that he had now reduced all the facts to such purely empirical conjunctions that he did not see how to get any tie between them. Any cause, so far as we have gone, might lead to any effect ; and even when we have

[1] *Logic*, p. 306 (bk. iii. ch. xii. § 2). See Chalmers's *Natural Theology*, bk. ii. ch. i.
[2] *Logic*, pp. 377-85 (bk. iii. ch. xxii.).

seen a case of conjunction, we can give no reason for its recurrence. Induction enables us to predicate attributes of a class ; but a logical class is itself merely a bundle of attributes arbitrarily selected, and it remains to see why, from a thing's possession of some of the class attributes, we can infer that it has the others. Why should not the same set of attributes form part of different bundles? and if so, what is the justification for the primary logical procedure? From featherless bipedism we infer mortality. But why may not some class of featherless bipeds be immortal? If we admit the possibility, all induction becomes precarious. The 'theory of kinds' was, it seems, intended as an answer to these obvious difficulties.

VI. REAL KINDS

Mill's account of 'real kinds' corresponds, as he tells us, to the old logicians' distinction between genus and species. Though our classification may be arbitrary and nothing properly deducible from it, except the mere fact that we have chosen to give names to certain clusters of attributes, there is also a real difference. Some of our classes do not correspond to 'real kinds,' and are mistaken for them. Others, however, correspond to a real or natural kind. The difference is this: a 'real kind' has an 'indeterminate multitude of properties, not derivable from each other,' whereas an arbitrary or merely logical 'kind' may only differ in respect of the particular attribute assigned. Thus, to say that Newton is a man is to attribute to him the 'unknown multitude of properties' connoted by 'man.' To say that Newton

is a Christian is only to attribute to him a particular belief and whatever consequences may follow from having that belief.[1] One classification, as he says, 'answers to a much more radical distinction in the things themselves, than the other does' ; and a man may thus fairly say, if he chooses, that one classification is made 'by Nature' and one 'by ourselves,' provided that he means no more than to express the distinction just drawn. Now, it is easy to understand why Mill felt that this assertion entitled him to a 'real' bond which would keep phenomena together in a more satisfactory way. All things had become so loose and disconnected that it was difficult to explain any extension of knowledge even by induction. Yet, whatever the reason, things do stick together in coherent and many-propertied clusters. The bond seems to be real when it is stated 'objectively,' not 'subjectively'—as a property of the things observed, not of the classes made by the mind itself. I take the remark to be both true and important ; and, moreover, that Mill deserves credit for perceiving so clearly this weak joint in his armour. His application, however, suggests, when he had hit upon an apparent escape from his 'inextricable' difficulties, he was too much relieved to work out its full effect upon his general theory. The 'theory of kinds' is inserted rather than embodied in his philosophy, and makes rents in the attempt to fill a gap. It plays, however, so important a part in the doctrine that it requires some further consideration.

A real kind, we see, has two characteristics ; it has innumerable properties, and those properties are not 'derivable' from the others. In fact, a derivative

[1] *Logic*, pp. 79-81 (bk. i. ch. vii. § 4).

property would be merely a modification of a primitive property. A geometrical 'kind,' a curve of the second order, for example, has innumerable properties, but they are all derivative from the simple properties expressed in the axioms and definitions. They reciprocally imply each other. But can we say the same of the properties of a thing—of a plant or of water or of an atom? Here we have the distinction already noticed. The so-called 'thing' may be merely a collection of separate things, and we can discover the 'laws' applicable to all by combining the laws applicable to each. From a given 'collocation' we can infer past or future 'collocations,' and one set of results can be added to or superposed upon the other. But when we proceed to chemical or organic compounds, we have 'heteropathic' laws. The compound may be analysed into elements, but we cannot derive the properties of the compounds from the properties of the elements. Hydrogen and oxygen can be combined into the form of water; but we could not infer the properties of water from the properties of the hydrogen and oxygen taken apart. In organic compounds, the problem is still more intricate. We have to consider a series of inter-related changes taking place within the organism, and dependent partly upon the 'environment' and partly upon the complex constitution of the organism itself. It is a unit in so far as all its properties manifest an organic law or a system of organic laws. Individuals may differ from external causes as plants, for example, in different soils, and in that case we may regard the differences as simply derivative. Differences which belong to the organic law itself indicate differences of kind; and these are

ultimate for us, so long as we cannot trace the way in which they are dependent upon differences of constitution. These, roughly stated, are the facts which Mill recognises. Now, in any case whatever, we can only 'explain' a fact by assuming both 'collocation' and 'causation'; or, in other words, we must have a statement of facts and of laws. Our analysis of the phenomena will in all cases come to showing how a given state results from, or results in, a previous or succeeding state. If new properties appear from the combination of simpler elements, we should infer that they result, though we may be quite unable in the existing state of knowledge to show how they result, from the properties of those elements. The properties do not manifest themselves, and are therefore not discoverable, till the combination is formed; and are thus only known to us 'empirically.' No process of reasoning, that is, can be adduced to show that they must result from the combination. But, in the case supposed, we do not doubt that they do result, and we assume that the elements had certain latent properties not previously discoverable. This, however, is the point upon which Mill diverges, owing, as I think, to his imperfect view of causation.

The doctrine of 'kinds,' in fact, gives the answer to Mill's old problem, why a single instance is sometimes conclusive, whereas any number of instances may sometimes fail to give certainty. It is this reciprocal connection between the properties of a 'kind' which justifies the inference from one set of attributes to another attribute—the inference implied in all induction. But Mill's interpretation of the fact seems strangely inconsistent. His favourite instance is the black crow. I have seen a

million black crows. Can I say that the million and oneth crow will be black? To answer this we must ask whether blackness is a property of 'kind.'[1] If the blackness be, 'as it were, an accident,' or not a property of kind, it must, he says, be a case of causation. If not a case of causation, it must be a property of kind. Hence we have the singular result, that if the coexistence be casual, it is caused, and if invariable, not caused. As 'causation' means according to him simply unconditional connection, the statement seems to be especially paradoxical. It is, however, explicable.

The blackness of the crow may be regarded as 'accidental,' if it is due to the external cause. The crow, perhaps, has fallen into a paint-pot. The blackness is 'caused,' then, by the properties of paint and by the 'accidental' collocation. It is an 'accident' in the crow, though caused in respect of the general arrangements of the universe. But why, if a property of 'kind,' should it be called 'not caused'? Here we have a curious result of Mill's view of causation. Our natural reply would be that the colour is still caused as everything else is caused.[2] We assume, that is, that 'crow' implies such a constitution that under a given environment crows will be black. Change something outside the crow and he may turn white. Or find a white crow in the same 'environment,' and we infer some difference in his constitution. There is

---

[1] Logic, pp. 377-86 (bk. iii. ch. xxii.).
[2] It has been suggested that upon Mill's principles the change of a lobster's colour to red is 'caused' when he is boiled, but the colour before boiling uncaused. A case in the South Kensington Museum showing variously coloured crows is a tacit comment on Mill's illustration. The colour of crows is obviously considered by modern men of science as implying causal relations.

a relation, we assume, though we cannot specify its nature, which determines the colour, and as in all cases we have at once collocation and causation. Here is Mill's peculiar difficulty. Causation, as he is profoundly convinced, always means a beginning. It is only, as we have seen, concerned with changes, not with persistence. Therefore, if two things, like blackness and crowness, exist side by side, it is a case of collocation, and consequently, as he supposes, *not* a case of causation. He cannot recognise a reciprocal relation, although it is clear that if one thing is found always to accompany another, the argument is the same as though one always followed another. Indeed, his whole theory of induction implies the possibility of reasoning from one property or attribute to another. Make a change in one and the other must be changed. He sees this clearly in the case of organised bodies.[1] In that case, he says, there is a 'presumption' that the properties are 'derivable' and therefore 'caused,' because there we have sequences or one process following another. He thus seems to limit his 'natural kinds' chiefly to chemical compounds. There we have properties lying side by side and not 'derivable,' that is, not to be inferred by us from the properties of the elementary constituents. The very attempt to derive them is idle. As any event may cause any other, however unlike, so any set of properties may be simply stuck together. Bacon is again reproved[2] for assuming that 'every object has an invariable coexistent.' The ultimate properties, so far as we can conjecture, are 'inherently properties

---

[1] Logic, p. 382 (bk. iii. ch. xxii. § 6).
[2] Ibid. p. 381 (bk. iii. ch. xxii. § 4).

of many different kinds of things, not allied in any other respect.' They simply lie side by side, without reference to each other. Thus Mill pushes his empiricism to assuming not only that our knowledge of properties must rest upon direct observation, but that there is absolutely no connection or 'cause' to be known. The 'kind' after all, which was meant to be an essential bond, turns out to be itself a purely arbitrary collection of attributes, and we have to ask whether it does not lose all the significance which he attached to it. The 'collocation' means that the attributes simply lie side by side, and yet are always conjoined. The tie which combines them is undiscoverable, and therefore for us non-existent. It is, as he rightly insists, important that our classification should correspond to natural kinds. 'Kinds,' he says, are classes 'between which there is an impassable barrier'; the logical class is arbitrary, but the real class is an essential fact. His illustration is remarkable. He holds that the 'species of plants are not only real kinds, but are probably all of them real lowest kinds, *infimæ species*,' and that further subdivision would lead to no valuable results.[1] The doctrine that the species of botany must correspond to 'real kinds' is curious in a writer who was himself a botanist and familiar with the difficulty of making absolute divisions between kinds. The conflict with the conceptions implied in Darwinism is of the highest importance.[2] The distinction between 'kinds,' according to Darwin, is not absolute, for it is the product of gradual divergence from a single form. But,

[1] *Logic*, p. 470 (bk. iv. ch. vii. § 4). It is curious that this remains in the last edition, that is, after the first Darwinian controversies.
[2] See Sigwart's *Logik* (1889), ii. 456, etc.

on the other hand, the kinds existing at a given time are discrete. There are gaps between them, as Mill remarks; though, in so far as they have a common origin, not absolutely insuperable gaps. This implies that the organism does not correspond to a mere aggregate of disconnected attributes, so that the difference of kinds would be simply a difference of more or less, and each type pass into the other by imperceptible gradations. We are obliged to suppose a system of reciprocal relations, so that any change in one organ involves correlated changes in others; and thus species diverge along different lines instead of remaining constant or simply adding on new properties. Mill, it seems, has to admit of kinds in order to account for the possibility of inference; but then, as he wishes to avoid 'mystical bonds,' and inferences from 'definitions,' and the scholastic beggings of the question, he declares the relation between the attributes to be 'accidental' or 'uncaused.' Hence, though he sees the difficulty and recognises the probability of 'causation' in organised bodies, he really reduces the 'kind' to be a mere aggregate, and destroys the very organic bond of which he is in need.

VII. UNIFORMITY OF NATURE

The effect of thus contra-distinguishing 'collocation' from causation, and admitting that 'uncaused coexistences' cover a large part of all observable phenomena, is to make the uniformity of nature exceedingly precarious. Indeed, Mill denies it to be conclusively proved. The chapter in which he sums up 'the evidence of the law of universal causation'

leads to remarkable results. No one, he thinks, with a properly trained imagination will find any difficulty in conceiving that in remote parts of the universe 'events may succeed one another at random without any fixed law.' He concludes by asserting that it would be 'folly to affirm confidently' that the law does prevail in 'distant parts of the stellar regions.'[1] A truth which depends upon locality might, for anything one sees, break down in Australia and even at Paris as easily as at Sirius. Mill, accordingly, reaches a thoroughly sceptical conclusion,[2] and reduces the evidence for universal causation to an induction *per enumerationem simplicem*. The wider the generalisation, the greater the efficacy of such induction, upon which depends not only the law of causation but the principles of number and geometry. If the 'subject-matter of any generalisation' be so widely diffused that it can be tested at every time and place, and if it 'be never found otherwise than true, its truth cannot depend on any collocations, unless such as exist at all times and places, nor can it be frustrated by any counteracting agencies except such as never actually occur.'[3] Now no exception to the 'law of causation' has ever been found, and apparent exceptions have only confirmed it. It is no doubt true that if a law be universal, it will be confirmed by all our experiments; but it hardly follows that, because all our experiments have failed to detect an exception, it is true universally. All our experiments have covered but a small fragment of

[1] *Logic*, pp. 370-76 (bk. iii. ch. xxi. § 1, 4).
[2] *Ibid.* p. 372 (bk. iii. ch. xxi. § 2).
[3] *Ibid.* p. 373 (bk. iii. ch. xxi. § 3).

nature, and they do not justify us, as he expressly asserts, in reasoning about the stellar regions. It is difficult, moreover, to see how an 'exception' could ever be proved, since, wherever we do not see a 'cause,' we can always suppose, and do in fact suppose, an invisible cause. Finally, the theory of 'natural kinds,' as it has now been interpreted, seems to fail us in our need. He takes it to indicate, indeed, that there are connections in nature, which, if known, would justify certain general inferences; but it does not appear that we can know what are these connections, and as, moreover, we have been carefully told that they are ultimate or not 'derivative,' we have no right to be certain that they will recur. We do not know, for example, whether blackness be a property of kind. If we found a black crow among white ones, the property would be casual, and therefore 'caused.' If we found a race of white crows in Australia, we should simply say that there was a kind hitherto overlooked.[1] Such a discovery, he says, is not at all incredible. It might be proved by the evidence of a single credible witness. It merely supposes that there is a kind with a different set of attributes, and as the attributes are in no way 'derivative,' there is no improbability in this. The more general the rule, however, the greater the probability of its holding, because the greater the improbability of the exception being overlooked. We should easily believe in white crows, but not so easily in crows with a property 'at variance with any generally recognised universal property of birds,' and still less, if it were 'at variance with such a property of animals.'[2] We could hardly, that is, believe

[1] *Logic*, p. 382 (bk. iii. ch. xxii. § 5).   [2] *Ibid.* p. 384 (bk. iii. ch. xxii. § 8).

in crows with the stomachs of wolves, or in crows without stomachs at all. But the difficulty appears to depend upon nothing else than the improbability that such animals, had they existed, would have been unnoticed.

Without trying fully to unravel this logic, we may notice one characteristic. Mill, trying to refer everything to 'experience,' has gone far to make experience impossible. What has dropped out of this theory of knowledge is the constructive part. He substitutes for organisation combinations of disparate 'things.' He will admit of no logic, except that of an external connection of radically different objects. Attributes must be stuck together without any reciprocal relations. All causation becomes in his phrase 'collocation,' though he declares causation and collocation to be not only different but mutually exclusive. His one logical formula is the *nota notæ est nota rei ipsius*.[1] Things are marks of each other, not implied by each other. He forces this language even upon mathematics. Even a geometrical 'kind,' if we may use the word, an ellipse, or a curve of the second order, is treated by the formula applicable to purely empirical conjunctions. The equality of two straight lines, it seems, is simply a 'mark' that if applied to each other they would coincide; the fact that two things are sums of equals is a 'mark' that they are equal, and so forth.[2] He would apparently be inclined to say that a thing's existence is a mark of its not being nothing. Thus, even the 'natural kind' becomes merely a permanent combination. When the properties of a curve are merely connected by 'marks,' it is no wonder that

[1] As he says in the *Examination of Hamilton*, ch. xix.
[2] *Logic*, p. 142 (bk. ii. ch. iv. § 4).

the properties of crows should be mere bundles. If it is only on such terms that we can thoroughly get rid of 'intuitions,' the advantage is doubtful.

I will venture to say another word upon the uniformity of Nature difficulty. It is easy, says Mill, to conceive of things happening at random. It is, indeed, in one sense perfectly easy. 'Raw' things, or unanalysed concrete events, do happen at random, that is, without uniform antecedents. Nothing is easier than to think of things without thinking of their causes. The primitive mind, and even the cultivated mind, may simply watch the series of events without trying to find any connection or indulging in any reasoning. But this is quite different from thinking of things as positively uncaused. A phenomenon suddenly intrudes without warning. I may accept it without asking whence it comes, or why. But there is no really positive meaning in the statement that it is caused by 'nothing.' It does not imply a contradiction, such as occurs when I put together the words crooked and straight, round and square; but it represents no intelligible meaning. It corresponds to a simple absence of thought. When I speak of the uniformity of Nature, I mean simply to indicate a condition of thinking about Nature at all. I may cease to reason or to think; but if I think, I must think coherently, and assume what has been called the 'Universal Postulate.'[1]

[1] Some writers, especially G. H. Lewes, have tried to maintain that the statement of the uniformity of Nature is an 'identical proposition.' The attempt is unsatisfactory, and certainly does not seem to have found favour with later writers; but, though I am unable to discuss the question, I will suggest that it seems to indicate the ideal result of reasoning. We assume that, if our knowledge were complete, we could state all the laws of action and reaction of any element as necessary consequences of its primitive consti-

The phrase seems to me to be inadequate; and at any rate it is a postulate with this peculiarity, that we cannot make any other. To deny it is to allow contradictory statements on the most intimate tissue of our reasoning. It is as impossible to do without it as to do without the principle of contradiction in pure logic. It helps us to no positive statement; but it is a warning that our statements must be coherent. Hence, we must allow the mind to have this modest capacity for working up its experience. If it starts from so unprejudiced a point of view as to admit contradictions, or allow of inconsistent statements about things, it will never be able to get anywhere, and when Mill has reduced all our knowledge to the relations between ideas in the mind, it is really quite inconsistent to allow the mind no power of putting ideas together. Without such a power it is difficult to say what is even meant by the perception of 'coexistences' and 'sequences.' The progress of knowledge, then, must be understood as corresponding to the process by which the chaos of impressions and ideas is gradually reduced to cosmos; and as starting from a position in which no cause has been yet discovered for great masses of facts, not from a position in which ' no cause' is an equally probable alternative with 'some cause.' To reason at all about facts is to arrange them in order of causation, and to suppose them as having certain time- and space-relations. To get behind that primitive germ of reasoning is really to

tution, as we can deduce all the properties of number and space from primary principles. Though we can never attain such a consummation, we can reject any theory which contradicts it, and, therefore, such doctrines as the 'plurality of causes,' which come to supposing that an identical process may be analysed in two inconsistent ways.

make logic impossible from the start. Mill's dread of *a priori* intuitions and necessary results thus led him into perfectly gratuitous difficulties. Granting the 'necessity' of arithmetic or geometry, it is still a hypothetical necessity. It can never take us beyond experience. Such theorems cannot tell us of the existence of a single thing or of its nature. They can only say that if we see things in space they will have certain relations which are deducible from the special confirmation. Without that power the universe would be undecipherable, but with it our knowledge still has throughout a completely empirical base. Not a single statement of fact can be made which is not derived from, and justified by, experience; nor can our experience ever get beyond saying that any given section of the whole is developed out of, and develops into, preceding and succeeding sections.

VIII. THE FOUR METHODS

I have dwelt upon these misconceptions to show why Mill was driven in defence of experience to assume the burthen of proving paradoxes which would be destructive to our very capacity for obtaining experience. Mill prided himself with some reason on his 'four methods.' Although they have been severely criticised,[1] they have, I take it, a genuine value; and, if we ask how they can be valuable in spite of his errors, a satisfactory

[1] *E.g.*, by Mr. F. H. Bradley in his *Principles of Logic* (1883), pp. 329-42. Dr. Venn, who is much more favourable to Mill, discusses them in his *Empirical or Inductive Logic* (1889), pp. 400-31, and shows very clearly how they assume what he calls the 'popular,' as distinguished from the 'rigidly scientific,' view of causation. Elsewhere (p. 58) he remarks that the popular might be called the 'Brown-Herschel-Mill view,' as those writers popularised the doctrine first clearly set forth by Hume. See also Sigwart's *Logik* (1889), ii. 469-500.

answer may perhaps be given. In the first place, his assumptions represent one genuine 'moment' in all reasoning about facts. The primitive intellect may be supposed to regard facts as simply conjoined, and to be guided by 'association of ideas.' The early generalisations of which Mill speaks—'fire burns,' 'water drowns,' and so forth—are really of this kind, and are apparently formed even by dogs and monkeys. Mill is quite right, moreover, in holding that a purely empirical element runs through the whole fabric of knowledge. The error, I think, is in his failure to allow for the way in which it is modified in scientific construction. The ultimate element out of which that construction is developed is always an observation of fact, but the fact means a definite relation of time and space. We start from a 'fact,' but it is not as a simple unanalysable unit, but as something which already is the base of a relation. The unit which corresponds to the final cell out of which tissue is composed is not properly a fact, but a 'truth.' We do not say simply 'this is,' but this is so and so, and has a certain order and configuration. This is gradually elaborated into physical science by the help of the geometrical and numerical relations already implied. Thus, causation, or the connection between phenomena, is not simple collocation, but supposes continuity. The unconditional sequence which Mill identifies with 'causation' does not, and cannot, give the 'cause,' though it does indicate 'causal connection.' So long as two things are entirely separate and distinguishable, we cannot say, in the full sense, that one is the cause of the other; but the connection, if proved, proves that there is a cause which may or may not be discoverable. Brown was right

in thinking that something was still wanting, though his mode of filling the gap by an intuition was erroneous. Mill's answer that the 'intuition' was needless left the difficulty where Hume had put it. Two facts are supposed to be unrelated and yet always combined. That states a difficulty, and only pronounces it to be insoluble. It has, in fact, to be surmounted by scientific hypotheses. Thunder and lightning, for example, are causally connected, but not so that lightning can be properly called the cause of thunder. They are regarded as due to a common cause—to the processes which we call electric disturbance, and so forth. We cannot give the 'law' or state the casual connection adequately, but we regard them as indicating some common element, which is continuous and capable of being described in terms of pure number and geometry. Hence any observation, as soon as we begin to reason, may be regarded as a particular case of some general law, or rather, as being conceivably a case of an indefinite number of laws. Not only so, but any law under which it may be arranged is 'necessary' if all the conditions be restored. The process by which we select one of the possible formulæ, therefore, comes to eliminating all the formulæ which are incorrect when various conditions are altered. We all along assume that some coherent system of 'laws' is possible, or that the rule is there if only we can discover it. If lightning goes once with thunder, we are entitled to say not only that it may go with thunder hereafter, but that it must go with thunder under the same conditions. Therefore the simple inference from an empirical conjunction is justified by the 'law of causation' or the 'uniformity of nature.'

Now, Mill's 'four methods' are applicable to the merely empirical conjunctions, which form a large part of our knowledge, and are implied in every stage. The methods do, in fact, I take it, form an approximately accurate mode of dealing with such knowledge. His cases are, for the most part, selected from the sciences, chemistry in particular, where in point of fact our knowledge is still purely empirical, and we can only assert a collocation, or sequence, without bringing it under a more general rule. He also observes, and the remark must be remembered, that he is trying to give a method of proof, rather than of discovery.[1] If the scientific theory be true, these purely empirical truths will hold good, although from them alone the theory might not have been discoverable. The phenomenon which we call the fall of a stone will be presented when an unsupported stone is near the earth, although the law of gravitation requires an application of methods not summed up by simple observation of conjoined phenomena. The most unsatisfactory part of the 'four methods' results from this view.[2] The process of discovery is not sufficiently represented by the case of A occurring with or without B. The sciences which have risen to be quantitative advance by showing how a variety of cases can be brought within some general and precise formula, and every approximation to, or deviation from, the law be exactly measured. Mill pays too little attention to this essential characteristic, partly, perhaps, because he considers mathematics as simply one part of the 'inductive' or empirical sciences.

The final position may be shortly illustrated by Mill's

relation to his contemporaries. It will show briefly what were the alternatives between which he had to choose, and that, if that which he chose leads to error, there were at least equal errors on the other side. Mill frankly states in his preface that but for Whewell's *History of the Inductive Sciences* the corresponding part of his own book 'wou¹ⁱ probably not have been written.' He remarks with equal candour that Sir John Herschel, in his *Discourse on the Study of Natural Philosophy*,[1] had recognised the four methods. Herschel, however, was his only predecessor, and a more distinct and articulate exhibition of their nature was desirable. Herschel and Whewell had graduated at Cambridge in 1813 and 1816. Both of them were able mathematicians, and, with their contemporary Babbage, had done much to introduce at their university the methods of analysis developed on the Continent. The university was gradually roused; Herschel won a great name in astronomy, and Whewell took in earlier life a very active part in promoting scientific studies in England.[2] Both of them had much

[1] Herschel's *Discourse* first appeared in 1830 as the first volume of Lardner's *Cabinet Cyclopædia*. The 'four methods' are noticed, as Mill states, though with comparative vagueness, in chap. vi. of the *Discourse*. Jevons prefers the statement to Mill's. Whewell makes the obvious remark (*Philosophy of Discovery*, p. 284) that the four methods resemble some of Bacon's *Prærogativæ Instantiarum*.

[2] For Whewell, see the *Writings* so described as to form a biography by I. Todhunter (2 vols. 1876). The *Life and Correspondence*, by Mrs. Stair Douglas, appeared in 1888. Whewell's chief philosophical works are: *History of the Inductive Sciences* (3 vols. 8vo, 1837: second edition, 1840; third edition, 1857); *Philosophy of the Inductive Sciences* (2 vols. 1840: second edition, 1847). This book was afterwards divided into three:—*History of Scientific Ideas*, 2 vols. 1858; *Novum Organum Renovatum*, 1 vol. 1858; and *Philosophy of Discovery*, 1 vol. 1860. Whewell also wrote a pamphlet *Of Induction, with special reference to Mr. J. Stuart Mill's 'System of Logic.'* This is republished as chap. xxii. of the *Philosophy of Discovery*.

closer acquaintance with the physical sciences than Mill, for whom they provided a useful store of materials. Herschel, though a friend of Whewell, approximates to Mill. A 'famous' review of Whewell's two books in the *Quarterly* of June 1841[1] gives his position; but although he seems to perceive the source of Whewell's weakness, he scarcely comes to close quarters. It is enough for my purpose to speak briefly of the points at issue between Mill and Whewell. Whewell, like his most eminent contemporaries at Cambridge, was becoming aware that German speculation could no longer be overlooked. Herschel was son of a German; and Whewell's friends, Julius Hare (1795-1855) and Connop Thirlwall (1797-1875) were taking up the study of German. Their translation of Niebuhr's *History of Rome* (1828-1832) marked an epoch in English scholarship. Whewell meanwhile had read Kant, and been greatly impressed. Especially, as he says, he accepted Kant's theories of space, time, and, in some degree, causation, although he differed from Kant's doctrine as to other so-called 'fundamental ideas.'[2] He 'gladly acknowledges,' too, his obligations to the Scottish school.[3] In fact, it may be said that, like Sir W. Hamilton, he made a compromise between two modes of thought which very rapidly diverge from each other. Whewell begins his *Philosophy of the Inductive Sciences* by considering the fundamental antithesis of philosophy, which corresponds to the distinction between thoughts and things, necessity and experience, object and subject,

---

[1] Republished in Herschel's *Essays* (1857), pp. 142-256.
[2] *Scientific Ideas*, i. 88 (note added to this edition).
[3] *Philosophy of the Inductive Sciences* (1847), ii. 311.

---

and so forth. Time and space are, in his phrase, 'fundamental ideas,' upon which are founded the mathematical sciences. But there are other 'fundamental ideas'— 'cause,' 'media,' 'polarity,' 'chemical affinity resemblance,' 'excitability,' and 'final cause'—which in succession become the foundation of various sciences.

These fundamental ideas are, as he admits, something like 'innate ideas,' except that they can be 'developed.' They can somehow be 'superinduced upon facts,' and are not 'generated by experience.' I shall not attempt to explain a theory which seems to be radically incoherent, and which made no converts. It will be quite enough to notice two of the points of collision with Mill. Mill and Whewell agree[2] that the 'first law of motion' which asserts the uniform rectilinear motion of a body not acted upon by a force was unknown till the time of Galileo. Whewell admits further that, 'historically speaking,' it was made 'by means of experiment.' We have, however, attained a point of view in which we see that it might have been certainly known to be true, independently of experience. Mill naturally ridicules this doctrine, according to which we burden ourselves with 'truths independent of experience, and yet admit that they were proved 'by (or 'by means of') experiment.' The history is admitted on both sides. It had been observed that the motion of all bodies ceases unless they receive a new impulse. The statement was true, though vague, for all bodies upon the earth. But the progress of astronomy and exact sciences required a more

---

[1] *Philosophy of the Inductive Sciences*, i. 80.
[2] Whewell's *Philosophy of Inductive Sciences*, i. 216-21; Mill's *Logic*, pp. 160, 265 (bk. ii. ch. v. § 6, and bk. iii. ch. viii. § 7).

---

precise statement. Science has not simply to recognise that motion declines, but to show at what rate, and under what conditions it declines. Then, as we cannot measure 'absolute motion,' or assign any fixed point in space, we can obtain no rule as to absolute motion. If we assume, however, that we have to account not for motion but for change of motion, we can get a consistent 'law' which at once gives a sufficient account of many observed phenomena. We proceed to define force as the cause of change in motion. Then it becomes an identical proposition that all change of motion implies force, or that bodies not acted upon continue to move uniformly. Thus the definition of force takes the shape of an *a priori* axiom as to force. We imagine that instead of simply co-ordinating our experience we are 'applying a fundamental idea' to it, the idea, namely, of a 'cause' or 'force.'[1] The axiom is not 'independent of experience.' Rightly understood, the whole process is one of interpreting experience. Mill, however, is hardly correct in saying that the law was proved by experiment. We cannot observe a 'force' apart from the moving body. Force is one of Bentham's 'fictitious entities,' a word which enables us to state the relations of moving bodies accurately. It harmonises our conceptions. The old belief that all motions stop is not disproved by discovering cases in which force is absent, but by postulating the presence of force wherever we find change of motion. The real proof is

---

[1] Whewell, indeed, says that the 'necessary law' is that a change of velocity must have a cause; the 'empirical law' tells us that the time during which it has been moving is not a cause.—*Philosophy of the Inductive Sciences*, ii. 591. I need not go into this.

---

not in direct experiment but in the harmonising of an indefinite number of complex statements when once the principle is systematically applied. It can reveal no fact to us, for nothing but experience can show that there are such things as the planets fortunately are, bodies moving freely, so as to illustrate the law continuously. Mill puts the first law of motion on a level with the law that the period of the earth's rotation is uniform. Both 'inductions,' he says, are accurately true.[1] In fact, however, the earth's motion is not absolutely uniform, a truth which we discover by applying the laws of motion, though no direct experiment could exhibit the fact. The law of motion has the authority derived from its rendering possible a consistent interpretation of experiences, whereas the earth's rotation is simply a particular fact which might change if the conditions were altered. The 'law' implies, therefore, a reconstruction of experience not given by simple observation.

This applies to a controversy between Mill and Whewell as to Kepler's great discoveries. They both accept the familiar facts. Kepler's problem was to show how a simple configuration of the solar system would present the complex appearances which we directly observe. The old observations gave approximately correct statements of the movements of the planets, assuming the earth to be fixed, or, as we may say, neglecting the consideration of its motion. His theory shows how the apparent movements must result if we suppose the sun to be fixed, or rather (as the sun is not really fixed) if we measure from it as fixed. Whewell treats this as a case of 'induction.' It illustrates what he calls the 'colliga-

---

[1] *Logic*, p. 151 (bk. ii. ch. v. § 3).

tion of facts'—a happy phrase, accepted by Mill, for the arrangement of facts in a new order, and the application to the facts of the appropriate conceptions; in this case, of the theorems of conic sections and solid geometry. The argument takes the form of a discussion as to whether this should be called induction or an operation subsidiary to induction.[1] Kepler, as Mill urges, was simply describing facts. He discovered a fact in which all the positions of the planet agreed—namely, that they were in an ellipse. If he had been somewhere in space, or the planet had left a visible track, he might have actually seen it to be an ellipse. He had only to 'piece together' his observations, as a man who sails round an island discovers its insularity. The only induction, then, was that as Mars had been in an ellipse he would stay in an ellipse. Apart from the verbal question whether the process be rightly called induction or subsidiary to induction, the real issue is in Mill's complaint that Whewell supposed a 'conception to be something added to the facts.' The conception, Mill admits, is in the mind, but it must be a conception of 'something in the facts.' The ellipse was in the facts before Kepler saw it. He did not put it, but found it there. Whether Kepler's process was inductive or deductive or subsidiary, it was an essential part of scientific investigation. The man of science must, as Mill truly says, interpret the facts, and nothing but the facts; he must also, as Whewell truly replies, 'colligate' or arrange the facts in a new order. The constructive process which justifies me in saying this is an island, or this is an ellipse, is precisely what makes scientific knowledge possible, and involves

[1] *Logic*, p. 190, etc. (bk. iii. ch. ii. § 3, 4); *Ibid.* p. 423 (bk. iv. ch. i. § 4).

something more than a mere putting together of raw fact. Every fact, as Whewell sees, may be regarded as a case of countless laws, each of which may be true under appropriate conditions. To eliminate the irrelevant, to organise the whole system of truths, so as to make the order of nature (as Mill forcibly says[1]) deducible from the smallest possible number of general propositions, is the aim of science; and Mill obscures this so far as he regards such operations as Kepler's as mere observations of fact, in such a sense as to omit the necessity of a new organisation of the data.

I have gone into some detail in order to show what was the essential characteristic of Mill's doctrine, which was itself, as I have said, an explicit statement of the principles implicitly assumed by his predecessors in the same school. To do him full justice, it would be necessary to show what was the alternative presented by his opponents. The Scottish writers and Whewell brought back 'innate ideas,' or endeavoured to connect knowledge by beliefs and intuitions arbitrarily inserted into the fabric as a kind of supernatural revelation. To explain these intuitive dogmas into effects of 'association' was the natural retort. Meanwhile the transcendental school was taking the bolder line of rejecting experience altogether, treating it with contempt as a mere rope of sand, and inferring that the universe itself is incarnate logic—a complex web woven out of dialectic, and capable of being evolved from mixing 'is' and 'is not.' To Mill this appeared rightly, as I should say, to be mysticism and ontology, or a chimerical attempt to get rid of the inevitable conditions of all knowledge

[1] *Logic*, p. 207 (bk. iii. ch. iv. § 1).

of reality. The real problem of metaphysics appears to be the discovery of the right method of statement, which will explain what appeared to be the insoluble antithesis between empiricism and intuitionism (to take Mill's phrase), and show that they are attempts to formulate correlative and essential truths.

IX. THE MORAL SCIENCES

Happily, philosophical theories are not really important solely as giving tenable and definitive results, but as indications of the intellectual temperament of different schools, and of the methods of reasoning which they find congenial. Without further disquisition, I shall conclude by indicating briefly Mill's application of his principles to the 'Moral Sciences.' This is the subject of the last book of his treatise, and represents, as we have seen, the purpose of the whole. As, however, the full application will appear hereafter, I may here confine myself to certain critical points. Mill begins of course by arguing that the 'Moral Sciences' are possible, and are to be created by applying the method of the physical sciences. This suggests the free will difficulty. The doctrine of 'philosophical necessity' had 'weighed on his existence like an incubus' during his early depression.[1] He escaped by the solution which now forms a chapter in the *Logic*. He discovered that the Hume and Brown theory removed the misleading associations with the word 'necessity.' It would be truer, he thinks, to say that matter is free than that mind is not free.[2] The supposed external 'tie' which binds things together is a

[1] *Autobiography*, pp. 168, 173.   [2] *Logic*, p. 548 (bk. vi. ch. ii. § 2).

nonentity. In practice, however, Owen and his like had become fatalists rather than necessitarians. Holding that character is formed by circumstances, they had forgotten that our own desires are part of the 'circumstances,' and therefore that the mind has the power to co-operate in the 'formation of its own character.' This, Mill thinks, is the ennobling belief which is completely reconcilable with the admission that human actions are caused, although the two doctrines had been on both sides regarded as incompatible. Upon this endless controversy I can only suggest one hint. Mill, I think, was right in saying that the difficulty depends on the confusion of 'determinism' with 'fatalism'; that is, with the belief that the will is coerced by some external force. But he does not see that his doctrine of causation always raises the difficulty. He orders us to think of the succession of ideas as due simply to association, as in the external world events are to be regarded as simply following each other; and in either case it is impossible to avoid the impression that there must be some connecting link which binds together entirely disparate phenomena. We cannot help asking why 'this' should always follow 'that,' and inferring that there is something more than a bare sequence. The real line of escape is, I think, shown by an improved view of causation. If we hold that the theory of cause and effect simply arises from the analysis of a single process, we need no external force to act upon the will. There is no 'coercion' involved. Given the effect, there must have been the cause; as given the cause, the effect must follow. 'All the universe must exist in order that I must exist' is as true as that 'I must exist if all the universe exists.' There is not a man *plus* a law, but the law is already implied in the man ; or the distinction of cause and effect corresponds to a difference in our way of regarding the facts, and implies no addition to the facts. I must not, however, launch into this inquiry. I only note that Mill's view is connected with his favourite principle of the indefinite modifiability of character.[1] To Mill, as to his father, this seemed to hold out hopes for the 'unlimited possibility' of elevating the race. If J. S. Mill denied 'the freedom of the will,' or, rather, the existence of 'will' itself as a separate entity, actually originating active principles, he admitted that the desires erroneously hypostatised as 'will' could work wonders. As the causal link between events is a figment, so, in the sphere of mind, we are bound by no fixed mysterious tie. He thus escapes from the painful sense of coercion by holding that an infinite variety of results is made possible by the infinite combinations of materials, though, in each case, there is a necessary sequence. Association, in fact, is omnipotent. As it can make the so-called necessary truths, it can transform the very essence of character. Accordingly the foundation of the moral sciences is to be found in the psychology, for an exposition of which he refers to his father, to Mr. Bain, and to Mr. Herbert Spencer.[2] He thus drops, consciously or not, the claim of treating metaphysical doctrine as common ground, and assumes the truth of the association doctrine. To pass from these principles to questions of actual conduct requires a science not hitherto constructed—the science, namely, of human character, for which he proposes the name Ethology. This, as we have seen, occupied his thoughts for some time, till it was ultimately dropped for

[1] *Autobiography*, p. 108.   [2] *Logic*, p. 557 (bk. vi. ch. iv. § 3).

political economy. The difficulty of forming such a science upon his terms is obvious. It holds an ambiguous place between 'psychology' and the 'sociology' which he afterwards accepts from Comte ; and as Professor Bain remarks, his doctrine would not fit easily to any such science. He has got rid of 'necessity' only too completely. In fact, his view of the indefinite power of association, and his strong desire to explain all differences, even those between the sexes, as due to outward circumstances, seem to make character too evanescent a phenomenon to be subjected to any definite laws.[1] Ethology, however, is taken by him to be the science which corresponds to the 'art of education,' taken in its widest sense, and would, if constructed, be a 'deductive science,' consisting of corollaries from psychology, the 'experimental science.'[2] The utility of such a science from his point of view is obvious. It would be a statement of the way in which society was actually to be built up out of the clusters of associated ideas, held together by the unit Man.

His method in 'moral science' follows the lines now laid down. All inference, as he has urged, consists of 'inductions' and 'the interpretation of inductions.'[3] Deduction is the application to new cases of the laws observed in previous cases. As our knowledge of such laws multiplies, science tends to become more deductive. But the deduction is still an induction ; and the true

[1] See his view that the difference of character between the sexes is due to external circumstances, and therefore removable.—*Logic*, p. 566 (bk. vi. ch. v. § 3).
[2] *Logic*, pp. 567, 569 (bk. vi. ch. v. § 4, 5). (Art is misprinted 'act' in the last edition.)
[3] *Ibid.* p. 185 (bk. iii. ch. i. § 1).

antithesis is not between deductive and inductive but between 'deductive and experimental.'[1] Deductive reasoning, that is, simply applies a previous induction ; but reasoning becomes 'experimental' when we have to interrogate nature for a fresh rule. This has an important bearing upon the next step. Social phenomena of all kinds are so complex that we cannot apply his four methods. They belong to the region (in his phraseology) of the 'intermixture of laws' and 'plurality of causes' ;[2] and though the phrases be inaccurate, the example certainly illustrates their plausibility. Experimental reasoning is thus impossible. We have, therefore, to fall back upon the 'deductive' method, which, indeed, would lead to mere 'conjecture' were it not for the essential aid of Verification.[3] The meaning of this is explained in two chapters really directed against Macaulay and James Mill, and giving the theory which had been suggested by their controversy.[4] Macaulay used the 'chemical' method. If men in society formed a new product differing from the individual man, as water from oxygen and hydrogen, or, in Mill's phrase, if the social union afforded 'heteropathic' laws, we should have to study social science apart from the science of individual human nature. But as men even in society are still men, the social law is derivable from the laws of individual nature. It is a case of 'composition of causes.' Now the purely empirical reasoner neglects this obvious fact. He reasons from immediate

[1] *Logic*, p. 144 (bk. ii. ch. iv. § 5).
[2] *Ibid.* pp. 576, 585 (bk. vi. ch. vii. § 4 ; bk. iv. ch. ix. § 2).
[3] *Ibid.* p. 303 (bk. iii. ch xi. § 3).
[4] *Autobiography*, p. 159.

experience without connecting his conclusions with psychology. He argues offhand that because the English have flourished under the old parliamentary system, therefore the old parliamentary system was perfect. That gives the crude empiricism preached by Macaulay in the name of Bacon. James Mill, on the contrary, represents the 'geometrical method.' He argued about politics as if all constitutional questions could be settled like a geometrical problem by appeals to a single axiom. Therefore a doctrine applicable to the immediate question of parliamentary reform was put forward as a general theory of government. Mill tells us in the *Autobiography*[1] that his reflection upon this controversy led to a critical point of his doctrine. Science must be deductive, when the effects are simply the sum of those due to the operating causes ; inductive, when they are not the sum, that is, when 'heteropathic' laws appear. Hence, he inferred, politics must be treated deductively, though not as his father had done, geometrically.

Both the criticisms are much to the purpose. Here I need only remark one point which affects Mill's later conclusions. Was Mill's inference correct ? Is it true that the social phenomena represent simply the sum of the individual actions ? Undoubtedly, there is a good deal to be said for it. Society does not exist apart from the individuals of which it is constructed. Moreover, in a great many cases, if we know the average character of an individual, we can deduce the character of a number of individuals. The bulk of what is called knowledge of the world is made up from more or less

[1] *Autobiography*, p. 160.

shrewd conjectures as to the motives of the average man. If we know what the average man thinks, we can guess what will be the opinion of a majority of the House of Commons. There are, however, two points which are taken for granted. In the first place, if we are to deduce the social phenomena from the individual, we must know the individual, who is already a tolerably complex product. In Mill's language, we require an ethology ; and the name already indicates a difficulty. Can we consider the average man to be a constant? or must we not take into account the fact that he is also a product of society, and varies upon our hands as society develops? And beyond this there is the further question, whether, in so far as society can be properly regarded as an 'organism,' we can fully explain the laws of social combination by considering the laws of individual character. Are not the two sets of laws so intricately combined and blended that the analysis of a society into separate individuals becomes necessarily illusory? Can we explain the reciprocal actions and reactions of a social body by simply adding together the laws of individual conduct? These questions will meet us in considering Mill's practical application of his theories. They amount to asking whether 'sociology' can be constituted from a purely 'individualist' basis, and Mill's view of sociology is a vital point in his doctrine. The name had already been invented by Comte, and Mill at this time was greatly influenced by Comte, and especially was kindled to enthusiasm by the last two volumes of the *Philosophie Positive*, containing a connected view of history. Although Mill had, as he says, worked out his theory of induction

before reading Comte, he owed a great deal, as he fully acknowledges, to Comte's philosophy. The two lines of thought, however, could never completely coalesce, and the result appears in this part of Mill's book.

Admitting a deductive method to be necessary, Mill distinguishes the 'direct' and the 'inverse methods.'[1] The direct method is that of reasoning from one 'law of human nature,' considering, of course, the outward circumstances. This justifies the system of political economy, which considers men as acting solely from the desire of wealth. He points out that fallacies may here arise from applying to one state of society what is true of another ; but he also holds that one who knows the political economy of England, or even of Yorkshire, knows that of all nations, if he have good sense enough to modify his conclusions.[2] Mill admits fully that this method can only give us 'tendencies'—results which are true if certain conditions, never fully assignable, are actually secured ; and that it therefore requires to be constantly checked by verification, that is, by showing that the results are confirmed by direct observation. The admission, however, that such a method is in any case admissible separates him from Comte, who held that we must in all cases start from historical generalisations, not from independent 'laws of human nature.'[3] Comte, in fact, rejected Mill's psychology and political economy as pseudo-sciences, and the difference is really vital. Mill, however, was prepared to accept much of Comte's teaching, and in particular allows the legitimacy of the

[1] *Logic*, p. 583 (bk. vi. ch. ix. § 1).
[2] *Ibid.* p. 590 (bk. vi. ch. i. § 3).
[3] *Ibid.* p. 584 (bk. vi. ch. ix. § 1).

'historical method.' Upon this he writes a chapter,[1] which shows no want of appreciation of Comte or of the great French writers by whom, as his *Dissertations* show, he had been deeply impressed.[2] He complains of the English want of interest in such matters. They know nothing in French literature except the novels of Balzac and Eugène Sue, and are not aware that the French historians greatly surpass even the Germans.[3] He points out the importance of the conception of progress and of the great modifications of human character. Still, he charges the French with a misconception. History can never give us a 'law of nature,' only 'empirical laws,' which are not scientific till duly based upon psychology and 'ethology.' Comte alone has seen the necessity of a deeper foundation ; and he proceeds to give an admiring account of some of Comte's conclusions. Especially he insists upon the necessity of connecting the social pheno-mena with the intellectual development of mankind. This Comte alone has attempted systematically, and he ends by emphatically adhering to the doctrine of the three stages—theological, metaphysical, and positive. The essential difference, however, remains. Comte held that we must not explain humanity by man, but man by humanity.[4] To Mill, of course, this savoured of mysticism. In any case, it marks the divergence of the two : Mill is a thorough individualist. He thinks it absolutely necessary to base sociology upon 'ethology,'

[1] Bk. vi. ch. x.
[2] See especially the reviews of Tocqueville, Michelet, and Guizot in the *Dissertations*.
[3] *Dissertations*, ii. 121.
[4] *Lettres inédites de Mill à Comte* (1899), p. xxxv. Mill's letters to Comte upon his view of ethology are significant.

that is, a theory of the individual character, and this again must be based upon psychology. Sympathising with Comte's general purpose, and warmly admiring some of his results, Mill adheres to a doctrine which was sure to bring him into conflict with his master. To create the moral sciences, we must start from a scientific psychology. This means that we must work on the lines of Hartley, James Mill, and his own younger con-temporaries, Professor Bain and Mr. Herbert Spencer. The corollary from psychology is ethology, or the science of character. This view does not conflict with the admission of the great importance of some historical method. At present, it needs only to be said that Mill accepts that method very cordially, subject to two conditions. First, he holds that some social sciences—political economy being, in fact, the only one to be clearly specified—can be deduced from ethology and psychology independently of history, though requiring verification from history. Secondly, he holds that the historical method cannot reveal true 'laws of nature' unless it is properly connected with psychological data. How far Mill really appreciated the significance of the historical method, or perceived its true relation to other depart-ments of thought, must be left for consideration.

CHAPTER III

POLITICAL ECONOMY[1]

I. MILL'S STARTING-POINT

MILL's decision to abandon 'ethology' in favour of 'political economy' had one clear advantage. The function of a philosophical pioneer in the vast and vague region indicated by the new science was beset with difficulty. It was doubtful whether the proposed science could be constructed at all; and any conclusions attainable would certainly have belonged to a region remote from specific application to the questions of the day. Political economy offered a field for inquiry with a narrower aim of easier achievement. The greatest problems of the time were either economical or closely connected with economical principles. Mill had followed the political struggles with the keenest interest: he saw clearly their

[1] Mill's *Political Economy* reached a sixth edition in 1865. A popular edition was first reprinted in 1865 from this sixth edition. I quote from the popular edition of 1883 by chapter and section. This is applicable, with very slight exception, to all editions. The 'table of contents' is almost identical from the first to the last edition. Some sections were expanded by adding later information as to land-tenures and co-operation. The early chapter upon Ireland was altered on account of changes which, Mill thought, made it no longer appropriate. An addition was made to the chapter on 'International Values'; and book ii. chap. i. was rewritten in order to give a more favourable estimate of Socialism. On the whole, the changes were remarkably small.

connection with underlying social movements; and he had thoroughly studied the science—or what he took to be the science—which must afford guidance for a satisfactory working out of the great problems. The philosophical Radicals were deserting the old cause and becoming insignificant as a party. But Mill had not lost his faith in the substantial soundness of their economic doctrines. He thought, therefore, that a clear and full exposition of their views might be of the highest use in the coming struggles. Hence arises one broad characteristic of his position. Mill was steeped from childhood in the principles of Malthus and Ricardo. In that capacity he had been a champion of their views against the followers of Owen. But he had come to sympathise with the aims, though he could not accept the theories, of the Owenites. Hence he was virtually asking how, given Ricardo's premises, are we to realise Owen's aspirations? The groundwork of argument, however, remained throughout. Though a more favourable estimate of Socialism was introduced in one chapter of his book, as I have already noticed, no corresponding changes were made in the remainder.

The *Political Economy* speedily acquired an authority unapproached by any work published since the *Wealth of Nations*. In spite of many attacks, it still holds a position among standard textbooks; and in the case of textbooks, fifty years may be counted as remarkable longevity. During the first half of that period, a large school looked up to Mill as an almost infallible oracle. If in the later half that belief has vanished, we ought to recognise merits, sometimes overlooked by his assailants. The most undeniable is the singular skill of

exposition. Mill had an admirable sense of proportion; each topic is taken up in intelligible order and treated with sufficient fulness; general principles are broadly laid down and clearly illustrated; and applications to actual cases are sufficiently indicated, without those superfluous digressions into minuter details which often entangle or break the main thread of an argument. The style is invariably lucid, and Mill, while free from arrogance and singularly courteous to opponents, wears his magisterial robes with the dignity of acknowledged authority. Whatever fallacies lie beneath the equable flow of didactic wisdom, we can understand what was the charm which concealed them from early readers. The book seemed to be a unique combination of scientific reasoning and practical knowledge, while the logical apparatus, so harshly creaking in the hands of Ricardo, not only worked smoothly but was in the hands of one whose opposition to 'sentimentalism' was plainly no cynical mask for coldness of heart.

Mill states his aim in the preface. He wished to expound the doctrine of Adam Smith with the 'latest improvements.' But he would take Smith for his model in combining economics with 'other branches of social philosophy.' Smith, he says, by never losing sight of this aim, succeeded in attracting both the general reader and the statesman. Mill certainly achieved a similar result. If he did not emulate Smith's wide researches into economic history, and had not Smith's curious felicity of illustration, he took a comprehensive view of the great issues of the time, and spared no pains in filling his mind with the necessary materials. His surprising power of assimilating knowledge had been strengthened by

official experience. No one had a more vigorous digestion for blue-books, or—what is perhaps rarer—less desire to make a display by pouring out the raw material.

Although Mill's work upon 'pure political economy' lies mainly beyond my province, it illustrates one important point. Mill speaks as one expounding an established system. The speed with which the book was written shows that it did not imply any revision of first principles. Mill is working in general upon Ricardo's lines, in whose 'immortal *Principles*,' for example, he finds the first philosophical account of international trade.[1] He assumes too easily that a mere modification of old doctrines is needed, where later writers have demanded a thoroughgoing reconstruction. He has incurred some ridicule, for example, by an utterance characteristic of his position. He says,[2] that 'there is nothing in the laws of Value which remains for the present or any future writer to clear up; the theory of the subject is complete.' The phrase was rash. Apparently unassailable theories have an uncomfortable trick of suddenly exploding. Later economists often take this for a case in point. They have, they think, made a specially successful breach in this part of Mill's doctrine, and his confidence was singularly infelicitous. Mill's luckless boast was suggested by his rectification of an ambiguity in the terminology of the science. How, he asked, could there be a 'proportion' between two disparate things, a 'quantity' (supply) and a 'desire' (demand)?[3] He

[1] See *Unsettled Questions* (1877), p. 1.
[2] *Political Economy*, p. 265 (bk. iii. ch. i. § 1).
[3] *Ibid.* p. 270 (bk. iii. ch. ii. § 3).

proceeds to remove the ambiguity by an account of the 'equation' between demand and supply, explaining the process by which values adjust themselves so that the quantity supplied at the current price will be equal to the quantity demanded at that price. I take it that his account of the facts is substantially correct, and that, by removing certain inconsistencies of language, he had purified the theory from one set of fallacies. But he himself seems to regard the improvement as merely one of terminology. He thinks that his predecessors meant to state the same facts, and, indeed, that they must have seen the truth, though he could not find in them an express statement. We may ask whether later improvements of Mill himself amount to a substantial change in the theory, or merely to a better mode of expression. I do not doubt that modern economists have much improved the language in which the theory is expressed. Nor, again, can it be doubted that the logic is rectified by rectifying the language. The only question can be as to the importance of the improvement. What strikes the sceptic is that, after all, when we approach any practical application of the theory, the old and the new theorists seem to be guided by pretty much the same reasoning. The improvement in elegance and consistency of the language does not bring with it a corresponding improvement in the treatment of actual problems. The obvious reason is that political economy has not reached, if it ever will reach, the stage at which the application of a refined logical method is possible or fruitful. The power of using delicate scientific instruments presupposes a preliminary process. We must have settled distinctly what are the data to be observed

and measured ; and the use of mathematical formulæ is premature and illusory till we know precisely what we have to count and how to count it. The data and the psychological assumptions of economists are still far too vague and disputable to admit of such methods, except by way of illustration. Meanwhile rough and even inaccurate statements may be adequate to convey the knowledge which we can really apply. We are really making use of facts admitted on all hands, and known with sufficient accuracy, though the principles upon which they depend have not been clearly defined.

II. CONTEMPORARY MOVEMENTS

To appreciate Mill's position, it is necessary briefly to notice the prejudices which he had to encounter and the sympathies upon which he could reckon. Political economy had been exultant in the days of James Mill. He and his allies were entering the promised land. They took the science to be in the same stage as astronomy just after the publication of Newton's *Principia*. The main truths were established, though prejudice and sentiment still blinded the outside world to the clearest demonstration. A narrow and unpopular circle naturally retorts dislike by fanaticism. The Utilitarians were, and knew themselves to be, bitterly hated ; though they took the hatred to be an unconscious tribute to their real authority—the homage of the stupid to irresistible logic. Richard Jones in the preface to his *Treatise on Rent* (1831), says, that the Ricardians had not only put forward 'startling and in some instances, unhappily, disgusting and most mischievous paradoxes,' but that

they had thus alienated mankind and caused a distrust of political economy. When J. S. Mill's treatise appeared, this position was modified. The 'philosophical Radicals' had declined as a party ; but the assault upon protectionism in which they had acted as forlorn hope had conquered a much wider circle. Their ideas had spread, whether by stress of argument or congeniality to the aspirations of the newly enfranchised classes. The conspicuous instance, of course, is the free trade movement. The triumph over the corn - laws seemed to establish the truth of the economic theory. Doctrines preached by professors and theorists had been accepted and applied by politicians on a grand scale. The result, as Cairnes, one of Mill's chief followers observes, was not altogether an advantage to the science.[1] The popular mind identified political economy with free trade, and thought that all difficulties could be solved by a free use of the sacred words 'supply and demand.' The strict economic doctrine had been, as Cairnes held, adulterated in order to suit the tastes of the exoteric audience. This remark suggests the problem, not strictly soluble, as to the causes of the free trade victory. Did it mark a triumph of logic, or was it due to the simple fact that the class which wanted cheap bread was politically stronger than the class which wanted dear bread? Cobden admitted fully that the free trade propaganda was a 'middle-class agitation.'[2] The genuine zealots were the manufacturers and merchants; and it was so far a trial of strength between the leaders of industry and the owners of the soil—a class struggle not between rich and poor, but

[1] *Logical Method of Political Economy* (1875), p. 4.
[2] See Morley's *Life of Cobden* (1881), ii. 249.

between the 'plutocracy' and the 'aristocracy.' Cobden was proud of the order to which he belonged, and held that the aristocracy represented blind prejudice. Some verses often quoted by popular orators declared that the landowners' motto was 'down with everything' (including health, wealth, and religion) 'and up with rent' ; and Bright in 1842 told the workmen that 'the greatest enemy of the remorseless aristocracy of Britain must almost of necessity be their firmest friend.'[1] As usual in such cases, a legend arose which regarded the victory as due exclusively to the force of truth. Beyond all doubt, argument played its part as well as class prejudice. Cobden, though little interested in abstract theories, was an admirable, cogent, and clear reasoner. He was fully competent to assimilate so much political economy as was required for his purpose, and used it most effectively. Later history, however, has shown that in such matters pure reason cannot by itself win the battle against interested prejudice. For the time, the victory, taken by the winners to be a victory of reason, reflected glory upon the economists who from the days of Adam Smith had been labouring to indoctrinate the public mind. The triumph of the agitation was thus due to sheer force of argument and the consequent recognition of the principles of justice to the poor and goodwill to all mankind. Science and philanthropy had joined hands. The enthusiasm which soon afterwards greeted the Exhibition of 1851 showed the widespread conviction that the millennium of peace and liberty, of which the *Wealth of Nations* marked the dawn, was at last appearing in full daylight. And Mill was

[1] Prentice's *Anti-Corn Law League*, i. 77, 378.

regarded as the authorised representative in philosophy of the principles now at last fully applied to practice.

Mill himself did not fully share the optimistic exultation which helped to strengthen his authority ; nor was it accepted by the class most immediately affected. The 'big loaf' was a cry, it might be thought, which should appeal most strongly to the hungriest. Yet the Chartists, whose agitation was beginning when the Anti-Corn Law League was founded, were lukewarm or positively hostile. They interrupted free trade meetings and looked askance at the agitation.[1] The Chartists thought that the middle class, having got into power by their help, were throwing them over and monopolising all the fruits of victory. Their ablest leaders admitted, indeed, that free trade would be desirable, but desirable only on condition that the charter should first be conceded and democracy invested with political power to guard against misappropriation of the economic advantages. The employers, as they suspected, wanted cheap bread, because, as Lord Shaftesbury once put it, 'cheap bread means low wages.'[2] The freetraders, indeed, had constantly to meet this argument. Cobden constantly and earnestly denied the imputation. He desired free trade, as he asserted with unmistakable sincerity, above all in justice to workmen, and ridiculed the notion that wages sank with the price of corn.[3] Cobden, however, appeals rather to obvious

[1] Cobden's famous debate with Feargus O'Connor, the Chartist leader, took place on 5th August 1844. Cobden's victory is admitted even by the Chartist historian, who regards it as a proof of O'Connor's incapacity.—R. C. Gammage's *Chartist Movement* (1894), p. 254. Prentice has much to say of the perverseness of the Chartist leaders.

[2] Hodder's *Shaftesbury*, p. 341. This was in 1841. Shaftesbury afterwards accepted free trade.   [3] See, *e.g.*, Cobden's *Political Speeches*, i. 119, 197.

facts than to economic theorems ; and Chartists who read Ricardo and M'Culloch might find some excuse for their opinion. If the 'iron law' held good, free trade in multiplying the labourers might only multiply the mass of misery. It might increase the aggregate wealth without raising the average welfare. The economical purists might reply that the poor would profit by the change on condition of also accepting the gospel according to Malthus. But the very name of Malthus stank in the nostrils of all Chartist leaders.

Another agitation gave special importance to this view. The credit which accrued to political economists from free trade was affected by their responsibility for the new poor-law. The passage of this measure in 1834 might be taken as a victory not merely of the economists in general, but specifically of the hated Malthus. He and his followers had denounced the old system most effectually, and had denounced it in the name of his principles. To Malthus and to Ricardo the only remedy seemed to be the ultimate abolition of the poor-laws. Their disciples were prominent in carrying the new law. Nassau Senior (already mentioned) had resolved when a young man to reform the poor-laws. He had lectured in 1828 on the Principles of Population as an adherent (with some modification) of Malthus. As an early member of the Political Economy Club he was at the very focus of sound doctrine. He was an active member of the commission of 1832, and is said to have drawn up the famous report upon which the new measure was founded.[1] The measure itself had therefore the highest credentials that strict political economists could desire.

[1] Reprinted in 1884.

Brougham as Lord Chancellor helped Miss Martineau, a most orthodox adherent of the school, and a personal friend of Malthus, to prepare the public mind by a continuation of her *Tales*.

The new poor-law, though placed to the credit of Malthusians, was by no means a pure and simple application of the Malthus theory. The gross abuses, rate-aided wages, and so forth, were suppressed in accordance with his views ; but the complete abolition of the poor-law, to which he had looked forward, was out of the question. The position was already critical. An experienced magistrate told the commission[1] that if the system went on for another ten years 'a fearful and bloody contest must ensue.' A generation of superfluous labourers, he said, had grown up demanding support. To maintain the system was dangerous, but simply to abolish it was to provoke a social war. The alternative was a cautious and gradual remodelling of the system ; and the transmutation of a demoralising into a disciplinary system. This meant so great a deviation from the extreme proposals that it might even tend to perpetuate the system by removing its abuses. Many of the evils resulted from the very fact which, in the eyes of Ricardo, was its chief palliation—the obligation of each parish to keep its own paupers. It had produced not economy but chaos. The commission recommend that the power of making regulations, now exercised 'by upwards of fifteen thousand unskilled and (practically) irresponsible authorities liable to be biased by sinister interests' (Bentham's sacred phrase) should 'now be confided to the central board of control, on which responsibility is most strongly concentrated,

[1] *Report of* 1834, p. 73.

and which will have the most extensive information.'[1] The competition between the parishes had produced the tangled laws of settlement, leading to endless litigation : the depopulation of some places, the overcrowding of others, the peculations and jobbery due to the 'sinister interests' of petty local authorities, and the utter absence of any uniform or rational system. To compel the fifteen thousand bodies to substitute co-operation for competition, to check their accounts, and to enforce general rules, it was necessary to create a central board with wide administrative authority. For such a scheme, now obvious enough, the commissioners found their only precedent in a measure by which a barrister had been appointed to inspect savings banks and friendly societies.[2]

The new poor-law was thus a 'centralising' measure, and marked a most important step in that direction. It was denounced for that reason on both sides, and among the orthodox economists by M'Culloch. J. S. Mill defended it warmly against this 'irrational clamour'; and but for certain restraining influences, especially the teaching of Tocqueville, would he thinks have gone into the opposite excess.[3] It seems, however, that the Utilitarians generally accepted the law as a judicious application of Malthus, tempered by proper regard for circumstances. They were indeed bound in principle to be shy of the direct application of *a priori* formulæ. Yet it may also be briefly noted that this was one of the cases on which the Utilitarians unconsciously forwarded a tendency to which they objected in general terms. They wished to codify and simplify the poor-law, and found it necessary to introduce a central regulating body. Though

[1] *Report of* 1834, p. 169.   [2] *Report*, p. 167.   [3] *Autobiography*, p. 193.

they meant to stimulate local activity, they were calling the central authority into fresh activity.

Meanwhile their opponents were equally ready to see nothing in it but Malthus, and to denounce it with corresponding bitterness. It was contrary to Christianity, to the rights of man, and to the good old laws of England. It was a part of the machinery by which cold-blooded economists were enslaving the poor. The operative, says the Chartist historian,[1] thought that it broke the last link in the chain of sympathy between rich and poor. Prison-like workhouses were rising to remind the poor of their 'coming doom.' They could expect nothing but 'misery in the present, and the Bastille in the future, in which they were to be immured when their rich oppressor no longer required their services.' The historian of the factory movement[2] confirms this statement. The poor man was to work or starve. Poverty, then, was to be treated as a crime. The parochial system was to be broken up, and the clergy thus separated from the poor. The whole system was anti-Christian: had not the commissioners put out a warning against almsgiving?[3] The commissioners again proposed the emigration of pauperised agricultural labourers into manufacturing districts, and were so playing into the hands of the capitalists.

[1] Gammage's *Chartist Movement*, p. 54.
[2] Alfred's *Factory Movement*, pp. 70-78. Alfred is a pseudonym for Samuel Kydd.
[3] Archbishop Whately is said to have thanked God that he had never given a penny to a beggar. The view suggests some confusion between the Political Economy Club and the Christian Church. In Newman's *Idea of a University* (1875, p. 88, etc.) there is an interesting passage upon the contrast between Christianity and the doctrine of the first professor of Political Economy at Oxford (Senior), that the accumulation of wealth was 'the great source of *moral* improvement. The contrast was undeniable.

Cobbett's view gave the keynote to another version of the case. He saw as clearly as any one the evils of pauperisation, but the old law at least admitted the poor man's right to support. In good old times he had been supported by the church. The great robbery at the Reformation had been partly compensated by the poor-law. To abolish or restrict the old right was to consummate the abominable robbery and to fleece the poor man more thoroughly at the bidding of 'parson Malthus.' Cobbett's view not only commended itself to his own class, but was more or less that of the 'Young Englanders,' who aspired to a reconstruction of the old social order. The *Times* denounced the new law bitterly, and its proprietor, Walter, thought (as Kydd says), and no doubt thought rightly, that the indignation roused by the measure had done much to foster Chartism.[1] Meanwhile, to Mill and his friends the whole of this declamation came under the head of the later 'sentimentalism.' They held with Malthus that an unlimited right to support meant an indefinite multiplication of poverty. To admit the right was to undertake an impossible task and provoke a revolution on its inevitable failure. Right must be based upon fact; and it is idle to neglect the inevitable conditions of human life. This position might be logically unassailable; and the measure supported on the strength of it is now admitted to have been a vast reform. It came to be cited as one of the claims to gratitude of the economists. Their science had arrested an evil which appeared to be almost incurable.

[1] Miss Martineau attributes the apostasy of the *Times* to the desire of the proprietors to please the country justices. See *History of the Peace* (1877), ii. 508.

Sound reason had again triumphed over vague sentimentalism. The new law was, however, still given as an illustration of the heartlessness of political economists. Mill, who might claim justly that he was as anxious as any one to raise the poor, had sorrowfully to admit that the masses were too ignorant and their leaders too sentimental to recognise his good intentions. They took the surgeon for an assassin.

Among the enemies of the new poor-law were the keenest agitators for factory legislation. The succession of leaders in that movement is characteristic. The early measures introduced by the first Sir Robert Peel and supported by Owen had been tentative and of limited application. As a demand arose for more drastic measures, the first bill was introduced in 1831 by John Cam Hobhouse (1786-1869), afterwards Lord Broughton. Hobhouse's election for Westminster in 1820 had been a triumph for the Benthamites; and he was afterwards one of the members through whom Place tried to influence legislation. Hobhouse was too much of the aristocrat to be up to Place's standard of Radicalism, and on this point he was too much of an economist to lead the movement. He declared the demands of the agitators to be hopelessly unpractical; or, as Oastler put it, gave in to 'the cold, calculating, but mistaken Scottish philosophers,' who had an overwhelming influence on the country.[1] The lead passed to Michael Thomas Sadler (1780-1835). Sadler, a Tory and an evangelical, had proposed to introduce the poor-law system into Ireland. He had attacked Malthus (1830) in a book to be presently noticed. He declared that Hobhouse had

[1] Alfred's *Factory Movement*, i. 138, 141.

surrendered to the economists, who were 'the pests of society and the persecutors of the poor.'[1] He now proposed a more stringent measure, which led to the appointment of a committee of the House of Commons in 1832. The report (presented 8th August 1832) startled and shocked the public. A royal commission was appointed in 1833 to collect further evidence. Sadler had meanwhile been defeated by Macaulay in a sharp contest for Leeds. His health soon afterwards broke down, under the strain of carrying on the agitation, and the lead fell to Lord Shaftesbury (then Lord Ashley). Shaftesbury, again, as an aristocrat and an evangelical, was a natural enemy of the Utilitarian. He was heartily approved by Southey, from the study of whose works he professed himself to have 'derived the greatest benefit.' He thought that the country was 'drooping under the chilly blasts of political economy,' and regarded the millowner as 'the common enemy of the operatives and the country-gentleman.'[2] Richard Oastler, the most effective and popular organiser of the agitation outside of parliament, was also a Tory, a churchman, and a protectionist. He had joined in the anti-slavery movement, and now thought that the factory system involved a worse slavery than that of the negro. He accepted the title of 'king of the factories,' given in ridicule by his enemies.[3] He became a martyr to his hatred of the new Poor-law by resigning his place as agent to an estate rather than enforce its provisions. He, too, hated the economists, and denounced 'the horrible Malthusian doctrine,' which

[1] See his life in *Dictionary of National Biography*.
[2] Hodder's *Shaftesbury*, i. 161, 339.
[3] Alfred's *Factory Movement*, i. 258.

he took to be that the 'Creator sent children into the world without being able to find food for them.'[1] John Fielden, who became the parliamentary leader in 1846, upon Shaftesbury's temporary retirement from the House, had been brought up as a Quaker and a Tory. He became a Utilitarian and a Radical. The typical Radical for him was not Place but Cobbett, his colleague for Oldham in the first reformed parliament. 'Honest John Fielden' made a fortune by cotton-spinning, but wrote a tract called the *Curse of the Factory System*, and no doubt shared Cobbett's hatred of the Scottish 'philosophers' and Parson Malthus.

These brief indications may be sufficient for one point. The agitators on behalf of the factory movement took the political economists, 'Malthusians,' and Utilitarians to be their natural and their most dangerous enemies. They assumed that the economist doctrine might be condensed into the single maxim 'do nothing.' Whether it were a question of encouraging trade or supporting the poor, or putting down 'white slavery' in a factory, government was to leave things alone or, in other words, to leave them to the devil. Chalmers, though an ultra-Malthusian in some respects, approved the factory movement, because, as he said, it was a question between free trade and Christianity.[2] Christianity orders us to help our neighbours, and political economy to let them alone. Mill, of course, would have repudiated this doctrine. Political economy, he would have replied, does not forbid us to do good, or it would be opposed to Utilitarianism as well as to Christianity. It only shows us what will do good by pointing out the consequences of our actions,

[1] Alfred's *Factory Movement*, i. 229.   [2] *Ibid.* ii. 251.

and Christianity can scarcely forbid us to disregard consequences. Nor, in fact, was it true that the economists unequivocally condemned the factory acts. Malthus had approved them, and M'Culloch wrote warmly to Shaftesbury to express his sympathy.

Undoubtedly, however, the opposition to the factory legislation appealed to the principles accepted and most vigorously enforced by the Utilitarians. It came from the free-traders, and from the inner circle of orthodox theorists. In the later debates, Bright and Cobden, Villiers and Milner-Gibson, Bowring, Bentham's trusted disciple, Roebuck, a wayward, though at first an eager, follower, and the sturdy Joseph Hume were zealous opponents. The *Edinburgh* and the *Westminster Reviews* rivalled each other in orthodoxy.[1] The *Edinburgh* declared (July 1835) that Sadler's famous report was full of false statements, if not wholly false; and the *Westminster* (April 1833) thought that it was 'a stalking horse' to divert attention from the agitation against the corn-laws and slavery. *Fraser's Magazine*, on the contrary, which was attacking the economists in a series of articles, made a special point of the horrors revealed by the report. They might be summed up as 'child murder by slow torture.' The Tory organs, the *Quarterly* and *Blackwood*, took the same side. The manufacturers denied the existence of the evils alleged, complained of spies and unfair reports, and taunted the landowners with neglect of the suffering agricultural labourers.   Shaftesbury

[1] See *Westminster Review* for April and October 1833; *Edinburgh Review* for July 1835 and January 1844; *Blackwood's Magazine* for April 1833; *Fraser's Magazine* for April 1833; and the *Quarterly Review* for December 1836.

says[1] that the argument most frequently used was a famous statement by Senior. That high authority had declared that all the profits of manufacturers were made in the last two hours of the twelve. Cut down the twelve to ten, and profits would disappear, and with them the manufacturing industry.[2] The same doctrine, in fact, worked into a variety of forms, sometimes fitted for practical men, and sometimes seeking the dignity of scientific formulation, was the main argument to be met. This is, in fact, typical of the economists' position. Some of them made concessions, and some of the Whigs shrank from the rigid doctrine.[3] But it was more in their way, at least, to supply 'chilling blasts' of criticism than to give any warm support. One qualification must be noticed. The agitation began from the undeniable cruelty to children. The enthusiast's view was put into epigrammatic form by Michelet. The monster Pitt had bought the manufacturers' support by the awful phrase, 'take the children.'[4] In reality the employment of children had at first appeared desirable from a philanthropic point of view; but it had developed so as to involve intolerable cruelty. The hideous stories of children worked to death, or to premature decrepitude, revealed by the commissions had made a profound impression. So far the Utilitarians as moralists were bound and willing to protest. They hated slavery, and to do nothing was to permit the most detestable slavery.

[1] Hansard, lxxiv. 911.
[2] The passage was quoted in full by Milner-Gibson, 15th March 1844.
[3] Macaulay's speech, 22nd May 1846 (in *Miscellaneous Works*, 1870, pp. 207-17), arguing that the moral question cannot be answered by pure economists, and defending the Ten Hours' Bill, is worth notice.
[4] See Alfred's *Factory Movement*, i. 2.

A child of tender years might be worked to death by brutal employers with the help of careless parents. This was fully admitted, for example, by Cobden, who said that he entirely approved of legislation for children, but held equally that adults should be encouraged to look for help to themselves and not to government.[1] Even the straitest economists seem to have admitted so much. The problem, however, remained as to the principle upon which the line must be drawn. If helpless children should be protected, have not women, or even working men in dependent positions, an equal right to protection? Moreover, can interference in one case be practically carried out without involving interference in the whole system?

The economic position was thus assailed on many points, though by enemies mutually opposed to each other. The general tendency of the economists was against government interference, and their most popular triumph on application of the do-nothing principle. In the free-trade agitation, their main opponents were the interested classes, the landowners, and the merely stupid Conservatives. Elsewhere they were opposed by a genuine, even if a misguided, philanthropy; by Conservatives who wished to meet revolution not by simple obstruction, but by rousing the government to a sense of its duties. Southey's 'paternal government' might be ridiculed by Macaulay and the Whigs; Cobbett's good old times might be treated as the figment of an ignorant railer; the Young Englanders who found their gospel in Disraeli's *Sibyl* might be taken to represent mere fanciful antiquarianism masquerading as serious politics; and

[1] See Cobden's letter at the end of the first volume of Mr. Morley's *Life*.

Carlyle, with his fierce denunciations of the 'dismal science' in *Chartism* and the *Latter-Day Pamphlets* set down as an eccentric and impatient fanatic naturally at war with sound reason. The appropriate remedy, as Mill thought, was a calm, scientific exposition of sound principles. His adversaries, as he thought, reproduced in the main the old sentimentalism against which Bentham and James Mill had waged war, taking a new colouring from a silly romanticism and weak regrets for a picturesque past. But there was a perplexing fact. Churchmen and Tories were acting as leaders of the very classes to whom Radicals look for their own natural allies. Shaftesbury complained that he could not get the evangelicals to take up the factory movement.[1] They had been the mainstay of the anti-slavery movement, but they did not seem to be troubled about white slavery. The reason, no doubt, was obvious; the evangelicals were mainly of the middle class, and class prejudices were too strong for the appeals to religious principles. On the other hand, the Radical artisans would accept men like Sadler or Shaftesbury for leaders as a drowning man may accept help from an enemy. The point of agreement was simply that something should be done, and that was enough to alienate the poor man from Whigs and Utilitarians, who were always proving that nothing should be done.

While these controversies were in the foreground the remarkable movement of which Mr. and Mrs. Sidney Webb[2] are the first historians, was developing itself.

[1] Hodder's *Shaftesbury*, i. 300, 325.
[2] *History of Trades-Unionism* (1894). See especially chaps. iii. and iv. (from 1829 to 1860).

Workmen were learning how to organise effective trades-unions, and co-operators were turning into a more practicable channel some of the aspirations of which Owen had been the prophet. What Mill thought of such movements will appear presently. Meanwhile it is enough to say that the economists generally confined themselves to throwing cold water upon what they held to be irrational schemes. The working classes could not raise their position by combination, though they had an undeniable right to try fruitless experiments. They were going astray after false prophets, and blind to the daylight of a true science. The co-operative movement, indeed, received a warmer welcome when it came to be known. But the remarkable point is once more the wide gap between the 'philosophical Radicals' and the classes whom they aspired to lead. The aspirations of the poorer class took a form condemned as simply absurd and illogical by the theories of their would-be leaders.[1]

III. MALTHUSIAN CONTROVERSY

Popular instinct recognised its natural enemy in Malthus. 'Malthusian' was a compendious phrase for anti-Christian, hard-hearted, grovelling, materialist, fatalistic. The formal controversy was dying out. One of the last 'confutations' was by the enthusiastic Sadler, which provoked a slashing attack in the *Edinburgh* by the rising light Macaulay.[2] Alison had prepared a ponderous

[1] For the view of the economists, especially Nassau Senior, and of a Whig government 'pledged to the doctrines of philosophical Radicalism,' see Mr. and Mrs. Sidney Webb's *Trades-Unionism*, pp. 123, etc., and the same writers' *Industrial Democracy*, p. 249.
[2] Sadler's *Law of Population*, 2 vols. 8vo, appeared in 1830, and was reviewed in the *Edinburgh* for July by Macaulay, who in the number for

treatise[1] by 1828, which, however, did not appear till 1840, when his popularity as a historian encouraged its publication. Thomas Doubleday (1790-1870), an amiable man and a sturdy reformer, published his *True Law of Population* in 1841.[2] Sadler, the churchman and philanthropist, Alison, the ponderous Tory, and Doubleday, the Radical, are agreed upon one point. They are all defending the beneficence of the deity, and take Malthus to be a devil's advocate. Sadler, who was a mathematician, devotes the greatest part of his book to a discussion, helped by elaborate tables, of the famous geometrical progression. Alison, of course, rambles over all the articles of the Tory faith, defending the corn-laws, protection, and slavery along with the factory acts, the poor-law, and the allotment system, and expounding his simple philosophy of history and the inevitable currency question. The real difficulty is to assign the precise point at issue. If Malthus is taken as asserting that, as a matter of fact, population actually and invariably doubles every twenty-five years, or at any rate

January 1831 published a 'refutation' of Sadler's 'refutation.' The articles were first collected in Macaulay's *Miscellaneous Works*.
[1] *Principles of Population and their Connection with Human Happiness*, 2 vols. 8vo, 1840.
[2] *The True Law of Population shown to be connected with the Good of the People*, 1 vol. 8vo, 1841 (second edition, 1847). G. Poulett Scrope (1797-1876), better known as a geologist than an economist, declares in his *Political Economy* (1833) that if every nation were to be freed from all checks and 'to start off breeding at the fastest possible rate,' very many generations would pass 'before any necessary pressure *could* be felt' (p. 276). The doctrine that there is an 'iron necessity' for resorting to inferior soils is in contradiction to 'every known fact' (p. 266). Scrope was a sentimentalist who starts from the 'natural rights' of man to freedom, the 'bounties of creation,' 'property,' and 'good government.' Given these 'simple and obvious principles,' everything will go right.

always multiplies to starvation point, it is easy to 'confute' him; but then he had himself repudiated any such doctrine. If, on the other hand, you only say that over-population is in fact restrained by some means, Malthus had said so himself. It was common ground, for example, that great towns were unfavourable to population; and Macaulay could fairly tell Sadler that this was admitted by Malthus, and was really a case of the famous 'positive checks.'[1] Alison takes similar ground in much of his argumentation. The difference seems to be that Sadler and Doubleday assume a pre-established harmony where Malthus traces the action of 'checks.' Sadler,[2] for example, agrees with the opinion of Muret, ridiculed by Malthus, that God had made the force of life 'in inverse ratio to fecundity.' Sadler and Doubleday agree that 'fecundity' is diminished by comfort. Men multiply less as they become richer, instead of becoming richer as they multiply less. J. S. Mill says that Doubleday alone among the Anti-Malthusians had some followers, but thinks that this argument is sufficiently confuted by a glance at the enormous families of the English upper classes.[3] Macaulay had taken more trouble to reply by statistics drawn from the *Peerage*. The one obvious point is that none of the disputants could properly talk of 'scientific laws.' What Malthus had indicated was a 'tendency,' or a consequence of the elasticity of population which might arise under certain conditions, and to

[1] *Miscellaneous Works*, p. 193.   [2] Sadler's *Population*, ii. 387.
[3] *Political Economy*, bk. i. ch. x. § 3 n. W. T. Thornton, in his *Over Population* (p. 121), though a professed disciple of Malthus, agrees with Doubleday. Mr. Herbert Spencer criticises Doubleday in his *Biology*, chap. xii. (§ 366 n.) in course of an elaborate discussion of the general question of fertility.

which it was important to attend. But this gives no approach to a formula from which we can infer what will be the actual growth under given conditions. Macaulay showed clearly enough the futility of Sadler's reasoning. It was hopeless to compare areas, taken at random, large and small, heterogeneous or uniform, in different countries, climates, and social states, and attempt by a summary process to elicit a distinct 'law.' All manner of physiological, psychological, and sociological questions are involved ; not to be set aside by a hasty plunge into a wilderness of statistics. To discover a tenable 'law of population' we shall have to wait for the constitution of hitherto chaotic sciences.

Meanwhile, it may be noticed that the Whigs as represented by Macaulay were upon this matter as dogmatic as James Mill himself, whose dogmatism Macaulay had censured as roundly as he censured Sadler. Malthus, in fact, had triumphed ; and Mill's Malthusianism dominates his whole treatise. He had been brought up as an uncompromising Malthusian ; in youth he had become something of a martyr in the cause, and he never flinched from upholding the general principle. What was it ? In an early chapter[1] of his treatise he lays down the Malthusian propositions. 'Twenty or thirty years ago,' he says, they might have been in need of enforcement. The evidence is, however, so incontestable that they have steadily made way against all opposition, and may now be regarded as 'axiomatic.' This incontestable doctrine, as Mill here explains, is, firstly, that the human race can double itself in a generation ; and, secondly, that the obvious consequences can be avoided only by limiting

[1] Bk. i. ch. x.

this power through Malthus's positive or preventive checks—that is, by prudence on the one hand, and starvation and disease on the other.[1] This prudential restraint, then, is, if not the one thing necessary, the universal condition without which no other scheme of improvement can be satisfactory. It is the focus upon which his whole argument converges. Mill, however, gives a characteristic turn to the argument. The doctrine that the progress of society must 'end in shallows and in miseries'[2] was not, as had been thought, a 'wicked invention' of Malthus. Implicitly or explicitly, it was the doctrine of his 'most distinguished predecessors, and can only be successfully combated on his principles. The publication of his essay is the era from which better views of this subject must be dated.'[3] It gives the really fundamental principle. Mill agrees with Malthus that the root of social evil is not the inequality of property. Even an unjust distribution of wealth does not aggravate, but at most accelerates, the advent of misery. 'With the existing habits of the people' an equal division of property would only cause them to populate down to the former state.[4] And yet Mill here parts company from Malthus in the spirit, if not in the logic, of his argument. Malthus no doubt was thoroughly benevolent, and like many amiable country clergymen desired to see the spread of savings banks, friendly societies, and schools ; but he was painfully conscious of the difficulty of infusing ideas into the sodden, sluggish labourers of his time, and

[1] *Political Economy*, p. 212 (bk. ii. ch. xi. § 3).
[2] One of Mill's rare quotations. See Shakespeare's *Julius Cæsar*, act iv. sc. iii.
[3] *Political Economy*, p. 452 (bk. iv. ch. vi. § 1).
[4] *Ibid.* p. 118 (bk. i. ch. xiii. § 2).

hoped rather for the diminution of abuses than for the regeneration of mankind. Mill, on the contrary, sympathised with the revolutionists who had alarmed Malthus. He tells them, indeed, with Malthus, that their schemes must conform to actual and inevitable conditions. But he also holds that the 'existing habits' of the 'people' can be materially modified ; and believes that a 'just distribution of wealth' would tend to modify them. Malthus emphasises the point that nothing can be done unless the standard of life be raised. Mill dwells on the other aspect : *if* the standard be raised, an indefinite improvement can be effected. What Malthus took to be a difficult though not impassable barrier Mill took to represent a difficulty which men might be trained to recognise and surmount. His sanguine belief in the educability of mankind enabled him to regard as a realisable hope what to Malthus in his early days had seemed a mere vision, and even in later days a remote ideal. The *vis medicatrix* is the same for Mill as for Malthus, but Mill has a far more vivid expectation of the probability of curing the patient.

IV. PEASANT-PROPRIETORSHIP

One of Mill's most characteristic doctrines shows conspicuously this relation. Malthus had found in Norway and Switzerland communities which flourished because they spontaneously practised his principles. 'It is worthy of remark,' says Mill,[1] 'that the two countries thus honourably distinguished are countries of small landed proprietors.' This coincidence was not acci-

[1] *Political Economy*, p. 99 (bk. i. ch. x. § 3).

dental ; and Mill's Malthusianism falls in with his admiration for peasant-proprietorship. He diverged in this respect from the orthodox economical tradition. The economists generally left it to sentimentalists to regret the British yeoman, and to weep musically with Goldsmith over the time 'when every rood of ground maintained its man.' Wordsworth had dwelt pathetically upon the homely virtues of the North-country statesman.[1] Cobbett had in his happiest passages dwelt fondly upon the old rural life, and denounced in his bitterest invectives the greedy landowners and farmers who had plundered and degraded the English peasant. The economists looked at the matter from the point of view represented by Arthur Young. Enclose commons ; consolidate small holdings ; introduce machinery ; give a free hand to enterprising landlords and substantial farmers, and agriculture will improve like commerce and manufactures. Small holders are as obsolete as handloom weavers ; competition, supply and demand, and perfect freedom of trade will sweep them away, new methods will be adopted, capital introduced, and the wages of the labourer be raised. M'Culloch, for example, took this view ;[2] denounced small holdings, and prophesied[3] that France would in fifty years become the greatest 'pauper-warren in Europe.' A remarkable advocate of a similar view was Richard Jones (1790-1855), who in 1835 succeeded Malthus at Haileybury.[4]

[1] See Mill's reference to Wordsworth, *Political Economy*, p. 155 (bk. ii. ch. vi. § 1 *n.*).
[2] See, *e.g.*, his note to the *Wealth of Nations*, p. 565 *seq.*
[3] As quoted by W. T. Thornton, *Plea for Peasant Proprietors* (1874), p. 133.
[4] Jones's *Essay on the Distribution of Wealth and on the Sources of Taxation* :

Jones admired Malthus and accepted with qualifications the account of rent given by Malthus and West. But he denounced Malthus's successors, Ricardo, James Mill, and M'Culloch for preferring 'anticipation' to 'induction,' and venturing to start with general maxims and deduce details from them. Jones deserves the credit of perceiving the importance of keeping historical facts well in view. He shows sufficiently that Ricardo's theory, if taken to be a historical statement of the actual progress of events, is not correct. He refuses to define rent, but treats historically of the various payments made in respect of land. After classifying these, he decides that rent of the Ricardian kind prevails over less than a hundredth part of the earth's surface. He considers it, however, as representing a necessary stage of progress. It is far superior to the early stages, because it supposes the growth of a class of capitalists, able to direct labour and introduce the best methods of cultivation. Hence Jones comes by a different route to an agreement with M'Culloch. He prophesies that peasant-proprietors will rapidly fall into want and their numbers be limited only by the physical impossibility of procuring food. They were precisely in the position least favourable to the action of prudential checks.[1]

Book I., *Rent*, appeared in 1831. Though constantly pressed by his intimate friend, Whewell, to complete the book, Jones never found time for the purpose. In 1859, Whewell published Jones's *Literary Remains*—chiefly notes for lectures—with a life.

[1] *Rent*, pp. 68, 146. Whewell in his preface to Jones's *Remains* (p. xvii.), seems to charge Mill with appropriating Jones's classification without due recognition of the merits. Mill used the book freely, and calls it a 'copious repertory of valuable facts' (*Political Economy*, bk. ii. ch. v. § 4). If he did not speak more strongly of the merits of Jones's classification (into 'labour,' 'metayer,' 'ryot,' and 'cottier' rents) it was probably because he thought Jones responsible for a fatal confusion between 'cottiers' and 'peasant-pro-

Mill upon this matter dissented most emphatically both from the 'classical' and the historical champion. The point is with him of vital importance. His French sympathies had prepared him to see the other side of the question. The most unequivocal triumph claimed, with whatever truth, for the French revolution was the elevation of the cultivators of the land. Mill, at any rate, held emphatically that the French revolution had 'extinguished extreme poverty for one whole generation,'[1] and had thereby enabled the French population to rise permanently to a higher level. Contemporary English history gave the other side. Poor-law controversies had brought into striking relief the degradation of the English agricultural labourer. The *Morning Chronicle* articles, to which he had devoted six months, combined with an advocacy of peasant-proprietorship an exposition of the inadequacy of poor-laws. The excellent W. T. Thornton (1813-1880) had been from 1836 Mill's colleague in the India House, and was one of the few friends who communicated freely with him during his seclusion.[2] In 1846 Thornton published a

prietors.' In the *Rent* this distinction is ignored. In the *Remains*, which Mill had not seen, Jones speaks (pp. 208, 217, 438, 522, 537) of 'peasant-proprietors' as an interesting class, but pronounces no definite judgment upon the system.

[1] *Political Economy*, p. 230 (bk. ii. ch. xiii. § 3).

[2] Bain speaks of Thornton as one of the friends who, like Sterling, maintained a close intimacy with Mill in spite of differences of opinion. These differences certainly did not prevent Thornton from speaking and writing of Mill in the tone of an ardent and reverential admirer. As little has been told of Thornton's private life, I will venture to say that, as a young man, I used often to see him, when he visited Fawcett and Fawcett's great friend, Mr. C. B. Clarke, at Cambridge. Thornton's extreme amiability, his placid and candid, if slightly long-winded, discussions of his favourite topics, won the affection of his young hearers, and has left a charming impression upon the survivors.

book upon *Over Population and its Remedy*, in which he declares himself to be a thoroughgoing Malthusian, and rebukes M'Culloch for saying that Malthus's work exemplified the 'abuse' of general principles. Thornton, like Mill, follows Malthus in thinking that over-population must be checked by preventing imprudent marriages;[1] but he makes a special point of the doctrine that misery is not only the effect but the 'principal promoter' of over-population.[2] Hence he is not content with Malthus's negative position. The evil will not die out of itself. His favourite remedy at this time was the 'allotment system.' From this Mill dissents.[3] They agree, however, upon the merits of peasant-proprietorship, upon which Thornton published a book in 1848, shortly before the appearance of Mill's treatise.[4] Mill says that this ought to be the standard treatise on that side 'of the question.'[5] Neither Mill nor Thornton had any first-hand knowledge of agriculture; but they forcibly attacked the assumptions then prevalent among English agriculturists. Thornton had been especially impressed by the prosperity of the Channel Islands—a rather limited base for a wide induction; but both he and Mill could refer to experience on a much larger scale throughout wide districts on the Continent. The pith of Mill's position is condensed in Michelet's picturesque passage, where the peasant is described as unable to tear himself away even on Sunday from the contemplation of his beloved plot of land. The three periods when the

[1] *Over Population*, p. 268.
[2] *Ibid.* p. 121.
[3] *Political Economy* (bk. ii. ch. xii. § 4).
[4] *Plea for Peasant Proprietors* (1874), p. 261 *n.*
[5] *Political Economy*, p. 223 (bk. ii. ch. vi. § 6).

peasant had been able to buy land were called the 'good King Louis XII.,' the 'good King Henry IV.' and the revolution. Arthur Young's famous phrase of the 'magic of property' which 'turns sand to gold' was a still more effective testimony, because Young was the Coryphæus of the modern 'English school of agriculturists.'[1]

France, then, represented the good effects of Malthusianism in action. The French peasantry, as Thornton says after Lavergne,[2] had not read Malthus, but they instinctively put his advice in practice. Mill triumphantly quotes the figures which showed the slow rate of increase of the French population.[3] The case of Belgium, as he remarks, showed that peasant-proprietorship might be consistent with a rapid increase, but the French case proved conclusively that this was not a necessary result of the system. The 'pauper-warren' theory at least is conclusively disproved. M'Culloch's unfortunate prediction might be explained by his *a priori* tendencies; but it is curious to find Mill confuting Jones, the advocate for a historical method, by an appeal to experience and statistics. The possession of the soundest method does not make a man infallible. Jones and M'Culloch, as Mill said, had confounded two essentially different things. They had argued simply as to the economic advantages of production on a large and small scale without reference to the moral effect upon the cultivator. Their criterion is simply the greatness

[1] *Political Economy*, pp. 168, 171, 182 (bk. ii. ch. vi. § 67; vii. § 1, 5).
[2] *Peasant Proprietors* (1874), p. 159, referring to Lavergne's *Économie Rurale* (1860).
[3] *Political Economy*, p. 177 (bk. ii. ch. vii. § 4).

of the return to a given amount of capital on different systems. They had therefore treated the cases of France and Ireland as identical, whereas in one vital circumstance they are antithetical. France represented the observance of Malthus's true principle, because the peasant was moved by the 'magic of property'; he had absolute security in his little plot; and the *vis medicatrix* or desire to save was raised to its highest point. Ireland represents the defiance of Malthus, because the Irish cottiers, with no security, and therefore no motive for saving, multiplied recklessly and produced a true 'pauper-warren.' Mill accordingly reaches the conclusion that while peasant-proprietorship does not of necessity involve rude methods of cultivation, it is more favourable than any other existing system to intelligence and prudence, less favourable to 'improvident increase of numbers,' and therefore more favourable to moral and physical welfare.[1]

Jones would admit small culture as a natural stage towards the development of the English system. Mill considers it to be in advance of that system, but neither does he consider it to represent the absolutely best system. In a later passage he repudiates an opinion which, he says, might naturally be attributed to him by readers of the earlier chapters.[2] Though the French peasant is better off than the English labourer, he does not hold that we should adopt the French system, nor does he consider that system to be the ideal one. To cover the land with isolated families may secure their independence and promote their industry, but it is not

[1] *Political Economy*, p. 182 (bk. ii. ch. vii. § 5).
[2] *Ibid*. p. 460 (bk. iv. ch. vii. § 4).

conducive to public spirit or generous sentiment. To promote those qualities we must aim at 'association, not isolation, of interests.' This view is significant. Peasant-proprietorship, we are constantly told, is the great barrier against Socialism. It represents, in fact, 'individualism' in its highest degree. It stimulates the Malthusian virtues, prudence, industry, and self-help, and makes each man feel the necessity of trusting to his own energy. Yet Mill, with all his Malthusianism, thinks that such virtues might be stimulated too much; and, after preaching the merits of individualism, shows a leaning towards the antagonistic ideal of Socialism. He says little—perhaps it would hardly have been relevant to say much—of the historical aspect of the question. But there is a tacit implication of his argument of no little importance. According to him, the English labourer had been demoralised, and the whole Irish peasantry brought to the edge of starvation, while the French and other peasantries were prosperous and improving. To what historical causes was this vast difference due? The French revolution, however important, can only be understood through its antecedents. Systems of land-tenure, it is obvious, have been connected in the most intricate way with all manner of social, industrial, and political phenomena. Commerce and manufactures may seem in some sense a kind of natural growth—a set of processes at which government can look on from outside, enforcing at most certain simple rules about voluntary contracts. But, in the case of land, we have at every point to consider the action and reaction of the whole social structure and of the institutions which represent all the conflicts and combinations

of the great interests of the state. Consequently neither the results actually attained, nor those which we may hope to attain, can be adequately regarded from the purely industrial side alone. Systems have not flourished purely because of their economical merits, nor can they be altered without affecting extra-economical interests. To do nothing is to leave agricultural institutions to be perverted by political or 'sinister' interests. Mill was very little inclined to do nothing. He saw in the superiority of the foreign to the British systems a proof of the malign influence of the 'sinister interests' in our constitution. The landed aristocracy were the concrete embodiment of the evil principle. The nobility and the squirearchy represented the dead weight of dogged obstructiveness. They were responsible for the degradation of the labourer; and the Ricardian doctrine of rent explained why their interests should be opposed to those of all other classes. Although Mill attributed enormous blessings to the revolution in France, he was far too wise to desire a violent revolution in England, and he was far too just to attribute to individual members of the class a deliberate intention to be unjust. Yet he was prepared to advocate very drastic remedies; and if there were any human being of moderate cultivation from whom he was divided by instinctive repulsion and total incapacity to adopt the same point of view, it was certainly the country squire. The natural antipathy was quaintly revealed when Mill found himself in the House of Commons opposed to thick rows of squires clamouring for protection against the cattle-plague.

So far Mill's position is an expansion or adaptation of Malthus. Obedience to Malthus makes the prosperous

French peasant; disobedience, the pauperised English labourer. Malthus, as Mill interprets him, means that all social improvement depends upon a diminished rate of increase, relatively to subsistence[1]; and to diminish that rate the prudential check must be strengthened. 'No remedies for low wages,' therefore, 'have the smallest chance of being efficacious which do not operate on and through the minds and habits of the people';[2] and every scheme which has not for its foundation the diminution of the proportion of the people to the funds which support them, is 'for all permanent purposes a delusion.'[3] The two propositions taken together sum up Mill's doctrine. Social welfare can be brought about only by stimulating the *vis medicatrix* or sense of individual responsibility. Every reform which does not fulfil that condition is built upon sand. The application to England is a practical comment. The true remedies for low wages[4] are first an 'effective national education' so designed as to cultivate common-sense. This will affect the 'minds of the people' directly. Secondly, a 'great national measure of colonisation.' This will at once diminish numbers. Thirdly, a national system for 'raising a class of peasant-proprietors.' This will provide a premium to prudence and economy affecting the whole labouring class. Besides this, Mill approves of the new poor-law, which has shown that people can be protected against the 'extreme of want' without the

[1] *Political Economy*, p. 217 (bk. ii. ch. xi. § 6).
[2] *Ibid*. p. 225 (bk. ii. ch. xii. § 4).
[3] *Ibid*. p. 211 (bk. ii. ch. xi. § 3).
[4] *Ibid*. p. 230, etc. (bk. ii. ch. xiii. § 31, 34). Mill, in the later editions, observes that he has left this as it was written, although the rapid increase of means of communication has made the case 'no longer urgent.'

demoralising influence of the old system.[1] Mill here accepts, though he does not often insist upon, the doctrine upon which Thornton had dwelt in his *Over Population* : that poverty is self-propagating so far as it makes men reckless : education, as he remarks, is ' not compatible with extreme poverty.'[2] Hence the remedies themselves require another condition to make them effective. He declares emphatically that in these cases small means do not produce small effects, but no effect at all.[3] Nothing will be accomplished, unless comfort can be made habitual to a whole generation. The race must be lifted to a distinctly higher plane, or it will rapidly fall back. Mill, I fancy, would have been more consistent if he had admitted that great social changes must be gradual. But in any case, he was far from accepting the do-nothing principle. Political economy, he says, would have ' a melancholy and a thankless task ' if it could only prove that nothing could be done.[4] He holds that a huge dead lift is required to raise the labourers out of the slough of despond, and he demands therefore nothing less than great national schemes of education, of home and foreign colonisation. He speaks, too, with apparent approval of laws in restraint of improvident marriages.[5] It is, indeed, true that upon his schemes government is to interfere in order to make the people independent of further interference. Whether such a compromise be possible is another question.

[1] *Political Economy*, p. 221 (bk. ii. ch. xii. § 2).
[2] *Ibid.* p. 230 (bk. ii. ch. xiii. § 3).   [3] *Ibid.* p. 232 (bk. ii. ch. xiii. § 4).
[4] *Ibid.* p. 225 (bk. ii. ch. xiii. § 1).   [5] *Ibid.* p. 213 (bk. ii. ch. xi. § 4).

V. CAPITALISTS AND LABOURERS

Meanwhile a wider problem has to be considered. Unless some remedy can be found for the existing evils, he says, the industrial system of this country—the dependence, that is, of the whole labouring class upon the wages of hard labour—though regarded by many writers as the *ne plus ultra* of civilisation, must be ' irrevocably condemned.'[1] The agricultural labourer can be taken out of that position. By making him a proprietor he can be brought within the range of new motives. The independent peasant has in visible form before his eyes the base from which he and his family must draw supplies. It requires no abstract reasoning to show him that, if he brings more mouths into existence, his fields will not therefore bear double crops. But for the artisan who is a minute part of a vast organisation, whose wages come out of an indefinite, unexplored reservoir which may be affected by changes in commerce of the origin and exact nature of which he is completely ignorant, there is no such palpable limit. The springs from which his subsistence flows may, for anything he sees, be inexhaustible. He is a unit in a large multitude, which, taken as a whole, must undoubtedly be somehow dependent upon the general resources of the nation. But how to explain the intricate relations of the different classes is a problem puzzling to the best economists, and capable of all manner of fallacious solutions. As an individual, the artisan might learn like other people to be prudent ; but to know what is prudent he must understand his position. Can the labourer rightfully demand or reasonably expect

[1] *Political Economy*, p. 229 (bk. ii. ch. xiii. § 2).

to get a larger share of the wealth which he produces, or must he confine himself to limiting his numbers, and trusting to supply and demand to bring his right share ? Here the workman was misled by all manner of false lights ; and it became incumbent upon Mill to explain the position.

A population entirely dependent on wages never, says Mill,[1] refrains from over-population unless from ' actual legal restraint,' or some ' custom ' which ' insensibly moulds their conduct.' The English agricultural labourer seems to multiply just as far as he can.[2] All ' checks ' have gone or are going. If the artisan is better off, it is due to the rapid expansion of our trade. Should the market for our manufactures—not actually fall off but—cease to expand as rapidly as it has done for fifty years, we may fall into the state of Ireland before 1846. He hopes, indeed, that the factory population may be intelligent enough to adapt itself to circumstances. The fact that so large a part of our population is composed of middle classes or skilled artisans is the only security for some restraint. Yet Mill's opinion even of the artisan was low. English experience confirms the evidence of Escher of Zürich.[3] The head of the English artisan is turned by the idea of equality. ' When he ceases to be servile, he becomes insolent.'[4] There is nowhere, he says elsewhere,[5] any friendly sentiment between labourers

[1] *Political Economy*, p. 213 (bk. ii. ch. xi. § 4).
[2] *Ibid.* pp. 213, 216 (bk. ii. ch. xi. § 3, 5).
[3] Quoted from the report of the Poor-law Commission in 1840.—*Political Economy* (bk. i. ch. vii. § 5).
[4] *Political Economy*, p. 68 (bk. i. ch. vii. § 5).
[5] *Ibid.* p. 460 (bk iv. ch. vii. § 4), where he speaks of the total want of fairness and justice on both sides.

and employers. The artisan, swamped by the growing multiplication of unskilled labour, will too probably, we may infer, take a false view of the situation, and ascribe his poverty not to his own neglect of Malthus, but to the greed and hard-heartedness of the capitalist. Such an anticipation was likely enough to be realised.

This leads to the great problem of the true relation between capital and labour. The distinctive peculiarity of England was the dependence of the masses upon wages. How, as Mill has asked, is this state of things reconcilable with improvement? He will assume, as his predecessors had substantially done, that the capitalist and labourers are separate classes, and that the labourer derives his whole support from the capitalist. Though this is not everywhere true, it is for him the really important case. Moreover, he seems to think that the rule derived from considering the classes separately will not be altered when the two characters are united in individuals. The labourer, so far as he has ' funds in hand,' is also a capitalist ; and that part of his income is still decided by the general law of profits.[1] The assumption of a complete separation, made for convenience of argument, might no doubt be confounded with a statement of fact. At any rate, it is merely an explicit avowal of the tacit assumption of the orthodox economists.

Here, then, we pass from Malthus to Ricardo. Mill adopts the Ricardian scheme, though trying to make it more elastic. Ricardo's doctrine of a ' minimum ' rate of wages to which the ' general rate ' constantly approximates has enough truth for the ' purposes of abstract

[1] *Political Economy*, p. 252 (bk. ii. ch. xv. § 6).

science.'[1] The rate indeed varies with the standard of living, and that, as we have seen, is a critical point. Yet the main outlines of the theory remain. As population presses upon the land, the landlord gets the benefit of his 'monopoly of the better soil,' and capitalist and labourer divide the remainder. Profits and wages, as Ricardo had said, vary inversely: a 'rise of general wages falls on profits; there is no possible alternative.'[2] Here, indeed, an important modification must be made in Ricardo's words, in order to state what Ricardo 'really meant.'[3] Profit depends, not upon wages simply, but upon the 'cost of labour.' The labourer is not a fixed quantity, representing so many 'foot-pounds' of energy; his efficiency, as Mill argued, may vary indefinitely with his moral and intellectual qualities;[4] it may be profitable to pay for the effective labour double the wages of the ineffective; and, in point of fact, 'the cost of labour is frequently at its highest where wages are lowest.'[5]

Thus interpreted, Ricardo, like Malthus, admits of progress. By improving in efficiency, and by maintaining his standard of life, the labourer's position may be improved. Still, however, improvement supposes a due regard to the interests of the capitalists, who make all the advances and receive all the produce. Here we have the old doctrine of the 'tendency of profits to a minimum.'[6] This theory, admitted though inade-

[1] *Political Economy*, p. 209 (bk. ii. ch. xi. § 2).
[2] *Ibid.* p. 418 (bk. iii. ch. xxvi. § 3).   [3] *Ibid.* p. 253 (bk. ii. ch. xv. § 7).
[4] *Ibid.* bk. i. ch. vii.   [5] *Ibid.* p. 254 (bk. ii. ch. xv. § 7).
[6] *Ibid.* bk. iv. ch. iv. Cf. *Unsettled Questions*, pp. 105-6. The article by Ellis, on the effect of improvements in machinery (*Westminster Review* for January 1826), though rather awkwardly stated, with the old capitalist and his quarters of corn illustration, puts the point clearly.

quately explained by Adam Smith, had been illustrated by E. G. Wakefield, and as Mill thinks, most scientifically treated by his friend Ellis. Another writer, to whom Mill refers with his usual generosity, was John Rae, whose *New Principles of Political Economy* had, he thinks, done in regard to accumulation of capital what Malthus had done in regard to population.[1] The necessity of resorting to inferior soils, which enriches the landowner, causes the difficulty of raising the labourer's 'real wages.' Profits are lowered not by the 'competition of capitalists,' but by the limitation of the national resources. As the difficulty of raising new supplies becomes more pressing, the 'cost of labour' rises, and the capitalist's profits diminish. Now, in every country, as Rae had shown, there is a certain 'effective desire of accumulation.'[2] It varies widely, and corresponds, we may say, to the principle which limits population—the 'effective desire' of propagation. There is a certain rate of profit which will induce men to save, and saving is the one source of capital. Hence, if the rate obtainable falls to this point, saving will cease, the capital which supports labour will not increase, and the country will be in the 'so-called stationary state.' Such a state, no doubt, is possible and often actual. Given a nation forced to draw its resources from a fixed area, and unable to improve its methods of cultivation, it is obvious that it may reach a point at which it can only just maintain its actual position. Mill holds not only that such a result is possible, but that it is always imminent. In an 'old country,' he says, 'the rate of profit is habitually within, as it were, a hair's-

[1] *Political Economy*, p. 102 (bk. i. ch. xi. § 2).
[2] *Ibid.* p. 103 (bk. i. ch. xi. § 3).

breadth of the minimum, and the country therefore on the very verge of the stationary state.'[1] He does not mean, he explains, that such a state is likely soon to be reached in Europe, but that, if accumulation continued and nothing occurred to raise the rate of profit, the stationary state would be very quickly reached. We have still the Malthusian view. We are always 'within a hair's-breadth' of the dead wall which will absolutely limit progress. Improvements are in fact constantly staving off the impending catastrophe. We are drifting, so to speak, towards a lee-shore, where, if not wrecked, we shall at least come to a standstill. Again and again we manage to make a little way, and by new devices to weather another dangerous point. By prudence, too, we may turn each new advantage to account, and improve our condition by refraining from increasing our numbers. But the danger is always threatening.

One noteworthy result is Mill's chapter upon the stationary state.[2] He has, it seems, been so impressed by the probability that he will find refuge from his fears by facing the worst. After all, are not the grapes sour? If we are unable to grow richer, is the loss of wealth so great a misfortune? He turns to think of the 'trampling, crushing, elbowing, and treading on each other's heels which form the existing type of human life.'[3] Is such a state desirable? In America, where all privileges are abolished, poverty unknown, and the six points of the Chartists accepted, the main result achieved is that 'the whole of one sex is devoted to dollar-hunting and

[1] *Political Economy*, p. 443 (bk. iv. ch. iv. § 4).
[2] *Ibid.* bk. iv. ch. vi.
[3] *Ibid.* p. 453 (bk. iv. ch. vi. § 2).

the whole of the other to breeding dollar-hunters.'[1] Coarse stimuli are needed for coarse minds; but a better ideal should be possible. We might aim at an order quite compatible with the 'stationary state,' where labourers should be comfortable, no enormous fortunes accumulated, and a much larger part of the population free from mechanical toil and enabled to 'cultivate freely the graces of life.' Nor is it desirable that cultivation should spread to every corner of the world, every flowery waste ploughed up and all wild animals extirpated. 'A world from which solitude is extirpated is a very poor ideal.'

Mill agreed with Ruskin, though Ruskin did not agree with Mill, and, indeed, called him a goose. A stationary state of wealth need not, says Mill, imply a stationary state of the 'art of living.' That art was more likely to improve when we were not all engrossed by the 'art of getting on.' How far that is true I do not presume to say. It seems possible that in such a state the struggle to be stationary might be as keen, though advance would be hopeless. But, without criticising a theory which represents rather a temporary protest than a settled conviction, we may be content to notice how far removed was this typical economist from the grovelling tendencies often ascribed to his kind. Mill, as even Carlyle would have admitted, was not a mere devotee of 'pig's-wash.'

This vision of a stationary state comes in the book in which Mill passes from the 'statics,' as he calls it, to the 'dynamics' of political economy. His purpose is

[1] *Political Economy* (1862), ii. 323. In the later editions this passage is replaced by a reference to the civil war, which showed that the struggle for wealth is not necessarily fatal to the 'heroic virtues.'

to trace the influence of industrial progress. His first chapter[1] notices the vast mechanical discoveries, the increased security of society and greater capacity for united action, which give reasons for hoping indefinite growth of aggregate wealth. There is, he thinks, ' not much reason to apprehend' that population will outrun, though we must sadly admit the possibility that it will keep up with, production and accumulation. This leads to the chapters in which he discusses the effect of progress upon the various classes concerned.[2] How does the ' progress of industry' affect the three classes—landowners, capitalists, and labourers? Land is a fixed quantity ; but population may increase, capital may increase, and the arts of production may improve by supposing each to increase separately and then together. A long and careful analysis gives us the general result. It is enough to notice the conclusion.[3]

Land represents the fixed ' environment' of the race. The proprietors of the land will be enriched by economical progress and the growing necessity for resort to inferior soils. The cost of raising the labourer's subsistence increases, and profits therefore tend to fall. The improvement of the arts of agricultural production acts as a ' counteracting force.' It relaxes the pressure and postpones the stationary state. For the moment the improvement may diminish (as Ricardo had argued), but in the long run must promote, the ' enrichment of landlords,' and, if population increases, will transfer to them the whole benefit. Mill, as we have seen, was fully alive to the enormous increase in past times of the

[1] *Political Economy*, bk. iv. ch. i.   [2] *Ibid.* bk. iv. ch. iii.
[3] *Ibid.* p. 439 (bk. iv. ch. iii. § 5).

general efficiency of labour and to the indefinite possibilities of the future. Yet the improvement seems here, again, to be regarded rather as checking the gravitation towards the stationary state, than as justifying any confident hopes of improvement. Meanwhile the elevation of the labouring classes depends essentially upon their taking advantage of such improvements to raise their standard, instead of treating an addition to their means ' simply as convertible into food for a greater number of children.'[1]

VI. THE WAGE-FUND

This doctrine led to one of the strangest of controversial catastrophes. In his chapter upon ' wages '[2] Mill had begun with an unlucky paragraph. He introduced the word ' wage-fund' to describe the sums spent in ' the direct purchase of labour'; and stated that wages necessarily depended upon the proportion of this fund to the labouring population. This doctrine was assailed by Thornton in 1869.[3] Mill, reviewing Thornton, astonished the faithful by a complete recantation ; and, though a disciple or two—especially Cairnes and Fawcett —continued to uphold the doctrine, or what they took to be the doctrine, political economists have ever since been confuting it, or treating it as too ridiculous for confutation. If we are to assume that the wage-fund was at once an essential proposition of the old ' classical' economy and a palpable fallacy, the whole structure

[1] *Political Economy*, p. 436 (bk. iv. ch. iii. § 4).
[2] *Ibid.* p. 207 (bk. ii. ch. x. § 1).
[3] Thornton's *On Labour ; its Wrongful Claims and Rightful Demands*. Another work generally mentioned in regard to this controversy is Longe, *Refutation of the Wages-Fund Theory* (1866).

collapses. The keystone of the arch has crumbled. Nor, again, is it doubtful that this catastrophe marked a critical change in the spirit and methods of political economy. And yet, when the actual discussion is considered, it seems strange that it should have had such importance. What was this ' wage-fund theory'? The answer is generally given by quoting the passage already mentioned from M'Culloch, a paragraph from Mill, and Fawcett's reproduction of Mill. Mill's sentences, says Professor Taussig, ' contain all that he ever said directly and explicitly on the theory of the wage-fund.'[1] It is strange that so vital a point should have been so briefly indicated. Then Mill's ablest follower, Cairnes, declares that though he had learned political economy from Mill, he had never understood the wage-fund theory in the sense which Thornton put upon it and which Mill accepted.[2] But for Mill's admission, he says, he would ' have confidently asserted' that not only no economist but ' no reasonable being' had ever asserted the doctrine. We are left to doubt whether it be really a corner-stone of the whole system or an accidental superstructure which had really no great importance. At any rate it was rather assumed than asserted ; and yet is so closely connected with the system that I must try to indicate the main issue.

In the first place, the ' wage-fund' is Mill's equivalent for Adam Smith's ' fund which is destined for the main-

[1] Professor Taussig, *Wages and Capital* (1896), p. 23. Professor Taussig gives a very thorough and candid discussion of the question, to which I am glad to refer. To follow the many controversies which he notices would take me into technicalities beyond the purpose of this book, and, I fear, beyond my competence.
[2] Cairnes's *Leading Principles*, etc., p. 214.

tenance of servants';[1] and Mill, again, starts from a proposition inherited from Smith. ' Industry,' he says, ' is limited by capital'—a doctrine, as he adds, perfectly obvious though constantly neglected.[2] Undoubtedly an industrial army requires its commissariat : its food, clothes, and weapons. Its very existence presupposes an accumulation of such supplies in order to the discharge of its functions. A more doubtful assumption is stated by Adam Smith. ' The demand,' he says,[3] ' for those who live by wages naturally increases with the increase of national wealth, and cannot possibly increase without it.' The growth of the national wealth, that is, ' naturally' involves the growth of the wealth of every class. Machinery increases the efficiency of labour and therefore increases the power at least of supporting labourers. Moreover, in the long run, and generally at the moment, this power will certainly be exercised.[4] The interests of the capitalist will lead him to support more labourers. The identity of interest between the classes concerned might thus be taken for granted. Hence, we may trust to the spontaneous or ' natural' order of things to bring to all classes the benefit of improved industrial methods. This natural order, again, including the rate of wages, is understood to imply, at least, the absence of state interference. Political rulers must not tamper with the industrial mechanism. It will spontaneously work out

[1] *Wealth of Nations* (M'Culloch), p. 38. Ricardo (*Works*, p. 59) and Senior (*Political Economy*, p. 153) call it the ' fund for the maintenance of labour.'
[2] *Political Economy*, p. 39 (bk. i. ch. v. § 1).
[3] *Wealth of Nations* (M'Culloch), p. 31. I do not consider what was Adam Smith's general doctrine.
[4] This is the gist of Ellis's article (see above, p. 200 n).

the prosperity of the whole nation and of each class. Left to itself the industrial organism generates those economic harmonies upon which the optimist delighted to dwell. 'Natural' seems to take the sense of 'providential.' The 'economic harmonies' are, like the harmonies perceived by Paley or the Bridgewater Treatise writers in external nature, so many proofs of the divine benevolence; any attempt to interfere with them could only lead to disaster. To show in detail the mischiefs involved, to expose the charlatans whose schemes implied such interference, was the grand aim of most economists. Mill, as we shall see, was very far from accepting this view without qualification. He thought with the Utilitarians generally that the 'sovereign' had enormous powers, and moreover was bound to apply them for the redress of social evils. Society, he held, was full of injustice. Laws aggravated many evils and could suppress others. Still the normal function of government is to prevent violence, see fair-play, and enforce voluntary contracts. When it exceeds these functions, and tries by sheer force to obtain results without considering the means, it may do infinite mischief. It acts like an ignorant mechanic, who violently moves the hands of the clock without regard to the mechanism. Erroneous conceptions of the very nature of the machinery had led to the pestilent fallacies which Smith and his successors had been labouring to confute. The freetraders[1] had often to expose one sophistry which deluded the

[1] Mill scandalised the staunch freetraders by admitting an exception to the doctrine in the case of new countries 'naturalising a foreign industry' by a moderate duty (*Political Economy* bk. v. ch. x. § 1). Such incidental consequences are obviously possible. A prohibition to import a material of industry might lead to the discovery of mines at home or to new methods of manufacture. But such results seem to lie outside of pure political economy.

vulgar. Its essence is, as Mill puts it, that we attend to one half of the phenomenon and overlook the other.[1] The protectionist thinks of the producer and forgets the consumer. Half the popular fallacies imply the failure to take into account all the actions and reactions which are implied by a given change. The processes by which industry adapts itself to varying conditions—compensating for an ebb in one quarter by a flow in another—is mistaken for a change in the whole volume. From the neglect to trace out the more remote, though necessary consequences, all manner of absurd doctrines had arisen. The doctrine of 'gluts' and 'over-production' confounded the case of a production of the wrong things with an excess of production in general. Improved machinery was supposed not merely to displace one class of labourers for a time, but to supersede 'labour' in general. We should forbid the substitution of power-looms and steam-ploughs for hand-weaving and spades, or try to increase wealth by depriving workmen of their tools. A strange confusion of ideas is involved. People, said Whately,[2] ask for 'work' when what they want is really 'wages.' They assume that because more labour is required, more wages will be forthcoming. The fire of London, as Mandeville observed, was an excellent thing for the builders. If their wages had simply dropped out of the skies, it might have been good for everybody. So, again, Mill has to labour the point[3] that society does not gain by unproductive expenditure, that is, by the support of horses and hounds, but by

[1] *Political Economy*, p. 209 (bk. ii. ch. xi. § 2).
[2] As quoted by Cairnes's *Leading Principles*, p. 302.
[3] *Political Economy*, bk. i. ch. v. § 5.

'production'; that is, by expenditure on mines and railways. He lays down a principle which, he says, is most frequently overlooked, that 'demand for commodities is not demand for labour.' His doctrine has been ridiculed and treated as paradoxical. It implies at any rate an important distinction. It is intended to draw the line between changes which merely mean that a different employment is being found for labourers, and changes which mean that a greater sum is being devoted to the support of labourers in general.[1] The argument against such fallacies might naturally be summed up by saying that the real point to be considered was the effect of any change upon the 'wage-fund.' The error, common to all, is the confusion between the superficial and the more fundamental—the functional, we may say, and the organic changes. They are exposed by tracing the secondary results, which have been overlooked in attending to the more palpable but less conspicuous part of the phenomenon. Then we see that some changes imply a change in the quantity of labour supported; only a redistribution of the particular energies. They do not affect the 'wage-fund.' The phrase was useful as emphasising this point; and useful, though it might be in some sense a truism. Truisms are required so long as self-contradictory propositions are accepted. But a further problem is suggested. What, after all, is the wage-fund? What determines its amount? If this or that phenomenon does not imply a change in the fund, what does imply a change, and what are its laws?

[1] Cairnes's *Leading Principles*, p. 222, explains the principle. Taussig (pp. 107 and 274) agrees with Brentano that Mill's doctrine is simply a corollary from the theory that wages 'are paid out of capital.'

To this we get, in the first place, the old Malthusian answer. Whatever the fund may precisely be, the share of each man will be determined by the whole number depending upon it. This is obviously true, but does not answer the question, What actually fixes the sum to be divided? That problem seems to drop out of sight or to be taken as somehow implicitly answered. The answer should, however, be indicated by Mill's treatment of the most important cases.

The distribution problem, made prominent by Ricardo, was emphasised by controversies over the poor-law or the factory acts and trades-unionism. The economists had been constantly endeavouring to expose quack remedies for poverty. The old attempts to regulate wages by direct legislation had been too long discredited to be worth powder and shot. Mill, in discussing 'popular remedies for low wages,'[1] argues that competition 'distributes the whole wage-fund among the whole labouring population.' If wages were below the point at which this happens there would be 'unemployed capital'; capitalists would therefore compete and wages would be raised. If, on the other hand, law or 'opinion' fixes wages above the point, some labourers will be unemployed, or the 'wage-fund' must be forcibly increased. 'Popular sentiment,' however, claimed that 'reasonable wages' should be found for everybody. Nobody, he says, would support a proposal to this effect more strenuously than he himself, were the claim made on behalf of the existing generation.[2] But when the claim extends to all whom that generation or

[1] *Political Economy*, p. 219 (bk. ii. ch. xii. § 1).
[2] *Ibid.* p. 219 (bk. ii. ch. xii. § 2).

its descendants chooses 'to call into existence' the case is altered. The result would be that the poor-rate would swallow up the whole national income, and the check to population be annihilated. Here, again, instead of hearing clearly why or how the wage-fund is fixed, we are at once referred to Malthus. The factory legislation suggests the same question. The rigid economists had maintained that here again the attempt to interfere must be injurious. It would hamper the growth of capital, and therefore injure those dependent upon capital. Mill treats the case with remarkable brevity. He apparently regarded the whole movement as savouring of quackery. But he discusses the question briefly from the moral point of view. Children, he says, should of course be protected from overwork, for in their case 'freedom of contract is but another word for freedom of coercion.'[1] Women, he notes, are protected by the factory acts; but this is only excusable, if excusable at all, because, as things now are, women are slaves. If they were free, it would be tyrannical to limit their labour. The old political economy still suffices. Meanwhile the problem was coming up in other shapes. The Utilitarians have been active in procuring the repeal of the laws against combination. They had thought, indeed, that the workmen, once set free, would find combination needless, and would learn to act by means of individual competition. Trades-unionism, on the contrary, had developed, and was producing long and obstinate struggles with the capitalist. Were these struggles attempts to interfere with a 'natural' order? Were they wasteful modes of attempting to secure a share

[1] *Political Economy*, p. 578 (bk. v. ch. xi. § 9).

of the 'wage-fund' which would come to them in any case by the spontaneous play of the industrial machinery? Socialists were beginning to declare that instead of an identity there was a radical opposition of interests. The answer made by orthodox economists implies some wage-fund theory. They were never tired of declaring that all attempts to raise wages by combination were fallacious. The struggle was always costly, and, even if successful, could only benefit one section of workmen at the expense of others. What precise assumption might underlie this doctrine is another question not so easily answered. It is taken for granted that there is a definite fund, such that no struggling can wring more from the capitalist; and all the rugging and riving of labourers and unions can only succeed in one body getting a larger share out of the mouth of the others. Mill's final view seems to be given in his discussion of erroneous methods of government interference. Legislation against combinations to raise wages is most vigorously condemned.[1] The desire to keep wages down shows 'the infernal spirit of the slave-master,' though the effort to raise them beyond a fixed limit is doomed to failure. We ought to rejoice if combination could really raise the rate of wages; and if all workmen could combine such a result might be possible. But even then they could not obtain higher wages than the rate fixed by 'supply and demand'—the rate which distributes the 'whole circulating capital of the country among the labouring population.'[2] Combinations are successful at times, but only for small bodies. The

[1] *Political Economy*, p. 563 (bk. v. ch. x. § 5).
[2] *Ibid.* p. 564 (bk. v. ch. x. § 5).

general rate of wages can be affected by nothing but the 'general requirements of the labouring people.' While these requirements (corresponding to the standard of living) remain constant, wages cannot long fall below or remain above the corresponding standard. The improvement, indeed, of even a small portion would be ' wholly a matter of satisfaction' if no general improvement could be expected. But as such improvement is now becoming possible, it is to be hoped that the better artisans will seek advantage in common with, or 'not to the exclusion of, their fellow labourers.' The trades-union movement, therefore, is taken to be equivalent to the formation of little monopolies through which particular classes of labourers benefit at the expense of others. Yet Mill is evidently anxious to make what concessions he can. Strikes, he thinks, have been the 'best teachers of the labouring classes' as to the 'relation between labour and the demand and supply of labour.' They should not be condemned absolutely—only when they are meant to raise wages above the 'demand and supply' limit; and, even then, he remembers that 'demand and supply' are not 'physical agencies'; that combinations are required to help poor labourers to get their rights (the 'demand and supply' rate) from rich employers; and, that trades-unions tend to advance the time when labourers will regularly 'participate in the profits derived from their labour.' Finally, it is desirable, as he characteristically adds, that 'all economical experiments, voluntarily undertaken, should have the fullest licence.'

Mill, unlike his rigid predecessors, is anxious to make out as good a case as he can for trades-unions. His sympathies are with them, if only the logic can be

coaxed into approval. To elevate the labouring class is the one worthy object of political action. Yet he is hampered by the inherited scheme. However modified, it always involves the assumption of a fixed sum to be distributed by 'supply and demand.' Limit the supply of labour, and you raise the price. No other plan will really go to the bottom of the problem. The rate of wages is fixed by 'supply and demand'; and the phrase seemed to imply that the rate of wages was fixed by a bargain, like the price of corn or cloth at a given time and place. Error, as Mill truly observes,[1] is often caused by not 'looking directly at the realities of phenomena, but attending only to the outward mechanism of buying and selling.' Are we looking directly at realities when we take for granted that 'labour' is bought and sold like corn and cotton? Are we not coming in sight of more fundamental changes, questions of the structure as well as the functions of industrial organism, which cannot be so summarily settled? Thornton argues as though workmen secreted 'labour' as bees secrete honey, and the value of the product were fixed by the proportion between the quantity in the market and the quantity which purchasers are prepared to take at the price. He only tries to show that the price may still be indeterminate. The 'equation' between supply and demand of which Mill had spoken might be brought about at varying rates of exchange. The whole supply might conceivably be taken off either at a high or at a low price. We need not go behind the immediate motives which govern a set of buyers meeting a set of sellers at an auction. Mill accepts the same assumptions. It is

[1] *Political Economy*, p. 56 (bk. i. ch. v. § 10).

quite true, he says, that in the case of wages various rates may satisfy the 'equation.' The whole labouring population may be forced to put up with starvation allowance or may be able to extort enough to raise their standard of life. This, he says, upsets the 'wage-fund' doctrine, hitherto taught by nearly all economists 'including myself.'[1] Moreover, the employer has the advantage in the 'higgling,' owing to what Adam Smith had already called 'the tacit combination of employers.'[2] This depressing influence can be resisted by a combination of the employed; and therefore the doctrine which declared the necessary incapacity of trades-unions to raise wages must be thrown aside.

Mill has received, and fully deserves, high praise for his candour in this recantation. We must, however, regret the facility with which he abandoned a disagreeable doctrine without sufficiently considering the effects of his admission upon his whole scheme.[3] To what, in fact, does the argument amount to which he thus yielded? He says that the capitalist starts with the 'whole of his accumulated means, all of which is potentially capital.' Out of this he pays both his labourers and his family expenses. No 'law of nature' makes it impossible for him to give to the labourer all 'beyond the necessaries of life,' which he had previously spent upon himself. The only limit to possible expenditure on wages is that he must not be ruined or driven out of business.[4]

[1] *Dissertations*, iv. 47 (reprint of article in *Fortnightly Review* of May 1869).   [2] *Ibid.* iv. 67.
[3] Since no edition of the *Political Economy* appeared between this time and Mill's death, he had no opportunity of making alterations in his treatise. His review of Thornton, however, seems to indicate a failure to appreciate the full bearing of his concessions.   [4] *Dissertations*, iv. 46.

This surely is obvious. No law of nature or of man forbids me from giving all that I have to my labourers, though I cannot give more than I have. If I have a balance at my bankers, I may pay my wage-bill by a cheque for any smaller sum, and live on the difference. Difficulties at once arise when we look at the 'realities' of the phenomena and turn from 'money wages' to 'real wages.' It is easy for an individual to give what he pleases, but not so easy to make such a change in the whole concrete industrial machinery as to apply it all to the production of labourers' commodities. What, in any case, was precisely the economical dogma inconsistent with Mill's statement? According to him, it was the doctrine that, at any given time, there is a certain fund in existence which is 'unconditionally devoted' to the payment of wages. This was taken to 'be at any given moment a predetermined amount.'[1] But how was it supposed to be predetermined? All events are predetermined by their causes, and to treat political economy as a possible science is to assume that wages, among other things, are somehow determinate. Mill means apparently to deny a determination by something in the nature of the capital itself. The capital might mean something which could not, even if everybody wished it, be applied in any other way. The circulating might bear to the fixed capital the same relation as wool, for example, to mutton. Save at all, and a certain part of your savings will be wages, as a certain part of the sheep will be wool. Unless you waste it, you will employ it on the only purpose for which it is adapted.

[1] *Dissertations*, iv. 43.

Such a 'predetermination' is of course a fiction. Was it ever taken for a fact?[1] It was rather, I believe, an assumption which has slipped into their reasoning unawares. Starting from the old proposition that 'industry is limited by capital,' and remarking that some capital did not go directly to wages, they simply amended the proposition by saying that wages depended on 'circulating' capital, and thought that the corrected formula would do as well as the old. Perhaps they assumed roughly that 'circulating' must bear a fixed proportion to capital in general; or that, at any rate, the proportion was somehow determined by general causes. The doctrine thus understood tends to become a merely identical proposition: the 'wage-fund' means simply the wages, and the rate of wages is given by the total paid divided by the number of receivers. The economists continued to lecture the labourers upon the futility of their aims with the airs of professors exploding the absurdity of schemes for perpetual motion. It must, however, be observed that neither Mill nor his disciples held that the rate of wages was unalterable. They had the strongest belief that it could be raised, and raised through the agency of trades-unions. Mill's disciple, Fawcett, as Professor Taussig remarks,[2] lays down the old wage-fund formula, and yet proceeds to argue about strikes raising wages without reference to this supposed impossibility. In an early article,[3] highly praised by Mill, Fawcett discussed strikes. He appeals to the wage-fund doctrine throughout, and

[1] See Taussig, pp. 211-45 for the vagueness of such writers as M'Culloch and Torrens. 'The point,' he says, 'was hardly ever raised in terms.'
[2] Taussig, p. 238.
[3] Article in *Fortnightly Review* for July 1860. See Mill, *Political Economy*, p. 565 (bk. v. ch. x. § 5).

yet he approves of trades-unions, and only exhorts men to strike when trade is improving, instead of striking when it is falling off. It does not for a moment occur to him that 'supply and demand' or the wage-fund theory determine every particular case. Undoubtedly men, by combining and taking advantage of the 'conjuncture,' may get the best of a bargain. Fawcett holds, indeed, that the immediate advantage will be temporary or limited to one trade. Still combination will, for the time, enable the men to get an earlier share of the improved profits. Then, he argues, and it is of this that Mill approves, that such a system, by interesting the men in business and letting them perceive the conditions of success, will lead to the consummation most ardently desired by Mill and himself; to a perception of an ultimate identity of interests and a final acceptance of some system of co-operation. Thus, by listening to Malthus and raising the standard of life, the artisan will himself become a capitalist or a sharer in profits.

The wage-fund doctrine, so understood, included a reference not to the immediate bargain alone but to a more remote series of consequences. The 'predetermination' refers to the whole set of industrial forces which work gradually and tentatively. The ablest defender of the wage-fund, understood in this sense, was J. E. Cairnes (1823-1875),[1] who, like Thornton, was a personal friend of Mill; and, though an acute and independent thinker, was an admiring disciple. He met Mill's recantation by applying Mill's earlier faith. He does not believe in that 'economic will-o'-the-wisp,'[2] as Thornton calls

[1] See *Dictionary of National Biography* for a short notice.
[2] *On Labour*, p. 292.

it, the wage-fund, which supposes that in the bargain between men and masters there is a 'predetermined' amount which must be spent in wages. It is only predetermined, he says, in so far as all men act from certain motives which, under given circumstances, must bring about certain results. Thornton, he says, has talked as if 'supply and demand' meant a power which forced men to act in a certain way, instead of being merely a general phrase indicating the normal operation of these motives. To determine the general rate of wages we have to look at the whole mechanism, not at the special bargain. To explain that action Cairnes starts again from the Ricardian scheme. On the one hand we have, of course, Malthus; and on the other, the relation between wages and profits, the effective desire of accumulation, the necessity of resorting to inferior soils, with the consequent 'tendency of profits to a minimum' (for the proof of which he refers to Mill himself), and the accepted statement that profits are already within a hand's-breadth of the minimum.[1] Cairnes modifies the scheme in various ways, upon which I need not dwell: as by admitting 'non-competing industrial groups,' and arguing that the amount of the fixed and circulating capital is more or less determined by the direction of the national industries. Such conditions, he argues, determine the permanent rate of wages, though for a time oscillations within comparatively narrow limits may of course take place. Mill, in his unregenerate days, had argued, as we have seen, that the whole 'wage-fund' must be distributed, without giving any precise reason for the necessity. He now held, with Thornton, that a 'conspiracy of employers' might retain

[1] *Leading Principles*, p. 257.

any part of it. Cairnes holds this conspiracy to be a fiction. It is not, as is often said, a question of rich men bargaining with poor men, but of rich men competing with each other. The competition of capitalists, as he holds, will always take place, not from any mysterious characteristic of 'circulating capital,' but because, as things are, they are always on the look-out for profitable employment of their capital. That process keeps wages up as the competition of labourers keeps them down, and, though it may act slowly, will inevitably keep wages approximating to an average.[1]

In this view Cairnes takes himself to be only expanding the doctrine which pervades Mill's whole treatise: in spite of the occasional *obiter dicta* about the wage-fund. He does not abandon—he declares that nobody ever held— the 'will-o'-the-wisp'—the absolute predetermination.[2] Certainly a doctrine which struck so thorough a student as one of which he had never even heard, and which appeared to him to be palpably absurd, could hardly have had the prominence usually assigned to it. When it has disappeared, the real point at issue is changed. Cairnes maintains that Thornton, though denouncing the sham doctrine, still virtually holds the old doctrine. Thornton said[3] that 'unionism could not keep up the rate (of wages) in one trade without keeping it down in others.' And this, as Cairnes says, implies some

[1] *Leading Principles*, p. 277.
[2] 'Historically,' says Professor Taussig (p. 242), 'there may be ground for that contention,' viz., that the wage-fund never meant more than Ricardo's doctrine that profits were the 'leaving of wages,' and that accumulation depended on profits. This, he adds, is held by many writers who reject the 'wage-fund' proper, that is, Thornton's 'will-o'-the-wisp.'
[3] *On Labour*, p. 288.

sort of 'predetermination,' though not the absolute predetermination of the abandoned wage-fund. The main difference is that Cairnes holds that capitalists will always compete; whereas Thornton holds that they will ultimately combine and then be certain of victory.[1]

This, I think, indicates the true underlying difficulty. The 'natural' rate of wages, said the economists, is fixed by 'supply and demand.' 'Supply and demand' suggests the ordinary processes which level prices in the market. Thornton declares that 'labour' is bought and sold like corn or cotton. The analogy might be denied. Mr. Frederic Harrison observed that 'labour' is not 'a thing' which can be bought and sold. Thornton treats this as a purely verbal distinction, and expects even his antagonist to admit that 'hiring' is simply a case of 'buying,' and therefore governed by the same laws.[2] If so, we may apply formulæ derived from the case of the market. Then we tacitly introduce the ordinary economic assumptions. The proposition that wages are fixed by 'supply and demand' is taken to mean that the rate can be deduced from the simple process of bargaining. The whole theory of distribution can be worked out by considering the fluctuations of the labour market: the value of labour being fixed by the number of labourers, and the demand for capital being represented by the rate of profit. The doctrine, it may be admitted, is approximately true at a given time and place. It simply generalises the arguments used in every strike. Capital may be driven from a trade if wages are excessive; the influx or efflux of capital will raise or lower wages in a given district, and

[1] *On Labour*, p. 274.　　　[2] *Ibid.* pp. 86, 87.

so forth. The facts may often be inaccurately stated by interested parties, but their relevance is undeniable. The forces of which Cairnes speaks, the competition of capitalists for profits, of labourers for wages, and their effect upon accumulation and population are undoubtedly the important factors. It was precisely because the economists recognised these obvious phenomena that they convinced themselves and persuaded others. They talked a great deal of undeniable common-sense. They could, again, fairly demand that some allowance should be made for 'friction'—for the fact, that is, that competition and the various changes which it implies do not take place so rapidly and automatically as they assumed. They took, it is true, considerable liberties; they spoke as if capital could be changed by magic, and a thousand quarters of corn transformed into a steam-engine; or as if the population could instantaneously expand or contract in proportion to its means of support. They could forget at times that such phrases involve a kind of logical shorthand, and suppose a 'fluidity' of capital, a rapidity in the processes by which adaptations are carried out, which is unreal, and may cover important errors.

Still, with whatever allowances, we may accept the approximate truth of the assumptions, as describing the process by which immediate variations in wages are actually determined. The real difficulty comes at the next stage. Granting the approximate truth of the formulæ at any given time and place, can they give us a general theory of 'distribution'—formulæ which can be applied to determine generally what share of the total produce will go to labourers and what to capitalists? That is, in other words, can the purely economic formula become also a 'sociological' formula? Will it not only assign the conditions which govern the particular bargains, but enable us to determine the whole process by which the industrial mechanism is built up? That, as I take it, is the point at which the old economists broke down. Their doctrines, applicable and important within the appropriate sphere, become totally inadequate when they are supposed to give a complete theory of industrial development.

The unreality of the whole theory becomes obvious when we give it the wider interpretation. The excuse of 'friction' becomes insufficient. That may be applicable when the error is simply due to a permissible simplification of the data; not when the data are themselves wrongly stated. Ricardo, we have seen, had virtually made an assumption as to the social order. The labourers, we may say, are a structureless mass; a multitude of independent units, varying in numbers but otherwise of constant quality; the value of labour was thus dependent simply on the abundance or scarcity of the supply, and the labourers were assumed to be wholly dependent for support upon the capitalist. The formulæ applicable upon such a hypothesis might be correct so far as the data were correct. They would require a complete revision when we consider the actual and far more complex social state. Every difference of social structure will affect the play of competition; the degree in which population is stimulated or retarded; and the general efficiency of industry. A lowering of wages instead of producing an increase of profit and an accumulation of capital may lead to social degeneration, in which labour is less efficient and the whole organism is slack and

demoralised. Conversely, rise of wages may lead to a more than corresponding increase of production. The effect, again, of accumulation of capital cannot be expressed simply by the increased demand for labour. That seems plausible only so long as capital is identified with money. It really implies an alteration of the industrial system and conditions under which the bargain is made. It may, again, be true that in any particular trade, capital will be attracted or repelled by fluctuations in the rate of profit; but it is by no means clear that we can infer that a general rise or fall of profit will have the same effect upon accumulation generally. For such reasons, as I take it, an investigation of the laws of distribution would require us to go beyond the abstractions about 'supply and demand,' however appropriate they may be to immediate oscillations or relatively superficial changes. No such short cut is possible to a real sociological result. 'To follow out all the causes or conditions involved would be,' as Professor Taussig says,[1] 'to write a book not only on distribution but on social philosophy at large.' Mill, and especially Cairnes, were sensible of the need of taking a wider set of considerations. Still no satisfactory conclusion could be reached so long as it was virtually attempted to solve the problem by bringing it under the market formula, instead of admitting that the play of market is itself determined by the structure behind the market. You have really assumed an abnormally simple structure, and erroneously suppose that you have avoided the necessity of considering the structure at all. The wage-fund controversy brought out the inadequacy of the method. One result has

[1] Taussig, p. 122.

perhaps been to encourage some writers to fall back into simple empiricism; to assume that because the supposed laws were not rightly stated there are no laws at all; that the justice of the peace can after all fix wages arbitrarily; and that political economy should shrink back to be 'political arithmetic,' or a mere collection of statistics. The more desirable method, one must hope, would be to assign the proper sphere to the old method, and incorporate the sound elements in a wider system.

VII. SOCIALISM

Meanwhile, the over-confidence of the economists only encouraged Socialists to revolt against the whole doctrine. It might be a true account of actual facts; but, if so, demonstrated that the existing social order was an abomination and a systematic exploitation of the poor by the rich. The 'iron necessity' was a necessity imposed by human law—not, that is, a legitimate development of social order, but something imposed by force and fraud. In some directions Mill sympathised with such doctrines. He professed to be in some sense a 'Socialist,' though he was not acquainted with some of the works published during his lifetime. He makes no reference to Marx or Lassalle and other German writers. Possibly a study of their writings might have led to modifications of his teaching. To him the name suggested Owen, Fourier, St. Simon, or his friend Louis Blanc.[1] Socialism, as understood by

[1] See the posthumous articles in the *Fortnightly Review* for February, March, and April 1879. They were obviously imperfect, and scarcely justified publication.

the early leaders, commended itself to Mill, because it proposed the formation of voluntary communities, like Fourier's Phalansteries or Owen's New Harmony. They are capable of being tried on a moderate scale, with no risk to any one but the triers.[1] They involve simply social experiments which could only injure those who tried them. But a different view was showing itself. Cairnes, commenting upon his master's so-called Socialism, says that the name now implies the direct interference of the state for the instant realisation of 'ideal schemes.'[2] He objects to this, and therefore, by anticipation, to 'state Socialism.' Here Mill's position is ambiguous. In the first place, while agreeing with the aims of the Socialists, he 'utterly dissents from the most conspicuous and vehement part of their teaching, their declamations against competition.'[3] 'Where competition is not,' he adds, 'monopoly is'; and monopoly means 'the taxation of the industrious for the support of indolence, if not of plunder.' Competition raises wages, if the supply of labourers is limited, and can never lower them, unless the supply is excessive. As Cobden is reported to have said, the real question is simply whether two masters are running after one man, or two men after one master. No one could speak more emphatically or forcibly upon this point, nor does he seem to have ever abandoned it. Both Mill and his disciples saw the only solution in a different direction. Co-operation is their panacea; and they are never tired of appealing to the cases of its successful operation,

[1] *Political Economy*, p. 133 (bk. ii. ch. i. § 4).
[2] *Leading Principles*, p. 316.
[3] *Political Economy*, p. 476 (bk. iv. ch. vii. § 7).

beginning with M. Leclaire's experiment in France and the Rochdale pioneers in England. The pith of the doctrine was already given in the famous chapter[1] upon 'the probable futurity of the labouring class' due to Mrs. Mill's influence. His hope for them lay in co-operation, and later editions only differed from the first by recording new experiments. Cairnes deduces the same conclusion from his wage-fund. The labourer can only improve by ceasing to be a 'mere labourer'; profits must 'reinforce' the wage-fund; co-operation shows how this is to be done, and 'constitutes the one and only solution of our present problem.'[2] Thornton reaches the same conclusion, co-operation giving the only compromise which can end the internecine contest. He can only express his feelings in poetry, and his last chapter upon 'labour's Utopia' is written with credit-able skill in the difficult *terza rima*. Fawcett fully shared this enthusiasm; and the reason is sufficiently obvious. Co-operation, in their sense, means simply the joint effort of independent individuals. Competition is assumed to remain in full force. All combinations, as Mill says of trades-unions, must be voluntary. That is an 'indispensable condition of tolerating them.'[3] The member of a co-operative society is as free to join or to leave as the shareholder in any commercial company. The societies compete with each other and with capi-talists at every point. 'Supply and demand' regulate

[1] *Political Economy*, p. 476 (bk. iv. ch. vii.). Mill refers to Babbage's *Economy of Machinery and Manufacturers* for an incidental reference to applications of profit-sharing in Cornish mines, and a suggestion that it would be applicable elsewhere. Babbage gives little more than a passing suggestion.
[2] *Leading Principles*, pp. 339, 344.
[3] *Political Economy*, p. 566 (bk. v. ch. x. § 5).

every part of their transactions. The motive for joining is simply the desire of each member to invest his savings, and therefore the *vis medicatrix* is duly stimulated. Each man can thrive better by working in concert; but he resigns none of his rights as an individual. He has not enlisted in an army bound by discipline, but has joined in a voluntary expedition.

So far we have what seems to be the logical and con-sistent result of the individualist view. But Mill, though he remains an 'individualist' philosophically, is also led to conclusions very far from the ordinary individualist theory. The last part of his treatise is devoted to a discussion of the limits of government interference. He urges energetically that there should be some space in human 'existence entrenched round and sacred from authoritative intrusion,'[1] a doctrine inherited from his teachers and eloquently expanded in his *Liberty*. It marks the point of transition from his economic to his ethical and political teaching. After repeating the ordinary arguments against excessive interference by way of protection, usury laws and the like, he states as a general principle that the burden of proof is on the advocates of interference, and that 'letting alone should be the general practice.'[2] All coercion, as Bentham had said, is an evil, but, in certain cases, it is the least possible evil; and Mill, as becomes an empiricist, declining to lay down an absolute rule, only asks what are the particular cases in which the evil is overbalanced by the good of interference. But, here, if we consider the list of exceptions, we must admit that the general

[1] *Political Economy*, p. 569 (bk. v. ch. xi. § 2).
[2] *Ibid.* p. 573 (bk. v. ch. xi. § 7).

principle is remarkably flexible. Some cases have been already noticed. Mill not only allowed but strongly advocated a national system of education.[1] He approved a great national scheme of emigration[2] and a scheme for home colonisation, and this expressly with a view to lifting the poor, not gradually but immediately into a higher level of comfort. He held that laws in restraint of imprudent marriage were not wrong in principle, though they might be inexpedient under many or most circumstances. He approved of measures tend-ing to equalisation of wealth. He proposed that the right of bequest should be limited by forbidding any one to acquire more than a certain sum, and so counteracting the tendency to the accumulation of large fortunes.[3] He held that government should take measures for alleviating the sufferings of labourers displaced by new inventions or the excessive change of 'circulating' into 'fixed capital.'[4] He not only approved of measures for form-ing a peasant-proprietary, but, in his last years, became president of an association for altering the whole system of land tenure. He thought that government should retain a property in canals and railways, though the working should be leased to private companies. He approved, as I have said, of the poor-law in its new form. The factory legislation alone was still uncongenial to his principles, though on moral grounds he accepts the protection of children. Even in this direction he inci-dentally makes a remarkable concession. A point to

[1] He qualifies this to some extent in the *Liberty*. The state should enforce education and pay for it, but not provide schools. The line is hard to draw.
[2] See especially *Political Economy*, p. 585 (bk. v. ch. xi. § 14).
[3] *Political Economy*, p. 138 (bk. ii. ch. ii. § 4).
[4] *Ibid.* p. 61 (bk. i. ch. vi. § 3).

which political economists had not, he thinks, sufficiently attended is illustrated by the case of the 'Nine Hours Bill.'[1] Assuming, though only for the sake of argu-ment, that a reduction of labour hours from ten to nine would be to the advantage of the workmen, should the law, he asks, interfere to enforce reduction? The do-nothing party would reply, No; because if beneficial, the workmen would adopt the rule spontaneously. This answer, says Mill, is inconclusive. The interest of the individual would be opposed to the interest of the 'class collectively.' Competition might enforce the longer hours; and thus classes may need the assistance of the law 'to give effect to their deliberate collective opinion of their own interest.' Here again Mill seems to be admitting as an 'exception' a principle which goes much further than he observed. He is mainly interested by the ethical problem, Is it ever right to force a man to act against his own wishes in a matter primarily concern-ing himself alone? He concludes that it may be right, because each man may wish for a rule on condition that every one else obeys it. In that case, the law only gives effect to the universal desire. But the argument really involves an exception to the beneficent action of com-petition. The case is one in which, upon his assumptions, free competition of individuals may lead to degeneration instead of a better development. In such cases, it is possible that association, enforced by law, may lead to benefits unattainable by the independent units. This admission would go far in the Socialist direction. It would justify the principle of 'collective bargaining' to sanction the collective interests. In the same way his

[1] *Political Economy*, p. 581 (bk. v. ch. xi. § 12).

justification of the factory acts in the case of children leads beyond the moral to economic grounds. Mill's view, so far as he goes, would fall in with the opinion that there was here a necessary conflict between Christian morality and political economy; or the admission that economic loss must be incurred for moral considerations. But, in the long run, the two views coincide; for practices which stint and degrade the breed must be ultimately fatal to economic efficiency. As was often said at the time, to forbid interference for economic reasons was to suppose that the country could only flourish by treating children as it might conceivably be necessary to treat them under stress of some deadly and imminent peril. When economists looked beyond the instantaneous advantage of the market, and remembered that children were made of flesh and blood, it was obvious that on the purest economic grounds, a system which implied the degradation of the labourer must be in the end pernicious to every interest. In this case, therefore, the interference of the law was desirable from the economic as well as from the moral point of view.

Nobody, of course, would have admitted this more cordially than Mill, and the admission would imply that we must here look beyond mere 'supply and demand' or individual competition. When we sum up these admissions, it appears that Mill was well on the way to state Socialism. Lange, the historian of materialism, praises him warmly upon this ground.[1] Lange is enthusiastic about Mill's *Liberty*, as well as about his *Political Economy*. He praises the *Economy* on the ground that

[1] J. S. Mill's *Ansichten über die Sociale Frage*, etc. (1866).

Mill's great aim is to humanise the science; and, especially, that in the various proposals which I have noticed Mill desires an active interference of government towards raising the moral level of society. Mill, in short, would have sympathised, had he come to know it, with the Socialism of the Chair, which was beginning at the time of his death to make a mark in Germany. Lange's appreciation was, I think, in great part correct; and suggests the question, How or how far was Mill consistent? Could a system essentially based upon Malthus and Ricardo be reconciled with modern Socialism?

Mill once more was an individualist in the philosophical sense. He assumes society to be formed of a number of independent units, bound together by laws enforced by 'sanctions.' The fundamental laws should be just; and justice presupposes equality; equality, at at least in this sense, that the position of each unit should depend upon his own qualities, and not upon mere outward accidents. In his articles upon Socialism Mill declared most emphatically that in the present state of society any idea of such justice was 'manifestly chimerical';[1] and that the main conditions of success were first birth, and secondly accident. In his first edition his discussion of Socialism ends by justifying 'private property.' The best scheme is that which lets every man's share of the produce depend on his own exertions. He complains, however, that the principle has 'never yet had a fair trial in any country.' Inequalities have been created and aggravated by the law.[2] This passage disappeared when he rewrote his views of Socialism.

[1] *Fortnightly Review* for February 1879.
[2] *Political Economy* (first edition) i. 252-53.

From the first, however, he asserts a principle for which he gives the chief credit to his wife.[1] Laws of production, he says, are 'real laws of nature'; methods of distribution depend on the human will, or, as he says in the *Political Economy*, 'the distribution of wealth depends on the laws and customs of society.'[2] Can the laws secure a just distribution?

Here, then, is a critical problem. As a Utilitarian he would reply that government should make fair rules for the general relations of individuals, and trust to the best man winning in an open competition. Mill's point of difference from the Socialists was precisely that he believed in competition to the last, and was so far a thorough 'individualist.' Yet, as a matter of fact, vast inequalities of wealth and power had developed, and exiled justice from the world—if, indeed, justice had ever existed there. So far as this could be attributed to laws, unjust because made by force and fraud, the remedy might lie in reforming the laws. That case was exemplified by land. 'Landed property,' he says, in Europe, derives 'its origin from force.'[3] English land-laws were first designed 'to prop up a ruling class.'[4] By force, in fact, the landowners had secured the best places at Malthus's feast, and were enabled to benefit by, without contributing to, the growth of the national wealth. Rent, says Cairnes, is 'a fund ever growing, even while its proprietors sleep.'[5] Mill, of course, admitted that part of rent is due to the application of

[1] *Autobiography*, p. 246.
[2] *Political Economy*, p. 123 (bk. ii. ch. i. § 1).
[3] *Dissertations*, iv. 59.   [4] *Ibid.* iv. 240.
[5] *Leading Principles*, p. 333.

capital; and he does not propose to confiscate the wealth of the actual proprietors who had acquired their rights fairly under the existing system. But he is convinced that land differs radically from movable property. Capital diminishes in value, as society advances; 'land alone . . . has the privilege of steadily rising in value from natural causes.'[1] Hence we have the famous proposal of taking the 'unearned increment.'[2] If the landowner was dissatisfied, he should be paid the selling price of the day. A good many landlords may regret that they had not this offer at the time that it was proposed (1873). Thus land was to be nationalised; the state was to become the national landlord, as in India,[3] and at any rate nothing was to be done by which more land could get into private hands. He seems, indeed, still to believe in a peasant-proprietary,[4] but does not ask how far the doctrine is compatible with nationalisation.

If, then, the forcible acquisition of land by its first owners be still a taint upon the existing title, is property in other wealth altogether just? Mill admits in his discussion of Thornton's book that something is to be said against capitalists. 'Movable property,' indeed, has, on the whole, a purer 'origin than landed property.' It represents industry, not simply force. There has, indeed, been a good deal of fraud, and many practices at which 'a person of delicate conscience' might scruple.[5] This is a gentle adumbration of the view of some recent

[1] *Dissertations*, iv. 263.   [2] *Ibid.* iv. 285.
[3] *Ibid.* iv. 274.   [4] *Ibid.* iv. 269.
[5] *Ibid.* iv. 60. The whole doctrine that the sanctity of property depends upon the mode of acquisition by remote proprietors seems to be scarcely reconcilable with sound Utilitarianism.

Socialists. Is not capital, they would say, precisely the product of fraud, and stained through and through by cheating? If Mill was far from the doctrine of Marx, and did not hold that capital was a mere name for the process of exploitation, he admitted at least that there was no such thing as justice in the actual industrial order. Wealth clearly represents something very different from a reward given in proportion to industry. In the first place, it is inherited, and Mill, as I have said, proposed therefore to limit inheritances; and, in the next place, nobody can suppose that a poor man who grows rich, even by purely honourable means, gets a prize proportioned to his virtue or to his utility; while, finally, the poor man certainly does not start on equal terms with his richer rival. He that hath not may not lose that which he hath; but he has small chances of climbing the ladder, and if he climbs, his success means devotion to his private interest.[1] Mill's abandonment of the wage-fund, again, involved the acceptance of the 'tacit conspiracy.' The poverty of the mass is not due to a 'law of nature'; and therefore it is due, partly at least, to the combination of capitalists, which enables them to bring their power to bear in keeping down the rate of wages to an indefinite extent.

The social injustice against which he protests exists under a system in which the laws are substantially equal. They no longer recognise class distinctions explicitly; they have ceased to forbid combinations or to fix the rate

[1] After giving Adam Smith's famous account of the causes of the varying rates of wages, Mill points out 'a class of considerations' too much neglected by his predecessors: cases, namely, in which unskilled labourers are insufficiently paid; and remarks that there is almost a 'hereditary distinction of caste.'—*Political Economy*, p. 238 (bk. ii. ch. xiv. § 2).

of wages; the paternal theory of government is gone, as he says, for ever, and the old relation of protector and protected supplanted by a system of equality before the law.[1] And yet monstrous inequalities and therefore injustices remain. What is the inference? Here we have the real inconsistency or, at least, failure to reconcile completely two diverging principles. Mill and all his disciples place their hopes in 'co-operation.' Co-operation can, they think, be reconciled with the 'liberty' which they regarded both as desirable in itself and as equivalent to the absence of law. Co-operation, on this showing, implies first absolute freedom to join or to leave the co-operative body. The individual joins with other individuals, but does not sacrifice his individuality. The relation is still, so to speak, 'external,' and the various associations compete with each other as fully and unreservedly as the component individuals. And yet there is an obvious difficulty. Co-operation must involve a loss of 'liberty,' though the loss may be compensated. If I co-operate, I undertake obligations, enforcible by law, though not originally imposed by law. Mill throws out the conjecture that the choice between Socialism and individualism will 'depend mainly on one consideration, viz., which of the two systems is consistent with the greatest amount of human liberty and spontaneity.'[2] Now all association limits action in fact. When great companies take up an industrial function of any kind, they put a stress upon the individual, not necessarily the less forcible because not legally imposed. A great railway, for example, soon

[1] *Political Economy*, p. 456 (bk. iv. ch. vii. § 1).
[2] *Ibid.* p. 129 (bk. ii. ch. i. § 3).

destroys other private enterprises, and makes itself practically necessary. It is equally governed by a body in which most individual shareholders exercise as little influence as though they were appointed by the state. As the industrial machinery, human or material, is developed, it becomes as much a part of social order as if it were created by the legislature. The point upon which Mill insists, that all associations must be 'voluntary,' then becomes insignificant. I may be legally at liberty to stand aside; but, in fact, they become imperative conditions of life. That is to say, that the distinction drawn by the old individualism between the state institutions and those created by private action ceases to have the old significance. When a society once develops an elaborate and complex structure, it becomes almost pedantic to draw a profound distinction between a system which is practically indispensable and one which is legally imperative.

I will not inquire further whether Mill's position could be made logically coherent. One thing is pretty clear. If his views had been actually adopted; if the state educated, nationalised the land, supported the poor, restrained marriage, regulated labour where individual competition failed, and used its power to equalise wealth, it would very soon adopt state Socialism, and lose sight of Mill's reservations. Mill, as I believe, had been quite right when he insisted on the vast importance of stimulating the sense of individual responsibility. That is, and must always be, one essential moment of the argument. His misfortune was, that having absorbed an absolute system in his youth, and accepting its claims to scientific validity, he was unable when he saw its defects

to see the true line (if any one yet sees the true line) of conciliation. His doctrine, therefore, contained fragments of opposite and inconsistent dogmas. While fancying that he was developing the individualist theories, he adopted not only Socialism, but even a version of Socialism open to the objections on which he sometimes forcibly insisted. Mill and the Socialist are both individualists; only the Socialist makes right precede fact, and Mill would make fact precede right. Every individual, says the Socialist, has a right to support; the consequences of granting the right must be left to Providence. This, says Mill following Malthus, would be fatal, because the individual would have no motive to support himself. He must only have such a right as implies personal responsibility. But then, as facts also show, many individuals may be unable to support themselves even if they wish it, and their responsibility becomes a mockery. If we enforce duties on all, must we not make the duty possible? Must not every one be so trained and so placed that work will be sure of reward? There is the problem, which he sees and feels, though his answer seems to imply a doubtful shifting between antagonistic theories.

VIII. LOGICAL METHOD

I must glance finally at the relation of Mill's method to his general principles. In an early essay[1] he declares that the method must be '*a priori*,' that is, as he

[1] 'On the Definition of Political Economy, and on the Method of Investigation proper to it.' Reprinted in *Unsettled Questions*, and quoted in the *Logic*, p. 388 (bk. vi. ch. ix. § 3).

explains, 'reasoning from an assumed hypothesis.'[1] In the *Logic* it is treated as a case of the 'direct deductive method.' This involves an important point in his system. He had derived from Comte, as he tells us,[2] only one 'leading conception' of a purely logical kind, the conception, namely, of the 'historical' or 'inverse deductive method.' This method, implied in Comte's sociology, starts, as Mill says, from the 'collation of specific experience.' Now Mill agrees that this 'historical' method was appropriate to sociology in general. He agrees, too, with Comte that it was not the method used by economists. But, whereas Comte had inferred that political economy must for that reason be a sham science,[3] Mill holds that economists were justified in using a different method. Comte, he thought, had failed to see that in certain cases the method of 'direct deduction' was applicable to sociological inquiry. One such case, though he will not undertake to decide what other instances there may be, is political economy.[4] He decides that the difficulties, regarded by Comte as insuperable, may be overcome. His early account is still valid; and he therefore explicitly rejects the 'historical' method.

I confess that the use of these technical phrases appears to me to be rather magniloquent, and to lead to some confusion. Setting them aside, Mill's view may be briefly stated. He argues, in the first place, that we cannot apply the ordinary method of experiment

[1] *Unsettled Questions*, p. 143.   [2] *Autobiography*, p. 210.
[3] See, *e.g.*, Comte's *Philosophie Positive*, iv. 266–78. The fourth volume of Comte disappointed Mill, as he says; and this probably explains one reason.
[4] *Logic*, p. 590 (bk. vi. ch. ix. § 4).

to economic problems. To settle by experience whether protection was good or bad, we should have to find two nations agreeing in everything except their tariffs; and that, of course, if not impossible, is exceedingly difficult.[1] It follows that if there be a true science of political economy, it must have a different method. We might indeed adopt Comte's answer: 'There is no such science'; a view for which there is much to be said. Mill, however, being confident that the science existed had to justify its methods. Political economy, he says, considers man solely as a wealth-desiring being; it predicts the 'phenomena of the social state' which take place in consequence; and makes abstraction of every other motive except the laziness or the desire of present enjoyment which 'antagonise' the desire of wealth. Hence it deduces various laws, though, as a fact, there is scarcely any action of a man's life in which other desires are not operative. Political economy still holds true wherever the desire of wealth is the main end. 'Other cases may be regarded as affected by disturbing causes'—comparable, of course, to the inevitable 'friction'—and it is only on account of them that we have an 'element of uncertainty' in political economy. Otherwise it is a demonstrable science, presupposing an 'arbitrary definition' of a man as geometry presupposes an 'arbitrary definition' of a straight line.'[2]

The relation of this doctrine to Mill's general views on logic is clear, but suggests some obvious criticisms. 'Desire for wealth,' for example, is not a simple but a highly complex desire, involving in different ways every

[1] *Unsettled Questions*, p. 148.
[2] *Ibid.* pp. 137–50.

human passion.[1] To argue from it, as though its definition were as unequivocal as that of a straight line, is at least audacious. Mill, no doubt, means to express an undeniable truth. Industry, in general, implies desire for wealth, and the whole mechanism supposes that men prefer a guinea to a pound. The fact is clear enough, and if proof be required can be proved by observation. We must again admit that whatever psychological theorem is implied in the fact must be assumed as true. But it does not follow that because we assume the 'desire for wealth' we can deduce the phenomena from that assumption. That inference would confound different things. If we were accounting for the actions of an individual, we might adopt the method. In some actions a man is guided by love of money, and in others by love of his neighbour. We may 'deduce' his action in his counting-house from his love of money, and consider an occasional fit of benevolence as a mere 'disturbing cause' to be neglected in general or treated as mere 'friction.' A similar principle might be applied to political economy if we could regard it as the theory of particular classes of actions. But we have to consider other circumstances to reach any general and tenable theory. We have to consider the whole social structure, the existence of a market and all that it implies, and the division of society into classes and their complex relations: the distribution of functions among them and the creation of the settled order which alone makes commerce possible. We cannot argue to the action without understanding the structure of which the agent is a constituent part,

[1] Mill makes this remark himself in writing to Comte about phrenology.

and which determines all the details of his action. The building up of society implies the influence not of any single desire, but of all the desires, modes of thought, and affections of human beings. If, therefore, a comprehension of existing institutions be necessary to political economy, the deductive method is clearly unequal to the task which he, partly following Comte, regards as implied in 'sociology' generally. To deduce, not the social structure at large, but any social organ, from such an abstraction is hopeless, because every organ is affected through and through by its dependence upon other organs. Mill virtually supposes that because the particular function can be understood by abstracting from accidental influences, the organ of which it is a function can be understood by abstracting from its essential relations to the organism.

Here, in fact, is the error which I take to be implied in Mill's individualism. Given the social structure as it is, you may fairly make some such abstraction as the postulates. You may consider large classes of actions, exchange of wealth, and all the normal play of commercial forces, as corresponding to the rather vague 'desire for wealth,' and ask how an individual or a number of individuals will act when under the influence of that dominant motive. That is legitimate, and applies to what is called 'pure political economy' —the relatively superficial study of the actual working of the machinery without considering how the machinery came to have its actual structure. But directly you get beyond this, to problems involving organic change, you get to 'sociology,' and can only proceed—if progress be possible—by the 'historical method,' or, in other words, by studying the growth of the institutions of which we form a part, and of which we may be considered as the product. This again means that the general conception of the Utilitarians, which recognises nothing but the individual as an ultimate unit, though capable of combining and grouping in various ways, omits one essential element in the problem. It regards all social structures as on the same plane, temporary and indefinitely alterable arrangements; and involves a neglect of the historical or general point of view which is essential not only to an understanding of society, but also of the individuals whose whole nature and character is moulded by it. I have tried to show the results upon the legal and political conceptions of Mill's teachers. We now see how the conception of political economy as a 'deductive' or *a priori* science naturally misled the school. When they mistook their rough generalisations for definitive science, they brought discredit upon the theory, and played into the hands of their enemies, the sentimentalists, who, finding that the science was not infallible, resolved to trust to instincts and defy 'laws of nature' in general. Read as common-sense considerations upon social questions, the writings of Mill and his followers were generally to the point and often conclusive. When read as scientific statements, they fail from their obvious inadequacy, and the vague terminology which takes the airs of clearly defined conceptions. Yet it is impossible to conclude without noticing two admirable characteristics of Mill and his disciples. The first is the deep and thorough conviction that the elevation of the poorer classes is the main end of

all social inquiries. The second and the rarer is the resolution to speak the plain truth, and to denounce all sophists who, professing the same end, would reach it by illusory means. Mill's sympathies never blinded him to the duty of telling the whole truth as he saw it.

CHAPTER IV

POLITICS AND ETHICS

I. MILL'S PROBLEM

In the *Political Economy* Mill had touched upon certain ethical and political questions. These are explicitly treated in a later group of works. The first and most important was the essay upon *Liberty* (1859). I have already spoken of the elaborate composition of this, his most carefully written treatise.[1] The book, welcomed by many even of his opponents, contains also the clearest statement of his most characteristic doctrine. The treatises on *Representative Government* (1861), upon the *Subjection of Women* (written at the same time, but not published till 1869), and upon *Utilitarianism* (in *Fraser's Magazine*, 1861, and as a book in 1863), are closely connected with the *Liberty*, and together give what may

---

[1] *Autobiography*, p. 50. The most elaborate attack upon the *Liberty* is contained in *Liberty, Equality, Fraternity* (1873), by my brother, Sir James FitzJames Stephen, in whose life I have given an account of the book. I shall not here go into the controversy. I am content to say that, though I cannot agree with my brother, I think that he strikes forcibly at some weak points in Mill's scheme. The most remarkable point is that the book is substantially a criticism of Mill's from the older Utilitarian point of view. It shows, therefore, how Mill diverged from Bentham.

be called his theory of conduct.[1] I shall try to bring out their leading principles.

The *Liberty*, says Mill, could have no claim to originality except in so far as thoughts which are already common property receive a special impress when uttered by a thoughtful mind. Hymns to liberty, indeed, have been sung so long and so persistently that the subject ought to have been exhausted. The admission that liberty can be in any case an evil is generally evaded by a device of touching simplicity. Liberty, when bad, is not called liberty. 'Licence, they mean,' as Milton puts it, 'when they cry liberty.' Bentham exposes the sophistry very neatly as a case of 'sham-distinctions' in the book of 'Fallacies.'[2]

The general sentiment is perfectly intelligible from the Jacobin point of view. At a time when legislators were supposed to have created constitutions, and priests to have invented religions, history was taken as a record of the struggle of mankind against fraud and force. War is simply murder on a large scale, and government force organised to support tyrants. All political evils can be attributed to kings, and superstition to priests, without blaming subjects for slavishness and stupidity. Such language took the tone of a new gospel during the great revolutionary movements of the eighteenth century. Men who were sweeping away the effete institutions upheld by privileged classes assumed 'Liberty' to be an absolute and ultimate principle. The Utilitarians, though political allies, were opposed in theory to this

---

[1] I refer for the *Liberty* and the *Representative Government* to the People's Editions of 1867.

[2] *Works*, ii. 451.

method of argument. Liberty, like everything else, must be judged by its effects upon happiness. Society, according to them, is held together by the sovereign. His existence, therefore, is essentially necessary, and his power almost unlimited. The greater was the importance of deciding when and where it should be used. Bentham and James Mill assumed that all ends would be secured by making the sovereign the servant of the people, and therefore certain to aim at the greatest happiness. They reached the same conclusions, therefore, as those who reached them by a rather shorter cut, and their doctrine differed little in its absolute and *a priori* tendency. Thorough democracy would give the panacea. J. S. Mill had become heretical. I have noticed in his life how he had been alarmed by the brutality and ignorance of the lowest classes, and had come to doubt whether 'liberty,' as understood by his masters, would not mean the despotic rule of the ignorant. The doubts which he felt were shared by many who had set out with the same political creed.

Here we come once more to the essentially false position in which the philosophical radicals found themselves. The means which they heartily approved led to ends which they entirely repudiated. They not only approved, but were most active in advocating, the adoption of democratic measures. They demanded, in the name of liberty, that men should have a share in making the laws by which they were bound. The responsibility of rulers was, according to James Mill, the one real principle of politics; and it followed that, to use the sacred phrase, the 'sinister interests' which distract them should be destroyed. The legislation

which followed the Reform Bill gave an approximate sanction to their doctrine. The abolition of rotten-boroughs destroyed the sinister interest of the land-owners; the reform of municipalities, the sinister interest of the self-elected corporations; the new poor-law, the sinister interest of the parish vestries; and the ecclesiastical reforms showed that great prelates and ancient cathedrals were not too sacred to be remodelled and made responsible. The process inevitably smoothed the way for centralisation. The state, one may say, was beginning to come to life. The powers which, in a centralised government, are exercised by an administrative hierarchy, had been treated under the category of private property. To introduce responsibility was to remove the obstacles to uniform machinery. Vigorous action by a central authority had been impossible so long as power had been parcelled out among a number of different centres, each regarding its privileges as invested with all the sanctity of private property. The duke, who claimed that he 'might do as he would with his own'—including his boroughs—had surrendered that part of his property to the new voters. They enjoyed their rights not as a personal attribute, but in virtue of satisfying some uniform condition. For the time, indeed, the condition included, not simply a ripe age and masculine sex, but 'ten-pound householdership.' Power held by men as members of a class is, at any rate, no longer private property, but something belonging to the class in general, and naturally used in the interests of the class collectively. The legislature could make general rules where it used rather to confirm a set of distinct bargains made with each proprietor

of ultimate authority. So far, the generalising and centralising process was both inevitable and approved by the Utilitarians. Nor could they, as prominent advocates of codification and law-reform generally, object to the increased vigour of legislation no longer trammelled by the multitude of little semi-independent centres. But a further implication often escaped their notice. 'Liberty' is increased by destroying privilege in the sense that the individual acquires more influence upon the laws that bind him. But it does not follow that he will be 'freer' in the sense of having fewer laws to bind him. The contrary was the case. The objection to the privileges was precisely that the possessors retained them without discharging the correlative functions. The nobles and the corporations had not been too active, but too indolent. They had left things undone, or left them to be done after a haphazard fashion by individual energy. The much-lauded 'self-government' implied an absence of government, or precisely the state of things which was no longer possible when the old privileges were upset. The newly organised municipalities had to undertake duties which had been neglected by the close corporations, and others which had been clumsily discharged by individuals. The result was that the philosophical radicals found that they were creating a Frankenstein. They were not limiting the sphere of government in general, only giving power to a new class which would in many ways use it more energetically. The difference came out in the economic matters where the doctrine of non-interference had been most actively preached. The Chartists and their allies claimed their 'rights' as indisputable possessions, whatever might be

the consequences. To the Utilitarians this meant that the Chartists were prepared in the name of *a priori* principles to attack the most necessary institutions, and fly in the face of 'laws of nature.' The old system had tended to keep the poor man down. The Chartist system would help him to plunder the rich. The right principle was to leave everything to 'supply and demand.' As the contrast became clearer, some of the philosophical radicals subsided into Whiggism, and others sank into actual Tories. Mill remained faithful, but with modified views. He had seen in the hostility of the lower classes to sound economy an illustration of the ignorance, selfishness, and brutality of the still uneducated mass.[1] But he drew a moral of his own. The impression made upon him by Tocqueville's *Democracy in America* is characteristic. That remarkable book led him to aim at a philosophical view of the whole question. It was an impartial study of the whole question of the social and political tendencies summed up in the phrase, 'democracy.' The general result was to open Mill's eyes to both the good and evil sides of democracy, to regard democracy in some shape as inevitable instead of making it a religion or denouncing it as diabolical; and to consider how the evils might be corrected while free play might be allowed to the beneficial tendencies. It enlightened him, he says, more especially on the great question of centralisation, and freed him from the 'unreasoning prejudices' which led some of the radicals to oppose even such measures as the new Poor Law.[2] So much may indicate Mill's general attitude; and, if his

[1] *Autobiography*, p. 231.
[2] *Ibid.* pp. 191-95.

conclusions were questionable, the main purpose was so far eminently philosophical.

Mill begins his *Liberty* by insisting upon the danger to which his attention had been roused by the course of events. The conflict between liberty and authority led to the demand that rulers should become responsible to their subjects ; and when this result was secured, a new evil appeared. The tyranny of the majority might supplant the tyranny of rulers ; and, if less formidable politically, might be even worse spiritually. 'Social tyranny' may be more penetrative than political, and enslave the soul itself.[1] In England the 'yoke of law' may be lighter, but the 'yoke of opinion' is perhaps heavier than elsewhere in Europe. When the masses have learned their power, they will probably be as tyrannical in legislation as in public opinion.[2] The purpose of his essay is to assert 'one very simple principle' by which this tendency may be restrained. That principle is (briefly) that the sole end which warrants interference with individual action is 'self-protection.' He will argue not from 'abstract rights,' but from 'utility' understood in its largest sense, and corresponding 'to the interests of a man as a progressive being.'

II. INTELLECTUAL LIBERTY

The principle thus formulated is applicable both in the sphere of speculation and in the sphere of conduct. Mill first considers 'liberty of thought and discussion.' He has here the advantage of starting from a generally admitted principle. Every one now admits, in words at

[1] *Liberty* (People's Edition, 1867), p. 3.   [2] *Ibid.* p. 5.

least, the doctrine of toleration. Mill might have adduced a catena of authorities beginning with the seventeenth century writers who, having themselves suffered persecution, were slowly perceiving that persecution even of error was objectionable. It is a proof of his ability that he could give fresh interest to so old a topic. In the previous generation indeed it had still been a practical question. The early Utilitarians had to attack the disqualifications imposed upon dissenters, and had remonstrated against the persecution of Carlile. That incident had started Mill's literary career. Moreover, as he points out, the prosecutions of Pooley, Truelove, and Mr. Holyoake showed that the old spirit was not extinct in 1857.[1] Still, these were but 'rags and remnants of persecution.' In denouncing them Mill was going with the tide. The ground upon which he plants his argument is more significant. The older writers had chiefly insisted upon the question of right. It cannot be just to punish a man for acting rightly, and it must surely be right for me to speak what I conscientiously believe to be true. One of James Mill's articles in the *Westminster* took this ground. Samuel Bailey had argued that a man cannot be responsible to men for his beliefs, inasmuch as they are beyond his own control. He may be foolish, but he cannot be immoral—a thesis which James Mill defended against certain theological opponents.[2] J. S. Mill, taking the ground of 'utility,' is led to wider considerations. He argues in substance that the suppression of opinions or of their free utterance

[1] *Liberty*, 17 *n.* The Bradlaugh case showed that the old spirit was not extinct twenty-five years later.
[2] See Bain's *James Mill*, p. 304.

is always opposed to the most vital interests of society. Hence the question as to liberty of thought connects itself with the whole question as to liberty of conduct. It comes under his general principle as to the rightful provinces of collective and individual action. His general conclusion upon freedom of dismission is summed up in four propositions.[1] The opinions suppressed may, in the first place, be true. To deny that possibility is to assume infallibility. Secondly, if not wholly, they may be partly, true ; and to suppress them is to prevent necessary corrections of the accepted beliefs. Thirdly, even a true opinion which refuses to be tested by controversy will be imperfectly understood. And fourthly, an opinion so held will become a dead formula, and only 'cumber the ground,' preventing the growth of real and heartfelt convictions.

The general validity of the arguments is unimpeachable, and the vigour of statement deserves all commendation. Mill puts victoriously the case for the entire freedom of thought and discussion. The real generosity of sentiment, and the obvious sincerity which comes from preaching what he had practised, gives new force to well-worn topics. The interest of the race not only requires the fullest possible liberty to form and to communicate our own opinions, but rather makes the practice a duty. Though Mill gives the essential reasons, his presentation of the case has significant peculiarities. Even if an opinion be true, he says, it ought to be open to discussion. He proceeds to urge the more doubtful point, that contradiction, even when the truth is contradicted, is desirable in itself. Free discussion not only destroys

[1] *Liberty*, pp. 30, 31.

error, but invigorates truth. It preserves a wholesome intellectual atmosphere, which kills the weeds and stimulates the healthy growths. In mathematical reasoning, indeed, the evidence is all on one side. There are no objections, and no answers to objections. But as soon as we reach any question of the truths even of physical, and still more of the moral, sciences, truth must be attained by balancing 'two sets of conflicting reasons.'[1] The doctrine, true or false, which is not contradicted, comes to be held as a 'dead belief.' An objector is supposed to observe that on this showing, the existence of error is necessary to the vitality of truth, and that a belief must perish just because it is unanimously accepted. Mill 'affirms no such thing.' He admits 'that the stock of accepted truths must increase.' But the growth of unanimity, though 'inevitable and indispensable,' has its drawbacks. It would be desirable to encourage contradiction even by artificial contrivances. The Socratic dialectics and the school disputations more or less supplied a want which we have now no means of satisfying.[2] By systematic discussion of first principles, men are forced to understand the full bearing and the true grounds of their professed beliefs. This doctrine is illustrated, and no doubt was derived in part from the early discussions in which Mill had trained his logical powers. It suggests a valuable mode of mental

[1] *Liberty*, p. 21. The excellent Abraham Tucker remarks that if he met 'a person of credit, candour, and understanding,' who denied that two and two made four, he would give him a hearing.—*Light of Nature* (1834), p. 125.
[2] *Liberty*, pp. 25, 26. 'To become properly acquainted with a truth,' says Novalis (quoted in Carlyle's essay upon him), 'we must first have disbelieved and disputed against it.' But Novalis also observed that 'my faith gains infinitely the moment I see it shared by some one else.'

discipline; but as a statement of the conditions of belief, it seems to confuse the accident with the essence. The bare fact of sincere contradiction surely tends to weaken belief; and resistance to contradiction, though it measures the strength of belief, is not the cause of its strength. No doubt a truth may be strengthened in passing through the ordeal of contradiction, so far as we are thus forced to realise its meaning. The same result may be produced by other means, and, above all, by applying belief to practice. We believe in arithmetical truths, partly because the oftener we have to count the more we realise the truth that two and two make four. Whatever the original source of our beliefs, the way to make them vivid is to act upon them. Mill himself incidentally observes that men have a living belief in religious doctrines, 'just up to the point to which it is usual to act upon them.'[1] That, I take it, hits the point. The doctrine, for example, that we should turn the second cheek is practically superseded, not because it is never contradicted, but because it does not correspond to our genuine passions or actions. Beliefs, true or erroneous, preserve their vitality so long as they are put into practice, and not the less because they are held unanimously. What is true is that they are then rather instincts than opinions. Beliefs do not die when un-challenged, but are the more likely to be 'dormant' or held implicitly without conscious formulation.

This leads to a further result. As Mill insists in the *Logic*, 'verification' is an essential part of proof. To act upon a belief is one way of verifying. The fact that we apply a theory successfully is also a valid proof that

[1] *Liberty*, p. 24.

it is true in the great mass of everyday knowledge. But a religious belief is not verified in the same sense. The fact that I act upon it, and am satisfied with my action, proves that it is in harmony with my emotions, not that it is a true statement about facts. The persuasive force often remains, though the logic has become unsatis-factory. This suggests the question as to the nature of a satisfactory 'verification.' We clearly hold innumer-able beliefs which we have not fully tested for ourselves. Mill supposes his opponent to urge that simple people must take many things on trust.[1] We might rather say that even the wisest has to take nine-tenths of his beliefs on trust. We may rightly believe many truths which we are incompetent either to discover or to prove directly because we can verify them indirectly. We can accept whole systems of truth, though we are unable to follow the direct proofs. A belief in astro-nomical theories, for example, is justified for the vast majority, not because they can understand the arguments of Laplace or Newton, but because they may know how elaborately and minutely the conclusions of astronomers are daily verified. The question is not whether we should take things on trust; we cannot help it; but upon what conditions our trust becomes rational. Authority cannot simply justify itself; but it is reasonable to trust an authority which challenges constant examination of its credentials and thorough verification of its conclusions.

Mill's tendency is not, of course, to deny, but to treat this too slightly. He is inclined to regard 'authority' as something logically opposed to reason, or, in other words, to accept the old Protestant version of the 'right of

[1] *Liberty*, p. 22.

private judgment'; or to speak as if every man had to build up his whole structure of belief from the very foundations. There is, he would admit, a structure of knowledge erected by the convergence of competent inquirers, and tested by free discussion and careful veri-fication at every point of its growth. New theories give and receive strength from their 'solidarity' with established theories; and 'authority' is derived from the reciprocal considerations of various results of investiga-tion. Mill is apt to speak as if each thinker and each opinion were isolated. The 'real advantage which truth has, consists,' he says, 'in this, that though a true opinion may be often suppressed, it will be generally rediscovered, and may be rediscovered at a favourable moment, when it will escape persecution and grow strong enough to defend itself.'[1] Persecution may succeed and often has succeeded. The doctrine that it cannot succeed is a 'pleasant falsehood' which has become commonplace by repetition. The statement is surely incomplete. Errors, like truths, may be 'rediscovered' or revived. There are 'idols of the tribe'—fallacies dependent upon per-manent weaknesses of the intellect itself, which appear at all ages and may gain strength under favourable circum-stances. Truth becomes definitively established when it is capable of fitting in with a nucleus of verified and undeniable truth. Mill seems to have in mind such a truth as the discovery of a particular fact. If the exist-ence of America had been forgotten, it would be redis-covered by the next Columbus. If the dream of an Atlantis had once vanished, we need never dream it again. But the statement is inadequate when the truth

[1] *Liberty*, p. 17.

discovered is some new law which not merely adds to our knowledge, but helps to systematise and to affect our whole method of reasoning.

This position affects Mill's view of the efficacy of per-secution. He argues, rather oddly, from the suppression of Lollards, Hussites, and Protestants. Mill certainly did not hold that the suppressed opinions were true; and he does not attempt to prove that they would not have died out of themselves. If Protestantism was suppressed in Spain, the reason may have been that it was so little congenial to the Spanish people, that the persecutions were on the side of the really dominant tendencies of the majority. That a tree without roots may fall the quicker when the wind blows needs no proof; but is not con-clusive as to the effect upon a living tree. The true view, I venture to think, is different.[1] Opinions are not a set of separate dogmas which can be caught and stamped out by themselves. So long as thought is active it works by methods too subtle to be met by such coarse weapons. It allows the dogma to persist, but evacuates it of meaning. The whole structure becomes honey-combed and rotten, as when in France sceptics had learned to say everything without overtly saying anything. Persecution directed against this or that separate theory only embitters and poisons a process which is inevitable if people are to think at all; and persecution can only succeed, either where it is superfluous, or where it is so systematic and vigorous as to suppress all intellectual

[1] Note in *Liberty* Mill's theory that the impulse given at 'three periods'—the Reformation, the last half of the eighteenth century, and the 'Goethean and Fichtean' period in Germany—have made Europe what it is. Yet each 'period' is only the product of the preceding periods. Has Europe owed nothing to the seventeenth century?

activity. In either case the result is most lamentable, and the admission only strengthens the case against persecuting. Persecution can only succeed by paralysing the whole intellectual movement.

I think, then, that Mill, though essentially in the right, has an inadequate perception of one aspect of the question. Elsewhere[1] he complains that we have substituted an apotheosis of instinct for an apotheosis of reason, and so fallen into an infinitely more 'degrading idolatry.' Here, he seems inclined to attack all beliefs not due to the individual reason acting independently. He accentuates too decidedly the absolute value, not of freedom, but of its incidental result, contradiction. He seems to hold that opposition to an established opinion is good in itself. He would approve of circle-squarers and perpetual-motion makers because they oppose established scientific doctrines. He admires originality' even when it implies stupidity. Intelligence shows itself as much in recognising a valid proof as in rejecting a fallacy; and the progress of thought is as dependent upon co-operation and the acceptance of rational authority as upon rejecting errors and declining to submit to arbitrary authority. A man after all ought to realise the improbability of his being right against a consensus of great thinkers. Mill himself remarks, when criticising Bentham, that even originality is not 'a more necessary part of the philosophical character than a thoughtful regard for previous thinkers and for the collective mind of the human race.'[2]

[1] Subjection of Women, p. 6.
[2] Dissertations, p. 351. So in Subjection of Women (second edition, 1869, p. 129) he remarks that originality generally presupposes 'elaborate discipline,' and agrees with F. D. Maurice that the most original thinkers are those who know most thoroughly what has been done by their predecessors.

That, I take it, is perfectly true, but is apt to pass out of sight in his argument. The ideal state is not one of perpetual contradiction of first principles, but one in which contradiction has led to the establishment of a rational authority.

III. THE DECAY OF INDIVIDUALITY

I have insisted upon this chiefly because a similar error seems to intrude into the more difficult problems which follow. The real difficulty of toleration arises when we have to draw the line between speculation and action. Is it possible to discriminate absolutely? to give absolute freedom to thought and yet to maintain institutions which presuppose agreement upon at least some general principles? If men, as Mill asks, should be free to form and to utter opinions, should they not be free to act upon their opinions—to carry them out, so long at least as it is 'at their own risk and peril'—in their lives?[1] How does the principle present itself in this case? Mill has declined[2] to take advantage of any assumption of absolute right. He wishes to give a positive ground; to show that the liberty which he demands corresponds in point of fact to a necessary factor of human progress. His own doctrine is that the 'development of individuality is one of the leading essentials of wellbeing'; and he adopts as identical the doctrine of Wilhelm von Humboldt,[3] that the right end of man is 'the highest and most harmonious development

[1] Liberty, p. 32.   [2] Ibid. p. 7.
[3] Humboldt's Sphere and Duties of Government was translated by Joseph Coulthard in 1854. Though originally written in 1791 it did not appear in a complete form till published in the collected edition of his works by his brother

of his powers to a complete and consistent whole.' Humboldt considers this end to be 'prescribed by the eternal or immutable dictates of reason.' Mill would prefer, we may suppose, to have regarded it as the uniform teaching of experience. In either case, it is a broad and elevated doctrine which few thinkers would deny in general terms. It is, moreover, eminently characteristic of Mill in his best mood. He never wrote more forcibly than in his exposition of this doctrine. He is now stimulated by the belief that he is preaching in painfully deaf ears. In advocating freedom of thought or denouncing despotism he was enforcing the doctrines most certain of popular applause. But nobody cared much for 'individuality' or objected to the subtler forms of moral tyranny. The masses are satisfied with their own ways; and even 'moral and social reformers' want as a rule to suppress all morality but their own. Mill is uttering forebodings common to the most cultivated class. The fear lest the growth of democracy should imply a crushing out of all the higher culture has been uttered in innumerable forms by some of our most eloquent writers and keenest thinkers. The course of events since Mill's death has certainly not weakened such fears. The problem is still with us, and certainly not solved. Mill's view is eminently characteristic of his whole doctrine. How, starting as a democrat, he had been led to a strong

Alexander in 1852. The book shows the influence of Kant and Rousseau. Humboldt was at the time a kind of philosophical antinomian objecting to all external law as injurious to spontaneous spiritual development. Marriage should be left to individual contract, because 'where law has imposed no fetters morality most surely binds.' In Bentham's phrase 'external sanctions' weaken the internal. The state should provide 'security,' and leave religion and morality to themselves. Humboldt's philosophy is not Mill's, though on most points the practical application coincides.

sense of the possible evils of democracy, I have already tried to show. I have now to inquire into the relation of this view to his general theory.

'Custom' in conduct corresponds to tradition in opinion. So far as you make it your guide, you need no faculty but that of 'ape-like imitation.'[1] You cultivate neither your reason nor your will when you let the world choose your plan of life. You become at best a useful automaton—not a valuable human being; and of all the works of man, which should be perfected and beautified, the first in importance is surely man himself. Obedience to custom implies condemnation of 'strong impulses' as a snare and a peril. And yet strong impulses are but a name for energy, and may be the source of the 'most passionate love of virtue and the sternest self-control.' Individual energy was once perhaps too strong for the 'social principle.' Now 'society' has fairly got the better of individuality. We live in dread of the omnipresent censorship of our neighbours, desire only to do what others do, bow even our minds to the yoke, shun 'eccentricity' as a crime, and allow our human capacities to be starved and withered. Calvinism, he says, preaches explicitly that self-will is the 'one great offence of men.' Such a creed generates 'a pinched and hidebound type of human nature.' Men are cramped and dwarfed, as trees are clipped into pollards. It has lost sight of qualities belonging to a different type of excellence. 'It may be better to be a John Knox than an Alcibiades; but it is better to be a Pericles than either.'

[1] It would be curious to compare Mill's theory with the very interesting books in which M. Tarde has shown the vast importance of 'imitation' in sociology.

Clipping and cramping means loss of 'individuality,' and 'individuality' may be identified with 'development.' This, he says, might close the argument; but he desires to give further reasons to prove to those who do not desire liberty for themselves that it should be conceded to others. His main point is the vast importance of genius, which can only exist in an atmosphere of freedom. The 'initiation of all wise and noble things comes, and must come, from individuals.' He is not such a 'hero-worshipper' as to desire a heroic tyrant, but he ardently desires a heroic leader; and where eccentricity is a reproach, genius will never be able to expand. Press all people into the same mould, condemn tastes which are not the tastes of the majority, and every deviation from the beaten path becomes impossible. Yet public opinion tends to become more stifling. 'Its ideal of character is to be without character.' 'Already energetic characters on any large scale are becoming merely traditional.' The greatness of England is now all collective. We are individually small, and capable of great things only by our 'habit of combining.' 'Men of another stamp made England what it has been, and men of another stamp will be needed to prevent its decline.' The evil is summed up in the 'despotism of custom.' China is a standing warning. It had the 'rare good fortune' of possessing a particularly good set of customs. But the customs have become stereotyped, the people all cast into the same mould, and China therefore is what England is tending to become.

Hitherto European progress has been due to the diversity of character and culture of the various nations. It is losing that advantage. Nations are assimilated; ranks

and professions are losing their distinctive characters; we all read the same books, listen (not quite all of us?) to the same sermons, and have the same ends. The process is accelerated by all the past changes. The extension of education, the extension of means of communication, the extension of manufactures, and, above all, the supremacy of public opinion, are all in its favour. With 'so great a mass of influences hostile to individuality' it is 'not easy to see how it can stand its ground.'

When Mill, as a young man, suddenly reflected that, if all his principles were adopted, he should still be unhappy, he did not doubt their truth. But now he seems to be emphatically asserting that the victory of all the principles for which he and his friends had contended would be itself disastrous. 'Progress' meant precisely the set of changes which he now pronounces to lead to stagnation. Democracy in full activity will extinguish the very principle of social vitality. And yet, when at a later period Mill became a politician, he gave his vote as heartily as the blindest enthusiast for measures which inaugurated a great step towards a democracy. His sincerity in both cases is beyond a doubt, and gives emphasis to the problem, how his practical political doctrine can be reconciled with his doctrine of development.

The first question provoked by such assertions is the question whether this is a correct, still more, whether it is an exhaustive, diagnosis of the social disease? May not Mill be emphasising one aspect of a complex problem, and seeing the extinction of that 'individuality' which is really an element of welfare, in the extinction

of such an 'individualism' as is incompatible with social improvement? His general aim is unimpeachable. The harmonious development of all our faculties represents a worthy ideal. The first or most essential of all human virtues, as Humboldt had said, is energy; for the greater the vitality, the more rich and various the type which can be evolved by cultivation. Yet it may be doubted whether the two aims suggested will always coincide. Energy certainly may go with narrowness, with implicit faith and limited purpose. The stream flows more forcibly in a defined channel. If Knox was inferior to Pericles or, say, the Jew to the Greek, the inferiority was not in energy or endurance. The efflorescence of Greek culture was short lived, it has been said, because there was too much Alcibiades and too little of Moses.[1] Culture tends to effeminacy unless guarded by 'renunciation' and regulated by concentration upon distinct purpose. As in the question of toleration, Mill overestimates the value of mere contradiction, so in questions of conduct he seems to overestimate mere eccentricity. Yet eccentricity is surely bad so far as it is energy wasted; expended upon trifles or devoted to purposes which a wider knowledge shows to be chimerical. To balance and correlate the various activities, to direct energy to the best purposes, and to minimise a needless antagonism is as essential to development as to give free play to the greatest variety of healthy activities.

Mill's doctrine may thus be taken as implying a historical generalisation. Historical generalisations are wrong as

[1] Mill, in his *Representative Government* (p. 17), argues that the Hebrew prophets discharged the functions of modern liberty of the press; and that the Jews were therefore the 'most progressive people of antiquity' after the Greeks. Still, their 'culture' was hardly so wide.

a rule; and one defect in this seems to be evident. Are energetic characters really rarer than of old? We may dismiss the illusion which personified whole processes of slow evolution in the name of some great prophet or legislator. It may still be true that the importance of the individual has really been greater in former epochs. The personal qualities of William the Conqueror or of Hildebrand may have affected history more than the personal qualities of Bismarck or of Pius IX. The action of great men, indeed, at all periods whatever, is essentially dependent upon their social environment; but personal idiosyncrasies may count for more in the total result at one period than another. The fortunes of a rude tribe may be, not only more obviously but more really, dependent upon the character of its chief than the fortunes of a civilised nation upon the character of its prime minister. And, therefore, it may be, the individual as a more important factor in the result, seems to represent greater individual energy. Yet the energy of the old feudal baron, who could ride roughshod over his weaker neighbours or coerce them with fire and sword, is not necessarily greater than the energy of the modern statesman, who has by gentler means slowly to weld together alliances of nations, to combine and inspirit parties, to direct public opinion, and to act therefore with constant reference to the national or cosmopolitan order.

Mill's[1] lamentation over the pettiness of modern English statesmen is familiar. What is really implied? England, as Mill the democrat would have said, was once a country of castes: the priest, the noble, the

[1] *Liberty*, p. 41.

merchant, the peasant, represented distinct types. Each class was bound by an unalterable custom and conforms to inherited traditions; each, again, discharged some simple or general function now distributed among many minor classes. In later phrase, modern England has been made by processes of 'differentiation' and 'integration.' The old class lines have disappeared, the barriers of custom have been broken down, the old functions have been specialised, and instead of independent individual action, the whole system of life depends upon the elaborate and indefinitely ramified systems of co-operation, deliberate or unconscious. The obvious result is a growth of organic unity, accompanied by an equal development of diversity. Each unit can be assigned to a more special function, because other functions are assigned to co-operating units, and greater mutual dependence is implied in the greater variety of careers and activities. In his democratic phase, Mill blesses this process altogether; he approves the destruction of privilege and caste distinctions; he approves the 'division of labour,' the increased diversity of occupation, and the consequent growth of co-operation; he desires the fuller responsibility of the ruling class or the closer dependence of government upon the people. But in the later phase, when he emphasises the evils of democracy, does he not condemn what is a necessary implication in the very process which he approves? The division of labour, he now observes, narrows a man's life and interests; the necessity of co-operation narrows the sphere of 'individuality'; and the process which gives diversity to society as a whole implies certain uniformities in the social atoms. The less the variety in the units,

the greater is the facility of arranging them in different configurations. The eccentric man is a cross-grained piece of timber which cannot be worked into the state. 'Individuality' is so far a hindrance to the power of entering into an indefinite number of combinations. And yet so far as 'individuality' diminishes, the responsibility of government means the subordination of rulers to the average commonplace stupidity. What, then, is the 'individuality' which may be called unconditionally good? How are we to define the danger so as to avoid condemning the conformity which is a necessary implication of progress? How are we to manage 'differentiation' at the expense of 'integration'; to exalt such 'individuality' as is incompatible with 'sociality'; and to regard 'eccentricity' and 'antagonism' and contradiction as valuable in themselves instead of accidental results in particular cases of originality which in some sense is priceless? Here, I think, is the real difficulty. Have we to deal with forces necessarily 'counteracting' each other, in Mill's phrase, or with forces which can be combined in a healthy organism? Mill undoubtedly supposes that some conciliation is possible. The historical view has shown the evil. We have now to consider the remedy to be applied to the various forms in which it affects economic, political, and ethical conditions. The general principle has been given. 'Self-protection' is the only justification for the interference of society with the individual. Although absolute liberty would mean anarchy, we may still demand a maximum of liberty, and suppress such a use of liberty by one man as would in fact restrain the liberty of another. Mill, like Bentham, holds to the purely empirical view. Inter-

ference is bad when the harm caused by the coercion is not counterbalanced by the good.

Bentham's doctrine is not only plausible but, within a certain sphere, points to one of the most obvious and essential conditions of useful legislation. The Utilitarians were always affected by the legal principles from which they started. In the case of criminal law, Mill's principle marks the obvious minimum of interference. A state must suppress violence. If I claim liberty to break your head, the policeman is bound to interfere. If you and I claim the same loaf, the state, even if it be a communistic state, must either settle which is to eat it, or leave us to fight for it. And, again, if the principle does not fix the maximum of legislation, it points to the most obvious limiting considerations. The state means the judge and the policeman, who cannot look into the heart, and must classify criminal action by its definable external characteristics. It can reach the murderer but not the malevolent man, who would murder if he could. It is therefore incompetent to punish wickedness except so far as wickedness is manifested by overt acts. If it went further it would be unjust, because acting blindly, as well as intolerably inquisitorial. Nor can it generally punish actions which produce no assignable injury to individuals. To punish a man for neglecting definite duties is necessary; but to try to punish the idleness which may have caused the neglect would be monstrous. The state would have to be omniscient and omnipresent, and at most would favour hypocrisy instead of virtue. Briefly, the law is far too coarse an instrument for the function of enforcing morality in general. It must generally confine itself to cases where injury is inflicted

upon an assignable person and by conduct defined by definite outward manifestations. This had been clearly stated by Bentham. Mill, in his chapter on the 'limits of the authority of society upon the individual,' insists upon objections obvious in the legal case. Can we deduce from these legal limits a general principle defining the relation between society and its units? I notice first the difficulty already suggested by the *Political Economy.*

IV. ECONOMIC APPLICATION

How, as Mill had asked, in speaking of the economic aspects of government interference, are we to mark out the space which is to be sacred from 'authoritative intrusion'? So long as the social state is simple, the application is easy. When one savage catches the deer, and another the salmon, each may be forbidden to take the other's game by force. Each man has a right to the fruits of his own labour. In the actual state of things there is not this charming simplicity. A man's wealth is not a definable material object, but a bundle of rights of the most complex kind; and rights to various parts of the whole national income, which are the product of whole systems of previous compacts. The possessor has not even in the vaguest sense 'created' his wealth; he has more or less contributed the labour of brains and hands to the adaptation of things to use, or enjoys his rights in virtue of an indefinite number of transactions, bargains made by himself, or bequests transferring the rights to new generations. To protect his property is to protect a multifarious system of rights accruing in all manner of ways, and to sanction the

voluntary contracts in virtue of which the whole elaborate network of rights corresponds to the complex social
order. The tacit assumption of the economists was
that this order was in some sense 'natural' and law
an artificial or extra-natural compulsion. Can the line
be drawn? The legal regulation has been an essential
though a subordinate part of the whole process. Law,
at an early stage, is an undistinguishable part of customs,
which has become differentiated from mere custom as
settled governments have been evolved and certain
definite functions assigned to the sovereign power.
We cannot say that one set of institutions is due to
law and another to customs or to voluntary contracts.
The laws which regulate property in land or inheritance
or any form of association have affected every stage of
the process and have not affected it as conditions imposed from without, but as a part of the whole elaboration. The principle that 'self-protection' is the only
justification of interference then becomes hard of application. I am to do what I like with my own. That
may be granted, for 'my own' is that with which I
may do what I like. But if I am allowed in virtue of
this doctrine to make any contracts or to dispose of my
property in any way that I please, it follows that the
same sanctity is transferred to the whole system which
has grown up by voluntary action at every point, and
which is therefore regarded as the 'natural' or spontaneous order. Now the actual course of events, as
Mill maintains, produced a society with vast inequalities
of wealth—a society which, as he declares, does not even
show an approximation to justice, or in which a man's
fortunes are determined not by his merits but by accident.

On this interpretation of the principle of non-interference, it follows that in the name of legal 'liberty' you
approve a process destructive of 'liberty' in fact. Every
man is allowed no doubt by the laws to act as circumstances admit ; but the circumstances may permit some
people to enjoy every conceivable pleasure and to develop
every faculty, while they condemn others to find their
only pleasure in gin, and to have such development as
can be acquired in 'London slums.' A famous judge
pointed out ironically that the laws of England were the
same for the rich and the poor ; that is, the same price
was charged for justice whether the applicants could
afford it or not. Is it not a mockery to tell a man
that he is free to do as he pleases, if it only means that
he may choose between starvation and the poorhouse?
Mill had himself been inclined to remedy the evils by
invoking an omnipotent legislature to undertake very
drastic measures of reform. Equal laws will produce
equal results when, in point of fact, they apply to men
under equal conditions. If a society consists of mutually
independent and self-supporting individuals, the principle
of non-interference may work smoothly. Each man has
actually his own secret sphere, and the law only affects
the exchange of superfluous advantages among independent units. But that is to say that to make your rule
work, you must prevent all that process of development
which is implied in civilisation. Society must be forced
to be 'individualistic' in order that the formula may be
applicable. Self-protection means the protection of
existing rights. If they are satisfactory, the result of
protecting them will be satisfactory. But if the actual
order, however produced, is essentially unjust, the test

becomes illusory. Yet, if the laws are to interfere to
prevent the growth of inequality, what becomes of the
sacred sphere of individuality ?

Here we have the often-noted conflict between equality
and liberty. Leave men free, and inequalities must arise.
Enforce equality and individuality is cramped or suppressed. And yet inequality certainly means a pressure
upon the weaker which may lead to virtual slavery. We
must admit that neither liberty nor equality can be laid
down as absolute principles. The attempt to treat any
formula in this fashion leads to the perplexities exemplified
in Mill's treatment of the 'liberty' problem. His doctrines
cannot be made to fit accurately the complexities of the
social order. 'Equality' and 'liberty' define essential
'moments' in the argument, though neither can be made
to support an absolute conclusion.

The difficulty was indicated in Bentham's treatment of
'security' and 'equality.' Both, he said, were desirable,
but when there was a conflict 'equality' must give way
to 'security.' Here we come to another closely allied
doctrine. 'Security' implies 'responsibility.' A man
must be secure that he may be industrious. He will not
labour unless he is sure to enjoy the fruit of his labour.
This gives the Malthusian *vis medicatrix*. But, stated
absolutely, it implies pure self-interest. Robinson Crusoe
was responsible in the sense that if he did not work he
would starve. And, if we could, in fact, mark off each
man's separate sphere, or regard society as a collection of
Robinson Crusoes, the principle might be applied. Each
man should have a right to what he has himself 'created.'
But when a man 'creates' nothing; when his 'environment' is not a desert island but an organised society, the

principle must be differently stated. 'Responsibility,'
indeed, always implies liberty—the existence of a sphere
within which a man's fortunes depend upon his personal
character, and his character should determine his fortune.
But, as Mill can most clearly recognise, social responsibility means something more. One most 'certain incident'
of social progress is the growth of co-operation, and that
involves, as he says, the 'subordination of individual
caprice' to a 'preconceived determination' and the performance of parts allotted in a 'combined undertaking.'[1]
The individual, then, is part of an organisation, in which
every individual should play his part. The over-centrali-
sation which would crush him into an automaton is not
more fatal than the individual independence which would
be incompatible with organisation. The desirable 'responsibility' is not that of a Robinson Crusoe but that of
the soldier in an army. It should be enforced by other
motives than mere self-interest, for it affects the interests
of the whole body corporate. Now Mill, believing even
to excess in the power of education, included in education
the whole discipline of life due to the relations of the individual to his social environment ; and it is his essential
principle that this force should be directed to enforcing
a sense of 'responsibility' in the widest acceptation of
the word.

V. POLITICAL APPLICATION

A similar doctrine is implied in his political writings,
of which the *Representative Government* is the most
explicit. The book is hardly on a level with his best
work. Treatises of 'political philosophy' are generally

[1] *Political Economy*, bk. iv. ch. i. § 2.

disappointing. The difficulty lies, I suppose, in combining the practical with the general point of view. In some treatises, the 'philosophy' is made up of such scraps about the social contract or mixture of the three forms of government as excited Bentham's contempt in Blackstone's treatise. They are a mere juggle of abstractions fit only for schoolboys. Others, like James Mill's, are really party pamphlets, masquerading as philosophy, and importing obvious principles into the likeness of geometrical axioms. A good deal of wisdom no doubt lurks in the speeches of statesmen; but it is not often easy to extricate it from the mass of personal and practical remarks. Mill's treatise might suggest some such criticism; and yet it is interesting as an indication of his leading principles. Some passages show how long experience in a public office affects a philosophic thinker. Mill's exposition, for example, of the defects of the House of Commons in administrative legislation,[1] his discussion of the fact (as he takes it to be) that governments remarkable for sustained vigour and ability have generally been aristocratic,[2] and his panegyric upon the East India Company,[3] record the genuine impressions of his long administrative career, and are refreshing in the midst of more abstract discussions. I have, however, only to notice a general principle which runs through the book.

Mill starts by emphasising the distinction applied in the *Political Economy* between the natural and the artificial. Political institutions are the work of men and created by the will. The doctrine that governments

[1] See chap. v.   [2] *Representative Government*, p. 45.
[3] *Ibid.* p. 104.

'are not made, but grow,' would lead to 'political fatalism' if it were regarded as true exclusively of the other. In fact, we might reply, there is no real opposition at all. 'Making' is but one kind of 'growing.' Growing by conscious forethought is still growing, and the antithesis put absolutely is deceptive. Mill is striving to enlarge the sphere of voluntary action. He wishes to prove that he can take the ground generally supposed to imply the doctrine of 'freewill.' Institutions, he fully admits, presuppose certain qualities in the people; but, given those qualities, they are 'a matter of choice.'[1] In politics, as in machinery, we are turning existing powers to account; but we do not say that, because rivers will not run uphill, 'water-mills are not made but grow.' The political theorist can invent constitutions as the engineer can invent machinery, which will materially alter the results; and to inquire which is the best form of government 'in the abstract' is 'not a chimerical but a highly practical employment of the scientific intellect.' The illustration is difficult to apply if the 'river' means the whole society, and the 'water-mill' is itself, therefore, one part of the 'river.' The legislator is not an external force but an integral part of internal forces.

In the next place, Mill rejects a distinction made by Comte[2] between order and progress. Comte had made a distinction between 'statics' and 'dynamics' in sociology, which are to each other like anatomy and physiology. The conditions of existence, and the conditions of continuous movement of a society correspond to

[1] *Representative Government*, p. 5.
[2] Coleridge, he observes, had also distinguished 'permanence' and 'progression.'—*Representative Government*, p. 8.

'order and progress.'[1] Mill replies that 'progress' includes 'order,' and that the two conditions cannot give independent criteria of the merits of the institutions. Comte, in any case, regarding sociology as a science, considers the dependence of political institutions upon social structure to be much closer than Mill would admit. The power of the legislator to alter society is strictly subordinate and dependent throughout upon its relation to the existing organism. In his study of Comte,[2] Mill declares emphatically that Comte's work has made it necessary for all later thinkers to start from a 'connected view of the great facts of history.' He speaks with enthusiasm of Comte's great survey of history, and fully accepts the principle. Yet, in fact, he scarcely applies the method in his political system, and accepts a doctrine really inconsistent with it. His anxiety to give a far wider sphere to the possibilities of modifying, leads him to regard institutions as the ultimate causes of change, instead of factors themselves strictly dependent upon deeper causes. Hence he substitutes a different distinction. We are to judge of institutions by their efficiency as educating agencies, on the one hand, and as the means of carrying on 'public business' on the other. Institutions should do their work well, and turn the workers into good citizens.[3]

The educative influence of government is thus his characteristic point. The 'ideally best form of government,' as Mill of course admits, is not one applicable 'at all stages of civilisation.'[4] We have to suppose certain

[1] See *Philosophie Positive*, iv. 318, etc.
[2] *Auguste Comte and Positivism* (reprinted from the *Westminster Review*, 1865), p. 36.
[3] *Representative Government*, p. 14.   [4] *Ibid.* p. 22.

conditions, and he takes pain to show in what cases his ideal would be inapplicable.[1] But, given the stage reached in modern times (as he practically assumes), there is 'no difficulty in showing' the ideal form to be the representative system; that in which 'sovereignty is vested in the entire aggregate of the community,' every citizen having a voice and taking at least an occasional part in discharging the functions of government.[2] This applies the doctrine already expounded in the *Liberty*. Citizens should be 'self-protecting and self-protective';[3] the 'active,' not the 'passive' type of character should be encouraged. The striving, go-ahead character of Anglo-Saxons is only objectionable so far as it is directed to petty ends; the Englishman says naturally, 'What a shame!' when the Frenchman says, '*Il faut de la patience!*' and the institutions which encourage this energetic character by giving a vote to all, by permitting freedom of speech, and by permitting all men to discharge small duties (to act on juries for example) are the best. I will only note that this tends to beg the important question, Are the institutions really the cause or the effect? Has the energy of the English race made their institutions free? or have the free institutions made them energetic? or are the institutions and the character collateral effects of a great variety of causes? When so much stress is laid upon the educational effect — of serving upon a jury, for instance—we are impelled to ask what is the ultimate cause. Are people so much morally improved by serving on juries? If the institution like the 'water-mill'

[1] *Representative Government*, ch. iv.   [2] *Ibid.* p. 21.
[3] *Ibid.* p. 22.

only directs certain instincts already existing, we must not speak as if the mill made the water-power ; and Mill's arguments suggest a liability to this fallacy. It becomes important at the next stage.

The ideal form of government has its infirmities, as Mill insists. Two are conspicuous : the difficulty of inducing a democracy to intrust work which requires skill to those who possess skill;[1] and the old difficulty —the 'tyranny of the majority.' Mill's contention that the 'Demos' may be stupid, mistake its own interests, and impress its mistaken views upon the legislation, needs no exposition. We are thus brought to the question how the ideal government is to be so constituted that the interests of a section—even if it be the majority —may not be so powerful as to overwhelm the other sections even when backed by 'truth and justice.'[2] Danger of popular stupidity and danger of class legislation indicate two great evils to be abated as far as possible by 'human contrivance.'[3] A sufficient 'contrivance' was in fact revealed at the right moment. A discovery of surpassing value had been announced by one of his friends. Hare's scheme of representation, says Mill with characteristic enthusiasm, has the 'almost unparalleled merit' of securing its special aim in almost 'ideal perfection,' while incidentally attaining others of almost equal importance. He places it among the very greatest 'improvements yet made in the theory and practice of government.'[4] It would, for example, be almost a 'specific' against the tendency of republics to ostracise their ablest men.[5] And it would

[1] Representative Government, p. 47.   [2] Ibid. p. 52.   [3] Ibid. p. 53.
[4] Ibid. p. 57.   [5] Ibid. p. 59.

be the appropriate organ of the great function of 'antagonism'[1] which now takes the place of contradiction in intellectual development. There will always be some body to oppose the supreme power, and thus to prevent the stagnation, followed by decay, which has always resulted from a complete victory.

Is not the 'water-mill' here expected to work the river ? The faith in a bit of mechanism of 'human contrivance' becomes sublime. Hare's scheme may have great conveniences under many circumstances. But that Hare's scheme or any scheme should regenerate politics seems to be a visionary belief, unworthy of Mill's higher moods. He seems to fall into the error too common among legislative theorists, of assuming that an institution will be worked for the ends of the contriver, instead of asking to what ends it may be distorted by the ingenuity of all who can turn it to account for their own purposes. There is a more vital difficulty. If Hare's scheme worked as Mill expected it to work, one result would be necessarily implied. The House of Commons would reflect accurately all the opinions of the country. Whatever opinion had a majority in the country would have a majority in the House. Labourers, as he suggests when showing the dangers of democracy, may be in favour of protection, or of fixing the rate of wages. Now in this scheme the majority in the country may enforce whatever laws approve themselves to the ignorant. I do not say that this would actually be the result ; for I think that, in point of fact, the change of mere machinery would be of comparatively little importance. The power of

[1] Representative Government, p. 60.

the rich and the educated does not really depend upon the system of voting, or the ostensible theory of the constitution, but upon the countless ways in which wealth, education, and the whole social system affect the working of institutions. Mill can fully admit the fact at times. But here he is taking for granted that the effect of the scheme will be to secure a perfectly correct miniature of the opinions of all separate persons. The wise minority will therefore be a minority in the land. It will be able to make speeches. But the speeches, however able, are but an insignificant trickle in the great current of talk which forms what is called 'public opinion.' The necessary result upon his showing would be, that legislation would follow the opinions of the majority, or, in other words, facilitate the 'tyranny of the majority.'

This suggests one vital point. Mill, as I have said, has endeavoured to enlarge as much as possible the sphere of operation of the freewill—of the power of individuals or of deliberate conscious legislation. The result is to exaggerate the influence of institutions and to neglect the forces, intellectual and moral, which must always lie behind institutions. We can admit to the full the importance of the educational influence of political institutions, and the surpassing value of energy, self-reliance, and individual responsibility. The sentiment is altogether noble, and Mill expresses it with admirable vigour. But the more decidedly we hold his view of the disease, the more utterly inadequate and inappropriate appears his remedy. The tendency to levelling and vulgarising, so far as it exists, can certainly not be cured by ingenious arrangements of one part of

the political machinery. I take this to mark Mill's weakest side. The truth was divined by the instinct of his democratic allies. So long as he voted for extending the suffrage, they could leave him to save his conscience by amusing himself with these harmless fancies.

VI. WOMEN'S RIGHTS

Mill's *Subjection of Women* brings out more clearly some of the fundamental Utilitarian tenets. None of his writings is more emphatically marked by generosity and love of justice. A certain shrillness of tone marks the recluse too little able to appreciate the animal nature of mankind. Yet in any case, he made a most effective protest against the prejudices which stunted the development and limited the careers of women. Mill declares at starting, that till recently the 'law of force' has been 'the avowed rule of general conduct.' Only of late has there been even a pretence of regulating 'the affairs of society in general according to any moral law.'[1] That moral considerations have been too little regarded as between different societies or different classes is painfully obvious. But 'force' in any intelligible sense is itself only made applicable by the social instincts, which bind men together. No society could ever be welded into a whole by 'force' alone. This is the Utilitarian fallacy of explaining law by 'sanctions,' and leaving the 'sanctions' to explain themselves. But the argument encourages Mill to treat of all inequality as unjust because imposed by force. The 'only school of genuine moral senti-

[1] Subjection of Women (1869), p. 16.

ment,' he says, ' is society between equals.' Let us rather say that inequalities are unjust which rest upon force alone. Every school of morality or of thought implies subordination, but a subordination desirable only when based upon real superiority. The question then becomes whether the existing relations of the sexes correspond to some essential difference or are created by sheer force.

Here we have assumptions characteristic of Mill's whole logical method ; and, especially, the curious oscillation between absolute laws and indefinite modifiability. His doctrine of ' natural kinds' supposed that two races were either divided by an impassable gulf, or were divided only by accidental or superficial differences. He protests against the explanation of national differences by race characteristics. To say that the Irish are naturally lazy, or the Negroes naturally stupid, is to make a short apology for oppression and for slavery. Undoubtedly it is wrong, as it is contrary to all empirical reasoning, to assume a fundamental difference ; and morally wrong to found upon the assumption an apology for maintaining caste and privilege. But neither is it legitimate to assume that the differences are negligible. The ' accident of colour ' has been made a pretext for an abominable institution. But we have no right to the a priori assumption that colour is a mere accident. It may upon Mill's own method be an indication of radical and far-reaching differences. How far the Negro differs from the white man, whether he is intellectually equal or on a wholly lower plane, is a question of fact to be decided by experience. Mill's refusal to accept one doctrine passes imperceptibly into an equally unfounded acceptance of its contradictory. The process

is shown by the doctrine to which, as we have seen, he attached so much importance, that political science must be deductive, because the effect of the conjoined causes is the sum of the effects of the separate causes. When two men act together, the effect may be inferred from putting together the motives of each. ' All phenomena of society,' he infers, ' are phenomena of human nature generated by the action of outward circumstances upon masses of human beings.' [1] We can therefore deduce scientific laws in sociology as in astronomy. This tacitly assumes that man, like molecule, represents a constant unit, and thus introduces the de facto equality of human beings, from which it is an inevitable step to the equality of rights. The sound doctrine that we can only learn by experience what are the differences between men becomes the doctrine that all differences are superficial, and therefore the man always the same. The doctrine becomes audacious when ' man ' is taken to include ' woman.' He speaks of the ' accident of sex ' and the ' accident of colour ' as equally unjust grounds for political distinctions.[2] The difference between men and women, Whites and Negroes, is ' accidental,' that is, apparently removable by some change of ' outward circumstances.'

Mill, indeed, does not admit that he is begging the question. He guards himself carefully against begging the question either way,[3] though he thinks apparently that the burthen of proof is upon those who assert a natural difference. Accordingly he urges that the so-

[1] Logic, p. 572 (bk. vi. ch. vi. § 2).
[2] Representative Government, p. 76. Cf. Political Economy, p. 493 (bk. iv. ch. vii. § 2).
[3] Subjection of Women, pp. 41, 104.

called ' nature of women ' is ' an eminently artificial thing '; a result of ' hothouse cultivation ' carried on for the benefit of their masters.[1] He afterwards[2] endeavours to show that even the ' least contestable differences ' between the sexes are such as may ' very well have been produced merely by circumstances without any differences of natural capacity.' What, one asks, can the ' circumstances ' mean ? Pyschology, as he truly says, can tell us little ; but physiology certainly seems to suggest a difference implied in the whole organisation and affecting every mental and ·physical characteristic. It is not, apparently, a case of two otherwise equal beings upon which different qualities have been superimposed, but of a radical distinction, totally inconsistent with any presumption of equality.[3] When we are told that the legal inequality is an ' isolated fact '—a ' solitary breach of what has become a fundamental law of human institutions '[4]—the reply is obvious. The distinction of the sexes is surely an ' isolated fact,' so radical or ' natural ' that it is no wonder that it should have unique recognition in all human institutions. Mill has, indeed, a further answer. If nature disqualifies women for certain functions, why disqualify them by law ? Leave everything to free competition, and each man or woman will go where he or she is most fitted. Abolish, briefly, all

[1] Subjection of Women, pp. 48-9.
[2] Ibid. p. 105. In one of the letters to Carlyle Mill asks whether the highest masculine, are not identical with the highest feminine, qualities. I should like to see Carlyle's answer.
[3] This argument is put by Comte in his correspondence with Mill. So far, Comte seems to have the best of it ; and Mill's inability to appreciate the doctrine is characteristic. At this time Mill seems to have been undecided upon the question of divorce. See the discussion in the Letters, pp. 208-73.
[4] Subjection of Women, p. 36.

political and social distinctions, and things will right themselves. If ' inequality ' is due to ' force,' and the difference between men and women be ' artificial,' the argument is plausible. But if the difference be, as surely it is, ' natural,' and ' force ' in the sense of mere muscular strength, only one factor in the growth of institutions, the removal of inequalities may imply neglect of essential facts. He is attacking the most fundamental condition of the existing social order. The really vital point is the bearing of Mill's argument upon marriage and the family. He thinks[1] that the full question of divorce is ' foreign to his purpose '; and, in fact, seems to be a little shy of what is really the critical point. He holds, indeed, that the family is a ' school of despotism,'[2] or would be so, if men were not generally better than their laws. Admitting that the law retains traces of the barbarism which regarded wives as slaves, the question remains whether the institution itself is to be condemned as dependent upon ' force.' Would not the ' equality ' between persons naturally unequal lead to greater instead of less despotism ? If, as a matter of fact, women are weaker than men, might not liberty mean more power to the strongest ? Permission to the husband to desert the wife at will might be to make her more dependent in fact though freer in law. Whatever the origin of the institution of marriage, it may now involve, not the bondage but an essential protection of the weakest party. This is the side of the argument to which Mill turns a deaf ear. We are to neglect the most conspicuous of facts because it may be ' artificial ' or due to ' circum-

[1] Subjection of Women, p. 59. Cf. Liberty, p. 61.
[2] Subjection of Women, p. 81.

stances,' and assume that free competition will be an infallible substitute for a system which affects the most vital part of the whole social organism. To assume existing differences to be incapable of modification is doubtless wrong; but to treat them at once as non-existent is at least audacious. Finally, the old difficulty recurs in a startling shape. If differences are to disappear and the characteristics of men and women to become indistinguishable, should we not be encouraging a 'levelling' more thoroughgoing than any which can result from political democracy?

VII. THE SELF-PROTECTION PRINCIPLE

These special applications raise the question: What is the interpretation of his general principle? 'Self-protection' is the only justification for social interference. Where a man's conduct affects himself alone society should not 'interfere'[1] by legislation. Does this imply that we must not interfere by the pressure of public opinion? We may, as Mill replies, approve or disapprove, but so long as a man does not infringe our rights, we must leave him to the 'natural and, as it were, the spontaneous consequences of his faults.' We may dislike and even abhor anti-social 'dispositions'—cruelty and treachery—but self-regarding faults and the corresponding dispositions are not subjects of 'moral reprobation.' A man is not accountable to his fellow creatures for prudence or 'self-respect.'[2] Mill anticipates the obvious objection. No conduct is simply 'self-regarding.' 'No one is an entirely isolated being';

[1] *Liberty*, p. 44.   [2] *Ibid.* p. 46.

and injuries to myself disqualify me for service to others. 'Self-regarding' vices, as his opponent is supposed to urge, are also socially mischievous; and we must surely be entitled to assume that the experience of the race has established some moral rules sufficiently to act upon them, however desirous we may be to allow of 'new and original experiments in living.'[1] Mill's reply is that we should punish not the fault itself but the injuries to others which result. We hang George Barnwell for murdering his uncle, whether he did it to get money for his mistress or to set up in business. We should not punish him, it is implied, for keeping a mistress; but we should punish the murder, whatever the motive. The criminal lawyer, no doubt, treats Barnwell upon this principle. But can it be morally applicable? Mill admits fully that self-regarding qualities may be rightfully praised and blamed. We may think a man a fool, a lazy, useless, sensual wretch: we may, and are even bound to, tell him so frankly, avoid his society, and warn others to avoid him. My judgment of a man is not a judgment of his separate qualities but of the whole human being. I disapprove of George Barnwell himself, not simply his greediness or his vicious propensities. I think a man bad in different degrees if he is ready to murder his uncle, whether from lust or greed or even with a view to a charitable use of the plunder. The hateful thing is the character itself which, under certain conditions, leads to murder. As including prudence, it may be simply neutral or respectable; as implying vice, disgusting; and as implying cruelty, hateful. Still, I do not condemn the abstract qualities—interest in oneself,

[1] *Liberty*, p. 47.

or sexual passion or even antipathy—each of which may be desirable in the right place—but the way in which they are combined in the concrete Barnwell. No quality, therefore, can be taken as simply self-regarding, for it is precisely the whole character which is the object of my moral judgment of the individual. I have spoken of the inadequate recognition of this truth by Bentham and James Mill. It makes J. S. Mill's criterion inapplicable to the question of moral interference. If, as he argues, we are to impress our moral standard upon others, we cannot make the distinction; for our standard implies essentially an estimate of the balance of all the man's qualities, those which primarily affect himself as much as those which primarily affect others. Here is the vital distinction between the legal and the moral question, and the characteristic defect of the external view of morality. Keeping, however, to the purely legal question, where the criterion is comparatively plain, we have other difficulties. We are only to punish Barnwell as an actual, not as a potential, murderer. We should let a man try any 'experiment in living' so long as its failure will affect himself only, or, rather, himself primarily, for no action is really 'isolated.' We are, says Mill, to put up with 'contingent' or 'constructive' injury for the sake of 'the greater good of human freedom.'[1] 'Society,' he urges, cannot complain of errors for which it is responsible. It has 'absolute power' over all its members in their infancy, and could always make the next generation a little better than the last. Why, then, interfere by the coarse methods of punishment to suppress what is not directly injurious to itself? The

[1] *Liberty*, p. 48.

strongest, however, of all reasons against interference, according to him, is that it generally interferes wrongly and in the wrong place. In proof of this he refers to various cases of religious persecution: to Puritanical laws against harmless recreation: to Socialist laws against the freedom to labour: to laws against intemperance and on behalf of Sunday observance: and, generally, to laws embodying the 'tyranny of the majority.' We may admit the badness of such legislation; but what is the criterion by which we are to decide its badness or goodness? Is it that in such cases the legislator is usurping the province of the moralist? that he is trying to suppress symptoms when the causes are beyond his power, and enforcing not virtue but hypocrisy? Or is it that he really ought to be indifferent in regard to the moral rules which are primarily self-regarding—to leave prudence, for example, to take care of itself or to be impressed by purely natural penalties; and to be indifferent to vice, drunkenness, or sexual irregularities, except by suppressing the crimes which incidentally result? Mill endeavours to adhere to his criterion, but has some difficulty in reconciling it to his practical conclusions.

Mill holds 'society' to be omnipotent over the young. It has no right to complain of the characters which it has itself concurred in producing. If this be so, can it be indifferent to morality? Indeed, Mill distinguishes himself from others of his school precisely by emphasising the educational efficiency of the state. Institutions, according to him, are the tools by which the human will—the will of the sovereign—moulds the character of the race. Mill's whole aim in economic questions is to encourage prudence, self-reliance, and energy. He wishes the state to interfere to strengthen and enlighten ; and to promote an equality of property which will raise the standard of life and discourage wasteful luxury. What is this but to stimulate certain moral creeds and to discourage certain 'experiments in living'? How can so powerful an agency affect character without affecting morals—self-regarding or extra-regarding? The difficulty comes out curiously in his last chapter. He has recourse to a dexterous casuistry to justify measures which have an obvious moral significance. Are we to legislate with a view to diminishing drunkenness? No : but we may put drunkards under special restrictions when they have once been led to violence. We should not tax stimulants simply in order to suppress drunkenness ; but, as we have to tax in any case, we may so arrange taxation as to discourage the consumption of injurious commodities. May we suppress gambling or fornication ? No : but we may perhaps see our way to suppressing public gambling-houses or brothels, because we may forbid solicitations to that which we think evil, though we are not so clear of the evil as to suppress the conduct itself. We may enforce universal education, though he makes the condition that the state is only to pay for the children of the poor, not to provide the schools. And, once more, we are not forbidden by his principle to legislate against imprudent marriages ; for the marriage clearly affects the offspring, and, moreover, affects all labourers in an over-populated country. Yet, what interference with private conduct could be more stringent or more directly affect morality ?

A principle requiring such delicate handling is not well

suited to guide practical legislation. This timid admission of moral considerations by a back-door is the more curious because Mill not only wishes to have a moral influence, but has the special merit, in economical and in purely political questions, of steadily and constantly insisting upon their moral aspect. He holds, and is justified in holding, that the ultimate end of the state should be to encourage energy, culture, and a strong sense of responsibility. It is true that, though he exaggerates the influence of institutions, he insists chiefly upon the negative side, upon that kind of 'education' which consists in leaving a man to teach himself. Yet his political theory implies a wider educational influence. Every citizen is to have a share both in the legislative and administrative functions of the government. Such an education must have a strong influence upon the moral characteristics. It may promote or discourage one morality or another, but it cannot be indifferent. And this impresses itself upon Mill himself. The principles of 'contradiction' in speculation and of 'antagonism' in politics ; the doctrines that each man is to form his own opinions and regulate his own life, imply a society of approximately equal and, as far as possible, independent units. This, if it means 'liberty,' also means a most effective 'educational' process. One lesson taught may be that 'any one man is as good as any other.' Mill sees this clearly, and declares that this 'false creed' is held in America and 'nearly connected' with some American defects.[1] He persuades himself that it may be remedied by Hare's scheme, and by devices for giving more votes to educated persons.

[1] *Representative Government*, p. 74.

One can only reply, *sancta simplicitas!* In fact, the 'educational' influence which implies levelling and equalising is not less effective than that which maintains ranks or a traditional order. It only acts in a different direction. Here, once more, Mill's argument seems to recoil upon his own position. When, in the *Liberty*, he sums up the influences hostile to individuality, including all the social and intellectual movements of the day, he is describing the forces which will drive his political machinery. The political changes which are to break up the old structure, to make society an aggregate of units approximately equal in wealth and power, will inevitably facilitate the deeper and wider influences of the social changes. If, in fact, 'individuality' in a good sense is being crushed by the whole democratic movement—where democracy means the whole social change—it will certainly not be protected by the political changes to be made in the name of liberty. Each man is to have his own little sphere ; but each man will be so infinitesimal a power that he will be more than ever moulded by the average opinions. In the *Liberty*[1] Mill puts his whole hope in the possibility that the 'intelligent part of the public' may be led to feel the force of his argument. To believe that a tendency fostered by every social change can be checked by the judicious reasoning of Utilitarian theorists, implies a touching faith in the power of philosophy.

Mill's doctrines, I believe, aim at most important truths. 'Energy' is, let us agree, a cardinal virtue and essential condition of progress. It requires, undoubtedly, a sphere of individual freedom. Without freedom, a man is a tool

[1] *Liberty*, p. 41.

—transmitting force mechanically, not himself co-operating intelligently or originating spontaneously. Every citizen should be encouraged to be an active as well as a passive instrument. Freedom of opinion is absolutely essential to progress, social as well as intellectual, and therefore thought should be able to play freely upon the sway of irrational custom. The tyranny of the commonplace, of a mental atmosphere which stifles genius and originality, is a danger to social welfare. That Mill held such convictions strongly was the source of his power. That he held to them, even when they condemned some party dogma, was honourable to his sincerity. That he failed to make them into a satisfactory or consistent whole was due to preconceptions imbibed from his teachers. Perhaps it is truer to say that he could not accurately formulate his beliefs in the old dialect than that his beliefs were intrinsically erroneous.

Upon his terms a clear demarcation of the sphere of free action is impossible. Mill, as an 'individualist,' took society to be an 'aggregate' instead of an 'organism.' To Mill such phrases as 'organic' savoured of 'mysticism' ; they treated a class name as meaning something more than the individuals, and therefore meant mere abstractions parading as realities,[1] and encouraged the fallacies current among Intuitionists and Transcendentalists. And yet they point at truths which are

[1] See in *Representative Government*, p. 62, his argument against the objection to Hare's scheme that it would destroy the local character of representation. The objectors think, he says, that 'a nation does not consist of persons but of artificial units, the creation of geography and statistics' ; that 'Liverpool and Exeter are the proper objects of a legislator's care in contradistinction to the population of those places.' This, he thinks, is 'a curious specimen of delusion produced by words.' The local interests and affections which bind neighbours and townsmen together may thus be simply set aside.

anything but mystical. It is a plain fact that society is a complex structure upon which every man is dependent in his whole life; and that he is a product, moulded through and through by instincts inherited or derived from his social position. Conversely it is true that the society is throughout dependent upon the character or the convictions and instincts of its constituent members. To overlook the reciprocal action and reaction, and the structure which corresponds to them, is necessarily to make arbitrary and inaccurate assumptions and to regard factors in a single process as independent entities. The tendency of the Utilitarian was to regard society as a number of independent beings, simply bound together by the legal or quasi-legal sanctions. Morality itself was treated as a case of external 'law.' The individual, again, was a bundle of ideas, bound together by 'associations which could be indefinitely modified.' In both cases, the unity was imposed by a force in some sense 'external,' and therefore the whole social structure of individual character became in some sense 'artificial.' It is the acceptance of such assumptions which hinders Mill in his attempt to mark out the individual sphere.

We have seen the difficulties. In morality, it is impossible to divide the 'extra-regarding' from the 'self-regarding' qualities, because morality is a function of the whole character considered as a unit. Mill, therefore, has to concede a considerable sphere to moral pressure. The fact that in positive law it is not only possible but necessary to distinguish 'self-regarding' actions from 'extra-regarding' actions marks the sphere within which legislation can work efficiently. But the same fact proves also that the direct legal coercion is

only a subordinate element in the whole social process. Though it is only called into play to suppress certain overt actions, it indirectly affects the whole character: it may help to stimulate all the qualities, 'self-regarding' or otherwise, which form a good citizen; and to argue that it should be indifferent to these broader results is to omit a reference to the wider 'utility' which is identical with morality. Mill is thus driven to awkward casuistry by trying to exclude the moral considerations where they are obviously essential, or to admit them under some ingenious pretext. In economic problems the difficulty is more conspicuous; for we have there to do with the whole industrial structure, which is affected throughout by institutions created or confirmed by law. It is, again, impossible to distinguish the spheres of the 'natural' and the 'artificial'—or of individual and state action. The industrial structure is a product of both. Consider all state action to be bad because 'artificial,' and you are led to such an isolation of the 'individual' as reduces all responsibility to a name for selfishness. You are to teach men to be prudent simply by leaving the imprudent to starvation. Mill, revolted by this consequence, admits that the state must have regard to the injustice for which it is, at least indirectly, responsible. He then inclines to exaggerate the power of the 'artificial' factor because it embodies human 'volition' and leans towards the crude Socialism which assumes that all institutions can be arbitrarily reconstructed by legislative interference. Hence when we come to the political problem, to the organ by which the legal bond is constructed, Mill exaggerates the power of 'making' as contradistinguished from the

'growing.' He seems to assume that institutions can 'create' the instincts by which they are worked: or to forget that they primarily transmit instead of originating power, though indirectly they foster or hinder the development of certain tendencies. Mill would guard against the abuse of political power by dividing it among the separate individuals. He then perceives that he is only redistributing this tremendous power instead of diminishing its intensity. By isolating the 'individual' he has condemned him to narrow views and petty ideals, but has not prevented him from impressing them upon the mass of homogeneous units. Hence, he is alarmed by the inevitable 'tyranny of the majority.' He has put a tremendous power into the hands of Demos, and can only suggest that it should not be exercised.

It is, if I am right, the acceptance of this antithesis, put absolutely, the 'individual,' as something natural on one side, and law, on the other side, as a bond imposed upon the society, which at every step hampers Mill's statement of any vital truths. He cannot upon these terms draw a satisfactory distinction between the individual and the society. When man is taken for a ready-made product, while his social relation can be 'made' offhand by the sovereign, it is impossible to give a satisfactory account of the slow processes of evolution in which making and growing are inextricably united, and the individual and the society are slowly modified by the growth of instincts and customs under constant action and reaction. The difficulty of course is not solved by recognising its existence. No one has yet laid down a satisfactory criterion of the proper limits of individual responsibility. The problem is too vast and complex

to admit of any offhand solution; and Mill's error lies chiefly in underestimating the difficulty.

The contrast to Comte is significant. The inventor of 'sociology' had seen in the 'individualism' of the revolutionary school a transitory and negative stage of thought, which was to lead to a reconstruction of intellectual and social authority. Mill could see in Comte's final Utopia nothing but the restoration of a spiritual despotism in a form more crushing and all-embracing than that of the mediæval church. They went together up to a certain point. Comte held that 'contradiction' and 'antagonism' were not ultimate ends, though they may be inseparable incidents of progress. In the intellectual sphere we should hope for the emergence of a rational instead of an arbitrary authority, and a settlement of first principles, not a permanent conflict of opinion. The hope of achieving some permanent conciliation is the justification of scepticism in speculation and revolutions in politics. Comte supposed that such a result might be achieved in sociology. If that science were constituted, its professors might have such an authority as now possessed by astronomers and teachers of physical sciences. Society might then be reconstructed on sound principles which would secure the responsibility of rulers to subjects, and the confidence of the subjects in rulers. Mill in his early enthusiasm had admitted the necessity of a 'spiritual power' to be founded on free discussion.[1] He had, with Comte, condemned the merely critical attitude of the revolutionary school. When he saw Comte devising an elaborate hierarchy to govern speculation, and even depreciating the reason in com-

[1] See *Correspondence with Comte*, p. 414.

parison with the 'heart,' he revolted. Comte was a great thinker, greater, even, he thought, than Descartes or Leibniz,[1] but had plunged into absurdities suggestive of brain disease. The absurdities were, indeed, flagrant, yet Mill still sympathises with much of Comte's doctrine; with the positivist religion ; and the general social conceptions. Even a 'spiritual authority ' is, he thinks, desirable. But it must be developed through free discussion and the gradual approximation of independent thinkers, not by premature organisation and minute systematisation.[2] The regeneration of society requires a moral and intellectual transformation, which can only be regarded as a distant ideal. We may dream of a state of things in which even political authority shall be founded upon reason : in which statesmanship shall really mean an application of scientific principles, and rulers be recognised as devoted servants of the state. Even an approximation to such a Utopia would imply a change in moral instincts, and in the corresponding social structure, to be worked out slowly and tentatively. Yet Mill is equally over-sanguine in his own way. He puts an excessive faith in human 'contrivances,' representation of minorities, and the forces of 'antagonism' and 'individuality.' If Comte's scheme really amounts, as Mill thought, to a suppression of individual energy, Mill's doctrine tends to let energy waste itself in mere eccentricity. As originality of intellect is useful when it accepts established results, so energy of character is fruitful when it is backed by sympathy. The degree of both may be measured by their power of meeting opposition ; but the positive stimulus comes from co-

[1] Auguste Comte, p. 200. [2] Ibid. pp. 94-100.

operation. The great patriots and founders of religion have opposed tyrants and bigots because they felt themselves to be the mouthpiece of a nation or a whole social movement. And, therefore, superlative as' may be the value of energy, it is not generated in a chaos where every man's hand is against his neighbour, but in a social order, where vigorous effort may be sure of a sufficient backing. When the individual is regarded as an isolated being, and state action as necessarily antagonistic, this side of the problem is insufficiently taken into account, and the question made to lie between simple antagonism and enforced unity.

VIII. ETHICS

The problem must be left to posterity. Mill's doctrine, if I am right, is vitiated rather by an excessive emphasis upon one aspect of facts than by positive error. He seems often to be struggling to express half-recognised truths, and to be hampered by an inadequate dialect. I have already touched upon the morality more or less involved in his political and economic views. His ethical doctrine shows the source of some of his perplexities and apparent inconsistencies. His position is given in the little book upon *Utilitarianism*, which is scarcely more, however, than an occasional utterance.[1] In a more systematic treatise some difficulties would have been more carefully treated, and assumptions more

[1] I refer to the second edition (1864). Mill's *Utilitarianism*, and some other parts of his writings referring to the same subject, have been republished in 1897 by Mr. Charles Douglas as *The Ethics of John Stuart Mill*. He has prefixed some interesting 'Introductory Essays.' Mr. Douglas had previously published *John Stuart Mill; a Study of his Philosophy*, 1895. Both are valuable studies of Mill.

explicitly justified. The main lines, however, of Mill's Utilitarianism are plain enough. The book is substantially a protest against the assertion that Utilitarian morality is inferior to its rivals. 'Utilitarians,' he says, 'should never cease to claim the morality of self-devotion as a possession which belongs by as good a right to them as to the Stoic or to the Transcendentalist.'[1] The Utilitarian standard is 'not the agent's own happiness, but the happiness of all concerned.' The Utilitarian must be 'as strictly impartial as a disinterested and benevolent spectator ' in determining his course of action. The spirit of his ethics is expressed in 'the golden rule of Jesus of Nazareth.' Mill insists as strongly as possible upon the paramount importance of the social aspect of morality. Society must be founded throughout upon justice and sympathy. Every step in civilisation generates in each individual 'a feeling of unity with all the rest.'[2] Characteristically he refers to Comte's *Politique Positive* in illustration. Though he has the 'strongest objections' to the system of morals and politics there set forth, he thinks that Comte has 'superabundantly shown the possibility of giving to the service of humanity, even without the aid of belief in a Providence, both the psychical power and the social efficacy of a religion.' Nay, it may 'colour all thought, feeling, and action, in a manner of which the greatest ascendency ever exercised by any religion may be but a type or foretaste.' The danger is that the ascendency may be so marked as to suppress 'human freedom and individuality.' The love of the right is to become an all-absorbing passion, and selfish motives admitted only so far as subordinated to

[1] *Utilitarianism*, p. 24. [2] *Ibid.* p. 48.

desire for the welfare of the social body. Clearly this is a loftier line than Bentham's attempt to evade the difficulty by ignoring the possibility of a conflict between private and public interest. The only question, then, is as to the logic. Can Mill's conclusions be deduced from his premises ?

We must first observe that Mill's argument is governed by his antipathy to the 'intuitionist.' The intuitionist was partly represented by his old antagonist Whewell, who in a ponderous treatise had set forth a theory of morality intended not only to give first principles but to elaborate a complete moral code. Mill attacked him with unusual severity in an article in the *Westminster Review*.[1] Whewell, in truth, appears at one time to be founding morality upon positive law—a doctrine which is at best a strange perversion of a theory of experience ; and yet he denounces Utilitarians by the old arguments, and brings in such an 'intuitionism' as always roused Mill's combative propensities. Mill defends Bentham against Whewell, and his *Utilitarianism* starts essentially from Bentham's famous saying, ' Nature has placed mankind under the governance of two sovereign masters, pain and pleasure.' Happiness, says Mill, is the 'sole end of human action ' ; to 'desire' is to find a thing pleasant ; to be averse from a thing is to think of it as painful ; and, as happiness gives the criterion of all conduct, it must give 'the standard of morality.'[2] To 'prove' the first principle may be impossible ; one can only appeal to self-consciousness in general ; but it seems to him so obvious that it will 'hardly be disputed.'[3] It still requires explicate statement in order to

[1] October 1852, reprinted in *Dissertations*, ii. 450, etc. [2] *Utilitarianism*, pp. 17, 58. [3] *Ibid.* p. 59.

exclude a doctrine held by many philosophers. Mill[1] refers to Kant, whose formula that you are to act so that the rule on which you act may be law for all rational beings, is the most famous version of the doctrine which would deduce morality from reason. It really proves at most, as Mill says, the formal truth that laws must be consistent, but it fails 'almost grotesquely' in showing which consistent laws are right. Absolute selfishness or absolute benevolence would equally satisfy the formula. For Mill, then, all conduct depends on pain and pleasure; every theory of conduct must therefore be based upon psychology, or consequently upon experience, not upon abstract logic. Every attempt to twist morality out of pure reason is foredoomed to failure; logical contradiction corresponds to the impossible, not to the immoral, which is only too possible. That is a first principle, which seems to me, I confess, to be unassailable.

It follows, in the next place, that Mill's argument is substantially an interpretation of facts, a sketch of a scientific theory of certain social phenomena. We find that certain rules of conduct are as a matter of fact generally approved; and we have to show that those rules are deducible from the assumed criterion. The rule, 'act for the greatest happiness of the greatest number,' coincides with the conduct approved in the recognised morality, and we need and can ask for no further explanation of the 'criterion.' Mill answers the usual objections. The criterion, it is said, can only justify the 'expedient' not the 'right.' The Utilitarian must act from a calculation of 'consequences,' and consequences are so uncertain that no general rule can be

[1] *Utilitarianism*, p. 5.

framed. To this, as urged by Whewell, Mill replied that his adversary had proved too much.[1] The argument would destroy 'prudence' as well as morality. We can make general rules about the interests of the greatest number as easily as about our own personal interests. And, if it be urged that such general rules always admit of exceptions, all moralists have had to admit exceptions to moral rules. Exceptions, however, as James Mill had said, can only be admitted in morality, when the exception itself expresses a general rule. All moralists admit of lying in some extreme cases, but only where the obligation to speak truth conflicts with some higher obligation. If something be wanting in this defence, it may perhaps be supplied from Mill himself. The importance of cultivating a sensitive love of truth is, he says, so great as to possess a 'transcendent expediency'[2] not to be violated by temporary considerations. When discussing the question of justice Mill insists upon the importance of the confidence in our fellow-creatures as corresponding to the 'very groundwork of our existence.' The general rule, that is, corresponds to an individual quality which is essential to the social union. A strong sense of veracity is unconditionally good, though circumstances may require exceptions to any rule when stated in terms of outward conduct. Lying may be necessary, but should always be painful. This is familiar ground on which it is needless to dwell. But another criticism of the 'criterion' is more important and leads to one of Mill's most characteristic arguments. The greatest happiness criterion, it is often said, will be interpreted differently as men form different judgments of

[1] *Dissertations*, ii. 474.   [2] *Utilitarianism*, p. 33.

what constitutes happiness. The 'felicific calculus' will give different results for the philosopher and the clown, the sensualist and the ascetic, the savage and the civilised man; and it is part of the empiricist contention that in fact the standard has varied widely. Mill himself observes, and he is only following Locke[1] and Hume, 'that morality has varied widely; has in some cases sanctioned practices the most revolting' to others, and that the 'universal will of mankind is universal only in its discordance.'[2] It is indeed precisely for that reason that the Utilitarian has declined to accept the authority of the 'moral sense' and appealed to facts. The belief that our feeling is right, simply because it is ours, is the 'mental infirmity which Bentham's philosophy tends to correct and Dr. Whewell's to perpetuate.'[3] That is to say, Bentham can lay down an 'objective criterion' because he calculates actual pains and pleasures. But will not this criterion be after all 'subjective' because our estimate of pains and pleasures is so discordant? Mill tries to meet this by a famous distinction between the qualities of pleasures. Bentham had insisted that one pleasure was as good as another. 'Quantity of pleasure being equal, push-pin is as good as poetry.'[4] Mill now declares that it is quite compatible with the principle of utility to recognise the fact that some kinds of pleasure are more desirable and more valuable than others.' We must consider 'quality' as well as 'quantity.'[5] The 'only competent judges,' he argues,

[1] See Locke's *Essay* (bk. i. ch. iii. § 9) upon the 'Caribbees' and 'Tououpinambos.'
[2] *Dissertations*, ii. 198.   [3] *Ibid.* ii. 389.   [4] *Ibid.* ii. 389.
[5] *Utilitarianism*, p. 12. It is rather odd to find Mr. Ruskin making the same remark.—*Fors Clavigera*, xiv. 8.

are those who have known both. Now, it is an 'unquestionable fact' that those who have this advantage prefer the higher or intellectual to the lower or sensual pleasures. It is better to be a Socrates dissatisfied than a fool satisfied. If the fool or the pig dissents it is because he only knows his own side of the question.[1]

Answers are only too obvious. What is 'quantity' as distinguished from 'quality' of pleasure? The statement, 'A cubic foot of water weighs less than a cubic foot of lead' is intelligible; but what is the corresponding proposition about pleasure? Can we ask, How much benevolence is equal to how much hunger? The 'how much' is strictly meaningless. Moreover, are not both Socrates and the pig right in their judgment? Pig's-wash is surely better for the pig than dialogue; and dialogue may be better for Socrates than pig's-wash. If 'desirable' means that pleasure which each desires, each may be right. If it means some quality independent of the agent, we have the old fallacy which in political economy makes 'value' something 'objective.' All 'value' must depend upon the man as well as upon the thing. And this again suggests that neither Socrates nor a Christian saint would really make the supposed assertion. It is not true absolutely that 'intellectual' pleasures are simply 'better' than sensual. Each is better in certain circumstances. There are times when even the saint prefers a glass of water to religious musings; and moments when even a fool may at times find such intellectual pleasures as he can enjoy better than a glass of wine. This seems to be so obvious that we must suspect Mill of hastily

[1] *Utilitarianism*, p. 14. The argument is virtually Plato's. See *Republic*, book ix. (581-83).

stopping a gap in his argument without duly working out the implications. Indeed, he seems to be making room for something very like an intuition. He assumes the proposition, doubtful in itself and apparently inconsistent with his own position, that all competent people agree, and then makes this agreement decisive of a disputable question.

Bentham, from his own point of view, was, I think, perfectly right in his statement. To calculate pleasures, the only question must be which are the greatest pleasures, and the only answer, those which, as a fact, attract people most. If a man is more attracted by 'push-pin' than by poetry, the presumption is that push-pin gives him most pleasure. We are simply investigating facts; and cannot overlook the obvious fact that estimates of pleasure vary indefinitely. Some things are pleasant to the refined alone, while others are more or less pleasant to every-body, and others, again, cease to be pleasant or become disgusting as men advance. To introduce the moral valuation in an estimate of facts—to change the 'desir-able' as 'that which is desired' into the 'desirable' as 'that which ought to be desired' is to beg the question or to argue in circle.

Yet Mill was aiming at an obvious truth. As men advance intellectually, intellectual pleasures will clearly fill a larger space in their ideal of life. The purely sensual pleasures will have their value as long as men have bodies and appetites; but they will come to have a subordinate place in defining the whole ends of human conduct. The morality of the higher being will include higher aspira-tions. We have then to inquire, In what sense is a 'felicific calculus' possible or required? The moral rule

is, as Mill holds, a statement of certain fundamental con-ditions of social life, giving, as he puts it, the 'ground-work' upon which all social relations are built up. This again supposes essentially a society made of the most varying elements, poets and men of science, philosophers and fools, nay, according to him, including both Socrates and the pig. In criticising Whewell, for example, he quotes[1] with most emphatical approval that 'admirable passage' in which Bentham includes animal happiness in his criterion. We are to promote the pig's happiness so far as the pig is 'sentient,' little as he may care for a Socratic dialogue. But if so, the 'greatest happiness' rule must have for its end the conditions under which the most varying types of happiness may be promoted and each kind of happiness promoted according to the character of the subject. And in point of fact, the actual moral rules, 'Love your neighbour as yourself,' be truthful, honest, and so forth, do not as such define any special type of happiness as good. They assume rather that happiness, as happiness, is so far good; and that we ought to promote the happiness of others if our action be not objectionable upon some other ground. This indicates a really weak point of the old Utilitarianism, which Mill was trying to remedy. If, as Bentham would seem to imply, we are to form our estimate of happiness simply by accepting average estimates of existing human beings, we shall be tempted to approve conduct conducive to the lower kinds of happiness alone. I should reply that this is to misunderstand the true nature of morality. If morality, as Mill would admit, corresponds essentially to the primary relations of social life, it is defined

[1] *Dissertations*, ii. 482.

not by any average estimates of happiness, but by a statement of the conditions of the welfare of the social organism. It states the fundamental terms upon which men can best associate. It gives the fundamental 'social compact' (if we may accept the phrase with-out its fallacious connotation) implied in an ordered system of society. The happiness of each is good, so far as it does not imply anti-social characteristics. But morality leaves room for the existence of the most varied types of character from the saint to the pig, and aims at producing happiness—not by taking the existing average man as an ultimate unalterable type, but—by leaving room for such a development of men themselves as will alter their character and therefore their views of happiness. As the society progresses the individual will himself be altered, and the type which implies a greater development of intellect, sympathy, and energy come to prevail over the lower, more sensual, selfish, and feeble type. Though happiness is still the ultimate base, the morality applies immediately to the social bond, which contemplates a general development of the whole man and a modification of the elements of happiness itself. Mill, perceiving that something was wanted, makes the unfortunate attempt at supplying the gap by his assumption of an imaginary consensus of all the better minds. What is true is that all men may consent to conditions of society which leave a free play to the higher influences: that is, are favourable to the more advanced type with greater force of intellect and richness of emotional power.

Here we return to the old Utilitarian problem: What is the 'sanction' of morality? The 'sanction' can be

nothing else than the sum of all the motives which in-duce men to act morally. What, then, are they? The Utilitarians, starting from the juridical point of view, had a ready answer in the case of positive law. The sanction, briefly, is the gallows. Law means coercion, and as everybody (with very insignificant exceptions) objects to being hanged, the gallows may be regarded as a sanction of universal efficacy. If the moral law be taken in the same way as implying a rule of conduct to be enforced by an external sanction, the correlative to the gallows was hell-fire. This satisfied Paley, but as the Utilitarians had abolished hell, they were at some loss for a substitute.

Here Mill accepts the principles laid down by his father. He defends the Utilitarians upon the ground that they 'had gone beyond all others in affirming that the motive has nothing to do with the morality of the action, though much with the morality of the agent.'[1] They based morality upon 'consequences,' and the con-sequences of an action are no doubt independent of the motive. If I burn a man for heresy, the 'consequences' to him are the same whether my motive be love of his soul or the hatred of a bigot for a free-thinker. To estimate the goodness or badness of an action, we must consider all that it implies. We must inquire whether a society in which heretics are repressed by the stake is better or worse than one in which they are left at liberty; and that cannot be settled by simply asking whether the persecutor is benevolent or male-

[1] *Utilitarianism*, p. 26. Mill is answering the criticism that Utilitarianism puts the standard of morality too high if it assumes that every man is to be prompted by desire for the 'greatest happiness of the greatest number.' I have spoken of this in considering James Mill's ethical position.

volent. The purest benevolence may be misguided if it is directed by erroneous belief. The 'sentimentalism,' denounced by Utilitarians, implied refusal to look at consequences, and the justification, for example, of corrupting charity on the ground that it was pleasant to the sympathy of the corrupter. Their especial function was to warn philanthropists that misguided philanthropy might stimulate the greatest evils. But to infer from this the general principle that the 'motive' was indifferent involves the characteristic fallacy. The true inference is that sound morality has an intellectual as well as an emotional basis; it supposes a just foresight of consequences as well as a desire for happiness. Conduct depends throughout upon character; it cannot be altered without altering character, though the alteration may imply enlightenment of the intellect rather than development of the feelings. When we come to the moral 'sanction' the motive becomes all important. The legislator may be contented if he can induce a bad man to act like a good man or to refrain from murder in the presence of the policeman. He can take the policeman and the gallows for granted; and assume the existence of the fundamental social instincts upon which the judicial machinery depends. But it is precisely with those instincts that the moralist is concerned. He has to ask what are the forces which work the machinery and cannot be indifferent to the question of 'motive.' Mill only half recognises the point when he admits that the 'motive' has much to do with the 'morality of the agent.' If 'motive' be interpreted widely enough it constitutes the agent's morality. An action is moral in so far as it implies a

character thoroughly 'moralised' or fitted to play the right part in society. The distinction between the morality of the conduct and the morality of the agent vanishes. A good act is that which a good man would perform. If a bad man, under compulsion, acts in the same way, he acts from fear, and his act is therefore morally neutral, and to call him good on account of his action is therefore a mistake. He simply shows that he is a man, and dislikes hanging even more than he hates his fellow-men.

An 'external sanction' really means a motive for acting as though you were good even if you are not good. That such sanctions are essential to society, that they provide a shelter under which true morality may or must grow up, is obvious. It is true, also, that in early stages the distinction between the law which rests upon force and that which rests upon the character is not manifest. But ultimately morality means nothing but the expression of the character itself. Hence to find a universal 'sanction' for morality is chimerical. Such a sanction would be 'a motive' which would apply to all men good or bad; that is, it would not be a moral motive. Fear of hell or the gallows may indirectly help (or hinder) the development of a moral character; but in itself the fear is neither good nor bad. The very attempt, therefore, to find such a 'sanction' implies the 'external' or essentially inadequate view of morality, into which the Utilitarians with their legal prepossessions were too apt to fall. The law, resting upon external sanctions, may be useful or prejudicial to morals, but must always be subordinate; for its application depends upon instincts by which it is guided and which it cannot create.

Mill recognises this, virtually, though not explicitly, in his discussion of the 'Utilitarian sanction.' He declares in rather awkward phrase that the 'ultimate sanction of all morality (external motives apart)' is 'a subjective feeling in our own minds.' (Where else can such a feeling be, and what is 'an objective feeling'?) These feelings exist, as he argues, equally for the Utilitarian and the 'Transcendentalist,' though the 'Transcendentalists' think that their existence 'in the mind' implies that they have a 'root out of the mind.'[1] The 'conscience,' that is, pain in breaking the moral law, exists as a fact, whatever its origin. If 'innate' it can still be opposed, and the question, 'Why should I obey it?' is equally difficult to answer. Even if innate, again, it may be an innate regard for other men's pains and pleasures, and so coincide with the Utilitarian view. He argues accordingly, that, in point of fact, we may acquire that 'feeling of unity' with others which gives the really 'ultimate sanction' to the 'Happiness morality.'[2] With this result I at least can have no quarrel. I hold it to be perfectly correct and as good an account of morality as can be given. The fault is in placing the 'external sanction' on the same level with the 'internal' and failing to see that it is not properly 'moral' at all. But here, once more, it is necessary to look at the difficulty of deriving his conclusion from the premises inherited from his teachers. The essential difficulty lies in the psychological analysis and the theory of association. We are again at James Mill's point of view. Conduct is determined by pain and pleasure. An action supposes an end, and that 'end' must be a pleasure. If we ask,

pleasure to whom? the answer must be, pleasure to the agent. All conduct, it would seem, must be directly or indirectly self-regarding, for the 'end' must always be my own pleasure. Mill maintains that 'virtue' may, for the Utilitarian as well as for others, be a 'thing desirable in itself.'[1] That is a 'psychological fact,' independently of the explanation. But at this point he lapses into the old doctrine. Virtue, he admits, is not 'naturally and originally part of the end.' Virtue was once desired simply 'for its conduciveness to pleasure' and especially 'to protection from pain.' It becomes a good in itself. This is enforced by the familiar illustration of the 'love of money' and of the love of power or fame. Each passion aimed originally at a further end, which has dropped out while the desire for means has become original. The moral feelings, as he says in answer to Whewell,[2] are 'eminently artificial and the product of culture.' We may grow corn, or we may as easily grow hemlocks or thistles. Yet, as he declares in the Utilitarianism,[3] 'moral feelings' are not 'the less natural' because 'acquired.' The 'moral faculty' is a 'natural outgrowth' of our nature. The antithesis of 'natural' and 'artificial' is generally ambiguous; but Mill's view is clear enough upon the main point. Virtue is the product of the great force 'indissoluble association.' Now 'artificial associations' are dissolved 'as intellectual culture goes on.' But the association between virtue and utility is indissoluble, because there is a 'natural basis of sentiment' which strengthens it—that basis being 'our desire to be in unity with our fellow-creatures.'[4] One further

---

[1] *Utilitarianism*, p. 42.   [2] *Ibid.* p. 48.

[1] *Utilitarianism*, p. 54.   [2] *Dissertations*, ii. 472.
[3] *Utilitarianism*, p. 45   [4] *Ibid.* p. 46.

corollary deserves notice. To become virtuous, it is necessary to acquire virtuous habits. We 'will' at first simply because we desire. Afterwards we come to desire a thing because we will it. 'Will is the child of desire, and passes out of the dominion of its parent only to come under that of habit.'[1] Thus, as he had said in the *Logic*,[2] we learn to will a thing 'without reference to its being pleasurable'—a fact illustrated by the habit of 'hurtful excess' and equally by moral heroism. It would surely be more consistent to say that habit is a modification of character which alters our pains and pleasures but does not enable us to act against our judgment of pains and pleasures. He is trying to escape from an awkward consequence; but the mode of evasion will hardly bear inspection.

Mill's arguments imply his thorough adherence to the 'association psychology.' They really indicate, I think, an attempt to reach a right conclusion from defective premises. The error is implied in the analysis of 'ends' of action. When a man acts with a view to an 'end' the true account is that his immediate action is affected by all the consequences which he foresees. This or that motive conquers because it includes a perception of more or less remote results. But what determines conduct is not a calculation of some future pains or pleasures, but the actual painfulness or pleasurableness of the whole action at the moment. I shrink from the pain of a wound or from the pain of giving a wound to another person. Both are equally my immediate feelings; and it is an error to analyse the sympathetic pain into two different factors, one the immediate action and the other

[1] *Utilitarianism*, p. 60.   [2] *Logic*, bk. vi. ch. iii. § 4.

the anticipated reaction. It is one indissoluble motive, just as natural or original as the dislike to the unpleasant sensation of my own wound. To distinguish it into two facts and make one subordinate and a product of association is a fallacy. We can hardly believe that 'association' accounts even for 'love of money' or 'fame.' Avarice and vanity mean an exaggerated fear of poverty or regard to other people's opinions. They do not imply any forgetfulness of end for means, but an erroneous estimate of the proportion of means to ends. The really noticeable point, again, has already met us in James Mill's ethics. When Mill speaks of 'virtue' as 'artificial' or derivative, he is asserting a truth not to be denied by an evolutionist. Undoubtedly the social sentiments have been slowly developed; and undoubtedly they have grown up under the protection of external 'sanctions.' The primitive society did not distinguish between law and morality; the pressure of external circumstances upon character and the influence of the character itself upon the society. A difficulty arises from the defective view which forces Mill to regard the whole process as taking place within the life of the individual. The unit is then a being without moral instincts at all, and they have to be inserted by the help of the association machinery. Sympathy is not an intrinsic part of human nature in its more advanced stages, but something artificial stuck on by indissoluble association. Mill, himself, when discussing the virtue of justice in his last chapter, substantially adopts a line of argument which, if not satisfactory in details, sufficiently recognises this point of view. And, if he still fails to explain morality sufficiently, it is in the main

because he never freed himself from the unsatisfactory assumptions of the old psychology. Here, as in so many other cases, he sees the inadequacy of the old conclusions, but persuades himself that a better result can be reached without the thorough revision which was really necessary.

CHAPTER V

HISTORICAL METHOD

I. JOHN AUSTIN

I HAVE spoken more than once of the paradox implied in the Utilitarian combination of appeals to 'experience,' with indifference to history. The importance of historical methods already recognised by Mill has become more obvious in later years. It was, as he saw, clearly desirable that the Utilitarians should annex this field of inquiry and apply appropriate methods. I have said something of Mill's view of the problems thus suggested; but the attitude of the Utilitarians in regard to them may be more fully indicated by the writings of some of his allies.

John Austin (1790-1859)[1] was accepted as the heir-apparent to Bentham in the special department of jurisprudence. Five years' service in the army was a unique apprenticeship for a Benthamite; and, as his widow tells us, helped to develop his chivalrous sense of honour. It may also help to explain a want of sympathy for the democratic zeal of most of his comrades. In any case, it did not suppress a delight in intellectual activity. Austin left the army, and in 1818 was called to the bar, but ill-health compelled him to retire in 1825. He was

[1] See Memoir by Mrs. Austin prefixed to the edition of his *Lectures*, edited by Mr. R. Campbell (1869).

thus qualified to be a jurist by some knowledge of practice, and forced to turn his knowledge to theoretical application. Upon the foundation of the London University he became the first professor of jurisprudence. With the true scholar's instinct for thorough preparation, he went to Bonn, studied the great German writers upon jurisprudence, and made the acquaintance of eminent living professors. The insular narrowness of Bentham and James Mill was thus to be corrected by cosmopolitan culture. Austin returned amidst the highest expectations. A clear voice, a perfect delivery, and a courteous and dignified manner were suited to give effect to his teaching ; and unanimous tradition tells us that his powers in conversation were unsurpassed. Why did he not acquire such an intellectual leadership in London as Dugald Stewart had enjoyed in Edinburgh ? Some reasons are obvious. English barristers and law students were serenely indifferent to the 'philosophy of law.' They had quite enough to do in acquiring familiarity with the technicalities of English practice. The University itself turned out to be chiefly a high school for boys not yet ripe for legal studies. Though J. S. Mill attended his lectures and took elaborate notes, few men had Mill's thirst for knowledge. Moreover, Austin thought it a duty to be as dry as Bentham, and discharged that duty scrupulously. The audiences dwindled, and the salary, derived from the fees, dwindled with it. Austin, a poor man, could not go on discoursing gratuitously to empty benches, and gave his last lecture in 1832.

Admiring friends did their best to find a sphere for his talents. Brougham placed him on the Criminal Law Commission, where he soon found that there was

no serious chance of being employed, as he desired, in active codification. A course of lectures promoted by the sound Utilitarian, Henry Bickersteth (Lord Langdale), at the Inner Temple fell as flat as the former. Austin retired to France, saying that he was born out of time and place, and should have been a 'schoolman of the twelfth century or a German professor.' He was afterwards on a Commission at Malta, with his friend Sir. G. Cornewall Lewis for a colleague. A change of government brought this employment to an end. Austin gave up active work. He passed some years in Germany and France in the enjoyment of intellectual society. After the revolution of 1848 he returned to England, and led a quiet country life at Weybridge. His sole later publication was a pamphlet against parliamentary reform in 1859. He died in the following December. Weak health and a fastidious temperament partly account for his silence. After publishing his early lectures he could never be induced to bring out a second edition. He suffered from scholar's paralysis—preference of doing nothing to doing anything short of the ideal standard. He had not strength to satisfy the demands of German professors, and cared nothing for the applause of the British public. His 'estimate of men was low,' says Mrs. Austin, 'and his solicitude for their approbation was consequently small.' His want of success did not embitter, though it discouraged him ; and he was constantly, we are told, 'meditating on the sublimest themes that can occupy the mind of man.' He kept the results for his own circle of hearers. Utilitarian zeal for democracy was impossible for him. He had the scholar's contempt

for the vulgar, and dreaded political changes which could increase the power of the masses. It is the more remarkable that Austin's Utilitarianism is of the most rigid orthodoxy. A thorough Benthamite training gave absolute immunity to even the germs of transcendental philosophy. He speaks with the profoundest respect of the great German professors, especially of Savigny. He cordially admires their learning and acuteness. But when they deviate into philosophy he denounces their 'jargon' as roundly as Bentham or James Mill. Austin became the typical expounder of Benthamite jurisprudence. His lectures long enjoyed a high reputation : partly, I cannot help guessing, because, good or bad, they had the field to themselves ; partly, also, because their dry, logical articulation fits them admirably for examination purposes ; and partly, I do not doubt, because they represent some rare qualities of mind. Their fame declined upon the rise of the 'historical school.' Austin's star set as Maine's rose. Yet Austin himself claimed that his was the really historical method. The historical school, he says,[1] is the school which appeals to 'experience,' and holds that a 'body of law cannot be spun out of a few general principles, considered a priori.' Bentham clearly falls under the definition, for Bentham considered the reports of English decisions to be 'an invaluable mine of experience for the legislator.' If this be an adequate criterion, how does Bentham differ from the school which claimed the historical method as its distinctive characteristic ? Austin aims at giving a 'philosophy of law.' The phrase at once indicates two correlative lines of inquiry. A 'law' supposes a law-giver

[1] *Jurisprudence*, p. 701.

—an authority which lays down or enforces the law. We may then inquire what is implied by the existence of this authority, or what is its origin, growth, and constitution ? That is a problem of 'social dynamics.' We may, again, take the existence of the state for granted ; inquire what are the actual laws ; how they can be classified and simplified ; and what are the consequent relations between the state and the individual. That is a problem of 'social statics,' and corresponds to the ordinary legal point of view. The conception of 'law' is common to both, though it may be approached from opposite directions, and may require modification so as to bring the results of the two lines of inquiry into harmony. The problems, and therefore the methods of inquiry, must be distinct, but each may be elucidated by the other.

Austin's position is given by his definition of law. It implies what has been called the 'Austinian analysis,' and is considered by his followers to dissolve all manner of sophistries. It is already implied in Hobbes.[1] A law, briefly, is the command of a sovereign enforced by a sanction. The definition gives the obvious meaning for the lawyer. Murder is punishable by death. That is the law of England. To prove that is the law, we need only go to the statute-book. The statute rests upon the absolute authority of the legislature. It assumes the existence, then, of a sovereign ; an ultimate authority behind which the lawyer never goes. It is for him infallible. The English lawyer accepts an act of parliament as a man of science accepts a law of nature. If

[1] For Austin's admiration of Hobbes see especially the long note in *Jurisprudence*, p. 286, etc.

there be any law which has not these marks it is for him no law. Conduct is illegal when the state machinery can be put in force to suppress it. Therefore the sphere of law is precisely marked out by the conception of the sovereign and the sanction.

The definition, then, may be true and relevant for all the lawyer's purposes. But a definition, as J. S. Mill would point out, is not a sufficient foundation for a philosophy. It may provisionally mark out some province for investigation; but we must always be prepared to ask how far the definition corresponds to an important difference. Now Austin's definition has important implications. It excludes as well as includes. Having defined a law, he argues that many other things which pass by that name are only 'metaphorically' or 'analogically' laws; and this raises the question, whether the fact that they do not conform to his definition corresponds to a vital difference in their real nature? Is he simply saying, 'I do not call them laws,' or really pointing out an essential and relevant difference of 'kind'? An important point is suggested by one exclusion. We are not to confound the so-called laws proper with the 'laws of nature' of scientific phraseology. Such a law of nature is simply a statement of a general fact. The astronomer asserts that the motion of bodies may be described by a certain formula. In saying so, he does not assert, even if he believes the inference to be legitimate, that their motion is caused by a divine command or enforced by a sanction. The actual uniformity is all that concerns him. The uniformity produced by law proper led, as Austin holds, to a confusion between different conceptions. Austin was clearly right in pointing out the difference;

and scientific thinkers, before and since his time, have had to struggle with a fallacy, singularly tenacious of life. A 'law of nature' in the scientific sense is not a law in the jurist's sense. The difference may be regarded in another way. The two senses of law differ as a 'command' differs from a proposition; the imperative from the indicative mood. The command, 'Do not murder,' is not a simple proposition. It belongs rather to action than to belief. It utters a volition and therefore creates a fact, instead of simply expressing a truth. Yet a command is also a fact, and may be regarded as part of the general system of fact. The command, 'Do not murder,' implies the fact, 'murder is forbidden.' We might show that in certain social conditions murder becomes punishable by death. That is a property of society at certain stages. If the social machinery worked with perfect accuracy, it would be as much a law of nature that a society kills murderers as that a wolf kills lambs or that fire burns straw. From this point of view, then, a 'law proper' falls under the conception of a 'law of nature,' though a law of nature is not a 'law proper.' It is a law of nature in the making, or a law of nature which is only fulfilled when a number of complex conditions of human conduct are satisfied. Austin, denying that free-will means a really arbitrary element, would no doubt have admitted that the 'law proper' was a product of the general laws (in the scientific sense) of human nature. This aspect of the case, however, passes out of sight. The law is something created; 'set,' as he calls it, or laid down by the sovereign at his own will, and is thus perfectly arbitrary. That is the ultimate fact, and makes a radical difference. We stop at the

'command,' and do not ask how the command itself comes into existence. This corresponds to J. S. Mill's distinction between 'making' and 'growing.' Law belongs to the region of 'making.' It originates in the will of the sovereign. Whatever he wills and 'sanctions,' and nothing else, is therefore law in the proper sense of the term.

Another class of 'laws' is excluded by the definition. A 'custom' is not a law proper. I obey many rules, which are not 'commands' and not enforced by legal sanctions. I conform to countless rules of conduct, though no assignable person has ever made them, and though the sovereign will not punish me for breaking them. In such rules the disapproval of society may act in the same way as a sanction, though not annexed by a sovereign. The resemblance may pass into identity. Customs become laws, as they receive the sanction of the legislator or of the courts. This includes Bentham's 'judge-made' law; and Austin diverges from Bentham by recognising this as a legitimate mode of legislation. The question then arises whether the distinction between laws and customs is essential or superficial—a real distinction of kinds or only important in our classification. From the lawyer's point of view, again, the importance is obvious. He always wishes to know precisely at what point the law can be brought to bear; whether a rule will be enforced by the courts, or generally under what circumstances a custom will be accepted as a law. The answer necessarily leads to much legal subtlety. The custom may be treated as constructively a law. The sovereign has not actually made nor 'sanctioned' it; but virtue has somehow gone out of him by

implication, and his recognition is equivalent to imposition of the rule. Though the 'sovereign' has not really 'made' the law, he may be considered as having made it by a metaphysical fiction. In this direction Austin becomes the twelfth century schoolman, and has to split hairs to force his definition upon the facts. The inquiry, though necessary from the lawyer's point of view, becomes irrelevant from the sociologist's. The social action is the same, whether the rule obeyed be a custom or a law strictly so called. Confusion therefore follows when the question of legal validity is substituted for the question of real efficacy. Primitive societies obey implicitly a variety of elaborate 'laws' or 'customs,' though they have no conception of legislation. The obedience to the rule is instinctive, and the rule regarded as absolutely unalterable. Are such rules 'laws'—though not made by a sovereign—or mere 'customs,' though obeyed as strictly as the most effective 'laws'? Austin answers consistently that they are not laws at all. There are people, he says, in 'a state of nature,'[1] such as the savages in New Holland or North America. Their life, in Hobbes's famous phrase, is 'solitary, poor, nasty, brutish, and short.' Their laws correspond to mere 'positive morality or the law set by public opinion,' which is necessarily so uncertain that it cannot serve as a complete guide of conduct, nor can it be sufficiently minute or detailed.[2] Savages, it seems, form herds not societies, and may be simply left out of consideration by the philosophical jurist. Austin, of course, could not be expected to anticipate more recent investigations into archaic institutions; but he was un-

[1] Jurisprudence, p. 238.   [2] Ibid. p. 791.

lucky in thus summarily condemning them by anticipation. In any case the position indicates an important gap in his system. What was the legal bond which converted the herds into political societies? The problem of the formation of society had been solved not by historical inquiry but by the 'social contract theory.' Austin follows Bentham and Hume. They had shown conclusively not only that the contract was a figment historically, but that it could not supply what was wanted. It professed to add the sanctity of a promise to the social bond, whereas the sanctity of a promise itself requires explanation. The theory simply amounted, as Bentham had urged, to a roundabout way of introducing utility. Any sort of contract, as Austin urges,[1] presupposes a formed political society. Clearly it cannot otherwise be a contract in his sense—an obligation enforced by a sanction—when it is itself to be the foundation of sovereignty or sanctions. Austin therefore rejects contemptuously the doctrine of natural law accepted by his German teachers. The theory that there is somehow or other a body of law, deducible by the pure reason, and yet capable of overriding or determining the 'law proper,' is his great example of ontological 'jargon' and 'fustian.' Austin's disciples hold[2] that his main service to the philosophy of law was precisely his exposure of the fallacy. The 'Natur-Recht' is 'jargon.' It is most desirable to discuss ideal law as meaning the law which it would be useful to adopt; but to speak as if it had already some transcendental reality is to confuse 'ought' with 'is' or, as Austin would say, the question of utility with the question of actual existence. The

[1] *Jurisprudence*, p. 336.   [2] Cp. Mill's *Dissertations*, iii. 237, etc.

'natural law' corresponds to the legal fictions denounced by Bentham, under which, when really making law, judges pretended to be only applying an existing law; and to the theories attacked in the *Anarchical Fallacies*, according to which this ideal law could override the actual law. Austin's polemic was no doubt directed against a theory fertile in confusion and fallacies.

Still the social contract, though exploded, leaves a problem for solution. Somehow or other the social organism has been put together, or, in Austin's phrase, the sovereign has come into existence. To explain this is the sociological problem. Austin recognises a difficulty. Generally speaking, he says, 'the constitution of the supreme society has grown.'[1] It should then, we might expect, be studied like other growths, as the physiologist studies the growth of plants and animals and tries to formulate the processes. Austin, however, protests by anticipation. He does not use the 'fustian but current phrase,' Growth, to cover anything mysterious. He only means that governments have in fact been put together by unsystematic processes;—'by a long series of 'authors' and 'successive sovereigns.' They did not, that is, spring ready-made from the hand of a supernatural legislator, but they were made by a series of patchings and cobblings carried out by ignorant and short-sighted rulers. The 'growing,' then, was really 'making,' however blundering and imperfect. Thus we have no 'mystical' social bond. Society has been constructed all along by the same method. The ultimate cause has always been 'the perception of the utility of political government, or the preference by the bulk of the com-

[1] *Jurisprudence*, p. 330.

munity of any government to anarchy.'[1] The theory thus appears to be that men in fact made such an agreement as the social contract supposes, though the agreement had not the force of a contract. Men have always seen, as they see now, that government is useful; and thus 'perception of utility' (not utility simply) is the sole force which holds society together and supports the sovereign and the sanctions.

A practical lawyer has little concern with savages and the origin of civil society. Austin's principles, however, apply to the modern society also. Law, as he seems to think, excludes or supersedes custom, so that the whole fabric of the state is entirely dependent upon the 'sovereign,' and the social union upon the 'perception of utility.' As a rule, one might observe, the question hardly arises. Men accept the social constitution into which they are born, because they can't help it. They never ask whether it is useful because they have no alternative of joining or separating. I may ask whether I shall belong to this or that club; but no one can choose whether he shall or shall not be a member of society. This leads to the point already noticed under Bentham. Custom is not really the creature of law, but law the product of custom. The growth of a society does not imply the disappearance of instinct, but implies on the contrary that certain fundamental instincts and the corresponding modes of action have become so thoroughly settled and organised that the society is capable of combining to modify particular regulations. When the English people passed the Reform Bill and the Americans

[1] *Jurisprudence*, p. 303. Austin makes certain qualifications which I need not notice.

accepted the constitution of the United States they altered very important laws, but it was precisely because they had been so thoroughly imbued with certain habits of combined action, involving the acceptance of complex legislative processes, that they were able to make changes in the less essential parts of the constitution. The 'sanction' no doubt determines the conduct of the individual. But when we ask upon what then does the sovereign power depend, we must go behind the law, and ask what are the complex instincts, beliefs, and passions which in fact bind men together and constitute the society as a moral organism.

The weak side of the 'Austinian analysis' is this transference of a legal conception to a sociological problem. Distinctions valid and important in their own sphere become irrelevant and lead to idle subtleties beyond that sphere. What, in fact, is the sovereign? He stands for an undeniable fact. Law presupposes a state and political unity. Political order implies some supreme and definite authority which can be invoked in all controversies as to what is or is not the law. The simplest case would be an irresponsible despot who could command whatever he pleased, and whose commands would be implicitly obeyed. If he does not exist he must be invented, as Voltaire said of the Deity. He is a 'fictitious entity,' or the incarnation of legal authority. This corresponds to the truth implied in the Utilitarian polemic against the supposed balance of powers and the mixture of the three abstract forms, monarchy, aristocracy, and democracy. The existence of the state implies unity of authority and the agreement that the validity of laws shall depend upon their elaboration by definite constitutional processes. But then we have to ask, Who precisely is the sovereign? The answer would be simple in the case of the individual despot. When the sovereign is not a single man but an organised body of men, such phrases as 'will' and 'command' become metaphorical. The will is not one will, but the product of multitudinous wills acting in complex though definable ways. The sovereign is not an entity distinct from the subjects, but is composed of the subjects themselves, or some fraction of them, according to a definite set of regulations. Can the state be treated as the embodiment of an external force? Austin is greatly puzzled to say who, in a given case, is the sovereign? Is parliament, or the House of Commons, or the electoral body the ultimate sovereign of England? Who is the true sovereign in a federal government such as the United States, where sovereign powers are distributed in complex ways? The legal question, What are the recognised forms by which valid laws are nominally constructed? is again confounded with the question of fact, What are the real forces which, in fact, produce obedience? The British Constitution has been steadily altering from remote times as a certain understanding has been developed. The centre of power has imperceptibly shifted without definite legislation; and the legal theory has remained unaltered, or has only conformed to customs already established. The question, therefore, what forms must be observed in conformity to precedent or explicit legislation, is entirely different from the question, What are the really dominant forces? The crown can undoubtedly veto an act of parliament in the legal sense of 'can'; whether it 'can' do so in the practical sense is a question only to be solved by saying

what are the real forces which lie beneath the constitutional machinery.

I have already noticed the tendency of the Utilitarians to confuse the legal doctrine of the sovereign's omnipotence with the doctrine of his omnipotence in fact. Macaulay had sufficiently pointed out to Mill that the sovereign was limited: limited by his own character and by the impossibility of enforcing laws not congenial to the public sentiment. Austin illustrates a further result. Customs are legally invalid till recognised and sanctioned by the sovereign. That is important for the lawyer. But interpreted as a law of 'social dynamics,' it leads to the inversion by which custom is supposed to be created by the law, and the sovereign made the ultimate source of power, instead of being himself the product of a long and intricate process of development of custom. Here, therefore, is the point at which the Utilitarian view becomes antithetic to the historical. It seeks to explain the first state of society by the last, instead of explaining the last by the first. We can see, too, the main reason for this mode of conceiving the case. To Austin the reference to the underlying forces by which political society is built up seemed to be 'mysticism.' A fully developed 'law' is intelligible: the customs which grow up in the twilight before the full light of day has appeared are too incoherent and shadowy for scientific treatment. The mode of analysing all phenomena into independent and uniform atoms leads to this result. Causation itself had been reduced to mere sequence to get rid of a 'mystic bond,' and the same method is applied to social phenomena.[1] We have the difficulty which occurs so

[1] Austin refers his readers to Brown's essay on 'Cause and Effect'; and

often in the Utilitarian theories. They desire on the one hand to be scientific, and on the other hand to be thoroughly empirical. The result is to divide the two spheres: to enlarge as much as possible the variability of human society in order to be 'empirical'; and to regard the constituent atoms as unchangeable. Hence they have always a difficulty of conceiving of growth or 'evolution,' in which variation is supposed to be compatible with the existence of law, or to combine the two aspects of change and uniformity. That always appears to them to be 'mystical.' Though they deny 'freewill,' they give the widest possible range to the sphere of voluntary action. 'Making' is radically distinguished from 'growing,' instead of being simply growth directed by conscious foresight. There is nothing really more 'mystical,' though there is something much more complex, in the growth of a society than in the growth of a natural species. But as it supposes a change due to something in the constitution of the man himself, not to merely 'external circumstances,' it has to be rejected as much as possible. Hence we get our omnipotent sovereign creating laws and customs and to be taken as an ultimate fact.

I need not point out at length the relation of these views to Utilitarianism in general, and to the belief in the indefinite modifiability of human nature and the transcendent importance of political machinery. It is enough to note that Austin's position involves one assumption remarkable in a Utilitarian. The empiricism of the Utilitarians is interpreted to mean that everything

takes Brown to have proved 'beyond controversy' that the faculty called the 'will' is just nothing at all.—*Jurisprudence*, pp. 424-25.

must be explained by circumstances, and conduct therefore by 'external' sanctions. Austin feels that, after all, some bond must be required to hold men together. The legislative sanctions cannot be quite ultimate. In fact, we want 'morality'; and he therefore includes the 'laws of God' among the laws which are really, not metaphorically, laws. He thus accepts the Paley view, though with a certain reserve. 'Utility' is the sole criterion or 'index,' as he calls it, to the moral law. Still, the law requires a sanction. The sanction is left in judicious vagueness; but we are told that God must be benevolent, and must therefore be held to approve the conduct which promotes the happiness of his creatures. This, it would seem, is essential to Austin's position.[1] Whether he was practising some 'economy,' and what his fellow-Utilitarians would have thought of it, and how precisely he would have justified his position logically, are questions which I cannot discuss.

The application of Austin's principles to the purely legal sphere lies beyond my purpose. His aim is to analyse the primary conceptions of jurisprudence in accordance with his principles, and to obtain a rational classification of law in general. Whether the result was satisfactory, or how far satisfactory, I cannot inquire. The lectures were reviewed in the *Edinburgh* both by J. F. Stephen[2] and by J. S. Mill.[3] Both of them speak warmly of the merits of Sir Henry Maine, then beginning to be famous, and both regard the two

[1] Mill touches this point characteristically in his review of Austin, but does not discuss the validity of the logic.
[2] *Edinburgh Review*, October 1861.
[3] Mill's *Dissertations*, iii. 206-74, from *Edin. Rev.* of Oct. 1863.

methods as correlative rather than antagonistic. That they ought to be correlative is clear. A sound theory of origins and growth should be perfectly compatible with a sound theory of the actual order. But whether the two systems actually present that harmony is another question.

The political application of Austin's principles might be illustrated from the writings of his friend and disciple, Sir George Cornewall Lewis (1806-1863).[1] Strong sense, unflagging industry, and the highest integrity won for Lewis high authority in parliament. A boundless thirst for knowledge, supported by a remarkable memory, enabled him to discuss many topics of historical criticism. He was intimate with Grote, who accepted his suggestions upon Greek history respectfully; and his intellect was of the true Utilitarian type. His writings are as dry as the most thoroughgoing Utilitarian could desire. He will not give his readers credit for understanding the simplest argument till it is set down at full length in plain black and white. He was sceptical, and practical experience had impressed him, even to excess, with the worthlessness of human testimony. In politics scepticism naturally becomes empiricism; and as a thoroughgoing empiricist he rejects altogether James Mill's absolute methods. He is as convinced as Macaulay that political theories must be based upon observation, and is entirely free from the error of supposing that a constitution can be devised without reference to time, place, and circumstance. Yet he could write a dialogue

---

[1] For Lewis see especially the very interesting article in Bagehot's *Works* (by Forrest Morgan), 1891, iii. 222-68. His chief political treatise is *A Treatise on Methods of Reasoning and Observation in Politics* (1852).

upon the best form of government, which seems to imply that some real meaning can be given to the problem without reference to the stage of social development, that is, to the one condition which makes the problem intelligible.

One reason is that Lewis was a practical man, and he shows very clearly why the practical man was inclined to Utilitarianism. A chancellor of the exchequer knows that the fate of a budget depends upon him, and refuses to regard himself as a mere tool of fate. A scientific treatment of history would lead, he thinks, to fatalism.[1] Everything is intrinsically uncertain where the human will is concerned.[2] Such events as the French revolution, therefore, must be regarded as controllable by statesmanship, and not, with some historians, declared to have been 'inevitable.' When we have got to the statesman or to the sovereign we have the ultimate cause, and need not ask whether he be not himself a product. Thus all laws, constitutional or otherwise, may be compared to machinery,[3] and suppose contrivance or design. All institutions have been made, and he assumes that even polygamy and slavery were 'dictated by unsound practical arguments.'[4] The tendency of such a doctrine is clear. All institutions, from the most organic to the most superficial, are regarded as equally a product of conscious manufacture. Their relation to the processes of social growth is tacitly disregarded, and the whole organism can be modified by a simple shuffling of the cards. We can therefore attack the problem of the best form of government

---

[1] *Methods of Observation*, etc., i. 448.   [2] *Ibid.* i. 357.
[3] *Ibid.* ii. 356.   [4] *Ibid.* ii. 370.

without emphasising the necessary reference to historical conditions. Lewis's wide reading supplied him with any number of judicious remarks, drawn from all authorities between Aristotle and Comte. Undoubtedly such remarks deserve respect; they are apt to be commonplace, but are not therefore useless. Only, to apply them to any purpose, it is necessary to have a more definite understanding of the processes of social development which limit and define their value at any given stage. Empiricism, thus understood, really makes scientific method, as well as any definite scientific conclusion, impossible. Even in the purely practical sphere, the most important of all problems for a statesman is to know what are the limits of his powers, and to recognise what is really 'inevitable' in the great changes. Otherwise, he is in the position of Mrs. Partington fighting the Atlantic. Lewis became a Whig instead of a Utilitarian Radical; but it may be doubtful whether Whig 'opportunism' was not the most natural development of the Utilitarian empiricism.

II. GEORGE GROTE

The great representative of Utilitarian history is George Grote (1794-1871).[1] In some respects he was the most typical Utilitarian. Grote had been introduced to James Mill by Ricardo in 1817. He had yielded after some struggle to Mill's personal influence; and, though a

---

[1] Mrs. Grote's *Personal History of George Grote* is neither adequate nor quite accurate. Compare a very useful life by G. Croom Robertson in *Dictionary of National Biography*, and the article in the *Encyclopædia Britannica* by William Smith.

student of Kant, had become an unhesitating proselyte. He had edited *Philip Beauchamp*, had defended radical reform against Mackintosh in 1821, and had joined J. S. Mill and other young friends in their systematic logical discussions. He fully sympathised with J. S. Mill's philosophy, and, as Professor Bain tells us,[1] hardly any man 'conned and thumbed' the *Logic* as he did. He was more of a Millite than Mill. Their friendship survived in spite of Mill's seclusion, and of certain doubts in Grote's mind of his friend's orthodoxy. The articles upon Coleridge and Bentham, marking Mill's sentimental backslidings, alarmed the more rigid adherent of the faith. During the political career of the 'philosophical Radicals' Grote was the faithful Abdiel. He defended their pet nostrum, the ballot, until the party became a vanishing quantity. 'You and I,' said Charles Buller to him in 1836, 'will be left to "tell" Molesworth.'[2] On the fall of the Melbourne ministry he gave up parliament, and in 1843 retired from the bank in which he had been a partner. His continued interest in the old Utilitarian principles was shown by his lifelong activity in the management of University College and the University of London. Happily, he could occupy himself in a more productive enterprise. He had been long interested in Greek history, and his great work appeared at intervals from 1846 to 1856. His study of *Plato* appeared in 1865, and he was still labouring upon *Aristotle* at the time of his death.

Of the substantial merits of Grote's History I shall not presume to speak. It took its place at once, and

---

[1] Bain's *J. S. Mill*, p. 83.
[2] Mrs. Grote's *Philosophical Radicals of 1832* (1866), p. 28.

gives a conclusive proof that the Utilitarian position was no disqualification for writing history. It seems, indeed, to prove a good deal more ; namely, that the Utilitarian who was faithful to his most vital principles was especially qualified to be a historian.

The true position may perhaps be suggested by a remark in a recent book[1] by MM. Langlois and Seignobos. In laying down the conception of history as now accepted by the best writers, they remark that Grote 'produced the first model of a history' in the class to which it belongs. The principle illustrated is significant. 'The aim of history,' we are told, 'should now be not to please, nor to give practical maxims of conduct, nor to arouse the emotions, but [to give] knowledge pure and simple.' History should be a descriptive science. Historians must be content to give political facts as a writer upon a natural science gives the ascertained facts about physiology or chemistry. Nothing, it may be said, could be more in accordance with Utilitarian doctrine. It was their very first principle to rely upon fact pure and simple, and to make it precede speculation and to minimise 'sentiment,' 'vague generalities,' and a priori theories. If Grote wrote a model history, it was because he thoroughly embodied the Utilitarian spirit. He studied the evidence with immense knowledge, unflagging industry, and thorough impartiality. He resembled an ideal judge investigating evidence in a trial. That was the method which, upon their own showing, the Utilitarians were bound to apply to all subjects, and Grote applied it to Greece with triumphant success.

[1] *Introduction to the Study of History* (English translation, 1898), p. 310.

The Utilitarian principle, again, was opposed to the errors most seductive to earlier historians. The classical histories were meant to be works of art. The artistic aim is incompatible with scientific history, so far as it interferes with the primary aim of giving the unadulterated facts. To give a clear, coherent, and distinct narrative of a complex series of events requires, indeed, powers of literary expression even of the highest order. The artistic purpose must be strictly subordinate rather than absent. A writer must not disguise or embellish or omit with a view to artistic effect of the whole ; and must often sacrifice the impressive to the truthful. Sometimes, indeed, the historian must be dull — but that is a condition against which neither Grote nor the Utilitarians generally protested. It had been the aim of a different school to avoid dulness and to rival the *Waverley Novels* in making past history live. The errors of such men as Thierry and Michelet, or Carlyle, Macaulay and Froude, show the dangers of the method. The severe historian may perhaps forgive them in consideration of the interest which they excited in their studies. May he not also admit that the aim is, in some sort, legitimate ? The people, after all, were once alive, and that truth has some bearing upon their history. If imagination means a faculty of generating illusions, as the Utilitarians generally thought, it is no doubt mischievous. But even for the bare purpose of judging evidence and perceiving truth the imagination is essential. The error of transposing modern standards of thought into previous epochs is too obvious to require illustration ; but it is really the fault less of an excess than of a defect of imagination. The writer must be able, at every turn, to put himself in the

place of his heroes, and of their contemporaries, if he would understand the meaning of their actions, or even judge the weight to be attributed to the evidence. That requires a trained and duly subordinate faculty of imagination. Even for mere annals—simple statements of hard facts—imagination is required, and it is required the more as we endeavour to rise from annals to history, or to make history more than an 'old calendar.'

A sound Utilitarian might be expected to make the proper compromise. No one could be more on his guard against the error of subordinating truth to poetic fancy. But he would not deny the importance of so much imaginative sympathy as is implied in a clear apprehension of the mental and moral condition of past epochs. He might find a sufficient substitute for the dangerous faculty of picturesque imagination in the more sober faculty which Grote possessed—massive commonsense ; the 'knowledge of human nature,' as it is called, which corresponds not to poetic imagination or to a set of established formulæ, but to the practical insight acquired by intimate acquaintance with actual affairs. If Grote was able to rival or to surpass German professors on their own ground, it was because his want of some of their special training was more than counterbalanced by his experience of business and public life. In Threadneedle Street and at Westminster he had acquired an instinctive perception which served him in describing the political and economical conditions of Athenian life. When joined with an ardour for research that power gave a value to his judgments of fact which enabled him to write a model history.

The 'graphic' or 'artistic' type of history may be

objectionable ; is not the philosophical worse ? Nothing distorts facts so much as theory ; and a scientific historian should be on his guard against the philosopher of all men. But how to draw the line ? Stick to bare fact and you can only write annals. History proper begins as you introduce causation, and the mere series is transformed into a process. It is impossible to get a bare fact without some admixture of theory. The Utilitarian principle, again, suggests the right aim. It excludes the mischievous didacticism of older historians. The question of fact must everywhere precede the question of right. In politics, economics and ethics Bentham and Malthus and the Mills had in various relations applied the principle which applies equally to history. The historian may adopt Spinoza's great saying. His business is to understand, not to approve or denounce. A historian treats of some great event such as the French revolution. His one legitimate and dominant purpose should be to explain its causes, and he should inquire with absolute impartiality how it came to pass, not whether it was right or wrong. The old method of writing history attributed events to individuals, and consistently applied a moral estimate. If the action of this or that man, Mirabeau or Robespierre, was the ultimate cause of the events, we may ask whether the action was good or bad, and infer that the event ought or ought not to have happened. The scientific view fixes attention simply on the causes. What were the conditions which determined the event ? We must inquire as impartially as a pathologist examining the causes of a disease. The category of causation is the sole category relevant. Ethical judgments may follow : we may decide that certain processes implied progress or decay ; we may go on to judge of the individuals, making allowance for their motives after estimating what view of the facts was possible for them, and we shall generally find that there were good men and bad men on both sides, and that it is out of place to apply such words as right or wrong to the events themselves. The moral question is transferred to another sphere, and human conduct is treated as a case of natural causation. This method is implied in the very conception of scientific history and was fully in accordance with Utilitarianism. Men had been complaining of the inadequacy of the old history, which dealt exclusively with political intrigues and the military incidents. As history became more scientific the necessity of attending to social conditions was daily more evident, though the extent of the change implied is scarcely even yet realised. The history, for example, of political or religious changes cannot be fully written without reference to the economic conditions of the country, and whole systems of investigation are requisite before those conditions can be tolerably understood. Nothing could be more in accordance with Utilitarianism than a thorough acceptance of this view. Nor, again, should any men have been more free from the temptation of allowing *a priori* theories and hasty generalisations to colour their view of facts. The true attitude of the historical inquirer should be that which was illustrated in science by Darwin. On the one side, he must collect as large as possible a store of facts, observed as impartially and accurately as possible. On the other side, he must be constantly but cautiously generalising ; endeavouring to fit the facts in their true order ; to discover what formulæ serve to 'colligate' them satisfactorily ; and always to assign causes which are

both real and adequate, such that their existence can be verified, and that, if they exist, they will fit into a reasoned theory. But his theories must be tentative and liable to constant revision. They may be suggestive even if not established, but in so complex an inquiry they must be regarded as being only a relative or approximate truth.

Briefly, then, the historian should aim at providing materials for a 'sociology,' but be on his guard against supposing for a moment that such a science now exists or can ever be raised to a level with the fully developed sciences. The word corresponds to an ideal aim, not to an established fact. It is important to regard history scientifically, though we cannot hope for a complete science of history. It simply means that we must regard the history of man as the history of the gradual development of the individual and of society by forces dimly perceived, not capable of accurate measurement, but yet working regularly and involving no abrupt or discontinuous intervention.

If Grote's history be really a 'model,' it was because he virtually accepted such limitations. Historians should admit that they are still in the stage of collecting the facts upon which any wide generalisations are still premature. Grote was a student of philosophy ; he had, like Mill, been impressed by Comte, though he never, like Mill, took Comte for a prophet. He discussed early beliefs and institutions, and he certainly supposed his history to have important political implications. But a cautious intellect and a desire for a solid groundwork of fact restrained him from excessive theorising, and prevented his prejudices from overpowering his candour. So far, he represented the best Utilitarian spirit, and

obeyed what was, or at least should have been, their essential canon : to make sure of your facts before you lay down your theories. They wished to apply scientific methods to history, as to law, political economy, ethics, and psychology : and, upon their view, the first condition of success was a sufficient accumulation of facts. Yet, as has abundantly appeared, they had been little disposed to confine themselves to this preliminary stage. They were too ready to assume that the sciences could be constituted offhand, and to accept convenient postulates as absolute truths. They had not only pointed out, but taken possession of, the promised land. Their premature dogmatism showed the weakness of their trusting their assumptions. The result to philosophy of history may be illustrated from the remarkable writer, who, in the period of Mill's philosophic supremacy, attempted to lay its foundation.

III. HENRY THOMAS BUCKLE

Henry Thomas Buckle (1821-1862) represents this aspiration by his *History of Civilization in England*.

Buckle[1] had some qualifications of the rarest kind.

[1] Buckle's *Life*, by Alfred Henry Huth, appeared in 1880. I have also to call attention to the very able and learned work, *Buckle and his Critics*, by John Mackinnon Robertson (1895). Mr. Robertson passes a severe judgment upon a criticism of Buckle which I contributed to the *Fortnightly Review* for May 1880, and takes the opportunity of pointing out some of my manifold shortcomings. Though his tone is not such as to make an apology easy, I must state my position frankly. Mr. Robertson points out the measureless inferiority of a book of mine upon the eighteenth century to Buckle's great performance. He thinks, too, that my attack was 'unchivalrous,' considering the pathetic circumstances of Buckle's death, and the fact that his work 'seemed to be sufficiently discredited already.' Now I can quite agree upon

He had been prevented by delicate health from coming into contact with contemporaries at school and college, and his intellectual tastes made him abandon a business career. He had from an early age devoted himself to a life of study. He absorbed enormous masses of knowledge, learned many languages, and had ranged over the most varied fields of literature. A most retentive memory

one point. It never entered my head to compare my own abilities to Buckle's. I could no more have rivalled his history than have encountered him at chess. It is impossible to speak more strongly. Why, then, did I presume to criticise ? Because I was not giving my own unaided opinion. I had been interested by a problem. Like all young men of my time I had been impressed by the controversial storm which followed the publication of Buckle's book, and by that which soon afterwards was roused by the publication of Darwin's *Origin of Species*. Many years later, when Buckle's *Life* appeared, I was struck by a contrast. Darwin's speculations had affected every department of thought, and his influence was still spreading. Buckle's, on the other hand, had lost much of their interest—what was the reason ? Briefly, as I thought, and as I still think, that Darwin had supplied a fruitful suggestion suited to the general movement of thought ; and that Buckle, for want of it, had struck into a wrong path. I tried in my article to point out the nature of his error. Mr. Robertson's book confirms the truth of my impression as to facts. Had Buckle continued to interest the leaders of thought, Mr. Robertson would not have given so prominent a position to an old review article never republished, and which, so far as I know, had never attracted any particular attention. Mr. Robertson's elaborate survey of recent sociology shows that while some distinguished writers more or less coincide with Buckle, they scarcely recognise any indebtedness. That is, I think, because there was little to recognise. Buckle, in short, as it appeared to me, had not produced an effect at all comparable to those produced by Darwin or by Mr. Herbert Spencer ; and I cannot think that Mr. Robertson accounts for the fact. My own explanation may of course have been wrong ; but I do not see that there was anything 'unchivalrous' in trying to explain why a man of genius has not produced an effect proportionate to his powers. Nor can I see that Buckle's pathetic death made it necessary for me to modify my language in discussing his philosophy. Upon re-reading my article I recognise faults which may partly justify Mr. Robertson's resentment. I should certainly have avoided anything savouring of contempt. I did recognise Buckle's extraordinary powers, but I forgot clearly to distinguish condemnation of his opinions from depreciation of the power displayed. Substantially my view is not changed.

and methodic habits of work gave him a full command of his materials, and the consciousness of intellectual force suggested a daring ambition. He proposed to write a general history of civilisation, though his scheme, as he gradually became aware of the vastness of his task, narrowed itself to a history of civilisation in England, with preliminary surveys of other civilisations. Buckle had been educated in the religious and political atmosphere of the average middle-class type. Foreign travel and wide reading had sapped his prejudices, and he had become a Liberal in the days when J. S. Mill's influence was culminating. Buckle shared the enthusiasm of the period in which the triumph of Free Trade and the application of Adam Smith's principles seemed to be introducing a new era of peace and prosperity and the final extinction of antiquated prejudice. He cannot be reckoned as a simple Utilitarian, but he represents the more exoteric and independent allies of the chief Utilitarian thinker. He accepts the general principles of Mill's *Logic*, though his language upon metaphysical problems implies that his intellect had never been fully brought to bear upon such questions. The general sympathy with the Utilitarians is, in any case, unmistakable, and the most characteristic tenets of the Mill school of speculation are assumed or defended in his writings. Buckle was thus fitted to interpret the dominant tendencies of the day, and his literary ability was fully adequate to the office. He has much of the clearness and unflagging vivacity of Macaulay, and whatever defects may be discoverable in his style, no writer was better qualified to interest readers outside the narrow circle of professed philosophers. The book was accepted by many readers as an authoritative manifesto of

the scientific spirit which was to transform the whole intellectual world.

Buckle's aim is to fill the gap in the Utilitarian scheme by placing historical science upon a basis as firm as that of the physical sciences. Statistics, he argues, reveal regularities of conduct as marked as those which are revealed by the observation of natural phenomena. He gives a fatalistic turn to this statement by speaking as though the 'laws' somehow 'overrode' the individual volitions, instead of simply expressing the uniformity of the volitions themselves. Fate, it seemed, went round and compelled a certain number of people every year to commit suicide or post undirected letters in spite of themselves. Without asking how far this language, which not unnaturally startled his readers, might be corrected into a legitimate sense, we may pass to a further application. The laws by which human conduct is governed may, he says, be either 'physical' or 'mental,' the physical having more influence in the early, and the mental in the later, stages of development. This corresponds to the distinction, now familiar, between the 'organism' and the 'environment,' and requires an obvious correction. The two sets of laws refer to two factors present at every stage of human development. The 'organism' is, from first to last, dependent upon its 'environment,' but the action of the environment depends also upon the constitution of the organism. The 'mental' and 'physical,' therefore, do not act separately, but as parts of a single process. Buckle's language, however, expresses an obvious truth. As civilisation advances, the importance of the 'mental' laws in explaining the phenomena increases. The difference between

two savage races may be explained simply by the difference of their surroundings; but the civilised man may vary indefinitely, while his dwelling-place remains constant. The earlier stages are those which, in Buckle's language, are under the predominant influence of physical laws. Climate, food, and soil on the one hand, and the 'general aspects of nature' on the other hand, represent these influences. To show their action at the dawn of civilisation, Buckle points to India, Egypt, and the ancient empires in America. In those regions arose great governments, displaying remarkable coincidences of structure, and thus suggesting the operation of some ascertainable causes. If we possessed a complete 'sociology,' these phenomena would clearly illustrate important laws, working with great uniformity, though in complete independence, and therefore, it may be inferred, revealing some general principles upon the origin of governments. Nothing can present a more legitimate field of inquiry. A great despotism implies an abundant population, and therefore certain physical conditions, geographical and climatic—as the existence of a whale implies an open sea and plenty of food. The problem, then, is how do the conditions lead to the observed phenomenon? How do the physical conditions lead to the formation of these early civilisations? Here Buckle makes a remarkable assumption. He finds a solution in the teaching of the economists. An increase of population means a lowering of wages; or, as he puts it, the question of wages is, 'in the long run,' a question of population.[1] Now, in cold countries more food is required, and the food is harder to procure than in the hot.[2] Hence population will

[1] *Civilisation*, i. 49. Note the 'wage fund' in the next page.   [2] *Ibid*. i. 58.

increase faster in hot countries, and wages will in them tend to be low. The case of Ireland confirms or extends the theory. There, cheap food does what general fertility does in India. The potato, more than the 'scandalous misgovernment,' is the most active cause of Irish poverty. Cheap food, then, means low wages. The result, startling for an enthusiastic freetrader, suggests a confusion. An increase of population on a given area may lower wages; but it does not follow that a larger population must be worse off when the area is more productive. He ought to show that the Indian population must be in greater excess; he has only shown that it may be positively greater. There is no proof that it will increase at all when the 'checks' are once operative, or increase in a greater ratio to its support. What is the real relation of cause and effect? Did Irishmen become poor because they had cheap food, or take to cheap food because they were poor? The food enabled them, no doubt, to support a larger number of poor, and in a more precarious position. When the potato failed they could not substitute wheat. That is enough to confute the hasty assumption that cheap food is a panacea for poverty, but does not prove that plenty necessarily causes poverty. There is another step to be taken. Ricardo now supplements Malthus. He had shown that the whole wealth of a country must be divided into wages, rent, profit, and interest, while interest is proportional to profit. Now, in India, interest and rent have been enormously high; therefore wages are low and profits high.[1] A high rate of interest, however, may show that capital is scarce and payment precarious. The

[1] *Civilisation*, p. 69.

moneylender may extort high interest from the peasant, and yet the aggregate of profits may be small, and the whole country miserably poor. Ricardo's doctrine assumes that the wages of the labourer are advanced by the capitalist. It does not apply to a population of village communities, where the differentiation of classes has not yet taken place.[1]

Buckle, however, does not trouble himself with such difficulties. The great empires are supposed to have arisen from the growth of a rich class, whose wealth has enabled them to gain political power. No doubt the despots had great wealth in poor countries; but it does not appear that they owed it to the development of a great class of rich capitalists, or even that such a class existed. The objection to Buckle's method is apparent. In the first place, it takes for granted the existence of a complex industrial organisation as an antecedent to the growth of the despotism. The system under which the capitalist, the labourer, and the landowner share profits, wages, and rent, the whole machinery of exchange and

[1] Mr. Robertson holds that Buckle's 'generalisation' is not, as I 'strangely' represent it, an 'arbitrary application of the Ricardian law of rent to the society of Ancient India, but constitutes an elevation of Ricardo's other law of the subsistence of labour into a broad historic principle.' He points out, too, that Buckle supposed a previous stage of development, and thinks that he had appreciated Jones's correction of Ricardo, in regard to Indian rent (*Buckle and his Critics*, pp. 49, 59, and see p. 138). I can only say that I adhere to my statement. Buckle expressly quotes Ricardo, and makes the origin of the civilisations depend upon the threefold division. That I hold to be unjustifiable, and to be false in fact. The 'broad historic principle' seems to be simply the fact that great empires rose where physical conditions, including, of course, fertility, were favourable. Buckle may deserve credit for dwelling upon the fact. I only say that his explanation does not explain; and that it is impossible to lay down as unconditionally true that cheap food involves cheap wages. If one is to have a theory, why should we not say that empires were made by conquerors instead of by capitalists?

competition, is postulated as though it represented a necessary state, even in the early stages of civilisation. That was a natural application of the necessary assumption of the orthodox political economy. It professed to deduce its conclusions from the laws of human nature common to all men in all ages. They were therefore as valid in the earliest as in the latest time, and explain the causes as well as the consequences of social development; and hence it follows that the 'mental laws' can be excluded. Since the organism is constant, all differences are due to differences of environment, or, in Buckle's language, to the 'physical laws.' 'In India,' he says, 'slavery, abject slavery, was the natural state of the great body of the people; it was the state to which they were doomed by physical laws utterly impossible to resist.'[1] In Europe, as he elsewhere puts it,[2] man is stronger than nature; out of Europe nature is stronger than man. Man is in one case the slave, and in the other the master of the physical forces. That is to say, that in the earlier stages we may argue directly from the 'environment' to the 'organism.' The hopeless slavery to which so many millions have been doomed is a direct and inevitable result of the 'physical laws,' that is, of the climate, soil, and food. We are therefore dispensed from any inquiry into the character of the organism itself and the 'mental' laws implied in its constitution; or we take for granted that the laws which regulate the more developed organism are absolute and permanent, and may therefore explain the earliest stages of growth.[3]

[1] *Civilisation*, i. 73.   [2] *Ibid.* i. 222.
[3] Buckle, I may notice, thinks Brown's essay upon Causation one of the greatest works of the century and a statement of the principles, derived ulti-

Thus the inquiry into the nature of the social organisation, into the primitive institutions out of which the empires have grown, is virtually set aside. Because the 'mental laws' work so uniformly they may be neglected. We are left with the bare result that great empires have grown up under appropriate physical conditions, and they are all lumped together as 'despotisms.' That is to emphasise a remarkable set of facts, but not to make them more intelligible. The facts, that is, reveal a remarkable uniformity in the social organism; but that does not show what is the nature of its organisation. If we know that, we shall be able to understand the differences and the way in which similar forces have worked under varying conditions. Buckle's leap at a generalisation so far distracts attention from the most fruitful line of inquiry. Malthus and Ricardo will solve the problem offhand. The simple coincidence of despotism and fertility entitles us to set them down as cause and effect, without further analysis of the precise mode of operation.

Buckle's next step illustrates the same point. The 'physical' laws have thus determined the distribution. They also influence religion, art, and literature by the action of 'aspects of nature' upon the imagination. The powers of nature, as he oddly puts it,[1] 'have worked

mately from Hume, upon which the 'best inquirers into these matters take their stand' (*Civilisation*, ii. 460 n). This, I take it, explains his tendency to take a simple statement of fact for a 'law.' The most curious instance of the confusion is the remark (*Civilisation*, i. 155) that physiologists have never been able to discover the cause of the equality in the number of male and female births. Statisticians have now answered the question by showing that the proportion is 20 to 21. Obviously they have not answered the question at all. They have only ascertained the facts. Buckle partly admits this; and yet he seems to think that the statement somehow indicates a new method of historical inquiry.   [1] *Civilisation*, i. 136.

immense mischief.' They generate superstition on one side, as they generated slavery on the other. Here Buckle's doctrine is connected with Comte's. He accepted, as he says elsewhere,[1] Comte's conclusions as to the earliest stage of the human mind. The man ignorant of scientific laws attributes all phenomena to 'supernatural causes.' Comte was only putting into a compact formula a theory more or less assumed by his predecessors. Superstition represents a necessary stage in the intellectual development of the race. It embodies the crude hypotheses of an early stage which have been falsified by later experience. They continue to exist, however, when they have long been untenable to educated minds; and Buckle's remarks may help to explain their vitality. The 'aspects of nature' represent the impression made by apparently irregular phenomena. Superstition thrives where men's lives are at the mercy of events which cannot be foreseen. One special and characteristic instance is the influence of earthquakes. Spain, Portugal, and Italy are the European countries in which earthquakes are most frequent, and are also the countries in which superstition has been most rife. The excessive stimulus to the imagination has led to the collateral result that while these countries have produced all the greatest artists, they have (with the partial exception of Italy) produced no great names in science.[2] The principle that superstition is fostered by such conditions may well be illustrated by these facts. Hume had remarked that the events which to good reasoners were the 'chief difficulties in admitting a supreme intelligence' were to the

[1] *Civilisation*, i. 342 n.   [2] *Ibid.* i. 112.

vulgar 'the sole arguments for it.'[1] Buckle might well extend the argument. But to say that earthquakes 'cause' Spanish superstition is a bold generalisation. It is an application of Mill's canon of simple agreement. Earthquakes and superstition coexist in two or three districts; therefore earthquakes are the cause of superstition.[2] On Buckle's own showing, earthquakes are only one of countless conditions which may produce superstition. Why is this special condition to be isolated? If Spain is now superstitious, must not that be due to the concurrence of innumerable causes? Have not other countries been steeped in the profoundest superstition though they had no earthquakes? How, indeed, is the amount of superstition in a country to be measured? If we were to explain a particular superstition by the apparent irregularity of the phenomena concerned—the belief in an

[1] *Natural History of Religion*, sec. vi. Mr. Robertson attacks me for my criticisms of Buckle's assertions of the deductive character of Scottish philosophers. I cannot go into the question, but I make one remark. He quotes the first sentence of Hume's *Natural History* to prove that Hume was a deist when he wrote it, and says that this is implied through the whole essay. Now Hume's most serious attack upon theology, the *Dialogues*, was written by 1751, though posthumously published. The *Natural History* appeared in 1757. The deistic phrases obviated the necessity for leaving it also for posthumous publication.

[2] A curious illustration is given by Mr. Robertson (p. 140). The Japanese, it had been said, are less superstitious than their neighbours, and yet more exposed to earthquakes. If Buckle's theory means that superstition necessarily follows earthquakes, the fact seems to contradict the theory. So Mr. Robertson seems to take it, for he gives an explanation. The Japanese do not suffer from earthquakes because they build slighter houses. If so, earthquakes, it surely might be urged, do not produce superstition, but rational precautions. If, on the other hand, the Spaniards have not modified their architecture, that would surely prove that they have not been much impressed by earthquakes. The case seems to me to prove simply the rashness of any such hasty guesses. Buckle's early critics were misguided enough to deny the facts alleged, and so gave him a triumph.

earth-shaking deity, for example—the explanation might be adequate. The objection rises when it is presented as a general scientific formula. Since 'superstition' is a universal incident of early stages of human thought, it is clearly not explicable by the phenomena of special districts. That may be an instructive example, but cannot give the general law. It is illegitimate to single out the particular condition as if it were the sole cause. The main point, however, is again the mode of arguing from the environment to the organism. The argument from the environment to the organism, from the earthquakes to superstition, has then an obvious limit. The constant condition can only explain the constant qualities. The palpable fact is that the same country has been occupied by races of most different characters. Freethinking flourishes where there was once abject superstition, and therefore the country cannot by itself explain the superstition. When, for example, Buckle explains the artistic temperament of Greeks or Italians by the physical characteristics, he is no doubt assigning a real cause, but obviously a cause insufficient to explain the singular changes, the efflorescence and the decay of artistic production in either country. One result is characteristic. The differences are often explained by 'heredity' or the inheritance by races of qualities not developed by their present environment, and essentially dependent upon the previous social evolution. Buckle fully admits that the question of 'heredity' is not settled by scientific inquiry.[1] He infers, and I suppose rightly, that we cannot assume that there is any organic difference between an infant born in the most civilised country and one born in the

[1] *Civilisation*, i. 161.

most barbarous region. Still, he 'cordially subscribes' to Mill's protest against explaining differences of character by race.[1] So far as this excludes all the influences by which a society is moulded through inherited beliefs and customs, it sanctions an erroneous inference. Because race differences are not ultimate, or indicative of absolute organic distinctions, they are altogether cast out of account. The existing differences have to be attributed entirely to the physical surroundings; and the influence of 'aspects of nature' is summarily adduced to explain much that is really explicable only through the history of the organism itself.[2]

How far this may have led Buckle to exaggerate the

[1] *Civilisation*, i. 37 n.

[2] Mr. Robertson reproves me for not quoting the passage in which Buckle says that the question of hereditary influence is still unsettled. Probably I should have recognised this more clearly. I did, however, say that Buckle held that the superiority of the civilised to the barbarian infant was 'not proved.' I said also that I thought that Buckle was justified for his purposes in neglecting the possibility of a superiority. He says, in the passage quoted above, that we have no right to assume such a change as an increase of brain capacity. I took it that for any historical period we may assume equality. The brain of a modern Englishman is not presumably superior to the brain of an Athenian. Evolution of that kind may be neglected by the historian of civilisation. The evolution, which I did take him to neglect, was the moral or social evolution, which is compatible with approximate identity of the brain or the innate faculties. Buckle, I said, shared the error of the Utilitarians who assumed moral progress to consist, not in a changed estimate of happiness, but simply in a better knowledge of the means of attaining it. Buckle's identification of progress with increase of knowledge involved, I said, the same error. The change is regarded as superficial or 'external.' Meanwhile my argument, which Mr. Robertson attacks, about the fallacy of arguing from the fixed environment to the varying organism applied to such cases as the inference from earthquakes to superstition or from climate to æsthetic tendencies. Such a generalisation, taken as an explanation of superstition, generally implies, as I held, an inadequate appreciation of the social or moral evolution. Perhaps I did not put the point clearly or accurately, and, if so, I regret it.

direct efficacy of mere physical surroundings I cannot further inquire. At any rate, his whole purpose is to explain the growth of civilisation, which must, as he perceives, be done by introducing a variable element. Here, therefore, we have to consider the state in which the 'mental' become more influential than the physical laws. Buckle begins by expounding a doctrine of critical importance. In general terms, he holds that progress depends upon the intellectual factor. A similar doctrine had been emphatically asserted by Comte, and was, indeed, implied as a fundamental conception in his whole work. Ideas, he says, govern the world: 'Tout le mécanisme social repose sur les opinions.'[1] The law of the 'three stages' is a systematic application of this doctrine. The doctrine, again, recognises an undeniable truth. Man is dependent throughout upon his environment. That, in a sense, remains constant. The savage lives in the same world as the civilised man. But every step of knowledge implies a change in the man's relations to the world. His position is determined not simply by the 'physical laws,' but by his knowledge of the laws. The discovery of iron or of electricity makes his world, if not the world, different; and the whole system of knowledge corresponds to an ultimate condition of his life. His knowledge, therefore, is an essential factor in the problem. The rationalism of the eighteenth century and the later progress of science had of course emphasised this truth. The natural sciences represent the intellectual framework, which steadily grows and at every stage gives a final determinant of all human activity. Superstitions and theology in general correspond to the

[1] *Philosophie Positive*, 1852, i. 44, and cp. *Ibid.* iv. 648, etc.

erroneous theories which are gradually dispelled as we construct a definitive and verifiable base of solid knowledge. But is the scientific progress not only the ultimate but the sole factor in all social development? Man is a complex being, with an emotional as well as an intellectual nature, which, proximately at any rate, determines his conduct. How are we to allow for this factor of the inquiry?[1]

Buckle's version of the principle is significant. He begins by distinguishing 'progress' into 'moral' and 'intellectual.'[2] Which of these is the important element? Do men progress in the moral or in the intellectual element? Since, as we have seen, we cannot assume an improvement in the individual, the later differences must be ascribed to the 'external advantages'—to the opinions and so forth of the society in which the child is educated. In the next place, the opinions are constantly varying, whereas the 'moral motives' are singularly constant.[3] A 'stationary element,' when surrounding circumstances are unchanged, can only produce a stationary effect, and hence we must explain civilisation by the variable agent. Buckle argues that the moral code recognised has remained unaltered since distant times. The same general rules are accepted, and no additional articles have been inserted. Then the great stages of progress—especially the growth of religious toleration and of peace—have been due to intellectual, not to moral

[1] Mr. Herbert Spencer raises this question in a criticism of Comte, contained in a pamphlet upon the 'Classification of the Sciences.' See Mill's remarks upon this in his *Auguste Comte and Positivism*, pp. 34, 43, 102, 114. The controversy between Mr. Spencer and Comte lies beyond my province.
[2] *Civilisation*, p. 152.   [3] *Ibid*. pp. 160-63.

changes; and, finally, as he thinks, the average man remains pretty much the same. Some men are good and some bad; but the good and the bad actions neutralise each other. Their effects are temporary, while the 'discoveries of great men' are 'immortal,' and contain the 'eternal truths which survive the shock of empires, outlive the struggles of rival creeds, and witness the decay of successive religions.'[1] Buckle, that is, reserves for the 'eternal truths' of scientific discovery the enthusiasm which others had lavished upon the eternal truths of the great religious teachers. The doctrine agrees with the Utilitarian theories in one respect. Man is supposed to remain on the whole constant, in his natural capacities and in his moral qualities. On the other hand, Buckle dwells more emphatically than Mill upon the spontaneous growth of scientific ideas as the sole but sufficient force which moulds the destinies of mankind. From Mill's constant insistence upon the power of association and the empirical character of all knowledge, it might be inferred that even scientific progress is precarious and unstable. To Buckle the development of scientific knowledge seems to be inevitable, if only the mind is allowed to work freely. The most conspicuous facts of the day gave force to his conviction. The enormous changes in the whole constitution of society were due to the advance of mechanical discoveries and to the triumph of freetraders. Watt and Adam Smith, not the religious preachers, represent the real transforming force. The steam-engine has altered the whole position of the human race. The sermons of Methodists and Catholics have left the

[1] *Civilisation*, p. 206.

average man just where he was. Napoleon was a great criminal, and Wilberforce, perhaps, a great philanthropist. Their influence has been transitory, while the scientific inventors have set up changes which will continue to gather force as the ages roll.

The truth contained in this, again, seems to be undeniable. Modify the 'environment' and your organism is modified throughout. Alter the climate, the soil, the amount of fertile land, and the whole state of mankind will be altered. That, again, has been virtually achieved by modern discoveries. Though the natural forces may be the same, our relation to them has been altered; and, if more fertile soil has not been brought into existence, the fertile soil has been brought, we may say, nearer to our doors. Moreover, the change has been primarily due to scientific discovery and not to any moral change; or the moral changes, whatever they may be, have been the consequence, not the cause. So far as Buckle emphasised this aspect, he was clearly insisting upon a truth which requires recognition. The question is what bearing this has upon the philosophy of history, and whether it justifies us in discarding the influence of the 'moral' element in building up the social structure.

The general doctrine leads to the conclusion that the essential difference between two stages of history is the difference between the quantity of knowledge possessed and its diffusion throughout all classes. That is really Buckle's contention, from which all his conclusions are deducible. The 'totality of human actions,' as he says, is 'governed by the totality of human knowledge;'[1] or, as he elsewhere puts it,[2] the history of every 'civilised

[1] *Civilisation*, p. 209.   [2] *Ibid*. p. 354.

country is the history of its intellectual development.' If early societies are governed by the 'physical laws,' later societies are governed by the action of those laws upon our minds, and the action is thus profoundly modified as our knowledge of the laws extends. The 'environment' has a different relation to us, but remains the ultimate and independent determinant. If this be the whole truth, it would follow that we might write the history of mankind by writing the history of science. All other phenomena would be simply deducible as corollaries from the state of knowledge. Comte had suggested that history might be written without mentioning the names of individuals. On Buckle's assumption, history may deal simply with the growth of scientific ideas; and, therefore, we need not take into account the moral ideas or all the complex system of actions which come under the head of the will and the emotions in psychological treatises.

Is it possible to write a history upon such terms? Granting that knowledge defines the base upon which the whole structure must repose, can we abstract from all this considerations of the way in which men's beliefs are brought to bear upon the constitution of society? The difficulty becomes obvious as soon as Buckle turns from his general principle to the historical application. Mark Pattison,[1] in his review of the History on its first appearance, puts the point. Buckle, he says, after insisting upon the utter inadequacy of the old historical and metaphysical methods, proceeds to 'exemplify the very method of writing history which he had con-

[1] *Essays* (1889), ii. 422. (Essay on Buckle, reprinted from *Westminster Review* of 1857.)

demned.' His account of French society is, as Pattison says, a 'masterly sketch,' unequalled in breadth and comprehensiveness of view by any English writer. But, then, it brings in precisely the elements of individual influence, and so forth, which Buckle expressly professed to exclude. I will add nothing to the commendation possessing a higher authority than my own. Buckle's surveys, not only of French, but of English, Spanish, and Scottish, I believe, may fully justify the opinion that his abilities, rightly directed, might have produced a history surpassing the achievement of any of his rivals. But the only question with which I am concerned is the relation of the history to the philosophy. Buckle, if he had simply written a history of England, might have eclipsed Hallam or Macaulay in their own line. Did he really inaugurate a better method of writing history in general ? or, if not, what caused the failure of a man possessed of such singular qualifications ?

A difficulty is suggested even in regard to the purely scientific development. Buckle speaks with the warmest enthusiasm of great men, such as Descartes, whose scientific discoveries revolutionised thought, or Adam Smith,[1] who, by publishing a single work, contributed more to human happiness than all the statesmen and legislators of whom we have an authentic record. How can this be reconciled with the insignificance of the individual ? A great discovery is necessarily the work of an individual. No combination of second-rate men could have supplied the place of a single Newton. It therefore occurs to Buckle that, after all, the individual has to be taken into account. If Descartes and Smith

[1] *Civilisation*, i. 197.

had died of the measles in infancy, progress would have been arrested. To escape this conclusion, he refers to the 'spirit of the age,' which would have made the discovery fruitless at a different period. What is covered by that phrase ? The social influence does not supersede the necessity for individual genius. Everything that is done must of course be done by individuals. The 'spirit of the age' must mean such a social order as fosters discovery ; an order, for example, in which so many men are devoted to scientific inquiry that discovery becomes certain. The man of genius is still first in the race ; but he is first of many competitors, who, even if he were to die, would achieve the same result a little later. The individual is still required, but the importance of any particular individual is so far diminished. The growth of science cannot be explained, in the historical sense, without reference to the social order which leads to the cultivation of science. It is not something which grows of its own accord outside of society, but supposes the whole social structure and the moral factor which we are endeavouring to discard.

The difficulty affects Buckle's mode of dealing with the great historical problems. Since progress depends absolutely upon the growth of science, the one essential is the spirit of inquiry, or, as he calls it, 'scepticism.' Its natural antagonist is the 'protective' spirit, which implies servile submission to authority in matters of opinion or practice. The disastrous effects of such a spirit are traced in Spain and Scotland. The 'inquisition' and the tyranny of Puritan ministers are its natural fruits. No one, of course, will deny the evils due to a suppression of intellectual activity. To exhibit and to denounce those

evils is a task which Buckle performs with admirable vigour. But, so far, he is merely writing an effective pamphlet on a large scale. He is denouncing the protective spirit as the Whig historian denounces Toryism, or rival religious historians find the evil principle in Protestantism or Popery. The protective spirit is an abstraction which means a quality of the whole society considered from one point of view ; its relation, namely, to scientific progress. It cannot be an ultimate cause— a power in itself—but is a product of many complex conditions. To consider it impartially, to form an accurate diagnosis of the disease is the problem for the scientific historian. He should discover the uniform laws whose working is manifest in the morbid condition, and, in the case of Spain, render the intellectual paralysis permanent and incurable. Here Buckle's method becomes that of the ordinary historian. He refers to the earthquakes and various physical conditions which apply to the case of Spanish superstition. We now learn, however, that these physical influences are 'interwoven with a long chain of other and still more influential events,' which enable us to trace the steps of decline with 'unerring certainty.'[1] We go back, therefore, both in Spain and Scotland to the political history ; to the play of party and class-interests, which have forced a priesthood at one time to ally itself with despots, and at another to throw itself upon the people. The history may be accurate and the facts alleged are no doubt relevant ; but they leave the difficult problems unsolved. Why, for example, was the Spanish people at the head of European races in the sixteenth century, and why did it then suddenly sink into

[1] *Civilisation*, ii. 9.

decay ? Why did Scotland, sunk in superstition in the seventeenth century, become, though still the most superstitious country in Europe, the most energetic and progressive part of the British empire ? To attack such problems it would, I take it, be necessary to study impartially a vast variety of social and of what Buckle calls moral questions ; to give weight to a number of 'interwoven' causes, determining the history of the two races. The facts—the intellectual stagnation of Spain and the intolerance of Scottish Puritanism—imply, as Buckle urges, some general causes. The history shows them at work, and Buckle's survey brings out many significant facts. Still, when the protective spirit is hypostatised and made a kind of independent cause, determining and not determined by the general social state, we miss the most interesting problem, or take the solution for granted. What, after all, is the true secret of this mysterious power ? Whence came its vitality ? The evil principle appears like the supernatural sovereign in 'Philip Beauchamp' or the Demogorgon of Shelley's *Prometheus*, a cruel tyrant enforcing false belief—even so, he requires to be explained as well as denounced, and we are at least tempted to ask whether the church and the king must not have discharged some useful social function ; and the creed have embodied some element of thought and emotion congenial to human nature. That is the aspect neglected by Buckle.

One or two conspicuous examples of the result may be indicated. Buckle has to deal with the French revolution.[1] Nobody has been more emphatic in insisting that

[1] On this point Mr. Robertson virtually agrees with me, though he attaches less importance to it.

history should deal with the facts which illustrate the state of the people instead of confining itself to court intrigues. Nor could any one speak more strongly of the misery of the French population before the revolution. Yet the whole explanation has to be sought in the purely intellectual causes. The social causes are simply dropped out of account. The revolution was due to the French philosophers. Intellectual activity had been entirely suppressed by the despotism of Louis XIV. The philosophers, he holds, learned the new doctrine from England. The persecution of the freethinkers by the later rulers and a servile priesthood forced the philosophers to attack both the despots, and (unfortunately, as Buckle holds) to attack Christianity as well. Hence both the achievements and the incidental evils caused by the final outbreak. The theory, though strangely inadequate, is a natural corollary from the doctrine that the history of a nation is the history of its intellectual development. Voltaire's study of Locke becomes the efficient cause of a gigantic social change.. A single characteristic, itself the product of many factors, is made to account for the whole complex process. Still more significant is his account of the decreasing influence of the warlike spirit. That, too, must be a product of purely intellectual causes. Divines have done nothing by preaching, but intellectual movement has operated in 'three leading ways.'[1] The discoveries of gunpowder, of free trade principles, and of the application of steam to travelling have produced the peaceable tendencies, which, in Buckle's day, were apparently so near a final triumph. Let us fully grant what I hope is true, that this corresponds to a truth; that the

[1] *Civilisation*, i. 185.

various forces which have brought men together may ultimately conduce to peace; and, moreover, that the discoveries of science are among the ultimate conditions of the most desirable of all changes. Does this enable us to abstract from the social movement? Gunpowder, according to Buckle, facilitated the differentiation of the military from the other classes. That already assumes a process only intelligible through the social history. Buckle tells us that 'divines' have done nothing. If he means that they have not persuaded nations, or not even tried to persuade them, to turn the second cheek, he is unanswerable. Religion, as he says elsewhere,[1] is an 'effect,' not a cause of human improvement. It can, in fact, be an original cause only on the hypothesis of a supernatural intervention. It must be an 'effect' in the sense that it is a product of human nature under all the conditions. If by religion is meant simply the belief in fictitious beings, it may be considered as simply an obstruction to scientific advance; and the priesthood, as Buckle generally seems to hold, is the gang of impostors who turn it to account. In any case, the 'moral' teaching of priests cannot be the ultimate cause of moral improvement. Yet no one, it might be supposed, could explain the history of the warlike sentiment in Europe without taking into account the influence embodied in the church. That the Catholic church represented a great principle of cohesion; that it was an organisation which enabled the men of intellect to exercise an influence over semi-barbarous warriors, are admitted facts which the historian is at least bound to consider. At whatever period the body may have become corrupt, it is an essential fact in

[1] *Civilisation*, p. 235.

the social processes which preceded the invention of gunpowder, and certainly the discoveries of Watt and Adam Smith. Buckle, as a rule, treats the church simply as an upholder of superstition. He ridicules the historians who believed in absurd miracles in 'what are rightly termed the dark ages,'[1] and declares summarily that 'until doubt began, progress was impossible.' Yet Buckle would certainly have admitted that there was some progress between the heptarchy and the reformation.

The truth which his method compels him to neglect seems to be obvious. The movement of religious thought represents forces not to be measured by the quantity of effete superstitions which it contains. The religion corresponds to the development of the instincts which determine the whole social structure. The general moral axioms—love your neighbour, and so forth—may, as Buckle urges, remain unaltered; but the change in the ideals of life and the whole attitude of men to each other takes place in the religious sphere. If Christianity does not correspond to a force imposed from without, it may still correspond to the processes of thought by which sympathy has extended and men been drawn into comparative unity and harmony. To treat the power of religion as simply a product of ignorant superstition is to be unable to understand the history of the world. So much Buckle might have learned from Comte in spite of the later vagaries of positivism.

Another collateral conclusion marks Buckle's position. As a historian of political progress he is constantly dwelling upon the importance of individual action. The

[1] *Civilisation*, pp. 248, 283, 289, 306. He occasionally admits that the church protected the poor and was useful in its time. *Ibid.* pp. 462, 559.

tolerant policy of Richelieu, the despotic system of Louis XIV., and so forth, are the great aids or impediments to human progress. How is this reconcilable with the doctrines that individual action is nothing and the spontaneous growth of knowledge everything? In answer we are referred to the great general causes, or to the protective spirit or the spirit of the age, which really govern the whole process in spite of superficial and transitory causes. What precisely is meant by these abstractions? To what does the protective spirit in politics owe its malign persistence? What, in short, is the source and true nature of the power of government? The answer is, that to Buckle, as to the Utilitarians, government represents a kind of external force; something imposed upon the people from without; a 'sovereign,' in Austin's sense, who can never originate or impel, though he can coerce and suppress. He chooses the history of England for his subject, as he tells us, because England has been 'less affected than any other country by the two main sources of interference, namely, the authority of government and the influence of foreigners.'[1] Both are treated as 'interferences' from without, which distort the natural development. English history is interesting not because its political constitution is a most characteristic outgrowth of its social state, but because all government is simply an interference, and in England has had a minimum influence. Consistently with this, he attacks the opinion that progress has ever been due to government. Government is, of course, necessary to punish crime and prevent anarchy;[2] but even its successful efforts are 'altogether negative'; and, even where its intentions have

[1] *Civilisation*, i. 213.　　　　[2] *Ibid.* i. 257.

been good, it has been generally injurious. Briefly, government is powerful for evil, and the one principle is that rulers should have a 'very little' power and exercise it 'very sparingly.'[1] At times he is inclined to deny all influence to government. Speaking of Scotland, he remarks that though bad government can be extremely injurious for a time, it can 'produce no permanent mischief.'[2] 'So long as the people are sound,' he says, 'there is life and will be reaction. . . . But if the people are unsound all hope is gone and the nation perishes.' What, then, makes the people 'sound'? Is not this a tacit admission of the importance of the moral factor? Has not the religion of a nation some influence, and sometimes perhaps an influence for good, upon its morality? Puritanism in Scotland was associated with gross superstition; was it not also an expression of the moral convictions which preserved the 'soundness' of the race? Catholicism in Spain is still, according to Buckle, associated with a high moral standard; but this has 'availed the Spaniards' nothing,[3] because it has suppressed intellectual progress. It has surely been of some use if it has preserved their virtue. But, in any case, what is the explanation of the power of government which can thus destroy the 'soundness' or morality and ruin the fortunes of a people? Buckle's theory might apply to the case of a nation conquered by a foreign tyrant. He denounces conquerors in the old tone as pests and destroyers of men, who pass their whole lives in increasing human misery.[4] Yet conquest has been a factor in the development of all nations, and Buckle

[1] *Civilisation*, i. 264.   [2] *Ibid.* ii. 274.
[3] *Ibid.* ii. 145, 146.   [4] *Ibid.* i. 729.

himself argues that the Norman conquest was an essential step in establishing the liberties of Englishmen.[1] It is still more difficult to suppose that a government which is the growth of a people's own requirements can be simply mischievous. Without trying to solve such puzzles, we may say that the whole doctrine seems to imply a misconception of the relations between the political and the social and moral constitution of a nation. No satisfactory theory can be formed, when it is assumed that the function of government is simply to keep the peace instead of inquiring historically what functions it has actually discharged. When Buckle regards government like the 'physical laws' as the cause of pure mischief, he ceases to be scientific and becomes after a fashion a moralist, denouncing instead of explaining.

The connection of this with the do-nothing doctrine which Buckle accepts in its fullest form is obvious. The less government the better is the natural formula for a disciple of Adam Smith. What is here important is the connection of the doctrine with Buckle's first principles. The political order cannot be thus treated as if it were an independent power impinging from without upon a natural order; it is a product of the whole organism, and to denounce it as simply bad is really meaningless. It is part of the essential structure, and therefore we cannot properly abstract from the other parts of the system. This or that regulation, or this or that wheel of the political machinery may be superfluous or mischievous; but the question can only be decided by regarding the system as a whole, and not by treating the ruling power as something separable. Its interference

[1] *Civilisation*, i. 563.

has to be treated as abnormal or as simply mischievous, and yet as of vital importance in history. It becomes a mystery simply because we do not investigate its nature with due reference to its functions in the body politic. In other words, Buckle becomes incoherent because his method induces him from the start to neglect what is implied when society is described as organic. He was speaking an indisputable truth when he said that society depends throughout upon the 'environment' in the physical laws. It is not less true to say that as the intellectual progress developed, the recognition of those laws supplies an ultimate and unchangeable condition of the whole process of social growth. All civilisation depends absolutely, as he asserts, upon the corresponding state of knowledge. The error is in the assumption that we can therefore omit the consideration of the complex laws which govern the growth of the organism itself. The individualism which he shares with the Utilitarians makes him blind to the importance of the line of inquiry which was to show its power in the following period. If the primitive despotisms are set down simply as a necessary result of 'physical laws,' it is superfluous to inquire into the real nature of the institutions which they imply, or to gain any light upon the working of similar principles elsewhere. When the whole ecclesiastical and political constitution of later ages is set down simply as a relic of barbarism, and the religious and social instincts which are elaborated through them as simply products of ignorance, the process becomes unintelligible. If, therefore, Buckle was recognising a real condition of sound investigation, he condemned in advance the very kind of inquiry which has proved most fruitful. If he did more in his purely

historical inquiries it was because he then forgot his philosophy and had to take into account the considerations which he had pronounced to be irrelevant. That, I believe, is the reason why Buckle, in spite of his surpassing abilities, did not make any corresponding mark upon later investigations. He was trying to frame a philosophy of history upon principles which really make the formation of a coherent philosophy impossible. Briefly, then, Buckle shared the ambition of the Utilitarians to make all the moral sciences scientific. So far as his writing strengthened the leaning to a scientific tendency he was working in the right direction. Unfortunately he also shared their crude assumptions: the 'individualism' which ignores the social factor, and deduces all institutions from an abstract 'man'; the tendency to explain the earlier from the later stages; and the impression that 'laws of nature' are to be unravelled by a summary method of discovering co-existences of concrete phenomena; and was therefore led to substitute hasty generalisations for that elaborate study of the growth of institutions and beliefs which has been the most marked tendency of sociological inquiry during the last generation. So far he shares and illustrates the real weakness of the Utilitarians, the premature attempt to constitute a science when we can only be labouring effectually by trying to determine the data.

Here I may try to indicate, though I cannot develop, a general conclusion. What was the true significance of the Utilitarian paradox—the indifference to history combined with the appeal to experience? History in the narrower sense is a particular case of evolution; and if it could be made scientific, would formulate the laws by which the existing institutions, political, ecclesiastical, and industrial, have grown out of earlier states. The importance of taking into account the 'genetic' point of view, of inquiring into the growth as well as the actual constitution of things, is obvious in all the sciences which are concerned with organic life. Though we cannot analyse the organism into its ultimate constituent factors, we can learn something by tracing its development from simpler forms. The method is applicable to biology as well as to sociology; and as sciences extended, its importance became manifest. Some theory of evolution was required in every direction, and must obviously be necessary if we are to carry out systematically the principles of the uniformity and continuity of nature. The difficulty of the Utilitarians was all along that theories of evolution appeared to them to involve something mystical and transcendental. They proposed to analyse everything till they could get to single aggregations of facts, or in their sense ideal, that is, to a thoroughgoing atomism. This leads to the paradox indicated by Hume's phrase. The atoms, things and thoughts, must be completely separate and yet invariably conjoined. Causation becomes mere sequence or conjunction, and 'experience' ceases to offer any ground for anticipation. I have tried to show how this affected the Utilitarians in every subject; in their philosophical, legal, ethical, and economical speculations; and how they always seem to be in need of, and yet always to reject by anticipation, some theory of evolution. To appeal to 'experience' they have to make the whole universe incoherent, while to get general laws they have to treat variable units as absolutely constant. 'External circumstances' must account for all variation, though it is difficult to see how everything

can be 'external.' The difficulty has now appeared in history proper, and the attempt to base a sociology upon a purely individualist assumption. This may help to explain the great influence of the Darwinian theories. They marked the point at which a doctrine of evolution could be allied with an appeal to experience. Darwin appealed to no mystical bond, but simply to verifiable experience. He postulated the continuance of processes known by observation, and aimed at showing that they would sufficiently explain the present as continuous with the past. There was nothing mystical to alarm empiricists, and their consequent adoption of Darwinism implied a radical change in their methods and assumptions. The crude empiricism was transformed into evolutionism. The change marked an approximation to the conceptions of the opposite school when duly modified, and therefore in some degree a reconciliation. 'Intuitions' no longer looked formidable when they could be regarded as developed by the race instead of mysteriously implanted in the individual mind. The organic correlations were admissible when they were taken to imply growth instead of supernatural interference, and it was no longer possible to regard 'natural kinds' as mere aggregates of arbitrarily connected properties. I need not ask which side really gained by the change, whether Darwinism inevitably leads to some more subtle form of atomism, or whether the acceptance of any evolution does not lead to idealism—to a belief in a higher teleology than Paley's—and the admission that mind or 'spirit' must be the ultimate reality. Such problems may be treated by the philosopher of the future. Without anticipating his verdict, I must try to indicate the final outcome of what passed for philosophy with the Utilitarians.

CHAPTER VI

PHILOSOPHY

I. MILL'S OPPONENTS

MILL's logic embodies the cardinal principles of his philosophy. The principles implied that little of what is called philosophy could be valid. Mill necessarily held that many of the most pretentious speculations were, in reality, nothing but words; cobwebs of the brain to be swept into the dustbin, finally, though politely, by the genuine thinkers. His view of the consequences to theology and religion could for a long time be inferred only from incidental remarks. Gradually he came to think that the reticence was undesirable, and had given his final conclusions in the *Essays*, which were published after his death. The philosophical position which underlies them is most clearly exhibited in his *Examination of Hamilton* (1865).[1] This included a criticism of Mansel's application of Hamilton's metaphysical doctrines to theology. Mansel's doctrine, stated in the

---

[1] Mill's *Examination of Sir William Hamilton's Philosophy and of the Principal Philosophical Questions discussed in his Writings* was first published in 1865. I refer to the fourth edition (1872). The book was more changed than any of Mill's other writings in consequence of the insertion of replies to various criticisms. A list of these replies is given in the preface to the third and fourth editions. The essays on 'Religion' appeared in 1874.

Bampton Lectures of 1858, had provoked some sharp and many-sided controversies. He defended himself against Mill's criticism. Other writers joined the fray, and in one way or other a perplexing set of intellectual encounters resulted. The leading champions were Mill, representing the pure Utilitarian tradition, Mansel, who represented the final outcome of what Mill called 'intuitionism,' and F. D. Maurice, who may be briefly called the intellectual heir of Coleridge; while another line of inference was represented by Mr. Herbert Spencer's *First Principles*. Many of the arguments have already a strangely obsolete sound; but they may serve to illustrate the direction of the main currents of opinion.

The writings of Sir William Hamilton provided the ostensible battle-ground. Mill had seen in Hamilton certain symptoms of a hopeful leaning towards the true faith. Upon taking up the study more seriously, he discovered that Hamilton was really an intuitionist at bottom, and even a 'chief pillar' of the erroneous philosophy. I shall therefore inquire, in the first place, into the true nature of this version of the evil principle. It has been so often 'lucidly expounded' that it is hard to say what it really means.

Hamilton,[1] born 8th March 1788, was grandnephew, grandson, and son of three successive professors of anatomy at Glasgow. While still an infant, he lost his father, and was ever afterwards on terms of the tenderest affection with his mother, who died in 1827. After studying at Glasgow, he went to Balliol as a Snell exhibitioner in 1807, and there startled his examiners by

---

[1] See Veitch's *Life of Hamilton* (1869), and an article by Hamilton's daughter in the *Encyclopædia Britannica*.

his portentous knowledge of Aristotle.[1]   After some
medical study, he decided to join the Scottish bar.   He
took, however, more interest in the antiquarian than in
the practical branches of the laws ; and spent a great deal
of time and labour on abstruse genealogical researches to
establish his claim to a baronetcy.   He had to show that
he was heir to a Sir Robert Hamilton, who died in 1701,
through a common ancestor who died before 1552.   His
love of obscure researches, or his want of aptitude for
speaking, together with his adherence to Whig principles,
kept him out of the road to professional success.   He
was known, however, as a ' monster of erudition.'   He
visited Germany with his college friend J. G. Lockhart
in 1817, and on a second visit in 1820 began a systematic
study of the language.

In 1820 Hamilton was a candidate for the chair of
Moral Philosophy at Edinburgh, vacant by the death
of Thomas Brown.   To the scandal of philosophers, it
was given to Wilson, or ' Christopher North,' mainly on
political grounds.   Probably it was also held that anybody
could talk Moral Philosophy.   Hamilton was appointed to
a small professorship in 1821, but the salary, payable from
a duty on beer, was stopped and he ceased to lecture.

In 1829, Macvey Napier, upon succeeding Jeffrey as
editor of the *Edinburgh Review,* applied to his friend

[1] A letter from Hamilton to Dr. Parr in 1820 (Parr's *Works,* vii. 194-
202), on occasion of the contest at Edinburgh, gives an account of his studies.
He was personally unknown to Dugald Stewart, to whom he desires Parr to
write a letter upon the advantages of studying ancient philosophy, to be shown
to the Town Council (who then elected the professor).   Hamilton says that
he took up nearly all Aristotle, most of Plato, and of Cicero's philosophical
works ; that he had read many Greek commentators upon Plato and Aristotle,
and that many of his books were declared to be too metaphysical for the schools
and were forbidden to be taken up again.   Veitch gives a similar account.

Hamilton for an article.   The result was the review of
Cousin, which appeared in the number for October 1829.
Jeffrey was rather scandalised by this novelty in his
old organ ; the writer showed an unholy familiarity with
the Absolute and the Infinite and the jargon of German
metaphysics ; he could not, said Jeffrey, be a ' very clever
man,' and the article was the 'most unreadable thing that
had ever appeared in the *Review.*'[1]   The average reader,
however, was awed if not interested ; and a select few,
including Cousin, were greatly impressed.   Hamilton's
reputation was made ; he wrote other articles which confirmed the impression, and in 1836 was appointed to the .
Edinburgh professorship of ' Logic and Metaphysics.'
He was at length in his proper place ; and many students
of that generation became ardent disciples.   For the next
twenty years he was regarded with an enthusiasm like
that which had surrounded Dugald Stewart in the previous period and Reid at an earlier date.   His impressive
appearance and force of character contributed to increase
the respect due to his vast reading and tone of rightful
authority.   He was unmistakably upright, a lover of
speculation for its own sake, and a man of warm and
pure affections.   No one could be happier in domestic
life.   In 1828, after his mother's death, he married his
cousin, Janet Marshall, by whom he had four children.
He is described as gentle and kindly in his family ; joining in childish games, writing in the general room, and
amusing himself with extravagant romances.   He possessed
great physical strength till, in 1844, his imprudent habits
of study brought on a paralytic stroke.   He recovered
partially, but became weaker and died on 6th May 1856.

[1] Napier's *Correspondence,* p. 70.

With all Hamilton's claims to respect, there was a
very weak side to his character.   A queer vein of
pedantry ran through the man.   A philosopher ought
surely not to spend two years unearthing a baronetcy.
Hamilton stickled for his rights in other cases in a way
which one feels to have been scarcely worthy of him.
His real magnanimity was combined with a mental
rigidity which made him incapable of compromise.   He
is undeniably candid and always speaks generously of his
opponents ; but his own logic always appears to him to
be infallible, and neither in practical matters nor in argument would he yield a jot or a tittle of his case.   His
self-confidence was unfailing, and he speaks even in his
first article with the air of an intellectual dictator.   He
was resolved, it seems, to justify his position by knowing
everything that had ever been written upon philosophy.
Like Browning's old grammarian, he would ' know all,'
both text and comment, and when the ' little touch ' of
paralysis came, he was still preparing and accumulating.
He had read a vast mass of obscure literature and helped
a powerful memory by elaborate commonplace books.
His passion for imbibing knowledge, indeed, was out of
proportion to his giving out results.   He has left comparatively little, and much of that is fragmentary.   His
writings are all included in the *Discussions* (from the
Edinburgh Review and elsewhere), the often elaborate
notes to his edition of Reid, and the *Lectures.*   The two
first volumes of these lectures (on Metaphysics), as we
are told by the editors, were written in the course of five
months for his first session.   They were repeated for
twenty years without serious alteration.   The lectures
upon logic, filling two volumes more, were written in

the same way for the second session.   Writing in such
haste, Hamilton naturally eked out his work by making
very free use of his commonplace book, and, in the
course upon logic, by long quotations from previous
textbooks.   The notes to Reid consist in part of long
chains of quotations.   They show one palpable weakness.
The extracts, detached from their context, lose their true
significance.   He gives a list of 101 authorities from
Hesiod to Lamennais, with quotations, in which an appeal
of some kind is made to ' common-sense.'   He might
have collected a thousand ; but instead of showing
approval of the special Scottish doctrine, they really show
that the phrase may be used more or less freely by
holders of every doctrine.   He seems to share the
opinion of old writers that every statement in a printed
book is an ' authority.'   The results are sometimes
grotesque.   It was natural enough that Hamilton should
note an unfavourable opinion of mathematical study
expressed by Horace Walpole ; but a grave citation
of Horace Walpole as an authority upon mathematical
studies would have amused nobody more than Walpole
himself.   On such a method the fuel too often puts out
the fire, and Hamilton's direct expositions are few and
his opinions often to be inferred from fragmentary
criticisms.   They naturally vary as he places himself at
different points of view ; and we are left to guess how he
would have tried to combine them.

Henry Longueville Mansel (1820-1871),[1] Hamilton's
most noteworthy interpreter, was a typical Oxford don,
as became his birth.   He was the descendant of an old

[1] Notice by Lord Carnarvon prefixed to *Gnostic Heresies* (1875), and
Burgon's *Twelve Good Men.*

family of country-gentlemen, the younger members of which had entered the army or navy or held the family living. He had been a brilliant schoolboy, had distinguished himself in Oxford examinations, and became known as a wit in common-rooms, a writer of vivacious squibs, and a sound Tory and high Churchman. He had a clear intellect, a forcible style, and had studied theology and German metaphysics with remarkable energy. He apparently began as a Kantian; but he was greatly impressed by Sir William Hamilton, with whom he had no personal relations; and he adopted from Hamilton the peculiar theory which was to enlist Kant in the service of the church of England. His Bampton Lectures in 1858 made him famous as a champion of orthodoxy. In 1868 he was appointed to the deanery of St. Paul's; but his labours had been too much for his brain, and he died suddenly in 1871.

Hamilton started under the double influence of the Scottish philosophy and of Aristotle. Formal logic was to him the most congenial of studies. He would have been thoroughly in his element in the mediæval schools, syllogising to the death. According to an enthusiastic pupil, he laid the top stone on the fabric founded by the 'master hand of the Stagirite.'[1] He was in his element when dividing, subdividing, and cross-dividing all manner of philosophical tenets. The aim was admirable. To have all opinions properly articulated and correlated would be the final result of a history of philosophy and a step to further progress. The danger of accepting such a classification prematurely is equally obvious. The technical terms of metaphysics have the most provoking

[1] See Mill's *Examination of Hamilton*, p. 496.

habit of shifting their meaning; they shade off imperceptibly into each other, and sometimes even change places; they represent aspects of truth caught from a particular point of view, which become inapplicable or carry different implications as the point of view imperceptibly shifts. What appear to be contradictory utterances may be merely qualifications of each other, or may mean the same thing in different dialects. A system built of such unsubstantial and slippery materials is apt to crumble into mere chaos without extreme care and penetration. Hamilton, most fully aware of this in general terms, was nevertheless not sufficiently on his guard. He always seems to fancy that he can avoid all ambiguities by a definition, and does not remember that the words by which he defines are as shifting in their sense as the word defined. The consideration is especially important because it is Hamilton's main purpose to mediate between conflicting opinions. He starts from Reid's 'common-sense,' and has to show how the position can be protected against scepticism on the one side and mysticism on the other.

Cousin, as a disciple of the Scottish philosophers, represented one line of deviation from the judicious mean. Beginning with Reid, he had become, with certain reserves, a follower or developer of Schelling. Coleridge's 'genial coincidence' with Schelling had led to no very tangible result; but Cousin's systematic development showed the philosophy diverging into a false track, and wasting itself upon the pursuit of utterly chimerical aims. Hamilton, therefore, endeavoured to expose the fallacies involved in the whole procedure. He agreed, as we shall see, with an important part of Kant's doctrine; but

thought that by certain oversights Kant had opened the door to Schelling's empty speculations. There was an opposite danger to which Hamilton was equally awake. He insisted upon it in an article published October 1830 upon the 'Philosophy of Perception.' This is, in the main, a fierce attack upon Brown—the one philosophical writer of whom he cannot speak without betraying prejudice. Hamilton's antipathy has been already explained. Brown shows Scottish philosophy lapsing into mere empiricism and 'inductive psychology.' Hamilton never mentions him without accusing him of blunders and of crass ignorance.

Hamilton thus stands up for the orthodox commonsense theory of Reid, and resents backslidings into transcendentalism on the right hand and sensationalism on the left. Like the excellent David Deans, he would keep the 'ridge of the hill, where wind and water shears.' When, however, he set about the edition of Reid's works, he began to discover inconsistencies. He doubted whether Reid had really taught the true faith; and he was led to restate more articulately his own view. To the end of his life, however, Hamilton called himself a Natural Realist; and held, though with increasing qualifications, that Reid's doctrine was an approximate statement of the same doctrine. What Natural Realism may be is another question.

The two essays just mentioned[1] give the pith of Hamilton's philosophical theories. His other writings on philosophy are mainly remodelled versions of the same views, or classifications of other solutions of the

[1] Reprinted as the first two chapters in the *Discussions* on the 'Philosophy of the Unconditioned' and the 'Philosophy of Perception.'

problems. His speculations in logic, whatever their value, belong to a sphere which fortunately lies outside my province. In treating of perception, Hamilton gives the rationale of our belief in the external world; and in treating of the 'Unconditioned' the rationale of our belief in a deity. The results are in both cases remarkable.

II. HAMILTON ON PERCEPTION

What is the relation between the world of matter and the world of mind? That had been Reid's problem, and Hamilton starts from the acceptance of Reid's common-sense reply. We have to steer between opposing difficulties. Give too much to the mind and you will drift into mysticism, idealism, or ultimately to 'nihilism.' Give too much to matter and you will become a materialist or a mere sensationalist. Commonsense gives the true answer. Reid was in the right path when he declared himself to be on the side of the 'vulgar.'[1] Things are just what they seem to be. It is the philosophers who, in Berkeley's famous phrase, have raised a dust, and complain that they cannot see. This doctrine gives the principle of an elaborate classification of philosophers generally, and supplies the test of their soundness.[2] The truth lies with the 'Natural Realists' or 'Natural Dualists,' who do justice to both sides. They believe both in mind and matter 'in absolute co-equality'; in a 'duality' which presents the elements of consciousness in 'equal counterpoise and

[1] Reid's *Works*, p. 823.
[2] See in *Discussions*, p. 55; *Lectures*, i. 295, etc.; Reid's *Works*, p. 817 (the most elaborate).

independence.'[1] Unluckily, there is a mock dualism which virtually makes the true position untenable. It surrenders the real key of the position. This is the unfortunate case of the 'Cosmothetic Idealists,' whose theory represents an illogical compromise. They assert that the mind perceives—not matter but—something which 'represents' matter. It is conscious only of its own 'ideas.' These form the visible imagery, an unreal screen, somehow 'representing' a real world behind. The sceptic, then, had only to point out that the world behind was a superfluity, and our whole world turns out to be illusion. Reid had answered Hume by sweeping away all this superfluous machinery, and proving (or at least asserting) that what we see is itself real. Reid's analysis of consciousness, when duly corrected, showing that 'we have, as we believe we have, an immediate knowledge of the material world, accomplished everything at once.'[2] 'Natural Realism' and 'Absolute Idealism' are the only systems worthy of a philosopher.[3] The Cosmothetic Idealist occupies a position from which he can be driven at any moment by the more thoroughgoing idealist. Yet, as Hamilton declares, Cosmothetic Idealism has been held in various forms by the immense majority of philosophers,[4] indeed, by almost all who have not been driven by its absurdity into materialism or scepticism. A few 'stray speculators'[5] alone have found the narrow way. The list is apparently exhausted by the names of Peter Poiret, Reid, and Sir William Hamilton,[6] and even

[1] Lectures, i. 292.   [2] Discussions, p. 93.   [3] Reid's Works, p. 817 n.
[4] Discussions, p. 56.   [5] Ibid. p. 192.
[6] Lectures, i. 230, 293. Peter Poiret corresponds to 'Johnny Dodds of Farthingsacre,' the one orthodox friend of Davie Deans.

Reid may be said with much plausibility to have held a version of the creed which would make his whole philosophy 'one mighty blunder.'[1] What has caused this universal apostasy?

The answer is remarkable. It is due to a 'crotchet of philosophers'[2]—a crotchet, moreover, not only unsupported by, but opposed to, all the evidence. It appeared first with Empedocles; it produced the 'gnostic reasons' of the Platonists; the 'pre-existing species' of Avicenna; the common intellect of Themistius and Averroes; the 'intentional species' of the schools; the 'occasional causes' of the Cartesians; the predetermined harmony of Leibniz; the plastic medium of Cudworth and the phenomena of Kant. When so many masters of thought have invented theories it is unhappily easy to believe that they have all gone wrong; but one would at least infer that there was some difficulty to be solved. And yet all these fabrics of sham philosophy are founded upon a 'baseless fancy,' which Reid alone was too independent to take for granted. That 'fancy' was that the 'relation of knowledge inferred an analogy of existence.'[3] Norris of Bemerton had urged that a direct perception of matter was impossible because 'material objects' are removed from the mind 'by the whole diameter of Being.' Reid, with 'an ignorance wiser than knowledge,' confessed his inability to understand this argument. Seeing no difficulty in supposing an immediate perception of a totally disparate thing, he did not make an 'irrational attempt to explain what is in itself inexplicable.'[4] We can no more know how the mind is conscious of itself

[1] Lectures, i. 331.   [2] Discussions, p. 61.
[3] Discussions, p. 61; Lectures, i. 225.   [4] Discussions, i. 62.

than how it is percipient of its contrary. The whole puzzle, then, is gratuitous;—which is a consoling result for ordinary common-sense.

Philosophers had thus bewildered themselves by refusing to admit a plain, though ultimate, fact. There is a gulf between mind and matter over which no bridge can be thrown, but no bridge is wanted. The attempt to construct one is superfluous. Yet in a different form the question is still prominent, and modern science has invested it with fresh interest. How are we to conceive of the relation between the mental and the material spheres? How, after all, do we draw the line between things and thoughts, object and subject, ego and non-ego? Where do we reach the impassable gulf, and what, therefore, is the precise sense in which we must pronounce all attempt at bridging it to be preposterous? Hamilton's first position is that we are bound to stand by 'consciousness.' The 'watchword' of the Natural Realist is 'the facts of consciousness, the whole facts and nothing but the facts.'[1] He constantly appeals to the 'deliverance of consciousness,' and assures us again and again that unless we can believe this deliverance, we must suppose man to have been formed only to 'become the dupe and victim of a perfidious creator.'[2] The error of the Cosmothetic Idealists consisted precisely in the arbitrary rejection of a truth given by the testimony of consciousness. An original conviction is to be distinguished from derivative knowledge, as he tells us, by various characteristics, among which is especially its 'necessity.' We cannot really resist it.[3] If a disbelief in consciousness be impossible, why argue against it? If not impossible,

[1] Discussions, p. 64.   [2] Reid's Works, p. 745.   [3] Ibid. p. 754.

how can you assert that the belief is necessary? You have only to state the belief and, on your showing, it will prove itself. To this Hamilton answers that 'necessity' may be of two kinds. We cannot believe a self-contradictory statement; and we are therefore sufficiently guarded by logic against errors which are in this sense impossible. But there are other assertions which may be denied without self-contradiction, and of which, notwithstanding this, the denial would lead to universal scepticism. This corresponds apparently to the difference between a statement of fact and a statement of judgment. A false statement of facts may be as consistent as a true statement, and can only be met by somehow appealing to experience.[1] So far, then, as consciousness assures us of a fact, we may deny it without contradicting ourselves; but yet, by denying it, we 'make God a deceiver and the root of our nature a lie.'[2] We may thus say without self-contradiction, that memory in general is an illusion, and the world a mere dream or bundle of baseless appearances;[3] but we cannot say so without denying the primary deliverance of consciousness, and striking at the base of all knowledge. Certain truths, though not logically self-supporting, so run through the whole fabric of belief, as to be essential to its existence. If I am conscious, I cannot doubt the fact of consciousness. The knowledge of the fact and the fact become identical. The possibility of error begins with judgment, or with the interpretation of the fact. It is undeniable, again,

[1] Hamilton admits the distinction between 'primary truths of fact' and 'primary truths of intelligence,' but says that as their sources are not different, he will not give them different names.—Reid's Works, p. 743 n.
[2] Reid's Works, p. 743.   [3] Lectures, i. 294.

that, in some sense or other, I believe in an external world. Every philosopher, as Hamilton says, admits this to be a fact, and Berkeley appeals to the common sense of mankind when denying, as confidently as Reid when affirming, the existence of matter. We must inquire, then, what precisely is this ultimate deliverance. Does consciousness testify merely to the fact of the belief, or also to the truth of the belief; and, in either case, of what belief? This is what Hamilton has to answer, before summoning us to admit the truth on penalty of making God a liar.

The highwater mark of his opinion seems to be given in a passage of the *Lectures*. He there tells us that, though it is a strange, it is a correct, expression to say, ' I am conscious '—not merely of perceiving the inkstand but—' of the inkstand.' [1] Reid's blunder—which, if he really made it, would convert his whole philosophy into one mighty blunder—lay in misunderstanding this. Reid had been startled at his own boldness in asserting the immediacy ' of our knowledge of external things ' ; [2] and therefore weakly admitted that we are conscious of perceiving the rose, not conscious of the rose itself. This comes of distinguishing ' consciousness ' from perception, and would end in philosophical suicide. It would seem, then, that according to this doctrine we are bound either to assert that the rose—the visible, coloured, scented object, is revealed in consciousness as part of the ' material world ' and therefore exists independently of us, or to admit that God is a liar. It is ' palpably impossible that we can be conscious of an act without being conscious of the object to which the act is relative.' [3]

[1] *Lectures*, i. 228.   [2] *Ibid.* i. 224.   [3] *Ibid.* i. 212.

To carry out this theory is the central aim of Hamilton's ' Natural Realism.' Reid's statement might seem to be not a blunder, but a truism. ' I am conscious of the rose ' means precisely ' I have certain sensations which I regard as implying the existence of a permanent external reality.' But this is to interpret perception as involving an ' inference,' and therefore, according to Hamilton, is to abandon the essential doctrine of Natural Realism.[1] It may seem strange, he admits, but it is true, ' that the simple and primary act of intelligence should be a judgment, which philosophers in general have received as a compound and derivative operation.' [2] ' Knowing ' and ' knowing that we know ' are the same thing ; as conceiving the sides and angles of a triangle are the same process, distinguishable in thought, but ' in nature, one and indivisible.' [3] What, then, is this essential judgment? In an act of sensible perception, says Hamilton, I am conscious of myself and of something different from myself.[4] This might seem to define the distinction between ' consciousness ' and ' perception.' The object of my thought may, as Hamilton remarks, be a ' mode of mind ' as well as a ' mode of matter.' [5] Consciousness of self, we should infer, differs from consciousness of the notself, and it is just the presence of the notself which distinguishes perception from simple consciousness. Hamilton, however, argues that perception is simple consciousness ; or that the distinction, for his purpose, is irrelevant. There is a ' logical ' but not a ' psychological ' difference.[6] Every act of conscious-

[1] Reid's *Works*, p. 822.   [2] *Lectures*, i. 204.   [3] *Ibid.* i. 194.
[4] Reid's *Works*, p. 744.   [5] *Ibid.* p. 806.
[6] *Discussions*, p. 50, etc.; *Lectures*, i. 225, etc.

ness implies a conception of the ego. But ' the science of opposites is one.' Therefore consciousness of the ego involves consciousness of the non-ego, or, in the simplest possible act of intelligence I must be taken to affirm the existence both of an ego and a non-ego.

If I cannot even think about myself without affirming the existence of an external world, it would be superfluous to look about for further proofs of its existence. But here occurs a singular difficulty. Hamilton has to guard against the transcendentalist as well as against the sceptic. He is therefore not only a ' realist,' but with equal emphasis a ' relativist.' That our knowledge is essentially relative is one of the points upon which he insists most emphatically, and confirms as usual by a catena of authorities. It is, he says, the truth ' most harmoniously re-echoed by every philosopher of every school, except the modern Germans.' [1] The phrase relativity has more than ône meaning ; but according to Hamilton means at least this : ' our whole knowledge of mind and matter is relative—conditioned—relatively conditioned.' Of mind and matter ' in themselves ' we only know that they are ' incognisable.' ' All that we know is therefore phenomenal—phenomenal of the unknown.' This, then, is a cardinal doctrine. How is it compatible with the doctrine that the ego and non-ego are given in every act of consciousness? Mind and matter, as we have seen, are separated ' by the whole

[1] *Discussions*, p. 639. This is the passage welcomed by Mill. Hamilton, as Mr. Stirling notices, applies to the Cosmothetical Idealist Virgil's *Rerumque ignarus, imagine gaudet*, and elsewhere uses the same words to give the position of the true philosopher (*Discussions*, pp. 57, 640 ; *Lectures*, i. 138). The inability to get beyond the phenomenon is ridiculed in one case and accepted in the other.

diameter of being.' They express ' two series of phenomena, known less ' (? not) ' in themselves than ' (? but) ' in contradistinction from each other.' [1] What is given is not two facts, the ego and the non-ego, but the ' relation.' Somehow, the conscious act implies the presence of two factors, unknowable in themselves. The ' science of opposites ' may be ' the same,' but, if I know neither opposite, there can be very little science. Strangely, Hamilton seems to confuse the difference between knowing a relation and knowing the two things related. He tells us as a rough illustration, that if we consider the perception of a book to be made up of twelve parts, four may be given by the book, four by the sight, and four by ' all that intervenes.' [2] He infers, presently, that the ' great problem of philosophy ' is to ' distinguish what elements are contributed by the knowing subject, what elements by the object known.' [3] Between these statements we have a renewed and emphatic assertion of the ' relativity of knowledge.' Hamilton, that is, speaks as if from the fact that life supposes breathing we could infer how far life depends upon the lungs and how far upon the air. From a relation between two things, unknowable in themselves, we can surely learn nothing as to the things separately. Equality of two quantities is compatible with indefinite variation in the equal quantities.[4] The difficulty is increased when we ask how the line is actually drawn. The distinction between subjective and objective corresponds to the distinction between the primary and secondary qualities of which Berkeley had denied the validity. Both, he held,

[1] *Lectures*, i. 225.   [2] *Ibid.* i. 147; ii. 129.   [3] *Ibid.* i. 160.
[4] Mill puts this in the *Examination*, p. 35.

are on the same plane, and exist only 'in our minds.'
Hamilton holds that the so-called 'secondary qualities'
are only 'subjective affections.' They are not properly
qualities of Body at all, but sensations produced in the
mind by the action of bodies on the nervous system.[1]
The opinion that these secondary qualities belong to the
non-ego is the 'vulgar or undeveloped form of natural
realism.' Hence, when we say that we are conscious of
the 'rose' or the 'inkstand,' we ought to regard the
colour, fragrance, temperature, and so on, as affections of
the ego. To the non-ego belong the primary qualities
alone; and these are substantially nothing but extension
and solidity.[2] In other words, the rose belongs to the non-
ego as space-filling; to the ego, as coloured and fragrant.
Upon this, it is easy to remark with Mill, that as the
vulgar admittedly consider the whole rose to belong
to the non-ego, and the distinction to have been first
drawn by philosophers, we at once admit an illusion in
what, on Hamilton's principles, is apparently a 'deliverance of consciousness.' Why are we forbidden to make
the same hypothesis as to the primary qualities? 'Falsus
in uno,' as Hamilton somewhere says, 'falsus in omnibus.'
If my judgment of colour be illusory, why not my judgment of extension? The veracity of the Creator is
equally concerned in both cases.

But, in the next place, we now reach a more serious
difficulty. The non-ego, we see, corresponds simply to
the qualities fully assignable in terms of space. But

[1] Reid's *Works*, pp. 854, 857.
[2] *Lectures*, ii. 112. In the more elaborate discussion in Reid's *Works*,
Note D, he concludes (p. 857) that the primary 'may be roundly characterised
as mathematical, the secundo primary as mechanical, the secondary as
physiological.'

Hamilton has read Kant, and moreover been convinced
by him. Kant has proved beyond 'the possibility of
doubt,'[1] the truth that space is a 'fundamental condition'
of thought, and therefore belongs to the ego. This at
once throws us back into idealism. The whole rose has
become a thought, not a thing. So long as he roundly
asserts that mind perceives matter, that matter means
solid space, and that this truth is implied by the very
simplest act of intelligence, we may wonder at his audacity,
but we may admit his consistency. But to combine this
with the most positive assertions of the 'relativity' of
knowledge, that is, of our inability to know either mind
or matter, and then to accept as conclusive Kant's theory
that space is a mental form, is to land us in a hopelessly
inconsistent position. What Kant precisely meant, or
whether he had not various and inconsistent meanings, is
happily a question beyond my purpose. Hamilton's view
of Kant is clear. 'The distinctive peculiarity' of Kant's
doctrine, he says, is 'its special demonstration of the
absolute subjectivity of space, and in general of primary
attributes of matter.'[2] He argues that if Reid virtually
held the same view, he abandoned the principle of Natural
Realism.[3] If, then, Kant's theory was conclusively proved,
was not Hamilton bound to give up his essential principle?
He tells us that the primary qualities are 'unambiguously
objective (object—objects),' whereas the secondary are
'unambiguously subjective (subject—objects).'[4] Yet, he
admits that Kant proves the primary to be absolutely
subjective. 'I have frequently asserted,' he says again,
that in 'perception we are conscious of the external

[1] *Lectures*, ii. 113, 114.   [2] Reid's *Works*, p. 845.
[3] *Ibid.* p. 820.   [4] *Ibid.* p. 858.

object immediately and in itself.' This is the doctrine of
Natural Realism.' But he explains that by speaking of
a thing 'known in itself' he does not mean known 'out
of relation to us,' but known 'as the necessary correlative of an internal quality of which I am conscious.'[1]
That is, apparently, knowing a thing 'in itself' is knowing it 'not in itself,' but only in its effect; which again
is to abandon 'Natural Realism.'

Hamilton finds a way out of these apparent contradictions which satisfies himself. Both theories, he suggests,
may be true. We have clearly an *a priori* knowledge
of space 'considered as a form or fundamental law of
thought,' but also an empirical knowledge of what, in this
relation, may be called 'extension.'[2] He agrees, he says,
with Kant that an '*a priori* imagination' of space is a
'necessary condition of the possibility of thought'; but
differs from Kant by holding that we have an '*a posteriori*
percept' of space 'as contingently apprehended in this
or that actual complexus of associations.'[3] It is most
natural to interpret this as a virtual acceptance of Kant's
doctrine. It falls in with what he says elsewhere: 'the
notion of space is *a priori*, the notion of what space
contains, adventitious or *a posteriori*. Of this latter class
is that of Body or Matter.'[4] If I merely fill up space
by the sense of resistance, as he thinks, that is a subordinate operation, in no way affecting the subjective
character of space generally. If, on the other hand, I can
acquire an empirical notion of space independently, it
seems impossible to see why I should admit the *a priori*
notion. Hamilton starts from the assertion that we

[1] Reid's *Works*, p. 866 n.   [2] *Lectures*, ii. 114.
[3] Reid's *Works*, p. 882.   [4] *Ibid.* p. 846.

actually perceive facts, and comes to admit that we simply
organise sensations.[1]

Finally, Hamilton turns to yet another theory. His
essential point is the necessity of believing consciousness.
When we inquire what is the sphere within which consciousness is infallible, we have to accept something very
like the condemned 'crotchet' of the Cosmothetic Idealists.
The infallibility of consciousness has, after all, to be
limited. The summary assertion that the mind can leap
the gulf which separates it from matter insists upon
some explanation. Consciousness is infallible when it is
its own object. But it is plain, as Hamilton agrees, that
this primary, direct, or presentative knowledge is only,
as it were, the limiting case of knowledge. Accordingly
he condemns Reid for speaking of memory as an 'immediate knowledge of the past.'[2] The 'object' in this
case is not the past event, but some picture of the past
event; not (in his illustration) George IV. landing at
Leith, but a mental image of the landing, 'including a
conviction' that it somehow represents a past reality. It
is natural, then, to inquire whether my belief in an external world may not be a consciousness of a modification
of myself, including a conviction that it merely 'represents' an external world,[3] and is not in direct contact
with the 'non-ego.' Immediate knowledge of the past

[1] Mr. Hutchison Stirling, in a severe examination of Hamilton's *Philosophy
of Perception* (1865, p. 79 n.), thinks that Hamilton never understood that,
according to Kant, space was a 'perception,' not a 'conception'; and infers
that he knew little of Kant except from the 'literature of the subject.'
[2] *Lectures*, i. 218.
[3] Mill's argument about this in the *Examination* (ch. x.) is entangled in the
question about the opinions of Thomas Brown and 'Cosmothetic Idealists,'
which perhaps lays him open to a reply made by Veitch. I cannot go into
this, which illustrates one confusion in the controversy.

is 'a contradiction in terms.' And this, he adds, applies equally to an 'immediate knowledge of the distant.'[1] It is false to say with Reid that .en men all see the same sun. Each sees a different object, because each sees a different set of rays from which he infers the object.[2] We perceive only modifications of light, or, as he has said before, the 'rays of light in relation to and in contact with the retina.'[3] There is, as he adds, no greater marvel in our perception of the external world than in the admitted fact that mind is connected with body. Therefore, in his final statement,[4] it is laid down as an essential principle that consciousness is a 'knowledge solely of what is now and here present to the mind.' What is meant by the 'here'? 'It is the condition of intuitive perception,' he says, that a sensation is actually felt 'there where it is felt to be.' To suppose that a pain in the toe is felt really in 'the brain is conformable only to a theory of representationism.'[5] If the mind is not itself extended or in any way a subject of space-relations, does this not imply that the whole external world is somehow outside the sphere of immediate knowledge—a construction, not a mode of consciousness? To this Hamilton replies that the 'nervous organism . . . in contrast to all exterior to itself, appertains to the concrete human ego, and is in this respect *subjective, internal*; whereas in contrast to the abstract, immaterial ego, the pure mind, it belongs to the nonego, and in this respect is *objective, external.*'[6]   This

[1] *Lectures*, i. 218 and 221 *n*.   [2] *Ibid*. ii. 153.   [3] *Ibid*. ii. 130.
[4] Reid's *Works*, Note B, p. 810.   [5] Reid's *Works*, p. 821.
[6] Reid's *Works*, p. 858 *n*.; cf. p. 880 *n*. The 'organism' is 'at once objective and subjective,' 'at once ego and non-ego.' Unless we admit this we must be materialists or idealists.

view leads him into pure physiology. He asks whether the mind is conscious of sensations at the periphery of the nerves, or at a 'central extremity in an extended *sensorium commune.*' He declares, lest such language may appear suspicious, that the question of materialism is not raised by this assumption.[1] Anyhow, since the body is now in some sense part of the concrete human ego, our consciousness of the primary qualities is in this sense part of our consciousness of ourselves. They are given as existing in our own organism, or, in other words, as we occupy space, we have an 'immediate' knowledge of space.[2] I only note the peculiar interpretation now put upon the deliverance of consciousness. I fancy myself to perceive the sun; what I really 'perceive' is the action of rays of light on my retina. Yet it is obvious that I only learn of the existence of 'rays' or 'retina' long after the perception. Nobody's 'consciousness,' we may be sure, ever told him that he perceived not the sun but the action of rays of light on his eye. Hamilton has diverged from a consideration of the consciousness itself to a consideration of the physical conditions of consciousness. Having started with Reid, he next admits Kant to be conclusive, and ends by escaping to what is only expressible in terms of materialism. The deliverance of consciousness has come to be a statement that my fingers are different from my toes, and

[1] Reid's *Works*, p. 862.
[2] Mr. Stirling (pp. 80-110) thinks this 'exceedingly ingenious,' though really fallacious. Mansel accepts it in his *Metaphysics* (1860), p. 114; and in the *Philosophy of the Conditioned* (pp. 72, 75, 83) tries to reconcile it with other phrases. He talks of matter being 'in contact with mind,' and the object of perception being 'partly mental and partly material.' The composition is like the chemical fusion of an acid and an alkali.

that, as I am fingers and toes, I am aware of the fact. I will not ask whether it is possible by any interpretation to put a tenable construction upon Hamilton's language. Hamilton begins by discarding the philosopher's crotchet that the difference between mind and matter prevents them from affecting each other; and now he seems to admit its force so fully that he conceives of the nervous organism as a kind of amalgam of mind and matter.[1]

I have followed Hamilton so far in order to illustrate the way in which, by superposing instead of reconciling two different sets of dogma, he became hopelessly confused. The old Scottish doctrine really becomes bankrupt in his version. Hamilton is still struggling with Reid's old problem, and attacking the 'cosmothetic idealism' as Reid attacked the ideal system. How are we to cross the gulf between mind and matter, especially when we know nothing about either mind or matter taken apart from matter or mind? The problem is insoluble on these terms because it is really meaningless. The answer suggested by Kant was effective precisely—as I take it—because it drew the line differently, and therefore altered the whole question. Kant did not provide a new bridge, but pointed out that the chasm was not rightly conceived. To try to settle whether the 'primary qualities' belong to 'things external to the mind' is idle. It leads to the inevitable dilemma. If the 'primary qualities' belong to the things or the object, geometry becomes empirical and deducible only from particular

[1] Veitch tries to make a coherent doctrine from these utterances. All that Hamilton requires, he thinks, is that the object perceived has the 'quality of a non-ego.'—Veitch's *Hamilton*, p. 191. As the non-ego is a merely negative conception, this tends to coincide with the doctrines of Tracy and Brown.

experiments, like other physical sciences. Then we cannot account for its unique character and its at least apparent 'necessity.' If, on the other hand, the primary qualities belong to the mind, we can understand how the mind evolves or constructs, but it is at the cost of admitting them to be after all unreal, because 'subjective,' or deriving knowledge of fact from a simple analysis of thought. But the dilemma is really illusory. We cannot say that the truths of geometry refer either to things 'out of the mind' or to things 'in the mind.' They are 'subjective' in the sense that they are constructed by the mind in the very act of experiencing. They are not subjective in the sense of varying from one experience to another or from one mind to another. They belong to perception as perception, or to the perceiver as perceiving. It is, therefore, meaningless to ask whether they are 'objective' or 'subjective,' if that is to be answered by deciding, as Hamilton would decide, what part is due to the subject and what part to the object. That feat could only be performed if we could get outside of our minds, which we always carry about with us, or outside of the universe to which we are strictly confined. Then we might perhaps understand what each factor is, considered apart from the other. As it is, we can only say that the truths are universal as belonging to experience in general, and necessary as corresponding to identical modes of combining our experience. But we must abandon the fruitless attempt to separate object from subject, and then to construct a bridge to cross the gulf we have made.

III. MILL ON THE EXTERNAL WORLD

Upon this I have spoken sufficiently in considering Mill's *Logic*. Mill's failure to appreciate the change in the real issues made by the Kantian doctrine in this and other questions is a source of perplexity in his criticism of Hamilton.[1] His straightforward statement of his own view is a relief after Hamilton's complex and tortuous mode of forcibly combining inconsistent dogmas. He is able, moreover, to expose very thoroughly some of Hamilton's inconsistencies. But though he can hit particular errors very hard, he has not a sufficient clue to the labyrinth. Metaphysicians for him are still divided into two great schools—intuitionists and empiricists, or, as he here says, the 'introspective' and the 'psychological' school.[2] The Scottish and the Kantian doctrines are still lumped together, and therefore more or less misunderstood. Hence in treating of our belief in an external world he is still in the old position. Kant, according to him, supposes the mind not to perceive but itself to 'create' attributes, and then by a natural illusion to ascribe them to outward things.[3] The mind, on this version, does not simply organise but adds to, or overrides, experience. Consequently the external world would become subjective or unreal; and unless we admit a quasi-miraculous intuition, we are under a necessary

[1] Mill had by this time read Kant, and makes frequent references to him. He may perhaps be excused for not appreciating the Kantian view by Kant's own inconsistencies and obscurities. This is a very ticklish point, which I cannot discuss, but which, as I think, does not really affect the argument.

[2] *Examination*, etc., p. 176. Mill here uses 'introspective,' which might be applied to psychology, as equivalent rather to logical; or to the *a priori* method which attempts to discover fact by analysis of pure reasoning.

[3] *Examination*, etc., p. 456; cf. p. 194.

illusion. Mill substantially starts from Berkeley's position. The distinction between the primary and secondary qualities is, he holds, illusory. We know nothing of 'object' or 'subject,' 'mind' or 'matter' in themselves.[1] Our knowledge is therefore 'subjective.' Our whole provision of material is necessarily drawn from sensations. The problem occurs, how from mere sensations we make an (at least) apparently external world. Mill endeavours to show that this is possible, though he thinks that Berkeley's attempt was inadequate.[2] We can leap the gulf without the help of any special machinery invented for the purpose, such as Reid's 'intuitions' or Kant's forms of perception. He offers his own theory as an 'antagonist doctrine to that of Sir William Hamilton and the Scottish school,'[3] and it certainly has the advantage of simplicity.

Mill lays down at starting[4] the postulates from which he is to reason. Here, of course, we appeal to association. Association, he tells us, links together the thoughts of phenomena which are like each other, or which have been contiguous or successive; the link strengthens as the association is repeated, and after a time becomes 'inseparable.' Now belief in an external world means the belief that things exist when we do not think of them; that they would exist if we were annihilated; and further, that things exist which have never been perceived by us or by others. This belief is explicable by the known laws of association. For at any moment a

[1] *Examination*, etc., p. 266.

[2] Cf. Mill's interesting article upon Berkeley.—*Dissertations*, vol. iv. pp. 154-87.   [3] *Examination*, p. 248.

[4] *Ibid.* p. 225.

given sensation calls up 'a countless variety of possibilities of sensation.' They are regarded, that is, as sensations which I might experience if circumstances were altered. Again, these possibilities of sensation (which, he adds, are 'conditional certainties') are permanent, because they may be called up by any of the fleeting sensations. This permanence is one of the characteristics of the outside world; and we thus have always in the background, or as a 'kind of permanent substratum,' whole groups of 'permanent possibilities' suggested by the passing sensations. These become further consolidated when fixed orders of succession have suggested the ideas of cause and effect—themselves a product of association. Hence, we get our external world, and can define Matter to be a 'Permanent Possibility of sensation.' The phrase became famous.

This involves the metaphysical question which was reserved or evaded in the *Logic*. His whole purpose there is to show that thoughts should conform to things. But how things differ from thoughts was never made clear. 'Attributes,' we were then told, were the same as 'sensations.' The sensations somehow cohere in clusters. But what makes them cohere in different forms? When a sensation is not accompanied by the sensation previously associated, why is not the association simply weakened or destroyed instead of suggesting a 'conditional certainty'? I learn that fire is hot because the sensations of brightness and heat have occurred together; but when I see the brightness without feeling the heat, why does not the association simply become fainter? Why should I interpret the experience to mean, 'If I were nearer I should feel the heat'?

Does not the interpretation imply that I have already some system of combining my impressions and a need of making the two experiences consistent instead of contradictory? Upon the single assumption of sensations occurring together or successively, and related in time alone, there seems to be no need for any external world whatever. The hypothesis would be exemplified in the case of an animal which, though capable of sensations, had no capacity for arranging them so as to represent space at all. And, again, the statement suggests no distinct reference to any criterion of truth or falsehood. It accounts for illusions as well as for true beliefs. What is the difference? The fact that certain sensations adhere in clusters is not the same thing as the belief in their regular recurrence; and considering the vast variety and intricacy of our sensations, the question which I have mentioned in connection with James Mill arises again: Why should any two people have the same clusters or (on this showing) the same belief—or how one association can be said to be (not real but) true, and another (not unreal but) false?

This difficulty shows itself when Mill proceeds to investigate the 'primary qualities.' They are to be simply 'attributes' co-ordinate with other attributes. With the help of Professor Bain and Mr. Herbert Spencer, in whose then recent writings he saw a most encouraging development of his father's principles, Mill makes out a case to show how the perception of space may be developed. The problem discussed by those authorities and their successors is clearly a legitimate part of psychology; their investigations, though still on the threshold of a vast and difficult inquiry, are at least valuable beginnings ; and when the experts have all agreed, we shall be ready to accept their conclusions. There is, however, a difficulty which exposes Mill to another criticism.[1] Briefly, it is that his so-called explanation of space-conception really presupposes space. Hamilton had pointed this out in his Kantian moods.[2] The difficulty is obvious. In a scientific theory a statement in terms of space is an ultimate statement. We do not try, nor does it appear to be possible, to get behind it. When I have said that a body moves in an ellipse, I do not go on to express the ellipse in terms of ' muscular sensation.' That would be to substitute for a definite measure one essentially fluctuating and uncertain. I can define a given muscular sensation as that which corresponds to a certain distance ; but to reverse the definition—to express the distance in terms of the pure sensation, excluding all reference to distance, is surely impossible. Now, it may seem that Mill is here attempting just this impossible feat. Therefore he is really still on the same side of the gulf, though he supposes himself to have crossed it. His ' pigtail '—according to the famous apologue—still ' hangs behind him.' In other words, he is mistaking a psychological for a metaphysical explanation ; an account of how it is that we come to perceive space, assuming space to exist, with an explanation of what space is ; and a resolution of the perception into a set of sensations associated in time. Here, again, he is under the great disadvantage of supposing the space-perception to have been made within the limits of a lifetime. If it were possible to look into the mind

[1] Made especially familiar in recent English speculations by T. H. Green's criticism of Hume.   [2] e.g. Reid's *Works*, p. 869.

of an infant we could, he thinks, see how the idea was formed.[1] A modern psychologist can at least help himself by looking indefinitely further back and tracing the whole history of the organism to the earlier forms of life ; and the space-perception ceases to imply a preternatural or *a priori* capacity. Something more is surely wanted, though I do not venture to say precisely what. Mill's doctrine that my belief in a external world is a belief in ' a permanent possibility of sensation ' may be accepted in some sense. When, for example, I believe in the existence of Calcutta, I mean that I believe that if I were transported to the banks of the Hoogly, I should have the sensations from which Calcutta is inferrible.[2] In other words, in making a statement about the external world, I construct a hypothetical and universal consciousness. When I exchange the geocentric for the heliocentric view, I am imagining what I should see if I were upon the sun instead of the earth. Instead of regarding my own series of sensations as the base from which to measure, I regard them as deducible from the series which would be presented to a different and, of course, incomparably more extended consciousness. I can thus fill up the gaps in my own experience and get a regular series instead of one full of breaches and interruptions. That I do this somehow or other is Mill's view, and I should admit with him that I do no more. But, then, the question remains whether Mill can account for my doing even this. It supposes, at least, a power of forming what Clifford called 'ejects,' as distinguished from ' objects.' I must be able to think not of things outside consciousness but of my own consciousness under

[1] *Examination*, pp. 146-47.   [2] *Ibid.* p. 235.

other conditions, and of other centres of consciousness than mine. But this ability is not explicable from sensations, as ultimate atoms, combined in various ways by ' association ' ; for that process, it would seem, might take place without in any way suggesting an external world or a different consciousness. Here Mill, like his father, is trying to explain thoughts by dealing with sensations as things and refusing to admit any action of the mind in order to keep to the unsophisticated facts. He will not allow the mind to have even an organising power, even though it be a power which cannot be separately revealed or give rise to independent truths, but appears simply as implied in its products. The mind *is* the cluster of atomic sensations. It must not tamper with the facts in any way, on penalty of causing illusion. I can only associate simple atoms, and the world remains a chaos of independent and incoherent fragments. They stick together somehow, but the division into the external and the internal world still remains an unsolved problem. The ' attribute ' will not distinguish itself from the ' sensation.' We are still unable, that is, to explain the metaphysical puzzle left unsolved in the *Logic*.

Another question arises : If the world is still an incoherent heap of ' attributes ' or ' sensations,' what are we to say of the mind? With his usual candour Mill applies his principles to the problem. We get, as he admits, to a real difficulty. The mind, in the phrase adopted from his father, is a ' thread of consciousness.' It is a series of feelings with the curious peculiarity that besides ' present sensations ' it has ' memories and expectations.' What are these? he asks. They involve beliefs in something ' beyond themselves.' If we call the mind

' a series of feelings,' we have to add that it is a series which is ' aware of itself as past and future.' Is it, then, something different from the feelings, or must we accept the paradox that something ' which in hypothesis is a series of feelings can be aware of itself as a series?' Here is the final ' inexplicability ' which must arrive, as he admits with Hamilton, when we get to an ultimate fact. The ' wisest thing we can do is to accept the inexplicable fact without any theory of how it takes place.'[1] That what we call personal identity is ' inexplicable ' will hardly be denied. Yet Mill's position seems to make the paradox something nearly approaching to a contradiction. If the mental processes are to be described as feelings, separable but simply forming clusters more or less complicated and linked to each other, we seem to get rid not only of a something which organises experience, but of organisation itself. It becomes difficult to understand not merely what the mind or soul can be, but what are the mental processes to which the conception corresponds. This, however, leads to a different set of questions and one of far greater interest.

IV. THEORIES OF THE ABSOLUTE

Discussions such as I have touched often seem to be little more than a display of dialectical skill. Hamilton and Mill probably believed equally and in the same sense in the reality of Edinburgh or London. When a belief is admitted, the question why we believe is of interest chiefly in so far as the answer may give canons applicable to really disputable questions. Now the application of

[1] *Examination*, p. 248.

Hamilton's theories to theology certainly involved issues in regard to which men generally suppose themselves to be profoundly interested. We clearly believe in an 'external world,' whatever precisely we mean by it. But do we believe in God? or, if we believe, what precisely is meant by believing in God? That is a problem upon which turn all the most important controversies which have divided men in all ages—and the controversy which now raged over Hamilton's theory between Mill and Mansel corresponded to vital issues. Hamilton's essential position was given in the famous Cousin article in 1830. He frequently repeats, but he never much modifies or develops the argument. In the course of lectures repeated for twenty years, he divides his subject into three departments: 'empirical psychology' and 'rational psychology'; or the facts and laws of consciousness; and thirdly, 'ontology,' which was to deal with the ideas of God, the soul, and so forth.[1] This third department was never written; and though we may guess at its general nature, his doctrine is chiefly indicated by his criticism of Cousin.

One result is unfortunate. I doubt whether so many sayings capable of different interpretations were ever brought together in the same space. The art of writing about 'ontology' is, it would seem, to disguise a self-evident truism by pompous phrases till the words are vague enough to allow the introduction of paradoxical meaning. Schelling and Cousin between them had provided a sounding terminology; and Hamilton, though his main purpose is to show that these fine phrases were only phrases, takes them up, tosses them about as if they had a

[1] Lectures (Preface).

real meaning, and leaves us in some doubt how far he is merely using the words to show their emptiness, or suggesting that, when the bubbles are burst, there is still some residuum of solid matter. 'The unconditioned,' he says (giving his own view), 'is incognisable and inconceivable.'[1] What, then, is 'the unconditioned'? 'The Unconditioned is the genus of which the Infinite and the Absolute are species.'[2] These technical phrases are the balls with which the metaphysical juggler plays his tricks till we are reduced to hopeless confusion. Mill gives the straightforward and, I think, conclusive criticism.[3] What is the sense of talking about 'The Absolute' or 'The Infinite' as hypostatised abstractions? Apply the epithets to concrete things or persons and we may understand what is really meant. A predicate going about at large cannot be really grasped; and the discussion would only be relevant if we were speaking of something which is absolute and nothing but absolute. The words themselves have meanings which become different when they are parts of different assertions. 'Inconceivable' is a word which varies from self-contradictory to mere difficulty of imagining. 'Absolute,' according to Hamilton, has two chief meanings, one of which is not opposed to the Infinite and the other contradictory of the Infinite. Mansel takes Mill to task for not seeing that Hamilton uses the word in two 'distinct and even contradictory senses,' and for not perceiving which meaning is implied in which cases.[4] It may be very wrong of Mill, but Hamilton's practice is certainly confusing. There is Cousin's 'Absolute' and Hamilton's 'Absolute' and

[1] Discussions, p. 12. [2] Ibid. p. 13.
[3] Examination, pp. 58, 73. [4] Philosophy of the Conditioned, p. 95.

Mansel's own 'Absolute';[1] and the difference is to be inferred from the nature of the argument. There is a false Infinite and a true Infinite; and this suggests another difficulty. The obvious 'contradictory' of infinite is finite; but words cannot be really contradictory at all till they form part of a proposition. It is contradictory to call a thing finite and infinite in the same sense; but, if we admit of infinite divisibility, a thing must be at once infinite in comparison with an infinitesimal, finite in relation to other things, and infinitesimal in relation to those which in relation to it are infinite. Some words, again, refer to our knowledge of things, and are meaningless when predicated of objects. A fact may be 'certain' to me and only 'probable' to you, simply because the probability to each depends upon the evidence which he possesses. When this is supposed to correspond to some difference in the facts themselves, endless fallacies are produced. 'The certain' is contradictory of the 'uncertain'; but a given fact may be both 'certain' and 'uncertain.' A discussion naturally becomes perplexed, which is really treating a question of logic in terms appropriate to a question of fact.

I will not attempt to follow a controversy so perplexed in itself and in which the antagonists seem to be normally at cross purposes. I must try to bring out the main issue which is obscured by the singular confusions of the contest; and to this there seems to be a simple clue. Hamilton's theory is admittedly a 'modification of that of Kant,'[2] and intended to eliminate the inconsistency by which Kant had left an opening for the systems

[1] Philosophy of the Conditioned, pp. 108, 147.
[2] Ibid. p. 67.

of Schelling and Hegel. Now Kant's famous argument, given in the Critique of Pure Reason, is a most crabbed piece of writing. It makes an English reader long for David Hume. Still, beneath its elaborate panoply of logical technicalities, it contains a very clear and cogent argument, which gives the real difficulty and which is strangely distorted by Hamilton.

According to Kant there are three Ideas of the pure Reason—the Soul, the World, and God. Nobody really doubts the existence of the world; but doubts as to the existence of the soul or of God are possible and have been met by professedly demonstrative arguments. The 'dogmatists' whom Kant criticised had, as they thought, proved the existence of a monad, an 'indiscerptible' unit called the soul; and of a Supreme Being, or 'Ens Realissimum,' who is taken to be in some sense absolute and simple. Kant holds these arguments to be essentially a misapplication of logical method. It is the function of the reason to unify our knowledge. The ideal would be reached if all knowledge could be regarded as a system of deductions from a single principle. This, in reasoning about the soul, produces a 'paralogism.' All our thoughts and faculties are bound together into a unity which is consistent with multiplicity. We interpret this unjustifiably as implying the existence of an absolutely simple unit. We hypostatise the unity and regard it as a thing when, in truth, it represents a complex system of reciprocal relations. The arguments upon the supposed proofs of the existence of a supreme Being, though they are expanded and considered in many different forms, reach a similar conclusion. We are perfectly right in unifying as much as possible our whole knowledge of the world, but though we may continue the process in-definitely, we can never logically arrive at the knowledge of a single Being existing independently as the founda-tion of all other being. In this sense, Kant calls the idea 'regulative.' It corresponds to the legitimate pro-cess of thought; we must unify, but no reasoning can reveal an entity lying beyond all experience. We are thus led to 'irresistible illusions,' from which, however, we can escape, though only 'by the severest and most subtle criticism.' Kant compares this to the illusion produced by a mirror, which makes objects really in front appear to be behind it, or to the apparent increase of the moon's size when near the horizon. Still, it is impossible, as he emphatically says, that reason should be itself undeserving of confidence. It is only from its misuse in an inappropriate sphere, or, in other words, from its attempt to transcend experi-ence, that the fallacy arises.[1]

It is needless to ask how this argument can be recon-ciled with the theism which Kant accepts. Hamilton's criticism of Cousin is essentially a statement of the con-verse argument. Schelling and Cousin had taken up

[1] Hamilton strangely declares that Kant makes the speculative reason an 'organ of mere delusion' (*Discussions*, p. 18, *Lectures*, i. 402), and Mansel says that if we accept Kant's doctrine we must believe 'in a special faculty of lies, created for the express purpose of deceiving those who believe in it.' For Kant's statement that the reason cannot be itself untrustworthy, see Appendix to *Transcendental Dialectic* (section on 'the ultimate end of the natural dialectic of human reason,' and for the comparisons above quoted the same Appendix (section on 'the regulative employment of the ideas of pure reason') and the Introduction to the *Transcendental Dialectic*. Bolton (*Inquisitio Philosophica*, ch. iv.) quotes many passages from Kant to illustrate this point, which seems to confirm Stirling's opinion of the superficiality of Hamilton's knowledge of his author.

Kant's challenge, not by inferring the simple being from the complex of experiences, but by professing to show how multiplicity might be evolved out of absolute simplicity. This feat, as Hamilton held, and as Mill of course held with him, could only be accomplished by a palpable juggle. Clearly you cannot count, if you are restricted to the use of an absolute 'one.' The germ from which an organic system is developed cannot be itself absolutely simple. Knowledge can only be made out of rules; and a simple 'is' gives no rule. Hamilton tries to express the principle implied in such instances in the proper pomp of metaphysical language. Cousin starts by admitting that knowledge supposes 'plurality,' that is, an object and a subject. Now, says Hamilton,[1] the 'absolute' must be identified with the subject or with the object, or with the 'indifference of both' (whatever that may be). On the first or second hypothesis, the absolute is not, as it ought to be, a unit, for it is one of a pair; on the other hypothesis, you suppose that con-sciousness does not imply plurality. A man, let us say in humbler language, if he thinks, must think about something. If so, we start from a man and a something. But suppose him to think about himself. Then there must be something to say about himself; and he will have nothing to say if he is absolutely simple. That seems to be true enough. Every proposition asserts a relation of some kind, and a proposition cannot be got at all if no relation be given. This, therefore, is one meaning of the 'relativity' of thought. 'To think is the condition'; that is, you cannot affirm or deny unless you deny or affirm something. If you try then to get

[1] *Discussions*, p. 33.

to the absolute by stripping off all relations, you really get to zero. We think only by the attribution of certain qualities, and the negation of these qualities and of this attribution is so far a negation of thinking at all. Kant's arguments duly carried out prove 'the unconditioned,' says Hamilton, to be a mere 'fasciculus of nega-tions.'[1] Clearly, we reply, if the unconditioned is reached by unsaying all that we have said. A plain person is, indeed, chiefly astonished that such arguments should be required. Schelling's system, says Hamilton himself, is only fit for 'Laputa on the Empire,'[2] but Schelling at least invented a supernatural faculty to perceive an 'incogitable' hypothesis. Cousin's hypothesis, which tried to omit this faculty, is worse, for it is self-con-tradictory.[3] The spectacle of three of the most dis-tinguished men in Germany, France, and England joining in this game, and even of Hamilton winning a 'European reputation' by declaring that we cannot believe two contradictory propositions at once, or make something out of nothing, is not edifying to a believer in philosophy.

V. ANTINOMIES

Mill does not want all this apparatus to get rid of the transcendental world. It is for him too obviously superfluous to require to be exploded. How then does he come into conflict with Hamilton? We must turn for explanation to another of Kant's arguments. The universe must be regarded as in some sense one, though that does not prove the existence of a simple and absolute Being as its ground or principle. On the other

[1] *Discussions*, p. 17.   [2] *Ibid.* p. 20.   [3] *Ibid.* p. 32.

hand, the universe is an indefinitely complex multitude of reciprocally dependent things. We can bring the 'laws' into unity and harmony; but the things through which the laws are manifested are themselves infinitely numerous. We may then ask whether the universe is not only one but a whole; whether its unity entitles us to call it a single object. This leads to the famous 'antinomies.' They have been familiar enough in many forms since speculation began. The universe is given in space and time. Now, we cannot think of space and time either as finite or infinite. We cannot think of space as finite because, however far we go, there is still space beyond. We cannot think of space as infinite, because to imagine infinite space would require an in-finite mind and infinite time. Space must be either infinite or finite, because one of two contradictories must be true, and yet each is 'inconceivable.' I must confess with due humility that I could never see any antinomy at all. In this I agree with Mill,[1] though I cannot agree with his attempt to explain our beliefs in the infinity of space by an 'inseparable association.' The apparent antinomy is due, I fancy, to a shift in the meaning of 'infinite.' The mathematician calls space 'infinite' because space is limited by space, and there cannot be a 'whole' of space. If by 'infinite' I mean the comple-tion of a process which *ex hypothesi* cannot be completed, I become self-contradictory. There is no meaning in 'a whole' of space, though every particular space is a whole. Acuter reasoners, however, can see the difficulty, and we will therefore admit the 'antinomy.' Then we must observe that, according to Kant, the antinomies apply

[1] *Examination*, p. 103.

solely to the cosmological idea. There is nothing, he says,[1] antinomial in the psychological and theological ideas; for they 'contain no contradiction.' He infers that their reality can be no more denied than affirmed. If from the organism I infer a soul I fall into a 'paralogism,' but not into an 'antinomy.' We do not prove that soul and no-soul are necessary alternatives and both 'inconceivable,' but simply that the soul, as a monad, is a superfluity which explains nothing—a thought interpreted as a thing. The antinomy occurs only when we deal with the perceived universe, and ask whether it has or has not limits. It has no application to the argument about God or the soul. Since they are not in space they have no concern with the antinomies involved in the conception of space.

Hamilton's misappropriation of this argument is the master fallacy of his system. In the Cousin essay he lays down a dogma without the slightest attempt to prove it. 'The conditioned is the mean between two extremes—two inconditionates—exclusive of each other, *neither of which can be conceived as possible*, but of which, on the principles of contradiction and the excluded middle, *one must be admitted as necessary*.'[2] He adds that our faculties are thus shown to be weak, but not deceitful. We learn, moreover, the 'salutary lesson' that the capacity of 'thought is not to be constituted into the measure of existence,' and we are warned from 'recognising the domain of our knowledge as necessarily coextensive with the horizon of our faith.' In a note we are invited to accept as true the declaration ' of a pious

[1] 'An ultimate end of the natural dialectic,' etc.
[2] *Discussions*, p. 14.

philosophy—a God understood would be no God at all'; and we are told that 'the last and highest consecration of all true religion must be an altar to the unknown God,'—which does not appear to have been St. Paul's opinion. This doctrine was repeated again and again in various lectures and notes. It was applied by Mansel to defend Christianity, and was in a sense accepted by Mr. Herbert Spencer as a support of Agnosticism.[1] Yet it is sprung upon us in this abrupt fashion, not only without proof, but without any clear statement of its meaning; and, as I think, is really the expression of a confusion of two lines of argument. An exposition of this great axiom, he says,[2] would show that 'some of the most illustrious principles' are only its 'subordinate modifications applied to certain primary notions.' Among such notions are those of 'cause and effect' and 'substance and phenomenon.' The discussion of Cause and Effect[3] illustrates sufficiently the curious shifting of the argument. Our inability to conceive a beginning either of time or of the existence of things in time gives the apparent necessity of causation. But as we cannot suppose an infinite regress, the necessity corresponds only to an 'impotence' of our minds. Hence, he argues, in the case of the human will, we must admit the possibility, though not the conceivability, of an absolute beginning, and therefore of freewill. The argument, if sound, is applicable to cause in general as

[1] I may say that although I am an 'Agnostic' I cannot accept Mr. Spencer's version of Hamilton's doctrine. But I must not attempt here to estimate the value of Mr. Spencer's theory.
[2] Reid's *Works*, p. 743 *n*.
[3] *Lectures*, ii. 376-413; *Discussions*, pp. 604-28.

well as to the will. Hamilton may mean that since an absolute beginning is possible at some time, it is possible at any time. We might then have an antinomy. One of the propositions, 'things are caused' and 'things are not caused,' must be true, and both are inconceivable. But this would be to destroy the axiom of causation. The appearance of an antinomy is obtained by changing the question. Instead of asking why we take things to be caused, we ask whether we can imagine an infinite series of causes. The antinomy in this case is simply the old formula over again. This central position of Hamilton's philosophy is thus an illegitimate application of Kant's argument. Kant admits an antinomy only where it is at least plausible, namely, as applied to the universe which we clearly have to extend indefinitely if not to absolute infinity. But no such difficulty is involved in the problem of unity. Hamilton seems to have been so delighted with the 'antinomy' that he 'enounces' it as a general law; applies it where it has no meaning whatever, and invariably 'illustrates' it by repeating the case in which it is plausible.

Hamilton thus contrives to blend two arguments into one. His view is the germ of inextricable confusions, and, one might have thought, too obvious a bit of logical legerdemain to impose even upon a metaphysician. It plays, however, a most important part in the attempt made by Mansel to bring Hamilton to bear against the unbeliever. Mansel's whole aim is to put his antagonists in a dilemma. They must not be allowed to say simply that an argument becomes meaningless; they must be taken to say that it leads to a balance between two alternatives. We therefore get a double result. On

the one hand, we are reduced to complete scepticism— that is, reason is made impotent in regard to a question which necessarily arises. On the other hand, we are left with an impression that we are compelled to take some position in this region of inconceivables, and this is translated into the pious assertion that 'belief' extends beyond 'knowledge.' Thus Hamilton emphatically declares that it is the 'main scope' of his speculation to show articulately that we 'must believe as actual much that we are unable (positively) to conceive as actual.'[1]

To follow him through the maze of 'inconceivables,' 'absolutes,' 'infinites,' 'unconditioneds' and so forth would be idle.[2] I shall be content with one argument which in Mansel's hands led to an important conflict with Mill. The Infinite, says Mansel, 'if it is to be conceived at all, must be conceived as potentially' everything and actually nothing; for if there is anything in general which it cannot become, it is

[1] Letters to Calderwood in *Lectures*, ii. 530-35.
[2] One specimen of Hamilton's method may be given for those who care for such things. In the essay on Cousin he opposes ' the Infinite' as the 'unconditionally unlimited' to the 'Absolute' as the 'unconditionally limited.' In both cases we have simple negations of thought, and therefore reach the inconceivable. If I say a thing and then unsay it, I get simple zero. That is obvious. If, again, the absolute asserts the same limit which is denied by the 'infinite,' they are of course contradictory. And, in this case, we get the old antinomy, which he accordingly introduces in the next sentence about the impossibility of conceiving space either as infinite or finite. But here the contradictory of infinite ought to be—not 'absolute' but 'finite.' Having thus got an 'antinomy' by making 'the absolute' equivalent to 'the finite,' Hamilton apparently assumes an antinomy between absolute and its contradictory everywhere. But I am not compelled to think of a thing either as being some quality and so far 'conditioned,' or as being no quality at all. The alternative is either to think of it or not think of it and that leads to no antinomy. So again (pp. 29, 30) infinite time is identified with endless time, and absolute with ended time.

thereby limited; and if there is anything in particular which it actually is, it is thereby excluded from being any other thing.[1] It must also be conceived as 'actually everything and potentially nothing; for an unrealised potentiality is likewise a limitation.' Hamilton had put the same argument. 'The infinite is conceived only by thinking away every character by which the finite was conceived.'[2] That is, the 'infinite' is equivalent to the 'indeterminate,' or the result of unsaying all that you have said. This logically leads to pure nothing, not to an antinomy. We are told that we must believe something where we get not to a contradiction but to an absolute vacuum. Mill makes an obvious criticism.[3] When I talk of infinite space, I do not 'think away' the character of space, but I only think of an indefinite extension of space. To believe in infinite space would otherwise be to disbelieve in geometry. We cannot think at all about an utterly indeterminate object, but we can think of space without asking how much space there is in the universe. 'The Infinite' may be meaningless, but to predicate infinity of space does not destroy the space conception. If, then, the infinity of space does not hinder us from obtaining a perfectly accurate knowledge of its properties, does the infinite or absolute nature of the Deity prevent us from understanding his attributes? Here is the real problem; and it leads to the odd spectacle of the sceptic arguing on behalf of theology against the divine. There is no contradiction, as Mill argues, in speaking of an infinitely knowing or powerful or good being. A being has infinite knowledge if

nothing is unknown to him; and is infinitely powerful if nothing is impossible to him. That gives a plain meaning on the human side, though we are of course unable adequately to imagine the result on the divine side. Infinite goodness is, indeed, a less natural phrase than 'absolute,' because absolute does not suggest a numerical measure of 'goodness.' Goodness is a quality, not a quantity. But, understood as meaning the absence of even an infinitesimal degree of badness, it may be called infinite, and the 'limit' which is denied is not that implied by 'good,' but by the degree of goodness. Infinite, if it means anything, must mean an infinite amount or degree of something definite.

Mill thus appears to argue that theology is not as irrational as its defender supposes. The introduction of such predicates as infinite and absolute do not make knowledge of their subject impossible. It would have cleared the matter if Mill had gone on to explain his own view of the 'Absolute.' We may guess what he ought to have said in conformity with his principles. If all knowing is essentially a knowledge of relations, it is idle to seek for an 'absolute' in the sense of a thing which (on Mansel's definition) 'exists in and by itself, having no necessary relations to any other being.'[1] Since, in saying anything about it, we assert a relation, we cannot even speak of such an 'absolute' without contradiction. 'Absolute,' like certain, necessary, and so forth, is a name referring to our knowledge. An assertion about facts may be 'absolutely' true, however trifling the fact. It may be as absolutely true that a sparrow fell to the ground at 9 A.M. on the 1st of January last as that

---

[1] *Bampton Lectures* (3rd edition, 1859), p. 71.
[2] *Lectures*, iii. 103.
[3] *Examination*, p. 105.

[1] *Bampton Lectures*, p. 45.

the sun exists or that two and two make four. Knowledge implies not an 'absolute fact' but an 'absolute truth'—a truth which requires no qualification not explicitly given in the proposition asserted. To say that a thing exists absolutely is to add nothing but emphasis to the statement that it exists. Nor does the statement that it exists 'conditionally' alter the case. It is conditional in so far as it has a cause, or as from its existence we may infer some previous state of things. If, however, it exists, the conditions have *ex hypothesi* been fulfilled. It exists now 'absolutely,' however it came to exist. It is a part of the whole system of interdependent and continuous processes which make up the universe.[1] If we know that anything, then, is part of the actual world, we have all 'the absolute' required; and this is an 'absolute' which is perfectly compatible with any complexity of relations. The clue is given by getting hold of any bit whatever of the actual web, not by getting into some transcendental world beyond. The error of supposing that we must find an 'Absolute' somewhere, and that we cannot find it in any part of our experience, is the same as would be the error of supposing that because we cannot fix a point in absolute space, we cannot get any valid space measures. The centre of the sun or Greenwich observatory will do equally well, though we cannot even speak intelligibly of their absolute position in the universe. To give a scientific account of astronomy we do not require an absolute centre of space.

This is what I take to be implied in Kant's argument about the idea of God. We cannot get to an 'absolute' Being outside of the universe, but the whole must be regarded as a single and self-supporting system. This argument is distorted in the elaborate argumentations of Hamilton and Mansel against the attempts to get to an absolute Being outside of things in general. Such an absolute as they attack is doubtless an absurdity; but neither are we, as they urge, compelled to believe in it. If we still use theological language, we must say that God is not a Being apart from the universe, but implied in the universe; the ground of all things, the immanent principle whose 'living raiment is the world.' Mill of course holds that we must abandon 'transcendentalism' or the search for 'things in themselves' outside of the phenomenal world. Mansel often seems to agree. Philosophers who indulge in these freaks try, he says, to lift up the curtain of their own being to view the picture which it conceals. 'Like the painter of old, they knew not that the curtain *is* the picture.'[1] That sounds like good positivism or phenomenalism. It should give the deathblow to all 'ontology.' He assures us over and over again that the 'Infinite' is a 'mere negation of thought';[2] that contradictions arise whenever we attempt to transcend the limits of experience; that human reason is so far from being able to construct a 'Scientific Theology, independent of and superior to Revelation, that it cannot even read the alphabet out of which that Theology must be framed.'[3] We can know the laws of nature or the phenomena, but we can know nothing of the substance or noumenon which lies behind

---

[1] Cf. Tennyson's 'Flower in the Crannied Wall'—
'. . . If I could understand
What you are, root and all, and all in all,
I should know what God and man is.'

[1] *Bampton Lectures*, p. 89.   [2] *Ibid.* p. 72.   [3] *Ibid.* p. 61.

them. Then, is the natural query, why not leave it out of account altogether? Why venture into this region, where, as Mansel admits, we find only 'antinomies' or 'contradictory inconceivables'? Why not, in short, be agnostics like Mr. Herbert Spencer, who based his *First Principles* on the Hamilton - Mansel doctrine? This gives the secret of the whole procedure.

'The cardinal point,' says Mansel, 'of Sir W. Hamilton's philosophy . . . is the absolute necessity, under any system of philosophy whatever, of acknowledging the existence of a sphere of belief, beyond the limits of the sphere of thought.'[1] Faith, then, remains when reason disappears, though faith cannot solve the doubts suggested by reason.[2] What 'faith' tells us, in fact, is that we must believe one of two propositions, though we cannot conceive the possibility of either. Can it possibly, we ask, much matter whether we believe that there is or is not an X of whom nothing more can be intelligibly said? A belief which extends beyond 'the sphere of thought' is a belief which we can afford to leave to itself. But Mansel has to declare that we are forced to believe where we cannot even properly think. 'We are compelled by the constitution of our minds to believe in the existence of an absolute and infinite Being,'[3] though, as we learn, to 'think of the infinite' is really a negation of thought. A decision to accept one of the contradictory beliefs is yet of the highest practical importance. The schemes of Freewill and Fatalism, says Hamilton,[4] are 'theoretically balanced,' though the fatalist inconceivability is the 'less obtrusive'; but

[1] *Philosophy of the Conditioned*, p. 51.   [2] *Bampton Lectures*, p. 8.
[3] *Ibid.* pp. 67, 68.   [4] Reid's *Works*, p. 974.

'practically' we must accept freewill on penalty of admitting the moral law to be 'a mendacious imperative.' That is, right and wrong become meaningless unless you accept one of two equally inconceivable doctrines. So Mansel declares freewill to be 'certain in fact' though 'inexplicable in theory.'[1] Why 'certain,' if, as he also declares, it is part of the 'fundamental mystery' of the coexistence of the Finite and the Infinite?[2] According to Mansel, again, the denial that an infinite Being exists, is simply the acceptance of one of two 'equally inconceivable alternatives.'[3] It is, he declares, 'our duty' to think of God as 'personal' and to believe that he is 'infinite.'[4] It is a duty, then, to accept as a certainty what reason declares to be only one of two equally probable alternatives.

The general attitude is familiar enough. Pascal has put it in his famous 'wager.' Believe a thing because it is impossible. You must back one side; and reason is too imbecile to settle which. Then give up reasoning. The argument is persuasive if not logically convincing. Hamilton was too much of a philosopher and a rationalist to accept it in that form. His application remained ambiguous. Probably he would have approved a rather vague theism, which might be interpreted in terms of many religious creeds. Mansel, unluckily, had to get from his philosophy to the position of strict Anglican orthodoxy; from the contradictory inconceivables to the Thirty-nine Articles. His method of performing this

[1] *Bampton Lectures*, p. 228. Yet he positively asserts (*e.g.* p. 220) that freewill is a 'fact of consciousness.'   [2] *Ibid.* p. 217.
[3] *Ibid.* p. 121. Though, as he adds, of that alternative which renders that very inconceivability 'itself inexplicable.'
[4] *Ibid.* p. 89.

feat has little interest now; but I must notice it enough to show the relation to Mill.

VI. REVEALED RELIGION

How is this Infinite and Absolute Being to be brought into any relation whatever with facts? How, by accepting one of two equally inconceivable alternatives, can we throw any light upon the truth of a historical statement? Mansel protests that he is not arguing as to the truth of any particular revelation. Though he is not bound to prove the truth of the Christian revelation, he is clearly bound to show that a revelation is probable, and to suggest the criterions by which its reality must be tested. A religion, as Kant had said, could not be true which conflicted with morality.[1] If morality binds me to be merciful, and a god orders me to be cruel, he cannot be the true God. The deist Tindal had argued long ago that Joshua could not be justified by a divine command in exterminating the Canaanites.[2] In answering this difficulty, Mansel hit upon the unlucky phrase 'Moral Miracles.'[3] A 'moral miracle,' a conversion of a bad act into a good one, was, he admitted, not the kind of experiment to be used too often. Every scoundrel can work 'miracles' of that kind. He can break the divine law though he cannot break the 'law of nature.' How are we to know that in a given case the divine law has been suspended by the supreme ruler and not really broken by the wicked subject? By what logical feat can we show the identity of Jehovah with the Absolute and Infinite? The deity of Joshua was frankly anthropomorphic; the

[1] *Bampton Lectures*, p. 202.   [2] *Ibid.* p. 12.   [3] *Ibid.* p. 244.

(generally) invisible deity of a tribe. We can judge of his character as we can judge of the character of Joshua himself, or of the character of Baal, or Moloch, or Zeus. If we argue that all the deities represent an imperfect feeling after a supreme Being, our judgment would not be affected. The deity would still be imperfect. The commands obeyed were still cruel and immoral, as conceived at the time. To argue that they were good because somehow or other Jehovah was the Inconceivable seems to be too obvious a fallacy even for a Bampton Lecturer. Mansel denounces the 'morbid horror of what they (philosophers) are pleased to call Anthropomorphism.' 'Fools, to dream that man can escape from himself, that human reason can draw aught but a human portrait of God.'[1] They really argue that the portrait has at any rate very ugly features, and doubt whether it is possible to draw any portrait whatever of the Inconceivable.

Mansel makes play with this 'antinomy.' The God of his philosophy is too inconceivable to be a moral lawgiver. But, says Mansel, he is also Jehovah. Jehovah, it is replied, is immoral. But, says Mansel, he is also the Inconceivable. This singular mode of eluding difficulties can of course be expressed in edifying language. The 'caviller,' for example, had objected to 'vicarious punishment.' Mansel says[2] that this supposes that nothing can be compatible 'with the boundless goodness of God, which is incompatible with the little goodness of which man may be conscious in himself.' The ingenious argument, in spite of this way of putting it, excited Mill's very justifiable wrath. 'I,' he said,

[1] *Bampton Lectures*, pp. 17, 18.   [2] *Ibid.* p. 212.

'will call no being good, who is not what I mean when I apply that epithet to my fellow-creatures; and if such a being can sentence me to hell for not so calling him, to hell I will go.'[1] Mansel is amazed at this 'extraordinary outburst of rhetoric'; he will not 'pause to comment on its temper and good taste'; but he suggests a parallel.[2] It is that of an 'inexperienced son' taking moral advice from an 'experienced father,' or believing that the elder man is acting rightly though his motives are not fully intelligible to the younger. This, as Mill replies,[3] assumes that the father is 'good' in the human sense, although with more wisdom or knowledge. To make the parallel close we should have to suppose a son who only knows that it is an equal chance whether his father exists or not, and is told by somebody who is equally ignorant that the father desires him to cut a man's throat and appropriate his wife. If the morality of God be absolutely inscrutable, we must fall back upon the conclusion that we are entitled to criticise not the moral contents but the external evidences of a religion.[4] Mansel tries to compromise. We may argue from the morality of religion within limits; the argument may prove that a religion cannot be divine; but not that it is divine. For that we must go to 'external facts.'[5] Our knowledge of God, he still asserts, is derivable from our 'moral and intellectual consciousness'; from the 'constitution and course of nature' and from revelation. These generally agree. When they appear to differ, we must not settle à priori which is to

[1] Examination, p. 129.
[2] Philosophy of the Unconditioned, p. 167 (also quoted in Mill's note to above).
[3] Examination, p. 123 n.   [4] Bampton Lectures, p. 234.
[5] Ibid. p. 239.

give way.[1] Mr. Herbert Spencer, as Mansel thinks, went wrong because he took only the 'negative position' of Hamilton's philosophy, and did not see, for example, that the belief 'in a personal God is imperatively demanded by the facts of our moral and emotional consciousness.'[2] Mansel was trying to escape from his own logic under the shelter of 'vague generalities.' Mr. Herbert Spencer, I think, was perfectly right in holding that when our Deity is the 'Unknowable,' he cannot be made to take sides even in a moral controversy and certainly not identified with the anthropomorphic deities of popular mythology.

The Hamilton-Mansel controversy has become a weariness to the flesh. The interest which it still possesses is only in the illustration of the conflict between different lines of development. The position of Hamilton and his disciple means a desperate attempt to escape from a pressing dilemma. Kant's theology represents the deistic rationalism of the eighteenth century. The metaphysical argument necessarily tends to some form of pantheism, such as that of which Spinoza is the most complete representative. Carry out the logic and God is identified with Nature, and is not a being who can be conceived as interfering with the laws of Nature. The growth of science had made it essential to widen the theological conceptions, and to invest the supreme ruler with attributes commensurate with the new universe, which had been growing both in vastness and regularity. The result of attempting to fulfil that condition was inconsistent with the common-sense theology of the Scottish philosophy, which tried, by help of 'intuitions,' to preserve a 'personal

[1] Philosophy of the Conditioned, p. 245.   [2] Ibid. p. 39 n.

deity,' a being still individual and therefore conceivable as interfering; and which, finding the metaphysical argument dangerous, was inclined to fall back upon the merely empirical argument of Paley. I have shown, at fully sufficient length, how by substituting an antinomy for a paralogism, Hamilton manages verbally to evade this difficulty; and by extending the sphere of belief beyond the sphere of reason, justifies belief in a God who is at once unknowable and yet may be an object of worship. Mansel's audacious extension of this to the historical and mythological creeds, and the consequent identification of Jehovah with the Absolute and Infinite, can only be regarded as a logical curiosity. The only results were, on the one hand, Mr. Herbert Spencer's agnosticism, and on the other, perhaps, some impulse to the speculation of the rising generation. Hamilton and Mansel did something, by their denunciations of German mysticism and ontology, to call attention to the doctrines attacked. The Germans might after all give the right clue; and it might be possible, by substituting a new dialectic for the old logic, to regard the universe as still woven out of reason, and to preserve a theological or at least an idealist mode of conception. With that, however, I have no concern.

VII. MILL ON THEOLOGY

Hamilton's theory at least recognised the inevitable failure of the empirical or Paley theology which virtually makes theology a department of science. Mill, as a thorough empiricist, might have been expected to abandon theology along with all transcendentalism and ontology. In fact, however, his position was different. I

have already pointed out that at one part of his argument he appears to be defending orthodox views of theology as against Mansel. This argument might appear to be merely ad hominem, as intended to show the absurdity of Mansel's doctrine of inconceivability; not to deny the inconceivability itself. Mill, however, really goes further. He approves Hamilton's strange assertion that 'religious disbelief and philosophical scepticism are not merely not the same, but have no natural connection,'[1] and holds that all the real arguments for the existence of God and the immortality of the soul remain unaffected by the association theory. In his Logic Mill had accepted Comte's 'law of the three stages'; but in his later study of Comte he expressly declares that this doctrine is reconcilable with the belief in a 'creator and supreme governor of the world.' It implies a belief in a 'constant order,' but that order may be due to a primitive creation, and even consistent with the continual superintendence of an 'intelligent governor.'[2] In the posthumous essays this position was developed in such a way as to give some scandal to his disciples.[3] He not only leaves room for theistic beliefs, but he seems even to sanction their acceptance.

In the Three Essays on Religion Mill is clearly treading unfamiliar ground. He refers to the arguments of Leibniz, Kant, and Butler, but, as Professor Bain remarks,[4] was a comparative stranger to the whole

[1] Examination, pp. 170, 240; Hamilton's Lectures, i. 394. I do not try to reconcile Hamilton's 'Obiter dictum' in this passage with his assertion in his second lecture that 'philosophy' and 'psychology' give the only possible proofs of theology; or with his claim to have met Kant's scepticism.
[2] Auguste Comte (1865), pp. 14, 15.
[3] See Mr. John Morley's article in Critical Miscellanies (second series).
[4] Bain's J. S. Mill, p. 139.

sphere of speculation. He is not so much at home with his subject as he was in the *Logic* or the *Political Economy*; and therefore scarcely appreciates certain conditions of successful navigation of these regions made sufficiently obvious by the history of previous adventurers. Yet his candour and his resolution to give fair consideration to all difficulties are as conspicuous as his wish to appreciate the highest motives of his antagonists.

Of the three essays, the first two, written before 1858 (on 'Nature' and the 'Utility of Religion'), show less disposition than the last (upon 'Theism') to compromise with orthodoxy; and yet their principles are essentially the same. Mill, of course, is still a thorough empiricist. One version of theology is therefore inconsistent with his most essential tenets. The so-called *a priori* or ontological argument is for him worthless. It involves, he thinks, the unjustifiable assumption that we can infer 'objective facts from ideas or convictions of our minds.' The 'First Cause argument,' again, can only upon his view of causation suggest an indefinite series of antecedents, and one in which the 'higher' as often follows the 'lower' cause, as the lower the higher. Matter may be the antecedent of mind, as well as mind of matter. Moreover, no 'cause' is wanted for that which has no beginning; and as our experience shows a beginning for mind but no beginning for force or matter, the presumption is against mind.[1] If, indeed, the world be simply a series of separate phenomena, connected solely as preceding and succeeding, there is no possibility, it would seem, of inferring any unity or underlying cause or ground. The very attempt to reach unity is as hope-

[1] *Three Essays*, pp. 142-54.

less as is the proverbial problem of weaving ropes from sand. The possibility of philosophical theism is thus destroyed; for the God of philosophy corresponds to the endeavour to assert precisely the unity thus denied in advance. By 'God' Mill must really mean, not Spinoza's necessary substance nor Kant's 'Idea of the pure Reason,' but a being who is essentially one factor of the universe. The confusion is of critical importance. It is constantly assumed, as Mill assumes, that the '*a priori*' and the empirical arguments are different modes of proving the same conclusion. The word 'God' is no doubt used in both cases; but the word covers entirely different senses. The existence of Jehovah might be proved or disproved like the existence of Moses. The God of Spinoza is proved from the logical necessity of the unity and regularity of the universe. One Being may interfere or superintend because he is only part of a whole. The other corresponds to the whole, and interferences or miracles become absurd. Mill, therefore, by calmly dismissing the *a priori* argument is really giving up the God of philosophy, and trying what he can do with the particular or finite being really implied in Paley. Theology on this showing can be only a part of natural science, and precisely that part in which we know nothing.

To know anything of God, in whatever sense, we must go to 'Nature.' In the first essay Mill discusses the question whether anything can be made of the various systems which prescribe 'imitation of Nature' or obedience to the laws of Nature. If Nature be taken in the widest sense, as including man, such systems are nugatory. Disobedience to a 'law of Nature' is not

wrong but impossible. We may, however, take Nature in the narrower sense in which it is the antithesis of art; or, as he puts it, as meaning 'that which takes place without human intervention.'[1] It is plain that, in this sense, the whole aim of all human endeavour must be to improve Nature. Mill emphasises this by expanding the indictment against Nature, which has become more familiar in discussions of the 'struggle for existence.' The 'absolute recklessness of the great cosmic forces,'[2] the variety of torments, such as the worst tyrants have hardly used, inflicted upon all living beings without the slightest regard to justice, are amply sufficient reasons for not 'imitating Nature.' Hence Mill protests emphatically against the notion that 'goodness is natural.'[3] All the virtues are in his sense 'artificial.' Sympathy begins as a form of selfishness—selfishness for two—and the sentiment of justice is developed by the necessity of external law. It is the pressure from without, the interest of each in the goodness of others, which has really created the moral world. The 'germs' of all these virtues must, it is true, have been present; the species could not have existed had it not been endowed with desire for useful ends; but then, we must also admit the existence of bad instincts, producing 'rankly luxuriant growths' of vice against which a long and precarious struggle must be carried on.[4]

Mill is thus saying emphatically much that has been said by later evolutionists. One remark is obvious. The distinction between 'Natural' and 'Artificial' in this sense is clearly arbitrary for one who, like Mill, rejects the doctrine of Freewill. If Nature makes men

[1] *Three Essays*, p. 19. [2] *Ibid.* p. 28. [3] *Ibid.* p. 46. [4] *Ibid.* p. 53.

with certain capacities, Nature must also be taken to be the cause of all human 'intervention.' The sphere of the 'artificial' is merely one part of the sphere of the 'natural.' 'Sympathy' and 'justice' are not the less natural because they are in this sense artificial. Mill is, of course, fully aware of the fact that his 'nature' is here at most a department of Nature in the wider sense. Yet the illegitimate distinction seems more or less to affect his conclusions. He comes to speak as if the distinction corresponded to a line between different worlds. In the non-human world we appear to catch 'Nature' alone and unaided; we can see what it can do by itself, and judge, if not of its justice, at least of its benevolence. He is thus led to use language about men amending Nature or 'co-operating with the beneficent powers,'[1] which would be more consistent in a thoroughgoing advocate of Freewill, but which in his mouth must be taken as a metaphorical or provisional mode of speech. To one who uses 'nature' in the widest sense as implying a conception of the universe as a whole, the narrower use would be meaningless. But, as we shall now see, the unity of nature is a conception which Mill virtually rejects.

Mill has shown conclusively that it is impossible to interpret Nature as the work of omnipotent Benevolence. So far, he agrees with many predecessors, including Hume and Mansel;[2] but he does not with Hume become

[1] *Three Essays*, p. 65.
[2] 'Why,' asks Hume, 'is there any misery in the world? Not by chance, surely. From some cause, then? Is it by the intervention of the Deity? But he is perfectly benevolent. Is it contrary to his intentions? But he is Almighty. Epicurus's old questions,' he says, 'are yet unanswered.' 'If,' says Mansel, 'an infinitely powerful Being wills evil, he is not perfectly good. If he wills it not, his will is thwarted and his sphere of action limited.'—Hume's *Works* (1874), ii. 440, 442; *Bampton Lectures*, p. 51.

simply sceptical, nor follow Mansel in pronouncing that we must believe a doctrine which we are unable to ' construe to the mind' as conceivable. He suggests an alternative view. It is possible to believe in a God who is benevolent though not omnipotent. This, he declares, is the only ' religious explanation of the order of Nature,' which is neither self-contradictory nor inconsistent with facts.[1] He ' ventures to assert,' moreover, that it has been the real faith of all who have drawn a worthy support from trust in Providence ; ' they have always saved [God's] goodness at the expense of His power.' This, for example, is the true meaning of Leibniz's ' best of all possible worlds.'[2] Mill declares that the doctrine of the Manichæans, which he knows to have been ' devoutly held by at least one cultivated and conscientious person of our own day,' is the only ' form of belief in the supernatural which stands wholly clear both of intellectual contradiction and moral obliquity.'[3] He points out, too, that even Christianity admits a devil, though it places upon the Creator the responsibility of not annihilating him.[4] Now Manichæism is a clear confession of philosophical bankruptcy. The whole aim of reasoning is to reduce the universe to unity, and this is to admit that there is an ultimate and insoluble dualism. From the point of view of the ontologist, indeed, the moral difficulty which Manichæism is supposed to meet is irrelevant. God is the ground or First Cause. Evil is caused as much as good, and if a first cause or an absolute substance be a necessary assumption, we must ascribe to it the whole system of things, good or bad,

[1] *Three Essays*, p. 39.   [2] *Ibid.* p. 40.   [3] *Ibid.* p. 116.
[4] *Ibid.* p. 184. Friday asks Robinson Crusoe why God did not kill the devil.

painful or pleasurable, without trying to separate what is inextricably intertwined. An argument from causation leaves no *locus standi* for any moral objection. Mill, however, denies the necessity for, or indeed the possibility of, such reasoning. He is fully prepared to admit that in the last resort we come to independent and equally uncaused factors. The question, then, remains, what positive ground we can assign for a belief in any first cause or causes or ' supernatural entities.'

Having rejected the metaphysical arguments for a Deity, we reach at last, says Mill, an argument of a really scientific character—the argument, namely, from design.[1] That is to say, he tries to find room for an empirical deity, who must therefore correspond to a part of nature, not to the whole. He does not hold that the knowledge of nature anywhere involves antinomies or contrary inconceivables. It is a coherent and throughout intelligible system, but it would correspond to the ideal of completed science, not to any metaphysical belief. Within this system there is room for a being who, though he is limited by something external to himself, may yet be an object of worship. In fact, there can be no *a priori* objection to the theory of a powerful being, who may be discovered, like any other beings known to us, by his action in particular cases. Metaphysicians may decline to call such a being God ; but a proof of superhuman wisdom and power may be enough for practical purposes.[2]

The proof, then, that such a being exists, must be made

[1] So in the *Examination of Hamilton* (p. 567) he says that this is ' by far the best' and ' by far the most persuasive argument.'
[2] *Examination*, p. 246.

by induction ; and, as Mill explains, by the first of the famous ' four methods,' namely, by that of Agreement.[1] This argument, though generally the weakest, is in this case ' strong of its kind.' He illustrates it by the familiar case. The eye is a complex structure which, as it began in time, must have had a cause or causes. ' Chance' is eliminated by the number of instances, and therefore there must be some causal connection between the ' cause' which brought the elements together and the ' fact of sight.' Mill, that is, thinks it necessary to prove what science takes for granted. No man of science disputes that there is some cause of eyes and of every eye. But here we have the curious transition into another order of thought, which corresponds to the passage from the empirical to the transcendental meaning. It is clear that so long as we are in the sphere of science, the only ' cause' of the existence of an eye is the sum of the preceding organic processes. A given animal has eyes because the processes of reproduction involve resemblance to its parents. If we go back to eyeless ancestors, we have the problem how eyes were developed ; but the purely scientific answer would still consist in assigning the previous conditions or the precedent stage in the whole process of nature. How do we get out of this series? The argument, according to Mill, would proceed by saying that, as sight follows the eye, the cause must be a ' final' cause ; or, in other words, correspond to an ' intelligent Will.' But what is the relation of this Will to the admitted series of events? Causation always sends me back along an indefinitely producible series. Am I to interpret this cause as an ' alternative' to what may be

[1] *Three Essays*, p. 170.

called the natural cause ; or as corresponding to a general power, which is manifested through the whole series? In the latter case we may consider the God of nature as an ' immanent' power. His operation is manifest in the general wisdom of the whole system. It is not only consistent with, but implies, the persistence of the ' laws of nature,' and therefore the evolution of eyes, if there was a period before eyes existed. If that view be tenable, we may save ' teleology' by applying it to nature as a whole, but there is no intervention in the actual series of natural events. On the view which Mill accepts, we have an intervention, at some particular point. But how is this to be inferred, or what can it mean? I have already noticed the familiar difficulties in speaking of ' Philip Beauchamp.' The philosophical objection is clear,[1] and in science ' creation' can be only a word ; it introduces an arbitrary and unmeaning interruption, and, under the form of explaining, declares explanation to be impossible.

In fact, when such conceptions are brought into the argument, when ' creation' is used as an alternative hypothesis to a permanent order, the answer of the evolutionist is conclusive. Here, accordingly, Mill finds himself confronted by Darwin. He admits that the doctrine of the ' survival of the fittest' would ' greatly attenuate,' though it would be in ' no way whatever inconsistent with creation.'[2] This means, apparently, that Darwinism does not prove that there was not a ' creation' at some indefinite time ; though it does show that there is no need for supposing a creation since the existing order began.

[1] The ' ingenious simile,' says Mansel, ' by which God is compared to a mechanic fails only in this particular, that both its terms are utterly unlike the objects which they profess to represent.'—*Bampton Lectures*, p. 188.
[2] *Three Essays*, p. 174.

I have already noticed Mill's view of this 'remarkable speculation.' Here he virtually admits that his theology, such as it is, and, indeed, his whole conception of nature, is virtually opposed to evolution. Science, he says, most truly, leads us to regard nature as 'one connected system, not a web of separate threads in passive juxtaposition with one another, but rather, like the human or animal frame,' in perpetual 'action and reaction'; and the natural version of this, he adds, is theism. The unity of nature, that is, has enabled monotheism to supersede polytheism, because it corresponds to the scientific view.[1] Yet, while saying this in general terms, he cannot reconcile it to his own theories; he still talks of 'laws of nature' counteracting each other;[2] he can speak of some things as 'uncaused'; and of a 'permanent' and 'a changeable' element in nature, as though persistence was not a case of causation. He is willing, as we have seen, to assume that anything may be the cause of anything else.   The universe is therefore ultimately a struggle between independent forces, and God becomes a being who has to struggle against antecedent or independent things. When science is regarded, not as a system of interdependent truths, where the value of every theory must be judged by the way in which it affects and is affected by all other ascertainable truth, but as an aggregate of purely empirical observations of the order of succession of otherwise unrelated facts, it is easy to introduce such conceptions as 'creation,' which virtually deny the continuity and reasonableness of the order

[1] *Three Essays*, p. 133.
[2] *Ibid.* pp. 16, 17. Observe the language about 'conforming to the laws of equilibrium among bodies,' instead of 'conforming only to the law of gravitation,' as though we did not necessarily 'conform' to all 'laws of nature' in all cases.

generally, and tend to confuse, as his antagonists would say, Nature with a particular element in Nature; and to make noumena take a side in the struggle between phenomena.

Mill is thus able to hold that the adaptations 'in nature afford a large balance of probability in favour of creation by intelligence.'[1] It is, he grants, only a probability, and not strengthened by any independent arguments.   It still remains to consider whether we can find reasons to believe that the creator is moral. He thinks that most 'contrivances' are for the preservation of the creatures, and that there is no reason for attributing the destructive agencies to one Being, and the preserving agencies to another. We may therefore give up Manichæism, or a conflict between good and evil powers; but we may still have an uncreated set of things with which the good being must struggle. We must be content to believe in a Being of great but limited power—how limited we cannot even conjecture; whose intelligence may be unlimited though it may also be more limited than his power; who desires the happiness of his creatures but has probably other motives. If he shows benevolence, there are no traces of justice.[2] Of immortality we can learn nothing, unless from revelation. He denies that a revelation, conflicting with morality, can be divine; but this forces him to limit the power of the Deity. His God desires morality. How can we discover that he desires it? Can these vague surmises be helped by any direct revelation or miraculous intervention? Mill

[1] *Three Essays*, p. 174.
[2] Mill has here come to speak of 'Nature' in the narrower sense, as opposed to art or to nature working through man.

discusses the argument of Hume's essay and reaches, what I take to be the true conclusion, that the real question is whether we have independent reasons for believing in a Deity whose intervention is conceivable.[1] Considering that we have some reason for believing in such a being, he at last concludes that, in spite of most serious difficulties, historical and philosophical, we are 'entitled to say that there is nothing so inherently impossible or absolutely incredible in the supposition that the "extremely precious" gift of Christianity came from a divinely commissioned man as to preclude any one from hoping that it may be true.' He can go no further, for he sees no 'evidentiary value' even in the testimony of Christ himself. The best men are the readiest to ascribe their own merits to a higher source. Mill, of course, does not believe in the divinity of Christ; he holds that Christ himself would have regarded such a pretension as blasphemous; but it remains possible that 'Christ actually was what he supposed himself to be . . . a man charged with a special, express, and unique commission from God to lead mankind to truth and virtue.'[2]

Mill, we see, declared positivism to be reconcilable with theism. Comte himself, who declared atheism to be the most illogical form of theology, would have agreed that positivism does not disprove God's existence. But Comte would have said that an unverifiable hypothesis about an inconceivable being was simply idle or 'otiose.' Mill seems to treat the absence of negative proof as equivalent—not indeed to the presence of positive, but—to the existence of a probability worth entertaining. His

[1] *Three Essays*, p. 232.   [2] *Ibid.* p. 255.

theism, if so vague and problematical a doctrine can be called theism, is defended as neither self-contradictory nor inconsistent with fact. Now a theory which is self-contradictory is really no theory at all. Nor is a theory scientifically valuable simply because 'consistent' with facts. A theory must have some definite support in facts. It must at lowest be not only consistent with the known facts, but inconsistent with some otherwise imaginable facts. If it fits every conceivable state of things, it can throw light upon none. But this is obviously the case with Mill's theory. He makes way for a good being by an arbitrary division of nature into two sets of forces. He saves the benevolence by limiting the power of the deity; but then the limits are, by his own admission, utterly unknowable. A power, restrained by unknowable bounds, is a power from which nothing can be inferred. Whatever its attributes, we do not know whether they will affect any state of things. The goodness may be indefinitely frustrated. In fact, on Mill's showing, a power omnipotent but not benevolent, or an indefinite multitude of powers of varying attributes, or a good and a bad power eternally struggling, or, in short, any religious doctrine that has ever been held among men, would suit the facts. Mill's 'plurality of causes' might have suggested this difficulty. I see a corpse. The death may have been due to any one of an indefinite number of causes. What right have I to select one? I am in the same position when I regard the whole of nature as what Hume called a 'unique effect.' The four methods of induction become inapplicable, for there are no other universes and I have no compass to steer by in the region of the unverifiable.

What, then, can be the advantage of any belief where conflicting hypotheses must be all equally probable? The question is partly discussed in the second essay upon the utility of Religion. Here Mill takes up the old argument of 'Philip Beauchamp,' the 'only direct discussion' of the point with which he is acquainted,[1] and endeavours to state the case more fairly and in a less hostile spirit. His argument, however, is in general conformity with Bentham and Grote, and is very forcibly put. One point may be noticed. He virtually identifies 'religion' with a belief in 'the supernatural.'[2] He compares the efficacy of such beliefs with the efficacy of education (which, as he characteristically says, is 'almost boundless')[3] and of public opinion, and shows with 'Beauchamp' that when conflict occurs, these influences are stronger than those derived from supernatural sanctions. Now when we believe in a revelation it is intelligible to ask, What is the influence of a creed? It represents a new force influencing men's minds from without. But when the creed is supposed to be generated from antecedent beliefs, the argument must be altered by considering what are the true causes of the belief. How did it come to prevail? An admirer of Comte might have brought out more distinctly the fact that such beliefs mark an essential stage of progress, that what are now sporadic superstitions were once parts of a systematic religion and represented the germs of science. They were approximate hypotheses which had to be remodelled by extricating or dropping the 'supernatural' element. A full recognition of this would diminish the paradoxical appearance of the statement from which he starts, that 'a religion

---

[1] *Three Essays*, p. 76.   [2] *Ibid.* p. 100.   [3] *Ibid.* p. 82.

may be morally useful without being intellectually sustainable.' The truth surely is that we cannot separate the two elements of a creed. Doubtless there were no such beings as the Zeus or Apollo of popular belief; but polytheism may still have provided the only form in which certain truths could be presented; and was, as Comte would have said, a stage in the process from fetishism towards monotheism and positivism. A discussion of the utility of belief in the 'supernatural' without reference to the place of the supernatural in the whole system of belief must be necessarily inadequate. Mill admits this in substance, and argues that the moral truth may survive the superstitions in which it was bound up.[1] He goes on to argue, as Comte had argued, that the instincts which once found their sanction in the supernatural world might find their embodiment in the 'Religion of Humanity.'[2] This he holds to be not only entitled to the name of religion, but to be 'a better religion than any of those ordinarily called by that title.' It is disinterested and does not tend to cramp the intellect or degenerate into a worship of mere power. Mill says emphatically that the Bentham mode of considering religion as a supplement to police by providing 'sanctions' is inadequate; and that religion, like poetry, is valuable as suggesting higher ideals and gratifying the craving for knowledge of corresponding realities. To the selfish, supernatural religion offers heaven; and to the 'tender and grateful' it offers the love of God. He points out that it does not follow that we must 'travel beyond the boundaries of the world we inhabit' in order to obtain such consolation.[3] And the essay con-

---

[1] *Three Essays*, p. 97.   [2] *Ibid.* p. 111.   [3] *Ibid.* p. 104.

cludes by saying that, though the 'supernatural religions' have always the advantage of offering immortality, the value set upon immortality may diminish as life becomes higher and happier and annihilation may seem more desirable.[1]

Yet in the middle of this argument we have the defence of Manichæism as a possible creed,[2] and in the last essay we seem to reach the true account of his leanings to such a belief. He still, that is, requires a breathing-space for the imagination. 'Truth is the province of reason,' but 'in the regulation of the imagination literal truth of facts is not the only thing to be considered.'[3] Reason must keep the fortress, but the 'imagination may safely follow its own end and do its best to make life pleasant and lovely inside the castle.' Thus, though we are only entitled to hope as to the government of the world and a life after death, the bare hope may have a beneficial effect. 'It makes life and human nature a far greater thing to the feelings, and gives greater strength and solemnity to all the sentiments which are awakened in us by our fellow-creatures and mankind at large.' Aspirations are no longer checked by the disastrous feeling of 'not worth while.' Religion, too, has set before us a 'Divine Person, as a standard of excellence and a model for imitation.'[4] The ideal, it is true, would remain, even if the person were held to be imaginary; and would not be encumbered by theological difficulties. Yet there is an advantage in the belief that a perfect being really exists and represents the ruler of the universe, which cannot be shared by the rationalist.[5] Hence as, after all, the truth of the

---

[1] *Three Essays*, p. 122.   [2] *Ibid.* p. 116.   [3] *Ibid.* pp. 248-49.
[4] *Ibid.* p. 253.   [5] *Ibid.* p. 252.

belief is possible, it may be combined with the Religion of Humanity. That religion, 'with or without supernatural sanctions,' will be the religion of the future; but it will be strengthened by the feeling that we are 'helping God' and supplying 'co-operation' which 'he, not being omnipotent, really needs.'[1] Truly, Mill was nearly qualified for a place among the prophets.

Mill's arbitrary assumptions, like the metaphysical wiredrawings of Mansel, are rather unprofitable in themselves: few people will care to follow them in detail; and neither could boast of many converts. Believers soon became aware of the real scepticism of Mansel's position; and positivists saw that Mill left an opening for superstition. Both Mansel and Mill were troubled about the Religion of Nature. It is abundantly clear, as Mill might have foreseen, that such a theology as he contemplates could be of no real value. It depends essentially upon compromises and arbitrary distinctions. It is still within the sphere of science, though doomed to disappear as science advances, and from the first is inconsistent with the very aims which are proposed by theology. God is admittedly not omnipotent, and his existence is no guarantee for morality or optimism. And hence there is an odd approximation between Mill and Mansel.

Mill observes[2] that the moral character of an alleged revelation cannot be of itself a proof of its divinity. The importance of the 'internal evidence' is therefore 'principally negative.' So says Mansel. 'The evidence derived from the internal character of a religion, whatever may be its value within its proper limits, is, as

---

[1] *Three Essays*, pp. 256-57.   [2] *Ibid.* p. 216.

regards the divine origin of the religion, purely negative.'[1]
Where is the difference? If the morality of a revelation
be bad, Mill argues that the revelation must be at once
rejected. Mansel thinks that although the morality be
not clearly good, it may in some way represent a divine
command. Immoral laws cannot be divine, says Mill,
though a good law may be human. A law apparently
bad, replies Mansel, may be divine, though, of course,
the badness can only be apparent. Here, as elsewhere,
the believer in the empirical character of morality appears
to attribute most certainty to the moral judgment. The
solutions differ accordingly. Mill supposes that God
must be good, but reconciles this to facts by assuming
that God is not all-powerful. Mansel will not give up
the power, and to preserve the goodness has to assume
a radical incapacity in the intellect—a necessity of believing where there is an impotence of conceiving.
Mill, that is, is content with the empirical deity, who
is necessarily limited; and Mansel keeps the deity of
ontology but admits that he cannot be known. Mill's
conception is purely arbitrary, though he keeps within
the limits of conceivable experience; while Mansel preserves the language appropriate to the conception of
absolute unity, and yet admits that it can mean nothing
for us. 'Agnosticism' seems to be an easier and more
rational alternative; if it means an open admission that
we know nothing, when we can only save our appearance
of knowledge by arbitrary assumptions or by the use of
meaningless words. Of Mill's position it must be frankly
admitted that his desire for a religious and even supernatural belief is a proof of dissatisfaction with his own

[1] *Bampton Lectures*, p. 238.

position. He felt here, as elsewhere, that something was
wanting in his philosophy. What that really was may
partly appear by considering other contemporary solutions. Mansel represents a particular phase of thought
which is already extinct, and views differing both from
theirs and from Mill's had in practice a far wider influence than either.

The Utilitarian view naturally identifies a religious
creed with a belief in certain historical statements of fact.
If the facts be provable the religion is true; if disproved it is false. If there was such a being as Jehovah,
it was desirable to worship him; and the creed would
then be useful. If there was no such being, worship
was folly. The test of the utility of a religion was,
therefore, simply the truth or falsehood of its historical
statements. If its gods were made by the fancy, not by
the reason, the result is a condemnation of religion in
general. That is simple and logical, and recognises an
indisputable truth. So far as a religion makes false
statements, they must be abandoned; and so far as its
influence depends upon the falsity, it is pernicious.

A religion, however, represents more than can be
estimated by this simple test. The poetical value of
Homer is not destroyed by disproving the existence of
the Pagan deisms, nor the value of the Hebrew Scrip-
tures by disproving the existence of Jehovah. The
facts alleged may be fabulous and absurd; but they are
also symbols for setting forth views of the world and
of conduct, and so giving emphatic utterance to important truths. The old religions were attempts of
men, in early stages of thought, to embody ideals of
conduct which may really have been of the highest value

to mankind. They were essential, again, to the social
bonds which have, in fact, determined the formation of
society and facilitated the growth of sympathy and philanthropy. Therefore, if a religious creed be false when
interpreted as a simple statement of fact, we have not
exhausted its significance or even touched the really most
important significance of the religion itself. Believers
felt more or less clearly that such attacks as 'Philip
Beauchamp' affected only externals, and left the need for
religion unsatisfied. Only as the actual creed was
pledged to maintain the truth of certain statements,
which were daily becoming more incredible, the necessity
appeared of finding some stronger position than the old
Paley scheme, which virtually regarded religion as a mere
statement of historical fact, or as a department of natural
science. To trace the consequences would be to write a
history of modern theology. I shall try only to indicate
the relation to the Utilitarians of a few thinkers. Two main
lines of thought were conspicuous in Mill's generation,
and correspond to what Newman called 'liberalism' and
'dogmatism.'

VIII. LIBERALISM

A very instructive example of one phase of liberal
thought was Frederick Denison Maurice (1805-1872).
Before Mill's attack upon Mansel, Maurice had been
engaged in a sharp controversy invoked by the Bampton
Lecturer. No two men could be more thoroughly at
cross-purposes. In their arguments each word bears a
different signification for the two disputants. Each, of
course, vehemently disapproved the other; and Mansel

was provoked to call Maurice a liar[1] in direct terms.
The real difficulty is to reduce the argument to any
common measure; and Maurice's position, though not
easy to define, is significant. Maurice,[2] as I have said,
was one of Mill's friendly adversaries in the early
debating society. His references to Mill are always
respectful, little as could be their intellectual sympathy;
while Mill's judgment was that 'more intellectual power
was wasted in Maurice than in any one else of my
generation.' Deep respect for Maurice, admiration of
his subtlety and power of generalisation, only increased
Mill's wonder that he could find all truth in the Thirty-
nine Articles.[3] Maurice had been brought up as a
Unitarian, and was profoundly impressed by the barren
wrangling over the dogmatic partitions of various sects.
After long hesitation he at last found satisfaction in the
Church of England and, as he declared, by accepting the
Anglican formulæ in their obvious and most natural
sense. To men of other persuasions, his interpretation
appeared on the contrary to amount to a complete transformation of their natural meaning. Maurice was
therefore excluded from all the higher preferment, and
passed for an insidious heresiarch. He replied by a full
and frank, though hardly a lucid, assertion of his own
convictions; and gradually proved, even to his enemies,

[1] *Examination of the Reverend F. D. Maurice's 'Strictures'* (1859), p. 80.
This is a reply to Maurice's *What is Revelation?* (1859). Maurice in a *Sequel*
(1860) answers this and other accusations with dignity; though his remarks
upon Mansel were certainly sharp enough.
[2] Maurice's most complete book, the *Kingdom of Christ* (1838, enlarged
1842), is less rhetorical and more logical than its successors. The *Theological
Essays* (1853) gives his teaching in the shortest compass.
[3] Mill's *Autobiography*, p. 153.

his entire superiority to any worldly motives. He was expelled in 1853 from his professorship at King's College for denying the truth of the popular version of hell, a little before the denial had become a commonplace. Disciples had already gathered round him and regarded him with the reverence due to the purity and loftiness of his character. As the head of the Christian Socialists in the critical period of 1848, he had at least given a proof that divines could take a genuine interest in the great social problems of the day. Maurice himself was little qualified for business details, and the whole movement failed for the time, like most others which start from the sympathy of the outsiders instead of the actual experience of the actual sufferers. It was, however, significant of a most important change, more easily underestimated than exaggerated. Maurice deserves all respect, as Mill observes, for his action, of which, moreover, it is only just to say that it was really characteristic of his whole position.

What, then, was Maurice's position in theology? In the first place he recognised most fully a truth which, in various forms, gives the real strength to all great religious teachers. He held that the value of a religion depends upon its congeniality to the highest parts of human nature. He is thus at the opposite pole to the Philip Beauchamp doctrine, according to which the essence of religion is to create a spiritual police, and to add the sanction of hell to the sanction of the gallows. Maurice is equally opposed to the sacerdotalism which makes the essence of religion consist in a magical removal of penalties instead of a 'regeneration' of the nature. He takes what may be vaguely called the 'subjective' view

of religion, and sympathises with Schleiermacher's statement that piety is 'neither a knowing nor a doing, but an inclination and determination of the feeling.'[1] It is evident, again, that Maurice could as little base his belief upon external evidence as his morality upon external sanctions. So far he may be said to coincide with the philosophical view. A religion must be an expression of general truths accessible to all men, and independent of time and place. Maurice had been a wide reader of philosophy; he spent much time upon a history of 'Metaphysical and Moral philosophy'[2] which, if vague in the statement of definite theories, shows wide sympathy and desire to enter into the spirit of the various schools. In the *Kingdom of Christ*[3] he declares that 'eclecticism is a necessity of the age'; meaning by eclecticism a doctrine which shall discover what is the truth contained in all the partial systems and creeds of all ages. Here, again, Maurice was sharing the best liberal impulses of the day, and sharing them because they were congenial to a generous and tender-hearted nature. The same tendency makes him averse to any definite system of metaphysical dogmas. The dialectical wranglings over dogmas which disgusted him in his youth appeared again in Mansel's metaphysics. The Bampton Lectures showed, according to him, that we cannot leave the ground of solid fact for the 'logical ground without being involved in a series of hopeless quibbles which no human being ought to trouble himself with, unless he means to abandon the business of

[1] i.e. *eine Neigung und Bestimmtheit des Gefühls*, quoted in *What is Revelation?* p. 316. Maurice defends this against Mansel.
[2] Begun about 1835 for the *Encyclopædia Metropolitana*. The whole collected in an edition of 1871-72.
[3] *Kingdom of Christ* (1842), p. 253.

existence and to give himself up to feats of jugglery.'[1] In such regions no lasting foundation can be found. Nor, on the other hand, can we be satisfied with the mere historical critics who, like Strauss, pick holes in the gospels or, like Strauss's opponents, manage to mend them; or with the philologists who argue whether 'the line in the O can be detected with the aid of spectacles or not.'[2] A religion which is to move men's hearts must have some wider and deeper basis.

So far Maurice's teaching would command the sympathy of all who called themselves liberal. But what becomes of Logic? Can philosophy dispense with it altogether? Maurice professedly appeals to the heart. The appeal is made over and over again in a great variety of forms: to the 'great human heart,' to 'bedridden sufferers,' to 'peasants, women, and children,'[3] and we are told that it is the 'office of the theologian' to appeal not to his own judgment or that of the ages, but to the 'conscience, heart, reason of mankind.'[4] Nothing can be more to the purpose if we are considering the efficacy of a religious belief; but we must ask how this appeal is related to the question of its truth. The emotions are not reason, though they are bound to be reasonable. The position is that of all mysticism. The mystic is one who virtually dethrones reason in favour of the heart. Therefore mysticism leads to all the varying beliefs which are suggested by our unguided feelings. When Maurice was charged with being himself a mystic or neoplatonist, his reply

[1] *What is Revelation?* (1819), p. 275.
[2] *Theological Essays*, pp. 65, 119.
[3] *Ibid.* pp. 113, 338, 465.
[4] *What is Revelation?* p. 232.

was that the error of the mystic is not in recognising an 'inner light,' but in supposing that his intuition is something personal and private, and not a universal faculty of the human heart.[1] He admits, that is, that all religion implies the direct recognition of divine influences by the human heart, though it is terribly apt to confound the true intuition with certain erroneous doctrines. By what test, then, are we to separate the true light from the misleading gleams of human passion and prejudices? How can we know that it is the divine Logos which is speaking to us, and not some sophist substituting a mere human theory?

This gives Maurice's characteristic doctrine, repeated in countless forms with most genuine fervour, and yet leaving the painful impression that we can never get a distinct meaning. He tells us again and again that we require not a system but a revelation; that we are to believe in God, not in a theory about God; not in 'notions' but in principles; that a theology is groundless which 'accepts as a tenet what is revealed as a truth,'[2] and that we shall be 'driven to creeds' by 'weariness of tenets.'[3] These, and countless variations upon the same theme, involve a puzzling distinction. How, precisely, does the belief in God differ from the acceptance of a theory about God? Maurice, I may perhaps say, takes the belief in God to be an operation, not a mere bit of logic; an act of the man's whole nature, not a purely intellectual process such as the deduction of

[1] *Kingdom of Christ*, i. (1842) 41. This book, first published as a series of letters to a Quaker, is an exposition of the way in which the mystical doctrine of Fox and Barclay degenerated from the confusion between a valid, because universal, principle and a claim to a private or individual application.
[2] *What is Revelation?* p. 228.
[3] *Theological Essays*, p. 316.

the conclusion of a syllogism. It is the apprehension of the 'inner light,' always perceptible if the eye be opened, and which is in the same indissoluble moment not merely enlightening but life-giving. The vision is also 'dynamical': the submission of ourselves to a force as well as the recognition of the existence of certain outward facts. It implies not merely the admission of a new theory about the universe, but the bringing ourselves into harmony with the one central force of the universe—that is with the God who is Love as well as power and wisdom. This is the true mystical doctrine; and that doctrine, if not the most logical, is the most unanswerable form of religious belief. If a man believes that he has the 'inner light,' he is in his own court beyond appeal. But the difficulty of making his decisions valid for others cannot be evaded, and implies some use of logic. If the inner light implies knowledge as well as an emotion, it should be expressible in forms true for all men. The mere formula by itself may be barren, or merely subordinate; but if any definite creed is to emerge, it must include tenets capable of logical expression. This is, in fact, the problem round which Maurice is always turning.

The result is indicated in his little book upon the *Religions of the World*.[1] It embodies one of the most marked tendencies of modern thought. No divine can now speak of strange religions as simply devil-worship, or limit divine truth to his own set of dogmas. The simple or logical rationalist had inferred that the true creed must be that which is common to all religions. But to reject all special doctrines was to leave a blank

[1] Originally the Boyle Lectures for 1846. Fourth edition in 1861.

residuum of mere abstract deism, if even deism could survive. It was but another road to the 'religion of nature.' Yet that was the tendency of most liberal divines within the church. The 'broad church' party, as it was called, was getting rid of 'dogma' by depriving the creed of all meaning. Maurice's method is therefore different. The element of truth in all religions is not any separable doctrine common to all. It is to be found by regarding all creeds as partial or distorted expressions of the full truth revealed in Christ. On this showing therefore Buddhism testifies to the truth of Christianity, but Christianity does not testify to the truth of Buddhism. Or, to take a trifling but characteristic argument,[1] Wilberforce and the Unitarian, W. Smith, were colleagues in a great benevolent work. Does that show that the doctrine of the Trinity is unimportant? No; Smith should have seen that the zeal of Wilberforce 'manifestly flowed out of the faith' in the divinity of Christ. Wilberforce, on the other hand, should see that Christ might rule in the heart of the Unitarian though the Unitarian knew it not. The divine influence may operate upon the heart which does not recognise its true nature. Thus Wilberforce, instead of becoming 'latitudinarian,' could escape 'latitudinarianism.' This may be true, but it would clearly not convince Smith. If you appeal to your heart, why may I not appeal to mine? Is not your conviction, after all, 'subjective' —as representing your own personal prejudices—and would it not be just as easy, with equal skill, to invert the argument? Or is not the real source of action in both cases the benevolence which has nothing to do with

[1] *Theological Essays*, p. 211.

either set of dogmas? This unintentional shifting is implied in the process by which Maurice manages to accept the Thirty-nine Articles. Taken as truths, they utter the voice of the heart, or imply an apprehension of the divine light. Taken as merely logical, they are but tenets or 'notional' dogmas. The doctrine of the Atonement, for example, as made into a quasi-legal theory by Archbishop Magee, is simply horrible: it deserves all that Paine could have said of it, and actually 'confounds the evil spirit with God.' But take it in another sense—not as proclaiming the supremacy of a harsh and unjust ruler, but as declaring the process by which the love of God and of his son reconciles men to himself—and it becomes infinitely comforting, and expresses the feelings of 'tens of thousands of suffering human beings.'[1] So the doctrine of 'endless' punishment is horrible and revolting. But eternity has properly nothing to do with time. 'Eternal punishment is the punishment of being without the knowledge of God.'[2] That knowledge does not procure but constitutes the life. This is no metaphysical theory, but gives the natural meaning which commends itself to 'peasants, women, and children.'[3] To the ordinary mind, the natural inference would be that we should throw aside dogmas so capable of misinterpretation, and which admittedly have, as a historical fact, covered a confusion between God and the devil. The Athanasian Creed appears to be at least an awkward and ambiguous mode of expressing a universal benevolence and an aversion to metaphysical

[1] *Theological Essays*, p. 145.
[2] Maurice, as I remember Carlyle saying, thought that you might be eternally damned for five minutes.
[3] *Theological Essays*, pp. 430, 450, 480.

dogma. But to reject it would be, as Maurice thinks, to fall into mere rationalism. The formulæ which are so revolting in the mouth of the mere dogmatist are essential when read as utterances of the deepest feelings of the human heart. We can only hold to their true meaning and denounce their misapplication.

After all comes the real difficulty of fitting a 'subjective' religion to a historical religion. The Christian creed does assert facts, and facts to which historical evidence is applicable. A dogma can be made into an utterance of sentiment. A statement that there was a deluge in the year 4004 B.C. must be decided by evidence. Maurice was painfully shocked when the excellent and simple-minded Colenso brought up this plain issue.[1] Though Colenso had stood by him generously in the King's College time, Maurice, who had fully recognised the generosity, felt himself bound to protest. The dilemma was, in fact, most trying. To declare that historical evidence is irrelevant, that our faith is independent of the truth of the Old Testament narrative, is really to give up historical Christianity. On the other hand, to argue that the criticisms are trifling or captious is to stake the truth of the religion upon the issue of facts. Maurice complains of Colenso for beginning at the wrong end.[2] As, however, Colenso has made certain statements, whatever his method, the truth must be either denied or admitted. Are they true but irrelevant, or relevant but false? Maurice cannot unequivocally take either side. He appears to hold that we may accept the deluge

[1] Maurice's criticism is in a little book called *The Claims of the Bible and of Science* (1863).
[2] *Claims of Science*, etc., pp. 76, 125.

because it teaches us a good lesson (that bad people will be drowned, apparently), that is, to accept whatever is edifying ; or to think perhaps the deluge was a little one, that is, to put himself on the ground of historical criticism. Here, in fact, was the growing difficulty. Mansel could still speak scornfully of the quibblings of Strauss. But historical criticism had now to be reckoned with, and subjective religion must consent to be merely subjective, or submit to have its results tested by the broad daylight of common sense.

From Maurice I turn to Carlyle, the beacon-light of the age, according to his disciples—the most delusive of wildfires, according to his adversaries ; but in any case the most interesting literary figure of his time. Extraordinary force of mind and character are manifested in the struggles with inward difficulties and external circumstances, which made much of his life tragic and his teaching incoherent. With the imagination of a poet he yet cannot rise above the solid ground of prose : a sense of pervading mystery blends with his shrewd grasp of realities ; he is religious yet sceptical ; a radical and a worshipper of sheer force ; and a denouncer of cant and yet the deviser of a jargon. Such contrasts are reflected in his work, and are not really hard of solution. A spiritual descendant of John Knox, he had the stern sense of duty, the hatred of priestcraft, and the contempt for the æsthetic side of things which had been bred in or burned into the breed. He came into the outer world, like his hero Teufelsdröckh,[1] as a ' Baptist living on locusts and wild honey,' and occasionally presented himself to others as a dyspeptic polar bear.[2] He had im-

[1] *Sartor Resartus*, ch. iv. ; cf. Froude, i. 334.   [2] Froude, iii. 67.

bibed radicalism in a home of sturdy peasants, pinched by all the sufferings of the poorer classes in the war time. When the yeomanry was called out in 1819 he was more disposed to join the sufferers than the guardians of order.[1] So far, Carlyle was in sympathy with James Mill, whose career also illustrated one mode of passage from Puritanism to political radicalism. Nor would Carlyle differ from Mill widely on certain religious points. The conventional dogmatism of the kirk had lost its savour for both, and meant a blind tradition, not a living force. Carlyle only went with the general current of youthful intellect in abandoning the dogmatic creed. When Irving made a painful effort to put life into the dead bones, Carlyle recognised the hopelessness of the enterprise. But he was no nearer to Mill. Carlyle's ' conversion' took place in Leith Walk in June 1821.[2] It followed three years of spiritual misery ; and it is recorded in the famous chapter in *Sartor Resartus* on the ' Everlasting No.'[3] That passage is, indeed, the keynote to Carlyle's history. Briefly, he had found himself face to face with materialism and atheism. The weapons of defence afforded by such teachers as Brown were futile. Carlyle felt that he too was drifting towards the abysses whither they were being dragged by Hume. The word duty, so sceptics would persuade him, had no meaning, or was the name for a mere calculation of pleasure ; an exhortation to build not on morality but on cookery. The universe seemed to be ' void of Life, of Purpose, of Volition, even of Hostility : it was one dead, unmeasurable steam-engine, rolling on in its dead indifference, to grind me limb from limb. O

[1] Froude, i. 73.   [2] *Ibid.* i. 101.   [3] *Sartor Resartus*, ch. vii.

the vast solitary Golgotha and Mill of Death !' The nightmare was broken by an act of will. The ' Everlasting No' pealed ' authoritatively through all recesses of my Being, of my Me ; and then it was that my whole Me stood up in native God-created majesty and with emphasis recorded its protest.' The result is noteworthy : ' Even from that time the temper of my misery was changed : not Fear or whining sorrow at it, but Indignation and grim fire-eyed Defiance.'

Carlyle had won not peace but a ' change of misery.' He could look at the enemy with ' fire-eyed defiance' but not with the calm of settled victory. His emancipation was not won by a reasoned answer to doubt. In the earlier essays Carlyle shows apparent sympathy with German philosophy.[1] He speaks with profound admiration, though in general and popular language, of the doctrines of Kant, Novalis, and Fichte, and seems to accept Coleridge's theory of a Reason superior to the Understanding.[2] Carlyle, however, was still less of a metaphysician proper than of a poet. He is a man of intuitions, scorning all logical apparatus in itself, and soon afterwards appears to regard metaphysics in general as a hopeless process of juggling which tries to educe conviction out of negation and necessarily ends in scepticism.[3] To him Goethe rather than any metaphysician presented the true solution. No two men of genius, indeed, could be more unlike. The rugged, stormy Puritan could hardly, one would have thought,

[1] Essays on 'State of German Literature' (1827) ; 'Novalis' (1829) ; 'Signs of the Times' (1829).
[2] Novalis, *Essays*, ii. 76.
[3] 'Characteristics' (1831) ; *Essays*, iii. 20.

breathe the serene atmosphere of the prophet of culture. But the very contrast fascinated him. Goethe had cast aside all the effete dogmas, and had yet reached the victorious position in which symmetrical development was possible. Carlyle remained to the end desperately struggling, full of ' fire-eyed defiance,' but never getting outside the chaotic elements. The metaphysical systems of Kant's successors attracted him as protests against materialism, but he preferred a shorter cut to the end, and his Scottish common sense was always whispering that philosophy was apt to be mere ' transcendental moonshine.'

Carlyle therefore was essentially protesting against the mechanical doctrines embodied in Utilitarianism. But he saw the hopelessness of meeting the attack in the old-fashioned armour of theology. The dogmas of the churches were dead, beyond all hopes of resuscitation. The verse in *Past and Present* gives his view :—

> ' The builder of the Universe was wise,
> He planned all souls, all systems, planets, particles ;
> The plan He shaped all worlds and æons by,
> Was—Heavens !—was thy small nine-and-thirty Articles.' [1]

An earlier version of these lines speaks of the ' logic of Maurice,' who had characteristically proved that the articles were a charter of religious liberty.[2] Carlyle rejected formulas. The Maurician rehabilitation led to mere cant. Like Maurice, he was in principle a mystic, and holds that mysticism may be taken in a true sense,[3] in which it seems to be much the same with an Idealist as contrasted with a materialist doctrine. When he first

[1] *Past and Present*, ch. xv.   [2] Froude, iii. 40.
[3] 'Novalis,' in *Essays*, ii. 72, etc.

made Mill's acquaintance, it was under the erroneous impression that Mill too was a mystic.[1]

I have spoken of Carlyle's personal relations to Mill. His judgment of the Utilitarians generally is significant. Froude publishes some entries from Carlyle's journal of 1829-30, a time when the prophet was only preluding his fuller utterances.[2] The Utilitarians, he holds, exhibit tendencies spread over the whole intellect and morals of the time. Utilitarianism must collapse, because the reason will triumph over the senses, and the angel at last prevail over the brute. The moral nature of man is deeper than the intellectual; the significance of Christ, he says, is altogether moral, and the significance of Bentham 'altogether intellectual, logical.' Where logic is the only method, the resulting system can be only mechanical. 'Alas! poor England! Stupid, purblind, pudding-eating England,' Bentham with his *Mills*[3] grinding 'thee out morality—and some Macaulay, also be-aproned and a grinder, testing and decrying it.' The mention of Macaulay reminds him that the Utilitarians have a relative merit. 'They *have* logical machinery,' and do grind 'fiercely and potently on their own foundation, whereas the Whigs have no foundation. . . . The Whigs are amateurs, the radicals are guild-brethren.'[4] The public utterances are versions of the same doctrines. In *Sartor Resartus* Teufelsdröckh would consent that the 'monster *Utilitaria*' should trample down palaces and temples 'with her broad hoof,' that new and better might be built.[5] So in the

[1] Mill's *Autobiography*, p. 175, etc.
[2] The journals have been separately printed in America for the Grolier Club (edited by Prof. Norton).　　[3] Carlyle, I fear, is punning.
[4] Froude, ii. 79, 90.　　　[5] *Sartor Resartus*, bk. iii. ch. iv.

Hero-Worship[1] he calls 'this gross steam-engine Utilitarianism' an approach towards a new faith. It is at least a 'laying down of cant,' an honest acceptance of the belief in mechanism : 'Benthamism is an *eyeless* heroism ; the human species, like a hapless blinded Samson, grinding in the Philistine mill, clasps convulsively the pillars of its mill, brings huge ruin down, but ultimately deliverance withal. Of Bentham I meant to say no harm.' In later years Carlyle insists more emphatically upon the bad side of Utilitarianism. He had grown more bitter, and was more alienated personally. In the *Chartism* (1839) he attacks the 'Paralytic Radicalism'—paralytic being substituted for 'philosophical'—which has sounded statistically a 'sea of troubles' around us, and concluded that nothing is to be done but to look on. Paralytic Radicalism, accordingly, is 'one of the most afflictive phenomena the mind of man can be called upon to contemplate !'[2] The summary of his later view is given in the famous summary of the 'Pig Philosophy' in the *Latter-day Pamphlets*. The universe is regarded as an 'immeasurable swine's trough,' and the consequences deduced in a kind of Swiftian catechism.[3] Utilitarianism means mere sensualism. Carlyle's interpretation, true or false, reduces the issue to the simplest terms. Will you accept the mechanical or the mystical view? Carlyle's metaphysical leanings were to some forms of transcendental idealism. Time and space, as he says in the *Sartor Resartus*, are the canvas on which our life-visions are painted. They are mysterious 'world-embracing phantoms,' to be rent asunder

[1] Lecture v.　　　　　　　　[2] *Chartism*, ch. x.
[3] *Latter-day Pamphlets*, 'Jesuitism.'

by the seer who would pierce to the Holy of Holies. They are illusions, though while we are on earth we try in vain to strip them off. Men are spirits ; the earth but a vision. We issue from and fall back into mystery. 'We are such stuff,' in his favourite quotation,

'As dreams are made of, and our little Life
Is rounded with a sleep.'[1]

This is poetry rather than philosophy ; and though the thought is always present to Carlyle and constitutes one secret of his most powerful passages, it would be impossible to grasp it as a logical theory or imprison it in any formula whatever. All systems and formulas are suspicious to him. He is a 'seer' who not only does not require any logical apparatus, but holds that to require one is to give up the point. It is the sense of the ephemeral nature of man, of his suspension in the midst of infinities, which stimulates or overpowers him. That sentiment lies deeper than all reasoning. The 'mechanical' view has the advantage derived from the authority of the physical sciences ; but the sciences, he holds, lie in a superficial region ; they belong to the world of appearance, not to the world of reality. When the mystic ventures into the ordinary daylight and fights the man of science with his own weapons, he will get the worst of it. Science must have its rights on its own ground ; and to suppose the supernatural intruding here and there into natural phenomena is to court defeat. There are no 'miracles,' but the universe is itself miraculous. His great message, given in *Sartor Resartus*, is that the natural *is* the supernatural.[2] We are not to pick up 'intuitions' here and

[1] *Sartor Resartus*, bk. i. ch. viii. ; bk. iii. ch. viii.　　[2] Froude, ii. 345.

there ; but we have one intuition, that the world is not a mechanism but a revelation of God. No set of words can hold the great mystery. They are hopelessly inadequate, and the sooner they are swept into oblivion the better. But the one profound mystery remains.

Even such a vague indication of Carlyle's general meaning is an attempt to define an imaginative tendency which shrinks from definite formulation. The more practical application is perhaps more definable. The 'Everlasting No' means : I will not believe that the world is a mere dead mechanism, nor that the sole forces by which society is moulded are the sensual appetites. Rightly or wrongly, Carlyle attributed those views to the Utilitarians. They had a certain negative merit, in so far as they took their own line directly and consistently. The ordinary theology was a mass of 'shams' and 'cants'—a collection of subterfuges by which men could blind themselves for the time to the necessary drift of the current. The way to meet the Utilitarian was not to compromise or to argue, but to leave the world of outward fact and to plant yourself on a deeper base : the direct, imperative, and unassailable conviction or intuition of the divine order implied everywhere beneath the 'living raiment.' The issue then becomes simple and absolute. No set of creeds and 'formulas' can matter ; 'evidences' are an absurdity ; the one formula is the divinity of the universe ; the only evidence, the direct intuition of the eternal verities. The religions of the world are good so far as they recognise this truth ; bad so far as they try to imprison it in any sort of formula or make it dependent upon any particular fact. To Maurice, as to others, this attitude seemed to be hopeless. Does it not become mere pantheism—a sentiment too vague to be efficient?

Pantheism is a phrase scarcely appropriate for Carlyle's creed. If Carlyle believed in God, he also believed for practical purposes in the devil. He might have been expected to accept some such pessimistic scheme as Schopenhauer's. He was deterred by his innate Puritanism. The voice of God for him, however vaguely defined, is heard in morality. God is essentially the giver of the supreme laws of human conduct, however much the legislator may be wrapped in mystery. The 'simple creed,' according to his chief disciple, which was the 'central principle' of all Carlyle's thought, was the creed of the Jews and the Puritans, namely, that obedience to the divine law is the one condition of human welfare, and that nations who worship Baal even in the guise of art or of material prosperity are on the road to destruction.[1]

Carlyle, then, is so far like Coleridge and Maurice, that he feels that a religion must find some deeper and more universal base than can be discovered in the region of empirical fact. It must correspond to an imperative dictate of the whole heart or the intellect. He carries out the principle with incomparably more vigour by rejecting all historical supports and particular formulas. Neither the Thirty-nine Articles nor the decrees of councils or popes can be adequate to express the mystery; nor can the religious sentiment be dependent upon particular events and 'miracles.' It is the difficulty of all such methods that the appeal to the heart comes to be the appeal to the prejudices

[1] Froude, iii. 12.

of the individual prophet. In a man of such marked idiosyncrasies as Carlyle's this is of course conspicuous. His version of history and of philosophy reflects his inherited prepossessions. It is enough here to mark one or two of the main points upon which he came into conflict with contemporaries. A characteristic result is his theory of hero-worship. The divine element in the world cannot be enshrined in one sacred book or a single supernatural order. The revelation comes not only through Moses or Christ, but through every great man. Odin, Mahomet, Dante, Shakespeare, Luther, John Knox, Johnson, Rousseau, Burns, Cromwell, and Napoleon are his chief instances in the 'lectures': each, more or less perfectly, was the vehicle of a more or less partial revelation. But then, may we not see gleams of the same light in all the multitudinous strugglings of the poor human beings who have more or less consciously co-operated in the world's progress? Here and there his shrewd commonsense leads him to recognise the value even of the stupid and the formula-ridden.[1] But, as a rule, he thinks of the world as a collection of 'dull millions' who 'as a dumb flock roll hither and thither,' led by little more than 'animal instincts.' Among them at rare intervals are scattered men of intellect and will.[2] The great men, as he says elsewhere, are 'children of the idea'—such a one as Ram Dass, who set up for a god because he had 'fire enough in his belly to burn up all the sins in the world.'[3] Inspiration belongs to the inspired few, who have to struggle amid the vast

[1] e.g. Past and Present, bk. ii. ch. xvii., and bk. iii. ch. v., with the humorous description of John Bull, who manages to settle down with his centre of gravity lowest.
[2] Essays, iii. 69 (Boswell).   [3] Essays, iv. 146 (Scott).

chaotic masses incapable of originating thought or action. To Carlyle, the essence of history was biography; the personal influence of a small minority of great men. The view condemns scientific modes of history. To disbelieve in the importance of great men is supposed to show materialistic principles. A 'law' of human development denies the importance of individual peculiarities. To hold that Cromwell or a Napoleon was a relatively insignificant accident, the mere fly on the wheel of great evolutionary processes, seems to be to lead to the exclusion of all action of the will or of thought. To Carlyle accordingly the historical method in some of its tendencies was profoundly antipathetic. To diminish the power of the individual was, in his view, to deny the spiritual forces upon which society is dependent. Inspiration, therefore, though no longer confined to a particular church, is still confined to the elect who stand out as burning and shining lights in the dim twilight of his Rembrandtesque pictures.

The great movements, then, of modern times correspond to the blind 'animal instincts' of the 'dumb flock.' They are good as the Utilitarians were good, or as the French revolutionists were good, so far as their blind action leads to the deposition of the false leaders and the destruction of their effete systems. The French Revolution is 'the crowning phenomenon of our modern time; the inevitable stern end of much: the fearful but also wonderful, indispensable, and sternly beneficent beginning of much.'[1] This is a brief summary of the great prose epic, than which no book, as he truly declared, had for a hundred years come more direct and flamingly 'from the

[1] Chartism, ch. v.

heart of a living man.'[1] The passage from which I have quoted, however, indicates a further point. The French Revolution, he holds, was essentially part of the revolt of the oppressed classes of Europe against their oppressors. But the positive doctrine of the 'rights of man,' theories which denied the need of government or demanded simply to throw the reins upon the neck of the governed, could lead only to chaos. The reconstruction must be by a new government; by a government of wisdom or, what to him seems the same thing, a government by the wise. The 'new Downing Street,' as he puts it, is to be a Downing Street inhabited by the 'gifted of the intellects of England.'[2] Nothing therefore could seem more contemptible than the doctrine of laissez faire. That is simply to leave the fools to themselves. Modern parliaments, with twenty-seven millions mostly fools listening to them, fill him with amazement.[3] A definition of 'right,' then, which makes it ultimately depend on the wishes of the fools, is simply absurd. Not the 'animal instinct' but the conformity to the divine law is the test of morality; and therefore not obedience to the majority but loyalty to the 'hero.' But how is the hero to be known? Could he tell us that, he replies, he would be a Trismegistus. No 'able editor' can tell men how 'to know Heroism when they see it that they might do reverence to it only, and loyally make it ruler over them.'[4] Here is, however, the difficulty. Obedience to the hero is our only wisdom, and obedience to the quack is the road to

[1] Froude, iii. 84.
[2] Latter-day Pamphlets, 'The new Downing Street.'
[3] Ibid., 'Stump Orators.'   [4] Past and Present, bk. i. ch. 19.

destruction. One is, it may be said, obedience to right, and the other obedience to might. How are we to tell right from might? The statement that Carlyle confused the two, that he admired might in reality, while professing to admire right simply, was the most popular and effective criticism of his opinions. He is constantly accused of approving mere brute-force. Nothing could less correspond to his intention; but he is puzzled in particular cases. He declares again and again that they coincide in a sense. 'Might and right do differ frightfully from hour to hour; but give them centuries to try it in, they are found to be identical.'[1] 'That which is just endures,' is an edifying statement, and one which he constantly emphasises; but may we not infer that that which endures is right, and be led to admire very questionable proceedings? Does the success of a Cromwell for his life-time, or the more permanent success of a Frederick, justify their proceedings? Carlyle may have often begun at the wrong end; but the curious point is that this part of Carlyle's teaching approximates so closely to a doctrine which he first detested. Froude tells us that he fought against Darwinism, but apparently 'dreaded that it might turn out true.'[2] Yet is not the doctrine of the 'survival of the fittest' just the scientific version of Carlyle's theory of the 'identity of Right and Might'? Was not evolution really in harmony with his conclusion? To him, according to Froude, it seemed that Science led to 'Lucretian Atheism.' He still believed in God, but when Froude once said that he could only believe in a God who did something, Carlyle replied 'with a cry

[1] *Chartism*, ch. viii.   [2] Froude, iv. 259.

of pain which I (Froude) shall never forget, He does nothing!'[1] The reconstruction which was to follow the destruction was indefinitely delayed. The hero did not come; and Carlyle was a prophet who had led his followers into the desert, but found that the land of promise always turned out to be a mirage. Carlyle held that hypocrisy was still worse than materialism; but, as he grew older and watched modern tendencies, he became less hopeful of the 'Exodus from Houndsditch,' and sometimes wished the old shelter to remain standing. He shrank even from the essayists and reviewers and from Colenso, though he had rejected historical creeds far more summarily than they had done.

Carlyle, then, and Maurice might both be called 'mystics' in the sufficiently vague sense used by Carlyle himself. They object to logic on principle. They appeal to certain primitive instincts which can be overridden by no logical manipulations or by any appeal to outward facts. Both, after all, are forced in the end to consider the plain, simple, 'objective' test. Maurice finds that he must answer the question of the historical critic: are the statements of fact true or false? Carlyle, not seeking for a base to support any particular creed, can throw the Thirty-nine Articles overboard, but finally comes into conflict with scientific conceptions in general. He finds himself opposed to the scientific view of historical evolution, and sees in the most conspicuous tendencies of modern thought the disappearance of all the most ennobling beliefs. The 'supernatural' and 'transcendental' have, after all, to conform to the prosaic matter of fact understanding. Accepting, as I do, what I suppose to be the scientific view, I fully believe that Carlyle's

method is erroneous; that in denouncing scientific methods as simply materialistic, he is opposing the necessary logic of intellectual development, and that his hero-worship and theory of right really lead to arbitrary and chaotic results.

There is, however, another remark to be made. If Carlyle's view of a scientific doctrine be correct; if its legitimate result be the destruction of morality, of all our highest aspirations, even of any belief in the reality of the mind or the emotions; if the universe is to be made into a dead mechanism or a huge swine's trough, we are certainly reduced to a most terrible dilemma. It was really the dilemma from which Carlyle could never escape, and the consciousness of which tormented him to the last. He had to choose between allegiance to morality and allegiance to truth. Scientific tendencies, especially as embodied in Utilitarianism, seemed to many men, and, as Carlyle's case shows, to the men of the highest abilities, to have that tendency. The absolute sincerity of that conviction is unmistakable. I do not doubt that men, holding the conviction sincerely, were bound to seek some escape; nor could I condemn them if under so terrible a dilemma they allowed their love of truth to be partly obscured. In fact, too, I think that it cannot be denied that many of the men to whom we owe most, whose morality was the highest and most stimulating, and who, moreover, were most hostile to the lower forms of superstition, did in fact take this position. Though Maurice was far from clear-headed, I fully believe that his liberal and humane spirit was of the greatest value, and that he did more than most men to raise the social tone in regard to the greatest problems. Carlyle's

doctrine is, I equally believe, radically incoherent; but I am also convinced that Carlyle's impetuous and vehement assertion of certain great social, ethical, and political principles was of the highest value. It must be allowed, I think, that such men as Carlyle and Emerson, for example, vague and even contradictory as was their teaching, did more to rouse lofty aspirations and to moralise political creeds, though less for the advancement of sound methods of inquiry, than the teaching of the Utilitarians. There was somewhere a gap in the Utilitarian system. Its attack upon the mythological statements of fact might be victorious; but it could not supply the place of religion either to the vulgar or to the loftiest minds. Then the problem arises whether the acceptance of scientific method, and of an empirical basis for all knowledge, involves the acceptance of a lower moral standard, and of a materialism which denies the existence or the value of all the unselfish and loftier elements of human nature? Can we adhere to facts without abandoning philosophy; or adopt a lofty code of ethics without losing ourselves in dream-land? Some thinkers sought a different line of escape.

IX. DOGMATISM

The 'Oxford Movement,' according to Newman, was really started on the 14th July 1833 by Keble's sermon on 'National Apostasy.' The 'movement' has become the subject-matter of vast masses of literature, as becomes a movement among a cultivated class. While Mill and his friends were under the impression that reason was triumphant and theology effete, the ghost of the old doctrinal disputes suddenly came abroad. Learned scholars once more plunged into dogmatic theology, renewed the old claims of the church, and seriously argued as to what precise charm would save an infant from the wrath of a righteous God. What explanation can be given of this singular phenomenon? There was clearly a 'reaction,' but why should there be a reaction? The Evangelical movement had been mainly ethical or philanthropical. It protested against evils when the national conscience was already in advance of the actual practice. That was its strength; its weakness was that it accepted, without examination, the current beliefs of the day, and simply did without philosophy. The Oxford movement, though many of its leaders were keenly awake to social evils, did not start primarily from a desire for social reform. Nor can its origin be traced directly to a philosophical development. Its leaders had, of course, been influenced by literary and speculative developments. They had, as Newman tells us, been stirred by Scott and Wordsworth and by Coleridge's philosophy. And yet it is plain enough that the impulse did not start from philosophical speculation. The movement corresponded to changes which would be part of the whole history of European thought. I have said enough of the Utilitarians to indicate the special English conditions. The Utilitarians saw in the established church the most palpable illustration of a 'sinister interest.' Bentham was attacking 'Church of Englandism'; James Mill was proposing to apply Bentham's principles by substituting an ethical department of the State for a church, and replacing the sacrament by tea-parties; the radicals of all varieties

regarded disestablishment and disendowment as the natural corollary from the Reform Bill, and a Whig statesman significantly advised the prelates to put their house in order. It was taken as a hint to prepare for confiscation.

Yet the Church was enormously strong; it was interwoven with the whole political and social organisation, and the genuine radical represented only a fraction of the population. Oxford in particular, the very focus of conservative and aristocratic interests, the favourite place for such culture as was popular with the landowners, the clergy, and all the associated classes, was startled and alarmed, and began to rouse its latent energy. Into Oxford no serious philosophical movement had penetrated. It had been slowly amending its system, but it still adhered in substance to the ancient traditions. Dimly it knew that infidels and rationalisers were preaching dangerous theories. Pusey had visited Germany in 1825-27, and had come back with some knowledge of German thought. He was even accused, very superfluously, of rationalism. Of that there was no real danger[1] for a man thoroughly steeped in the Oxford spirit. A sufficient illustration of Oxford education may be found in the curious controversy between Copleston, who had done much to rouse his University, and the Edinburgh Reviewers. Copleston replied vigorously, and yet his boast is a tacit confession. He declares that Oxford possesses good classical scholars, and we need not inquire how far they were really abreast

[1] See Pusey's (afterwards suppressed) *Historical Inquiry* into German rationalism (1828). H. J. Rose had attributed the evil to want of bishops. Pusey thought it was due to 'dead orthodoxism.' He looked leniently for the moment upon the attempt to infuse a little philosophy into the creed, but soon perceived that the Thirty-nine Articles would be more to the purpose.

of the day. Oxford men had to get up logic in Aldrich and make some acquaintance with Aristotle; and he argues that the mathematical studies of the place were more than 'elementary.' They were even beginning to include 'fluxions.' If this were a matter for boasting, it could not be seriously held that Oxford was doing anything comparable to the German universities as an adequate organ of the national intellect.[1] In point of fact, the system allowed the great majority to remain in complete ignorance of any recent movements of living speculation, a century or two behind-hand in philology, and absolutely indifferent to science. Naturally, when the champions of the Church came out to fight, they were armed with antiquated weapons. Yet many of them were men of great ability, and one at least a man of most indisputable genius.

The alarm spread by radical assaults upon the Church was equally felt by the liberal divines. No one, for example, was more alarmed than Dr. Arnold. But Arnold, a man of lofty and generous instincts and strong political interests, took the essentially liberal view. The Church, as all active-minded men agreed, was in danger. It was threatened by 'the godless party,' the radicals and revolutionists who were the heirs of Jacobinism, and were as hateful to him as to the high-

[1] Oxford had been incidentally attacked in the *Edinburgh Review* in an article upon 'Laplace' by Playfair; in a review by R. Payne Knight of an Oxford edition of Strabo; and by Sydney Smith in a very amusing review of a book upon education by Edgeworth. Copleston replied, and was answered in an article by the three conjointly. The controversy wandered into various small points. Newman, in his *Idea of a University*, quotes Copleston with deserved respect for his general principle. But the application to the Oxford system is less cogent.

churchmen. But here his diagnosis becomes essentially different. Arnold thought that the Church had become a separate sect because it adhered to old prejudices and to sacerdotalism. His remedy was to make it truly national, by widening its borders, admitting dissenters, and encouraging philosophic thought. The Church should be, as Coleridge urged, an essential part of the State organism; not a close corporation belonging to a priestly order. It was properly identical with the State. It must be liberalised that the State might be made religious, and drop the antiquated claims to magical authority which opposed it to the common sense of the masses and the reason of the thinkers.[1] This was precisely the antithesis to the view taken by the leaders of the 'movement.' They held that the Church was weak, precisely because it had been unfaithful to its higher claims and made an alliance with the State, which had passed into a bondage. This, then, is one aspect of the division between the liberals and the dogmatists; and what I have now to do is to endeavour to indicate the dogmatical view.

I confine myself to two representatives of the movement: Newman, whose literary genius needs no emphasis; and W. G. Ward, conspicuous as one who never shrank from an inference, and who, to do him bare justice, was incapable of supporting logic by misrepresenting his opponents. He represents the forlorn Hope, and

[1] See especially Arnold's pamphlet on *Principles of Church Reform* (1833), reprinted in *Miscellaneous Works* (1845), pp. 257-359. Arnold's aversion to sacerdotalism was most vigorously expressed in an article in the *Edinburgh* for April 1836, entitled (by the *Edinburgh*) 'The Oxford Malignants and Dr. Hampden.' It was not reprinted in his works. See Stanley's *Life of Arnold*, ii. 9.

reveals the tendencies which frightened his less daring comrades.

The true starting-point of the 'movement' can hardly be given more distinctly than in Ward's *Ideal of a Christian Church*.[1] It represents the stage at which Ward was becoming fully aware of the consequences of his own logical position. The *Ideal* has ceased to be lively reading; it is like an echo from old common-room disputations of young men intensely interested in the ecclesiastical movements of the day. Ward contrasts the actual Church of England with the ideal Church of Christ, and already finds in the Church of Rome a more promising embodiment of the true spirit. The true Church is of divine institution, the channel of super-natural graces, and independent of all human authority. The Church of England, if not the creature, has become in fact the slave, of the State. It claims a parliamentary title, and in return for privileges has abandoned its rightful authority. Above all, a true church is known by its discipline. It should be the incarnate conscience of the society, and should superintend, enforce by its sanctions and stimulate by its example, the spiritual nature of its members. A true church should exercise an omnipresent spiritual authority, reaching every detail of life and organising the perpetual warfare against the world, the flesh, and the devil. The utter decay of any such power is the most fatal symptom of the Anglican body. From a contemporary book,

[1] The *Ideal* (1844) was a defence of articles contributed by Ward to the *British Critic* against the 'Narrative' of William Palmer (1803-1885). It led to the final catastrophe, and was soon followed by the conversions to Catholicism of Ward and Newman.

Ward extracts a ghastly account of the misery, vice, and spiritual degradation of the mass of the population.[1] To remedy such evils, he declares, the 'science of dogmatic theology' is more essential than the science of political economy.[2] Dogmatic theology is in fact the basis of 'ascetic theology,' or of the whole theory of religious discipline. If, indeed, the Christian theology be taken seriously, if spiritual degeneration has an importance altogether out of proportion to material progress, and the salvation of souls be the one thing necessary, the con-clusion is inevitable. To enforce those truths upon the reason, to impress them upon the imagination, and to ensure a constant reference to them in all our conduct, must be the essential work of an authoritative church. Ward expatiates enthusiastically upon the ceaseless activity of the Church of Rome; upon the elaborate training of the priesthood; upon the catechising of children, the daily meditations, the constant practice of confession, and the various methods by which the church fixes the eyes of believers steadily upon spiritual realities. A church incapable of this can no longer be the salt of the earth, and, in fact, the Church of England, though it has boasted of being 'the poor man's church,' has been utterly blind to the 'accumulated mass of misery which has been gradually growing to a head for the last sixty years.' 'Through no agency of hers,' attention has been roused by such men as Lord Ashley; and yet the church has shown no symptoms of shame at such im-portant neglect.[3] What else can you expect from the organ of the comfortable classes?

[1] *Ideal*, p. 27. The *Perils of the Nation* (1843) is the book quoted.
[2] *Ibid.* p. 416.   [3] *Ibid.* p. 420.

The social evils were serious enough. Dogmatic theology may not seem at first sight to be the most appropriate remedy; but, if it were, it certainly needed a better army of defenders. The ideal church must have a theological school, a body of trained teachers capable of meeting the assaults of unbelievers, of pointing out the true results of biblical criticism, of scientific and historical inquiries, and of defining the attitude of the church in regard to them.[1] Ward is awake to the growth of a new infidelity, more dangerous than that of the last century. Carlyle, Kant, Michelet, and Milman are mentioned as representing different manifestations of this evil spirit. Strauss, too, is selling more rapidly than any foreign work.[2] Moreover, 'Protestantism,' as he maintains, is utterly effete and unable to cope with the antagonist. The 'theory of private judgment' involves doubt, and will tend inevitably to 'Comte's philosophy.'[3] Comte was represented in England by Mill, who was accordingly the butt of Ward's sharpest attacks.

If Ward thus expresses the seminal principle of the movement, Newman was the most efficient leader. Newman, as he tells us in the *Apologia*, held three doctrines: first, the 'principle of dogma,' which was the 'fundamental principle' of the movement of 1833, and was the antithesis of 'liberalism'; secondly, the principle, implied by this, of a 'visible church'; and thirdly, the doctrine that the Pope was antichrist.[4] The last, of course, vanished; but the two others remained and only took a sharper form in his mind. The history of his

[1] *Ideal*, pp. 34-44.   [2] *Ibid.* p. 266.
[3] *Ibid.* p. 504.   [4] *Apologia*, p. 121.

thought is simply the history of his growing conviction that the true authority was that of Rome, not of the Anglican Church.[1] The 'principle of dogma' is equiva-lent to the statement that 'religion as a mere sentiment' was to him 'a dream and a mockery.' The liberal principle applied to theology means the substitution of vague feeling for definite truth. But to speak absolutely of a 'principle of authority' is to raise a difficulty. To believe in authority is to ground my belief on the belief of some one else. Therefore the questions remain: why does the authority believe, and why should I accept its belief as authoritative? The Church must be com-petent to judge, and I must be able to judge of its competence.

The special answer given by Ward and Newman to these points gives their true position. First of all the dogmatists, agreeing so far with the liberals, were convinced that the ordinary opinions of the day led to infidelity or to complete scepticism. A perfectly consistent mind must, as Newman declared, accept Catholicism or Atheism. Anglicanism is 'the half-way house to Rome, and Liberalism is the half-way house' to Atheism.[2] Protestantism, again, as involving the right of private judgment, must lead, as Ward agreed, to Comte. Taken simply, such sayings amount to pure scepticism. To admit the consistency of Atheism is to admit that you have no grounds of confuting the Atheist. Upon the assumptions common to both, the sceptic would get the better of the Protestant. The rationalised theology of Paley had really given away the key of the position. It could not permanently hold out against

[1] *Apologia*, p. 205.   [2] *Ibid.* pp. 322, 329.

the legitimate development of the eighteenth century infidelity. 'As a sufficient basis for theism,' says Ward, the argument from final causes is 'absolutely and completely worthless';[1] and he declares that Paley's argument is quite unable to prove God's love, or goodness, or justice, or personality.[2] But Paley and his contemporaries had explicitly given up any other argument. A Protestant, then, was logically bound to Atheism. Newman agrees. 'I have ever viewed this argument with the greatest suspicion,' he says, and for good reasons. It may prove the power and, in lower degrees, the wisdom and the goodness of God; but it does not prove his attributes as judge and moral legislator.[3] So again, Newman declared[4] that it was 'a great question whether atheism is not as philosophically consistent with the phenomena of the physical world, taken by themselves, as the doctrine of a creative and governing power.' Paley's proof of Christianity is naturally as unsatisfactory as his proof of theology. In one of the *Tracts for the Times*,[5] Newman applied what he called a 'kill-or-cure' remedy. He argued, that is, that if his antagonists rejected his doctrines for want of Scripture proof, they would have to abandon their own for the same reason. After recalling and enforcing a number of the objections made by sceptics to the historical evidence, he concludes that the evidence is by itself insufficient. Shall we for

---

[1] *Ideal*, p. 277.
[2] *Ibid.* p. 499. Ward would apparently have modified these statements at a later period.
[3] *Idea of a University* (1875), p. 453.
[4] *University Sermons* (1843), p. 186. In the later edition this phrase is carefully qualified as referring only to an illegitimate use of reason.
[5] No. 85 (1838), reprinted in *Discussions and Arguments*, 1872.

that reason refuse to believe? No, we must begin by believing. If we refuse 'to go by evidence in which there are (so to say) three chances for revelation and only two against it, we cannot be Christians.'[1]

Hume, then, or Mill or Comte, can at least hold his own upon empirical ground. Unaided reason, as Newman says in the *Apologia*,[2] can indeed discover sound arguments for theology, but historically and in practice it will tend towards simple unbelief. The 'liberals' endeavoured to meet the enemy by appealing to some philosophical or quasi-mystical doctrine; but in so doing they either dropped dogmatic and historical creeds altogether, or saved them by non-natural interpretations. Religion sublimated into philosophy becomes a mere sentiment, or a system of subtle metaphysics. It cannot effectively discipline the ordinary mind or inspire a church to meet the world. Yet some philosophical principle is necessary. To the Oxford men philosophy meant chiefly some modification of Aristotle. They held, of course, that the necessity of a first cause was demonstrable, and that a theology could be constructed by the pure reason.

This, however, leads to the old difficulty, the perplexity which runs through Christian theology in general. It is forced to combine heterogeneous elements. Philosophy must be combined with mythology; and the first cause identified with the anthropomorphic deity. Your metaphysic proves the existence of God in one sense, and your concrete creed assumes the existence to

---

[1] In *Discussions and Arguments*, p. 249, the curious correction is made of substituting twelve for three. That marks without mending the blot.
[2] *Apologia* (1864), p. 380.

be proved in a sense quite inconsistent. By calling inconsistency mystery, you verbally force contradictions into a formula, and speak of a God-man; but the difficulty of getting from the metaphysical to the historical theology is thus only masked. How is it to be overcome?

Ward, laying the greatest stress upon the metaphysical argument, came into conflict with Mill. Ward and Mill always spoke of each other with marked respect. They communicated their writings to each other before publication. Ward reviewed Mill's *Logic* in the *British Critic* in the most complimentary terms. Mill wrote to Comte in hopeful terms of the services to be rendered to speculation by the new school of divines. Ward thought Mill by far the most eminent representative of the 'antitheistic school,' and spoke with generous warmth of his high moral qualities.[1] The point, however, upon which Mill specially valued himself was just the point upon which Ward took him to be utterly in the wrong. Mill denied the existence of 'necessary truths.' Ward believed in the existence of a great body of 'necessary truth.' Ward argues forcibly for the 'necessity' of mathematical truths, and denies the power of association. Ward, in short, is Mill's typical 'intuitionist.' Intuitions, he says, are truths which, 'though not parts of present consciousness, are immediately and "primarily" known with certitude.'[2] He adopts from Lewes the word 'metempirical,' as expressive of what lies beyond the sphere of phenomena;[3] and holds that all 'intuitions' give us 'metempirical' knowledge.

---

[1] Ward's *Essays on the Philosophy of Theism* (1884), pp. 120-125.
[2] *Philosophy of Theism*, pp. 143 n., 304.   [3] *Ibid.* ii. 87.

Lewes invented the phrase to express the difference between the legitimate 'intuitions' implied in experience and the illegitimate, which are 'metempirical' as professing to transcend experience. Ward holds that 'metempirical' truths are valid and essential to reason.

Morals, again, says Ward, are as certain as mathematical intuitions; the truth that 'malice and mendacity are evil habits' is as necessary as the truth that 'all trilateral figures are triangular.'[1] Further, I 'intue' that 'all morally evil acts are prohibited by some living Personal Being'; and from this axiom it follows 'as an obvious inference' 'that this Person is the supreme Legislator of the Universe.'[2] The obvious difficulty is that Ward proves too much. His argument is leading to an independent theism, not a theism reconcilable with an historical creed. Accordingly he has to limit or resist his own logic. He admits the uniformity of nature as 'generally true,' but makes two exceptions, in favour, first, of 'an indefinite frequency' of miracles, and secondly of the freedom of 'human volitions.'[3] The Freewill doctrine leads to an elaborate and dexterous display of dialectic, though he must be a very feeble determinist who could not translate Ward's arguments into his own language. Beyond this we have further difficulties. If the creed be as demonstrable as Euclid, how can anybody deny it? Ward has to account for the refusal of those who do not accept his intuitions by some moral defect; they are like blind men reasoning upon colours. Mill's 'antitheism' shows that he was guilty of 'grave sin'; for, on the Catholic doctrine, there can be no 'invincible ignorance of the one true

---

[1] *Philosophy of Theism*, i. 50.   [2] *Ibid.* i. 90, 94.   [3] *Ibid.* i. 315.

God.'[1] Many men, however, condemn the creed of revelation precisely upon the moral ground. The Utilitarians denounced the profound immorality of the doctrine of hell and of vicarious punishment. Ward's argument requires such a conscience as will recognise the morality of a system which to others seems radically immoral. The giver of the moral law is also the giver of the natural law. But it seems to be as hard to show that Nature is moral in this sense as to show that the moral legislator, if omnipotent, can also be benevolent. The one great religious difficulty, as Ward allows, is the existence of evil. He quotes Newman's statement that it is a 'vision to dizzy and appal; and inflicts upon the mind a sense of a profound mystery, which is absolutely beyond human solution.'[2] Plainly, it comes to this : the 'intuitions' are in conflict with experience. They assert that the creator is omnipotent and infinitely just and benevolent. The admitted facts are incompatible with the theory, and are therefore declared to imply an 'insoluble mystery.' Ward intimates that he can show the true place of this difficulty after setting forth the 'impregnable basis on which Theism reposes.' But he does not appear to have found time for this ambitious enterprise.

This introduces the more special problem. How from your purely metaphysical position do you get to the historical position ? What is the relation between the authority of the Church and the authority of the pure reason ? Though Ward was perfectly satisfied with his

[1] *Philosophy of Theism*, i. 121. Ward, we are told, subsequently ceased to hold this opinion 'with any confidence,' or abandoned it altogether. *Ibid.* ii. 132.   [2] *Ibid.* i. 359.

own metaphysics, it was of course evident to him that such reasoning was altogether beyond the reach of the mass of mankind. If you are to prove your creed by putting people right about Freewill and the uniformity of nature, you will adjourn the solution till the day of judgment. An essential point of his whole argument is the utter incapacity of mankind at large to form any judgment upon such matters. The Protestant 'right of private judgment' means scepticism. Everybody will have his own opinion if nobody trusts any one else. If the truth of Christianity is to be proved by the evidences after Paley's fashion, nobody has a right to believe who has not swallowed whole libraries and formed elaborate canons of criticism. The peasant who holds opinions about history, to say nothing of science and philosophy, must obviously take them on trust. Hence we must either give up the doctrine that 'certitude' is necessary, or we must find some proof accessible to the uneducated mind. But it is an essential point of Catholicism, if not of Christianity, that faith is necessary to salvation. If wrong belief be sinful, right belief must be attainable. But men by themselves are utterly impenetrable to right reason. We have, then, to combine scepticism as to the actual working of the human intellect with dogmatism as to the faith. How is that feat to be accomplished ?

Ward replies, by the doctrine of 'implicit reasoning.' Acceptance of the intuitions implies acceptance of all legitimate deductions. But this position is more fully 'drawn out' (in his favourite phrase) by Newman. It runs through a whole series of the writings in which the delicacy and subtlety of his style are most fully

displayed,[1] and the difficulty of the position most fully exhibited. Chillingworth had stated the Protestant argument. To admit the infallibility of the Church, he had said, takes the individual no further, unless he is infallibly certain of the infallibility. To this Newman replies[2] that I may be certain without claiming infallibility. Certainty that two and two make four is quite consistent with a power of mathematical blundering. Perhaps it should rather be said that, if there be necessary truths, every one must, within their sphere, be infallible. But no one asserts that the infallibility of the Church is a necessary truth. If real, it is a concrete fact to be proved by appropriate evidence. After exhausting your eloquence in proving the fallibility, and indeed the inevitably sceptical result of 'private judgment,' you are bound to show how, in this case, the individual can attain certitude. The judgment that 'the Church is infallible' has been disputed by reasonable people. How are we to show that, in this case, their doubts are unreasonable, if not wicked? Why do not the proofs of the weakness of private judgment apply to this as to every other judgment? Have you not really cut away the foundation on which sooner or later your argument must be based? Yet certitude is made out to be a moral duty even for the average believer.

The theory is most explicitly worked out in the *Grammar of Assent*. Newman exerts all his skill in expounding a very sound doctrine. As a matter of fact, we form innumerable judgments by what he calls the

[1] Especially the *University Sermons*, the *Essay upon Miracles*, the *Essay upon Development*, and the *Grammar of Assent*.
[2] *Grammar of Assent* (1870), p. 219.

'illative sense '; that is to say, not by formal argument, but by a complex system of 'implicit' reasonings. 'Logic,' as he says, 'does not really prove. It enables us to join issue with others . . . it verifies negatively '; and for 'genuine proof in concrete matter we require an organism more delicate, versatile, and elastic, than verbal argumentation.'[1] Logic is a chain which 'hangs loose at both ends,'[2] for the first principles must be assumed, and the abstract concept never fits the actual complexity of concrete fact. By the 'illative sense,' again, we reach innumerable truths. We hold that England is an island, or that the man whom we see is our brother, with a faith indistinguishable from absolute conviction. We go further; we believe that a friend is honest, or, say, that Cæsar crossed the Rubicon, without admitting the slightest scruple of doubt. All knowledge whatever of fact plainly implies something different from formal logic ; and, so far, the only question seems to be why so palpable a truth needs so elaborate and graceful an exposition. The answer is indicated by the polemic against Locke. Locke had proposed, as a test of a love of truth, the refusal to hold any proposition 'with a greater assurance than the proofs it is built on will warrant.'[3] The statement seems to be not only unassailable but in conformity with Newman's doctrine. Should we believe England to be an island? When Julius Cæsar landed, it was not proved; and he would have been wrong to be certain. When did it become right to be certain? Surely at whatever moment it was adequately proved. It is never so proved that to deny it would be self-contradictory, but

[1] *Grammar of Assent* (1870), p. 264.   [2] *Ibid.* p. 277.
[3] *Ibid.* p. 155. See also *Essay on Development*, p. 328.

by this time it is as much proved as any fact can be proved. Locke would simply justify himself by saying that in this case our 'assurance' does not exceed the 'proofs on which it is built.' The approximation to demonstration is indefinitely close, though never absolute, and the difference becomes too small to be perceptible. A difficulty emerges only if we at once admit the rightness of belief and deny the sufficiency of the evidence.

Newman, having shown that we believe in concrete truths not proved by abstract logic, argues that we also assume many truths not proved even by sufficient empirical evidence. We have what Locke called a 'surplusage of assurance.' The fact, again, is undeniable. We believe implicitly in countless things upon insufficient evidence. This, as Locke would add, is one main explanation of the prevalence of error, and also a proof that error may be innocent. It is a duty to be candid; it cannot be a duty to be right. We must listen to reason; but the effect of reasoning must depend upon the constitution of our minds, and the various beliefs with which they are already stored. Now to Newman this doctrine always seems to be sceptical. It amounts to the 'liberalising' view that all creeds are equally good if only they be equally sincere. Hence he lays stress upon the doctrine that 'assent' is a volitional as well as an 'intellectual act.' It is our duty to obey the reason; and when the 'illative sense' declares the truth of a proposition, we are bound to an 'active recognition' of the truth.[1] Locke, on the contrary, holds that if we listen to reason, the assent follows automatically by a non-voluntary act.

[1] *Grammar of Assent*, p. 337.

On Newman's showing, an element of volition intrudes into logic. Belief belongs to action as well as to pure speculation. 'To act you must assume,' he says, 'and that assumption is faith.'[1] If acting upon an hypothesis is the same thing as believing the truth to be demonstrated, this leads to a singular result. A judge, says Newman, acts upon the assumption that a criminal's guilt is proved.[2] Yet, as it is never mathematically demonstrated, he has a 'surplusage of assurance.' The judge may be of opinion that the prisoner's guilt is highly probable and yet be bound to acquit. Is he to believe that the prisoner's innocence is demonstrated? The case really shows the opposite : simply that as we have to act upon probabilities, we are not the less, but the more, bound to guard against the illusion that they are certainties. At every moment and in every relation of our lives, we are forced to act upon imperfect knowledge. The obvious inference is that we are bound to keep in mind that it is imperfect; or otherwise we shall be morally bound to commit intellectually error. If, therefore, a creed be not demonstrably true, we may wisely act as if it were true, but have no right to deny that we are acting upon probability. Butler's famous doctrine that 'probability must be the guide of life,' is true if 'properly explained.' But the difficulty is that, in religious questions, 'certitude' is declared to be essential; it must correspond to something more than a 'balance of arguments';[3] and yet the certitude rests upon faith, and faith is 'assumption.' The probability must be somehow converted into certainty. In the *Essay on Development*, Newman meets Locke by declaring that 'calculation never made a hero,'

[1] *Grammar of Assent*, p. 92. [2] *Ibid.* p. 320. [3] *Ibid.* p. 231.

and praising the Fathers for 'believing first and proving afterwards.'[1] Though calculation does not make a hero, it is essential to making heroism useful. The true hero is the man who is ready to act, though he fairly estimates the chances and knows perhaps that they mean a probability of death.

This gives the real dilemma. Allow conviction to be influenced by the will, and you must admit that a belief morally right may be intellectually wrong. You justify the judge for mistaking presumption for demonstration, and the child for believing that a drunken parent is strictly sober. If so, you sanction erroneous beliefs. And this admittedly applies in particular to religious beliefs. The world, it is granted, is full of false beliefs, attained precisely by your method. Not one man in ten of all that have lived has belonged to the true Church. Newman, in fact, admits that his ultimate proof is 'subjective.' There is no ultimate test of truth beside 'the testimony borne to truth by the mind itself.'[2] He does not, indeed, deny the possibility of demonstration : he often asserts it; but he holds that the demonstration will not in fact convince. Men differ in their first principles, and he cannot change a man's principles more than he can make a crooked man straight or a blind man see.[3] Hence we have the final answer. We have really to desert a logical ground and to take our stand upon instinct. Our instincts are in one respect infallible. Belief in revealed religion depends upon belief in natural religion. Natural religion is founded on the conscience. The conscience means the sense of

[1] *Development*, pp. 328, 331.
[2] *Grammar of Assent*, p. 343. [3] *Ibid.* pp. 405, 408.

sin, and therefore the desire for intercession which is satisfied by the priesthood. The religion of philosophy ignores the conscience, though it recognises the moral sense.[1] The order of the world, indeed, seems to contradict this. What strikes the mind 'so forcibly and so painfully' is God's absence from His own world. He has left men in ignorance, and is a 'hidden God.' We are forced to the conclusion that 'either there is no Creator or He has disowned His creatures.'[2] Such doubts 'call for the exercise of good sense and for strength of will to put them down with a high hand as irrational or preposterous.'[3] Why 'irrational,' if they cannot be answered? Newman, indeed, declares that he is as certain of the existence of God as of his own, although he has a difficulty in putting the grounds of his certitude into 'mood and figure.'[4] The position is illustrated by a remarkable sermon[5] in which, after his conversion, he again applies the old 'kill-or-cure' remedy. He puts the various difficulties of theistic belief with his usual force. He declares that there are 'irrefragable' demonstrations of the doctrine; but he admits the difficulties.[6] They are so great, indeed, that if you once believe in God you need not shrink from accepting any of the mysteries of the Catholic creed. The result seems to be that while Newman declares that 'demonstrations' exist, he also emphatically declares

[1] *Grammar of Assent*, p. 391. [2] *Ibid.* p. 392. [3] *Ibid.* p. 211.
[4] *Apologia*, p. 377. [5] *Sermons to Mixed Congregations*, No. xiii.
[6] In one of his famous phrases, Newman says that ten thousand difficulties do not make one objection (*Apologia*, p. 374). This is clearly true in a sense. I may find it impossible to solve a mathematical problem without doubting that a solution exists. But it suggests a very convenient logical device. An unanswerable objection can always be met by calling it a difficulty.

that they will not practically convince. The proof for the ordinary mind must depend upon the 'illative sense'; and the illative sense implies the existence of the conscience, and, moreover, of the conscience as distinguished from the 'moral sense.' The 'moral sense' leads only to the hollow morality of 'so-called civilisation' and of superficial philosophy. To convince men we must appeal to their conscience. But for the conscience he would be 'an atheist, a pantheist, or a polytheist when he looked into the world,' that is, if guided by experience alone.[1]

What, then, is, as he puts it, the 'burdened conscience' which is my true informant?[2] The conscience is the sense of sin. It tells us of a judge; of one who is 'angry with us and threatens evil.' It tells us of the need of atonement, and yet of the absence of God from the world. Natural religion, the foundation of revealed religion, is therefore, as Lucretius said, a yoke; it 'burdens and saddens the religious mind.' It proves, too, the doctrine of which Butler was the 'great master,' the absolute necessity of 'vicarious punishment.'[3] Thus, as he says, in another famous passage, natural religion teaches gloom and horror of ourselves. To be 'superstitious . . . is nature's best offering, her most acceptable service, her most mature and enlarged wisdom, in the presence of a holy and offended God. They who are not superstitious without the gospel, will not be religious with it.'[4]

This is, indeed, the real pith of the doctrine. Without asking what may be the logical demonstration, the actual persuasive force is the appeal to the conscience as a

[1] *Apologia*, p. 377.
[2] *Grammar of Assent*, p. 392.
[3] *Ibid.* p. 401.
[4] *University Sermons* (1872), p. 118.

'sense of sin.' Starting from the conception of the Church implied in Ward's *Ideal*, that is the foregone conclusion. We accept the Church theology, because we feel the terror which the Church soothes. Newman, as was inevitable from the confusion between rules of conduct and canons of logic, has given us the real cause of belief, but not a good reason for believing. And here the apologists are precisely at one with the ordinary deist of the eighteenth century. They agree that the doctrine was accepted because it fell in with 'natural religion' in 'superstition.' The power of the Church, or the power of priest-craft, depends essentially upon the belief in its power of pardoning sin and reconciling man to God. The difference is that the deist asserted the superstition to be false, and pardon a quack remedy; whereas Newman sees a fundamental truth in the superstition, and the full explanation in the revelation committed to the Church. How, then, is the issue to be decided? You are wrong, says Newman, as a blind man judging of colours is wrong. You have quenched the conscience, and therefore have no guide. Yet, if a blind man can never realise what sight is, no blind man ever doubts that sight exists. Nothing is easier than to prove to him that I have means of knowledge which he does not possess. Why, if conscience reveals truths, cannot the truths be impressed even upon those who have no conscience? Why should I believe that your theory is right, when the ultimate test is one which, by its nature, can appeal only to its own authority? If men have radically different instincts which can be brought to no common measure, scepticism is the inevitable result, unless a supernatural authority can be applied. That is

precisely Newman's conclusion; leave men to themselves, he says, and they will have no 'common measure,' unless controlled by a supreme power. The 'absolute need of a spiritual supremacy' is the 'strongest argument in its favour.'[1]

This gives Newman's relation to the philosophy of the time. The 'irrefragable demonstrations' of the schools are left in the background. Granting them to be irrefragable, do they prove or disprove his point? Does the 'first cause' argument properly lead to Nature or to the God of Catholicism? To overlook this is to assume that your reasoning is confirmed by the very logic to which it is radically opposed. Is Newman really sceptical when he denies the validity of the scientific view, or the man of science when he denies the validity of Newman's? What is the relation of 'science' to philosophy? Private judgment is said to lead, in religion, to scepticism. The obvious reply is that in the physical sciences it has led to indisputable truths. Whence the difference? Newman speaks as though the proofs of scientific truths rested exclusively upon the arguments for each proposition separately. Men of science accept Newton's theory, he says, without rigidly testing it each for himself, and assume that it conforms to the facts, even if the conformity be not obvious.[2] Believers in theology should make similar assumptions. But this omits the real ground of conviction. We believe in Newton's theory of gravitation, not simply because we have read the *Principia*; not even simply because the

[1] *Development*, pp. 127, 128.
[2] *Essays on Development*, p. 129. Laplace and Lagrange had a different opinion.

argument is part of a whole system of consistent and independent truths; but also because it can be verified by proofs intelligible to all, and because it can predict facts open to the severest tests. The enormous authority of science is not due to the fact that it is believed by this or that expert or body of experts, but because it manifests its power by working wonders which are not miracles. It can appeal to a criterion which is not supernatural, and is as valid for the sinner as for the saint.

Here is one result of the Oxford indifference to science. When Newman was invited by innocent people to appear as the champion of faith against science, he refused, for the reason (among others) that he could not tell what was the position to be assailed. He would not deny that 'science grew, but it grew by fits and starts,' and threw out hypotheses which 'rose and fell.'[1] He supposes science to represent a fluctuating set of guesses. Even if it appeared to contradict revelation, the contradiction could be evaded by an easy device. Science and Scripture contradict each other as to the motion of the earth. We cannot decide till we know what motion is, and then it may turn out that science is false or reconcilable to Scripture.[2] This saying alienated Froude and Kingsley, and, I fancy, with good reason; but we can see how Newman came to it. Theology, he thought, rested on a deeper foundation than science. It represented a single body of deductive truth; while science represented a set of detached conclusions formed upon particular facts.

This appears to reverse the truth. 'The scientific

[1] *Apologia*, p. 404.
[2] *University Sermons* (1872), p. 348.

principle, in the first place, is at issue with the theology not upon this or that point, not on the conflict between particular statements, but all along the line. Two differing conceptions of the universe are at issue, and one must be accepted. Newman substantially replies that science has its own—a lower—sphere.[1] In the *Idea of a University* he argues that theology must be admitted into the course, because it deals with the realities underlying phenomena, and is therefore the rightful queen of sciences. The history of the actual relations of science and theology would supply a curious commentary upon this opinion. Newman meanwhile holds that the conflict arises from a scientific misconception. The latest infidel device, he says, is to leave theology alone. The man of science trusts to the interest of his own pursuits to distract the mind from theology, which then perishes by inanition.[2] His error consists in leaving the higher study out of sight, or applying methods legitimate in one sphere to those of the other sphere. Science, then, does not give certainty, or gives certainty which has no bearing upon the higher orders of truth.

The reply is obvious. The physical sciences, in the first place, give a body of consistent and verifiable truth, and the only such body of truth. In the next place, it is impossible to assign science and philosophy to two different provinces. The scientific doctrines must lay down the base to which all other truth, so far as it is discoverable, must conform. The essential feature of contemporary thought was just this: that science was passing from purely physical questions to historical,

[1] *Idea of a University* (1875), pp. 428-455.   [2] *Ibid.* pp. 401, 402.

ethical, and social problems. The dogmatist objects to private judgment or free thought on the ground that, as it gives no criterion, it cannot lead to certainty. His real danger was precisely that it leads irresistibly to certainty. The scientific method shows how such certainty as is possible must be obtained. The man of science advocates free inquiry precisely because it is the way to truth, and the only way, though a way which leads through many errors. His test is that which so impressed Newman himself, *Securus judicat orbis terrarum*; only *orbis terrarum* must not be translated one European Church during a few centuries. The man of science fully agrees with Newman that there is a true 'illative sense'; that men can reason implicitly before they can reason in logical form, and make approximately true formulæ though involved in innumerable superstitions and errors. The ultimate criterion is the power of verifying conclusions, of testing truth by its capacity to explain phenomena, and by its conformity to the scientific truth already established beyond dispute. But there is no royal road to truth in philosophy any more than in science; or, rather, it must be far longer and more difficult to reach it. Therefore we must not lay down rules as absolutely certain, but subject them to perpetual examination, to what Newman calls 'the all-corroding force' of the intellect, in the conviction that by that process we are slowly approximating to sounder belief. The errors have to be 'corroded.' This is admittedly true of all the natural sciences; we have to puzzle out the truth in every development of thought, from astronomy to physiology, by a slow and painful process. Moreover, it is true of all the religions of the world

except, as Newman would say, the Catholic. Why is that to be an exception? Newman candidly admits a difficulty. The suggestion that a religion to be universally accepted should be universally revealed, as though written 'on the sun,' is, he admits, plausible.[1] He urges that there always was a revelation somewhere, though a revelation in Jerusalem was not of much use in Peking. Yet the admitted fact seems to be a fatal objection to the *a priori* probability which he assumes of a revelation. To nine-tenths of the world there has been only a 'virtual,' that is to say, no revelation. How, then, does he try to make room for the one exceptional case? The secret is to keep to the geocentric point of view. Shut yourself up within the Church, interpret the world by reference to it, instead of interpreting it by its place in the world; pronounce the instincts by which it has been supported to be ultimate and infallible, instead of listening to the obvious explanation, and you can certainly escape self-contradiction—as it is still always possible on the same terms to hold to the Ptolemaic astronomy. You have only to assume as a first principle that the earth does not move, and the facts can always be forced into conformity. To outsiders this is to confuse the causes with the reasons of belief. So Newman in his famous development theory provides a kind of parallel to the scientific theory. He shows with the greatest clearness how a certain body works out the properties implied in the type, and so obeys an implicit logic. He illustrates the case by analogies with other bodies, such as the Anglican Church.[2] But why stop there? How did

[1] *Grammar of Assent*, pp. 372, 426.
[2] *Essay on Development*, pp. 102, 108, 170.

the first beliefs arise from which the full theological doctrine expanded? Newman again suggests the answer. They arise from the 'natural religions' or superstitions, many of which were admittedly embodied in the Church.[1] We have only to carry out his view logically, and the 'supernatural' element becomes needless. Christian and Hebrew legends take their place in the general process of human thought, and the assertion of the ultimate authority of one particular body is simply the description of the arbitrary claims which it developed under natural conditions. If we keep the earth in the centre of our system, we require a supernatural force to make the sun revolve. Let things fall into their right order and all becomes harmonious.

The positions thus occupied by the leading writers of the time indicate the true issues. The 'dogmatists,' the 'liberals,' and the 'Utilitarians' are virtually agreed upon one point. The Paley theology was in a hopeless position. Protestantism could only lead to infidelity. The arguments from design and from miracles are radically incoherent. They confuse a scientific with a philosophical argument, and cannot lead legitimately to proving the existence of a supreme or moral ruler of the universe. While accepting scientific methods they are radically opposed to scientific results, because they tend to prove intervention instead of order, and disappear as scientific knowledge extends. Mill's attempt to suggest some kind of tentative and conjectural theology was obviously hopeless, and interesting only as showing his sense of the need of some kind of religion which would embody high ethical ideals and stimulate the purest

[1] *Essay on Development*, pp. 358-365.

emotions. Empiricism was destructive of the historical creeds, but could not of itself supply the place of the old faiths.

Here then we come to the great problems by which men are still perplexed. The Utilitarian, which is the scientific view, lays down an unassailable truth. A religious creed, so far as it is a statement of fact, must state facts truly, and be in conformity with the results of scientific teaching. Moreover, no theology can be legitimately constructed upon this basis. The gods become figments ; and theology is relegated to the region of the unknowable. If that be the whole truth, religious creeds are destined to disappear as knowledge is extended and organised systematically. 'Philip Beauchamp' gives the true Utilitarian position. Religion, however, as J. S. Mill felt, is a name for something far wider. It means a philosophy and a poetry ; a statement of the conceptions which men have formed of the universe, of the emotions with which they regard it, and of the ethical conceptions which emerge. It has played, as it still continues to play, a vitally important function in human life, which is independent of the particular statements of fact embodied in the historical creed. The 'mystical' doctrine, represented by Carlyle, corresponds to this element of religion. Men will always require some religion if religion corresponds not simply to their knowledge, but to the whole impression made upon feeling and thinking beings by the world in which they live. The condition remains that the conceptions must conform to the facts ; our imagination and our desires must not be allowed to override our experience ; or our philosophy to construct the universe out of *a priori* guesses. What doctrine can be developed upon those terms, whether a 'religion of humanity' in some shape be possible, is still an open question. To the dogmatist this view seemed to be equivalent to the simple evaporation of all religion into mere vague emotional mist. To him a religion appeared essentially as a system of discipline or a great social organism, governing men's passions and providing them with a cult and a concrete vision of the universe. The difficulty is that such a creed cannot be really deduced from a general philosophy. The dogma has to be based upon 'authority,' instead of basing the authority upon proof. That is a radically incoherent position, and leads to the acceptance of the dogmas and traditions which have become essentially incredible, and to a hopeless conflict with science. To found a religion which shall be compatible with all known truth, which shall satisfy the imagination and the emotions, and which shall discharge the functions hitherto assigned to the churches, is a problem for the future. I must be content with this attempt to indicate what was the relation to it of the Utilitarian position.

INDEX